FISKE GUIDE TO COLLEGES 2005

FISKE GUIDE TO COLLEGES 2005

EDWARD B. FISKE

former Education Editor of
the *New York Times*
with Robert Logue
and
the *Fiske Guide to Colleges* Staff

SOURCEBOOKS, INC.®
NAPERVILLE, ILLINOIS

Published by Sourcebooks, Inc.
P.O. Box 4410
Naperville, Illinois 60567-4410
(800) 432-7444
FAX: (630) 961-2168
www.sourcebooks.com

ISBN 1-4022-0229-6
Twenty-First Edition

Your comments and corrections are welcome.
Please send them to:

Fiske Guide to Colleges
P.O. Box 287
Alstead, NH 03602
Fax: (603) 835-7859
Email: editor@fiskeguide.com

Printed and bound in the United States of America
DR 10 9 8 7 6 5 4 3 2 1

To Sunny

Contents

Index by State and Country

The colleges in this guide are listed alphabetically and cross-referenced for your convenience. Below is a list of the selected colleges grouped by state. Following this listing, you will find a second listing in which the colleges are categorized by the yearly cost of attending each school.

Index by Price

	PUBLIC	PRIVATE
$$$$	More than $16,000	More than $38,000
$$$	$14,000–$16,000	$34,000–$38,000
$$	$11,000–$14,000	$30,000–$34,000
$	Less than $11,000	Less than $30,000

PUBLIC COLLEGES AND UNIVERSITIES

Inexpensive—$

Moderate—$$

Expensive—$$$

Very Expensive—$$$$

PRIVATE COLLEGES AND UNIVERSITIES

Inexpensive—$

Albertson College, ID, 6
Albion College, MI, 8
Alfred University, NY, 10
Alma College, MI, 15
Alverno College, WI, 17
Antioch College, OH, 24
Bard College, NY, 47
Baylor University, TX, 54
Beloit College, WI, 57
Birmingham-Southern College, AL, 61
Brigham Young University, UT, 74
Calvin College, MI, 110
Centre College, KY, 124
Cooper Union, NY, 174
Cornell College, IA, 176
Dallas, University of, TX, 182
Dayton, University of, OH, 191
Deep Springs College, CA, 193
DePaul University, IL, 203
Drexel University, PA, 213
Eckerd College, FL, 221
Elon University, NC, 224
Gordon College, MA, 265
Guilford College, NC, 273
Gustavus Adolphus College, MN, 275
Hampden-Sydney College, VA, 281
Hendrix College, AR, 297
Hiram College, OH, 299
Hood College, MD, 309
Hope College, MI, 311
Houghton College, NY, 314
Howard University, DC, 316
Illinois Institute of Technology, 321
Kalamazoo College, MI, 360
Marlboro College, VT, 397
Millsaps College, MS, 424
Morehouse (Atlanta University Center), 34
Oglethorpe University, GA, 488
Prescott College, AZ, 520
Principia College, IL, 526
Randolph-Macon Woman's College, VA, 533
Rhodes College, TN, 548
Rice University, TX, 550
Ripon College, WI, 555
Rochester Institute of Technology, NY, 560
Saint Louis University, MO, 581
Spelman College (Atlanta University Center), 36
St. John's University and St. Benedict, MN, 572
Sweet Briar College, VA, 636
Texas Christian University, 648
Trinity University, TX, 655
Tulsa, University of, OK, 664
Wabash College, IN, 688
Wake Forest University, NC, 691
Warren Wilson College, NC, 693
Wells College, NY, 709
Wheaton College, IL, 717
Wofford College, SC, 740
Xavier University of Louisana, 748

Moderate—$$

Agnes Scott College, GA, 1
Austin College, TX, 42
Case Western Reserve University, OH, 118
Catholic University of America, The, DC, 121
Clark University, MA, 145
Clarkson University, NY, 148
Denison University, OH, 198
Denver, University of, CO, 201
DePauw University, IN, 205
Earlham College, IN, 219
Emerson College, MA, 226
Florida Institute of Technology, 239
Furman University, SC, 248
Georgia Institute of Technology, 260
Goucher College, MD, 267
Grinnell College, IA, 270
Hollins University, VA, 304
Illinois Wesleyan University, 324
Ithaca College, NY, 352
Kenyon College, OH, 368
Knox College, IL, 371
Lake Forest College, IL, 376
Lawrence University, WI, 379
Lewis & Clark College, OR, 384
Loyola University New Orleans, 389
Macalester College, MN, 391
Manhattanville College, NY, 395
Marquette University, WI, 400
Muhlenberg College, PA, 441
Ohio Wesleyan University, 495
Pacific, University of the, CA, 504
Presbyterian College, SC, 518
Redlands, University of, CA, 535
Richmond, University of, VA, 553
South, University of the (Sewanee), TN, 597
Southern Methodist University, TX, 603
Southwestern University, TX, 606
St. Olaf College, MN, 577
Stetson University, FL, 627
Susquehanna University, PA, 631
Washington and Jefferson College, PA, 698
Washington and Lee University, VA, 701
Whittier College, CA, 724
Wittenberg University, OH, 738
Wooster, The College of, OH, 743

Expensive—$$$

Allegheny College, PA, 12
American University, DC, 19
Amherst College, MA, 21
Atlantic, College of the, ME, 38
Babson College, MA, 44
Bates College, ME, 52
Boston College, MA, 64
Brandeis University, MA, 71
Bryn Mawr College, PA, 80
Bucknell University, PA, 83
California Institute of Technology, 107
Carleton College, MN, 113
Carnegie Mellon University, PA, 115
Claremont McKenna College (Claremont Colleges), CA, 134
Colby College, ME, 152
Colorado College, 171
Colorado School of Mines, 163
Columbia College (Columbia University), NY, 165
Connecticut College, 171
Davidson College, NC, 188
Drew University, NJ, 210
Fairfield University, CT, 233
Fordham University, NY, 243

PRIVATE COLLEGES AND UNIVERSITIES

The Best Buys of 2005

Following is a list of forty-three colleges and universities that qualify as Best Buys based on the quality of the academic offerings in relation to the cost of attendance.

Public

University of British Columbia (Canada)
University of Florida
University of Kansas
Mary Washington University
University of Massachusetts
McGill University (Canada)
University of North Carolina at Asheville
University of North Carolina at Chapel Hill
University of Oregon
Queens University (Canada)
SUNY–Albany
SUNY–Binghamton
SUNY–Buffalo
SUNY–Geneseo
SUNY–Stony Brook
University of Texas
Texas A&M University
University of Toronto (Canada)
College of William and Mary
University of Wisconsin–Madison

Private

Antioch College
Bard College
Brigham Young University
Centre College
Clark University
Cooper Union
Deep Springs College
Earlham College
Elon University
Grinnell College
Hendrix College
Kenyon College
Lawrence University
Macalester College
Redlands, University of
Rhodes College
Rice University
St. Olaf College
University of the South (Sewanee)
Trinity University
Wake Forest University
Warren Wilson College
Washington and Lee University

Introduction

THE *FISKE GUIDE TO COLLEGES*—AND HOW TO USE IT

The 2005 edition of the *Fiske Guide to Colleges* is a revised and updated version of a book that has been a best-seller since it first appeared two decades ago and is universally regarded as the definitive college guide of its type. Features of the new edition include:

- Updated write-ups on more than three hundred of the country's best and most interesting colleges and universities
- A section titled "Sizing Yourself Up," with a questionnaire that will help you figure out the kind of school that is best for you
- A Guide for Preprofessionals that lists colleges and universities strong in nine preprofessional areas
- A list of schools with strong programs for students with learning disabilities
- Designation of the forty-three schools that constitute this year's Best Buys
- Statistical summaries that give you the numbers you need, but spare you those that you do not
- Authoritative rankings of each institution by academics, social life, and quality of life
- The unique "If You Apply..." feature, which summarizes the vital information that you need about each college's admission policies—including deadlines and essay topics
- A section on the top Canadian and British universities in response to the fact that a growing number of students and families in the United States have become aware of the educational bargains that are lurking just across the border to the north. These universities offer first-rate academics—easily the equivalent of the flagship public institutions in the U.S.—but at a fraction of the cost.

Picking the right college—one that will coincide with your particular needs, goals, interests, talents, and personality—is one of the most important decisions that any young person will ever make. It is also a major investment. Tuition and fees alone now run at least $3,500 at a typical public university and $17,500 at a typical private college, and the tab at the most selective and expensive schools tops $27,500. Obviously, a major investment like that should be approached with as much information as possible.

That's where the *Fiske Guide to Colleges* fits in. It is a tool to help you make the most intelligent educational investment you can.

WHAT IS THE *FISKE GUIDE TO COLLEGES?*

The *Fiske Guide to Colleges* mirrors a process familiar to any college-bound student and his or her family. If you are wondering whether to consider a particular college, it is logical to seek out friends or acquaintances who go there and ask them to tell you about their experiences. We have done exactly that—but on a far broader and more systematic basis than any individual or family could do alone.

In using the *Fiske Guide*, some special features should be kept in mind:

- The guide is *selective*. We have not tried to cover all four-year colleges and universities. Rather, we have taken more than three hundred of the best and most interesting institutions in the nation—the ones that students most want to know about—and written descriptive essays of one thousand to twenty-five hundred words about each of them.
- Since choosing a college is a matter of making a calculated and informed judgment, this guide is also *subjective*. It makes judgments about the strengths and weaknesses of each institution, and it contains a unique set of ratings of each college or university on the basis of academic strength, social life, and overall quality of life. No institution is right for every student. The underlying assumption of the *Fiske Guide* is that each of the colleges chosen for inclusion is the right place for some students but not a good bet for others. Like finding the right husband or wife, college admissions is a matching process. You know your own interests and needs; the *Fiske Guide* will tell you something about those needs that each college seems to serve best.

• Finally, the *Fiske Guide* is *systematic*. Each write-up is carefully constructed to cover specific topics, from the academic climate and the makeup of the student body to the social scene, in a systematic order. This means that you can easily take a specific topic, such as the level of academic pressure or the role of fraternities and sororities on campus, and trace it through all of the colleges that interest you.

HOW THE COLLEGES WERE SELECTED

How do you single out "the best and most interesting" of the more than twenty-two hundred four-year colleges in the United States? Obviously, there are many fine institutions that are not included. Space limitations simply require that some hard decisions be made.

The selection was done with several broad principles in mind, beginning with academic quality. Depending on how you define the term, there are about 175 "selective" colleges and universities in the nation, and by and large these constitute the best institutions academically. All of these are included in the *Fiske Guide*. In addition, an effort was made to achieve geographical diversity and a balance of public and private schools. Special efforts were made to include a good selection of three types of institutions that seem to be enjoying special popularity at present: engineering and technical schools, those with a religious emphasis, and those located along the Sunbelt, where the cost of education is considerably less than at its northern counterparts. This current edition also includes several colleges that in recent years have significantly increased their academic quality and appeal to students.

Finally, in a few cases we exercised the journalist's prerogative of writing about schools that are simply interesting. The tiny College of the Atlantic, for example, would hardly qualify on the basis of superior academic program or national significance, but it offers an unusual and fascinating brand of liberal arts within the context of environmental studies. Likewise, Deep Springs College, the only two-year school in the *Guide*, is a unique institution of intrinsic interest.

HOW THE *FISKE GUIDE* WAS COMPILED

Each college or university selected for inclusion in the *Fiske Guide to Colleges* was sent a packet of questionnaires. The first was directed to the administration and covered topics ranging from their perception of the institution's mission to the demographics of the student body. Administrators were also asked to distribute a set of questionnaires to a cross-section of students.

The questions for students, all open-ended and requiring short essays as responses, covered a series of topics ranging from the accessibility of professors and the quality of housing and dining facilities to the type of nightlife and weekend entertainment available in the area. By and large, students responded enthusiastically to the challenge we offered them. The quality of the information in the write-ups is a tribute to their diligence and openness. American college students, we learned, are a candid lot. They are proud of their institutions—but also critical in the positive sense of the word.

Other sources of information were also employed. Administrators were invited to attach to their questionnaires any catalogs, in-house research, or other documents that would contribute to an understanding of the institution and to comment on their write-up in the last edition. Also, staff members have visited many of the colleges, and in some cases, additional information was solicited through published materials, telephone interviews, and other contacts with students and administrators.

The information from these various questionnaires was then collated by a staff of journalists and freelance writers and edited by Edward B. Fiske, former Education Editor of the *New York Times*.

THE FORMAT

Each essay covers certain broad subjects in roughly the same order. They are as follows:

Academics	**Housing**
Campus setting	**Food**
Student body	**Social life**
Financial aid	**Extracurricular activities**

Certain subtopics are covered in all of the essays. The sections on academics, for example, always discuss the departments (or, in the case of large universities, schools) that are particularly strong or weak, while the sections on housing contain information on whether the dorms are coed or single-sex and how students get the rooms they want. Other topics, however, such as class size, the need for a car, or the number of volumes in the library, are mentioned only if they constitute a particular strength or weakness at that institution.

We paid particular attention to the effect of the twenty-one-year-old drinking age on campus life. Also, we noted efforts some schools' administrations have been making to change or improve the social and residential life on campuses by such measures as banning fraternities and constructing new athletic facilities.

BEST BUYS

One of the lesser-known facts of life about higher education in the U.S. is that price and quality do not always go hand in hand. The college or university with the jumbo price tag may or may not offer a better education than the institution across town with much lower tuition. The relationship between the cost paid by the consumer and the quality of the education is affected by factors ranging from the size of an institution's endowment to judgments by college officials about what the market will bear.

In the face of today's skyrocketing tuition rates, students and families in all economic circumstances are looking for ways to get the best value for their education dollar. Fortunately, there are some bargains to be found in higher education; it just takes a bit of shopping around with a little guidance along the way.

Since its inception nearly two decades ago, the *Fiske Guide* has featured an Index by Price that groups public and private institutions into four price categories, from inexpensive to very expensive. Now we have gone one step further: we have combined the cost data with academic and other information about each college and university, and have come up with forty-three institutions—twenty public and twenty-three private—that offer remarkable educational opportunities at a relatively modest cost. We are calling them Best Buys, and they are indicated by a Best Buy graphic next to the college name. (A list of the 2005 Best Buys appears on page xv.)

All of our Best Buys fall into the inexpensive or moderate price category, and most have four- or five-star academic ratings. But there are bargains to be found among all levels and types of institutions. For example, some of the best values in American higher education are public colleges and universities that have remained relatively small and offer the smaller classes and personalized approach to academics that are typically found only in expensive private liberal arts colleges. Several of these are included as Best Buys.

STATISTICS

At the beginning of each write-up are basic statistics about the college or university—the ones that are relevant to applicants. These include the address, type of location (urban, small town, rural, etc.), enrollment, male/female ratio, SAT or ACT score ranges of the middle 50 percent of the students, percentage of students receiving need-based financial aid, relative cost, whether or not the institution has a chapter of Phi Beta Kappa, the number of students who apply and the percentage of those who are accepted, the percentage of accepted students who enroll, the number of freshmen who graduate within six years, and the number of freshmen who return for their sophomore year. For convenience, we include the telephone number of the admissions office and the school's website and mailing address.

Unlike some guides, we have intentionally not published figures on the student/faculty ratio because colleges use different—and often self-serving—methods to calculate the ratio, thus making it virtually meaningless.

A word about several of these items:

You will sometimes encounter the letters "N/A." In most cases, this means that the statistic was not available. In other cases, however, such as schools that do not require standardized tests, it means "not applicable." The write-up should make it clear which meaning is the relevant one.

We have included information on whether the school has a chapter of Phi Beta Kappa because this academic honorary society is a sign of broad intellectual distinction. Keep in mind, though, that even the very best engineering schools, because of their relatively narrow focus, do not usually qualify under the society's standards.

Tuition and fees are constantly increasing at American colleges, but for the most part, the cost of various institutions in relation to one another does not change. Rather than put in specific cost figures that would immediately become out of date, we have classified colleges into four groups ranging from inexpensive ($) to very expensive ($$$$) based on estimated costs of tuition, fees, and housing for the 2002–2003 academic year. Separate scales were used for public and private institutions, and the ratings for the public institutions are based on cost for residents of the state; out-of-staters should expect to pay more. If a public institution has a particularly low or high surcharge for out-of-staters, this is noted in the essay. The categories are defined as follows:

	PUBLIC	PRIVATE
$$$$	More than $16,000	More than $38,000
$$$	$14,000–$16,000	$34,000–$38,000
$$	$11,000–$14,000	$30,000–$34,000
$	Less than $11,000	Less than $30,000

We also include an index that groups colleges by their relative cost (see Index by Price pages xii–xiv).

SAT and ACT SCORES

A special word needs to be said about SAT and ACT scores. Some publications follow the practice of giving the median or average score registered by entering freshmen. Such figures, however, are easily misinterpreted as thresholds rather than averages. Many applicants forget that if a school reports average SAT-Verbal scores of 500, this means that, by definition, about half of the students scored below this number and half scored above. An applicant with a 480 would still have lots of company.

To avoid such confusion, we report the range of scores of the middle half of freshmen—or, to put it another way, the scores achieved by those in the twenty-fifth and seventy-fifth percentiles. For example, that college where the SAT-Verbal average was 500 might have a range of 440 to 560. So if you scored within this range, you would have joined the middle 50 percent of last year's freshmen. If your score was above 560, you would have been in the top quarter and could probably look forward to a relatively easy time; if it was below 440, you would have been struggling along with the bottom quarter of students.

The reporting of ranges rather than a single average is an increasingly common practice, but some colleges do not calculate ranges. These are indicated by "N/A." Keep in mind, as well, that score ranges (and averages, for that matter) are misleading at colleges such as Bates, Bowdoin, and Union, which do not require test scores from all applicants. The ranges given for these colleges represent the range of scores of students who choose to submit their test scores, although they are not required to do so.

Unfortunately, another problem that arises with SAT and ACT scores is that, in their zeal to make themselves look good in a competitive market, some colleges and universities have been known to be less than honest in the numbers they release. They inflate their scores by not counting certain categories of students at the low end of the scale, such as athletes, certain types of transfer students, or students admitted under affirmative-action programs. Some colleges have gone to such extremes as reporting the relatively high math scores of foreign students, but not their relatively low verbal scores. Aside from the sheer dishonesty of such practices, they can also be misleading. A student whose own scores are below the twenty-fifth percentile of a particular institution needs to know whether his profile matches that of the lower quarter of the student body as a whole or whether there is an unreported pool of students with lower scores.

Even when dealing with a range rather than a single score, keep in mind that standardized tests are an imprecise measure of academic ability, and comparisons of scores that differ by less than 50 or 60 points on a scale of 200 to 800 have little meaning. According to the laws of statistics, there is one chance in three that the 550 that arrived in the little envelope from ETS should really be at least 580 or no more than 520. On the other hand, median scores offer some indication of your chances to get into a particular institution and the intellectual level of the company you will be keeping—or, if you prefer, competing against. Remember, too, that the most competitive schools have the largest and most sophisticated admissions staffs and are well aware of the limitations of standardized tests. A strong high school average or achievement in a field such as music will usually counteract the negative effects of modest SAT or ACT scores.

SCHOLARSHIP INFORMATION

Since the first edition of the *Fiske Guide to Colleges* appeared, the problems of financing college have become increasingly critical, mainly because of the rising cost of education and a shift from grants to loans as the basis for financial-aid packages.

In response to these developments, many colleges and universities have begun to devise their own plans to help students pay for college. These range from subsidized loan programs to merit scholarships that are awarded without reference to financial need. Most of these programs are aimed at retaining the middle class.

We ask each college and university to tell us what steps it has taken to help students pay their way, and their responses are incorporated in the write-ups. Also indicated is whether a candidate's inability to pay the full tuition, room, and board charges is a factor in admissions decisions. Some colleges advertise that they are "need blind" in their admissions, meaning that they accept or reject applicants without reference to their financial situation and then guarantee to meet the "demonstrated need" of all students whom they accept. Others say they are need blind in their admissions decisions, but do not guarantee to provide the financial aid required of all those who are accepted. Still others agree to meet the demonstrated need of all students, but they package their offers so that students whom they really want receive a higher percentage of their aid in the form of outright grants than in repayable loans.

"Demonstrated need" is itself a slippery term. In theory, the figure is determined when students and families fill out a needs-analysis form, which leads to an estimate of how much the family can afford to pay. Demonstrated need is then calculated by subtracting that figure from the cost at a particular institution. In practice, however, various colleges make their own adjustments to the standard figure.

Students and parents should not assume that because their family has even a six-figure income they are automatically disqualified from some kind of subsidized financial aid. In cases of doubt, they should fill out a needs-analysis form to determine their eligibility. Whether they qualify or not, they are also eligible for a variety of awards made without regard to financial need.

Inasmuch as need-based awards are universal at the colleges in this guide, the awards generally singled out for special mention in the write-ups in the *Fiske Guide to Colleges* are the merit scholarships. We have not mentioned awards of a purely local nature—restricted to residents of a particular county, for example—but all college applicants should search out these awards through their guidance offices and the bulletins of the colleges that are of interest to them. Similarly, we have not duplicated the information on federally guaranteed loan programs that is readily available through both high school and college counseling offices, but we cite novel and often less-expensive variants of the federal loan programs that are offered by individual colleges.

For more information on the ever-changing financial-aid scene, we suggest that you consult the companion book to this guide, *Fiske Guide to Getting into the Right College*.

RATINGS

Much of the controversy that greeted the first edition of the *Fiske Guide to Colleges* revolved around its unique system of rating colleges in three areas: academics, social life, and quality of life. In each case, the ratings are done on a system of one to five, with three considered normal for colleges included in the *Fiske Guide*. If a college receives a rating higher or lower than three in any category, the reasons should be apparent from the narrative description of that college.

Students and parents should keep in mind that these ratings are obviously general in nature and inherently subjective. No complex institution can be described in terms of a single number or other symbol, and different people will have different views of how various institutions should be rated in the three categories. They should not be viewed as either precise or infallible judgments about any given college. On the other hand, the ratings are a helpful tool in using this book. The core of the *Fiske Guide* is the essays on each of the colleges, and the ratings represent a summary—an index, if you will—of these write-ups. Our hope is that each student, having decided on the kind of configuration that suits his or her needs, will then thumb through the book looking for other institutions with a similar set of ratings.

The categories are defined as follows.

Academics ✎

This is a judgment about the overall academic climate of the institution, including its reputation in the academic world, the quality of the faculty, the level of teaching and research, the academic ability of students, the quality of libraries and other facilities, and the level of academic seriousness among students and faculty members.

Although the same basic criteria have been applied to all institutions, it should be evident that an outstanding small liberal arts college will by definition differ significantly from an outstanding major public university. No one would expect the former to have massive library facilities, but one would look for a high-quality faculty that combines research with a good deal of attention to the individual needs of students. Likewise, public universities, because of their implicit commitment to serving a broad cross-section of society, might have a broader range of curriculum offerings but somewhat lower average SAT scores than a large private counterpart. Readers may find the ratings most useful when comparing colleges and universities of the same type.

In general, an academics rating of three pens suggests that the institution is a solid one that easily meets the criteria for inclusion in a guide devoted to the top 10 percent of colleges and universities in the nation.

An academics rating of four pens suggests that the institution is above average even by these standards and that it has some particularly distinguishing academic feature, such as especially rich course offerings or an especially serious academic atmosphere.

A rating of five pens for academics indicates that the college or university is among the handful of top institutions of its type in the nation on a broad variety of criteria. Those in the private sector will normally attract students with combined SAT scores of at least 1300, and those in the public sector are invariably magnets for the top students in their states. All can be assumed to have outstanding faculties and other academic resources.

For the 2005 edition, in response to the suggestion that the range of colleges within a single category has been too broad, we have introduced some half-steps into the ratings.

Social Life ☎

This is primarily a judgment about the amount of social life that is readily available. A rating of three telephones suggests a typical college social life, while four telephones means that students have a better-than-average time socially. It can be assumed that a college with a rating of five is something of a party school, which may or may not detract from the academic quality. Colleges with a rating below three have some impediment to a strong social life, such as geographic isolation, a high percentage of commuting students, or a disproportionate number of nerds who never leave the library. Once again, the reason should be evident from the write-up.

Quality of Life ★

This category grew out of the fact that schools with good academic credentials and plenty of social life may not, for one reason or another, be particularly wholesome places to spend four years. The term "quality of life" is one that has been gaining currency in social science circles, and, in most cases, the rating for a particular college will be similar to the academic and/or social ratings. The reader, though, should be alert to exceptions to this pattern. A liberal arts college, for example, might attract bright students who study hard during the week and party hard on weekends, and thus earn high ratings for academics and social life. If the academic pressure is cut-throat rather than constructive, though, and the social system is manipulative of women, this college might get an apparently anomalous two stars for quality of life. By contrast, a small college with modest academic programs and relatively few organized social opportunities might have developed a strong sense of supportive community, have a beautiful campus, and be located near a wonderful city—and thus be rated four stars for quality of life. As in the other categories, the reason can be found in the essay to which the ratings point.

OVERLAPS

Most colleges and universities operate within fairly defined "niche markets." That is, they compete for students against other institutions with whom they share important characteristics, such as academic quality, size, geographical location, and the overall tone and style of campus life. Not surprisingly, students who apply to College X also tend to apply to the other institutions in its particular niche. For example, "alternative" colleges such as Bard, Bennington, Hampshire, Marlboro, Oberlin, Reed, and Sarah Lawrence share many common applications, as do those with an evangelical flavor, such as Calvin, Hope, and Wheaton (IL).

As a service to readers, we ask each school to give us the names of the five colleges with which they share the most common applications, and these are listed in the Overlaps section at the end of each write-up. We encourage students who know they are interested in a particular institution to check out the schools with which it competes—and perhaps then check out the "overlaps of the overlaps." This method of systematic browsing should yield a list of fifteen or twenty schools that, based on the behavior of thousands of past applicants, would constitute a good starting point for the college search.

IF YOU APPLY...

An extremely helpful feature is the If You Apply... section at the end of each write-up. This is designed for students who become seriously interested in a particular college and want to know more specifics about what it takes to get in.

This section begins with the deadlines for early admissions or early decision (if the college has such a program), regular admissions, and financial aid. If the college operates on a rolling-admissions basis—making decisions as the applications are received—this is indicated.

If You Apply... gives a snapshot of the institution's financial-aid policies. It indicates whether the college or university guarantees to meet the demonstrated need of applicants and, if so, the percentage of students whose financial need is actually met. The phrase "guarantees to meet demonstrated need" means that the institution for all practical purposes makes every effort possible to come up with the aid for which all of its students qualify.

Colleges have widely varying policies regarding interviews, both on campus and with alumni, so we indicate whether each of these is required, recommended, or optional. We also indicate whether reports from the person doing the interview are used in evaluating students or whether, as in many cases, the interview is seen only as a means of conveying information about the institution and answering applicants' questions.

This section also tells what standardized tests—SAT, ACT, or achievement—are required, and whether applicants are asked to write one or more essays. In the latter case, the topics are given.

The admissions policies of most colleges are fairly similar, at least among competing clusters of institutions. In some cases, however, a school will have its own special priorities. Some don't care that much about test scores. Others are looking for students with special talent in math or science, while others pay special attention to personal characteristics such as leadership in extracurricular activities. We asked each institution to tell us if its admission policies are in any ways "unique or unusual," and their answers are reported.

CONSORTIA

Many colleges expand the range of their offerings by banding together with other institutions to offer unusual programs that they could not support on their own. These options range from foreign-study programs around the world to semesters at sea, and keeping such arrangements in mind is a way of expanding the list of institutions that might meet your particular interests and needs. The final section of the *Fiske Guide* describes sixteen of these consortia and lists the member institutions.

MOVING FORWARD

Students will find the *Fiske Guide* useful at various points in the college-selection process—from deciding whether to visit a particular campus to selecting among institutions that have accepted them. To make it easy to find a particular college, the write-ups are arranged in alphabetical order in the index. Indexes by state and price can be found on pages ix and xii, respectively.

While most people are not likely to start reading at Agnes Scott and keep going until they reach Yale (though some tell us they do), we encourage you to browse. This country has an enormously rich and varied network of colleges and universities, and there are dozens of institutions out there that can meet the needs of any particular student. Too many students approach the college-selection process wearing blinders, limiting their sights to local institutions, the pet schools of their parents or guidance counselors, or to ones they know only by possibly outdated reputations.

But applicants need not be bound by such limitations. Once you have decided on the type of school you think you want—a small liberal arts college, an engineering school, or whatever—we hope you will thumb through the book looking for similar institutions that might not have occurred to you. One way to do this is to look at the overlaps of schools you like and then check out those schools' overlaps. Many students have found this worthwhile, and quite frankly, we view the widening of students' horizons about American higher education as one of the most important purposes of the book. Perhaps the most gratifying remark we hear comes when a student tells us, as many have, that she is attending a school that she first heard about while browsing through the *Fiske Guide to Colleges*.

Picking a college is a tricky business. But given the current buyer's market, there is no reason why you should not be able to find the right college. That's what the *Fiske Guide to Colleges* is designed to help you do. Happy college hunting.

Sizing Yourself Up

The college search is a game of matchmaking. You have interests and needs; the colleges have programs to meet those needs. If all goes according to plan, you'll find the right one and live happily ever after——or at least for four years. It ought to be simple, but today's admissions process resembles a high-stakes obstacle course.

Many colleges are more interested in making a sale than they are in making a match. Under intense competitive pressure, many won't hesitate to sell you a bill of goods if they can get their hands on your tuition dollars. Guidance counselors generally mean well, but they are often under duress from principals and trustees to steer students toward prestigious schools regardless of whether the fit is right. Your friends won't be shy with advice on where to go, but their knowledge is generally limited to a small group of hot colleges that everyone is talking about. National publications rake in millions by playing on the public's fascination with rankings, but a close look at their criteria reveals distinctions without a difference.

Before you find yourself spinning headlong on this merry-go-round, take a step back. This is your life and your college career. What are you looking for in a college? Think hard, and don't answer right away. Before you throw yourself and your life history on the mercy of college-admissions officers, you need to take some time to objectively and honestly evaluate your needs, likes and dislikes, strengths and weaknesses. What do you have to offer a college? What can a college do for you? Unlike the high school selection process, which is usually predetermined by your parents' property lines, income level, or religious affiliation, picking a college isn't a procedure you can brush off on dear ol' Mom and Dad. You have to take some initiative. You're the best judge of how well each school fits your personal needs and academic goals.

We encourage you to view the college-selection process as the first semester in your higher education. Life's transitions often call forth extra energy and focus. The college search is no exception. For the first time, you'll be contemplating a life away from home that can unfold in any direction you choose. Visions of majors and careers will dance in your head as you sample various institutions of higher learning, each with hundreds of millions of dollars in academic resources; it is hard to imagine a better hands-on seminar in research and matchmaking than the college search. The main impact, however, will be measured by what you learn about yourself. Piqued by new worlds of learning and tested by the competition of the admissions process, you'll be pushed as never before to show your accomplishments, clarify your interests, and chart a course for the future. More than one parent has watched in amazement as an erstwhile teenager suddenly emerged as an adult during the course of a college tour. Be ready when your time comes.

DEVELOP YOUR CRITERIA

One strategy is to begin the search with a personal inventory of your own strengths and weaknesses and your "wish list" for a college. This method tends to work well for compulsive list-makers and other highly organized people. What sorts of things are you especially good at? Do you have a list of skills or interests that you would like to explore further? What sort of personality are you looking for in a college? Mainstream? Conservative? Offbeat? What about extracurriculars? If you are really into riding horses, you might include a strong equestrian program in your criteria. The main problem won't be thinking of qualities to look for—you could probably name dozens—but rather figuring out what criteria should play a defining role in your search. Serious students should think carefully about the intellectual climate they are seeking. At some schools, students routinely stay up until 3:00 A.M. talking about topics like the value of deconstructing literary texts or the pros and cons of free trade. These same students would be viewed as geeks or weirdos on less cosmopolitan campuses. Athletes should take a hard look at whether they really want to play college ball, and if so, whether they want to go for an athletic scholarship or play at the less-pressured Division III level. Either way, intercollegiate sports require a huge time commitment.

Young women have an opportunity all to themselves—the chance to study at a women's college. The *Fiske Guide* profiles fourteen such campuses, a vastly underappreciated resource on today's higher education scene. With small classes and strong encouragement from faculty, students at women's colleges move on to graduate study in significantly higher numbers than their counterparts at coed schools, especially in the natural sciences. Males seeking an all-male experience will find two options in the *Fiske Guide*, Hampden-Sydney College and Wabash College.

Students with a firm career goal will want to look for a course of study that matches their needs. If you want to major in aerospace engineering, your search will be limited to schools that have the program. Outside of specialized areas like this, many applicants overestimate the importance of their anticipated major in choosing a college. If you're interested in a liberal arts field, your expected major should probably have little to do with your college selection. A big purpose of college is to develop interests and set goals. Most students change their intentions regarding a major at least two or three times before graduation, and once out in the working world, they often end up in jobs bearing no relation to their academic specialty. Even those with a firm career goal may not need as much specialization as they think at the undergraduate level. If you want to be a lawyer, don't worry yourself looking for something labeled prelaw. Follow your interests, get the best liberal arts education available, and then apply to law school.

Naturally, it is never a bad idea to check out the department(s) of any likely major, and occasionally your choice of major will suggest a direction for your search. If you're really into national politics, it may make sense to look at some schools in or near Washington, D.C. If you think you're interested in a relatively specialized field, say, oceanography, then be sure to look for some colleges that are a good match for you and also have programs in oceanography. But for the most part, rumors about top-ranked departments in this or that should be no more than a tie-breaker between schools you like for more important reasons. There are good professors (and bad ones) in any department. You'll have plenty of time to figure out who is who once you've enrolled. Being undecided about your career path as a senior in high school is often a sign of intelligence. Don't feel bad if you have absolutely no idea what you're going to do when you "grow up." One of the reasons you'll be paying megabucks to the college of your choice is the prospect that it will open some new doors for you and expand your horizons. Instead of worrying about particular departments, try to keep the focus on big-picture items like, What's the academic climate? How big are the freshman classes? Do I like it here? and Are these my kind of people?

KEEP AN OPEN MIND

The biggest mistake of beginning applicants is hyper-choosiness. At the extreme is the "perfect-school syndrome," which comes in two basic forms.

In one category are the applicants who refuse to consider any school that doesn't have every little thing they want in a college. If you're one who begins the process with a detailed picture of Perfect U. in mind, you may want to remember the oft-quoted advice, "Two out of three ain't bad." If a college seems to have most of the qualities you seek, give it a chance. You may come to realize that some things you thought were absolutely essential are really not that crucial after all.

The other strain of perfect-school syndrome is the applicant who gets stuck on a "dream" school at the beginning and then won't look anywhere else. With those twenty-two hundred four-year colleges out there (not counting those in Canada), it is just a bit silly to insist that only one will meet your needs. Having a first choice is OK, but the whole purpose of the search is to consider new options and uncover new possibilities. A student who has only one dream school—especially if it is a highly selective one—could be headed for disappointment.

As you begin the college search, don't expect any quick revelations. The answers will unfold in due time. Our advice? Be patient. Set priorities. Keep an open mind. Reexamine priorities. Again, be patient.

To get the ball rolling, move on to the Sizing-Yourself-Up Survey.

FISKE'S SIZING-YOURSELF-UP SURVEY

With apologies to Socrates, knowing thyself is easier said than done. Most high school students can analyze a differential equation or a Shakespearean play with the greatest of ease, but when it comes to cataloging their own strengths, weaknesses, likes, and dislikes, many draw a blank. But self-knowledge is crucial to the matching process at the heart of a successful college search. The thirty-item survey below offers a simple way to get a handle on some crucial issues in college selection—and what sort of college may fit your preferences.

In the space beside each statement, rate your feelings on a scale of 1 to 10, with 10 = Strongly Agree, 1 = Strongly Disagree, and 5 = Not Sure/Don't Have Strong Feelings. (For instance, a rating of 7 would mean that you agree with the statement, but that the issue is a lower priority than those you rated 8, 9, or 10.) After you're done, read on to Grading Yourself to find out what it all means.

Size

_____ 1) I enjoy participating in many activities.

_____ 2) I would like to have a prominent place in my community.

_____ 3) Individual attention from teachers is important to me.

_____ 4) I learn best when I can speak out in class and ask questions.

_____ 5) I am undecided about what I will study.

_____ 6) I want to earn a Ph.D. in my chosen field of study.

_____ 7) I learn best by listening and writing what I hear.

_____ 8) I would like to be in a place where I can be anonymous if I choose.

_____ 9) I prefer devoting my time to one or two activities rather than many.

_____ 10) I want to attend a college that most people have heard of.

_____ 11) I am interested in a career-oriented major.

_____ 12) I like to be on my own.

Location

_____ 13) I prefer a college in a warm or hot climate.

_____ 14) I prefer a college in a cool or cold climate.

_____ 15) I want to be near the mountains.

_____ 16) I want to be near a lake or ocean.

_____ 17) I prefer to attend a college in a particular state or region.

_____ 18) I prefer to attend a college near my family.

_____ 19) I want city life within walking distance of my campus.

_____ 20) I want city life within driving distance of my campus.

_____ 21) I want my campus to be surrounded by natural beauty.

Academics and Extracurriculars

_____ 22) I like to be surrounded by people who are free-thinkers and nonconformists.

_____ 23) I like the idea of joining a fraternity or sorority.

_____ 24) I like rubbing shoulders with people who are bright and talented.

_____ 25) I like being one of the smartest people in my class.

_____ 26) I want to go to a prestigious college.

_____ 27) I want to go to a college where I can get an excellent education.

_____ 28) I want to try for an academic scholarship.

_____ 29) I want a diverse college.

_____ 30) I want a college where the students are serious about ideas.

Grading Yourself

Picking a college is not an exact science. People who are total opposites can be equally happy at the same college. Nevertheless, particular types tend to do better at some colleges than others. Each item in the survey is designed to test your feelings on an important issue related to college selection. Sizing Up the Survey (below) offers commentary on each item.

Taken together, your responses may help you construct a tentative blueprint for your college search. Statements 1–12 deal with the issue of size. Would you be happier at a large university or a small college? Here's the trick: add the sum of your responses to questions 1–6. Then make a second tally of your responses to 7–12. If the sum of 1–6 is larger, you may want to consider a small college. If 7–12 is greater, then perhaps a big school would be more to your liking. If the totals are roughly equal, you should probably consider colleges of various sizes.

Statements 13–21 deal with location. The key in this section is the intensity of your feeling. If you replied to No. 13 with a 10, does that mean you are going to look only at schools in warm climates? Think hard. If you consider only schools within a certain region or state, you'll be eliminating hundreds of possibilities. By examining your most intense responses—the 1s, 2s, 9s, and 10s—you'll be able to create a geographic profile of likely options.

Statements 22–30 deal with big-picture issues related to the character and personality of the college that may be in your future. As before, pay attention to your most intense responses. Read on for a look at the significance of each question.

Sizing Up the Survey

1. **I enjoy participating in many activities.** Students at small colleges tend to have more opportunities to be involved in many activities. Fewer students means less competition for spots.

2. **I would like to have a prominent place in my community.** Student-council presidents and other would-be leaders take note: it is easier to be a big fish if you're swimming in a small pond.

3. **Individual attention from teachers is important to me.** Small colleges generally offer more one-on-one with faculty both in the classroom and the laboratory.

4. **I learn best when I can speak out in class and ask questions.** Students who learn from interaction and participation would be well-advised to consider a small college.

5. **I am undecided about what I will study.** Small colleges generally offer more guidance and support to students who are undecided. The exception: students who are considering a preprofessional or highly specialized major.

6. **I want to earn a Ph.D. in my chosen field of study.** A higher percentage of students at selective small colleges earn a Ph.D. than those who attend large institutions of similar quality.

7. **I learn best by listening and writing what I hear.** Students who prefer lecture courses will find more of them at large institutions.

8. **I would like to be in a place where I can be anonymous if I choose to be.** At a large university, the supply of new faces is never-ending. Students who have the initiative can always reinvent themselves.

9. **I prefer devoting my time to one or two activities rather than many.** Students who are passionate about one activity—say, writing for the college newspaper—will often find higher quality at a bigger school.

10. **I want to attend a college that most people have heard of.** Big schools have more name recognition because they're bigger and have Division I athletic programs. Even the finest small colleges are relatively anonymous among the general public

11. **I am interested in a career-oriented major.** More large institutions offer business, engineering, nursing, etc., though some excellent small institutions do so as well (depending on the field).

12. **I like to be on my own.** A higher percentage of students live off campus at large schools, which are more likely to be in urban areas than their smaller counterparts.

13. **I prefer a college in a warm or hot climate.** Keep in mind that the Southeast and the Southwest have far different personalities (not to mention humidity levels).

14. **I prefer a college in a cool or cold climate.** Consider the Midwest, where there are many fine schools that are notably less selective than those in the Northeast.

15. **I want to be near the mountains.** You're probably thinking Colorado or Vermont, but don't zero in too quickly. States from Maine to Georgia and Arkansas to Arizona have easy access to mountains.

16. **I want to be near a lake or ocean.** Oceans are only on the coasts, but keep in mind the Great Lakes, the Finger Lakes, etc. Think about whether you want to be on the water or, say, within a two-hour drive.

17. **I prefer to attend a college in a particular state or region.** Geographical blinders limit options. Even if you think you want a certain area of the country, consider at least one college located elsewhere just to be sure.

18. **I prefer to attend a college close to home.** Unless you're planning to live with Mom and Dad, it may not matter whether your college is a two-hour drive or a two-hour plane ride.

19. **I want city life within walking distance of my campus.** Check out the neighborhood(s) surrounding your campus. Urban campuses—even in the same city—can be wildly different.

20. **I want city life within driving distance of my campus.** Unless you're a hardcore urban-dweller, a suburban perch near a city may beat living in the thick of one. Does public transportation or a campus shuttle help students get around?

21. **I want my campus to be surrounded by natural beauty.** A college viewbook will take you only so far. To really know if you'll fall in love with the campus, visiting is a must.

22. **I like to be surrounded by free-thinkers and nonconformists.** Plenty of schools cater specifically to students who buck the mainstream. Talk to your counselor or browse *The Fiske Guide to Colleges* to find some.

23. **I like the idea of joining a fraternity or sorority.** Greek life is strongest at mainstream and conservative-leaning schools. Find out if there is a split between Greeks and non-Greeks.

24. **I like rubbing shoulders with people who are bright and talented.** This is perhaps the best reason to aim for a highly selective institution, especially if you're the type who rises to the level of the competition.

25. **I like being one of the smartest people in my class.** If so, maybe you should skip the highly selective rat race. Star students get the best that a college has to offer.

26. **I want to go to a prestigious college.** There is nothing wrong with wanting prestige. Think honestly about how badly you want a big-name school and act accordingly.

27. **I want to go to a college where I can get an excellent education.** Throw out the *U.S. News* rankings and think about which colleges will best meet your needs as a student.

28. **I want to try for an academic scholarship.** Students in this category should consider less-selective alternatives. Scholarships are more likely if you rank high in the applicant pool.

29. **I want a diverse college.** All colleges pay lip service to diversity. To get the truth, see the campus for yourself and take a hard look at the student-body statistics in the *Guide*'s write-ups.

30. **I want a college where students are serious about ideas.** Don't assume that a college necessarily attracts true intellectuals merely because it is highly selective. Some top schools are known for their intellectual climate—and others for their lack of it.

Putting It All Together

We hope the survey will help you get started on a thorough self-assessment that will continue throughout the college search. After thinking about your priorities, the time is right to begin looking at the colleges. Hundreds of them await!

Use the state-by-state index to search geographically if you like, or simply browse to find those that interest you. When you find a likely candidate, look to the Overlaps at the end of the article to find additional possibilities.

A Guide for Preprofessionals

The lists that follow include colleges and universities with unusual strength in each of nine preprofessional areas: engineering, architecture, business, art/design, drama, dance, music, communications/journalism, and film/television. We also offer lists covering two of today's hottest interdisciplinary majors: environmental studies and international studies. In compiling the lists, we drew on data from the thousands of surveys used to compile the *Fiske Guide*. We examined the strongest majors at each college as reported in student and administrative questionnaires, and then weighed these against the selectivity and overall academic quality of each institution. After compiling tentative lists in each subject, we queried our counselor advisory group, listed at the back of this volume, for additional suggestions and feedback. In order to make the lists as useful as possible, we have included some schools that do not receive full-length write-ups in the *Fiske Guide*. Moreover, while the lists are suggestive, they are by no means all-inclusive, and there are other institutions in the *Fiske Guide to Colleges* that offer fine programs in these areas. Nevertheless, we hope the lists will be a starting place for students interested in these fields.

If you are planning a career in one of the subjects below, your college search may focus largely on finding the best programs for you in that particular area. But we also recommend that you shop for a school that will give you an adequate dose of liberal arts. For that matter, you might consider a double major (or minor) in a liberal arts field to complement your area of technical expertise. If you allow yourself to get too specialized too soon, you may end up as tomorrow's equivalent of the typewriter repairman. In a rapidly changing job market, nothing is so practical as the ability to read, write, and think.

ARCHITECTURE

Private Universities Strong in Architecture

Carnegie Mellon University
Catholic University of America
Columbia University
Cooper Union
Cornell University (NY)
Drexel University
Hobart and William Smith Colleges
Howard University
Lehigh University
Massachusetts Institute of Technology
University of Miami (FL)
New Jersey Institute of Technology
Northeastern University
University of Notre Dame
Princeton University
Rensselaer Polytechnic Institute
Rice University
Temple University
Tuskegee University
Tulane University
Washington University in St. Louis

Public Universities Strong in Architecture

University of Arizona
University of California–Berkeley
University of Cincinnati
Clemson University
University of Florida
Georgia Institute of Technology
University of Illinois–Urbana-Champaign
University of Kansas
Kansas State University
University Maryland
Miami University (OH)
University of Michigan
University of Nebraska
State University of New York–Buffalo
University of Oregon
Pennsylvania State University
Texas A&M University
University of Texas–Austin
Virginia Polytechnic Institute and State University (Virginia Tech)
University of Washington

A Few Arts-Oriented Architecture Programs

Barnard College
Bennington College
Pratt Institute
Rhode Island School of Design
Savannah School of Art and Design
Wellesley College
Yale University

ART/DESIGN

Top Schools of Art and Design

Art Center College of Design
California College of the Arts
California Institute of the Arts
Cooper Union
Kansas City Art Institute
Maryland Institute, College of Art
Massachusetts College of Art
Moore College of Art and Design
North Carolina School of the Arts
Otis Institute of Art and Design
Parsons School of Design
Pratt Institute
Rhode Island School of Design
Ringling School of Art and Design
San Francisco Art Institute
Savannah College of Art and Design
School of the Art Institute of Chicago
School of the Museum of Fine Arts (MA)
School of Visual Arts (NY)

Major Universities Strong in Art or Design

American University
Boston College
Boston University
Carnegie Mellon University
University of Cincinnati
Cornell University
Drexel University
Harvard University
University of Michigan
New York University
University of North Carolina/
  Greensboro
University of Pennsylvania
Syracuse University
Washington University in St. Louis
University of Washington
Yale University

Small Colleges and Universities Strong in Art or Design

Alfred University
Bard College
Brown University
Centre College
Cornell College
Dartmouth College
Furman University
Hollins University
Kenyon College
Lake Forest College
Lewis and Clark
Manhattanville College
Mills College
State University of New
  York–Purchase
Randolph-Macon Woman's College
University of North
  Carolina–Greensboro
Sarah Lawrence College
Scripps College
Skidmore College
Smith College
Southwestern University
Vassar College
Wheaton College (MA)
Willamette University
Williams College

BUSINESS

Major Private Universities Strong in Business

American University
Baylor University
Boston College
Boston University
Carnegie Mellon University
Case Western Reserve University
University of Dayton
Emory University
Fordham University
Georgetown University
Howard University
Ithaca College
Lehigh University
Massachusetts Institute of
  Technology
New York University
University of Notre Dame
University of Pennsylvania
Pepperdine University
Rensselaer Polytechnic Institute
University of San Francisco
Santa Clara University
University of Southern California
Southern Methodist University
Syracuse University
Texas Christian University
Tulane University
Villanova University
Wake Forest University
Washington University in St. Louis

Public Universities Strong in Business

University of Arizona
University of California–Berkeley
University of Cincinnati
University of Connecticut
University of Florida
University of Georgia
University of Illinois–Urbana-
  Champaign
Indiana University
James Madison University
University of Kansas
University of Maryland
University of
  Massachusetts–Amherst

Miami University (OH)
University of Michigan
University of Missouri
University of North
  Carolina–Chapel Hill
Ohio State University
University of Ohio
University of Oregon
Pennsylvania State University
University of Pittsburgh
Rutgers, The State University of
  New Jersey
University of South Carolina
SUNY–Albany
SUNY–Binghamton University
SUNY–Buffalo
SUNY–Geneseo
University of Tennessee
Texas A&M University
University of Texas–Austin
University of Vermont
University of Virginia
University of Washington
University of Wisconsin
College of William and Mary

Small Colleges and Universities Strong in Business

Agnes Scott College
Babson College
Bucknell University
Calvin College
Claremont McKenna College
Clarkson University
Eckerd College
Fairfield University
Franklin and Marshall College
Furman University
Gettysburg College
Guilford College
Hendrix College
Lafayette College
Lake Forest College
Lehigh University
Lewis and Clark College
Millsaps College
Morehouse College
Muhlenberg College
Oglethorpe College
Ohio Wesleyan University

Presbyterian College
Rhodes College
University of Richmond
Ripon College
Skidmore College
Southwestern University
Stetson College
Susquehanna University
Trinity University (TX)
Washington and Jefferson College
Washington and Lee University
Whittier College
Wofford College
Worcester Polytechnic Institute
Xavier University of Louisiana

COMMUNICATIONS/ JOURNALISM

Major Universities Strong in Communications/Journalism

American University
Arizona State University
Boston University
University of California–Los
  Angeles
University of California–San Diego
University of Florida
University of Georgia
University of Illinois–Urbana-
  Champaign
Indiana University
Ithaca College
University of Kansas
University of Maryland
University of Michigan
University of Missouri–Columbia
University of Nebraska
University of North
  Carolina–Chapel Hill
Northwestern University
Ohio University
University of Oregon
Pepperdine University
St. Lawrence University
University of San Francisco
University of Southern California
Stanford University
Syracuse University
Texas Christian University
University of Utah
University of Wisconsin–Madison

ENGINEERING

Top Technical Institutes

California Institute of Technology
California Polytechnic Institute–San
  Luis Obispo
Colorado School of Mines
Cooper Union
Florida Institute of Technology
Georgia Institute of Technology
Harvey Mudd College
Illinois Institute of Technology
Massachusetts Institute of
  Technology
Michigan Technological University
Montana Tech of the University of
  Montana
New Jersey Institute of Technology
New Mexico Institute of Mining
  and Technology
Rensselaer Polytechnic Institute
Rochester Institute of Technology
Rose-Hulman Institute of
  Technology
Stevens Institute of Technology
Worcester Polytechnic Institute

Private Universities Strong in Engineering

Boston University
Bradley University
Brigham Young University
Brown University
Carnegie Mellon University
Case Western Reserve University
Catholic University of America
Columbia University
Cornell University
Drexel University
Duke University
George Washington University
Johns Hopkins University
Northeastern University
Northwestern University
University of Notre Dame
University of Pennsylvania
Princeton University
University of Rochester
Rochester Institute of Technology
Santa Clara University
University of Southern California
Southern Methodist University

Stanford University
Syracuse University
Tufts University
Tulane University
University of Tulsa
Vanderbilt University
Villanova University
Washington University in St. Louis

Public Universities Strong in Engineering

University of Arizona
University of California–Berkeley
University of California–Davis
University of California–Los
  Angeles
University of California–San Diego
University of Cincinnati
Clemson University
University of Connecticut
University of Delaware
University of Florida
University of Illinois–Urbana-
  Champaign
Iowa State University
University of Kansas
McGill University
University of Maryland
University of
  Massachusetts–Amherst
University of Michigan
Michigan State University
University of Missouri–Rolla
University of New Hampshire
College of New Jersey
North Carolina State University
Ohio State University
Oregon State University
Pennsylvania State University
Purdue University
Queen's University (CA)
University of Rhode Island
Rutgers, The State University of
  New Jersey
SUNY–Binghamton University
SUNY–Buffalo
Texas A&M University
Texas Tech University
University of Texas–Austin
University of Toronto
Virginia Polytechnic Institute and
  State University (Virginia Tech)

University of Virginia
University of Washington
University of Wisconsin

Small Colleges and Universities Strong in Engineering

Alfred University
Bucknell University
Butler University
Calvin College
Clarkson University
Dartmouth College
Lafayette College
Lehigh University
Loyola University (MD)
University of the Pacific
Rice University
Smith College
Spelman College
Swarthmore College
Trinity College (CT)
Trinity University (TX)
University of Tulsa
Tuskegee University
Union College

FILM/TELEVISION

Major Universities Strong in Film/Television

Arizona State University
Boston University
University of California–Los Angeles
University of Cincinnati
Drexel University
University of Florida
Ithaca College
University of Kansas
Memphis State University
University of Michigan
New York University
Northwestern University
Quinnipiac University
Pennsylvania State University
University of Southern California
Syracuse University
University of Texas–Austin
Wayne State University

Small Colleges and Universities Strong in Film/Television

Bard College
Beloit College
Brown University
California Institute of the Arts
Columbia College (CA)
Columbia College (IL)
Emerson College
The Evergreen State College
Hampshire College
Hofstra University
Hollins University
Occidental College
Pitzer College
Pomona College
Sarah Lawrence College
School of Visual Arts
SUNY–Purchase
Wesleyan University

PERFORMING ARTS—MUSIC

Top Music Conservatories

Berklee College of Music
Boston Conservatory
California Institute of the Arts
Cleveland Institute of Music
Curtis Institute of Music
Eastman School of Music
Juilliard School
Manhattan School of Music
New England Conservatory of Music
North Carolina School of the Arts
Peabody Conservatory of Music
San Francisco Conservatory of Music

Major Universities Strong in Music

Baylor University
Boston College
Boston University
University of California–Los Angeles
Carnegie Mellon University
Case Western Reserve University
University of Cincinnati
University of Colorado–Boulder

University of Denver
Depaul University
Florida State University
Harvard University
Indiana University
Ithaca College
Miami University (OH)
University of Miami (FL)
University of Michigan
University of Nebraska–Lincoln
New York University
Northwestern University
University of Oklahoma
University of Southern California
Southern Methodist University
Vanderbilt University
Yale University

Small Colleges and Universities Strong in Music

Bard College
Bennington College
Bucknell University
Butler University
DePauw University
Furman University
Gordon College
Illinois Wesleyan University
Knox College
Lawrence University*
Loyola University–New Orleans
Manhattanville College
Mills College
Oberlin College*
University of the Pacific
Rice University
St. Mary's College of Maryland
St. Olaf College
Sarah Lawrence College
Skidmore College
Smith College
University of Southern California
Stetson University
SUNY–Geneseo
SUNY–Purchase
Wesleyan University
Wheaton College (IL)

*These two schools are unusual because they combine a world-class conservatory with a top-notch liberal arts college.

PERFORMING ARTS—DRAMA

Major Universities Strong in Drama
Boston College
Boston University
University of California–Los Angeles
Carnegie Mellon University
The Catholic University of America
DePaul University
Emerson University
Florida State University
Fordham University
Indiana University
University of Iowa
Ithaca College
University of Minnesota
New York University
Northwestern University
University of North Carolina–Chapel Hill
University of Southern California
Southern Methodist University
Syracuse University
Texas Christian University
University of Washington
Yale University

Small Colleges and Universities Strong in Drama
Beloit College
Bennington College
Centre College
Colorado College
Connecticut College
Drew University
Ithaca College
Juilliard School
Kenyon College
Lawrence University
Macalester College
Middlebury College
Muhlenberg College
Occidental College
Otterbein College
Princeton University
Rollins College
Sarah Lawrence College
Skidmore College

SUNY–Purchase
Vassar College
Whitman College
Wittenberg University

PERFORMING ARTS—DANCE

Major Universities Strong in Dance
Arizona State University
University of California–Irvine
University of California–Los Angeles
University of California–Riverside
Case Western Reserve University
Florida State University
George Washington University
Howard University
Indiana University
University of Iowa
University Minnesota
New York University
Ohio University
Southern Methodist University
Texas Christian University
University of Texas–Austin
University of Utah
Washington University in St. Louis

Small Colleges and Universities Strong in Dance
Amherst College
Barnard College
Bennington College
Butler University
Connecticut College
Dartmouth College
Goucher College
Hollins University
Juilliard School
Kenyon College
Middlebury College
Mills College
Muhlenberg College
North Carolina School of the Arts
Princeton University
Sarah Lawrence College
Smith College
SUNY–Purchase

ENVIRONMENTAL STUDIES
Allegheny College
College of the Atlantic
Bowdoin College
University of California–Davis
University of California–Santa Barbara
Clark University
Colby College
University of Colorado–Boulder
Dartmouth College
Deep Springs College
Eckerd College
The Evergreen State College
Hampshire College
Hiram College
Hobart and William Smith Colleges
McGill University
Middlebury College
University of New Hampshire
University of New Mexico
University of North Carolina–Asheville
University of North Carolina–Greensboro
Oberlin College
Prescott College
St. Lawrence University
Tulane University
University of Vermont
University of Washington
Williams College
University of Wisconsin–Madison

INTERNATIONAL STUDIES

American University
Austin College
Brandeis University
University of British Columbia
Brown University
Bucknell University
Claremont McKenna College
Clark University
Colby College
Connecticut College
Dartmouth College
Davidson College

Denison University
University of Denver
Dickinson College
Earlham College
Eckerd College
Georgetown University
George Washington University
Goucher College
Hiram College
The Johns Hopkins University
Kalamazoo College
Lewis and Clark College

Mary Washington College
University of
  Massachusetts–Amherst
Middlebury College
Mount Holyoke College
Occidental College
University of the Pacific
University of Pittsburgh
Pomona College
Princeton University
University of Puget Sound
Randolph Macon Woman's College

Reed College
Rhodes College
University Richmond
St. Olaf College
Scripps College
University of South Carolina
Sweet Briar College
Tufts University
Wesleyan University
College of William and Mary

Learning Disabilities

Services for students with learning disabilities have proliferated in recent years. Following is a list of major universities and small colleges with strong support for such students.

Major Universities with Strong Support for Students with Learning Disabilities

American University
University of Arizona
University of California–Berkeley
Clark University
University of Colorado–Boulder
University of Denver
DePaul University
University of Georgia
Hofstra University
Purdue University
Rochester Institute of Technology
Syracuse University
University of Vermont
University of Virginia

Small Colleges with Strong Support for Students with Learning Disabilities

Bard College
Curry College
Landmark College
Loras College
Lynn University
Marist College
Mercyhurst College
Mitchell College
Muskingum College
University of New England
St. Thomas Acquinas College (NY)
Southern Vermont College
Westminster College (MO)
West Virginia Wesleyan College

Agnes Scott College

141 East College Avenue, Decatur, GA 30030

Combines the tree-lined seclusion of Decatur with the bustle of Atlanta. More money in the bank than most Ivy League schools, and enrollment is up 50 percent since 1990. Small classes, sisterhood, and a more exciting location than the Sweet Briars of the world.

Agnes Scott College, founded in 1889, seeks "to educate women to think deeply, live honorably and engage the intellectual and social challenges of their times." Known for strength in the sciences and math, the school also produces skilled writers and artists, and continues to be one of the South's leading women's institutions. ASC's small size leads to close student–faculty relationships, and the lack of men on campus helps students focus on their own academic and extracurricular priorities. "Everyone tends to support each other, and there is a sense of community," says a biochemistry and molecular biology major. "Students complain about petty things because everything is pretty great!"

The Agnes Scott campus sits on one hundred acres in the historic district of Decatur, just outside Atlanta. The well-maintained Gothic and Victorian buildings are surrounded by gardens filled with rare shrubs, bushes, and trees—all evidence of strong alumnae support. A $125 million capital campaign has paid for a new campus center, library expansion and renovation, new tennis courts, and three renovated theme houses, all in the past two years. The $36.5 million Science Center at Agnes Scott includes an x-ray spectrometer, nuclear magnetic resonance imaging equipment, and a scanning tunneling microscope. The school's Delafield Planetarium has a computer-controlled Zeiss projector, one of only ten in the United States.

Aside from outstanding instruction in the sciences, Agnes Scott provides students with solid grounding in the liberal arts. First-year students may choose seminars on special topics such as U.S. foreign policy, religion and human rights in Atlanta, or living in Roman Pompeii. To graduate, students must complete one semester of English composition and literature, plus courses in math, historical studies, and classical civilization, fine arts, science, and physical education. Students must

"Agnes Scott students are hard-working, but also know how to cut loose and have fun."

also attain intermediate-level proficiency in a foreign language, and because ASC is affiliated with the Presbyterian Church, take one course in religion or philosophical thought. Eighty-two percent of the classes taken by first-years have twenty-five students or less, though this doesn't cause problems at registration time. Even so, "almost everyone graduates in four years or less," a senior says. "Only exceptional circumstances cause a fifth year to be necessary."

Academically, Agnes Scott excels in biology and math, producing five Goldwater scholars in the past five years. The school is also strong in German, with five Fulbright scholars since 1993. "Professors come to ASC because they want to teach," one student says. "TAs don't teach classes." Fine and performing artists have their own facility, while aspiring authors can rub elbows with real-life practitioners each spring when the college sponsors a writers' festival. Those participating in research

Website: www.agnesscott.edu
Location: Urban
Total Enrollment: 910
Undergraduates: 869
Male/Female: 0/100
SAT Ranges: V 570–680
  M 540–650
ACT Range: 26–30
Financial Aid: 61%
Expense: Pr $ $ $
Phi Beta Kappa: Yes
Applicants: 743
Accepted: 73%
Enrolled: 43%
Grad in 6 Years: 72%
Returning Freshmen: 82%
Academics: ✍ ✍ ✍
Social: ☎ ☎
Q of L: ★ ★ ★ ★
Admissions: (404) 471-6285
Email Address:
  admission@agnesscott.edu

Strongest Programs:
English
Psychology
Astrophysics
German
Biology
Mathematics

in any field may attend or present results at an annual conference held in the spring. Entrepreneurs and students interested in nonprofit work may take advantage of the Kauffman and Hubert internship programs. The academic climate is cooperative, students say. "Everyone strives for their personal best, but helps her peers along the way," says a biochemistry and molecular biology major.

When Agnes Scott's idyllic campus feels too small, students may enroll in the Atlanta Semester, focusing on women, leadership, and social change, or the Global Awareness and Global Connections programs, which offer a semester of cross-cultural study before sending students out around the globe. If it's sun and fun you want, take a term at all-female Mills College in Oakland, California. Engineers and architects may complete their degrees through a 3–2 program with Georgia Tech or a 3–4 program with Washington University in St. Louis. As a member of the Atlanta Regional Consortium for Higher Education, Agnes Scott shares facilities and resources with twenty other schools in the area through a cross-registration program.

The ASC student body hails mainly from the Southeast; half are Georgia natives. While most students had conservative upbringings, they tend to champion liberal causes. "An acceptance of homosexuality and racial diversity is a must for all students," says one student. "Agnes Scott students are hard-working, but also know how to cut loose and have fun," agrees another. "We care deeply about others, and most are actively involved with one to many organizations on campus." Despite the school's small size, its campus is amazingly diverse, with 21 percent of the student body African-American, 3 percent Hispanic, and 5 percent Asian-American. An honor system, enforced by a student judiciary, allows for self-scheduled and unproctored exams. Agnes Scott awards merit scholarships of $3,000 to $28,230 a year, based on academic performance, leadership, or musical ability.

Ninety percent of Agnes Scott students live in the dorms, which are linked by tree-lined brick walks. "Students are required to stay on campus all four years, unless you have a relative in the area or are married," a senior explains. "After the first year, rooms are done by lottery; everyone gets one. Dorms are great and much better

"Professors come to ASC because they want to teach. TAs don't teach classes."

than other colleges," with high ceilings and hardwood floors. Juniors and seniors can live in Avery Glen, the college-owned apartment complex, while first-years are assigned to the two dorms (out of six total) that tend to be more "chummy." The "Agnes Scott Convent" has no sororities, but with only 910 students, 5 percent of whom are typically studying off-campus, the college itself is a close-knit sisterhood. Wherever they bunk, students can grab a bite at the snack bar or the renovated dining hall. "Vegetarianism is huge," one student says. "We have tofu and hummus and vegan entrees everyday, with soy milk available. The food is good and tasty."

ASC has many campus clubs and events, but when the weekend comes, "all partying is off-campus, usually at Georgia Tech," one says. A college-run shuttle and taxi service also takes students to Emory and other locations around Atlanta, while convenient public transportation serves cultural landmarks like the High Art Museum. "Atlanta is very alive with arts, clubbing, and restaurants," one student says. "Decatur is small and quaint. A lot of ASC students get involved with community service both on and off campus, with Habitat for Humanity, the DeKalb Rape Crisis Center, Girl Scouts, Hands Across Atlanta and Best Buddies."

Back on campus, underage students may not imbibe, in accordance with Georgia state law; enforcement falls under the honor code. Still, "the alcohol policies seem almost not relevant," says a biochemistry major. "Nobody drinks on campus; everyone just goes to Buckhead or Georgia Tech." Popular road trips include Stone Mountain and Six Flags, or New Orleans for Mardi Gras. Every October, students invite men to a formal dance known as Black Cat, which follows a week of class competitions that marks the end of new-student orientation. Other quaint old traditions survive, too, such as throwing recently engaged classmates into the alumnae pond. And seniors who get into grad school or find jobs go to the top of the college bell tower, pealing out chimes to share the good news.

Varsity sports are improving with the formation of the Great South Athletic Conference, and the Agnes Scott tennis team brought home the conference trophy in 2003. Also strong are soccer, swimming, basketball, softball, and cross-country. Intramural activities include the standard roundup of sports plus a few more exotic options, such as studio dance.

Feminists used to sing a song that started out "I am woman, hear me roar/In numbers too big to ignore." While the genteel women of Agnes Scott probably would not roar, and while their numbers are tiny among the legions of college students in Atlanta, ASC understands the importance of independence, intellectual growth, and strong voices for smart women. Small classes encourage quick thinking, and off-campus internship and study opportunities make it easy to explore new ideas.

If You Apply To ➤

Agnes Scott: Early decision: Nov. 15. Regular admissions: Mar. 1 (Jan. 15 for scholarship applicants). Financial aid: Feb. 15. Meets demonstrated need of 80%. Campus interviews: recommended, evaluative. Alumni interviews: optional, informational. SATs or ACTs: required. SAT IIs: optional. Accepts the Common Application and electronic applications. Essay question: impact of significant experience, risk or ethical dilemma; issue of personal, local, national or international concern; influential person, fictional character, historical figure, or creative work; topic of your choice.

University of Alabama

Box 870132, Tuscaloosa, AL 35487-0166

Roll, Tide, Roll says it all. Not exactly a hotbed of intellectual energy, 'Bama has been left in the dust by University of Georgia and its Hope Scholarship. Look for pockets of excellence in the professional programs, the Blount Undergraduate Initiative, and honors programs.

Tuscaloosa, Alabama, only looks like a place where time stands still. Sure, the city's landmarks include those that have largely faded from view in other Southern towns: well-preserved antebellum homes, down-home Dreamland barbecue, and world-renowned blues music. And devotion to the University of Alabama and its Crimson Tide football team remains as strong as ever. But Tuscaloosa has also grown to include the only Mercedes-Benz plant outside of Germany, JVC, and other international companies that provide internship opportunities for students. And the state's first university, which dates to 1831, is diversifying itself and looking to make the education it offers more global and high-tech, and increase offerings for honors students and undergraduate researchers.

'Bama's one-thousand-acre campus combines classical, revival-style buildings (several of which survived the 1865 burning of the university by Union troops) with modern structures. One of the most stunning in the South, the campus wraps around a shaded quadrangle, the home of the main library and "Denny Chimes," a campanile carillon that rings the Westminster Chimes on the quarter hour. A building for engineering students' projects, tennis courts, and a multipurpose building are among the newer additions to campus. A newly expanded student recreation center offers state-of-the art facilities for personal fitness and intramural sports.

Website: www.ua.edu
Location: Small city
Total Enrollment: 19,584
Undergraduates: 15,441
Male/Female: 47/53
SAT Ranges: V 490–620
 M 490–620
ACT Range: 21–26
Financial Aid: N/A
Expense: Pub $
Phi Beta Kappa: Yes
Applicants: 7,322
Accepted: 85%
Enrolled: 36%
Grad in 6 Years: 63%
Returning Freshmen: 84%
Academics: ✍ ✍ ✍

(Continued)

Social: ☎ ☎ ☎
Q of L: ★ ★ ★
Admissions: (205) 348-5666
Email Address:
   admissions@ua.edu

Strongest Programs:
Communications
Dance
Commerce
Business Administration
Engineering
Psychology
English
Philosophy

In part because the recent athletic scandals have made Alabama something of an academic laughingstock, administrators are no longer satisfied with being a purely athletic and social school.

Alabama is a leader among Southern flagship universities with 16 percent minority enrollment: 14 percent African-American, 1 percent Asian-American, and 1 percent Hispanic.

The University of Alabama is organized into eight undergraduate colleges and schools, which together offer eighty-four undergraduate degree programs. The Culverhouse College of Commerce and Business offers strong programs in marketing, information systems, and accounting; marketing and finance are the most popular majors on campus, followed by public relations. Alston Hall, an imposing classroom–administrative building, provides state-of-the-art instructional technology for budding tycoons. Online databases in the Bruno Business Library and Bashinsky Computer Center offer search and retrieval of information from a wide variety of sources. The College of Communication and Information Sciences has one of the country's top ten journalism schools, while respected programs in the College of Human Environmental Sciences include nutrition and hospitality management. The School of Music is a regional standout, attracting guest artists such as Jean-Pierre Rampal and Midori.

"Football is the major tradition at U of A."

Students who receive academic scholarships, or who score at least 28 on the ACT or at least 1240 on the SAT, may enroll in the honors program, which features smaller classes, better professors, and the opportunity to write a senior thesis. Additionally, twenty talented students of any major—mostly engineers—may participate in the computer-based honors program, which pays them to develop software programs in their field of study. The Blount Undergraduate Initiative is a living/learning program within the College of Arts and Sciences, where freshmen are housed with a faculty director and fellows. Other innovative offerings include 'Bama's Weekend College, the continuing education division, which has attracted a large undergraduate following, and the May interim term, when students focus on one course in depth.

About 20 percent of Alabama freshmen take part in the Arts and Sciences Mentoring Program, which pairs them with faculty mentors who ease the adjustment to college through informal counseling and enrichment activities such as concerts, movies, or lectures. All students may also enroll in the two-credit Academic Potential Seminar, which covers self-assessment, motivation, personal responsibility, time management, memory, textbook reading, note-taking, and test preparation. The only course 'Bama requires students to take during the first year on campus is a two-term English composition sequence. Before graduation, students must also take courses in

"The student body is extremely diverse. There is really no stereotypical student."

writing, natural sciences, math, humanities and social sciences, and either two semesters of a foreign language or one of computer science.

While UA's core curriculum has been streamlined and the math requirement has been reduced, don't expect to party all the time and still pass, students say. "Certain classes and students are very competitive, while other courses and professors are laid-back," says a freshman. "It's a good mix. Most courses are very rigorous." Professors teach lectures and many seminar courses, and UA is home to the Carnegie Foundation's 2001–2002 National Professor of the Year, Cornelius Carter. "Most of the teachers are very well educated and fluent in their areas of expertise," another freshman says. "Half the freshman classes are taught by full professors."

Seventy-five percent of 'Bama's students are homegrown, 20 percent hail from elsewhere in the United States, and 5 percent are international, from more than ninety countries. "The student body is extremely diverse," says a freshman biology major. "There is really no stereotypical student." Alabama is a leader among Southern flagship universities with 16 percent minority enrollment: 14 percent African-American, 1 percent Asian-American, and 1 percent Hispanic. "Racism and homosexuality often occupy editorial pages in the campus newspaper," says a senior. "Greek versus non-Greek issues are also very big, especially around Homecoming and Student Government Association elections," partially because the black and white Greek systems remain separate. 'Bama awards athletic scholarships in eleven women's sports and nine men's sports, as well as merit scholarships.

Most Alabama students live in off-campus apartments in the Tuscaloosa area; only 23 percent remain in campus residence halls, where options range from apartment-style living to private rooms and suites. "Most of the dorms are nice," says a freshman. "Getting a room in one of the smaller dorms can be a challenge but it isn't hard to get a dorm room in general." Another freshman gives high marks to the living/learning communities, some of which are for first-year students and others that bring together students from a particular school or college. Sixteen percent of men pledge fraternities and 24 percent of women join sororities, and they may live in chapter houses. 'Bama's campus is safe, thanks to visible school police, though "most students feel nervous about the areas just off campus at night," one student says. Students may use a free school escort service, 348-RIDE, to reach their destinations after dark.

On the weekends, much of 'Bama's social life revolves around the Greek system. Participation has been steady in recent years, despite administrators' efforts to weaken it by prohibiting fraternities and sororities from having parties on campus. Those under twenty-one can't have alcohol in the dorms—or elsewhere, for that matter, per state law—but a freshman says "this is hardly effective, as underage students can get beer rather easily." Those who don't go Greek, or who don't wish to drink, will find everything from the Society for Creative Anachronism (medievalists) to Bible study groups. City Fest, featuring music, food, beer, and a German theme, is a popular annual event, as is Capstone, a Saturday dedicated to community service. A modern trolley service connects the 'Bama campus to the city's thriving downtown. Road trips to New Orleans (for Mardi Gras and Greek weekend formals), Atlanta, Nashville, Birmingham, and the Gulf Coast and Florida beaches are popular, too.

Legendary coach Bear Bryant is long gone, and the program that he once led has been rocked by a series of scandals involving sexual favors, hard partying, and recruiting violations that have landed the football team on NCAA probation. Nevertheless, the annual Auburn–Alabama game—the Iron Bowl, one of the most intense rivalries in college sports—is the highlight of the school year. "Football is the major tradition at U of A," says a freshman. Alabama competes in Division I, and the gymnastics team brought home an NCAA championship in 2002. Football, baseball, and men's basketball also attract fans, as does the women's softball team.

In part because the recent athletic scandals have made Alabama something of an academic laughingstock, administrators are no longer satisfied with being a purely athletic and social school. (In fact, they brag, the school's debate team has won fourteen national championships—two more than the football team!) 'Bama is emphasizing technology, merit scholarships, global perspectives, and undergraduate research to raise its academic profile. But students hope that won't change the welcoming atmosphere. "It's a large university but at the same time it's small," a freshman says. "I feel as though I belong here and can make a difference on campus."

The annual Auburn–Alabama game—the Iron Bowl, one of the most intense rivalries in college sports—is the highlight of the school year.

Overlaps

Auburn, University of Georgia, Florida State, University of Tennessee–Knoxville, University of Mississippi

If You Apply To ➤

'Bama: Rolling admissions: July 1. Financial aid and housing: Mar. 1. Meets demonstrated need of 98%. Campus interviews: recommended, informational. Alumni interviews: optional, informational. SATs or ACTs: required. SAT IIs: optional. Accepts the Common Application and electronic applications. No essay question.

Caldwell, Idaho 83605

Got a map? You'll need a sharp eyes to spot Albertson, the *Fiske Guide*'s only liberal arts school (along with Colorado College) in the interior of the Mountain West. Innovative programs include Leadership Studies and the Center for Experiential Learning.

Website: www.albertson.edu
Location: Small town
Total Enrollment: 778
Undergraduates: 778
Male/Female: 46/54
SAT Ranges: V 500–620
  M 520-620
ACT Range: 22–27
Financial Aid: 67%
Expense: Pr $
Phi Beta Kappa: No
Applicants: 631
Accepted: 62%
Enrolled: 33%
Grad in 6 Years: N/A
Returning Freshmen: 71%
Academics: ✍ ✍ ✍
Social: ☎ ☎ ☎
Q of L: ★ ★ ★
Admissions: (800) 224-3246
Email Address:
  admission@albertson.edu

Strongest Programs:
Biology
Business
History
Mathematics
Political Science

The college cooperates with Columbia University, the University of Idaho, Boise State University, and Washington University in St. Louis to offer a five-year course of study in engineering.

Emphasizing technology, education, and experiential learning, Albertson College of Idaho, the state's oldest four-year university, offers students an opportunity to earn a solid liberal arts education through small classes in a small town. Outside class, the school's scenic environment allows sports and nature enthusiasts to romp freely before heading back into the classrooms.

The college is located in the small town of Caldwell where the atmosphere is calm and serene. For those looking for a little excitement, the state capitol of Boise is a short drive from campus. Also nearby are some of Idaho's most scenic locations such as beautiful mountains, deserts, and whitewater rivers. The school, originally a Presbyterian college, first planted roots in downtown Caldwell in 1891 and then moved to its present site in 1910, where its twenty-one buildings now inhabit forty-three acres. For more than eighty years, it was called the College of Idaho, but officials changed the college's name to honor the Albertson family, which gave $13.5 million for new facilities. The McCain Center, a $3 million student union, features a snack bar, coffee shop, student theater, movie theater, and outdoor eating area. New offices and labs are planned to accommodate the growing student population.

Most classes at Albertson have twenty-five or fewer students, and all are taught by full professors. Students agree its small size is the school's strongest asset, allowing students to usually get into the classes they want. "Teaching is incredible and outstanding," says one senior. Students appreciate being able to get to know their professors. "I love it because there's a real sense of community, it's so small. Professors are on a first-name basis," says a junior.

"Advisors are incredible. They are always willing to help sort out your academic program."

The school's academic schedule is composed of twelve-week semesters, spring and fall, separated by a six-week winter session, during which students can assist professors with research, take an internship, volunteer, or travel abroad. Offerings run from "creative writing and backcountry skiing in the Sawtooth Mountains" to "history of art in London." The general education requirements include natural sciences, writing, mathematics, physical education, and cultural diversity. Freshmen go through a first-year program that includes a specialized curriculum and intensive two-semester writing course. First-year students demonstrating leadership potential are invited to a series of seminars to draw them into the leadership studies program, a business minor. The two libraries have 178,000 volumes and are accessible online twenty-four hours a day.

Biology, English, and history are among the majors recommended by students, and preprofessional majors, such as premed, prevet, and prelaw are also popular and strong. Weaker departments are the smaller ones, such as foreign languages, music, business, and education. To improve business offerings, the school is revising the curriculum and increasing internship opportunities. Students can choose such specializations as sports and fitness-center management. It has also overhauled education and is adding a five-year master's degree program. The college cooperates with Columbia University, the University of Idaho, Boise State University, and Washington University in St. Louis to offer a five-year course of study in engineering. The new Center for Experiential Learning coordinates out-of-classroom experiences, such as international education and service learning. For those who want to venture abroad (physically or mentally), the International Education Program offers several options, including attending a foreign university, traveling overseas during the summer and winter breaks, and taking international studies on campus. Travel has really taken off, with 25 percent of students accepting opportunities to study in such places as Cuba, Greece, and Germany. Advising is available to help students make good academic choices. "Advisors are incredible. They are always willing to help sort out your academic program," says a senior majoring in politics and economics.

The school's price tag is lower than that of most private colleges. It offers 474 merit scholarships ranging from $500 to $16,700, as well as 174 athletic scholarships in Albertson sports. Not surprisingly, some of those scholarship dollars are set aside for skiers. Seventy-six percent of the students are from Idaho; 82 percent are white. Only 2 percent hail from foreign nations. "PC is an issue," says a junior. "Our campus is concerned about environmental issues and we're evenly divided between conservatives and liberals."

Fifty-six percent of students live on campus. Each room in the five residence halls has individual heating and cooling and hookups for Internet access, and each hall has a computer lab. Dorms are "decent-sized, not any better or worse than a typical college," a junior comments. For safety, the college recently implemented a round-the-clock escort system.

Nineteen percent of men and women participate in the Greek system, which dominates campus social life. Annual social highlights include Winterfest and Spring Fling and Homecoming Week. Games against rival Northwest Nazarene also attract attention. Caldwell, with 24,000 people, is not a great spot for college students. "Finals breakfasts" offer something for bleary-eyed students to look forward to during finals week. At midnight on Tuesday, faculty and staff cook breakfast for students. Nearby Boise is a popu-

> **"Our campus is concerned about environmental issues and we're evenly divided between conservatives and liberals."**

lar destination for shopping, dining, cultural events, and volunteering. Many students take advantage of hiking, kayaking, and skiing in the surrounding area, and many hit the road during a weeklong break taken every six weeks.

Basketball is a crowd-pleaser, and the team has made Albertson students proud, chalking up victories in NAIA Division II competition. The women's team was a runner-up in 2001. The men's baseball team won the 1999 NAIA Division II national championship and competed in the conference World Series in 2002. The women's ski team competed for the national championship during the 1999–2000 season. For those who enjoy the game but might not make the team, there is an active intramurals program, including Frisbee football, volleyball, basketball, and softball, and the large J.A. Albertson Activities Center. Beyond sports, extracurricular activities include Bible study, choir, student government, an environmental club, and a rejuvenated Hispanic club.

Albertson College has much to offer the "Yotes" (translation: "We are the coyotes"). They enjoy a solid liberal arts education and personal academic attention on a campus striving to keep its offerings on the cutting edge.

First-year students demonstrating leadership potential are invited to a series of seminars to draw them into the leadership studies program, a business minor.

Overlaps

Boise State, University of Idaho, Linfield, Gonzaga, Willamette

If You Apply To ➤ **Albertson:** Early action: Nov. 15. Regular admission: June 1. Does not guarantee to meet demonstrated need. Campus interviews: recommended, informational. Alumni interviews: optional, informational. SATs or ACTs: required. SAT IIs: optional. Accepts the Common Application and electronic applications. Essay question: fictional character, sentimental possession, important issue.

Next to evangelical Hope and Calvin and out-there Kalamazoo, Albion is Michigan's middle-of-the road liberal arts college. Think Gerald Ford, the moderate Republican president who is the namesake of Albion's signature Institute for Public Service. Future doctors, lawyers, and business-people will be well served.

Website: www.albion.edu
Location: Small town
Total Enrollment: 1,548
Undergraduates: 1,548
Male/Female: 45/55
SAT Ranges: V 510–640
   M 520–630
ACT Range: 22–27
Financial Aid: 60%
Expense: Pr $
Phi Beta Kappa: Yes
Applicants: 1,297
Accepted: 87%
Enrolled: 40%
Grad in 6 Years: 72%
Returning Freshmen: 86%
Academics: ✍ ✍ ✍
Social: ☎ ☎
Q of L: ★ ★ ★
Admissions: (800) 858-6770
Email Address:
   admissions@albion.edu

Strongest Programs:
Economics and Business
Ford Institute for Public
   Service
Environment Institute
Premed
Prelaw

Albion is a small, private college in Michigan whose motto is "Liberal arts at work." The school's motto emphasizes the importance Albion places on combining learning with hands-on experience. Students at Albion often participate in leadership and service-learning seminars. And when the work is through, students here enjoy a close-knit social life. "Albion is where I have built lifetime friendships," admits a senior. Another student says, "Since Albion is a small school, it gives each student personal attention in every aspect of their education while having all of the advantages of a larger school due to all the resources available to the students."

Founded in 1835 by the Methodist Church, Albion is located near the banks of the Kalamazoo River. In addition to its newer Georgian-style architecture, the college has retained and restored several of its nineteenth-century buildings. The campus is spacious with statuesque oaks and a beautiful nature center. Robinson Hall, the campus centerpiece, houses myriad departments, including the Ford Institute for Public Service, the Gerstacker Liberal Arts Program in Professional Management, and the Anna Howard Shaw Women's Center. The campus continues to expand with the addition of the Ferguson Student Services Building.

Academically, Albion is as sound as its buildings. It was the first private college in Michigan to have a Phi Beta Kappa chapter (1940) and has produced three Rhodes Scholars. On their journey to becoming Rhodes Scholars, students are required to take core courses distributed among humanities, natural sciences, social sciences, fine arts, and math. They must also satisfy requirements in environmental science and gender and ethnicity studies. Freshmen must take first-year seminars designed to provide a "stimulating learning environment" in a small-class setting, while seniors participate in a capstone experience.

Albion's most distinguishing feature is the emphasis placed on citizenship and service. The Gerald R. Ford Institute for Public Service takes a unique approach for future civic leaders. Students participate in a simulation of city government in which they play the roles of community leaders. Visiting speakers include senators and congressmen, governors and state legislators, and interest group representatives. The premedical and prelaw programs draw dedicated undergrads, and the English and economics departments are well respected. Another option is the Summer Research Program, which allows students to remain on campus during the summer to work with faculty members on different projects.

The academic climate at Albion is described as competitive but not cut-throat. One student says, "The average student who attends is the high achiever who is involved in school." Top-notch academic and career counseling and low student/faculty ratios keep students on track and motivated. Class size varies, but the average class is under twenty-five students. Professors are interested in students' academic performance and their emotional well-being. While "the courses are carefully prepared and the professors expect diligence from the students, the professors really care and take an interest in the students" and it is not "uncommon to have class at a professor's house with pizza and holiday cookies." The professors seem to know the secret to motivating college students—feed them and they will work.

Teaching assistants are used for tutoring, not teaching. Albion's libraries feature computer facilities, an interlibrary loan service, a listening lab for language or music study, and a helpful staff. If you can't find what you need at Albion's libraries, weekly bus trips to the University of Michigan libraries in Ann Arbor provide access to even more resources.

Albion continues to attract an ambitious, involved group of students. Michigan residents make up 90 percent of the student population. Eighty-five percent are Caucasian, 2 percent African-American, and 1 percent Hispanic. The remainder come from abroad. Up to now, there has been little deviation from the white, upper-middle-class norm. In an effort to change this, a new host-family program matches minority students with families from within the community. There are a number of merit scholarships available, based on academic records, extracurricular involvement, and demonstrated leadership abilities. There are no athletic scholarships.

Eighty-nine percent of Albion students call the residence halls home, which are described as "sufficient" and "not exactly modern." The majority of the freshman class inhabits Wesley Hall. During their sophomore year, many students move to Seaton or Whitehouse halls; seniors enjoy apartment-style housing called The Mae. Dorms are co-ed by hall or floor, and the information each student provides in their housing

"The average student who attends is the high achiever who is involved in school."

request form is used to assign rooms and roommates. One student claims, "The dorms are extremely well maintained and have maintenance boards located on every floor so that the students can voice their concerns. Most of the concerns are taken care of by the next day." Other housing options include apartment annexes and fraternity houses. Sororities do not have houses; they hold their meetings in lodges. Two large dining rooms feed campus residents on an "eat all day" meal plan.

Forty percent of Albion men and women belong to one of the school's six national fraternities and seven sororities. Greek parties draw large crowds, composed of Greeks and non-Greeks, making them a primary part of many students' social lives. Controlling the alcoholic intake of students has become a priority of the administration. Students say "underage drinking does happen" but the college "has strict consequences if caught." Those who insist on imbibing can do it at Gina's or Cascarelli's, popular bars in town.

Road trips are a big part of weekends for many students. Ann Arbor, East Lansing, and Canada are frequent destinations. A well-run union board organizes all sorts of activities—films, lectures, plays, comics, and concerts—to keep students occupied in their spare time. Several students report that the town movie theatre shows "free movies if you show a valid student ID!"

Still, students complain that there are not many social outlets available at Albion. Students focus some of their energy on work for groups supported by the Student Volunteer Bureau; in fact, half of the students volunteer on a regular basis. They are very involved in the community, including "city clean-up day, Habitat for Humanity, and volunteering at nursing homes and schools." Some traditional events that offer a nice break from academics are the Briton Bash, a fair that familiarizes students with clubs and organizations, and the Day of Woden, which is a picnic held in the spring on the last day of class.

The varsity football team has won nine conference championships in the past decade. Recently, the women's soccer team brought home the Conference MIAA Championship. Men's track, baseball, and golf, along with women's swimming, also receive a lot of attention on campus. Hope College is a hated rival, as is Alma College.

At Albion, professors are accessible and interested, and academics are challenging without being overwhelming. Students agree that the "small campus with

Albion was the first private college in Michigan to have a Phi Beta Kappa chapter (1940) and has produced three Rhodes Scholars.

The college's Foundation for Undergraduate Research, Scholarship, and Creative Activity is providing students with funding for the summer so that they can remain on campus and work with faculty members on different research projects.

friendly students, caring faculty, and kind staff members" make this college an appealing place.

Alfred University

Alumni Hall, Saxon Drive, Alfred, NY 14802-1205

Talk about an unusual combination—Alfred combines a nationally renowned college of ceramics, a school of art and design, an engineering program, and a business school wrapped up in a university of just more than two thousand students. It takes elbow-grease to pry coastal types to the hinterlands of western New York.

Website: www.alfred.edu
Location: Rural
Total Enrollment: 2,367
Undergraduates: 2,055
Male/Female: 48/52
SAT Ranges: V 500–600
    M 500–600
ACT Range: 23–28
Financial Aid: 90%
Expense: Pr $ $
Phi Beta Kappa: Yes
Applicants: 2,169
Accepted: 69%
Enrolled: 32%
Grad in 6 Years: 65%
Returning Freshmen: 82%
Academics: 🖊 🖊 🖊
Social: 🐻 🐻 🐻
Q of L: ★ ★ ★
Admissions: (607) 871-2115
Email Address:
    admwww@alfred.edu

Strongest Programs:
Ceramic Engineering
Art

When you think of ceramics, what comes to mind? Sculptures or semiconductors? Either way, Alfred University has a top-notch program to satisfy your educational needs. This small school boasts highly respected programs in art and design, as well as ceramic engineering. Innovation not only shapes the curriculum, but also has a profound effect on campus life. Small classes and friendly competition support this diversity while encouraging individuals to succeed. With just under 2,400 students, Alfred isn't a bustling academic factory; it's a quiet, cloistered, self-described "educational village" in a tiny town wholly dedicated to the "industry of learning."

Alfred's campus consists of a charming, close-knit group of modern and Georgian brick buildings, along with a stone castle. The Kanakadea Creek runs right through campus, and the town of Alfred consists of two colleges (the other is the Alfred State College) and a main street with one stoplight. There are a few shops and restaurants, but certainly no malls, parking lots, or tall buildings.

The university and its students share a no-nonsense approach to education. Although prospective students apply directly to one of four colleges and declare a tentative major, half of all requirements for a bachelor's degree are earned in the liberal arts college. Requirements are quite different in each school. However, the mix usually includes coursework in oral and written communication, foreign language and culture, social sciences, history, literature, philosophy, and religion.

Alfred, though private, is actually the "host" school for the New York State College of Ceramics, which is a unit of the state university system and comes with a public university pricetag. Ceramic engineering (the development and refinement of ceramic materials) is the undisputed king of the academic castle and the program that brings Alfred international recognition. All engineering programs have been consolidated into one School of Engineering, and students may choose from six engineering majors. The art department, with its programs in ceramics, glass, printmaking, sculpture, video, and teacher certification, is also highly regarded. The

School of Art and Design offers a graphic design major in which students use electronic and computer equipment. The business administration school also gets good reviews from students and provides undergraduates with work experience through a small-business institute where students have real clients.

Many majors also offer a co-op program that alternates semesters of work and study. "It is competitive enough to make you work hard, but not enough to drive you to suicide," says one ceramic engineering major. Recently, health planning and management has moved from a major to a career emphasis within the College of Business. The major in foreign language and culture sponsors trips abroad, and exchange programs are available in England, Germany, Italy, France, Japan, China, and the Czech Republic. The Track II program enables students to design their own interdisciplinary majors with personal guidance from top faculty members.

Whatever their major, all students enjoy small classes (average size is eighteen students), and the quality of teaching is described as very high. "All the profs are down to earth and very approachable," explains a senior. Most classes are taught by full professors, with graduate students and teaching assistants helping out only in lab sessions.

"Professors are very involved with the students and clearly interested in teaching."

The university stresses its commitment to helping undergrads plan their future, and the academic-advising and career-planning services are strong enough for Alfred to deliver on its promise. Students say faculty members really want to see them succeed, both in class and in the "real world." "Professors are very involved with the students and clearly interested in teaching," brags one junior.

"I feel that there is a cloning process going on at schools across America," opines one student. "Students look alike, act alike, think alike, and dress alike. Alfred is a refreshing exception to this rule." Sixty-seven percent of the students at Alfred are from New York State, and 23 percent graduated from high school in the top tenth of their class. Students are mostly white and from public schools. Minority enrollment is growing: 5 percent are African-American, 4 percent are Hispanic, and 2 percent are Asian-American. Students praise the financial aid packages they receive. "Financial aid is great. Without it, I would not be here," says a junior. The university is holding freshman tuition steady under the "Alfred Plan." Outstanding students can apply for many merit scholarships ranging from $2,500 to a full ride, and National Merit finalists receive Alfred's Award of Merit. There are no athletic scholarships.

No one seems to mind the two-year, on-campus residency requirement because the rooms are large and comfortable, and the dorms are equipped with lounges, kitchens, and laundry facilities; some even boast such extras as computers and saunas. Upperclassmen have a choice of dorms that are co-ed by floor, with single rooms, suites, or apartments. Freshmen enjoy their own housing divided into doubles. The favorite freshman dorm is Barresi. Sixty-seven percent of all students choose to live on campus, but some juniors and about half of the seniors opt to live off campus. The school has two dining halls and a choice of six meal plans. Freshmen and sophomores are required to subsist on cafeteria cuisine, which features an enormous variety of regular buffets, plus a salad bar, a deli line, and daily international lines. Campus security is good, according to most. "This town is very safe," says one female student. "I do not even think twice about walking around at night."

Alfred's location in the Finger Lakes region, almost two hours from Buffalo and an hour and a half from Rochester, is isolated. Social life is difficult due to the rural atmosphere, but the Student Activities Board brings many events to campus, including musicians, comedians, lecturers, and movies. Favorite road trips are to Letchworth and Stony Brook state parks, and to Ithaca, Rochester, Buffalo, and Toronto. Many students are skiing, hunting, camping, and rock-climbing enthusiasts.

(Continued)
Business
Sciences
Psychology
English

Ceramic engineering (the development and refinement of ceramic materials) is the undisputed king of the academic castle and brings Alfred international recognition.

Friendly games of hackeysack, Frisbee, football, softball, and other sports can often be found somewhere on campus. Fraternities and sororities, which had been attracting a declining proportion of students in recent years and facing repeated sanctions, were eliminated last year following the death of a fraternity member near the campus. The alcohol policy is enforced on the campus, but students say it is not impossible to get alcohol. "The alcohol policies are very strict for freshmen, but after freshmen year, they don't work very well," says a sophomore.

Because Alfred shares the town with Alfred State University, the dominant student population makes Alfred a good college town. "This town is dead when college is not in session," observes a communications major. The downtown scene provides students with an adequate number of movie theaters and eateries. Every spring brings the annual Hot Dog Weekend, a big fund-raising event that fills Main Street with game booths, bands, and lots and lots of hot dog stands. Alfred's Division III Saxons are ominous opponents on the football, soccer, and lacrosse fields, and alpine skiing, equestrian, and men's swimming have all won spots in the top ten nationally.

If you want to spend four years concentrating on your ABCs (that's arts, business, or ceramic engineering), then small, secluded Alfred University is a good choice. But bring your heavy coat and gloves, because upstate New York winters can be brutal.

Although prospective students apply directly to one of four colleges and declare a tentative major, half of all requirements for a bachelor's degree are earned in the liberal arts college.

"Financial aid is great. Without it, I would not be here."

Overlaps

Rochester Institute of Technology, Ithaca, SUNY–Geneseo, SUNY–Buffalo, Hartwick

If You Apply To ➤ | **Alfred:** Early decision: Dec. 1. Regular admissions: Feb. 1. Campus interviews: recommended, informational. Alumni interviews: optional, informational. SATs or ACTs: required. SAT IIs: recommended. Accepts the Common Application and electronic applications. Essay question: write article about yourself; build a personal web page; how has technology shaped you; why Alfred?

Allegheny College

520 North Main Street, Meadville, PA 16335

An unpretentious cousin to more well-heeled places like Dickinson and Bucknell. Draws heavily from the Buffalo–Cleveland–Pittsburgh area. The college's powerhouse athletic teams clean up on Division III competition. If you've ever wondered what lake-effect snow is, you'll find out here.

Website: www.allegheny.edu
Location: Small city
Total Enrollment: 1,924
Undergraduates: 1,924
Male/Female: 48/52
SAT Ranges: V 550–650
   M 550–650
ACT Range: 23–27
Financial Aid: 94%
Expense: Pr $ $ $
Phi Beta Kappa: Yes
Applicants: 2,612

Allegheny College is a down-to-earth Eastern liberal arts school boasting a rich history of academic excellence in an intimate setting. Administrators here understand the importance of providing students with real-world experience to complement their classroom work. The school's innovative May term offers time for internships or other off-campus work and study. Allegheny's small size means students don't suffer from lack of attention, and despite the heavy workload, anyone struggling academically will get help before the situation becomes dire. "There are great one-on-one relationships between students and professors," one student says.

Tucked away in tiny Meadville, Pennsylvania, ninety miles north of Pittsburgh, lies Allegheny's seventy-two-acre campus. Founded in 1815, nestled in the Norman Rockwell–esque rolling hills of northwestern Pennsylvania, the campus is home to

"The students do a lot of volunteer work and help immensely throughout the community."

traditional, ivy-covered buildings and redbrick streets, as well as new apartment-style housing for upperclassmen. A nationally acclaimed science complex supports already-strong programs, and students who wish to pump iron can visit the new fitness center. The college also owns a 182-acre outdoor recreational complex, a 283-acre research reserve, and an 80-acre protected forest.

Students at Allegheny work hard and do well, as evidenced by the fact that 33 percent of a recent senior class immediately went on to graduate or professional school. "Allegheny is a very challenging institution, however, I would not describe it as a highly competitive school," says an English and political science major. The school's strongest programs are in environmental studies, the sciences, writing, and civic engagement, and students give high marks to English, too. Though the college eliminated its degree program in education some years ago, it enjoys a strong articulation program with the University of Pittsburgh School of Education, allowing graduates to have that much sought-after graduate degree. There is a new minor in values, ethics, and social action, and a new major in biochemistry. Co-op programs include a 3–1, 3–2, 3–4 option leading to degrees in engineering, nursing, and allied health. The Allegheny College Center for Experiential Learning (ACCEL) is a clearinghouse for internship opportunities, service learning, and overseas study.

Allegheny has two fifteen-week semesters each year, and its general education requirements keep students busy. Freshmen take the first seminar in their first semester and the second seminar in their second. Sophomores have a writing and speaking seminar, while juniors take a seminar in their major field, and seniors complete an intensive capstone project in their major. All students must take courses in each of three major divisions (humanities and the natural and social sciences) and must finish a minor in a subject area outside their major. Despite Allegheny's small size—94 percent of courses have fewer than fifty students—most of those enrolled graduate in four years, although it can be tough to get into communication arts courses, students say.

Students praise Allegheny's faculty for their passion, knowledge, and accessibility. Says one, "Whenever I need help with an assignment, I feel extremely comfortable talking to my professors." You won't find a TA at the lectern in any Allegheny classroom, and the college's honor code allows students to take unproctored exams. Off campus, Allegheny offers study in several U.S. cities or abroad, an on-campus independent study option, and semester internships or "externships" (a chance to observe a professional at work during the winter vacation). There's also a three- or four-week Experiential Learning term following spring semester for study abroad and internships not available during the year. The library holds more than 776,000 volumes and the campus offers more than 330 computer workstations.

Sixty-seven percent of Allegheny's students hail from Pennsylvania, and sizable contingents come from nearby Ohio, New York, and New England. While Allegheny isn't a terribly diverse campus—minority students make up only 5 percent of the total—the school is committed to increasing awareness of and appreciation for diversity. "Some people aren't politically conscious or aware at all. However, if it's your passion to be an activist, there are plenty of organizations to get involved with," comments one senior. The college's new Center for Political Participation engages students by fostering an appreciation for the vital link between an engaged, active citizenry and a healthy democracy. Merit scholarships are available, ranging from $500 to $12,500.

Eleven residence halls and twenty-one houses (including TV and study rooms) accommodate undergraduates in relative style and comfort with a variety of living situations: all-freshmen dorms; co-ed and single-sex halls; small houses; and single, double, and triple rooms and suites. Dorms are "clean and of reasonable size," says a senior, and "there is no trouble getting a room," says a sophomore. Housing is

(Continued)

Accepted: 80%

Enrolled: 26%

Grad in 6 Years: 71%

Returning Freshmen: 85%

Academics: ✍ ✍ ✍

Social: ☎ ☎ ☎

Q of L: ★ ★ ★

Admissions: (814) 332-4351

Email Address:
  admiss@allegheny.edu

Strongest Programs:
Writing
Sciences
Civic Engagement
Environmental Science

A nationally acclaimed science complex supports already-strong programs, and students who wish to pump iron can visit the new fitness center. The college also owns a 182-acre outdoor recreational complex, a 283-acre research reserve, and an 80-acre protected forest.

guaranteed for four years, and 73 percent of students stay on campus. The most popular dorm is the new, townhouse-style College Court complex, which holds eighty students in suites with four single bedrooms each. Students want more variety in food services and more parking because cars are a necessity for trips to the factory outlets in nearby Grove City, Pennsylvania, or the bright lights of Pittsburgh, Buffalo, or Cleveland. Officers from campus security are available twenty-four hours a day, but they aren't much needed. "Meadville is a safe, quite town," says a senior.

Greek organizations draw 26 percent of the men and 29 percent of the women, and provide a great deal of nightlife. Four fraternities have their own houses, while the four sororities are relegated to special dorm suites. There are also two campus theater series, two-dollar movie nights, and comedians, ventriloquists, and

"If it's your passion to be an activist, there are plenty of organizations to get involved with."

live bands provided by the center for student activities. Large-scale philanthropic events like Make a Difference Day and the Month of Service, in March, are also popular. "There is a mix of on- and off-campus social life," says a junior. College policy states that students must be twenty-one to have or consume alcohol on campus. Homecoming, Springfest (a day full of bands, activities, and food), and Winter Carnival break up the monotony of studying for exams.

Downtown Meadville, lovingly referred to as Mudville, is a ten-minute walk from campus and has a four-screen movie theater and several community playhouses, as well as schools, hospitals, children's homes, animal shelters, and other organizations that benefit from the more than 22,000 hours of service students contribute each year. "The students do a lot of volunteer work and help immensely throughout the community," says an economics major. When more time in Meadville is too much to bear, students hit the road. Nearby state parks at Conneaut Lake and Lake Erie offer water-skiing and boating in warm weather and cross-country skiing in the winter.

As for Allegheny traditions, there's the somewhat suspect "13th Plank" ritual, which states that all freshman women must be kissed on the thirteenth plank of the campus bridge by an upperclassman to be considered a "true Allegheny co-ed." Of course, a group of freshmen men steal the plank every year at the beginning of the first semester to prevent that from happening. Athletics play a big role in Allegheny life, although there are no athletic scholarships, and the recent addition of a $13 million sports and fitness complex gave students new reason to cheer. Twenty-five percent of Allegheny students participate in varsity athletics, while 50 percent participate in intramural sports. The men's and women's indoor and outdoor track and field and cross-country teams claimed five out of six North Coast Athletic Conference championships in 2002–2003.

Allegheny College boasts a rich history of academic excellence in an intimate setting, augmented by a new emphasis on extracurricular experiences designed to produce well-rounded alumni. The campus's natural beauty and the genuine affection students feel for it and for each other remain unchanged. Indeed, the Allegheny experience "urges you to be well rounded and grow as a person, not just as a student," proclaims a proud junior.

The men's and women's indoor and outdoor track and field and cross-country teams claimed five out of six North Coast Athletic Conference championships in 2002–2003.

Overlaps

Penn State, University of Pittsburgh, Washington and Jefferson, Bucknell, College of Wooster

If You Apply To ➤ **Allegheny:** Early decision: Jan. 15. Regular admissions and financial aid: Feb 15. Does not guarantee to meet full demonstrated need. Campus interview: recommended, evaluative. Alumni interviews: optional, informational. SATs or ACTs: required. SAT IIs: recommended. Accepts the Common Application and electronic applications. Essay question: significant experience, important issue, or person of significant influence.

Alma College

Alma, MI 48801

The college that put the "Alma" back in "alma mater." As friendly a campus as you'll find, Alma combines the liberal arts with distinctive offerings in health-related fields. Diversity is an issue and few out-of-staters enroll. If central Michigan drives you stir-crazy, join the hordes who go abroad.

The mission of Alma College, a tiny gem on Michigan's lower peninsula, is fourfold: "To prepare graduates who think critically, serve generously, lead purposefully and live responsibly as stewards of the world they bequeath to future generations." To that end, the school provides a liberal arts education with lots of close, personal attention—along with a global perspective. Alma students have taken part in everything from the U.S. mission to the United Nations to the reclamation of a Jewish cemetery in Poland. And the college's annual Highland Festival, with kilt-wearing bagpipers and competitions, has led some to dub the school "Scotland, USA." "I like the people and the small size," says a math major. An increasing emphasis on collaborative research and scholarship doesn't hurt, either.

Alma's campus features twenty-five Prairie-style buildings of redbrick and limestone surrounding a scenic central mall. There are lots of trees and open places to sit, at least in the warmer months. Administrators are looking at how best to expand toward the Pine River, because the current campus is bounded by residential neighborhoods, making it difficult to find room for new academic, athletic, and residential facilities. The Alan J. Stone Center for Recreation opened in August 2001.

The Alma experience begins with the seven-day Preterm Orientation, built around a one-credit academic seminar, which includes readings, discussions, and research, and introduces students to computer resources, on-campus life, and extracurricular activities. To graduate, students must demonstrate proficiency in communication, computation, and foreign language, and must complete sixteen credits in each of three areas: arts and humanities, social sciences, and

> **"All classes are taught by professors, and many, even freshman courses, by full professors."**

natural sciences. In addition, students must complete a comprehensive series of English courses. "Courses are pretty rigorous, but there is not a lot of competition," says a freshman. "Math and political science are both good," while administrators say economics, modern languages, philosophy, and religious studies are weaker.

Alma's top majors, by student enrollment, are business administration and education. Next on the list are exercise and health science, and biology, both of which prepare students for work with wellness intervention programs and public health agencies, or graduate study in medicine, nursing, or physical therapy. Alma's Service Learning Program gives students academic credit for work with nonprofit economic development organizations or educational, environmental, and social service agencies. The annual Honors Day features presentations of scholarly work from nearly 10 percent of the student body, and $2 million from the Lilly Endowment has enabled Alma to create a program called "Discovering Vocation" to help students find meaning and purpose in their choice of career.

Despite Alma's small size and the fact that 96 percent of students are Michigan natives, the terms "provincial" and "insular" just don't apply here. In fact, one of the college's selling points is its wide variety of study abroad opportunities. During the one-month spring term, students enroll in a single intensive course that often includes off-campus study. Past programs have taken students to Australia to study

Website: www.alma.edu
Location: Rural
Total Enrollment: 1,317
Undergraduates: 1,317
Male/Female: 43/57
ACT Range: 22–27
Financial Aid: 76%
Expense: Pr $ $
Phi Beta Kappa: Yes
Applicants: 1,502
Accepted: 79%
Enrolled: 28%
Grad in 6 Years: 68%
Returning Freshmen: 83%
Academics: ✍ ✍ ✍
Social: ☎ ☎ ☎
Q of L: ★ ★ ★
Admissions: (800) 321-ALMA
Email Address:
   admissions@alma.edu

Strongest Programs:
Education
Business Administration
Exercise and Health Science
Biology
English
History
Psychology
Communication

A $2 million grant from the Lilly Endowment has enabled Alma to create a program called "Discovering Vocation" to help students find meaning and purpose in their choice of career.

culture and trade in the Pacific Rim, to Paris to learn language and culture, and to Israel for archaeological fieldwork. Alma also offers foreign study programs in eight other countries, including Bolivia, Ecuador, England, and Peru.

Back on campus, Alma's professors win praise. "All classes are taught by professors, and many, even freshman courses, by full professors," says a math major. None of the classes taken by freshmen have more than one hundred students; 58 percent have twenty-five or less. "The classes are small enough for the teachers to know your name," says a psychology major. Students say graduating in four years is seldom a problem, except for education majors, who may need a ninth semester to complete their student teaching.

Alma students "are very involved around campus," says a freshman. "People are active with a lot of different organizations and activities." That said, state residency isn't the only point of homogeneity. The campus is 94 percent white, with African-Americans and Hispanics each comprising 1 percent of the student body, and Asian Americans 2 percent. "The administration is trying to recruit more people of diverse backgrounds, more international students and out-of-staters," reports a senior. "Bursting the Bubble" weekend, which occurs each January around Martin Luther King Jr. Day, is part of the effort to increase diversity. Brainy types can vie for an unlimited number of merit scholarships, ranging from $500 to full tuition.

Only fifty seniors may live off-campus, so 85 percent of Alma's students take beds on campus, in the "decent" and "well-maintained" dorms. Freshmen are assigned rooms in single-sex and co-ed halls (some co-ed by room, others by floor), while upperclassmen play the lottery and usually get suites. Other options include two international houses, a multicultural house, and fraternities and sororities, at least for the 25 percent of the men and 39 percent of women who go Greek. Everyone buys fourteen or nineteen meals a week, and chows down at the all-you-can-eat Commons or at Joe's Place, a snack bar. "The food is great!" cheers a freshman. "Also, there is a lot of variety—always something for everyone."

Alma students may live in a small town, but "there are lots of things to do socially," says a math major, thanks to the student-run union board. "Many people also go to clubs," and there's a movie theater, bowling alley, and three bars close to campus, too. Officially, the campus alcohol policy follows Michigan law: No one under twenty-one can drink. But "it is not that difficult to get some beer as an underage student," one reports. Underage students caught imbibing are written up and fined, though "no matter where you go, you can find a way to buy" booze if you want it, says a premed.

"Courses are pretty rigorous, but there is not a lot of competition."

Town–gown relations at Alma are strong, with students volunteering, taking part-time jobs, and otherwise getting involved in the community. The annual Highland Festival features bagpipers and Scottish dancing; for members of the Alma marching band, who strut in kilts stitched from the college's own tartan, every performance might as well be a festival. Almost all Alma students welcome St. Paddy's Day with Irish Pub, a thunderous celebration sure to rouse the leprechauns for a celebratory toast. Students with wheels will find diversions within easy reach, as Mt. Pleasant, Saginaw, and the East Lansing campus of Michigan State are less than an hour away, and ski slopes are just a bit farther. The Alma softball team has taken first place in the Michigan Intercollegiate Athletic Association since 1997, and the volleyball and football teams have also brought home titles in recent years.

Helpful advisors and caring faculty members help Alma students chart a course on campus and in the broader world, allowing them to leave well prepared for today's competitive job market. Though the school's small size and rural location may take some getting used to, Michigan natives are sure to find a warm welcome—and perhaps a friendly face from their own hometown.

Overlaps
Michigan State, Central Michigan, Grand Valley State, Western Michigan, Albion

Alma: Rolling admissions and financial aid. Early action: Nov. 1. Housing: May 1. Meets demonstrated need of 94%. Campus interviews: recommended, informational. No alumni interviews. SATs or ACTs: required (ACT preferred). SAT IIs: optional. Accepts electronic applications. Optional essay question: creatively introduce yourself, discussing something important to you or why Alma is a good fit.

Alverno College

3401 South 39th Street, P.O. Box 343922, Milwaukee, WI 53234-3922

At last, a college that evaluates students on what they can do rather than how well they can memorize. Forget oval-blackening; students here show mastery in their chosen fields. Practical and hands-on, Alverno is at its best in preprofessional programs. Only women need apply.

At Alverno College, you can forget about striving for an A. That's because this small Roman Catholic women's college emphasizes ability-based learning instead of letter grades. Students are required to show "mastery" in a range of liberal arts courses, as well as demonstrated ability in eight broad areas: communications, analysis, problem solving, values in decision making, social interaction, global perspectives, effective citizenship, and aesthetic responsiveness. Students move through interdisciplinary progressive levels toward a degree by being "validated" in these areas. For example, a course in sociology might contribute to validation in communication and social interaction, as well as in making independent value judgments. The learning environment isn't competitive, though the ability-based method can "create a lot of work requiring much thought," says a professional communications major. As one senior puts it: "We learn in a way that gives us a cutting edge."

Alverno is located in a quiet, well-kept residential area. The parklike forty-six-acre campus is just fifteen minutes from downtown Milwaukee and a ten-minute walk from shops and restaurants. Its three main academic buildings, of 1950s and '60s vintage, feature brick and stone exteriors and stained-glass windows. The Teaching, Learning, and Technology Center houses 73,000 square feet of science labs, multimedia production areas, and computer facilities.

Alverno is really two colleges rolled into one. There is a regular weekday program that attracts mostly traditional college-age women, the majority of whom are from Milwaukee. The Weekend College allows women, most of them older with full-time jobs, to earn a degree in four years by attending classes every other weekend. Students in the weekday college may earn credit by spending four to eight hours a week in internships related to their field of study. First-year

"We learn in a way that gives us a cutting edge."

students take an orientation seminar and introductory courses in the arts and humanities, science, psychology and sociology, communications, and math. The student body is diverse—in age, ethnic background, and religion. "It would be very hard to make generalizations," one junior says. Religious studies aren't required, but for those who seek it, a Catholic liturgy is available on a daily basis.

Alverno's business and management programs are well established. "The level of professionalism that Alverno students have compared to those at other colleges or universities is amazing," one junior says. Students praise the professional communications and teacher education programs and its strong nursing program. Newer majors include computer studies, global studies, and community leadership and

Website: www.alverno.edu
Location: Suburban
Total Enrollment: 1,952
Undergraduates: 1,779
Male/Female: 0/100
ACT Range: N/A
Financial Aid: 89%
Expense: Pr $
Phi Beta Kappa: No
Applicants: 511
Accepted: 80%
Enrolled: 50%
Grad in 6 Years: 57%
Returning Freshmen: 78%
Academics: ✍ ✍ ✍
Social: ☎
Q of L: ★★★★
Admissions: (414) 382-6100
Email Address: admissions@alverno.edu

Strongest Programs:
Nursing
Education
Business and Management
Psychology
Biology
Professional Communication
Interdisciplinary Arts and Humanities

development. One art education major says the art department "has produced some of the best art instructors, local artists, and art therapists that Milwaukee has to offer." The library holds 350,000 titles, and for major research projects students can use the online library/media center catalog made available through a consortial arrangement with five Milwaukee colleges. Bali, Paris, Tokyo, and London are just a few of the places where students have taken advantage of the school's study abroad program.

Many professors at Alverno teach all levels of classes, so "there is no distinct difference" in the quality of teaching for freshmen or seniors, one international business major says. The instructors don't generally focus on publishing research. "The faculty and staff really care whether you are successful," says a social science major.

"The level of professionalism that Alverno students have compared to those at other colleges or universities is amazing."

"They want to see you achieve and are willing to go over and beyond to make sure you do." Academic counseling and individual attention run throughout students' academic careers to keep them on track. "We couldn't have more help," one junior says.

Many students are older than the traditional college age and quite a few have children. There are dozens of student groups and cultural groups, like Women of Color, active on campus. Students and faculty often engage in roundtable discussions to look at political or social issues, according to a sophomore. With so many different kinds of people on campus, the college "is open-minded to all views but does not allow hate or anything that might hurt any specific group," one senior says. The vast majority of the students receive financial aid, and merit scholarships ranging from $2,100 to $5,800 are awarded based on a personal evaluation of each incoming student.

A three-day orientation program serves freshmen, transfer, resident, and commuter students. The majority of students are commuters, though there are a limited number of dorm rooms. Students say the residence halls offer clean, spacious rooms with fully equipped lounges, laundry, and cooking facilities available on each floor. "Dorms are comfortable and well maintained every day, including weekends," says one junior. Male visitors are allowed, but they must sign in and be out by midnight on weekdays and 2:00 a.m. on weekends.

Most of the social life takes place off campus at local clubs, bars, coffee bars, and nearby colleges, but the student union, called the Pipeline, frequently offers on-campus activities. The campus also has an on-site day-care center, a fitness center, and a jogging track, and sponsors dance and theater groups. "Milwaukee is a thriving city of the arts—visual, theatrical, and performance—not to mention the festivals that go on every year," says one art education major. There are also myriad parks and shopping centers, a Performing Arts Center, professional sports teams, ethnic festivals, and free outdoor concerts. Students look forward to the annual Rotunda Ball and homecoming festivities. When it comes to alcohol on campus, the combination of strict policies and a generally low amount of drinking means Alverno is rarely the home of the *Animal House* booze fest.

Alverno competes in Division III and fields varsity basketball, volleyball, softball, soccer, and cross-country teams. Intramurals are popular as well. Nonsporting annual events include Student Seminar Day, which allows students and faculty to change places so that students can "share their experiences" with the Alverno community.

Attending a school like Alverno promises an experience far afield in some ways from the traditional college world. The lack of grades and emphasis on real-world applications builds confidence in one's actual ability to perform, rather than ability to score an A. Students and faculty are often on a first-name basis from the start and build relationships that help students find their "own unique style of learning," one senior says. It's a method that obviously works.

If You Apply To ➤

Alverno: Rolling admissions. Does not guarantee to meet demonstrated need. Campus interviews: optional, informational. No alumni interviews. ACTs: required. Accepts the Common Application and electronic applications. Essay question: recent activities and/or work history, academic goals and abilities, and most important reason for applying to Alverno.

American University

4400 Massachusetts Avenue NW, Washington, DC 20016-8001

If the odds are against you at Georgetown and you can't see yourself on GW's highly urban campus, welcome to American University. The allure of AU is simple: Washington, D.C. American has a nice campus in a nice neighborhood with easy access to the Metro. It is about a third smaller than GW.

Some people might take the moniker "budding politician" to be an epithet, but not so with students at American University. Located just a few miles from where our nation's leaders make decisions of global impact, AU is a breeding ground for the next generation of reporters, diplomats, lobbyists, and political leaders who will shape domestic and international policy. Alongside these eager buzz hounds is a host of students taking advantage of AU's strong programs in the arts and sciences. If it sounds like the leafy AU campus has all the bustle of downtown D.C., take heart. "Students who go to AU are super-friendly and outgoing," an international studies major says, "and they are more than happy to point a lost freshman in the right direction."

AU's eighty-four-acre residential campus is located in the northwest corner of Washington, D.C., in a neighborhood called Tenleytown just minutes from downtown; free shuttle buses transport students to the nearby Metro (subway) station. There's a mix of classical and modern architecture and flower gardens alongside the parking lots. The quads have numerous sitting areas for reflection and study. Indeed, now that the campus has gone totally wireless, students can study outdoors and enjoy AU's lush landscaping during Washington's balmy fall and splendid spring. The University Center has been renovated, with offices for student clubs, casual lounges, and a wireless cybercafe. The three-hundred-seat Greenberg Theater has opened and construction has begun on the Katzen Arts Center for studio and performing arts.

All AU undergraduates must demonstrate competency in writing and English, either through two courses or an exam; for math or statistics, it's one semester of class or placing out through a test. The required general education program draws thirty credit hours from five areas: the creative arts, traditions that shape the Western world, international and intercultural experience, social institutions and behavior, and the natural sciences. The requirements are typically completed during the first two years so that students can study abroad or participate in an internship or co-op—of which there are many, thanks to the school's relationships with more than nine hundred private, nonprofit, or government institutions. The school also uses these connections in its Washington Semester* program, which attracts a wide range of majors.

In the classroom, AU has outstanding programs in political science and

> **"I enjoy being able to discuss current events with students who actually know what is going on."**

Website: www.american.edu	
Location: Urban	
Total Enrollment: 11,052	
Undergraduates: 5,872	
Male/Female: 39/61	
SAT Ranges: V 560–670	
M 550–650	
ACT Range: 24–29	
Financial Aid: 62%	
Expense: Pr $ $ $ $	
Phi Beta Kappa: Yes	
Applicants: 9,879	
Accepted: 63%	
Enrolled: 21%	
Grad in 6 Years: 66%	
Returning Freshmen: 87%	
Academics: ✍ ✍ ✍ ½	
Social: ☎ ☎ ☎	
Q of L: ★ ★ ★	
Admissions: (202) 885-6000	
Email Address:	
afa@american.edu	

Strongest Programs:
International Studies
Political Science/Government
Justice, Law, and Society
Studio Art
Premed
Journalism

Now that the campus has gone totally wireless, students can study outdoors and enjoy AU's extensive flower gardens and lush landscaping during Washington's balmy fall and splendid spring.

government, international studies, and history. An honors program offers the top 15 percent of entering students small seminars, special sections of many courses, and designated floors in the residence halls, plus specialized work in the major and a senior capstone experience. There are new majors in communications studies and audio production. Classes are "competitive but not to the point of driving you insane," says a freshman. "Professors expect students to read, discuss, and do assignments, but there isn't much busywork." On the quality of teaching, students' opinions are mixed. American has a reputation for bringing in adjunct professors who are well known outside academia, which "is good since they have real experience and good contacts, but bad because they are never around," one student says. Freshmen are taught by professors, but often they are nontenured assistants or visitors who leave after a year or two, "making it hard to make connections," says an international relations and Spanish major. "The quality of teaching that I have received is poor in comparison to what I had been expecting." But one student says that the professors "bring a lot of real-world knowledge" to the classroom. AU's career center offers counseling and a career fair. Students must meet with academic advisors before registering for classes, though that's often difficult because of everyone's busy schedules, one student says. AU does offer significant support services for students with disabilities, whether physical or learning-related.

AU prides itself on drawing students from every state and more than 140 foreign countries; just 15 percent hail from the District of Columbia. Six percent of the student body is African-American, 5 percent is Hispanic, and 4 percent are Asian-American. Unlike many college campuses where apathy reigns, AU is very active politically—after all, this is Washington, D.C., and causes are what the city is all about. AU's price tag is hefty, but the school offers 549 merit scholarships ranging from $500 to full tuition. The number of athletic scholarships has skyrocketed to 169 in ten women's and nine men's sports.

AU's World Capitals Program sends students to seventeen countries on four continents, while the Washington Semester Program keeps them local with study opportunities within the federal government or at one of Washington's premier museums.

About two-thirds of AU's students, mostly freshmen and sophomores, live on campus. The dorms are air-conditioned—a must during D.C.'s muggy early fall and late spring—with kitchens and laundry facilities on each floor and carpeting and built-in furniture in the rooms. There is also new off-campus housing for upperclassmen in newly renovated luxury apartments, and a shuttle bus connects them to campus. "Housing draw is difficult, since it not only goes by current dorm status, but also by credits, making it more difficult for those with fewer credits," says a junior. Students say they generally feel safe on campus, noting that public safety officers are visible, and that AU is adding more blue-light emergency telephones.

A good deal of the social life at AU revolves around campus-related functions, such as room and frat parties; 17 percent of men and 18 percent of women go Greek, though the women lament that the bottom-heavy male–female ratio is "a little ridiculous." The immediate area around AU has restaurants and shops, but you need to get a bit farther away for true nightlife in Dupont Circle and Georgetown. While greater D.C. certainly has its share of clubs and bars, they're largely off-limits to students under twenty-one. Students of legal age may imbibe at AU's Tavern; otherwise, the campus is officially dry. Happily, there is so much other stuff to do in D.C.—from the new art house movie theaters to gallery openings, pro soccer games, and funky live music. Each year, Family Weekend brings games, rides, and popular bands to campus, along with a carnival on the quad.

"Professors expect students to read, discuss, and do assignments, but there isn't much busywork."

Homecoming and Founder's Week are also campus favorites. D.C. also has plenty of monuments, museums, and other free attractions. "You just jump on the Metro to get anywhere in the city," says a communication major. Popular road trips include Baltimore, Annapolis, the Ocean City shore, and nearby amusement parks.

American competes in Division I, but sports are an afterthought for most students. There's no football team, but students are enthusiastic about Eagles basketball, where games against Bucknell and the Naval Academy top the schedule. In 2003, AU boasted an All-American swimmer who made the Olympic trials, while the men's soccer and tennis teams won the 2002 tournaments. The women's volleyball and tennis teams took home the 2002 NCAA Division I titles.

Even if you're not a C-SPAN junkie, AU and Washington, D.C., are still a top combo for a rich college life. The opportunities for real-world experience—in fields ranging from museum studies to dance to political science—are outstanding, and the school's facilities continue to improve. Of course, there are some other pluses to being in Washington, says one student: "I enjoy being able to discuss current events with students who actually know what is going on."

Overlaps

George Washington, Syracuse, Georgetown, Boston University, NYU

If You Apply To ➤

American: Early decision: Nov. 15. Regular admissions: Feb. 1. Financial aid: Mar. 1 (Nov. 15 for early decision). Housing: May 1. Meets demonstrated need of 23%. Campus and alumni interviews: recommended, informational. SATs: required. SAT IIs: recommended. Accepts the Common Application and electronic applications. Essay question: cover story for a national news magazine on Jan. 1, 2025, an event or individual instrumental in shaping who you are, or a sample of creative or fiction writing produced for a class.

Amherst College

Amherst, MA 01002-5000

Original home to the well-rounded, superachieving, gentle-person jock. Compare to Williams, Middlebury, and Colby. Not Swarthmore, not Wesleyan. Amherst has always been the king in its category—mainly because there are four other major institutions in easy reach to add diversity and depth.

At Amherst College, the focus isn't on racking up high grade point averages. Instead, students focus on becoming people who base their thinking on a strong foundation in the liberal arts. Emphasizing "freedom to explore," the spotlight here is on learning, not competing for grades. "The lack of a core curriculum means I choose, and therefore I like, most of my classes and actually look forward to going to them," says a sophomore. While there is little time left for partying or playing games, a weekly student-sponsored keg bash, known as TAP (The Amherst Party), and any athletic contest against arch rival Williams will draw students away from their books.

Amherst's 964 acres overlook the picturesque town of Amherst and the Pioneer Valley and offer a panoramic view of the Holyoke Range and the Pelham Hills. On campus, a plot of open land housing a wildlife sanctuary and a forest shares space with academic and residential buildings and athletic fields and facilities. While Amherst's predominant architectural style remains nineteenth-century academia—redbrick is key—everything from a "pale yellow octagonal structure to a garish, modern new dorm" can be found here. Amherst looks like a college is supposed to look, with trees and paths winding through the buildings to offer long, contemplative walks. Of course, the flip side is snowy winters that don't end soon enough when spring break has come and gone. All of the first-year housing is getting an upgrade, and three other buildings have recently been renovated—Fayerweather Hall, the Fine Arts building, and the Mead

"Students enjoy an unprecedented level of independence."

Website: www.amherst.edu
Location: Small town
Total Enrollment: 1,618
Undergraduates: 1,618
Male/Female: 51/49
SAT Ranges: V 660–770
  M 650–770
ACT Range: 28-33
Financial Aid: 46%
Expense: Pr $ $ $ $
Phi Beta Kappa: Yes
Applicants: 5,238
Accepted: 18%
Enrolled: 43%
Grad in 6 Years: 96%
Returning Freshmen: 98%
Academics: ✏ ✏ ✏ ✏ ✏
Social: ☎ ☎ ☎
Q of L: ★ ★ ★ ★
Admissions: (413) 542-2328

(Continued)

Email Address:
admission@amherst.edu

Strongest Programs:
English
Psychology
Political Science
History
Economics
Dance

All of the first-year housing is getting an upgrade, and three other buildings have recently been renovated. A new geology museum is planned, along with renovations for upperclass dorms.

Art Museum. A new geology museum is planned, along with renovations for upper-class dorms.

Amherst's curriculum emphasizes education as a process or activity rather than a form of production. There is no core program and there are no distribution requirements; to graduate, students must only take a first-year seminar, declare a major at the end of sophomore year, fulfill departmental program requirements, pass the requisite number of electives, and perform satisfactorily on comprehensive exams in their major field. First-year seminars, taught by two or more professors, help foster interdisciplinary approaches across topics and are offered in several subject areas. Of this approach to education, administrators say, "A student should be free at this stage to make choices—even foolish choices." Says a senior political science student: "Amherst has a rich and intense academic environment. Students do not compete since everyone takes their own unique set of courses through the open curriculum."

The most popular majors—English, economics, political science, psychology, and biology—and what Amherst calls its unique "law, jurisprudence, and social thought" major are top-notch, and students may mix and match among these subjects to form dual-degree programs. (About one-third of students pursue double majors, and a few overachievers even triple major, administrators report.) Students may create their own courses of study from Special Topics classes if the subject of their interest is not available. The dance program is also strong, although it requires courses at each school in the Five College Consortium.* To house all of these programs, Amherst has spent millions of dollars in recent years renovating facilities, upgrading technological capabilities, and improving spaces for studying, exhibits, performances, and sports.

On such a small campus without graduate students, interaction with professors is constant and friendly. "The professors are definitely one of the best things about Amherst College," a freshman says. "They are flexible, accessible and truly engage their students." Even as freshmen, students can become involved in a professor's research. But Amherst believes teaching is a professor's highest priority, more important even than research. "They come to a school like Amherst because they enjoy teaching and they're good at it," a senior says.

In addition to being one of the Five Colleges—the others are Smith, Mount Holyoke, the University of Massachusetts at Amherst, and Hampshire—Amherst also belongs to the Maritime Studies Program* and the Twelve College Exchange.* With three other liberal arts colleges and a major state university a brief shuttle bus ride away, cross-registration in any one of a host of fields—like basic accounting at UMass or "something experimental" at Hampshire—is a godsend about the middle of sophomore year. All-female Smith and Mount Holyoke also add to the social life,

Amherst is located in "the quintessential college town, full of academics, old hippies, small shops, and cheap restaurants."

and numerous cultural and artistic events at the other schools are open to Amherst students. Each year, about one-third of the junior class spends a semester or year abroad; in the past two years, students enrolled in seventy-two programs in thirty-five countries, ranging from a math program in Budapest to analyzing architecture in Rome. Amherst also has a program in Kyoto, Japan, where one of the college's Colonial-style buildings has been duplicated.

Amherst is working hard to shake off its image as a homogenous, elitist, male-dominated school, and one freshman says the students don't let the school's prestige go to their heads. But economic diversity is still a concern, says a senior: "Many students feel that the social scene revolves around money and those with money. However, there's currently a group—FACE—that's addressing class issues; the group has wide campus support from those from all backgrounds." The college dealt a major blow to the old-boy network when it abolished fraternities in the mid-'80s. Minority enrollment includes 9 percent African-Americans, 8 percent Hispanics, and 12 percent Asian-Americans, sizable fractions for a school of this size. A new Diversity Educators group teaches first-years about race issues and invites speakers to campus. The campus is liberal and discussions on political issues and hot topics are common. "Students are always trying to present fresh and new perspectives on their concerns," says one political science major. A senior says Amherst "brings in students who get bored very easily," and that "makes for a more interesting classroom and social environment."

Housing at Amherst is guaranteed for four years, and 98 percent of students live on campus. There has been a housing crunch and complaints about underclassmen's housing, but that is being addressed with extensive renovations. One student says, "Upperclass residences are first-rate, often in large Victorian mansions" that once belonged to the frats, complete with ballrooms, pianos, hardwood floors, and stained-glass windows. "Sophomore housing sucks (many triples)," says a senior. "However, juniors and seniors typically live in fantastic singles," often in the apartment-style social dorms. Everyone who lives on campus, and anyone else who wants to, eats in Valentine Hall, which includes a central serving station and five dining rooms. The selection is diverse but the food overall gets mixed reviews.

The legacy of beer-drenched partying at Amherst lingers even after the demise of the frats. "The school respects students enough to let them make their own decisions and understands when mistakes happen," a freshman says. "At the same time, students are made to understand that their actions have consequences." Thursday Night TAP, complete with kegs, dancing, and security monitors, is the place to see and be seen, with popular theme nights such as Madonna TAP and Motown TAP. Not everyone has to drink plain-old beer to have fun, as one junior describes: "My friends and I organized 'anti-parties' in our substance-free dorm. The college paid for our root-beer keg."

While much of Amherst's social life takes place on campus, the four other schools in the area also provide diversions. The biggest party of the year, thrown in February, is Casino Night, which includes gambling with real money. The weekend-long Bavaria festival in the spring offers a pig roast and big-wheel joust, while a lip-sync contest that offers winners their first pick during room draw usually attracts hilarious entries. The relatively new Campus Center includes outdoor terraces, a formal living room, a game room, a snack bar, a small theater, and a student-run co-op coffeehouse, open three nights a week, with live entertainment.

Amherst is located in "the quintessential college town, full of academics, old hippies, small shops, and cheap restaurants," says an interdisciplinary studies major. "The town is also much more diverse than usual in western Massachusetts. There are large Vietnamese, Cambodian, and Puerto Rican populations." For the many outdoorsy types, good skiing in Vermont is not far, and Boston (an hour and a half) and New York (almost four) are close enough to be convenient road trip destinations.

Sports are taken seriously, both varsity and intramurals, and the admissions office frankly acknowledges that seventy-five spots in each year's freshman class are reserved for student-athletes who are recruited by coaches and who may or may not meet the academic standards demanded of other admits. Amherst competes in Division III, but the strong baseball team takes on Division I opponents as well. During the 2001–2002 season, Amherst women's soccer and cross-country teams were NESCAC champions. In 2002–2003, the men's swimming and women's lacrosse teams claimed the NESCAC championship, and the women's golf coach was named the NCGA Division III national coach of the year. Any showdown with archrival Williams is inevitably the biggest game of the season, drawing fans from all corners of campus.

Overlaps

Yale, Harvard, Brown, Williams, Stanford

Combine a lack of restrictive requirements with a cadre of professors who are focused on teaching, and it becomes clear why students here so love their institution. "Students enjoy an unprecedented level of independence," says a senior, which prepares them well for whatever challenges they undertake after graduation.

If You Apply To ➤	**Amherst:** Early decision: Nov. 15. Regular admissions: Dec. 31. Financial aid: Nov. 1. Guarantees to meet demonstrated need. No campus or alumni interviews. SATs or ACTs: required. SAT II: any three required of applicants who take the SAT. Accepts the Common Application and electronic applications. Essay question: one Common Application question and respond to one of five quotations.

Antioch College

795 Livermore Street, Yellow Springs, OH 45387

Part Goth, part granola, and part anarchist—with plenty of none-of-the-above mixed in—Antioch is a haven for square pegs. Yet Antioch offers something very practical: the chance for sixteen-week co-op experiences interspersed with academic study. March and protest, then get a job. Cool.

Website: www.antioch-college.edu

Location: Rural

Total Enrollment: 589

Undergraduates: 581

Male/Female: 39/61

SAT Ranges: N/A

ACT Range: N/A

Financial Aid: 97%

Expense: Pr $ $

Phi Beta Kappa: No

Applicants: 504

Accepted: 75%

Enrolled: 51%

Grad in 6 Years: 45%

Returning Freshmen: 78%

Academics: ✍ ✍ ✍

Social: ☎ ☎

Q of L: ★ ★ ★ ★

Admissions: (937) 769-1100

Email Address: admissions@antioch-college.edu

Strongest Program:
Cooperative Education

Come to Yellow Springs, Ohio, and you may think you've stepped out of a time machine. But no, you haven't spun back to 1969—you're simply at Antioch College, where the humanistic messages of that generation are still taken to heart and put into action. The students, many of them products of "alternative" high schools, discuss feminism, gay rights, and nuclear proliferation over vegetarian meals, and they are more likely to take road trips to Washington for an environmental rally than to show up at a neighboring school's fraternity party.

Founded in 1852 by abolitionist and social reformer Horace Mann, Antioch remains a haven for outspoken and independent students who thrive under the rigors of a refreshingly nontraditional education. Antioch pioneered the idea that students should alternate time in the classroom with jobs in the "real world," and this idea has remained the foundation for Antioch's unique approach to training students. Under the college's famed co-op program, students spend nearly half of their college years out in the real world,

> **"The co-op program is amazing; it's the reason to come to Antioch."**

be it selling fresh-squeezed orange juice on a street corner in California, studying Buddhism in India, or working in a Fortune 500 company in New York City.

Antioch does not use standardized test scores for admission. In classes, written faculty evaluations take the place of grades, and students are required to submit self-evaluations of their class performance. "Antioch is for the independent learner," notes a junior. A senior adds, "Any student with self motivation and a desire to learn can find the resources to succeed academically."

In completing Antioch's thirty-two-credit general education program, students spend their first year pursuing a core of courses that blends the traditional liberal arts with examination of the "social, historical, philosophical, and economic" nature of work. In addition, there are distribution requirements in the humanities, social and behavioral sciences, natural sciences, and cultural studies. Physical education is also required. Students report that the academic climate is laid-back yet rigorous. Because classes are usually no larger than twenty, students must always be prepared to participate. Close relationships often develop between students and faculty; representatives of both groups sit on several of the influential governing committees, including the administrative council, the housing board, and the community council. "Because students evaluate each professor and class, we have helped to keep some very talented professors," says one student. Each student is assigned a co-op advisor to help with the nearly continuous job hunt, and a network of alumni offering jobs is one major resource that students can depend on in their search. You can't miss with the career counselors. "It's not just counseling, it's cooperative education that teaches you more about yourself than you could imagine. It's the best reason to come to Antioch," says a student.

Antioch's trimester system lasts fifteen weeks, with co-op terms lasting sixteen weeks. The college helps place students in co-op programs and credit is earned after the student completes a paper or project demonstrating what he or she learned during the co-op experience. Antioch's mission lies in its "commitment to undergraduate experiential learning and to preparing students to face the challenges and opportunities of the twenty-first century." In order to receive a "cross-cultural" experience, Antioch has all students spend three to twelve months in a significantly different cultural environment. In addition to those offered by the school, study-abroad options are available through the

> **"If I characterize the 'typical' Antioch student, I invariably misrepresent those who are not queer, vegan, feminist, environmentalist, cynical, or political activists."**

Great Lakes College Association.* There is a downside to this: students blame the high attrition rate on the rigors of the co-op program. One student explains that "students often move every three or six months because of co-op—this is both financially and emotionally draining." Friendships and involvement in extracurricular activities at the Yellow Springs campus often suffer because of the on-again, off-again attendance schedules. But the co-op program wouldn't have been there for so long if it didn't have its fans, such as a senior who says, "The co-op program is amazing; it's the reason to come to Antioch. It's made me as confident and clear about my life goals as can be."

Antioch's traditional academic programs are somewhat uneven. Although there are only eight official majors, each allows a student to in a more specialized area. The major in physical sciences has traditionally been strong, especially with its heavily stocked research laboratory. Concentrations in political science, psychology, and many of the arts offerings are also established strongholds. Environmental and life sciences is excellent, in part because of the proximity of a one-thousand-acre forest preserve, Glen Helen, and a nature museum. Students complain mostly about the history department. The communications program benefits from a major public radio station operated by Antioch, which gives students experience in the broadcasting field.

Being different may be the only thing Antioch students have in common, and diversity is a given on this campus. "If I characterize the 'typical' Antioch student, I invariably misrepresent those who are not queer, vegan, feminist, environmentalist, cynical, or political activists," says a senior, who describes his peers as "bright, quirky, passionate students." Twenty-three percent of the students come from Ohio; the rest hail from points throughout the nation. Six percent of students are African-American, 5 percent are Asian-American, and 1 percent are Hispanic. A variety of merit scholarships ranging from $5,000 to $10,000 are renewable for four years.

Ninety-nine percent of the students are housed on campus in apartment-style dorms. "To get financial aid, you have to live on campus," says one resident. In contrast to the college's democratic creed, room assignments are determined by the whim of "a much-courted administrator." Co-ed and single-sex dorms are available, and all come equipped with kitchens. Everyone is guaranteed on-campus housing if

Without Greek organizations, social life tends to be rather spontaneous and limited to on-campus activities. Drinking is said to be less of a problem among students than among the high school students who make the scene at campus parties.

Antioch does not use standardized test scores for admission. In classes, written faculty evaluations take the place of grades, and students are required to submit self-evaluations of their class performance.

they want it, and students can choose from a number of special options that include a quiet hall, a moderate-noise hall, and even a substance-free hall, which bars smoking and drinking. The Spalt International Center, just a few years old, houses sixty students in foreign language living/learning halls. Seven- and nineteen-meal-a-week plans are available at the Caf, which features vegetarian entrees, a salad bar, and a popcorn machine.

Without Greek organizations, social life tends to be rather spontaneous and limited to on-campus activities. Drinking is said to be less of a problem among students than among the high school students who make the scene at campus parties. There is a student coffeehouse, which "is the best hangout space," while stargazers frequently congregate on the roof of the science building. Each fall, a three-day blues festival hits town. "Community Day" is actually two days a year where everyone takes the day off to mellow out and relax. Many student organizations, including the Anarchist Study Group and Third World Alliance, draw widespread student interest. A noteworthy tradition on this untraditional campus is the Quasi-Prom, an annual dance put on by the Lesbian/Gay Center.

Traditionally considered taboo, varsity sports have nevertheless enjoyed a rousing resurgence, thanks to the women's rugby team. Gym classes are offered in kayaking, rafting, and horseback riding. Camelot, a one-hundred-lap bicycle race, is an annual event: a team of two people races around a muddy track while the audience slings yogurt, mud, and "anything else that isn't hard" at them. The one-thousand-acre nature preserve ("the glen") across the street "lets you forget the boring flatlands of Ohio." Behind the glen is John Bryan State Park. A nearby reservoir is a popular place for swimming and windsurfing, and Clifton Gorge offers rock climbing.

The town of Yellow Springs is "a bubble of liberalism in Bible Belt Southern Ohio," according to one student. The town hosts a variety of health food stores, a pizza joint that makes its pies with whole wheat crust, and an assortment of bars and restaurants. Yellow Springs may become limiting for some students, but that problem is usually solved by the next co-op trimester.

For those who think cooperative education would be a "far out" experience, Antioch offers a unique opportunity to discover themselves in both the working world and among the college's bright, opinionated, and cooperative student body. Horace Mann once implored his students to "be ashamed to die until you have won some victory for humanity." The Antioch community takes this message to heart. "We are here to educate ourselves about social and political injustices so that we can change our world," says a health and human development major.

Overlaps

Oberlin, Hampshire, Earlham, Evergreen State, Bard

If You Apply To ➢

Antioch: Rolling admissions. Financial aid: Feb. 1. Does not guarantee to meet demonstrated need. Campus interviews: recommended, informational. No alumni interviews. SATs: optional. SAT IIs: optional. Accepts the Common Application. Essay question: important experience; significant personal, local, or national issue; or portfolio. Looks for independent, self-directed students who are willing to take risks.

University of Arizona

Robert L. Nugent Building, Tucson, AZ 85721

Tucson is an increasingly popular destination, and it isn't just because of the UA basketball team. A well-devoted honors program attracts top students, as do excellent programs in the sciences and engineering. Bring plenty of shorts and sunscreen.

With a campus that's encircled by mountain ranges and the beautiful Sonoran Desert, lined with palm trees and cacti, and set against a backdrop of stunning Tucson sunsets, it's no surprise that students at the University of Arizona love to hang out at the mall. Of course, that's not the shopping center—but a huge grassy area in the middle of campus where nearly 35,000 Wildcats gather between classes. Judging by numbers alone, that's enough people to fill a medium-sized town. But students are quick to point out that UA has a strong sense of community and offers a genuinely friendly campus. "Nobody else has a huge central meeting place like we do," says a senior marketing major. "I always see familiar and friendly faces around the mall area." With all the natural beauty that surrounds them, many Wildcats simply purr through four satisfying years.

Architecturally, the UA campus distinguishes itself from the city's regiment of adobe buildings with a design that seems a study in the versatility of redbrick. Old Main, the university's first building, is into its second century, but others verge on high-tech science facilities. Hard hats and heavy machinery have become commonplace on campus; recent construction includes a new student union, facilities for first-year students and learning-disabled students, the Athletic Hall of Fame and weight training facility, a residence hall, and a 1,300-space parking structure.

Sciences are unquestionably the school's forte—the astronomy department is among the nation's best, helped by those clear night skies. Students have access not only to leading astronomers, but also to the most up-to-date equipment, including a huge 176-inch telescope operated jointly by the university and the Smithsonian. A $28 million aerospace and mechanical engineering building has a state-of-the-art subsonic wind tunnel and rocket-combustion test facility. The history and English departments are standouts, as are several of the social science programs. Eager shutterbugs can pore through photographer Ansel Adams's personal collection, and the Center for Creative Photography offers one of the leading photographic collections in the world. Students in the popular business and public administration school can pick racetrack management as their area of expertise, while interested anthropology students can delve into garbage research. Two new programs are optics and public health. Areas getting low marks from students are the language programs and the journalism department.

Under the core curriculum, students take ten general education courses in common. They fall under the broad categories of arts, humanities, traditions and cultures, natural sciences, and individuals and societies. In addition, almost everyone gets a healthy dose of freshman composition, math, and foreign language. Academic competition, according to most students, is left up to both the individual and the specific concentration. "The courses can range in difficulty from somewhat challenging to impossible," explains one senior. The University Honors Center offers one of the nation's largest and most selective honors programs (students must maintain a grade point average of 3.5 to remain in the program). In addition to offering two hundred honors courses per year, the center features smaller classes, personalized advising, special library privileges, and great research opportunities.

> **"I always see familiar and friendly faces around the mall area."**

Website: www.arizona.edu
Location: Urban
Total Enrollment: 36,847
Undergraduates: 28,278
Male/Female: 47/53
SAT Ranges: N/A
ACT Range: 21–27
Financial Aid: 70%
Expense: Pub $ $ $
Phi Beta Kappa: Yes
Applicants: 24,026
Accepted: 83%
Enrolled: 39%
Grad in 6 Years: 55%
Returning Freshmen: 78%
Academics: ✏ ✏ ✏ ½
Social: ☎ ☎ ☎ ☎
Q of L: ★ ★ ★ ★
Admissions: (520) 621-3237
Email Address:
  appinfo@arizona.edu

Strongest Programs:
Management Information
  Systems
Nursing
Astronomy
Pharmacy
Creative Writing
Aerospace Engineering

Sciences are unquestionably the school's forte—the astronomy department is among the nation's best, helped by those clear night skies.

The Undergraduate Biology Research Program also has a national reputation. Teaching is well regarded, with some freshman courses taught by graduate students. "Each of the professors and TAs have something special to bring to the classes and show an exceptional amount of enthusiasm," a sophomore says.

One student describes his peers as "go-getters" who "bleed red and blue." Despite tougher admission standards, the administration cites a sharp increase in freshman applications over the past few years, especially out-of-staters, who constitute 29 percent of the student body. In addition to various merit scholarships, all the athletic scholarships allowed by the NCAA are available. Hispanics account for 13 percent of the enrollment, African-Americans for 3 percent, and Asian-Americans for 5 percent. A diversity action council, a newly developed student minority advisory committee, and cultural resource centers help students deal with race-relation issues. An active and popular student government runs a free legal service and a tenants' complaint center, and the university has instituted many programs to help those with learning disabilities.

Dorm rooms tend to be small but well maintained, the major problem being getting a room rather than living comfortably in it. "It's important to send your housing application in early," advises a veteran. Only 20 percent of undergraduates live in the dorms, while most upperclassmen flock to the abundant and inexpensive apartments near the school. The best way to enjoy the excellent food service at the student union's seven restaurants is to use the university-issued All Aboard credit card, which helps students take advantage of the wealth of different gustatory options and frees them from carrying cash.

Despite the high percentage of off-campus residents, students stream back onto campus on weekends for parties, sports, and cultural events. Fifteen percent of the men and women belong to fraternities or sororities. The campus is technically alcohol free, though some question whether the frats have realized that yet. Still, most social life takes place off campus. There are a lot of different dance clubs around town, and some do have after-hours for underage people. Those who feel they must go elsewhere need only head to the Mexican town of Nogales (one hour away), where there is no drinking age. Many students are content remaining in Tucson because it offers "the most incredible sunrises and sunsets, and delightful temperatures year-round."

One of the UA's most time-honored traditions is Spring Fling, said to be the largest student-run carnival in the country. Athletics is also somewhat of a tradition here. The basketball Wildcats have been among the nation's leaders in recent years. Division I football and baseball enjoy national prominence, generate lots of money

"The courses can range in difficulty from somewhat challenging to impossible."

for other men's and women's sports teams, and provide great weekend entertainment, especially when the opposing team is big-time rival Arizona State. UA's battle cry "Bear Down!" frequently heard at sporting events dates back to the 1930s, when a campus football hero, fatally injured in a car crash, whispered his last message to his teammates: "Tell them, tell them to bear down." More than sixty years later, the enigmatic slogan still appears on T-shirts and in a gym on the central campus.

The University of Arizona offers a wide variety of academic opportunities along with spectacular weather. Prospective students are warned to honestly evaluate how that will affect their ability to concentrate. UA is the place to go to engage in the pursuit of truth, knowledge, and a good tan.

Overlaps

Arizona State, Northern Arizona, UCLA, University of Colorado, UC–Santa Barbara

If You Apply To ➢   **Arizona:** Early action: Sept. 1. Regular admissions: Apr. 1. Financial aid: Feb. 1. Housing: Mar. 1. Campus interviews: optional, informational. Alumni interviews: optional. SATs or ACTs: required. SAT IIs: optional. Accepts electronic applications. No essay question.

Arizona State University

Box 870112, Tempe, AZ 85287-0112

Want to get lost in the crowd? ASU is the biggest university in the Southwest— apologies to UCLA. No matter how appealing the thought of forty-four thousand new faces, you'd better find the right program to get a good education. Try the professional schools and the honors college.

There's no doubt about it—Arizona State University is big. In fact, as the largest school in the Southwest, it's inevitable that some people will be just a number. But most students don't come here just to work on their tans. ASU's anthropology department is ranked within the top five nationwide, and its Barnett Honors College allows exceptional students to live, work, and study among their peers, and to write a senior thesis, creating a small-school atmosphere on this mammoth campus. While the perennial sunshine, low humidity, and balmy afternoons vie with lectures, labs, and reading for students' attention, the combination seems to keep everyone in a good mood.

ASU's north Tempe campus offers a beautiful blend of palm-lined walkways, desert landscapes, and public art displays. Architectural styles range from modern to turn-of-the-century historic, as the school renovates and expands Memorial Union to add four restaurants and more seating and program space. Lattie F. Coor Hall, with state-of-the-art classroom space, is slated to open in January 2004, while the 17,000-square-foot Arizona Biodesign Institute will provide lab and office space for research in neural rehabilitation, genomics, molecular biophysics, and neutraceuticals. The campus is officially listed as an arboretum, and ASU groundskeepers tend to more than 115 species of trees that thrive in Arizona's arid climate.

> "I love the large student body. There's so much to do."

ASU has eight undergraduate schools—business, liberal arts and sciences, engineering and applied sciences, architecture and environmental design, education, fine arts, nursing, and public programs (justice studies, leisure studies, communication, social work, and public affairs)—though students apply to the institution as a whole. The most popular majors are business, psychology, and communication, followed by interdisciplinary studies, a flexible and popular program that includes concentrations such as social welfare, American public policy, international studies, civic education, and Southeast Asian studies. The college of business ranks second in placing graduates with the Big Four accounting firms, while the fine arts college features an innovative child drama program, and nationally recognized majors in art, music, and dance. Engineering programs, especially microelectronics, robotics, and computer-assisted manufacturing, are sure bets; the facility for high-resolution microscopy allows students to get a uniquely close-up view of atomic structures.

The sciences (including solar energy, physical science, geology, and biology) and social sciences also boast first-class facilities, notably the largest university-

Website: www.asu.edu
Location: Urban
Total Enrollment: 47,359
Undergraduates: 36,802
Male/Female: 48/52
SAT Ranges: V 480–590
  M 490–610
ACT Range: 20–26
Financial Aid: 34%
Expense: Pub $ $
Phi Beta Kappa: Yes
Applicants: 18,155
Accepted: 85%
Enrolled: 41%
Grad in 6 Years: 52%
Returning Freshmen: 77%
Academics: ✍ ✍ ✍
Social: 🐿 🐿 🐿 🐿
Q of L: ★ ★ ★ ★ ★
Admissions: (480) 965-7788
Email Address:
  askasu@asu.edu

Strongest Programs:
Business
Anthropology
Music
Landscape Architecture
Geography
Engineering
Nursing
Communication and
  Journalism

Lattie F. Coor Hall, with state-of-the-art classroom space, is slated to open in January 2004, while the 17,000-square-foot Arizona Biodesign Institute will provide lab and office space for research in neural rehabilitation, genomics, molecular biophysics, and neutraceuticals.

owned meteorite collection in the world. Planetary science is out of this world; a team of ASU students, faculty, and staff, led by geology professor Philip Christensen, designed the Thermal Emission Imaging System and are conducting research with the system as it orbits Mars. ASU is also a founding member of the NASA Astrobiology Institute, which will focus on studying the origin of life on Earth and elsewhere. Anthropology benefits from its association with the Institute of Human Origins' Donald C. Johannson, who discovered the 3.2-million-year-old fossil skeleton named Lucy. The Walter Cronkite School of Journalism and Telecommunication has posted top ten finishes in the annual Hearst writing competition every year for the past decade and in the broadcast journalism competition seven times in that period. Each year, the legendary CBS newsman visits campus to lecture in individual classes.

New options at ASU include undergraduate concentrations, certificate programs, and minors in topics such as Islamic studies, acting, scenography, movement science, and tourism management. Regardless of major, students must fulfill requirements in literacy and critical inquiry (including composition), mathematical studies (including college-level algebra or higher), humanities and fine arts, social and behavioral sciences, and natural sciences. Students must also complete courses in three awareness areas: global, historical, and U.S. cultural diversity. An automated phone system helps speed registration. If courses are full, "I've had no problems asking professors to be allowed to register," a senior says. "Or, if I couldn't get into the course, it was easy to find an alternate class."

The most popular majors are business, psychology, and communication, followed by interdisciplinary studies, a flexible and popular program that includes concentrations such as social welfare, American public policy, international studies, civic education, and Southeast Asian studies.

Three-quarters of the students at Arizona State come from elsewhere, including many Chicagoans fleeing miserable winters. And they must meet tougher standards for automatic admission: While in-state students need to be in the top quarter of their class or have a 3.0 GPA, as well as a total SAT score of 1040 or an ACT score of

"I loved living on campus. Apply early!"

22, out-of-staters must meet the same class-rank or GPA requirements and have a cumulative SAT score of 1110 or ACT score of 24. Because ASU draws so heavily from within Arizona, 11 percent of the student body is Hispanic; African-Americans contribute 3 percent, and Asian-Americans add 5 percent. The Intergroup Relations Center works to overcome racial, religious, gender, and other differences, including the gulf between Greeks and independents, and athletes and academics. ASU offers merit scholarships as well as money for athletes in ten men's and eleven women's sports.

Seventeen percent of ASU students live in the co-ed dorms, which fill up quickly and are generally available only to freshmen. "I loved living on campus," says a senior. "Apply early!" After freshman year, students live off campus in nearby apartments and houses. Those lucky enough to get a bed on campus jockey for one of the three residence halls with their own swimming pools and volleyball courts. No matter where they live, students don't have to buy a meal plan.

New options at ASU include undergraduate concentrations, certificate programs, and minors in topics such as Islamic studies, acting, scenography, movement science, and tourism management.

ASU's Greek system attracts 6 percent of the men and 7 percent of the women, though the campus is officially dry. The underage are also warned: "Tempe is very tough on serving," says a kinesiology major. Perhaps that's why students head off campus on weekends—often way off campus. Many have cars, giving them access to the mountains of Colorado, the beaches of California, the natural beauty of the Grand Canyon, or the bright lights of Las Vegas. Students can fly from Phoenix to San Diego for as little as $60, and they love to follow the Division I football team to games at the University of Arizona and elsewhere. In 2002–2003, nine Sun Devil teams turned in top twenty national finishes, and ASU produced six Academic All-American student athletes.

Students who know what they're getting into revel in ASU's size, calling it an opportunity rather than a liability. "I love the large student body," says a senior.

"There's so much to do." Sure, it may take a little extra effort to get faculty members to learn your name, or to get into the section or class you want. But those who persevere will find a "devil" of a good time—and a more-than-decent education, too.

If You Apply To ➢

ASU: Early action: Nov. 1. Rolling admissions. Financial aid: Feb. 15. Housing: Mar. 1. Does not guarantee to meet demonstrated need. Campus interviews: optional, informational. No alumni interviews. SATs or ACTs: required. SAT IIs: optional. Accepts the Common Application and electronic applications. No essay question.

University of Arkansas

200 Hunt Hall, Fayetteville, AR 72701

University of Arkansas rates in the second tier of Southern public universities alongside Alabama, LSU, and Ole' Miss. With traditional strength in agriculture, U of A has also developed programs in business, engineering, and other professional fields. U of A's highest-ranked program takes the field on Saturday afternoons.

Want to really make your mark for posterity? Then consider the University of Arkansas, where every graduate's name is etched into the five-mile network of sidewalks on campus. To date, the Senior Walk lists more than 120,000 alumni, including former Sen. J. William Fulbright, founder of the international scholarship program that bears his name, as well as the namesake of the U of A College of Arts and Sciences. Arkansas is also the place where former President Bill Clinton and his wife Hillary, now New York's junior senator, held their first faculty posts. No political aspirations? No problem—you'll still find something to study, as Arkansas also offers more than 150 undergraduate degree programs along with abundant school spirit.

The Arkansas campus is nestled among the mountains, lakes, and streams of the Ozarks, in the extreme northwest corner of the state. Architectural styles range from modern concrete buildings to those dating from the Depression. The center of campus is the stately brick Old Main, which once housed the entire university. Recent renovations and additions have expanded and improved many facilities, from the science and poultry labs to the west section of Razorback Stadium. A new housing complex, health center, and parking deck are now under construction. When completed, the $46 million North Quadrant Residence Halls will house six hundred students and some faculty members in luxury apartments near the campus core. The complex will also include classrooms, computer labs, dining facilities, and other amenities.

Established as a land-grant institution in 1871, the university has blossomed beyond its agricultural and mechanical roots to include six colleges and professional schools. Regardless of the college they choose, students must complete the university's core curriculum, which includes six hours each of English and fine arts or humanities, three hours each of math and history or government, and eight hours of

Website: www.uark.edu
Location: Small city
Total Enrollment: 16,035
Undergraduates: 12,889
Male/Female: 51/49
SAT Ranges: V 510–640
  M 520–650
ACT Range: 22–28
Financial Aid: 43%
Expense: Pub $ $
Phi Beta Kappa: Yes
Applicants: 5,025
Accepted: 86%
Enrolled: 52%
Grad in 6 Years: 46%
Returning Freshmen: 82%
Academics: ✎ ✎ ✎
Social: 🐧 🐧 🐧 🐧
Q of L: ★ ★ ★
Admissions: (479) 575-5346
Email Address:
  uofa@uark.edu

Strongest Programs:
Marketing

science. Arts and sciences students must also achieve foreign language proficiency. The Sam M. Walton College of Business offers some of the most popular majors at Arkansas—marketing and finance; it's named for the founder of Wal-Mart Stores, the world's largest retailer, whose family foundation gave a record $300 million to the school in April 2002. Two-thirds of that amount has been used to endow the new undergraduate Honors College, in which 13 percent of the student body was enrolled by fall 2002. The honors program offers independent study and research opportunities and the chance to design interdisciplinary courses. The remaining $100 million of the Walton grant was earmarked for U of A's graduate school.

Other popular programs at Arkansas include psychology, journalism, and childhood education; English and history, especially Southern history, are likewise strong. The Dale Bumpers College of Agricultural, Food and Life Sciences, another part of the institution named for a former senator, includes the Poultry Health Center, a national leader in research on the containment of poultry epidemics. Students in the Bumpers College may also take a term at the Scottish Agricultural College in Edinburgh. Bachelors' degrees are no longer available in botany, microbiology, and zoology, but students may concentrate in those areas as part of a related major. Despite the school's size, most students report few problems getting into classes they want or need; registration is done by phone, using an automated system. Each academic college also offers freshman seminars.

U of A students tend to be of the small town variety, and 85 percent are Arkansas natives. A fine art major insists that "diverse voices and opinions are equally represented and well-balanced on campus," but the numbers tell a different story. African-Americans make up 6 percent of the student body, while Hispanics add 2 percent and Asian-Americans add 3 percent. The university is striving to improve race relations, and the chancellor has personally chaired a campus task force on diversity to help boost success rates of students from underrepresented minority groups. In addition, increasing diversity is one of the school's top five priorities in its state budget request for the next biennium. Campus dress is "laid back," with students wearing T-shirts and jeans most of the time, says a journalism major. Arkansas awards nearly 700 merit scholarships each year, ranging from $554 to $16,398, and about 450 athletic scholarships in ten women's and six men's sports. The Good Neighbor program lets students from nearby states with GPAs of 3.0 or higher and ACT scores of at least 24 enroll at in-state rates.

The chancellor has personally chaired a campus task force on diversity to help boost success rates of students from underrepresented minority groups. In addition, increasing diversity is one of the school's top five priorities in its state budget request for the next biennium.

Forty-one percent of undergrads live in the dorms, where rooms tend to be cramped and some buildings still lack air-conditioning, though they are maintained well. "The housing at U of A is very uncomfortable because you have to share a small room, and there is only one bathroom for several people," says a biology major. All halls are single-sex, except for one that's co-ed by floor. Students recommend Gregson and Holcombe halls for freshmen. When it comes to chow, "two of three dining facilities are excellent," says an advertising and public relations major. "They are clean and roomy, with wonderful food, including veggie meals."

Arkansas' twenty-five Greek chapters attract 18 percent of the women and 14 percent of the men, and aside from the revelry that accompanies Razorback football and basketball, their parties are pretty much the only game in town on weekends, students say. "Most socializing takes place off-campus, on a street nearby," says a senior. The town of Fayetteville (population 55,000) is "a medium-sized college town, rich in cultural diversity, with frequent events in the arts," says a junior. Aside from the usual restaurants and shopping, "there are interesting social outlets and a tolerant atmosphere, plus a beautiful natural environment." Students participate in community service through Greek organizations and other groups.

The Good Neighbor program lets students from nearby states with GPAs of 3.0 or higher and ACT scores of at least 24 enroll at in-state rates.

And, of course, who could forget Razorback sports? Cries of "Wooooooo! Pig sooie!" ring out during home football and basketball games, and red Razorback logos are all over town—on T-shirts, napkins, book covers, license plates, and on game day, the cheeks of ecstatic fans. "Everyone in the state comes to football games," says a senior. The football team brought home the SEC Western Division crown in 2002, and in 2003, the track team won the SEC indoor and outdoor championships and the NCAA indoor title. In fact, their coach has won more national titles than any other in NCAA history.

Poultry science students aren't the only ones flocking to Arkansas for a solid education at a bargain price. Northerners may feel out of their element, and those who dislike football should keep their feelings quiet. For everyone else, if its alumni are any guide, this student-centered research university is a launching pad to success in disciplines from politics to business, and beyond. "With so many activities and events taking place," says a freshman, "it's very easy to find something that I like."

If You Apply To ➤ | **Arkansas:** Rolling admissions: Feb. 15 for priority consideration (Feb. 1 for scholarship applicants). Early action: Nov. 15. Financial aid: March 1. Does not guarantee to meet demonstrated need. Campus interviews: optional, evaluative. Alumni interviews: optional, informational. SATs or ACTs: required. SAT II: recommended. Accepts the Common Application. Essay question: one-page personal statement.

Atlanta University Center

Atlanta is viewed as the preeminent city in the country for bright, talented, and successful African-Americans. It became the capital of the civil rights movement in the 1960s—a town described by its leaders as "too busy to hate."

At the heart of this extraordinary culture is the Atlanta University Center, the largest African-American educational complex in the world, replete with its own central library and computing center. The seven component institutions have educated generations of African-American leaders. The Reverend Martin Luther King Jr. went to Morehouse College; his grandmother, mother, sister, and daughter went to Spelman College. Graduates spread across the country in a pattern that developed when these were among the best of the few colleges to which talented African-Americans could aspire. Even now, when the options are almost limitless, alumni continue to send their children back for more.

The center consists of three undergraduate colleges (Morris Brown, Morehouse, and Spelman) and three graduate institutions (Clark Atlanta University, the Interdenominational Theological Seminary, and the Morehouse College of Medicine) on adjoining campuses in the center of Atlanta three miles from downtown. Students at these affiliated schools can enjoy the quiet pace of their beautiful magnolia-studded campuses or plunge into all the culture and excitement of this most dynamic of Deep South cities. The six original schools—all but the medical school—became affiliated in 1929 using the model of California's Claremont Colleges, but they remain fiercely independent. Each has its own administration, board of trustees, and academic specialties, and each maintains its own dorms, cafeterias, and other facilities. There is cross-registration among the institutions (Morehouse students, for example, go to Spelman for drama and art courses) and with Georgia State and Emory University as well. The governing body of the consortium, the Atlanta University Center, Inc., administers a center-wide dual-degree program in engineering in conjunction with Georgia Tech—and it runs campus security, a student crisis center, and a joint institute of science research. There is also a center-wide service of career planning and placement where recruiters may come and interview students from all six of the institutions.

Dating and social life at the coeducational institutions tend to take place within the individual schools, though Morehouse, a men's college, and Spelman, a women's college, maintain a close academic and social relationship. The Morehouse–Spelman Glee Club takes its abundance of talent around the nation, and its annual Christmas concert on the Spelman campus is a standing-room-only event.

Morehouse and Spelman (see full write-ups) constitute the Ivy League of historically African-American colleges. The following are sketches of the other two institutions offering undergraduate degrees.

Clark Atlanta University (www.cau.edu)

Formed by the consolidation of Clark College, a four-year liberal arts institution, and Atlanta University, which offered only graduate degrees, CAU is a comprehensive coeducational institution that offers undergraduate, graduate, and professional degrees. The university draws on the former strengths of both schools, offering quality programs in the health professions, public policy, and mass communications (including print journalism, radio and television production, and filmmaking). Graduate and professional programs include education, business, library information studies, social work, and arts and sciences. Undergraduate enrollment: 4,000.

Morris Brown College (www.morrisbrown.edu)

An open-admission, four-year undergraduate institution that is related to the African Methodist Episcopal Church, MBC lost most of its students in the spring of 2003 after the college lost its accreditation. A new president and a restructured board of trustees, including the Reverend Jesse Jackson, is working hard to restore its financial and academic viability. Its most popular programs are education and business administration. Morris Brown also offers evening courses for employed adults, as well as a program of co-op work–study education.

Morehouse College

830 Westview Drive, Atlanta, GA 30314

Along with sister school Spelman, Morehouse is the most selective of the historically black schools. Alumni list reads like a Who's Who of African-American leaders. Best known for business and popular 3–2 engineering program with Georgia Tech. Built on a Civil War battlefield, Morehouse is a symbol of the new South.

Website:
   www.morehouse.edu
Location: Urban
Total Enrollment: 2,970
Undergraduates: 2,970
Male/Female: 100/0
SAT Ranges: V 440–680
   M 470–680
ACT Range: 19–32
Financial Aid: N/A
Expense: Pr $
Phi Beta Kappa: Yes
Applicants: 2,079
Accepted: 75%
Enrolled: 36%
Grad in 6 Years: 63%
Returning Freshmen: 83%
Academics: ✍ ✍ ✍
Social: ☎ ☎ ☎ ☎
Q of L: ★ ★ ★ ★
Admissions: (404) 215-2632
   or (800) 851-1254

Founded in 1867, Morehouse College has the distinction of being the nation's only historically African-American, four-year liberal arts college for men. If its sister school, Spelman, was once the "Vassar of African-American society," Morehouse was the Harvard or Yale, attracting male students from the upper echelons of society around the country. Top students come to Morehouse because they want an institution with a strong academic program and a supportive atmosphere in which to cultivate their success-orientation and leadership skills without facing the additional barriers they might encounter at a predominantly white institution. "Morehouse is a college of young, assertive, ambitious black men," says a psychology major. Notable alumni include the Reverend Martin Luther King Jr., Samuel L. Jackson, Spike Lee, and Dr. Louis Sullivan, current president of the Morehouse School of Medicine and former U.S. Secretary of Health and Human Services.

Located near downtown Atlanta, the sixty-one-acre Morehouse campus is home to thirty-five buildings, including the Martin Luther King Jr. International Chapel. In a little more than a decade, the college has enriched its academic program, conducted a successful multimillion-dollar national fund-raising campaign, increased student scholarships and faculty salaries, doubled its endowment, improved its physical plant, and acquired additional acres of land.

The general education program includes not only sixty-eight semester hours in four major disciplines (humanities, natural sciences, math, and social sciences), but also the study of "the unique African and African-American heritage on which so much of our modern American culture is built." In fact, appreciation of this culture is one of the college's main drawing cards. "Many students are here to get a greater understanding of their heritage and to promote it," attests one student. The academic climate at the House can get intense, with students learning and challenging themselves for the sake of learning and not just to bust a curve. "Morehouse offers an academic structure that is both competitive and rigorous," states a freshman. Counseling, including career counseling, is considered quite strong.

Undergraduate programs include the traditional liberal arts majors in the humanities and social and natural sciences. While the sciences have been traditionally strong at Morehouse, business courses have risen in prominence. The college has obtained accreditation of the undergraduate business department by the American Assembly of Collegiate Schools of Business, and current students are linked to graduates who serve as mentors in the ways of the business world. The most popular major is business administration. Engineering, which trails shortly behind in popularity, is actually a 3–2 program in conjunction with Georgia Tech and other larger universities. The school also runs a program with NASA that allows students to engage in independent research.

(Continued)
Email Address:
admissions@morehouse
.edu

Strongest Programs:
Economics
Business
Biology
Political Science
Psychology

"Morehouse offers an academic structure that is both competitive and rigorous."

dent research. Programs that receive less favorable reviews from students are English, art, and drama, and the administration admits that physical education and some of the humanities offerings could use some strengthening. Study abroad options include programs offered through the Associated Colleges of the South consortium.* The school also offers courses and additional resources as a member of the Atlanta Regional Consortium for Higher Education.* Newer options include a major in applied physics and minors in public health sciences and telecommunications.

Sixty-seven percent of Morehouse students come from outside the state, with a sizable number from New York and California. Sixty-seven percent graduated in the top quarter of their high school class. More than six hundred merit scholarships are available, many providing full tuition. There are 121 scholarships for athletes in football, basketball, track, soccer, and tennis.

There's limited housing, leaving half of the student body to find their own off-campus accommodations. For freshmen, students recommend Graves Hall, the college's oldest building, built in 1889. Those who do get campus housing sometimes wish they hadn't. Complaints range from "too small" to "not well-maintained." Most upperclassmen live off campus. The meal plan at Morehouse is mandatory for students living on campus and draws its share of complaints.

While the sciences have been traditionally strong at Morehouse, business courses have risen in prominence.

Morehouse's Homecoming, the centerpiece of Spike Lee's movie *School Daze*, is a joint effort between Morehouse and Spelman. The queen elected by Morehouse men has traditionally been a Spelman woman, as are the cheerleaders and majorettes. The four fraternities, which sign up a very small percentage of the students, hold popular parties; "drinking is not a big deal here," most students concur. Going out on the town in Atlanta is a popular evening activity, and on-campus football games, concerts, movies, and

"Morehouse is a college of young, assertive, ambitious black men."

religious programs all draw crowds. In its early years, Morehouse left much to be desired in the area of varsity sports, but it now competes well in NCAA Division II. Track, cross-country, tennis, basketball, football, and soccer are all strong, but it is the strong intramural program that allows students a chance to become the superstar they know is lurking within them. During football season, Morehouse men road-trip to follow the games at Howard, Hampton, and Tuskegee universities.

Morehouse is well equipped to serve the modern heirs of a distinguished tradition. Morehouse students don't just attend Morehouse. They become part of what amounts to a network of "Morehouse Men" who share the bonds of having had the Morehouse experience, and graduates find previous alumni stand ready and willing to help them with jobs and other needs.

Overlaps

Clark Atlanta, Howard, Georgia Tech, Hampton

Spelman College

350 Spelman Lane, Atlanta, GA 30314

The Wellesley of the black college world. Reputation draws students from all corners of the country. Unusually strong in the sciences with particular emphasis on undergraduate research. Wooded Atlanta campus offers easy access to urban attractions.

Website: www.spelman.edu
Location: Urban
Total Enrollment: 2,065
Undergraduates: 2,065
Male/Female: 0/100
SAT Ranges: V 490–590
   M 470–560
ACT Range: 20–24
Financial Aid: 86%
Expense: Pr $
Phi Beta Kappa: No
Applicants: 3,266
Accepted: 53%
Enrolled: 33%
Grad in 6 Years: 75%
Returning Freshmen: 91%
Academics: ✍ ✍ ✍
Social: 🐿 🐿 🐿 🐿
Q of L: ★ ★ ★ ★ ★
Admissions: (800) 982-2411
Email Address:
   admiss@spelman.edu

Strongest Programs:
Biology
Engineering
Natural Sciences
Premed
Prelaw

As one of only two surviving African-American women's colleges in the United States, Spelman College is far and away the most prestigious. And it's certainly found a friend in comedian Bill Cosby. His $20 million gift helps keep tuition low and quality academics available. Cosby is not alone in his generosity; Spelman recently completed a campaign that raised what is said to be the largest amount ever raised by a historically African-American university. These contributions—as well as a strong academic department—are sure to produce promising young African-American women who will become leaders in fields ranging from science to the arts.

Founded in 1881 by two Caucasian women from New England (it was named after John D. Rockefeller's mother-in-law, Mrs. Harvey Spelman), the school was traditionally the starting point for teachers, nurses, and other African-American female leaders. Today's emphasis is on getting Spelman grads into the courtrooms, boardrooms, and engineering labs. Honing women for leadership is the main mission, and that nurturing takes place on a classic collegiate-green thirty-two-acre campus with a $140 million endowment.

These are heady times for Spelman. Although the college finds itself competing head-on with the Seven Sisters and other prestigious and predominantly Caucasian institutions that are eager to recruit talented African-American women, the college is holding its own. Students still flock here for that something special that the predominantly Caucasian schools lack: an environment with first-rate academics where African-American women can develop self-confidence and leadership skills before venturing into a world where they will once again be in the minority.

The college offers a well-rounded liberal arts curriculum that emphasizes the importance of critical and analytical thinking and problem solving. Usually by the end of sophomore year, students are expected to complete thirty-four credit hours of core requirements, including English composition, foreign language, health and physical education, mathematics, African diaspora and the world, African-American women's studies, and computer literacy. In addition, freshmen are required to take First Year Orientation, and sophomores must take Sophomore Assembly. Spelman's liberal arts program introduces students to the principal branches of learning, specifically languages, literature, English, the natural sciences, humanities, social sciences, and fine arts.

Spelman's established strengths lie in the natural sciences (especially biology) and the humanities, both of which have outstanding faculties. Over the last decade, the college has greatly strengthened its offerings in math and the natural sciences;

extensive undergrad research programs provide students with publishing opportunities, and many end up attending grad school to become researchers. Many students have discarded the popular majors of the early '70s—education and the fine arts—in favor of premed and prelaw programs, and these programs remain strong. The dual-degree program in engineering (in cooperation with Georgia Tech) is also a standout. The Women's Research and Resource Center specializes in African-American women's studies and community outreach to African-American women.

Individual attention is the hallmark of a Spelman education. About 70 percent of the faculty have doctorates, and many are African-American and/or female—and thus excellent role models, ones the students find very accessible. One political science major reports that the majority of instructors are "very well learned. Their lectures are tactful and effective," and she is "often challenged to put forth the best effort." Except for some of the required courses, classes are small; most have fewer than twenty-five students. Students who want to spread their wings can venture abroad through a variety of programs, or try one of the domestic exchange arrangements with Wellesley, Mount Holyoke, Vassar, or Mills. The school also offers courses and additional resources as a member of the Atlanta Regional Consortium for Higher Education.*

"Atlanta is a great college town! If there is any place that a student can be academically enriched, it is here."

Spelman's reputation continues to attract African-American women from all over the country, including a high proportion of alumnae children. Three-quarters of the students come from outside Georgia. Students represented here include high achievers looking for a supportive environment and those women with high potential who performed relatively poorly in high school. Only 4 percent of the student body are not African-American. Spelman does not guarantee to meet the financial need of all those admitted, but it does offer 120 merit scholarships worth up to $18,015. There are no athletic scholarships.

Fifty-seven percent of students live on campus, and housing is "well kept and quite comfortable," reports a mathematics major. Because Spelman is an old school and it has tried to keep up the original buildings, most of the dorms are relatively old. But that certainly can add to the school's historical charm, and students report having little trouble in getting a room. There are eleven dorms, and students recommend that freshmen check out the Howard Harreld dorm. The meal plan is mandatory for campus-dwellers.

Largely because of the Atlanta University Center, students also have plenty of chances for social interaction with other nearby colleges. "Students mingle in the student centers of all four schools all the time, especially on Fridays," a veteran explains. "Atlanta is a great college town!" gushes one junior. "If there is any place that a student can be academically enriched, it is here." Spelmanites do take advantage of the big-city nightlife; they attend plays, symphonies, and the hot Atlanta nightclubs such as Ethiopian Vibrations, Fat Tuesdays, and Lenoxx. Sororities are present but only in small numbers—3 percent of the students go Greek. The attitude on drinking leans toward the conservative. Says one student, "No alcohol on campus—period." The most anticipated annual events include sisterhood initiation ceremonies and the Founders Day celebration. Although varsity sports are not the highlight here, the school boasts fine volleyball, basketball, and tennis teams. Synchronized swimming is the specialty, however. Athletic facilities are poor, but there are several organized intramurals, including flag football and bowling.

Spelman College has spent a century furthering the education and opportunities of African-American women. It has adapted its curriculum to meet the career aspirations of today's youth, built up its bankroll, and successfully met the challenge posed by affirmative action in other universities. Still an elite institution in

Extensive undergrad research programs provide students with publishing opportunities, and many end up attending grad school to become researchers.

Overlaps

Clark Atlanta, Howard, Hampton, Georgia State, Florida A&M

African-American society, Spelman is staking its future on its ability to provide a unique kind of education that allows its graduates to compete with anyone.

If You Apply To ➢

Spelman: Early action: Nov. 15. Regular admissions: Feb. 1. Housing: May 1. Does not guarantee to meet demonstrated need. Campus interviews: optional, informational. No alumni interviews. SATs or ACTs: required. SAT IIs: optional. Accepts the Common Application. Essay question: personal statement reflecting achievements, interests, personal goal; or issue of personal, local, or national concern. Seeks women who are active in school, church, or community.

College of the Atlantic

105 Eden Street, Bar Harbor, ME 04609

In the conservative world of today, COA is as out-there as it gets. A haven for communal, vegetarian types who would rather save the world than make a buck. Cozy is an understatement; with fewer than three hundred students, it is the second-smallest institution in the *Fiske Guide*.

Website: www.coa.edu
Location: Small town
Total Enrollment: 283
Undergraduates: 280
Male/Female: 36/64
SAT Ranges: V 570–670
  M 550–640
ACT Range: 25–29
Financial Aid: 77%
Expense: Pr $ $ $
Phi Beta Kappa: No
Applicants: 287
Accepted: 70%
Enrolled: 37%
Grad in 6 Years: 71%
Returning Freshmen: 89%
Academics: ✍ ✍ ✍
Social: ☎ ☎
Q of L: ★ ★ ★
Admissions: (800) 528-0025
Email Address:
  inquiry@ecology.coa.edu

Strongest Programs:
Education
Environmental Studies
Organic Agriculture

The College of the Atlantic attracts rugged individualists troubled by the same issues that so worried the founders of this "mission-oriented" school, such as pollution, environmental damage, and troubled inner cities. Today, the tiny college's curriculum is focused on human ecology—the study of the relationship between humans and their natural and social environments—which is the only major offered. The goal, says a senior, is "to educate people to do something good with their lives—to make the little corner of their world, wherever they end up, a little better off."

The thirty-one-acre campus, covered in lush flowers, vegetable gardens, and lawns, sits on the island of Mount Desert, along the shoreline of Frenchman Bay and adjacent to the magnificent Acadia National Park. In addition, the college has recently acquired two offshore island research centers and an eighty-six-acre organic farm, and opened the new Witch Cliff residence hall.

Most courses focus on a single aspect of humans' relationships with the world. Instead of traditional academic departments, the school has three broad resource areas: environmental science, arts and design, and applied human studies. Many students choose to concentrate on more narrowly defined topics within human ecology, such as marine studies, biological and environmental sciences, public policy, visual and performing arts, environmental design, or education. With advisors and resource specialists, each student designs an individual course of study drawing from different programs. "I really appreciate the school's encouragement in designing an academic program that suits me," says a junior human ecology/teacher certification student.

> **"COA hippies are passionate about life, politics, and environment and know how to live well and have fun."**

Given COA's location, the natural sciences are stellar, with excellent instruction in ecology, zoology, and marine biology. The arts are catching up, with a more formal video and performance art program created in recent years. Allied Whale, the school's marine study arm, offers hands-on research opportunities, while another course prepares exhibits for the college's natural history museum. COA also offers more than ninety courses in human studies, with significant concentrations in literature, philosophy, economics, history, law, and anthropology. Unusual offerings include study on an organic farm and in a taxidermy lab.

Student life at COA is intense and semi-communal, beginning with a rugged five-day wilderness orientation preceding first trimester. Before graduating, students must also complete a ten-week off-campus internship and support at least one "campus-building" activity, such as the student government or newspaper. Requirements are few: freshmen must take a human ecology course and a writing course, and juniors must write a human-ecology essay, expanding it during the following year until it grows into their senior project, a major independent work. Students also must take two courses from each of the following categories: environmental studies, human studies, and art and design.

Some departments only have a professor or two. Since the student body is small, scholars can become close to faculty members. "The teachers here are awesome. You have the chance to develop great relationships with professors from the moment you enter the school," says a junior. A freshman adds: "The quality of teaching and attention is brilliant...truly inspiring." In lieu of grades, students receive in-depth written evaluations of their work, although they may request grades as well. They must reciprocate with an evaluation of the course and their performance in it. The unusual advising system, a three-person student–faculty team chosen by the advisee, further promotes close contact between students and professors.

Students attracted to the quirky College of the Atlantic and its unique curriculum are often bright and idealistic; many worked with Americorps or traveled the world before beginning school. "COA hippies are passionate about life, politics, and environment and know how to live well and have fun," says a junior. COA is predominantly Caucasian, with African-American, Hispanics, and Asian-Americans collectively comprising 5 percent of the student body. However, 14 percent of the students are international students. "Most students get along very well and there is a huge diversity of cultures, religions, countries, beliefs, financial status, and thought," says a freshman. The college's governance system gives students and administrators almost equal voices in how it's run; anyone may voice concerns or vote on policy-change proposals or the hiring of new faculty at the All College Meeting. Students aren't shy about also speaking out on more worldly issues, "from 'students for a free Tibet,' to antiwar protests, to environmental justice, to the global AIDS campaign," says a sophomore.

"The quality of teaching and attention is brilliant...truly inspiring."

Forty percent of students—freshmen, international students, and upper-class resident advisors—live on campus, while the balance find cozy, inexpensive apartments or houses in the nearby town of Bar Harbor. Campus-dwellers may choose from small cooperative houses with five to twenty students or a fairly new dorm with space for sixty students, "which looks like a beautiful ski chalet," says one resident.

Though the tiny tourist town of Bar Harbor is packed with visitors during the summer, it largely shuts down in the winter. Students get to know the townspeople through the required forty hours of community service. "People do lots of stuff for local organizations, including work on farms, parks, the downeast AIDS network, and the YMCA," writes a student. On weekends, few students leave campus, since Portland, the nearest urban center, is three hours away. Campus social functions revolve around nature and the seasons, including biking, hiking, boating, cross-country skiing, skating, and rock climbing, often in Acadia National Park. Some students take road trips to Canada. There are no fraternities or sororities, and stu-

(Continued)
Land Use Management
Visual and Performing Arts
Public Policy/Law
Marine Biology

In lieu of grades, students receive in-depth, written evaluations of their work, although they may request grades as well.

The tiny college's curriculum is focused on human ecology—the study of the relationship between humans and their natural and social environments—which is the only major offered.

dents kick back at off-campus house parties, which are generally alcohol free. There's no drinking on campus, and it's tough for underage students to get served in town. COA's new men's and women's soccer teams, known as the Blackflies and nicknamed the "Swarm," have already earned strong student support, and students also keep in shape by joining community teams that compete with the local YMCA.

The College of the Atlantic is a place where Earth Day really is a cause for celebration, where students ride nude through the cafeteria and on nearby streets during Bike Week, and where everyone from students to trustees jumps into frigid Frenchman Bay on the first Friday of the fall term, trying to swim from the school's docks to Bar Island. The long snowy winters and shrunken winter population make for an atmosphere that is cozy to some, dreary to others. "The school is a special place because I can be myself, engorge myself in an education that I personalize, and have great conversations with like-minded individuals," says a sophomore.

Overlaps

Colby, Hampshire, University of Maine, Warren Wilson, Reed

If You Apply To ➤

COA: Early decision: Dec. 1, Jan. 10. Regular admissions: Feb. 15. Financial aid: Feb. 15. Housing: May 1. Guarantees to meet demonstrated need. Campus interviews: recommended, evaluative. Alumni interviews: optional, informational. SAT I or ACT: optional. SAT IIs: optional. Accepts the Common Application and electronic applications. Essay question: does your academic record accurately reflect your ability and potential?; most rewarding nonacademic experience; how COA fits with your goals; and an essay on any topic (four suggested topics are provided). Looks for students committed to improving the quality of life on Earth.

Auburn University

202 Mary Martin Hall, Auburn, AL 36849

Sweet Home Alabama, where the skies are so blue and the spirit of football lasts year-round. Auburn was once called Alabama Polytechnic, and today AU's programs in engineering, agriculture, and the health fields are still among its best.

Website: www.auburn.edu
Location: Small town
Total Enrollment: 23,276
Undergraduates: 19,603
Male/Female: 52/48
SAT Ranges: V 490–600
  M 510–610
ACT Range: 21–27
Financial Aid: 26%
Expense: Pub $
Phi Beta Kappa: Yes
Applicants: 13,264
Accepted: 83%
Enrolled: N/A
Grad in 6 Years: 68%
Returning Freshmen: 84%
Academics: ✍ ✍
Social: ☎ ☎ ☎
Q of L: ★ ★ ★
Admissions: (334) 844-4080

Auburn University may be home to more than twenty thousand football-crazy students, but students know they're here for more than the games. Once known as Alabama Polytechnic, Auburn is a public land grant university, which still excels in professional and technical fields, such as engineering and architecture. But the school also welcomes students with warm and cozy hospitality and charm. "Auburn means family to me, not just because my father is an alumnus, but because of the embracing Auburn spirit," says a senior. "It is easy to get lost in the crowd at a big university, but at Auburn, I found my place," a classmate agrees. "I have loved every minute."

The town of Auburn, which grew up amid miles of forest and farmland largely to serve the university, is depicted in an Oliver Goldsmith poem as the "loveliest village of the plain." The campus stretches for nearly two thousand acres, graced by mossy trees, lush lawns, and majestic colonnades. Most buildings are redbrick and

"I have loved every minute." Georgian in style with some more modern facilities grouped in a compact central location. New additions include the Jule Collins Smith Museum of Fine Art, a 39,000-square-foot facility with eight exhibition galleries. A fifteen-acre botanical garden opened as part of the museum in 2003–2004, with large-scale sculpture, a three-acre lake, and a landscape of walking paths.

Auburn's core curriculum requires six semester hours of composition; six semester hours each of history, literature, and social sciences; three semester hours each of philosophy and fine arts; three semester hours of math; and eight semester hours of a lab science. "Freshman math, English, and some science classes are taught by TAs who have a hard time speaking English," a senior warns. To ease the transition, an optional seminar called the Auburn Experience helps acquaint freshmen and transfer students with university resources. The academic climate "is as competitive as you want it to be," says a senior. "Half of our students do not care, and the other half work hard to compete against one another." The difficulty of courses increases as students progress through their majors, and it can be tough to get into some programs. "Registration is a stressful time," sighs a communication major. "It was for me all four years, and I was told it would get better every year. It never did."

Many Auburn students are eager to get started on their careers, so the co-op program, which provides pay and credit in several professional fields, is increasingly popular. Auburn has also established a first-of-its-kind program in wireless engineering for students who want to design network hardware or software for cell phones and other mobile devices. (The school's Samuel Ginn College of Engineering is named for a former top executive at AirTouch Cellular, now part of Verizon Wireless.) Students also give high marks to the colleges of human science and of business, though they say the liberal arts suffer from a lack of funding and the perception that they're less useful than other majors after graduation. Seven areas designated as Peaks of Excellence compete for millions of dollars in special funding; these include cell and molecular biosciences, food safety, fisheries and allied aquacultures, and forest sustainability. The quality of teaching varies. "There will always be the one who tries to fail students or may be a genius, but can't teach other people at all," says a senior, "but even freshmen are given the opportunity to learn from accomplished, inspired professors."

"Even freshmen are given the opportunity to learn from accomplished, inspired professors."

Sixty-eight percent of Auburn students are Alabama natives, and many are legacies—the second or third generation in their families to attend the school. African-Americans account for 7 percent of the total, while Hispanics and Asian-Americans add 1 percent each. The conservative tone of this Bible Belt campus makes it hospitable for many Christian groups, and Auburn is home to one of the largest chapters in the United States of the Campus Crusade for Christ. Students are also among the friendliest you'll find anywhere, and a public relations major, already putting to use what he learned, claims "Auburn women are probably the best-looking in the South!" Each year, the university awards over 1,500 merit scholarships and more than 180 athletic scholarships in seven men's and nine women's sports, including gymnastics and equestrian teams.

Auburn's twenty-five dorms are single-sex, and visiting hours are restricted to weekends. Fourteen of the halls have been renovated, but only 16 percent of the students live in them. "For freshmen, especially women, it can be difficult to get housing," says a nursing major, since first-years compete on a first-come, first-served basis with returning students. Almost 22 percent of Auburn men join fraternities, and nearly 37 percent of the women join sororities, perhaps because chapters get space in the best dorms. There are food courts at each end of campus and dining facilities in the Foy Student Union as well, though "the food is too routine," says a senior. "It is expensive, and often just not worth the money."

Aside from sporting events and fraternity parties, Auburn sponsors concerts, free movies, and plenty of intramural sports. "Everyone finds their niche," says a senior. "Some go off campus, some just hang out in random places on campus with friends. The best road trips are Atlanta, Montgomery (where Auburn has a branch campus), and Birmingham, or—for a long weekend—the Gulf Coast beaches, Chicago, D.C., or New Orleans." The campus is officially dry, except on game days,

(Continued)
Email Address:
admissions@mail.auburn.edu

Strongest Programs:
Information Systems
    ManagementEngineering
Agriculture
Architecture
Prehealth Programs
Education

New additions include the Jule Collins Smith Museum of Fine Art, a 39,000-square-foot facility with eight exhibition galleries. A fifteen-acre botanical garden opened as part of the museum in 2003–2004, with large-scale sculpture, a three-acre lake, and a landscape of walking paths.

Auburn has established a first-of-its-kind program in wireless engineering for students who want to design network hardware or software for cell phones and other mobile devices.

and students say the alcohol policy is enforced. Long-standing traditions include the Burn the (Georgia) Bulldogs Parade and Hey Day, when everyone wears a name tag and walks around saying, "Hey!"

Auburn is a football powerhouse, and on fall Saturdays, 86,000 screaming fans turn the place into Alabama's fourth-largest city. The rallying cry "Warrrrr Eagle!" reverberates each time an Auburn back runs to daylight. Whenever there's a Tiger victory, regardless of the sport, Toomer's Corner (in downtown Auburn) will surely be rolled in toilet paper. The annual Auburn–Alabama football game is known as the Iron Bowl, and "you can't fully understand it until you have been here on game day," says a senior. "It is so much more than a sports event," attracting 150,000 rabid fans, only half of whom actually get into the stadium. Fans camp out in trailers and Winnebagos some two weeks advance. The men's and women's swimming and diving teams brought home Division I-A national championships in 2003, while men's basketball made it to the Sweet 16 round of the NCAA tournament. The McWhorter Center for Women's Athletics is one of the finest gymnastics training facilities in the country.

Auburn is working hard to increase the caliber of its students and academic programs, and especially to achieve a top twenty national ranking for its college of engineering. But students say certain key characteristics have stayed the same—and hopefully will continue to do so. "While Auburn has grown in many ways, the heart of Auburn remains unchanged," says a senior. "We are a family."

If You Apply To ➤

Auburn: Rolling admissions: Aug. 1. Does not guarantee to meet demonstrated need. Campus and alumni interviews: optional, informational. SATs or ACTs: required. Accepts electronic applications. Out-of-state enrollment is capped on a year-to-year basis; there are no set limits. No essay question.

Austin College

900 North Grand Avenue, Sherman, TX 75020-4440

The second-most famous institution in Texas with Austin in its name. Half the size of Trinity (Texas), runs neck-in-neck with Southwestern to be the leading Texas college under two thousand students. Combines the liberal arts with strong programs in business, education, and the health fields.

Website:
  www.austincollege.edu
Location: Small town
Total Enrollment: 1,281
Undergraduates: 1,241
Male/Female: 43/57
SAT Ranges: V 560–660
  M 570–660
ACT Range: 22–28
Financial Aid: 61%
Expense: Pr $ $
Phi Beta Kappa: Yes

Only an hour away from the ten-gallon hats and gleaming skyscrapers of Dallas is Austin College, a small but warm institution where students know their professors personally and take advantage of a broad array of majors. AC's preprofessional programs, most notably premed and prelaw, are among the strongest in the state. With about twelve hundred undergraduates, no one is just a number at Austin. Professors here even serve students breakfast at 10:00 p.m. the night before finals. It's just another example of the personal style that is typical of this charming Southern institution.

Austin's sixty-five-acre campus is located in a residential area outside the city of Sherman. The campus is designed in the traditional quadrangle style and hosts beige sandstone buildings, tree-lined plazas, decorative fountains, and an impressive seventy-ton sculptured solstice calendar. Dorms are conveniently located approximately two hundred yards from most classrooms, which eases the pain of first-period classes. The new Robert T. Mason Athletic/Recreation Complex includes the Sid Richardson Center, Hannah Natatorium, Hughey Gym, and the Verde Dickey Fitness Pavilion for student athletes and the fitness-conscious. Other new additions to campus include the Jackson Technology Center, Roo Suites residence hall for upperclassmen, and a new College Green, which provides students and their families a place to relax outdoors.

Austin College challenges its students, but the atmosphere is far from cut-throat. Says a political science/philosophy major, "It is competitive but friendly. Students are willing to study together and collaborate in their effort to succeed." The core curriculum begins with a freshman seminar called Communication/Inquiry. Each professor who teaches the course becomes the mentor for the twenty freshmen in his or her class. Next is a three-course sequence on the Heritage of Western Culture. Then comes a slew of optional courses in seven categories, including social policy, values, and decision-making, and historical or social perspectives. Nearly three-quarters of all classes have twenty-five students or fewer, and no class has more than a hundred. Students report that they rarely have problems getting the classes they want, but sometimes it's necessary to plan early.

Preprofessional areas are Austin College's specialties. When it comes time to apply to grad school, premed and predental students at this little college have one of the highest acceptance rates of any Texas school, and aspiring lawyers also do well. AC's five-year teaching program grants students both a bachelor's and a master's degree. Science and education receive high marks from students, as do international studies and political science. Business is among the school's most popular majors. The Jordan Language House boards forty-eight students studying French, German, Japanese, and Span-ish, along with a native speaker of each language. Students can

"Students are willing to study together and collaborate in their effort to succeed."

also earn a double major or combine three of the school's twenty-six majors into an interdisciplinary degree. A cooperative engineering program links the college with other schools. Southwestern and Mexican studies minors have been added.

A January term option lets students take an "experiential learning" course, usually outside their major, on a pass/fail basis. An international studies concentration provides opportunities to study abroad. The college also offers its students independent study, directed research, junior year abroad, and departmental honors programs. The Leadership Institute is open to just fifteen students of each entering class, and five more can get in after their first year. Participating students enjoy a suite of privileges, from study abroad options to working with mentors outside the college. Austin also provides three research areas located in Grayson County: the Barry Buckner Biology Preserve, the Lee Harrison Bratz Field Laboratory, and the Clinton and Edith Sneed Environmental Research Area.

Ninety percent of Austin students hail from the Lone Star State. Hispanics and African-Americans comprise 7 and 4 percent of the student body, respectively, and Asian-Americans make up 9 percent. Students say the campus, like the surrounding area, is fairly conservative. Political correctness tends to be a nonissue. "We're politically active for a small town in North Texas, but we're no Berkeley," one senior says. Austin has been tied to the Presbyterian Church in the United States since 1849; this affiliation manifests itself in the emphasis on values in the core courses, participation in service activities, and limited residence-hall visitation hours. AC offers three hundred merit scholarships, ranging from $500 to just more than $17,000.

As for dorm life, there are six residence halls, and 70 percent of undergraduates live in traditional dorm housing. Students say dorms are clean and well-maintained—a selling point because off-campus living is almost exclusively restricted to seniors. "Dorms are comfortable and homey," a senior says. One dorm is co-ed, one

(Continued)
Applicants: 1,140
Accepted: 78%
Enrolled: 39%
Grad in 6 Years: 78%
Returning Freshmen: 83%
Academics: ✏ ✏ ✏
Social: ☎ ☎ ☎
Q of L: ★ ★ ★
Admissions: (903) 813-3000
Email Address:
  admission@austincollege
  .edu

Strongest Programs:
Biology
Chemistry/Biochemistry
Austin College Teachers
  Program
International Studies
Religion and Philosophy

Political correctness tends to be a nonissue. "We're politically active for a small town in North Texas, but we're no Berkeley," one senior says.

houses language studies students, two are men-only, and two are women-only. Dean (the only co-ed residence hall) seems to be a popular choice for freshmen, despite (or perhaps because of) its reputation as being loud and social. Others say Clyce is the best bet for freshman women, and Luckett for freshman men. Residence hall access is computerized, and security officers are on duty twenty-four hours a day. Nearly all students take advantage of the three-meal-a-day plan, though not all take advantage of the all-you-can-eat option. Then there's the Pouch Club, an on-campus joint that serves beer and wine for those students twenty-one and over.

"Dorms are comfortable and homey."

Most of the social life is either on or near campus, with the Greeks taking the lion's share of credit. Seventeen percent of the men and 20 percent of the women belong to fraternities and sororities, but the Greeks are not school-funded and are not allowed to advertise off-campus parties without the college's permission. Not everyone depends on the Greek system for a good time. Students get an eyeful during the Baker Bun Run, in which the men of Baker Hall strip to their boxers and cavort around the campus on the Monday night before finals. Students can have alcohol in dorm rooms only if they are twenty-one or older, and school policy prohibits booze at campus organization events. Popular weekend excursions are a drive to Dallas or to the college's twenty-eight-acre recreational spot on Lake Texoma (a half-hour north). Some students say having a car is an absolute must. "Sherman is horrible for college students," a theater major says. "There are very few outlets for the students. All of them go to Dallas to do anything fun. But that is an hour by car."

Even without athletic scholarships, varsity sports are generating increasing support. The school's teams compete in Division III, and the women's soccer team has won recent championships. Football, men's and women's soccer, men's baseball, and women's basketball and volleyball are popular.

At Austin, students find the personal attention they desire. They are challenged at every turn by top professors who work closely with all their students. While Sherman may be a sleepy little town, Austin College certainly isn't a sleepy little institution.

Overlaps

Trinity University, Texas Christian, Baylor, Texas A&M, Southern Methodist

If You Apply To ➤

Austin: Early decision: Dec. 1. Early action: Jan. 15. Regular admissions: Mar. 1. Financial aid: Apr. 1. Housing: May 1. Campus and alumni interviews: recommended, evaluative. SATs or ACTs: required. SAT IIs: optional. Accepts the Common Application and electronic applications. Essay question: political, social, or economic issue of personal concern; significance of a "defining moment" in your life.

Babson College

Babson Park, MA 02457-0310

The only college in the *Fiske Guide* devoted entirely to business. Only fourteen miles from College Student Mecca, a.k.a. Boston, and tougher to get into now than at any time in its history. The one college in Massachusetts where it is possible to be a Republican with head held high.

Website: www.babson.edu
Location: Suburban
Total Enrollment: 3,407

The budding corporate leaders who choose Babson College can be summed up in a single word: driven. For four years, they shoulder a demanding workload focused on business and put up with a lackluster social life, all to gain the hands-on experience they hope will give them an edge in the job market after graduation. What makes them different from students at similar schools? "We will be the bosses of the students who attend rival institutions," smirks a junior. After all, how many other undergrads get school funding to start businesses during their first year, or hone stock-picking skills by managing part of their college's endowment?

Founded in 1919, Babson sits on a 370-acre campus near the sedate Boston suburb of Wellesley. The tract features open green spaces, gently rolling hills, and heavily wooded areas. Buildings are gently shaded and parking lots relatively hidden. Architectural styles vary, but are mainly neo-Georgian and modern. A recent addition is the Sorenson Visual Arts Center, with new studios for painting, ceramics, and sculpture, labs for photography and digital art, a student art gallery, and a studio for artists in residence.

Although Babson is a business school, about half of students' classes are in the liberal arts, and in 2002, Babson won the Hesburgh Award for curricular innovation. The school's general education requirements focus on competence in five areas: rhetoric; numeracy; ethics and social responsibility; international and multicultural perspectives; and leadership, teamwork, and creativity. All students take a five-semester sequence of integrated management courses, including the Foundation Management Experience. In the FME, working in groups of thirty, first-years get up to $3,000 in seed money to launch, manage, and liquidate a business, with profits going to charity. In past years, classes have donated more than $30,000.

"If it affects business, we talk about it."

All Babson students major in business and then select a concentration, such as management, finance, or marketing. The entrepreneurship program is one of Babson's strongest, bringing prominent venture capitalists and executives (from companies such as Dunkin' Donuts and Jiffy Lube) to campus for how-to lectures. Courses are rigorous and most are small—a senior says the largest he's taken had sixty students and puts the average at twenty-six. "The academic climate is "very competitive," a classmate agrees. "We are business geeks." Still, as the corporate world has moved to emphasize working in groups, so has Babson, says a student concentrating in management. "Teamwork is huge and integrated into nearly every course." For all those group projects, students can use more than two hundred and fifty workstations in five computer labs—except for the twenty-four-hour quiet lab, where no talking is allowed. Incoming students also get a brand-new IBM laptop computer on lease, included with tuition, and they're guaranteed an upgrade midway through their time at school.

In the classroom, Babson relies on the case-study approach, more typically employed by MBA programs. This method has students address specific business situations in groups or as officers of pseudo corporations. "Students are expected to learn beyond the textbooks and participate in class discussions," says a freshman. While upperclassmen get priority

"Teamwork is huge and integrated into nearly every course."

in registration, students say it's not hard to get into required courses. Accounting may take longer than four years to finish, but a junior says most students pursuing that major get paid internships at the Big Four accounting firms, helping make up for the extra time. Babson doesn't have teaching assistants; professors teach all courses, and they have "very impressive educational and industry backgrounds," says a senior.

Babson remains largely white and wealthy, despite administrators' efforts to diversify. African-Americans comprise 3 percent of the student body, Hispanics 4 percent, and Asian-Americans 9 percent. About a third of the undergrads are Massachusetts natives, and 19 percent come from abroad. "Students here are more motivated, focused, and creative than other schools," says a senior. Politically, the

(Continued)
Undergraduates: 1,735
Male/Female: 61/39
SAT Ranges: V 550–630
   M 590–600
Financial Aid: 42%
Expense: Pr $ $ $ $
Phi Beta Kappa: No
Applicants: 2,402
Accepted: 48%
Enrolled: 35%
Grad in 6 Years: 83%
Returning Freshmen: 92%
Academics: ✏ ✏ ✏
Social: ☎ ☎
Q of L: ★ ★ ★
Admissions: (781) 239-5079
   or (800) 488-3696
Email Address:
   ugradadmission@babson
   .edu

Strongest Programs:
Accounting
Economics
Entrepreneurship
Finance
International Business
Marketing
Management

Although Babson is a business school, about half of students' classes are in the liberal arts, and in 2002, Babson won the Hesburgh Award for curricular innovation.

campus leans conservative, and "if it affects business, we talk about it," says a junior. Otherwise, "we're too worried about money to get involved in much else."

Babson guarantees housing for four years, and 85 percent of undergraduates live on campus, resulting in high demand for singles and suites. Dorms are air-conditioned and carpeted, and most upper-class rooms have their own bathrooms. "Rooms are larger than other schools," says a senior, and there are kitchens on every floor. Most halls are co-ed, but one dorm is reserved for men, and floors and wings of other buildings are reserved for women. After the first year, rooms are assigned by lottery, where standing is based on credits earned. Every Wednesday is gourmet night at the dining hall, and the menu may include fresh lobster, Italian specialties, or turkey with all the trimmings.

Social life at Babson is improving, but still consists mainly of "drinking games in the suites and nightlife in Boston," says a junior. The Campus Activities Board brings in comedians and organizes parties, as do Greek organizations, which attract 12 percent of the women and an equal fraction of the men. The school also sponsors trips to local events such as Celtics and Red Sox games. If you're caught with booze while underage, it's three strikes and you're out of the dorms; fines of $75 each for underage drinking and open containers have helped cut down on illegal imbibing, but haven't curbed it entirely. (In fact, some enterprising students recently worked up T-shirts parodying the school motto, "Always Thinking," as "Always Drinking.") Two miles from campus, a subway stop gives students access to greater Boston, where they participate in mandatory first-year volunteer projects. Those with cars will find easy access to the beaches of Cape Cod and Martha's Vineyard, as well as the ski slopes of Vermont and New Hampshire. New York City and Montreal are also popular weekend getaways.

The town of Wellesley is a "wealthy suburban town," says a senior. It has "coffee shops, ice cream shops, and other stores, but Natick and Boston are close enough to make up for areas Wellesley lacks," a junior adds. Wellesley is also home to Wellesley College, and it's not uncommon for Babson students to socialize with Wellesley women. Each year, Babson students look forward to Homecoming (great networking opportunities), Oktoberfest, Winter and Spring Weekends, and Greek Week. April 8th is Founders Day, and classes are cancelled so that everyone can celebrate entrepreneurship.

While making money may be the most competitive "sport" at Babson, the Beavers participate in NCAA Division III athletics, too. Any match against archrival Bentley and soccer games against Brandeis and Colby are the most popular spectator events, and the men's lacrosse team brought home a conference championship in 2003. Babson's upper athletic fields were completely renovated and improved in the summer of 2002, and the field hockey and lacrosse field got new lights.

Babson encourages students to develop their management skills with hands-on experience. The school's focus on all things financial and its relatively small size offer students ample opportunity to make their mark. "Babson is a great place for me because on top of the great education I am receiving, I am a member of the women's soccer team, the women's leadership program, and Women Giving Back," says a junior. For many, the first step up the corporate ladder—and the first lesson in how to balance work with everything else that's important in life—occurs in the halls of Babson College.

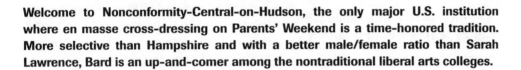

If You Apply To ➤ | **Babson:** Early decision and early action: Nov. 15. Regular admissions: Feb. 1. Financial aid: Feb. 15. Campus interviews: recommended, evaluative. Alumni interviews: optional, evaluative. SATs or ACTs: required. SAT IIs: recommended (writing and math Ic or IIc). Accepts the Common Application and electronic applications. Essay questions: Common Application essay and another specific to Babson; past questions have included how Babson will help you achieve personal and career goals; significant experience or achievement; issue of concern; influential person, fictional character, historical figure, or creative work; or a topic of the student's choice.

Bard College

Annandale-on-Hudson, NY 12504

Welcome to Nonconformity-Central-on-Hudson, the only major U.S. institution where en masse cross-dressing on Parents' Weekend is a time-honored tradition. More selective than Hampshire and with a better male/female ratio than Sarah Lawrence, Bard is an up-and-comer among the nontraditional liberal arts colleges.

The first class at Bard College, founded in 1860, consisted of twelve men studying to enter the seminaries of the Episcopal Church. They would no doubt be surprised at the eclectic mix of students that now populate Bard, which has become a hotbed of artsy intellectualism. "At Bard, you can be whoever or whatever you want to be," says a senior. The professors are highly praised and the courses are rigorous but don't fuel intense competition. "Even with its rigorous environment, the climate is not competitive, rather one of support," says a first-year photography and American studies major.

Bard was once known mainly as a school for the performing arts, and creative types have long flocked to its lovely campus, which occupies six hundred well-landscaped acres in New York's Washington Irving country. The hodgepodge of architectural styles leaves each ivy-covered brick building with a character all its own, especially the dorms, which come in every variety, from cottages in the woods to one Russian Colonial–style dorm. Nine new houses for upperclassmen opened recently, accommodating 190 students. The $62 million performing arts center, which opened in spring 2003, was designed by renowned architect Frank O. Gehry. As part of a new emphasis on math and science, a new science facility is planned.

Freshmen show up three weeks before classes start for the unique required Workshop in Language and Thinking, organized around the quaint notion that good writing and clear thinking are necessary tools for higher learning. Bard's general education requirements include a yearlong multidisciplinary freshman seminar. At the end of their second year, all students write their educational autobiography and declare a major program of study. These are presented before a board of professors in the relevant area and discussed with the student. Junior year includes a tutorial in preparation for the senior project, **"Bard is at once intense and laid back."** and during senior year students do the project, equivalent to an undergraduate dissertation—an original work that could materialize in a one-hundred- to three-hundred-page critical analysis of literature, a show, opening of artwork, a series of dances, a novel, or a scientific experiment.

Students agree that the academic climate is intense and classes are rigorous, but add that students rarely compete with each other. "Bard is at once intense and laid back. Students are academically driven due to their own desire to learn, and not for the sake of competition," says a senior literature major. Ninety-seven percent of classes have twenty-five or fewer students, and independent studies and tutorials

Website: www.bard.edu
Location: Rural
Total Enrollment: 1,713
Undergraduates: 1,513
Male/Female: 43/57
SAT Ranges: V 650–750
     M 590–690
Financial Aid: 61%
Expense: Pr $ $ $ $
Phi Beta Kappa: No
Applicants: 3,118
Accepted: 35%
Enrolled: 32%
Grad in 6 Years: 71%
Returning Freshmen: 89%
Academics: ✍ ✍ ✍ ✍
Social: ☎ ☎ ☎
Q of L: ★ ★ ★ ★
Admissions: (845) 758-7472
Email Address:
    admission@bard.edu

Strongest Programs:
Photography
Visual and Performing Arts
Social Sciences
Literature
Creative Writing
Languages

are the soul of the curriculum. Students have the opportunity to draw up their own course description, find a professor to sponsor it, and produce a custom-designed program. Bard also makes a point of recognizing visual and performing arts as equals among academic disciplines, and all faculty members are full professors. "They are all helpful and approachable and have a true love of teaching that I think makes a Bard education so unique," says a senior. Adds a classmate: "Professors challenge students and seem to gain a genuine satisfaction from watching us develop."

With distinguished authors such as John Ashbery, Chinua Achebe, and Bradford Morrow teaching seminars in creative writing, it is no wonder that some students feel the best programs at the school are literature and writing. "The longer I spend in the department, the more impressed I am by the faculty. I'm on a first-name basis with Pulitzer-prize winning authors," a lit major says. Natural sciences and physics are surprisingly good for their size, and the distinguished-scientist scholars program offers full tuition to the top applicants who will major in the Division of Natural Science and Mathematics. Bard recently established what administrators believe is the first collegiate program in human rights.

"I'm on a first-name basis with Pulitzer-prize winning authors."

Students say the history and dance departments need improvement, and the administration admits archaeology is small in offerings and enrollment. A new collaborative program with Rockefeller University allows Bard undergrads to study at this premier science research institution. The library has 280,000 volumes, plus 13,000 online journals and ninety online databases.

Bard offers combined programs with other schools in engineering, architecture, city planning, social work, public health, business and public administration, forestry, and environmental science. Students can take part in special Bard programs in China, Greece, India, Senegal, and South Africa, and study language in France, Germany, Italy, or Mexico. Bard Globalization & International Affairs in New York City offers classes and internships in international affairs organizations.

Diversity, be it racial, ideological, or even regarding fashion, is a hallmark at Bard. "Bard students are a strange mix, the artsy, the brainy, and the eccentric," a senior political studies major says. "There's no shortage of wierdos here, but most interactions are pretty interesting as a result." Three percent of students are African-American, 5 percent are Hispanic, and 4 percent are Asian-American. Three-quarters of students are from out of state, and 28 percent attended private school. Bardians are "incredibly politically active" says a senior political studies major, who complains "Bard is so liberal that the conservative students on campus are still staunch leftists." Although Bard does not guarantee financial aid for all four years, 61 percent of the students receive some form of financial assistance and 90 percent have their full demonstrated need met.

"Bard students are a strange mix, the artsy, the brainy, and the eccentric."

Bard offers up to twenty merit scholarships of $5,000 to $28,249. Under Bard's unique Excellence and Equal Cost program, qualified high school students can apply to Bard at the cost of their state university's tuition. Admission to this program is not automatic; about two hundred students vie for forty spots.

Freshmen are required to live on campus in dorms, which include converted mansions. "Housing is really varied here," says a freshman. "You could find yourself living in a cottage, co-op, more traditional dorm, or a Hudson Valley mansion." One student boasts, "My room has four diamond-paneled bay windows that face west with sunsets like a Monet painting. It has oak walls, carved ceilings, and its own bathroom with a marble shower." The room draw system can be chaotic, driving 15 percent of the students to rent rooms off campus. All residential students eat on campus. "There are probably as many students who eat meat as don't, and the dining service is quite accommodating," a senior says.

Social life at Bard is far from an endless party, but Bardians enjoy films, concerts (a lot of indie rock and hip hop), dances, student art exhibits, and lectures, as well as local coffee shops. "At Bard parties, I've ridden a mechanical bull, dressed up like one of the four horsemen of the apocalypse, and danced on stage with George Clinton (though not all at once). And one time, a mentalist made my hand bleed with voodoo," says a senior. There are no fraternities or sororities on campus. Drag Race, which happens on Parents' Weekend, is a cross-dressing, performance-based extravaganza bearing the theme "Dress in Drag or Don't Dress At All."

Having a car on this lovely but rural campus does much to prevent occasional attacks of claustrophobia. Some students say Bard's hometown of Annandale-on-Hudson is "in the woods." But the town is less than twenty miles away from great shopping in Woodstock and within striking distance of ski slopes in the Catskills or Berkshires. Plus, New York City is just a two-hour Amtrak ride away. Students also cite the Upstate Films movie theater in Rhinebeck as one of the best cinematic experiences around.

Bard is part of the Hudson Valley Athletic conference, and the men's soccer and tennis teams and women's soccer and cross-country teams have claimed recent conference championships. Fencing, basketball, squash, and women's volleyball are also popular, but Bard is virtually devoid of dedicated jocks. "Athletics is definitely not a popular activity," says one student. But another notes "there are plenty of pseudo jocks and intellectuals in good shape." There's always Ultimate Frisbee in the fall, and intramural softball competition is "a staple in the spring," for which most majors—and faculty and staff—form teams. Nearby, there are five miles of trails through the woods along the Hudson that are perfect for myriad outdoor activities, from raspberry picking to skiing, jogging, or hiking.

Over the last two decades, this small school has carved out a significant niche for itself in higher education, mainly due to the iconoclastic vision of its president, Leon Botstein (known to everyone simply as Leon) who, when not running the college, can often be found conducting the American Symphony. Under his direction, students at Bard can decide what they want to learn, how they want to learn it, and the ways to use their newfound knowledge after college. "Every student at Bard really wants to learn. It's a refreshing thing," says a freshman.

> **Overlaps**
>
> NYU, Vassar, Oberlin, Wesleyan, Brown

If You Apply To ➢

Bard: Early action: Nov. 1. Regular admissions: Jan. 15. Financial aid: Feb. 15. Meets demonstrated need of 90%. Campus and alumni interviews: optional, informational. SATs and ACTs: optional. SAT IIs: optional. Accepts the Common Application and electronic applications. Essay question: important issue; list three topics you are interested in and explain why one piques your curiosity and how you would learn more about it.

Barnard College

3009 Broadway, New York, NY 10027-6598

With applications running double what they were ten years ago, Barnard has eclipsed Wellesley as the nation's most popular women's college. Barnard women are a little more artsy and a little more city-ish than their female counterparts at Columbia College. Step outside and you're on Broadway.

"Imagine the smartest four or five girls at a high school—strong-willed, accomplished, convinced of their own self-worth. Now imagine 2,300 of them. That's

> **Website:** www.barnard.edu

(Continued)

Location: Urban
Total Enrollment: 2,297
Undergraduates: 2,297
Male/Female: 0/100
SAT Ranges: V 630–710
M 620–700
ACT Range: 27–30
Financial Aid: 53%
Expense: Pr $ $ $ $
Phi Beta Kappa: Yes
Applicants: 3,686
Accepted: 35%
Enrolled: 43%
Grad in 6 Years: 86%
Returning Freshmen: 93%
Academics: ✍ ✍ ✍ ✍ ✍
Social: ☎ ☎ ☎
Q of L: ★ ★ ★
Admissions: (212) 854-2014
Email Address:
admissions@barnard.edu

Strongest Programs:
English
Psychology
Political Science
Biology
Economics
History
Sociology

The Senior Scholars program allows students to substitute a single extensive research project for a semester or year of classes. And the Centennial Scholars program gives ten especially able students $4,000 stipends to be spent on independent projects.

Barnard," says an American history major at this New York City women's college. "We have many very divergent girls, but whatever they are, they are very sure about it." Barnard students get the best of both worlds—the small, close-knit atmosphere of a liberal-arts school, along with the limitless opportunities of Columbia University, an Ivy League research institution. Whether they are passionate about art and music or urban studies and politics, women seeking a high-energy environment with top-notch academics are likely to find a niche here.

Barnard's campus is on the Upper West Side of Manhattan, in the Morningside Heights neighborhood. It's just blocks from Riverside Drive, which has a lovely path running parallel to the Hudson River for running, biking, or roller-blading. Trees and other greenery shade grand prewar apartment buildings, and grassy medians break up the wide expanse of Broadway itself. Barnard's architecturally diverse buildings are more modern than Columbia's, and in recent years, the college has invested to upgrade labs, classrooms, animal research facilities, and the residence halls with new bathrooms, heat and air-conditioning systems, elevators, and windows. A campus master plan has been commissioned to focus on future space and building needs.

Barnard's requirements are designed to reflect the changing nature of our technological society, and the fact that graduates are increasingly pursuing law, business, and other professions rather than academic careers. To that end, students take two first-year foundation courses and fulfill nine "area requirements" in reason and value, social analysis, historical studies, cultures in comparison, laboratory science, quantitative and deductive reasoning, language, literature, and the visual and performing arts. Students must also take two physical education courses, though most get plenty of exercise running for the bus or dashing up and down subway stairs.

While curricular requirements guarantee Barnard graduates have intellectual breadth, the mandatory senior thesis project or comprehensive examination ensures academic depth. Barnard students may cross-register at Columbia if they find more courses of interest there, or enroll in graduate courses in any of Columbia's schools. Dual-degree and joint-degree programs are also available with Columbia and the Jewish Theological Seminary, and music students may also take classes at Juilliard and the Manhattan School of Music. Barnard's interdisciplinary majors include Jewish studies, medieval and Renaissance studies, and urban affairs, and another innovative program offers women the chance to concentrate on dance, music, theater, visual arts, or writing—while also completing a degree in liberal arts.

Barnard's most popular majors are English, psychology, and political science, all of which happen to be some of the school's best departments. Also well-subscribed are biology (there's a healthy contingent of premeds) and economics. "Learning at Barnard is constant and mind-opening," says an urban studies major. "Science classes are much more competitive than the humanities," says a religion major. "I have never felt competitive for grades or for a teacher's favor. The classes, however, are rigorous, and the academic atmosphere is one that expects students to try their hardest." Women's studies and education also draw praise, though students in these programs must also choose another major. Columbia's departments of math, physics, and computer science make up for weak offerings in these disciplines at Barnard.

Many students come to Barnard because of its low student/faculty ratio. "My first year, eight of my nine classes were taught by full professors," says a sophomore. "In art history, my professor led class tours at the Metropolitan Museum of Art in groups of fifteen or so. Availability and enthusiasm of professors is extraordinary." Another plus: Barnard has no graduate teaching assistants. In fact, Barnard professors enjoy Columbia's proximity almost as much as undergraduates, and each year one-third of the full-time faculty teaches in graduate departments throughout the university. Still, faculty members focus on their teaching responsibilities first. "Very often, students develop close connections to both faculty and staff," says an English major. Undergraduate research is also a priority at Barnard. The Senior Scholars program allows students to substitute a single extensive research project for a semester or year of classes. And the Centennial Scholars program gives ten especially able students $4,000 stipends to be spent on independent projects.

Thirty-five percent of Barnard students are New York natives, including a sizable contingent from the East Side of Manhattan, and 45 percent attended private high school. A whopping 98 percent ranked in the top quarter of their high school class. Asian-Americans make up 20 percent of the student body, while African-Americans add 5 percent and Hispanics make up another 6 percent.

Barnard now competes head-to-head with Columbia in admissions, an interesting dilemma because Barnard is just another division of the university, similar to the engineering school, the medical school, the business school—or Columbia College. In general, women looking for a more traditional "rah-rah" experience may prefer Columbia. Those seeking flexibility might do better at Barnard, a hotbed of liberalism where students don't shy away from rallies and protests. "The debate over the sexual misconduct policy was a big issue, as was the war in Iraq," says a senior. "Because of the

"My first year, eight of my nine classes were taught by full professors."

high Jewish population, the Israeli–Palestinian conflict is very apparent." Barnard students do share a first-year orientation program with Columbia, where they mix together in small groups and take tours of the campus and city. Students can also take part in a preorientation backpacking trip.

Eighty-eight percent of Barnard students live in the dorms, which have come a long way since the college's beginning as a commuter school: There's an eighteen-story Barnard dormitory tower, plus one dorm complex and five off-campus apartment buildings; nonresidents must be signed in by a resident, and entries are always guarded, so students say they feel safe. In addition, Barnard shares two co-ed dorms with Columbia. With New York's notoriously high rents and broker fees, demand for dorm beds remains high. "All first-years live in the Quad," says a music major. "Most people live in doubles, but there are a few triples and quads." Seniors get the best rooms, though an English major says housing "is a crap-shoot. I know many people who are unhappy, and maintenance is often irregular." Housing is guaranteed as long as you stay in the dorms; choose to move out for a year, and you may have difficulty getting back in. Dorm-dwellers must buy a meal plan, which may also be used at Columbia's John Jay cafeteria, though students say Barnard's food is better. "There is always a salad bar, a home-cooked section, a pizza section, a sandwich section, and a grill station," says a sophomore. "There are also Kosher, vegan, and vegetarian options."

When it comes to social life, "the college believes that it cannot compete with New York City," says a music major. "When there is something big on campus, everybody goes." That includes traditions such as Midnight Breakfast, the night before finals begin, when deans and administrators serve up eggs and waffles in the gym. Women in the arts are celebrated in the annual Winterfest, while the Books Etc. series brought Barnard alumnae authors like Jhumpa Lahiri '89 and Anna Quindlen '74 back to campus for lectures in the fall of 2003. Less academic pursuits are available, too. "There are about a half-dozen

"Learning at Barnard is constant and mind-opening."

bars within a ten-minute walk of campus, where many students spend a lot of time and money," says an English major. "More adventurous students can go downtown and find fantastic nightlife." Fake IDs are easy to come by in Manhattan, and while they often work, Barnard students aren't focused on drinking themselves into oblivion. Instead, "there is something for everyone," says a religion major. "Student tickets for performances on- and off-Broadway, museums, parks, clubs, bars, restaurants, music, dance, film festivals...you name it." Road trips are infrequent, but when they happen, destinations range from Washington, D.C., to Boston, easily reached by train and plane, to skiing and snowboarding in Vermont, or spring break on the beaches of South Carolina.

Barnard athletes compete alongside their peers enrolled at Columbia, and the field hockey, soccer, lacrosse, archery, and crew teams have the largest number of participants. The fencing team is also strong. Columbia's marvelous gym and co-ed intramurals are also available to Barnard women, but many prefer to exercise their minds.

Barnard offers the intimate attention of a small, independent women's college with the resources of a major research university. "Students and faculty truly watch out for one another and want everybody to feel comfortable and happy," says a sophomore. What makes Barnard a special place? "It is a women's college without being a girls' school," says an American history major. "I can have all-girls classes and activities without cloistering myself away from men."

Overlaps

NYU, Columbia University, Wellesley, Cornell, UC–Berkeley

If You Apply To ➤

Barnard: Early decision: Nov. 15. Regular admissions: Jan. 1. Financial aid: Feb. 1. Housing: Second Friday in June. Guarantees to meet demonstrated need. Campus interviews: recommended, evaluative. Alumni interviews: optional, evaluative. SATs or ACTs: required. SAT IIs: required with the SAT I, optional with the ACT (writing or literature and two others). Accepts the Common Application. Essay question: two pages on an important idea, influential person, or experience that has helped shape who you are.

Bates College

23 Campus Avenue, Lewiston, ME 04240

Bowdoin got rid of its frats, Bates never had them, and therein hangs a tale. With its long-held tradition of egalitarianism, Bates is a kindred spirit to Quaker institutions such as Haverford and Swarthmore. A month-long spring term helps make Bates a leader in studying abroad.

Website: www.bates.edu
Location: Small city
Total Enrollment: 1,738
Undergraduates: 1,738
Male/Female: 49/51
SAT Ranges: V 630–710
  M 630–720
Financial Aid: 39%
Expense: Pr $ $ $ $
Phi Beta Kappa: Yes
Applicants: 4,012
Accepted: 28%
Enrolled: 37%
Grad in 6 Years: 87%
Returning Freshmen: 94%

While Bates, Bowdoin, and Colby share a rugged Maine location, a mania for ice hockey, and popularity among prep-schoolers clad in Patagonia and L.L. Bean, Bates has more in common ideologically with Quaker colleges such as Haverford and Swarthmore. Founded by abolitionists in 1855, Bates takes pride in its heritage as a haven for seekers of guidance, freedom, and justice. Its 4–4–1 calendar offers ample opportunity for study abroad, even for just one month at year's end. The school's small size also means student/faculty interaction is plentiful, and close friendships are easily formed. "My loyalty is unending," sighs a nostalgic senior. "I'll support Bates however I can."

The Bates campus features a mix of Georgian and Federal buildings and Victorian homes spread out over grassy lawns in the "recovering mill town" of Lewiston,

"My loyalty is unending. I'll support Bates however I can."

says a biology major. Lewiston is about two and a half hours from Boston, and very close to Maine's picturesque coast, but that's about all there is to recommend it. "Auburn, across the river, is more of a town, with restaurants and shops," the student says. "Community service and volunteering is huge, with Big Brothers, tutoring, and two hospitals within walking distance."

Bates emphasizes the liberal arts, and to graduate, all students must complete a comprehensive exam in the major field, a senior thesis, or both. The Ladd Library is often crowded, as 85 percent of students write a thesis or produce an equivalent research, service, performance, or studio project. Ladd has more than five hundred thousand volumes, plus an all-night study room, a typing room, and "an audio room with everything from Bach to Bruce Springsteen." In their first year, students must satisfy a physical education requirement through intercollegiate or club sports or two ten-week activity courses. They may also take first-year seminars, capped at fifteen students each. General education requirements include at least three courses in the natural sciences and another three in the social sciences; at least one course that emphasizes quantitative analysis; and at least five courses in the fine arts, music, theater, or a foreign language. Despite the school's size, and the fact that "some courses are more popular than others," it's usually easy to register for most classes. If the one you need is full, professors will usually "let you in on petition," says a senior.

"The school provided a mentor for me."

While Bates doesn't require standardized tests for admission, don't expect to coast through. "People here take their studies very seriously," says a biology major. Still, "classes do not feel competitive" because "people are always willing to help one another." A senior gives high marks to political science, biology, economics, and psychology, which also happen to be the four most popular majors, and says art is "small, but quite good." Indeed, the music and art departments benefit from the Olin Arts Center, which houses a performance hall, gallery, recording studio, art studios, and practice rooms. Interdisciplinary programs at Bates include American cultural studies, neuroscience, and women and gender studies. The school's rhetoric program has produced a nationally ranked debate team, popular among future lawyers. Professors teach all courses, including lab and discussion sections.

Bates offers study abroad opportunities in locations such as China, India, South America, France, Ecuador, and Japan. The school also participates in the Washington Semester,* the ten-college Venture Program,* and the American Maritime Studies Program at Mystic Seaport*—all attractive options for students seeking real-world experience. Only two short-term courses are required for graduation, though many students take more. After all, who wouldn't want to spend a month studying the Philosophy of Star Trek? Or how about Cult and the Community, which led two students to a five-week tour with the Grateful Dead? The fall semester study abroad program is even open to first-year students, giving them a chance to acclimate to college through home stays and tours with families in other countries. They join their classmates in Lewiston in the winter.

Eighty-nine percent of Bates students come from outside Maine, many from Massachusetts, Connecticut, and New York. "We are laid-back, easy-going, and friendly," says a freshman. "The people are the main reason I chose Bates," a senior agrees. "We're an intellectual, motivated group, while maintaining a sense of connectedness to strong ideals like environmentalism, and an open, unpretentious campus." While the administration is trying to make Bates more diverse, minorities remain a tiny fragment of the student population, with African-Americans and Hispanics adding 2 percent each, and Asian-Americans 3 percent. Politically, the "campus is somewhat left-leaning, but activities are balanced well," says a biology major, noting that pacifist civil rights leader Howard Zinn spoke on campus one fall, and conservative Dinesh D'Souza followed in the spring. Admission is not need-blind and no merit or athletic scholarships are awarded.

Ninety percent of Bates students live on campus, where there is "great variety in dorm rooms, from brand-new suite living to immaculately maintained college

(Continued)
Academics: ✐ ✐ ✐ ✐ ½
Social: ☎ ☎ ☎
Q of L: ★ ★ ★
Admissions: (207) 786-6000
Email Address:
  admissions@bates.edu

Strongest Programs:
Economics
Biology
Psychology
History
Political Science

The Ladd Library is often crowded, as 85 percent of students write a thesis, or produce an equivalent research, service, performance, or studio project.

The fall semester study abroad program is even open to first-year students, giving them a chance to acclimate to college through home stays and tours with families in other countries. They join their classmates in Lewiston in the winter.

houses," says a senior. "The school-owned houses directly on and off campus are gorgeous, and dorm rooms are huge," enthuses a freshman. Dorms even include weekly maid service. Housing is guaranteed for four years, but awarded by lottery after the first year, causing some student angst. Food in the Commons, where everyone eats, is "great, but it gets monotonous," says a biology major. There's a vegan bar every day.

Since there's not much to do in Lewiston, parties, concerts, and other weekend diversions mostly occur on campus. Without a Greek system, college alcohol policies are fairly loose, one student says: "If you got admitted, you should be a responsible adult, but if not, get ready for the consequences." Barbecues and clambakes are big when the weather is nice, and the annual Winter Carnival includes ice skating, snow sculpting, and a semiformal dance. During the St. Patrick's Day Puddle Jump, students of Irish descent—and all those who want to be Irish for the day—cut a hole in the ice on Lake Andrews and plunge in. Students with cars can easily road-trip to the outlet stores in Freeport and Kittery, Maine. Other popular destinations include Bar Harbor in Acadia National Park, or "Portland, for great food," says a senior. Montreal and Boston are not far, and neither are the ski slopes of Vermont and New Hampshire.

Bates' varsity teams compete in Division III, except for the ski team, which is Division I. Everyone gets excited for matches against Bowdoin and Colby, especially when they involve ice hockey. Basketball, football, and lacrosse are also popular among spectators. The intramural program, organized by the students and supervised by faculty members, is "strong and spirited," sparking lively dorm rivalries.

Bates isn't for everyone, but if you can stand the cold and the silent, starry nights, it may be a good choice. With caring professors, a small student body, and a focus on the liberal arts, students quickly become big fans. "The school provided a mentor for me," says a women and gender studies major. "The friendly people and atmosphere here are great."

Overlaps

Colby, Middlebury, Bowdoin, Dartmouth, Williams

If You Apply To ➤

Bates: Early decision: Nov. 15, Jan. 1. Regular admissions and financial aid: Jan. 15. Guarantees to meet demonstrated need. Campus and alumni interviews: recommended, evaluative. SATs and ACTs: optional. SAT IIs: optional. Accepts the Common Application and electronic applications. Essay question: Why Bates? Encourages applicants to send additional material.

Baylor University

Waco, TX 76798

Come to Baylor and Mom can rest easy. Baylor is Southern Baptist, which means less of the debauchery prevalent at many schools. Dad will like it, too: Baylor is one of the least expensive private universities in the country. Prayers come in handy on the football field; the team is still praying to beat UT.

Website: www.baylor.edu
Location: Center city
Total Enrollment: 14,159
Undergraduates: 11,987
Male/Female: 42/58

Baylor University's Baptist heritage remains a campus mainstay, but students and faculty at this Texas institution are also looking forward, aiming to become one of America's elite universities. The school's 2012 vision plan includes twelve strategic imperatives, such as lowering the student/teacher ratio and building new residence halls to house 1,600 students—half the study body—on campus. One thing that won't change is the sense of community that students say makes the school a special place. "Baylor offers students a unique opportunity to grow academically, socially, physically, and most of all spiritually, thereby developing the whole person," says a history and environmental studies major.

The 432-acre Baylor campus, nicknamed Jerusalem on the Brazos, abuts the historic Brazos River near downtown Waco, Texas (population 110,000). The architectural style emphasizes the gracious tradition of the Old South, and the central part of campus, the quadrangle, was built when Baylor moved from Independence, Texas, in 1886. The 130,000-square-foot Sheila & Walter Umphrey Law Center recently opened, along with the 80,000-square-foot George Truett Theological Seminary, housing one of the nation's fastest growing theological schools. The new Stacy Riddle Forum provides meeting space for sororities and a new science building will help enhance undergraduate research opportunities.

Waffling on what to study? Not to worry. Except for those in the school of music, all freshmen enter the college of arts and sciences, where they complete the Baylor Interdisciplinary Core. After the core, students pursue their majors—in arts and sciences or one of Baylor's five other schools: business, education, engineering and computer sciences, music, and nursing. All students also take two religion courses and two semesters of Chapel Forum, a series of lectures and meetings

> "Baylor offers students a unique opportunity to grow academically, socially, physically, and most of all spiritually, thereby developing the whole person."

on various issues or Christian testimonies. In the fall of 2002, the Honors College began to oversee the honors program (which offers opportunities for course integration and independent research), the University Scholars Program (which waives most distribution requirements), the Core, and the new Great Texts of the Western Tradition program. Students may major or minor in Great Texts, an interdisciplinary program exploring "the richness and diversity of the Western intellectual heritage."

Biology is Baylor's most popular major, followed by psychology, journalism, teacher education, and forensic science (the school has the only such program in Texas). The business school's programs in accounting, professional selling (one of only two worldwide), and entrepreneurship also draw praise. More unusual options include church–state studies and museum studies, and institutes focusing on environmental studies and childhood learning disorders. The archeology and geology departments benefit from fossil- and mineral-rich Texas prairies. An increasing number of Baylor students are traveling on study abroad programs, which send them to fifteen countries, including England, Mexico, Costa Rica, and Brazil.

One of Baylor's greatest strengths is the sense of campus community, fostered by the emphasis on Christianity and by the administration's efforts to focus faculty members on teaching, rather than on research and other activities outside the classroom, students say. Baylor also strives to keep classes small—students say most have fifty or fewer enrolled—which can make it difficult to fulfill requirements on time. "Many people don't graduate in four years without summer school," says a sophomore. The level of rigor varies with the course, a classmate adds: "The basic classes are laid-back. The major classes are more in-depth and difficult." Professors teach most courses, but not all instructors are of equal quality, cautions a speech communication major: "Finally, in my fourth semester here, do I have those great teachers you always hear about."

Baylor students are largely middle- to upper-middle-class Christians. Eighty-one percent are Texans, and most "are more conservative than the rival institutions around our area," says a Spanish major. "It is a bit conformist," agrees another student. "Here, 'different' isn't always so cool." Minorities total nearly one-fifth of the student body, with Hispanics the largest group at 8 percent, Asian-Americans at 6 percent, and African-Americans at 5 percent.

(Continued)

SAT Ranges: V 530–630
  M 550–650
ACT Range: 22–27
Financial Aid: N/A
Expense: Pr $
Phi Beta Kappa: Yes
Applicants: 7,432
Accepted: 81%
Enrolled: 43%
Grad in 6 Years: 72%
Returning Freshmen: 84%
Academics: ✍ ✍ ✍
Social: ☎ ☎ ☎
Q of L: ★ ★ ★
Admissions: (254) 710-3435
Email Address:
  Admission_Serv_Office@
  baylor.edu

Strongest Programs:
Premed
Math
Theater Arts
Entrepreneurship
Engineering
Classics
Music

The 130,000-square-foot Sheila & Walter Umphrey Law Center recently opened, along with the 80,000-square-foot George Truett Theological Seminary, housing one of the nation's fastest growing theological schools.

As might be expected on a conservative and religious campus like Baylor's, dorms are single sex and have restrictive visitation privileges, which can be frustrating. The "very comfortable and well-kept" halls have lounges, computer labs, and gyms, and house 29 percent of the student body—mainly freshmen, says a sophomore. The dining facilities "really have something for everybody, even vegetarians" and "are always trying new things and requesting student input." Upperclassmen look off campus for cheaper housing with private rooms and fewer rules, says a junior. Those who've moved out of the dorms appreciate the presence of twenty fully commissioned police officers patrolling the area on bikes and in patrol cars. "Waco is not a safe town, but I feel safe on campus," says a speech communication major.

Thirteen percent of Baylor's men and 17 percent of the women belong to a fraternity or sorority, providing a party scene for those who want it, and community service outlets for those who don't participate in the school-sponsored Steppin' Out service days that occur once a semester. Baylor is "very social with tons of on-campus opportunities for fun," says a sophomore. Easy road trips include Dallas, Austin, San Antonio, Bryan/College Station, and beaches at Galveston, South Padre Island, and Corpus Christi. Most destinations are within two-and-a-half hour drive, students say, making a set of wheels a big help, if not a necessity. "Waco gets boring," laments a sophomore. "Some weekends there is nothing to do but go out to eat." Alcohol isn't served on campus or at campus-sponsored events, "but you can find it off campus," says a senior. "Baylor strictly looks down on alcohol consumption," adds a junior. But "if you desire to drink, it is not hard to get."

Highlights of Baylor's social calendar include the annual Halloween Monster Bash (complete with a ghost story told by the university president), and the Dia del Oso (Day of the Bear), when classes are cancelled for a day in April in favor of a campus-wide carnival. The Fiesta on the River, organized by the Residence Hall Association, lets student-run organizations set up booths to raise funds for the causes they support. The school also has the largest collegiate homecoming parade in the nation.

When it comes to football, remember: You're in Texas. Freshmen wear team jerseys to games and take the field before the players, then sit together as a pack. "It's a very awesome part of the freshman experience," one student says. Baylor is in Division I, and both the men's and women's tennis teams brought home recent championships. Women's track and field also draws fans. For weekend warriors, the McLane Student Life Center offers the tallest rock-climbing wall in Texas. The university maintains a small marina for swimming and paddle boating, and several lakes with good beaches are nearby. Generally, though, religious groups are more popular than the intramural sports program, with chapters of Campus Crusade for Christ and the Fellowship of Christian Athletes very much alive and well.

For all its emphasis on conservative, traditional Christianity, Baylor also recognizes that it must remain open to new ways of thinking to achieve its goal of becoming a top-tier university by 2012. Baylor's president took a step in that direction by giving his wife a whirl in public, signaling an end to the school's unwritten but long-standing ban on dancing. "Baylor is emphasizing the 2012 vision that will send Baylor on a path to even more greatness," says a sophomore.

Overlaps

University of Texas, Texas A&M, Texas Tech, Rice, Texas Christian

If You Apply To ➤ **Baylor:** Rolling admissions. Does not guarantee to meet demonstrated need. SATs or ACTs: required. Campus and alumni interviews: optional. Accepts electronic applications. Essay question: How your value system would help you succeed as a Baylor student and throughout your lifetime. Looks for students who want a "Christian education with academic excellence."

Tiny Midwestern college known for free-thinking students and international focus. Has steered back toward the mainstream after its heyday as an alternative school in the '60s and '70s. Wisconsin location makes Beloit easier to get into than comparable schools in sexier places.

Beloit College urges students to "Invent Yourself," urging intellectual curiosity and personal initiative by giving students freedom to explore. Known for attracting liberal, freethinkers in the 1960s and '70s, the school is now steering back toward the mainstream. What hasn't changed is its emphasis on tolerance, understanding, and the world beyond the United States. "We are one big family that grows, interacts, and learns from each other, as much as from our professors," explains a sophomore majoring in studio art and business administration. "Beloit offers endless opportunities for every student to pursue his or her individual goals."

Beloit's forty-acre campus is a Northeastern-style oasis an hour's drive from Madison and Milwaukee and ninety minutes from Chicago. Academic and administrative buildings sit on one side, with residence halls on the other. Two architectural themes dominate, says one student: "1850s Colonial and obtuse 1930s." In 2001, the college's Turtle Creek Bookstore opened three blocks away in downtown Beloit. A cozy coffee bar, selection of general books and maga-

> **"We don't feel scared to ask questions, to slow class down a little so that everyone is caught up."**

zines, and a patio for relaxing, reading, or studying augment the typical stacks of textbooks. A new dorm opened in the fall of 2002, offering apartment-style living for forty-eight upperclassmen.

All Beloit freshmen complete a First Year Initiative (FYI) seminar led by a faculty member who serves as their advisor until they declare majors the next year. Courses under the recent FYI theme "Here, There, and Everywhere" included "Personal Choice and Global Responsibility" and "Enemies Among Us: Communists and Cosmopolitans in Cold War Culture." The FYI program flows into the Sophomore Year Program, which offers a retreat, Exploration Week, and the charting of a Comprehensive Academic Plan for the final two years, which often includes internships, research, and off-campus study. If fact, 80 percent of Beloit students undertake some type of independent project, presenting their findings in the annual Student Symposium.

All students must also complete three writing courses, at least two units in each of three subject areas (natural science and math, social sciences, and arts and humanities), and a unit of interdisciplinary studies. Students are likewise required to complete at least two units involving a different culture or language, or focusing on relations between nations. "Classes are rigorous, but students and faculty work collaboratively to learn," says a senior.

Teaching is the faculty's first priority, and the vast majority of classes have twenty-five or fewer students. "We don't feel scared to ask questions, to slow class down a little so that everyone is caught up," says a psychology and drama major. Anthropology is the most popular major, followed by English language and literature, biology, economics, and psychology, which students say are among Beloit's best departments. Among more unusual options are a museum studies minor, with hands-on restoration experience, and the rhetoric and discourse major, which asks students to reflect on current nonfiction writing while producing their own prose.

Website: www.beloit.edu
Location: Small city
Total Enrollment: 1,281
Undergraduates: 1,281
Male/Female: 41/59
SAT Ranges: V 590–690
  M 560–650
ACT Range: 25–29
Financial Aid: 72%
Expense: Pr $ $
Phi Beta Kappa: Yes
Applicants: 1,677
Accepted: 69%
Enrolled: 30%
Grad in 6 Years: 70%
Returning Freshmen: 94%
Academics: ✍ ✍ ✍
Social: ☎ ☎ ☎
Q of L: ★ ★ ★ ★
Admissions: (800) 356-0751
Email Address:
  admiss@beloit.edu

Strongest Programs:
Anthropology
Economics
English
Geology
Modern Languages and
  Literatures
Natural and Social Sciences
Theatre Arts

Physics is Beloit's one weak spot, students and administrators say; education majors should be prepared to spend an extra semester because of complexities related to certification.

To satisfy Beloit's experiential learning and global diversity requirements, Venture Grants offer $500 to $1,500 for "entrepreneurial, self-testing activities" that benefit the community; one recent awardee is repairing and distributing used bikes in Beloit, while another created a photographic portfolio of the culture, tradition, art, and architecture of her native Bhutan. An exchange program sends five Beloit students and a faculty member to China's Fudan University and brings their counterparts to Beloit. Other options include student teaching in Britain or Australia, or studying marine biology in Tahiti. More than half of Beloit's students study or do research abroad through the World Outlook Program, where

"Students at Beloit are not numbers; each student is a name, a face, a set of values, and a smile."

destinations include African and South American nations. The Center for Language Studies complements Beloit's own foreign language programs with intensive summer study in Chinese, Japanese, Russian, Hungarian, and English as a second language. Beloit is also a member of the Associated Colleges of the Midwest* consortium, increasing students' choices.

Beloit's Wisconsin location makes it easier to get into than similar schools in sexier places, but only 20 percent of the student body is homegrown; 70 percent hail from out of state, and 10 percent come from abroad. African-Americans and Hispanics each comprise 4 percent of the total, and Asian-Americans are 5 percent. Women's rights, gay rights, and the war in Iraq were hot-button issues in recent months—"to shave or not to shave is the final question," quips one student. The environment, domestic violence, homosexuality, and world peace continue to arouse concern. "We don't take anything too seriously, but we're very involved and very conscientious," says another.

Ninety-three percent of Beloit students live on campus, where they're required to remain for three years. The Haven, Wood, and 815 residence halls boast new carpeting, furniture, and central air-conditioning and heat; one student says other good choices include Chapin and Aldrich. Four fraternities attract 15 percent of the men, and two sororities draw 5 percent of the women; members may live in their chapter houses. Special-interest houses cater to those interested in foreign languages, music, anthropology, and other disciplines.

On-campus movies, concerts, art shows, dance recitals, and parties at the frats and special-interest houses tie up many Friday and Saturday nights at Beloit. Two all-campus festivals liven up the calendar: the Folk and Blues Fall Music Festival brings jazz, reggae, folk, and blues bands to campus, while on Spring Day, classes give way to concerts and everyone kicks back to enjoy the (finally!) warmer weather. The school's alcohol policy is lax, students say. "They will treat you as an adult who can make good, responsible choices," explains a junior. "They trust you, but they take action when you are harming yourself or others."

Having wheels here will definitely raise your social standing, as they make it easier to take off for Chicago or the college town of Madison, also easily reached through a cheap local bus service. For the outdoors-minded, the nearby Dells offer camping and water parks. "Beloit is a friendly community with lots of hidden jewels," says one student. "But it is facing economic hardship after the closing of several local factories." That said, the town has basic necessities, such as a few bars (check out the excellent burgers at Hanson's Pub, says a senior), a bowling alley, a movie theater, and a Wal-Mart. "Groups such as Habitat for Humanity, Beloit Interaction Committee, and the Outreach Center work hard to integrate students into the community," says a sophomore.

Sports at Beloit are played more for fun than glory. Among the school's Division III squads, standouts include baseball, men's and women's basketball, men's and women's cross-country, and football, especially against rival Ripon College. The women's tennis team won Midwest Conference championships in 2001 and 2002, and intramural Ultimate Frisbee typically draws hundreds of players and spectators.

Beloit is a bundle of contradictions: a small liberal-arts college in the heart of Big Ten state university country, where the academic program has an East Coast rigor but the laid-back classroom vibe reflects the free-and-easy spirit of the Midwest. The school is also the source of the "mindset list" that circulates nationally among university administrators each fall, helping them relate to their new charges. (Tips on the class of 2005, born in 1983, include the fact that they're younger than the first DOS and Mac computers, have always had the choice of drinking Diet Coke, and think of *Survivor* as a TV show rather than a band.) "People are accepting of new ideas, attitudes, and beliefs," a sophomore says. "Students at Beloit are not numbers; each student is a name, a face, a set of values, and a smile."

Overlaps

Oberlin, Macalester, Grinnell, Lawrence, Knox

If You Apply To ➤

Beloit: Early action: Nov. 15, Dec. 15. Rolling admissions: Feb. 1. Financial aid: Mar. 1 (priority). Housing: May 1. Guarantees to meet demonstrated need. Campus interviews: recommended, informational. Alumni interviews: optional, informational. SATs or ACTs: required. SAT IIs: optional. Accepts the Common Application and electronic applications. Essay question: How you heard about Beloit, factors that have led you to apply, and topic of your choice.

Bennington College

One College Drive, Bennington, VT 05201

Known for top-notch performing arts and lavish attention to every student. Arts programs rely heavily on part-time faculty who are practitioners in their field. Less competitive than Bard and Sarah Lawrence, comparable to Hampshire. Enrollment is robust after a dip in the '90s.

Bennington College just might be the best example of "quirky" among American colleges and universities. Students learn by doing, and that's about the only thing that hasn't been tweaked or adjusted since classes began in 1932. Courses are as rigorous as you make them, since faculty members require a personal meeting with each prospective student before they grant a seminar seat. Academic advising is stellar; rather than grades, students get detailed feedback from a self-selected faculty committee that meets as often as once a week. And forget about career counseling, says a sophomore: "There is not much; Bennington students tend to do strange things after graduation." Whether they're painters or writers, musicians or scientists, sculptors, dancers or some combination thereof, what Bennington students have in common is self-motivation and a real thirst for knowledge. "I get treated like a thinker, and am allowed to respond and grow as such," a junior says.

Bennington sits on 550 acres at the foot of Vermont's Green Mountains. The campus was once an active dairy farm, and a converted barn houses the main classroom and administrative spaces. But don't let the quaint, New England setting fool you. The Dickinson Science Building offers high-tech equipment for aspiring chemists, biologists, environmental scientists, and geneticists. The building is also home to a media lab dedicated to the study of languages, including Chinese, French, German, Italian, Japanese, and Spanish. Recent campus additions include

Website: www.bennington.edu
Location: Rural
Total Enrollment: 787
Undergraduates: 627
Male/Female: 32/68
SAT Ranges: V 580–690
M 500–630
Financial Aid: 54%
Expense: Pr $ $ $ $
Phi Beta Kappa: No
Applicants: 701
Accepted: 71%
Enrolled: 25%
Grad in 6 Years: 83%
Returning Freshmen: 84%
Academics: ✍ ✍ ✍
Social: ☎ ☎ ☎

(Continued)

Q of L: ★ ★ ★ ★
Admissions: (800) 833-6845
Email Address:
admissions@bennington
.edu

Strongest Programs:
Literature
Writing
Music
Dance
Sciences

Recent campus additions include three new student houses featured in the February 2002 issue of Architectural Record magazine.

three new student houses, featured in the February 2002 issue *of Architectural Record* magazine.

Thanks to its focus on experiential learning, Bennington's academic structure differs from that of a typical college or university. Each student designs a major and there are few academic requirements other than a seven-week internship each January and February in a field of interest and a location of the student's choice. "All professors are also working professionals, as well as great people," a music major explains. "We know them all on a first-name basis, eat dinner with them, stay at their houses if we need to. Faculty are more like mentors." Even without grades, students push themselves to learn, grow, and achieve, says an international relations and religion major: "Bennington fosters creative problem-solving and commitment to the work—your work. Classes are collaborations."

> **"This is place where students come to make friends and colleagues, not to attend keg parties."**

Without academic departments, the Core Faculty works to provide students with a well-rounded academic foundation. Since the school's size limits standard course offerings, more than 175 tutorials fill in the gaps. The most popular area of study is visual and performing arts, followed by multidisciplinary or interdisciplinary studies, including such unlikely combinations as biology and set design. Another popular program, English language and literature, focuses on creative writing supervised by actual poets, novelists, short story writers, essayists, and playwrights, rather than critical analysis of existing work. Social and biological sciences are likewise popular.

Bennington's "fluid and free-form" climate appeals to a "diverse, motley bunch," says a literature and writing major. They're "very artsy, but not exclusively so." Five percent are from Vermont and 8 percent are foreign nationals. While a microbiology major insists that "the students here can't be categorized," a recent grad calls them "those students who are smart and creative, and who never quite fit in at high school." Curiosity and excitement about exploration and experimentation will take you far here, and if you lean liberal in the voting booth, so much the better. (The recent war in Iraq sparked some protests and rallies, though a photography and literature major says that students tend to be "politically apathetic, and more interested in campus-related social issues or their own work.") Together, African-Americans, Hispanics, and Asian-Americans account for 4 percent of the student body.

As Bennington lacks traditional departments, requirements, and even faculty tenure, it's probably not surprising that the school also lacks dorms. Most students live in one of the college's eighteen co-ed houses; fifteen are white New England clapboard and three are more modern. Each holds twenty-five to thirty people with an elected chair to govern house affairs. "Each house has a living room with a fireplace, a kitchen, wood floors," says a sophomore. "There is a great sense of shared community." Freshmen and sophomores share rooms—those of the opposite sex may live together if both parties request it—and juniors and seniors are guaranteed singles. The college food service provides plenty of options, from vegetarian and vegan choices to a salad bar, wok station, and pizza machine.

> **"Bennington fosters creative problem-solving and commitment to the work—your work. Classes are collaborations."**

Although the vibe on Bennington's campus is liberal, sophisticated, and cosmopolitan, the neighboring town of the same name—four miles away—is far more conservative, typical of rural New England. "It is a relatively small, rural, blue-collar town, and not a mecca of culture," sighs a photography and literature major. "However, there are movie theaters, a few great restaurants, and beautiful scenery—

the way most students want it." Students are trying to mend the town–gown rift through volunteer work in local schools and homeless shelters, though such programs can be tough because of the mandatory mid-year internship term, which takes many students away from campus. Social life centers on rehearsals, performances, films, and lectures. "This is place where students come to make friends and colleagues, not to attend keg parties," says a recent grad. That said, the annual theme parties always draw raves—recent themes have included "Gatsby's Funeral" and "Mods vs. Rockers." Road trips to Montreal and New York are fun but infrequent diversions.

Given Bennington's rugged location, hiking, rock climbing, caving, camping, and canoeing keep students moving. Ski slopes beckon in the winter, when the college turns part of its huge Visual and Performing Arts complex into an indoor roller rink for the Rollerama party. "Imagine several hundred pairs of roller skates, a disco ball, at least half of the student body, and lots of '80s music," says a writing and literature major. "Lots of people wear costumes." For twelve hours one day each May, the campus celebrates spring with Sunfest, which includes "amazing, crazy bands, a foam pit, sometimes Jello wrestling, and other games," says a sophomore. Transvestite Night livens things up during Parents' Weekend. And during finals week, the blaring of fire-truck sirens tells weary students to head to the dining hall, where professors and the college president serve up French toast. Sports aren't a big focus, but Bennington does compete in an intramural co-ed soccer league that also includes other Northeastern colleges.

As the first school in the nation to grant the arts equal status with other disciplines, Bennington offers a novel, participatory, and hands-on approach. The emphasis on self-direction, field work, and personal relationships with professors sets it apart even from other liberal arts colleges of similar (small) size. Crossing disciplines is encouraged, and forget about taking the road less traveled; each student here charts his or her own course. "I'm given a lot of freedom and support—it's both a challenging and welcoming place," says a senior. And besides, there's a tree house—and milk and cookies served at every meal. Who says going to college means growing up?

Curiosity and excitement about exploration and experimentation will take you far here, and if you lean liberal in the voting booth, so much the better.

Overlaps

Bard, Oberlin, Sarah Lawrence, Hampshire, Reed

If You Apply To ➤ | **Bennington:** Early decision: Nov. 15. Regular admissions: Jan. 1. Financial aid: Mar. 1. Does not guarantee to meet demonstrated need. Campus interviews: recommended, evaluative. Alumni interviews: optional, informational. SATs or ACTs: required. SAT IIs: optional. Accepts the Common Application. Essay question: create and describe your own "experiment of living," a reference to Henry David Thoreau's Walden, or turn an image into a piece of writing (and include the picture with your application).

Birmingham-Southern College

Box A18, Birmingham, AL 35254

One of the deep South's best liberal arts colleges. The vast majority of students come from Alabama and the surrounding states. At 1,407 students, BSC is roughly the same size as Rhodes (Tennessee) and Millsaps (Missouri). Strong fraternity system and a throwback to the way college used to be.

BSC, once an old-school conservative Southern institution, is now striving to prepare students for all aspects the modern world, with high-tech facilities and a more global curriculum. Birmingham-Southern stresses service, effectively preserving the

Website: www.bsc.edu
Location: Urban

(Continued)

Total Enrollment: 1,407
Undergraduates: 1,316
Male/Female: 42/58
SAT Ranges: V 540–650
    M 540–640
ACT Range: 23–29
Financial Aid: 32%
Expense: Pr $
Phi Beta Kappa: Yes
Applicants: 1,040
Accepted: 90%
Enrolled: 36%
Grad in 6 Years: 74%
Returning Freshmen: 86%
Academics: ✏ ✏ ✏
Social: ☎ ☎ ☎
Q of L: ★ ★ ★
Admissions: (205) 226-4696
Email Address:
    admission@bsc.edu

Strongest Programs:
Biology
English
Business
Humanities

Recent additions to campus include a new Humanities Building, six-house Fraternity Row, and the $24 million Elton B. Stephens Science Center, a 100,000-square-foot facility for biology, chemistry, physics, psychology, and environmental science.

school's image as a strong liberal arts institution with its own brand of community involvement. More than half the student body participates in community service through Southern Volunteer Services, as well as claiming active membership in fraternities and sororities. Caring and attentive faculty add to a sense of commitment to both personal and community growth. Says a junior: "Southern has this incredible atmosphere in which students meet great friends, delve into different areas of academics, become involved in the community, and feel proud of their school."

Known as the Hilltop for obvious reasons, BSC is the result of the 1918 merger of two smaller colleges: Birmingham College and Southern University. The campus, a green and shady oasis in an urban neighborhood, contains a pleasing hodgepodge of traditional and modern architecture, all surrounded by a security fence for added safety. Recent additions to campus include a new Humanities Building, six-house Fraternity Row, and the $24 million Elton B. Stephens Science Center, a 100,000-square-foot facility for biology, chemistry, physics, psychology, and environmental science.

The academic climate at BSC is described as rigorous by most. "Students can generally handle the workload," says a junior, "but must remain dedicated and diligent in their studies to succeed." Each student is assigned a faculty member who serves as his or her academic advisor from freshman convocation to graduation, an arrangement that students praise for its effectiveness. Equal praise goes out to faculty in the classrooms, where 93 percent of classes have fewer than thirty students. "The professors at Southern are very interested in the students and provide a very good learning environment," reports a political science major. Half of the students go on to professional or graduate school.

"It's a small, unique campus where the strongest friendships grow."

Business is the biggest major, followed by biology, which premeds cite as a major drawing card. English, the next largest major, is one of the school's strongest programs, and The Stephens Science Laboratory gives this program, as well as the chemistry and physics departments, a further boost. About a quarter of the students major in business, a division that includes programs ranging from accounting to international issues. The art, drama, dance, and music programs are all among the best in the South. A recent group of students traveled to Florida to help conceptual artist Christo wrap an island, while back at 'Southern students stage several major productions each year, often including American and world premieres.

The new Foundations general education program, launched in fall 2001, encompasses half of the credits needed to graduate. Students are required to take three first-year courses, five arts units, five science units, one unit in each of the following: creative or performing arts, foreign language and culture, math and writing, an intercultural course, and a Senior Conference course, which can be a scholarly seminar, term project, or independent study.

Students also must attend forty approved intellectual and cultural events, thirty of which must be on campus. BSC, a member of the Associated Colleges of the South* consortium, also offers a wide variety of special programs. The January term allows students to explore new areas of study from cooking lessons to travel in China. The international studies program offers students the chance to study abroad in several different countries, and the honors program allows twenty-five exceptional first-year students to take small seminars with one or more professors.

Seventy percent of the students are homegrown Alabamians, and practically all the rest hail from Deep South states, many with family ties to 'Southern. Though moderate by Alabama standards, the student body is quite conservative. Thirty-eight percent of the students belong to the Methodist Church, and the school chaplain heads the personal counseling program. Despite their geographic homogeneity, students of color do exist at BSC: 6 percent are African-American, 1 percent are Hispanic, and 2 percent are Asian-American. "Birmingham-Southern is a conservative Southern school," says a student. "There is not a great amount of mixing of ideas, but there is no obvious racism, homophobia, or anything of the sort." There is an honor code at BSC that students take very seriously. In addition to need-based awards, BSC offers various merit scholarships to 85 percent of students, with grants ranging from $500 to $24,000. National Merit Scholars who list 'Southern as their first choice receive an automatic scholarship of $500 to $2,000, and up to ten get full-tuition awards. Athletes compete for scholarships in fourteen Division I sports.

Eighty-eight percent of the students live on campus, including many of those whose families reside in Birmingham. Co-ed housing hasn't filtered down to 'Southern yet, so all seven dorms are single-sex with a variety of visitation policies depending on student preferences. Daniel Hall and New Mens are generally the most desired men's residences, while Bruno Hall is the preferred choice for women. "The rooms are not large, but more than adequate," says a student. The new six-house Fraternity Row opened in fall 2003. Campus security is quite visible and students praise its effectiveness in keeping the campus safe.

Fifty-three percent of the men and 74 percent of the women are members of Greek organizations, which means that much of the social activity at BSC revolves around the Greek system. "We often have jazz and blues bands on Sunday afternoons on the Dorm Quad, and the SGA sponsors fall and spring concert weekends as well," a history major reports. As for alcohol, it's not allowed on the quad, and elsewhere it must be in an opaque container, a policy most students find reasonable. The biggest social event of the year is Southern Comfort, a four-day festival that is "always a wild time," notes one satisfied customer. Another popular music celebration is E-Fest. When social opportunities on campus dry up, many students take advantage of the shuttle to Birmingham for the city's nightlife—cultural events, bars, and the rather bohemian (at least for Alabama) South Side. Road trips to Auburn, Nashville, and Atlanta are popular, and beaches and mountains are less than five hours away.

In a state where the late Bear Bryant of 'Bama is practically a saint, BSC is a school without a football team. Men's basketball partially fills the void, as does the baseball team, which at one point had twenty winning seasons in a row. The men's soccer team is also top-notch, and both the men's and women's tennis teams are of championship caliber. There are eight women's varsity sports and intramurals are popular, although dominated by the Greeks.

BSC is proud of its close ties to the Deep South and its ever-expanding academic challenges that keep students on their intellectual toes. In the meantime, the close relationships between faculty and students ensures that nobody at 'Southern is ever left out in the cold. "It's a small, unique campus," says a freshman, "where the strongest friendships grow."

Overlaps

Rhodes, Auburn, University of Alabama, Vanderbilt, University of Alabama–Birmingham

If You Apply To ➤

'Southern: Rolling admissions (after Jan. 15.) Early action: Dec. 1. Regular admissions: Jan. 15 (priority). Financial aid: March 1. Housing: May 1. Does not guarantee to meet demonstrated need. Campus interviews: recommended, informational. Alumni interviews: Optional, informational. SATs or ACTs: required. SAT IIs: optional. Accepts the Common Application and electronic applications. Essay questions: topic of interest; two pages of autobiography; choose fictional characters from literature as TV guests.

Many of the students clamoring for a spot at Boston College are surprised to learn that it is affiliated with the Roman Catholic church. Set on a quiet hilltop at the end of a "T" (subway) line, BC's location is solid gold. A close second in the pecking order among true-blue Catholics.

Website: www.bc.edu

Location: Suburban

Total Enrollment: 14,700

Undergraduates: 8,900

Male/Female: 47/53

SAT Ranges: V 600–680
   M 610–690

ACT Range: N/A

Financial Aid: 46%

Expense: Pr $ $ $ $

Phi Beta Kappa: Yes

Applicants: 16,680

Accepted: 38%

Enrolled: 33%

Grad in 6 Years: N/A

Returning Freshmen: N/A

Academics: ✍ ✍ ✍ ½

Social: ☎ ☎ ☎ ☎

Q of L: ★ ★ ★

Admissions: (617) 552-3100

Email Address: N/A

Strongest Programs:
Chemistry
Music
Art
Drama

The Jesuit appeal for tolerance means that students can find support and interaction even when approaching hot-button issues that Catholicism will not condone.

Boston College is a study in contrasts. Academics are well respected, but so are the athletic teams. The environment is safely suburban, but barely twenty minutes from Boston, the hub of the collegiate Eastern seaboard. The Jesuit influence on the college, the largest Roman Catholic school in the country, really does provide a guiding spirit for campus life, but the social opportunities still seem endless. If you're looking for the best of all possible worlds, you just might find it here.

Don't let the name fool you. Boston College is actually a university with nine schools and colleges. It has two campuses: the main campus at Chestnut Hill and the Newton campus a mile and a half away. The dominant architecture of the main campus (known as "the Heights") is Gothic Revival, with modern additions over the past few years, including new dining hall facilities and Fulton Hall for the Carroll School of Management. There's lots of grass and trees, not to mention a large, peaceful reservoir (perfect to jog around) right in the front yard.

The college's mission is to "educate skilled, knowledgeable, and responsible leaders within each new generation." To accomplish this goal, the Core Curriculum requires not only literature, science, history, philosophy, social science, and theology, but also writing, mathematics, the arts, and the study of other cultures, in addition to specific requirements set by each undergraduate school. "Core Curriculum forces you to take classes you might not want to take but end up enjoying," says a senior. Students in arts and sciences must

"The courses are rigorous but intellectually stimulating."

also show proficiency in a modern foreign language or classical language before graduation. Freshmen are required to take a writing workshop in which each student develops a portfolio of personal and academic writing and reads a wide range of texts. Seniors participate in the University Capstone program, a series of seminars aiming to give a "big picture" perspective to the college experience.

The climate here is challenging. A senior says, "The courses are rigorous but intellectually stimulating." A junior adds, "In general, other students and all teachers are very supportive and motivated." Professors are described as "phenomenal" and "unbelievable." The Jesuits on BC's faculty (about sixty out of nine hundred) exert an influence out of proportion to their numbers. "The philosophy, theology, and ethics departments are the most important in setting the tone of the campus because they keep the students encouraged to be open minded," says a freshman. Another student says, "Our teachers are dedicated to students and scholarly research, and they are easily accessible through regular office hours." Registration is made painless through a computerized system, and students report that getting required classes is "never much of a problem."

The schools of arts and sciences, management, nursing, and education award bachelor's degrees. In the College of Arts and Sciences—the largest undergraduate division—English, biology, and psychology are popular. Future Massachusetts politicians will benefit from the strong political science program. Outside the traditional classroom, at the Boston College Museum of Art in Devlin Hall, students find exhibitions, lectures, and gallery tours. The Music Guild sponsors professional concerts throughout the year, and music students emphasizing performance can take advantage of facilities equipped with Steinways and Yamahas. Theater majors find a home in the six-hundred-seat E. Paul Robsham Theater Arts Center, which produces eight student-directed productions each year.

Students searching for out-of-the-ordinary offerings will be happy at BC. The student-run PULSE program provides participants with the opportunity to fulfill their philosophy and theology requirements while engaging in social service fieldwork at any of about thirty-five Boston organizations. Perspectives, a four-part freshman program, attempts to illustrate how great thinkers from the past have made us who we are. There's also a Freshman-Year Experience program, which offers seminars and services to help students adjust to college life and take advantage of the school and the city. An honors program allows students to work at a more intensive pace and requires a senior thesis.

Thirty percent of BC students come from the greater Boston area, and Catholics comprise about 80 percent of the student body. Blacks now constitute 4 percent of the student body, while Asian-Americans make up another 8 percent and Hispanics 5 percent. According to a marketing major, BC's "biggest problem is the lack of minorities on campus." Still, the Jesuit appeal for tolerance means that students can find support and interaction even when approaching hot-button issues that Catholicism will not condone.

Housing is plush compared to most colleges. When students are admitted, they are notified whether they will get on-campus housing for three or four years, and most juniors with three-year guarantees live off campus or study abroad that year. The city of Boston has a fairly reliable bus and subway system to bring distant residents to campus; if students want to drive to school, there's a lottery for parking stickers. Another lottery system determines where on-campus residents hang their hats. Freshman dorms are described as "not great and not very modern," but accouterments in upper-class suites include private baths, dishwashers, and full kitchens. Students pay in advance for a certain number of dining hall meals, served a la carte.

BC students are serious about their work, but not excessively so. There is time and plenty of places to party. Yet BC's reputation as a hard-core party school is diminishing, now that no kegs or cases of beer are allowed on campus grounds. Those of legal age can carry in only enough beer for personal consumption. Bars in Boston ("The best city!" gushes a freshman, when asked how Boston rates as a college town) are a big draw because it's easier to get served there. On weekends, especially in the winter, the mountains of Vermont and New Hampshire beckon outdoorsy types who like to hike and

Professors are described as "phenomenal" and "unbelievable."

ski. The campus is replete with sporting events, movies, festivals, concerts, and plays. And as far as social life is concerned, "BC is not a dating school," laments one lonesome student. As at other Jesuit institutions, there is no Greek system at BC.

Athletic events become social events too, with tailgate and victory parties common. Although the Doug Flutie era is over, football games remain a big draw—the annual contest with Notre Dame is jokingly referred to as the "Holy War." The football program has been recognized for achieving the highest graduation rate in the College Football Association, and the women's field hockey team made it to the quarterfinals of the NCAA Tournament. The Silvio O. Conte Forum Sports Arena is well attended, and BC meets fierce competition from Big East rivals Georgetown, Syracuse, Pitt, Villanova, and Miami. Students even get the day off from classes to line the edge of campus and cheer Boston Marathon runners up "Heartbreak Hill." Intramural sports are huge here, and students rave about BC's marvelous recreational complex.

BC students spend four years fine-tuning the art of the delicate balance, making

Although the Doug Flutie era is over, football games remain a big draw—the annual contest with Notre Dame is jokingly referred to as the "Holy War."

old-fashioned morals relevant to life in the twenty-first century, finding time for fun while keeping an eye on their academic averages.

If You

Apply

To ➤

BC: Early action: Nov. 1. Regular admissions and housing: Jan. 1, Jan. 15. Financial aid: Feb. 1. No campus or alumni interviews. SATs or ACTs: required. SAT IIs: required (English, math, and one other). Apply to particular schools or programs. Meets demonstrated need of 94%. Essay question: why Boston College; a flash of revelation you have had; how a piece of art impacted you; or an important issue facing today's teens.

Boston University

121 Bay State Road, Boston, MA 02215

One of the nation's biggest private universities, but easy to miss amid the bustle of the city. Boston's Back Bay neighborhood is the promised land for hordes of students nationwide seeking a funky, artsy, youth-oriented urban setting that is less in-your-face than New York City.

Website: www.bu.edu
Location: Center city
Total Enrollment: 28,982
Undergraduates: 17,860
Male/Female: 39/61
SAT Ranges: V 590–680
   M 610–690
ACT Range: 25–29
Financial Aid: 49%
Expense: Pr $ $ $ $
Phi Beta Kappa: Yes
Applicants: 27,038
Accepted: 58%
Enrolled: 29%
Grad in 6 Years: 75%
Returning Freshmen: 89%
Academics: ✐ ✐ ✐ ✐
Social: 🍷 🍷 🍷 🍷
Q of L: ★ ★ ★
Admissions: (617) 353-2300
Email Address:
   admissions@bu.edu
International admissions:
   intadmis@bu.edu

Boston University is an integral part of the city it calls home. The school's mammoth collection of nondescript high-rises straddles bustling, six-lane Commonwealth Avenue—and so do thousands upon thousands of students. The school draws them in with something for everyone, from aspiring actors, musicians, journalists, and filmmakers to doctors, dentists, and hotel managers. And the quality of its programs is catching up to their quantity. "I've found the perfect blend of terrific academics, varied social and sport activities, and volunteer and internship positions," says a geophysics and planetary sciences major with a French minor.

Like George Washington University and NYU, the BU campus is practically indistinguishable from the city that surrounds it. Indeed, Boston may be the quintessential college town, but be warned that BU is anything but bucolic; as a history major says, "Our campus blends into the city, and works as part of it." A measure of relief is available on the tree-lined side streets, which feature quaint Victorian brownstones. The School of Management uses a team-based curriculum, so its new Rafik B. Hariri Building has a soaring, light-filled atrium, breakout rooms, a library,

"BU has been a place for me to open up and find who I really am."

and four thousand places to get your laptop computer online. The curriculum lab at the Photonics Center helps professors transform research in chemistry, physics, biology, medicine, and engineering into coursework, lectures, and student experiments.

The caliber of preprofessional offerings for aspiring lawyers and doctors in the College of Arts and Sciences is unmatched, and is the university's largest undergraduate division. The College of Communication combines theory and hands-on training, some by adjunct professors with day jobs at major newspapers and TV networks, and houses the nation's only center for the study of political disinformation. The School of Theatre Arts is strong, while the School of Music benefits from its own concert hall in which members of the Boston Symphony Orchestra teach. A dance minor has been added, and the School of Theatre Arts has instituted a freshman core for the performance and design production programs. The Sargent College of Health and Rehabilitation Sciences now offers a nutritional science program, while physical therapy has been converted to a six-year program, leading to BS and DPT degrees. Students in the School of Education can teach in local classrooms from their first year on campus.

The School of Management, already regarded as one of BU's top colleges, now has a four-year honors program, while the College of Engineering has a robotics and biomedical engineering lab. Companies seeking to employ graduates from the School of Hospitality Administration are supporting scholarships for future workers who may also choose to intern in exotic locales such as Brussels and Britain. (Students in other fields who wish to work abroad may vie for internships from Australia to Moscow.) Also intriguing is the University Professors Program, which begins with a two-year integrated core focusing on major authors and central themes of Western thought. As juniors and seniors, students in the program create individualized, interdisciplinary courses of study, unbounded by departmental divisions. The College of General Studies provides an alternative path into BU; after a two-year introduction to college academics, successful students may continue into one of the school's four-year programs. BU also offers seven- and eight-year programs admitting qualified students to both an undergraduate program and the university's medical or dental school.

Each of BU's eleven schools sets its own general-education requirements, but every students must take the two-semester Freshman Writing Program. These theme-oriented seminars are limited to eighteen students each, and include readings from the classics, natural and social sciences, and the arts and humanities. When Boston's winters get too brutal, BU offers study abroad and exchange programs in countries from France, Spain, and the United Kingdom to Ecuador, Greece, Israel, and Italy. There's also the Semester at Sea,* a program welcoming students from many schools to spend a term living and studying on a cruise ship.

The academic climate at BU requires students to hit the books, but is relaxed enough that they don't hit one another. "Courses are rigorous from the very beginning," says a senior. "Reading, class attendance, and careful note-taking are needed to succeed." Amazingly for such a large school, administrators say that 88 percent of the classes taken by freshmen have twenty-five or fewer students. Though introductory courses in psychology, biology, and other disciplines may have hundreds enrolled in the main lecture, graduate students lead smaller workshop sections where students can ask questions and get help. "Except for an introductory writing series, all classes are taught by BU professors at the top of their field," says a senior. "I've even had a couple classes in which the textbook we used was written by the professor."

Diversity extends from academics to the student body, of which a majority is female. About 68 percent of BU students hail from outside Massachusetts, and 8 percent come from foreign countries. Minorities comprise 18 percent of the total. "The student body is so diverse that it would be difficult to simply characterize it," says a senior. "We do not have a certain kind of student multiplied by the thousands; it's quite fun exploring and learning about so many different cultures." Significant campus issues include rape prevention and integration of cultural groups. The university offers more than 4,200 merit scholarships each year, from $500 to full tuition and fees, and 244 athletic scholarships in seven men's and nine women's sports.

Three-quarters of BU students live in campus housing, which is guaranteed for four years. There's little trouble getting a room, though sophomores often find that—thanks to the lottery system—it may not be the room they want. "There are large dorms with doubles, triples, and quads, suites with four to six people sharing

The School of Management uses a team-based curriculum, so its new Rafik B. Hariri Building has a soaring, light-filled atrium, breakout rooms, a library, and four thousand places to get your laptop computer online.

The new Residences at 10 Buick Street, an eighteen-story high-rise, represent the lap of luxury. The building holds 814 students in apartments with four single bedrooms each. Each bedroom is wired for phone and fast Internet service, and each air-conditioned unit also includes a kitchen, living and dining area, and two full bathrooms.

a common area and their own bathroom, and brownstone apartments, which are singles, doubles, or triples," says a geophysics and planetary sciences major. The new Residences at 10 Buick Street, an eighteen-story high-rise, represent the lap of luxury. The building holds 814 students in apartments with four single bedrooms each. Each bedroom is wired for phone and fast Internet service, and each air-conditioned unit also includes a kitchen, living and dining area, and two full bathrooms. There are six dining halls on campus, one of which is Kosher, plus a food court with chains such as Burger King, Starbucks, and D'Angelo's, a local sub shop. "I actually enjoy and sometimes crave the dining hall food," says a senior. "For vegetarians and vegans, however, choices seem very limited."

The city of Boston, also known as America's College Town, plays a major role in social life at BU. "Fenway Park, downtown, Landsdowne Street, and Boston Common are all within walking distance," says a marine biology major, and the subway system's Green Line squiggles through the center of campus, putting the rest of city within easy reach. "There are on-campus events, but they aren't extremely popular—unless it is a hockey game." Parties at neighboring schools are an option, and owing to Boston's heavily Irish heritage, St. Patrick's Day is also an occasion for revelry. Three percent of the men and 5 percent of the women go Greek, so their parties hardly dominate the social scene. Drinking is fairly common, though BU strictly enforces liquor laws in dorms, and violators may find themselves kicked out of university housing. Boston's bartenders and stores also have an eagle eye for underage students with fake IDs. The Splash party in September, Homecoming in October, and Spring Thaw in April round out the social calendar. The best road trips are Cape Cod, Cape Anne, and Providence, Rhode Island.

The annual Beanpot hockey tournament pits BU against Boston College, Harvard, and Northeastern. It's the athletic highlight of the school year, and an event that BU often wins. Most any game against arch rival BC also draws a crowd, as do hockey match-ups against the University of New Hampshire and basketball games against Northeastern. The Head of the Charles regatta, which starts at BU's crew house each fall, draws college crews from across the country. BU competes in the Division I America East conference, and the men's and women's basketball and women's tennis teams are perennial championship winners. The school does not, however, field a football team. A 60,000-square-foot Track and Tennis Center has recently opened as well.

The influence of John Silber, the pugilistic and moralistic president and Kant scholar who helped build BU's academic reputation as president from 1971 through 1996, appears to be on the wane—which should make for a happier BU faculty. Boston University urges students to just "Be You." Accomplishing that goal is made easier by its nearly three hundred degree programs, and almost four hundred clubs and organizations. While students may need help to stay focused on just who it is that they are, or are becoming, BU's rich mix of cultural resources and social events are sure to keep most students happily distracted from their studies.

Overlaps

NYU, Boston College, Northeastern, George Washington, Tufts

If You Apply To ➤

BU: Early decision: Nov. 1. Regular admissions: Jan. 1 (Dec. 1 for the BA/MD and BA/DMD programs and applicants for some scholarships). Financial aid: Feb. 15. Housing: May 1. Meets demonstrated need of 58%. Campus interviews: required, evaluative for B.A./M.D. and B.A./D.M.D. programs and some theatre arts programs; not available to other students. Alumni interviews: optional, informational. SATs or ACTs: required. SAT IIs: required (vary by program). Apply to particular school or program. Accepts the Common Application and electronic applications. Essay question: 500 words on a personally meaningful topic; 500 words on the experiences that have led you to select your professional field and objective; how you became interested in BU.

Rates with Amherst, Williams, and Wesleyan for liberal arts excellence and does not require SAT I. Bowdoin has strong science programs, and outdoor enthusiasts benefit from proximity to the Atlantic coast. Smaller than some of its competitors, with less overt competition among students.

For more than two centuries, Bowdoin College has been dedicated to making nature, art, friendship and the world of books integral to the student experience. This is, after all, the alma mater of the great American poets Longfellow and Hawthorne. In fact, when they matriculate, new students sign their names in a book on Hawthorne's very desk. Yes, the winters are cold. But students say great food and "friendships that transcend labels," to include faculty and staff as well as other students, help keep campus a warm and friendly place.

Bowdoin's two-hundred-acre campus sits in Brunswick, Maine, the state's largest city. Hidden amid the pine groves and athletic fields are 117 buildings, in styles from German Romanesque, Colonial, Medieval, and neoclassical to neo-Georgian, modern, and postmodern. Former fraternity houses now house academic and administrative offices, after Greek groups were phased out. The newest addition is the

> "It's a very friendly campus of mostly white, upper-middle-class students wearing polo shirts."

Schwartz Outdoor Leadership Center, home to the Bowdoin Outing Club. The college is repairing the towers of its Chapel, a historic landmark, and plans are underway for a new academic building.

To graduate, Bowdoin students must complete thirty-two courses, including two each in natural sciences and math, social and behavioral sciences, humanities and fine arts, and non-Eurocentric studies. Freshmen also have their choice of seminars, capped at sixteen students each, which emphasize reading and writing; recent topics included "Mass Media and American Politics" and "Players and Spectators: History, Culture and Sports." Academic strengths include the sciences, specifically biology, chemistry and environmental studies. "The facilities are fantastic," says a sophomore. "The college's Coastal Studies Center and Coleman Farm are great for ecology labs and geology field trips." Bowdoin also offers coursework in Arctic Studies (its mascot is the polar bear), as well as opportunities for Arctic archeological research in Labrador or ecological research at the Kent Island Scientific Station in Canada. Premeds of all persuasions will find top-of-the-line lab equipment and outstanding faculty; the field of microscale organic chemistry was developed and advanced here.

Students also praise the art history and English departments, and say the popularity of government and economics, the majors with the highest enrollment, is well deserved. The physics department is notoriously difficult. New interdisciplinary majors include Latin American studies, Eurasian and East European studies, and English and theater. There's also a

> "Professors are enthusiastic and know what they are teaching."

minor in gay and lesbian studies, and an emphasis on service-learning; a third of all departments offer courses letting students apply their classroom work to real-world problems faced by local community groups. Undergraduate research is a priority, and it's common for juniors and seniors to conduct independent study with faculty members, then publish their results in professional journals.

Those same professors teach all Bowdoin classes—there are no graduate students here, and thus no TAs—and their skills in the classroom draw raves. "The

---

Website: www.bowdoin.edu
Location: Mid-size town
Total Enrollment: 1,657
Undergraduates: 1,657
Male/Female: 49/51
SAT Ranges: V 640–730
  M 640–720
Financial Aid: 40%
Expense: Pr $ $ $ $
Phi Beta Kappa: Yes
Applicants: 4,505
Accepted: 25%
Enrolled: 41%
Grad in 6 Years: 90%
Returning Freshmen: 95%
Academics: ✏ ✏ ✏ ✏ ✏
Social: ☎ ☎ ☎
Q of L: ★ ★ ★
Admissions: (207) 725-3100
Email Address:
  admissions@bowdoin.edu

Strongest Programs:
Natural Sciences
Classics
German
Anthropology
Economics
English
Government
Environmental Studies

The recent shift to a plus-minus grading system has made things more competitive. "There is a bit more emphasis on grades, and students think more about them, as they try to figure out where they currently stand," says a biology major.

department chair taught my introductory physics course," says a chemistry major. "The quality of teaching is beyond great," agrees a sociology and psychology major. "Professors are enthusiastic and know what they are teaching." Academically, students "strive for personal satisfaction, not doing better than our roommates or friends," says a senior. Still, the recent shift to a plus-minus grading system has made things more competitive. "There is a bit more emphasis on grades, and students think more about them, as they try to figure out where they currently stand," says a biology major. "While there may be a great difference between a B-plus and a B-minus student, it was far simpler and de-emphasized before."

Before school begins, about 70 percent of the entering class takes pre-orientation hiking, canoeing, or sea kayaking trips, which teach them about the people and landscape of Maine. There's a community-service experience in Brunswick for students less interested in the outdoors. The entering class also reads the same book before arriving, to start the year with a common academic experience.

Eighty-six percent of students hail from outside Maine; most are generally hard-working, fun-loving, athletic types. "It's a very friendly campus of mostly white, upper-middle-class students wearing polo shirts with upturned collars and Patagonia fleeces, and carrying Nalgene water bottles," says a sophomore. "The New England schools are similar, although I think we smile more than Bates, Colby, Middlebury, and Williams." African-Americans and Hispanics each make up 4 percent of the student body, and Asian-Americans add 8 percent. Bowdoin was the first U.S. institution to make SAT I scores an optional part of the admissions process, shifting the emphasis to a student's whole body of work.

Ninety percent of Bowdoin students live on campus, where "freshmen start off in a two-room triple (or if you're lucky, a two-room double), so you'll never be kept up by your roommate typing a paper at 3 a.m.," says a chemistry major. After that, students try their luck with the lottery, although members of the social houses, which have replaced sororities and fraternities, can escape by living with these groups. Upperclassmen may choose four-bedroom quads—co-ed, apartment-style suites with single bedrooms, a bathroom and a common room. The two campus dining halls always have two to four entrée choices, plus soups, breads, cereal and a salad bar, says a chemistry major. "Theme dinners range from Chinese New Year to a New Orleans fish fry," says a biochemistry major, and there's also a "just like home" dinner, with winning parents' recipes. Students also love the lobster bake that kicks off each school year.

"The two campus dining halls always have two to four entrée choices, plus side dishes, soups, breads, cereal and a salad bar," says a chemistry major. "Theme dinners range from Chinese New Year to a New Orleans fish fry," says a biochemistry major, and there's also a "just like home" dinner, with winning parents' recipes.

With the Greeks gone, social life at Bowdoin centers around two groups, says a sophomore: sports teams and social houses. "The college does bring in campus-wide entertainment, such as hypnotists, bands, and comedians," says a senior. "In addition, there is usually a party open to the entire campus at one or more of the social houses every weekend." While all parties and kegs must be registered, "unless the parties create havoc in the neighborhood by being too loud or rambunctious, security tends not to intrude," says an art history major. "If you don't drink," agrees a freshman, "forget about coming to Bowdoin." Students look forward to Homecoming, the BearAIDS benefit concert and Ivies Weekend, one last blast of fun before spring finals. The latter celebrates the fact that Bowdoin didn't join the Ivy League, with bands and games in the quad.

Students say Brunswick (population 21,000) is "a cute coastal town" with "a funky feel, nice restaurants, and a little shopping." A car comes in handy, for the fifteen-minute drive to the outlets of Freeport (including L.L. Bean's 24/7 factory store) or a quick trip to Portland for a "real" night out. A school shuttle takes students to Boston, which is less than three hours' away, and ski bums will find several resorts even closer. Habitat for Humanity and various mentoring programs help build bridges between local residents and students. For those who get really stir-crazy, study abroad programs are available in more than one hundred countries, including warm ones like Ecuador (a welcomed treat when you consider the normally brutal New England winters).

While "the long winters are certainly not a favorite," according to a senior, they do bring out school spirit, with any sporting event against Colby—especially hockey games—inspiring excitement. "That rivalry is almost out of control," says a biology major. "The chanting is brutal, and dead fish have been known to fly onto the ice." Bowdoin's Bears compete in the Division III New England Small College Athletic Conference, and students "get blacked out" to demonstrate support, wearing all black when they attend games. Bowdoin's athletic facilities also include a sixteen-lane swimming pool, a two-hundred-meter track, tennis courts, exercise rooms, and a fitness center with free weights and Cybex stations.

Outdoorsy types and those who can brave the cold will find warm and inviting academics at Bowdoin, where close friendships with peers and professors are easily forged. "Being able to make friends with my professors is something I'll treasure forever," says an art history major. Agrees a chemistry major: "The outstanding education and the great friends make Bowdoin a special place for me."

Overlaps

Williams, Dartmouth, Middlebury, Amherst, Brown

If You Apply To ➤

Bowdoin: Early decision: Nov. 15. Regular admissions: Jan. 1. Financial aid: Nov. 15 (early-decision candidates), Jan. 1 (international applicants), Feb. 15 (regular-admissions candidates). Guarantees to meet demonstrated need. Campus and alumni interviews: recommended, evaluative. SATs or ACTs: optional (SATs preferred). SAT IIs: optional. Accepts the Common Application and electronic applications. Essay question: influential secondary-school teacher; your greatest challenge; significant work of art, book, or experience. Places less emphasis on test scores than comparable colleges.

Brandeis University

Waltham, MA 02454-9110

Founded in 1948 by Jews who wanted an elite institution to call their own. Now down to 55 percent Jewish and seeking top students of all faiths. Academic specialties include the natural sciences, the Middle East, and Jewish studies. Competes with Tufts in the Boston area.

Brandeis University, founded to provide educational opportunities to those facing discrimination, has always had a reputation for intense progressive thought. Now, it's being recognized as a rising star among research institutions. The only nonsectarian Jewish-sponsored college in the nation, Brandeis continues its struggle to maintain its Jewish identity while attracting a well-rounded, eclectic group of students.

Set on a hilltop in a pleasant residential neighborhood nine miles west of Boston, Brandeis's attractively landscaped 270-acre campus boasts many distinctive buildings. The music building, for example, is shaped like a grand piano; the theater looks like a top hat. The new 24-hour Carl and Ruth Shapiro Campus Center includes a student theater, electronic library and bookstore, and the Rose Art Museum recently got a 7,300-square-foot addition that doubled its exhibition space. The Village, which added 220 undergraduate beds to the campus, was completed in 2003, along with the Lemberg Academic Center at the Brandeis International Business School.

At Brandeis, biochemistry, chemistry, neuroscience, and physics are top-notch,

> "Classes here are designed to challenge, and they do."

Website: www.brandeis.edu
Location: Suburban
Total Enrollment: 4,852
Undergraduates: 3,057
Male/Female: 43/57
SAT Ranges: V 627–710
  M 630–710
Financial Aid: 70%
Expense: Pr $ $ $ $
Phi Beta Kappa: Yes
Applicants: 6,080
Accepted: 42%
Enrolled: 33%
Grad in 6 Years: 85%
Returning Freshmen: 94%

(Continued)
Academics: ✍ ✍ ✍ ✍
Social: ☎ ☎ ☎
Q of L: ★ ★ ★
Admissions: (781) 736-2000
Email Address:
sendinfo@brandeis.edu

Strongest Programs:
Neuroscience
Biochemistry
East Asian Studies
Politics
Psychology
English
Near Eastern and
Judaic Studies
Biology

Newly approved interdepartmental programs include international and global studies; health: science, society, and policy, biological physics; and educational studies.

benefiting from the $41.5 million Volen Natural Center for biological, cognitive, and computational research. Several other departments, including English, history, theater arts, music, and political science offer nationally ranked graduate programs. Dedicated premeds are catered to hand and foot, with special advisors, internships, and their own Berlin Premedical Center, with specialized laboratories designed to provide would-be MDs with research opportunities. Biology, economics and psychology are the most popular majors here, followed by politics and sociology. Grad school acceptance rates are impressive; 80 percent of those who apply to medical school are accepted.

With the largest faculty in the field outside of Israel, the university is virtually unrivaled in Near Eastern and Judaic studies; Hebrew is a Brandeis specialty. East Asian Studies, recently added as a major, gives students a broad yet intimate knowledge of the history, politics, economics, art, and language of the major areas of East Asia. A growing number of popular interdisciplinary programs includes Latin American, medieval, Russian, peace, and women's studies, add spice to the academic menu. Brandeis also maintains a commitment to the creative arts, with strong theater offerings and a theory-based music program founded by the late Leonard Bernstein. Nearly two-thirds of the classes have 25 or fewer students.

The Brandeis core curriculum is rooted in a commitment to developing strong writing, foreign language, and quantitative-reasoning skills and an interdisciplinary and cross-cultural perspective. Newly approved interdepartmental programs include international and global studies; health: science, society and policy; biological physics; and educational studies. Women's studies and creative writing were recently expanded from minors to majors, and rising sophomores and juniors now have the opportunity to earn credit through summer internships related to their studies. More than 260 study abroad programs are offered in 63 countries, and 20 percent of each class takes advantage of these opportunities.

> **"Everyone at Brandeis wants others, even those different from them, to feel accepted and comfortable."**

Twenty-six percent of the Brandeis student population are in-staters and heavily bicoastal otherwise, with sizable numbers of New York, New Jersey, and California residents. The group is also very bright; 93 percent graduated in the top quarter of their high-school class, and professors want them to continue working hard. Students say the academic climate here is intense. "Brandeis takes its academic integrity seriously," notes a creative writing and English major. "Our programs are highly competitive and professors here expect great things from their students. Classes here are designed to challenge, and they do." There is an out, though; the Flex 3 option allows students to take three classes one semester if an especially rough course is required, and five the next, to stay on track for four-year graduation.

Though more than half the student body is Jewish, there are three chapels on campus—Catholic, Jewish, and Protestant—built so that the shadow of one never crosses the shadow of another. It's an architectural symbol that students say reflects the realities of the campus community. African-Americans make up 3 percent of the student body, Hispanics 3 percent, and Asian-Americans 9 percent. "Everyone at Brandeis wants others, even those different from them, to feel accepted and comfortable," says a senior. Gays and lesbians have an established presence, and throw some of the liveliest parties. The unofficial fraternities and sororities that have colonized at Brandeis are clamoring for recognition from the school. Other hot-button issues include political correctness, rape awareness, and environmental causes.

Even with one of the highest tuition rates in the country, Brandeis does not guarantee to meet each student's full demonstrated need, but help is generally available to those who apply on time. The level of support remains fairly constant over four years, students report. The university also offers four hundred merit scholarships, ranging from $5,000 to $27,000. The six-day freshman-orientation program is one of the most extensive in the nation, including a broad spectrum of events, such as a Boston Harbor cruise and special programs for minority, international, commuter, and transfer students.

As befits its mold-breaking heritage, Brandeis is the only school in the nation where you can live in a replica of a Scottish castle with pie-shaped rooms and stairways leading to nowhere. More pedestrian housing options include traditional quadrangle dormitories, where freshmen and sophomores live in doubles, and juniors live in singles. The Foster Living Center, or the "Mods," are coed, university-owned town houses reserved for seniors. According to a junior, "Ziv Quad, with its air-conditioning and modern suites, is the hope of many sophomores." The newest option is The Village, which offers singles and doubles clustered around family-style kitchens, semi-private bathrooms and lounges. Freshmen and sophomores are guaranteed housing, while upperclassmen play the lottery each spring. Eighty-two percent of students live on campus, and the rest find affordable off-campus housing nearby. Brandeis boasts the best college food in the Boston area, as well as the most appetizing set-ups, students say, thanks to a decision to outsource dining services. Campus meal tickets buy lunch or dinner in a fast-food joint, the pub, a country store, a kosher dining hall with vegetarian selections, or the Boulevard, a cafeteria where "the salad bars are huge."

Social life at Brandeis offers lots of options for those ready to relax. There are 207 campus clubs to keep students busy, but "Brandeis is not the type of school where there are parties at every corner," a student adds. Weekends begin on Thursday, with live entertainment at the on-campus Stein pub. Students can party at will in the dorms so long as they don't get

"Waltham is a blue-collar town containing a university of students with champagne backgrounds and caviar aspirations."

too rambunctious, but suites are officially "dry" unless a majority of the residents are over twenty-one. Major events on the campus calendar include a Tropics Night dance (where beachwear is required in February), the massive Bronstein Weekend festival just before spring finals, and the "Screw Your Roommate" dance, where dormies set up their roommates on blind dates. Also well attended are the Homecoming soccer match and the annual lacrosse tilt against cross-town rival Bentley College. The possibilities for off-campus diversion are nearly infinite, thanks to the proximity of Boston and Cambridge, which are accessible by the free Brandeis shuttle bus or a nearby commuter train. (A car is more trouble than it's worth.) And what about Waltham, Brandeis's host town? "We have a hugely successful volunteer/community-service program called the Waltham Group," says a senior. But, quips a history major, "Waltham is a blue-collar town containing a university of students with champagne backgrounds and caviar aspirations." Another student sees it differently: "There's a lot of fun things to do in Waltham. You just have to look for them."

Though the school does not field a football team, Brandeis has developed strong men's baseball and swimming and women's swimming, fencing and cross-country squads, all of which have taken regional championships in recent years. The athletic program gets a boost from its membership in the University Athletic Association, a neo–Ivy League for high-powered academic institutions such as the University of Chicago, Johns Hopkins, and Carnegie Mellon. Brandeis's sports facilities include the seventy thousand-square-foot Gosman Sports and Convocation Center, reportedly the largest multipurpose indoor athletic facility on the East Coast.

Few private universities have come as far as Brandeis so quickly, evolving from a bare 270-acre site with the leftovers of a failed veterinary school to a modern research university of more than 100 buildings, $406 million endowment and ever-evolving academic opportunities. Landscaping, dining services, health services, and the campus computer network have all been dramatically improved in the past few years, students say, adding to their feelings of pride in the school. One student sums it up this way: "Brandeis is not only an awesome place to get an education, it's also an open, accepting place where anyone can feel at home."

Overlaps

...nell, Brown, NYU, ...Washington, Tufts

If You Apply To ➤

Brandeis: Early decision: Jan. 1. Regular admissions and financial aid: Jan. 31. Does not guarantee to meet demonstrated need. Campus and alumni interviews: recommended, evaluative. SATs or ACTs: required (SAT preferred). SAT IIs: required (writing and two others). Accepts the Common Application and electronic applications. Essay question: Personal statement.

Brigham Young University

A-153 ASB, Provo, UT 84602

From the time they are knee-high, Mormons in all corners of the country dream about coming to BYU. Most men and some women do a two-year stint as a missionary. The atmosphere is generally mild-mannered and conservative—and goes absolutely bonkers for its sports teams.

Website: www.byu.edu
Location: City outskirts
Total Enrollment: 32,408
Undergraduates: 29,379
Male/Female: 50/50
SAT Ranges: V 540–650
    M 560–670
ACT Range: 25–30
Financial Aid: 36%
Expense: Pr $
Phi Beta Kappa: No
Applicants: 7,329
Accepted: 73%
Enrolled: 79%
Grad in 6 Years: 73%
Returning Freshmen: 93%
Academics: ✑ ✑ ✑
Social: ☎ ☎ ☎
Q of L: ★ ★ ★ ★
Admissions: (801) 422-2507
Email Address:
    admissions@byu.edu

Strongest Programs:
Accounting
Law
Economics

You don't have to be Mormon to attend Brigham Young University, but it helps. The school's strong bond with the Church of Jesus Christ of Latter-Day Saints means that "there is a real feeling of respect and freely given friendship," says a psychology major. A sense of the spiritual pervades most everything at BYU, where faith and academia are intertwined, and life is governed by a strict code of ethics, covering everything from dating to academic dishonesty. Indeed, the school's commitment to church values is the reason most students choose it. "Students at BYU are goal-oriented and academically secure and confident," says an illustration major. "However, more than that, we are happy. We have testimonies of Jesus Christ, and we try to live with high moral standards."

Mormon values of prosperity, chastity, and obedience are strongly in evidence on BYU's 638-acre campus, where the utilitarian buildings, like everything else, are "clean, modern, and orderly." The campus sits 4,600 feet above sea level, between the shores of Utah Lake and Mount Timpanogos, with breathtaking sunsets and easy access to magnificent skiing, camping, and hiking areas. Days begin early; church bells rouse students at 6 a.m. with the first four bars of the church hymn "Come, Come Ye Saints." (The same bells also peal every hour throughout the day.) A student athletic center and indoor practice facility were slated for completion in late 2003, to be followed by the Joseph F. Smith Building in 2004.

The church's influence continues when students set their schedules; students must take one religion course per term to graduate, and offerings include, of course, the Book of Mormon. BYU requires students to demonstrate proficiency in math, writing (first-year and advanced), and advanced languages, a catch-all category that can be satisfied with coursework in a foreign language or in statistics, advanced math or advanced music. Students must also complete an extensive liberal arts core, which includes work in civilization, American heritage, biology, physical sciences, and wellness (three physical education or dance activity courses), and electives in the natural sciences, social and behavioral sciences, and arts and letters.

"The academic climate is very competitive," says a senior. "You won't make it without becoming good friends with your books," a classmate agrees.

BYU's academic offerings run the gamut, from liberal arts to range management and clothing and textiles. Students say the strongest offerings include engineering and most departments in the Marriott School of Management, especially accounting. Elementary education, visual arts, and biology also get high marks, and while some students avoid economics because of its difficulty, one student calls the department's faculty "incredible." New majors include actuarial sciences and animation; programs in veterinary sciences and interior design have been dropped. New concentrations include jazz studies within the music major, mid-eastern studies within the international relations major, and advertising and marketing within the communications major. Aside from the

(Continued)
Engineering
Music
Languages
Chemistry
Education

"Students at BYU are goal-oriented and academically secure and confident. However, more than that, we are happy."

main campus in Provo, Brigham Young has campuses in Idaho and Hawaii, a center in Jerusalem, and study-abroad programs in Vienna, London, and elsewhere.

Seventy-one percent of the courses taken by BYU freshmen have twenty-five or fewer students, and the honors program, open to highly motivated students, offers even smaller seminars with more faculty interaction. "Freshmen are very often taught by full professors, sometimes the department's best," says a psychology major. In fact, the strength of the faculty is one reason BYU has more full-time students than any other church-sponsored university in the U.S. Still, with thousands of students to accommodate, registration can be a chore. "Most classes, especially in the art fields, fill up fast," says an illustration major. "The physical education courses are difficult to get into unless you are an upperclassman, at least for the times you would like to take them," a senior reports. Eighty percent of the men and 12 percent of the women interrupt their studies—typically after the freshman year—to serve two years as a missionary.

Twenty-three percent of BYU students are from Utah. Many others hail from California and Idaho, and about 6 percent come from more than one hundred other countries, testifying to the effective and far-flung Mormon missionary effort. Despite the heavy international presence, the student body remains largely white, with Asian-American and Hispanic students contributing about 3 percent each, and African-Americans less than 1 percent. "The students here are the cream of an already creamy crop," says a senior. "They differ because of the honor code and their religious pursuit." That code requires students to eschew drinking, smoking, and drugs; a city ordinance in Provo takes care of the "vice" of dancing. Politically, "everyone seems to be pretty conservative," says an illustration major. "We

BYU requires students to demonstrate proficiency in math, writing (first-year and advanced), and advanced languages, a catch-all category that can be satisfied with coursework in a foreign language or in statistics, advanced math or advanced music.

"The academic climate is very competitive."

all support America for better or worse. There was some tension and debates during the recent conflict with Iraq, but it was still pretty low-key." More important are issues within the student "wards," or mini-congregations, involving marriage, family, and the proper way to prepare for and raise children. Tuition for church members is lower than for nonmembers, because Mormon families contribute to BYU through their tithes. Academic scholarships and 365 athletic scholarships are available.

Twenty percent of BYU students—primarily freshmen—live in the single-sex residence halls, where the Freshman Academy program allows them to take courses and eat meals with fellow dorm-dwellers and professors. A senior says the Helaman Halls are the nicest bet for freshmen, since "the other campus freshman housing is old." Upperclassmen typically opt for cheaper off-campus apartments, which are also single-sex (remember the honor code?) When it comes to chow, there are several fast-food outlets on campus, plus dining halls for the freshman dorms, and the Creamery, a "don't miss" ice cream spot.

New majors include actuarial sciences and animation; programs in veterinary sciences and interior design have been dropped.

A student athletic center and indoor practice facility were slated for completion in late 2003, to be followed by the Joseph F. Smith Building in 2004.

Whether it's work with the homeless or disabled, dances, concerts, plays or sporting events, most of BYU's social life is organized through or linked to the church. Community service is big, with students visiting patients at hospitals and care centers, performing at local festivals, and building and refurbishing houses. Dating is common, within the church's bounds of propriety. There are no fraternities and sororities to provide housing or parties, which is just fine with most students, since alcoholic and caffeinated drinks are both banned. Campus traditions include Tuesday-morning devotional prayers, and the Fall and Spring Fling festivals. The town of Provo, about

> **"The students here are the cream of an already creamy crop. They differ because of the honor code and their religious pursuit."**

forty-five miles south of Salt Lake City, satisfies students' basic needs, but a better bet is the mall in Orem, accessible by bus. For those with wheels, "some of the best ski resorts in the world are within an hour," says one student. Moab, Las Vegas, and Zion's and Yellowstone National Parks are also popular destinations.

Physical fitness is big here, and the intramural facilities are some of the country's best, with indoor and outdoor jogging tracks; courts for tennis, racquetball, and handball; a pool; and a golf course. Also important are varsity sports; the church philosophy of obedience has worked wonders for Cougar teams. The football team has a national reputation, and annual contests with the University of Utah or Utah State transform the mild-mannered BYU student body into the gracious but raucous BY Zoo (hence their nickname, "Zoobies"). One of the most popular course offerings at BYU is ballroom dancing, partly because many participants aspire to join BYU's award-winning dance team. The ESPN television network has dubbed the BYU-Utah rivalry the "Holy War."

To most Americans, BYU probably seems like a step back in time—a "clean-scrubbed complacency farm," in one student's words. But for young members of the Church of Latter-Day Saints, that may be just what the elder ordered.

Overlaps

BYU–Idaho, Utah State, Utah Valley State, University of Utah, Arizona State

---

If You Apply To ➤

BYU: Rolling admissions: Feb. 15. Housing: First-come, first-served; students are encouraged to apply a year in advance, with housing contingent on acceptance at the university. Meets demonstrated need of 8 percent. Campus and alumni interviews: optional, informational. SATs or ACTs: required (ACTs preferred). SAT IIs: optional. Accepts electronic applications. Essays: significant life experience that has strengthened your character; additional information the admissions committee should consider. Looks for college prep courses versus overall GPA.

University of British Columbia: See page 331.

Brown University

45 Prospect Street, Providence, RI 02912

To today's stressed-out students, the thought of taking every course pass/fail is a dream come true. In reality, nobody does, but the pass/fail option, combined with Brown's lack of distribution requirements, gives it the freewheeling image that students love. Bashed by conservatives as a hotbed of political correctness.

Brown University is a perennial "hot college," with an overwhelming number of happy students and many more clamoring to join their ranks. Once here, students not only receive a prestigious and quality education, but a chance to explore their creative sides at a liberal arts college that does not emphasize grades and preprofessionalism and shuns required courses. Brown's environment and policies have drawn both praise and criticism over the years, but its students thrive on this discussion and lively debate. "The freedom of shaping one's own education is both frightening and exhilarating, since the possibilities for good and ill are almost endless," says one student.

Located atop College Hill on the east side of Providence, Brown's 140-acre campus affords an excellent view of downtown Providence that is especially pleasing at sunset. Campus architecture is a composite of old and new—plenty of grassy lawns surrounded by historic buildings that offer students refuge from the city streets beyond. One student describes it as a "melting pot of architecture's finest. We have a building that resembles a Greek temple [and] buildings in the Richardsonian tradition." The engineering building was recently expanded, and the MacMillan Center for Sciences and Watson Institute for International Studies are new to the campus. The neighborhoods that surround the campus lie within a national historic district and boast beautiful tree-lined streets full of ethnic charm.

Brown's faculty has successfully resisted the notion that somewhere in their collective wisdom and experience lies a core of knowledge that every educated person should possess. As a result, aside from completing courses in a major, the only university-wide requirements for graduation are to demonstrate writing competency and complete the thirty-course minimum satisfactorily. (The assumption is that students will take four courses a term for a total of thirty-two in four years.) Freshmen have no requirements. Those with interests in interdisciplinary fields will enjoy Brown's wide range of concentrations that cross departmental lines and cover everything from cognitive science to public policy. Indeed, there are bona fide departments in cognitive

> "The freedom of shaping one's own education is both frightening and exhilarating, since the possibilities for good and ill are almost endless."

and linguistic sciences and media and modern culture. Students can also create their own concentration from the array of goodies offered. Brown also offers group independent-study projects, a popular alternative for students with the gumption to take a course they have to construct primarily by themselves. Particularly adventurous students can choose to spend time in one of Brown's 57 study abroad programs in 18 countries, including Brazil, Great Britain, France, Tanzania, Japan, Denmark, and Egypt. Closer to home, students can cross-register with Rhode Island School of Design, also on College Hill, or participate in the Venture Program.*

Students can take their classes one of two ways: for traditional marks of A, B, C, or No Credit; or for Satisfactory/No Credit. The NC is not recorded on the transcript, while the letter grade or Satisfactory can be supplemented by a written evaluation from the professor. A habit of NCs, however, lands students in academic hot water. Any fewer than seven courses passed in two consecutive semesters makes for an academic "warning" that does find its way onto the transcript, and means potential dismissal from the university.

The most popular majors are biology, international relations, and history, followed by business economics and psychology. History and geology are some of the university's best, and students also praise computer science, religious studies, and applied math. Other top-notch programs include comparative literature, classics, modern languages, and the writing program in the English department. Among the sciences, engineering and the premed curriculum are standouts. Future doctors can try for a competitive eight-year liberal medical education program where students

---

Website: www.brown.edu
Location: City center
Total Enrollment: 7,892
Undergraduates: 6,030
Male/Female: 45/55
SAT Ranges: V 640–750
  M 650–750
ACT Range: 26–32
Financial Aid: 38%
Expense: Pr $ $ $ $
Phi Beta Kappa: Yes
Applicants: 14,612
Accepted: 17%
Enrolled: 59%
Grad in 6 Years: 94%
Returning Freshmen: 96%
Academics: ✑ ✑ ✑ ✑ ✑
Social: ☎ ☎ ☎ ☎
Q of L: ★ ★ ★ ★ ★
Admissions: (401) 863-2378
Email Address:
  admission_undergraduate@
  brown.edu

Strongest Programs:
History
Geology
Computer Science
Religious Studies
Film and Television
Engineering
Art and Design
Writing
International Relations

The size of the faculty ranks was recently increased by 20 percent, and investment in university libraries has also risen.

can earn an M.D. without having to sacrifice their humanity. The political science department is said to be rapidly improving, as is the international relations concentration. Sociology, psychology, and math, however, still receive thumbs down from students. Fields related to scientific technology have very good facilities, including an instructional technology center, while minority issues are studied at the Center for Race and Ethnicity.

Brown prides itself on undergraduate teaching and considers skill in the classroom as much as the usual scholarly credentials when making tenure decisions. Younger professors can receive fellowships for outstanding teaching, and the administration's interest in interdisciplinary instruction and imaginative course design help cultivate high-quality instruction. The size of the faculty ranks was recently increased by 20 percent, and investment in university libraries has also risen. The advising system reflects the administration's commitment to treat students as adults. The lack of predetermined requirements is supposed to challenge students, so "no one is going to tell you what to take." The advising system pairs each freshman with a professor and a peer advisor, and resident counselors in the dorms are also available to lend an ear. "As an Asian, I have an Asian advisor as well as a woman's peer counselor, a resident counselor, a minority counselor, and a head counselor who lived on my floor in the dorm," reports one well-advised student. Sophomores utilize special advising resources, upperclassmen are assigned an advisor in their concentration, and a pool of interdisciplinary faculty counselors is on hand for general academic advising problems.

Brown offers more than a hundred freshman courses via the Curricular Advising Program (CAP), and the professors in these courses officially serve as academic advisors for their students' first year. This program receives mixed reviews, but some professors are highly praised by students for their abilities and availability. "They are very casual about open office hours, and welcome students to pop in for a chat," one student says. Upper-level classes are usually in the teens, CAP courses are limited to 20, and only 13 percent of introductory lectures have more than 50 students. Especially popular courses are usually jammed with students, and often there aren't enough teaching assistants to staff them effectively. Some popular smaller courses, especially writing courses in the English department and studio art courses, can be nearly impossible to get into, although the administration claims that perseverance makes perfect—in other words,

"Students are self-motivated, study often, and learn a great deal, because they want to do the work, not compete with others."

show up the first day and beg shamelessly. Compared with the other Ivies, Brown's academic climate is relatively casual, or at least seems to be. "Students are self-motivated, study often, and learn a great deal, because they want to do the work, not compete with others," one student says.

"Brown is ideally suited to two kinds of people," offers one student, "someone who wants to sample many different departments before deciding what they want to do...and someone who wants to examine a certain area in their studies and not worry about core requirements." With a mere 4 percent of students hailing from Rhode Island, geographical diversity is one of Brown's hallmarks. Brown is one of the few remaining hotspots of student activism in the nation; nary has a semester passed without at least one demonstration about the issue of the day. Students of color account for at least 27 percent of the population, and foreigners make up 9 percent. Minorities rarely miss an opportunity to speak out on issues of concern. The gay and lesbian community is also prominent. "They throw the best dances on campus," says one science major. Ninety-seven percent of students were in the top quarter of their high school class, and 40 percent hail from private or parochial schools.

In 2002, Brown began admitting all students regardless of their financial need, and although it doesn't offer athletic or academic merit scholarships, it does guarantee to meet the full demonstrated need of everyone admitted. Fifteen Starr National Service scholarships, ranging from $1,000 to $2,000, are awarded each year to students who devote a year or more to volunteer public-service jobs. About 120 other "academically superlative" students, called University Scholars, will find their financial-aid package sweetened with extra grant money. Brown's use of binding early decision, also used by Princeton, has made some waves.

"I feel safer here than I do at home."

Freshmen arrive on campus a few days before everyone else for orientation, which includes a trip to Newport, and there is also a Third World Transition Program. About half the freshmen are assigned to one of the eight co-ed Keeney Quad dorms, in "loud and rambunctious" units of thirty to forty with several sophomore or junior dorm counselors. The other half live in the quieter Pembroke campus dorms or in a few other scattered locations. After the freshman year, students seeking on-campus housing enter a lottery. The lottery is based on seniority, and sometimes the leftovers for sophomores can be a little skimpy, though there are some special houses set aside to give them a chance at some decent rooms.

The dorms themselves are fairly nondescript. "There are no fireplaces or engraved wood trim a la Princeton," observes one student, but nevertheless there are many options from which to choose, including apartment-like suites with kitchens, three sororities, two social dorms, and three co-ed fraternities. Brown guarantees housing all four years, and a dorm with suites of singles ensures that there is room for all. A significant number of upperclassmen get "off-campus permission." Places nearby are becoming more plentiful and more expensive as the area gentrifies. Brown's food service, which gets high marks from students for tastiness and variety, offers meal plans ranging from seven to twenty meals a week. Everyone on a meal plan gets a credit card that allows the student to do what students at every other school only wish they could: use the meal ticket for nocturnal visits to snack bars should they miss a regular meal in one of Brown's two dining halls. Campus security is described as "very good." Says a junior, "I feel safer here than I do at home."

Providence is an old industrial city that recently underwent a renaissance. It is still the butt of student jokes—"Be prepared to wear your proletarian disguise," cautions one—but extensive renovations of the downtown area have had a positive impact. Providence is Rhode Island's capital, so many internship opportunities in state government are available, as are a few good music joints, lively bars, and a number of fine, inexpensive restaurants. For the couch-potato set, there are plenty of good things right in the neighborhood. "Downtown is a ten-minute walk, but why bother when you can buy anything from Cap'n Crunch to cowboy boots on Thayer Street, which runs through the east side of campus?" asks a philosophy major. For a change of scenery, many students head to Boston or the beaches of Newport, each an hour away.

The few residential Greek organizations are generally considered much too unmellow for Brown's taste (only 11 percent of the men and 9 percent of the women sign up), and hence freshmen and sophomores are their chief clientele. The nonresidential black fraternities and sororities serve a more comprehensive student-life function. Tighter drinking rules have curtailed campus drinking somewhat. The university sponsors frequent campus-wide parties, and plays, concerts, and special events abound. Funk Nite every Thursday night at the Underground, a campus pub, draws a mixed bag of dancing fools. The biggest annual bash of the year is Spring Weekend, which includes plenty of parties, and a big-name band. Strong theater and dance programs, daily and weekly newspapers, a skydiving club, political organizations, "even a Scrabble club and a successful croquet team," represent just a few

Brown's use of binding early decision, also used by Princeton, has made some waves.

of the ways Brown students manage to keep themselves entertained. One other is the campus student center, which has been thoroughly renovated. For those interested in community outreach—and there are many at Brown who are—the university's nationally recognized public-service center helps place students in a variety of volunteer positions. The Brown Community Outreach, in fact, is the largest student organization on campus.

Brown isn't an especially sports-minded school, but a number of teams nevertheless manage to excel. Of the 36 varsity teams, recent Ivy League champions include the volleyball, women's crew, men's tennis and men's soccer teams. The women's cross-country squad finished third in the NCAA Regional Championships in 2002. Athletic facilities include an Olympic-size swimming pool and an indoor athletic complex with everything from tennis courts to weight rooms. There's also a basketball arena for those trying to perfect their slam dunks. The intramural program is solid, mixing fun with competitiveness.

Ever since the days of Roger Williams, Rhode Island has been known as a land of tolerance, and Brown certainly is a twentieth-century embodiment of this tradition. The education offered at this university is decidedly different from that provided by the rest of the Ivy League, or for that matter, by most of the country's top universities. Brown is content to gather a talented bunch of students, offer a diverse and imaginative array of courses, and then let the undergraduates, with a little help, make sense of it all. It takes an enormous amount of initiative, maturity, and self-confidence to thrive at Brown, but most students feel they are up to the challenge. "You get four years of choice," says one student. "Deal with it."

Overlaps

Harvard, Yale, Princeton, Stanford, Columbia

If You Apply To ≫

Brown: Early decision: Nov. 1. Regular admissions: Jan. 1. Financial aid: Nov. 1 for early decision, Feb. 1 for regular admissions. Guarantees to meet demonstrated need. No campus interviews. Alumni interviews: recommended, evaluative. SATs or ACTs: required. SAT IIs: required (any three). Accepts electronic applications. Essay question: personal statement.

Bryn Mawr College

101 North Merion Avenue, Bryn Mawr, PA 19010-2899

BMC has the most brainpower per capita of the elite women's colleges. Politics range from liberal to radical. Do Bryn Mawrters take themselves a little too seriously? The college still benefits from ties to nearby Haverford, though the relationship is not as close as in the days when Haverford was all male.

Website: www.brynmawr.edu
Location: Suburban
Total Enrollment: 1,744
Undergraduates: 1,322
Male/Female: 0/100
SAT Ranges: V 630–730
   M 600–690
ACT Range: 26–30
Financial Aid: 59%

Leafy suburban enclaves are a dime a dozen around Philadelphia. But only one is home to Bryn Mawr College, a top-notch liberal arts school. On this campus, students find a range of academic pursuits from archeology to film studies to physics, and a diverse yet community-oriented student body. Founded in 1885, Bryn Mawr has evolved into a place that prepares students for life and work in a global environment. Although students here abide by a strict academic honor code and participate in a host of loopy and long-standing campus traditions, they remain doggedly individualistic.

Bryn Mawr's lovely campus is a path-laced oasis set among trees (many carefully labeled with Latin and English names) and lush green hills, perfect for an afternoon walk, bike ride, or jog. Just a twenty-minute train ride to downtown Philadelphia,

Bryn Mawr provides a country setting with a vital and exciting city nearby. The predominant architecture is collegiate Gothic, a style that Bryn Mawr introduced to the United States. Ten of Bryn Mawr's buildings are listed in the National Register of Historic Places. The M. Carey Thomas Library, which was named after the school's first dean and second president, a pioneer in women's education, is also a National Historic Landmark. Variations on the collegiate Gothic theme include a sprinkling of modern buildings, such as Louis Kahn's slate-and-concrete residence hall and the redbrick foreign language dormitory. Recent campus additions include a new 30,000-square-foot building for the departments of education and psychology and a renovated student activity village called Cambrian Row.

Students don't discuss their grades out of respect for their academic honor code, but they freely admit that they work hard. "There is a lot of trust and sense of responsibility wrapped up in the honor code," says a student. A classmate adds, "The courses are always extremely challenging." Most departments are strong, especially the sciences, classics, archaeology, art history, and the foreign languages, includ-

> **"There is a lot of trust and sense of responsibility wrapped up in the honor code."**

ing Russian and Chinese. The Fine Arts Department, however, is cited as weaker than most because of its small size. Mawrters who want to do serious work in music, art, photography, or astronomy hike over to Haverford, Bryn Mawr's nearby partner in the "bi-college" system. Bryn Mawr handles the theater, dance, creative writing, geology, art history, Italian, and Russian programs for the two colleges, and the departments of German and French are joint efforts. Bryn Mawr also offers a rich variety of special programs. Approximately one third of students study overseas during their junior year. Projects include fieldwork in the Aleutian Islands with the Anthropology Department and studying Viennese architecture with the Growth and Structure of Cities Department.

The general education requirements include two classes in each of the three divisions (social sciences, natural sciences, and the humanities), one semester of "quantitative" work, an intermediate level of competency in a foreign language, and the requirements of a major. Students are also required to take eight half-semesters of physical education and must also pass a swimming test. In addition, all freshmen are required to take two College Seminars to develop their critical thinking, writing, and discussion skills.

The quality of teaching at Bryn Mawr is unquestionably high. "My professors have been brilliant," a junior says. "the professors have always been available and willing to help. Besides, "If a professors stinks, word gets out fast," asserts a sophomore. Freshmen are initiated to the Bryn Mawr experience during Customs Week, which includes a variety of seminars and workshops as well as a tour of the campus and town. To help first-year students acclimate, Bryn Mawr has developed the OWLS (Orientation Workshop Leaders) program, which begins during orientation and continues throughout the first year. A wide range of topics, from going home for the first time to the honor code and dealing with stress, are discussed by first-year and upperclass students, administrative staff, and faculty. For those looking ahead to see what the steep tuition will buy in the long term, the campus has a career resource center that offers information on interviewing and building a résumé. It also brings recruiters to campus, offers mock interviews, and keeps students posted on internships.

"Bryn Mawr women are sharp, intellectual, and well-read," says a student. Another adds, "Students are internally motivated, smart, passionate about learning, and compete with themselves—not with their classmates." The student body is fairly diverse—African-Americans make up 3 percent, Hispanics 3 percent, and Asian-Americans 13 percent. To encourage diversity and harmony on campus,

(Continued)

Expense: Pr $ $ $ $
Phi Beta Kappa: No
Applicants: 1,744
Accepted: 50%
Enrolled: 35%
Grad in 6 Years: 82%
Returning Freshmen: 92%
Academics: ✐ ✐ ✐ ✐ ✐
Social: ☎ ☎ ☎
Q of L: ★ ★ ★
Admissions: (610) 526-5152
Email Address:
  admissions@brynmawr.edu

Strongest Programs:
Archaeology
Growth and Structure of Cities
Physics
Mathematics
Art History
Classics
Foreign Languages

"Every type of person is seen and accepted here," says an economics major. "Everyone from BMW princesses to militant vegan lesbians."

freshmen can take an intensive four-hour session during orientation on pluralism, which teaches students to examine assumptions about class, race, and sexual orientation. "Every type of person is seen and accepted here," says an economics major. "Everyone from BMW princesses to militant vegan lesbians." Scholarships are not available but the school does guarantee to meet the demonstrated financial need of every admit.

Even though the much-prized fireplaces do not operate, housing at Bryn Mawr is "beautiful," says one student. "Almost all rooms have nice perks: hardwood floors, a window seat, a nice view, a bay window," a student says. Seventy percent of the rooms are singles. The college has added dining halls to two dorms, and the rooms have high-speed Internet access. Dorms have quotas for students from all four classes, so freshmen mix freely with upperclassmen. Though housing is a little tighter than it was a few years ago, it is still guaranteed for four years, and most students can expect singles after freshman year. All those who live on campus—98 percent of the student body—must subscribe to the twenty-meal-a-week plan, and most seem to really like it. In fact, the food service has even received a national award from *Restaurants and Institutions Magazine*.

"My professors have been brilliant."

Bryn Mawr is located on suburban Philly's wealthy Main Line (named after a railroad), and the campus is two blocks from the train station. "The people who live here are yuppies with BMWs," a sophomore notes. "Bryn Mawr equals suburbia." Shopping at national chain stores is nearby, and there are cute places to eat, but, like college students around the world, Mawrters duck out of town and head to the city for nightlife. The twenty-minute train ride provides students with easy access to cultural attractions, as well to social and academic events at the nearby University of Pennsylvania. "We really have the best of both worlds," a junior says.

"The social life at Bryn Mawr is largely a campus energy spurred by a strong sense of community and the many Bryan Mawr traditions," says a chemistry major. The social life at Bryn Mawr is, well, different due to the fact that it is basically a women's college. There are no sororities and little pressure to "go with any flow," a student says. Of course, party opportunities abound off campus at Swarthmore, Haverford, or Penn. What social life there is at Bryn Mawr generally includes Haverford men who, one junior gripes, "regress to apes when drunk." Top road trips include New York, Atlantic City, the Jersey shore, and even Hershey Park.

Tradition is a very important part of the social scene on campus. The Elizabethan-style May Day festivities are held the Sunday after classes end in May. Everyone wears white, eats strawberries, and watches Greek plays. Students are known to skinny-dip in the fountains and drink champagne on the lawn. The presentation of lanterns and class colors to incoming freshmen on Lantern Night, and regal pageants, such as Parade Night, Hell Week, and Step-Sings, fill life with a Gothic sense of wonder and school spirit. Says a student, "They play a big role in uniting all four classes and give students a role in the greater history of the college." As for athletics, Bryn Mawr students are active in twelve intramural sports including rugby, cross-country, volleyball, and field hockey. And, of course, there's always the champion badminton team.

Bryn Mawr is a study in paradox: the campus is in suburbia, but steps from a major city. The academic foundation is based on the liberal arts, but science majors are enormously popular. The students are independent but revel in college traditions. The result is overwhelmingly positive. Says a sophomore, "When I sit in a math or science course with fifteen other women who are smart and eager to learn, I realize that I am surrounded by women who are going places." Taken together, it all means that Bryn Mawr is one unique place.

"Bryn Mawr women are sharp, intellectual, and well-read."

Bryn Mawr: Early decision: Nov. 15. Regular admissions: Jan. 15. Housing: Jun. 1. Guarantees to meet demonstrated need. Campus and alumnae interviews: recommended, evaluative. SATs: required. SAT IIs: required (English and two others). Accepts the Common Application and electronic applications. Essay question: Common Application; what will you gain from the Bryn Mawr experience?

Bucknell University

Lewisburg, PA 17837

Bucknell, Colgate, Hamilton, Lafayette—all a little more conservative than the Ivy schools and nipping at their heels. Bucknell is the biggest of this bunch and the only one with engineering. (Perhaps Lehigh is a better comparison.) The central Pennsylvania campus is isolated but one of the most beautiful anywhere.

Where some schools might be easily typecast as too focused on partying or too religious about studying, Bucknell University strikes a healthy balance. In the pastoral setting of central Pennsylvania, Bucknellians seek out live music, outdoor activities, and plenty of socializing. But when it comes to their work, they delve into research programs in chemical engineering, intense theatre performances, and numerous opportunities to study abroad in places like France and Barbados. "I've never met so many students who can handle all their academic, extracurricular, and social responsibilities as well as Bucknell students," says a junior. "They are the most well-balanced people I know."

In addition to being comfortable and friendly, Bucknell is physically beautiful. Located on a hill just south of quaint Lewisburg, the campus overlooks the scenic Susquehanna River valley, and features a landscape of leafy nooks and grassy expanses of playing fields. Greek Revival architecture dating from the nineteenth century provides a picture-book setting, blended with modern residential complexes, a magnificent science center and a performing arts center. Newer additions to campus include a 4,000-seat gymnasium to go with the $31.5 million recreation center. The university has completed five years of a seven-year project to renovate 82 classrooms and 10 auditoriums. And, a new $5 million art building is in the works.

All freshmen in Bucknell's College of Arts and Sciences start with Interdisciplinary Foundation seminars, designed to strengthen research, computing, and writing skills. Arts and Sciences distribution requirements include four courses in the humanities, two in social sciences, and

> **"Bucknell students...are the most well-balanced people I know."**

three in natural sciences and mathematics. Two of these courses must address "broadened perspectives" on the natural and fabricated world, and on human diversity. All students enrolled in the College of Engineering have a common first semester, including a special course that exposes them to all five engineering disciplines. Along with major-related requirements, each student completes a capstone project during senior year, and must demonstrate competence in writing in order to graduate. Arts and Sciences students complete at least thirty-two credits in their four years, while engineering students complete at least thirty-four.

After fulfilling Bucknell's many requirements, students select from a variety of courses, including the popular Management 101, where students create and sell a product and donate their profits to charity. Thirty-seven percent of each graduating class studies abroad. The school has its own programs in England, France, and

Website: www.bucknell.edu
Location: Rural
Total Enrollment: 3,586
Undergraduates: 3,439
Male/Female: 51/49
SAT Ranges: V 590–670
 M 620–700
ACT Range: 25–30
Financial Aid: 45%
Expense: Pr $ $ $ $
Phi Beta Kappa: Yes
Applicants: 7,760
Accepted: 39%
Enrolled: 31%
Grad in 6 Years: 88%
Returning Freshmen: 95%
Academics: ✍ ✍ ✍ ✍
Social: 🏮 🏮 🏮 🏮
Q of L: ★ ★ ★
Admissions: (570) 577-1101
Email Address:
 admissions@bucknell.edu

Strongest Programs:
Humanities
English
Music
Theater
Engineering and Natural
 Sciences
International Relations
Psychology

Barbados, led by Bucknell professors, and through relationships with other colleges and universities, students may travel to more than sixty other nations, ranging from Japan and Sweden to China, Argentina, and Australia. Independent research projects often pair students and professors with common interests. The two-summer Institute of Leadership in Technology and Management, for example, allows engineering and business students to learn new ways to solve problems while enhancing critical thinking, teamwork, and communication skills. Several departments have arranged special research programs with various centers around the country; the physics department has a National Science Foundation grant to fund eight undergraduate research projects every summer through 2005. On-campus study the first summer is followed by an off-campus internship during the second.

Back on campus, 95 percent of courses have fewer than fifty students, and the emphasis is on classroom discussion. "Many courses utilize group projects that facilitate learning from one's peers," says a sophomore. "The professors are demanding, but they don't seek to overwork their students." Courses are rigorous, but not cut-throat, and there's little competition among students. "There are no pages torn out of books in the library," says an international relations major. Students often build tight bonds with their profs, too. To wit: "I even helped one of my professors pick out windowpanes for her new house," says a political science major. Programs in economics, engineering, management, and biology get especially high marks from students. Some fields are just downright neat: the undergraduate animal behavior program has its own outdoor naturalistic primate facility for teaching and research—that's usually found at the graduate level.

"The professors are demanding, but they don't seek to overwork their students."

Bucknell students tend to be ambitious and goal-oriented, says an economics major. "They all wear J.Crew, Banana Republic, or Abercrombie and Fitch clothes, and listen to the Dave Matthews Band," sighs a chemistry major. "There is very little variation." Though less than one-third are from Pennsylvania, 85 percent are white, with Asian-Americans accounting for 5 percent, African-Americans accounting for 3 percent, and Hispanics for 2. The campus is growing increasingly more politically active, as groups on campus "push each other's buttons, but keep everyone aware," says a French major. Other big issues include improving ethnic, socioeconomic, and religious diversity, and deciding whether to go Greek. (Ten fraternities and seven sororities attract 41 percent of the men and 45 percent of the women.) "Students here tend to use their four years wisely, and make the most of them," one student says. "The activities offered on campus allow students to develop as well-rounded individuals."

All first-year students must live in the dorms, and housing is guaranteed for four years, so 89 percent of the student body stays on campus. Most of the residence halls are either new or have recently been renovated, students happily report. They all have laundry facilities, lounges with cable TV, study areas, and rooms wired for Internet access. "Dorms are nice—especially the newer ones, which are like four-star hotels," says a junior. "The older ones have new furniture, and have a lot of character." Seniors who want to move off campus must apply for the privilege, which is a hassle, so more than three hundred upperclassmen live in five college-owned apartment buildings. About 25 percent of each entering class affiliates with one of the six intellectually focused "colleges": Environmental, Global, Social Justice, Humanities, Arts, and Society and Technology. Some upperclassmen live in the colleges too, but most enter a lottery based on seniority for rooms in traditional dorms.

Social life at Bucknell is centered on campus, where "we have more than 120 clubs and organizations, and new ones are springing up all the time," one student says. Activities and Campus Events books events ranging from carnivals to hypnotists to religious retreats, while the nonalcoholic, school-run Uptown nightclub offers dancing 'til dawn. The school sponsors road trips to Washington, Baltimore, Philadelphia, and New York City, and movie theaters and malls offer diversion closer to home. "There is

"Dorms are nice—especially the newer ones, which are like four-star hotels."

always more to do than time allotted!" says a junior. Bucknell has a ten-point program to reduce alcohol abuse; alcohol-related incidents fell 32 percent during the 2001–2002 academic year, and it's getting more difficult for the underage to be served, especially at fraternity parties, students say. For those who choose not to imbibe, there's support to be found with the substance-free organization C.A.L.V.I.N. and H.O.B.B.E.S. The meaning of the longest acronym ever seen? Creating a Lively, Valuable, Ingenious, and New Habit of Being at Bucknell and Enjoying Sobriety. The Greek scene is lively, attracting 41 percent of the men and 45 percent of the women, respectively.

Even as the focus of socializing shifts away from drinking, students still look forward to annual traditions like Homecoming, Parents' Weekend, and the springtime House Party Weekend, planned by the Greeks, with food, music, and fun for all. Apparently, the deans are there to give out free hot dogs. The black-tie Chrysalis Ball, the last weekend of April, is open to faculty, staff, students, and alumni. At graduation, the whole university community gathers under a huge tent to fete new alumni. Town-gown relations between Bucknell and the quaint, beautiful town of Lewisburg are good. The town is "our little secret," says a senior. Another student adds that "Market Street is very cute, with old-fashioned buildings and shops that have been there for years. There is also an old-style movie theatre that has booths and serves food, though it shows regular movies." Community-service opportunities include work at the local hospital and projects organized by B.I.S.O.N., Bucknellians In Service to Our Neighbors. For those seeking more excitement, parties and concerts at Penn State's main campus are just an hour away, and the nearby town of Bloomsburg offers ethnic eateries with Indian and Thai cuisine.

A six-time winner of the Patriot League Presidents Cup for overall athletic excellence, Bucknell boasts recent championships in men's and women's cross-country, women's indoor and outdoor track, women's volleyball, and men's lacrosse and baseball. Two new women's teams are water polo and golf. Bucknell's biggest rivalries are with Lafayette and Lehigh, though these aren't a tremendous focus.

When parking is listed as a major concern on campus, you know you've got a pretty good thing going. That's the case at Bucknell, where the students bask in close relationships with professors, tons of unusual undergraduate research programs, and a group of peers who can always been convinced to take a study break and relax. And all of this in a beautiful setting. "I can walk around and see friends, both students and faculty, and always find something to do," says a sophomore. "But most importantly, the campus just puts me at ease."

Overlaps
Colgate, Lehigh, Boston College, Lafayette, Cornell University

If You Apply To ➤

Bucknell: Early decision: Nov. 15. Regular admissions, financial aid, and housing: Jan. 1. Does not guarantee to meet demonstrated need. Campus and alumni interviews: recommended, informational. SATs or ACTs: required. SAT Is: optional. Accepts the Common Application and electronic applications. Essay question: significant experience or achievement; issue of personal, local, or national concern; influential person, fictional character, historical figure, or creative work; or topic of choice.

California Colleges and Universities

California's three-tiered system of colleges and universities has long been viewed as a model of excellence by other public higher education institutions nationwide and even around the world. Many have attempted to emulate its revered status, which offers a wealth of educational riches including world-class research universities, enough Nobel Prize winners to fill a seminar room, and colleges on the cutting edge of everything from film to viticulture. Underlying the creation of this remarkable system was a commitment to the notion that all qualified Californians, whatever their economic status, were entitled to the benefits of a college education. In pursuing this ideal, California led the nation in opening up access to higher education for African-Americans, Hispanics, and other previously disenfranchised groups.

Unfortunately, in the early 1990s, this golden dream started fading due to the state's recession, population growth, and many other contributing factors. As a result, California's public universities and colleges received reduced tax support, student charges and user's fees shot up, student/faculty ratios increased, fewer classes were offered, and, in some cases, entire academic programs were eliminated. Although it still remained relatively lower than most states, tuition started to climb. The good news is that California has made a brave attempt to counteract this quandary despite an unprecedented budget deficit in 2002–2003, and total enrollment swelling to sixty thousand students over the next decade. Tuition increases are a likelihood on the horizon.

The system is composed of the nine combined research and teaching units of the University of California (UC), with a tenth campus, UC Merced, expected to open this year with one thousand students, and twenty-three state universities and colleges (CSUC), including the newest CSU campus at Channel Islands, that focus on undergraduate teaching. It also includes 106 two-year community colleges that offer both terminal degrees and the possibility of transferring into four-year institutions.

Admissions requirements to the three tiers and the institutions within them vary widely. Community colleges are open to virtually all high school graduates. The top third of California high school graduates (as measured statewide by a combination of SAT scores and grade-point average) may attend units of the state university and college system; all applicants must have taken a course in the fine or performing arts to be considered for admission. In the past, students in the top 12.5 percent of their class have been eligible to attend the University of California. In-state students graduating in the top 4 percent of their high school class will be guaranteed admission to the UC system, although not to a particular campus. The 4 percent proposal is part of a plan to broaden the representation of California applicants and to give more weight to GPA and SAT II subject tests. Out-of-state students continue to face ferocious competition for a limited number of spots, and still pay more.

Although one university system, the nine campuses each offer a full range of academic programs, and each has its own distinctive character. In recent years, UC has moved from relying primarily on statistical academic information to a "comprehensive review" that takes into consideration not only course work and test scores but also leadership, special talent, and the educational opportunities available to each student. Despite state laws that prohibit the university from considering race in admission, the system remains dedicated to achieving a diverse student body. The university offers a number of outreach programs designed to assist low-income or educationally disadvantaged students who have promising academic potential with admissions and support services.

To apply for admission to the University of California, complete the electronic application available at UC's PATHWAYS Application Center or submit the printed version to UC's Undergraduate Application Processing Service. Prospective students may apply to as many as eight UC campuses using the same application form. It should be noted that UC does not base admission on the applicant's campus choice, so students cannot request a campus preference. However, it is possible to be accepted at more than one school; in that case, the applicant is free to choose between those campuses. Each of the major undergraduate UC campuses receives a full-length summary in the following pages.

The California State University and College System is totally separate from the University of California; in fact, the two institutions have historically competed for funds as well as students. The largest system of senior higher education in the nation, Cal State focuses on undergraduate education; while its members can offer master's degrees, they can award doctorates only in collaboration with a UC institution. Research in the state-university system is severely restricted, a blow to Cal State's national prestige but a big plus for students. Unlike UC, where the mandate to publish or perish is alive and well, teachers in the state system are there to teach. Cal State's biggest problem is the success of UC, and its frequent lament—"Anywhere else we'd be number one"—is not without justification.

The twenty-three-campus system caters to more than 350,000 students a year. And while most of the campuses serve mainly commuters, Chico, Humboldt, Monterey Bay, San Luis Obispo, and Sonoma stand out as residential campuses. While a solid liberal arts education is offered, the stress is usually on career-oriented professional training. Size varies dramatically, from about thirty thousand students at San Diego and Long Beach to fewer than six thousand at several other branches like San Marcos, Channel Islands, and Monterey Bay. Each campus has its own specific strengths, although in most cases a student's choice of school is dictated by location rather than by academic specialties. For those with a wider choice, some of the more distinctive campuses are profiled below.

Chico (enrollment 14,983), situated in the beautiful Sacramento Valley, draws a large majority of its students from outside a one-hundred-mile radius. The on-campus undergraduate life is strong and the social life is great. Bakersfield (5,594) and San Bernardino (12,000) boast residential villages along with more conventional dorms. The former is in a living/learning center with affiliated faculty members; the latter has its own swimming pool. California Polytechnic at San Luis Obispo is the toughest state university to get into. It provides excellent training in the applied branches of such fields as agriculture, architecture, business, and engineering. Enrollment: 16,735. Fresno, located in the Verdant Central Valley, has the only viticulture school in the state outside of Davis, and undergraduates can work in the school winery. Yosemite, Kings Canyon, and Sequoia national parks are nearby. Enrollment: 18,113.

San Diego State is the biggest and balmiest of the campuses, and since it has a more residential and outdoorsy, campus-oriented social scene, it appeals more to traditional-age undergraduates. "You could go for the weather alone—some do," says one former student. Contrasted with other state schools, athletics are very important, and the academic offerings are almost as oriented to the liberal arts as at its UC neighbor at San Diego. Enrollment: 30,776.

Humboldt State is perched at the top of the state near the Oregon border in the heart of the redwoods. Humboldt's forestry and wildlife departments have national reputations, and the natural sciences are, in general, strong. Students have the run of excellent laboratory facilities and Redwood National Park. Most in-staters come here to get away from Los Angeles and enjoy the rugged coastline north of San Francisco. Enrollment: 7,475.

California Maritime Academy, located thirty miles northeast of San Francisco with six hundred students, specializes in marine transportation, engineering, and maritime technology, and requires summer cruises on the T.S. Gold Bear. Monterey Bay, one mile from the beach with three thousand students, 65 percent of whom live on-campus, offers an interdisciplinary focus with global perspective and opportunities for internships.

To apply to California State University, complete either the electronic application available at their website, which will be routed to the campus of the applicant's choice, or the paper application, which should be mailed to the admissions office of the campus to which the applicant is applying. It should be noted that Cal Poly and San Diego State require electronic applications. The prospective student can list a first and alternate campus choice on the application. If the first choice can't accommodate the applicant, it automatically sends the application to the alternate campus. However, for competitive campuses and programs, it is wiser to send separate applications to avoid delays.

UC–Berkeley

110 Sproul Hall # 5800, Berkeley, CA 94720-5800

Mention Berkeley and even down-to-earth students get stars in their eyes. Students who come here want the biggest and best of everything, though sometimes that ideal runs head-long into budget cuts, tuition increases, and housing shortages. Never mind. Berkeley is where the action is.

If you want a quick indicator of Berkeley's academic prowess, look no farther than the parking lot. The campus is dotted with spots marked "NL"—spots reserved for

Website: www.berkeley.edu

(Continued)

Location: Urban
Total Enrollment: 31,347
Undergraduates: 22,705
Male/Female: 49/51
SAT Ranges: V 580–710
    M 620–730
ACT Range: N/A
Financial Aid: 48%
Expense: Pub $ $ $ $
Phi Beta Kappa: Yes
Applicants: 31,108
Accepted: 27%
Enrolled: 43%
Grad in 6 Years: 83%
Returning Freshmen: 94%
Academics: ✍ ✍ ✍ ✍ ✍
Social: ☎ ☎ ☎ ☎
Q of L: ★ ★ ★
Admissions: (510) 642-3175
Email Address:
    ouars@uclink4.berkeley.edu

Strongest Programs:
Engineering
Architecture
Business
Theoretical Physics
Molecular and Cell Biology
Political Science
English

Berkeley is a quintessential college town ("kind of a crazy little town"), and of course, there's always the people-watching; where else can an individual meet people trying to convert pedestrians to strange New Age religions or revolutionary political causes on every street corner?

resident Nobel laureates. The last time anyone counted, Berkeley boasted seven Nobel Prize winners, 140 Guggenheim fellows, and a bevy of Pulitzer Prize recipients, MacArthur fellows, and Fulbright scholars. Is it any wonder that this radical institution of the '60s still maintains the kind of reputation that makes the top private universities take note? Engineering, architecture, and business are a few of the best of the fine programs at this mother of UC schools. The social climate is not as explosive as it once seemed to be, but don't expect anything tame on today's campus. Flower children and granola chompers still abound, as do fledgling Marxists, young Republicans, and body-pierced activists.

Spread across twelve hundred scenic acres on a hill overlooking San Francisco Bay, the Berkeley campus is a parklike oasis in a small city. The sometimes startlingly wide variety of architectural styles ranges from the stunning classical amphitheater to the modern University Art Museum draped in neon sculpture. Large expanses of grass dot the campus and are just "perfect for playing Frisbee or lying in the sun." The oaks along Strawberry Creek and the eucalyptus grove date back to Berkeley's beginnings nearly 130 years ago. Sproul Plaza, in the heart of the campus, is one of the great people-watching sites of the world.

Like everything else, the academic side of Berkeley can be overwhelming. With more than twenty-two thousand undergraduate overachievers crammed into such a small space, it is no wonder that the academic climate is about as intense as you can get at a public university. "Everyone was the top student in his or her high-school class so they can't settle for anything less than number one," says one student. A classmate concedes that "it can be a stressful environment, especially during the first years." Another says tersely, "Expect very little sleep." Some introductory courses, particularly in the sciences, have as many as eight hundred students, and professors, who must publish or perish from the university's highly competitive teaching ranks, devote a great deal of time to research. After all, Berkeley has made a large part of its reputation on its research and graduate programs, many of which rank among the best in the nation.

And while the undergraduate education is excellent, students take a gamble with the trickle-down theory, which holds out the promise that the intellectual might of those in the ivory towers will drip down to them eventually. As a political science major explains, "This system has allowed me to hear outstanding lectures from amazing professors who write the books we read, while allowing far more personal attention by the graduate-student instructors." Another student opines, "It's better to stand fifty feet from brilliance than five feet from mediocrity." Evidence of such gravitation is seen in the promising curriculums designed specifically for freshmen and sophomores that include interdisciplinary courses in writing, public speaking, and the history of civilization, and an offering of small student seminars (enrollment is limited to fifteen) taught by regular faculty. Despite these attempts at catering to undergraduates, the sheer number of students at Berkeley makes it difficult to treat each student as an individual. As a result, such things as academic counseling suffer. "Advising? You mean to tell me they have advising here?" asks one student.

"Everyone was the top student in his or her high-school class so they can't settle for anything less than number one."

Each college or school has its own set of general education requirements, which are generally not extensive, and many can be fulfilled through advanced-placement exams in high school. All students, however, must take English composition and literature, and one term each of American history and American institutions. Also, undergrads have an American Cultures requirement for graduation—an original approach (via courses offered in several departments) to comparative study of ethnic groups in the United States.

Most of the departments here are noteworthy, and some are about the best anywhere (like engineering and architecture). Sociology, mathematics, physics, chemistry, history, and English are just a handful of the truly dazzling departments. Engineering is also strong, and Berkeley offers a 3–2 engineering program with UC–Santa Cruz. The biological sciences department integrates several undergraduate majors in biochemistry, biophysics, botany, zoology, and others into more interdisciplinary programs such as integrative biology and molecular and cell biology. The College of Natural Resources has streamlined its eight departments into four, and established an Institute for Natural Resource Systems.

Special programs abound at Berkeley, though it's up to the student to find out about them. "Our class enrollment system is much like playing a low-risk lottery," opines one undergrad. "Maybe you'll win, or maybe you won't. If anything, adding courses will definitely toughen up any person." Students may study abroad on fellowships at one of fifty centers around the world, or spend time in various internships around the country. If all you want to do is study, the library system, with more than eight million volumes, is one of the largest in the nation and

"Social life at UC–Berkeley is killer!"

Just about everyone turns out for the "Big Game," where the favorite activity on the home side of the bleachers is bad-mouthing the rival school to the south: Stanford.

maintains open stacks. The system consists of the main library (Doe-Moffitt) and more than twenty branch libraries, one of which (Bancroft) houses rare books and Western Americana.

Forty-five percent of the student population is Asian-American, 4 percent African-American, and 9 percent Hispanic. The Coalition for Excellence and Diversity in Mathematics, Science and Engineering, which provides women and minorities with undergraduate mentors in these fields, received the Presidential Award for Excellence in Science, Mathematics, and Engineering in 1998. The university also provides a variety of other programs to promote diversity, including Project DARE (Diversity Awareness through Resources and Education), the Center for Racial Education, and a Sexual Harassment Peer Education Program. Despite Berkeley's liberal reputation, the recent trend is away from the legacy of the free-speech movement. Business majors and fraternity members increasingly outnumber the young Communists and peaceniks, though the school does produce a large number of Peace Corps volunteers. The main issue concerning every group on campus? Cost. In the past few years, outrageous fee hikes and severe budget cuts had some students wondering if a first-rate, affordable education had gone the way of the dinosaurs.

Though dorms have room for only a quarter of the students, freshmen are guaranteed housing for their first year. After that, the Community Living Office is a good resource for finding an apartment in town. Many students live a couple of miles off campus, where "apartments are cheaper," says one student. About two-thirds of the university's highly prized dorm rooms are reserved for freshmen, and the few singles go to resident assistants. Doubles are likely to become crowded triples, albeit at a reduced fee. Losers in the May lottery automatically go on a long waiting list to vie for rooms in subsequent monthly lotteries. In the absence of a mandatory meal plan, everybody eats "wherever and whenever they wish," including in the dorms.

Though the housing shortage can get you down, the beautiful California weather will probably take your mind off it in time. The BART subway system provides easy access to San Francisco, by far one of the most pleasant cities in the world and a cultural and countercultural mecca. The Bay Area boasts myriad professional sports teams, including the Oakland A's and the San Francisco 49ers. From opera to camping, San Francisco has a wide variety of activities to offer. Get yourself a car, and hike in Yosemite National Park, ski and gamble in Nevada, taste wine in the Napa Valley, or visit the aquarium at Monterey. But be advised that a car is only an asset when you want to go out of town—students warn that parking in Berkeley is difficult, to say the least.

Despite Berkeley's liberal reputation, the recent trend is away from the legacy of the free-speech movement. Business majors and fraternity members increasingly outnumber the young Communists and peaceniks, though the school does produce a large number of Peace Corps volunteers.

"Social life at UC–Berkeley is killer!" exclaims one geography major. Weekends are generally spent in Berkeley, hanging out at the many bookstores, coffeehouses, and sidewalk cafés, heading to a fraternity or sorority party, or taking advantage of the many events right on campus. Berkeley is a quintessential college town ("kind of a crazy little town," opines one anthropology major), and of course, there's always the people-watching; where else can an individual meet people trying to convert pedestrians to strange New Age religions or revolutionary political causes on every street corner? Nearby Telegraph Avenue is famous (infamous?) for such antics every weekend. More than three hundred student groups are registered on campus, which ensures that there is an outlet for just about any interest and that no one group will ever dominate campus life.

Despite all this activity, many students use the weekend to catch up on studying. Greeks have become more popular, with 9 percent of the men and 6 percent of the women in a fraternity or sorority. Varsity athletics have always been important, with strengths in the men's gymnastics and crew teams. A surge in popularity for the basketball team probably has to do with its great performance in the PAC 10. And just about everyone turns out for the "Big Game," where the favorite activity on the home side of the bleachers is badmouthing the rival school to the south: Stanford. Intramurals are popular, and the personal fitness craze is fed by an extensive recreational facility and gorgeous weather year-round.

The common denominator in the Berkeley community is academic motivation, along with the self-reliance that emerges from trying to make your mark among upward of twenty-two thousand peers. Beyond that, the diversity of town and campus makes an extraordinarily free and exciting college environment for almost anyone. "It makes one feel free to dress, say, think, or do anything and not be chastised for being unorthodox," explains a student. "At Berkeley, it is worse to be dull than odd."

Overlaps

UCLA, Stanford, UC–San Diego, UC–Davis, Harvard

If You Apply To ➢

Berkeley: Regular admissions: Nov. 30. Financial aid: Mar. 2. Guarantees to meet demonstrated need of in-state students. No campus or alumni interviews. SATs or ACTS: required. SAT IIs: required (writing, math I or II, and one other). Essay question: personal statement. Apply to particular school or program.

UC–Davis

175 MRAK Hall, Davis, CA 95616

The agricultural and engineering branch of the UC system. Premed, prevet, food science—you name it. If the subject is living things, you can study it here. A small-town alternative to the bright lights of UC–Berkeley and UCLA. As is often true of science-oriented schools, the work is hard.

Website: www.ucdavis.edu
Location: Small city
Total Enrollment: 26,094
Undergraduates: 20,388
Male/Female: 44/56
SAT Ranges: V 510–630
  M 550–660

At the University of California–Davis, environmental studies and most everything that has to do with agriculture or biological science is noteworthy. The Aggies' cup truly runneth over. Originally known as the University of California Farm, the campus maintains its sprawling, verdant beauty, replete with native and imported forestry, charming bike paths, and mooing cows. But lest you assume this environmentally oriented university is full of quaint country folk, think again. Davis has become an international leader in the agricultural, biological, biotechnical, and environmental sciences.

Located fifteen miles west of Sacramento and seventy-two miles north of San Francisco, the six-thousand-acre campus is in the middle of a stretch of flat farmland that even Dorothy and Toto could mistake for Kansas. It features nearly one thousand buildings with a blend of architectural styles, from traditional dairy barn to modern concrete. The hub of the university is a central area known as the Quad, one of many grassy open spaces on campus. Newer facilities include the Center for Comparative Medicine and a variety of seismic renovations.

Though it has added programs in many disciplines over the past few years—including Chinese, Japanese, food engineering, and biological systems engineering—its biological and agricultural science departments are still the ones that shine. Animal science and engineering are strong departments, and the botany program is one of the best in the country. The school is "the number-one choice for any pre-vet," and it's great for premeds, too. The food sciences major is also stellar, and not for the faint of heart or those afraid of chemistry. It was Davis food scientists who gave us the square tomato (better for packing into boxes), as well as more useful things such as the method for

"It is not rare to find many students in the library on Saturday night."

creating orange-juice concentrate. Studio art, boasting several internationally known artists, is also among the top in the nation, while history and English are generally good but not up to par with the sciences. Noteworthy special programs include the Inter-Disciplinary Electronics Arts (IDEA) Lab, which allows students to create electronically based productions by integrating photography, video, digital editing, and the Internet. Internships and co-op programs are well established, which is why many students remain for more than four years.

Faculty members here are expected to do top-level research as well as teach, so Davis is charged with both education and research. These two are uniquely blended when undergraduate students contribute to first-class research groups as paid technicians or volunteer interns. Davis also offers the innovative Washington Program, which gives undergraduates academic credits for internships in Congress, at federal agencies, and the like. Many introductory courses are quite large, but Davis also offers forty freshman seminars taught by the best instructors. The academic advising system gets generally high marks, but you must seek out their assistance. "They helped me plan a four-year college schedule and always kept me on track."

General education requirements stipulate that all students take courses in three broad areas: topical breadth, social-cultural diversity, and writing experience. These areas include courses in the arts and humanities, science and engineering, and the social sciences. Students may elect to take a general education theme option (sets of general education courses that share a common intellectual theme).

The academic demands are intense, and the students are high achievers. Many students describe the atmosphere as competitive if not cut-throat (especially in the biological sciences). "It is not rare to find many students in the library on Saturday night," testifies one student. Another student reports, "Professors expect students to learn vast amounts of information in a ten-week span." For students who still want more, the Davis Honors Challenge is designed for highly motivated, academically talented first- and second-year students who want to enhance their education through special courses. A famous campus saying claims that "Davis students take notes at graduation." Maybe they're taking notes for job interviews: 64 percent of Davis students get jobs after college and 38 percent prefer more class time in graduate school. African-Americans account for 3 percent of the students, Asian-Americans 35 percent, and Hispanics 10 percent. Students are slightly more conservative than in past years, and most are characterized as "friendly and open-minded." Campus hot topics include fair labor practices and political correctness. In its pledge to foster awareness of diversity issues, the university has established an Office of Campus

(Continued)
ACT Range: 22–27
Financial Aid: 62%
Expense: Pub $ $ $
Phi Beta Kappa: Yes
Applicants: 22,224
Accepted: 63%
Enrolled: 27%
Grad in 6 Years: 73%
Returning Freshmen: 90%
Academics: ✍ ✍ ✍ ✍
Social: ☎ ☎ ☎
Q of L: ★ ★ ★ ★
Admissions: (530) 752-2971
Email Address:
thinkucd@ucdavis.edu

Strongest Programs:
Environmental Studies
Botany
Animal Science
Viticulture
Agricultural Sciences
Studio Art
Biological Sciences
Engineering

It was Davis food scientists who gave us the square tomato (better for packing into boxes), as well as more useful things such as the method for creating orange-juice concentrate.

Diversity and a Cross-Cultural Center. UC–Davis boasts the highest graduation rate in the UC system. Davis awards merit scholarships, but there are no athletic awards.

Virtually all freshmen inhabit campus housing, which is well maintained and includes a number of theme houses. The vast majority of upperclassmen live off-campus in nearby houses or apartments. Housing is guaranteed for freshmen and transfer students if applications are received by the deadline. Six different meal plans for the dining halls are available, and one student says, "The dorm food is very good (better than at most colleges)." A variety of nearby eating establishments serve the student clientele, but a car can come in handy if you are looking for a good meal in Sacramento (fifteen minutes) or a great one in San Francisco (a little more than an hour). Beaches are a two-hour drive from the campus, and the ski slopes and hiking trails of Lake Tahoe and the Sierra Nevada are a little closer. But if you feel, as most Davis students do, that studies are too important to be abandoned on weekends, the town has restaurants, activities, and entertainment enough to keep the stay-at-homes happy.

In between quizzes and cram sessions, the outlying countryside offers a welcome change of pace. The town of Davis itself is small, about fifty thousand, and students make up half the population. If some call it a cowtown, others call it peaceful, with its tree-lined streets and quiet nights. The relationship between college and town is one of rare cooperation (partly because the students are a significant voting bloc in local elections). Health and energy consciousness runs high in town and on the vast,

"There's no free ride. You are going to have to work for everything you get."

architecturally diverse campus, where bicycles are the main form of transportation on the incredible forty-six miles of bike paths that crisscross the campus and environs. "Bicycles are the norm at Davis. Don't come without one," advises one psych major. The university has encouraged environmental awareness by sponsoring solar energy projects and promoting such novelties as contests between dorms for the lowest heating and electric bills.

On-campus activities are varied, and many university-sponsored events fill the calendar. One rhetoric major points out that "social functions are hard to avoid at Davis." Active drama and music departments provide frequent entertainment, and there is plenty of room for homegrown talent in the coffeehouses, which offer mellow live entertainment and poetry readings on a regular basis. The new eighteen-hundred-seat Mondavi Center for the Arts features international and local groups. Fraternities and sororities attract 7 percent of the men and 6 percent of the women. Alcohol is allowed in the dorms for those over twenty-one years old; those too young to imbibe have trouble finding booze, unless it's supplied by peers. Major annual social events include Picnic Day, in which alumni join current students in a massive outdoor shindig; African-American Week; and the Whole Earth Festival, "an earthy, tie-dyed sort of event" in celebration of the '60s.

The university's varsity athletic teams compete in Division II and attract relatively scant attention compared to those at most other state universities. Nevertheless, Davis won the Sears Directors' Cup, a trophy symbolic of overall excellence in intercollegiate athletics, and cross-country, basketball, and track and field have brought home NCAA championships. The annual Causeway Classic against rival Sacramento State does create a measure of excitement. Intramurals, however, are much more popular than spectator sports, with 65 percent of students participating. On this outdoor campus, almost everyone does something athletic—jogging, softball, tennis, swimming, or Frisbee—if only to break up the monotony of studies with a different kind of competition.

Proud of its small-town atmosphere, Davis is not for the lazy or faint of heart. As one man says, "There's no free ride. You are going to have to work for everything

Overlaps

UC–Berkeley, UCLA, UC–San Diego, UC–Santa Barbara, UC–Irvine you get." And most students get a lot out of their four or more years at Davis. It's the ideal spot to combine high-powered work in science and agriculture with that famous easygoing California lifestyle.

<table>
<tr><td>**If You Apply To ➤**</td><td>**Davis:** Regular admissions: Nov. 30. Financial aid: Mar. 3. Does not guarantee to meet demonstrated need. No campus or alumni interviews. SATs or ACTs: required. SAT IIs: required (writing, math, and one other). Accepts the Common Application and electronic applications. Essay question: personal statement. Apply to particular program.</td></tr>
</table>

UC–Irvine

260 ADM, Irvine, CA 92697

Irvine sits in the midst of one of the nation's biggest suburbs, combining funky modern architecture with perhaps the most conservative student body in the UC system. Premed is the featured attraction, along with various other health-related offerings. Not quite as close to the beach as Santa Barbara—but close enough.

On the surface, UC–Irvine's clean, contemporary campus appears to be home to students who study diligently in the busy library, wear sensible shoes to biology lab, and resist that double shot of espresso at the local coffeehouse. But that image starts to dissipate as soon as you hear that bizarre noise: "Zot! Zot! Zot!" Then a UCI student explains that "it's the sound that an anteater supposedly makes when it swipes an ant with its tongue." Hey, any school that has an anteater as a mascot can't be completely straight-laced. The university is, however, straight on its reputation as a school with stellar programs in biology and creative writing. The current academic climate can be quite serious and challenging, but as one UCI student swears, the Anteaters are "also surprisingly cooperative."

Located in the heart of Orange County, UCI (founded in 1965) is among the newest of the UC campuses. Although enrollment is up and the administration has dreams of further expansion, "it is the perfect size," says one English major. UCI is liberally supplied with trees and shrubs

> **"UCI is fairly competitive and the courses are moderately rigorous."**

from all over the world. Futuristic buildings are arranged in a circle around a large park, "giving it the appearance of a relaxed art school," says one observer. Undergraduates have long quipped that UCI stood for "Under Construction Indefinitely," and current campus construction does little to challenge the moniker: new additions include the Anteater Recreation Center and new parking structures.

A "premed mentality" reigns at Irvine, since the School of Biological Sciences is the best and most competitive academic division. The School of Arts offers nationally ranked programs in dance, drama, music, studio art, and musical theatre, as well as a minor in digital arts. The Beall Center for Art and Technology in the Claire Trevor School of the Arts enables students to explore the relationship between digital technology and the arts and sciences. The popular interdisciplinary School of Social Ecology offers courses combining criminology, environmental and legal studies, and psychology and social behavior, strongly emphasizes teacher-student relationships, and offers one of two B.S. degrees in business administration, one of only two such programs in the UC system. Like most of the other UC campuses, UCI is on a ten-week quarter system, so the pace is fast and furious. Students should

Website: www.uci.edu
Location: Suburban
Total Enrollment: 21,885
Undergraduates: 17,865
Male/Female: 48/52
SAT Ranges: V 520–610
  M 550–660
ACT Range: N/A
Financial Aid: 48%
Expense: Pub $ $
Phi Beta Kappa: Yes
Applicants: 29,178
Accepted: 59%
Enrolled: 23%
Grad in 6 Years: 72%
Returning Freshmen: 92%
Academics: ✍ ✍ ✍ ✍
Social: ☎ ☎
Q of L: ★ ★ ★
Admissions: (949) 824-6703
Email Address: oars@uci.edu

Strongest Programs:
Biology
English
Dance
Chemistry
Computer Science

face registration with the same determination, too; it's a tough fight to get into the science classes of choice as a sophomore.

Languages are strong at UCI, as are the biggest nonbiology majors: English, economics, political science, psychology, and a fiction-writing program that is gaining national recognition. UCI has added a plethora of new programs, including majors in global cultures, literary journalism, biomedical engineering, and German studies.

"UCI is fairly competitive and the courses are moderately rigorous," says a junior. Students may be overwhelmed by the size of most classes. Even seniors find their classes packed with one hundred undergrads, which leaves little time for personal attention. "Graduate students teach lower-division writing courses," says one student, adding that "most classes are overcrowded, leaving little room for personal attention." The Center for Health Sciences focuses on five areas of research, including: neuroscience, genetics, cancer, infectious diseases, and aging. The university also houses the Reeve-Irvine Research Center, which supports the study of spinal-cord trauma and disease with emphasis on finding a cure. The "breadth requirement" means that students must take three courses each in writing, natural sciences, social and behavioral sciences, and humanities in order to graduate. There is also a language requirement (though students can substitute linguistics, logic, math, or computer science) and requirements in multicultural and international/global issues. Honors programs are available in humanities, economics, psychology, and political science.

Ninety-one percent of the student body are in-staters, the majority from Southern California and many of those from wealthy Orange County. The students are in general "much more conservative than at the other UC campuses," says one applied math major. Minorities account for well over half the student body, with Asian-Americans comprising 52 percent, African-Americans 2 percent, and Hispanics 14 percent. "Cultural groups seem to segregate from each other more than I really like," says a senior.

Condominium-style dorms, both single-sex and co-ed, are "exceptional compared to the high-rise dormitories of other institutions," says one senior. Others agree that the homey campus dwellings provide a good experience for freshmen, though finding a room can be a challenge. "If you really want on-campus housing," warns a student, "you need to make sure you meet the deadlines." Newly added housing, including those with academic themes and ones especially for fraternities and sororities, opens more rooms for students, but most opt to move off-campus after their first year. Currently, 70 percent of freshmen live off-campus—many on the beach—giving the campus a commuter-school atmosphere. One student laments, "You have to find the social life on this campus. It won't find you."

Still, the Greek scene is vigorous. There are eighteen sororities and eighteen fraternities, and each has something going on every weekend. As for booze, UCI is a dry campus and students say finding a drink on campus without proper ID is difficult. Irvine touts many festivals that seem to attest to a celebration of diversity: the Rainbow Festival (cultural heritage), Asian Heritage week, Black History month, Cinco de Mayo, and rush week. The one event that brings everybody out is the daylong Wayzgoose, when the campus is transformed into a medieval fair complete with mimes, jugglers, and performers dressed up in medieval costumes.

"If you really want on-campus housing you need to make sure you meet the deadlines."

But if life on-campus is slow, life off-campus is not. That's because the campus is located just fifty miles from L.A., five miles from the beach, and a little more than an hour from the ski slopes. Catalina Island, with beaches and hiking trails, is a quick boat trip off Newport Harbor; Mexico is two hours away. While some students treasure the quiet setting of Irvine, others lament its "lackluster, homogeneous communities." Notes one student, "UCI and the city of Irvine seem like completely different entities; the former is slightly liberal while the latter is ultraconservative."

Irvine fields twenty athletic teams and competes in Division I of the NCAA. Tennis and cross-country are perennial Big West powerhouses, and men's water polo has been ranked in the top five nationally for twenty-three of the last thirty-one years. There is no football team, but intramurals are extremely popular, as is the five thousand-seat multipurpose gym.

What lures students to UCI is its top-name professors, innovative academic programs, and the chance to be a part of its cutting-edge research. For the students who come here prepared to keep their heads buried in a book for a few years, the ultimate reward will be an exceptional education.

If You Apply To ➤

Irvine: Regular admissions: Nov. 30. Financial aid and housing: May 1. No campus or alumni interviews. SATs or ACTs: required. SAT IIs: required (English composition, math, and one other). Accepts electronic applications. Essay question: autobiographical statement.

UC–Los Angeles

1147 Murphy Hall, 405 Hillgard Avenue, Los Angeles, CA 90095

Tucked into exclusive Beverly Hills with the beach, the mountains, and chic Hollywood hangouts all within easy reach. Practically everything is offered here, but the programs in arts and media are some of the best in the world. More conservative than Berkeley and nearly as difficult to get into.

With stellar programs in music, film and television, journalism/communication, dance, and drama, you'd think UCLA was some kind of incubator for truly talented and gifted people. Or with alumni such as Kareem Abdul-Jabbar, Troy Aikman, and Arthur Ashe, maybe UCLA's some sort of farm that grows superstar athletes. Well, UCLA is all that and more. A superb faculty, a reputation for outstanding academics, and a powerful athletics program make this university the ultimate place to study. "There are endless opportunities and unlimited resources because of the size of this university," says an English major. "There's nothing you can't do at UCLA."

UCLA's prime location—sandwiched between two glamorous neighborhoods (Beverly Hills and Bel Air) and a short drive away from Hollywood, the Sunset Strip, and downtown Los Angeles—makes it appealing for students who want more from their college experience than what classes alone can offer. The university's beautifully landscaped 419-acre campus features a range of architectural styles, with Romanesque/Italian Renaissance as the dominant motif, providing only one of a number of reasons students also enjoy staying on campus. A wealth of gardens—botanical, Japanese, and sculpture—adds a touch of quiet elegance

> **"My professors have been dynamic and inspirational and genuinely interested in the student's success."**

to the campus. Planned facilities include additional student apartments, a physics and astronomy building, and the Luck Center, which will house research activities in orthopedics and related fields.

Strong programs abound at UCLA, and many are considered among the best in the nation. The School of Engineering and Applied Science, especially electrical engineering, is generally regarded as the leading department. As befits a university next door to Hollywood, the School of Film, Theater, and Television is first-rate, and its students have the opportunity to study in Verona, Italy, with the Theater Overseas program. The dance and drama departments are excellent, and the popular music department offers a course in jazz studies. The biological sciences are also highly regarded; new majors include plant biology, marine biology, ecology, and behavior and evolution. Research opportunities abound at UCLA, and the university ranks seventh in the nation in federal funding for research. In the Student Research Program, more than fourteen hundred undergrads work side-by-side with professors on cutting-edge research. Students say that the math department doesn't add up to the sum total of its parts.

Freshmen are encouraged to participate in a three-day summer orientation, which provides workshops, counseling, and a general introduction to the campus and community. During their first two years, most students take required core classes that are sometimes jammed with three hundred to four hundred people. But administrators are quick to point out that nearly two-thirds of all undergraduate classes have fewer than fifty students. Savvy students come to UCLA with advanced courses in their high-school backgrounds and test out of the intro courses. First-year students are required to take a course involving quantitative reasoning unless they hit 600 or higher on their math SAT, and English composition requirements should also be met

"There are endless opportunities and unlimited resources because of the size of this university. There's nothing you can't do at UCLA."

during the freshman year. Lab science and a language requirement are also required for a liberal arts degree.

Simply getting into classes here can be a big challenge. Students register by phone in a sequence of two scheduled "passes" based on their class standing. UCLA's academic environment is extremely intense. "Depending on your major, the courses can be very time-consuming," says a senior. The faculty is also impressive. "My professors have been dynamic and inspirational and genuinely interested in the student's success," says an English major. On the other hand, there is a widespread sense here that undergraduate teaching is often sacrificed on behalf of scholarly research. "Some professors considered their research primary and teaching their students secondary," says a mechanical engineering major. The UCLA library ranks in the top ten of all research libraries, public or private, and actually consists of the College Library and nine specialized libraries containing more than 7.2 million volumes. The campus newspaper, the *Daily Bruin*, is the third-largest daily in Los Angeles.

"We have some very interesting and eccentric students at our school," says a freshman. "Most are social, trendy, and tanned." Asian-Americans account for 39 percent of UCLA's student population, Hispanics make up 15 percent, African-Americans 4 percent, and Native Americans 1 percent. "Affirmative action and minority representation are the largest political issues on campus," says a sophomore. UCLA has several student-run newsmagazines as alternatives to the *Daily Bruin,* including the feminist *Together* and the Asian-American newsmagazine *Pacific Ties.* UCLA is also one of the few universities in the nation with a gay fraternity and a lesbian sorority. These groups, as well as GALA (Gay and Lesbian Association) and TenPercent, have helped foster a rising feeling of empowerment among the campus's gay and lesbian students and faculty.

Freshmen are guaranteed housing, but for everyone else it's strictly a waiting list. "Dorm life is awesome!" says one student. "It spawns lifelong friendships." Overcrowding is a concern, though future housing construction should give students a bit more elbow room. The campus is philosophically divided into North

As befits a university next door to Hollywood, the School of Film, Theater, and Television is first-rate, and its students have the opportunity to study in Verona, Italy, with the Theater Overseas program.

and South. North attracts more liberal arts aficionados, while those in math and science tend to favor South. Fifteen dining halls, restaurants, and snack bars serve average meals.

UCLA has won a nation-leading number of collegiate championships, including eighty-six NCAA titles, and has produced more than 250 Olympians. The men's football, basketball, baseball, and tennis teams are the undeniable superstars as are the women's gymnastic and water-polo teams. Beating USC is the name of the game in any sport; UCLA fans regard their intracity rivals with passionate feelings. ("Bruins are forever, but a Trojan is good only once.")

If you would rather be a doer than a watcher, the opportunities awaiting you are superb. "UCLA has an awesome social setting!" exclaims a junior. "Since we're based right here in L.A., there's too much to do." The hopping Westwood suburb, which borders the university, has at least fifteen movie theaters and scores of restaurants, but the shops cater to the upper class. UCLA's Ocean Discovery Center, located on the Santa Monica Pier, is an innovative, hands-on ocean classroom for students and the public. The beach is five miles away, and the mountains are only a short drive. Although public transportation is cheap, it's also inconvenient, making a car almost a necessity for going outside of Westwood. Unfortunately, parking is expensive and difficult to obtain. The easiest solution is to live close to campus and bike it.

With all the attractions of the City of Angels at its doorstep, the campus tends to empty out on the weekends (except when the football Bruins have a home game). Eleven percent of the men and 10 percent of the women join one of UCLA's fifty fraternities and sororities. The university's alcohol policy is similar to that of other UC schools—open consumption is a no-no. But according to one student, "It is extremely easy for undergrads to be served, especially at fraternities." Top-name entertainers, political figures, and speakers of all kinds come to the campus; film and theater presentations are frequent, and the air is thick with live music, usually every week.

A leading research center, UCLA's broad range of innovative academic programs, distinguished faculty members, and outstanding athletics make it one of the most prestigious universities in the nation. In order to make the most of this university, a student must have stamina, self-reliance, and willpower.

Freshmen are encouraged to participate in a three-day summer orientation, which provides workshops, counseling, and a general introduction to the campus and community.

Overlaps

UC–Berkeley, UC–San Diego, UC–Irvine, UC–Santa Barbara, USC

If You Apply To ➤

UCLA: Regular admissions: Nov. 30. Does not guarantee to meet demonstrated need. No campus or alumni interviews. SATs or ACTs: required. SAT IIs: required (writing, math I or II, and one other). Apply to particular school or program. Accepts electronic applications. Essay question: personal statement.

UC–Riverside

Riverside, CA 92521

While multitudes of students throng other UC campuses, Riverside offers a more personal touch. A unique biomedical studies program is a major drawing card. The town of Riverside is not—but it is an hour from L.A. Without big-time athletics or a marquee location, Riverside is rarely a first choice.

Website: www.ucr.edu

Location: City outskirts

Total Enrollment: 15,934

Undergraduates: 14,124

Male/Female: 46/54

SAT Ranges: V 450–560
    M 500–620

ACT Range: 18–23

Financial Aid: 60%

Expense: Pub $ $ $ $

Phi Beta Kappa: Yes

Applicants: 18,162

Accepted: 81%

Enrolled: 20%

Grad in 6 Years: 66%

Returning Freshmen: 85%

Academics: ✍ ✍ ✍ ½

Social: ☎ ☎

Q of L: ★ ★ ★

Admissions: (909) 787-3411

Email Address:
    discover@pop.ucr.edu

Strongest Programs:

Plant Sciences and
    Entomology
Engineering
Natural Sciences
Social Sciences
Biomedical Sciences
Humanities and Arts
Business
Education
Engineering

Research is an institutional priority for faculty, but professors continue to dedicate must of their time and attention to their students. Plus, UCR has a tradition of undergraduate and faculty interaction with a wide range of undergraduate research grants available during the academic year.

Lacking the big-name reputation and booming athletic programs of the other UC schools, UC–Riverside has chosen to place its emphasis on something that not all institutions consider to be an important component of higher education: the student. Riverside offers one of the lowest student/faculty ratios in the UC system, strong programs with personalized attention, and a sense of academic community that seems to have been forgotten at other UC schools. "Students are well taken care of and get personal attention," says one satisfied senior. Though part of the UC system, UC–Riverside is a breed apart.

Located sixty miles east of Los Angeles, UCR is surrounded by mountains on the outskirts of the city of Riverside. The beautifully landscaped,1,200-acre campus consists of mainly modern architecture, with a 160-foot bell tower (with a 48-bell carillon) marking its center. Wide lawns and clusters of oaks create "a veritable botanical garden," where students and faculty enjoy relaxing between classes. Acres of citrus groves form a half-circle on the outer edges of campus, which means the place smells great every spring. New facilities include residence halls, an international village, a large lecture hall, a plant genomics research center, an entomology building, and science laboratories. In 2005, construction will be completed on a four-story student commons area housing entertainment venues, dining services, and office space for student organizations.

Decades ago, researchers at the Citrus Experiment Station in Riverside perfected the growing methods for the imported navel orange, making discoveries to protect the fruit from disease and pests and saving California's citrus industry. Riverside continues to excel in plant sciences and entomology. But the campus has grown since its founding in 1954 to include excellent programs in engineering, natural sciences, social sciences, humanities, the arts, business, and education. The biomedical sciences program, unique in California, is UCR's most prestigious and demanding course of study, and its most successful students can earn a seven-year B.S./M.D. in partnership with the medical school at UCLA. Students who want a more traditional path can still pursue their graduate studies at a normal pace. The engineering program also is quite selective, more so than the campus as a whole, which generally accepts students who are ranked in the top 12 percent of the state's high school graduates. One of the few undergraduate environmental engineering programs is at UCR, as is an undergraduate program in creative writing, the only one in the UC system. Graduate programs in the arts are strong, with an M.F.A. in writing for the performing arts and the nation's only doctoral program in dance history and theory. Academic weaknesses include journalism and geography. The

"Students are well taken care of and get personal attention."

campus has abolished its PE department, which means that recreation classes such as aerobics and yoga can no longer be taken for class credit. The University Honors Program offers exceptional students further academic challenges in addition to extracurricular activities and special seminars for freshmen. A new program in new media that combines art and computer science is in the planning stages. And talented student singers, dancers, and actors can earn stipends for performing in the community through an arts outreach program funded by the Maxwell H. Gluck Foundation.

All students are required to meet extensive "breadth requirements" that include courses in English composition, natural sciences and math, humanities, and social sciences. Some majors include a foreign language requirement. Students do not encounter much difficulty in getting the courses they want. "As a freshman and sophomore, classes always filled up quick," one business major explains. "But as a junior, classes are much easier to get into." The campus libraries have an impressive two million volumes, an interlibrary loan system within the UC system, and vast electronic databases. A specialized research collection in science fiction is world-class.

UCR's museum of photography, located in a downtown Riverside mall and available on the Web, has grown in stature. A "Digital Studio" complete with the latest Apple computers and software is available free for students working on digital films.

Research is an institutional priority for faculty, but professors continue to dedicate must of their time and attention to their students. "From my very first quarter I had professors who inspired me with the passion they had for the subjects and areas of expertise, and who made me feel like a person—not a number!" raves one psychology major. Plus, UCR has a tradition of undergraduate and faculty interaction with a wide range of undergraduate research grants available during the academic year. This may be why one in six graduates goes on to get a Ph.D.

Ninety-seven percent of the UCR student body are from California, mainly L.A., Riverside, San Bernardino, and Orange counties. Ninety-four percent of the students graduated in the top tenth of their public high school class. Asian-Americans account for 38 percent of the students, and Hispanics and African-Americans 21 percent and 5 percent respectively. As part of the UC commitment to diversity, Riverside upholds policies prohibiting sexual harassment, hazing, and physical and verbal abuses. It supports centers for various ethnicities, for women and for gay and lesbian students. "UCR is one of the most diverse universities in the nation," a political science major says. "Because of this, there is a wide range of students at UCR that make a blended environment of different cultures, nationalities, and social statuses." Numerous merit scholarships, ranging from $500 to $12,000, are doled out every year, as well as Division I athletic scholarships in baseball, softball, basketball, tennis, volleyball, track, soccer, and golf. Scholarships also are available in specific academic departments.

Housing is a breeze, reasonably priced and relatively easy to obtain. Thirty percent of the students live in the well-maintained dorms, where freshmen are guaranteed a spot. Twenty-eight percent of the students live in off-campus apartments and another third commute from home. Many complain about the scarcity and cost of parking. The co-ed dorms are clean and comfortable, and provide a social context as well as a living atmosphere. Social life is

"UCR is one of the most diverse universities in the nation."

relatively tame, since so many of the students commute. While some complain of a lack of nightlife in Riverside, they readily agree that activities on campus make up for it. Returning students are welcomed back every year with a campus-wide block party, and Spring Splash brings in hot bands. Fraternities and sororities lure 3 percent of men and women on campus. The groups usually hold campus-wide parties once a quarter. "There is always something going on, whether it be a concert, lecture, or sorority/fraternity party," one sophomore says. Campus hangouts known as "The Barn" and "Bear Grounds" have live bands and comedy nights. Every Wednesday the campus can enjoy a "nooner," where live bands play during lunch. University Village is a new commercial center offering a movie theater, restaurants, and an arcade right on the edge of campus. The campus runs a cultural arts program that brings professional shows to campus, such as Laurie Anderson and Margaret Cho.

Riverside weather is temperate except during the summer months, when the heat and haze combine to make a trip to the coast look really inviting. The coast is only about 45 minutes by freeway and the desert is an hour east. Big Bear and numerous ski resorts are also within an hour's drive.

Athletics is generating more interest on campus since the switch to NCAA Division I competition. The baseball team boasts the first success, earning a ranking in the top twenty-five in the nation in the 2003 season. Other sports on the rise include women's volleyball, men's and women's golf, and men's basketball. A recreational program in men's and women's karate has turned out national champions. For weekend athletes, a student recreation center offers a health-club atmosphere with sand volleyball, weight machines, and intramural leagues.

Acres of citrus groves form a half-circle on the outer edges of campus, which means the place smells great every spring.

Social life is relatively tame, since so many of the students commute. While some complain of a lack of nightlife in Riverside, they readily agree that activities on campus make up for it. Returning students are welcomed back every year with a campus-wide block party, and Spring Splash brings in hot bands.

Overlaps

UC–Irvine, UCLA, UC–San Diego, UC–Santa Cruz, UC–Santa Barbara

All in all, Riverside is growing and improving. While it isn't UCLA or Berkeley, it is half the size of those sister campuses and offers more personal attention to its students. UCR is fast becoming a nationally recognized research institution, from which students surely will benefit. "UCR has grown immensely over the past few years," one sophomore says. "The emphasis for the future is to establish a name for UCR, to let the nation know what a wonderful university this is."

<table>
<tr><td>If You
Apply
To ≫</td><td>Riverside: Regular admissions: Nov. 30. Financial aid: Mar. 2. Housing: June 1. Guarantees to meet demonstrated need. Campus and alumni interviews: optional, informative. SATs or ACTs: required. SAT IIs: required (writing, math, and one other). Accepts electronic applications. Essay question: personal statement.</td></tr>
</table>

UC–San Diego

9500 Gilman Drive, Department 0021-A, La Jolla, CA 92093-0021

Applications have doubled in the past ten years at this seaside paradise. UCSD now rivals better-known Berkeley and UCLA as the Cal campus of choice for top students. Five undergraduate colleges break down UCSD to a more manageable size. Best known for science and engineering.

Website: www.ucsd.edu
Location: Suburban
Total Enrollment: 22,939
Undergraduates: 19,088
Male/Female: 48/52
SAT Ranges: V 540–650
  M 600–700
ACT Range: 26–29
Financial Aid: 50%
Expense: Pub $ $ $ $
Phi Beta Kappa: Yes
Applicants: 41,354
Accepted: 41%
Enrolled: 25%
Grad in 6 Years: 82%
Returning Freshmen: 94%
Academics: ✑ ✑ ✑ ✑ ✑
Social: ☎ ☎ ☎ ☎
Q of L: ★ ★ ★ ★
Admissions: (858) 534-4831
Email Address:
  admissionsinfo@ucsd.edu

Strongest Programs:
Biology
Engineering and
  Bioengineering

Some say that looking good is better than feeling good, but at UC–San Diego, they're doing a lot of both. Set against the serene beauty of La Jolla's beaches, students catch as much relaxation time as they do study time. But it's not all fun and games around this campus. The research star of the UC system, UCSD's faculty is rated number one nationally among public institutions in science productivity. And within each of the five undergraduate colleges, a system that offers undergraduates more intimate settings, students are honing their minds with the classics and the cutting edge in academics. Sure, San Diegans tend to be more mellow than the average Southern Californian, and UCSD students follow suit. But beneath the frown-free foreheads and bright smiles, UCSD's bubbling with intellectual energy and the healthy desire to be at the top of the UC system.

San Diego's tree-lined campus sits high on a bluff overlooking the Pacific in the seaside resort of La Jolla. Each of the six colleges has its own flavor, but the predominant architectural theme is contemporary, with a few out-of-the-ordinary structures, including a library that looks like an inverted pyramid. Another tinge of the postmodern is the nation's largest neon sculpture, which wraps around one of the high-rise academic buildings and consists of seven-foot-tall letters that spell out the seven virtues superimposed over the seven vices. Construction is taking place all around campus, with new buildings and a parking structure in the works.

> "Professors here are brilliant and conduct research throughout the year, but they also have a desire to share their knowledge with their students."

UCSD's programs in science and engineering are "not for the faint of heart," says one student. Engineering requires a B average in entry-level courses for acceptance into the major. The Scripps Institute of Oceanography is also excellent, due to the university's advantageous location. Computer science and chemistry also get strong recommendations, but you really can't go wrong in any of the hard sciences. Although the humanities and social sciences are not as solid in comparison, political science and psychology get strong backing from students. The math department, however, is less than adequate. To address its lack of a business program, the new School of Management began accepting students in its M.B.A. program in 2004. Imaginative interdisciplinary offerings include computer music, urban planning, ethnic studies, and a psychology/computer science program in artificial intelligence, as well as majors devised by students themselves. The School of Pharmacy and Pharmaceutical Sciences enrolled its first students in 2002. UCSD has also opened a new, 109,000-square-foot building for the Jacobs School of Engineering, called the Powell-Focht Bioengineering Hall, a state-of-the-art research and teaching facility.

(Continued)
Cognitive Science
Economics
Political Science
Applied Mechanics & Engineering
Economics
Oceanography
Communication
Psychology

Like most of the UC campuses, San Diego operates on the quarter system, which makes for a semester's worth of work crammed into ten weeks. Science students find the load intense. "The courses here are challenging and intellectually stimulating, but there are also a lot of fun classes too," says one senior. Students have a choice of six libraries, some good for research, others better for socializing. Despite the quality of research done by the faculty, half a dozen of whom are Nobel laureates, students find that the typical scenario of research over teaching seen at most large research universities is not as common at UC–San Diego. "Professors here are brilliant and conduct research throughout the year, but they also have a desire to share their knowledge with their students," says a communication major.

"The residence halls are very nice, with all the amenities, including Ethernet hookups in every room."

UC–San Diego's six undergraduate colleges have their own sets of general education requirements, their own personalities, and differing ideals upon which they are based. Prospective freshmen apply to UC–San Diego—the admissions requirements are identical for each college—but students must indicate their college preference. Revelle College, the oldest, is the most rigorous and mandates that students become equally acquainted with a certain level of coursework in the humanities, sciences, and social sciences, as well as fulfill a language requirement. Muir allows more flexibility in the distribution requirements. Thurgood Marshall College was founded to emphasize and encourage social awareness; like Revelle, it places equal weight on sciences, social sciences, and humanities. However, it stresses a liberal arts education based on "an examination of the human condition in a multicultural society." Warren has developed a highly organized internship program that gives its undergraduates more practical experience than the others do. Eleanor Roosevelt College ("Fifth"), devotes its curriculum to international and cross-cultural studies. The newest college—appropriately dubbed Sixth College—focuses on art, culture, and technology. Its goal is to graduate multicultural students who can work collaboratively and enjoy working in their communities.

A theater major notes that UCSD's academic intensity "does not mean that all the students here are nerdy. They enjoy athletics and extracurricular activities, but academic excellence is their priority." A short walk to the beach, however, reveals the student body's wild and crazy half-surfers and their fans, who celebrate the "kick back." Students jumping curbs on skateboards are common on this campus. Yet these beach babies are no scholastic slouches. All of them placed in the top 10 percent of their high school class. The average student pulls a 3.0 GPA while at UCSD. Many students here choose to take five years to graduate in order to gain a higher GPA, and many of the scientists continue their studies after graduation. UCSD also ranks high among public colleges and universities in the percentage of graduates who go on to earn a Ph.D., and in the percentage of students accepted to medical school. Only 2 percent of students are from out of state, and another 3 percent are foreign students. Minority representation is high, with 39 percent of the student body Asian-American, 10 percent Hispanic, and 1 percent African-American. Affirmative action programs have been abolished in the UC system, but "UCSD is still

Although San Diego is the farthest thing imaginable from a rah-rah school, it is rapidly becoming a Division II powerhouse, most notably in women's sports.

Annual festivals include the Open House, Renaissance Faire, UnOlympics, and the Reggae Festival. Another annual festival pays tribute to a hideously loud and colorful statue of the Sun God, which is the unofficial mascot for this sun-streaked student body.

Students jumping curbs on skateboards are common on this campus. Yet these beach babies are no scholastic slouches. All of them placed in the top 10 percent of their high school class. The average student pulls a 3.0 GPA.

Overlaps

UCLA, UC–Berkeley, UC–Davis, UC–Santa Barbara, University of Southern California

shaping its new admissions policy to maintain ethnic diversity on campus," notes the administration. Efforts include a Cross-Cultural Center for students, faculty, and staff that provides activities, brown-bag luncheons, and programs on race relations.

Each of the university's colleges has its own housing complex, with either dorms or apartments. Most freshmen live on campus and are guaranteed housing for their first two years. "The residence halls are very nice, with all the amenities, including Ethernet hookups in every room," says an animal physiology major. By junior year, students usually decide to take up residence in La Jolla proper or nearby Del Mar, often in beachside apartments; only 26 percent of all the students live on campus. But that can be costly: the price ends up being inversely proportional to proximity to the beach. If you are willing to relinquish the luxury of a five-minute walk to the beach, a short commute will bring you relatively affordable housing.

The immediate surroundings of UCSD, however, are definitely not affordable. "La Jolla equals rich, conservative, retired, white, snobbish community," one sophomore says. "Not a college town!" Cars are, of course, an inescapable part of Southern California life, and owning one—many people do—makes off-campus living even more pleasant. "No car equals no fun," one international studies major says. Unfortunately, trying to park on campus can be difficult, though at least one student says that "parking is not nearly as bad here as it is at other schools." Dorm residents are required to buy a meal card, which gets them into any of the four campus cafeterias as well as the campus deli and burger joints.

The university is dry, so most of the real socializing seems to take place off-campus. "Most students hang out at the dance clubs, jazz bars, and great restaurants in the Gaslamp Quarter," says a senior. Annual festivals include the Open House, Renaissance Faire, UnOlympics, and the Reggae Festival. Another annual festival pays tribute to a hideously loud and colorful statue of the Sun God, which is the unofficial mascot for this sun-streaked student body. Ten percent of both the men and the women try to beat the blahs by joining a fraternity or sorority. Alcoholic parties are banned in the residence halls, though students say lax RAs and good fake IDs make for easy underage drinking. Although campus life is relatively tame, students rely heavily on the surrounding area—but not La Jolla—for their entertainment. Students go to nearby Pacific Beach, and downtown San Diego with the zoo, Sea World, and Balboa Park only twelve miles away. Torrey Pines Natural Reserves are great for outdoor enthusiasts. Mexico—and the $5 lobster—is a half-hour drive (even nearer than the desert, where many students go hiking), and the two-hour trip to Los Angeles makes for a nice weekend jaunt.

Although San Diego is the farthest thing imaginable from a rah-rah school, it is rapidly becoming a Division II powerhouse, most notably in women's sports. Women's volleyball and tennis teams have won numerous national championships, and the men's water polo and volleyball teams have also done well. For weekend competitors, classes are available in windsurfing, sailing, scuba diving, and kayaking at the nearby Mission Bay Aquatic Center. Everyone participates in one intramural league or another, and if you're not on a team, "you're not a true UCSD student." The RIMAC, an impressive sports facility for students, gets even the couch potatoes off their BarcaLoungers.

The students at UCSD are exceptionally serious and out for an excellent education. But the pace (study, party, relax, study more) and the props (sun, sand, Frisbees, and flip-flops) give the rigorous curriculum offered by UCSD's six colleges an inimitable flavor that undergraduates would not change. Indeed, many believe they have the best setup in higher education: "a beautiful beach-front environment that eases a life of academic rigor."

If You Apply To ➤

San Diego: Regular admissions: Nov. 30. Financial Aid: Mar. 3. Does not guarantee to meet demonstrated need. Campus and alumni interviews: optional, informational. SATs or ACTs: required. SAT IIs: required (English, math level 1 or 2). Essay question: personal statement.

UC–Santa Barbara

Santa Barbara, CA 93106

Willpower is the word at UC–Santa Barbara. On a beautiful day with the sound of waves crashing in the distance, it takes willpower to hang in there with pen, paper, and book. Fairly or not, Santa Barbara is known as the party animal of the UC system. In the classroom, science is the best bet.

For students at UC–Santa Barbara, California's famed beaches serve as both classroom and playground. On weekends, sun-worshipping students don surfboards and bikinis and head for the water to have some serious fun. During the week, those same students can likely be found studying technology rather than tan lines. UCSB provides a comfortable mixture of work and play that is unique to the UC system and draws praise from its students. Says a senior, "I love the fact that I am getting a highly rated UC education in such a relaxing location." Recent construction includes student housing and the School of Environmental Science and Management.

Located just a stone's throw from the beach, UC–Santa Barbara's 989-acre campus is bordered on two sides by the Pacific Ocean, with a clear view of the Channel Islands. On the landward side are a nature preserve and the predominantly student community of Isla Vista (I.V.), and five miles to the north lie the Santa Inez Mountains. "We are definitely a college town," one senior says. "Isla Vista is almost all college students, and it is a really relaxed atmosphere." The campus itself features mainly 1950s Southern California architecture with a Southern California atmosphere to match.

Not surprisingly, the marine biology department capitalizes on the school's aquatic resources and stands out among the university's best. Other favorites include physics, ecology, engineering materials, and chemistry. The accounting program is also very strong, and the courses are geared toward taking and passing the CPA exam, so graduation is usually followed by a mass recruit-

> **"Our students differ from students at other UC's because we are probably the most relaxed UC campus."**

ment by California's big accounting firms. In addition, history, English, communications, and geological sciences are solid, but students say political science and math are considerably weaker. The College of Creative Studies offers an unstructured curriculum to about four hundred self-starters ready for advanced and independent work in the arts, math, or the sciences. An interdisciplinary program called the Global Peace and Security Program combines aspects of physics, anthropology, and military science. The National Science Foundation provides funding for the $5.5 million National Center for Geographic Information and Analysis program. The Bren School of Environmental Science and Management is open for business, and the science departments are world-renowned—the college boasts Nobel prize winners in chemistry and physics.

Website: www.admit.ucsb.edu
Location: City outskirts
Total Enrollment: 20,559
Undergraduates: 17,714
Male/Female: 46/54
SAT Ranges: V 510–620
  M 550–660
ACT Range: 23–28
Financial Aid: 88%
Expense: Pub $ $ $ $
Phi Beta Kappa: Yes
Applicants: 34,703
Accepted: 51%
Enrolled: 22%
Grad in 6 Years: 72%
Returning Freshmen: 91%
Academics: ✑ ✑ ✑ ✑
Social: ☎ ☎ ☎ ☎
Q of L: ★ ★ ★ ★
Admissions: (805) 893-2881
Email Address:
  appinfo@sa.ucsb.edu

Strongest Programs:
Marine Biology
Physics
Engineering
Chemistry
Geology
Religious Studies
Accounting
Environmental Studies

UCSB's general education program requires all students to fulfill four subject areas: writing, non-Western cultures, quantitative relationships, and ethnicity. Other required courses include English reading and composition, foreign languages, social sciences, and art. For those who crave time away, Santa Barbara is the headquarters of the UC system's Education Abroad program, which sends students to any of one hundred host universities worldwide. In order to graduate, all students must take courses in English Composition and American History and Institutions, must fulfill a unit requirement, and must also meet the requirements of their individual majors. In addition, students must be registered at UCSB for a minimum of three regular quarters.

UCSB students are traditionally public-spirited; the fraternities and sororities, which attract 8 percent of men and 10 percent of women, are known for their philanthropy. The students, 94 percent of whom are California residents, are laidback. "Everyone says 'hi' to other students, we ride bikes around our campus and people are generally really friendly," one senior says. "Our students differ from students at other UC's because we are probably the most relaxed UC campus." Minorities make up 39 percent of the student body, with Asian-Americans at 16 percent and Hispanics at 17 percent. "Being of Latino background, I have never felt like a minority on campus," one student says. "I associate with a lot of Latinos. We are a huge family, all know each other, and create great programs that help other Latinos get hyped up for college." The campus's beach locale inspires many students to be environmentally friendly. Merit scholarships and various athletic scholarships are available for those who qualify.

University housing, which includes both dorms and privately run residence halls, is comfortable, well maintained, and much sought after. "Our on-campus housing is amazing, right in front of the beach" a junior says. "They come fully furnished, with high-speed Internet, cable, telephone lines, and a great atmosphere." Unfortunately, there is a waiting list to get into the dorms—even with the addition of the new Manzanita Village Student Housing. Only 20 percent of the students, most of whom are freshmen, snag on-campus housing. The rest find a home in neighboring Isla Vista, which has welcomed its student population—after all, most of its population is UCSB students. As a result, students are very active in the community. "Community service and maintaining our little community of Isla Vista is very important to students," one film studies/Chicano studies major says. "Isla Vista is the best college town." Meals in the dorms are available to residents and nonresidents alike, and are, according to most students, more than simply edible. "When one thinks of cafeteria food they think of nasty food, but not at UCSB's dining commons," one student says. While all students say they feel extremely safe on campus, one frequently used motto is "four years, four bikes," because of the frequency of bicycle thefts.

"Isla Vista is the best college town."

Because Isla Vista is predominantly made up of students, it's become what some students consider Party Central. But don't call UCSB a party school—students bristle at what they say is a misnomer. "It's just because we have so many students living in such a small area," one senior says. Alcohol isn't allowed on campus, but many students say the rule is easy to get around. The local bars are off-limits to those under twenty-one, but when the long-awaited birthday arrives, students celebrate with a quaint little ritual known as the State Street Crawl, imbibing at all the numerous establishments up and down the "main drag" of Santa Barbara. Movies and concerts are also available, and the mountains, Los Padres National Forest, and L.A. are all an easy drive away. The annual Extravaganza is an all-day, free concert, and students are known to go wild on Halloween and dress up for the entire weekend.

Although the Greeks are strong and growing, there's an ample selection of other organizations from which to choose. A never-ending rotation of intramurals is available on and off the beach. The most successful varsity teams include water polo, baseball, volleyball, swimming, and basketball. All of UCSB's varsity teams compete in the NCAA's Division I. Ultimate Frisbee is also quite popular, as well as nationally competitive. And students brag their football team has been undefeated since 1992. Of course, that was the last year UCSB *had* a football team.

UCSB students love to work and play. They rave about their professors and the academic challenges they face. But they also know a good thing when they see it: not everyone gets to spend four years on the beach. "No matter what college you go to, you find people who you relate with," one student says. "At UCSB you find the social, happy, outgoing crowd. I love it here."

Overlaps

UC–San Diego, UCLA, UC–Irvine, UC–Davis, UC–Berkeley

If You Apply To ➤

Santa Barbara: Regular admissions: May 1. Financial aid: Mar. 2. Does not guarantee to meet demonstrated need. Campus interviews: required for dramatic arts and dance, evaluative. No alumni interviews. SATs or ACTs: required. SAT IIs: required (writing). Common application not accepted; College of Creative Studies requires additional application. Essay question: personal statement.

UC–Santa Cruz

1156 High Street, Santa Cruz, CA 95064

With its flower-child beginnings, UC–Santa Cruz has come back toward the mainstream. The distinctive flavor is still there, but the students are a lot more conventional than in its earlier incarnation. Santa Cruz's relatively small size and residential college system give it a homey feel.

UC–Santa Cruz, still a baby in the UC system, grew up during the radical '60s when it reigned as the ultimate alternative school. The founding vision of an integrated learning environment remains to this day, and every undergraduate affiliates with one of the residential colleges. Overcrowding has become a problem, especially in terms of housing and the school's innovative Narrative Evaluation System. Still, progressive thought continues to flourish, as does an excellent academics program devoted to undergraduate education. Students still come to UCSC to do their own thing.

The campus, among the most beautiful in the nation, is set on a two-thousand-acre expanse of meadowland and redwood forest overlooking Monterey Bay. Bike paths and hiking trails wind throughout the campus and the beach is only a few minutes away. The buildings range from 1860 Cowell Ranch farm structures to the multi–award-winning modern colleges, whose styles range from Mediterranean to Japanese to sleek concrete block. Thanks to a unique building code, nothing can be built taller than two-thirds the height of the nearest redwood tree. Newest additions include a new student union, an interdisciplinary sciences building, and an expanded bookstore.

The surroundings are deceptive. "Courses are very rigorous, in my experience," warns one undergrad. Santa Cruz's academic offerings range as widely as its architecture, and feature both traditional and innovative programs. In an effort to become what one official calls a "near-perfect hybrid" between the large university and the small college, campus life revolves around the residential colleges, each of which includes between 900 and 1,300 students and specializes in a broad academic area.

Whatever one's specialty, the curriculum is demanding. Led by marine sciences and biology, the sciences are Santa Cruz's strongest suit, and frequently give students

Website: www.ucsc.edu
Location: Suburban
Total Enrollment: 14,997
Undergraduates: 13,660
Male/Female: 45/55
SAT Ranges: V 510–630
M 520–640
ACT Range: N/A
Financial Aid: 44%
Expense: Pub $ $ $
Phi Beta Kappa: Yes
Applicants: 21,525
Accepted: 80%
Enrolled: 19%
Grad in 6 Years: 64%
Returning Freshmen: 86%
Academics: ✍ ✍ ✍ ✍
Social: ☎ ☎ ☎
Q of L: ★ ★ ★ ★ ★
Admissions: (831) 459-4008
Email Address:
admissions@cats.ucsc.edu

the opportunity to coauthor published research with their professors. Science facilities include state-of-the-art laboratories; the Institute of Marine Sciences, which boasts one of the largest groups of experts on marine mammals in the nation; and the nearby Lick Observatory for budding stargazers. Santa Cruz boasts the top linguistics division in the country, and the psychology department is also praised. In the past, computer engineering wasn't up to par, but that has changed with the addition of the Jack Baskin School of Engineering, which was developed to accommodate the growing needs of engineering students. UCSC has recently added majors in astrophysics, bioinformatics, and plant sciences.

While the majority of students now pursue traditional majors, the possibility is still there for eclectically minded students to pursue just about anything they can get a faculty member to OK. One of UCSC's most unique features is that professors provide written evaluations for each student in their class and also provide letter grades to every undergraduate student who requests them. UCSC boasts more than the average number of interdisciplinary programs, including environmental, community, and women's studies; creative writing; and modern society and social thought. Field and independent study are encouraged. Overall, the emphasis is on the liberal arts, and students will find few programs with a vocational emphasis.

"The NES and the setting may appear casual, but there is a strong pressure for individual achievement."

The school has devised a few ingenious ways to accommodate its students, including converting lounges into dorm rooms and offering students the option of living in an on-campus trailer park.

To meet general education requirements, students must complete courses in quantitative methods, ethnic/Third World studies, arts, writing, humanities and arts, natural sciences, social sciences, and three topical courses. In addition, American History and Institutions and English Composition are required, as is a senior thesis or comprehensive exam. The main library, McHenry, houses more than a million books and thirteen thousand periodicals, and students have access to books at other UC campuses through an online catalog system and interlibrary loans. The science library houses an additional three hundred thousand volumes.

Though the curriculum is demanding and the quarter system keeps the academic pace fast, the atmosphere is emphatically noncompetitive. Such competition as there is tends to be internalized. "The NES and the setting may appear casual, but there is a strong pressure for individual achievement," says one history major. The majority of the students eventually go on to graduate study. All UC campuses insist on faculty research, but most Santa Cruz professors are there to teach. "I've been very impressed with how accessible professors are," says a sophomore. "Whether it's via email or regular office hours, I feel very comfortable approaching and talking to all of my professors."

Santa Cruz remains the most liberal of the UC campuses, and, according to one student, "still a school with a social conscience."

Santa Cruz remains the most liberal of the UC campuses, and, according to one student, "still a school with a social conscience." "Before I came here I was told that UCSC was a 'hippie-dippie' college," says one student, "but this is not true at all." Ninety-four percent of the students are Californians, though Santa Cruz has managed to lure a few Easterners. Nearly one-third of the students are members of minority groups, with Asian-Americans accounting for 16 percent of the students, Hispanics 13 percent, and African-Americans 2 percent. "Racial, ethnic, and cultural diversity is celebrated and strongly encouraged by the majority of the students here," reports a politics major. Santa Cruz offers more than four hundred merit scholarships ranging from $1,759 to $2,781, but there are no athletic scholarships.

Forty-two percent of the student population live in the residential colleges. Overcrowding is a problem but new housing is on the way. Until then, the school has devised a few ingenious ways to accommodate its students, including converting lounges into dorm rooms and offering students the option of living in an on-campus trailer park. "I lived in the trailer park for two years and loved it," says a language studies major. "It was a tight-knit community complete with potluck dinners." Some dorms have their own dining halls with reasonably good food; students may also opt to join a food co-op. Freshmen and transfer students are guaranteed on-campus housing and are free to choose among the colleges. Upperclassmen can take their chances in the lottery or move off campus, though higher enrollment means that nearby apartments are becoming increasingly scarce and expensive in this "tourist" town.

The beach and resort town of Santa Cruz, with its boardwalk and amusement park, are only ten minutes away from campus by bike. Those looking for city lights will have no trouble getting to San Jose (thirty-five miles away) or San Francisco (seventy-five miles) by public transportation. If you have a car, places like Carmel, Big Sur, the Napa Valley, and the Sierras are easily accessible.

There are a dozen fraternities and sororities, as well as countless established student groups, to provide an active social life. One senior boasts, "With eight colleges, you have eight times as many opportunities for concerts, dances, films, speakers, and so on." Although Santa Cruz fields only a few varsity teams, students love the school mascot, Sammy the banana slug. The men's tennis team is nationally ranked and won the NCAA Division III championship last year, as did the men's swimming team. Participation in intramurals ("Friendship through Competition" is the motto) is widespread, with rugby in particular growing in popularity. The student recreation department sponsors everything from white-water rafting to cooking classes.

> "Before I came here I was told that UCSC was a 'hippie-dippie' college, but this is not true at all."

Santa Cruz is a progressive school where the main priority is the education of undergraduates. Many students are concerned that UCSC is growing too fast, and with powerful lures such as a gorgeous campus and innovative academic programs, that's likely to continue. Still, as the student population grows, so does the college itself. As long as UCSC retains its belief in "to each his or her own," it will always remain uniquely Santa Cruz.

Although Santa Cruz fields only a few varsity teams, students love the school mascot, Sammy the banana slug.

Overlaps

**UC–Santa Barbara,
UC–San Diego,
UC–Davis, UCLA,
UC–Berkeley**

If You Apply To ➢

Santa Cruz: Regular admissions: Nov. 30. Financial aid: Mar. 2. Housing: May 1. Does not guarantee to meet demonstrated need. No campus or alumni interviews. SATs or ACTs: required. SAT IIs: required (writing, math I or II, and one other). Essay question: personal statement.

California Institute of Technology

Mail Code 328-87, 1200 East California Boulevard, Pasadena, CA 91125

If you're a distractedly brilliant techie with a 1600 on the SAT, maybe you'll have a fighting chance of getting into Caltech. With fewer than one thousand undergraduates, Caltech is a quarter the size of MIT but just as muscular academically. From day one, freshmen have access to the best Caltech has to offer.

If you've got a perfect SAT score, a burning desire to study math, science, or engineering, and some independent research or published papers already under your belt, maybe you'll have a fighting chance of getting into Caltech. The school counts twenty-seven Nobel Prize winners among its faculty and alumni, and with

Website: www.caltech.edu
Location: Suburban
Total Enrollment: 2,120

(Continued)

Undergraduates: 939

Male/Female: 67/33

SAT Ranges: V 710–780
    M 760–800

Financial Aid: 57%

Expense: Pr $ $ $

Phi Beta Kappa: No

Applicants: 2,615

Accepted: 21%

Enrolled: 45%

Grad in 6 Years: 85%

Returning Freshmen: 95%

Academics: ✍ ✍ ✍ ✍ ✍

Social: ☎

Q of L: ★ ★ ★

Admissions: (626) 395-6341

Email Address:
    ugadmissions@caltech.edu

Strongest Programs:
Engineering
Physics
Applied Sciences

Expectations are high; "Techers" are fond of saying that "the admissions office doesn't make mistakes," and it's fairly common to take time off to deal with stress and avoid burnout.

administrators' permission—which is easy to obtain—students may tap into that brilliance by taking as many classes as they can cram in each semester. Expectations are high; "Techers" are fond of saying that "the admissions office doesn't make mistakes," and it's fairly common to take time off to deal with stress and avoid burnout. "The atmosphere promotes a love of science, learning, and discovery that is truly exhilarating," says a biology major. "There are absolutely no limits as to how much I can push myself academically," agrees a computer science major.

Caltech's 124-acre campus is located in Pasadena, "A wealthy suburban town about fifteen miles outside Los Angeles," says a senior. "It's not a college town at all." The distance from downtown mean the school is relatively isolated from the glitz, glamour, and good times that many people associate with "La La Land." Outside the classroom, at least, tranquility prevails, with olive trees, lily ponds, and

> **"The atmosphere promotes a love of science, learning, and discovery that is truly exhilarating."**

plenty of flowers breaking up clusters of older Spanish-mission style buildings. Leafy courtyards and arcades link these with the more modern, "block institutional" structures. The new Broad Center for the Biological Sciences offers 120,000 square feet of lab, classroom, and office space at the northwest corner of campus. It was designed by Pei Cobb Freed & Associates, the firm behind the U.S. Holocaust Memorial Museum in Washington, D.C.

Caltech's mission, one official says, is "to train the creative type of scientist or engineer urgently needed in our educational, governmental, and industrial development." After all, it was here that Albert Einstein abandoned his concept of a static cosmos and endorsed the expanding-universe model. This is also where physicist Carl Anderson discovered the positron. With these luminaries as their models, students plunge right into the demanding general requirements, which include five terms each of math and physics, three terms of chemistry with lab, one term of biology, two terms of science communication, and courses in the humanities and social sciences to round things out. Students complain about these, "and usually take no more than absolutely required," says a biology major. Still, they can be tough to get into come registration time, says a computer science major, since enrollment is limited "to allow for discussion among a small group." The pass/fail grading system in the freshman year goes a long way toward easing the acclimation period for new arrivals. And the honor system, which mandates that "no one shall take unfair advantage of any other member of the Caltech community," helps discourage competition for grades. Professors give take-home exams, and if violations of the honor code are suspected, "students decide if a violation was indeed made," one student explains.

Caltech made its name in physics, and students say that program remains strong. An economics major also gives high marks to geology, noting that everyone in the major "seems euphoric." Since Caltech is a research institution, "The departments that typically require the most research—as opposed to, say, training for industrial work—are the best," a junior explains, mentioning chemistry, biology, and astronomy as programs that fit the bill. Regardless of major, Caltech students benefit from state-of-the-art facilities, including the Beckman Institute, a center for fundamental research in biology and chemistry, and the Keck telescope, the largest optical telescope in the world. The Moore Laboratory has ninety thousand square feet of the latest equipment for engineering and communications majors studying fiber optics and the like. Summer Undergraduate Research Fellowships give three hundred undergraduates the chance to get a head start on their own discoveries, with help from a faculty sponsor. Some 20 percent of these students publish results from their endeavors in scientific journals.

Despite Caltech's reputation for brilliance, students say the quality of teaching is hit or miss. "At times, you get lucky and get amazing professors," says a computer science major. "Other times, you get professors who either don't care about the class they teach, or are so advanced in their field that they are unable to convey 'simple' concepts." A senior goes farther, calling instruction "not so much poor as nonexistent." Here, the student says, professors in the humanities and social sciences really shine, since they actually want to teach, rather than hole up in a lab with gas spectrometers and computer simulations of atomic fission. Another student calls courses "incredibly rigorous," noting that "if you don't know your stuff, you won't make it." Perhaps that's why collaboration between students is encouraged and embraced. While teaching assistants do lead some recitation sections affiliated with large lectures, it's not uncommon for professors to lead them, too—even for freshmen, says a sophomore. "If you don't like your TA, switching sections is a breeze," the student says.

Twenty-nine percent of Techers come from California, and the same fraction are Asian-American; other minorities are less well-represented, with Hispanics making up 7 percent of the student body and African-Americans 1 percent. Students are "brilliant, young, sheltered, driven, interesting, and socially awkward," says a biology major. "The girls aren't catty or ditzy,

"The departments that typically require the most research—as opposed to, say, training for industrial work—are the best."

the guys aren't macho or aggressive. There's room for everyone." Foreign students account for 8 percent of the student body, but even in a year of political strife and war, "social and political issues are not a big deal on campus, period," says a junior. "People live in a 'Tech bubble,' where they care about nothing more than 50 meters from campus," a sophomore agrees. The school awards merit scholarships of $11,000 to $23,000 a year, but "unless you're absolutely at the top of the incoming freshman class—which many think they are, yet most are not even close—you won't get any," a junior says.

Caltech guarantees on-campus or school-affiliated housing for all four years, and 87 percent of students live in the "comfortable and convenient" dorms. While there are no fraternities or sororities, the seven co-ed on-campus houses inspire a loyalty worthy of the Greeks. The four older houses, which have been renovated, offer mostly single rooms, while the three newer dorms have doubles. Freshmen select their house during Rotation Week, after spending an evening of partying at each one, and indicating at week's end the four they like the most. Resident upperclassmen take it from there in a professional-sports-type draft, which places each new student in one of his or her top choices. Business-minded types, for example, may choose Avery House, which focuses on entrepreneurship. Each dorm has a dining hall, and those who live on campus must buy a meal plan, which a junior calls "quite expensive for the quality of food." A vegetarian calls the chow "awful," and says that "by the end of the week, I am often wondering if we're being served the same spinach for five days in a row."

The houses are the emotional center of Caltech life, and the scene of innumerable practical jokes. On Ditch Day, seniors barricade their dorm rooms using everything from steel bars to electronic codes, leave clues as to how to overcome the obstacles, and disappear from campus. Underclassmen spend the day figuring out how to break in, using "cleverness, brute force, and finesse," to claim a reward inside, which can range from the edible to...well, anything is possible. Perhaps the best student prank occurred during the 1984 Rose Bowl game, when cross-town rival UCLA played Illinois. A group of Caltech whiz kids spent months devising a radio-control device that would allow them to take control of the scoreboard in the second half, to gain national exposure for Caltech by flashing pictures of their school's mascot, the beaver, and a new version of the score that had Caltech leading MIT by a mile.

The new Broad Center for the Biological Sciences offers 120,000 square feet of lab, classroom, and office space at the northwest corner of campus. It was designed by Pei Cobb Freed & Associates.

*The annual design competition that's the culmination of Mechanical Engineering 72 helped inspire the TV shows **Battle Bots** and **Robot Wars**.*

While drinking might seem a reasonable escape from the pressure of all that work, Caltech requires any organization hosting a party to hire a professional bartender—"and they card," says a senior. "Ask any local bartender for a Caltech Cocktail and you will get three ounces of straight water," quips a sophomore. Social life at Caltech "is horrible," agrees a junior. "There are occasional parties, but the administration does not allow students from other colleges to attend, unless accompanied by a Caltech student." So students head off-campus—to Old Pasadena, nearby schools like USC, Occidental, and the Claremont colleges, or to downtown L.A., now easily reachable on the Metro's gold line. Disneyland and Hollywood are always an option, and road trips to the beach, mountains, or desert—or south of the border, to Tijuana—are options for those with cars. "From yoga studios to death metal concerts, L.A. has it all," one student says. But some Caltech students still prefer to make their own fun. The annual Pumpkin Drop (on Halloween, of course) involves immersing a gourd in liquid nitrogen, and then dropping it from the library roof, so that it shatters into a zillion frozen shards. During finals week, stereos blast "The Ride of the Valkyries" at seven o'clock each morning, just the thing to get you going after that all-nighter.

Caltech fields eighteen Division III teams, and the most popular include men's soccer, men's and women's track and field, and men's cross-country. The school also offers more unusual sports such as water polo and fencing. Perh'aps more popular than varsity competition, though, are the intramural matches between the houses, in nine sports every year. Also popular is the annual design competition that's the culmination of Mechanical Engineering 72; it helped inspire the TV shows *Battle Bots* and *Robot Wars*.

Caltech students may not be happy in the traditional sense, thanks to the school's tremendous workload and lackluster social life. But students say they appreciate the freedom to think and explore—and the trust administrators place in them because of the honor code. "The unique student body, how available professors are (I call almost all of them by their first names) and how much we learn make Caltech a special place," says a sophomore. So long as your interests tend toward the technical, this high-powered and demanding school may be a good fit.

Overlaps

MIT, Stanford, Harvard, UC–Berkeley, UCLA

If You Apply To ➤

Caltech: Early action: Nov. 1. Regular admissions: Jan 1. Guarantees to meet demonstrated need. No campus or alumni interviews. SATs: required. SAT IIs: required (writing, math, and either physics, biology, or chemistry). Accepts electronic applications. Looks for math/science aptitude as well as research orientation or unusual academic potential. Essay question: areas of interest; personal statement.

Calvin College

3201 Burton, Grand Rapids, MI 49546

An evangelical Christian institution that ranks high on the private-college bargain list. More than half the students are members of the Christian Reformed Church. Archrival of Michigan neighbor Hope and Illinois cousin Wheaton. Best-known in the humanities.

Website: www.calvin.edu
Location: Suburban

Christian values are as central to the Calvin College experience as academics. Students explain their religious beliefs on the admissions application, and a spiritual mentorship program offers to link students with "wise Christian friends" such as professors and staff. Religion also permeates the classroom environment. Along with Wheaton College in Illinois, Calvin is regarded as one of the country's top two evangelical colleges. "Calvin is all about community, in word and deed," says a sophomore.

The educational wing of the Christian Reformed Church in North America, Calvin was founded in 1876. After outgrowing its first home, the college bought a large tract of land on the city's edge and built the present campus of more than 370 beautifully landscaped acres that encompass three ponds, playing fields, and a nature preserve. The campus includes an 80-acre woodland and wetland ecosystem preserve used for classwork, research, and recreation. Campus facilities are less than 35 years old and were designed by a student of famed architect Frank Lloyd Wright. The new east campus, dedicated in fall 2002, includes the Prince Conference Center, DeVos Communications Center, and Gainey Athletic Facility. The college is in suburban Grand Rapids, and "businesses and communities do a good job of catering to students," says a senior.

> "As a freshman, I had respected authors, philosophers, and theologians as my teachers."

Calvin students describe the overall academic environment as challenging but supportive. "The coursework is demanding and students are held to a high standard," says one nursing student. "While Calvin is somewhat laidback in its acceptance policy, once you're there, you work your tail off!" Every subject, the school believes, can be approached from a Christian perspective, integrating faith and learning. For instance, first-year students take courses such as Developing a Christian Mind. The Communication Arts and Sciences department is highly respected for its reformed Christian perspective on the mass media and popular culture.

A new core curriculum, called Engaging God's World, mandates Core Gateway courses, Core Capstone courses, Core Studies courses such as Physical World and Biblical Foundation, and Core Skills courses. Strong high school preparation and advanced-placement tests can help reduce these requirements. Minors in Asian studies, medieval studies, and writing are new, along with a major in environmental geology. A criminal justice major was recently dropped.

Traditionally, the school's strongest programs have been English and history, and the departments of math and the natural sciences are outstanding. Calvin graduates have few problems getting accepted to graduate schools of law, medicine, or business. Students also recommend the education, social work, and nursing programs, as well as the engineering and communication arts departments, but cite the art department, housed in a basement, as weak. Students in the general business program can opt for a wide range of specializations, including marketing, human resources management, operations management, finance, and economics. Internships and small-business consulting opportunities are also integral parts of a student's program—Calvin is a member of the Christian College Consortium*—and there's a five-year co-op plan. The bachelor's degree in accounting has resulted in students passing the CPA exam at rates of 15–20 percent above the national average. Education is the most popular major, followed by business and engineering.

Class size is small—more than half have fewer than twenty-five students—and faculty members, all of whom must be committed to Christian teachings, are especially helpful. "As a freshman, I had respected authors, philosophers, and theologians as my teachers," says a sophomore. "Not only do my professors demonstrate excellent scholarship, but they are also superb instructors." There are no teaching assistants, and professors are expected to reserve about ten hours per week for advising outside of class. Most devote more time than that to their students. "The profs are very approachable and accessible. They want you to do well," a junior says. Students use the interim month of January to pursue a variety of creative, low-pressure

(Continued)

Total Enrollment: 4,324
Undergraduates: 4,286
Male/Female: 44/56
SAT Ranges: V 520–640
  M 530–660
ACT Range: 22–28
Financial Aid: 63%
Expense: Pr $
Phi Beta Kappa: No
Applicants: 1,862
Accepted: 98%
Enrolled: 56%
Grad in 6 Years: 73%
Returning Freshmen: 87%
Academics: ✍ ✍ ✍
Social: ☎ ☎ ☎
Q of L: ★ ★ ★ ★
Admissions: (616) 526-6106
Email Address:
  admissions@calvin.edu

Strongest Programs:
English
History
Math
Natural Sciences
Education

Minors in Asian studies, medieval studies, and writing are new, along with a major in environmental geology.

alternatives on- or off-campus and Calvin profs teach more than 25 off-campus courses. For those who opt for travel, there are opportunities for studying art and theater in England, and languages in Germany, Canada, and the Dominican Republic.

The administration reports that more than half of Calvin students are members of the Christian Reformed Church, though that proportion is dwindling. The school has a strong Dutch heritage but is becoming more diverse. The population is 85 percent white, 1 percent African-American, 1 percent Hispanic, and 2 percent Asian-American. "There are a lot of different people at Calvin, but everyone seems to be real with who they are and what they believe," says a student. Fifty-four percent are students are from Michigan and 8 percent are foreign-born. The Entrada Scholars program brings high school students from ethnic minorities to campus for a residential summer program. The school offers more than 2,500 merit scholarships worth $400 to $12,000 each, and a tuition gift-certificate program that allows families to prepay tuition, but there are no athletic awards.

Freshmen and sophomores under twenty-one who do not live at home with their parents must live on campus, and dorms are home to 58 percent of students. "The dorms are my favorite thing about Calvin," says a senior. "It is a 'suite' setup, no pun intended." Each residence hall and two apartment buildings have computer rooms in their basements. The "MOSAIC Community" lets students live in a residence hall designed to be multicultural. Calvin's social life includes on-campus concerts and Thursday open-mike nights at Cave Cafe. "There are tons of social events both on- and off-campus. Students are only bored if they choose to be," a senior says. There is no Greek scene, and many of the social activities revolve around the housing units. Calvin maintains an officially dry campus, but a junior says "there is a definite party scene to plug yourself into, but there are a lot of students who are not into that." Road trips include the beaches of Lake Michigan (a one-hour drive) or Chicago (three hours distant). A popular annual event is Chaos Day, when each dorm (both the male and female wings) competes in athletic games. The huge Airband lip-sync competition in February is also a favorite activity, as are athletic contests versus Hope College. "Calvin's basketball rivalry with Hope College is the biggest in Division III sports...very intense!" says a Calvin senior. The Festival of Faith and Writing has drawn authors such as Maya Angelou.

"There are tons of social events both on- and off-campus. Students are only bored if they choose to be."

While the Knights don't field a football squad, students love almost all other sports, with men's soccer and basketball and women's basketball and volleyball yielding the most participation. The men's basketball team and cross-country team each took the national championship in the NCAA Division III in 2000. Calvinites can also come face to face with each other in intramural competition.

Calvin's sense of community and the opportunity to serve meshes well with the strong Christian faith of most students. They come here looking for an environment that would combine faith-based learning with academic rigor, and they find it. "I feel connected with professors and students, and I love being able to learn with, worship with, and have healthy debates with people who want to do these things," a sophomore says.

Overlaps

Hope, Grand Valley State, Michigan State, University of Michigan, Wheaton (IL)

If You Apply To ➤

Calvin: Rolling admissions. Financial aid: Feb. 15. Housing: Jun. 1. Regular admissions: Aug. 15. Campus interviews: optional, informational. No alumni interviews. SATs or ACTs: required. ACTs preferred. SAT IIs: optional. Accepts Common Application and electronic applications. Essay question: interest in Calvin, academic experiences, religious beliefs, impact of involvement in activities.

Carleton College

100 South College Street, Northfield, MN 55057

Less selective than Amherst, Williams, and Swarthmore because of its chilly Minnesota location. Yet Carleton retains its position as the premier liberal arts college in the upper-Midwest. Predominately liberal, but not to the extremes of its more antiestablishment cousins.

Minnesota is many things: the land of ten thousand lakes, home to the massive Mall of America, birthplace of lore from Hiawatha to Paul Bunyan, and proud parent of the Mississippi River. Beyond all that history-book stuff, tucked into a small town in the southeastern corner of the state, is Carleton College, arguably the best liberal arts school in the expansive Midwest. Classes are tiny, professors are enthusiastic, and students are itching to explore academia and the world beyond their doorstep. "I love this place!" says a freshman.

Surrounded by rolling farmland, Carleton's 955-acre campus is in the small town of Northfield, whose one-time status as the center of the Holstein cattle industry brought it the motto "The City of Cows, Colleges, and Contentment." Lakes, woods, and streams abound, and you can traverse them on twelve miles of hiking and cross-country skiing trails. The city boasts of fragrant lilacs in spring, rich summer greens, red maples in the fall, and glistening blanket of white in winter. There's even an eight-hundred-acre arboretum, put to good use by everyone from jogging jocks to bird-watching nature lovers. When it's –8 degrees, the new indoor recreation center provides a rock-climbing wall, gym, putting green, sports courts, track, and dance studio. Carleton's architectural style is somewhat eclectic— everything from Victorian to contemporary, but mostly redbrick.

Carleton's top-notch academic programs are no less varied: the sciences—biology, physics, astronomy, chemistry, geology, and computer science—are among the best anywhere, and scores of Carleton graduates go on to earn Ph.D.s in these areas. Of all the liberal arts schools in the country, Carleton's undergrads were recently awarded the highest number of National Science Foundation fellowships for graduate studies. English, history, economics, and biology get high marks, too. Engineers can opt for a 3–2 program with Columbia University or Washington University in St. Louis, and for geologists seeking fieldwork—and maybe wanting to thaw out after a long Minnesota winter—Carleton sponsors a program in Death Valley. Closer to home at the "arb," as the arboretum is affectionately known, environmental studies majors have their own wilderness field station, which includes a prairie-restoration site. At the opposite end of the academic spectrum, the arts also flourish. Music and studio art majors routinely get into top graduate programs, even though Carleton lacks a conservatory and doesn't emphasize performance, a music major says.

Distribution requirements ensure that a Carleton education exposes students not only to rigor and depth in their chosen field, but also to "a wide range of subjects and methods of studying them," administrators say. All students must show proficiency in English composition and a foreign language while fulfilling requirements in four broad areas: arts and literature; history, philosophy, and religion; social sciences; and math and natural sciences. There's also a Recognition of Affirmation and Difference requirement, under which students must take at least one course dealing with a non-Western culture, and a senior comprehensive project is required in every major field. Carleton offers interdisciplinary programs in Asian, Jewish, urban, African and African-American, and women's studies. A concentra-

Website: www.carleton.edu
Location: Small city
Total Enrollment: 1,932
Undergraduates: 1,932
Male/Female: 48/52
SAT Ranges: V 640–740
   M 640–720
ACT Range: 27–31
Financial Aid: 56%
Expense: Pr $ $ $ $
Phi Beta Kappa: Yes
Applicants: 4,170
Accepted: 35%
Enrolled: 35%
Grad in 6 Years: 86%
Returning Freshmen: 96%
Academics: ✍ ✍ ✍ ✍ ✍
Social: ☎ ☎ ☎
Q of L: ★ ★ ★
Admissions: (507) 646-4190
Email Address:
  admissions@acs.carleton
  .edu

Strongest Programs:
Mathematics
Computer Science
Chemistry
Physics
English
History
Economics
Psychology

tion in Cross-Cultural Studies brings in foreign students to discuss global issues and dynamics with their American counterparts. Nearly 70 percent of students spend at least one term abroad, and many take advantage of programs available either through numerous organizations, including Carleton and the Associated Colleges of the Midwest.* The school's 799,000-volume library is bright, airy, and—much to the delight of caffeine-stoked night owls—open until 1:00 a.m. Students love the four-year-old center for mathematics and computing, which brought together all campus computing functions for the first time.

With highly motivated students and a heavy workload, Carleton isn't your typical mellow Midwestern liberal arts college. The trimester calendar means finals may be just three months apart, and almost everyone feels the pressure. The six-week Christmas vacation is Carleton's way of dealing with the cold winters. "The courses are extremely rigorous," says a student. "Classes take up a lot of time and are quite demanding." Ninety percent of all classes have twenty-five students or fewer, so Carls are expected to participate actively. Carleton's faculty members are very committed to teaching. "Professors are here to teach," says a senior, "and they are dedicated to the task."

"Carleton students cover the range of stereotypical types of students," says a student, "but as I've gotten to know each, I've found intelligence and passion for learning among them all." Seventy-four percent of Carleton's students hail from outside Minnesota, half are from outside the Midwest, and most attended public schools. Both coasts are heavily represented, and more than fifteen foreign countries send at least one student. African-Americans and Hispanics account for 8 percent of the total student body, and Asian-Americans for another 8 percent. But most Carls have a few things in common, such as being intellectually curious, yet laid-back; individualistic, but into building a community feel on campus. Their earthy dress and attitude are very distinguishable from their more traditional crosstown cousins at rival St. Olaf College. The Carleton campus is rather left of center, concerned with issues including the environment, multiculturalism, and affirmative action, gay rights, and sexism. Qualified students receive Carleton-sponsored National Merit and National Achievement scholarships every year, and students call financial-aid packages "definitely adequate."

> **"Carleton students cover the range of stereotypical types of students but as I've gotten to know each, I've found intelligence and passion for learning among them all."**

Campus accommodations range from comfortable old townhouses to modern hotel-like residence halls. "The dorms are nice and kept in very good condition," says a sophomore. Everyone is guaranteed a room for four years, although "it can be difficult to get the exact room you want," a wise senior explains. Best of all are the ten college-owned off-campus "theme" houses, which focus on special interests such as foreign languages, the outdoors, or nuclear-power issues. With the exception of the Farm House, an environmental studies house sitting on the edge of the arb, all the theme houses (including Women's Awareness House) are situated in an attractive residential section of town close to campus. Dorms are co-ed by room, but there are two halls with single-sex floors. Davis is the recommended dorm, although Burton enjoys a "fun" reputation. Everyone who stays on campus must be on a meal plan, and dining-room fare is "getting better," a music major says.

Absent a Greek system, Carleton's social life tends to be relaxed and informal, and often centers around going out with friends. People go to parties on campus, or if they are of drinking age, bar hop around town. "There are very diverse happenings on any given weekend evening," says a senior. There are activities for those who pass on imbibing; a group called Co-op sponsors dances and Wednesday socials every two weeks, free movies, and special events like Comedy Night. Students agree that Carleton makes little more than token efforts to enforce the drinking age. "A few people are problem drinkers, a few never drink, most drink responsibly and socially," which goes for underage students, too. And a history major adds, "there is no pressure to participate in anything you don't want to do."

Northfield itself is a quaint, history-filled town with a population of about seventeen thousand. There are old-style shops and a beautiful old hotel. "It's a great place to feel safe and sound," a senior sighs. "It's steeped in tradition and Minnesota friendliness." Students often frequent the St. Olaf College campus and a night spot known as the Reub'n'Stein. Minneapolis–St. Paul, thirty-five miles to the north, is a popular road-trip destination. Since students aren't allowed to have cars on campus, Carleton charters buses on weekends.

> **"It's a great place to feel safe and sound. It's steeped in tradition and Minnesota friendliness."**

About a third of the students play on varsity teams, but about two-thirds play intramurals. The track, swimming, tennis, basketball, and baseball teams are competitive, as are the championship cross-country ski teams. Popular events include the Winter Carnival, the Spring Concert, and Mai-F'te, a gala celebrated on an island in one of the two lakes on campus. Traditions include the week-long freshman orientation program, where—during opening convocation—students bombard professors with bubbles as the faculty members process. There's also the annual spring softball game that begins at 5:30 a.m. and runs as many innings as there are years in Carleton's existence. The all-campus 10:00 p.m. scream on the eve of final exams keeps fatigued studiers awake. Notorious outlaw Jesse James failed to rob the Northfield Bank lo those many years ago, and Northfield still celebrates with a Wild West bank raid reenactment every year. (The robbery was thwarted by brave townsfolk, and the gang broke up immediately afterward.)

It can be cold in Minnesota, in a face-stinging, bone-chilling kind of way. And the classes are far from easy. But Carleton is a warm campus, and the academics are challenging without being impossible. Carls toe the line between individuality and community, which makes for personal growth and lifelong friendships. "The people you debate with in the dining hall on Friday afternoon are the same people you party with on Friday night," a senior says. It seems Carleton provides all the ingredients for a promising college career.

Overlaps

Macalester, Williams, Brown, Harvard, Middlebury

If You Apply To ➤ | **Carleton:** Early decision: Nov. 15, Jan. 15. Regular admissions and financial aid: Jan. 15. Guarantees to meet demonstrated need. Campus interviews: recommended, informational. Alumni interviews: optional, informational. SATs or ACTs: required. SAT IIs: recommended. Accepts the Common Application and electronic applications. Essay question: turning points in your life; influential people; lunch with anyone; integrating classroom learning into daily life; or your own question.

Carnegie Mellon University

5000 Forbes Avenue, Pittsburgh, PA 15213-3890

CMU is the only premier technical university that also happens to be equally strong in the arts. Applications have more than doubled in the past ten years, so it must be doing something right. One of the few institutions that openly matches better financial-aid awards from competitor schools.

Website: www.cmu.edu

Location: City outskirts

Total Enrollment: 8,514

Undergraduates: 5,106

Male/Female: 64/36

SAT Ranges: V 600–700
   M 680–760

ACT Range: 27–32

Financial Aid: 80%

Expense: Pr $ $ $

Phi Beta Kappa: Yes

Applicants: 14,621

Accepted: 36%

Enrolled: 25%

Grad in 6 Years: 77%

Returning Freshmen: 93%

Academics: ✐ ✐ ✐ ✐

Social: ☎ ☎ ☎

Q of L: ★ ★ ★

Admissions: (412) 268-2082

Email Address:
   undergraduate-
   admissions@andrew.cmu
   .edu

Strongest Programs:
Computer Science
Engineering
Drama
Music
Industrial Management
Business
Architecture

Students at Carnegie Mellon don't have to choose between soaking up the high drama of Shakespeare and experiencing the fast-paced dot-com world. The university is known for both its science offerings and strong drama and music programs. But scholars can't be too focused on their particular course of study—Carnegie Mellon continues to make every effort to offer both its technical and liberal arts students a well-rounded education that requires a lot of hard work, but promises great results.

Carnegie Mellon was formed by the merger of Carnegie Tech and the Mellon Institute, resulting in a self-contained 103-acre campus attractively situated in Pittsburgh's affluent Oakland section. Next door is the city's largest park and its major museum, named after—you guessed it—Andrew Carnegie. Campus buildings range from early-1900s Beaux Arts style to contemporary eyesores. Construction was recently completed on the Purcell Center for the Arts, and work continues on an addition for the School of Computer Science and an addition to the Graduate School for Industrial Administration.

Carnegie Mellon is divided into six undergraduate colleges: Fine Arts, Humanities and Social Sciences, the Carnegie Institute of Technology, the Mellon College of Science, the School of Computer Science, and the School of Industrial Management. Each has its own distinct character and admission requirements, so applicants may want to contact the admissions office to find out about the varying policies. All the colleges, however, share the university's commitment to what it calls a "liberal-professional" education, which makes the liberal arts extremely relevant while stressing courses that develop technical skills and good job prospects.

"Carnegie Mellon is very intense, so lots of time is dedicated to class assignments and group projects."

Humanities and social science types can major in applied history, professional writing, or public policy, for example, instead of traditional disciplinary concentrations. Under the University Choice Program, a select group of students is allowed to design an individualized freshman-year course of study directed toward their particular interest, and can defer the selection of a major until sophomore year. In addition, the Fifth-Year Scholars program provides full tuition for outstanding students who want to remain at CMU for an additional year to pursue a course of study that interests them.

Most departments at Carnegie Mellon are strong, but exceptional ones include chemical and electrical engineering. While some humanities courses are praised, most students agree that CMU is definitely more of a science-oriented school. Each college requires core work from freshmen; in the College of Humanities and Social Science, for example, students are introduced to computers in a required first-year philosophy course, using the machines to work on problems of logic. Two majors—logic and computation in the philosophy department and cognitive science through the psychology department—combine computer-science technology with such fields as artificial intelligence and linguistics. The university created a Department of Modern Languages and a Bachelor of Science and Arts degree program was added recently along with a Science and Humanities Scholars Program.

As one student bluntly puts it, the courses at CMU are "extremely rigorous with many hours expected outside of the classroom. Expect to work hard if you come here." The College of Fine Arts' drama department, the first and still one of the best in the country, concentrates on performance, and its faculty is made up of highly regarded working professionals. While the program embraces the art of performance, freshmen must take English and history, as well as a basic computer course. After that it's drama all day, every day. Students at CMU work hard, no doubt about it. "Carnegie Mellon is very intense, so lots of time is dedicated to class assignments and group projects," a student says. However, nearly all the classes are small, with fewer than thirty students. Most students agree that the Carnegie Institute of Technology is by far the most difficult college. Professors rate high with most students, who praise their availability and willingness to help. "Most professors are very eager to help and make sure that material is understood," says a sophomore psychology major.

Carnegie Mellon's professional focus shows through in its internship program. A number of five-year, dual-degree options exist, including a joint B.S./M.S. or a co-op program in metallurgical engineering and materials science that places students in the metals industry. Other engineers and scientists vie for a spot in the Junior Year in Switzerland Program. Humanities and social sciences students can spend a semester in England, and political science majors can go to Washington. One innovative program allows students to receive a bachelor's degree, teaching certificate, and master's degree within five years. But to counteract the tendency toward a narrow, preprofessional focus, the university-wide core curriculum requires courses such as Fundamentals of the Art of Communication, Fundamentals of Computing, and Foundations of Human Thought and Values. The idea is to give students with diverse interests a shared intellectual background. As the late Herbert Simon, the Nobel Prize–winning economist who helped design the core curriculum, puts it, "We want to provide some common topics of conversation besides sports, the weather, and sex."

Nevertheless, Carnegie Mellon remains one of the most fragmented campuses in the nation. Students divide themselves between actors, dancers, and other artsy types and engineers, scientists, and architects. In any case, students are united in their quest for a good job after graduation. Still, many complain about the fact that students will give up sleep to study, and that this kind of academic orientation can often hinder social life. "Sometimes there just isn't very much social life, but many students prefer it that way," says one student.

Once a very regional institution, drawing mostly Pennsylvania residents, Carnegie Mellon now counts about 70 percent of its students from out of state. Nearly one-third are from minority groups, including 20 percent Asian-American, 3 percent African-American, and 5 percent Hispanic. "We are very diverse and therefore very culturally aware," a biology major says. Censorship of Internet newsgroups, because some provide access to "cyberporn," has garnered national headlines and stirred up student protests. Other students say a big issue is the nearly two-to-one male to female ratio. The university says it remains committed to need-blind admissions, but it provides larger proportions of outright grants in financial-aid packages to "academic superstars." CMU has also stopped guaranteeing to meet the financial need of all accepted students, but now offers an early evaluation of financial-aid eligibility for interested prospective students. The financial aid office encourages students who have received more generous packages from competing schools to let CMU know so they have an opportunity to match or better them.

"Sometimes there just isn't very much social life, but many students prefer it that way."

Housing, which is guaranteed for all four years, offers old and newer buildings, the most popular being university-owned apartments. Upperclassmen get first pick, with freshman assignments coming from a lottery of the remainder. "The dorms are generally very comfortable and well maintained, with ample living space," says one student. The best dorms for freshmen are Donner, Resnik, and Morewood Gardens. Most halls are co-ed, but a few are men-only. Students can remain in campus housing as long as they wish, and nearly 70 percent do so each year. Meal plans are said to be restrictive and expensive.

With all the academic pressure at CMU, it's a good thing there are so many opportunities to unwind, especially with the entire city of Pittsburgh close at hand. The Greek system provides the most visible form of on-campus social life, and 22

Carnegie Mellon remains one of the most fragmented campuses in the nation. Students divide themselves between actors, dancers, and other artsy types and engineers, scientists, and architects.

Once every four years, the College of Fine Arts sponsors the Beaux Arts Ball, an absolutely amazing all-night masquerade party.

*A number of five-year,
dual-degree options exist,
including a joint B.S./M.S.
or a co-op program in
metallurgical engineering
and materials science.*

percent of the students belong. For those who choose not to fraternize, coffee-houses, inexpensive films, dances, and concerts in nearby Oakland, plus downtown Pittsburgh itself (opera, ballet, symphony, concerts, and sporting events just twenty minutes away by bus) provide plenty of alternatives. Once every four years, the College of Fine Arts sponsors the Beaux Arts Ball, an absolutely amazing all-night masquerade party. The administration is desperately trying to curtail underage drinking, so far with only modest success. Some students say the penalties for being caught are harsh, but others maintain that the rules are "vaguely known."

One event that brings everyone together is the Spring Carnival, when the school shuts down for a day and a big top is constructed in a parking lot. Students set up booths with electronic games, and fraternities race in buggies made of lightweight alloys designed by engineering majors. Students put on original "Scotch and Soda" presentations, two of which—*Pippin* and *Godspell*—went on to become Broadway hits. But in a sports-crazed town like Pittsburgh, Carnegie Mellon's Division III varsity teams often have trouble getting attention. "I had to pass out flyers to try to get people to attend the football game Homecoming weekend!" laments a cheerleader. Both the men's and women's soccer teams recently won divisional championships.

CMU appeals to those yearning for the bright lights of Broadway or the glowing computer screens of the scientific and business worlds. And with a broad range of liberal arts and technical courses available and required, there's no doubt students leave CMU with a well-rounded education as well as an impressive diploma. "It's driven, but there's no better place to be interacting with people of so many disciplines who are so focused," says one senior.

Overlaps

MIT, Cornell University, Penn, Stanford, Northwestern

If You Apply To ➤

Carnegie Mellon: Early decision: Nov. 15 (Nov. 1 for fine arts applicants). Regular admissions: Jan. 1. Financial aid: Feb. 15 (priority). Does not guarantee to meet demonstrated need. Campus interviews: recommended, evaluative. Alumni interviews: optional, evaluative. SATs or ACTs: required. SAT IIs: required (varies by college). Essay question: personal statement.

Case Western Reserve University

P.O. Box 128016, Cleveland, OH 44112-8016

The Cleveland Browns always lose to the Pittsburgh Steelers and CWRU is still trying to catch up with Carnegie Mellon. Students may sing its praises, but Cleveland isn't exactly Boston, or even Pittsburgh. On the plus side, students get an outstanding technical education at Case with solid offerings in other areas.

Website: www.cwru.edu
Location: Urban
Total Enrollment: 9,097
Undergraduates: 3,457
Male/Female: 61/39
SAT Ranges: V 590–710
   M 630–730
ACT Range: 26–31
Financial Aid: 51%
Expense: Pr $ $ $

Forget Atari, typewriters, and cassette players—Case Western Reserve University offers students the chance to learn and live on a high-tech, computer-savvy campus. Cutting-edge equipment and strong arts and science programs create a comprehensive, intellectually stimulating environment. Though known for turning out brainy leaders in technology, CWRU is just as strong in the arts. But "that isn't to say we don't have fun here," says one student. "Far from it."

Case Western Reserve is located on the eastern edge of Cleveland at University Circle, an artistic 550-acre area of parks and gardens that is home to more than forty cultural, educational, medical, and research institutions. The buildings represent an eclectic mix of architectural styles, and several are listed on the National Register of Historic Places. The $33 million science education and research center was completed in 2002, and the new Silver Spartan classic diner is now open for late-night study breaks. A new campus center is on the drawing board; it will house space for offices, dining, and retail outlets.

The product of a marriage between Case Institute of Technology and Western Reserve University in 1967, the university is composed of the College of Arts and Sciences and the Case School of Engineering. Students take one of four core curricula to fulfill their general education requirements, depending on their major. Only after students declare their majors are they formally enrolled in one of the colleges. A newer, growing program called SAGES (Seminar Approach to General Education and Scholarship) allows two hundred freshmen to learn through seminars, community service, internships, research projects, and some traditional classes, with an emphasis on communication, information technology, diversity, and ethics.

Among the strongest academic programs in the College of Arts and Sciences are anthropology, art history (conducted with the adjoining Cleveland Museum of Art), management, music (linked with the nearby Cleveland Institute of Music), and psychology. The Case School of Engineering boasts one of the world's first departments in biomedical engineering. Other leading programs include mechanical and aerospace engineering, macromolecular science, mathematics, and physics. As testimony to CWRU's outstanding programs in polymer science and in materials science and engineering, the university received a grant from NASA for the study of materials in space. There are new minors in Judaic studies and Italian, as well as a major in evolutionary biology. Students cite English, philosophy, and the languages as being weak and "often overshadowed by engineering and science." The classic program might only have three full-time professors, but two of them received research fellowships from Harvard. The College Scholars Program takes twenty outstanding undergraduates in the arts, humanities, and sciences or engineering who want to take what they learned in the classroom into the real world. Some of the past emphases have been on medical ethics, Africa, dreams and fantasy, and urban design.

"The courses are very rigorous and challenge students regardless of background."

Classes tend to be smaller and professors more available at the College of Arts and Sciences than at the Case School of Engineering. The administration explains that engineering students find their professors more accessible as they move out of the introductory courses and focus on a specialty. The typical advanced class is limited to twenty students, and students often participate in research.

While it would seem that mixing engineering types with liberal arts majors would be chemically and intellectually impossible, all insist that the groups mix, especially when students load up with double (and even triple) majors. "The students here are eager to learn, excited about class, and take their time here very seriously," one student says. "The courses are very rigorous and challenge students regardless of background." Some even take six or seven courses in one semester. Academic competition exists, but does not rule the campus. "Case is not cut-throat, but there is a definite sense of curiosity and awareness of how your classmates are doing," notes a sophomore.

Most CWRU students have their eyes on the prize that comes after graduation, which makes preprofessional majors a big hit. The university offers integrated B.A./M.A., B.S./M.S., and B.S.E./M.S. degree programs, and the Senior Year in Absentia program lets enterprising students substitute their final undergrad year for their first year of professional school. The best bet of all may be the Preprofessional Scholars program, in which top freshmen who plan careers in law, medicine, or dentistry are given conditional acceptance into the CWRU professional schools in their fields. Between 65 and 75 percent of students participate in independent research, and a spring Senior Capstone Fair offers cash prizes for solo work.

(Continued)
Phi Beta Kappa: Yes
Applicants: 4,428
Accepted: 78%
Enrolled: 24%
Grad in 6 Years: 76%
Returning Freshmen: 92%
Academics: ✍ ✍ ✍ ✍
Social: ☎ ☎
Q of L: ★ ★ ★
Admissions: (216) 368-4450
Email Address:
admission@cwru.edu

Strongest Programs:
Engineering
Accounting
Anthropology
Biology
Physics
Music
Psychology
Nursing

When CWRU students pledge their undying love and devotion, it can as easily be to their computers as to a hottie of the opposite sex.

Sixty-six percent of the freshmen come from the top tenth of their high school class, and 40 percent come from outside Ohio. Asian-Americans make up 14 percent of the student body, African-Americans make up 5 percent, and Hispanics make up 2 percent. The school stresses respect for diversity, and has developed a university-

"Students here are bright, engaging, and conscientious."

wide program called Share the Vision, designed to foster respect for different values, ideas, opinions, and ethnic, cultural, and racial differences. Although CWRU students are highly motivated toward their careers, it doesn't prevent them from donating their time to a worthy cause or two. Habitat for Humanity and activities organized through Alpha Phi Omega are popular options. Case Western Reserve offers students a wide variety of possibilities for meeting costs. The university distributes more than four hundred merit scholarships per year, ranging from $500 to full tuition. No athletic scholarships are offered.

All freshmen are now housed together on the campus's North side. Students seem generally satisfied with the housing situation at CWRU (78 percent live on campus), but some complain that dorms are old and rooms are small. But that will change as Case begins building new residences. Upperclassmen seeking more sophisticated living quarters enter a room draw for better choices. Housing is coed, save for several off-campus men's fraternity houses. Apartments are available, but expensive and often a long trek from campus, and financial aid awards are trimmed if students move off-campus. Most students living on-campus take their meals in one of three cafeterias, which do not exactly draw gastronomic raves. "The vegetarian options make me want to eat meat again," says a Spanish major. When the munchies hit, snacks are available at one of the twelve food operations on campus.

Forget all those things you heard in the past about Cleveland. It has made a smashing comeback and is a "cultural cornucopia" of art galleries, theaters, restaurants, bars and clubs, and many areas for shopping, says a senior. "There's Little Italy for great food; Coventry for vegetarians, milkshakes, and a bohemian atmosphere; Cedar-Fairmount for pool, bagels, and cheap Middle-Eastern cuisine; and the downtown/flats area for clubs, bars, concerts, and malls," says a nursing major. Having a car helps, but bus service has lately been beefed up and students can pay $25 a semester for unlimited rides. Cleveland is home to the Rock & Roll Hall of Fame, as well as to the Indians baseball team. On the downside, crime is a potential problem, but a veritable fleet of police officers, security guards, and campus escorts has the campus covered. "Campus security is fantastic," gushes a computer engineering student. The sandy beaches of a rejuvenated Lake Erie are just a few minutes away, and a university-owned farm is a great picnic place. Quaint Chagrin Falls is about a half-hour away and boasts some sweet restaurants and shops.

When CWRU students pledge their undying love and devotion, it can as easily be to their computers as to a hottie of the opposite sex. Rationalizes one student: "You may have trouble finding a date on most weekends, but if your computer crashes on a Friday night, it will be up and running by Saturday morning." And even though there are nearly twice as many boys as girls, many women say it works like this: "The odds are good, but the goods are odd," says a biology major. The annual sci-fi movie marathon is a virtual rite of passage, while Engineering Week features competitions such as the Mousetrap Car Race (all cars must run on a one-mousetrap engine) and the Egg Drop (a foolproof protective package for the tossed egg is key). The Film Society's weekend movies are popular, as are the frequent events sponsored by the University Program Board. Alcohol policies are relatively strict, and students say they have further worsened social life. "But it's easy to wet your whistle at some of the famous east-side Cleveland dives/bars," says an international studies major. A Peer Helper Network trains student volunteers to be nonjudgmental listeners and sources of referral for students with problems ranging

Engineering Week features competitions such as the Mousetrap Car Race (all cars must run on a one-mousetrap engine) and the Egg Drop (a foolproof protective package for the tossed egg is key).

from alcohol abuse to sexual harassment. About one-third of the men and about 15 percent of women are Greek. "Social life is what you want to make it at CWRU," a senior says.

Sports are welcomed at CWRU, though they don't dominate campus. The track and field, women's softball, basketball, and swimming teams have done well recently, along with male swimmers, tennis players, and wrestlers. Case can also now boast a UAA Women's Basketball Player of the Year and eleven All-Americans in swimming. The twenty-six-mile Hudson Relays, held the last week of the spring semester to commemorate the school's relocation from Hudson to Cleveland, pits teams of runners from the four classes against one another. There's a spiffy racquetball and squash complex and a field house with an Olympic-size pool.

There's nothing like a hearty dose of undergraduate research opportunities, interdisciplinary work, and challenging classes to turn out a great engineer, scientist, or even artist. But there's more to Case than that. "Students here are bright, engaging, and conscientious, and they are every bit the academic all-stars that go to rival institutions," says an economics student. "But they are still down-to-earth, practical, and considerate." Well, we should hope so.

Overlaps

Washington University, Carnegie Mellon, Ohio State, University of Michigan, Cornell

If You Apply To ➤ **CWRU:** Early action: Nov. 15. Regular admissions: Jan. 15. Financial aid: Feb. 15. Does not guarantee to meet demonstrated need. Campus interviews: recommended, informational. Alumni interviews: optional, informational. SATs or ACTs: required. SAT IIs: recommended. Accepts the Common Application and electronic applications. Essay question: writing sample. Audition required for artists and musicians.

The Catholic University of America

Washington, DC 20064

There are other Roman Catholic–affiliated universities, but this is *The* Catholic University. Catholics make up 80 percent of the student body here (versus roughly half at nearby Georgetown). If you can't be in Rome, there is no better place than D.C. to work and play. CUA even has a Metro stop right on campus.

Founded in 1887 under a charter from Pope Leo XIII, The Catholic University of America was the brainchild of United States bishops who wanted to provide an American institution where the curriculum was guided by the tenets of Christian thought. Over time, the university has garnered a reputation as a research-oriented school that also provides a strong undergraduate, preprofessional education and an appreciation for the arts.

Catholic's campus comprises 145 tree-lined acres, an impressive layout for an urban university. Buildings range from ivy-covered brownstone and brick to ultramodern, giving the place a true collegiate feel. Catholic is one of the few colleges in the country that began as a graduate institution, and grad students still outnumber their younger counterparts. Six of its ten schools (arts and sciences, engineering, architecture, nursing, music, and philosophy) now admit undergrads, while two others (social service and religious studies) provide undergraduate programs through arts and sciences.

Students have excellent options in almost any department at CUA. Apart from politics (which all agree sets the tone on campus), the history, English, drama, psychology, and physics departments are very strong. Philosophy and religious studies

Website: www.cua.edu
Location: City outskirts
Total Enrollment: 5,493
Undergraduates: 2,609
Male/Female: 46/54
SAT Ranges: V 540–640
 M 520–630
ACT Range: 22–29
Financial Aid: 58%
Expense: Pr $ $ $
Phi Beta Kappa: Yes
Applicants: 3,117
Accepted: 87%
Enrolled: 20%
Grad in 6 Years: 70%
Returning Freshmen: 84%

are highly regarded and have outstanding faculty members as well. The School of Nursing is one of the best in the nation, and engineering and architecture are also highly regarded. Architecture and physics have outstanding facilities, the latter enjoying a modern vitreous-state lab, a boon for both research and hands-on undergraduate instruction. Also, a high-speed fiber-optic network connects the entire campus to the Internet. For students interested in the arts, CUA's School of Music offers excellent vocal and instrumental training, and there's also a program in musical theater. Students cite communications and business as weaker than others. The library is modest for a school of this size.

Students at CUA need at least forty courses in order to graduate. In the School of Arts and Sciences, approximately twenty-five of these must be from a core curriculum spread across the humanities, social and behavioral sciences, philosophy, environmental studies, religion, math and natural sciences, and languages and literature. English composition also is required. The brightest students can enroll in a twelve-course interdisciplinary honors program that offers sequences in the humanities, philosophy, and social sciences. CUA's library offers approximately 1.49 million volumes.

Standard off-campus opportunities are augmented by internships at the British and Irish parliaments, NASA, the National Institutes of Health, the Pentagon, and the Library of Congress. The School of Architecture and Planning hosts summer classes for seniors and grad students to study in Italy and a host of European and Mediterranean countries. The Rome study abroad program for design students incorporates design studio, field study, history, theory, and the Italian language. Finally, two students are chosen each year to spend a fall semester at the Fondazione Architetto Rancilio (FAAR) in Milan to study themes including architecture, urban studies, and technology. CUA also offers accelerated degree programs in which students can earn bachelor's and master's degrees in five years, or six years for a joint B.A.-J.D. CUA is part of the eleven-university Consortium of Universities of the Washington Metropolitan Area and the Oak Ridge Associated Universities

> "The teachers push us to work hard but at the same time apply the subjects to everyday living."

consortium. The latter is comprised of eighty-seven U.S. colleges and a contractor for the federal Energy Department. The program gives students access to federal research facilities.

Although Catholic University is research-oriented, most classes have fewer than twenty-five students. That means special attention from faculty members. It also means that there's no place to hide. "The teachers push us to work hard but at the same time apply the subjects to everyday living," a history major reports. The faculty is given high marks by students. "The quality of teaching is excellent. Professors are usually very willing to help students," praises a veteran. Clergy are at the helm of certain graduate schools, but the School of Arts and Sciences has a primarily lay faculty, with priests occupying less than 16 percent of the teaching posts. Its chancellor is the archbishop of Washington, and Catholic churches across the country donate a fraction of their annual collections to the university. One downside of being the only Catholic school with a papal charter is that officials in Rome, who do not always warm up to American traditions of academic freedom, keep a sharp eye on the theology department.

Catholicism is clearly the tie that binds the student body. Sunday Masses are so well attended that extra services must be offered in the dorms. Says one administrator, "We like students to leave with Catholic values, but most of them come here with those values in the first place." Eighty percent of the students belong to the faith. Most are from the Northeast, and are primarily white. African-Americans and Hispanics comprise 7 and 4 percent of the student body, respectively. Another 4

A fifteen-minute Metro ride brings students to the center of downtown D.C. and the capitol. Georgetown, bustling with great shopping, bars, restaurants, and art galleries, is only a half-hour away.

percent are Asian-American, and foreign students account for 3 percent. Ninety percent are from out of state, and 54 percent of freshmen rank in the top quarter of their high school class. Politically, students are fairly conservative, and the big issues on campus include abortion and gay/lesbian rights. "Everyone is basically the same at Catholic—white, upper-middle-class Catholics," says one student.

The university maintains a need-blind admissions policy. It does not guarantee to meet the full demonstrated need of all admitted, but 64 percent of aid recipients are offered full demonstrated need. Thirty-one lucky students—one from each archdiocese in the nation—receive a full-tuition merit scholarship. There are 450 additional merit scholarships available ranging from $1,000 to full tuition, along with various types of financial aid. There are no athletic scholarships.

Fifty-eight percent of the students live in the dorms, seven of which are co-ed by floor. The spacious and ultramodern Centennial Village (eight dorms and six hundred beds laid out in suites) is available to all students, many of whom flee CUA's strict visitation (no guests past 2:00 a.m.) and alcohol policies and move into apartments of their own. The best dorms for freshmen are Spellman and Flather (coed), and Conaty (women). Dorm food is fairly tasty, and there's always the Rathskeller (or "Rat") the campus bar and grill where students can get a late-night meal or brunch and dinner on weekends. Emergency phones, shuttle buses, and escort services are provided as part of campus security, and students agree that they always feel safe on campus as long as they are careful.

> "We like students to leave with Catholic values, but most of them come here with those values in the first place."

When students want to explore the city, they need only walk to the campus Metro stop and then enjoy the ride. Capitol Hill is fifteen minutes away; the stylish Georgetown area, with its chic restaurants and nightspots, is only a half-hour away.

CUA students do indulge in some serious partying. Some of their favorite locales include the Irish Times, Colonel Brook Tavern, the Tune Inn, and Kitty's. It's no wonder most students agree that the social scene is "off-campus at various bars, clubs, and coffeehouses in D.C." Only 1 percent of the men and women join the Greek system. No one under twenty-one can drink on campus, and most students agree that this policy is effective in curbing underage drinking. Also, alcohol "abuse" has been added as an offense in addition to use, possession, and distribution. For those eager to repent the weekend's excesses, there are student ministry retreats. Annual festivals on the campus calendar include a week-long Homecoming celebration, Beaux Arts Ball, Christmas Holly Hop (held in New York City), and Spring Fling. A time-honored winter tradition is sledding down Flather Hill on cafeteria trays.

Sports on campus means varsity and intramural competition. CUA's athletic teams compete in Division III, and the men's basketball team won the 2001 championship. Other solid men's teams include baseball, swimming, and lacrosse. Volleyball, field hockey, softball, and swimming are the strongest women's teams. Intramural and varsity athletes alike enjoy the beautiful $10 million sports complex. Many students use their strength for community service, including the Christian-based Habitat for Humanity, in which they build houses for needy families.

When discussions first raised the idea of a Catholic university, the man who would become the university's first rector, Bishop John Joseph Keane, argued for an institution that would "exercise a dominant influence in the world's future" with a superior intellectual foundation. Now, more than one hundred years later, CUA offers students a wealth of preprofessional courses spanning the arts and sciences. The founders' quest for "a higher synthesis of knowledge" is constantly being realized at CUA, a unique university and a capital destination.

Design students can study in Rome for one semester accompanied by a design studio critic from the School of Architecture and Planning. The program focuses on history, theory, design, and the Italian language.

Overlaps

American, Villanova, Loyola (MD), Boston College, Georgetown

If You Apply To ➤

Catholic: Early action: Nov. 15. Regular admissions: Feb. 15. Financial aid: Feb. 1. Housing: June 1. Does not guarantee to meet demonstrated need. SATs or ACTs: required. SAT IIs: required (writing and foreign language). Accepts the Common Application and electronic applications. Essay question: local, national, international issue of concern; historical figure to meet. Music applicants must audition.

Centre College

600 West Walnut, Danville, KY 40422

Centre is college the way it used to be—gentleman scholars, football games, and fraternity pranks (preferably done in the nude). There is also the unparalleled closeness between students and faculty that comes with a student body of 1,055. Compare to Sewanee, DePauw, and Kenyon.

Website: www.centre.edu
Location: Small town
Total Enrollment: 1,055
Undergraduates: 1,055
Male/Female: 47/53
SAT Ranges: V 590–670
  M 580–660
ACT Range: 25–29
Financial Aid: 66%
Expense: Pr $ $
Phi Beta Kappa: Yes
Applicants: 1,354
Accepted: 78%
Enrolled: 28%
Grad in 6 Years: 75%
Returning Freshmen: 85%
Academics: ✎ ✎ ✎ ½
Social: ☎ ☎ ☎
Q of L: ★ ★ ★
Admissions: (800) 423-6236
Email Address:
  admission@centre.edu

Strongest Programs:
English
History
Biology
Biochemistry
Economics
Art

Centre College is the only independent school in Kentucky with a Phi Beta Kappa chapter, and it's produced two-thirds of the state's Rhodes Scholars over the last forty years. But Centre is not all work and no play. It's also a throwback to the way college used to be, with Friday night parties on fraternity row, and Saturday afternoon football games, dressed in your Sunday best. Centre's small size offers "the ability to get involved and have a direct hand in making improvements," says a biology major. And its liberal arts focus means that despite Centre's Southern location, students are progressive, intellectual, and perhaps more well-rounded than their peers at neighboring schools.

Located in the heart of Kentucky Bluegrass country, Centre's campus is a mix of old Greek Revival and attractive modern buildings. More than fourteen of them are listed on the National Registry of Historic Places, a fact that's less surprising when you know that Centre is the forty-eighth oldest college in the U.S. In April 2003, the school broke ground on the College Centre, a renovation and expansion of library, classroom, and athletic facilities, as well as faculty offices.

Speaking of faculty, they receive high marks from students for accessibility and knowledge. "Virtually every class is taught by a full professor, and usually a well-experienced and accomplished one at that," says a junior. General education requirements include basic skills in expository writing, math, and foreign language, as well as a freshman seminar and two courses in each context (aesthetic, social, scientific, and fundamental questions). Students must also take one more course in math, a foreign language, or computer science. The freshman seminar is offered during the three-week January "CentreTerm," which began in 2001–2002. These courses are capped at fifteen students each, and offer a chance to explore unusual and interdisciplinary topics, such as cloning, leadership, Duke Ellington, and baseball in American politics.

> **"Virtually every class is taught by a full professor, and usually a well-experienced and accomplished one at that."**

Centre's most popular majors are economics, biology, history, English, and government; not coincidentally, these are also the school's best departments. Art is also strong, and glassblowing enthusiasts will find one of the few fully equipped undergraduate facilities for their pursuit in the nation. Administrators say foreign languages, especially German, are among their weaker offerings. No course taken by a Centre freshman has more than fifty students, and the vast majority has twenty-five or fewer. Still, students report few problems with scheduling. "Students always get the classes they want because each semester they switch what students get to register first," says a biology major. "If you don't graduate within four years, the school pays for a fifth year."

Two-thirds of students take advantage of Centre's study abroad programs, which offer travel to London, France, Mexico, Japan, and Ireland during the semester, and to Vietnam, Cameroon, Turkey, and the Bahamas during the January term. Centre also belongs to the Associated Colleges of the South,* through which students may select programs in Central America. A 3–2 program sends aspiring engineers on to one of four major universities, including Columbia and Vanderbilt.

Almost two-thirds of Centre students hail from Kentucky, and three-quarters graduated from public high school. Just 2 percent are African-American; another 2 percent are Asian-American, and less than 1 percent are Hispanic. The lack of diversity doesn't seem to

"If you don't graduate within four years, the school pays for a fifth year."

generate much concern, though. "We are all open-minded, and support each other's right to voice our opinions," says a junior. Centre does not offer athletic scholarships, though it does award 150 merit scholarships a year, ranging from $4,500 to full tuition.

Ninety-four percent of students live in Centre's dorms, where "the rooms are decent in size, and there aren't any maintenance problems," says a biology major. There are three main clusters of halls on campus—North Side, Old Centre, and the Old Quad. Each has all of the necessities of college life—washers and dryers, a computer lab, kitchen facilities, lounges, and study rooms—and all rooms are wired for cable TV, voice mail, Internet access, and air-conditioning. Freshmen live in single-sex halls, while upperclassmen may choose buildings that are co-ed by floor. Hillside offers six-person suites, each with three bedrooms and a living room. Centre has also purchased and remodeled an apartment building to provide additional upperclass housing, though the 55 percent of men and 55 percent of women who go Greek may bunk in one of ten new fraternity and sorority houses. Everyone eats together in Cowan Dining Commons, which has made-to-order stir-fry and deli stations, plus a pasta bar, pizza line, grill (for burgers and fries), and a soup and salad bar. Meal plan credits are also good at the Grille in the student union, and the House of Brews coffee shop.

Social life at Centre revolves around Fraternity Row. "The parties are open to all students, including the other fraternities," says a junior. "The Student Activities Council is always trying to offer alternatives, but the majority of people still go to the frat houses every weekend." When it comes to alcohol, Centre follows federal and state law—no one under twenty-one can drink. "However, if a student has a beverage in a non-original container, the RAs and department of public safety will not guess what is in the cup," one student explains. "It is a very lax system." That said, the town of Danville is located in a dry county, and local restaurants only recently won permission to serve alcohol. Thankfully, Lexington and Louisville are within an hour's drive, and it's easy to get to the countryside for camping, fishing, and other outdoor pursuits. Students also get free admission to Centre's separately endowed Norton Center for the Arts, which brings touring musicals, plays, and other performances to campus. Eighty percent of the student body does community service.

Centre's football team has been around for more than a century, and while it now competes against regional opponents in Division III, that wasn't always the case. In 1921, Centre beat then-powerhouse Harvard, 6–0, an event that has been called the greatest sports upset in the first half of the 20th century. The women's basketball team was among the best in the nation in 2000–2001, and remains one of the most popular sports on campus, along with men's and women's soccer, track and cross-country. Centre's archrival is nearby Transylvania University, but it's

In April 2003, the school broke ground on the College Centre, a renovation and expansion of library, classroom, and athletic facilities, as well as faculty offices.

Freshman seminars are capped at fifteen students each, and offer a chance to explore unusual and interdisciplinary topics, such as cloning, leadership, Duke Ellington, and baseball in American politics.

other traditions that really get students going. Those include a serenade for the president by senior women clad in bath towels, and faculty Christmas caroling for the freshmen. And don't forget "Running the Flame," which has students dashing from the fraternity houses, around a sculpture and back—"naked, of course."

What Centre College lacks in size, it more than makes up for in quality. With a safe, bucolic campus, an emphasis on academic excellence, and faculty and students who care about forming lasting friendships with each other, this undiscovered gem may be worth a look.

If You Apply To ➤

Centre: Early action: Dec.1. Regular admissions: Feb. 1. Financial aid: Mar. 1. Meets demonstrated need of 80%. Campus interviews: recommended, informational. Alumni interviews: optional, informational. SATs or ACTs: required. SAT IIs: optional. Accepts the Common Application and electronic applications. Essay question: experience, achievement, or risk you have taken; issue of local, national, or international concern; influential person; or influential fictional character or historical figure.

College of Charleston

Charleston, SC 29424

The College of Charleston, a public school about half the size of the University of South Carolina that offers business, education, and the liberal arts. It compares to William and Mary in both scale and historic surroundings but is far less rigorous academically. Must address its housing crunch to reach the next level.

Website: www.cofc.edu
Location: Urban
Total Enrollment: 11,716
Undergraduates: 10,044
Male/Female: 37/63
SAT Ranges: V 550–640
    M 550–630
ACT Range: 22–26
Financial Aid: 76%
Expense: Pub $ $
Phi Beta Kappa: No
Applicants: 8,635
Accepted: 60%
Enrolled: 25%
Grad in 6 Years: 54%
Returning Freshmen: 82%
Academics: ✍ ✍ ✍
Social: ☎ ☎ ☎ ☎
Q of L: ★ ★ ★ ★
Admissions: (843) 953-5670
Email Address:
    admissions@cofc.edu

Strongest Programs:
Intermodal Transportation

Whether sampling the traditional Low Country cuisine or delving into a wide range of courses offered at this 232-year-old school, students at the College of Charleston know they are getting a quality education in a beautiful setting. Founded as Colonial South Carolina's first college, C of C has moved beyond its traditional roots to become a well-respected institution throughout the Southeast.

Located in Charleston's famous Historical District, the campus features many of the city's most historic and venerable buildings. More than eighty of its buildings are former private residences ranging from the typical Charleston "single" house to the Victorian. The campus has received countless regional, state, and local awards for its design, and has been designated a national arboretum. But the campus is undergoing somewhat of a transformation. In the past two years, two modern dorms, two restaurants and a food court, a fitness center, and a wireless computing network were added to the campus. A new library is nearly complete, and several more projects are in the wings: a business center, arts wing, multicultural center, and education building.

"The professors at C of C are not only knowledgeable and caring, they are inspirational."

C of C has a core curriculum based strongly in the liberal arts and focused on the development of writing, computing, language acquisition, and thinking skills. Each student is required to complete six hours in English, history, mathematics or logic, and social science; eight hours in natural sciences; and twelve hours in humanities and a modern or classical foreign language. Biology and chemistry are two of the strongest programs; many of the graduates end up at the Medical University of South Carolina a few blocks down the street. Marine biology is also strong, and students use the South Carolina marshes and beaches for a research laboratory. The most popular major is communication, followed by business administration, biology, elementary education, and psychology. Many of the new performing arts majors take advantage of internship opportunities with Charleston's annual Spoleto Music Festival. Study abroad options include the International Student Exchange Program and the Sea Semester.* The academic climate at C of C is challenging but not cut-throat. Students report the quality of teaching is excellent. "The professors at C of C are not only knowledgeable and caring, they are inspirational," boasts a Spanish major.

More than a third of the students hail from out of state, and one-quarter graduated in the top tenth of their high school class. Asian-Americans and Hispanics together make up less than 2 percent of the student body, and African-Americans make up 9 percent. The college offers hundreds of merit scholarships, as well as athletic scholarships in nine sports. A payment plan allows students to spread the cost of tuition over the course of the semester, a handy option some 20 percent of the students use.

Lack of dorm space has been one of C of C's biggest challenges as of late—only a quarter of students live on campus—but the campus has addressed that with the purchase of two new dorms and renovations of an existing residence hall. "You pay for what you get. If you pay more, you get a better room, and the opposite is true also," a sophomore points out. In order to get a room, students advise applying early. Commuters complain parking is scarce and expensive. "It's hard to get to class on time because of the lack of parking spaces," laments a sophomore.

"Charleston is amazing for all its variety."

No matter where they live, students enjoy Charleston, with its festivals, plays, and scenic plantations and gardens. "Charleston is amazing for all its variety," an economics major says. Students party off-campus in local clubs and apartments as well as on campus, where 13 percent of the men and 18 percent of the women belong to frats and sororities, respectively. Due to a well-enforced policy on drinking, students report that it is difficult to be served on campus if you are not twenty-one, but off-campus is not a problem. Women far outnumber men, but females looking to beat the odds can always go to the Medical University of South Carolina or the Citadel Military College, which are both in Charleston.

A very old tourist town, Charleston has a "hostile attitude toward college kids," complains one student. "We are taken advantage of every day. City ordinances severely limit the nightlife and try to force kids out of the downtown area." Based on your tastes, however, you may find the historic quality charming and inspiring. On weekends, students can head to beaches such as Folly Beach, Sullivan's Island, and Isle of Palms, which are merely minutes away. For those who don't mind a drive, there's "the Grand Strand," Myrtle Beach, ninety miles north, or Savannah and Hilton Head to the south. Others enjoy taking a journey out of state to Georgia or North Carolina.

The absence of a football team is a common gripe among students, but other athletics are relatively popular. Several teams have claimed recent conference championships—volleyball, men's basketball, golf, and tennis, and women's tennis and softball.

The College of Charleston has set its sights on becoming the finest public liberal arts and sciences institution in South Carolina, and it seems to be on its way. With a strong liberal arts foundation, an honors college, and opportunities to do research and study abroad, students at C of C can take advantage of big opportunities at this small school. "It is not too big or too little. Classes are small and teachers know your names!" exclaims one pleased sophomore.

(Continued)
Marine Biology
Business
Communications
Psychology
Education

Students enjoy Charleston, with its festivals, plays, and scenic plantations and gardens.

The historic campus is undergoing somewhat of a transformation. In the past two years, two modern dorms, two restaurants and a food court, a fitness center, and a wireless computing network were added to the campus and several more projects are in the wings.

Overlaps

Clemson, University of South Carolina, University of Georgia, University of North Carolina, Furman

University of Chicago

1116 East 59th Street, Chicago, IL 60637

Periodically, the news media reports that students at the University of Chicago are finally loosening up and having some fun. Don't believe it. This place is for true intellectuals who don't mind working hard for their degrees. Less selective than the top Ivies, but just as good. Social climbers apply elsewhere.

Website: www.uchicago.edu
Location: Urban
Total Enrollment: 12,327
Undergraduates: 3,917
Male/Female: 59/41
SAT Ranges: V 620–730
   M 630–730
ACT Range: 27–31
Financial Aid: 59%
Expense: Pr $ $ $ $
Phi Beta Kappa: Yes
Applicants: 5,361
Accepted: 33%
Enrolled: 57%
Grad in 6 Years: N/A
Returning Freshmen: 95%
Academics: 🖉 🖉 🖉 🖉 🖉
Social: ☎ ☎
Q of L: ★ ★ ★
Admissions: (773) 702-8650
Email Address:
   college-admissions@
   uchicago.edu

Strongest Programs:
Economics
English
Sociology
Anthropology
Political Science
Geography
Geophysical Science
History
Linguistics

The University of Chicago attracts a very specific kind of student: one eager to eschew the superficial trappings of Ivy League prestige; one who is much more passionate about physics or Plato than about finding a great party. "This is a place that has always been very proud of its nerdiness," boasts a senior. To make the school more attractive to high school seniors, U of C's administration has responded by launching a controversial campaign. The core curriculum has been reduced, and plans include increasing the undergraduate population, building new recreational facilities, and expanding student activities. "The administration has taken many steps to make the college a more fun place to go to school," says a sophomore.

Chicago's 190-acre tree-lined campus is located in the integrated neighborhood of Hyde Park, an eclectic community on the South Side of Chicago surrounded by low-income communities on three sides and Lake Michigan on the fourth. Town–gown relations are said to be calm, and crime is no more a problem than in any other urban setting, but African-American students complain that they are too often mistaken for trespassers by local police. The campus itself is self-contained and architecturally magnificent. The main quads are steel-gray Gothic—gargoyles and all—and the newer buildings are by Eero Saarinen, Mies van der Rohe, and Frank Lloyd Wright.

Historically, Chicago has been recognized for its graduate programs. But administrators and faculty members alike are beginning to realize that they must concentrate on the holistic experience the school offers undergraduates if Chicago has any hope of remaining competitive with schools like Stanford, Harvard, and Princeton. On the undergraduate level, though, Chicago remains unequivocally committed to the view that a solid foundation in the liberal arts is the best foundation for any walk of life, and that theory is better than practice. Thus, music students study musicology but learn calculus along with everyone else. Indeed, half of a student's forty-two courses at Chicago, regardless of major, are taken as part of general education requirements called the common core. Dubbed by one student as the "hallmark of a Chicago education," the core curriculum has undergone a controversial reduction, down from twenty-one courses to fifteen or eighteen (depending on the foreign language requirement) and the replacement of long-standing Western civilization courses with others focusing on European civilization. What used to account for half of a student's total coursework now takes up only one-third. Requirements include courses in science and

"This is a place that has always been very proud of its nerdiness."

math, humanities and civilization, social sciences, and a foreign language. Sound intense? It is, students say, especially because courses are crammed into eleven-week quarters, rather than thirteen- or fourteen-week semesters. In addition to the core, seniors are encouraged to undertake final-year projects, which need not be in their area of concentration (although 99 percent of the time they are).

(Continued)
Mathematics

Chicago's brilliant and distinguished faculty is certainly its greatest asset. Although U of C was founded in the tradition of the German research universities, professors here take their teaching role quite seriously. "I have had renowned professors with years of study and experience in their fields," says a student. "In addition, lectures are informative and enjoyable." The university's dedicated professors get more time to teach and do research than they would elsewhere, since Chicago is one of the few schools in the country with full-time advisors to help students with academic and other matters. Most classes have about twenty-five students, and practically none are larger than fifty. A computerized enrollment system makes getting into sought-after classes a little less grueling. Although classes are small, students say graduating in four years is not a problem.

"Political correctness is pointedly ignored. Students simply treat each other fairly."

The economics department, a bastion of neo-liberal or New Right thinkers, is Chicago's main academic claim to fame and the most popular major. But biology, English, history, psychology, and political science also draw crowds. Chicago was father to both sociology and political science as scholarly disciplines, and these two programs remain among the best anywhere. The university also prides itself on outstanding interdisciplinary programs and area studies, such as East Asian, South Asian, Middle Eastern, and Slavic. The New Collegiate Division of the university offers popular interdisciplinary programs such as Fundamentals: Issues and Texts, and newer majors include computer science and cinema and media studies. Students cite art and design, psychology, and foreign languages as weaker than most.

If Chicago gets too cold and snowy, students may study abroad on one of seventeen programs that reach most corners of the globe. A combined degree program also allows the most motivated premeds to earn a B.A. and an M.D. in eight years, with acceptance to Chicago's medical school occurring after the second undergrad year. Other qualified undergrads are able to register for courses in all of the university's graduate and professional schools—law, divinity, social service, public policy, humanities, social sciences, biological and physical sciences, and business. "Those who are ready can accelerate as fast as the faculty and facilities permit," explains an administrator.

Since Chicago is committed to the quarter system it pioneered, the first term starts in late September and is over by Christmas. For practical purposes, this means virtually uninterrupted work straight through the school year, a long summer vacation, and three exam weeks a year. The one concession to the work ethic is a two-day reading period between the end of classes and the beginning of exams. All five of the university's libraries are excellent, containing one of the most extensive collections in the country; "much bigger than an undergrad would ever need."

Chicago has more graduate and professional students than undergraduates, and the climate on campus reflects the lopsided ratio. Some describe it as a high-pressure "grind," but it also translates into an enormous number of research projects and a better-than-even chance that an ambitious undergraduate can get a diploma having coauthored a journal article or two. "Chicago students care about their time here, which means that a lot of students are concerned about grades, curriculum, and the quality of their education," says one student.

Only 21 percent of Chicago's student body come from Illinois; a high percentage hail from the East Coast, and many were raised in academic homes; 87 percent

A combined degree program also allows the most motivated premeds to earn a B.A. and an M.D. in eight years, with acceptance to Chicago's medical school occurring after the second undergrad year.

were in the top fifth of their high school class. Fifty-nine percent go on to further study of some kind, which is why the university is known as "teacher of teachers." Asian-Americans account for a sizable 27 percent of Chicago's students, while blacks contribute 4 percent and Hispanics represent 5 percent. Both conservatives and liberals are "ably present and vocal," and interests run the gamut from government and politics to music. "Political correctness is pointedly ignored. Students simply treat each other fairly," says one junior. Most students dress in a come-as-you-are style. Freshman orientation, which the administration says was invented at U of C in 1924, is known as O Week, and it's a time when students make lasting friendships.

"We have incredible housing," boasts one student. And he's got a point, considering that one dorm, Shoreland, is a former luxury hotel located on the shore of Lake Michigan. There are twelve dorm complexes on campus, some new and sterile, others old and modeled after Cambridge or Heidelberg, and all co-ed by room or floor. Shoreland is the largest and most social, but it's also half a mile from campus, a definite hike when the wind is howling off the lake (from November to April). All rooms are connected to a campus-wide computer network, and some are equipped with kitchens. About two-thirds of the students live on campus, and housing is guaranteed for four years. Food is said to be "mediocre but plentiful," and while freshmen and residents of certain dorms are required to be on a full-meal contract, others can buy a meal plan or purchase individual meal coupons.

The nine fraternities and two sororities don't play a very large role in campus life, although frat parties are reasonably well attended. "Social life is very individualistic," says one student. There are two campus bars, both of which are fairly strict about not serving anyone underage, but the administration has never really cracked down on drinking, which "really isn't a social necessity here," says a student. Other weekend entertainment options on campus include low-cost flicks in the five hundred-seat movie theater, dorm parties, and a plethora of cultural activities. Still, one student asks, "We're in Chicago, where else should we go?" He's referring, of course, to downtown, with its internationally acclaimed symphony, museums, and other cultural facilities. Though everything is accessible by public transportation, cars are a nice luxury if you can find a parking place. With over one hundred extracurricular clubs and programs, everyone should be able to find something of interest on campus.

Robert Maynard Hutchins, the famous president of Chicago from 1929 to 1951, once opined that "having fun is a form of intelligence." As evidence that such views are acceptable, the university belongs to the University Athletic Association, which includes other academically minded schools, such as Johns Hopkins and New York University. To everyone's surprise, the recently resurrected football team has already had a couple of winning seasons. Chicago fans often fill Stagg Field to its 1,500-seat capacity to support the school's teams, and the Scholarly Yell they shout out is one of the best cheers around: "Themistocles, Thucydides/The Peloponnesian Wars/X-squared, Y-squared, H2SO4/Who for, what for/Who the hell are we cheering for?/Go Maroons!"

Athletes here are well respected, and—remember, this is the University of Chicago—have a higher overall GPA than the student body as a whole; the wrestling team and women's soccer squad sport All-Americans. Both men's and women's soccer teams have been to the Division III Final Four, while the softball team has won the UAA championship in the past. The basketball team, which has been playing since 1896, posted a 22–12 record a couple of years ago, its greatest number of victories in a single season ever. Even weekend warriors get in on the action at Chicago; intramurals attract an enthusiastic three-quarters of the student body. Hans Brinker types flock to the Midway, site of the 1893 World's Fair, which

With one hundred-plus extracurricular clubs and programs, everyone should be able to find something of interest on campus.

is flooded every winter for skating. In addition, there's Kuviasungnerk (the Eskimo term for happiness), an esoteric winter carnival that features ice sculptures, hockey, poetry readings, and fireside lectures on Arctic food and the meteorology of cold fronts. Only at the University of Chicago!

U of C students take pride in both their individuality and their intellectual prowess. They come to college to flex their scholarly muscle, not raise their alcohol tolerance. They place a premium on academics, not extracurriculars, and at graduation they are rewarded for their efforts—as one student says, "Once this is over, you'll be good enough to tackle anything." Film director Mike Nichols described his own years as an undergraduate here as "wide open," adding, "Everybody was strange at the University of Chicago! It was paradise." Current students would likely agree.

If You Apply To ➤

Chicago: Early action: Nov. 15. Regular admissions: Jan. 1. Financial aid: Feb. 1. Guarantees to meet demonstrated need. Campus interviews: recommended, evaluative. Alumni interviews: optional, evaluative. SATs or ACTs: required. No SAT IIs. Essay question: something that reminds you of your past; why a newspaper story of importance interests you; improvise a story, play, or dialogue; a creative work that's a key to your worldview.

University of Cincinnati

P.O. Box 210091, Cincinnati, OH 45221-0091

In most states, UC would be the big enchilada. But with Ohio State two hours up the road and Miami U even closer, Cincinnati has to hustle to get its name out there. The inventor of co-op education, it offers quality programs in everything from engineering to art—and a top-ranked men's basketball team to boot.

Many first-time visitors to Cincinnati are surprised to find an attractive and very livable city. As they traverse the city's hilly roads, they are in for another surprise— its university. Not only is the University of Cincinnati renowned for its extensive research programs, the school's co-op program is also one of the largest of any public college or university in the country.

The compact campus nudges up to the edge of the downtown area and is centered at the top of a hill. Ultramodern buildings rise up next to traditional ivy-covered Georgian halls. A $300 million construction project is underway to create a "Main Street" in the center of campus that will consolidate all student activities. A new dorm under construction is one of several planned. A new medical research facility and performing arts complex recently joined the campus. Research is a UC specialty. Campus scientists have given the world anti-knock gasoline, the electronic organ, antihistamines, and the U.S. Weather Bureau. UC is also the place where, in 1906, cooperative education was born, allowing students to earn while they learn. Across the Cincinnati curriculum, there is an abundance of co-op opportunities available. Nearly four thousand students take advantage of them. In all, forty-two programs offer the popular five-year professional-practice option.

The colleges of engineering; business administration; and design, architecture, art, and planning (the schools with the most co-op students) are the best bets at UC. The university's music conservatory, one of the best state-run programs in the field, also offers broadcasting training. The schools of nursing and pharmacy are well known and benefit from UC's health center and graduate medical school. The most popular major is marketing. In addition, education is a strong program. The

Website: www.uc.edu
Location: City outskirts
Total Enrollment: 27,327
Undergraduates: 20,039
Male/Female: 51/49
SAT Ranges: V 460–590
    M 470–600
ACT Range: 19–25
Financial Aid: 48%
Expense: Pub $ $
Phi Beta Kappa: Yes
Applicants: 10,745
Accepted: 82%
Enrolled: 41%
Grad in 6 Years: 45%
Returning Freshmen: 70%
Academics: ✍ ✍
Social: ☎ ☎ ☎
Q of L: ★ ★ ★
Admissions: (513) 556-1100
Email Address:
    admissions@uc.edu

Cincinnati Initiative for Teacher Education requires all education majors to complete a five-year program that ends in an entire year of internships in different education environments. Education students earn two bachelor's degrees: one in education and one in a liberal arts subject. The two-year University College is Cincinnati's open-admissions unit, which prepares less-qualified students to transfer into four-year programs and offers a variety of vocational degrees, including paralegal technology and robotics. A new Department of Biomedical Engineering was founded in 2001. Inventureworks is a new program for design and business students that allows them to brainstorm on new products for international companies.

The academic grind is determined largely by the major. Fields such as engineering, business, and nursing require a substantially larger academic commitment. "Most classes are laid-back until you are admitted to your degree program," says a sophomore. But another student notes "UC harbors a certain competitive spirit." Some courses end up being quite large (in popular design courses, two people to a desk is not unusual), and students say about 20 percent of their classes have up to one hundred students. One fine asset is the school's huge library, which has 1.9 million volumes and is completely computerized.

UC has taken steps to improve the quality of the undergraduate education by strengthening its general education requirements to focus on critical thinking and expression, and expanding its honors program.

"Most classes are laid-back until you are admitted to your degree program."

Additionally, UC has adopted its Pedagogy Initiative, which allows students to interact with professors and encourages them to develop questions in the classroom. Freshmen must take English and math as well as a contemporary issues class; other requirements vary by college. A third of the faculty members hold outside jobs, bringing fresh practical experience to the classroom.

More than 1,500 students receive more than $11 million in scholarships each year, but are required to participate in a service-learning program each year.

All but 8 percent of the student body comes from within the state, but the student body is fairly diversified. "Students at UC are very diverse, and represent all different levels of academic ability, experience, and interests," says one student. There are art types and business types, liberals and conservatives. African-Americans, Asian-Americans, and Hispanics comprise 15, 3, and 1 percent of the student body, respectively. Diversity, feminist issues, campus construction, and rising tuition are the hot topics on campus. The school offers over 1,500 merit scholarships ranging from $1,500 to full tuition, and 370 athletic scholarships for men and women. While students say they have noticed the budget squeeze in terms of services being cut and the hiring of new personnel curtailed, the school is growing. "Our school is constantly changing," says a triple major who notes a campus-wide joke is that UC stands for "Under Construction."

A mere 10 percent of UC students live on campus. Noncommuting freshmen and athletes are required to live in the six co-ed and single-sex dorms, which are described as adequate but crowded. Students say the lack of parking facilities is a much bigger deal than housing conditions. Many upperclassmen, especially the older and married students, consider off-campus living far better than dorm life, and inexpensive apartments can usually be found. Food in the two cafeterias located on opposite ends of the campus is "bland and unappetizing," and many students find stopping at the plastic village of fast-food joints surrounding the campus a tastier, cheaper, and more convenient option.

Students can participate in international co-op experiences, alternating their studies with work assignments in countries including Japan and Germany.

Merchants have turned the area surrounding UC, called Clifton, into a mini college town with plenty to do. A bus line running by the campus takes undergraduates into the heart of the "Queen City" of Cincinnati in minutes. There the students find museums, a ballet, professional sports teams, parks, rivers, hills, and as many large and small shops as anyone could want. Still, the students advise caution, especially at night, when maneuvering through the campus and the "somewhat run-down" urban neighborhood surrounding it. On-campus activities include everything from a mountaineering club to Internat (the international students association) to clubs in various majors. Fraternities and sororities are small, but are still the most active places to party on campus, usually opening their functions to everyone. The university sponsors some events, such as the massive but still wacky Springfest, which spotlights local bands playing all day and lots of "crafts and food and beer." The most popular road trips are the city of Cleveland and white-water rafting in West Virginia.

In sports, men's basketball, track, and swimming teams have captured recent titles, along with the volleyball and women's swimming teams. Football, track, soccer, baseball, and women's crew are also popular. Everyone mentions the football rivalry with Miami (of Ohio) as a game you won't want to miss, and the same holds true when the men's basketball squad takes on Xavier University. Weekend athletes also take advantage of UC's first-rate sports center.

The University of Cincinnati and the surrounding city offer students opportunities for a hands-on education and the full college experience. Students who attend UC not only get a good education at a reasonable price, they also get a chance to put what they've learned into practice outside the halls of academia.

Overlaps

Ohio State, Miami University (OH), Ohio University, Bowling Green State, Toledo

If You Apply To ➤

UC: Rolling admissions: Jan. 15. Does not guarantee to meet demonstrated need. Campus interviews: optional, informational. No alumni interviews. SATs or ACTs: required. SAT IIs: optional. Accepts the Common Application and electronic applications. No essay question. Apply to particular program.

Claremont Colleges

In 1887, James A. Blaisdell had the vision to create a group of colleges patterned after Oxford and Cambridge in England. More than a century later, the five schools that comprise the Claremont Colleges thrive as a consortium of separate and distinct undergraduate colleges with two adjoining graduate institutions, a theological seminary, and botanical gardens. As families can sometimes get, the colleges coexist, interact, and experience their share of both cooperation and tension. Ultimately, however, the Claremont College Consortium forms a mutually beneficial partnership that offers its students the vast resources and facilities one might only expect to find at a large university.

The colleges are located on 317 acres in the Los Angeles suburb of Claremont, a peaceful neighborhood replete with palm trees, Spanish architecture, and the nearby San Gabriel Mountains. The picture-perfect California weather can sometimes be marred by smog, courtesy of the neighbors in nearby L.A., but the administration claims the smog level has declined dramatically in the past few years.

None of the five undergraduate colleges that make up the Claremont Colleges Consortium—Claremont McKenna, Harvey Mudd, Pitzer, Pomona, and Scripps—is larger than a medium-size dorm at a state school. Each school retains its own institutional identity, with its own faculty, administration, admissions, and curriculum, although the boundaries of both academic work and extracurricular activities are somewhat flexible. Each of the schools also tends to specialize in a particular area that complements the offerings of all the others. Claremont McKenna, which caters mainly to students planning careers in economics, business, law, or government, has eight research institutes located on its campus, while Harvey Mudd is the choice for future scientists. Pitzer, the most liberal of the five, excels mainly in the behavioral sciences, and at the all-women Scripps, the best offerings are in art and foreign languages. The oldest of the five colleges, Pomona ranks as one of the top liberal arts colleges anywhere, and is the one Claremont school that is strong across the board, with the humanities especially superb.

Collectively, the colleges share many services and facilities, including art studios, a student newspaper, laboratories, an extensive biological field station, a health center, auditoriums, a 2,500-seat concert hall, a 350-seat theater, bookstores, a maintenance department, and a business office. The Claremont library system makes more than 1.9 million volumes available to all students, though each campus also has a library of its own. Faculties and administrations are free to arrange joint programs or classes between all or just some of the schools. Courses at any college are open to students from the others (approximately twelve hundred courses in all), but each college sets limits on the number of classes that can be taken elsewhere. Perhaps the best example of academic cooperation is the team-taught interdisciplinary courses, which are organized by instructors from the different schools and appeal to a mix of different academic interests.

The Claremont Colleges draw large numbers of students from within California, although their national reputation is growing. These days, about half the students hail from other Western and non-Western states, with a sizable contingent from the East Coast. The tone at Claremont is decidedly intellectual—more so than at Stanford or any other place in the West—and graduate programs in the arts and sciences are more common goals than business or law school. Anyone who is bright and hardworking can find a niche at one of the five schools. Unfortunately, despite their excellence, the Claremonts are also among the most underrated colleges in the nation.

The local community of Claremont is geared more to senior citizens than college seniors. "Quiet town of rich white people—boring," yawns an English major. A sophomore says, "Most of the stores have strange granny knick-knacks or cosmic aura trinkets." Still, "the Village," a quaint cluster of specialty shops (including truly remarkable candy stores), is an easy skateboard ride from any campus, though the shades come down and the sidewalks roll up well before sunset. Students report that the endless list of social activities offered at the colleges make up for the ho-hum town of Claremont. For hot times, Hollywood's glamour and UCLA-dominated Westwood are within sniffing distance, and a convenient shuttle bus makes them even closer for Claremont students without cars. Nearby mountains and the fabled surfing beaches make this collegiate paradise's backyard complete. Mount Baldy ski lifts, for instance, are only fifteen miles away, and you'll reach Laguna Beach before the end of your favorite CD. For spring break, Mexico is cheap and a great change of pace.

On campus, extracurricular life maintains a balance between cooperation and independence. Claremont McKenna, Harvey Mudd, and Scripps field joint athletic teams, and the men's teams especially are Division III powers, due to the exploits of CMC athletes. Pomona and Pitzer also compete together. Each of the five colleges has its own dorms, and since off-campus housing is limited in Claremont proper, the social life of students revolves around their dorms. "Scripps itself is quiet but parties at Harvey Mudd and Claremont McKenna can get pretty wild," admits a Scripps student. There are no fraternities, except at Pomona, where joining one is far from de rigueur. All cafeterias are open to all students, and most big events—films, concerts, etc.—are advertised throughout the campus. Large five-school parties are regular Thursday, Friday, and Saturday night fare. Social interaction among students at different schools, be it for meals or dates, is not what it might be. Pomona is seen as elitist, and its admissions office has been known to try to distance itself from the other colleges. Occasional political squabbles break out between liberal faculty and students at Pitzer and their conservative counterparts at Claremont McKenna. For the most part, students benefit not only from the nurturing and support within their own schools, each of which has its own academic or extracurricular emphasis, but also from the abundant resources the Claremont College Consortium offers as a whole.

Following are profiles of each undergraduate Claremont College.

Claremont McKenna College

890 Columbia Avenue, Claremont, CA 91711

Make way, Pomona—this up-and-comer now has the lowest acceptance rate in the Claremont Colleges and is no longer content with being a social sciences specialty school. CMC is half the size of a typical liberal arts college and 50 percent smaller than Pomona. Still developing a national reputation.

Website:
www.claremontmckenna
.edu

At Claremont McKenna College, the students not only have parties, they study them, too. Political parties, that is. As a member of the Claremont Colleges consortium, CMC boasts top programs in government, economics, business, and international relations. In addition, Claremont McKenna has eight research institutes located on campus, which offer its undergraduates ample opportunities to study everything from political demographics to the environment. The arts and humanities are also available, but Claremont McKenna is better suited to those with high ambitions in business leadership and public affairs.

The fifty-acre campus, located thirty-five miles east of Los Angeles, is mostly "California modern" architecture with lots of Spanish tile roofs and picture windows that look out on the San Gabriel Mountains. Described by one student as "more functional than aesthetic," the physical layout fits right in with the school's pragmatic attitude. Roberts Hall is a state-of-the-art academic center housing classrooms, seminar rooms, a computer laboratory, and faculty offices.

Claremont McKenna offers top programs in economics and government, but the international relations, prelaw, premed, and business programs are also considered strong. The biology, chemistry, and physics departments are greatly enhanced through the use of Keck Science Center, an outstanding facility providing students

> **"Students at CMC are competitive, critical, pragmatic, and mostly goal-oriented."**

with hands-on access to a variety of equipment. In addition, the eighty-five-acre Bernard Biological Field Station is located just north of the CMC campus and is available to students for field work. The administration candidly admits that computer science and engineering are not as fully developed as most departments.

CMC's extensive general education requirements include two semesters in the humanities; three in the social sciences; two in the natural sciences; a semester each in mathematics, English composition and literary analysis, and Questions of Civilization; and a Senior Thesis. The college offers popular 3–2 programs in management engineering and a 4–1 M.B.A. program in conjunction with the Claremont Graduate University. Nearly 40 percent of Claremont McKenna students take advantage of its study abroad programs to countries including Australia, Brazil, Costa Rica, Japan, and numerous others. CMC also offers active campus exchange programs with Haverford, Colby, Spelman, and Morehouse, and universities in Quebec, Canada, and Germany. Another popular program is the Washington Semester program, in which students can intern with E-Span, the State Department, the White House, and lobbying groups.

The academic climate is fairly strenuous at Claremont McKenna, but not overwhelming. "Students usually average 100–200 pages of reading each week plus regularly assigned papers," says a senior. "Studying until the wee hours is usual." The students at CMC give most professors high marks with the exception of the occasional prof who "should have chosen the field over the classroom." Freshmen are always taught by full professors in classes that rarely exceed twenty-five students. "We don't do the whole 'TA' thing here," asserts a junior.

"Students at CMC are competitive, critical, pragmatic, and mostly goal-oriented," says one student. "Student government, publication, sports, and getting involved in leadership roles tends to be the norm." The CMC student body is 46 percent Californian, with most everyone else from west of the Mississippi. Many attended public high school and 83 percent graduated in the top tenth of their class. The student body is 65 percent white; Asian-Americans comprise the largest minority at 14 percent. Hispanics comprise 9 percent, while African-Americans make up 4 percent. A junior says, "We have a very equal split between conservative and liberal students. So, while they are not always politically correct, they are politically active." All freshmen take part in a five-day orientation program that includes a beach trip and a reception with the president and department chairs. The school guarantees to meet the demonstrated need of accepted applicants and offers thirty merit scholarships of up to $5,000 a year. There are no athletic scholarships.

Almost all CMC students (96 percent) live on campus "because of the social life." The maid service probably doesn't hurt. "They dust and vacuum our rooms

(Continued)

Location: Suburban
Total Enrollment: 1,040
Undergraduates: 1,040
Male/Female: 56/44
SAT Ranges: V 650–740
  M 660–740
ACT Range: 28–32
Financial Aid: 71%
Expense: Pr $ $ $ $
Phi Beta Kappa: Yes
Applicants: 2,892
Accepted: 31%
Enrolled: 32%
Grad in 6 Years: 86%
Returning Freshmen: 97%
Academics: ✍ ✍ ✍ ✍½
Social: ☎ ☎ ☎
Q of L: ★ ★ ★
Admissions: (909) 621-8088
Email Address: admission@
  claremontmckenna.edu

Strongest Programs:
Economics
Government
International Relations
Premed
Prelaw
Business
Accounting
Sciences

and clean our bathrooms! We do nothing (except study, of course)!" declares a happy resident. All the residence halls are co-ed; freshmen are guaranteed a room. Stark Hall, an eight-story residence hall, gives students more living options. A cluster of on-campus apartments equipped with kitchen facilities is a popular option for upperclassmen. Dorm food is said to be adequate, and students can eat in dining halls at any of the other four colleges, though the best bet may be CMC's Collins Dining Hall.

Most students agree that the social life at CMC is more than adequate, thanks to the five-college system. "Needless to say, our parties usually center on alcohol," admits one student. Another student adds, "You could easily lead a full and crazy social life without ever leaving campus." In addition to the usual forms of revelry, a calendar full of annual bashes includes Monte Carlo Night, Disco Inferno, Oktoberfest, Chez Hub, and the Christmas Madrigal Feast. Enthuses a junior, "Beer golf is also an interesting tradition. Golf clubs, tennis balls, and beer...need I say more?" "SYRs—Screw or Set Up Your Roommate dances—are also pretty popular," a government major says. Ponding, another unusual CMC tradition, involves being thrown

"Student government, publication, sports, and getting involved in leadership roles tends to be the norm."

into one of the two campus fountains on one's birthday. The college sponsors an outstanding lecture series at the Marion Minor Cook Athenaeum on Monday through Thursday nights each week. Before each lecture, students and faculty can enjoy a formal gourmet dinner together and engage in intellectual debates. Road trips to Joshua Tree, San Francisco, Las Vegas, and Mount Baldy are highly recommended by the students.

Athletics are an important part of life at Claremont McKenna. A third of the students play varsity sports, and CMC men tend to dominate the teams jointly fielded with Harvey Mudd and Scripps (for women). Recent conference championships have been won by women's soccer, swimming, and tennis and men's track, basketball, and cross-country. Top rivalries include Pomona, both in athletics and academics, one student claims. "Basketball games rock this campus," another student says.

CMC may be a small college, but its mission is to produce great leaders. "Leadership pervades almost everything that goes on here," says a junior. "Claremont McKenna builds character, fosters a sense of ambition among its students, and drives them to set their sights high." Indeed, this up-and-coming West Coast college is developing a national reputation.

Overlaps

UC–Berkeley, UCLA, Pomona, Stanford, Georgetown

If You Apply To ➤ **Claremont McKenna:** Early decision: Nov. 15, Jan.1. Regular admissions: Jan. 1. Financial aid: Feb 1. Guarantees to meet demonstrated need. Campus interviews: recommended, evaluative. Alumni interviews: optional, evaluative. SATs or ACTs: required. SAT IIs: optional. Accepts the Common Application. Essay question: personal statement and issue of importance. Places "strong emphasis on caliber of an applicant's extracurricular activities."

Harvey Mudd College

301 East 12th Street, Kingston Hall, Claremont, CA 91711

The finest institution that no one outside of the techie world has ever heard of. Future Ph.D.s graduate from here in droves. Rivals Caltech for sheer brainpower and access to outstanding faculty. Offers more exposure to the liberal arts than most technically oriented schools.

A top-ranked technical institution, Harvey Mudd College strives to give its students a sense of balance. Although it's a leading provider of high-quality programs in science and engineering, it also emphasizes a well-rounded education with knowledge in the humanities. Harvey Mudd also encourages balance in work and play, and manages to maintain a community feeling in both realms. Although the academic climate is challenging here, the students go out of their way to assist each other, says one engineering major. This desire to help is fostered by the faculty's encouragement of cooperation and team projects.

HMC's mid-'50s vintage campus of cinder-block buildings even "looks like an engineering college; it's very symmetrical and there's no romance." In addition, the buildings have little splotches all over their surfaces that students have dubbed "warts"—not a very attractive picture. Future campus additions include two new dorms and a student dining facility.

While most technical schools tend to have a narrow focus, HMC has come up with the novel idea that even scientists and engineers "need to know and appreciate poetry, philosophy, and non-Western thought," says an administrator. Students here take a third of their courses in the humanities, the most of any engineering college in the nation. Up to half of them can be taken by walking over to another Claremont school. To ensure breadth in the sciences, students take another third of their work in math, physics, chemistry, biology, engineering design, and computer science. The last third of a student's courses must be in one of six major areas: biology, computer science, chemistry, physics, engineering, or math. And finally, to cap off their HMC experience, all students must complete a research project in their major, as well as a senior thesis in the humanities and social sciences.

Of the six majors, engineering is considered not only the strongest but the most popular by students, with physics not far behind. In the past few years, the number of biology faculty has more than doubled, and with the completion of the Olin Science Center, HMC's program in science is a strong one. Students rave about the engineering clinic program, which plops real-life engineering tasks (sponsored by major corporations and government agencies to the tune of more than $30,000 per project) into the laps of students. There's also a Freshman Project that allows neophytes to tackle "some real-world engineering problems." The biology program "is not as popular on campus," according to a student. "It's very small so you'll get a lot of attention."

Whatever department students end up in, the workload at HMC is no cakewalk. One student says the academics are a bit like "drinking from a fire hose...this is one tough school." A peer adds, "I have been pushed and challenged academically more than I ever have before and I am amazed at what I've learned." Still, most agree that the atmosphere is supportive. "Students are still willing to help each other out," says a junior. The absence of graduate programs means that undergraduates get uncommon amounts of attention even from top faculty. Students love the small-college atmosphere. "We're spoiled with small classes taught by Ph.D.s," says a student. "Their dedication is amazing and their knowledge immense." The campus-wide honor code is strongly supported by the student body. These budding technicians are also top achievers: 88 percent graduated in the top 10 percent of their high school class.

"Prospective students should know that it can be temporarily damaging to their egos to come to a school with so many bright students," says a junior. Forty-three percent of the students are homegrown Californians. African-Americans and Hispanics combine for 11 percent of the student body, while Asian-Americans weigh in at 20 percent. The administration advises that prospective applicants should be "passionate" about some aspect of math, science, or engineering. Political awareness

> **"I have been pushed and challenged academically more than I ever have before and I am amazed at what I've learned."**

Students here take a third of their courses in the humanities, the most of any engineering college in the nation. Up to half of them can be taken by walking over to another Claremont school.

Website: www.hmc.edu
Location: Suburban
Total Enrollment: 703
Undergraduates: 703
Male/Female: 67/33
SAT Ranges: V 670–750
   M 720–750
Financial Aid: 80%
Expense: Pr $ $ $ $
Phi Beta Kappa: No
Applicants: 1,773
Accepted: 39%
Enrolled: 30%
Grad in 6 Years: N/A
Returning Freshmen: 99%
Academics: ✏ ✏ ✏ ✏ ½
Social: ☎ ☎ ☎
Q of L: ★ ★ ★
Admissions: (909) 621-8011
Email Address:
   admission@hmc.edu

Strongest Programs:
Engineering
Math
Physics
Chemistry

is not prevalent on campus, and "political correctness is only an issue for a very small group of people," according to one senior.

Five older dorms and two newer, more modern ones are all co-ed and mix the classes. "They are definitely the engineering-school type—functional and efficient," notes a freshman. They range from Atwood ("study hard, party hard") to North ("way cool, so very"). The dorms are also ideal for computer whizzes: all are wired for online access to the HMC mainframe. Campus security is considered ample, especially with the school's recent installations of campus phones, additional lighting, and fences. Workshops in self-defense are also offered for those who are interested.

The college has no fraternities, and most social life takes place in and around the dorms where there are parties every weekend. "On the weekends there is always some sort of on-campus party," says an engineering major. "People tend to know each other so there is plenty of social life." Despite their heavy workload, most HMC students find abundant social outlets, even if it's just joining the parade of unicycles that has overrun the campus. A student describes the town of Claremont as "a wonderful place if you're married or about to die." However, most students say there is always fun to be had at one of the five campuses. Down-and-dirty types often frequent the Mudd Hole, a pizza/pinball/Ping-Pong hangout. Underage drinking is "compliments of a peer over twenty-one," as one student puts it. For a school so young, Mudd is rife with tradition, including the annual "pumpkin caroling" trip at Halloween, in which students serenade professors' homes with doctored-up Christmas carols. Another night of screwball fun is the Women's Pizza Party, in which men don dresses and crash a meeting of the Society of Women Engineers. There is also an annual Five Class competition among the four classes and the handful of fifth-year students, complete with amoebae soccer and relay races that include unicycles (backward), peanut butter and jelly, and slide-rule problem-solving.

> "Prospective students should know that it can be temporarily damaging to their egos to come to a school with so many bright students."

Mudd fields varsity sports teams with Claremont McKenna and Scripps, and mainly because of all the CMC jocks, the teams do extremely well. The men's teams in soccer, track, cross-country, tennis, water polo, and swimming are nationally ranked in NCAA Division III. Women's teams in soccer, basketball, swimming, tennis, and track are perennial high achievers. Not long ago, some enterprising Mudders stole archrival Caltech's cannon, elevating the Mudd-Caltech rivalry to include a soccer game dubbed the Cannon Bowl. Intramurals, also in conjunction with Scripps and CMC, are even more popular. Traditional sporting events include the Black and Blue Bowl, an interdorm game of tackle football, and the Freshman-Sophomore Games, which climax in a massive tug-of-war across a pit of vile stuff.

A common student complaint is "too much work," and there's no denying that students here spend countless hours buried in textbooks. Perhaps that's why HMC is right on the heels of Caltech as the best technical school in the West. Mudd doesn't promise you'll end up the owner of your own mining company—or president of anyone else's—within a decade of graduation, but it does offer a gem of a technical education perfectly blended with a dash of humanities and social sciences. HMC's intimate setting also offers something bigger schools can't: a sense of family.

Overlaps

MIT, Caltech, Stanford, Princeton, UC–Berkeley

If You Apply To ➤

Harvey Mudd: Early decision: Nov. 15. Regular admissions: Jan. 15. Guarantees to meet demonstrated need. Campus interviews: recommended, informational. No alumni interviews. SATs: required. SAT IIs: required (writing, math II, and one other). Accepts the Common Application and electronic applications. Essay question: personal statement; recent difficult decision; what troubles you about the world?

Offers a haven for the otherwise-minded without the hard edge of nonconformity at places like Evergreen and Bard. Traditional strengths lie in the social and behavioral sciences. Still more than 60/40 female, but much more selective than it was ten years ago.

As the most laid-back of the Claremont colleges, Pitzer College offers students a creative milieu, abundant opportunities for intellectual exploration, and a sense of fierce individualism. Founded in the '60s, this small school has changed with the times but continues its tradition of progressive thought and open social attitude.

Even the campus is, well, different. The classroom buildings are modernistic octagons, and the grass-covered "mounds" that distinguish the grounds "are perfect for sunbathing and Frisbee," says one student. In keeping with Pitzer's freewheeling style, each student has the maximum freedom to choose which classes he or she would like to take. A lively freshman seminar program sharpens students' learning skills, especially writing. Students select from forty majors in sciences, humanities, and social sciences. Almost anything in the social and behavioral sciences is a sure bet, especially sociology (the most popular major), anthropology, psychology, political science, and biology. A psych course, Sexual Deviance, wins the most-popular-class award hands down. The art department also garners praise, while most courses in Pitzer's weaker areas can be picked up at one of the other Claremont schools.

> "People work together with their professors to create a classroom climate that is supportive and engaging."

Interdisciplinary inquiry is encouraged and original research is common. Pitzer students take advantage of Claremont's abundant foreign-study options, including a program in international and intercultural studies combining language proficiency, cultural study, and an off-campus Challenge semester. Class size is generally small, promoting close interaction between students and faculty. "People work together with their professors to create a classroom climate that is supportive and engaging," says a psychology major. "The professors rock!" gushes a senior. "They are all dynamic, brilliant teachers." Academic advising gets the thumbs-up as well. A student says that advisors are "profs in our own majors, so they are knowledgeable."

Individualism is a prized characteristic among Pitzer students, half of whom are from California. Pitzer has a substantial minority community: African-Americans and Hispanics make up 21 percent of the student body, and Asian-Americans make up 12 percent. A senior describes his peers as leaders. "These kids design their own majors, coordinate student protests, devise community education programs, and ultimately tend to fight for what they believe in." Lest anyone

> "These kids design their own majors, coordinate student protests, devise community education programs, and ultimately tend to fight for what they believe in."

get the idea that Pitzer students are too far out in left field, many of them eventually go on to graduate or professional school. Adequate financial aid is guaranteed to those students in need, and Pitzer offers scholarships to twenty outstanding students.

Seventy percent of students live on campus. One student describes the dorms as "livable but outdated." Boarders can choose from a variety of meal plans in the dining hall (which never fails to have a vegetarian plate), join a food co-op, or cook

Website: www.pitzer.edu
Location: Suburban
Total Enrollment: 954
Undergraduates: 954
Male/Female: 38/62
SAT Ranges: V 570–670
  M 550–670
ACT Range: 25–27
Financial Aid: 50%
Expense: Pr $ $ $ $
Phi Beta Kappa: No
Applicants: 2,323
Accepted: 56%
Enrolled: 18%
Grad in 6 Years: 66%
Returning Freshmen: 85%
Academics: ✍ ✍ ✍
Social: ☎ ☎ ☎
Q of L: ★ ★ ★
Admissions: (909) 621-8129
Email Address:
  admission@pitzer.edu

Strongest Programs:
Psychology
Sociology
Film and Television
Media Studies
English
Biology

Interdisciplinary inquiry is encouraged and original research is common.

on their own. Campus security is ever-present; a student says, "Pitzer seems to be more safe than other campuses because campus security is so effective." One interesting campus curiosity is Grove House, a structure students saved from the wrecking ball nearly two decades ago and moved to campus. It houses a dining room, study areas, and art exhibits.

Pitzer has no Greek organizations, nor does it want any, and social life tends to be fairly low-key. Kohoutek is the big party: "A weeklong art-music fest celebrating the comet that never came," says a senior. Activities include bands, food, and a "whole week of hoopla." The college enforces the twenty-one-year-old drinking age, and all parties that serve alcohol must be registered. Dances, cocktail parties, and cultural events do much to occupy students' leisure time, but without a car things can get claustrophobic.

According to one student, Pitzer "doesn't have enough athletic spirit," but the Pomona-Pitzer football team—"The Sage Hens"—has had winning seasons and the school fields a variety of teams within the Southern California Intercollegiate Athletic Conference. Students play a large role in Pitzer's community government and sit on all policy committees, including those on curriculum and faculty promotion.

Pitzer attracts open-minded students looking for the freedom to go their own way. Notes one student: "Pitzer is the only Claremont school that can claim to be genuinely different, in terms of race, religion, sexual orientation, and political belief. Pitzer is an amalgamation of every color of the spectrum."

Overlaps

UC–San Diego, UC–Santa Barbara, UCLA, University of Southern California, UC–Berkeley

If You Apply To ➤

Pitzer: Regular admissions: Jan. 15. Financial aid: Feb. 1. Guarantees to meet demonstrated need. Campus interviews: recommended, informational. No alumni interviews. SATs or ACTs: optional. SAT IIs: optional (English and two others). Accepts the Common Application and electronic applications. Essay question: significant social issue; how do you represent your generation; greatest life lesson.

Pomona College

333 North College Way, Claremont, CA 91711

The great Eastern-style liberal arts college of the West. Offers twice the resources of stand-alone competitors with its access to the other Claremonts. Location an hour east of LA would be ideal except for the choking smog that hangs over the area during the warmer parts of the year.

Website: www.pomona.edu
Location: Suburban
Total Enrollment: 1,555
Undergraduates: 1,555
Male/Female: 51/49
SAT Ranges: V 700–760
  M 690–760
ACT Range: 29–34
Financial Aid: 53%
Expense: Pr $ $ $ $
Phi Beta Kappa: Yes

Pomona College, located just thirty-five miles east of the glitz and glamour of Hollywood, is the undisputed star of the Claremont College Consortium and one of the top small liberal arts colleges anywhere. This small, elite institution is the best liberal arts college in the West, and its media studies program (film and television) gets top billing. But the school's prestigious reputation doesn't get to the heads of Pomona's friendly students. "Students here are very open about different types of people—[Pomona] prides itself on its diverse community," chirps one Sage Hen (the school's mascot).

The architecture is variously described as Spanish Mediterranean, pseudo-Italian, or, as a sophomore puts it, "a perfect mix of Northeastern Ivy and Southern California Modern." The administration building, Alexander Hall, is described as "postmodern with Mediterranean influences," and one notices more than one stucco building cloaked in ivy and topped with a red-tile roof on campus, as well as eucalyptus trees, canyon live oaks, and an occasional "secretive courtyard lined with flowers." By virtue of its location and beauty, Pomona's campus has served as the quintessential collegiate milieu in various Hollywood movies, including *Beaches* and, appropriately enough, *How I Got into College*. Current construction includes a new life sciences facility, and several more buildings are in final planning stages.

> **"Students here are very open about different types of people—[Pomona] prides itself on its diverse community."**

Classes at Pomona are challenging. "Most courses are very rigorous," says a student. "Professors expect students to participate actively in class discussions." Another student asserts, "I'm surrounded by so many brilliant students, but students here are not consumed by their academics as they have an uncanny ability to balance the fine line between academics and social life." One undergrad estimates the average student spends twenty to thirty hours a week studying outside the classroom.

Biology, economics, English, politics, and psychology are the most popular majors at Pomona. Newer programs include media studies and cognitive science, and a reorganized self-study curriculum in the history department. One Pomona student reports that the history, chemistry, and politics departments are "rigorous and familial in that students are challenged to their limits by figures (professors) who are somewhat parental but very professional." As for weak spots, the administration candidly admits that dance could be stronger. Students say they tend to avoid a "small number of professors as opposed to entire departments or programs."

A required freshman seminar offers an introduction to critical inquiry through intensive writing on subjects such as Space: To Boldly Go? and Myths, Frauds, and Mysteries. Freshman seminars are designed to "teach students well and early how to use the classroom, foster discussion, step away from destructive competitive behaviors, and push to work collaboratively and supportively." Although no specific course or department is prescribed for graduation, students must take courses that meet the Perception, Analysis, and Communication requirement. Students must also enroll in at least two courses that are writing-intensive, and one course designated speech-intensive, and must demonstrate proficiency in a foreign language.

Educational opportunities abound at Pomona. Students can spend a semester at Colby or Swarthmore, pursue a 3–2 engineering

> **"I know many of my professors on a personal level and feel that even after graduation, I can call them up for advice, good conversation, and possibly a free lunch!"**

plan with the California Institute of Technology, or spend a semester in Washington, D.C., working for a congressperson. Nearly one-half of the students take advantage of study abroad programs offered in twenty-two foreign countries, and many others participate in programs focusing on six cultures and languages at the Oldenborg Center. In addition, the Summer Undergraduate Research Program (SURP) provides students with the opportunity to conduct funded research with a faculty member in their area of study.

Classes are small at Pomona—the average is fourteen students—and the faculty makes a point of being accessible. It's not uncommon for professors to hold study sessions at their houses. "My professors have managed to combine their extensive experience and their research with continually inspired teaching and new ideas," a junior waxes. An ever-popular take-a-professor-to-lunch program gives students free meals when they arrive with a faculty member in tow, and there is even a prof who leads aerobics classes open to all interested parties. "For the most part, my professors are engaging and intelligent," a senior says. A classmate adds, "I know many

(Continued)
Applicants: 4,539
Accepted: 21%
Enrolled: 41%
Grad in 6 Years: 92%
Returning Freshmen: 98%
Academics: ✍ ✍ ✍ ✍ ✍
Social: ☎ ☎ ☎
Q of L: ★ ★ ★ ★
Admissions: (909) 621-8134
Email Address:
    admissions@pomona.edu
Strongest Programs:
English
International Relations
Economics
Neuroscience
Foreign Languages
Media Studies

This small, elite institution is the best liberal arts college in the West, and its media studies program (film and television) gets top billing.

A required freshman seminar offers an introduction to critical inquiry through intensive writing on subjects such as Icons of America: The Madonna Factor, Deviance and the Devil, and What is Wrong with Killing People?: An Introduction to Ethics.

of my professors on a personal level and feel that even after graduation, I can call them up for advice, good conversation, and possibly a free lunch!"

Pomona tends to attract "people who produce work of exceptionally high quality, but who also know how to relax and have fun," notes one student. Thirty-four percent of the students are Californians, and a growing percentage venture from the East Coast. Pomona is proud of its diverse student body: 6 percent are African-American, 8 percent are Hispanic, and 16 percent are Asian-American. "We want to move beyond debates about statistics and make real integration happen among different ethnic groups," says a politics major. There is a healthy mix of liberals and conservatives on campus, though the leftists, especially the feminist wing, are much more vocal. "There is a high degree of political correctness on campus," claims one student, "though this does not preclude students from speaking their minds." One interesting way students voice their issues is by painting the Walker Wall. Anyone is allowed to paint any message they want on the wall, and four-letter words and descriptions of alternative sexual practices show up on a regular basis. The student government is active, and the administration is credited with respecting students' opinions.

Pomona is need-blind in admissions and meets the full demonstrated need of all those who attend. Admissions officers are on the lookout for anyone with special talents and are more than willing to waive the usual grade-and-score standards for such finds. A five-day freshman orientation program divides the new arrivals into groups of six to twelve students headed by a sophomore. "We provide a great deal of support in acclimating students to a college environment," says a senior.

The vast majority of Pomona students (97 percent) live on campus all four years. The dorms are co-ed, student-governed, and divided into two distinct groups. Those on South campus are family-like, fairly quiet, and offer spacious rooms and those on the North end have smaller rooms with a livelier social scene. Housing "kicks a** for freshmen," according to one blunt student, while "sophomores kind of get screwed." Freshmen must live on campus and are placed in a "sponsor group" with two guardian upperclassmen, creating a "quasi family away from home." Upperclassmen generally get single rooms or spacious two-room doubles that sometimes include fireplaces. The open courtyards and gardens are popular study spots. A handful of students isolate themselves in Claremont proper, where apartments are scarce and expensive. Boarders must buy at least partial meal plans. The food is good, with steak dinners on Saturday and ice cream for dessert every day. Students

"Every freshman participates in a traditional ceremony involving gates and bird noises...the rest is a secret!"

with common interests can occupy one of the large university houses; there is a vegetarian group and a kosher kitchen, both of which serve meals to other undergraduates. Pomona has a well-established language dorm with wings for speakers of French, German, Spanish, Russian, and Chinese, as well as language tables at lunch. Campus security is ever-present: "Officers are approachable and easy to find," says a student, "and they create a reassuring presence on campus." Another adds, "The biggest nuisances are occasional incidents of bike theft or theft from dorm rooms."

Students at Pomona often spend Friday afternoons relaxing with friends over a brew at the Greek Theater. Social life begins in the dorms, where barbecues, parties, and study breaks are organized. There are movies five nights a week, and students also enjoy just tossing a Frisbee on the lawn. One student wanted to be sure that incoming freshmen and transfers knew of the Coop's (student union) "best milkshakes west of the Mississippi" and its "game room, with pool, Ping-Pong, pinball, and assorted video games." "With the five-college system, there's always something going on somewhere," asserts another Pomona enthusiast. Five-college parties happen nearly every weekend. During midterms and finals, however, the campus is a "social ghost town." Of more concern is the poor air quality, described by a junior as "oppressive on hot days during the fall semester." Most students are willing to live with the smog, but at least one student complains, "I'd prefer to breathe clean air."

Pomona is unique among the Claremont Colleges in that it has six non-national fraternities (four co-ed; there are no sororities), each with its own party rooms on campus. There is "no peer pressure to join frats," and no fraternity rivalry. As for booze, "Kegs are not allowed in dormitories, but there is an 'out of sight, out of mind' policy in which students can have as much alcohol in their rooms as they want," reports one student. Alcohol is not much of a problem, according to another student: "At Pomona no one feels pressured to drink or not drink. I've had a great time at parties completely sober, no one looks at me like I'm a nerd, and I respect others even if they drink." Harwood dorm throws the five-college costume party every Halloween, and interdorm Jell-O fights keep things lively. Freshman orientation gets interesting, too. "Every freshman participates in a traditional ceremony involving gates and bird noises," reports a student. "I can't say too much because the rest is a secret!"

There was a time when Pomona was an athletic powerhouse; the football team even knocked off mighty USC on Thanksgiving Day back in 1899. Currently, women's basketball, tennis, soccer, and swimming, and men's football, baseball, soccer, track, and water polo are strong programs. Intense rivalry exists between the colleges in the Claremont consortium; basketball games between Pomona, Pitzer, and CMS are "particularly heated." Intramurals, including hotly contested inner-tube water polo matches, attract many participants, and Pomona's $14 million athletic complex makes its facilities the best of the Claremonts.

"Pomona offers a unique and desirable juxtaposition of rigorous academics and comfortable social atmosphere," says a student. Another student says, "Once you take advantage of the five-college system, you realize how cool it is." The strongest link in an extremely attractive chain, Pomona continues to symbolize the rising status of the Claremont Colleges—and the West in general—in the world of higher education. There are few regrets about coming to Pomona. Says a senior, "We're in California. The sun is always shining. What's the problem?"

Classes are small at Pomona—the average is fourteen students—and the faculty makes a point of being accessible.

Overlaps

Stanford, Brown, UC–Berkeley, Yale, UCLA

If You Apply To > **Pomona:** Early decision: Nov. 15, Dec. 28. Regular admissions: Jan. 2. Financial aid: Feb. 1. Guarantees to meet demonstrated need. Campus interviews: strongly recommended, evaluative. SATs or ACTs: required. SAT IIs: required (writing and two others). Accepts the Common Application and electronic applications. Essay question: personal statement and choice of most important scientific development; influential character; or how diversity affects college experience.

Scripps College

1030 Columbia Avenue, Claremont, CA 91711

Scripps is a tiny, close-knit women's college with co-ed institutions literally right next door. Only Barnard and Spelman offer the same combination of single-sex and co-ed. Innovative Core Curriculum takes an interdisciplinary approach to learning.

Scripps College offers a solid, well-rounded education with a distinctly female sense of community. Founded in 1926 by newspaper publisher Ellen Browning Scripps, the college continues to pursue the mission of its founder: "to educate women by

Website:
www.scrippscollege.edu

(Continued)
Location: Suburban
Total Enrollment: 750
Undergraduates: 750
Male/Female: 0/100
SAT Ranges: V 620–720
    M 600–690
ACT Range: 26–30
Financial Aid: 51%
Expense: Pr $ $ $ $
Phi Beta Kappa: Yes
Applicants: 1,371
Accepted: 58%
Enrolled: 28%
Grad in 6 Years: 68%
Returning Freshmen: 88%
Academics: ✍ ✍ ✍ ½
Social: ☎ ☎ ☎
Q of L: ★ ★ ★ ★
Admissions: (909) 621-8149
Email Address: admission@
    scrippscollege.edu

Strongest Programs:
English
Studio Art
Biology
Psychology
Foreign Languages
Music
Politics/International Relations

developing their intellects and talents through active participation in a community of scholars." "Scrippsies," as they are sometimes called, are by and large a moderate to liberal group, with a sprinkling of radical feminists (who will kill you if you call them Scrippsies). All are interested in "proving their worth and combating sexism, stereotypes, and sexual assault."

Scripps's scenic thirty-acre campus, listed in the National Register of Historic Places, offers a tranquil, safe, and comfortable environment. The architecture is Spanish and Mediterranean, with Roman roof-tiled buildings and elegant landscaping. "We have more than twenty courtyards and a dozen fountains," says one student. A new performing arts complex is the most recent addition to the Scripps campus.

At the heart of the Scripps academic offerings is the Core Curriculum, a closely integrated sequence of three interdisciplinary courses focusing on ideas about the world and the methods used to generate these ideas. All students are required to take one course in each of the four disciplines: fine arts, letters, natural sciences, and social sciences. In addition, there is a foreign language, mathematics, and multicultural requirement, and all students must complete a senior thesis or project in their chosen field. "The courses here are definitely challenging and rigorous," says one student, noting that "we do a lot of work here but we also have a ton of fun." Although competitive, students tend to help one another through the academic challenges. "The climate here is more collaborative than competitive," says a sophomore.

Anything in the humanities is a good bet at Scripps. The languages (especially French and Spanish) are particularly strong; history and psychology are also good. The strong fine arts program gets an additional boost with the Millard Sheets Art

"The climate here is more collaborative than competitive."

Center, which includes a state-of-the-art studio and a freestanding museum-quality gallery. English tops the list of most heavily enrolled majors, followed by psychology, studio art, and biology. Physics is weaker than most departments, but students are quick to point out that the five-college system makes it easy to find solid offerings in every field. The Keck Science Center, a joint facility for students studying the sciences at Scripps, Claremont McKenna, and Pitzer, is a prime example of the camaraderie among Claremont schools. Media studies is now available as a major through cross-registration as well.

The Career Planning and Resources Center helps Scripps women integrate elements of their college experience in setting goals relevant to their lives at Scripps and beyond. Computers appear across the curriculum and are located in dorms for convenience. Students usually have no problem getting the courses they want. Inside those courses, students are lavished with attention from professors. "The teachers here are very dedicated to women's education and most will schedule time to meet with you outside of class or office hours," says a biology major.

Forty-six percent of Scripps women are from California. African-Americans account for 3 percent of the student body, Hispanics 6 percent, and Asian-Americans make up another 14 percent. As for relations between various ethnic groups on campus, a sophomore notes that "most people seem to mingle without a fuss." Gay rights, race issues, and women's issues are always a hot topic and "liberalism is generally expected," says a student. The college holds several programs on cultural diversity and has adopted "Principles of Community." The college doles out forty-three merit scholarships annually to outstanding students. Freshmen take part in a week-long orientation, and all are assigned to a peer mentor for the whole year.

Ninety-three percent of the students live in one of the eight small, home-style dorms, which are well maintained, luxurious, and even have "character," according to one chemistry major. "The dorms are amazing," says a sophomore. Many of the dorms boast their own reflecting pools and inner courtyards; a number of the rooms have balconies and are furnished with antiques and beautiful rugs. Students

Anything in the humanities is a good bet at Scripps.

praise the dining facilities, which serve vegetarian alternatives at every meal. Students agree that campus security is good. "Scripps is a very safe campus," says a student, "because campus security is good and because we take precautions."

Campus social life centers around the residence halls, which take turns throwing parties. Scripps is adamant about stopping underage drinking, and the school's alcohol policy is rather strict but it isn't foolproof. One student reports, "Underage students can still get alcohol through their older friends if they want it." Students hang out in the Motley, a coffeehouse, relax at $2 movies on Friday or Saturday nights, or attend the five-college parties that take place nearly every weekend. For male companionship, "Claremont McKenna is just across the street," cheers one sophomore. As far as traditions go, "at the end of orientation week there's Scripps Under the Stars, an exercise in shared humiliation for first-year women," reports a senior. "Everyone does skits or songs on the Wood Steps; it is followed by an ice cream social." Scripps fields joint Division III athletic teams with CMC and Harvey Mudd, and conference championships have been won by the soccer, tennis, swimming, cross-country, and basketball teams.

> "Scripps is dedicated not only to education but also to the empowerment and success of women."

The Career Planning and Resources Center helps Scripps women integrate elements of their college experience in setting goals relevant to their lives at Scripps and beyond.

Scripps has the appeal of being both a women's college with its supportive environment and part of the diverse academic and social university environment of Claremont. As a lit major sums up: "I feel supported and encouraged to be outspoken and confident with myself as a student and a woman. Scripps is dedicated not only to education but also to the empowerment and success of women."

Overlaps

UCLA, Occidental, Smith, University of Southern California, Wellesley

If You Apply To >

Scripps: Early decision: Nov. 1, Jan. 1. Regular admissions: Feb. 1. Guarantees to meet demonstrated need. Campus and alumni interviews: recommended, evaluative. SATs or ACTs: required. SAT IIs: recommended. Accepts the Common Application and electronic applications. Essay question: personal statement.

Clark University

950 Main Street, Worcester, MA 01610-1477

If Clark were located an hour to the east, it would be the hottest thing since Harvard. Worcester is not Boston, but Clarkies bring a sense of mission to their relationship with this old industrial town. Clark is liberal, tolerant, and world-renowned in psychology and geography.

A classic Clark University poster distills the school's philosophy into a single photograph: A normal green peapod, filled with multicolored peas. "Categorizing people," the poster says, "isn't something you can do here." And indeed, it's not. Clark started as an all-graduate school, excelling in disciplines such as psychology and geography. (It was the only American university where famed psychoanalyst Sigmund Freud lectured, as well as the birthplace of the American Psychological Association, and the concept of adolescence as distinct from childhood.) Now, Clark welcomes undergraduates of all backgrounds and interests, with small classes and lots of faculty attention. "It is a small community, where I feel right at home," says a senior. "I can get the attention I need, yet I still have the freedom and possibility to do whatever I want."

Website: www.clarku.edu
Location: Center city
Total Enrollment: 3,035
Undergraduates: 2,167
Male/Female: 39/61
SAT Ranges: V 540–650
  M 540–640
ACT Range: 22–27
Financial Aid: 51%
Expense: Pr $ $ $

(Continued)

Phi Beta Kappa: Yes

Applicants: 3,694

Accepted: 68%

Enrolled: 23%

Grad in 6 Years: 71%

Returning Freshmen: 87%

Academics: 🖋🖋🖋🖋

Social: ☎ ☎ ☎

Q of L: ★ ★ ★

Admissions: (508) 793-7431

Email Address:
admissions@clarku.edu

Strongest Programs:

Psychology

Geography

Physics

Chemistry

Biology

Government and International
Relations

Economics

Holocaust and Genocide
Studies

The Traina Center for the Arts opened in fall 2002. A former city elementary school, the center now houses recital, classroom, and office space, along with a darkroom, multimedia center and gallery.

Clark's compact, fifty-acre campus has "enough ivy, tall maples, and collegiate brick buildings to make a traditionalist happy," even though it's located in the gritty Main South section of Worcester. Buildings range from remodeled Victorian-era residences, former homes of prosperous merchants, to the award-winning Robert Hutchings Goddard Library. Clark is always renovating something—in the past decade, half of the fifty campus buildings have been completely renovated or newly constructed—and careful restoration has also brought a renewed sense of history to the area. A statue of Freud stands stoically in the center of the campus, marking the spot where he spoke. New additions include the Traina Center for the Arts, which opened in fall 2002. A former city elementary school, the center now houses recital, classroom, and office space, along with a darkroom, multimedia center, and gallery.

"I can get the attention I need, yet I still have the freedom and possibility to do whatever I want."

While Clark now serves primarily undergraduates, its history of graduate education is clearly evident in its classrooms. Most courses are seminars, and 80 percent have twenty-five or fewer students. First-year seminars are even smaller, limited to sixteen students each. They permit students to explore issues in depth in their first or second semesters, and the faculty member teaching the course acts as an academic adviser until students declare a major. In those seminars, students have isolated strands of DNA, explored the workings of the brain, discussed origins of modern sports, and interned at local elementary schools. "Students learn to compete against themselves, to be the best that they can be," a freshman says.

The foundation of a Clark education is the Program of Liberal Studies, which promotes the habits, skills, and perspectives essential to lifelong learning. Each student must complete eight courses: one in verbal expression, one in formal analysis, and six in perspectives—aesthetic, comparative, historical, language, scientific, and values. International studies majors take courses in those areas with a focus on the foreign. Interdisciplinary programs are popular, with women's studies especially good, and students also may design their own majors. Those who finish with a grade point average of 3.25 or better may take a fifth year for free, to obtain a master's degree. "There are people like me here, with common goals and values," says a senior. "There are professors who encourage me constantly. I am academically inspired."

Clark's historically strong psychology and geography departments continue to burnish their national reputations, the latter having churned out more Ph.D.s in the field than any other school in the nation, plus four members of the National Academy of Science (the most of any geography program). Also strong are the sciences, whose majors have high acceptance rates at medical and dental schools, and programs in management, government and international relations, and communication and culture. A relatively new and unusual concentration is urban development and social change. Students in the program have helped to revitalize Clark's own Worcester neighborhood. Concentrations in environment and society, and cultural identities and global processes, are no longer offered.

Regardless of major, Clark encourages students to take internships, through the university itself or the fourteen-college Worcester Consortium.* More than 20 percent of all Clark students spend at least one semester studying abroad at one of fifteen programs in ten countries. Even those who don't go abroad can get a taste of foreign culture, by taking courses or attending international research conferences at the Clark University Center in Luxembourg. Back on campus, faculty members really make an effort to get to know their students, says a senior: "I had a professor who, for our first assignment, asked us to bring in a picture and a paragraph describing ourselves. In a class of 150, this biology professor takes the time to learn the names of every single student." In fact, department heads often teach introductory science courses, says a psychology major.

Thirty-seven percent of Clark students are from Massachusetts; another large contingent hails from New York and other parts of New England, and international students from about ninety foreign countries make up another 8 percent. "Students are aware of different cultures and lifestyles, and are very good about accepting and learning from them," says a senior. The university also has a collaborative educational program with historically African-American Howard University in Washington, D.C., and the Multicultural Center has a grant-funded director to host regular programs exploring race relations and diversity. Politically, Clark has a reputation for being "(very) liberal," says a Spanish major. "We have been sometimes criticized for not being accepting of conservative viewpoints." Clark also offers countless merit scholarships, plus special "Making a Difference" scholarships for students interested in community service, worth $44,000 each.

"In a class of 150, this biology professor takes the time to learn the names of every single student."

Freshmen and sophomores at Clark are required to live in the dorms, and all except one are co-ed by floor or wing. In all, 76 percent of the student body bunks on campus. The rest—mostly juniors and seniors—find apartments and group houses nearby. However, the dorms have become so popular, a senior warns, that "there is currently a shortage of rooms. Everyone that wants campus housing will receive it, though first-year students may be temporarily tripled or quadrupled." After the first year, students must play the lottery to get rooms. Campus dwellers must buy the meal plan, which always offers student favorites like hamburgers, pizza, and pasta.

A relatively new and unusual concentration is urban development and social change. Students in the program have helped to revitalize Clark's own Worcester neighborhood.

Clark has no Greek life, but eighty student-run organizations offer "concerts, dances, karaoke nights, ice cream socials, and other events," says a junior. The campus pub has become Grind Central, a performance space for live music, speakers, and performers. Caffeine addicts need not despair, though. The student union in Dana Commons has pool and foosball tables, chess and other board games, a large-screen TV, and the Moonlight Cafe, which sells snacks and coffee. As for booze, first-year dorms are dry, and mixed-class halls "are dry if you are under twenty-one," says a Spanish major. "It's quite common for students to get caught" with beer or liquor that they shouldn't have.

Worcester and the vicinity host fourteen colleges, but the area's history—a manufacturing and industrial hub that's fallen on hard times—means it's hardly a "college town," students say. That said, Worcester does have movie theaters, restaurants with every conceivable type of cuisine, and small clubs where bands can play, as well as the Centrum, a 13,000-seat arena. Students mix with the townspeople through volunteer programs such as Clark University Brothers and Sisters. "There is always a lot to be done in the community, and Clark students rise to the challenge," says a senior. When Worcester gets too depressing, Clarkies head to the larger cities of Boston and Providence, or the rural wilds of Vermont, New Hampshire, and Maine. All are easily reachable by car or public transit.

"College is a time for finding yourself, and students at Clark are generally open-minded to whoever it is that you become."

Coping with the frigid New England winters includes quaffing cups of hot chocolate and dreaming about Spree Day—"what every Clarkie lives for," one student says. On Spree Day, classes are spontaneously cancelled one spring day, and everyone celebrates spring with a carnival on the green, including food, music, and games (with prizes!). Completely different is Academic Spree Day, which celebrates undergraduate research. Clark competes in the Division III, and the men's basketball team reached the Elite Eight of the NCAA tournament in 2001 and 2002. Top women's teams include basketball, cross-country, field hockey and crew. The Dolan Field House opened in May 2003, providing facilities and locker rooms for spring and fall teams, plus lighted outdoor fields. The crew team has a new boathouse on Lake Quinsigamond.

Clark started out doing things differently, with its sole focus on graduate students. Though it now caters mainly to undergraduates, the school continues to challenge convention, pioneering new teaching methods, pursuing new knowledge, and finding new ways to connect thinking and doing. "I enjoy Clark because I do not have to fit into a certain group of people," says a freshman. "College is a time for finding yourself, and students at Clark are generally open-minded to whoever it is that you become."

If You Apply To ➢

Clark: Early decision: Nov. 15. Regular admissions, financial aid, housing: Feb. 1. Does not guarantee to meet demonstrated need. Campus and alumni interviews: recommended, evaluative. SATs or ACTs: required. SAT IIs: optional. Accepts the Common Application and electronic applications. Essay question: significant experience, achievement or risk and its impact on you; issue of personal, local, national, or intellectual concern; influential person, fictional character, historical figure, or creative work; or a topic of your choice.

Clarkson University

Holcroft House, Box 5605, Potsdam, NY 13699

You know you're in the north country when the nearest major city is Montreal. Over the river and through the woods lies Clarkson, one of the few small, undergraduate-oriented technical universities in the nation. The atmosphere is informal and close-knit. Compare to Lehigh, Bucknell, and Union.

Website: www.clarkson.edu
Location: Small town
Total Enrollment: 3,107
Undergraduates: 2,756
Male/Female: 75/25
SAT Ranges: V 520–620
   M 580–670
Financial Aid: 88%
Expense: Pr $ $ $
Phi Beta Kappa: No
Applicants: 2,556
Accepted: 82%
Enrolled: 35%
Grad in 6 Years: 73%
Returning Freshmen: 88%
Academics: ✍ ✍ ✍
Social: ☎ ☎
Q of L: ★ ★ ★
Admissions: (315) 268-6400
Email Address:
   admission@clarkson.edu

At Clarkson University, engineering and ice hockey reign supreme. More than half of the student body is enrolled in the engineering program, and the hockey team is a perennial contender for top honors. Students at this tiny school take advantage of a quality technical education and a small-town environment that offers plenty to do, especially during the sled dog days of winter.

The tiny town of Potsdam, New York, is cloistered away between the Adirondacks and the St. Lawrence River. The "hill campus," where most freshmen and sophomores live and take classes, relies mainly on modern architecture and lots of woods and wildlife. Personal computers are a must, and countless resources exist on the campus network, which can be accessed from dorm rooms. Among the most recent additions to campus is the Adirondack Lodge, which serves as headquarters for student outdoor recreation.

Engineering isn't the only thing at Clarkson, but it certainly gets top billing; 49 percent of the students are in the program. The combined programs in electrical/computer engineering and mechanical/aeronautical engineering earn the highest marks from students. Clarkson's School of Business has majors in business and technology management, e-business, financial information analysis, and information systems and business processes. Project Arete allows students to earn a double major in management and a liberal arts discipline. Physics and chemistry are the strongest offerings in the sciences, and would-be doctors have the benefit of a joint program combining biology and—you guessed it—engineering. The liberal arts and humanities are cited by students as being weaker than other departments.

As part of their Foundation Curriculum requirements, all students at Clarkson are required to take six liberal arts courses; two in mathematics; two in science; and one each in computing, engineering, and business. Freshmen are required to take a two-semester Great Ideas course along with a personal wellness course. A convocation program for new students is designed to introduce them to distinguished speakers and performers whose appearances may broaden their educational horizons. About thirty freshmen are invited to participate in the honors program, which offers specially developed courses and research experiences. New interdisciplinary majors have been added in biomolecular science and software engineering.

"The professors are excited by the subjects they teach and it shows."

Clarkson prides itself on intimacy and personalized instruction, and the fact that 80 percent of the Foundation courses are taught by full-fledged faculty members proves that it's no idle boast. "The professors here are very intelligent, readily available, and willing to help their students in any way they can," says an environmental science and policy major. Another student adds, "The professors are excited by the subjects they teach and it shows." Clarkson isn't the academic pressure cooker that many technical institutes are, but it really depends on whom you talk to. "The academic climate here is fairly rigorous but not to the point where it's overwhelming," says a business administration and social science double major. A senior adds, "Students mainly help each other out and have a laid-back demeanor." The bottom line of a Clarkson education is getting a job after graduation, and students uniformly praise the career counseling office and note with pride Clarkson's high placement rate. One junior says that the career center is "very good at getting students to think about their futures."

At Clarkson the students are friendly, serious-minded, and down-to-earth; radicals are notably absent. Seventy-two percent of the students graduated in the top quarter of their class. Seventy-seven percent are New Yorkers, and 3 percent are from abroad. Clarkson has trouble luring minorities to its remote locale; the combined total of African-Americans, Hispanics, and Asian-Americans is 7 percent. "Our campus definitely needs more minority students," says a senior. All accepted applicants demonstrating financial need are offered some aid, but not necessarily enough to meet full need. Clarkson awards a handful of merit scholarships each year, ranging from $1,000 to $9,000. Eighteen athletic scholarships are offered for ice hockey players only.

Seventy-seven percent of all students live in campus housing. Students are required to reside on campus all four years, unless exempted to live in a Greek house. Most dorms are centrally located and are cleaned every day. "The dorms are comfortable and very well maintained," says a student. Four of the dorms are all-men and the rest are co-ed by floor. All freshman are

"Our campus definitely needs more minority students."

housed with students in their major areas of study and in some instances in their department, giving them the chance to study and learn together. Many underclassmen are housed in conventional dorms, but university-owned townhouse apartments offer more gracious living. "The dorm situation is handled by the lottery, and housing improves based on your class year," a senior reports.

In keeping with Clarkson's "come as you are" atmosphere, the social scene is low key. "There are activities, such as comedians, picnics, and other types of entertainment on campus," says one senior. "However, a good deal of socializing also takes place off campus." Fifteen percent of the men and 12 percent of the women join the Greek system. Fraternity beer blasts are the staple of weekend life, and those not into the Greek scene (and over twenty-one) can head to the handful of bars in downtown Potsdam. Nearby SUNY–Potsdam is also a source of social life,

(Continued)

Strongest Programs:

Engineering

Chemistry

Management

Physics

Biology

Math

Computer Science

Seventy-seven percent of all students live in campus housing. Students are required to reside on campus all four years, unless exempted to live in a Greek house.

A convocation program for new students is designed to introduce them to distinguished speakers and performers whose appearances may broaden their educational horizons.

especially for men frustrated by Clarkson's three-to-one male/female ratio. Drinking is prohibited on campus, and residence-life staff are on the watch for violators; however, students report that it's still easy for the underaged to be served off campus. For those who crave the bustle of city nightlife, Ottawa and Montreal are each about an hour and a half away by car.

When it comes to sports, hockey is first and foremost in the hearts of Clarkson students—the only one in which the university competes in Division I. The team has been ECAC champ in recent years, and contends for the national championship with other blue-chip teams like archrivals Cornell and St. Lawrence. A Division I women's ice hockey program has been initiated. In addition, Clarkson offers nineteen Division III sports and a healthy dose of intramurals. The ski teams, Nordic and Alpine, are among the best in the nation, and men's baseball and golf and women's soccer and basketball are also strong. For weekend athletes, an abundance of skiing and other outdoor and winter sports is within easy driving distance.

For those seeking a technical education without having to worry about big-school problems, Clarkson will be like a breath of mountain-fresh air. Come January, you'll feel like an Eskimo, but at least you'll have a high-tech igloo.

Overlaps

Cornell University, Northeastern, Rochester Institute of Technology, Rensselaer Polytechnic, Syracuse

If You Apply To >

Clarkson: Early decision: Dec. 1, Jan. 15. Regular admissions: Mar. 15. Financial aid: Mar. 1. Does not guarantee to meet demonstrated need. Campus interviews: recommended, informational. Alumni interviews: optional, informational. SATs: required. Accepts the Common Application and electronic applications. Essay question: personal statement.

Clemson University

Sikes Hall, Box 345124, Clemson, SC 29634-5124

Calhoun College, Clemson's honors program—the oldest in South Carolina—is open to freshmen who scored 1200 or above on their SATs and ranked in the top 10 percent of their high school graduating class.

Website: www.clemson.edu
Location: Small town
Total Enrollment: 17,465
Undergraduates: 14,066
Male/Female: 54/46
SAT Ranges: V 525–620
  M 555–640
ACT Range: 23–27
Financial Aid: 11%
Expense: Pub $ $
Phi Beta Kappa: No
Applicants: 10,472
Accepted: 64%
Enrolled: 45%
Grad in 6 Years: 71%
Returning Freshmen: 84%
Academics: ✍ ✍ ✍

Clemson is a technically oriented university in the mold of Georgia Tech, Virginia Tech, and North Carolina State. Smaller than the latter two and more focused on undergraduates than Georgia Tech, Clemson serves up its education with ample helpings of school spirit and small-town hospitality.

Nestled in the foothills of the Blue Ridge Mountains, Clemson University is a place where Southern spirit continues to flourish. The campus occupies terrain that once was walked by John C. Calhoun, former Southern senator and a Civil War–era rabble-rouser of the first degree. Today Clemson features quality academics in technical areas such as engineering and biology, and big-time athletics supported by strong school spirit.

CU's fourteen-hundred-acre campus is situated on what was once Fort Hill Plantation, the homestead of Thomas Green Clemson. The campus is surrounded by seventeen thousand acres of university farms and woodlands and offers a spectacular view of the nearby lake and mountains. Architectural styles are an eclectic mix of modern and nineteenth-century collegiate. Newer additions to the campus include a student center.

Electrical engineering is the university's largest department, and computer engineering is among the nation's best in research on large-scale integrated computer circuitry and robotics. Chemists enjoy the impressive Hunter Laboratory. The College of Architecture, one of the school's most selective programs, offers intensive semesters at the Overseas Center for Building Research and Urban Study in Genoa, Italy. A fantastic resource for science enthusiasts and history buffs is the library's collection of first editions of the scientific work of Galileo and Newton. Because of the prevailing technical emphasis, most students interested in the liberal arts head "down country" to the University of South Carolina. Undergraduate teaching has always been one of Clemson's strong points, and for students interested in pursuing a liberal arts curriculum, the school has degrees in fine arts, philosophy, and languages and enjoys a strong regional reputation for its history program. "My favorite academic department has been the political science department," says a senior marketing major. "The professors have challenged me and really helped me to learn while showing me they care." Highly motivated students should consider Calhoun College, Clemson's honors program—the oldest in South Carolina—open to freshmen who scored 1200 or above on their SATs and ranked in the top 10 percent of their high-school graduating class. Clemson also offers exchange programs in Mexico, Scotland, Ecuador, Spain, England, Australia, and Italy.

> **"The professors have challenged me and really helped me to learn while showing me they care."**

General education requirements include courses in communication and speaking, computer skills, mathematical sciences, physical or biological science, humanities, and social science. Each student is assigned a faculty advisor for help and guidance. "My academic advisors are perfect," says a health science major. Academically, the level of difficulty varies. "Most intro courses are not that difficult," one senior says. However, "the upper-level courses are rigorous." Students report some problems finishing a degree in four years, and class registration can be a hassle.

Clemson's student body has a definite Southern air, as 70 percent of the undergrads hail from South Carolina, with most of the rest from neighboring states. The average Clemson student is friendly and conservative, and though, as a public institution, the school isn't affiliated with any church, there is a strong Southern Baptist presence on campus. "We are creative, hard working, and love to be challenged," says an economics major. Thirty-seven percent were in the top tenth of their high school graduating class. African-Americans make up 7 percent of the student body,

> **"Student athletes get to register for classes first and sometimes get priority treatment."**

and Hispanics and Asian-Americans account for less than 2 percent combined. The university offers three hundred academic scholarships and as many athletic scholarships as the NCAA allows. One students grumbles that "student athletes get to register for classes first and sometimes get priority treatment."

Housing gets positive reviews, and 47 percent of the students live on campus, usually during their first two years. Most of the dorms are single-sex, though co-ed university-owned apartment complexes are also an option. "It can be competitive to receive a room if you don't send your housing information on time," warns a student. Clemson House and Calhoun Courts, the co-ed halls, are considered the best places to be. The food is typical dorm fare. Upperclassmen can cook for themselves, and each dorm has kitchen facilities.

After class, many students hop on their bikes and head to nearby Lake Hartwell. The beautiful Blue Ridge mountain range is also close by for hiking and camping, and beaches and ski slopes are both within driving distance. Atlanta and Charlotte are only two hours away by car, and Charleston is four hours away on the coast. Aside from the sports teams, fraternities and sororities provide most of the social life. Fifteen percent of Clemson men and 22 percent of women go Greek. Though Clemson empties out a bit on away-game weekends, there are still plenty of off-campus

(Continued)

Social: ☎ ☎ ☎ ☎
Q of L: ★ ★ ★ ★
Admissions: (864) 656-2287
Email Address:
 cuadmissions@clemson.edu

Strongest Programs:
Engineering
Architecture
Biological Sciences
Business

No haven for carpetbaggers or liberals, Clemson is best at serving those whose interests lie in technical fields.

parties where the main activity is drinking beer. The town itself is pretty small, with a few bars and movie theaters, but some students love it. "Clemson is an awesome college town," a marketing major says.

Sports still help make the world go 'round at Clemson, and on weekends when the Tiger teams are playing there are pep rallies, cookouts, dances, and parties for the mobs of excited fans. The roads leading to campus are painted with large orange pawprints, an insignia that symbolizes great enthusiasm for Clemson sports. So, too, are half the fans at an athletic event, making the stands look like an orange grove. Football fever starts with the annual First Friday Parade, held before the first home game, and on every game day the campus dissolves into a sea of Tiger orange. Clemson has regained its former gridiron glory under the leadership of Coach Tommy Bowden. Hordes of Tiger fans cram "Death Valley" for every game and are especially rowdy when the reviled University of South Carolina Gamecocks are in town. Other very competitive athletic teams include basketball, baseball, and men's track.

No haven for carpetbaggers or liberals, Clemson is best at serving those whose interests lie in technical fields. School spirit is contagious, fueled by a love of big-time college sports, and becomes lifelong for many Clemson students. Everyone can become part of the Clemson family, from Southern belle to Northern Yankee, as long as they're friendly, easygoing, not aggressively intellectual, and enthusiastic about life in general and the Tigers in particular.

Overlaps

University of South Carolina, College of Charleston, UNC–Chapel Hill, University of Georgia, North Carolina State

If You Apply To ➤

Clemson: Rolling admissions: May 1. Does not guarantee to meet demonstrated need. Campus interviews: optional, informational. No alumni interviews. SATs or ACTs: required. SAT IIs: required (math II for math placement). No essay question.

Colby College

Lunder House, Waterville, ME 04901

The northernmost outpost of higher education in the East. Colby's picturesque small-town setting is a short hop from the sea coast or the Maine wilderness. No frats since the college abolished them twenty years ago. A well-toned, outdoorsy student body in the mold of Middlebury, Williams, and Dartmouth.

Website: www.colby.edu
Location: Small city
Total Enrollment: 1,830
Undergraduates: 1,830
Male/Female: 47/53
SAT Ranges: V 620–700
  M 640–710
ACT Range: 27–30
Financial Aid: 38%
Expense: Pr $ $ $ $
Phi Beta Kappa: Yes
Applicants: 3,873

Colby College draws students who like to work hard and play harder, whether in the classroom or on the ski slopes. The nearby town of Waterville, Maine (population 20,000), offers few distractions, and close friendships with peers and professors help ward off the bitter winter chill. Colby's top study abroad program offers some respite from the howling winds, and even those who don't spend a semester or year away can get a taste during the month of January, when Jan-Plan trips send Colby students far and wide. "Colby allows me to explore educational possibilities and experiences of all kinds, from taking a class with a top U.S. economist, to sea kayaking, to mentoring needy children in local schools," says a sophomore. "The setting is picturesque, and the faculty and students alike are friendly and warm."

Colby sits high on a hill, with beautiful views of the surrounding countryside. Its 714 acres include a wildlife preserve, miles of cross-country trails, and a pond used in winter as an ice-skating rink. Georgian architecture predominates, and the oldest buildings are redbrick with white trim, ivy, and brass nameplates above their hunter-green doors. The more contemporary buildings lend a touch of modernity. One of the most iconic Colby buildings is the library tower, which is topped with a blue light. No K-Mart special, students honor this light with a party each year, and they're fond of telling one another to "keep the blue light burning" as they catch up on reading and writing. A $44 million plan to renovate Colby's residence halls and three dining halls continues, with Averill Hall gutted and renovated in the summer of 2003. The trustees have approved a campus expansion, which will add four buildings in the next decade, centered around the new Colby Green.

As a small college with a history of innovation and educational excellence, Colby encourages students to learn for learning's sake, rather than for a good grade. "Students get their work done, and do it well, but it is not cutthroat or competitive," says a senior. "The pressure is self-induced." Students must complete distribution requirements in English composition, foreign language, "Areas" (one course each in arts, historical studies, literature, quantitative reasoning and social sciences, and two courses in natural sciences), "Diversity" (two courses focusing on how diversity has contributed to the human experience), and "Wellness" (five supper seminars over the first two semesters). Freshmen eager to fulfill that language requirement can ship off to Cuernavaca or Dijon to take care of it, delaying on-campus enrollment until the second semester. Other popular and well-regarded programs include economics, biology, English, and government, which also happen to be the four most popular majors. Music is strong, too. New minors include Italian studies and women's, gender, and sexuality studies; the major in philosophy and mathematics has been discontinued.

Colby's faculty is devoted to undergraduate teaching. "The main reason I chose to attend a small liberal arts college was that I wanted to be a name and not just a number to my professors," says an English major. "All the professors I have had are very passionate about teaching, and encourage student input and discussion," agrees an anthropology and religious studies major. While faculty advisors get high marks, students say career counseling could be improved, though the office does bring prospective employers up from Boston and New York to conduct on-campus interviews.

Colby was the first college to establish a special January term, back in 1962, and students must take three such terms for credit to graduate. Motivated students might use the month off to serve an internship, study abroad, or prepare an in-depth report. Less serious types head for the ski slopes or southern beaches, and write a

"Colby allows me to explore educational possibilities and experiences of all kinds."

quick paper at the end of the month. The school also sponsors Jan-Plan trips to everywhere from Nicaragua to Vietnam, including Bermuda (for biology), Connecticut's Mystic Seaport (for marine biology), Kyoto, Japan, and the great cities of Europe. For would-be engineers, there are joint 3–2 programs with Case Western Reserve, Dartmouth, and the University of Rochester, and exchange programs with Clark Atlanta and Howard. With all of these options, perhaps it's no wonder that nearly 75 percent of Colby students spend some time abroad.

Only 16 percent of Colby students are Mainers; the rest learn to act like natives during the COOT program (Colby Outdoor Orientation Trips). These four-day excursions by bicycle, canoe, or foot introduce them to the beauty of the Maine wilderness. The administration is trying to make Colby more diverse, but rural Maine can be a hard sell for students from urban centers. African-Americans account for 3 percent of the student body, Hispanics are 2 percent, and Asian-Americans contribute 5 percent. "People are aware of issues related to sexuality, race, religion, cultural differences," says a junior. "People are open-minded and welcome these differences. People are

(Continued)

Accepted: 33%
Enrolled: 37%
Grad in 6 Years: 88%
Returning Freshmen: 94%
Academics: ✍ ✍ ✍ ✍ ½
Social: ☎ ☎ ☎
Q of L: ★ ★ ★ ★
Admissions: (207) 872-3168
Email Address:
   admissions@colby.edu

Strongest Programs:
Economics
Government
English
International Studies
Environmental Studies
Natural Sciences
Music

The Trustees have approved a campus expansion, which will add four buildings in the next decade, centered around the new Colby Green.

similarly aware of environmental issues." The Oak Institute organizes symposia on international human rights; recently, an anti-child labor crusader from Pakistan, and a rural development advocate from the Congo, came to campus as fellows.

Ninety-four percent of Colby students live on campus, where residence halls have live-in faculty members. Dorms are co-ed, and come in varieties including "quiet, substance-free, and regular," says a computer science and music major. There are singles, doubles, and triples, and all halls have students from all four classes. While this enables students to make friends of all ages, "room draw can be stressful, due to gender and class quotas in each dorm," says an anthropology and religious studies major. About one hundred dred seniors live off campus each year, in new apartment-style buildings. Dining hall menus "are all online, so you can decide which dining hall to go to based on what they have that day," says an economics major. "For college, the food is really good, especially Sunday brunch."

"For college, the food is really good, especially Sunday brunch."

When the weekend comes, Colby students keep busy with "parties, shows, plays, talks and concerts," says a junior. The college's Greek system was abolished in 1984, when most current students were still learning their ABCs. But house parties and free-flowing booze still define the social life for many, even with prohibitions (and $250 fines) for open containers. "A moderate number of activities go on every weekend, and during the week, though the most successful are often the ones that involve alcohol," quips an English major. Popular road trips include Augusta, Portland, and Freeport, Maine (home to the L.L. Bean factory and store). Also easy to reach are the bright lights of Boston and Montreal, and the slopes of Sugarloaf, Vermont. Waterville itself is "an old factory town," a senior says. "There are many cute little lunch restaurants," and shops that cater to the college crowd, as well as community-service opportunities, but not much else.

The Colby administration likes to share two "big secrets" about Maine winters: they're beautiful, and they're a lot harsher and colder in the telling than in the living. Still, an enthusiasm for chilly weather and outdoor sports are the major non-academic credentials needed to find contentment here. Everyone looks forward to hockey and football games against archrivals Bowdoin and Bates, as well as the annual winter carnival and snow-sculpture contest. Athletics have come a long way since the first intercollegiate croquet game, played at Colby in 1860, and in recent years, Colby has produced ten All-Americans, including three in Division I alpine skiing, and seven in Division III sports. Nonvarsity athletes are eager participants in many of the twenty-six intramural sports.

Colby doesn't only look like the traditional New England liberal-arts college, with its small-town setting and historic, ivy-covered buildings. It feels that way, too, with long-standing traditions, tons of school spirit and caring faculty members, who focus on developing their charges' minds. "The best part about Colby is how friendly the students are," says a junior. "Everyone is really happy to be here, which creates a warm vibe."

Colgate University

13 Oak Drive, Hamilton, NY 13346

At less than three thousand students, Colgate is smaller than Bucknell and Dartmouth but bigger than Hamilton and Williams. Like the other four, it offers small-town living and close interaction between students and faculty. Greek organizations and jock mentality are still well-entrenched despite administrative efforts to neutralize them.

From the herbarium to the Devonian fossils to the sixteen-inch reflecting telescope, it's clear that the small Colgate University has more to offer its students than its picture-postcard setting. Indeed, behind the walls at this elite liberal arts college is a vibrant academic environment pumped up in tiny classes, matched with an equally vibrant sense of school spirit and overall eagerness. "I have soaked up every opportunity that has come my way," gushes a sophomore English major.

Back in 1880, toothpaste mogul William Colgate gave $50,000 to the fledgling university—enough to get its name changed from Madison to Colgate. Colgate's 515-acre campus is located on a hillside overlooking the village of Hamilton near Lake Moraine in rural New York. Its ivy-covered limestone buildings are all set amid tree-lined drives and lush green spaces, perfect for rugby, Frisbee, or a host of other outdoor diversions. The campus is surrounded by rolling hills and farmland, making "the view from the high ground part of the memories of

> "The student body is made up of driven, successful students who embody the philosophy of 'Work hard, play hard.'"

many Colgate people," a student says. Recent projects include a new university bookstore to allow the move of the current bookstore downtown. In 2001, Little Hall, a state-of-the-art building that houses the art and art history programs, provided needed extra work and teaching space for the growing department. There is an outdoor sculpture garden connecting Little Hall to the Eric J. Ryan Studio building.

Colgate's interdisciplinary first-year seminar program gives freshmen a chance to meet top faculty and congregate in small groups. The faculty first established an interdisciplinary core program in 1928, and, while it has been adapted over the years, the core has been a foundation of the curriculum ever since. The latest revision examines the development of Western and non-Western cultures and gives students a personal view of science and technology. The school also requires proficiency in a foreign language. Add to that one of fifty majors (or design your own), four physical education classes, and a swim test, and you have the Colgate version of a liberal arts education.

Among the concentrations in the liberal arts curriculum, English/writing, economics, psychology, philosophy/religion, history, and political science stand out. The college offers four concentration programs in environmental studies: environmental biology, geography, geology, and economics. The new minor in film and media studies encourages students to critically examine how mass media influence individuals' ideology, identity, and historical consciousness. All language instruction programs are linked to off-campus study groups led by Colgate professors, and the Lawrence Hall Language Labs and classrooms offer state-of-the-art language studies facilities. Colgate's curriculum has an international flavor, and more than half of all students take advantage of the school's off-campus study programs—which include three domestic programs, like the one in Bethesda, Maryland, at the National Institutes of Health. In addition to the Maritime Studies Program* and the Sea Semester,* Colgate's international study options, many led by their own professors, include England, Japan, Nigeria, Russia, Poland, Central America, France, Germany, Switzerland,

Website: www.colgate.edu
Location: Rural
Total Enrollment: 2,837
Undergraduates: 2,786
Male/Female: 49/51
SAT Ranges: V 610–700
    M 630–710
ACT Range: 27–31
Financial Aid: 45%
Expense: Pr $ $ $ $
Phi Beta Kappa: Yes
Applicants: 6,268
Accepted: 34%
Enrolled: 35%
Grad in 6 Years: 88%
Returning Freshmen: 94%
Academics: ✍ ✍ ✍ ✍ ½
Social: ☎ ☎ ☎
Q of L: ★ ★ ★
Admissions: (315) 228-7401
Email Address:
    admission@mail.colgate.edu

Strongest Programs:
Biology
Economics
Foreign Language and
    Literature
History
Philosophy
Political Science
Psychology

The new minor in film and media studies encourages students to critically examine how mass media influence individuals' ideology, identity, and historical consciousness.

and Spain. One of the most exciting off-campus study programs emphasizes the historical, environmental, and geographical diversity of Australia, and gives the students the opportunity to travel there. The Center for Ethics and World Studies brings nationally known authorities to campus to focus on different subjects each year.

Colgate works hard to keep its class sizes small; 99 percent of the courses have fewer than fifty students. Perhaps Colgate's greatest asset is a talented and dedicated faculty. "I have never been so challenged and richly rewarded in class," says one student. "Professors really care about getting to know their students," says a geography major, "whether talking during office hours or over coffee downtown." Undergraduate research is one of Colgate's greatest strengths, and its faculty receives accolades for involving students. Each summer, more than one hundred students assist professors in their work. Academic advising is administered through the First-Year Seminar instructor, giving all students a classroom relationship with their advisor. Career advisors receive praise, too. "They are organized and ready and willing to help you write a resume, contact alumni and network, look for a job or internship, or prepare for an interview."

Incoming freshmen get the campus to themselves for orientation, and some go on a week-long camping trip before that to make friends and see the Adirondacks. For the 78 percent of Colgate grads who go directly to jobs rather than graduate school, the career counseling center is a blessing. Many students credit both the center and Colgate's strong and loyal alumni network with helping them land their first job.

"The student body is made up of driven, successful students who embody the philosophy of 'Work hard, play hard,'" says a student. With a combined minority population of only 17 percent, many students lament Colgate's lack of diversity. "Our effort to create a more diverse student body is one of the main issues facing Colgate today," explains one underclassman. Colgate has implemented an honor code that was developed, written, and passed recently by the students. Though there are no merit

"Colgate has helped me define who I am as a person and who I want to be."

scholarships available, Colgate does meet the demonstrated financial need of all admitted students. "Financial aid is very competitive. Colgate will give you a great offer the first time around instead of making you squabble over the figures," says one sophomore. "The aid is above and beyond any I received at other schools." And student athletes need not worry: Colgate now offers thirty-one scholarships each year to qualified jocks.

Colgate's housing options range from traditional buildings with fireplaces to new ones that seem more like hotels than dorms. "Residence life is more appropriate than housing because of the all-encompassing nature of the services," one student explains. Another student adds, "All the rooms are a good size, and the beds are comfortable." The university offers various special-interest housing, including a substance-free dorm. About 250 upperclassmen are allowed to live off campus each year, and the remaining 87 percent live in university housing. Miss that home cookin'? No worries. You can give the campus chefs one of your favorite family recipes...and they'll make it. One dish some students remember loving was "Tony's Dad's Oatmeal Pancakes." There's also a number to call to get each dining hall's dinner menus by phone.

Miss that home cookin'? No worries. You can give the campus chefs one of your favorite family recipes...and they'll make it. One dish some students remember loving was "Tony's Dad's Oatmeal Pancakes." There's also a number to call to get each dining hall's dinner menus by phone.

There are some new additions to Hamilton—the Palace Theatre, new restaurants, a candy store—that have upped the town's appeal to college students. It's a friendly place where everyone says hello to one another, a student says, and folks are welcoming to the students. The town is not, however, a social mecca. "It's more of a village than a town," says one student. "Don't come here looking for NYC because you won't find it!" There's one very welcome addition to the town's main street, thanks to Colgate. The college opened the Barge Canal Coffee Company in a downtown storefront. The informal coffeehouse, open to faculty, students, and townspeople, has been very popular among Colgate students. "Besides serving up some mean Java, the atmosphere is terrific, cheap, and there are games, puzzles, magazines, and books to occupy your hours," gushes a junior.

Thirty-five percent of men and 32 percent of women belong to Greek houses, so these still provide many of the social options as well as considerable controversy over whether their values are conducive to a healthy campus environment. The university has increased its funding of student activities fourfold in the last decade, and has stepped up its efforts to offer alternatives to frat parties and alcohol. Such measures are the latest signs of a running battle between the faculty and alumni over the proper balance between academics and social life that has plagued Colgate for decades. Another big issue on campus: making Colgate more environmentally aware. Colgate is far from a "suitcase school," and for good reason. Luminaries, including Ed Harris, Dave Chappelle, and Mo Rocca, often speak and perform on campus, while there are free movies, cultural dinners, and improv comedy performances to keep students local. The campus pub and Edge Cafe offer on-campus social options, and dance parties have recently attracted enthusiastic participation. Spring Party Weekend and Winterfest are popular annual traditions as is Octoberfest, which features pumpkin carving and a huge bonfire. Under the category of clean fun are the traditional rites of passage that punctuate the Colgate calendar. Among them are torchlight processions in the fall for first-years and the spring for seniors, and, of course, the Colgate versus Cornell hockey game.

Colgate students love athletics. Colgate's teams play in Division I and, despite being a David among many Goliaths, win more than their share of games. Hockey, football, and basketball are the top varsity spectator sports, and the teams are fierce competitors in the Eastern leagues. Men's and women's soccer also draw great crowds. The men's football team has been league champ, and women's teams have also brought home trophies in field hockey, volleyball, and softball. Colgate also gives its students plenty of space to play and compete, including the Sanford Field House, the Lineberry natatorium, the nationally recognized Seven Oaks golf course, a trap range, a rock quarry for climbing, miles of trails for running and cycling, as well as sailing and crew facilities at scenic Lake Moraine, five minutes north of town.

In between the torchlight ceremony leading first-years to convocation to the same procession the night before graduation for seniors, Colgate students take a big bite of the world as their college changes with the times. But what stays steady is the school's dedication to elite academics, strong relationships between faculty and students, and the job of molding tomorrow's leaders. "Colgate has helped me define who I am as a person and who I want to be," a sophomore says. "There is no question in my mind that Colgate meets, and even exceeds, all of my hopes and expectations."

Colgate is far from a "suitcase school," and for good reason. Luminaries, including Ed Harris, Dave Chappelle, and Mo Rocca, often speak and perform on campus, while there are free movies, cultural dinners, and improv comedy performances to keep students local.

Overlaps

Cornell University, Dartmouth, Middlebury, Tufts, Boston College

If You Apply To ➢

Colgate: Early decision: Nov. 15, Jan. 15. Regular admissions: Jan 15. Financial aid: Feb. 1. Guarantees to meet demonstrated need. Campus and alumni interviews: optional, informational. SATs and SAT IIs (writing and two others) or ACTs required. Accepts the Common Application and electronic applications. Essay question: Common Application essays and supplemental essay on rotating topics.

Colorado College

14 East Cache La Poudre Street, Colorado Springs, CO 80903

The Block Plan is CC's calling card. It is great for in-depth study and field trips but less suited to projects that take an extended period of time. The allure of the Rockies draw outdoor enthusiasts and East Coasters who want to ski. CC is the only leading liberal arts college between Iowa and the Pacific.

Website:
www.ColoradoCollege.edu
Location: Urban
Total Enrollment: 1,930
Undergraduates: 1,902
Male/Female: 44/56
SAT Ranges: V 590–670
M 590–670
ACT Range: 26–30
Financial Aid: 40%
Expense: Pr $ $ $ $
Phi Beta Kappa: Yes
Applicants: 3,411
Accepted: 53%
Enrolled: 27%
Grad in 6 Years: 83%
Returning Freshmen: 92%
Academics: ✍ ✍ ✍ ✍
Social: ☎ ☎ ☎ ☎
Q of L: ★ ★ ★ ★
Admissions: (800) 542-7214
Email Address: admissions@
coloradocollege.edu

Strongest Programs:
Biology
Geology
English
Mathematics
Psychology
Neuroscience
Drama
Philosophy

Former Ohio Governor and Peace Corps Director Richard Celeste took over at Colorado College in July 2002, charged with using his diplomatic and fund-raising experience to raise the school's profile and endowment. One thing he has no plans to change is the academic program, which lets students focus on a single class at a time. CC is one of just three U.S. schools offering block scheduling, also known as the "One-Course-At-A-Time" method. For more than a century, CC's focus on academics, and its breathtaking location in the heart of the Rocky Mountains, has drawn liberal-leaning liberal arts enthusiasts who also like to go out and play.

Founded in 1874, the college campus lies at the foot of Pike's Peak, in the politically conservative town of Colorado Springs. The surrounding neighborhood is listed on the National Register of Historic Places, as are many CC buildings, including its first, Cutler Hall (1879), and Palmer Hall, named after town founder William J. Palmer. (He was also a major force behind establishment of the college.) The prevailing architectural styles are Romanesque and English Gothic, with some more modern structures thrown in. The Western Ridge dorm complex opened in fall 2002, offering apartment-style living for 290 students, plus a spacious courtyard, cafe, and meeting space. A 54,000-square-foot building for the psychology, math, and geology departments, and the environmental sciences program, was finished in the summer of 2003.

CC requires students to take thirty-two courses, at least half outside their major department. Within those thirty-two courses, two must focus on the Western tradition; two on the non-Western tradition, minority culture, or gender studies; and three on the natural sciences, including lab or field study. Foreign-language proficiency is also required, and students must complete either a six-course thematic minor, which examines an issue or theme, cultural group, geographic area or historical era, or six social-sciences courses outside their major. What really defines the academic climate, though, is the block schedule (also used by Cornell College in Iowa). Students take eight courses between early September and mid-May, but focus on each one, in turn, for three-and-a-half weeks. Four-and-a-half-day breaks separate the terms. The plan helps students stay focused, eliminating the temptation to let one course slide so that they can catch up in another. But there are trade-offs. Students say it can be hard to integrate material from courses taken one at a time. There's also the danger of burnout, because so much material is crammed into such a short span. Still, prevailing vibe is low-key. "You decide how rigorous the course is by how much effort you give," explains a freshman. "The only person you are ever really competing with is yourself." The First Year Experience program helps students adjust to this unorthodox academic setup. The FYE theme changes every two years; recently, it was "Order and Chaos."

> "The school could definitely be classified as 'hippie.'"

Students at Colorado tend to be bright and independent; they say the school's best programs include the sciences and English. "Writing and hands-on experience are strong priorities," says a biology major. The block schedule permits some classes at unique times and in unique places—for instance, astronomy at midnight, or coral biology work in the Caribbean. The college's popular program in Southwest studies includes time at its Baca campus, 175 miles away in the historic San Luis Valley. Other interesting interdisciplinary programs include Asian studies, North American studies, studies in war and peace, American-Ethnic studies, and neuroscience. CC also offers study abroad in locations ranging from France and Germany to Japan, China, Tanzania, and Zimbabwe. Yet more options are available through the Associated Colleges of the Midwest.* And for students who want to see more of the U.S., there are arts and urban studies programs in Chicago, a Washington Semester for budding politicos, and a science semester at Tennessee's Oak Ridge National Laboratory.

Back on campus, no CC class has more than fifty students, and 70 percent have nineteen or fewer. Required courses aren't hard to get, since spots are secured with an auction system. At the beginning of each year, students get eighty points to "bid" on the classes they want. Those who bid the most for a particular class get a seat. And if you're going to take only one class at a time, it helps to like the teacher. Students say that's no problem here. "The professors are very accessible, and it is easy to have a good working relationship," says a history and political science major.

Just 30 percent of Colorado College students are in-staters; 3 percent are foreign, and the rest are from elsewhere in the U.S. "Most students come from families that are well-off, but are trying to defy societal norms," says a German major. "The school could definitely be classified as 'hippie,'" agrees a freshman. "The students tend to be incredibly smart, but grades don't matter that much to them." Minorities account for about 13 percent of the student body—2 percent are African-American, 7 percent Hispanic, and 4 percent Asian-American—and the school is trying to attract more. The Bisexual, Gay, and Lesbian Alliance; the Feminist Collective; the College Republicans; the Jewish Chaverim; and the Black Student Union also provide support to students of varied backgrounds and viewpoints. "It's a very liberal campus, most are outdoor, tree-hugging types," says a biology major. The admissions office places great weight on the essay, and 10 percent of each year's freshmen enroll for summer school, take the fall term off, and then settle into the regular routine in January.

"I really enjoy the people and the unique learning environment."

Only seniors are permitted to live off campus at Colorado College, so the other 76 percent of the student body bunks in the dorms. And while seniors don't have to move, a junior says it's easy to see why they do: "There's housing for about 80 percent of our study body, but a lot of it sucks." Architecturally, dorms range from large brick halls to small wooden houses; some are for freshmen only, others are same-sex, and still others offer a language or cultural theme. Campus residents give the dining hall chow a universal thumbs-down: "There is a good variety of food, but almost all of it is horrible," quips a freshman. "Many times, it can make you physically ill, and it just doesn't taste good."

When the weekend comes, students stay on campus for parties in friends' rooms or events sponsored by the "low-key" Greek system, which attracts 13 percent of the men and the same percentage of women. Officially, no one under twenty-one is permitted to have alcohol, in the dorms or elsewhere, but students say enforcement is lax. "It's fairly easy to get alcohol from an upperclassman," says a biology major. For those who don't, won't, or can't imbibe, the campus center hangout, Benjamin's, serves great milkshakes. Each spring, the Llamapalooza festival brings about ten bands to play outdoors. For those seeking a bit of urban culture, Denver and Boulder are a short drive away. And most CC students love heading off campus to ski or hike, either at nearby resorts, or in Utah, New Mexico, or the Grand Canyon area. (Freshman Outdoor Orientation Trips help out-of-staters sort out the options, from backpacking and hiking to rafting, bicycling, and windsurfing. Students may even reserve a college-owned mountainside cabin.)

Former Ohio Governor and Peace Corps Director Richard Celeste took charge at Colorado College in July 2002.

The Western Ridge dorm complex opened in fall 2002, offering apartment-style living for 290 students, plus a spacious courtyard, café, and meeting space. A 54,000-square-foot building for the psychology, math and geology departments, and the environmental sciences program, was finished in the summer of 2003.

When it comes to sports, most Colorado College teams compete in Division III, except for the women's soccer and men's ice hockey squads, which are Division I. Women's lacrosse and volleyball, men's soccer, and men's and women's track and field all have made national tournament appearances in recent years. There's a huge rivalry with the University of Denver.

The block plan may have made Colorado College what it is today, but new president Richard Celeste will determine how the school looks and feels in years to come. Already, students say he's off to a good start. "He's made a lot of positive changes, and is more concerned with what students think and feel," says a junior. While CC is intense, and the schedule is not for everyone, "I really enjoy the people and the unique learning environment," a freshman says. "It's small and conducive to the way I learn."

Overlaps

University of Colorado, Middlebury, University of Denver, Whitman, Colby.

If You Apply To ➢ **Colorado College:** Early action: Nov. 15. Regular admissions: Jan. 15. Financial aid: Feb. 15. Housing: June 20. Guarantees to meet demonstrated need. Campus interviews: optional, informational. No alumni interviews. SATs or ACTs: required. No SAT IIs. Accepts the Common Application and electronic applications. Essay questions: why Colorado College, and design your own three-and-a-half week intellectual adventure.

University of Colorado at Boulder

Campus Box 30, Boulder, CO 80309-0552

Boulder is a legendary place that draws everyone from East Coast ski bums to California refugees. The scenery is gorgeous and the science programs are first-rate. The University of Arizona is the only public university of similar stature in the Mountain West. Check out the residential academic programs.

Website: www.colorado.edu
Location: Suburban
Total Enrollment: 30,983
Undergraduates: 25,158
Male/Female: 53/47
SAT Ranges: V 520–620
   M 540–640
ACT Range: 22–27
Financial Aid: N/A
Expense: Pub $ $ $
Phi Beta Kappa: Yes
Applicants: 19,152
Accepted: 80%
Enrolled: 35%
Grad in 6 Years: 67%
Returning Freshmen: 83%
Academics: ✑ ✑ ✑ ✑
Social: 🏮 🏮 🏮 🏮 🏮
Q of L: ★ ★ ★ ★ ★
Admissions: (303) 492-6301

Wild buffalo may be all but extinct on America's Great Plains, but they're in boisterous residence, proudly wearing gold and black, at Ski U—otherwise known as the University of Colorado at Boulder. The best of Colorado's public universities academically, CU has worked hard to shed its party-school image only to gain one as a symbol of the corrosible effects of big-time athletics run amuck. A raft of scholars' programs, learning communities, and academic neighborhoods help the campus feel smaller, and stress is no problem, thanks to the active social scene, which emphasizes nature, fitness, sports, and outdoor pursuits. "Most people are very friendly, and every time you look up, you see beautiful mountains," says a freshman, referring to the majestic Rockies. With more than three hundred days of sunshine a year, is it any wonder students here are a happy lot?

Tree-shaded walkways, winding bike paths, open spaces, and an incredible view of the dramatic Flatirons rock formation makes CU's 600-acre Boulder campus a haven

"Most people are very friendly, and every time you look up, you see beautiful mountains."

for students from both coasts and for Colorado residents eager to pursue knowledge in a snowy paradise. Campus buildings, in a rural Italian style, are Colorado sandstone with red-tile roofs. In fact, the campus tends to look and feel a bit Ivy League, which is not surprising when you know that CU's architect also worked for Yale and Princeton. The 45,000-square-foot Discovery Learning Center opened in fall 2002, giving engineering students nine new labs in which to tackle society's challenges with videoconferencing and other high-tech capabilities. The University Memorial Center has received a $27 million facelift and expansion, and Folsom Stadium is getting a 125,000-square-foot addition, including forty-one private boxes. The Williams Village residence hall complex is in progress, and will add 1,900 apartment-style beds when complete.

Entering freshmen at CU choose from five colleges: arts and sciences (the easiest), business and administration, architecture and planning, music, and engineering and applied science (the hardest, students say). Transfers may apply to two additional schools: journalism and education. Each has different entrance standards and requirements; music, for example, requires an audition. General education requirements for the 70 percent of students who enroll in arts and sciences are designed to provide a broad background in the liberal arts to complement their major specialization. The requirements cover four skills-acquisition areas—writing, quantitative reasoning and math, critical thinking, and foreign language—and seven content areas: historical context, culture and gender diversity, U.S. context, natural sciences, contemporary societies, literature and the arts, and ideals and values.

In a typical semester, CU may offer 2,500 undergraduate courses in one hundred fields. Among the best choices is molecular cellular developmental biology, which takes advantage of state-of-the-art electron microscopes. CU–Boulder also receives the second-most NASA funding of any university in the nation, leading to unparalleled opportunities for the design, construction, and flight of model spacecraft—and to fifteen CU alumni having worked as astronauts. CU distinguished professor Carl Weiman and adjunct professor Eric Cornell of the National Institute of Standards and Technology won the Nobel Peace Prize for Physics in 2001, for creating a new form of matter that occurs at a few hundred billionths of a degree above absolute zero. Business, engineering, sociology, and psychology are likewise strong, students say. "As a freshman, my lectures were always taught by full professors, and small recitation sections were taught by grad students," says a speech, languages, and hearing sciences major.

"More housing is needed, but more is currently being built."

Boulder has tried to make its mammoth campus smaller through "academic neighborhoods" focusing on topics such as leadership, diversity, natural or social sciences, international studies, engineering, music, and the American West. Through these programs, students take one or two courses, each limited to twenty-five students, in their residence halls. For students having trouble choosing from the CU smorgasbord, the FallFEST program simplifies course selection. Up to 250 freshmen may participate in FallFEST, which lets them register in groups of twenty-five for a prepackaged set of core courses. The groups meet for weekly discussions with a faculty member and peer advisor. The Presidents Leadership Class is a four-year scholarship program that exposes the most promising students to political, business, and community leaders through seminars, work and study trips, and site visits. The new Undergraduate Academy offers special activities and advising for 150 to 200 of CU's most "intellectually committed" students, chosen for their excitement about learning and academic success.

Two-thirds of CU's student body comes from in-state, and by state regulation that fraction can be no lower than 45 percent, on average, over a three-year period. There's a mix of "middle-class in-state students from several ethnic backgrounds, and rich white out-of-state kids," says a freshman. "I've heard people say there are beautiful people at CU, which is true, but there are also skaters and hippies and people with dreadlocks." Hispanics and Asian-Americans each comprise 6 percent of the total, and African-Americans are a paltry 2 percent. CU leans liberal, and important campus issues include environmental awareness, recycling, and the rationale for going to war in Iraq.

First-year students are required to live on campus, where rooms are "standard and well-maintained," says a psychology and Spanish major. "More housing is

(Continued)
Email Address:
apply@colorado.edu

Strongest Programs:
Physics
Psychology
Geography
Applied Mathematics
Molecular/Cellular/Developmental Biology
Kinesiology and Applied Physiology
Aerospace and Chemical Engineering
Music

Folsom Stadium is getting a 125,000-square-foot addition, including 41 private boxes. The Williams Village residence-hall complex is in progress, and will add 1,900 apartment-style beds when complete.

For students having trouble choosing from the CU smorgasbord, the FallFEST program simplifies course selection. Up to 250 freshmen may participate in FallFEST, which lets them register in groups of twenty-five for a prepackaged set of core courses.

needed, but more is currently being built." Until it's finished, most sophomores, juniors, and seniors find off-campus digs in Boulder. Those who want to stay on campus are advised to make early reservations for Farrand, Sewall, or Kittredge halls. All rooms come with microwaves, refrigerators, cable TV, and Internet hook-ups. Generally, students say campus is safe, helped by thirty emergency telephones along walkways and paths, and sixteen more in the parking structures. CU also offers walking and riding escorts at night. An alternative to the dining hall is the student-run Alferd Packer Memorial Grill, which provides fast food under innocent auspices. Boulder students and trivia buffs know, however, that Packer was a controversial nineteenth-century folk figure known as the "Colorado Cannibal." Still hungry?

Eight percent of CU men and 12 percent of women go Greek, though fraternity and sorority parties have changed dramatically since CU's chapters became the first in the nation to voluntarily make their houses dry. On campus, the ban on alcohol is taken seriously, and dorms are officially "substance-free"—get caught with booze three times while underage, and you'll be booted from school housing. Off campus, "the bars are very stringent with IDs," a junior says. Even if you don't drink, though, you'll surely find something to do. "The Residence Hall Association plans numerous on-campus events, and so does the recreation center," says a speech, hearing, and language sciences major. "Students can go bowling, to an arcade, or see movies from the International Film Series—all on campus."

For the culturally minded, the university and the city of Boulder offer films and plays, the renowned Colorado Shakespeare Festival, and concerts by top rock bands. Boulder "is a great college town," says freshman. "There are concert venues, restaurants, clubs, churches, parks, shops, and a great bus system, free to students, to get everywhere." Even better, Denver is only thirty miles southeast, reachable

"The Residence Hall Association plans numerous on-campus events, and so does the recreation center."

with that same bus service. Day trips to ski resorts like Breckenridge, Vail, and Aspen largely replace weekend getaways here, but for those who've got to get out of the cold, Las Vegas isn't so far, says one student. For a quick night out, the Eldora ski area—with twelve lifts, fifty-three trails, runs up to two miles long, and a vertical drop of as much as fourteen hundred feet—is just a half hour from campus.

Aside from skiing, exercise is the leading extracurricular activity at CU. The school's Triathlon Club has won the USA Triathlon National Challenge for six years running, and CU–Boulder has also captured national titles in cycling and mountain biking for the past four years. Mountain-climbing enthusiasts have even interpreted CU as "Climb with Us." Just sixty-eight dollars a year gives students access to the sprawling recreation center, with swimming pools, squash and racquetball courts, three weight rooms, and an ice-skating rink. (Over 90 percent of CU students use the facility regularly.) The football program, which competes in the Big 12, has had its share of success on the field but is now reeling from a national scandal involving allegations of sexual assault and recruiting violations. Each year, fans flock to Denver for the game against Colorado State, and any showdown with Nebraska is sure to get students riled up. Ralphie, the live buffalo who acts as CU's mascot, doesn't miss a game—and neither do many students.

CU–Boulder just may be the place to kick off your boots and stay awhile, if you can focus with the snow-covered Rockies just beyond your dorm-room window—and if you're willing and able to take the initiative required to become more than a number. If you want to exercise your body as well as your mind, forget the ivy-covered bricks and gray city skies endemic to so many eastern institutions, and consider going west instead.

Overlaps

Colorado State, UCLA, University of Arizona, University of Illinois, University of Minnesota

Colorado School of Mines

1811 Elm Street, Golden, CO 80401-1842

The preeminent technical institute in the Mountain West. Twice as big as New Mexico Tech, one-tenth the size of Texas Tech. Best-known for mining-related fields but strong in most areas of engineering. Men outnumber women three to one, and Golden provides little other than a nice view of the mountains.

If you're a bit of a geek whose only dilemma is what kind of engineer to become, and you want to spend your scarce free time hiking, biking and skiing with friends, Colorado School of Mines may be a perfect choice. The school's small size and rugged location endear it to the mostly male students who shoulder heavy workloads to earn their degrees—and starting salaries of around $49,000 a year. "I can actually talk to people with the same academic interests," gushes a freshman. "It's amazing!" Just down the road from Coors Brewing Co., which taps the Rockies for its legendary brews, students at Mines learn to tap the Rockies for coal, oil, and other natural resources.

CSM's 373-acre campus sits in the shadow of the spectacular Rocky Mountains, in tiny Golden, Colorado. Architectural styles range from turn-of-the-century gold dome to present-day modern, and native trees and greenery punctuate lush lawns. A $10 million research building was completed in 2003, and about $30 million of renovation and new construction started that same year. Those projects include renovation of the last two traditional residence halls and the cafeteria, and construction of three new sorority houses and more apartment-style student housing. Work on a $4 million all-weather athletic facility will begin this year.

Academics at Mines are rigorous. All freshmen take the same first-year program, which includes chemistry, calculus, physical education, physics, design, environmental systems, quantitative chemical measurement, and the Freshman Success Seminar, an advising and mentoring course designed to increase retention. Because of CSM's narrow focus, the undergraduate majors—or "options," as they're called—are quite good. There's plenty of variety, as long as you like engineering; programs range from geophysical, geological, and petroleum to civil, electrical, and mechanical. Courses in a student's option start in the second semester of sophomore year, after yet more calculus and differential equations. Mines also offers the only B.S. degree in economics in the state of Colorado.

> **"CSM is a highly competitive school with the best brains."**

Pass/fail grading is unheard of at Mines, but failing grades are not. "CSM is a highly competitive school with the best brains," says a senior. "It can be discouraging, as you may see yourself as average, instead of always at the top of the class." Professors are well-qualified, but a chemical engineering major warns that they expect students to do a great deal of learning on their own. "Some are better at research than teaching," a mechanical engineering major agrees. Adjunct professors, who work in the fields they teach, draw raves for bringing real-world application into the

Website: www.mines.edu
Location: Small town
Total Enrollment: 3,261
Undergraduates: 2,504
Male/Female: 76/24
SAT Ranges: V 540–650
  M 620–690
ACT Range: 24–29
Financial Aid: 74%
Expense: Pub $ $ $
Phi Beta Kappa: Yes
Applicants: 3,033
Accepted: 79%
Enrolled: 28%
Grad in 6 Years: 64%
Returning Freshmen: 84%
Academics: ✍ ✍ ✍ ½
Social: ☎ ☎ ☎
Q of L: ★ ★
Admissions: (303) 273-3220
Email Address:
  admit@mines.edu

Strongest Programs:
Geology/Geophysics
Mining Engineering
Petroleum Engineering
Metallurgy and Materials
  Engineering
Chemical Engineering
Math and Computer Science

classroom. The required two-semester EPICS program—the acronym stands for Engineering Practices Introductory Course Sequence—helps develop communications, teamwork, and problem-solving skills with weekly presentations and written reports.

CSM supplements coursework with a required six-week summer field session, enabling students to gain hands-on experience. Each year, two hundred students are chosen for the Guy T. McBride Honors Program in the humanities, which includes seminars and off-campus activities—including a summer trip to Washington, D.C., centered on public affairs—that encourage them to think differently about the implications of technology. CSM also offers the opportunity to live and study at more than fifty universities in Europe, Australia, Latin America, Asia, and the Middle East, and about 15 percent of each graduating class takes part. Each year, sixty to seventy undergraduates also participate in research with faculty members or on their own.

CSM is a state school, making it a good deal for homegrown students, who comprise 78 percent of the student body. "We all share something in common—discipline, drive, and hard work," a senior says. "One has to study, and study hard, to get a good grade." A classmate is more blunt, saying that Mines attracts "a lot of nerds." Minority enrollment continues to increase: Hispanics comprise 7 percent of the student body, Asian-Americans 5 percent, and African-Americans 1 percent. Politics aren't prevalent on campus, probably because the workload is so consuming, though the war in Iraq did generate some discussion.

Thirty percent of CSM students—mostly freshmen—live in the residence halls, most of which have been renovated. Most buildings are co-ed, though the preponderance of men results in a few single-sex dorms. The "old" dorms have conventional doubles, while the newer and more popular Weaver Towers offer five-room suites. Most upperclassmen move to fraternity or sorority housing, college-owned apartments, or off-campus condos and houses. Crime is nonexistent, students say. "Campus public safety has nothing better to do than pull people over for running stop signs," quips a senior.

There is life outside of the library here, though it is well hidden. "The social life at Mines is not like other college campuses," says a mechanical engineering major. "Parties are few and far between." That said, CU–Boulder offers plenty of partying, just twenty minutes away. And Mines does have an active Greek system, with fraternities and sororities attracting 20 percent of the men and the same percentage of women. Still, rush is dry, and, owing to Mines' small size, those serving the alcohol almost always know the age of those trying to obtain it, making it tough for the underage to imbibe.

"We all share something in common—discipline, drive, and hard work."

Social life also includes house parties, comedy shows, Homecoming, and Engineering Days—a three-day party with fireworks, a pig roast, tricycle races, taco-eating contests, and twenty-five-cent beers. The celebration includes the M-climb, in which freshmen hike up Mount Zion lugging a ten-pound rock, "and whitewash it, and each other," says one participant. The rock is added to an M formation atop the mountain, then "seniors return to take down a rock, completing the cycle."

CSM's location at the base of the Rockies means gorgeous Colorado weather (make sure to bring sunscreen) and easy access to skiing, hiking, mountain climbing, and biking. Denver is also nearby, and aside from its museums, concerts, and sports teams, the city is home to many government agencies and businesses involved in natural resources, computers, and technology, including the regional offices of the U.S. Geological Survey and Bureau of Mines. Golden hosts the National Earthquake Center, the National Renewable Energy Laboratory, and, of course, the Coors Brewery. (The three-thousand-foot pipeline that runs from the

Coors plant to campus is there to convert excess steam from the brewery into heat for the school—not to supply the frats with fresh brew.) The biggest complaints are too much homework and not enough girls, not exactly a recipe for weekend mayhem. Road trips to Las Vegas or Texas provide some respite.

Despite the abundance of wacky school traditions, CSM competes in Division II, so there aren't many true athletic rivalries. The men's soccer and tennis teams have recently brought home conference championships, and other popular sports include football, baseball, and wrestling, as well as women's track, swimming, and softball. "CSM is probably one of the last places where you will find true student athletes, " notes one student. "We play for fun."

While time spent in the classroom at Mines may not be fun, for those who are focused on engineering, educational options don't get much better than those offered here. "It is a diverse, unique, close community that makes me feel I am not just a number," says an already-nostalgic senior. Sure, a CSM education may not stretch students' cultural horizons. It does, however, enable them to support themselves well after graduation—as they seek new and better ways to power our world, uncover natural resources, shelter us from the elements, and move people and information.

If You Apply To ➤

CSM: Rolling admissions: June 1. Financial aid: Mar. 1. Housing: May 1. Guarantees to meet demonstrated need. Campus interviews: recommended, informational. Alumni interviews: optional, informational. SATs or ACTs: required. SAT IIs: optional. Accepts electronic applications. No essay question.

Columbia College

212 Hamilton Hall, New York, NY 10027

Columbia may soon leave Yale in the dust as the third-most selective university in the Ivy League. Applications have doubled in the past ten years for one simple reason: Manhattan trumps New Haven, Providence, Ithaca, and every other Ivy League city. But the heart of Columbia is still the core.

Though students entering Columbia College will, of course, expect the rigorous academic program they'll encounter at this Ivy League school, there's no room here in the heart of Manhattan for the bookish nerd. Students must be streetwise, urbane, and together enough to handle one of the most cosmopolitan cities in the world. "It's an Ivy League school with a campus in the leading cultural center of the United States," says a sophomore. CC lets its students experience life in the Big Apple, but serves as a refuge when it becomes necessary to escape from New York; ideally, Columbians can easily be part of the "real world" while simultaneously immersing themselves in the best academia has to offer.

Although Columbia is among the smallest colleges in the Ivy League, its atmosphere is far from intimate. With a total university-wide enrollment of 21,000 students, says one, "it's easy to feel lost." Still, the college is the jewel in the university's crown and the focus is "unquestionably oriented toward undergraduate education," reports a classics major. Columbia's campus has a large central quadrangle in front of Butler Library and at the foot of the steps leading past the statue of Alma Mater to Low Library, which is now the administration building.

Website: www.columbia.edu
Location: Urban
Total Enrollment: 21,547
Undergraduates: 7,593
Male/Female: 50/50
SAT Ranges: V 650–760
  M 650–740
ACT Range: 29–34
Financial Aid: 60%
Expense: Pr $ $ $ $
Phi Beta Kappa: Yes
Applicants: 14,135
Accepted: 12%
Enrolled: 63%
Grad in 6 Years: 90%

(Continued)

Returning Freshmen: 97%

Academics: 🖊 🖊 🖊 🖊 🖊

Social: ☎ ☎ ☎

Q of L: ★ ★ ★

Admissions: (212) 854-2522

Email Address: ugrad-
  admiss@columbia.edu

Strongest Programs:

English

History

Political Science

Economics

Dance

Drama

Chemistry

Biology

The redbrick, copper-roofed neoclassical buildings are "stunning," and the layout, says an undergrad, "is well thought out and manages to provide a beautiful setting with an economy of space."

Columbia is an intellectual school, not a preprofessional one, and even though 60 percent of the students aspire to law or medical school (they enjoy a 90 percent acceptance rate), "we are mostly content to be liberal artists for as long as possible," says an English major. Even the 30 percent of undergraduates who enroll in the School of Engineering and Applied Sciences pursue "technical education" with a liberal arts base. Almost all departments that offer undergraduate majors are strong, notably English, history, political science, and psychology. Chemistry and biology are among the best of Columbia's high-quality science offerings. The geology department owns two hundred acres in Rockland County, home to many rocks and much seismographic equipment. There are thirty-five offerings in foreign languages, ranging from Serbo-Croatian to Uzbek to Hausa. The fine arts are not fabulous but are improving thanks to departmental reorganization, new facilities, and joint offerings with schools such as the Juilliard School of Music. And while the administration admits that the economics and computer science departments are geared too much toward graduate students, at least the comp-sci undergrads benefit from an abundance of equipment. Columbia offers many challenging combined majors such as philosophy/economics and biology/psychology. The East Asian languages and cultures department is one of the best anywhere. New programs in Asian-American studies, Latino studies, and American studies have recently been added to the curriculum. There is also an African-American studies major and a women's studies major that delves into topics from the Asian woman's perspective to the lesbian experience in literature.

The kernel of the undergraduate experience is the college's renowned core curriculum. While these courses occupy most of the first two years and can become laborious, students generally praise them as worthwhile and enriching: "You learn how to read analytically, write sharply, and speak succinctly, and you are exposed to the greatest ideas in Western art, music, literature, and philosophy," exclaims an enlightened sociology major. A junior adds, "The core is the highlight of our education, providing the basis for all other classes and giving you an amazing familiarity with Western civilization....It's been one of the best parts of my experience." The value of the Western emphasis of the core, however, is a subject of perennial debate. "Why should we study the Western tradition when it represents sexism, racism, imperialism, and exploitation?" asks one incensed student. "The canon is composed almost exclusively of dead European males." Yet, as it has since World War I, the college remains committed to the core while at the same time expanding the diversity of the canon and requiring core classes on non-Western cultures. Engineering students take only half as many core courses as their Columbia College counterparts.

"Nearly everything I'd grown up believing was questioned in one way or another."

Two of the most demanding introductory courses in the Ivy League—Contemporary Civilization and Literature Humanities—form the basis of the core. Both are year-long and taught in small sections, generally by full profs. "Nearly everything I'd grown up believing was questioned in one way or another. They forced me to examine my life and to ponder how I fit into the big picture," states an art history major. LitHum (as it is affectionately called) covers about twenty-six masterpieces of literature from Homer to Dostoyevsky, usually with some Sappho, Jane Austen, and Virginia Woolf thrown in for alternative perspectives. CC examines political and moral philosophy from Plato to Camus, though professors have some leeway in choosing twentieth-century selections. One semester each of art and humanities is required and, while not given the same reverence as their literary counterparts,

To call Columbia diverse would be "a gross understatement. We make Noah's Ark look homogeneous," says a sophomore.

are eye-opening all the same. Foreign language proficiency is required as are two semesters of science; two semesters of "extended core" classes dealing in cultures not covered in the other core requirements; two semesters of phys ed; and logic and rhetoric, a one-semester, argumentative writing class that first-year students reportedly "either love or hate."

Columbia is tough, and students always have something to read or write. Student–faculty interaction is largely dependent on student initiative. Additional interaction stems from professorial involvement in campus politics and forums and from the faculty-in-residence program, which houses professors and their families in spruced-up apartments in several of the residence halls. First-year students are assigned a faculty advisor and receive a departmental advisor when they declare a major at the end of sophomore year. Columbia students can take classes at Barnard, which maintains its own faculty, reported to be "more caring and involved than Columbia's." As at Barnard, students can also take graduate-level courses in several departments, notably political science, gaining access to the resources of the School of International and Public Affairs and its multitude of regional insti-

"Columbia students are individualists."

tutes. For students wishing to spend time away from New York, there are summer, semester, and one-year programs at the Reid Hall campus in Paris; other programs include opportunities with Kyoto University in Japan, Howard University in Washington, D.C., Oxford or Cambridge in England, and The Free University of Berlin. Columbia University engineering students suffer through the core, too—they take almost all of their classes with CC students during their first two years.

To call Columbia diverse would be "a gross understatement. We make Noah's Ark look homogeneous," says a sophomore. In fact, Columbia has the largest percentage of students of color in the Ivy League; 10 percent are African-American, 8 percent are Hispanic, and 19 percent are Asian-American. About 17 percent of the students come from New York City and another 15 percent from elsewhere in the state, especially Long Island. Socially, the campus is also diverse. In a city such as New York, "diversity is assumed," says one student. Another adds, "We have Euros, WASPs, jocks, grinds, sorority bunnies, Deadheads, fashion plates, a sizable Jewish population, and plenty of sideburn-sporting, cigarette-smoking, espresso-sipping, angst-ridden folks who own only black clothing."

Columbia remains one of the nation's most liberal campuses. "Columbia has always been known for its tradition of social and political activism," says a junior. "Students are not afraid to protest to get what they want." No one group dominates campus life. Although 6 percent of the men and 6 percent of the women go Greek, Columbia is hardly a Hellenocentric campus, namely because, as a junior argues, "the frats are chock-full of athletic recruits, the organizations—even the co-ed ones—are deemed elitist and politically incorrect, and there are too many better things to do in NYC on a Friday night than getting trashed in the basement of some random house." The advent of co-ed houses has raised interest in Greek life as has the arrival of sororities open to both Columbia and Barnard women.

With the New York housing market out of control, 95 percent of Columbia students live in university housing, which is guaranteed for four years. Security at the dorms is rated as excellent by students, and every person entering has to flash an ID to the guard on duty at the front door or be signed in by a resident of the building. One exciting aspect of Columbia housing is that

"Students are not afraid to protest to get what they want."

many rooms are singles, and it is possible to go all four years without a roommate. Carman Hall is the exclusively first-year dorm and "the fact that you get to meet your classmates compensates for the noise and hideous cinder-block walls," says a music major. First-year students can also live in buildings with students of all years.

One exciting aspect of Columbia housing is that many rooms are singles, and it is possible to go all four years without a roommate.

"Living with upperclasspeople was great. They knew the ins and outs of the university and the neighborhood. It wasn't the blind leading the blind," offers a junior. First-year students are automatically placed on a nineteen-meal-a-week plan and take most of those meals at John Jay, an all-you-can-eat "binge-a-rama with salad bar, deli, grill, and huge dessert bar." Many soon-bloated students scale down their meal plans or convert to points, a buy-what-you-want arrangement with account information stored electronically on student ID cards. Several dorms have kitchens, allowing students to do much of their own cooking. Some students dine at the kosher dining hall at Barnard.

Social life on campus is best described as mellow. Rarely are there big all-inclusive bashes, the exceptions being fall's '60s throwback, Realityfest, and spring's Columbiafest. "The social scene here is well balanced between school events, concerts and dances, and the variety of activities the city offers," says a senior.

Columbia athletics don't inspire the rabid loyalty of, say, a Florida State, because "Columbia students are individualists," according to one sophomore. "This is not a school that rallies together at football games." Still, the fencing teams are superlative, and men's soccer and basketball are also strong. As an urban school, Columbia lacks team field facilities on campus; however, merely one hundred blocks to the north are the modern Baker Field, home of the football stadium, the soccer fields, an Olympic track, and the crew boathouse. On campus, the Dodge Gymnasium, an underground facility, houses four levels of basketball courts, swimming pools, weight rooms, and exercise equipment. The gym is often crowded and not all the stuff is wonderful. "It does the job, as well as providing for the best pickup basketball this side of Riverside Park," notes a sophomore. Intramural and club sports are popular, with men's and women's Ultimate Frisbee both national competitors.

Columbians are proud that they are going to college in New York City, and most would have it no other way. Explains an art history major: "Choosing to isolate oneself in the middle of nowhere for four years isn't what college is about. It's about taking one's place as an adult in an adult society. Columbia is the perfect place for that."

Overlaps

Harvard, Yale, Brown, Penn, Cornell

If You Apply To ➤

Columbia: Early decision: Nov. 1. Regular admissions: Jan. 1. Financial aid: Jan. 1. Housing: Jan. 1. Meets demonstrated need of 60%. Campus interviews: not available. Alumni interviews: optional, evaluative. SATs or ACTs: required. SAT IIs: required (writing and two others). Essay: personal statement.

University of Connecticut

Tasker Building, 2131 Hillside Road, Unit 3088, Storrs, CT 06269-3088

Squeezed in among the likes of Yale, Brown, Wesleyan, Trinity, and UMass—all within a two-hour drive—UConn could be forgiven for having an inferiority complex. But championship basketball teams, both men and women, have ignited Husky pride, and the university's mammoth rebuilding project is boosting its appeal.

Website: www.uconn.edu
Location: Rural
Total Enrollment: 21,427

Five years ago, as companies and schools throughout the U.S. prepared for the possible "Millennium Bug," UConn wrapped up a $1 billion facilities-renewal program called UConn 2000. The building boom would have been the envy of many private-school presidents, and helped make UConn the top public university in

New England. Success spurred state legislators to approve another $1.3 billion in funding, covering physical improvements for the next decade. Couple the new buildings with the glow of two championship basketball teams, a wealth of research opportunities, and more than 250 clubs and organizations, and it's clear why students who in the past would have dismissed it as a "cow college" are choosing UConn even when they have other options. "It's the perfect atmosphere to go to college in," says a communications major. "The academics are challenging and interesting, and the social setting is fun and diverse."

Squeezed in among the likes of Yale, Brown, Wesleyan, Trinity, and UMass—all within a two-hour drive—UConn's four-thousand-acre campus is about twenty-three miles northeast of Hartford. Building styles range from collegiate Gothic and neoclassical to half-century-old redbrick. Dense woods surround the campus, which also boasts two lakes, Swan and Mirror. Ongoing renovations are the norm, sparking jokes about the "University of Construction," but the results are evident: a new Co-op bookstore, biophysics building, and information technologies engineering building opened recently. Work is underway on a forty-thousand-seat football stadium, a state-of-the-art School of Pharmacy, and a $3.2 million addition to the Benton Museum. The Student Union and Neag School of Education are also being renovated.

Students say UConn's strongest offerings are preprofessional, including business, engineering, pharmacy, education, and allied health, including nursing and physical therapy. Also notable are basic sciences, history, linguistics, psychology, and, of course, agriculture. (UConn was founded more than a century ago as a farm school; it's where America learned to get more eggs per chicken by leaving the lights on in the coops.) Interesting interdisciplinary programs include neurosciences, American studies, aquaculture, survey research, and coastal studies. Engineering is demanding, and, as at many schools, it has a relatively high attrition rate, with many students switching to the less-rigorous major in management information systems. UConn is also the only public university in New England to offer majors in environmental engineering, computer engineering, computer science, and metallurgy and materials engineering. New majors in engineering physics and biomedical engineering bring the total number of undergraduate engineering specialties to fourteen. A special program in medicine and dentistry allows students to earn bachelor's degrees in any of UConn's more than one hundred disciplines, and guarantees admission to the School of Medicine or Dental Medicine if they meet all criteria. Fine arts are a weak spot, administrators say.

UConn's core requirements include expository writing; mathematics; literature and the arts; culture and modern society and non-Western/Latin-American studies; philosophical and ethical analysis; social scientific and comparative analysis; and science and technology. Also required are two foreign language courses, waived if a student has studied three years of a single language in high school. All freshmen take seminar-style writing classes, and the university also offers advising programs specifically for them. The First Year Experience encourages enrollment in a faculty–student seminar, a learning skills course, or a community skills seminar. The Academic Center for Exploratory Students helps freshmen and sophomores who are undecided about their majors, though on the whole, academic advising gets mixed reviews. "I felt a lack of connection with my advisors, and saw them only when I contacted them," says a senior. "Often, I felt like an inconvenience." Still, students applaud career counseling, and the enthusiasm of their professors—and the graduate teaching assistants who run labs and discussion groups. "Many of the professors I've had have sparked my interest in subjects I've previously disliked," a junior explains.

"It's the perfect atmosphere to go to college in."

(Continued)
Undergraduates: 14,716
Male/Female: 48/52
SAT Ranges: V 520–610
  M 530–630
Financial Aid: 79%
Expense: Pub $ $ $ $
Phi Beta Kappa: Yes
Applicants: 13,760
Accepted: 62%
Enrolled: 37%
Grad in 6 Years: 69%
Returning Freshmen: 88%
Academics: ✑ ✑ ✑ ✑
Social: ☎ ☎ ☎
Q of L: ★ ★ ★
Admissions: (860) 486-3137
Email Address:
  beahusky@uconn.edu

Strongest Programs:
Biosciences
Communication Sciences
Business
Education
Engineering
Pharmacy
History
Linguistics

Ongoing renovations are the norm, sparking jokes about the "University of Construction," but the results are evident: a new Co-op bookstore, biophysics building and information technologies engineering building opened recently. Work is underway on a forty-thousand-seat football stadium.

UConn's engineering, business, pharmacy, and honors students are required to undertake research projects, and each year two teams of finance majors run the $1 million student managed investment fund. Students who aspire to graduate school in academic fields, rather than professional certification, may win grants to work independently under faculty members through the undergraduate summer research program. The Eurotech Program offers overseas jobs for engineering students with interest or expertise in a foreign language. Students who qualify for the honors program gain access to special floors and dorms; several programs for disadvantaged or underprivileged students are also available. In addition, about three hundred students a year participate in the study abroad program, which lets them travel to more than thirty countries. UConn's five campuses around Connecticut offer the first two years of the undergraduate program, and some four-year degree programs. Students who satisfactorily complete work at these schools are automatically accepted at the Storrs campus for their last two years.

Three-quarters of UConn students are in-staters, and about 16 percent are minorities—5 percent African-American, 5 percent Hispanic, and 6 percent Asian-American. More than 1,700 merit scholarships, ranging from $1,500 to $12,500, are helping the school's efforts to diversity, and 437 athletic scholarships are available, too. There are cultural centers for African-American, Asian-American, Latin-American, and Puerto Rican students, as well as the new Rainbow Center, a resource for gay, lesbian, bisexual, and transgender students. "We occasionally have issues brought up, such as homosexuality, gay and lesbian rights, women's rights and diversity," says a junior. "Students like to express opinions, but it's not overwhelming or interfering," adds a senior.

Seventy-two percent of the students live in university housing, which is available to everyone who wants it. Options include traditional single and double rooms, as well as suites and apartments. Though a few dorms are single-sex, most are co-ed by floor. "We have awesome suites, and on-campus apartments," says a secondary education major, noting that 27 percent of students live off campus,

"Many of the professors I've had have sparked my interest in subjects I've previously disliked."

and 85 percent live within three miles. Those who stay in the dorms have access to "HUSKYvision," a data, voice, and video communication service that offers replays of class lectures, online course registration, and forty-two educational and information channels, including foreign news, culture, and entertainment. Thirteen dining halls offer plenty of choices, even for vegetarians and vegans, though many students would just as soon visit the snack bar for some ice cream, freshly made with help from the cows grazing nearby.

When the weekend comes, freshman dorms are officially dry, but students say it's easy to get alcohol from older friends. Still, those under twenty-one who are caught with booze may be evicted from their rooms. And if you're tempted to try a bogus ID at one of the three local pubs (Ted's, Huskie's, and Civic), a junior says beware, noting that they "are pretty good at carding and refusing fakes." A sophomore says on-campus parties, sporting events, club functions, and shows at the school auditorium keep underage students busy. The best road trips are to Boston and New York—or, a little closer to home, the Buckland Hills Mall or the Wal-Mart, says a secondary education major. Fraternities attract 7 percent of the men and sororities claim 7 percent of the women; members will be able to live in chapter housing at the new Husky Village.

The town of Storrs "is no college town, but it's rural and we're proud of it," says one student. "Everyone gets involved with something," agrees a sophomore, often through the Center for Community Outreach. Legend also holds that UConn also offers one diversion most other colleges can't: Cow tipping—that is, sneaking up on unsuspecting cows, who sleep standing up, and tipping them over. The administration contends that this is a myth, though students always claim to "know someone who did it." For most big-city needs, Hartford is only thirty minutes away, and Cape Cod and the Vermont ski slopes are within weekend driving distance.

UConn's teams are known as the Huskies (Get it? Yukon!). Basketball is by far UConn's most popular sport, and in a state without professional sports teams, the UConn women's team routinely sells out the Hartford Civic Center. In 2004, both the men's and women's teams won the ultimate prize: the NCAA national championship—the first time any university has pulled off this feat. The men also won in 1999; the women won in 2000, 2002, and 2003. In fact, the Lady Huskies are the only women's basketball team that operates in the black. Football isn't huge at UConn, but the team is getting a new stadium as it moves into Division I-A. Favorite annual campus events include Homecoming, Winter Weekend, and Midnight Madness—the first official day of basketball practice.

Despite the school's agricultural roots, UConn students aren't "cowed" by the plethora of offerings. Those seeking greener pastures will be hard-pressed to find a more dynamic public institution. "Because of private donations, we are up and coming; it's getting more competitive," says a junior. Adds a senior: "The people I've met here have made UConn the best place I could ever imagine!"

Overlaps

University of Massachusetts, Boston University, Northeastern, University of Rhode Island, Boston College

If You Apply To >

UConn: Early action: Dec. 1. Rolling admissions: Mar. 1. Campus interviews: optional, informational. No alumni interviews. SATs or ACTs: required. SAT IIs: optional. Accepts the Common Application and electronic applications. Essay question: what makes you unique and how that will benefit the UConn community, or an influential person or event.

Connecticut College

270 Mohegan Avenue, New London, CT 06320-4196

Like Vassar and Skidmore, Connecticut College made a successful transition from women's college to co-ed. The college is strong in the humanities and renowned for its study abroad programs. It is also an SAT I-optional school. New London does not offer much but at least it is on the water.

Connecticut College is a small liberal arts school where students aren't "led around by the hand," says a sophomore proudly. "We are treated and respected like adults and expected to act as such." The school's professors here focus on teaching, helping students follow the example of Conn College's camel mascot: to drink up and store knowledge. Thanks to a student-run honor code, students also feel comfortable leaving their doors and bikes unlocked on campus. They're tested on what they've learned during unproctored final exams scheduled at their convenience within a ten-day window. "Students are treated as equals by faculty and administration, and help make important decisions," says one sophomore.

Sitting majestically atop a hill, Conn College's lovely campus provides beautiful views of the Thames River (pronounced the way it looks, not like the "Temz" that Wordsworth so dearly loved) on one side, and Long Island Sound on the other. The campus is on a 750-acre arboretum with a pond, wetlands, wooded areas, and hiking trails. The granite campus buildings are a mixture of modern and collegiate Gothic, neo-Gothic, and neo-Classical architecture.

Website: www.connecticutcollege.edu
Location: Suburban
Total Enrollment: 1,912
Undergraduates: 1,890
Male/Female: 40/60
SAT Ranges: V 594–697
  M 605–698
ACT Range: N/A
Financial Aid: 42%
Expense: Pr $ $ $ $
Phi Beta Kappa: Yes
Applicants: 4,395

(Continued)

Accepted: 35%

Enrolled: 35%

Grad in 6 Years: 83%

Returning Freshmen: 88%

Academics: ✍ ✍ ✍ ✍

Social: ☎ ☎ ☎

Q of L: ★ ★ ★ ★

Admissions: (860) 439-5435

Email Address:

admission@conncoll.edu

Strongest Programs:

Psychology

Biology

English

International Studies

Dance

Government

Economics

Efforts to bring a diverse student body to Conn College have been helped by the school's decision to emphasize high school transcripts, rather than the SAT I, as a measure of achievement and potential in the admissions process. But the student body remains more than three-quarters Caucasian.

Since its 1911 founding as a women's college, Conn has been dedicated to the liberal arts, broadly defined. The school's dance and drama departments are superb, and talented dance students often take a few semesters off to study with professional companies. Theater majors may work with the Eugene O'Neill Theater Institute, named for New London's best-known literary son. Chemistry majors may use high-tech gas chromatograms and mass spectrometers from their very first day. The school's Ammerman Center for Arts and Technology lets students examine the links of theater, film, music, dance, writing, and other artistic pursuits to the world of math and computer science. Students also give high marks to the popular English, psychology, and government programs, and the college's four interdisciplinary programs. And the Study Away/Teach Away initiative allows groups of Conn College students and faculty members to spend a semester living and working together at a university abroad in locations as far-flung as Vietnam, South Africa, and Egypt. Conn College also participates in the Twelve-College Exchange* and Venture Program consortiums.*

The school's general education requirements include one course in each of eight academic areas: physical and biological sciences, mathematics and logic, social sciences, critical studies and literature and the arts, creative arts, philosophical and religious studies, historical studies and foreign language. Each student is guaranteed $3,000 from the school for a summer internship sometime during his or her four years. "Because the school will pay, some students are able to get internships at places that would not normally hire interns," says a chemistry major.

A French and philosophy student rates the teaching at Conn College as "excellent." "Professors are happy to be there and enjoy what they do," the sophomore says. Professors are always willing to provide extra help, and it's not uncommon to see them having coffee with students at the Student Center. "I know my professors on a very personal basis," says one senior who describes the faculty as

"Students are treated as equals by faculty and administration, and help make important decisions."

"always ready to help and challenge our minds." "Students are challenged every day by the faculty," adds another senior. Students say they work hard and are motivated to achieve but compete with themselves, rather than each other. "Students don't go around interrogating one another about how they did on the last test," says a sophomore.

Despite strenuous effort, diversity has been slow in coming to Conn College. The student body remains more than three-quarters Caucasian, mostly from New England and the mid-Atlantic States. African-Americans, Asian-Americans, and Hispanics each comprise 3 percent. Freshmen must attend a session on issues of race, class, and gender, run by a panel of peers representing different cultures, socioeconomic backgrounds, sexual orientations, and physical disabilities. Conn College's diversification efforts have been helped by the school's decision to emphasize high school transcripts, rather than the SAT I, as a measure of achievement and potential in the admissions process.

Ninety-six percent of Conn College students live on campus, where freshmen are assigned to doubles, triples, or quads. "The dorms are definitely well maintained, clean and comfortable," says a sophomore. Dorms house students of all ages, and are run by seniors who apply to be "house fellows." Roommates tend to be well matched, because incoming students complete a three-page questionnaire about personal habits before coming to campus, says a sophomore. Most upperclassmen get single rooms, perhaps in the River Ridge Apartments, though that's no longer guaranteed because the student body has grown. Buildings range from older, more traditional structures to newer facilities known as the "plex" dorms, which "are all very clean and sterile, and remind many of a hospital," says a chemistry major.

Among the seven specialty houses are Earth House (environmental awareness), the Abbey House co-op (where students cook their own meals), Unity House (fostering relationships across ethnic and racial boundaries), and houses dedicated to substance-free living, quiet lifestyles, and international languages. "Housing at Connecticut College is definitely one of its strengths," says a sophomore. "What Conn students call 'bad' housing is what other colleges would consider good housing."

Because Conn lacks a Greek system, most activities—including co-ed intramural sports—revolve around the dorms, which sponsor weekly keg and theme parties. Also keeping students busy are movie nights, comedy shows, student productions and dances—sometimes with out-of-town bands and DJs. "I've been entertained by a hypnotist, a world famous pianist, flamenco dancers from Spain, and plays on campus," says a sophomore. The alcohol policy fits under the honor code, so students under twenty-one can't imbibe at the campus bar. Conn is helping redevelop New London, which is home to defense-contractor General Dynamics and drug-maker Pfizer. "New London is a small city with lots of potential as Pfizer continues to help with its development," says a psych major. "There are lots of boutique shops and small coffee shops that only the native would know and rave about." Students do get involved in the life of New London through volunteer work, with about 50 percent participating in some way each year. A college van makes it easy to get to and from work sites. When students get the urge to roam, the beaches of Mystic and other shore towns are twenty minutes from campus. Farther away—yet still close enough for a weekend visit—are Providence, Rhode Island, New York City, Boston, and camping, hiking, and skiing in Vermont or upstate New York. Students eagerly anticipate two annual traditions: October's Camel Olympics, which pits dorms against each other in games ranging from Scrabble to Capture the Flag, and Floralia, an all-day music festival the weekend before spring finals, which the Dave Matthews Band recently headlined.

> "Because the school will pay, some students are able to get internships at places that would not normally hire interns."

The Conn Camels compete in Division III of the NCAA. Among the most popular sports, for both men and women, are track and field, lacrosse, rowing, soccer, and cross-country. Men's ice-hockey games against rival Wesleyan draw crowds, and a T-shirt brags that Conn football has been undefeated since 1911 (the joke's on you if you believe that, since Conn—as a former women's college—has never had a team!). Between classes or at the end of the day, students of all skill levels can enjoy the natatorium's pool and fitness center—though one student says complaints about its condition are common—and the field house's rowing tanks and climbing walls.

There are plenty of reasons to head to this little college on the hill—even if a great football team isn't one of them. On its friendly campus, Conn College fosters strong student–faculty bonds, and takes pride in its ability to challenge—and trust—students in the classroom. "I love that you are encouraged to pursue your dreams, no matter how big or small they are. I just love this place," raves one happy sophomore.

Students eagerly anticipate two annual traditions: October's Camel Olympics, which pits dorms against each other in games ranging from Scrabble to Capture the Flag, and Floralia, an all-day music festival the weekend before spring finals.

Overlaps

Tufts, Wesleyan, Middlebury, Vassar, Boston College

If You Apply To ➤

Conn College: Early decision: Nov. 15. Regular admissions: Dec. 15 (supplement), Jan. 1 (Common Application and other materials). Financial aid: Jan.15. Guarantees to meet demonstrated need. Campus interviews: recommended, evaluative. Alumni interviews: optional, informational. SAT Is: optional. SAT IIs: required (any three or the ACT). Accepts the Common Application and electronic applications. No essay question.

Cooper Union

30 Cooper Square, New York, NY 10003

As college costs skyrocket, so does the popularity of Cooper Union's free education in art, architecture, and engineering. Expect Ivy-level competition for a place in the class here. Instead of a conventional campus, Cooper Union has the East Village—which is quite a deal.

Website: www.cooper.edu
Location: Urban
Total Enrollment: 907
Undergraduates: 870
Male/Female: 65/35
SAT Ranges: V 510–760
    M 510–780
Financial Aid: 40%
Expense: Pr $
Phi Beta Kappa: No
Applicants: 2,216
Accepted: 13%
Enrolled: 69%
Grad in 6 Years: 80%
Returning Freshmen: 90%
Academics: ✍ ✍ ✍ ½
Social: ☎
Q of L: ★ ★ ★
Admissions: (212) 353-4120
Email Address: N/A

Strongest Programs:
Architecture
Electrical Engineering
Art

Some say the best things in life are free. In most cases, they're probably wrong. But not in the case of the Cooper Union for the Advancement of Science and Art. If you manage to get accepted into this top technical institute, you get a full-tuition scholarship and some of the nation's finest academic offerings in architecture, engineering, and art. With cool and funky Greenwich Village in the background and rigorous studying in the forefront, college life at Cooper Union may seem to be faster than a New York minute. Whatever the pace, though, no one can deny that a CU education is one of the best bargains around—probably the best anywhere. The only problem is that its acceptance rate is lower than most of the Ivies.

The school was founded in 1859 by entrepreneur Peter Cooper, who believed that education should be "as free as water and air." With hefty contributions from J.P. Morgan, Frederick Vanderbilt, Andrew Carnegie, and various other assorted robber barons, the school was able to stay afloat in order to recruit poor students of "strong moral character." Today, students must pay a few hundred dollars for nonacademic expenses, but tuition is still free.

In place of a traditional collegiate setting are three academic buildings and one dorm plunked down in one of New York's most eclectic and exciting neighborhoods. The stately brick art and architecture building is a beautiful historic landmark. Built of brick and topped by a classic water tower, the dorm blends right in with the neighborhood. The Great Hall was the site of Lincoln's "Right Makes Might" speech and the birthplace of the NAACP, the American Red Cross, and the national women's suffrage movement. Wedged between two busy avenues in the East Village, Cooper Union offers an environment for survivors. One mechanical engineering major describes the climate as "a tropical rain forest. Only the truly dedicated should come here."

The academic climate is intense, yet cooperation is critical, according to students. "We all feed off each other and strive for our best, but rivalry is low," says an architecture major. A junior adds, "You don't know the meaning of stress until you've been through Cooper." The curriculum is highly structured, and all students must take a sequence of required courses in the humanities and social sciences. The

"Only the truly dedicated should come here."

first year is devoted to language and literature and the second to the making of the modern world. In some special circumstances, students are allowed to take courses at nearby New York University and the New School for Social Research. The nationally renowned engineering school, under the tutelage of the nation's first female engineering dean, offers both bachelor's and master's degrees in chemical, electrical, mechanical, and civil engineering as well as a bachelor of science in general engineering. "Architecture and engineering are the most acclaimed, but then, these occupations are more mainstream, and graduates get big money and success," reflects an art major. "It's harder to measure success in the art school." The art school offers a broad-based generalist curriculum that includes graphic design, painting, sculpture, photography, and video but is considered weak by some students. The architecture school, in the words of one pleased participant, is "phenomenal—even unparalleled." Requirements for getting into each of these schools vary widely—each looks for different strengths and talents—hence the differences in test-score ranges.

The Cooper Union library is small (ninety thousand volumes), but contains more than one hundred thousand graphic materials. Classes are small and, with a little persistence, are not too difficult to get into. Professors are engaging and accessible. "One of the best aspects of this college is that everyone is taught by full professors," reports a junior. A professional counseling and referral service is available, as is academic counseling, but the school's small size and its rigorously structured academic programs set the classes the students take and eliminate a lot of confusion or decision making. Reactions on career counseling vary between "horrible" from an art major to "excellent" from an engineering major. Students "tend to talk to other students, recommending or insulting various classes and profs around registration time," notes a senior.

Strong moral character is no longer a prerequisite for admission, but an outstanding high school academic average most certainly is. Prospective applicants should note, however, that art and architecture students are picked primarily on the basis of a faculty evaluation of their creative works. For engineering students, admission is based on a formula that gives roughly equal weight to the high school record, SAT scores, and the SAT IIs in mathematics and physics or chemistry.

"The students here tend to be incredibly driven people."

"The students here tend to be incredibly driven people," says one student, noting that some classmates have spent "literally twenty-four hours at the drafting desk." Sixty-one percent of the students are from New York State, and more than half of those grew up in the city. Most are from public schools, and many are the first in their family to attend college. Forty-four percent of the students are from minority groups, most of them Asian-Americans (27 percent); 6 percent are African-American, and 8 percent are Hispanic. One student attests that diversity is not an issue at CU: "We are a racially mixed student body that stays mixed. There's no overt hostility and rare self-segregation. One of the officers of the Chinese Student Association is a large black man from Trinidad. Need I say more?" The campus is home to ethnically based student clubs, but, according to one student, membership is not exclusive: "In other words, you can be white and be a member of Onyx—a student group promoting black awareness." According to one senior, CU is a very liberal place: "If you can't accept different kinds of people, you shouldn't come here." For students who demonstrate financial need, help with living expenses is available.

Students love the dorm, a fifteen-story residence hall that saves many students from commuting into the Village or cramming themselves into expensive apartments. It is noteworthy that housing here is guaranteed only to freshmen. The facility is composed of furnished apartments with kitchenettes and bathrooms complete with showers or tubs and is "in great condition

"We are a racially mixed student body that stays mixed. There's no overt hostility and rare self-segregation."

and well maintained," states one resident. A less enraptured dweller notes, "Rooms are barely big enough to fit a bed, a table, and a clothes cabinet." Still, each apartment does have enough space for a stove, microwave, and refrigerator. So you can cook for yourself or eat at the unexciting but affordable school cafeteria or at one of the myriad nearby delis and coffee bars.

The combination of intense workload and CU's location means that campus social life is limited, though the administration hopes the dorm will promote more on-campus social activities. "Many students will say that Cooper social life is dead," notes a junior. "In many ways they are right." On the other hand, as one senior puts it, "The East Village is great place to be young, with tons of bars and culture." About 20 percent of the men and 10 percent of the women belong to professional societies. Drinking on campus is allowed during school-sponsored parties for adult students—otherwise, no alcohol on campus. But as one student puts it, "This is New York; one can be served anywhere." The intramural sports program is held in several different facilities in the city, and the games are popular. Students organize clubs and outings around interests such as soccer, basketball, skiing, fencing, Ping-Pong, classical music, religion, and drama. And of course, the colorful neighborhood is ideal for sketching and browsing. McSorley's bar is right around the corner, the Grassroots Tavern is just down the block, and nearby Chinatown and Little Italy are also popular destinations. The heart of the Village, with its abundance of theaters, art galleries, and cafes, is just a few blocks to the west. The Bowery and SoHo's galleries and restaurants are due south; all of midtown Manhattan spreads to the northern horizon.

Getting into Cooper Union is tough, and once admitted, students find that dealing with the onslaught of city and school is plenty tough as well. But most students like the challenge. "The workload, living alone in New York, and the administrative policies force you to act like an adult and take care of yourself," explains a senior. Surviving the school's academic rigors requires talent, self-sufficiency, and a clear sense of one's career objectives. Students who don't have it all can be sure that there are six or seven people in line ready to take their places. That's quite an incentive to succeed.

Overlaps

NYU, Columbia, Cornell University, MIT, Carnegie-Mellon

If You Apply To ➢

Cooper Union: Rolling admissions (for art applicants, by invitation). Early decision (for art and engineering applicants): Dec. 1. Regular admissions: Jan. 1 (architecture), Jan. 10 (art), Feb. 1 (engineering). Financial aid and housing: May 1. All students receive full-tuition scholarships. No campus or alumni interviews. (Portfolio Day strongly recommended for art applicants.) SATs: required. SAT IIs: required for engineering (math and physics or chemistry). Apply to particular program. Essay question: varies by school.

Cornell College

600 First Street West, Mount Vernon, IA 52314-1098

One-course-at-a-time model is Cornell's calling card. Cornell's main challenge: trying to lure students to rural Iowa. With a student body of about one thousand, Cornell lavishes its students with personal attention. Though primarily a liberal arts institution, Cornell has small programs in business and education.

Website:
www.cornellcollege.edu
Location: Rural
Total Enrollment: 1,001
Undergraduates: 1,001
Male/Female: 40/60
SAT Ranges: V 540–660
M 540–640
ACT Range: 23–28
Financial Aid: 80%
Expense: Pr $ $
Phi Beta Kappa: Yes

Cornell College, located in tiny Mount Vernon, Iowa, is actually eleven years *older* than Cornell University, located in slightly bigger Ithaca, New York. The college is as small as its hometown, with about one thousand students to the university's twenty thousand. And while the university has the traditional two semesters, separated by a three-week winter term, Cornell College is one of only three U.S. schools to use block scheduling, also known as One-Course-At-A-Time (OCAAT). College students focus on a single subject for eight three-and-a-half week terms, with four-day breaks in between. A ninth term can be used as vacation, or for another course. If you're not satisfied with easy answers, are adventurous enough to head to the rural midwest, and want loads of personal attention while you focus on one discipline, Cornell College may be worth a look.

Aside from its distinctive schedule, Cornell has the only U.S. college or university campus listed in its entirety on the National Register of Historic Places. The majestic bell tower of King Chapel offers an unparalleled view of the Cedar River valley. Palettes and paintbrushes have replaced hook shots in Cornell's former gymnasium, which underwent a fifteen-month renovation to become McWethy Hall for the visual arts. Also new are a pedestrian mall running through campus, an eight-lane, all-weather track, a strength-training facility for student-athletes, and an outdoor amphitheater. A state-of-the-art, 280-seat theatre has been added to the performing arts building.

Cornell offers four types of undergraduate degrees, and 86 percent of students choose the bachelor of arts. That requires thirty-two courses, including one each in English composition or writing, fine arts and math; two each in social sciences and natural sciences (one of which must have a lab); and fourth-term competence in a foreign language. The One-Course method can be problematic here, because "it is difficult to learn a language in three and a half weeks," a junior says. "And if you don't understand math, it's likely you won't understand it in three and a half weeks." Also available are bachelor of special studies, music and philosophy degrees.

Other than Cornell, Colorado College and Tusculum College are the only U.S. schools to use the One-Course-At-A-Time academic model, also known as the "block plan." The schedule makes it easier for some students to graduate early; others use the flexibility to finish with a double major. If that sounds intimidating, it can be. But administrators say block scheduling also improves the quality of Cornell's liberal arts education, by helping students acclimate to the business world, where "what needs to be done needs to be done quickly and done well." The One-Course method also helps in academic advising—with grades every four weeks, signs of trouble are quickly apparent. Block scheduling does have drawbacks, though. Courses are "very intense," says a senior. "They contain a lot of information in eighteen days."

Aside from the pressure created by the One-Course calendar, Cornell's academic atmosphere "is laid-back, and all students are encouraged to succeed," says an elementary education and psychology major. The most popular programs are education, psychology, economics and business, English, and history, and other strong options include biology, chemistry and geology. Weaker areas include German and medieval and early modern studies. Classes are capped at twenty-five students, and most have around sixteen; you won't find graduate students at the lectern, since Cornell doesn't hire them. Professors "frequently are available for one-on-one interaction, and in fact encourage it," says a physical education major—usually by giving out their home phone numbers.

When Mount Vernon gets too small, Cornell students may choose from study programs around the world, such as Marine Science Research in the Bahamas, Advanced Spanish in Spain, or Greek Archaeology in Greece. They can also spend a semester at sea or in one of thirty-six countries through the Associated Colleges of the Midwest* consortium. During the short

Courses "contain a lot of information in eighteen days."

breaks between courses, students can take advantage of symposia, Music Mondays, carnivals, and athletic events. The school's Cole Library is also the town of Mount Vernon's public library, one of only two such libraries in the country.

One of Cornell's biggest challenges is drawing students to its rural Iowa campus, but so far, administrators are doing well on that score: Only 31 percent of students are homegrown. African-Americans represent 3 percent of the total, Hispanics 2 percent, and Asian-Americans 1 percent. Politically, Cornell leans liberal; hot topics have included the 2004 presidential candidates (since the Iowa caucuses are the campaign's first) and President Bush's actions in Iraq. "Cornellians have views that developing minds setting out to change the world ought to have," says a junior.

Ninety-two percent of students live on campus, where "it can sometimes be difficult to get the room you want, but getting a room is not an issue," says a geology

(Continued)
Applicants: 1,625
Accepted: 62%
Enrolled: 31%
Grad in 6 Years: 68%
Returning Freshmen: 76%
Academics: ✍ ✍ ✍
Social: ☎ ☎ ☎
Q of L: ★ ★ ★
Admissions: (319) 895-4000
Email Address:
admissions@cornellcollege.edu

Strongest Programs:
Art
Biology
Economics
Education
English
Philosophy
Politics

There's a new pedestrian mall running through campus, an eight-lane, all-weather track, a strength-training facility for student-athletes, and an outdoor amphitheater.

and philosophy major. Two apartment buildings are available to upperclassmen, and about half of the dorms are co-ed. The largest co-ed residence hall, which houses Cornell's living and learning communities, has been renovated. Everyone eats together in the Commons, which is also being renovated. Sodexho Marriott runs the kitchen, and the food is "nothing like mom's cooking, but it is edible," a junior says. Vegetarian options are always available.

On campus, the Greek system draws 30 percent of the men and 32 percent of the women; frats and sororities sponsor many parties, which are open to all. Some dorms and floors are substance-free; on the others, only students over twenty-one may have alcohol. "These rules aren't enforced very strictly, as long as the students don't cause trouble and aren't loud and disrespectful," says a junior. Mount Vernon itself is "small, but very welcoming," says a physical education major. "Many students knit themselves into the community, whether it be with jobs downtown or going to the local churches," a junior agrees. "I am judging the middle school science fair tomorrow." Students either love the town's idyllic pace—a few local bars, an acclaimed restaurant, some funky shops, and a lot of peace, quiet, and safety—or long for more excitement. The latter is available in Cedar Rapids (home of archrival Coe College) or Iowa City (home to the University of Iowa), each less than half an hour away. Chicago is less than four hours' drive.

On the field or on the court, Cornell's competition with Coe "is intense, and the entire student body is involved," says one student, especially when it comes to football or basketball. "Every time a rival plays us at home in men's basketball, it's a tradition that we throw rolls of toilet paper out on the floor after we score our first basket," adds another—perhaps to show how Cornell plans to "clean up" its opponent. Cornell teams have competed in the Iowa Intercollegiate Athletic Conference since 1998 and have been to the NCAA men's basketball tournament five times. Recently, the women's tennis team brought home a conference championship.

> **"Many students knit themselves into the community, whether it be with jobs downtown or going to the local churches."**

For those with a "one-track mind," Cornell offers a top-notch education and a supportive community—if you can take the bitter winters and relative isolation of rural Iowa. "Cornell offers a friendly atmosphere, welcoming population and homelike environment," says a physical education major. "I've gained lifelong friends here, and a great education."

Overlaps

Coe, University of Iowa, Colorado College, Luther, Beloit

If You Apply To ➢ **Cornell:** Early action: Dec. 1. Rolling admissions and financial aid: Mar. 1. Housing: May 1. Meets demonstrated need of 30%. Campus interviews: recommended, informational. No alumni interviews. SATs or ACTs: Required. Accepts the Common Application and electronic applications. Essay question: how you've integrated classroom learning into your non-academic life; fictional character you would be for a day; or revealing possession or trait.

Cornell University

Ithaca, NY 14850

Cornell's reputation as a pressure cooker comes from its preprofessional attitude and "we try harder" mentality. Spans seven colleges—four private and three public. (Tuition varies accordingly.) Strong in engineering and architecture, world-famous in hotel administration. Easiest Ivy to get into.

Cornell has a long tradition for being the lone wolf among the Ivy League universities. So it should come as no surprise that Cornell has taken another huge step away from its Ivy League counterparts by announcing its intention to become the finest research university for undergraduate education in the nation. Cornell's president recently unveiled a $400 million, ten-year plan to improve undergraduate education by combining education and research and having all freshmen live in the same residential area. With rain, drizzle, slush, and snow known as "the four seasons of Ithaca," just walking to class across the vast and hilly campus can be challenging. Cornell's highly talented student body and notoriously competitive academics probably make it, in the words of one student, "the only place where you walk up a forty-five-degree incline in twenty-degree weather to get 30 percent on a prelim."

Aside from the great strides in undergraduate education, Cornell also has its stunning campus to lure students to upstate New York. Perched atop a hill that commands a view of both Ithaca and Cayuga lakes, the campus is breathtakingly scenic; or, as the saying goes, "Ithaca is gorges." Ravines, waterfalls, and parks border all sides of the school's campus. The Cornell Plantation, more than three thousand acres of woodlands,

> **"Our school of hotel administration is among the best in the world."**

natural trails, streams, and gorges, provides space for walking, picnicking, or contemplation. In addition to completing their north campus residential community, Cornell has also renovated both the Lincoln Hall and the Martha Van Renessaler Hall. Currently, they are working on improving the College of Industrial and Labor Relations and the College of Agriculture and Life Sciences.

At the undergraduate level, Cornell has four privately endowed colleges: architecture, art, and planning; arts and sciences; engineering; and hotel administration. "Our school of hotel administration is among the best in the world," raves one junior. Cornell is also New York State's land-grant university. Therefore, three other colleges are operated by Cornell under contract with New York State: agriculture and life sciences, human ecology, and the school of industrial and labor relations (ILR). Thirty-four percent of the students in these state-assisted colleges are New York State residents who pick up their Ivy League degrees at an almost-public price (tuition at these schools is slightly steeper than SUNY rates).

The College of Arts and Sciences boasts considerable strength in history, government, and just about all the natural and physical sciences. The English program has turned out a number of renowned writers, including Toni Morrison, Thomas Pynchon, and Richard Farina. Foreign languages, required for all arts and sciences students, are also strong, and the performing arts, mathematics, and most social science departments are considered good. Among the state-assisted units, the agriculture college is one of the best in the nation and a good bet for anyone hoping to make it into a veterinary school (there's one at Cornell with state support). The School of Hotel Administration is one of the best in the world, and ILR is also world-renowned. Students may sample a wine-tasting course. Human ecology is among the best in the nation in human service related disciplines, and the Department of Applied Economics and Management offers an undergraduate business major. The Johnson Museum of Art, designed by I. M. Pei, has been rated as one of the ten best university museums in America. Students enjoy the $22 million theater arts center, designed specifically for undergraduates. Students say the math department needs improvement.

Student–faculty relations at Cornell are a mixed bag, but for the most part students do have a lot of respect for their professors. "I am always impressed by the professors' real interest in helping students in addition to their research," says an Operations Research and Industrial Engineering major. First-year courses in the

Website: www.cornell.edu
Location: Small city
Total Enrollment: 20,334
Undergraduates: 18,655
Male/Female: 51/49
SAT Ranges: V 620–720
  M 660–750
ACT Range: 25–30
Financial Aid: 49%
Expense: Pr $ $ $ $
Phi Beta Kappa: Yes
Applicants: 20,441
Accepted: 31%
Enrolled: 51%
Grad in 6 Years: 91%
Returning Freshmen: 96%
Academics: ✍ ✍ ✍ ✍ ✍
Social: ☎ ☎ ☎ ☎
Q of L: ★ ★ ★
Admissions: (607) 255-5241
Email Address:
  admissions@cornell.edu

Strongest Programs:
Computer Science
English
Art and Design
Architecture
Hotel Administration
Industrial and Labor Relations
Engineering
Agriculture
Biology

Despite the intense academic atmosphere, Cornell social life beats most of the other Ivies hands down.

Cornell's highly talented student body and notoriously competitive academics probably make it, in the words of one student, "the only place where you walk up a forty-five-degree incline in twenty-degree weather to get 30 percent on a prelim."

sciences and social sciences are generally large lectures, though many are taught by "charismatic profs" who try to remain accessible. The largest course on campus, Psych 101, packs in more than one thousand, but students report that scintillating lectures make it a well-loved rite of passage. Some undergrads complain that it is difficult to get into popular courses unless you are a major. "There are times when students don't get into courses, but that's usually for classes with limited enrollment," explains one junior. The administration, however, is hoping that the decision to make undergraduates a priority will improve most of the problems in the lower-level courses. For now, first-year students do have access to senior faculty members, including such notables as novelists Alison Lurie and Dan McCall, through mandatory First-Year Writing Seminars.

The Fund for Educational Initiatives gives professors money to implement innovative approaches to undergraduate education, which have included a visual learning laboratory and a course on electronic music. Cornell was early among universities to add women's studies to the curriculum and continues to be an innovator, with programs in Asian-American studies and by offering its students programs like its Sea Semester.*

Cornell academics are demanding and foster an intensity found on few campuses. "The easiest Ivy to get into; the toughest to get out of," quips one student. "Students spend four to five hours per night on coursework, and at least half the weekend is spent hitting the books." Another student adds, "The courses here are very difficult but can be mastered if the student puts in enough effort." University-wide, 90 percent of Cornell students ranked in the top tenth of their high school class, so those who were the class genius in high school should be prepared for a struggle to rise to the top. To cope with the anxieties that the high-powered atmosphere creates, the university has one of the best psychological counseling networks in the nation, including an alcohol-awareness program, peer sex counselors, personal-growth workshops, and EARS (Empathy, Assistance, and Referral Service).

"The courses here are very difficult but can be mastered if the student puts in enough effort."

The library system is superb. Cornell students have access to more than 7.1 million volumes, 65,000 journals, and one thousand networked resources in the nineteen branches around campus. The resources on the Olin Graduate Library's first floor are available to anyone, and a pass from a professor gets you into the graduate stacks. Within the beautiful, underground Carl A. Kroch Library, students study in skylit atriums and reading rooms and move about the renowned Fiske Icelandic Collection and the Echols Collections, the finest Cambodian collection on display.

Academically, Cornell is a veritable plethora of opportunities offering more than four thousand courses in seven colleges and schools. A co-op program is available to engineering students, and Cornell-in-Washington, with its own dorm, is popular among students from all seven undergraduate colleges. Students looking to study abroad can choose from more than two hundred programs and universities throughout the world, including those in Indonesia, Belgium, Ireland, and Nepal. Research opportunities are outstanding at Cornell, and students can take part in some of the most vital research happening in the nation. Recent research findings include solving the mystery of how Jupiter's rings are formed and discovering a new technology to make computer software less vulnerable to bugs.

Prospective students apply to one of the seven colleges or schools through the central admissions office, and admissions standards vary by school. The mixture of state and private, preprofessional, and liberal arts at one institution provides a diversity of students rare among America's colleges. City slickers and country folk, engineers and those with an artsy flair all rub shoulders here. About two-thirds of Cornell's students are out-of-staters; another 7 percent are foreign. African-Americans and Hispanics account for 10 percent of the students, and Asian-Americans 16 percent more. "Cornell is open to all ideas as long as they do not harm another group or person," says one student. Cornell offers many workshops and discussion groups aimed at increasing tolerance. The state-assisted schools draw a large number of in-staters, as well as many students from New Jersey, Pennsylvania, and New England, while arts and sciences and engineering draw from the tristate metropolitan New York City area, Pennsylvania, Massachusetts, and California. Whatever their origin, students seem self-motivated and studious. Upon graduation, 50 percent of Cornell students take jobs, and 32 percent continue to graduate and professional schools.

Cornell is need blind in admissions and guarantees to meet the demonstrated need of all accepted applicants, but the proportion of outright grants—as opposed to loans that must be repaid—in the financial-aid package varies depending on how eager the university is to get students to enroll. The Cornell Installment Plan (CIP) allows students or their parents to pay a year's or semester's tuition in monthly interest-free installments. The university also takes pride in its three Cornell Commitment fellowship programs that recognize leadership and academic excellence, work and service, and research and discovery. Depending on financial need, Commitment students may receive up to $4,000 in loan replacement each year in addition to other financial rewards.

The mixture of state and private, preprofessional and liberal arts at one institution provides a diversity of students rare among America's colleges.

Many changes are in store for Cornell housing as a result of the new plan to transform undergraduate education. The university recently received a $100 million pledge from an anonymous donor to reach this goal. North Campus now has two new residence halls and a dining room and is the home of all freshmen. West Campus will be transformed into a post-freshman-year living and will have faculty leadership from all the undergraduate schools and colleges at Cornell. A few students are housed in two dorms on the edge of Collegetown, the blocks of apartments and houses within walking distance of the campus. There are dorms devoted to everything from ecology to music, and cultural houses include the International Living Center, Latino Living Center, Ujamaa Residential College, and Akwe:kon, a program house focusing on American Indian culture (the only facility of its kind in the nation). "Program houses and co-ops are wonderful alternatives to dorm life," says one student. Also available are a small number of highly coveted suites—six large double rooms with kitchens and a common living area. More than half of Cornell students—and most juniors and seniors—live off campus. Many try their luck in Collegetown, where demand keeps the housing market tight and rents high, while others live in fraternity and

"Program houses and co-ops are wonderful alternatives to dorm life."

sorority houses. Cornell's food service is reputedly among the best in the nation. There are seven dining halls that function independently, so, one student enthuses, "there are at least 28 different entrées for each meal." Milk products and some meats come right from the agriculture school, and about twice a semester a cross-country gourmet team—the staff of a famous restaurant—prepares its specialties on campus.

Despite the intense academic atmosphere, Cornell social life beats most of the other Ivies hands down. Once the weekend arrives, local parties and ski slopes are filled with Cornell students who have managed to strike a balance between study and play. Collegetown bars offer good eats and drinks, but those under twenty-one are barred. However, there is plenty to do at Cornell aside from drinking, students report. "We go to movies, plays, concerts, or just go out to dinner with friends," says a senior. With 30 percent of men and 25 percent of women pledging, fraternities and sororities also play a significant role in the social scene. Big events include Fun in the Sun (a day of friendly athletic competition), Dragon Day (architecture students build a dragon and parade it through campus), and Springfest (a concert on Libe Slope).

Students celebrate the last day of classes—Slope Day—by hanging out at Libe Slope. There are also innumerable concerts and sporting events. In addition, there are more than six hundred extracurricular clubs ranging from a tanning society to a society of women engineers.

Hockey is unquestionably the dominant sport on campus (the chief goal being to defeat Harvard), and camping out for season tickets is an annual ritual. Cornell boasts the largest intramural program in the Ivy League; it includes more than a dozen sports, including one hundred hockey teams organized around dorms, fraternities, and other organizations. The aforementioned "four seasons of Ithaca" can make walking to class across the vast and hilly campus challenging, but with the first snow of the winter, "traying" down Libe Slope becomes the sport of choice for hordes of fun-loving Cornellians. Ithaca boasts "wonderful outdoor enthusiast stores," says one student. It also hosts Greek Peak Mountain for nearby skiing, Cayuga Lake for boating and swimming, and lots of space for hiking and watching the clouds roll by.

Like most other Ivy League universities, Cornell is a premiere research institution with a distinguished faculty and outstanding academics. What sets it apart is the university's willingness to stray from the traditional Ivy League path as it did with the announcement of its plan to make undergraduates its highest priority. Cornell University is a pioneer in the world of education, and students unafraid to blaze their own trail will feel at home here. "There is no one way to characterize a Cornell student and I think that's what sets us apart," says one student. "Anyone is welcome here and anyone can find their niche."

Overlaps

Penn, Columbia, Northwestern, Brown, Yale

If You Apply To ≫ **Cornell:** Rolling notification (College of Agriculture and Life Sciences, School of Industrial and Labor Relations, and School of Hotel Administration only). Early decision: Nov. 1. Regular admissions: Jan. 1. Financial aid: Feb. 10. Housing: Processed upon admission. Campus interviews: required for school of Hotel Admin. and College of Architecture, Art, and Planning, informative. Alumni interviews: recommended, informational (varies by program). SATs or ACTs: required. SAT IIs: required (varies by program). Essay question: Common Application. Apply to individual programs or schools.

University of Dallas

1845 East Northgate Drive, Irving, TX 75062

Bulwark of academic traditionalism in Big D. Despite being a "university," U of D has only 1,200 undergraduates. Except for the Business Leaders of Tomorrow program, the curriculum is exclusively liberal arts. The only outpost of Roman Catholic education between Loyola of New Orleans and University of San Diego.

Website: www.udallas.edu
Location: Suburban
Total Enrollment: 3,542
Undergraduates: 1,200
Male/Female: 42/58
SAT Ranges: V 550–670
  M 540–660
ACT Range: 23–28
Financial Aid: 27%

While many universities around the nation have reexamined their Eurocentric core curriculums, the University of Dallas—the best Roman Catholic college south of Washington—remains proudly dedicated to fostering students in "the study of great deeds and works of Western civilization."

"Imagine a party where someone makes a joke about Plato or Dante, and everybody cracks up. That's UD in a nutshell," says one student. And appropriately for a Roman Catholic school, much of the focus is on Rome, where most of the sophomore class treks every year. The unique and intense program focuses on the art and architecture of Rome, the philosophy of man and being, classical literature, Italian, and the development of Western civilization.

UD's 744-acre campus occupies a pastoral home in a Dallas suburb on top of "the closest thing this region has to a hill." Texas Stadium, home of the Dallas Cowboys, is right across the street. A major portion of the campus is situated around the Braniff Mall, a landscaped and lighted gathering place near the Braniff Memorial Tower, the school's landmark. The primary tone of the buildings is brown, and the architecture, as described by one student, is "post-1950s, done in brick, typical Catholic-institutional." While it may not be a picture-perfect school, it does have a beautiful chapel and a state-of-the-art science building. A new four-building Art Village is home to enlarged sculpture, painting, printmaking, and ceramics creations.

The curriculum can be daunting for those unaccustomed to the rigors of a more traditional liberal arts education. There's a heavy dose of classics (which leads to those late-night Roman jam sessions). English is the most popular major, followed by politics, economics, math, and history. Political philosophy is also a popular major, although students claim that most courses tend to be slanted toward the conservative side. One junior reports "philosophy and politics set the tone of the campus." Students say the math and education departments need improvement. The Business Leaders of Tomorrow program can be completed in addition to any undergraduate major. It includes introductory courses in business management, an internship, a mentor who is a business professional, and a choice of electives from the Graduate School of Management—all designed to prepare students to be future leaders. Premed students are well served by the biology and chemistry programs, and a majority of UD graduates go on to grad school.

> "Imagine a party where someone makes a joke about Plato or Dante, and everybody cracks up. That's UD in a nutshell."

The Rome semester is considered part of the UD Western Civilization core curriculum, which takes up close to half the requirements for a bachelor's degree. Included in the core are heavy doses of philosophy, history, literature, science, and math, as well as a serious foreign language requirement. Two theology courses (including Scripture and Western Theological Tradition) are also required of all students. Those inclined toward the sciences may take advantage of the John B. O'Hara Chemical Science Institute, which offers a hands-on nine-week summer program to prepare new students for independent research.

Students report that the academic pressure and the workload can be intense. "The academic climate here is extremely rigorous," says a classics and drama double major. "You can either decide that the work is difficult and strive to accomplish, or get overwhelmed and crumble." A senior English major describes the school as "competitive and rigorous, based strongly on critical thinking, examination, writing, and discussion." The university uses no teaching assistants, and professors are easy to get to know. "We have outstanding faculty who are personally committed to students and to teaching them and not to advancing their own academic status," one student says. Getting into the small, personal classes is rarely a problem, and counseling receives high marks.

> "We have outstanding faculty who are personally committed to students and to teaching them and not to advancing their own academic status."

About 70 percent of UD students are Catholic, and many of them choose this school because of its religious affiliation. Fifty-six percent are from Texas, and 13 percent of the student body are Hispanic. Seven percent are Asian-American and 1 percent is African-American. Students say that racial tension is not a problem on campus.

UDers tend to lean to the right politically. "UD is an ultraconservative university," says one senior. "Liberals are not exactly welcomed with open arms, although

(Continued)
Expense: Pr $
Phi Beta Kappa: Yes
Applicants: 1,175
Accepted: 78%
Enrolled: 31%
Grad in 6 Years: 61%
Returning Freshmen: 83%
Academics: ✐ ✐ ✐
Social: ☎ ☎
Q of L: ★ ★ ★
Admissions: (972) 721-5266
Email Address: undadmis@ acad.udallas.edu

Strongest Programs:
Biology
English
Politics
Psychology
History

"UD is an ultraconservative university," says one senior. "Liberals are not exactly welcomed with open arms, although there are numerous forums for discussion."

there are numerous forums for discussion." Tradition and religion govern rules on dorms and conduct.

UD offers various merit scholarships, ranging from $1,000 to full tuition, but no athletic scholarships. Everyone under twenty-one who doesn't reside at home with their parents must live on campus in single-sex or co-ed-by-floor dorms, "where visitation regulations are relatively strict," one student reports. As for the dorms, they're "not luxurious, but they are comfortable," one student reports. The most popular dorms are Jerome (all-female) and Madonna (all-male). At Gregory, the dorm reserved for those who like to party, the goings-on are less than saintly. In addition to a spacious and comfortable dining hall with a wonderful view of North Dallas, there is Rathskeller, which serves snacks and fast food (and great conversation). A car is a must for off-campus life since there is virtually no reliable public transportation in the Dallas/Fort Worth Metroplex.

The University of Dallas is unusual for a Texas school in that its entire population does not salivate at the sight of a football or basketball. Save for the Groundhogs, UD's rugby team, students rarely mention their Division III athletics. "Athletics will always be overshadowed by the academic commitments of the students," says one student. Intramural sports, on the other hand, are well organized and very popular, and chess is a favored activity. With no fraternities or sororities at UD, the student government sponsors most on-campus entertainment. Three free movies a week, dances, and visiting speakers are usually on the agenda. Church-related and religious activities provide fulfilling social outlets for a goodly number of students. Annual events include Mallapalooza, a spring music festival, and Groundhog, a party on Groundhog's Day weekend. Then there's Charity Week in the fall, when the junior class plans a week's worth of fund-raising events. Each year

"UD is an ultraconservative university." students dread Sadie Hawkins Day and the annual Screw Your Roommate dance—dark nights of the soul, each. The university can be vigorous in enforcing restrictive drinking rules, and, as a result, it is difficult for a minor to drink at campus events.

Students describe Irving as "a suburb, just like any other," but the Metroplex offers almost unlimited possibilities, including a full agenda for bar-hopping on Lower Greenville Avenue, about ten minutes away. The West End and Deep Ellum offer a taste of shopping and Dallas's alternative music scene. And for the more adventurous, New Orleans isn't too far away.

UD is without a doubt the best Catholic-affiliated university south of Washington, D.C. Students pride themselves on being the "Philosopher Kings of the twenty-first century," but their roots go back to the Roman thinkers of an earlier era. The mix of religion and liberal arts can serve a certain breed of students well. In the words of one senior, "The best thing about the college is the amazing respect that professors have for their students, especially after Rome. It makes you feel like you can accomplish anything, and after four years at UD, you usually can."

Overlaps

University of Texas–Austin, Texas A&M, Notre Dame, Baylor, University of Texas–Arlington

If You Apply To ➤ **Dallas:** Early action: Dec 1. Regular admissions, financial aid, and housing: Feb. 15. Does not guarantee to meet demonstrated need. Campus interviews: recommended, evaluative. Alumni interviews: optional, informational. SATs or ACTs: required. SAT IIs: optional. Accepts the Common Application. Essay question: describe a character in fiction, a historical figure, or a creative work (as in art, music, science, etc.) that has had an influence on you, and explain that influence.

Dartmouth College

6016 McNutt Hall, Hanover, NH 03755

The smallest Ivy and the one with the strongest emphasis on undergraduates. Traditionally the most conservative member of the Ivy League, it has been steered leftward in recent years. Ivy ties notwithstanding, Dartmouth has more in common with places like Colgate, Williams, and Middlebury. Great place for those who like the outdoors.

Dartmouth is truly a different species of Ivy. The Big Green has the highest graduation rate in the United States; it is one of the safest campuses in the United States; it is a college among universities; it has the smallest total enrollment in the Ancient Eight; and it is the most undergraduate-friendly. All of this has resulted in a mad rush of high school students lining up for admission. The ones who make it in are thrilled. "Life seems perfect when I am sitting on the Green, with Baker Towner in the background and the sun gleaming down," says a nostalgic senior. "I am sad to be leaving."

As Dartmouth remains dedicated to tradition, it is also trying to grow. When former president James Freedman was hired in the 1980s, he was charged with the task of "leading Dartmouth out of the sandbox" and making it a hospitable place with a more scholarly feeling. He said then that he wanted students "whose greatest pleasures may not come from the camaraderie of classmates but from the lonely acts of writing poetry, or mastering the cello, or solving mathematical riddles, or translating Catullus." (The reference to Catullus may have been the president's little esoteric joke. The Latin poet Catullus wrote erotic, sometimes obscene, verse on topics that included his passion for his mistress Lesbia, a boy named Juventius, and the sexual excesses of Julius Caesar.)

> **"Dartmouth is inundated with so many intelligent people, so courses are very challenging no matter what the subject matter."**

Today's Dartmouth hardly resembles the Dartmouth of yesteryear, when liberal elements—mainly women and minorities—squared off against the self-proclaimed heirs of the Dartmouth tradition.

Set in the "small, Norman Rockwell town" of Hanover, New Hampshire, Dartmouth's picturesque campus is arrayed around a quaint green with the impressive Baker Library at one end and the college-owned Hanover Inn at the other. Although the campus architecture ranges from Romanesque to postmodern, the dominant theme is copper-topped Colonial frame. The nearest significant urban area (Boston) is two hours away, but major artists (including Itzhak Perlman) and groups visit the Hopkins Center for the Creative and Performing Arts, adding a touch of culture to the rural campus. Recent additions include the new $30 million Berry Library.

Much is questioned and considered at Dartmouth, and academic excellence is a given. "Dartmouth is inundated with so many intelligent people, so courses are very challenging no matter what the subject matter," says a history major. The Big Green also rates as one of the top in the country for undergraduate teaching. Three professional schools—business, engineering, and medicine—provide additional resources, but Dartmouth's passion still lies in undergraduate liberal arts. Most popular majors include government, history, English, biology, and economics. Students complain that teaching in the math department could improve. Intro biology classes are "the most feared and disliked 'weed out' classes," says a biophysical chemistry major, who should know. Dartmouth is perhaps best known for foreign languages, including Hebrew and Arabic, which are taught through the Intensive Language Model developed by John Rassias, a nationally renowned language

Website: www.dartmouth.edu
Location: Rural
Total Enrollment: 5,593
Undergraduates: 4,079
Male/Female: 51/49
SAT Ranges: V 650–750
   M 680–770
ACT Range: 27–33
Financial Aid: 46%
Expense: Pr $ $ $ $
Phi Beta Kappa: Yes
Applicants: 10,193
Accepted: 11%
Enrolled: 51%
Grad in 6 Years: 95%
Returning Freshmen: 96%
Academics: ✍ ✍ ✍ ✍ ✍
Social: 🍷 🍷 🍷 🍷 🍷
Q of L: ★ ★ ★
Admissions: (603) 646-2875
Email Address: admissions.office@dartmouth.edu

Strongest Programs:
Biological Sciences
Computer Science
Engineering
Economics
Languages
Psychological and Brain
   Sciences
Studio Art
Women's, Native American,
   and Environmental Studies

professor. Computer science is also among the best in the nation, thanks in no small part to the late John Kemeny, the former Dartmouth president who coinvented time-sharing and the BASIC language. With the most extensive undergraduate facilities in the nation, computer literacy is a way of life at Dartmouth; virtually every academic classroom and all residential dorms are networked.

Dartmouth also offers its students a wide variety of special programs, including the Presidential Scholars Program, which offers one-on-one research assistantships with faculty, and the Senior Fellowship Program, which empowers students to undertake interdisciplinary research projects. Another program, the Women in Science Project, encourages female students to pursue their interest in science, mathematics, and engineering, offering mentors, speakers, and even research apprenticeships for first-year students. Still another bonus is the Montgomery Fellowships, which bring well-known politicians, writers, and others to the campus for periods ranging from a few days to several months. The Visionary in Residence program invites notable thinkers to campus to share their talents and insights with students. Other innovative programs explore the intersections of gender and culture, including The Men's Project, Women of Color and Allies Collective, and Sex Week.

Students are quite enthusiastic about their professors. "They inspire brilliance," says a religion major. Another student adds, "Professors often hold study sessions during the weekend before exams and invite you for dinner in their homes." Academic and career counseling resources are abundant but vary in quality. "Advising for freshman is hit or miss," one student reports.

Incoming students receive immediate instruction for the use of the written word at the college level: a composition course followed by a mandatory freshman seminar with an emphasis on writing. Students must also take an interdisciplinary class, fulfill a world culture requirement, and take ten courses across the following areas: arts, literature, philosophy, religion or history, international studies, social analysis, technology or applied science, quantitative reasoning, and natural or physical science. Students are expected to become proficient in at least one foreign language. In addition, Dartmouth has a senior culminating activity—a thesis, public report, exhibition, seminar, production, or demonstration—which allows students to pull together the work of their major and add a creative and intellectual twist of their own.

The school's most notable eccentricity is the Dartmouth Plan, whereby the school operates year-round with four ten-week terms a year, including one during the summer. The D Plan allows students to take classes any of the four seasons they wish, with only the requirement that they be on campus during their entire freshman and senior years and the summer after their sophomore year. Students use their time off for jobs, internships, or travel. About 60 percent of the student body spends at least one term participating in one of Dartmouth's forty-four programs of foreign study, either for intensive language training or a departmental study (drama in London or environmental studies in Zimbabwe, for example). The college is also part of the Twelve College Exchange* and the Maritime Studies Program.* Nearly 20 percent go on to graduate schools.

Dartmouth was founded in 1769 to educate Native Americans, and since 1969 the college has made serious efforts to attract them. Dartmouth has the most outstanding Native American program in the country today, and 3 percent of the student body is made up of such students. The formerly all-male school went co-ed in 1972, and nearly half of the current student body is female. African-Americans account for 6 percent of the student body, Hispanics for 6 percent, and Asian-Americans for 12 percent. "Students are well-rounded and personable, and tend to be involved deeply and passionately in a variety of activities," says a senior. Dartmouth is need-blind in admissions and guarantees to meet the demonstrated financial need of all accepted students. It was the first of a growing number of privately financed institutions to go into the business of selling tax-exempt bonds through a state authority to underwrite loans to families at low interest rates. Within the last few years, Dartmouth has added roughly $4 million to its scholarship resources, mainly through reduced loan amounts for students. Additionally, Dartmouth is trying to lure more middle-class students to campus by offering bigger grants to students whose parents earn less than $60,000 per year. No merit scholarships are awarded, and athletic scholarships are prohibited at all Ivy League institutions.

On the housing front, the thirty-four dorms have been grouped into eleven clusters that organize activities and programs and provide a sense of community. There are also several academic affinity and special-interest housing options. Separate first-year housing will be provided as an alternative starting with the class of 2005. Rooms are large and homey—some of the older ones have working fireplaces, though students are no longer allowed to use them, one senior gripes—and the maintenance service even cleans the bathrooms. "Dorms are generally very comfortable, well maintained, and full of character," says an Italian and biochemistry major. Housing is guaranteed only for the first year, but some students say that getting a room can be a problem. Eighty-three percent of students live on campus. As at many schools, sophomores get the short end of the stick when it comes to getting on-campus housing—some go into town for lodging. Students entering the Class of 2007 will have the opportunity to take advantage of the latest communication craze: free long-distance telephone calls via their computers. It's just one more way that Dartmouth is integrating technology into the academic experience.

Dartmouth's Greek system is nationally famous for, among other things, having inspired the movie *Animal House*, cowritten by a 1963 Dartmouth grad; but membership in fraternities and sororities has fallen—only 24 percent of the men and 22 percent of the women belong. But the college's powerful and intensely loyal Greek alumni are the self-appointed keepers of the flame. This burgeoning family tree began to take root in the days before the interstate highway system, when Dartmouth males had nothing to do on Saturday nights but participate in male-bonding activities of the sort

"Dorms are generally very comfortable, well maintained, and full of character."

rarely seen these days outside beer commercials. Almost twenty years ago, the faculty recommended abolishing the fraternities and, according to one junior, they continue to be a point of contention. After an outcry from the alumni, the school compromised by putting the most boisterous on probation. Under the two-year Student Life Initiative, a Greek-life steering committee has developed a set of more rigorous standards for the system. While some see the administration as becoming too controlling in general, one student prophesies that the famous frats will disappear within a decade or so. The Initiative, however, has made significant progress in creating more social and residential alternatives for students throughout campus. Recent additions include a new dance club in the student center, a joint kosher-halal dining facility, and free athletic tickets.

The Big Green also has the most elaborately organized alumni associations in the country—testimony to the loyalty it inspires. "It is often said that Dartmouth students 'bleed green' because they love their school so much," says a religion major. It seems as if every other grad has a title like deputy assistant class secretary, and many return to Hanover when they retire, further cementing their bonds with the college (and driving local real-estate prices beyond the reach of most faculty members).

Greeks are no mean contributors to the college's longtime nickname of its surrounding city, "Hangover." In response to the excessive imbibing of some fraternity members, Dartmouth was one of the first to develop a counseling and educational program designed to combat the abuse of alcohol. The administration is trying to

One famous alum of the college is someone the students actually have known almost all their lives: Dr. Seuss.

curb the fraternity drinking scene and provide alternative student opportunities. A bar on campus called the Lone Pine Tavern is described by one student as a place "where students play everything from Scrabble and chess to checkers and Jenga while listening to jazz and acoustic groups."

Of all Dartmouth's traditions, perhaps the best known is Winter Carnival, an annual festival that draws seekers from all over the Eastern seaboard. During the spring, students celebrate Green Key weekend, which one student calls, "an excuse to drink under the guise of community service." Another unusual tradition, Tubestock, is a day when the entire sophomore class floats down the Connecticut River in rafts.

To the city dweller, Hanover is halfway to the North Pole, but to the outdoors lover it's nearly paradise. "In Hanover, it's odd when strangers don't smile at you as you pass them in town," admits a senior. Residents of Hanover flock to theater productions and women's basketball games alike. Dartmouth students serve as tutors, coaches, and role models for the children here. Dartmouth's own ski area is twenty minutes distant, the Connecticut River is even closer for canoeing and kayaking, and the great outdoors is literally steps away. More adventurous types take to the wilds of Dartmouth's 27,000-acre land grant in the northeast corner of the state, where cabins can be rented for five dollars a night. Most first-year students begin their Dartmouth career with a camping trip led by an upperclass student or faculty member, and the Outing Club is the most popular student organization.

Love of the outdoor life extends to varsity athletics. Recent success stories include the co-ed sailing team, the men's lacrosse, cross-country, rowing, soccer, skiing, and basketball teams, and the women's basketball, ice hockey, lacrosse, and soccer teams. Few Dartmouth students miss the biannual excursion to the Dartmouth–Harvard football game, when thousands of Big Green devotees descend upon Cambridge. Dartmouth's sports center boasts, among other things, a 2,100-seat arena, a four thousand square-foot fitness center, and the only permanent three-glass-wall squash court in North America. Recent construction includes the $3 million Scully-Fahey Field, an artificial-athletic-turf facility.

Even if you don't play squash, Dartmouth has the world to offer from the convenience of a beautiful, tight-knit campus where undergraduate excellence is the top priority. A powerful sense of tradition reigns while new ideas make up the stuff of daily conversation. "The peaceful nature of northern New England has really given me an opportunity to rethink who I am," philosophizes a history major. As another student puts it: "I have grown into myself here. I wish I could stay four more years." Of course, that might get a bit expensive.

Overlaps

Yale, Harvard, Princeton, Stanford, Brown

If You Apply To ➤ **Dartmouth:** Early decision: Nov. 1. Regular admissions: Jan. 1. Financial aid: Feb. 1. Housing: Jul. 1. Guarantees to meet demonstrated need. Campus and alumni interviews: optional, evaluative. SATs or ACTs: required. SAT IIs: required (any three). Accepts the Common Application and electronic applications. Essay question: significant experience or ethical dilemma; issue of concern; significant person; influence of a fictional or historical character; topic of your choice.

Davidson College

P.O. Box 1737, Davidson, NC 28036

"The Dartmouth of the South" is how Davidson has always been styled. Goes head-to-head with Washington and Lee (VA) for honors as the most selective liberal arts

college below the Mason-Dixon Line. At 1,644 students, it is slightly bigger than Rhodes and Sewanee and slightly smaller than W&L.

Davidson College boasts the Southern tradition and gentility of neighbors like Rhodes and Sewanee, with the athletic and academic prowess more common to northern liberal arts powerhouses such as Dartmouth and Colby. Often overlooked because of its small size and sleepy location, Davidson is one of the most selective liberal arts colleges below the Mason-Dixon Line, and might be best described as an "Ivy wannabe." The school's size, honor code, and strong interdisciplinary, international, and preprofessional programs distinguish Davidson from many of its contemporaries.

Located in a beautiful stretch of the North Carolina Piedmont, Davidson's wooded campus features Georgian and Greek Revival architecture. The central campus is designated as an arboretum, and college staff lovingly maintain a collection of the woody plants that thrive in the area. In fact, the arboretum serves as an outdoor laboratory for students, with markers identifying the varieties of trees and shrubs. Davidson retains its original quadrangle, which dates from 1837, plus two dorms and literary society halls built in the 1850s. The Alvarez College Union and Duke Family Performance Hall make up the Knoblach Campus Center, which opened in the fall of 2001. The old campus center was transformed into the Sloan Music Center, which opened in August 2002. Chambers Hall, the school's main academic building, is being renovated.

Davidson's honor code allows students to take exams independently and to feel comfortable leaving doors unlocked. "Everyone follows it in academics and life," says a senior. "It is not uncommon to see money taped to a bench or a pole, saying it was found there." Every entering freshman agrees to abide by the code, and all work submitted to professors is signed with the word "pledged." Core requirements include one course each in fine arts, literature, and history, and two courses each in religion and philosophy, natural sciences and math, and social sciences. Students must also take classes with significant writing and discussion in the first year to satisfy the composition requirement. Four physical education classes are required, as is third-semester proficiency in a foreign language. Many requirements, including in-depth or comparative studies of another culture, may be met through the two-year interdisciplinary humanities program.

Davidson's academic climate is rigorous, but not grueling. "Classes are highly competitive, in that they are challenging you as a student, but it is not cutthroat against peers," one student says. "There is a group-work mentality." The most popular majors are English, biology, economics, and political science; history and psychology tie for fifth place. While administrators say there are no weak spots in the curriculum, one student criticizes sociology as too easy, and says the chemistry major is "a little hard." Students here truly want to "learn and enjoy knowledge," says a math major. "It is common for academic discussions to occur just for fun." The quality of teaching "ranges from good to

> **"It is common for academic discussions to occur just for fun."**

excellent," another student says. "Freshmen are always taught by full professors." And a senior notes that faculty–student interaction is not limited to the classroom: "I've been to professors' houses for desserts, chicken dinners, and movies."

For those whose academic interests lie outside the mainstream, Davidson's Center for Interdisciplinary Studies allows students to develop and design their own majors. Environmental studies majors may apply to the School for Field Studies, to spend a semester studying environmental issues in other countries, or to work and conduct research at Biosphere 2. Aspiring diplomats can tap into the Dean Rusk Program for International Studies, named for the Davidson alumnus who served as Secretary of State to Presidents Kennedy and Johnson. The South Asia

Website: www.davidson.edu
Location: Small town
Total Enrollment: 1,644
Undergraduates: 1,644
Male/Female: 50/50
SAT Ranges: V 620–710
   M 630–720
ACT Range: 27–31
Financial Aid: 33%
Expense: Pr $ $ $ $
Phi Beta Kappa: Yes
Applicants: 3,387
Accepted: 35%
Enrolled: 40%
Grad in 6 Years: 89%
Returning Freshmen: 96%
Academics: ✍ ✍ ✍ ✍ ½
Social: ☎ ☎ ☎
Q of L: ★ ★ ★ ★
Admissions: (800) 768-0380
Email Address:
   admission@davidson.edu

Strongest Programs:
Biology
Psychology
English
Political Science
Theatre
Chemistry
International Studies
History

The old campus center was transformed into the Sloan Music Center, which opened in August 2002. Chambers Hall, the school's main academic building, is being renovated.

Studies program focuses on India, Pakistan, Bangladesh, Sri Lanka, Nepal, and Bhutan; study abroad is also available in countries from France, Germany, and England to Cyprus and Zambia, and more than 60 percent of the students go abroad. A 3–2 engineering program is available with five larger universities. A Sloan Foundation grant is helping Davidson integrate technology into the liberal arts, with courses such as From Petroleum to Penicillin and Sex, Technology, and Morality. On campus, class size is restricted; you won't find a room other than the cafeteria with more than fifty students, and 72 percent of all classes taken by freshmen have nineteen or less.

Most Davidson students come from affluent Southern families, though only 18 percent are native North Carolinians. Many students are Presbyterian, and the school has ties to the Presbyterian Church; their parents are doctors, lawyers, and ministers (as well as premed and prelaw preparation, Davison has a number of courses appropriate for students who aim to become clergy). Five percent of the student body is African-American, with 3 percent Hispanic and 2 percent Asian-American. Students are "highly motivated, involved, interesting individuals," says one. "They are also very diverse in experiences." An Andrew Mellon Foundation grant is helping the school add diversity programs in dorms, educate faculty on specific student populations, and host artist- or scholar-in-residence programs. Davidson also lures top students with merit scholarships averaging more than $6,000 a year. Athletic scholarships are available in twenty sports.

Ninety-two percent of Davidson's students live on campus in co-ed or single-sex dorms. Freshmen are housed together in two five-story halls and they eat in Vail Commons, where the "food is great—all you can eat, and lots of options," and the social climate is better. Upperclassmen may live in the dorms, off campus, or in college-owned cottages on the perimeter of campus, which hold about ten students each. Seniors get apartments with private bedrooms. "Campus rooms are highly available and pretty nice," says one student. Most upperclassmen take meals at one of the ten eating clubs—seven for men, three for women. These Greek-like groups have their own cooks, and serve meals family style.

The eating clubs are the center of social life on campus. All but one are in Patterson Court, which freshmen are not allowed to enter for the first three weeks of school. The dues charged by these clubs cover meals as well as parties and other campus-wide events. The fraternities, which claim 42 percent of Davidson's men, are not much different from the eating clubs, and freshmen simply sign up for the group they want to join on Self-Selection Night, with no "rushing" allowed. There are no sororities on campus. And even if you don't join up, don't despair; Davidson requires that most parties—"at least two per weekend" at the eating clubs—be open to the entire community. Alcohol policies comply with North Carolina law. Officially, no one under twenty-one can be served, but this is college—it's possible for most students to get booze. Still, says one student, "it's not being poured down your throat."

Students are "highly motivated, involved, interesting individuals."

Davidson's five-day freshman orientation includes a regatta, scavenger hunt, and the Freshman Cake Race. The program helps introduce students to the cozy town of Davidson, which has coffee shops and cafés, nearby Lake Norman for sailing, swimming, and waterskiing, and plenty of volunteer opportunities. The equally quaint town of Cornelius is only a ten-minute drive from campus, so it's a common destination for dinner and a movie, or a relaxed night out. When those diversions grow old, North Carolina's largest city, Charlotte, is just twenty miles away, with clubs and other attractions. A car definitely helps here, as Myrtle Beach and skiing are several hours from Davidson, in different directions. Intramural sports are popular, and the men's varsity basketball team won the Southern Conference championship in 2002.

Overlaps

Duke, Wake Forest, UNC–Chapel Hill, University of Virginia, Vanderbilt

Davidson is working to strengthen its position among liberal arts colleges by attracting more top students to its charming neck of the woods. From study-abroad and independent research to a strawberries-and-champagne reception with the college president for graduating seniors, students here combine tradition with forward thinking, to make great memories—and intellectual strides.

<table>
<tr><td>If You Apply To ➤</td><td>Davidson: Early decision: Nov. 15. Regular admission: Jan. 2. Financial aid: Feb. 15. Guarantees to meet demonstrated need. Campus and alumni interviews: optional, informational. SATs or ACTs: required. SAT IIs: recommended. Accepts the Common Application and students may complete a portion of the application online. Essay question: significant experience, important issue, influential person or character.</td></tr>
</table>

University of Dayton

300 College Park, Dayton, OH 45469-1300

Among a cohort of second-tier Roman Catholic institutions in the Midwest that includes Duquesne, Xavier (OH), U. of St. Louis, and DePaul and Loyola of Chicago. Drawing cards include business, engineering, education, and the sciences. The city of Dayton is not particularly enticing and UD's appeal is largely regional.

Anyone who thinks college students of today subscribe to postmodern cynicism ought to take a peek at Dayton, where optimism and Christian charity are alive and well. Students describe the campus as a welcoming, homey place, but say the school is large enough to continually expose them to new people and ideas. "It's just a very friendly, warm, comfortable atmosphere," explains one senior. "Everyone really wants to be here."

Founded by the Society of Mary (Marianists), Dayton continues to emphasize that order's devotion to service. More than one thousand students volunteer their time in thirty different public service areas. And like many religiously affiliated schools, Dayton prides itself on the closeness and sense of community among its students and faculty members. "One will never feel uncomfortable going to their professor about anything at all," says a junior.

UD's campus is on the southern boundary of the city, secluded from the traffic and bustle of downtown. The more historic buildings on the parklike campus make up the central core of the campus and blend architectural charm with modern technological conveniences. The sports arena recently got a major sprucing-up, along with the Baujan soccer field and a central campus hub; and a new baseball field, practice track, and football practice field are in the works at the arena. A $22 million expansion project provided 55,000 square feet of new science facilities, and five new five-person houses were recently added to the student housing lineup. A new four-hundred-bed residence hall with amenities such as a post office and credit union is going up in the heart of campus, and an arts-centered living and learning center called ArtStreet is in the works.

UD students take full advantage of the strong offerings found in business, engineering, education, communications, and the sciences—the most popular majors. Weaker offerings include theater and physical education. Most students agree the academic climate can be either demanding or laid-back, depending on the course and the major. "The workload at times can get overbearing, but most of the professors will work around your schedule to do what they can to help you out," says a junior.

Website: admission.udayton.edu
Location: City outskirts
Total Enrollment: 10,126
Undergraduates: 7,085
Male/Female: 50/50
SAT Ranges: V 500–610 M 510–630
ACT Range: 22–27
Financial Aid: 56%
Expense: Pr $ $
Phi Beta Kappa: No
Applicants: 7,496
Accepted: 84%
Enrolled: 27%
Grad in 6 Years: 76%
Returning Freshmen: 90%
Academics: ✍ ✍ ✍
Social: ☎ ☎ ☎ ☎ ☎
Q of L: ★ ★ ★
Admissions: (937) 229-4411 or (800) 837-7433
Email Address: admission@udayton.edu

Strongest Programs:
Business
Engineering

Dayton's general education requirements include courses in five "domains of knowledge": arts, history, philosophy and religion, physical and life sciences, and social sciences. Faculty members in the College of Arts and Sciences have developed a twelve-course core curriculum that satisfies the general education requirements through an interdisciplinary program that clumps mandatory classes into sequences pertinent to academic disciplines. The Barry Scholars program includes seminars, study-abroad opportunities, service and leadership projects, and a major independent research project. Students with at least a 1300 combined SAT score or a 30 ACT score and who place in the top 10 percent of their graduating class or have a 3.7 GPA may join the University Honors Program, which provides guest speakers in small classes and requires an honors thesis project.

"It's just a very friendly, warm, comfortable atmosphere."

The Interdepartmental Summer Study Abroad Program is a popular ticket to Europe's most exciting cities, while the Immersion Program in Third World countries is much praised by participants. Students can take advantage of the cooperative education opportunities, and benefit from the information science center, which houses computer classrooms and labs. All students purchase a notebook computer upon entering UD. Students speak enthusiastically about contacts with professors outside of the classroom. A senior history major describes the profs as "wonderful, willing to help students anytime, very accessible, very intelligent, well-known in their fields, very nice, genuinely concerned about students." New students unsure of their majors can take advantage of First Year Experience, a structured program where students are required to meet with their advisors once a week.

A new four-hundred-bed residence hall with amenities such as a post office and credit union is going up in the heart of campus, and an arts-centered living and learning center called ArtStreet is in the works.

Students are "mostly Caucasian, middle- to upper-class Catholic students" says a junior. Two-thirds of Dayton's students are from Ohio, and minorities make up just 7 percent of the student population. The Task Force on Women's Issues, the Office of Diverse Student Populations, and an updated sexual-harassment policy demonstrate UD's growing sensitivity to campus issues. More than three-quarters of incoming students rank in the top half of their high-school class. Dayton's athletic scholarships go to all sports except football. There are also many scholarship and leadership awards, from $1,000 to full tuition, that go to those with superior academic credentials.

Seventy-six percent of students are campus residents; those who live off-campus generally live adjacent to it. On-campus dwellers can choose from four residence halls, all smoke-free, and housing is available for all undergraduate students. Upperclassmen often enter the lottery for coveted university-owned apartments and houses located in an adjacent student neighborhood that also contains privately owned homes. Students praise the clean and well-maintained rooms. "Dorms are great, not the newest, but they are a lot of fun," says a senior. The best dorm for freshmen, according to many, is Marycrest, with "huge rooms and loads of storage space." Sophomores have an opportunity to live in Virginia Kettering, a residence hall whose amenities evoke luxurious apartments and is also known as "the Hilton on the Hill." The food in the dining halls that dot the campus is generally well received;

"One will never feel uncomfortable going to their professor about anything at all."

one dining hall is located in one of the first-year dorms, another in the sophomore complex, and the third is centrally located in the student union. A food emporium is in the newest dorm on campus, and a café will be in the new ArtStreet complex.

More than one thousand students volunteer their time in thirty different public service areas.

The student neighborhood (aka "the Ghetto") serves as a sort of continuous social center. A lit porchlight beckons party-seeking students to join the weekend festivities. Because the university owns most of the properties, a twenty-four-hour campus security patrol keeps watch over the area. The more adventurous weekend excursions are trips to Ohio State University, Ohio University, and Cincinnati or

Indianapolis. But the best road trip is the Dayton-to-Daytona trip after spring finals, a seventeen-hour trek that draws loads of students each year. Partying on campus is commonplace and controlled, but parties have sized down due to the university's enforcement of the twenty-one-year-old drinking age. Kegs are allowed only at parties where the legal drinking age of the partiers can be validated. Still, "There is a 'three strikes, you're out' policy regarding drinking," which students say makes them cautious. But on average they enjoy drinking and have no problem being served at off-campus parties. Greek organizations draw 15 percent of UD men and 18 percent of the women, with all chapters playing an active role in the community service and social life.

The Interdepartmental Summer Study Abroad Program is a popular ticket to Europe's most exciting cities, while the Immersion Program in Third World countries is much praised by participants.

More important, though, are sports, particularly basketball. "Our annual basketball games versus Xavier are always a big, spirited event," says a sophomore. The football team, which is Division I-AA, plays in the Pioneer Football League and was the 2002 league champion. UD is in the Atlantic 10 for Division I athletics in all other sports. In 2002, the men's basketball and women's soccer teams advanced to the NCAA tournament. When students aren't cheering, they can participate in an extensive intramural program. Other activities in the city include a minor-league baseball team and an art institute, aviation museum, and a symphony and ballet are in the new Schuster Performing Arts Center. A large shopping mall is also easily accessible. Those who hunger for a more cosmopolitan atmosphere can frequent Cincinnati and its restaurants, shops, and sports arenas.

The success of Dayton's attempts to provide its students with a high quality of life and a sense of cohesiveness is reflected in many of the students' comments about the terrific social life and family-like atmosphere among both students and faculty. As a mid-size

"Our annual basketball games versus Xavier are always a big, spirited event."

university where the undergraduates come first, Dayton has managed to maintain an exciting balance of personal attention, academic challenge, and all-American fun.

"It's an atmosphere of acceptance, and you feel like you're part of a big family," says one sophomore.

Overlaps

Miami University (OH), Ohio University, Ohio State, Xavier (OH), University of Cincinnati

If You Apply To ➤	**Dayton:** Rolling admissions: Jan. 1 (priority). Financial aid: Mar. 31. Housing: May 1. Campus interviews: recommended, informational. Alumni interviews: optional, informational. SATs or ACTs: required. No SAT IIs. Accepts electronic applications. Essay question: personal statement on an achievement, experience, or risk and its impact on you.

Deep Springs College

Deep Springs, CA Mailing address: Dyer, NV 89010-9803

Picture twenty-five Ivy League–caliber men living and learning in a remote desert outpost—that's Deep Springs. DS occupies a handful of ranch-style buildings set on fifty thousand acres on the arid border of Nevada and California. Most students transfer to highly selective colleges after two years.

At Deep Springs College, all work and no play doesn't make Jack a dull boy; it makes him one of twenty-five or so male students at this two-year institution that doubles as a working ranch. Bonding is easy here, and students enjoy a demanding and individualized education based on ranch life. Both, it seems, demand the same things:

Website:
    www.deepsprings.edu
Location: Rural

(Continued)

Total Enrollment: 26
Undergraduates: 26
Male/Female: 100/0
SAT Ranges: V 660–800
    M 690–800
Financial Aid: N/A
Expense: Pr $
Phi Beta Kappa: No
Applicants: 150
Accepted: 8%
Enrolled: 95%
Grad in 6 Years: N/A
Returning Freshmen: 95%
Academics: ✍ ✍ ✍ ✍½
Social: ☎
Q of L: ★ ★ ★
Admissions: (760) 872-2000
Email Address:
    apcom@deepsprings.edu

Strongest Programs:
Liberal Arts
Environmental Studies
Philosophy

hard work, commitment, and pride in a job well done. Deep Springs College students are also rewarded for their efforts in other ways: tuition is free and so is room and board. Students pay only for books, travel, and personal items; the average cost of one year at Deep Springs is $500.

Many of the men who work, study, and live at this college have shunned acceptance at Ivy League schools to embrace the rigors of a truly unique approach to learning. Deep Springs students tend to be of the academic Renaissance-man variety with wide-ranging interests in many fields. Almost all transfer to the Ivies or other prestigious universities after their two-year program, and 70 percent eventually earn a doctorate.

California's White Mountains provide a stunning backdrop for the Deep Springs campus, set on a barren plain 5,200 feet above sea level, near the only water supply for miles around. The campus is an oasislike cluster of trees and a lawn with eight "somewhat ramshackle" ranch-style buildings that were built from scratch by the class of 1919. Deep Springs is twenty-eight miles from the nearest town, a thriving metropolis known as Big Pine, population 950. The focal point of campus is the Main Building, a venerable ranch house that includes dorm rooms, a computer room, and offices. Faculty houses and the dining facilities are grouped around the circular lawn a few yards away, and the trappings of farm life surround the tiny settlement. The college has 170 acres under cultivation, mostly with alfalfa, and an assortment of barnyard animals. Once threatened with extinction (thanks to meager financial resources), the college launched a capital campaign that generated $18 million in only six years. True to its practical spirit, the school used much of the money to enhance facilities and put itself back on track to a long future.

Founded in 1917 by an industrialist who made a fortune in the electric-power industry, Deep Springs today remains true to its charter "to combine taxing practical work, rigorous academics, and genuine self-government." Ideals of self-government, reflectiveness, frugality, and community activity have weathered more than seventy-five years of a grueling academic climate. "Academics depend as much on the student here as the professor," says one student. "Nearly every class is discussion-based." Explains a freshman, "We take academics seriously but we're not at all competitive." Academic learning is the primary activity here, but students are also required to perform twenty hours per week of labor, which can include everything from harvesting alfalfa to cooking dinner. When asked which are the best majors, one wit exclaims, "Dairy is the most popular, but many students swear by irrigation."

The students' input carries a lot of weight at this school. They help choose the college's faculty and even elect one of their own to be a voting member on the board of trustees. They play a determining role in admissions and curricular decisions. And they abide by a spartan community code that bans all drugs, including alcohol, and forbid anyone to leave Deep Springs Valley (the fifty square miles of desert surrounding the campus) while classes are in session, except for medical visits and college business. Lest these rules sound unnecessarily strict, keep in mind that these are all decided upon and enforced by the student body, not the administration.

Like almost everything else about it, Deep Springs has an unorthodox academic schedule: two summer terms of seven weeks each, and a fall and spring semester of fourteen weeks each. Between seven and ten classes are offered every term. The faculty consists of three "permanent" professors (they sign on for five years), plus an average of four others who are hired on a temporary basis to teach for a term or two. The quality of particular academic areas varies as professors come and go. "The faculty turnover is so high it can be hard to stick with a stellar group of professors," says one student. Although the curriculum is altered yearly, students predict that literary theory and philosophy will always remain superior. The students control the academic program and quickly replace courses—and faculty—that do not work out. Foreign lan-

The college has 170 acres under cultivation, mostly with alfalfa, and an assortment of barnyard animals.

guage offerings are still sparse, and lack of high-tech lab equipment puts a damper on chemistry and physics courses. "In eighth grade at least I had a microscope," says a student. Currently, the only required courses are in public speaking and composition.

Deep Springers aren't much for the latest conveniences, but computers have taken the campus by storm; there's one in each student's room, plus several in a common area. With class sizes ranging from two to fourteen, there is ample opportunity for close student-faculty interaction. Close living arrangements have fostered a kind of kinship between faculty and students. Students routinely visit their mentors in their homes, sometimes to confer on academic matters and sometimes to play soccer with their children.

Deep Springers can truly boast of being hand-picked to attend; of the approximately two hundred applications received each year, only thirteen students are accepted. Most DS students are from upper-middle-class families and typically rank in the top 3 percent of their high school class. A freshman says his peers are "willing to take responsibility to manage a cattle ranch, to teach themselves what they don't know, to fix things that break, and clean up after themselves and others." Many Deep Springers are transplanted urbanites; the rest hail from points scattered across the nation or across the seas. Political leanings run the gamut, and there is diversity even among this small population: 76 percent of the student body is white; Asian-Americans make up 20 percent; and Hispanics account for 4 percent. "We all enjoy a comfortable level of deep brotherhood," says a student. The college's single-sex status is a source of much discussion, as well as "the extent to which we're justified in removing ourselves so thoroughly from mainstream culture," states a freshman.

Dorm selection and maintenance is entirely the responsibility of the students. "One cool thing about DS is that you can do anything you want to your room," says a student. "Our walls are painted mauve and there is a pink queen-sized bed hanging from the ceiling called the 'Love Loft.'" Students all pitch in preparing the meals, from butchering the meat to milking the cows to washing the dishes. "Even back home, I've never eaten better," says a student. Given the sequestered location of DS, crime is not an issue. Safety, however, is another matter. "Sometimes we get charged by bulls," admits one student.

"Academics depend as much on the student here as the professor."

Social life can be a challenge. "The lack of women, alcohol, and nightlife can at times be frustrating," reports one student. Still, "Despite work, fatigue, and over-philosophizing, spirits are generally high." When the moon is full, students go out en masse in the middle of the night to frolic in the seven-hundred-foot-high Eureka Sand Dunes with Frisbees and skis. "We slide down the Eureka Valley sand dunes *au naturel*," says one student. As for "recent technological advancement," they used to have one telephone line for the whole school; now they have six. Perhaps the most popular social activity on campus is conversation over a cup of coffee in the dining hall, where the chatter is usually lively until the wee hours of the morning. Other common activities are road trips to nearby national parks, hikes in the nearby mountains, and horseback riding. The Turkey Bowl, the potato harvest, the two-on-two basketball tournament, and Sludgefest, an annual event involving cleaning out the reservoir, are only some of the time-honored Deep Springs traditions. Critics of Deep Springs charge that DS cultivates arrogance and social backwardness among students who were too intellectual to be in the social mainstream during high school. They argue that students who come here are doomed to be misfits for life, citing a survey that shows many Deep Springers never marry. While that charge is debatable, even supporters of Deep Springs confess to a love-hate relationship with the college.

Tuition is free, and so is room and board. Students pay only for books, travel, and personal items; the average cost of one year at Deep Springs is $500.

When the moon is full, students go out en masse in the middle of the night to frolic in the seven hundred-foot-high Eureka Sand Dunes with Frisbees and skis. "We slide down the Eureka Valley sand dunes au naturel," says one student.

Perhaps more than any other school in the nation, Deep Springs is a community where students and faculty interact day-to-day on an intensely personal level. Though the financial commitment is small, the school demands an intense level of personal commitment. All must quickly learn how to get along in a community where the actions of each person affect everyone. Urban cowboys who dream of riding into the sunset are in for a rude awakening. For a select few, however, the camaraderie and soul-searching fostered in this tight-knit community can be mighty tempting—just stay clear of those bulls.

If You Apply To ➤

Deep Springs: Regular admissions: Nov. 15. Campus interviews: required, evaluative. No alumni interviews. SATs: required. SAT IIs: required. Essay questions: describe yourself; critical analysis of book or other work of art; and why Deep Springs?

University of Delaware

116 Hullihen Hall, Newark, DE 19716

Plenty of students dream of someday becoming Nittany Lions or Cavaliers—even Terrapins—but not many aspire to be Blue Hens. The challenge for UD is how to win its share of students without the name recognition that comes from big-time sports. Less than half the students are in-staters.

Website: www.udel.edu

Location: Small city

Total Enrollment: 18,673

Undergraduates: 15,808

Male/Female: 41/59

SAT Ranges: V 530–620
  M 550–650

ACT Range: 22–27

Financial Aid: 37%

Expense: Pub $ $

Phi Beta Kappa: Yes

Applicants: 20,365

Accepted: 47%

Enrolled: 35%

Grad in 6 Years: 72%

Returning Freshmen: 89%

Academics: ✍ ✍ ✍

Social: 🐱 🐱 🐱 🐱 🐱

Q of L: ★ ★ ★

Admissions: (302) 831-8125

Email Address:
  admissions@udel.edu

Strongest Programs:
Chemical Engineering

The University of Delaware is a midsized gem that boasts more than 124 solid academic programs, from engineering to education. Delaware also has a lush, tree-lined campus filled with friendly people, and a growing stable of spirited athletic traditions. It all adds up to "the small-school feel with the opportunities of a larger university," says a junior. "I couldn't picture myself anywhere else."

Delaware's one-thousand-acre campus has an attractive mix of Colonial and modern geometric buildings, set among one of the nation's oldest Dutch elm groves. The hub of the campus is a grassy green mall, flanked by classic Georgian buildings. New additions include the Delaware Biotechnology Institute, MBNA Career Services Center, and a $25.2 million addition to P.S. duPont Hall. The 35,000-square-foot studio arts building offers the latest in safety and ventilation features, plus new printmaking implements, kilns and sculpting tools. Along with the Clayton Hall conference center, hotel and restaurant management students benefit from a just-opened Courtyard by Marriott right on campus, which doubles as a learning and research facility.

Delaware's academic menu includes more than 124 majors ranging from the liberal arts and sciences, to more vocational programs such as apparel design and fashion merchandising. To graduate, students must pass Freshman English (critical reading and writing) with a minimum grade of C–, demonstrate proficiency in written communication, and take three courses stressing multicultural, ethnic, or gender-related content. Other requirements vary by college; Delaware has seven, and all except the College of Marine Studies award undergraduate degrees. Business administration and elementary education are most popular majors, followed by psychology, biology, and English. New programs include a major in ancient Greek and Roman studies.

Engineering, especially chemical engineering, is one of UD's specialties, and the school benefits from the close proximity of DuPont, which developed Lycra spandex.

The music department is upwardly mobile, with a 350-member marching band, and a number of faculty members holding impressive professional performance credits. For those seeking a change of scenery, more than sixty study abroad programs are available on all seven continents. These include a winter-term trip to Antarctica aboard a Russian icebreaker ship for journalism students, less surprising when you know that UD created the nation's first study abroad program in 1923. About six hundred UD students hold research apprenticeships with faculty members each year, and the Carnegie Endowment Reinvention Center at SUNY–Stony Brook has called Delaware the "national model" for undergraduate research.

(Continued)
Business Administration
Biological Sciences
Psychology
Nursing
English
History
Political Science

As UD has become more popular, academic standards have gotten more rigorous. Delaware routinely gets the highest number of nonresident applications for state-affiliated U.S. institutions. "Delaware is very competitive in all of its different colleges," says a senior. Still, says a junior, "Professors want to see students succeed, and are more than willing to provide additional help. Also, the students support each other—we're all in this together." About five hundred new students enter the University Honors Program each year, which offers interdisciplinary col-

"Professors want to see students succeed, and are more than willing to provide additional help."

loquia, priority seating in "honors" sections of regular courses, along with talented faculty, personal attention, and extracurricular and residence hall programming. Despite Delaware's size, students report little trouble registering for courses. "It's not difficult as long as you're persistent," says a finance major. "People get into the classes they need to graduate on time."

Forty-one percent of students at Delaware hail from the First State; many of the rest are from the Northeast. "Students understand the balance between great academics and a great social atmosphere," says a senior. They're also friendly, says a psychology major: "People smile at each other and hold doors for strangers." Minority enrollment is increasing; 6 percent of the student body is African-American, and Hispanics and Asian-Americans add 3 percent each. In spite of these advancements, "The racial divide needs to be addressed. It's getting better, but it still has a ways to go," a financial major said. Merit scholarships range from $1,000 to a full ride, and athletic scholarships are offered in five men's and nine women's sports. The university maintains a search program to ensure that deserving Delaware students are aware of the scholarships for which they are eligible.

Forty-eight percent of students live on campus, including all freshmen except those commuting from home. After that, dorm housing is guaranteed, and awarded by lottery, though many juniors and seniors move into off-campus apartments. Those who stay on campus find a range of accommodations: co-ed and single-sex halls with single and double rooms, as well as suites and apartment-style

"Students understand the balance between great academics and a great social atmosphere."

buildings. Smaller special-interest communities, such as French House, International House, and Martin Luther King Jr. House, are found within larger dorms. Campus dwellers must buy the meal plan, which offers plenty of variety. "Dinner includes three different hot-meal options, pizza, hamburgers, hot dogs, veggie burgers, chicken breast, grilled cheese, a deli, a salad bar, a pasta bar, a specialties bar, a dessert bar, and fresh fruit," says a junior.

When the weekend comes, Delaware students know how to let loose, though a ban on alcohol at campus parties has really taken things down a notch. "Campus has a three-strikes-and-you're-out underage drinking policy," says a psychology major. "The bars in Newark are very serious about underage drinking, too, so it's pretty much guaranteed that you won't frequent a bar there until you're twenty-one." Fraternities and sororities attract 15 percent of the men and the same fraction

More than sixty study-abroad programs are available on all seven continents. These include a winter-term trip to Antarctica aboard a Russian icebreaker ship for journalism students, less surprising when you know that UD created the nation's first study-abroad program in 1923.

of the women, and Greek groups often throw parties. But there are plenty of other options, too, from concerts, plays, and other on-campus performances to casual gatherings in friends' rooms or apartments.

Main Street, the heart of downtown Newark, "practically runs right through campus," one student says. "It's easy walking distance from anywhere, and there are tons of coffee shops, pizza places, restaurants, a movie theater, a bowling alley, bookstores, and shops—anything you could possibly want." For those seeking more excitement, New York, the Washington/Baltimore area, and Philadelphia are all within a two-hour drive. When the weather is warm, the beaches of Rehoboth and Dewey beckon, and in chilly months, the Pennsylvania ski slopes aren't far, either. Mallstock is the annual spring bacchanal, bringing music and a carnival to the central campus green.

Delaware's Blue Hens compete in Division IA, and on Saturdays in the fall, watch out. "Football is big," says one student. "Just wait for a game against West Chester."

"Football is big." Tailgate picnics are popular before and after the game. Aside from football, spectators love to cheer for men's lacrosse and for the women's crew and soccer squads. Intramural sports are popular, and there's space for six thousand to cheer on indoor events at Delaware's sports center.

Aspiring engineers and educators alike, and practically everyone in-between, can find something to delve into at the University of Delaware. With a challenging and stimulating academic environment, an increasingly smart student body, a healthy social scene, and up-and-coming athletic teams, UD offers a blend of strengths that would make many schools envious—and leads to many happy Blue Hens.

If You Apply To ➢

Delaware: Early decision: Nov. 15. Regular admissions: Jan. 15. Financial aid: Feb. 1. Housing: Feb. 15. Meets demonstrated need of 20%. No campus interviews. Alumni interviews: optional, informational. SATs or ACTs: required. SAT IIs: recommended. Accepts the Common Application. Essay question: a work of art, research project, or victory or defeat that's shaped your values, intellect, or academic and career goals; how your ethnic or cultural heritage has shaped your worldview; or a book, play, or film you've wanted to read or see, and why.

Denison University

Granville, OH 43023

Denison shut down its Frat Row in an effort to shift the spotlight from partying to academics. Not quite as selective as Kenyon, it draws more Easterners than competitors such as Wittenberg and Ohio Wesleyan. Denison has a middle-of-the-road to conservative student body and one of the most beautiful campuses anywhere.

Denison University aims to provide personalized education, to graduate independent thinkers who become active citizens of a democratic society. To that end, the school has shut down its Frat Row, part of a continuing effort to shift the spotlight from partying to academics. Its small size offers ample opportunity to interact (and do research with) professors, and the chance to form close relationships with peers. Not as selective as nearby Kenyon, and with more Easterners than in-state rivals such as Wittenberg and Ohio Wesleyan, Denison engages students in a study of the liberal arts. That focus, administrators say, fosters self-determination—and success.

Denison's campus is set atop rolling hills in the central Ohio town of Granville. Huge maples shade the sloping walkways, which offer a panoramic view of the surrounding valley. And don't be surprised if the place reminds you of New York's Central Park—Denison retained Park architect Frederick Law Olmsted for its first master plan back in the early 1900s. Many buildings are Georgian in style, redbrick with white columns, leading one religion major to compare Denison to "a small, private, liberal arts college in a New England setting." Not all facilities are antique, though. Higley Hall is being renovated to house the departments of economics, communication, and service learning after the biology department moved to the new Samson Talbot Hall. Talbot is located across from the new Burton D. Morgan Center, with space for various academic and administrative departments, plus a 385-car parking garage. The chemistry department's Ebaugh Laboratories are being renovated, and a new computer lab for the fine arts was added to Mulberry House.

In keeping with Denison's focus on the liberal arts, freshmen must take two first-year seminars to develop reading, writing, and critical-reasoning skills: Words and Ideas, and another course selected from an array of topics. Each is limited to eighteen students. Students must also fulfill requirements in life and physical sciences (with a lab component); a third lab science or math; writing; textual, social, and artistic inquiry; minority or women's studies; and oral communication. Additionally, students must pursue a foreign language through the intermediate level, and take classes from two of three areas: western studies, nonwestern studies, and American social institutions. Though this may sound intimidating, some courses eligible for general education credit include World Cinema, Human Sexuality, Computer Science, and Creative Writing.

Students say Denison's best programs include economics, history, computer science, English, and psychology. Also strong are the sciences, including biology, chemistry, and a neuroscience concentration, unusual at the undergraduate level. The departments of geology and geography, physics and astronomy, and math and computer science benefit from their modern building, finished in 1994 with funding from the F.W. Olin Foundation. Environmental

> "Denison gives you the opportunity to appreciate learning for what it is, to play with ideas and take intellectual risks."

studies majors can take advantage of Denison's 350-acre biological reserve. New programs include courses in Arabic and a major in athletic training education. The physical education program could use more academic muscle, say administrators, who are trying to beef it up. Also under review is the major in media, technology, and arts.

Denison encourages independent and collaborative research with faculty, giving summer research stipends to one hundred students each year. The school also takes pride in "Chowder Hour," where students and faculty gather for an informal presentation while dining on a faculty member's culinary specialty. "Denison gives you the opportunity to appreciate learning for what it is, to play with ideas and take intellectual risks," says a political science major. "Faculty are never too busy to answer your questions, and classes are never so large that your voice is drowned out." When Granville gets too small, internships and off-campus studies are available through the Great Lakes Colleges Association* and the Associated Colleges of the Midwest.* For the May Term, students select from more than two hundred internships around the country, including—as a sports-management major did—a position at German sneaker-maker Adidas in Portland, Oregon. About 30 percent of students participate in the honors program.

Geographically, 43 percent of Denison's population is homegrown, and 5 percent from abroad. Good portions "are wealthy and preppy," says a senior, though diversity is increasing. African-Americans and Asian-Americans each constitute 5 percent of the student body, and Hispanics 2 percent. Helping make campus less homogenous are more than eleven hundred merit scholarships, including the Wells, Dunbar, and Faculty Achievement awards, which cover full tuition. Politically, Denison students "are more conservative and mainstream" than their counterparts at

(Continued)

Phi Beta Kappa: Yes
Applicants: 3,289
Accepted: 61%
Enrolled: 31%
Grad in 6 Years: 76%
Returning Freshmen: 86%
Academics: ✍ ✍ ✍ ½
Social: 🍷 🍷 🍷 🍷 🍷
Q of L: ★ ★ ★
Admissions: (740) 587-6276
  or (800) DENISON
Email Address:
  admissions@denison.edu

Strongest Programs:
Natural and Social Sciences
Philosophy
Music and Theatre
Creative Writing
International Studies
Computer Science
Geology

The chemistry department's Ebaugh Laboratories are being renovated, and a new computer lab for the fine arts was added to Mulberry House.

nearby rivals Kenyon and Oberlin, says a philosophy major. "The college draws and recruits strong students, who also tend to be strong leaders," adds a senior. From student government to athletics to cultural clubs, "at times it seems like everyone is leading, and there is no one left to follow!"

Ninety-eight percent of Denison students live on campus; the only ones allowed to live elsewhere are those commuting from home. (One exception is the Homesteaders, who live in student-built, solar-paneled cabins on a farm a mile away, and raise much of their own food.) Housing is guaranteed for four years, and students applaud the sense of community this creates, though they complain about the lack of suites for upperclassmen. "The housing lottery is the worst day of the year," gripes a sports-management major. "Only seniors have a chance of getting into the apartment-style dorms, and still only half of seniors get into these." Crawford Hall, the freshman dorm, is geared to newcomers, with counseling, entertainment, and information on the premises. Former fraternity houses shelter those with common interests, such as service-learning (Morrow House) or the honors program (Gilpatrick House). Stone Hall and Curtis East got new carpet, paint, windows, and plumbing in 2002–2003. Entrees in the two dining halls change daily, and alternatives include salad and pasta bars, wok and grill stations, and made-to-order pizza and omelets.

> **"Faculty are never too busy to answer your questions, and classes are never so large that your voice is drowned out."**

For the May Term, students select from more than two hundred internships around the country, including—as a sports-management major did—a position at German sneaker-maker Adidas in Portland, Oregon.

When the weekend comes, Denisonians "have mastered the delicate balance of hard-core academics and partying," says a history major. The school provides plenty of alcohol-free entertainment, such as comedians, speakers, hypnotists, and magicians, though many underage students get beer and liquor from older friends, "almost as if they were returning the favor to those who did the same for them," says a senior. That said, "no one is left out of campus parties based upon whether they drink, or judged by how much they drink," says a religion major. While the fraternities are now nonresidential, 28 percent of men and 41 percent of women still go Greek. Students also look forward to two blowout parties each year—November's D-Day, and Festivus, on the last day of spring classes, which includes a big-name concert, such as Dave Matthews Band, Guster, Rusted Root, or the Samples.

The tiny town of Granville has four churches on the corners of its main intersection. It's "adorable, picturesque, friendly, and cozy," says a philosophy major, but also like "dating a model—it's pretty, but there's not a lot there." The sidewalks roll up early, with most stores and restaurants closing by 8 p.m., though students appreciate the feeling of safety and security that results. And the Denison Campus Association sends students into Granville and nearby Newark almost daily, says a religion major, "to provide tutoring, teach swimming lessons, participate in environmental

> **"The college draws and recruits strong students, who also tend to be strong leaders."**

cleanups, and help provide food and housing for those in need." Popular road trips include Ohio University, Ohio State, and Miami University in Oxford, Ohio.

Denison students are enthusiastic supporters of the Big Red, and "Denison–Kenyon swim meets and Denison–Ohio Wesleyan lacrosse games are always standing-room-only events," says an educational studies major. The school competes in the North Coast Athletic Conference, and has won the All Sports Championship for six straight years. Women's indoor track and field, women's softball, and women's tennis won conference crowns in 2002–2003, when sixteen of the school's twenty-two teams had top-three finishes. Enthusiasm reaches a fever pitch during Homecoming Weekend, when the all-campus gala always includes a chocolate volcano.

Denison University "encourages a 'horizontal education,'" says a history major. "It creates and sustains an environment where students and faculty are on the same level." The sense of community created by the school's small size has always lit up the weekend party scene—and now it's heating up the classrooms, too. A philosophy major says Denison's academic profile has been rising ever since the frats lost their houses. "Each incoming class is increasingly committed to placing academics first, while not ignoring other aspects of college life," the student says. "Denison is beginning to have more people with the 'complete package,' academic talent in addition to athletic ability, artistic merit or passion for some other extracurricular pursuit."

If You Apply To ➤ | **Denison:** Early decision: Nov. 15, Jan. 15. Regular admissions: Feb. 1. Financial aid: Jan. 1 for scholarships, Feb. 15. Meets demonstrated need of 70%. Campus and alumni interviews: recommended, evaluative. SATs or ACTs: required. SAT IIs: optional. Accepts the Common Application and electronic applications. Essay question: significant experience or achievement; issue of concern; influential person; most meaningful activity.

University of Denver

2199 South University Boulevard, Mary Reed Building, Denver, CO 80208

The only major middle-sized private university between Tulsa and the West Coast, DU's campus in residential Denver is pleasant but uninspiring. Brochures instead tout Rocky Mountain landscapes. DU remains a haven for ski bums and business majors.

The oldest private university in the Rocky Mountain region, the University of Denver provides plenty of options for students looking to hit the books or hit the slopes. DU boasts a strong business program, and the school's location offers ample opportunities for making job contacts and enjoying the beautiful Colorado landscape.

DU's 125-acre main campus is located in a comfortable residential neighborhood only eight miles from downtown Denver and an hour east of major ski areas. The north campus is home to the law school, the school of music, and several other programs, including the Women's College. Architectural styles vary, and include Collegiate Gothic, brick, limestone, Colorado sandstone, and copper. Special facilities on campus include centers for Judaic studies, Latin-American studies, the environment institute, and fine arts. Nearby Mount Evans (14,264 feet) is home to the world's loftiest observatory, a DU facility available to both professors and students.

DU is known for its business school, especially the hotel, restaurant, and tourism management offerings, and for its innovative core curriculum. The school's preprofessional programs are feeders for graduate schools (almost 60 percent of DU's student body are grad students) and new businesses in the booming West. International studies is another strength, backed by lots of opportunities for study abroad, while chemistry, atmospheric physics, music, psychology, and computer science have solid reputations. Students praise the School of Communications for its numerous internships, television studios, and computer lab. Outstanding undergrads can get early admittance to DU's graduate schools of business, international studies, and social work, completing both undergraduate and graduate degrees in five years. Despite the inherent pressure of a quarter system, the academic climate is relatively relaxed. Students say that there is little competition with each other, though students at DU routinely push themselves to do their best. Professors receive high marks for their intelligence and passion. "Many of the professors are invested in the lives of students and are genuinely concerned for them and their

Website: www.du.edu
Location: City outskirts
Total Enrollment: 9,188
Undergraduates: 3,751
Male/Female: 42/58
SAT Ranges: V 510–610
   M 500–610
ACT Range: 21–27
Financial Aid: 43%
Expense: Pr $ $ $
Phi Beta Kappa: Yes
Applicants: 3,303
Accepted: 84%
Enrolled: N/A
Grad in 6 Years: 69%
Returning Freshmen: 84%
Academics: ✍ ✍ ✍
Social: ☎ ☎ ☎ ☎
Q of L: ★ ★ ★ ★
Admissions: (800) 525-9495
Email Address:
   admission@du.edu

Strongest Programs:
Biological Sciences
Accountancy

Each student must enroll in the University of Denver Campus Connection, a seminar in which first-year students are introduced to college life and are paired with faculty mentors for advising.

education," says a senior. The Partners in Scholarship program pairs students and professors in research projects across the academic spectrum.

The DU core curriculum has received much praise from the National Endowment for the Humanities and is consistent with the national trend toward structured college curriculums. All undergraduates—poets and engineers alike—must take one year of English, arts and humanities, social sciences, and natural sciences; additional requirements include a quarter of oral communication and two quarters of mathematics. Each student must enroll in the University of Denver Campus Connection, a seminar in which first-year students are introduced to college life and are paired with faculty mentors for advising. The Student Orientation and Registration Program (SOAR) helps smooth the transition to freshman life, with programs in the summer as well as when classes begin.

University rules stipulate that all core courses must be taught by senior faculty. Course titles include The Making of the Modern Mind, Multiple Voices of America, and Understanding Human Conflict. "At first I thought, 'Who wants to take these science, art, and English classes?'" explains a business major. "But now that I've completed the core, I feel better about myself and my world knowledge. Now I can speak of Goya, Berlioz, and define my favorite artists with a knowledge of the period, styles, and works." The average undergraduate class size is twenty-one students, though introductory courses can be much larger. A rigorous honors program is available, as are numerous study-abroad options.

For the most part, students come from fairly affluent families. One student jokes that "the stereotypical DU student drives a brand-new SUV, wears only Abercrombie and Gap clothing, and skis every weekend." Forty-four percent of the students are from Colorado; minorities account for 15 percent of the student body, and on the whole, race relations are considered good. Because it is one of the few private colleges in the West, DU is also among

"Many of the professors are invested in the lives of students and are genuinely concerned for them and their education."

the most expensive in the region. In a nod to the diminishing importance of standardized test scores and GPAs, the university now conducts personal interviews of every candidate for undergraduate admissions, either in person or by phone. There are a number of merit and athletic scholarships available to help those who qualify. The financial-aid office is notorious for including parent loans in the packages offered to students.

Students are required to live their first two years on campus in the residence halls. "The dorms are comfortable enough," says a sophomore. "They have a beautiful view of the mountains, and at sunset or during lightning storms, students often crowd around lounge windows to watch." The Johnson-McFarlane hall ("J-Mac") is supposed to be the best place for freshmen, though another student says that the Towers are a much quieter on-campus option. Freshman and sophomore dorm residents must sign up for a fifteen- or nineteen-meal-a-week plan. Greeks can live and dine together in their houses. Since there are no restrictions concerning off-campus living for upperclassmen, many juniors and seniors opt for the decent quarters found within walking distance of campus.

In a nod to the diminishing importance of standardized test scores and GPAs, the university now conducts personal interviews of every candidate for undergraduate admissions, either in person or by phone.

With consistently beautiful sunny weather and great skiing, hiking, and camping less than an hour away in the Rockies, many DU students head for the hills on weekends. Besides various ski areas, one can explore Estes Park, Mount Evans, and Echo Lake. Additionally, DU is near Moab, Albuquerque, and Las Vegas, the mecca of all American road trips. Since Denver is not primarily a college town, many students with cars head for Boulder (home of the University of Colorado), about thirty miles away. For those staying home, the transit system makes it easy to get to downtown Denver. Once there, the options are tremendous and include great local restaurants, bars, and stores, many of which cater to students. About 15 percent of the men and 8 percent of the women join fraternities or sororities.

Greeks tend to dominate the social life, and several students mention the Border Bar as a hot spot. Wednesday is pub night at the $10 million student center. Drinking policies abound, and although DU enforces the law, students say it's no harder for an underage student to imbibe at DU than any other school in the country.

When it comes to sports, peace-loving '60s types and partyers unite when the DU hockey team, a national powerhouse, skates out onto the ice, especially against archrival Colorado College. Women's gymnastics also competes successfully in Division I, while men's and women's soccer, basketball, tennis, skiing, and swimming, along with men's baseball and women's volleyball, have returned to Division I play. Intramural sports, for those with less ability but just as much competitive spirit, also are popular. Every January, all thoughts of academics are put aside for the three-day Winter Carnival. Top administrators, professors, and students all pack off to Steamboat Springs, Crested Butte, or some other ski area to catch some fresh powder and see who can ski the fastest, skate the best, or build the most artistic ice sculptures. In the spring, the whole campus turns out for the annual Chancellor's Barbecue.

Students like DU for its modest size and friendly atmosphere. And while there remain some moneyed students with attitude problems, these types are balanced by more down-to-earth kids. As the school pushes for a more diverse student body, and emphasizes teaching and technology, the University of Denver is becoming better known for its intellectual rigor than its gorgeous setting in the Rocky Mountains.

Overlaps

University of Colorado, Colorado State, Colorado College, University of Northern Colorado, Puget Sound

If You Apply To >

DU: Rolling admissions. Financial aid: Feb. 15. Does not guarantee to meet demonstrated need. Campus interviews: recommended, evaluative. Alumni interviews: optional, informational. ACTs or SATs: required. SAT IIs: optional. Accepts the Common Application and electronic applications. Essay question: what are you thinking, feeling, or laughing about and why?

DePaul University

One East Jackson Boulevard, Chicago, IL 60604

Gets the nod over Loyola as the best Roman Catholic university in Chicago. DePaul's Lincoln Park setting is like New York's Greenwich Village without the headaches. Especially strong in business and the performing arts. The student body is about half Catholic.

Enrollment at DePaul University has doubled in the past fifteen years, but it still boasts a "small-school feel with big-school opportunities," according to one sophomore. The school's location in the heart of Chicago and a spate of campus construction has transformed DePaul from the "little school under the tracks" to Chicago's version of NYU. Moving beyond its Roman Catholic roots, DePaul values diversity and is largely a feeder to Chicago's business community. "It offers a great window to the real world because students are constantly surrounded by the working community of downtown," says a freshman.

DePaul has three residential campuses. The Lincoln Park campus, with its state-of-the-art library and new student center, is home to the College of Liberal Arts and Sciences, the School of Education, the Theatre School, and the School of Music, as well as residence halls and academic and recreational facilities. Lincoln Park itself is

Website: www.depaul.edu
Location: Urban
Total Enrollment: 23,227
Undergraduates: 14,343
Male/Female: 45/55
SAT Ranges: V 510–620
  M 490–610
ACT Range: 21–28
Financial Aid: 67%
Expense: Pr $ $
Phi Beta Kappa: No

(Continued)

Applicants: 8,932
Accepted: 78%
Enrolled: 33%
Grad in 6 Years: 59%
Returning Freshmen: 81%
Academics: ✍ ✍ ✍
Social: ☎ ☎
Q of L: ★ ★ ★
Admissions: (312) 362-8300
Email Address:
   admitdpu@depaul.edu

Strongest Programs:
Computer Science
Theater
Business
Education
Liberal Arts and Sciences

Founded in 1898 by the Vincentians, DePaul's president is a priest, and priests teach some courses, and hold (voluntary) Mass every day. But University Ministry hosts other religious services and leads programs to teach students about other faiths.

At the Loop campus, a 1,700-student residence hall is in the works and will include a rooftop garden, fitness center, and music, art, and study rooms.

a fashionable Chicago neighborhood with century-old brownstone homes, theaters, cafes, parks, and shops. The Loop, or "vertical" campus, twenty minutes away by elevated train in downtown Chicago, houses the College of Law, the School for New Learning, the College of Commerce, and the School of Computer Science, Telecommunications, and Information Systems in four high-rise buildings. The DePaul Center, a $70 million teaching, learning, and research complex, is the cornerstone of this campus. The Barat campus is in Lake Forest, north of Chicago, and offers a traditional small-college liberal arts education, emphasizing interdisciplinary studies. Old Main, at the heart of the campus, is being renovated to blend its historic nature with high-tech resources.

> **"All of my instructors have been friendly and very willing to help any student succeed."**

DePaul's name is closely associated with Midwestern business and law, and undergraduates can find internships with local legal and commercial institutions. The School of Accountancy draws many majors and is reported to be the most challenging department in the College of Commerce, which has added majors in e-business and management information systems. Programs in music and theater are renowned, while the School of Computer Science, the School of Education, and several of the science departments (including biology, chemistry, and physics) have been rejuvenated, and the impressive prelaw program balances the strong liberal arts and business offerings. According to students, the arts program is not well-developed and is avoided by some.

At DePaul, courses are small—77 percent have fewer than fifty students—and professors teach at all levels. In fact, the administration appoints student representatives from each school and college to faculty promotion and tenure committees. Social activities bring undergraduates and faculty members together, and students receive a phone book with all the profs' home numbers. "All of my instructors have been friendly and very willing to help any student succeed," says a student in the College of Commerce. Students take a common core, with a first-year program of courses in composition and rhetoric, quantitative reasoning and exploring, and discovering Chicago; a sophomore seminar on multiculturalism in the U.S.; and a junior-year program in experiential learning. Students also complete a series of "learning domains," consisting of arts and literature, philosophical inquiry, religious dimensions, scientific inquiry, social science, and history; and B.A. recipients are required to take three foreign language courses. The highly selective honors program includes interdisciplinary courses, a modern language requirement, and a senior thesis. Study abroad options include programs in France, Hungary, Italy, England, Germany, China, Japan, South Africa, Greece, and Mexico.

Founded in 1898 by the Vincentians, DePaul's president is a priest, and priests teach some courses, and hold (voluntary) Mass every day. But the University Ministry hosts other religious services and leads programs to teach students about other faiths. Eighty percent of DePaul students hail from Illinois. "Many of the students here are middle- to upper-middle-class. Some are in the upper echelons of society," says a junior. "The students who attend DePaul are very career-oriented. Many hold part-time jobs downtown," adds a freshman. Hispanics, African-Americans, and Asian-Americans are well represented in the student body—35 percent total—and DePaul wants to boost this figure by reaching out to disadvantaged inner-city students with academic potential. DePaul is said to be very liberal, and there's been an antiwar movement on campus.

> **"The students who attend DePaul are very career-oriented. Many hold part-time jobs downtown."**

Traditionally, DePaul has been a commuter school; only 20 percent of undergrads live on campus, but those who do like their digs. Two "traditional" dorms lack air-conditioning, but the dorms "are all very nice and well-maintained." Students advise applying early to secure a bed, especially after sophomore year. The university has eight modern co-ed dorms, and several townhouses and apartments on the Lincoln Park campus. At the Loop campus, a 1,700-student residence hall is in the works and will include a rooftop garden, fitness center, and music, art, and study rooms. While Chicago may have a high-crime reputation, students say campus security is visible, with officers patrolling in cars and on foot, emergency blue lights on campus, and dorms requiring students to swipe ID cards at two or three places before allowing entrance. "I believe students feel really safe," says a freshman.

Social activities bring undergraduates and faculty members together, and students receive a phone book with all the profs' home numbers.

Fraternities draw 43 percent of DePaul men, and sororities 57 percent of women. Not surprisingly, with the school's proximity to Chicago's clubs (especially on Rush Street), sporting events, and bars, most social life occurs off-campus. In the warmer months, the beaches of Lake Michigan beckon downtown students, while the annual outdoor Fest concert—suspended in 2001—and the Gamble (the biggest frat party) attract large crowds from both campuses. "There are plays to see all over the city, concerts happening all the time, and a lot of great restaurants, too," says a computer science major. "A fake ID is almost necessary," says a marketing major. On campus, the alcohol policy forbids beer in the dorms except for those over twenty-one behind closed doors.

> **"There are plays to see all over the city, concerts happening all the time, and a lot of great restaurants, too."**

On the sports scene, men's basketball is the headline story, beginning with the Midnight Madness of each fall's first practice in October. The game against Notre Dame always draws a capacity crowd, though Loyola is DePaul's oldest rival. The Lady Blue Demons softball team won an NCAA regional championship and a conference championship in 1999, and has made it to the NCAA tournament nine times in the past ten seasons. Basketball also rules in the solid intramural program.

DePaul's student body is becoming more diverse as it increases in size, an admirable achievement. The administration credits the school's "increased academic reputation" for growth, but students say DePaul's popularity is due as much to the special bonds they feel with fellow Blue Demons. "It sometimes feels like a network of community colleges, with a school-spirit feel of a big in-state college," says a junior.

Overlaps
Northwestern, University of Chicago, University of Illinois–Urbana-Champaign, Notre Dame, Loyola (IL)

If You Apply To ➤

DePaul: Rolling admissions. Early action: Nov. 15. Regular admissions: Feb. 1. Financial aid: Apr. 1. Does not guarantee to meet demonstrated need. Campus interviews: optional, informational. No alumni interviews. SATs or ACTs: required. SAT IIs: optional. Apply to particular schools or programs; music and theater require auditions. Accepts the Common Application and electronic applications. Essay questions: who or what influenced your decision to apply to DePaul; proudest accomplishment.

DePauw University

315 South Locust Street, P.O. Box 37, Greencastle, IN 46135

DePauw is a solid Midwestern liberal arts institution in the mold of Illinois Wesleyan, Ohio Wesleyan, Denison, and Dickinson. Its Greek system is among the strongest in the nation and full of students destined for Indiana's business and governmental elite.

DePauw brings together the best of a Big Ten university with the strengths of a small liberal arts school more often found in New England. Administrators have focused on pumping up school spirit and creating a close community, similar to

Website: www.depauw.edu
Location: Small town

those found at Midwestern peers like Illinois Wesleyan and Ohio Wesleyan. But they've also been raising DePauw's academic standards, emphasizing seminar-based learning, internships, independent research, and interdisciplinary work. Perhaps it's no surprise, then, that DePauw graduates populate the Indiana business and government elite. "The only way to predict the future is to be the one who writes it," reasons a senior.

DePauw is set amid the gently rolling hills of west-central Indiana. The lush green campus has a mix of older buildings and more modern redbrick structures, centered around a well-kept park with fountains and a reflecting pool. New additions include a $15 million art building, which provides studio space, a digital image library, classrooms, and galleries; and a $36 million technology and physical science center, which offers 200,000 square feet of classrooms and labs. DePauw has also invested $5 million to create space for students to socialize, $9 million in an indoor tennis and track facility, and $8 million in dorm renovations, plus $1 million for new on-campus duplex apartments.

DePauw's first-year program emphasizes intellectual engagement, building community, valuing difference, and goal assessment. The program helps students transition to college by combining academically challenging coursework with cocurricular activities and programs. When they arrive, students are assigned to mentor groups with ten to twelve peers, plus an upperclassman advisor and a faculty member who will teach their first-year seminar and serve as their academic advisor. In addition to the first-year seminar, students must demonstrate competence in expository writing, quantitative reasoning, and oral communication. And they must fulfill distribution requirements in six areas: natural science and math, social and behavioral science, literature and the arts, historical and philosophical understanding, foreign language, and self-expression through performance and participating.

Academically, the DePauw student body is as career-oriented as they come. Aspiring business leaders benefit from courses, speakers, and internships offered through the McDermond Center for Management and Entrepreneurship. Future reporters, editors, anchors, and producers will find a home in the Pulliam Center for Contemporary Media, which supplements DePauw's strong student-run newspaper, TV station, and radio stations. And DePauw's School of Music is also worth a mention, offering all students the chance to take lessons, join ensembles, and perform, in genres from orchestra to jazz to opera. For exceptionally motivated students, five programs of distinction offer the chance to focus on an area of interest, such as media, management, scientific research, or information technology. The latter program

"Intellectually curious, philanthropically minded, and socially active."

includes real-world work experience, both in IT departments at DePauw and with off-campus employers. New majors include black studies, biochemistry, and environmental geoscience; new minors have been added in Jewish, European, film, and jazz studies.

DePauw's calendar includes a January term, during which first-year students must remain on campus for a focused, interdisciplinary course. Upperclassmen may use the time for independent study, exchanges with other schools, or study and service trips, in the U.S. or abroad. Approximately 40 percent of DePauw students spend a semester off-campus, and when the January term is included, that fraction rises to more than 80 percent. The school offers its own programs, as well as those arranged by the Great Lakes Colleges Association.* Back on campus, the academic climate is becoming increasingly rigorous, but caring professors help students handle the workload. "I am aided by professors with years of experience," says a junior, one of whom "actually came to see my theater production!"

One student describes her peers at DePauw as "intellectually curious, philanthropically minded, and socially active." The minority presence is growing, thanks in part to recruitment of Posse Foundation students from New York and Chicago. African-Americans now account for 5 percent of the student body, with Hispanics adding 3 percent, and Asian-Americans 2 percent. Merit scholarships range from $3,000 to full tuition, though there are no athletic scholarships, since DePauw competes in Division III. Three-quarters of DePauw students volunteer with area churches and social-service agencies, making them eligible for another scholarship pool.

Ninety-two percent of DePauw students live in university housing, which is guaranteed for four years. Overcrowding is a thing of the past, since the school has opened seventeen new duplexes and renovated another forty-six apartments in the past two years. The homey buildings have computer labs, common areas, and TV lounges; students recommend Humbert

> **"The university, the faculty, and the staff are all amazing, and will give you stepping stones with which to build your path."**

Hall for freshmen, because of its hotel-like atmosphere. Only a few students are allowed to move off-campus, a privilege doled out by lottery. A whopping 74 percent of DePauw's men and 69 percent of the women go Greek, though they must wait until sophomore year to move into their chapter houses.

Perhaps because of the prevalence of Greeks on campus, these groups have worked hard to change the stereotypes of fraternities and sororities. They've devised a risk-management policy and instituted a community council to review conduct violations. In addition, rush is delayed until second semester, so freshmen can get their feet on the ground academically first, and fraternities still maintain the old custom of having "house moms." Still, students say it's easy for underage drinkers to imbibe, especially at fraternity parties. Forget about boozing it up off-campus, though; one student warns that fake IDs "get confiscated quicker than you can take them out."

Off campus in the town of Greencastle, students say there's not much to do. While the town has movie theater, bowling alley, and several pizza places, it "lacks a college-town atmosphere," says a recent grad. "It is fine for sustaining day-to-day living, but doesn't offer many alternatives to the university." In good weather, several state parks offer trails and grounds for hiking and picnicking, plus a lake for the sailing club; Indianapolis is only a forty-five-minute drive. When students have more time, St. Louis, Chicago, and Cincinnati make for good road trips. Another cherished tradition is a takeoff of Indiana University's famed Little 500 bike race, itself a takeoff of the Indianapolis 500 auto race. DePauw's version pits Greeks against independents on a forty-mile course.

Aside from Greek parties, social life at DePauw revolves around varsity athletics, especially the annual football game against archrival Wabash College. The Wabash-DePauw rivalry is the oldest west of the Alleghenies, and the winner of each year's content gets the much-cherished Monon Bell, hence the popular T-shirt: "Beat the bell out of Wabash." In 2003, DePauw hosted the NCAA Division III indoor track and field championships, and the women's golf team finished third nationally. Women's tennis has also had success, placing two players in the top ten at the national tournament, and bringing home a second-place finish in doubles play. In 2002, the women's basketball team advanced to the Division III Final Four, and men's basketball made it to the Elite Eight.

For a small school, DePauw offers a multitude of opportunities, balancing strong academics with a healthy dose of school spirit and a wealth of opportunities to lead—whether in one of the abundant extracurricular activities, or by blazing a trail through study abroad. "The university, the faculty, and the staff are all amazing, and will give you stepping stones with which to build your path," says a junior.

Three-quarters of DePauw students volunteer with area churches and social-service agencies, making them eligible for another scholarship pool.

Ninety-two percent of DePauw students live in university housing, which is guaranteed for four years. Overcrowding is a thing of the past, since the school has opened seventeen new duplexes and renovated another forty-six apartments in the past two years.

Overlaps
Indiana, Purdue, Miami University (OH), Northwestern, Vanderbilt

"Don't overlook or discount any of these opportunities, because there will never be another one just like it."

Dickinson College

P.O. Box 1773, Carlisle, PA 17013

Dickinson occupies an historic setting in the foothills of central Pennsylvania. Known foremost for study abroad and foreign languages, Dickinson's curriculum combines liberal arts with a business program that picks up the international theme. Competes head-to-head with nearby Gettysburg.

Website: www.dickinson.edu
Location: Small town
Total Enrollment: 2,261
Undergraduates: 2,261
Male/Female: 42/58
SAT Ranges: V 590–680
　M 590–680
Financial Aid: 57%
Expense: Pr $ $ $ $
Phi Beta Kappa: Yes
Applicants: 4,632
Accepted: 52%
Enrolled: 28%
Grad in 6 Years: 79%
Returning Freshmen: 89%
Academics: 🖋 🖋 🖋 🖋
Social: ☎ ☎ ☎
Q of L: ★ ★ ★
Admissions: (717) 245-1231
Email Address:
　admit@dickinson.edu

Strongest Programs:
Foreign Languages
Political Science
English
Biology
Psychology
International Business and
　Management

Dickinson College has occupied its pastoral plot of land in central Pennsylvania for more than two hundred years, but that's about all that has stayed the same at this small liberal arts school. It's safe to say that Dickinson's goal is to evolve along with the changing world as it infuses classes with a global perspective, packs off most of its students for study abroad in thirty-two programs, and encourages the questioning of authority. The students have not just accepted this; they have adopted it as their lifestyle. "Dickinson students are not content with mediocrity," says one student. "We come here in search of more than just a degree. We are determined to leave our mark."

Almost all of Dickinson's Georgian buildings are carved from gray limestone from the college's own quarry, which gives the place a certain continuity. Even the three-foot stone wall that encloses much of the wooded 86-acre Dickinson yard is limestone. The campus is part of the historic district of Carlisle, an economically prosperous central-Pennsylvania county seat nestled in a fertile valley. The newly renovated Community Studies Center fosters interdisciplinary, hands-on learning in the social sciences and humanities. Go there and you'll find a treasure trove of taped interviews, surveys, and videotapes produced by students and faculty engaged in field work.

Dickinson is best known for its workshop approach to science education, for its outstanding and comprehensive international education program, and for the depth of its foreign language program—Chinese, Japanese, Hebrew, Portuguese, and Italian are offered, along with seven other languages. A 3–3 program with the Dickinson School of Law (part of Penn State) allows students to accelerate their legal studies, and the international business and

> **"Teachers challenge us to reach beyond our comfort zones."**

management major exposes aspiring executives to economics, history, financial and business analysis, internships, and overseas education. The biochemistry and molecular biology major requires coursework in four departments and completion of an independent research project, a boon for aspiring physicians. The teaching certification program may become more popular with Dickinson's Teachers for Tomorrow program, which gives a $5,000 cash award and $5,000 grant for career advancement to students who teach high school for four years after graduation. The college has added majors in theater design, dance, music, and archaeology. About half of all Dickinson students get hands-on internships, such as learning about stock trading at a brokerage firm, assisting a judge in a common pleas court, or working with the editorial staff of a magazine.

To help students gain an appreciation for the liberal arts and the broader world, Dickinson requires two courses each in humanities, social sciences, natural and mathematical sciences, and cross-cultural studies. One course must be writing-intensive. In addition, the required Freshman Seminar Program introduces new students to college-level study and reflection, with widely varied courses such as Muslim Lives in the First Person, and You Call That Art? Controversies in Contemporary Visual Arts. Academics are rigorous, but not cut-throat. "Teachers challenge us to reach beyond our comfort zones," says a French major. There are no graduate students at Dickinson, so professors teach all classes. "Freshmen have the same access to the college's wealth as seniors do. And it is the professors who are the treasure of the college," another student adds.

Though Dickinson is trying to recruit more minority and international students, still, almost all Dickinsonians are white, upper-middle-class, and from suburban areas of the Northeast. Thirty-eight percent hail from the Keystone State. "It can be said that Dickinson is a rather preppy place," reports a international business major. But at least they're open-minded. Recent events, such as the war in Iraq, drew out opinions from all corners of campus. It is not uncommon, one student says, to find posters supporting military action next to fliers quoting Gandhi and the Reverend Martin Luther King Jr. "I do not ever feel a need to withhold my opinions," says a biology major. African-Americans, Hispanics, and Asian-Americans account for 7 percent of the student body. Partnerships with New York's Posse Foundation in New York and the Philadelphia Futures Foundation promise to help boost these numbers.

Dickinson guarantees housing for four years, so 93 percent of students live on-campus, though that number may decrease now that all seniors have the option of moving off-campus. Freshmen have their own dorms, including one for women only. Upperclass dorms are co-ed by floor except for a complex of townhouses with eight-person suites. The college recently transformed an abandoned factory into a combina-

> ## "It has become a home away from home. Dickinson is the perfect place for me."

tion of art studios and loft-style apartments with 118 beds for juniors and seniors. "The buildings themselves are old and traditional, but the interiors are renovated and up-to-date," says a junior. There is also a wide variety of special-interest housing, such as Spanish House, Arts House, Multicultural House, Equality House, and Tree House. As for safety, don't worry about it. The campus "is as safe as a Florida retirement community," one student says.

Most of Dickinson's social life occurs on campus, and the fraternities and sororities, which attract 21 percent of the men and 23 percent of the women, play a big role. "However, there are always alternatives, such as movies, concerts, and plays," says a freshman, as well as stand-up comics, dances, and performances of comedy troupes. There's also the Quarry, a former frat house turned into a coffeehouse/game room/dance club. You must be twenty-one to drink and monitors check IDs at parties. That said, "underage students can easily find alcohol," says a biochemistry and molecular biology major. Students look forward to annual traditions like Freshman Olympics, the Fall Fest arts festival, and the Spring Fest carnival. "Put down the book and carry a blanket to Morgan Field to hear some live music," explains one student. "Kick off the shoes, and enjoy the inflatable rides in the warm spring sun just in time before finals."

Carlisle is not a thriving metropolis or a one-stoplight dead zone. It has a sprinkling of restaurants, a movie theater, shops, and a Wal-Mart. Big Brother–Big Sister

Dickinson infuses most courses with a global perspective, part of the vision of the school's founder, Dr. Benjamin Rush, a signer of the Declaration of Independence and a scientist.

Recent events, such as the war in Iraq, drew out opinions from all corners of campus. It is not uncommon, one student says, to find posters supporting military action next to fliers quoting Gandhi and the Reverend Martin Luther King Jr.

programs, the Alpha Phi Omega community-service fraternity, and programs like Adopt-a-Grandparent help bring the school and community together. "Plus, it's really nice to go into one of the 'mom-and-pop' stores and actually know 'mom and pop,'" says a junior. In the spring and early fall, Maryland and Delaware beaches beckon; they're just a two- to three-hour drive. Come winter, good skiing is a half-hour away. Budding politicians can intern in Harrisburg, the state capital, which is twenty miles from campus, and nature lovers will enjoy hiking the Appalachian Trail, just ten minutes away. For those who crave urban stimulation, the best road trips are to Philadelphia, New York, and Washington, D.C. They're accessible by bus or train—a good thing, since freshmen can't have cars.

Dickinson students get riled up for any match against top rival Franklin and Marshall, which it battles each year for the coveted Conestoga Wagon trophy. The women's cross-country team and indoor and outdoor track and field squads have won Centennial Conference championships in 2002 and 2003. Dickinson also squares off each year with Gettysburg College for the Little Brown Bucket. Intramurals are a favorite of the fraternities, and dorms also organize teams. The twenty-nine-acre Dickinson Park provides teams with two soccer fields, two softball fields, and lighting for night games. Students may also assemble club teams to compete with other schools in sports where Dickinson doesn't field varsity squads, such as ice hockey.

Dickinson was founded more than two hundred years ago by Dr. Benjamin Rush, a signer of the Declaration of Independence and a scientist. He had a global vision, and his modern protégés are following suit. Dickinson professors ask their students to constantly challenge what is safe and comfortable, and to engage the world in enterprising ways. At the same time, faculty are known for treating students to lunch while offering help with coursework. This balance between pushing students out of the nest, yet nurturing them all along the way, leaves a deep impression. "It has become a home away from home," says a freshman. "Dickinson is the perfect place for me."

Overlaps

Gettysburg, Franklin and Marshall, Bucknell, Hamilton, Lehigh

If You Apply To ➤ **Dickinson:** Early decision: Nov. 15, Jan. 15. Early action: Dec. 15. Regular admissions and financial aid: Feb. 1. Meets demonstrated need of 98%. Campus interviews: recommended, informational. Alumni interviews: optional, informational. SATs or ACTs: optional. SAT IIs: optional. Accepts the Common Application and electronic applications. Essay question: uses Common Application questions, plus additional essay on why student is a good match for Dickinson.

Drew University

Madison, NJ 07940-4063

From Drew's wooded perch in suburban Jersey, Manhattan is only a thirty-minute train ride away. That means Wall Street and the UN, both frequent destinations for Drew interns. Drew is New Jersey's only prominent liberal arts college and one of the few in the greater New York City area.

Website: www.drew.edu
Location: Suburban
Total Enrollment: 2,487
Undergraduates: 1,558
Male/Female: 39/61

Some schools take the idea of a liberal arts education to the max. To wit: small Drew University sends its students abroad for month-long educational ventures, promotes internships on Wall Street, and encourages theater and the arts to thrive. Founded more than a century ago as a Methodist university, Drew has grown into a place where an emphasis on hands-on learning, research, independent studies, and internships take the same ranking as performance in the classroom.

The school occupies 186 acres of peaceful woodland in the upscale New York City suburb of Madison and is known as "The University in the Forest." Fifty-six campus buildings peek through splendid oak trees and boast classic and contemporary styles, a physical reflection of Drew's respect for both scholarly traditions and progressive education. The school is currently sprucing up the atmosphere through a reforestation project and the opening of the $20 million Dorothy Young Center for the Arts for the theater and studio arts departments.

Political science is Drew's strongest undergraduate department. Drew's president, former New Jersey governor Tom Kean, annually teaches a course titled Governing a State. Political science majors can also take advantage of off-campus opportunities in Washington, D.C., London, Brussels, and the United Nations in New York City. Other popular majors include behavioral science, economics, English, and psychology. The Dana Research Institute for Scientists Emeriti offers opportunities for students in biology, chemistry, physics, mathematics, and computer science to do research with distinguished retired industrial scientists. Even more impressive is a program whereby students can earn a B.A. and M.D. from Drew and the University of Medicine and Dentistry of New Jersey/New Jersey Medical School in seven years. Future financiers can follow in the

> "The classes are small, which allowed my professors to learn my name and help me personally grow."

footsteps of the school's founder and take advantage of Drew's Wall Street Semester, an on-site study of the national and international finance communities. Other recent program additions include minors in Holocaust studies, archeology, and linguistic studies; the Russian major was dropped.

Drew's commitment to liberal arts education includes a lofty goal: universal computer literacy. In fact, tuition for full-time students includes a notebook computer and supporting software, which students take with them when they graduate. The school's campuswide fiber-optic network links all academic buildings and many residence halls.

General education requirements, which take up a third of each student's total program, involve coursework in natural and mathematical sciences, social sciences, humanities, and arts and literature. Students must also show competency in writing, and each first-year student enrolls in seminars limited to sixteen people, 80 percent of which are taught by senior faculty. The theater arts department works closely with the Playwrights Theater of New Jersey (founded by faculty member Buzz McLaughlin) to produce plays that are written, directed, and designed by students. Drew has long been a proponent of study-abroad programs, including the Drew International Seminar program, where students study another culture in-depth on campus, then spend three to four weeks in that country. "It's one of the best things Drew has to offer," says a behavioral science major.

Maintaining a rigorous study schedule is key, according to many upperclassmen. The industrious grind of hard work is fueled by a cast of highly praised, interactive faculty who generate enthusiasm and ambition. "The classes are small, which allowed my professors to learn my name and help me personally grow," says a psychology major. Some students complain that professors can

> "There are democrats, republicans, gays, lesbians, middle class, upper class, all with a variety of interests."

be less than enthusiastic about teaching introductory classes, but students will only find teachers' assistants in the science labs. Drew's library complex, a cluster of three buildings, contains more than 450,000 titles and offers ample study accommodations, though some students complain that some collections are outdated.

Fifty-eight percent of Drew's students are from New Jersey, and most attended public high schools. The school is working on increasing its racial diversity—

(Continued)

SAT Ranges: V 560–670
M 540–640
Financial Aid: 45%
Expense: Pr $ $ $ $
Phi Beta Kappa: Yes
Applicants: 2,587
Accepted: 72%
Enrolled: 21%
Grad in 6 Years: 75%
Returning Freshmen: 81%
Academics: ✍ ✍ ✍
Social: ☎ ☎ ☎
Q of L: ★ ★ ★
Admissions: (973) 408-DREW
Email Address:
cadm@drew.edu

Strongest Programs:
Political Science
English
Biology
Psychology
Theater

The theater arts department works closely with the Playwrights Theater of New Jersey (founded by faculty member Buzz McLaughlin) to produce plays that are written, directed, and designed by students.

61 percent of the students are white, 6 percent are Asian-American, and 4 percent are African-American. And the differences extend past heritage: "There are democrats, republicans, gays, lesbians, middle class, upper class, all with a variety of interests," says a senior. Merit awards for incoming freshmen range from $8,000 to $27,000. Students can also win arts scholarships worth $10,000 each and minority scholarships ranging from $1,000 to $15,000.

Eighty-nine percent of the students live in university housing, which includes both single-sex and co-ed dorms and six theme houses. Themes have included Earth House, Umoja House, Womyn's Concerns, Asia Tree House, and Spirituality Home. Some students lament their quality, but the school is renovating many dorms. Several housing options are available to upperclassmen, from dorm rooms of all sizes to suites and townhouses. A lottery gives housing preference to seniors and juniors, and most freshmen reside in dorms situated at the back of campus, which aren't the best. "It's hard to get a nice room until junior year," a student says. Still, most students live on campus because housing prices in Madison are out of reach for collegians. Although the dorms have kitchenettes, everyone must buy the meal plan, which students say is improving and offering a wider range of eating options.

There is no Greek system, but social life mostly takes place on campus. Officially, nobody under twenty-one is allowed to drink, but alcohol is said to be easy to come by. There is a twenty-one-and-over pub on campus, but there are also two on-campus coffeehouses. On-campus social programming is extensive. "With more than one hundred clubs on campus and the Student Activity Board, there is always a concert, play, or lecture," a psychology major says. New York City's Pennsylvania Station is less than an hour away by commuter train, and Philadelphia, the Jersey Shore, and the Delaware River are close by.

The First Annual Picnic, held on the last day of classes and numbered like Super Bowls (FAP XVII), provides an opportunity to enjoy live music and food. On Multicultural Awareness Day, students are excused from one day of classes to celebrate cultural diversity by attending lectures, workshops, and social events. Drew also launched an initiative to give all students and staff opportunities to participate in diversity training.

The commuter town of Madison tends to get discouraging reviews as a college town by students who feel its wealthy residents don't take too kindly to Drewids, as they affectionately call themselves. However, Community Day—designed to bring students and residents together—has become an annual event, and approximately

> "With more than one hundred clubs on campus and the Student Activity Board, there is always a concert, play, or lecture."

50 percent of students volunteer in activities such as "Mentors at Drew" and "The Honduras Project," in which a group of Drew students travel to Honduras to help at an orphanage. Madison does provide several unique shops and restaurants within walking distance of campus, though the town is "populated with upper-class families so things tend to be expensive." Nearby Morristown is more of a college place. The New Jersey Shakespeare Festival is in residence part of every year, and offers both performances and internships.

Students used to seem more interested in intramural sports than in the school's Division III varsity teams, but interest has grown as the teams have become more successful. The $15 million athletic center is a 126,000-square-foot state-of-the-art facility that seats four thousand and is used by varsity sports teams and intramural programs. The fencing team has done exceptionally well, too.

From a tight-knit campus to far-flung study abroad programs, Drew offers its small body of students a wide range of opportunities in a classic liberal arts structure. "It's easy to get involved, make friends, and feel like you make a difference," says a senior. Pretty good for a school in the forest.

Overlaps

Muhlenberg, Skidmore, Lafayette, Vassar, Dickinson

Drexel University

3141 Chestnut Street, Philadelphia, PA 19104

Drexel is a streetwise, no-nonsense technical university in the heart of Philadelphia. Go to school, work an internship, go to school again, work again—that's the Drexel way. Like Lehigh, Drexel also offers programs in business and arts and sciences, and its most distinctive offering is a College of Media Arts and Design.

For career-minded students who want to bypass the soul-searching of their liberal arts counterparts, Drexel University offers both solid academics and an innovative co-op education that combines high-tech academics with paying job opportunities. "If you want a good job, you go to Drexel and you do co-op." It's easy to see why Drexel University is nicknamed "the Ultimate Internship."

"Drexel's campus is impressive for its downtown Philadelphia location, with gardens and greenery on every block," says a student, "but the campus is woven tightly into the fabric of the city." The buildings are simple and made of brick; most are modern and in good condition. Sitting just west of the city center and right across the street from the University of Pennsylvania, the campus is condensed into about a four-block radius. Students are encouraged to use a shuttle bus between the library and dorm at night, and access to dorms, the library, and the physical education center is restricted to students with ID, so most feel safe on campus.

Cooperative education is the hallmark of the curriculum, which alternates periods of full-time study and full-time employment for four or five years, providing students with six to eighteen months of money-making job experience before they graduate. And the co-op possibilities are unlimited: students can co-op virtually anywhere in this country, or in eleven foreign countries, and 98 percent of undergraduates choose this route. Freshman and senior years of the five-year programs are spent on campus, and the three intervening years (sophomore, prejunior, and junior) usually consist of six months of work and six months of school. A precooperative education course covers such topics as skills assessment, ethics in the workplace, résumé writing, interviewing skills, and stress management. Each co-oping student has the opportunity to earn from $7,000 to $30,000 while attending Drexel. And although some students complain that jobs can turn out to be six months of make-work, most enjoy making important contacts in their potential fields and learning while earning. "It starts out laid-back, but after a while you begin to feel the competitiveness," mentions one sophomore. "Keep in mind Drexel works on trimesters, so it keeps you on your toes."

> **"Drexel's campus is impressive for its downtown Philadelphia location."**

To accommodate the co-op students, Drexel operates year-round. Flexibility in requirements varies by college, but in the first year everyone must take freshman seminar, English composition, mathematics, and Cooperative Education 101; engineering majors must also complete the Drexel Engineering Curriculum, which integrates math, physics, chemistry, and engineering to make sure that even techies enter

Website: www.drexel.edu
Location: City center
Total Enrollment: 13,128
Undergraduates: 10,582
Male/Female: 63/37
SAT Ranges: V 520–620
   M 540–640
Financial Aid: 78%
Expense: Pr $ $
Phi Beta Kappa: Yes
Applicants: 10,355
Accepted: 65%
Enrolled: 34%
Grad in 6 Years: 54%
Returning Freshmen: 87%
Academics: ✍ ✍ ✍
Social: ☎ ☎
Q of L: ★ ★
Admissions: (215) 895-2400
Email Address:
   enroll@drexel.edu

Strongest Programs:
Engineering
Graphic Design
Architecture
Film and Video

It's easy to see why Drexel
University is nicknamed
"the Ultimate Internship."

the workforce well-rounded and able to write as well as they can compute and design. Students enjoy the 700,000-volume library, which features a computerized card catalog, good hours, and lots of room for studying. Professors receive high praise from most, and are noted for their accessibility and warmth. Says one student, "They take a great interest in the students and are always willing to offer assistance or direction outside of class."

Drexel's greatest strength is its engineering college, which churns out more than 1 percent of all the nation's engineering graduates, B.S. through Ph.D. The electrical and architectural engineering programs are particular standouts. The College of Arts and Sciences is well recognized for theoretical and atmospheric physics; chemistry is also recommended. The futuristic Center for Automated Technology complements the strong computer science program. Students mention that the biology and chemistry departments are weak, primarily due to lack of organization and foreign teachers who are hard to comprehend. One film and video major says, "The dramatic writing major is lacking in popularity due to its placement under the College of Design rather than Arts and Sciences."

The performance-oriented student body is 64 percent Pennsylvanian, with another large chunk of students from adjacent New Jersey. The foreign student population is 13 percent, while Asian-Americans and African-Americans account for 20 percent of the student body. Twenty-three percent of Drexel undergrads graduated in the top tenth of their high-school class, and the student body tends to lean right politically. "This is a science and technology school full of conservative students who don't really have the time to worry about liberal issues," says a student. In addition to need-based financial aid, a wide range of athletic and merit scholarships (the latter in amounts up to $10,000 per year) is offered.

To accommodate the co-op students, Drexel operates year-round.

Freshmen live in one of six co-ed residence halls, including a luxurious high-rise, but many upperclassmen reside in nearby apartments or the fraternities, which are frequently cheaper and more private than university housing. Overall, 28 percent of the students live in the dorms; another third commute to campus from home. The cafeteria offers adequate food and plenty of hamburgers and hot dogs, but it's far away from the dorms. While on-campus freshmen are forced to sign up for a meal plan, most upperclassmen make their own meals; the dorms have cooking facilities on each floor. If all else fails, nomadic food trucks park around campus providing quick lunches.

"In a single weekend, I may play paintball in the Poconos, swim at the Jersey shore, see an opera in Philadelphia, and go mountain biking in nearby Wissahickon Park."

With so many students living off campus and the city of Philadelphia at their disposal, Drexel tends to be a bit deserted on weekends. A student notes, "In a single weekend, I may play paintball in the Poconos, swim at the Jersey shore, see an opera in Philadelphia, and go mountain biking in nearby Wissahickon Park." Friday-night flicks are cheap and popular with those who stay around, and dorms sponsor floor parties. The dozen or so fraternities also contribute to the party scene, especially freshman year, but a handful of smaller sororities has little impact. Still, Greek Week is well attended by members of both sexes, as is the spring Block Party, which attracts four or five bands. The Greeks recruit 7 percent of the men and women. Drinking is "not a big deal to everyone," and campus policies are strict; dorms require those of age to sign in alcohol, and limit the quantities they may bring in.

Students take full advantage of their urban location by frequenting clubs, restaurants, cultural attractions, and shopping malls in Philadelphia, easily accessible by public transportation.

The co-op program often undermines any sense of class unity, and can strain personal relationships. Activities that depend on some continuity of enrollment for success—music, drama, student government, athletics—suffer most. "It's hard to get people involved because of the amount of schoolwork and co-ops," says one woman.

There is no football team, but men's basketball and soccer are strong. "Our biggest rivalry is our feud with Delaware," admits one frenzied student. "We delight in sacrificing blue plastic chickens!" Men's and women's swimming and women's volleyball also generate interest. An extensive intramural program serves all students, and joggers can head for the steps of the Philadelphia Art Museum, just like Rocky did in the movies. Students take full advantage of their urban location by frequenting clubs, restaurants, cultural attractions, and shopping malls in Philadelphia, easily accessible by public transportation.

Aspiring poets, musicians, and historians may find Drexel a bit confusing. But for future computer scientists, engineers, and other technically oriented minds, the university's unique approach to learning inside and outside the classroom could give your career a fantastic jumpstart. As one satisfied customer explains, "The terms are intense, the activities unlimited, but Drexel graduates are surely among the most capable and motivated individuals I have ever met. When I graduate, I will be prepared and proud of it."

Overlaps

Penn State, Temple, Villanova, Rutgers, LaSalle

If You Apply To ➤

Drexel: Rolling admissions. Financial aid: May. 1. Does not guarantee to meet demonstrated need. Campus interviews: recommended, informational and evaluative. No alumni interviews. SATs: required. SAT IIs: optional. Accepts electronic applications. Apply to particular schools or programs.

Duke University

2138 Campus Drive, Durham, NC 27708

What fun to be a Dukie—face painted blue, rocking Cameron Indoor Stadium as the Blue Devils score again. Duke is the most selective private university in the South, though not as tough for out-of-staters to get in as public archrival UNC. Duke is strong in engineering and offers public policy rather than business.

Duke University is one of the few elite U.S. colleges where solid academics and championship-caliber sports teams manage to coexist. It might be south of the Mason-Dixon Line, and may seem a bit wet behind the ears compared to the nation's oldest and most prestigious Northeastern schools, but Duke is competing with them and winning its fair share of serious students as well as athletes. A rising star in the South, Duke is now on even footing with the Ivies and Stanford.

Founded in 1838 as the Union Institute (later Trinity College), Duke University is young for a school of its stature. It sprouted up in 1924 thanks to a stack of tobacco-stained dollars called the Duke Endowment. Duke's campus in the lush North Carolina forest is divided into two main sections, West and East, and also includes an adjacent 8,300-acre forest and enough open space to satisfy even the most diehard outdoors enthusiast. West Campus, the hub of the university, is laid out in spacious quadrangles and dominated by the impressive Gothic chapel, a symbol of the university's Methodist tradition. Constructed in the 1930s, West includes residential and classroom quads, the administration building, Perkins Library (with 4.2 million volumes, nearly 8.9 million manuscripts, and two million public documents), and the student union. The West Edens Link residence hall complex opened there in 2002. East Campus, built in the 1920s, consists primarily of Georgian red-brick buildings. Most of Duke's arts facilities are here, as are dorms renovated in

Website: www.duke.edu
Location: Small city
Total Enrollment: 12,488
Undergraduates: 6,206
Male/Female: 52/48
SAT Ranges: V 650–740
M 670–770
ACT Range: 29–33
Financial Aid: 36%
Expense: Pr $ $ $ $
Phi Beta Kappa: Yes
Applicants: 15,047
Accepted: 24%
Enrolled: 44%
Grad in 6 Years: 93%
Returning Freshmen: 97%
Academics: ✎ ✎ ✎ ✎ ✎
Social: ☎ ☎ ☎ ☎

(Continued)

Q of L: ★★★★

Admissions: (919) 684-3214

Email Address: undergrad-
admissions@duke.edu

Strongest Programs:

Biology

Ecology

Neuroscience

Political Science

Public Policy

Economics

Literary Studies

Engineering

1995 to house all first-year students together "for a sense of class unity, which works quite well," says a freshman. East and West are connected by shuttle buses, though many students enjoy the mile-or-so walk between them along wooded Campus Drive. The new Center for Human Disease Models provides high-tech space for experimental psychology. Also new to the campus is the renovated Multicultural Center and Doris Duke Center at the Duke Gardens. The Perkins Library is being renovated and expanded and several new facilities are under construction, including the Nasher Art Museum; the Center for Interdisciplinary Engineering, Medicine, and Applied Sciences; and Smith Warehouse for Arts and Culture.

Duke includes two undergraduate schools: The Pratt School of Engineering and Trinity College of Arts & Sciences; the latter resulted from a merger of the previously separate men's and women's liberal arts colleges. The school's engineering programs—particularly electrical and biomedical—are national standouts. The natural sciences, most notably ecology, biology, and neuroscience, are also first-rate. The proximity of the Medical Center enhances study in biochemistry and pharmacology. Duke's literature, English, and romance studies programs have received heightened national attention and student interest. The English department has been successfully reconstructed after losing Stanley Fish and some of its other deconstructionist superstars.

Duke's Sanford Institute of Public Policy offers an interdisciplinary major—unusual at the undergraduate level—that trains aspiring public servants in the machinations of the media, nonprofit organizations, government agencies, and other bodies that govern our lives. Internships and apprenticeships are a big part of the program. Additionally, Duke offers more than one hundred interdisciplinary courses in areas such as genetics, statistics, and decision sciences and hemispheric studies, bolstered by the John Hope Franklin Center for International and Interdisciplinary Studies. Duke is looking to improve science and engineering even more, and increase its interdisciplinary offerings. More than 40 percent of Duke students study abroad, and for those

> **"Students are given considerable freedom, and with it, responsibility."**

who want a break from campus without leaving the country, Duke has arts and public policy programs in New York and a media arts and industries program in Los Angeles. Majors were recently added in documentary studies and policy, journalism, and media studies and, starting in the fall of 2004, eighteen Baldwin Scholars will be part of a program that offers women a single-sex education in the context of the overall coeducational environment.

Trinity College's Curriculum 2000, part of the traditional undergraduate coursework known as Program I, requires courses in four general areas of knowledge: arts and literature; civilizations; social sciences; and natural sciences and mathematics. Students must achieve competency in foreign language, writing, and research, while also fulfilling requirements in areas called modes of inquiry and focused inquiries. Curriculum 2000 gets mixed reviews from students. "Kids complain about the core curriculum, but I haven't found it hard to complete. In fact, it's helped make my academic experience a diverse one," says a junior. All students also must complete three Small Group Learning Experiences: one seminar course during the freshman year—offered in topics such as Narrative Politics and Jazz and American Culture—and two more as upperclassmen. Students must finish thirty-four courses to graduate; those who wish to explore subjects outside and between usual majors and minors may choose Program II, to which they are admitted after proposing a topic, question, or theme, for which they plan an individualized curriculum with faculty advisors and deans. "Students are given considerable freedom, and with it, responsibility," says a student.

When college counselors say Duke is hot, they're not referring to the temperatures in the South. Duke is up there with the Ivies and the select few other colleges

Duke's Sanford Institute of Public Policy offers an interdisciplinary major— unusual at the undergraduate level—that trains aspiring public servants in the machinations of the media, nonprofit organizations, government agencies, and other bodies that govern our lives.

that compete with them for students. Courses here are rigorous, and the academic atmosphere has become more intense, particularly in the sciences. "While many Duke students don't seem to be intellectually engaged, the atmosphere can still get pretty competitive," says a junior. In recent years, the university has focused resources on undergraduate education, reducing the number of nonprofessors who teach incoming students and having senior professors teach more classes. The nationally recognized FOCUS program, groups of seminars with fifteen or fewer students clustered around a single broad theme such as Biotechnology and Social Change, and Humanitarian Challenges at Home and Abroad, offer another way to get to know faculty members. Despite Duke's relatively large undergraduate population, 76 percent of courses have twenty-five or fewer students.

Only 15 percent of Duke students are from North Carolina, although a large fraction of the student body hails from the South, and the Northeastern corridor sends a fair-sized contingent, too. Ten percent of students are African-American, 6 percent are Hispanic, and 12 percent are Asian-American. Students of different ethnicities and races tend to "self-segregate," students say, producing little tension, but also little interaction. Overcoming these self-imposed barriers has been an ongoing quest for students and administrators, who conduct a diversity orientation program each year. A student-run Center for Race Relations was established recently.

Majors were recently added in Documentary Studies and Policy, journalism, and media studies.

Duke's southern gentility is reflected in the look here, which is generally neatly pressed on guys and maybe a bit outfitty on women, in contrast to the thrown-together anti-status uniform of jeans and sweats that dominate on some other campuses. Duke is also a culturally active campus; theater groups thrive, and the Freewater Film Society shows classic movies each week. During the summer, Duke is home to the splendid American Dance Festival. Undergraduates use the school's cable-television system to make and broadcast parodies of game shows and other entertainment.

Despite the imprimatur of wealth evident here, Duke admits students without regard to financial need, and guarantees to meet all accepted applicants' full demonstrated need. Dozens of merit scholarships are offered, ranging from $1,000 to $38,000, and some include six weeks of summer study at Oxford University, or simultaneously attend Duke and UNC. There are a number of scholarships earmarked for outstanding African-Americans. Unlike most other universities of its academic stature, Duke hands out hundreds of athletic scholarships annually, offering them in seven men's sports and eight women's sports.

Eighty-two percent of Duke undergrads live on campus, and each student is loosely affiliated with one of sixty "living groups," ranging in size from fourteen to 250 students, in a nod to the college- or house-based living units at some Ivy League schools. Student programmers and resident advisors plan lectures and social activities for these groups. On East Campus, the university operates residential houses for fifty to 120 students, led by a faculty member and his or her family, under the Faculty-in-Residence program. The decision to have all freshmen live on East Campus was aimed at insulating them from the wilder aspects of Duke's social scene and making it easier to introduce them to the life of the mind. A new housing plan requires all sophomores to live on West Campus, and everyone to live on campus for at least three years. There are also special-interest dorms, focused on themes such as women's studies, the arts, languages, and community service. University-owned apartment buildings popular with upperclassmen are located on two nearby satellite campuses. Students use prepaid meal cards to order chow, either from the main dining hall or from a full-service restaurant or an on-campus pizza shop, which delivers. Unused "money" is refunded at the end of the semester, an unusual and much-appreciated policy.

The new Center for Human Disease Models provides high-tech space for experimental psychology. Also new to the campus is the renovated Multicultural Center and Doris Duke Center at the Duke Gardens.

Durham "has charm in places but overall, it's not very good," a junior says. "As a college town, it has several of the requisite bars and pizza places, but compared to a place like Madison, Ann Arbor, or Boston, or even Chapel Hill, it's pitiful." Fraternities and sororities attract 29 percent of men and 42 percent of women, respectively. Fraternity parties are open to everyone, and the free shuttle-bus service that connects the school's various dorm and apartment complexes runs until 4 a.m., making it easy to socialize in rooms or suites. "Alcohol, it seems, is quite easy to find," says a freshman. During the basketball season, games always sell out, and in the off-season, movies are an option for those tired of the frat-party scene. Off-campus, the town boasts bars and clubs aplenty to feed and water them, as well as the beloved Durham Bulls, the local minor-league baseball team, which coined the term "bullpen." Popular road trips include nearby Chapel Hill, home of archrival UNC, or Raleigh, the state capital and home of North Carolina State University. In warm weather, the broad beaches on North Carolina's outer banks are two to three hours away, while ski slopes are three to four hours distant in winter. The popular Oktoberfest and Springfest bring in live bands and vendors peddling local crafts and exotic foods each fall and spring, and concerts are being brought back to Cameron Indoor Stadium, which one student says "is going to be awesome."

"Duke–Durham relations do leave something to be desired," says a student dismayed by the contrast between the school's wealth and the economic depression afflicting Durham. However, students take part in plenty of community-service projects, including tutoring in local schools. And Durham is adjacent to the Research Triangle Park, the largest research center

"By far, basketball season brings out the best of student support."

of its kind in the world, about fifteen minutes from campus. Duke, North Carolina State, and the University of North Carolina at Chapel Hill created the park for nonprofit, scientific, and sociological research. Many Silicon Valley technologies companies have East Coast outposts in the park, which has helped make the Raleigh–Durham area one of the most productive regions in the nation, with the highest percentage of Ph.D.s per capita in the U.S.

At the opposite end of the spectrum, Duke's official motto is Eruditio et Religio only to a few straight-laced administrators; everyone else knows it as "Eruditio et Basketballio," which translates more or less as "To hell with Carolina"—the University of North Carolina, Duke's archrival for supremacy in the Atlantic Coast Conference. At games, students get the best courtside seats, where they make life miserable for the visiting team. Their efforts paid off when the Blue Devils won the national Division I championship for the third time in a decade. "By far, basketball season brings out the best of student support," a senior says. Indeed, sports-crazed Blue Devils erect a temporary "tent city" to vie for the best seats. This is far from "roughing it"—students form groups to hold their places so that some fraction can go to class and keep their peers on track academically, while those who hold down the fort may check their email thanks to lampposts with Internet jacks. The women's basketball team has come on strong and is the perennial winner in the ACC. In 2003, women's golf and tennis and men's tennis were also conference champions. The men's cross-country team is also part of the unusually strong athletic program, while football is conspicuously weak. For part-time jocks, there are two intramural leagues, one for competitive types and one for strictly weekend athletes, which draw heavy participation from the Greeks.

Taking a walk around Duke's up-to-date campus, you can see the latest technology, but also can hear the whisper of the Old South through those big old trees. In addition to blending old and new, Duke also does an amazing job combining sports and academia, producing students who almost define the term "well-rounded." "It's attracting better students, shifting the focus away from basketball and fraternities, and trying to create a more intellectual environment on campus," says a junior. "I think it's great."

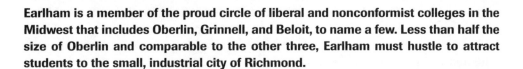

If You Apply To ➢ | **Duke:** Early decision: Nov. 1. Regular admissions: Jan. 2. Financial aid and housing: Feb. 1. Guarantees to meet demonstrated need. Campus interviews: optional, evaluative. Alumni interviews: recommended, evaluative. SATs or ACTs: required. SAT IIs: required (writing and two others, or writing, math, and one other for engineering applicants). Accepts the Common Application and electronic applications. Essay question: how you responded to someone doing something wrong, most profound or surprising intellectual experience, or a matter of importance to you.

Earlham College

801 National Road West, Richmond, IN 47374

Earlham is a member of the proud circle of liberal and nonconformist colleges in the Midwest that includes Oberlin, Grinnell, and Beloit, to name a few. Less than half the size of Oberlin and comparable to the other three, Earlham must hustle to attract students to the small, industrial city of Richmond.

Earlham is a study in contradictions—a top-notch liberal arts institution in a smart, conservative city few could place on a map, and an institution that even in the 21st century remains true to the traditions of community, peace, and justice that are hallmarks of its Quaker heritage. The school has "impressive connections throughout the world, and an academic approach that emphasizes cooperation, relatedness, and growth through new ways of thought," says a junior. "Students come to Earlham to be challenged, exposed to new experiences, and to find comfort in questions."

Earlham's eight-hundred-acre campus sits in the small city of Richmond, just a short distance from Cincinnati and Indianapolis. Georgian-style buildings dominate, surrounded by mature trees and plantings, while the Japanese gardens symbolize the college's long friendship and closeness with Japan. The most recent addition to campus is the $13.3 million, three-story Landrum Bolling Center for Interdisciplinary Studies and Social Sciences. It houses a computer lab, 150-seat lecture hall, and class and seminar rooms equipped with the latest technology.

Earlham's general education requirements were revised in 2002. During their first year, students now complete a course in interpretive practices (emphasizing interpretive reading and communication skills), an Earlham seminar (exploring a topic of interest), and a Living and Learning in Community Seminar (examining residential life and developmental psychology). In the second year, students take a Comparative Practices course, where they look at a set of challenging texts arranged around a particular question, theme, or historical period. Students must also complete courses in the arts, analytic reasoning, scientific inquiry, and perspectives on diversity and wellness. While the academic climate is demanding, it's characterized by "collaborative learning and research," says a human development and social relations major. That approach "teaches students as much about an area of study as about how to think."

Indeed, class discussion rather than lecture is the predominant learning style here. And Earlham faculty members are selected for their excellence in teaching and their ability to cross disciplinary lines. "In a sense, your professors become another group of friends, just as enthusiastic about debating philosophy as they are participating in intramural soccer," one student says. "Professors serve as passionate connections to new ideas, types of thought, and most importantly, caring communities." Academic advising

> **"In a sense, your professors become another group of friends."**

Website: www.earlham.edu
Location: City outskirts
Total Enrollment: 1,153
Undergraduates: 1,080
Male/Female: 44/56
SAT Ranges: V 550–690
  M 530–650
ACT Range: 23–29
Financial Aid: 65%
Expense: Pr $ $ $
Phi Beta Kappa: Yes
Applicants: 1,269
Accepted: 78%
Enrolled: 29%
Grad in 6 Years: 73%
Returning Freshmen: 85%
Academics: ✏ ✏ ✏ ✏
Social: ☎ ☎ ☎
Q of L: ★ ★ ★ ★ ★
Admissions: (765) 983-1600
Email Address:
  admission@earlham.edu

Strongest Programs:
Biology
English
Psychology
Interdisciplinary Studies

is also a strength. "During the first week of school, all freshmen eat dinner at their advisor's home," says a senior. Frequent meetings with advisors throughout the first year help guide students toward their eventual academic focus.

Aside from interdisciplinary programs, Earlham's top fields include the sciences, especially psychology and biology. A special stress is put on Japanese studies, a field in which Earlham is a national leader. (Notes one student: "Richmond, Indiana, is on all the U.S. maps in Japan because the Earlham presence is so strong there.") English is also well-regarded, as is Earlham's unique major in human development and social relations, which mixes sociology, anthropology, and psychology, to help students understand and work with other people, countries, and institutions. Twenty percent of recent graduates immediately pursue post-graduate study, and eventually that figure rises to 75 percent, as it's common for students to take some time off to participate in volunteer or service programs before continuing their education. Back on campus, when Richmond gets too small, more than two dozen study-abroad programs take students to far-flung locales, including Mexico, Kenya, and the American and Canadian wilderness. About 70 percent of Earlham students participate in at least one off-campus program, including those affiliated with the Great Lakes Colleges Association.*

Though the Earlham student body is small, it's relatively diverse. Only a quarter of the students are Hoosiers, and African-Americans make up 8 percent of the total, with Hispanics adding 2 percent, and Asian-Americans 3 percent. "Students at Earlham are conscious of their environment, of their beliefs and values, and especially of how their actions impact others," says a human development and social relations major. "Students are motivated to engage with passion in those activities they truly care about, whether academics, athletics, or activism." The campus is progressive and politically active, with globalization, war, and racism gaining attention right now. Rights of all kinds—women's, gay, animal, environmental—are also a big deal.

Earlham students are strongly encouraged to live on campus, and 87 percent do. Single, double, and triple rooms are available, and while some dorms may be

"Students are motivated to engage with passion in those activities they truly care about, whether academics, athletics, or activism."

old, all are "comfortable, fun, exciting and the center of much of Earlham's social life," says one student. Examples? "Olvey-Andis is loud and friendly. Earlham Hall and Barrett aren't very spacious. Hoerner has horribly thin walls but is cozy," says one student. "Some college houses are bordering on decrepit, but in general, housing is varied, accessible, and easy to obtain," says a recent graduate. Space in each dorm is reserved for freshmen, and upperclassmen enter a lottery for the remaining rooms, or petition to live together. All residence halls and academic buildings provide access to the campus computer network, and students may also tap into more than fifty databases from one of the six public computer labs, one of which is open twenty-four hours. Juniors and seniors may move into one of twenty-four college-owned apartments and houses, including a working farm, although demand for these beds usually exceeds supply. Most people eat at the college dining hall, where "numerous vegetarian options complement a very diverse menu, with everything from hamburgers to curried spinach soup, individually made omelettes, sandwiches, Moroccan couscous, and everyone's favorite—vegan peanut butter bars," says a senior.

Quaker beliefs and Indiana's liquor laws prohibit alcohol on campus, and Earlham approaches alcohol issues "through education and intervention, not hand-slapping judicial policies," says one student. Students generally appreciate the meaning behind the policy, and drinking is not a focus of social life here. There are no fraternities or sororities at Earlham, so fun includes "music and comedy shows, dances, movies, games and festivals, plays, and a lot of people just hanging out." In warmer months, students enjoy the wealth of trails, parks, and outdoor recreation areas nearby. Those with wheels can easily get to Dayton, Cincinnati, or Indianapolis to dine out, go shopping, or visit other colleges and universities. Campus traditions include Sunsplash (the fall reggae festival), Harumatsuri (the Japanese spring festival), International and Latino festivals, and the Reading Day Plays. An air-guitar and lip-sync contest keeps the winter blahs at bay.

City-oriented people may have to adjust to its slower pace of life, but Richmond, Indiana, does offer "restaurants, shopping malls, a real hospital, tremendous symphony orchestra, a large public school system, and numerous social service agencies," one student says. In fact, Earlham enjoys a close relationship with the city and with Wayne County, where it's one of the top ten employers. Each year, students give 29,000 hours of community service, supporting nineteen local agencies through the Earlham Volunteer Exchange. The school's seventeen varsity teams include nearly a third of the student body and compete in Division III. Strong squads include men's cross-country and basketball and women's soccer and basketball.

Earlham students may learn in an isolated location, but they graduate ready to take on the world, thanks to the school's cooperative, can-do spirit and caring student–faculty community. As one peace and global studies major puts it, "Earlham will take you around the world, but it'll make sure your feet are planted on the ground when you come home."

If You Apply To ➤

Earlham: Early decision: Dec. 1. Early action: Jan. 1. Regular admissions: Feb. 15. Financial aid: Mar. 1. Does not guarantee to meet demonstrated need. Campus and alumni interviews: recommended, evaluative. SATs: required. SAT IIs: optional. Accepts the Common Application and electronic applications. Essay question: choose one from five options: important issue, significant experience or valued relationship; significant book, piece of writing, or research article; support or refute H. L. Mencken's assessment of whether Christian faith can exist within a scientific framework; the definition of a good balance of freedom and responsibility; the importance of creativity as a means of expression.

Eckerd College

4200 54th Avenue South, St. Petersburg, FL 33711

There are worse places to go to school than the shores of Tampa Bay. Eckerd's only direct competitor in Florida is Rollins, which has a business school, but is otherwise similar. Marine science, environmental studies, and international studies are among Eckerd's biggest draws.

Attending Eckerd College demands a special sort of willpower. Why? In the words of an international business major: "We are right on the water, and it is like going to college in a resort." With free canoes, kayaks, boats, coolers, and tents always available for student use, it's a wonder anyone studies. But study they do, as the president and student affairs staff continue to lure capable students to Eckerd with small classes, skilled professors, renovated housing, and a reinvigorated social scene. "The standard of education and competition has improved dramatically," says a computer science major.

Founded in 1960 as Florida Presbyterian College and renamed a decade later after a generous benefactor (of drug store fame), Eckerd considers itself nonsectarian. Still, the school maintains a formal "covenant" with the major Presbyterian denomination, from which it receives some funds. The lush, grassy campus is on

Website: www.eckerd.edu
Location: City outskirts
Total Enrollment: 1,594
Undergraduates: 1,594
Male/Female: 46/54
SAT Ranges: V 510–620
   M 500–620
ACT Range: 20–26
Financial Aid: 53%
Expense: Pr $ $

(Continued)

Phi Beta Kappa: No

Applicants: 1,943

Accepted: 78%

Enrolled: 29%

Grad in 6 Years: 64%

Returning freshmen: 75%

Academics: ✍ ✍ ✍

Social: ☎ ☎ ☎

Q of L: ★ ★ ★ ★ ★

Admissions: (727) 864-8331

Email Address:
admissions@eckerd.edu

Strongest Programs:
Marine Science
Environmental Studies
International Relations
International Business
Biology
Economics
Creative Writing
Psychology

the tip of a peninsula bounded by the Gulf of Mexico and Tampa Bay, with plenty of flowering bushes, trees, and small ponds—and it's not unusual to spot dolphins frolicking in the adjacent waters. Campus buildings are modern, and none are taller than three stories. A new $15 million library and technology center is being built, and the outdoor athletic fields are being resurfaced.

Freshmen arrive three weeks early for orientation, where they take a one-credit seminar on the skills required for college-level work. First-years also take a year-long course called Western Heritage in a Global Context, which focuses on influential books, and they must meet composition, foreign language, information technology, oral communication, and quantitative skills requirements to graduate. Also required are one course in each of the four academic areas—arts, humanities, natural sciences, and social sciences—plus one course each in environmental and global perspectives. The capstone senior seminar, organized around the theme "Quest for Meaning," asks students to draw on what they've learned during college to find solutions to important issues. Popular departments include marine science, business management, biology, international business, and psychology. The Russian and German departments suffer because each has only one professor. Because the emphasis of Eckerd's music program is on vocal and keyboard performance, instrumentalists get short shrift.

> **"We are right on the water, and it is like going to college in a resort."**

Watery subjects such as marine science are especially strong. "Marine science is what Eckerd does best, no questions asked; there are great professors, classes, and experiences to be had in that program," says a junior majoring in the subject. Eckerd pioneered the 4–1–4 term schedule, in which students work on a single project for credit each January. Concentrating on a single subject sparks strong student–faculty bonds, and every student has a faculty mentor—there are no graduate assistants at the blackboards. "Teaching is excellent," a junior says. "Professors are also available outside the classroom to help students. They are amazing." The academic climate is "cooperative and laid-back," a sophomore says, adding "there is a sense of team-building." New majors include business administration, communications, and East Asian studies, and minors are now available in legal studies and leadership studies. A Freeman Foundation grant has funded significant new coursework in the Chinese and Japanese languages, and there are new opportunities to study in India, Vietnam, China, and Japan. The Russian studies major has been eliminated, but students can still study the Russian language.

While St. Petersburg isn't a college town—a senior calls it "old people central" and it closes up by 10 p.m.—a side benefit to the school's location is the Academy of Senior Professionals, a group of senior citizens who mentor undergrads. Academy members, who come from all walks of life, take classes with students, work with professors on curriculum development, help students with career choices, and lead workshops in their areas of expertise. About half of Eckerd's students study abroad, in countries from Austria and France to Bermuda and China. The school also has its own campus in London, England.

> **"Marine science is what Eckerd does best, no questions asked."**

Marine science programs include a Sea Semester* and the Eckerd College Search and Rescue, which performs more than three hundred marine rescues annually and inspires a popular campus T-shirt that tells students to "GET LOST! Support Eckerd Search and Rescue."

Eckerd students "are friendly, liberal, and laid-back," a junior says. "We have strong student leaders in our ranks, and a fair amount of student involvement in all aspects of college life." Nearly two-thirds of the student body hails from out of state; 10 percent are foreign. Hispanics are the largest minority group at 4 percent, African-Americans comprise 3 percent, and Asian-Americans account for 2 percent.

The annual Festival of Cultures has "amazing food, awesome dancing, and cultural activities from around the world," says a sophomore.

Seventy-two percent of students live in one of eight housing quads, separated from the rest of campus by the imaginatively named Dorm Drive. Some residence halls are single sex, and others are co-ed by floor. Rooms are fairly large and air-conditioned, and waterfront views and beach access are in-your-face—and free. Two trendy townhouse- and apartment-style residence halls provide suite living above and beyond the standards of other dorms, and other dorms have been renovated to add computer labs and kitchens in lounges. "Dorms are old but well-maintained, though they are very utilitarian," says a sophomore. Adds a junior: "Dorms also build an amazing community that makes Eckerd."

There are no Greek organizations at Eckerd, and a strict alcohol policy—no kegs on campus, no alcohol at university events—means wristbands at campus parties, even for those over twenty-one. The policy has been relaxed a bit to allow students of drinking age to imbibe at the campus bar, the Triton Pub, and to drink in public areas of the dorms. Students say those who are underage still manage to get booze and consume it in their rooms, away from prying eyes. Off-campus, it's next to impossible for underage students to be served at bars and restaurants, students say—though they do enjoy the new Baywalk shopping complex, about fifteen minutes from campus, with a stadium-seating movie theater, bars, and restaurants.

> "We have strong student leaders in our ranks, and a fair amount of student involvement in all aspects of college life."

Students who tire of hanging around the campus eschew the concerts, lectures, shows, and games arranged by the student activity board in favor of the nightclubs and bars of Latin-flavored Ybor City about thirty minutes away. Tampa and St. Pete also offer a Salvador Dali museum and professional baseball, football, hockey, and soccer teams. Tempting road trips include Orlando's Walt Disney World and Islands of Adventure theme parks, Miami's South Beach, and that hub of debauchery on the delta, New Orleans.

Eckerd doesn't have a football team, but intramural athletics range from flag football to the assassin game, in which students try to shoot their peers with dart guns, pit dorms against each other in serious contests. Varsity teams compete in NCAA Division II, and the men's basketball squad recently competed in the final Elite Eight. "Men's basketball is the only sport that attracts lots of fans and spectators," a senior says, and a night of Midnight Madness helps kick off the season. The co-ed sailing team has claimed several recent divisional and regional championships.

Eckerd is striving to add "experiential, service, and international learning" to the traditional classroom experience. That mission, combined with the fun to be had in the Florida sun, makes Eckerd a standout, students say. "I love what I'm learning," says a junior marine biology student. "The Eckerd community is amazing."

A new $15 million library and technology center is being built, and the outdoor athletic fields are being resurfaced.

Overlaps

University of Tampa, Rollins, University of Miami, University of Florida, Stetson

If You Apply To >

Eckerd: Rolling admissions: May 1. Financial aid: Apr. 15. Housing: May 1. Meets demonstrated need of 70%. Campus interviews: recommended, evaluative. Alumni interviews: optional, informational. SATs or ACTs: required. SAT IIs: recommended (writing and math I or II). Accepts the Common Application and electronic applications. Essay questions: significant concern and how you'll address it in college; influential event or person; book, movie, play, or piece of music that's impacted you.

A rapidly rising star among liberal arts colleges in the Southeast. With a welcoming environment and a supportive faculty, Elon is good at taking okay students and turning them on to academics. Strong emphasis on global perspectives and hands-on learning in the classroom.

Website: www.elon.edu

Location: Small town

Total Enrollment: 4,584

Undergraduates: 4,431

Male/Female: 39/61

SAT Ranges: V 530–620
  M 540–630

ACT Range: N/A

Financial Aid: 32%

Expense: Pr $

Phi Beta Kappa: No

Applicants: 7,053

Accepted: 45%

Enrolled: 38%

Grad in 6 Years: 71%

Returning Freshmen: 87%

Academics: ✍ ✍ ✍

Social: 🏳 🏳 🏳 🏳

Q of L: ★ ★ ★ ★ ★

Admissions: (336) 278-7655
  or (800) 334-8448

Email Address:
  admissions@elon.edu

Strongest Programs:

Business

Communications

Performing Arts

Psychology

Political Science

Biology

Education

Elon University derives its name from the Hebrew word for "oak." And with an emphasis on undergraduate research, group work, service learning, and study abroad, the university provides its students with plenty of opportunities to grow—intellectually and socially. Indeed, students here are encouraged to branch out into new areas of learning and to take an active role in their education. "There are so many opportunities to get involved or experience new things," says a junior. It's this engaged style of learning that keeps young men and women rooted here for many academic seasons.

Founded in 1889, Elon occupies a 575-acre campus set in the woods of North Carolina's Piedmont region and is arguably the most architecturally consistent campus in the nation. Buildings are Georgian-style brick with white trim, and newer buildings have been adapted to modern architectural lines while maintaining this classic collegiate feel. At the center of campus is Lake Mary Nell, which is home to an abundance of geese and ducks. Academic buildings are organized in two clusters: an arts and sciences quad near a fountain in the older section of the campus, and a newly constructed "academic village," complete with a colonnade and rotunda. Recent construction includes the Belk Library (which remains open twenty-four hours a day), a $17.2 million science center, and a new athletic complex that includes Rhodes Stadium.

All of the new facilities have been designed to support Elon's highly interactive academic programs. The university offers forty-nine undergraduate degrees, with strong programs in business, communications, psychology, and education (which also happen to be among the most popular). Students agree that the academic climate is rigorous but varies greatly, depending on your chosen major. "Classes are discussion-based and offer a great foundation in social skill and critical thinking," says a senior. A junior adds, "In the communications department, I have found the classes to be challenging, yet always doable and fun." The School of Communications is nationally recognized and benefits from two ultramodern digital television stations that broadcast seven hours of live programming each week. Weaker academic areas include nonviolence studies and Asian-Pacific studies.

Elon has an elaborate support system designed to ensure that first-year students don't fall through the cracks. Students begin general studies with a first-year course called The Global Experience, a seminar-style, interdisciplinary class that investigates challenges facing the world. First-year orientations include Move-In Day, in which faculty members literally help students lug their belongings from their cars to their new rooms, and an optional experiential learning program that partners 120 freshmen with returning students for activities ranging from whitewater rafting

> **"Classes are discussion-based and offer a great foundation in social skill and critical thinking."**

to volunteer work. Elon 101 is taken by nearly all first-years; students meet weekly in groups of about fifteen during the first semester and discuss academic, social, and personal concerns with a faculty member and an upper-level student.

Students must complete a core that includes English, mathematics, wellness, eight courses in liberal arts and sciences, three courses at the advanced level, and a general studies interdisciplinary seminar. Consistent with its theme of engaged—or hands-on—learning, the university places a big emphasis on service learning and service research. Fifteen percent of undergrads are engaged in research work with faculty members that leads to publication or presentations at conferences. Seventy-eight percent of students complete internships, 87 percent participate in volunteer service projects, and 62 percent study abroad, thanks to the 4–1–4 academic calendar. The Honors Program offers a series of demanding courses that focus on writing and critical thinking skills. Throughout the four-year sequence, students reside in the Honors Pavilion, an "academic village" with twenty-two international students and international studies majors. In addition, the university offers a variety of prestigious Fellows programs.

More than two-thirds of all classes have twenty-five or fewer students. Professors are highly praised and 85 percent hold the highest degree in their field. "Elon's faculty is simply wonderful," says a mathematics major. "They make themselves accessible through whatever means necessary." Not surprisingly, the academic and career advising programs are highly lauded by students.

Elon prides itself on attracting students who may not have been academic stars in high school—but have leadership potential—and turning them on to the life of the mind. "Elon students are exceptional students who are interested in both academics and leadership opportunities," says an education major. "Our students participate in service activities and are involved in the community." Nearly two-thirds come from outside North Carolina, mainly from Virginia, Maryland, and Washington, D.C. Ninety percent are white, 7 percent African-American, 1 percent Hispanic, and 1 percent Asian-American. Diversity is a hot campus issue and the university has developed a diversity education program to address this. It seems to be working, as the number of African-American freshmen enrollees doubled between 2002 and 2003. Qualified students can vie for more than four hundred merit scholarships ranging from $1,000 to $9,500, and there are 140 athletic scholarships available to student athletes.

Sixty-one percent of students reside on campus. "Residence halls are larger and more accessible than other campuses I have visited," says a senior. "They are all well-maintained." Elon's single-gender suites and flats house up to ten students in double bedrooms. Other options include traditional residence halls, an academic village complex where students and faculty live and study

> **"Elon students are exceptional students who are interested in both academics and leadership opportunities."**

together, and university-owned apartments. Campus dining includes a variety of options for the discerning palette. "The food is actually good," says a junior. A math major agrees, "Our food on campus is better than going to some restaurants." Campus security includes 24/7 escorts and emergency lights, but safety is not a big issue, according to most students.

When it's time to let off steam, students generally turn to the active Greek scene—the fraternities and sororities attract 26 percent of the men and 43 percent of the women, respectively—or the countless activities on campus. "Most of the student body is on campus every weekend so there is always something to do," says a student. Parties, sporting events, and more than one hundred student organizations keep students occupied, and students say that while alcohol is ever-present, there is little pressure to drink. Says a student, "Most of our students are responsible when partying." Road trips to the beach (three hours by car) and the mountains are popular diversions for those seeking to put distance between themselves and the campus.

The tiny town of Elon is virtually indistinguishable from the university, which even owns the two main restaurants. "There are a few bars and music lounges, a coffee shop, and several apartment complexes," says a senior. A junior agrees, "The

A Freeman Foundation grant has funded significant new coursework in the Chinese and Japanese languages, and there are new opportunities to study in India, Vietnam, China, and Japan.

First-year orientations include Move-In Day, in which faculty members literally help students lug their belongings from their cars to their new rooms, and an optional experiential learning program that partners 120 freshmen with returning students for activities ranging from whitewater rafting to volunteer work.

Consistent with its theme of engaged learning, the university places a big emphasis on service learning and service research. Fifteen percent of undergrads are engaged in research work with faculty members that leads to publication or presentations at conferences.

town is small but has the college essentials." Students take an active role in the community through volunteer projects both "through certain classes as well as on their own time," says a student. Back on campus, popular events include the Festival of the Oaks, Homecoming, and College Coffee, where students and faculty mingle over free breakfast and coffee.

And let's not forget the road trip to rival Furman University. "Six to eight chartered buses are filled and we tailgate at the university before the game," a student says. Elon competes in the Division I Southern Conference. Men's football, baseball, and soccer are strong, as are women's track and field, soccer, and softball.

Without a doubt, Elon University has come a long way in recent years. By emphasizing service learning, service research, and an active, engaged style of learning, this quality liberal arts university is quickly outgrowing its local reputation and making a name for itself as a college that, as one student puts it, "cares about its students and makes an effort to create a personal environment."

If You Apply To ➢ **Elon:** Rolling admissions: Nov. 15. Financial aid: Feb 15. Campus and interviews: optional, informational. SATs or ACTs: required. SAT IIs: optional. Accepts the Common Application and electronic applications. Essay question: significant influence; impact of significant achievement; what do you expect to contribute?

Emerson College

120 Boylston Street, Boston, MA 02116-4624

Emerson is strategically located in the heart of Boston's theatre district and within walking distance of the city's major sites. Communication and the performing arts head the list of strong programs. With roughly 4,300 undergraduates, Emerson is a smaller alternative to neighboring giants Northeastern and Boston U.

Those who aspire to a career in Hollywood may want to make a four-year pit stop in Boston first. There they will find Emerson College, a small liberal arts school that offers strong programs in communications and the performing arts. Here, students take notes from professors who also happen to be working directors, producers, actors, and writers. It's an approach that puts students in the spotlight and asks them, "Are you ready to be heard?"

Founded in 1880, Emerson is located on Boston Common in the heart of the city's theatre district and features a mix of nineteenth-century brownstones and modern high-rise buildings. Much of the surrounding city is accessible by foot, including the historic Freedom Trail and the Boston Public Garden. Recently, an eleven-story Tufte Performance and Production Center was completed that contains rehearsal space, a theatre design and technology center, and television studios. When most of the college was relocated to Boston's cultural district, part of that purchase included the historic Majestic Theatre, which in 2003 was reopened after being fully restored to its original 1903 appearance. A currently undeveloped site on the Boston Common will be used to build residence halls and a college center that will have new athletic facilities and offices for student staff.

Emerson was founded with an emphasis on communication and performance, and the school still offers a plethora of strong programs in this vein. Undergraduates may choose from more than twenty majors, including acting, broadcast journalism, print and multimedia journalism, film, communication sciences, television/video, and theatre design and technology. General education requirements consist of a combination of interdisciplinary seminars and traditional courses. All students must take courses in three areas: foundations, which includes courses in writing, oral communications, and quantitative reasoning; perspectives, which includes courses in history, literature, and scientific, social, and psychological perspectives; and multicultural diversity, which includes classes in global and U.S. diversity. Interdisciplinary seminars of no more than twenty students stress the interrelationships between different communication fields; recent seminars include Minds and Machines, The City, Ways of Knowing: Philosophy and Literature, and Words, Imagination, Expression.

The most popular major is film, followed closely by performing arts, journalism, television/video, and writing. Students say the atmosphere of the college can be competitive, but help can be found from instructors and peers. A marketing major says, "The classes here push the students to do more in and out of the classroom." The college provides students with access to state-of-the-art equipment and facilities—including digital editing labs, Avid composers, recording studios, and fully-equipped television studios—and the campus is home to the oldest noncommercial radio station in Boston.

For those seeking a spotlight and stage elsewhere, Emerson offers a semester-abroad program at Kasteel Well (The Netherlands), where students are housed in a restored thirteenth-century castle complete with moats, gardens, a gate house, and peacocks. Film students may attend a summer program in Prague, and approximately two hundred students vie annually for a semester-long internship at Emerson's Los Angeles Center. Those who are located at the Los Angeles Center

"The quality of teaching is excellent, very updated."

may be able to go to internships with companies such as Interscope Records, CNN, Warner Bros., Dreamworks, and NBC. Back on campus, students may cross-register with nearby Suffolk University, Wheelock College, and the six-member Boston ProArts Consortium.

Nearly two-thirds of all classes have less than twenty-five students, and professors receive high marks for their knowledge and accessibility. "Most faculty are professionals in their chosen fields and offer a unique approach to each course," says an acting major. Though adjunct professors teach a large portion of freshman classes, students seem to appreciate their real-world advice—especially considering the competitive nature of a career in the arts. "The quality of teaching is excellent, very updated," says a senior. The library holds 193,000 volumes, mostly related to communication and performing arts, and students may also take advantage of more than seven hundred thousand volumes in the collections of ten nearby academic and museum libraries.

Emerson students are "ambitious, intelligent, unique, and friendly" according to a junior. "Most of the students are more than willing to help out their classmates." Nearly two-thirds hail from outside of Massachusetts, and 76 percent come from public high schools. Whites account for 86 percent of the student body, African-Americans 2 percent, Hispanics 4 percent, and Asian-Americans another 3 percent. Hot campus issues include the presidential elections and the war in Iraq. One acting student says, "Emerson is a model for active student body. Most students and faculty march in rallies, protest outside the state house and some even get arrested for disturbing the peace." Emerson offers 202 merit scholarships to qualified applicants, ranging from $5,000 to a half-ride. There are no athletic scholarships.

Forty-eight percent of students live in one of four residence halls, some on special theme floors, including the Writer's Block (cute, huh?), and the Wellness and Digital Culture floors. Freshman are guaranteed on-campus housing, but a majority

(Continued)
Admissions: (617) 824-8600
Email Address:
  admission@emerson.edu

Strongest Programs:
Film
Performing Arts
Journalism
TV/Video
Writing/Literature/Publishing
Communication Sciences

Emerson was founded with an emphasis on communication and performance, and the school still offers a plethora of strong programs in this vein.

The social life on campus seems to be less party-oriented and more activity-oriented, with plays and film shoots taking place on a regular basis.

of the upperclassmen live off campus due to the limited housing. The current residence halls are "the nicest I've seen at any school in Boston," says one junior. Others seem to agree that the dorms are spacious and well-maintained. Campus dining is not only about eating but also, according to one sophomore, "the social mecca for kids on campus." The food rates well, with lots of options for vegans, vegetarians, and those with special diets. Students feel safe on campus. Each building requires an ID to enter and public safety officers regularly patrol the streets outside the buildings.

The social life on campus seems to be less party-oriented and more activity-oriented, with plays and film shoots taking place on a regular basis. According to a senior, "There are parties, but most of us go to BU or Northeastern since Emerson is not a big party school." More than fifty student organizations and performance groups offer students ample opportunity for involvement, including two radio stations, six humor and literary journals, ten performance troupes, and six production organizations. The Greek scene attracts 5 percent of Emerson men and 4 percent of the women, and its share of party animals. Though the campus is considered "dry," most of the partying takes place off-campus at apartments and if a student really wants to drink, it is possible if they know someone of age. "Alcohol is not a huge problem," says one sophomore.

"There are so many colleges in the Boston area that this city is crawling with young people."

When students tire of on-campus events, they can rush headlong into Boston, arguably the best college town in the nation. One student says, "There are so many colleges in the Boston area that this city is crawling with young people." Another gushes, "Emerson students live, study, work, and volunteer in almost every major neighborhood and area of the city." There are plenty of diversions, including museums, the Franklin Park Zoo, Freedom Trail, the Boston Symphony Orchestra, and major league baseball at Fenway Park. Back on campus, popular festivities include EVVY Awards, the largest student production/organization in the country. Also, there is Hand-Me-Down Night (during which outgoing club officers "hand down" their positions to incoming officers) Greek Week, and the New Student Revue.

Emerson fields twelve Division III athletic teams, and the Lions compete as a member of the Eastern College Athletic Conference. The college is also a charter member of the Great Northeast Athletic Conference; recent GNAC champions include the women's cross-country team and the men's basketball and golf squads. Emersonians also enjoy a strong intramural program and take advantage of a ten-thousand-square-foot fitness center featuring state-of-the-art fitness equipment, classes, and wellness workshops.

While you are not guaranteed to become the next Julia Roberts or Brad Pitt, the possibility for stardom exists at Emerson. And even if a lifestyle of fame is not for you, the excellent education, small classes, and attentive professors may teach you how to be the "star" of your own life.

Overlaps

New York University, Boston University, Syracuse, Northeastern, USC

If You Apply To ➤

Emerson: Regular admissions: Jan. 15. Financial aid: Mar. 1. Housing: May 1. Does not guarantee to meet demonstrated need. Campus interviews: optional, informational. No alumni interviews. SATs or ACTs: required. SAT IIs: recommended. Accepts electronic applications. Essay question: personal statement.

200 Boisfeuillet Jones Center, Atlanta, GA 30322-1950

Often compared to Duke and Vanderbilt, Emory may be most similar to Wash U. in St. Louis. Both have suburban locations in major cities and both tout business and premed as major draws. If the campus is uninspiring, the suburban Atlanta location is unbeatable.

Emory University is the best Southern example of an increasingly popular genre of schools: medium-sized universities whose identities are inseparable from the cities they call home. In this case the city is Atlanta, a globally oriented business and communications center whose corporate behemoths (read Coca Cola and the Woodruff family) have lavished hundreds of millions on their local university. Though lacking the across-the-board strength in the liberal arts of many of the Northeastern universities with which it competes, Emory is increasingly favored by bright preprofessional students from all regions of the country who like the mix of Underground Atlanta, big-time sports, and internships at CNN. As one senior put it, "I love the fact that I can have a blast, but still feel like I'm doing something with my life."

Set on 631 acres of woods and rolling hills, Emory's campus spreads out from an academic quad of marble-covered, red-roofed buildings. Contemporary structures dot the periphery of the lush, green grounds. Recent additions include the 90,000-square-foot Schwartz Center for the Performing Arts, with an 825-seat concert hall, 135-seat theater lab, and 135-seat dance studio. The central campus has also been closed to all car traffic except for Emory shuttles, as administrators try to create a pedestrian campus.

Emory's distribution requirements take up more than a third of every student's total coursework; they aim to develop competence in writing, quantitative methods, and foreign language, and include exposure to the humanities, social sciences, natural sciences, and physical education. Other required coursework helps broaden students' perspectives on national, regional, and global history and culture. Finally, students take two seminars—one as freshmen (fifty to sixty are available each term, limited to eighteen students each) and one at an upper level. Entering freshmen looking for an even more intimate environment may want to consider Emory's two-year Oxford College, where six hundred students earn associate's degrees in a "small-town" atmosphere, and transfer to the main campus to finish up. Emory also belongs to the Atlanta Regional Consortium for Higher Education,* allowing students to take courses at other area schools. To really get away, students can tap into the Center for International Programs Abroad, which offers more than sixty programs in other nations, with Emory credit, Emory grades, and even Emory financial aid. The school plans to add programs in Western Samoa, Denmark, and South America to its already extensive list.

As Emory has built and renovated academic buildings, the school has also spent lavishly to draw new faculty members, adding stars to key departments, such as Archbishop Desmond Tutu in the school of theology. Chemistry and biology benefit from physical proximity to the federal Centers for Disease Control, while many political science professors have ties to the Carter Center (named for the former president), and serve as regular guests on nearby CNN. The most popular majors are business, psychology, economics, and political science, and students say English is also strong. They likewise give high marks to biology and neuroscience and behavioral

"I love the fact that I can have a blast, but still feel like I'm doing something with my life."

Website: www.emory.edu
Location: Suburban
Total Enrollment: 11,617
Undergraduates: 5,587
Male/Female: 44/56
SAT Ranges: V 640–720
   M 660–740
ACT Range: 29–33
Financial Aid: 65%
Expense: Pr $ $ $ $
Phi Beta Kappa: Yes
Applicants: 10,372
Accepted: 42%
Enrolled: 32%
Grad in 6 Years: 90%
Returning Freshmen: 94%
Academics: ✍ ✍ ✍ ✍
Social: ☎ ☎ ☎
Q of L: ★ ★ ★ ★
Admissions: (800) 727-6036
Email Address:
   admiss@unix.cc.emory.edu

Strongest Programs:
Business
Psychology
Natural Sciences
Political Science
English
History
Art History

biology, which draw hordes of premeds. A 4–2 program enables students to earn bachelor's degrees at Emory, and then pursue a master's in engineering at Georgia Institute of Technology. Recent additions to the academic menu include Chinese studies (offering a major and minor in Chinese language and literature) and American studies.

Twenty percent of Emory students are Georgians, and a little over half are from the Southeast. Though it is in the South, students say Emory doesn't feel southern, because New York, New Jersey, California, and Florida are also well represented. "This is definitely a 'rich kids' school," says a sophomore. "People are driven and competitive. The people who party, party hard. The people who work all the time work really hard; it's difficult to find someone in-between the two extremes." African-Americans constitute 10 percent of the student body, Asian-Americans 16 percent, and Hispanics 3 percent. Politically, "Emory is pretty middle-of-the-road, and there is some campus activism," says a political science and anthropology major. Merit scholarships range from two-thirds of tuition to a full ride; there are no athletic scholarships.

Two-thirds of Emory students live on campus; freshmen and sophomores are required to do so. Juniors, seniors, and graduate students can snag beds in the one- to four-bedroom Clairmont Campus apartments, which opened in fall 2002, with private bedrooms, full kitchens and baths, and a washer-dryer in each unit. Clairmont residents also get an activity center with basketball, volleyball and tennis courts, a pool, and weight-training facilities. Housing is guaranteed for four years, and assignments are booked online, "so you can get your room in real-time," says a freshman. Campus dwellers are required to buy a meal plan, which can be used in the student center, or at other school restaurants, including a kosher deli, snack bar, and an ice-cream parlor.

Fraternities and sororities attract 28 percent of Emory's men and 31 percent of women, and Greeks had dominated the campus social scene, though "the current administration is kind of anti-frat," says a freshman. "Students spend Thursday nights in Buckhead or midtown Atlanta at dance clubs. The most popular weekend road trip is probably to UGA in Athens." Atlanta also offers a multitude of other diversions,

"I love the atmosphere—there are always new people to meet and new things to try."

from Braves baseball and Hawks basketball to plays at the Fox Theatre, exhibits at the High Museum of Art, or shopping at Underground Atlanta or the Lenox Mall, to which Emory provides a free shuttle every Saturday. Alcohol isn't allowed in the dorms, though that doesn't stop students from bringing it in. "If you want beer, you can get it," says a sophomore. "But if your resident advisor or a cop catches you and you are underage, you will be punished." A quirky highlight of the social calendar is Dooley's Week, a spring festival in honor of Emory's enigmatic mascot, William M. Dooley, a skeleton who reportedly escaped from the biology lab almost one hundred years ago. If Dooley walks into your class, "the professor has to let class out, or they'll get soaked with a water gun," says a freshman. The week culminates with a costume ball in Dooley's honor. Road trips range from New Orleans for Mardi Gras to Disney World and the beaches of Florida and Alabama to Memphis, Tennessee—home of Graceland, barbecue, and the Delta blues.

Emory doesn't field a varsity football team, though students show their spirit with T-shirts that proudly proclaim: "Emory Football: Still Undefeated (since 1836)." Last year, men's and women's tennis both finished first nationally in NCAA Division III, while men's and women's swimming placed third, softball placed fourth, and baseball fifth. Men's basketball competes in the University Athletic Association against such academic powerhouses as the University of Chicago, Johns Hopkins, and Carnegie Mellon. All around, Emory's athletic program is exceptionally strong, ranking second in the nation last year in the NACDA Director's Cup standings.

Overlaps

Duke, Washington University (MO), University of Pennsylvania, Vanderbilt, Georgetown

While many Southern schools suffer from a regional provincialism, the same can't be said of Emory, which draws students from all over with strong academics and study-abroad opportunities. "I love the atmosphere—there are always new people to meet and new things to try," says an international studies major. "Emory's brilliant faculty and genuinely nice and fun-loving students make it fun for me," agrees an anthropology and political science major. Throw in the sunny weather, and it's easy to see why Emory has a winning combination.

<table>
<tr><td>If You Apply To ≽</td><td>Emory: Early decision: Nov. 1, Jan. 1. Regular admissions: Jan. 15. Financial aid: Feb. 15. Housing: May 1. Meets demonstrated need of 98%. No campus or alumni interviews. SATs or ACTs: required. SAT IIs: optional. Accepts the Common Application and electronic applications. Essay question: half-page on both a meaningful activity or work experience, and why Emory is a good match; and one to three pages on any topic of genuine personal interest.</td></tr>
</table>

The Evergreen State College

Olympia, WA 98505

There's no mistaking Evergreen for a typical public college. Never mind the way-out garb favored by its students. Evergreen's interdisciplinary, team-taught curriculum is truly unique. To find anything remotely like Evergreen, you'll need to go private and travel east to places like Hampshire or Sarah Lawrence.

When it comes to bucking the mainstream, few schools are so insistent—and successful—as Evergreen State College. The school's unofficial motto: Omnia extares, Latin for "Let it all hang out," demonstrates the school's laid-back atmosphere. Founded in 1967 as Washington State's experimental college, Evergreen lacks grades, majors, and even departments. Students have almost unlimited control over their academic destinies, which a senior calls "the double-edged sword of choice and responsibility." This system may sound strange, but it works: among Evergreen's alumni is Matt Groening, creator of *The Simpsons*, *Futurama*, and *Life in Hell*.

Evergreen lies in a fir forest at the edge of the ninety-mile-long Puget Sound. The peaceful, thousand-acre campus includes a twenty-four-acre organic plant and animal farm, as well as 3,300 feet of undeveloped beach. It's a "beautiful, wooded location," says one student. "The students who attend TESC are independent thinkers," adds a classmate. "They are interested in synthesis rather than separation." That said, most of Evergreen's buildings are boxy concrete-and-steel creations, though the Longhouse Education and Culture Center is designed in the Native American style typical of the Pacific Northwest. Evergreen's Tacoma campus, for juniors and seniors, now has a science lab dedicated to public health and other environmental science studies, as well as a multimedia lecture hall seating 250 people.

At first glance, Evergreen's wide-open curriculum looks like Easy Street: no required classes and few traditional exams to slog through at the end of each ten-week quarter. And instead of signing up for a set of unrelated courses to fulfill requirements, students enroll in a coordinated "program," which may last as long as a year. Each program is team-taught by multiple professors; one recent program, Problems Without Solutions, for example, looked at topics like AIDS and homelessness from the perspective of political science, philosophy, anthropology, economics, statistics, and writing. Evergreen is a

"The students who attend TESC are independent thinkers."

Website: www.evergreen.edu
Location: City outskirts
Total Enrollment: 4,367
Undergraduates: 4,081
Male/Female: 44/56
SAT Ranges: V 520–650
  M 480–590
ACT Range: 20–26
Financial Aid: 40%
Expense: Pub $ $
Phi Beta Kappa: No
Applicants: 1,399
Accepted: 94%
Enrolled: 35%
Grad in 6 Years: 48%
Returning Freshmen: 72%
Academics: ✍ ✍ ✍
Social: ☎ ☎ ☎
Q of L: ★ ★ ★ ★
Admissions: (360) 867-6170
Email Address:
  admissions@evergreen.edu

Strongest Programs:
Environmental Studies
Media Arts

place where, when asked to list the best academic departments, a senior responded: "International Feminism, Reinhabitation, and Body Mind Soul." The integrated approach draws raves, but also warnings to expect a sizable workload. "I have been challenged to demonstrate my learning from a variety of perspectives," says a social sciences major. Freshmen select an interdisciplinary core program, while upperclassmen concentrate in more specialized areas, often concluding with a thesis or Individual Learning Contract developed with a faculty sponsor. Some students say the contracts can be a pain to write up.

Since Evergreen does not favor traditional departments, it's tough to assess the quality of various programs. But even without rankings and ratings, students say definite winners include expressive arts and film and media studies. The superb environmental science program invariably fills up fast, and offers classes in ornithology, marine biology, and wetlands studies. To supplement their coursework, students study marine animals while sailing the Puget Sound, or spend seven weeks at a bird sanctuary in Oregon. Other field studies may take students to tropical rainforests in Costa Rica or the Grand Canyon. "The science departments offer students the chance to do graduate work at the undergraduate level with hands-on lab time," says a freshman. The animation program is a big draw, too, with Hollywood studies like Disney quickly snapping up graduates. These programs, along with the general penchant for activism, set the tone on campus.

Because Evergreen attracts many nontraditional students, administrators take advising and career counseling seriously; they've also asked faculty members to do more to help students adjust to life on campus. "You get an amazing amount of support and advising from your actual professors," says a junior. "Academic advising has also been very helpful!" Students give professors high marks for teaching skill—and more. "Everyone develops personal relationships with the professors," says one student. "I hear rumors of it being competitive to *teach* here because many professors want that." Because there is no tenure at Evergreen, there's less pressure for professors to conduct research and publish their findings—and less to distract them from their undergraduates. Still, individual interest and motivation are the keys to getting the most from four years at Evergreen.

Not surprisingly, "Greeners" are an environmentally conscious, nonconformist lot, open-minded and liberal; many are community-college transfers. Ideologically,

Students can study marine animals while sailing the Puget Sound, or spend seven weeks at a bird sanctuary in Oregon. Other field studies may take students to tropical rainforests in Costa Rica or to the Grand Canyon.

"I hear rumors of it being competitive to teach here because many professors want that."

the school remains one of the best choices for students who think they were born thirty years too late. If the '60s was your decade, take heart: special admissions consideration is given to applicants twenty-five years of age and older, as well as Vietnam-era veterans and applicants whose parents have not graduated from college. Three-quarters of Evergreen's students are homegrown Washington residents, and 18 percent are minorities, with Native Americans and African-Americans accounting for 5 percent each, and Asian-Americans and Hispanics each accounting for 4 percent of the student body. Important campus issues include abortion, women's rights, and environmental issues. "You really need to be politically correct, so as not to look like a jackass," reports one freshman. Social activism is ubiquitous, adds another: "You can't walk around without seeing tons of flyers about various issues." There are 104 merit scholarships of up to $3,000 each, and athletic awards are once again available, as Evergreen is now part of Division II of the NAIA.

Twenty-one percent of Evergreen students, mostly freshmen and sophomores, live happily on campus, many in apartment complexes with single bedrooms, shared bathrooms—with bathtubs, not just shower stalls—and full kitchens, says a junior. Because housing can be expensive and sometimes tough to land, most students live off campus, especially after their first year. An efficient bus system brings nonresidents back to campus, though it helps to have a car, students say. The food service on campus, Bon Appetit, offers a wide variety of dishes including vegan options, all of which are organic. "It's funny because almost everything fits vegan or vegetarian, so the normal person has to conform to that," says a freshman.

Nearby Olympia (the state capital) doesn't really qualify as a college town, but it's progressive and open-minded. "It is a very community-oriented city and very welcoming to Evergreen students," says one student. Situated at the southernmost point of the Puget Sound, Olympia naturally offers a lot of water-related activities. The city also has "beautiful trees and mountains for hiking," kept lush and green by the (interminable) rain, which stops in time for summer break and begins again by October. Seattle (an hour away) and the rugged Oregon coast (three to four hours) provide changes of scenery for students with wheels. The college offers all types of outdoor equipment for rent, from backpacks and skis to kayaks and sailboats. Evergreen's large College Activities Building houses a radio station, the student newspaper, and space for student gatherings.

You may laugh at Evergreen's mascot, an eight-foot clam named "Gooeyduck," for the large geoduck clams found in Puget Sound, but the school is getting more serious about organized sports. When it switched to Division II, Evergreen expanded its athletic program, adding women's volleyball and cross-country to soccer, swimming, tennis, and basketball. While the college hasn't brought home championships yet, it has produced two All-American swimmers and one All-American men's basketball player. Many students also enjoy intramural Frisbee, volleyball, skiing, and sailing. As might be expected at this nonconformist mecca, fraternities and sororities don't exist; social life revolves around movies and parties with friends. The biggest annual event is Super Saturday, a huge community fair the day after graduation, featuring bands, arts and crafts, and ethnic foods.

Without the yoke of requirements and grades, students at Evergreen "can begin studying what they are passionate about immediately," raves a neuroscience student, adding that students are "personally engaged in carefully planning out their degree path and the most efficient, qualitative way of earning their degree." All that freedom could be a burden for some, but Greeners welcome the challenge. "Here, I can take my education in my own hands," says a freshman. "There isn't anywhere else in the world I'd rather be."

The animation program is a big draw, too, with Hollywood studies like Disney quickly snapping up graduates.

Overlaps

University of Washington, Western Washington, University of Oregon, Reed, Lewis and Clark

If You Apply To ➤ | **Evergreen:** Early action: Dec. 1. Rolling admissions: Mar. 1. Financial aid: Mar. 15. Housing: May 1. Guarantees to meet demonstrated need. No campus or alumni interviews. SATs or ACTs: required. Essay question (strongly recommended): academic goals.

Fairfield University

Fairfield, CT 06824

Fairfield is one of the up-and-coming schools in the Roman Catholic universe. Undergraduate enrollment has grown by more than one thousand in the past decade. Strategic location near New York City is a major attraction. Lack of big-time sports keeps Fairfield from the Boston College/Holy Cross echelon.

Website: www.fairfield.edu

Location: Suburban

Total Enrollment: 5,114

Undergraduates: 4,073

Male/Female: 44/56

SAT Ranges: V 560–650
    M 580–660

ACT Range: 25–28

Financial Aid: 57%

Expense: Pr $ $ $ $

Phi Beta Kappa: Yes

Applicants: 6,974

Accepted: 49%

Enrolled: 24%

Grad in 6 Years: 80%

Returning Freshmen: 90%

Academics: 🖉 🖉 🖉

Social: ☎ ☎ ☎ ☎

Q of L: ★ ★ ★ ★

Admissions: (203) 254-4100

Email Address:
    admis@mail.fairfield.edu

Strongest Programs:
Biology
International Studies
Art History
Religious Studies
Sociology
Accounting and Finance
Mechanical Engineering

Fairfield University, a comprehensive Jesuit school, focuses on "preparing students for lives of leadership and service in a constantly changing world." To provide a well-rounded education, the school combines solid academics, real-world opportunities in and outside of the classroom, and an abundance of community-service projects. No doubt about it, Fairfield is moving into the same class as older, more revered East Coast Jesuit institutions.

The university's physical beauty, a scenic, tree-lined campus just ninety minutes from Manhattan, is a source of pride. The administration takes pains to preserve a lush atmosphere of sprawling lawns, ponds, and natural woodlands. Buildings are a mix of collegiate Gothic, Norman chateau, English manor, and modern. The library, Campus Center, and Science Center have all undergone recent expansion, and the business school recently relocated to a new building with state-of-the-art teaching facilities, seminar rooms, and group study areas.

> "There are rigorous and challenging courses with a mildly competitive atmosphere, but there is a balance of peer support."

Students enjoy a twenty-four-hour computer lab, Geographic Information Systems lab, and a wireless 125-person computer lab in the School of Nursing. A 51,000-square-foot Athletic Center offers improved locker facilities for varsity players and an aerobics and free-weight area for weekend warriors.

Despite the beautiful facilities, students may find it difficult to squeeze a workout into their demanding class schedules. Everyone must complete the liberal arts core curriculum over four years, with two to five courses from each of five areas: math and sciences, history and social science, philosophy and religious studies, English and fine arts, and modern and classical languages. The core constitutes almost half of a student's total courseload.

Fairfield's main academic strengths are business (accounting, finance, and economics), the social sciences (sociology and psychology), and the natural sciences (biology and physics). "Fairfield is mainly known by reputation and in the literature as a liberal arts school, but I believe their biology program is underrated," says one biology major. Upperclassmen can now design their own majors.

Fairfield's academic climate is not cut-throat, but challenging nevertheless. "There are rigorous and challenging courses with a mildly competitive atmosphere, but there is a balance of peer support," says a psychology major. Recent additions to the curriculum include minors in information systems; operations management; classical studies; Irish studies, which has strong ties to the University of Galway; and Italian studies, which maintains strong ties to the Lorenzo de'Medici Institute in Florence. Engineering students may enroll in joint five-year programs with the Rensselaer Polytechnic Institute, Columbia University, or the University of Connecticut. MBA candidates can now have a concentration in e-business. Approximately two hundred students study abroad each year, through their choice of more than one hundred programs in fifty nations. In the past few years, sixteen Fairfield students have been awarded Fulbright Scholarships for studies abroad. About 8 percent are part of the four-year honors program. Students looking to travel abroad without committing a full semester can take a trip with one of several professors who lead educational summer tours—for credit—to locations including England, France, Russia, Latin America, and South America. Sophomores can join the Ignatian Residential College, in which they live together and, literally, explore the meaning of life. A new computer engineering program is developing.

Fairfield's advanced fiber optic network brings email, Internet, and video capabilities to classrooms, offices, and dorm rooms. There are no graduate teaching assistants, hence no teaching assistants, and 98 percent of the classes have fewer than forty students. "Professors are absolutely incredible," raves a politics major. "They care so much about making us better critical thinkers." The vast majority of Fairfield's students come from Roman Catholic families, and approximately one-quarter from Connecticut. Minority enrollment is small, with African-Americans constituting 2 percent of the student body, Hispanics 5 percent, and Asian-Americans another 3 percent. Students are somewhat self-conscious about their conservative, preppy image, referring jokingly to themselves as "J.Crew U," though some students say that profile is changing. Volunteerism abounds, and tensions with beach residents of Fairfield top the list of current issues at the college. "Our town–gown relations aren't great," one student says. The college canceled some more raucous beach events to calm relations. A peer group helps Fairfield deal with race issues and sexual harassment. Minority recruiting efforts include programs in Latin American, Asian, Women's, Judaic, and Black studies, and there are many diversity celebrations.

To help students with Fairfield's steep price, the school offers 160 merit scholarships annually, ranging from $8,000 to $13,500, and 163 athletic scholarships. Freshmen are introduced to Fairfield with a thorough orientation program. Two days of academic orientation and a parents' program occur in June, and a three-day orientation occurs in September before classes begin. All first-semester freshmen must complete the noncredit, nongraded First Year Experience Program, which provides first-year students with a chance to meet and discuss college transitional issues in a relaxed setting with two upperclass facilitators and a University faculty or staff resource person. The small group meetings take place once a week for the first eight weeks of school.

Fairfield's "comfortable and well-maintained" residence halls house 85 percent of the student body. One student admits some residences are better than others: "The dorms vary in quality depending on which building you are in." But the school recently built a new upperclassman apartment village, and four of the traditional halls have been renovated. In one of the more unusual housing arrangements in American higher education, upperclassmen can move off-campus to nearby beach houses, which they can rent at off-season rates. Meal plan options are available to all students, and many say the food is constantly improving.

Fairfield's proximity to the beaches of the Long Island Sound, a quick five-minute drive from campus, provides students with a scenic social space for everything from romantic retreats to rowdy parties. Still, students say much of the social life takes place on-campus, where sponsored events range from dances to hanging out at the coffeehouse and on-campus pub to concerts with stars like Blues Traveler and Billy Joel. Harvest Weekend at the end of October and Dogwoods Weekend at the end of April provide relief from the stress of studying. Road trips

"Professors are absolutely incredible. They care so much about making us better critical thinkers."

to New York (only an hour by train) and Boston are popular. The college recently instituted a new program for alcohol misuse or abuse. Students who violate rules must attend educational programs focused on substance abuse to remedy their records. "Students still drink though, regardless of penalties," a student says. Although Jesuits are very much in evidence and often live in the dorms, students say they do not hinder the social scene. The Campus Ministry draws a large following, with daily Masses, retreats about three times a semester, and regular community-service work, including two weeks of programs in the Caribbean and Latin America.

As for the surrounding area, some students say the quaint, wealthy Fairfield area can feel a bit "snobby," though there are plenty of shopping outlets and restaurants that fit college-student budgets. Beach residents don't always approve of beach-apartment students and their activities. "Most Fairfield residents use FU facilities, but they treat the students like garbage," complains one student. Community-service work in the less advantaged community of nearby Bridgeport is a common pastime for Fairfield students.

Students looking to travel abroad without committing a full semester can take a trip with one of several professors who lead educational summer tours—for credit—to locations including England, France, Russia, Latin America, and South America.

There are no graduate teaching assistants, hence no teaching assistants, and 98 percent of the classes have fewer than forty students.

Athletics have come of age at Fairfield, with a number of women's sports leading the way. Women's volleyball reached NCAA qualifiers during the 2000 and 2001 seasons, while women's basketball earned an at-large bid to the NCAA tournament in 2001. Men's soccer and women's lacrosse and field hockey have also brought home trophies. Men's and women's basketball both draw crowds, and the boisterous home-court fans, who come to games in full Fairfield regalia, have been dubbed the "Red Sea." The university recently moved varsity football and men's ice hockey into club sports as a budget-cutting move. Living up to the Jesuit motto of sound mind and sound body, many students play on intramural teams, whose exploits are copiously chronicled in the campus newspaper. The school also takes pride in its high graduation rate for athletes, regularly one of the highest rates in the country.

Fairfield University has combined several traditions to create a rich undergraduate experience, including close bonds with faculty, an emphasis on community involvement, challenging academics, and, of course, big fun on the beach. It can be such a good trip that one departing senior, when asked to name a top student complaint, simply said: "That we can only spend four years here."

If You Apply To ➤ **Fairfield:** Early decision: Nov. 15. Regular admissions: Jan. 15. Financial aid: Feb. 15. Does not guarantee to meet full demonstrated need. Campus and alumni interviews: optional, informational. SATs or ACTs: required. SAT IIs: optional. Accepts the Common Application and electronic applications. Essay question: from Common Application and a personal statement.

University of Florida

Gainesville, FL 32611

It should come as no surprise that UF is a world leader in citrus science. Throw in communications, engineering, and Latin American studies to the list of renowned programs. Among Deep South public universities, only the University of Georgia rivals UF in overall quality.

Set on two thousand acres of rolling, heavily forested terrain in north-central Florida, the University of Florida is an athletic powerhouse, and administrators are working hard to gain the same level of national recognition for their academic offerings. The school is massive and continues to grow, and in this case, bigger does seem to be better. While some students certainly get lost in the shuffle, those who can navigate the bureaucratic red tape will find resources including one of the nation's top ten natural history museums, one of the largest art museums in the Southeast, as well as a world-class bell carillon and the 99-rank Anderson Memorial pipe organ. Budding techies and Nobel Prize winners are accommodated, too, with the second-largest academic computing center in the South, and a micro-Kelvin laboratory capable of producing the coldest temperature in the universe.

UF's central campus has twenty-one buildings on the National Register of Historic Places; most are collegiate Gothic in style, redbrick with white trim. They're augmented by more modern facilities, including a 173,000-square-foot complex for nursing, pharmacy, and the health professions; and an honors dorm complex, which offers suite-style living, a computer lab, classrooms, and a full-time honors staff in residence. UF's research capabilities and equipment are likewise impressive, and a boon to aspiring physicians. The school has one of the nation's few self-contained intensive care hyperbaric chambers for treatment of near-drowning victims, and a world-class, federally funded brain institute. Media types flock to the school's public TV and radio stations, and its two commercial radio stations.

Academically, UF's strongest programs are those with a preprofessional bent, including engineering, tax law, and pharmacy. Popular majors include business administration, finance, elementary education, and advertising. Students also give high marks to the College of Journalism and Communications, the first in the nation to offer students an electronic newsroom. Students mention foreign languages and math as weaker, saying they rely too much on teaching assistants. Fine arts and music also suffer, probably because they're perceived as less helpful in the eventual job search. Students with high school GPAs of 3.9 or higher and SAT scores of at least 1350, gain access to the Honors Program, where classes are limited to twenty-five students. The program offers honors sections in standard academic subjects, and interdisciplinary courses such as masterworks of music, writing and love, and the history of rock and roll. The University Scholars Program offers $2,500 stipends to 175 students each year for one-on-one research with a faculty member. (Results must be published in the online *Journal for Undergraduate Research*.) Even if you don't qualify for those options, you should find something of interest, since only Ohio State and the University of Minnesota offer more degree programs on one campus than UF, the nation's fourth-largest university.

To balance students' preprofessional coursework, UF's general education program requires credits in composition, math, humanities, social and behavioral sciences, and physical and biological sciences. Students must also take six credits in the humanities, social or physical sciences that focus on themes of internationalism or diversity. Internships abound, along with volunteer and leadership opportunities, and foreign study in Latin America, Asia, the Middle East and more than a dozen cities in Eastern and Western Europe. UF has recently added a major in women's studies and an accelerated bachelor of science degree in nursing for students already holding B.A. or B.S. degrees in another

Students say Gainesville, a city of about 125,000 between the Atlantic Ocean and the Gulf of Mexico, is a great college town.

field. New minors include family, youth, and community sciences; urban and regional planning; aerospace studies and military science (for students in Air Force or Army ROTC); information technologies in agriculture; and organizational leadership for nonprofits.

While UF offers programs in every conceivable discipline, like many super-sized schools, it also forces students to climb a mountain of bureaucracy to get the courses and credits they need. Occasionally, for example, lectures in the College of Business Administration have to be videotaped and rebroadcast on the campus cable network, so that everyone can see them. Still, administrators are working to fix these problems, moving course registration to a telephone system and reserving some seats in many courses for first-year students. While academic advising can be impersonal, with so many students to serve, the university does provide personalized letters as students complete thirty, forty-five, and sixty credit hours, explaining the specific requirements they must meet to stay on track to graduate. Professors often have deep professional experience, and bring enthusiasm to their work, though academic pressure varies by major and student. As the university's academic standards rise, one student says, it's becoming more and more important to hit the books. An "incredible" career resource center allows students to research potential employers, work on resumes, and interview for jobs.

UF is one of Florida's three state universities, and 96 percent of students here hail from the Sunshine State. Despite the geographical homogeneity, they're an ethnically diverse bunch, with African-Americans adding almost 9 percent of the study

(Continued)
Social: ☎ ☎ ☎ ☎
Q of L: ★ ★ ★ ★
Admissions: (352) 392-1365
Email Address:
   freshman@ufl.edu

Strongest Programs:
Business
Engineering
Journalism/Communications
Citrus Science
Latin American studies

Sports are a year-round obsession here, and students say the best road trips are to UF away football games, especially against in-state rivals or the University of Georgia.

New minors include family, youth, and community sciences; urban and regional planning; aerospace studies and military science (for students in Air Force or Army ROTC); information technologies in agriculture; and organizational leadership for nonprofits.

body, Asian-Americans nearly 7 percent, and Hispanics 12 percent. UF has established the Latino-Hispanic Cultural Center to serve the largest minority on campus, and many African-American students belong to historically African-American fraternities and sororities. The multicultural celebration known as People Awareness Week has grown into a popular campus event, but students say that unfortunately, while there's no hostility between ethnic groups, there's also not much mixing. UF offers more than two hundred athletic scholarships, and 3,100 merit scholarships. National Merit Scholars automatically qualify if they list UF as their first choice.

About a fifth of Florida's undergrads live on campus, and students say rooms are tough to come by if you're not a first-year student. Doubles, triples, and suites in the co-ed dorms are awarded by lottery, based on Social Security numbers, and there just isn't enough room for everyone. Dorm-dwellers buy the campus meal plan, or use kitchens in their residence halls. Fifteen percent of men and the same fraction of women go Greek; rush is held before classes start in the fall, and again in the spring. The twenty-two traditional fraternities and sixteen Panhellenic Council sororities have privately owned houses in Gainesville, which also offer meal service. Nine historically African-American Greek groups and seven culturally based Greek organizations also recruit at various times during the year; they don't offer housing.

Students say Gainesville, a city of about 125,000 between the Atlantic Ocean and the Gulf of Mexico, is a great college town. There are plenty of stores, restaurants, and bars, as well as a sports arena and the Center for Performing Arts, which brings in world-class symphony orchestras, Broadway plays, opera, and large-scale ballet productions. The university owns a nearby lake, which is "great for lazy Sundays" and more vigorous water sports, and there's a plethora of parks, forests, rivers, and streams for backpacking, camping, and canoeing. Beaches are also a popular destination.

Sports are a year-round obsession here, and students say best road trips are to UF away football games, especially against in-state rivals or the University of Georgia.

The university owns a nearby lake, which is "great for lazy Sundays."

The annual Homecoming extravaganza, known as "Gator Growl," boasts a half-million-dollar budget and annual attendance averaging 78,000. Other sports are not forgotten, though; the university has one of the top intercollegiate programs in the nation, with varsity competition for men and women in sixteen sports, including nationally ranked teams in baseball, track, golf, tennis, gymnastics, volleyball, and swimming and diving. Men's and women's basketball are also powerhouses, and the school has also built a new women's softball stadium. Intramural sports are also popular, and for those who don't want to join a team, the 60,000-square-foot fitness park offers aerobics classes, martial arts, strength training equipment, and squash and racquetball courts.

For some students, Florida's sheer size is overwhelming. For others, it's a drawing card. Combine great weather with nationally recognized programs in engineering and business, and nationally ranked athletic teams, and it's easy to see why Sunshine State natives clamor to study here.

Overlaps

Florida State, University of Miami (FL), University of Central Florida, University of Georgia, UNC–Chapel Hill

If You Apply To ➤

Florida: Early decision: Oct. 1. Rolling admissions: Jan. 12 (for fall semester). Financial aid: Mar. 15. Campus interviews: optional, evaluative. No alumni interviews. SATs or ACTs: required. SAT IIs: required for placement in some programs. Accepts the Common Application and electronic applications; students apply to a particular school within UF. Essay question (choose two): meaningful activity, interest, experience, or achievement; how family history, culture, or environment has influenced you; qualities or unique characteristics.

Florida Institute of Technology

150 West University Boulevard, Melbourne, FL 32901-6975

FIT is practically a branch of the nearby Kennedy Space Center, so it should come as no surprise that aeronautics and aviation are popular specialties. The Atlantic Ocean is close at hand, also making the school an ideal spot for marine biology. With a total enrollment of about 4,500, FIT is the smallest of the major technical institutions in the Southeast.

Students at the Florida Institute of Technology can explore the endless depths of the ocean or shoot for the stars. With the sea nearby and Cape Canaveral only forty minutes away, it's natural that some of the most cutting-edge work in space and water-related sciences happens here. The combination of academic excellence and a bustling central Florida location—just an hour from the dizzying bustle of Walt Disney World—draws students to this unique and innovative school.

Founded in 1958 to meet the needs of engineers and scientists working at what is now Kennedy Space Center, Florida Tech's contemporary 130-acre campus features more than two hundred species of palm trees and botanical gardens in a tropical setting. Campus architecture ranges from modern to Georgian Gothic. Newer facilities include the state of the art F.W. Olin Engineering Complex, F.W. Olin Life Sciences Building, Charles Ruth Clemente Center for Sports & Recreation and seven new dorms.

If you're considering Florida Tech, the only independent technological university in the Southeast, make sure you have a strong background in math and science, especially chemistry and physics. Few students major in the less practical sciences. Though many students grouse that Florida Tech is too expensive for their tastes, those who plan their education well are able to get high-paying technical jobs as soon as they graduate. Fifty-six percent of students go into the workforce, and another 28 percent move on to graduate school. Prospective aviation students can major in aviation management, aviation meteorology, or aviation computer science,

> **"The professors are passionate about the subjects they teach at Florida Tech. They go out of their way to help their students understand the material."**

as well as aeronautics with or without a flight option. The flight school has a modern fleet of thirty airplanes and three flight-training devices, and the precision-flying team regularly wins titles. The computer and electrical engineering majors have gained popularity recently, and marine biology remains a popular major. Business administration, perhaps surprisingly, has grown, and programs have been added in business accounting, business information systems, and business environmental studies. Other new programs include software development and forensic psychology.

The academic climate at FIT is challenging. "People spend a lot of time studying," says a sophomore space science student. An aviation computer science major reports that "every class I go to people are comparing grades. If you don't study, you don't pass." Graduate teaching assistants are not overused. "The professors are passionate about the subjects they teach at Florida Tech," says one student. "They go out of their way to help their students understand the material."

All majors offer co-op programs and senior independent research at the Indian River Lagoon or on the RV *Delphinus*, a sixty-foot research boat the school owns. Recent marine research includes manatee preservation, beach erosion, and sea turtle studies. Everyone must take courses in communication, physical or life science, math, humanities, and social sciences, and be proficient in using computers.

Website: www.fit.edu
Location: Small city
Total Enrollment: 4,506
Undergraduates: 2,168
Male/Female: 71/29
SAT Ranges: V 500–610
  M 550–650
ACT Range: 22–27
Financial Aid: 61%
Expense: Pr $ $ $
Phi Beta Kappa: Yes
Applicants: 1,982
Accepted: 84%
Enrolled: 31%
Grad in 6 Years: 53%
Returning Freshmen: 74%
Academics: ✍ ✍ ✍
Social: ☎ ☎ ☎
Q of L: ★ ★ ★
Admissions: (321) 674-8030
Email Address:
  admission@fit.edu

Strongest Programs:
Aeronautics/Aviation
Computer Engineering
Electrical Engineering
Mechanical Engineering
Marine Biology
Computer Science

Forty-four percent of Florida Tech students are out-of-staters, while 22 percent arrive from out of the country. "One of our nicknames is 'Foreign Tech,'" says a sophomore. The student body is 56 percent white, yet political correctness and diversity-related issues seem to be taken in stride because of the preponderance of international students. Like any school, the students "vary from kooky to crazy and nerd to jock," says a political science major. One sophomore says the students have "character" and claims that this is what sets FIT apart from rival Embry-Riddle. Florida Tech offers 318 merit scholarships, ranging from $4,000 to $12,500, and 32 athletic scholarships in nine sports. Incoming freshmen are welcomed with a week-long orientation program highlighted by trips to Disney World and the beach, just three miles away. On campus, freshmen may take part in the University Experience Program, which helps first-years adapt to college life.

The growing selection of dorms at Florida Tech are modern, air-conditioned (whew!), and well-maintained. Forty-eight percent of students make their home on campus, though some complain about the price of it. "The rooms here are comfortable and convenient and much larger than in most college dorms," says a marine biology major. Freshmen are required to live on campus in large double rooms. Four-student apartments are available to a small percentage of qualifying upperclassmen by lottery. Students who live off campus are drawn by cheap rent and not much else, because Melbourne "is not much of a college town," reports an aviation major senior. The meal plan is an open, unlimited arrangement, and students report the food is survivable.

Most Florida Tech students who don't have cars choose bikes as their favorite mode of transportation. Diversions can be found in Orlando (with Epcot, MGM Studios, and Animal Kingdom abutting Disney World) or at the Kennedy Space Center. Students also hit the road for other Sunshine State cities, including Tampa, Key West, Miami, Daytona, and St. Augustine. Watching space shots from campus with a trained eye and a cold brew is a treasured pastime. The campus bar, the Rat, is a popular hangout. Otherwise, campus social life is predictably hampered by the low male/female ratio. "There's a greater influx of females to the school that will dramatically improve the social scene," says a molecular biology major.

Fraternities and sororities are slowly becoming more popular at Florida Tech, claiming 15 percent of the men and 11 percent of the women. "The Greek organizations offer excellent extracurricular activities that help you both socially and academically," says a sophomore. And while the campus is officially dry, every frat party has beer that the underage eagerly guzzle, students say. Besides partying, students spend their off time surfing, fishing, hanging out at the beach, shopping, or going for a "Sunday drive" (in the sky) with a flight school student. Every April, students brace for the invasion of other collegians on spring break. Techies also look forward to Greek Week and intramural sports competitions. Florida Tech is in Division II, and with so much water around, it's not surprising that crew is popular and awesome.

Whether it's surveying marine coral fifty feet below the sea or the sky thirty thousand feet above, students at Florida Tech get hands-on experience that serves to sharpen the school's already specialized, high-quality academics. The administration continues to focus on capital improvements, sponsor cutting-edge research, and embrace diversity. Under leadership of a new president, "it looks like FIT will have a promising future," a sophomore says. And with beaches and amusements close at hand, students can have some real fun in the sun while they prepare for high-flying—or low-lying—careers.

Overlaps

University of Florida, University of Central Florida, Embry-Riddle, Florida State, Georgia Tech

Florida State University

A2500 University Center, Tallahassee, FL 32306-2400

With an assist from its football program, FSU's popularity has burgeoned in recent years. Not that there weren't some quality programs to begin with. The motion picture school is among the best around, and business and the arts are also strong. So long as the football team beats the hated Gators, all is well.

Florida State University has long been synonymous with football, but students at this Sunshine State university enjoy success off the gridiron, too. Here, you could have a Nobel laureate for a professor, study in one of the finest science facilities in the Southeast, or get your feet wet in state government through an internship at the state capitol. The choices are plentiful at FSU, and the pace of life makes it possible to taste a little of everything: a wide array of academic choices, Florida sunshine, and some rowdy football.

FSU is located in Tallahassee, a land described as the "Other Florida": the one with rolling hills, flowering dogwoods and azaleas, and a canopy of moss-draped oaks. Glistening Gulf of Mexico waters are only half an hour away. The main campus features collegiate Georgian structures surrounded by plenty of shade trees, with some modern facilities sprinkled in. Situated on 463 compact acres, the campus is the smallest in the state university system—it's just a ten-minute walk from the main gate on the east side to the science complex on the west side. The University Center, which wraps around the football stadium, offers centralized services, including counseling, financial aid offices, undergraduate studies, and an active career center. Bicycling and skating are popular forms of transportation, though the parking garage provides spaces for more than one thousand cars and a free shuttle bus circles campus for those without wheels. A new freshman dorm is in the works and promises to ease the campus housing crunch.

FSU has outstanding programs in music, drama, art, and dance; it's moving up fast in the natural sciences with improved equipment and facilities in physics, chemistry, and biology. The College of Medicine, which focuses on serving the elderly and underserved communities, is the university's newest. FSU has twenty-five programs rated exemplary by the state university system, more than any of the other ten system schools. Communications, statistics, and business (especially accounting) have strong reputations in the Southeast. The most "wired" campus in the state, FSU has 1,700 computers available to undergraduates. The School of Motion Picture, TV, and Recording Arts has consistently won an impressive array of national and international awards. For gifted students, the honors program offers smaller classes and closer faculty contact, as well as forty special seminars each year. Certain students can even earn their degrees in three years. Directed Individual Study courses offer undergraduates the chance to participate in independent research projects with faculty direction. Internships and political jobs abound for tomorrow's politicians, since the state capitol and Supreme Court are nearby.

Website: www.fsu.edu
Location: City outskirts
Total Enrollment: 34,982
Undergraduates: 28,231
Male/Female: 43/57
SAT Ranges: V 530–630
  M 530–640
ACT Range: 22–27
Financial Aid: 40%
Expense: Pub $
Phi Beta Kappa: Yes
Applicants: 28,817
Accepted: 53%
Enrolled: 38%
Grad in 6 Years: 62%
Returning Freshmen: 87%
Academics: 🐾🐾🐾
Social: 🍷🍷🍷
Q of L: ★★★
Admissions: (850) 644-6200
Email Address:
  admissions@admin.fsu.edu

Strongest Programs:
Chemistry
Physics
Meteorology
Oceanography
Geology
Music
Dance
Theatre

Students report the academic climate is somewhat laid back but that "the courses are rigorous." Recently, liberal studies requirements were reduced from forty-nine to thirty-six hours, common prerequisites were established, and the total hours for a bachelor's degree were dropped to 120 (with a few exceptions). The general education requirements—courses in math, English, history and social sciences, humanities and fine arts, and natural sciences—are reported to be among the easier classes at FSU. Within FSU's liberal studies program, students must also complete six hours of multicultural understanding coursework—three focusing on diversity within the Western experience and three focusing on cross-cultural studies. Fresh-

"The quality of teaching is excellent."

men must take math and English, and may find a TA at the helm in these courses. But overall, faculty members do teach. "The quality of teaching is excellent," a senior says. For those with wanderlust, FSU offers extensive study abroad options. They include year-long placements in Italy, England, and Spain and summer programs in Greece, Vietnam, Switzerland, France, Costa Rica, Russia, the Czech Republic, and Barbados. The university is making strides in the world of distance learning, allowing some students with an associate's degree to earn their bachelor's degree online. Four undergrad and seven master's majors are online.

Perhaps not surprisingly, FSU's student body has a distinctly Floridian flavor: in-staters comprise 81 percent of the group. Nearly two-thirds of the student body are white; 13 percent are African-American, and 9 percent are Hispanic. There's little evidence of racial tension on the diverse campus. Seminoles are a mixture of friendly small-towners and city dwellers, and political tastes tend toward the conservative. While tuition is a hot topic of campus conversation, so are issues like voter registration, the environment, and student government concerns.

Sixteen percent of FSU's undergrads live in the university dorms, all of which are air-conditioned and wired for Internet access. Students may opt for typically spacious older halls or newer ones that tend to be more cramped. The dorms get mixed reviews, and the number of students who can live in them is limited; rooms are assigned on a first-come, first-served basis. Upperclassmen generally forsake the housing rat race and move into nearby apartments, houses, or trailers, where they take advantage of the city and campus bus systems (substantially cheaper and infinitely easier than driving and parking a car in FSU's infamously crowded lots) to get to school. The dorms are equipped with kitchens; meal plans that offer "good but expensive" food are also available.

When they're not studying, dorm parties, plays, concerts, and films keep FSU students busy. "The school has been known as the number-one party school, so the

"It is a place I can consider almost like my home."

social life is fine," a freshman says. Those with a good ID can head for one of Tallahassee's bars or restaurants, which fall somewhere between "college hangout" and "real world." Generally, though, students give the area a thumbs-up. As for Greek life, 14 percent of the men and 13 percent of the women join fraternities and sororities, which constitute another important segment of the social scene.

In sports, the big-time Seminole football team won two national titles in the '90s and was runner-up in 2000. Going to games is an integral part of the FSU social scene, especially when games are against FSU's two most hated rivals: the University of Florida and the University of Miami. FSU's baseball team also draws an enthusiastic following, as do the Lady 'Noles volleyball and softball teams.

While Florida State has all the elements of a party school, the merrymaking here doesn't seem to reach the riotous excesses for which some universities are known. FSU students take pride in their school and what it has to offer. "It is a place I can consider almost like my home," says a business major.

Overlaps

University of Florida, University of Central Florida, University of South Florida, University of Miami (FL), Florida International

Fordham University

Rose Hill Campus: 441 East Fordham Road, Bronx, NY 10458
Lincoln Center Campus: 113 West 60th Street, New York, NY 10023

New York City's Fordham has climbed a few notches on the selectivity scale. There is no better location than Lincoln Center in Manhattan, where the performing arts programs are housed. The Bronx campus is less appealing but better than the horror stories you may hear.

The Jesuit philosophy and motto of Fordham University, "Wisdom and learning," is borne out by the school's lasting emphasis on a quality liberal arts education offered in small classes and through individual attention to students. The Rose Hill campus in the Bronx is an oasis of trees, green grass, and Gothic architecture within the hectic and fast-paced Big Apple. But head to the university's Lincoln Center campus in Manhattan and you will feel the metropolitan, industrial setting of a fast-paced, no-nonsense city.

Although the university is an independent institution, its Jesuit heritage rings loudly through its concern for liberal values on both campuses. In the Jesuit tradition of "men and women for others," students travel as far away as Romania and Belize on their breaks for intensive service and study projects. For most students, the Roman Catholic influence is positive, and many students say that the Jesuit tradition is the school's best feature. If nothing else, the Catholic influence keeps the campus lively. "Because of the amount of Catholics here, there are differences in opinions concerning religious beliefs," says a junior theater major. "Yet I find the student body very liberal and free-thinking."

> **"Most Fordham students are liberal, open-minded, social, intelligent, and don't take themselves too seriously."**

The eighty-five-acre Rose Hill campus (aka the countryside in the city) is home to Fordham College as well as to the undergraduate schools of business administration and general studies. Fordham College at Rose Hill, the largest liberal arts school, is full-scale back to basics in the broadest sense. The eighteen-course core curriculum concentrates on developing a liberal arts foundation in three distinct but interlocking stages: the history of the Western world, the study of the contemporary world, and an introduction to the various disciplines scholars choose in studying both the past and the present. The popular business program is especially strong in marketing, accounting, and finance, and it provides hundreds of internships in all areas of Manhattan's business community, many leading to jobs. Freshmen are required to take courses in literature, English composition (which students cite as weak), foreign languages, history, philosophy, and theology.

The Lincoln Center campus, the Manhattan performing arts complex, has its own college as well as the law school and other graduate programs. Started as an alternative-style urban institution with no grades, it has become more traditional over the years and now shares the common core curriculum with Rose Hill. The

Website: www.fordham.edu
Location: Urban
Total Enrollment: 14,318
Undergraduates: 7,228
Male/Female: 41/59
SAT Ranges: V 530–630
  M 530–630
ACT Range: 23–27
Financial Aid: 65%
Expense: Pr $ $ $ $
Phi Beta Kappa: Yes
Applicants: 11,380
Accepted: 56%
Enrolled: 27%
Grad in 6 Years: 73%
Returning Freshmen: 90%
Academics: ✍ ✍ ✍
Social: ☎ ☎ ☎
Q of L: ★ ★ ★
Admissions: (800) FORDHAM
Email Address: enroll@fordham.edu

Strongest Programs:
Business
Theater and Drama
Psychology
English
Philosophy
Theology
History

university recently agreed to take over Marymount College, a small women's college in Tarrytown, New York, where Fordham has already leased space for graduate programs. Fordham has agreed to continue to operate Marymount as a women's college while looking for ways to integrate the two institutions.

Both colleges have strong humanities departments: Rose Hill's strengths include history, philosophy, psychology, and economics, while Lincoln Center's forte is, appropriately enough, theater. The B.F.A. in dance is offered in conjunction with Alvin Ailey; students must be accepted both by Fordham's admissions committee and Alvin Ailey's audition panel. Communications/media studies is praised at both schools, but some students cite the lack of an on-campus television studio as a major fault. Both colleges offer interdisciplinary majors, including black and Puerto Rican studies, and preprofessionals may enter 3–2 engineering programs at Columbia or Case Western Reserve. Rose Hill offers an innovative set of seminars, taught by the philosophy and theology departments, to help upperclassmen involved in community service analyze their experiences. The GLOBE Program in International Business includes an international internship or study-abroad assignment and requires proficiency in a foreign language. Programs have recently been added in Middle East studies and American Catholic studies. Classes are assigned to freshmen during their fall semester, but they have the option to change their given schedule. Overall, students say faculty members are accessible and knowledgeable. "I have had the best teachers of my life," a junior gushes.

Sixty-one percent of the students are from outside of New York, and more than two-thirds graduated in the top quarter of their class. Seventeen percent of Fordham's undergraduates are African-American or Hispanic, and the minority community is vocal. The atmosphere at both campuses is less intellectual than at nearby Columbia and New York universities, and Fordham students must motivate themselves. An American studies major says, "Most Fordham students are liberal, open-minded, social, intelligent, and don't take themselves too seriously." A large number of students receive financial aid. There are nearly one thousand merit scholarships, ranging from $7,500 to a full ride. Athletic scholarships are available as well in a wide array of sports. Responding to a declining commuter population and an increasing housing crunch, the university offers a $4,000 tuition discount for entering freshmen who continue to live at home and commute to the college.

The college has been seeking to build its national appeal and residential character, and 58 percent of students now live on campus (78 percent at Rose Hill and 46 percent at Lincoln Center.) Lincoln Center students gladly welcome the twenty-story, 850-bed dorm, so they don't have to deal with pricey rents in nearby apartments or in two specially priced hotels. One student says the dorms are "roomy and well-structured."

And what's there to say about the social life? "New York has so much to offer and it's right outside the gates," says a sophomore. The school sponsors some extracurricular activities, including an intramurals program in Central Park, but they pale against the city's vast cultural smorgasbord. Students say there's much happening on campus, too, including parties, movies, social events, bands, and plays, and there's a pub and coffeehouse. The university's cultural affairs program brings the Bronx campus students into Manhattan for a little high life; it is, after all, just half an hour away by train, subway, or college shuttle bus. Two of the most enjoyable events of the year are Spring Weekend and Homecoming. "The ten o'clock scream," a ritual every Thursday night in which everyone leans out their window and screams for one minute, is a favorite stress reliever.

"New York has so much to offer and it's right outside the gates."

The Bronx community plays a large role in Rose Hill students' lives, including volunteering. The Rose Hill campus is backed up against the Bronx Zoo, the beautiful botanical gardens, and Belmont, the "Little Italy" of the Bronx. Of course, students must constantly be aware of their surroundings, but guards at each entrance to the campus and roving security give Rose Hill a safe feeling.

The marvelous Lombardi Athletic Center (named for that famed alumnus) supports an active program of club sports and intramurals, while "grandstand athletes" especially enjoy rooting for the varsity basketball team, not to mention the rapidly improving football team—the 2002 Patriot League Champions—and the baseball team. The basketball team is competitive nationally, and one student says it is a source of pride on campus. "Opponents named the Fordham Gym one of the most feared in the whole nation. They view our loyalty to our team and having to come to the Bronx and face a Fordham home crowd as intimidating," a former student says. Fordham is a member of the Atlantic 10 Conference and has produced championship men's baseball and women's rowing teams. Says one sports-minded student, "Winning draws big crowds and gives the campus a new level of energy."

And it's that high level of energy that continues to propel Fordham University into the future. This service-oriented school, like its home city, is built on the ideas that diversity and a strong sense of community need not be mutually exclusive. "Although the volume and quality of our applicant pool have increased over the past 11 years, Fordham continues to prioritize small classes and individualized attention in keeping with the Jesuit mission of the university," administrators say.

Overlaps

NYU, Boston College, Boston University, St. John's, Fairfield

If You Apply To >

Fordham: Early action: Nov. 1. Regular admissions, financial aid, and housing: Feb. 1. Meets demonstrated need of 20%. Campus interviews: recommended, evaluative. Alumni interviews: optional, evaluative. SATs or ACTs: required. SAT IIs: recommended. Apply to particular school or program. Accepts the Common Application and electronic applications. Essay question: significant life experience; personal identification with a literary character; important issue.

Franklin and Marshall College

637 College Avenue, Lancaster, PA 17604-3003

F&M is known for churning out hard-working preprofessional students. Faces tough competition from the likes of Bucknell, Gettysburg, Lafayette, and Dickinson for Pennsylvania-bound students. Known for natural sciences, business, and internships on Capitol Hill.

At Franklin and Marshall College, set in the serene hills of Pennsylvania's Amish country, you can come nose to nose with a horse and buggy, but also enjoy the fruits of being in one of the country's fifty largest metro areas. While the city has modernized beautifully, parts of this historic town and many of its residents look much the same as they did when President James Buchanan insisted in 1853 that Marshall College merge with Franklin College in his hometown of Lancaster.

F&M's 125-acre campus is surrounded by a quiet residential neighborhood shaded by majestic maple and oak trees. The campus itself is an arboretum and boasts forty-seven buildings of Gothic and Colonial architecture. The College Square complex appeals to students seeking a study respite. Reflecting a recent focus on the arts, new additions to the campus include a new art museum, a revamped center for the performing arts, and the new Roschel Center for the Performing Arts, with a main-stage theater and dance performance spaces.

Website: www.fandm.edu
Location: Small city
Total Enrollment: 1,878
Undergraduates: 1,878
Male/Female: 52/48
SAT Ranges: V 570–660
M 590–680
Financial Aid: 43%
Expense: Pr $ $ $ $
Phi Beta Kappa: Yes
Applicants: 3,425
Accepted: 62%
Enrolled: 25%

Although there are no required courses freshman year, nine out of ten students enroll in First-Year Residential Seminars. Participating students live together in groups of 16 on co-ed freshman floors and study a major theme or concept within a discipline. Recently, the college curriculum was significantly revised. General education requirements include writing and language requirements, one course in three different "Foundation" areas (Mind, Self, and Spirit; Community, Culture, and Society; and the Natural World), and one course each in the arts, humanities, social sciences, natural sciences, and non-Western cultures. Collaborations are optional opportunities to get course credit for an experience that includes working with others.

F&M has traditionally been known for being strong in the natural sciences, and the school is now placing more emphasis on courses with a service-learning component. New majors have been added in astronomy, astrophysics, English/creative writing, environmental studies and environmental science, and all majors can be combined with an international studies concentration that requires students to study abroad and become proficient in a foreign language. Foreign languages offerings, once cited as weak, have been expanded. There are majors and minors in French, German, Spanish, ancient Greek and Latin, minors in Italian and Russian and small programs in Hebrew, Japanese and linguistics. About 40 percent of students engage in independent study or research with faculty during the academic year, and 70 percent have the chance to work one-on-one with a professor on a project. A preprofessional college in line with Lafayette and Bucknell, F&M has an excellent reputation for preparing undergrads for medical school, law school, and other careers.

Approximately fifty Marshall and seventy-five Presidential scholars are named each year. Marshalls receive a $12,500 tuition grant, a Macintosh computer, and the chance to apply for up to $3,000 in research travel funds. Presidential scholars receive a $7,500 tuition grant. F&M also offers two Rouse scholarships worth full tuition, books, and fees and about forty Buchanan community-service grants of $5,000 each. The school also offers merit-based financial aid to outstanding students of ethnic backgrounds that have been traditionally underrepresented in higher education. There are no athletic scholarships.

> "What makes us different from other schools is that we somehow manage to combine a casual attitude with a pretty killer workload."

Students uniformly describe the coursework as rigorous. The atmosphere at F&M can be competitive, and "the workload is always an issue," says a senior. Nonetheless, "what makes us different from other schools is that we somehow manage to combine a casual attitude with a pretty killer workload," says a history major. Students rate the quality of teaching as outstanding, and the relatively small student body and intimate class sizes—more than three-quarters of classes have fewer than twenty-five students—help create a strong sense of community between students and professors. "The faculty at F&M made my experience what it was—stimulating, intellectually maturing, open, insightful, and never redundant," says a senior. F&M offers cross-registration with two other small Pennsylvania colleges—Dickinson and Gettysburg—and several domestic-exchange and cooperative-degree programs. In the summer, the college sends students to countries such as Japan and Russia, and nearly 25 percent study in locations around the world during the junior year. Others participate in the Sea Semester.*

Seventy percent of students rank in the top quarter of their graduating high-school class, and students hail from forty states and sixty-two countries. Merely one-third are from Pennsylvania. Asian-American students comprise 4 percent of the student body; African-Americans 3 percent and Hispanics 2 percent. Although the student body is fairly homogeneous, students say it has become more diverse in

New majors have been added in astronomy, astrophysics, English/creative writing, environmental studies and environmental science, and all majors can be combined with an international studies concentration that requires students to study abroad and become proficient in a foreign language.

recent years. An occasional political debate may waft through the murmurs of light social exchanges during dinner, but according to one student, the big issue on campus is the lack of issues on campus. Fummers do, however, take an interest when it comes to extracurricular activities and social opportunities. The 115 clubs on campus attest to that, as does an unusually high level of participation in community-service activities.

Student housing, all co-ed, ranges from campus dorms to theme houses and private apartments near the campus. Although dorm rooms can vary greatly in size, students say they are very well maintained. "The dorms here are clean and comfortable," says a sophomore. All dorms also have heating, air-conditioning, carpet, hard wiring, and cable. Every student is guaranteed housing and about two-thirds of the student body takes advantage; freshmen and sophomores are required to live on campus, while many juniors and seniors live off campus in houses and apartments. Boarders eat most of their meals in the campus cafeteria under a flexible meal plan, but students are issued debit cards that they may use at a number of different food stops on campus. Food has been a common complaint in the past but seems to be improving.

Regarded by the college as independent social organizations, the nine fraternities, which attract 35 percent of men, and three sororities, joined by 20 percent of women, are integral to much of the nightlife, although the residence halls and special-interest groups offer a range of alternatives, including concerts, comedians, and Ben's Underground, a popular student-run nightclub. Hildy's, a tiny local bar, is a favorite campus meeting place. In recent years, the student-run and college-funded College Entertainment Committee has brought the Gin Blossoms, Rusted Root, Live, Ben Folds Five, and Vertical Horizon to the campus.

Lancaster is a historical and well-to-do city of 60,000 people located in a larger metro area of more than 400,000. Lancaster offers a sixteen-screen cinema, scores of shops, a farmer's market, brick-and-cobblestone streets (with hitching posts for the Amish horses and buggies that are almost never used), and a plethora of quaint restaurants and cafés. Students have a measured, realistic appreciation of its urban amenities and rural ambiance. The Amish culture draws the interest of some students, and many frequent the charming farmer's market to shop for handmade quilts. "People who complain that there is nothing to do just aren't looking hard enough," says one senior. Those with a hankering for contemporary action take road trips to Philly, Baltimore, Washington, D.C., and New York City. The biggest annual

> "People who complain that there is nothing to do just aren't looking hard enough."

event is Spring Arts, held the weekend before the last week of classes, which includes student air-band contests, live concerts, art exhibits, games, booths, and barbecues. Other highlights include the freshman Pajama Parade, the Sophomore Sensation, the Senior Surprise, International Day, Black Cultural Arts Weekend, and Flapjack Fest (when professors serve pancakes to students).

The college has a good selection of intramural sports, which include popular co-ed competitions. In addition to competing in Division I in wrestling, F&M boasts recent Centennial Conference championships in men's swimming, golf, and indoor track and field. Varsity squads are called the Diplomats, a name that is irresistibly abbreviated to "the Dips." The annual football game against Dickinson for the Conestoga Wagon trophy is always a crowd-pleaser.

Franklin and Marshall's small size and peaceful location could appear easily able to leave students feeling bored or isolated, but many students say on-campus activities have improved as of late, and they don't have to go far to find action. The atmosphere at F&M is warm and welcoming, and the campus is largely self-sufficient. While some students complain of being overworked or stressed, most tell tales revealing a college experience that blends rigorous academics with a healthy dose of fun.

About 40 percent of students engage in independent study or research with faculty during the academic year, and about 70 percent have the chance to work one-on-one with a professor on a project.

There are 115 clubs on campus and an unusually high level of participation in community-service activities.

Overlaps
Bucknell, Dickinson, Gettysburg, Lafayette, Penn

Furman University

3300 Poinsett Highway, Greenville, SC 29613-5245

Furman's campus is beautiful, and the swans are definitely a nice touch. At 3,252 total enrollment, Furman is nearly twice the size of Davidson and half the size of Wake Forest. As befits its Baptist heritage, Furman is a conservative place and still a largely regional institution.

Website:
www.engagefurman.com
Location: City outskirts
Total Enrollment: 3,208
Undergraduates: 2,772
Male/Female: 45/55
SAT Ranges: V 590–690
M 590–680
ACT Range: 24–29
Financial Aid: 41%
Expense: Pr $ $ $
Phi Beta Kappa: Yes
Applicants: 3,866
Accepted: 58%
Enrolled: 33%
Grad in 6 Years: 80%
Returning Freshmen: 91%
Academics: ✑ ✑ ✑ ½
Social: ☎ ☎ ☎
Q of L: ★ ★ ★
Admissions: (864) 294-2034
Email Address:
admissions@furman.edu

Strongest Programs:
Chemistry
Psychology
Political Science
Music
Biology
History

Students are fond of the "bubble" that develops around them at Furman University, insulating them from the harsh outside world. Some even call this school the "Country Club of the South." And if you're southern, white, Christian and conservative, y'all are likely to love it here. As a political science and communication major says, people aren't really involved in social and political issues, but "everyone is obsessed with perfection—academically, spiritually, socially, and physically." Beyond the lush lawns lie small classes led by caring faculty, and plenty of opportunities for independent research, all part of what administrators call "engaged" or "active" learning.

Furman's 750-acre campus is one of the country's most beautiful, featuring tree-lined malls, fountains, a formal rose garden and Japanese garden, and a thirty-acre lake, filled with swans and ducks. Flowering shrubs dot the well-kept lawns, which surround buildings in the classical revival, Colonial Williamsburg, and modern architectural styles. Many have porches, pediments and other southern touches, such as handmade Virginia brick. New additions include Hipp Hall, finished in 2002, with 38,000 square feet for the departments of economics, business administration, and education. Windows on three sides of the building have solar green glass, to keep out glare and ultraviolet rays. Phase one of the $25 million renovation of Duke Library was finished in 2003, adding a 48,000-square-foot wing for studying, reading and research.

Furman sees itself as a new type of liberal arts college, which recognizes how fast the world is changing. As such, general education requirements include freshman composition, four other humanities courses, one to three courses in math, two courses each in natural sciences and social sciences, and one course each in fine arts, health and exercise science, and the Asian-African program. Students must also achieve foreign-language proficiency, and attend nine events a year from the Cultural Life Program. High marks go to the departments of psychology, chemistry and music, but students reserve their most vocal praise for political science. "The department promotes the most involvement, through debate clubs, opportunities for foreign travel, and summer internships in D.C.," says one student. The academic calendar enables students to focus on topics in greater depth, with three courses each during the fall and spring terms, and two courses during the eight-week winter term.

"Most students here were at the very top of their high school classes, and we'd all like to stay there."

Perhaps because of the calendar, students say Furman's academic climate is intense. "Most students here were at the very top of their high school classes, and we'd all like to stay there," says a freshman. Three-quarters of the classes taken by freshman have fewer than twenty-five students, and virtually none of the rest has more than fifty, helping students get to know faculty members well. "Classes are small and interactive, and professors are nurturing and passionate," says a communication major. "Professors generally want students to talk with them outside of class more than the students take advantage of that opportunity," agrees a studio art major. The Furman Advantage program helps fund research fellowships and teaching assistantships for more than 125 students a year. Furman also typically sends one of the largest student delegations to the annual National Conference of Undergraduate Research. More than 250 students study abroad each year, through one of thirteen Furman-sponsored programs on five continents, including a special exchange with Japan's Kansai-Gaidai University. Furman also belongs to the Associated Colleges of the South.*

Furman is trying to diversify, but those efforts have been slow to bear fruit. African-Americans make up 6 percent of the student body, and Hispanics and Asian-Americans add 1 percent each. Students are "basically conservative, upper-middle-class, with high academic records from high school," says a freshman. "Many are focused on double majors and graduate school. They are politically knowledgeable, from religious backgrounds and two-parent families, concerned with physical health." There's also a lot of competition for leadership positions among this resume-conscious bunch, the student says. Although many denominations are represented, the Baptist influence is the strongest, though Furman broke with the South Carolina Baptist Convention in 1992 after 166 years. Each year, Furman awards a number of merit scholarships, from $500 to full tuition, plus 251 athletic scholarships.

Ninety-eight percent of students live on campus, and all soon will, as Furman is phasing in a four-year residency requirement. "The dorms vary in size, some extremely small, and others fairly large," says a political science major. "They are quite comfortable, well-maintained and easy to get." Furman is somewhat unusual in maintaining a dry campus. The policy is strictly enforced in freshman and sophomore dorms, where underage students shouldn't be imbibing anyway, though "plenty of drinking still occurs," one student says. The atmosphere is more relaxed in North Village, a new university-owned apartment building. If there are no noise complaints, students close the doors of their suites, and do what they wish. All dorms are equipped with telephone, cable TV, and Internet access, and students enjoy the camaraderie that results from a residential campus. Meal plan credits can be used in the dining hall or food court, which always offers student favorites like hamburgers and hot dogs. "The food is good," says a math and computer science major. "Vegetarians can always find something." Campus security is "ridiculously good," says another student. "I am never worried about leaving my apartment unlocked, or my belongings alone."

When the weekend comes, Furman's Student Activities Board sponsors "free movies, weekend trips, restaurant deal, huge concerts and basically always something to do," says a communication major. Fraternities claim 30 percent of the men and sororities 35 percent of the women, and off-campus Greek parties draw crowds. "Downtown Greenville is also a very popular destination," says a political science major, with a movie theater, restaurants, and other places to go out. The Peace Center for the Performing Arts, also downtown, brings in touring casts of Broadway shows, and other top-rated acts. More than 60 percent of Furman's students devote spare time to the Collegiate Educational Service Corps, which provides volunteers

New additions include Hipp Hall, finished in 2002, with 38,000 square feet for the departments of economics, business administration, and education. Windows on three sides of the building have solar green glass, to keep out glare and ultraviolet rays.

"You know just enough people to feel comfortable, but not everyone, which makes it interesting."

Furman's athletic teams compete in the Southern Conference, and in 2002–2003, the men's and women's soccer teams brought home conference titles for the third straight year. The rugby team, which competes in Division III, won a national championship in 2003.

to eighty-five community agencies and organizes the annual May Day-Play Day carnival, which converts the campus into a playground for underprivileged kids. The best road trips are to the mountains of Asheville (only forty-five minutes away), Atlanta (for the big city and shopping, about two hours), and Charleston or Myrtle Beach (four hours).

Furman's athletic teams compete in the Southern Conference, and in 2002–2003, the men's and women's soccer teams brought home conference titles for the third straight year. The rugby team, which competes in Division III, won a national championship in 2003, and Furman also fields a handball team, which was the runner-up in the national collegiate tournament that year. Students happily yell out the school's tongue-in-cheek cheer—"F.U. one time, F.U. two times, F.U. three times, F.U. all the time!"—during football games against archrivals Wofford and Georgia Southern. Almost 70 percent of the student body competes for the coveted All Sports Trophy by participating in intramurals, which range from flag football to horseshoes.

Furman may call itself a university, but its educational approach is closer to that of a liberal arts college, emphasizing problem solving, projects, and experience-based learning. More than a decade after severing its religious ties, the school continues to evolve, drawing more academically capable students from increasingly diverse backgrounds. "The involvement in all facets of life—community, classroom, intramural, Greek life—inspires enthusiasm," says one. "You know just enough people to feel comfortable, but not everyone, which makes it interesting."

If You Apply To ➤ **Furman:** Early decision: Nov. 15. Regular admissions and financial aid: Jan. 15. Housing: May 1. Meets demonstrated need of 85%. Campus and alumni interviews: optional, informational. SATs or ACTs: required. SAT IIs: optional, required for home-schooled students (math, writing and a third test of the student's choice). Accepts the Common Application and electronic applications. Essay question: personal statement on topic of genuine personal interest.

George Mason University

4400 University Drive, Fairfax, VA 22030-4444

Located in one of the richest suburbs in American, GMU is poised to become a major university. Though still mainly a commuter school, campus housing continues to grow. The presence of prominent conservatives such as Walter Williams have added cachet to economics and public policy.

Just forty minutes from the White House and the Smithsonian, smack in the middle of greater Washington, D.C.'s budding high-tech corridor, stands a fledgling university that is a leading center of conservative political and economic thought. George Mason University's urban campus and symbiotic relationship with the surrounding region contrast starkly with Virginia's two other major universities, which have held classes for a hundred years in the relative isolation of Charlottesville and Blacksburg. With just thirty years on its Fairfax campus—and only forty-five years of life experience—GMU is clearly the new kid on the block.

Founded as a sleepy outpost of the University of Virginia, GMU sits on a 583-acre, wooded campus in the Washington, D.C., suburb of Fairfax, Virginia. Campus architecture is modern and nondescript; most structures were erected after the mid-'70s. GMU's ten-thousand-seat arena, the Patriot Center, hosts both sporting and entertainment events. In addition, a new aquatic and fitness center, featuring two pools, a whirlpool, and co-ed saunas, was recently completed. And although GMU's campus doesn't have the Colonial ambiance or tradition of William and Mary or UVA, its namesake does have the same Old Virginia credentials. George Mason drafted Virginia's influential Declaration of Rights in 1776, and he later opposed ratification of the federal Constitution because there was no Bill of Rights attached.

Mason's general education requirements stipulate that all students take the equivalent of two courses in English composition, humanities, social sciences, and math and sciences. Students who prefer to find their own way can design a major under the Bachelor of Individualized Study program. The academic climate is intense but manageable. "The courses here are not too rigorous," says a sophomore, "but professors expect excellence from students." If they do fall behind or need some guidance, academic counseling is likely to put them back on course. Advisors "have been so helpful and really supportive," says a marketing major.

Mason has grown by leaps and bounds for most of the past two decades; recent additions to the curriculum include degree programs in classical studies, international transactions, computational sciences, public policy, and urban systems engineering. Another option is the New Century College degree program, which teams small groups of faculty and undergraduates on projects that can be easily connected to the world outside GMU. Though it is growing up fast, Mason's youth shows in a number of ways. First, programs taken for granted at more established universities are just hitting their stride here. Next, GMU's relatively small endowment means almost constant tuition increases. Last, some of the school's facilities are just plain inadequate for its more than twenty thousand students. The library, for example, has fewer than seven hundred thousand volumes, though it now subscribes to more than three hundred online databases and allows students to borrow books from all eight members of the Washington Research Library Consortium.

The lack of resources in the library may present less of a problem for GMU's career-focused students, who seem to like learning on the job: 70 percent enter the working world after graduation, and just 20 percent proceed to graduate and professional schools. Psychology tops the list of popular majors, and economics—which

> **"The courses here are not too rigorous, but professors expect excellence from students."**

boasts its own Nobel laureate—is probably the strongest department. Other well-regarded majors include computer science, nursing, engineering, and English; not surprisingly, given the school's location, the public policy department also receives accolades. The drama department, once a weak sister, is now part of the Institute of the Arts, created to make arts an intrinsic part of every student's GMU experience. The institute includes a professional theater company, which hosts actors and playwrights in residence.

Eighty-six percent of GMU students are home-grown, and Mason's student body is fairly diverse, likely due to the diversity of the surrounding area. Minorities make up 28 percent of the student population—9 percent African-American, 6 percent Hispanic, and 13 percent Asian-American. Students are politically aware and tend to lean rightward. That said, racial tensions haven't been a problem, perhaps thanks to the four-year-old Stop, Look, and Learn program. The program attempts to increase campus discussion on prejudice, discrimination, and harassment. Athletic and merit scholarships are available to those who qualify.

George Mason has been a commuter school for much of its short existence, but there is on-campus housing, and 19 percent of undergrads choose this option. Another several thousand live around campus in university-sponsored housing. The administration admits that room and board costs are inflated because the university's entire housing stock dates from 1978 or later, which means the buildings are modern and air-conditioned—but still being paid for. And though the dorms are

(Continued)
Accepted: 68%
Enrolled: 39%
Grad in 6 Years: 48%
Returning Freshmen: 76%
Academics: ✍ ✍ ✍
Social: ☎ ☎
Q of L: ★ ★
Admissions: (703) 993-2400
Email Address:
   admissions@gmu.edu

Strongest Programs:
Economics
Engineering
Public Policy
Business Administration
Government
English
Communications
Information Technology

The lack of resources in the library may present less of a problem for GMU's career-focused students, who seem to like learning on the job.

With barely a generation of history under its belt, Mason is notably lacking in traditions and annual events: "Come here and invent one!" a student urges.

comfortable and well-maintained, there's still a lot of building to do. "The dorms are nice enough, but most students still prefer to live off-campus," says a junior. Freshmen live together in Presidents Park, while other students get rooms on a first-come, first-served basis, based on class status. Those looking for an active social life should definitely consider a stint in the dorms, particularly in Presidents Park or the Freshman Center, but freshman dorms are dry, and you can get the boot if you're caught having a party with alcohol.

GMU's University Center, with its food court, movie theater, classrooms, computer labs, and study areas, has become the center of on-campus social life. The center is a convenience and a lure for students who commute to school and have gaps between classes. On the weekends, students find a predictable assortment of malls and shopping centers in Fairfax, just southwest of D.C., but off-campus parties and the sights and sounds of downtown Washington, Georgetown, and Old Town Alexandria beckon when the sun goes down. Best of all, these are only a short commute away via a free shuttle bus to the subway. Those searching for a more lively collegiate scene take road trips to other local schools, including James Madison and UVA.

With barely a generation of history under its belt, Mason is notably lacking in traditions and annual events: "Come here and invent one!" a student urges. Patriots Day and Mason Day are the two major bashes, in addition to Homecoming, Greek Week, and International Week. GMU competes in Division I, and basketball dominates the sports scene since there's no football team. Any game against James Madison University draws a big crowd. Other successful teams include women's soccer, men's and women's track, and women's volleyball. Intramurals are catching on, now that many games are held in the Patriot Center.

The name of George Mason may not have the cachet of George Washington, James Madison, or the other luminaries of Virginia history who have had universities named for them, but with improving academics, a growing and improving physical campus, and the rich cultural and economic resources of Washington, D.C., Mason's namesake looks like it's set to follow in those other schools' fine footsteps.

Overlaps

Virginia Tech, James Madison, Mary Washington, University of Virginia, University of Maryland

If You Apply To ➤

Mason: Regular admissions: Feb. 1. Meets demonstrated need of 40%. Campus interviews: required, informational. Alumni interviews: optional, informational. SATs or ACTs: required. SAT IIs: optional. Accepts the Common Application. Essay question: personal statement.

George Washington University

2121 Eye Street NW, Washington, DC 20052

Ten years ago, GW was a backup school with an 80 percent acceptance rate that was maligned for its lack of identity. But the allure of Washington, D.C., has proved to be a strong drawing card, and GW now accepts less than half who apply. Still not much for school spirit, GW is the nation's leader in internships per capita.

Website: www.gwu.edu
Location: Urban
Total Enrollment: 23,019
Undergraduates: 10,328

Like Washington itself, George Washington University draws students from all over America—and around the world. Upon arrival, they find a bustling campus in the heart of D.C. with ready access to Smithsonian Institution museums, the Folger Shakespeare Library and the Library of Congress, and other national treasures, including top political officials as guest speakers and visiting professors. Since Congress chartered GW in 1821, perhaps it's not surprising that the school has learned well from nearby government agencies how to create red tape. "GW is more like a business with consumers than a university with students," a senior laments. "Bureaucracy is huge, office staff is rude, and money is everything. However, it has made some wonderful expansion possible, and put us where we are today."

Where the school is today includes two campuses—the main, older campus in the Foggy Bottom neighborhood, on Pennsylvania Avenue near the White House, and the new Mount Vernon campus a few miles away, with five residence halls and some classroom buildings. The Foggy Bottom campus has a mix of renovated federal row houses and modern buildings, while the wooded Mount Vernon campus spans twenty-six acres near Georgetown, and also includes athletic fields, tennis courts, and an outdoor pool. Formerly a women's college, all GW students are now permitted to take classes and attend activities at Mount Vernon, though certain programs and academic initiatives are geared toward women. A new building for the Elliott School of International Affairs, with residence hall space and five floors of classrooms, as well as more dorms and a new hospital, have been completed.

Aside from the Elliott School, freshmen may enroll in the School of the Engineering and Applied Science, the School of Business and Public Management, the School of Media and Public Affairs, and the Columbian College of Arts and Sciences, which is the largest undergraduate division. During freshman year, all undergraduates take English composition. Other requirements vary by school. To graduate from the college, students fulfill requirements covering seven areas of knowledge: literacy, quantitative and logical reasoning, natural sciences, social and behavioral sciences, creative and performing arts, humanities, and foreign languages and cultures.

> "The threat of not getting a good job after graduation is a bigger motivator than a love of academia."

For highly motivated and capable undergraduates seeking a challenge, GW's honors program offers special seminars, independent study, and a university symposium on both campuses. The intensive Enosinian Scholars Program culminates with a written thesis and oral examination. The School of Engineering also offers an honors program, in which students work with professors on research projects; a team recently collaborated with America Online to create a wireless-technology lab. A new literacy requirement is being introduced into the undergraduate curriculum and the bachelor of music degree has been phased out. GW's political communications major, which combines political science, journalism, and electronic media courses, is one of the few undergraduate programs of its kind, and benefits from its Washington location. Students say history, English, political science, and international affairs are also among the school's best departments. Geology and statistics— "None of the profs speak English," a senior complains—need work, they say.

GW's academic climate has become more rigorous because the school is raising standards with each entering class, says a criminal justice major. "The overall climate is one of healthy competition," a history major reasons. "The threat of not getting a good job after graduation is a bigger motivator than a love of academia." Two-thirds of the classes taken by freshmen have twenty-five students or less; professors handle lectures and seminars, and TAs facilitate discussion or labs. "So many of my teachers have taught in interesting ways," says a history and psychology major. "They make it exciting to go to class." Still, almost half of GW's faculty members divide their time between the halls of academia and the corridors of power, with many holding high-level government positions. "Avoid the 'super-profs,'" says a junior history major. "They tend to cancel classes more, for things like an appearance on CNN." Then again, those connections allow students tremendous access to the bigwigs of D.C.—prominent figures such as President

(Continued)
Male/Female: 44/56
SAT Ranges: V 580–680
　M 590–680
ACT Range: 24–29
Financial Aid: 42%
Expense: Pr $ $ $ $
Phi Beta Kappa: Yes
Applicants: 16,910
Accepted: 40%
Enrolled: 34%
Grad in 6 Years: 73%
Returning Freshmen: 92%
Academics: ✍ ✍ ✍ ½
Social: 🐿 🐿 🐿
Q of L: ★ ★ ★
Admissions: (202) 994-6040
Email Address:
　gwadm@gwu.edu

Strongest Programs:
Political Communications
History
International Affairs
Electronic Media
International Business
English
Biology
Computer Science

A new building for the Elliott School of International Affairs, with residence-hall space and five floors of classrooms, as well as more dorms and a new hospital, are under construction on the main campus.

Bush, Virginia Governor Mark Warner, the Dalai Lama, and Larry King have all addressed GW students.

Given GW's location and its improving academic reputation, students "are smart, politically savvy, and ambitious," says a junior. "They are used to being leaders and achievers, not as much scholars." Six percent of the students are African-American, 5 percent are Hispanic, 10 percent are Asian-American, and 14 percent come from foreign countries. "The diversity of the campus sets it apart," says a senior. As you might expect, political issues important on the national stage are also important here. "Every issue big in the news is big on campus," says a mechanical engineering major.

Sixty-three percent of GW students live in campus housing, where "everyone is guaranteed a room, but it might not be the one they want," says a freshman, since sophomores get first pick in the lottery. Dorms are "palatial, mostly renovated former hotels or apartments," with private bathrooms and fast Internet links, says a junior. "D.C. rents are so high and the dorms so nice that many people stay." Those who move off-campus typically find group houses in Foggy Bottom, or go to nearby neighborhoods like Dupont Circle and Georgetown, just a short walk from campus. Some also choose the Maryland or Virginia suburbs, where housing stock is newer and a little more affordable, since they're just a short subway ride away. Most freshmen are assigned to suites with up to four roommates in Thurston Hall, the biggest and rowdiest dorm on campus. They may also choose one of twenty-four Living and Learning Communities, groups of students who share similar interests. These groups have gone to the Kennedy Space Center for a rocket launch and to New York City to tour the United Nations.

"Every issue big in the news is big on campus."

Fourteen percent of GW men and 16 percent of the women go Greek, though "the Greeks don't have lots of public parties because most of them don't have houses," says a junior. "People tend to gather with friends, either at apartments or bars." That said, a D.C. police crackdown on underage drinking has made it extremely difficult for those under twenty-one to be served at off-campus restaurants and pubs. Major annual events include the Fall Fest and Spring Fling carnivals, with free food and such nationally known entertainment as The Roots and Busta Rhymes. Popular road trips include the beaches of Ocean City, Maryland, and Virginia Beach, Virginia. Philadelphia and New York City are easily accessible by bus or train, a boon because most GW students don't have cars.

GW doesn't field a football team, but its men's and women's basketball teams have won Atlantic 10 conference championships in recent years. The gymnastics squad is also strong, and the men's and women's rowing teams compete on the Potomac River, right in GW's backyard. "Our rivalries with schools like Georgetown are more social than athletic," says a history major. The school's unofficial mascot is the hippopotamus.

A popular GW T-shirt proclaims: "Something Happens Here." Something certainly has happened on both of the school's campuses in the past five years, says a junior. "GW has gone up in status, scholarship, and quality of life, recruiting stellar students and becoming far more selective," a history major says. "We're expanding the physical campus while dramatically improving existing traditions of achievement and work." For students interested in urban living, in the heart of the nation's political establishment, GW may be a very good choice indeed.

Overlaps

Boston University, Georgetown, NYU, American, University of Maryland

If You Apply To ➤	**GW:** Early decision: Nov. 1, Dec. 1. Regular admissions: Jan. 15. Financial aid: Jan. 31. Housing: Jul. 1. Campus and alumni interviews: recommended, evaluative. SATs or ACTs: required. SAT II: recommended (math, writing, science). Accepts the Common Application and electronic applications. Essay question: why GW; how GW's strengths compare to your view of the "ideal" college experience; or a graded sample of creative or fiction writing. Media and public affairs applicants have an additional essay on political communication, electronic media, or journalism.

Georgetown University

37th and O Streets, NW, Washington, DC 20057

For everyone who wants to be a master of the political universe, this is the place. Only a handful of Ivy League schools and Stanford are tougher to get into than Georgetown. In all the excitement over D.C., students can forget the Jesuit affiliation, which adds a conservative tinge to the campus.

As the most selective of the nation's Roman Catholic schools, Georgetown University offers students an intellectual milieu that is among the nation's best. With unparalleled access to Washington D.C.'s corridors of power, aspiring politicos benefit from the university's emphasis on public policy, international business, and foreign service. For avid sports fans, there is a powerful basketball team. The national spotlight shines brightly on this elite institution, drawing dynamic students and athletes from around the world.

From its imposing, hilly location just blocks from the Potomac River, Georgetown affords its students an excellent vantage point from which to survey the world. The 104-acre campus reflects the history and growth of the nation's oldest Jesuit university. The Federal style of Old North, home of the school of business administration, which once housed guests such as George Washington and Lafayette, contrasts with the towers of the Flemish Romanesque–style Healy Hall, a post–Civil War landmark on the National Register of Historic Places. The new Southwest Quadrangle is currently underway and includes a student residence hall, dining facility, underground parking garage, and Jesuit Community Residence.

Although Georgetown is a Roman Catholic university, founded in 1789 by the Society of Jesus, the religious atmosphere is by no means oppressive. Just over half of the undergraduates are Catholic, but all major faiths are respected and practiced on campus. That's partially due to the pronounced international influence here. International relations, diplomatic history, and international economics are among the hottest programs, as evidenced by former Secretary of State Madeline Albright's return to the School of Foreign Service. Through its broad liberal arts curriculum, GU focuses on developing the intellectual prowess and moral rigor its students will need in future national and international leadership roles. The curriculum has a strong multidisciplinary and intercultural slant, and students can choose from several programs abroad to round out their classroom experiences.

> "Departments usually select their best faculty to teach introductory courses."

Would-be Hoyas may apply to one of four undergraduate schools: Georgetown College, School of Nursing and Health Studies, McDonough School of Business, and the Walsh School of Foreign Service (SFS), which gives future diplomats, journalists, and others a strong grounding in the social sciences. Prospective freshmen must declare intended majors on their applications, and their secondary school

Website:
  www.georgetown.edu
Location: Center city
Total Enrollment: 12,856
Undergraduates: 6,332
Male/Female: 47/53
SAT Ranges: V 640–730
  M 640–730
ACT Range: 27–32
Financial Aid: 55%
Expense: Pr $ $ $ $
Phi Beta Kappa: Yes
Applicants: 15,536
Accepted: 21%
Enrolled: 46%
Grad in 6 Years: 94%
Returning Freshmen: 97%
Academics: ✑ ✑ ✑ ✑ ½
Social: 🐾 🐾 🐾 🐾
Q of L: ★ ★ ★ ★
Admissions: (202) 687-3600
Email Address: N/A

Strongest Programs:
Government
Chemistry
Philosophy
Business
International Relations
Diplomatic History
International Economics

records are judged accordingly. This means, among other things, intense competition within the college for the limited number of spaces in Georgetown's popular premed program.

Georgetown's liberal arts program is also very strong: American studies gets favorable reviews, as do history, government, English, and, of course, theology. The School of Foreign Service stands out for its international economics, regional and comparative studies, and diplomatic history offerings. SFS also offers several five-year undergraduate and graduate degree programs in conjunction with the Graduate School of Arts and Sciences. The business school balances liberal arts with professional training, which translates into strong offerings in international and intercultural business as well as an emphasis on ethical and public policy issues. A new major, operations and information management, prepares students to understand business processes and the information systems that support them. The School of Nursing and Health Studies runs an integrated program combining the liberal arts and humanities with professional nursing theory and practice, and offers a major in health studies. The Faculty of Languages and Linguistics, the only undergraduate program of its kind nationwide, grants degrees in nine languages, as well as degrees in linguistics and comparative literature. The computer science department has been bolstered by the recruitment of a chair with a national reputation, but students continue to cite it and the anthropology department as weak.

Georgetown's general education requirements are of two types: applicable to all students (literature, philosophy, and theology), and specific to certain divisions (chemistry, biology, physiology, math, philosophy, and sociology for nursing students, for example). The library holds 2.2 million volumes and features quiet study areas, audiovisual equipment, and access to special collections. That GU views most subjects through an international lens is evidenced by the 38 percent of students who study abroad. University-sponsored study programs in eighty-five countries—in Asia, Latin America, Poland, Israel, France, Germany, and at the university's villas in Florence, Italy, and Alanya, Turkey—attract the culturally curious. First-years read the same novel during the summer and the author visits campus during the first few weeks for a daylong seminar. There are no special academic requirements for the freshman year, but about thirty Georgetown College freshmen are accepted annually into the liberal arts colloquium.

"We have all the opportunities of Washington, D.C., without the city streets cutting through our campus."

Georgetown likes to boast about its faculty, and well it should. "Departments usually select their best faculty to teach introductory courses," says a junior. Professors "really love teaching and have a passion for their area of expertise," adds an international politics major. Academically, the environment is tough but manageable. Says a biochemistry major, "most students are extremely motivated, but there is virtually no competition between students." A sophomore adds that GU students "pursue knowledge for the sake of knowledge."

The GU community includes students from all over the United States and abroad. Ninety-one percent are from outside the District of Columbia, and 7 percent are foreign. African-Americans and Hispanics make up 12 percent of the undergraduate group, and Asian-Americans comprise 9 percent. A student committee works with the vice president for student affairs to improve race relations and develop strategies for improving inclusiveness and sensitivity to issues of multiculturalism. Students take studying seriously; they also say that each faculty member likes to think you're majoring in his or her subject. Sixty-two percent of graduates move directly into the job market after graduation, helped by the more than 127 resume-building clubs, organizations, and student government activities available at this incubator for aspiring public leaders. Georgetown offers no academic merit scholarships, but it does guarantee to meet the full demonstrated need of every admit, and some 160 athletic scholarships draw male and female athletes of all stripes.

University-owned dorms, townhouses, and apartments accommodate two-thirds of students, and the university guarantees housing for three out of four years. All dorms are co-ed, and some have more activities and community than others. "All have great amenities like Ethernet and landscaping," says one student. Two dining halls serve "passable" food, but the popular student-run coffee shop offers more palatable options. Although D.C. has a high crime rate, GU students feel relatively safe on campus thanks to the school's ever-present Department of Public Safety and its walking and riding after-dark escort services. "The campus feels very safe. We are also in a self-contained community, so much of the D.C. crime stays out," an underclassman says.

Jesuits, who know a thing or two about secret societies, frown upon fraternities or sororities at their colleges, and so there are none at Georgetown. The university's strict enforcement of the twenty-one-year-old drinking age has led to a somewhat decentralized social life, which is not necessarily a bad thing. Alcohol is forbidden in undergrad dorms, and all parties must be registered. The dozens of bars, nightclubs, and restaurants in Georgetown—Martin's Tavern and the Tombs are always popular—are a big draw for students who are legal, but they can get pricey. The Hoyas, a campus pub in the spectacular student activity center, is a more affordable alternative. Popular annual formals such as the Diplomatic and the Blue/Gray Ball force students to dress up and pair off.

Washington offers unsurpassed cultural resources, ranging from the museums of the Smithsonian to the Kennedy Center. "We have all the opportunities of Washington, D.C., without the city streets cutting through our campus," says a biochemistry major. "Georgetown's location and its student body are its greatest assets." And given the city's excellent public transit system and the absence of on-campus parking, a car is probably more trouble than it's worth.

And speaking of Hoya basketball, should you notice the hills begin to tremble with a deep, resounding, primitive chant—"Hoya...Saxa...Hoya...Saxa"—don't worry; it's just another Georgetown basketball game. Their mascot, the Hoya, is derived from the Greek and Latin phrase, "hoya saxa" which means, "what rocks!" Some say it originated in a cheer referring to the stones that comprised the school's outer walls. The Hoya team is always tough, especially when Syracuse, Villanova, or UConn come to town, and GU often figures prominently in the NCAA postseason tournament in March. The thrill of victory in intramural competition at the superb underground Yates Memorial Field House is not to be missed, either.

For anyone interested in discovering the world, Georgetown offers an outstanding menu of choices. Professors truly pay attention to their undergrads and the diverse students who are "hard-working, diligent, caring individuals," says one sophomore. "Georgetown is a place where students of all backgrounds, all traditions, and all faiths come together for a common purpose of educating each other and making an impact on the world."

Overlaps

Boston College, University of Pennsylvania, Harvard, George Washington, NYU

If You Apply To >

Georgetown: Early action: Nov. 1. Regular admissions: Jun. 1. Financial aid: Feb. 1. No campus interviews. Alumni interviews: required, evaluative. SATs or ACTs: required. SAT IIs: recommended. Apply to particular schools or programs. Essay question: personal statement plus one additional question for each school.

University of Georgia

212 Terrell Hall, Athens, GA 30602-1633

What a difference free tuition makes. Top in-state students now choose UGA over highly selective private universities. Business and social sciences head the list of strong and sought-after programs. The college town of Athens boasts great nightlife and is within easy reach of Atlanta.

Website: www.uga.edu
Location: Small city
Total Enrollment: 32,941
Undergraduates: 24,983
Male/Female: 44/56
SAT Ranges: V 550–650
　M 560–650
ACT Range: 24–29
Financial Aid: 22%
Expense: Pub $ $
Phi Beta Kappa: Yes
Applicants: 12,786
Accepted: 65%
Enrolled: 52%
Grad in 6 Years: 70%
Returning Freshmen: 93%
Academics: ✎ ✎ ✎
Social: ☎ ☎ ☎ ☎ ☎
Q of L: ★ ★ ★
Admissions: (706) 542-2112
Email Address: undergrad@
　admissions.uga.edu

Strongest Programs:
Life Sciences
Ecology
Environmental Studies
Agriculture
International and Public Affairs
Business
Education
Journalism

The University of Georgia is a rapidly rising star that shines among the country's public universities. As recently as a decade ago, it was known primarily for its dynamite football team—a sleepy party school that would readily accept virtually anyone with a high-school diploma and a pulse. But Georgia's Hope Scholarship program, which pays tuition and fees for state residents with at least a B average, has turned UGA into a highly selective flagship public university that is able to pick and choose from among the region's best high school seniors. "Getting into UGA has gotten much more difficult," confirms a junior. The average SAT score and grade point average for entering freshmen has soared, and the university has moved aggressively to provide programs to challenge its new and brainier breed of students.

Situated on 706 acres, Georgia's attractive campus is speckled with greenery and wooded walks. The older north campus, which houses the administrative offices and law school, features nineteenth-century architecture and landscaping while more modern buildings and residence halls are found on the southern end of campus. Founded in 1785, Georgia is the nation's first chartered state university. The list of newer facilities includes a $43 million student learning center with an electronic library, a $34 million home for the Complex Carbohydrate Research Center with specialized labs, a $40 million Biomedical and Health Sciences Center, and four new residence halls.

Despite great strides toward improving education, some undergraduates still take a low-key approach to the life of the mind. Many of the toughest academic requirements are found in premedical, preveterinary, and other preprofessional concentrations, as well as in the highly regarded honors program. UGA's strongest programs include business (especially accounting and management), education, journalism, law, studio art, ecology, and genetics. Majors in international affairs, biochemical engineering, computer systems engineering, environmental engineering and environmental chemistry are among the recent additions to UGA's undergraduate program, and the school is investing more and more in the life sciences. The core curriculum requires students to complete forty-two semester hours in humanities and fine arts, English, science, mathematics, technology, social sciences, environmental literacy, and four to five hours of electives. Freshmen can spend a

"The students are incredibly friendly, outgoing, fun-loving, and overall well-rounded."

month on campus before the semester begins to become familiar with the campus and meet their new classmates, and even earn six hours of credit. Freshmen also have small seminars with senior faculty during the year, and Dawg Camp brings incoming students together in the summer for a weekend retreat.

The faculty at the University of Georgia receives high marks from the students. "All of my professors have been interested in their subject, fairly enthusiastic, and always knowledgeable," says a junior English and psychology major. "They are also very approachable." Registration for classes has been significantly simplified by a computerized registration system. First pick for all courses usually goes to honors students and varsity athletes, and the rest follow by seniority. The Center for Undergraduate

Research allows students to take research courses and conduct a research or service project, write a thesis, or develop a creative work. About 15 percent of students study abroad, using more than seventy-five programs offered in more than thirty countries.

The student body is overwhelmingly Georgian (90 percent) and 66 percent are public school graduates. "The students are incredibly friendly, outgoing, fun-loving, and overall well-rounded," says a junior. Many belong to the five-hundred-plus campus organizations. African-Americans account for 5 percent of the students, and Hispanics and Asian-Americans combine for 6 percent. Despite the lack of much cultural diversity, students say there's a wealth of political diversity, as evidenced by antiwar protesters. Georgia makes its admissions decisions without regard to student financial need. The school does not guarantee to meet the demonstrated need of every admit, but 45 percent of enrolled students are offered complete financial aid packages. Most in-state freshmen receive the Georgia Hope Scholarship, which covers tuition, books, and most fees (although benefits are being trimmed and academic requirements raised because of budget problems). Up to one hundred of the top undergraduates participate in the Foundation Fellows program, which provides a full scholarship plus international travel and research.

Tales of miscreant air-conditioning and elevators in some regular dorms often lure freshmen to the high-rise variety, where they find the smallest rooms on campus. Most upperclassmen prefer the roomier low-rise dorms, if they haven't already moved off campus. Only 17 percent live on campus, but expect that to change with the addition of new beds. One student says, "Housing is OK, but it could be better as far as being newer or nicer." Students aren't required to buy one of the two meal plans (for five or seven days a week), but most do. There are four dining halls plus the student union's snack bar.

On-campus activities are numerous. "Social life at UGA was a huge draw" recalls one junior. Downtown Athens—a well-known spot on the national rock map, having spawned such hit groups as R.E.M. and the B-52's—borders the university and provides bus service and an abundance of diversions. "We have

> "We have the best college town in the country! I think it is one of the best parts about going to UGA."

the best college town in the country! I think it is one of the best parts about going to UGA," says a junior. One nightclub enthusiast notes that many of the clubs in Athens cater to UGA students and admit those who are under twenty-one as long as they get a stamp saying they can't drink. It is difficult but not impossible to obtain and enjoy alcohol on campus.

Georgia's thirty-two fraternities and twenty-two sororities provide much of the social activity, though a campus policy banning open parties has put a damper on things. Only 16 percent of the men and 19 percent of the women go Greek, but almost everyone attends at least a couple of Greek bashes each year. Atlanta is only an hour away, and Savannah and Myrtle Beach are other popular getaways. Students descend on Florida en masse twice a year: first for the Florida football game and then for spring break.

Athens residents worship UGA's perennially fierce football team, which won the Sugar Bowl in 2002. "During the fall, a lot of the social life is centered around football," explains a junior. Other sports have been impressive lately as well, though the 2003 men's basketball season was cut short due to an ethics scandal. The men's tennis team, women's swimming and diving, and women's gymnastics teams won the 2001 national championships, and women's softball brought home a conference championship in 2003. The university has everything the weekend jock could want, including indoor and outdoor tennis and swimming; handball, racquetball, and tennis courts; and a jogging and exercise trail. Athletic rivalries with Auburn, Florida, and Georgia Tech make the hairs stand up on the Bulldogs' necks.

Majors in international affairs, biochemical engineering, computer systems engineering, environmental engineering, and environmental chemistry are among the recent additions to UGA's undergraduate program, and the school is investing more and more in the life sciences.

Overlaps

Georgia Tech, Georgia Southern, Florida State, Emory, University of North Carolina

With nearly 25,000 undergraduates, UGA is not a school where students are coddled, and recent cuts in state funding mean that they are even less so. Hundreds of faculty and staff positions have gone unfilled, classes are larger and likely to be taught by teaching assistants, and students report difficulty getting into classes they want. Nevertheless, outstanding educational opportunities—including scientific research, international study, and a top-notch honors program—await serious students, while football games and live music may appeal to the more easy-going. "UGA is the quintessential college experience—excellent academics, gorgeous campus, never-ending social opportunities, great sports," says a junior. "This is always what I pictured college to be. I love it."

Georgia Institute of Technology

Atlanta, GA 30332-0320

As the South's premier technically oriented university, Ma Tech does not coddle her young. That means surviving in downtown Atlanta and fighting through a wall of graduate students to talk with your professors. Architecture and big-time sports supplement the engineering focus.

Website: www.gatech.edu
Location: City center
Total Enrollment: 16,481
Undergraduates: 11,456
Male/Female: 72/28
SAT Ranges: V 600–690
  M 650–740
Financial Aid: 31%
Expense: Pub $ $ $ $
Phi Beta Kappa: No
Applicants: 8,953
Accepted: 59%
Enrolled: 43%
Grad in 6 Years: 68%
Returning Freshmen: 91%
Academics: 🐿 🐿 🐿 🐿 🐿
Social: ☎ ☎
Q of L: ★ ★
Admissions: (404) 894-4154
Email Address: admissions@ gatech.edu

If you're looking for lazy days on the college green and hard-partying weekends, look elsewhere. You won't find those at Georgia Institute of Technology, the South's premier tech university. What you will find are challenging courses that prepare you for a high-paying job as an engineer, architect, or computer scientist. "Tech is tough," reasons a graduate student. "You have to want to be here." Still, even those who want to be here are happy to finally arrive at graduation day. What makes Tech a special place? "The fact that I survived it and got out with a degree," says a computer science major, only partially joking.

Located just off the interstate in Georgia's capital city, Tech's 330-acre campus includes seven residence halls, an aquatic center, a sports performance complex, and an amphitheater. Newer additions include Technology Square, which will house the Dupree College of Management, the Economic Development Institute, and the Center for Quality, Growth, and Regional Development. The $45 million student athletic center will include a pool with water slide, hot tub and sundeck, among other amenities. Ford Motor Company is helping to fund the new Environmental Science and Technology Building, just one of the $483 million in construction projects now underway.

> **"Tech is tough. You have to want to be here."**

Courses at Tech are "extremely rigorous," says a senior, at least in the sciences and engineering. "Grading on a curve creates hyper-competitive situations because your absolute grade is largely irrelevant—you just have to do better than most of the others." Strong programs include math and computer science—"it's hard to have a life and be a CS student," one major quips—as well as most types of engineering, especially electrical, computer, and mechanical. (Tech also offers materials, ceramic, chemical, and nuclear engineering.) The school does offer liberal arts, but a grad student says history, philosophy, and English aren't the reason why most students enroll. "International affairs, while it has some interesting classes, seems to be a haven for people that can't hack the engineering stuff," another student adds.

Aside from the technical fare, Tech's management college is becoming more popular, and its school of architecture has done pioneering work in historic preservation and energy conservation. (Among the architecture program's alumni are Michael Arad, whose winning design for the September 11 memorial in lower Manhattan was selected from a field of more than 5,200.) The new prelaw certificate is a boon to aspiring patent attorneys, as is the new minor in law, science, and technology. As most courses require computers, the school requires students to bring their own desktops or laptops. Regardless of major, students must complete nine semester hours of social sciences, eight hours each of math and science, six hours each of English and humanities and fine arts, and three hours each of computer science and U.S. or Georgia history.

As students move from those core and required courses to upper-level options within their majors, the quality of teaching improves. "It's absolutely horrible for things like freshman math classes," says a computer science major. "You're typically taught by TAs (grad students), maybe half of whom have even the slightest grasp of English. Things get better as you progress and get to know professors." That's because those professors are indeed exceptional; some have worked on projects such as the Star Wars missile-defense system and the space shuttle. Still, classes are big—18 percent of those taken by freshmen have more than one hundred students—and the problem is getting worse rather than better. Massive cuts in state aid have forced Tech to lay off faculty members, cut course offerings, and increase class sizes. "Students are generally stressed and tired," sighs a grad student. "Not working hard is not an option here."

In fact, Tech's demanding workload means it's common to spend five years getting your degree. There's also the frustrating course selection process: "Sleep through your registration time ticket, and you may blow your semester because you won't get into anything," warns a senior. Also contributing to delayed graduation dates is the popular co-op program, through which more than three thousand students earn money for their education while gaining on-the-job experience. Those eager to experience another culture or environment can tap into the courses and resources of the Atlanta Regional Consortium for Higher Education,* or choose Tech study abroad programs in Paris, London, Australia, or England's Oxford University. By graduation day, 70 percent of Tech students have jobs, and 17 percent are in to graduate or professional school.

"I love a good challenge, and Tech is perfect for that."

Nearly two-thirds of Georgia Tech's mostly male students come from Georgia, and most are too focused on school or their co-op jobs to care about politics, causes or any of the issues that get their peers riled up on nearby campuses. "There are a lot of left-brain types here—high on the introspection and thinking, low on the social skills," says a senior. And though they may be united in their pursuit of technical expertise, the campus is hardly homogenous: One in four Tech students is a racial minority, with African-Americans accounting for 8 percent of the student body, Hispanics 3 percent, and Asian-Americans 14 percent. To limit burgeoning enrollment, out-of-state applicants must meet slightly higher criteria than their Georgia counterparts. The university awards 316 merit scholarships each year, ranging from $1,000 to $22,000, and 360 athletic scholarships.

Forty-seven percent of Tech students live in the dorms, where freshman are guaranteed a room. A senior says that despite the new construction and renovation that took place before 1996, when Tech was transformed into the Olympic Village,

(Continued)
Strongest Programs:
Engineering
Computer Science
Architecture

The $45 million student athletic center will include a pool with water slide, hot tub and sundeck, among other amenities. Ford Motor Company is helping fund the new Environmental Science and Technology Building, just one of the $483 million in construction projects now underway.

The new prelaw certificate is a boon to aspiring patent attorneys, as is the new minor in law, science, and technology.

the quality of residence halls varies widely. "Some dorms are new, apartment-style, and nice," the student says. "Others are foul dungeons." Many dorms have full kitchen facilities, though, and while most halls are single-sex, visitation rules are lenient. Off-campus housing is generally comfortable, but parts of the surrounding neighborhood are unsavory. "Far too many cars are broken into or stolen," says one student. "There's usually a couple of armed robberies (at least) a semester." The campus dining halls offer "little variety and less quality," according to another student.

Fortunately, even if mystery meat is on the day's menu at Tech, the school is smack-dab in the middle of "Hot-Lanta," with its endless supply of clubs, bars, movie theaters, restaurants, shopping and museums, both in midtown Atlanta and the Buckhead district. "Atlanta is not a college town," reasons a computer science major. "However, it is the best thing going in Georgia," with friendly, young residents, good cultural activities, beautiful green spaces, and a booming economy. The city also offers plenty of community service opportunities. Fraternities draw 23 percent of Tech's men and 22 percent of the women, and members may live in their chapter houses. Alcohol flows freely at frat parties, but otherwise, students say, Tech's policies against open containers and underage drinking are strictly enforced. "There's not much in the way of social life here outside of the frats," says a senior. "You have your group of friends and you do your own thing." The best road trips include Florida's beaches, which are a half-day's drive, and Athens, Georgia, for basketball or football games against the University of Georgia.

Tech's varsity sports have become as big-time as any in the South, and when the weekend comes, students throw off their lab coats and pocket protectors and become wild members of the "Rambling Wreck from Georgia Tech." In the past two years, fifteen of seventeen Tech varsity teams have qualified for postseason play, and the men's golf, women's softball, and women's indoor track teams have brought home conference championships. Among Tech's many other traditions are "stealing the T," in which students try to remove the huge yellow letter "T" from the tower on the administration building, and return it to the school by presenting it to a member of the faculty or administration. The addition of alarms, motion sensors, and heat sensors on the T has made the task more difficult, but "certainly not impossible for a Georgia Tech engineer," says an electrical engineering major. And then there's the Mini 500, a fifteen-lap tricycle race around a parking garage with three pit stops, a tire change, and a driver rotation.

Forget fitting the mold; the engineers of Georgia Tech are proud to say they make it. Self-direction, ambition, and motivation will take you far here, as will dexterity with a graphing calculator and a fondness for highly complex software algorithms. And despite their complaints about the workload, the social life (or lack thereof) the safety of their surrounding neighborhood, and the impact of budget cuts, Tech students do have a soft spot for their school. Says one student, "I love a good challenge, and Tech is perfect for that."

Overlaps

University of Georgia, MIT, Virginia Tech, University of Florida, Duke

If You Apply To ➤

Georgia Tech: Regular admissions: Jan. 15. Financial aid: May 1. Housing: July 1. Does not guarantee to meet demonstrated need. No campus or alumni interviews. SATs or ACTs: required. SAT IIs: optional. Accepts the Common Application and electronic applications. Essay question: the personal experience that gave you the feeling of greatest achievement or satisfaction because of the challenges you met. Looks for high math and science aptitude.

Gettysburg College

300 North Washington Street, Gettysburg, PA 17325-1484

The college by the battlefield is strong in U.S. history—that's a given. The natural sciences and business are also popular, and political science majors enjoy good connections in D.C. and New York City. Students can also take courses down the road at Dickinson and Franklin and Marshall.

Mention the word "Gettysburg," and patriotic heart palpitations and echoes of the "Battle Hymn of the Republic" are likely to result. Whether the reference is to the Pennsylvania town steeped in Civil War history or the small, high-caliber college located in the famed battlefield's backyard, a certain pride and reverence are immediately evident. This feeling is not lost on students at Gettysburg College, who come to southeastern Pennsylvania to acquaint themselves with American history while gearing up for the future.

Situated in the midst of gently rolling hills, Gettysburg's two-hundred-acre campus is "a historical treasure," an eclectic assemblage of Georgian, Greek, Romanesque, Gothic Revival, and modern architecture, plus several styles not easily categorized. One campus building—Penn Hall—was actually used as a hospital during the Battle of Gettysburg. Rumor has it that ghostly soldiers can still be seen walking the grounds. The new, 86,000-square-foot Science Center provides a new home and state-of-the-art equipment for the sciences, and the departments of English and Asian studies have new facilities.

Indoors, the English department, home of the *Gettysburg Review*, is among the strongest at Gettysburg, as are the natural sciences, which are well endowed with state-of-the-art equipment. The fine psychology department offers opportunities for students to participate in faculty research. The management major is the most popular. Also popular, of course, is the excellent history department, which is bolstered by the school's nationally recognized and prestigious Civil War Institute. The library system boasts nearly 400,000 volumes, a library/learning resource center, and an online computer catalog search. "The best academic departments are those that both educate and allow students to grow academically and personally," a senior says. These include physics and classics.

> **"I'm constantly amazed that I get to learn from the brilliant people here and that they're so willing to talk with me outside of class."**

The small class sizes make for close student–faculty relationships. "Teachers are for the most part amazing," a junior says. "I'm constantly amazed that I get to learn from the brilliant people here and that they're so willing to talk with me outside of class." Advising draws praise from students. "Academic counseling here helped me through any speed bumps I might have encountered," says one happy undergrad. The academic honor code contributes to the atmosphere of community and mutual trust. The popular first-year seminars focus on particular topics such as "Why Do People Dance"; participants live in the same residence hall and are in the same first-year residential college program. Another popular program is the Area Studies Symposium, which focuses each year on a different region of the world and offers lectures and films for the whole campus in addition to academic credit for participating students. There are disciplinary programs such as environmental studies, Latin American studies, and biochemistry and molecular biology. Japanese studies and anthropology are the two newest majors, and minors are now offered in neuroscience and peace studies. Bachelors of science degrees are also available in the health and exercise sciences and environmental studies programs.

Website: www.gettysburg.edu
Location: Small town
Total Enrollment: 2,597
Undergraduates: 2,597
Male/Female: 54/52
SAT Ranges: V 600–670
  M 600–670
Financial Aid: 61%
Expense: Pr $ $ $ $
Phi Beta Kappa: Yes
Applicants: 5,017
Accepted: 46%
Enrolled: 30%
Grad in 6 Years: 77%
Returning Freshmen: 92%
Academics: ✍ ✍ ✍ ½
Social: ☎ ☎ ☎
Q of L: ★ ★ ★
Admissions: (717) 337-6100
Email Address:
  admiss@gettysburg.edu

Strongest Programs:
English
History
Psychology
Natural Sciences
Business
Political Science

Gettysburg sponsors a Washington semester with American University, a United Nations semester through Drew University in New Jersey, and cooperative dual degree programs in engineering and forestry. Most departments offer structured internships, and the chemistry department offers a summer cooperative research program between students and professors in which most majors participate and work on a joint publication. Through the Central Pennsylvania Consortium, students may take courses at two nearby colleges—Dickinson and Franklin and Marshall. Outstanding seniors may participate in the Senior Scholar's Seminar, with independent study on a major contemporary issue, but all students have a chance to do independent work and/or design their own majors. Study abroad programs are global and popular with more than half of the students taking part during their college career.

The student body is 91 percent white and mostly middle- to upper-middle-class. Terrorism and the war in Iraq led to campus-wide discussions. "We are all socially conscious people and active members of the wider state, federal, and world communities who strive for a balance of liberty and equality for all," a philosophy major says. Though the administration is trying to lure more minorities with activities sponsored by the Intercultural Advancement Division, African-American, Asian-American, and Hispanic enrollment accounts for just 8 percent of the student body. Students are so interested in public service that the school set up a Center for Public Service to direct their community activities. Seventy percent of the students come from public high school and nearly two-thirds were in the top tenth of their high school class. No athletic scholarships are available, but academic scholarships run from $7,500 to $12,500.

Campus housing is guaranteed all four years, and students can choose from apartment-style residence halls, special interest halls, and the Quarry Suites. The top scholars in each class get first crack at the best rooms. Student rooms have been added in renovated historical properties (some reputed to be haunted) on campus,

"We are all socially conscious people and active members of the wider state, federal, and world communities."

and there are more options for interest housing and suite living. Off-campus apartments lure 8 percent of the student body while freshmen are required to remain in the residence halls. There are a variety of dining options, including the ever popular Cafe 101, the campus snack bar and grill room where many students take their regular meals. Kitchens are also available in the residences for upperclassmen.

Social life at the 'Burg involves the Greek system and other activities. Forty-four percent of the men belong to the dozen fraternities; the seven sororities draw 26 percent of the women. Greek parties are open and attract crowds eager to dance the night away, although students insist they're not the only source of fun on campus. A Student Activities Committee provides alternative social events, including concerts, comedians, bus trips to Georgetown, movies, and campus coffeehouses. Favorable reviews have come in for the Attic, an on-campus nightclub. Those who get the munchies can make the short walk to the Lincoln Diner or take a brief road trip to Stavros, a locally famous pizza parlor. Officially the campus is dry, but like many such campuses, drinking can be done, albeit carefully, students report. The orchards and rolling countryside surrounding the campus are peaceful and scenic, and there is a small ski slope nearby. Students also get free passes to the historic attractions in town. Many participate in the November 19 Fortenbaugh Lecture by noted historians commemorating the Gettysburg Address and in the yearly wreath-laying ceremony in front of the Eisenhower Admissions Office to commemorate the general's birthday. Tourist season is a common complaint among students. But those who want to escape can do so—the campus is within an hour and a half of Washington, D.C., and considerably closer to Baltimore, where students enjoy the scenic Inner Harbor area.

About a quarter of Gettysburg's students earn varsity letters, and the college boasts a strong athletic program. Thirty-seven teams have gone to the Division III playoffs over the past five years. The annual football game against Dickinson draws a good turnout, and the Little Brown Bucket, mahogany with silver handles, is passed to the team that wins. Both track and swimming frequently produce All-Americans. The college is a ten-time winner of the President's Cup, awarded to the top overall athletic program in the Centennial Conference.

At Gettysburg, students stay true to their slogan: "Work Hard, Play Smart." "Gettysburg is a challenging institution that delivers students the necessary tools to succeed," a political science/sociology major says. Students wanting personal attention from professors, solid academics, and an area rich with history might consider getting their education with a Gettysburg address.

Overlaps

Dickinson, Bucknell, Franklin and Marshall, Lafayette, Muhlenberg

If You Apply To ➤

Gettysburg: Early decision, regular admissions and financial aid: Feb. 15. Guarantees to meet demonstrated need. Campus interviews: strongly recommended, informational. No alumni interviews. SATs or ACTs: required. SAT IIs: optional. Accept Common Application and electronic applications. Essay question: Common Application questions.

Gordon College

255 Grapevine Road, Wenham, MA 01984

Gordon is the most prominent evangelical Christian college in New England and competes nationally with Wheaton (IL) and Calvin. Not quite in the Boston area, but close enough.

Christian values color almost all aspects of life at this Evangelical school where faith and spirituality are actually required classes. But while Gordon emphasizes moderation in life, it certainly doesn't skimp when it comes to its liberal arts education. The college is always evolving, sharpening its offerings across the board from neuroscience to music education. The students revel in the atmosphere. "We are interested in Christian community and don't worry about fashion or 'high society,'" says one chemistry major. "We emphasize comfort and being real with our peers."

Gordon is located on Massachusetts's scenic North Shore, three miles from the Atlantic Coast and twenty-five miles from Boston. The campus sits on hundreds of forested acres with five lakes. Academic buildings and dorms are clustered in one small section, so it doesn't take more than two or three minutes to walk anywhere on campus. Most structures are Georgian-influenced traditional redbrick, except for the old stone mansion that houses administration and faculty offices. The college has just finished its third new residence hall in five years; this one is located on a rocky rise near the school's main entrance.

Because religious commitment is seen as an enhancement to, not a threat against, serious academic inquiry, Gordon's core curriculum includes forty-six hours of instruction distributed among religion, the fine arts, humanities, social and behavioral sciences, natural sciences, math, and computer science. Freshmen also take a first-year "Christianity, Character, and Community" seminar to help them learn how to integrate faith into their academic experience. The conservative John Templeton

> **"We are interested in Christian community and don't worry about fashion or 'high society.'"**

Website: www.gordon.edu
Location: Suburban
Total Enrollment: 1,701
Undergraduates: 1,631
Male/Female: 36/64
SAT Ranges: V 580–640
   M 540–650
ACT Range: N/A
Financial Aid: 96%
Expense: Pr $
Phi Beta Kappa: No
Applicants: 1,100
Accepted: 74%
Enrolled: 49%
Grad in 6 Years: 65%
Returning Freshmen: 87%
Academics: ✍ ✍ ✍
Social: ☎ ☎
Q of L: ★ ★ ★ ★
Admissions: (800) 343-1379
Email Address: admissions@ hope.gordon.edu

Foundation has recognized the program for its academic excellence and character-building ability. The most popular major is philosophy, religion, and theology, followed by education, social science, the arts, and communication. There are no easy passes at Gordon. "Recreation and leisure sounded like a joke major, but from what I hear, the courses are no joke. They are actually challenging," reports a junior. Some students complain that some of the science departments, such as chemistry and physics, lack modern equipment.

Gordon's faculty receives high marks; a history major calls the quality of teaching "impeccable." One freshman says, "The faculty are thrilled when a student comes to them with a question." Off-campus opportunities include stints in Washington, D.C., for aspiring politicos, in Michigan for environmentalists, in Los Angeles for filmmakers, and trips abroad through the Council for Christian Colleges and Universities.* The college also has its own program in Orvieto, Italy, focused on the country's history, art, and language, and partners with programs around the world from Africa to England to Israel. Each year, about sixty-five students take cooperative-education jobs that offer work experience at high-tech firms, publishing houses, and service organizations in the area.

Gordon's core curriculum includes 46 hours of introduction to Christianity and the liberal arts. Freshmen also take a first-year "Christianity, Character, and Community" seminar to help them learn how to integrate faith into their academic experience.

> "Most of the students are white, middle-class, New Englanders."

Hard-working Christians come to Gordon from all over the U.S. seeking "a supportive environment without the strict rules of some Christian colleges," says a biology and Chinese studies major. Still, the regional diversity doesn't translate into ethnic diversity. "Most of the students are white, middle-class, New Englanders," says a sophomore. "Overall, they are open and very friendly, willing to help and cooperate in academics and campus endeavors." African-Americans constitute 1 percent of the campus, while Asian-Americans comprise 2 percent. Gordon students face the same campus issues as their peers at most colleges—homosexuality and tolerance, for example—but are required to sign a Statement of Faith promising acceptance of racial and gender equality, and moderation in behavior. "Abortion is a huge issue," says a junior. "Most of the campus leans Republican."

Eighty-six percent of Gordon students live in the co-ed dorms, where men and women live in separate wings of the same buildings—separated by a lobby, a lounge, and a laundry room. Persons of the opposite sex may traverse these barriers only at specified times. The administration is easing the housing crunch by going on a dorm-building spree. "Incoming students are able to request specific dorms and floors, a luxury that can cramp the plans of upperclassmen. The newest dorm, Wyland, opened in 2003. Permission to move off-campus is granted only after the dorms are filled.

Social life at Gordon is "nice and relaxing," says an economics major, though a business major complains it "needs more variety and participation." As drinking and smoking are forbidden on campus (and may result in suspension or expulsion), students focus on chapel services and Bible study outside of class. Those who are twenty-one or older may drink off campus, but are expected to do so responsibly. Other options include weekend excursions to Boston (twenty-five miles away by a five-minute walk to the T), the beach, church-related functions,

> "Most of the campus leans Republican."

When Wenham gets a bit small, students can hop the T into Boston or pile into a car and head to the beaches of Massachusetts's picturesque North Shore.

movies, and an occasional square dance. Everyone looks forward to homecoming, the Winter Ball formal (held in a castle), and the Last Blast spring party. Each year, the most popular guys in each class face off in the "hilarious" Golden Goose talent show, where the winner is crowned "Mr. Gordon."

For outdoorsy types, Gordon's setting on rugged Cape Ann is ideal, and it attracts its share of tourists. The campus has cross-country ski trails and ponds for swimming, canoeing, and skating. The ocean is a quick bike ride away, nice beaches are available on Cape Cod and in Maine, and students frequently ski New Hampshire's nearby White Mountains. Having a car is essential. Volunteering through prison ministry and in soup kitchens and local churches is popular, and missionary road trips take students to Tennessee, Florida, and Washington, D.C.

When it comes to sports, Gordon competes in NCAA Division III, and "a good portion of the student body comes out to the games" when the opponent is rival Endicott College, says a history major. Another adds: "The basketball games are standing-room-only when we play them." The women's soccer, men's and women's lacrosse, and volleyball teams all brought home the 2002 Commonwealth Coast Conference championships. Other popular sports are basketball and field hockey.

So the drunken toga parties are out—Gordon has no Greek system—and the dictates of the Bible are in. For many students, this is the perfect college environment. "Students who choose Gordon enjoy the strong spiritual atmosphere and close community offered to them," explains a freshman. Of course, the school can feel a bit small at times and escaping to Boston is often required to get that much-needed shot of city bustle. But those feelings don't rule the day. The college's drive for constant improvement "is attracting students of increasing caliber," a chemistry major says. "I think the school is working for recognition as a center for Christian scholarship and integration of faith and learning."

> ## Overlaps
> **Wheaton (IL), Messiah, Grove City, Houghton, Taylor**

> **If You Apply To ➤**
>
> **Gordon:** Early decision: Dec. 1. Rolling admissions: Mar. 1. Financial aid: Mar. 1. Meets demonstrated need of 12%. Campus interviews: required, evaluative. No alumni interviews. SATs: required. SAT IIs: optional. Accepts electronic applications. Essay question: Do you consider yourself a Christian?; Why a college like Gordon?; Your response to a meaningful educational experience or achievement, or a pressing issue in American life.

Goucher College

1021 Dulaney Valley Road, Towson, MD 21204

This is not your grandmother's Goucher. Once a staid women's college, Goucher has added men and a more progressive ambience, similar to places like Skidmore and Sarah Lawrence. Strategically located near Baltimore and not far from D.C., Goucher offers an excellent internship program.

Goucher is the kind of place where a student starts off with a dance class, then dashes to a lab to use a nuclear magnetic resonance spectrometer, and finally wraps up the afternoon chatting with a professor about studying abroad in Ghana. The constant intellectual nourishment will undoubtedly bear fruit, says one art major: "There are so many strong, independent personalities here. I just know they will make great contributions to our world."

Goucher, once a woman's college that went co-ed in 1987, has a long-standing history of excellence. Phi Beta Kappa established a chapter on campus only twenty years after the college was founded, and the college ranks among the nation's top fifty liberal arts colleges in turning out students destined for Ph.D.s in the sciences. Set on 287 landscaped acres in the suburbs of Baltimore, Goucher's wooded campus features lush lawns, stately fieldstone buildings, and rare trees and shrubs from all corners of the globe. New additions to the campus included an expanded alumni building and sixty-four-bed residential suite facility.

"There are great performance opportunities."

Website: www.goucher.edu
Location: Suburban
Total Enrollment: 2,102
Undergraduates: 1,270
Male/Female: 29/71
SAT Ranges: V 540–650
M 520–640
ACT Range: 22–28
Financial Aid: N/A
Expense: Pr $ $ $
Phi Beta Kappa: Yes
Applicants: 2,596
Accepted: 49%
Enrolled: 21%
Grad in 6 Years: 68%

The college received a Jesse Ball duPont grant to recruit minority faculty and students, as well as work on curriculum development and community outreach.

There's a host of student groups catering to specific slivers of the campus population: HOLA (Hispanic Organization for Learning and Awareness), Umoja-The African Alliance, B-GLAD (Bisexuals, Lesbians, and Straights for Diversity), and organizations for Asian and Pacific cultures, Jewish students, and those from the Middle East.

A rigorous general education program forms the foundation of every Goucher student's education. The core curriculum requires a first-year colloquium (Frontiers), one course in each of the humanities, social sciences, and mathematics, a lecture/lab course in the natural sciences, computer proficiency, a writing class, completion of the intermediate level of a foreign language, and two physical education courses. Of Goucher's offerings, the science department's are arguably the strongest, with a nuclear magnetic resonance spectrometer and scientific visualization lab available for student use. Other facilities include dedicated research space, a greenhouse, and an observatory with a six-inch refractor telescope. The dance department is especially strong. "There are great performance opportunities," says a junior. Administrators acknowledge that anthropology and cognitive studies are weaker than other majors.

An honors program offers special team-taught interdisciplinary seminars for participants from freshman through senior years. Interdisciplinary programs include international studies, peace studies, American studies, Judaic studies (in cooperation with Baltimore Hebrew University), and a program in theory, culture, and interpretation. There's also a German minor offered through Loyola College (MD), and a 4–1 program in international business ending with a Goucher B.A. and an M.A. with California's Monterey Institute of International Studies. Future engineers can take advantage of the 3–2 program offered in conjunction with the Whiting School of Engineering at Johns Hopkins University.

For those with wanderlust, Goucher sponsors working trips to numerous countries, including Israel, France, Spain, Ghana, and Germany, as well as an exchange program with a Ukrainian university. In addition, Goucher students may take courses at nearby Johns Hopkins and seven smaller area colleges. The campus library houses 280,000 volumes and draws complaints from some students, mainly because it closes at 6 p.m. on Saturdays. However, Goucher students have free access to the libraries at Hopkins and other nearby schools.

> **"Goucher has challenging academics without the competition."**

Faculty members here devote most of their time and energy to undergraduate teaching and have a good rapport with students. "The faculty are by far one of the 'selling points' of Goucher," says a theatre education major. "They are knowledgeable, experienced and well-spoken, and they really reach out and connect with students." Each freshman has a faculty advisor to assist with the academic and overall adjustment to college life, which are made easier by Goucher's trademark small classes and individual instruction. The top students strive for better, and many hold leadership roles. Another student says, "Goucher has challenging academics without the competition." In addition to their academic work, all Goucher students are required to do a three-credit internship or off-campus experience related to their major. Popular choices include congressional offices, museums, law firms, and newspapers. Another option is the three-week-long Public Policy Seminar in Washington, D.C., where students meet informally with political luminaries.

Thirty-five percent of Goucher's students are homegrown, and most of the rest hail from Pennsylvania, Virginia, New York, and New Jersey. African-Americans, Hispanics, and Asian-Americans together make up 10 percent of the student body. Diversity, one student says, "is discussed easily in the small Goucher community," and students agree that multiculturalism is an important campus issue. The administration hosts "campus conversations" with students, faculty, and the college president to discuss various subjects. One student complains that too many Goucher students are "liberals and feminists," while another says students are open-minded and accepting. "Many different views are represented at Goucher, and people are very accepting of others' opinions," a sophomore says. Goucher offers merit scholarships for those who are qualified, some providing full tuition, room, and board each year. And co-education seems to be working well; applications for recent classes have increased substantially, and enrollment is up. However, women still make up nearly three-quarters of the student body.

A new emphasis on global awareness requires students to fulfill a yearly requirement in international literacy, intercultural fluency, and ecological sustainability.

Goucher has four co-ed dormitories divided into thirteen residential units of about fifty students each. Sixty-two percent of students live on campus. Freshmen double up in spacious rooms, while upperclassmen select housing through lotteries; the available singles usually go to juniors and seniors, though a lucky sophomore may occasionally get one. While the freshman accommodations may be small, they are "pleasant and quite comfortable," reports a junior. The administration has been offering incentives to upperclassmen, encouraging them to move off campus to avoid a housing crunch; women who want an apartment closer to male-dominated Johns Hopkins can usually get one.

The social life on campus is improving, though it is often up to students to make their own fun. One student says, "Most people have small gatherings in their rooms instead of raging parties." Access to a car is a virtual necessity because many students travel to nearby universities (Loyola and Towson State) or Baltimore's Inner Harbor for entertainment. The CollTown Network, however, provides transportation to nearly twenty colleges in the area. Students who are of age frequent restaurants and bars in Towson, the small but bustling college town a five-minute walk away. Goucher has no sororities or fraternities, but the close-knit housing units hold periodic events, and the college hosts weekend movies, concerts, and lectures. Major annual social events include Rocktoberfest, Spring Fling, and the Blind Date Ball each fall ("It can be great, or your roommate can be dead at sunup," a junior quips). Biggest of all is GIG, Get-into-Goucher Day, when classes are canceled and the whole campus celebrates. Popular road trips include Ocean City, New York, Philadelphia, and Washington, D.C.

As Goucher was a women's college for so long, women's athletics are more highly developed than those at many co-ed schools. The women's lacrosse team is popular, along with men's basketball and lacrosse. The genteel sport of horseback riding is popular,

"Most people have small gatherings in their rooms instead of raging parties."

thanks to the indoor equestrian ring, stables, and beautiful wooded campus trails. Goucher also has several tennis courts, a driving range, practice fields, a swimming pool, and saunas.

Goucher is far from a stagnant place. Indeed, it is constantly rethinking its mission and redirecting its resources to broaden student experiences. With self-designed interdisciplinary majors, an emphasis on experiential learning, and several partnerships with other top schools, Goucher students find themselves sampling from a buffet of options. "Its intimate setting and small population has allowed me many opportunities I would not have otherwise sought out," says a junior. (And the guys don't seem to be a problem at all.)

Overlaps
Skidmore, University of Maryland, Towson, American

If You Apply To ➢

Goucher: Early action: Dec. 1. Regular admissions: Feb. 1. Financial aid: Feb. 15. Housing: May 1. Guarantees to meet demonstrated need. Campus interviews: recommended, informational. Alumni interviews: optional, informational. SATs or ACTs: required. SAT IIs: optional. Accepts the Common Application. Essay questions: significant experience or achievement; personal, local, national, or international issue and why it is important to you; significant person; topic of own choosing.

Iowa cornfields provide a surreal backdrop for Grinnell's funky, progressive, and talented student body. At just under fifteen hundred students, Grinnell is half the size of Oberlin. That translates into tiny classes and tutorials of thirteen students or fewer. Grinnell's biggest challenge is simply getting prospective students to the campus.

Website: www.grinnell.edu
Location: Small town
Total Enrollment: 1,485
Undergraduates: 1,485
Male/Female: 45/55
SAT Ranges: V 630–730
  M 620–710
ACT Range: 28–31
Financial Aid: 58%
Expense: Pr $ $ $
Phi Beta Kappa: Yes
Applicants: 2,067
Accepted: 65%
Enrolled: 28%
Grad in 6 Years: 84%
Returning Freshmen: 91%
Academics: ✑ ✑ ✑ ✑ ½
Social: ☎ ☎
Q of L: ★ ★ ★
Admissions: (641) 269-3600
Email Address:
  askgrin@grinnell.edu

Strongest Programs:
Foreign Languages
Biology
Chemistry
History
English
Political Science
Religious Studies

"Go West, young man, go West," Horace Greeley said to Josiah B. Grinnell in 1846. The result of Grinnell's wanderings into the rural cornfields, fifty-five miles from Des Moines and sixty miles from Iowa City, is the remarkable college that bears his name, and is second only to Carleton as the best liberal arts college in the Midwest. Despite its physical isolation, Grinnell is a powerhouse on the national scene. Ever progressive, it was the first college west of the Mississippi to admit African-Americans and women, and the first in the country to establish an undergraduate political science department. It was once a stop on the Underground Railroad, and its graduates include Harry Hopkins, architect of the New Deal, and Robert Noyce, inventor of the integrated circuit, two people who did as much as anyone to change the face of American society in the twentieth century.

The school's 108-acre campus is an attractive blend of collegiate Gothic and modern Bauhaus academic buildings and Prairie-style houses. (Architecture buffs should take note of the dazzling Louis Sullivan bank facade just off campus.) The Noyce Science Center, a technological showpiece, recently underwent a $15.3 million renovation, and a 75,000-square-foot addition to the Fine Arts Center—including gallery, studio, performing, and rehearsal space—has been completed. New dorms are in the works.

> **"All courses are rigorous—it's just on a scale of rigorous to more rigorous."**

True to its liberal arts focus, Grinnell mandates a first-semester writing tutorial, modeled after Oxford University's program, but doesn't require anything else. The more than thirty tutorials, limited to thirteen students each, help enhance critical thinking, research, writing, and discussion skills, and allow first-year students to work individually with professors. When it comes to declaring a major, students determine their own course of study with help from faculty. Strong departments include the natural sciences and foreign languages, including German and Russian, bolstered by an influx of research grants, including one from the National Science Foundation. Beware of language courses if you aren't planning to major in the field, though: "I took an intermediate class in Spanish first semester freshman year, and I spent three hours in class as well as about eight hours outside of class on homework, and two hours in Spanish lab," says a drained sophomore. The chemistry department (including a newer biological chemistry major) draws majors with independent research projects, and English, anthropology, sociology, and economics are popular, too.

Grinnell's standards are high—91 percent of students were in the top quarter of their high school class—and 30 percent of graduates move on to graduate and professional schools. Students who don't mind studying, even on weekends, will be happiest here. "All courses are rigorous—it's just on a scale of rigorous to more rigorous," says a senior. Adds a sophomore: "Even the art classes are demanding." During finals, perhaps to help ease the stress, costumed superheroes run around the library giving out candy, says a sociology major. Teaching is the top priority for Grinnell faculty members, and because the college awards no graduate degrees, there are no teaching assistants. "The profs act as responsible guides to our explorations of the texts," says an English major. "My current profs describe the expectations as difficult to meet, in that students expect magic in the classroom," reports a philosophy major.

Academic advising is also well-regarded, as students are assisted by the professor who leads their first-year tutorial, and then choose another faculty member in their major discipline: "Faculty really do take a great interest in the success of students inside and outside of the classroom," says a psychology major. It's rare to find classes with more than fifty students, and 88 percent of classes taken by freshmen have 25 or fewer. When campus becomes too stressful, students may study abroad in more than one hundred locations, through the Associated Colleges of the Midwest* consortium and Grinnell-in-London. Fifty percent of students spend some time away from campus, and financial aid extends to study abroad, administrators say, and there are opportunities for research across disciplines. Coops in architecture, business, law, and medicine, and 3–2 engineering programs are also available.

"There's a McDonald's in town now, so we can't claim to be that far outside of civilization, though most would like to."

Grinnell is a bit of Greenwich Village in corn country. Despite the rural environment, the college attracts an urban clientele, especially from the Chicago area. Only 13 percent are from Iowa, and 10 percent are foreign. "Students at Grinnell are very multitalented—athletes, musicians, actors, activists, writers, on and on," says a religious studies major. "I am amazed by the diversity of talent." The student body is 4 percent Hispanic, 4 percent Asian-American, 4 percent African-American, and 68 percent white. Women's rights, gay rights, labor rights, human rights, globalization, the environment, and groups such as PAFA (the Politically Active Feminist Alliance), GEAR (Grinnell Escalating AIDS Response), and Fearless (formed to combat gender-based violence) set the tone. Grinnell benefits from a hefty endowment, considering the school's size, thanks to portfolio managers who are among the best in the country.

The college guarantees four years of campus housing and 85 percent of students take advantage of the dorms, each of which has kitchen facilities, cable television, and a computer room. All but two dorms are co-ed, and after freshman year, students participate in a room draw, which can be stressful but usually works out. "Self-governance in the halls makes for tight communities," says a senior—as does some recent overcrowding, which has occasionally placed two students in a room designed for one. Students who move off campus, mostly seniors, live just across the street, and the smallness of campus means "you can't avoid embarrassing exes—ever," cautions a philosophy major. There are two dining halls, one on each side of campus, and meal plans range from full board to just dinner. Special family-style dinners are served every other Wednesday. Safety is a nonissue, quips a sophomore: "We live in a small town in the middle of Iowa!"

"Self-governance in the halls makes for tight communities."

That town, Grinnell (population 9,100), is "delightfully small," says a sophomore. "Everything you need is accessible by foot and within ten minutes (excepting Wal-Mart)." Still, a senior complains, "There's a McDonald's in town now, so we can't claim to be that far outside of civilization, though most would like to." Community service helps bridge the town–gown gap, with some students serving as tutors and student teachers at the local high school and others participating in mentoring programs and community meals, among other projects. Outdoor recreation is popular, and nearby Rock Creek State Park lends itself to biking, running, camping, kayaking, and cross-country skiing, as well as other pursuits sponsored by the Grinnell Outdoor Recreation Program, or GORP. There are a few bars and pizza joints downtown, but for those craving bright lights, Iowa City and Des Moines are

Fifty percent of students spend some time away from campus, and financial aid extends to study abroad, administrators say, and there are opportunities for research across disciplines.

Grinnell is a bit of Greenwich Village in corn country. Despite the rural environment, the college attracts an urban clientele, especially from the Chicago area.

within an hour's drive, and the college runs a shuttle service to them. Chicago and Minneapolis are each about four hours distant.

With no fraternities or sororities, intramurals and all-campus parties revolve mainly around the dorms. Each dorm periodically sponsors a party using wordplay from its name in the title. For instance, Mary B. James Hall puts on the Mary-Be-James party, for which everyone comes in drag. As for alcohol, a senior reports, "The policy is very relaxed." That said, there have been problems with excessive drinking and alcohol poisoning, leading to mandatory age identification and campus security supervision at all parties, explains a sophomore. "This is a pretty controlled drinking scene," adds a senior. "The policy is, don't have alcohol outside, don't drink underage, do take care of each other. As a self-governed institution, we pride ourselves on our community-oriented ways of addressing alcohol problems."

Nondrinkers need not sit home, however. Grinnell's social groups and activities range from the Society for Creative Anachronism and the Black Cultural Center to improvisational workshops, poetry readings, symposia, concerts, and movies— "You name it, it's all free to students," says a history and secondary education major. Highlights of the campus calendar include semiformal Winter and Spring Waltzes ("Yes, we really waltz"), where "most people wear formals and look very nice, not a common occurrence at a school where comfort is the usual standard and women rarely wear makeup," notes one student. At Disco, "everyone dresses up in clothes from the '70s and dances all night." Other noteworthy events include a band/tie-dyeing fest called Alice in Wonderland, Titular Head (a festival of five-minute student films), Pipe Cleaner Day ("May 5 generally brings upwards of twenty thousand of the sculptable wires to campus"), and the Zirkle Circle, described by a senior as "a spontaneous dance around a famous campus sculpture, usually after imbibing intoxicating liquids."

The Grinnell Pioneers compete in the Division III athletic conference, and the men's basketball team has won national attention for an unusual run-and-gun offense that uses waves of five players like hockey shifts in an effort to wear down opponents. The football and women's swimming teams attract the most athletes. Athletics aren't the focus here, though a senior does say the "honor G" letter on the uniforms of varsity athletes is "very cool."

Grinnell wouldn't put a grin on every prospective college student's face. "Most of us don't apologize for what at first turns people off about Grinnell," explains a senior. "We like being in the middle of Iowa, we like that you've probably never heard of us, we love that you won't come here because you want a big name." But there's no denying that Grinnell—a first-rate liberal arts college in the cornfields— is a real gem of a school.

Overlaps

Carleton, Macalester, Oberlin, Washington University (MO), Kenyon

If You Apply To ➤

Grinnell: Early decision: Nov. 20. Early action: Jan. 1. Regular admissions: Jan. 20. Financial aid: Feb. 1. Guarantees to meet demonstrated need. Campus interviews: recommended, evaluative. Alumni interviews: optional, informational. SATs or ACTs: required. SAT IIs: optional. Accepts the Common Application and electronic applications. Essay question: changed opinion; original essay on any subject (expository, fictional, or poetic, but descriptive of applicant's style and abilities); or why you favor a rural education.

5800 West Friendly Avenue, Greensboro, NC 27410

One of the few schools of Quaker heritage in the South. Emphasizes a collaborative approach and is among the most liberal institutions below the Mason-Dixon line. A kindred spirit to Earlham in Indiana. Guilford's signature program is justice and policy studies.

If you meet a student whose idea of a rousing road trip is protesting in Washington, D.C., you might be at Guilford. This generally left-leaning campus loves to debate just about any issue and get involved in the world around them. There's none of that college "bubble" that encompasses many other colleges. Instead, enrollment numbers are going up and the student body is becoming ever more diverse. "Intelligent, socially active, liberal students form the backbone of the school," says one senior, "but the Conservative Club is thriving." Founded in 1837 by the Religious Society of Friends (Quakers), Guilford is sticking to its original principles of inclusiveness as it constantly encourages its students to broaden their minds.

Located on 340 wooded acres in northwest Greensboro, Guilford's redbrick buildings are mainly in the Georgian style. The school is the only liberal arts college in the Southeast with Quaker roots, as well as the oldest coeducational institution in the South and the third oldest in the nation. During the Civil War, Guilford was one of a few Southern colleges that remained open—perhaps because it was also an embarkation point on the Underground Railroad. Newer additions include the Frank Family Science Center, with optical and radio telescopes.

In addition to their majors, Guilford students fulfill general education requirements in three areas: Foundations, Explorations, and Capstone. All students must also demonstrate quantitative literacy. Foundations consists of four skills and perspectives courses. The college has five areas of study—arts, business and policy, humanities, natural sciences and math, and social science—and the first set of Explorations courses provides academic breadth outside the area covered by a student's major and concentration. The second set of Explorations courses consists of three critical perspectives classes, one each from the categories of intercultural, social justice and environmental responsibility, and U.S. diversity. During the senior year, students take an interdisciplinary studies course to meet the Capstone requirement.

Students say Guilford's best programs include physics, religious studies, peace and conflict studies (owing to the Quaker influence), and political science. Newer majors include computer information systems, computing and information technology, health sciences, and forensic biology. Some students

"We have people with pink and blue hair."

avoid the highly regarded management program because they're "more interested in changing the world than doing business," says a political science major. One student says some of the literature classes can be "way out there," while on the other hand, another complains that some history profs are "narrow-minded." When it comes to teaching, Guilford has high standards—instruction should be "thorough, meaningful, applicable to real life, and most of all, interesting!" says a psychology and health sciences major. Students call professors by their first names and classes are generally more discussion-based than focused on the lecture-and-listen paradigm. The informality encourages tight bonds between profs and students. "Faculty here make the difference," says a psychology major. "They are unbelievably challenging but supportive, too." Guilford believes that experiential learning adds

Website: www.guilford.edu
Location: City outskirts
Total Enrollment: 1,800
Undergraduates: 1,800
Male/Female: 51/49
SAT Ranges: V 520–650
    M 520–620
ACT Range: 21–26
Financial Aid: 54%
Expense: Pr $
Phi Beta Kappa: No
Applicants: 1,650
Accepted: 69%
Enrolled: 28%
Grad in 6 Years: 72%
Returning Freshmen: 78%
Academics: ✍ ✍ ✍
Social: ☎ ☎
Q of L: ★ ★ ★ ★
Admissions: (800) 992-7759
Email Address:
    admission@guilford.edu

Strongest Programs:
Business Management
Education
English
Geology
Physics
Psychology

You are as likely to find a sporting event as you are to find a poetry slam at Guilford, where the student body is becoming more diverse by the year.

immeasurably to classroom work, so the college offers study abroad from China and Japan to Mexico, Germany, and France. In the summer, students may participate in a five-week seminar that includes hiking, camping, and geological and biological research in the Grand Canyon, or in a seminar on the East African rift, which includes a three-week trip to Africa.

Despite its small size, Guilford gives students the tools needed for groundbreaking work. Physics majors get professional-grade optics and robotics equipment, and students working on complex geology and chemistry projects have access to the Scientific Computation and Visualization Facility, with more than twenty Unix workstations for information-based modeling. Perhaps not surprisingly, Guilford publishes both the Journal of Undergraduate Mathematics and the Journal of Undergraduate Research in Physics. Wireless Internet connections are available in the Hege Library, where students may check out laptop computers from the circulation desk.

Guilford students are quite literally a colorful bunch, says a justice and policy studies major. "We have people with pink and blue hair," he says. "We have our share of hippies, and many athletes as well. Throw in the mix a couple of Republicans and some run-of-the-mill college students, and the result is a diversity of thought and conflict that makes Guilford an exciting place to spend four years." Students come from forty states, twenty-five countries, and a range of socioeconomic backgrounds; though most are liberal, there is a rising number of conservative students. "Political correctness is to an extreme here," says an art major. "Most students are concerned with hating Bush, saving the environment, and helping others." African-Americans comprise 12 percent of the student body, Hispanics 2 percent, and Asian-Americans 1 percent.

Ninety percent of students live in Guilford's dorms, which feature newer furniture and carpeting, big-screen TVs, remodeled kitchens, and upgraded heating and air-conditioning systems. One student says things only get fixed "if there is an emergency or you know the right people." On-campus apartments for juniors and seniors, are comparable in price to off-campus digs—a good thing, since getting permission to move off campus is tough. Bryan is the party dorm, and English (for men) and Shore (for women) are the single-sex quiet dorms. The female residents of

"Most students are concerned with hating Bush, saving the environment, and helping others."

Mary Hobbs, a co-op dorm built in 1907, do their own housekeeping in exchange for cheaper rent. Binford has a large freshman population and a substance-free floor that spawned a circus club. Food in the college cafeteria is awful, and unfortunately, students say, it's nearly impossible to opt out of the meal plan.

Guilford's social life revolves around various clubs and organizations, ranging from the Entrepreneur's Network and Strategic Games Society to Hillel and the African-American Cultural Society. "This is the place to find your niche!," says an economics major. No alcohol is allowed at college functions, but it remains pretty easy for underage students to drink—despite efforts to impose fines on those who are caught. Serendipity, a celebration of spring with games, mud wrestling, streakers, famed musicians such as the Violent Femmes, and "a sense of mass disorientation," is a cherished tradition. "If you love to drink and be loud, and throw chairs and trash cans off of balconies and buildings, then you will have a great time," says one student.

Beyond the campus gates, students find all of the essentials—Wal-Mart, some clubs in downtown Greensboro (only ten minutes away), the ethnic restaurants of Tate Street, and the college's Quaker Village, which has a $1 movie theater, pool hall, and a Starbucks. Getting off campus and back will be easier now that Guilford plans a free shuttle service, also stopping at some of the five other schools in the area, and running until 2 a.m. on weekends. Popular road trips include UNC–Chapel Hill (one hour), Asheville and the mountains (three-and-a-half hours), and the famous Outer Banks beaches (four hours).

Guilford's athletic teams compete as the "Fighting Quakers," and students love the oxymoron, as in their cheer: "Fight, fight, inner light! Kill, Quakers, kill!" Students root for the football team in the annual Soup Bowl against Greensboro College, while the men's golf team brought home the NCAA Division III national championship in 2002. The women's basketball team won conference championships in 2001 and 2002, and the women's rugby team plays in prom dresses once a year. Because of Guilford's emphasis on developing the whole person, physically, mentally, and spiritually, students are encouraged to participate in school-sponsored outdoor adventures, such as a ropes course, sailing, and white-water rafting.

"This is the place to find your niche!"

A popular Guilford mantra is "how are you going to change the world?" And with students who'd rather get involved than sit back and watch, you can expect some pretty passionate answers to that question. It all goes back to Guilford's traditional Quaker goal of "educating individuals not only to live, but to live well." As one student explains it, the college "supports me while allowing me to grow as a person." She then adds, in typical Guilford-speak: "It gives me the tools I need to make a change in the world when I leave."

Overlaps

Earlham, Goucher, Elon, Beloit, UNC–Chapel Hill

If You Apply To ➤

Guilford: Early action: Jan. 15. Regular admissions and financial aid: Mar. 1. Housing: Jun. 1. Does not guarantee to meet demonstrated need. Campus interviews: recommended, evaluative. Alumni interviews: optional, evaluative. SATs or ACTs: optional; personal portfolio or presentation may be substituted. SAT IIs: optional. Accepts the Common Application and electronic applications. Essay question: Use the quote "Nothing bears out in practice what it promises incipiently" to compare your experiences with another person's; relate the work of an admired or disliked artist, public figure, scientist, or writer to your own experiences; compare Palmer's concepts of "community" and "lifestyle enclave" to personal experience. Graded writing sample also required.

Gustavus Adolphus College

800 West College Avenue, St. Peter, MN 56082

A touch of Scandinavia in southern Minnesota, GA is a guardian of the tried and true in Lutheran education. With Minnesotans comprising three-quarters of the students, GA is less national than cross-state rival St. Olaf. Extensive distribution requirements include exploring values and moral reasoning.

The sidewalk running through the middle of the spacious Gustavus Adolphus College campus is nicknamed the "Hello Walk" because it's a tradition for students venturing down the path to greet one another—whether they've met or not. An emphatically Midwestern feel permeates the campus. "Students are laid-back, friendly, dedicated, and welcoming," says an English major. GA is named for Sweden's King Gustav II Adolph (1594–1632), who is credited with making Sweden a major European power and defending Lutheranism against the Catholics. While the king's battle victories earned him the title "Lion of the North," he was also an advocate of education and culture. Save for the women now attending classes, King Gustav would probably feel at home at the college that bears his name, where a not-so-subtle Swedish influence pervades everything from the buildings to the curriculum.

Website: www.gustavus.edu
Location: Small city
Total Enrollment: 2,509
Undergraduates: 2,509
Male/Female: 42/58
SAT Ranges: V 550–660
  M 540–670
ACT Range: 23–29
Financial Aid: 68%
Expense: Pr $ $

(Continued)

Phi Beta Kappa: Yes

Applicants: 2,203

Accepted: 77%

Enrolled: 39%

Grad in 6 Years: 80%

Returning Freshmen: 87%

Academics: 🖉 🖉 🖉

Social: ☎ ☎ ☎

Q of L: ★ ★ ★

Admissions: (507) 933-7676

Email Address:
admission@gustavus.edu

Strongest Programs:
Physics
Psychology
Classics
Spanish
Chemistry
Communications Studies

More than 70 percent of Gustavus students participate in community service projects ranging from elder friendships, Amigos and Big Partner/Little Partner, and after-school clubs.

The 330-acre GA campus is about sixty-five miles southwest of the Twin Cities. The campus architectural theme is, not surprisingly, Scandinavian, dominated by subdued, semi-modern to modern brown brick buildings. Highlights include the 113-year-old Victorian Old Main Building and the centrally located Christ Chapel, with spires and shafts resembling a crown. Thirty bronze works by sculptor-in-residence Paul Granlund are strategically placed, and the 130-acre Linnaeus Arboretum and Interpretive Center offers plant study and retreats. The campus boasts one thousand new trees and many new windows, carpets, computers, and roofs—all grim reminders of the March 1998 tornado that caused more than $60 million in damage. Students have clamored for more of the two apartment-style dorms that had to be built because the storm destroyed the college's oldest residence hall.

In the classroom, students will find an academic smorgasbord, as GA aims to offer an education both "interdisciplinary and international in perspective." Among more innovative programs, students may choose majors in Scandinavian studies, environmental studies, women's studies, or materials science—or they may design their own. GA's strongest programs include physics, chemistry, biology, classics, and communication studies. But "personal attention and small student numbers in less 'popular' majors such as environmental studies and religion allows students to get to know profs very well," a junior explains. Outside the classroom, learning opportunities come from several internationally renowned meetings held on campus each year, including the Nobel Conference, a two-day meeting of scientific experts from all over the world; the May Day peace conference, held the first Wednesday in May; and the International Festival, incorporating a diversity-focused conference called Building Bridges. One recent conference was titled "The Nature of Nurture."

To fulfill core requirements, Gustavus students have two options. Curriculum I includes twelve courses from seven areas of knowledge, plus a first-term seminar covering liberal arts skills such as critical thinking, writing, speaking, and recognizing and exploring values. Curriculum II is an integrated twelve-course sequence focused on related classic works from various disciplines. The sixty students who select this option—on a first-come, first-served basis—start with the first four courses in the liberal arts core: Historical Perspective I and II, The Biblical Tradition, and The Individual

"On campus you feel like you belong here, like you are an important asset and your presence and voice are making a greater Gustavus."

and Morality. In addition to the core courses, students must satisfy a "writing across the curriculum" requirement, with three courses that have a substantial amount of writing, and the first-term Values in Writing seminar, which explores questions of value while emphasizing critical thinking, writing, and speaking. Some new courses of study including criminal justice and women's studies.

Overall, academics at Gustavus are rigorous, but study groups are common. "Students want to do well, but are not willing to make others look bad in the process," says a classics major. Undergraduate research is a hallmark—despite the library's paltry 250,000 volumes—and Gustavus Adolphus students recently presented forty-two papers at the National Conference on Undergraduate Research, the third-highest total in the nation. That's not as surprising when you consider that each year, thirty-five freshmen are selected for the Partners in Scholarship program, which matches undergraduates with faculty research mentors and gives them annual grants of $7,500. For the professionally minded, Gustavus offers 3–2 engineering programs with the University of Minnesota and Minnesota State University Mankato.

When winter winds force almost everyone indoors during the January term, Gustavus students (known as Gusties) may take concentrated study on campus, or enjoy travel and co-op opportunities. Gustavus sponsors study abroad programs at five colleges and universities in Sweden, as well as in Japan, India, Malaysia, Australia, Russia, the Netherlands, and Scotland. About half the students study abroad. Back on campus, students find professors knowledgeable and friendly. "Professors' doors are open all the time, and some come back at night for office hours," raves a communications major.

For all its good points, though, this liberal arts college is hardly a model of diversity. In fact, the population is more reminiscent of Garrison Keillor's Lake Wobegon: 94 percent of students are white, 79 percent are Minnesotan, and about 55 percent are Lutheran. The school is trying to recruit more diverse students. The Greek system, the use of wind power, and U.S. politics are among the myriad issues and causes that occupy students' minds. "People are whiny about various things, but most of it is minor," says a biology and history major. One student says her biggest complaint is that "I want to be at three places at one time doing all the fun, free things Gustavus has to offer."

> "Students want to do well, but are not willing to make others look bad in the process."

Eighty percent of Gusties live in the dorms, and why not? The housing is guaranteed for four years, and have kitchenettes, twenty-four-hour computer labs, foosball tables, and free laundry machines (BYO detergent.) Substance-free floors are available, and smoking is prohibited in all residences. Norelius is exclusively for freshmen and sophomores, which helps them form friendships and encourages group activities. Two dorms with single rooms and apartment-style suites and some college-owned houses are exclusively for upperclassmen, who get priority at room draw. Juniors and seniors, and all students over twenty-one, may also request permission to live off campus.

Twenty-seven percent of the men and 22 percent of the women go Greek, but GA's social life is not centered around fraternities and sororities. More than 70 percent of Gustavus students participate in community service projects ranging from elder friendships, Amigos and Big Partner/Little Partner, and after-school clubs. There's a huge dining hall open from 7 a.m.–11 p.m. that offers everything from deli, grilled foods, pasta, Chinese, vegetarian fare, and the extremely popular Belgian waffles. There are always a ton of college-sponsored events, such as outdoor movies, concerts, and the annual Earth Jam outdoor concert. The multiple music ensembles all perform together at the Christmas in Christ Chapel concert, for which more than five thousand tickets are usually sold. The Dive is a popular on-campus dry bar, and the college offers periodic trips to Mankato—ten miles away—and to the Twin Cities, for shopping at the Mall of America and the Target headquarters, or a Minnesota Twins baseball game. "It gets to the point where there is almost too much to choose from," says an overwhelmed student.

> "On campus you feel like you belong here."

Because students twenty-one and older may drink in their rooms, with the door closed, underage students may easily get alcohol if they want it, but students say drinking isn't a popular pastime. The town of St. Peter, population 10,000, is quaint, but it has a great coffee shop and a hometown feel.

The GA football team has a loyal following, particularly in annual match-ups against St. Olaf, and that rivalry extends to men's swimming, which brought home a conference championship last year. Numerous GA teams participated in NCAA Division III national championship competition, with women's ice hockey and men's tennis placing third, and women's tennis and men's golf coming in fifth. When the men's basketball team made it to nationals for the first time in 2003, the school packed three coach buses with eager Gusties and drove them to the game—in Virginia, twenty-two hours away.

Though Gustavus is trying to keep up with the outside world by encouraging diversity and expanding its course offerings, perhaps what students like best about

When the college's basketball team made it to nationals for the first time in 2003, the school packed three coach buses with eager Gusties and drove them to the game—in Virginia, twenty-two hours away.

Overlaps

St. Olaf, University of Minnesota, University of St. Thomas, Luther, University of Wisconsin

this college is that some things don't change here. It's gorgeous in the spring, too cold in the winter, and warmhearted all year long. Small classes, one-on-one academic attention and a kickin' on-campus social life go a long way. "On campus you feel like you belong here," says a junior, "like you are an important asset and your presence and voice are making a greater Gustavus."

If You Apply To >

Gustavus Adolphus: Early action: Nov. 1. Rolling admissions and financial aid: Apr. 1. Housing: Jun. 1. Meets demonstrated need of 88%. Campus interviews: recommended, evaluative. Alumni interviews: optional, informational. SATs or ACTs: required. SAT IIs: optional. Accepts the Common Application and electronic applications. Essay question: significant experience; what you hope to gain from college; personal goals; or submit a writing sample from one of your classes.

Hamilton College

198 College Hill Road, Clinton, NY 13323

Hamilton is part of the network of elite, rural, Northeastern liberal arts colleges that extends from Colby in Maine through Middlebury and Williams to Colgate, about half-an-hour's drive to Hamilton's south. Hamilton is on the small side of this group and emphasizes close contact with faculty and a senior project requirement.

Website: www.hamilton.edu
Location: Rural
Total Enrollment: 1,851
Undergraduates: 1,851
Male/Female: 49/51
SAT Ranges: V 600–700
    M 610–700
Financial Aid: 54%
Expense: Pr $ $ $ $
Phi Beta Kappa: Yes
Applicants: 4,565
Accepted: 35%
Enrolled: 31%
Grad in 6 Years: 84%
Returning Freshmen: 93%
Academics: ✍ ✍ ✍ ✍ ½
Social: ☎ ☎ ☎ ☎
Q of L: ★ ★ ★
Admissions: (315) 859-4421
Email Address:
    admission@hamilton.edu

Strongest Programs:
Sciences
Social Science
Asian Studies

Back in 1978, Hamilton College seemed to have everything: money, prestige, and academic excellence. Everything, that is, except women. So, after 166 years of bachelorhood, Hamilton walked down the aisle with nearby Kirkland College, the artsy women's college founded under its auspices a decade before. The arrangement took some getting used to, but ultimately, it's been a success. Hamilton's student body is now evenly split between men and women, and students of both sexes benefit from the mix of old-boy tradition and right-brain flair. "You do have to sift through the stereotypical frat boys and sorority girls who popular the campus with their BMWs and clique mentality," sighs a government major. "Outside of those students are some truly interesting people, who are here to learn, meet new friends, and experience new things."

Set on a picturesque hilltop overlooking the tiny town of Clinton, the old Hamilton campus features collegiate Victorian architecture rendered in rich, warm brownstone. In fact, the only facility interrupting the rhythmic beauty of campus is the eyesore housing the library. By contrast, the adjacent Kirkland campus consists mostly of boxy concrete structures of a 1960s "brutalist" vintage, otherwise described as "faux I.M. Pei." Straddling the ravine that divides the campuses, joining them literally and figuratively, is a Student Activities Building with a diner, lounges, and areas for student and faculty relaxation. Surrounding the campuses are more than twelve hundred college-owned acres of woodlands, open fields, and glens, with trails for hiking or cross-country skiing. A new science building is slated to open this year.

In the classroom, Hamilton is pure liberal arts. Government, economics, and psychology are the most popular majors, and English is fifth on the list; computer science is fourth, showing the growing influence of techies here. Computer science students "seem to love the professors, especially because students and faculty interact in social settings regularly, and the professors are very qualified," say a junior. The student also cautions that despite the popularity of the economics major, the material is "very difficult" and "some professors do a poor job of explaining it."

Hamilton's Arthur Levitt Public Affairs Center, named for the former Securities and Exchange Commission chairman, is a working think tank where students can pursue research for local, regional, and state social-service groups and government agencies. A grant from the National Science Foundation helps send geology students to Antarctica for research each year, while Hamilton's rocky terrain provides fertile ground for those who remain. The nationally recognized physics department has been nominated for prestigious awards, though administrators say the rhetoric and communication department needs work.

> **"The smaller classes certainly demand more time and effort, because you cannot anonymously coast through."**

Hamilton overhauled its general education curriculum in the 2001–2002 school year to emphasize breadth and depth. Students are now required to take a total of four "proseminars" in their first and second years. These classes, limited to sixteen students each, focus on writing, speaking, discussion and intensive student–faculty interaction. Students must also pass three writing-intensive courses in the their first four semesters, and in the sophomore year, take an interdisciplinary seminar that culminates in an integrative project and public presentation. In fact, Hamilton is among a handful of schools requiring all seniors to produce an independent project in their area of concentration. Through this requirement, as many as seven outstanding seniors become Senior Fellows, letting them replace normal coursework with a project that culminates in a written thesis and a public lecture to the college community. Another interesting development is the administration's decision to let students choose which standardized tests to submit with their application for admission, including SAT I, the ACT, three SAT IIs, or three Advanced Placement (AP) or International Baccalaureate (IB) exams. Students may also select more than one type of test, so long as their portfolio includes an English test and a quantitative test, plus one other exam.

Academically, students say Hamilton is more laid-back than competitive, though a government major wants that "the smaller classes certainly demand more time and effort, because you cannot anonymously coast through." Three-quarters of the courses here have fewer than twenty students, and despite their size, you'll always find a professor at the lectern, not a teaching assistant. "The professors seem to embrace being at a small school, and provide the individual attention and abundant office hours that we expect," says a junior. Even with the intimate size of most classes, students report few problems getting needed courses, once they declare a major. (Electives are another thing entirely: "I've heard horror stories about people trying for two or three years to take drawing or photography," says one student.) When the

> **"The professors seem to embrace being at a small school, and provide the individual attention and abundant office hours that we expect."**

town of Clinton gets claustrophobic, students can spend a semester or year France, Spain, or China, or take a term in Washington, D.C.; about two-thirds of the students enroll. There are 3–2 programs in engineering with Columbia, Rensselaer Polytechnic Institute, and Washington University (MO), and a 3–3 program in law with Columbia.

Forty-two percent of Hamilton students are New York residents (most hail from downstate), and 60 percent were in the top 10 percent of their high school class. Most are social, outdoorsy, and fans of preppy clothing from L.L. Bean, J. Crew, and Abercrombie and Fitch. African-Americans and Hispanics each comprise almost 4 percent of the student body, and Asian-Americans add almost 5 percent. "Diversity is always an issue here," one student says. "There are some divides between minority students and the rest of the campus that have flared up over the past few years. But otherwise, students are pretty apathetic." Hamilton offers a few merit scholarships,

There are 3–2 programs in engineering with Columbia, Rensselaer Polytechnic Institute, and Washington University (MO), and a 3–3 program in law with Columbia.

of $5,000 to $10,000 each, but there are no athletic scholarships, as the school competes in Division III.

Ninety-six percent of the students reside on campus. Options range from old fraternity houses renovated and turned into dorms to stately mansions with posh amenities, and newer apartments, which accommodate three to four students each. All halls are co-ed and include residents from all four classes. "The dorms are decent, fairly well-maintained, although it differs, building to building," says a government major. "There is some really high-class housing for upperclassmen, but not enough of it." Smart students become resident assistants, which guarantees them a single and lets them bypass the hated lottery. The Hamilton side of campus is the place for party animals; Dunham gets cheers for being social, but some students liken it to a "dungeon." The Kirkland dorms have a more mellow reputation. Students may also choose to live in a co-ed cooperative house, or in houses that are substance free, smoke free, or quiet. A student food co-op offers opportunities to make your own chow, though the on-campus dining halls welcome student feedback and are trying to accommodate vegetarians.

Social life at Hamilton ranges from the campus pub, which occupies an old barn, to programming arranged by the campus activities board, such as comedy shows, a casino night, and concerts by big-name acts such as Blues Traveler, the Indigo Girls, and Barenaked Ladies. There's also the popular Greek system, which draws 34 percent of the men and 20 percent of the women, even though fraternities may not have on-campus houses. Clinton itself is "a very small town in a very rural area," says a junior. "The students definitely take over at night, although most of the town is shut down by then, unfortunately. Some students do get involved with the community, but Clinton–Hamilton relations have sometimes been rocky." Because there's relatively little to do, much of the social life does revolve around alcohol, one student says. "It's fairly easy for underage students to be served, although the college does crack down from time to time," the student explains. "This seems to drive people downtown, to the bars." The nearest small city, Utica, is only ten minutes away by car. Other popular road trips include Syracuse and New York City, while Boston, Toronto, and Montreal are all about five hours' drive.

> "There are some really great courses and professors that love what they do and show it, and who have had a great influence on me."

In athletics, Hamilton recently finished in the top twenty-five of the nearly four hundred colleges eligible for the Sears Cup, which recognizes overall athletic excellence. Men's basketball and men's lacrosse both scored UCAA championships and advanced to the NCAA Division III tournament. Hamilton has also started a very popular varsity crew team. School spirit often seems dormant (or maybe frozen?), but it comes out of hibernation at the annual Orange Bowl, where Hamilton students pelt the opposing goalie with oranges after the first goal of the first home hockey game. In football, a major event is the annual Rocking Chair Classic against Middlebury, where the winner keeps the chair. Class and Charter Day marks the last day of classes in the spring, with ceremonies, a picnic, and other festivities.

Hamilton students are, by necessity, hearty. They're used to the cold and the snow—and perhaps that's what leads to the strong sense of community evident on campus. "I know many of the people I pass when walking around," says a government major. "There are some really great courses and professors that love what they do and show it, and who have had a great influence on me." So much, indeed, for the battle of the sexes. As the Hamilton–Kirkland union proves, women may be from Venus and men from Mars, but with time, both sexes can find common ground.

Overlaps

Colgate, Colby, Bowdoin, Middlebury, Bates

Hamilton: Early decision: Nov. 15. Regular admissions: Jan. 1. Financial aid: Feb. 1. Guarantees to meet demonstrated need. Campus and alumni interviews: recommended, evaluative. SATs or ACTs: required. SAT IIs: recommended. (Students may also substitute three AP or IB exams, including one English, one quantitative, and one other.) Accepts the Common Application and electronic applications. Essay question: reasons for applying to Hamilton. Students must also submit a graded expository writing sample.

Hampden-Sydney College

P.O. Box 667, Hampden-Sydney, VA 23943

The last bastion of the Southern gentleman and one of two all-male colleges (without a coordinate women's college) in the nation. H-SC is a feeder school to the Virginia business economic establishment in Richmond. Picturesque rural setting evokes the old South.

Perhaps a bit of an anachronism in a society increasingly focused on diversity, all-male Hampton-Sydney College still aims to expose its small student body to a broad liberal arts education that is entirely focused on undergraduate success. H-SC is one of only two all-male colleges (without a coordinate women's college) in the nation. Tradition reigns here and students like to call themselves "Southern Gentlemen." Of course, there's plenty of fun to be had when you've got one thousand guys hanging around.

Hampden-Sydney's 660-acre campus, surrounded by farmland and woods, features mainly redbrick buildings in the Federal style. The nearby town of Farmville, population 6,600 and home to Longwood College, offers restaurants, stores, and a movie theater; it's just five miles from H-SC, but one student describes the town as "a black hole inside a time warp." Despite its lack of bright lights, the town does provide numerous community service and outreach opportunities. A campus volunteer group called Good Men, Good Citizens spearheads projects such as tutoring, highway clean-up, and Habitat for Humanity home-building.

Hampden-Sydney's most popular major is economics, which may help explain why more than half of the school's alumni have pursued business careers. The department offers concentrations, including managerial and mathematical concepts; instruction is "intensive," a junior says. History, English, and religion are also popular, and the rhetoric program has earned international recognition, administrators say. The Wilson Center for Leadership in the Public Interest puts a public-service focus on the study of political science, preparing students for government work and garnering high marks in return. The school's small size offers many opportunities to work closely with professors, but has some academic drawbacks, including few computer courses and fewer than thirty majors total. The fine arts program, with concentrations in music, theater, and visual arts, has begun emphasizing performance rather than the study of these disciplines, but it suffers from a lack of facilities and student interest.

> "When you come here, teachers challenge students to think deeper."

Students at Hampden-Sydney say they are no free passes when it comes to classwork. "The coursework is quite demanding," says an economics major. "It takes a lot of effort to make good grades and do really well." But as another student reports, "I am challenged, but not to the point of mental breakdown." To graduate, students must demonstrate proficiency in rhetoric and a foreign language, along with completing seven humanities courses, three in the social sciences, and four in

Website: www.hsc.edu
Location: Rural
Total Enrollment: 1,038
Undergraduates: 1,038
Male/Female: 100/0
SAT Ranges: V 510–620
  M 520–620
ACT Range: N/A
Financial Aid: 54%
Expense: Pr $ $
Phi Beta Kappa: Yes
Applicants: 1,028
Accepted: 71%
Enrolled: 29%
Grad in 6 Years: 61%
Returning Freshmen: 84%
Academics: ✍ ✍ ✍
Social: ☎ ☎ ☎ ☎
Q of L: ★ ★ ★ ★
Admissions: (800) 755-0733
Email Address:
  hsapp@hsc.edu

Strongest Programs:
Economics
Biology
Chemistry
Physics
English
Rhetoric

the natural sciences and mathematics. Classes are small; more than half have fewer than twenty-five students, and none have more than fifty. "Most courses require strict attendance," a history major says—after all, with a class of twelve or fourteen students, your presence or absence will certainly be felt. "It is not a cake walk," says a managerial economics major. "When you come here, teachers challenge students to think deeper." Most H-SC professors live on campus and encourage students to drop by their offices often. Some even make house calls to find out why a student missed class. "I have been invited to numerous dinners at professors' homes, and professors encourage us to contact them whenever we have a question, even if that means at nine o'clock on a Wednesday night," says a junior.

One thing you won't see a lot of at H-SC are students with long hair, body piercing, or much else that would not fit into a clean-cut profile. "Ninety-nine-point-nine percent of the students are conservative Republicans," one student says. "Left-wingers are seldom found here." Sixty-four percent of students are state

> **"I have been invited to numerous dinners at professors' homes, and professors encourage us to contact them whenever we have a question."**

residents, and 93 percent are white. African-Americans make up 4 percent of the student body, and Hispanics and Asian-Americans account for 1 percent each. "Political correctness is NOT an issue," says a political science major. The college has, however, added a director of intercultural affairs to help increase tolerance for diversity. As a Division III school, Hampden-Sydney offers no athletic scholarships. There are 168 merit awards, ranging from $3,000 to $18,000 a year.

Ninety-five percent of students live on campus, as housing is guaranteed for four years, and H-SC is renovating older residence halls with mostly single rooms to offer more apartment-style living. "The rooms—not all, however—are spacious and bright," says a psychology and music major. "There can be some trouble getting the room that a student wants, because everyone wants basically the same rooms." All rooms have Internet connections and cable. Cushing Hall, built in 1824, is the dorm of choice for first-year students, with "big rooms, excellent parties, and at least three ghosts."

Students praise the close-knit atmosphere fostered by Hampden-Sydney's all-male status. "Brotherhood amongst your peers" is what makes the place special, says a senior. One student reports that showering during the week is really optional: "We clean up on Fridays before the girls come." Men seeking members of the opposite sex can find them at four all-female schools nearby—Sweet Briar, Hollins, Mary Baldwin, and Randolph-Macon Woman's College. Those who make a love connection will be glad to know that H-SC's dorms have twenty-four-hour visitation. When rural Virginia gets too insular, H-SC students can be found on road trips to the University of Virginia and James Madison University, Virginia's beaches, or Washington, D.C. The ski slopes of Wintergreen are also within three hours' drive.

Hampden-Sydney's social nexus is the Circle, the site of eleven of the school's twelve fraternities, which claim 30 percent of the students. "Fraternities offer basically all of the entertainment," a history major says. Students under twenty-one

> **"Ninety-nine-point-nine percent of the students are conservative Republicans."**

can't drink, but where there's a will, there's a way. "To be honest, a three-year-old could drink here," reports one student. But campus security will crack down if students get wild. The annual spring Greek Week brings out the *Animal House* aspect of Hampden-Sydney's budding gentlemen. Homecoming and various music festivals are also eagerly anticipated.

Perhaps because of all that testosterone on campus, Hampden-Sydney men are competitive, and that spells excellence in athletics. Football is big; students attend games in coat and tie, and H-SC's football rivalry with Randolph-Macon (not the famed women's college!) is the oldest in the South. At the annual pre-game bonfire, the college rallies to sing songs and hear student and faculty leaders vilify the enemy and extol "the garnet and gray." While football has the most players, basketball draws the most spectators. The school's basketball, lacrosse, and soccer teams have recently won conference championships, and for weekend warriors, intramurals are available in seven sports.

So it's largely conservative and a bit homogenous. But Hampden-Sydney offers more than just a flat demographic profile. Two centuries of tradition and an incredibly tight-knit student body make for a rich undergraduate experience. "I like the small size because I don't feel like a number," a junior says. "And I have lived all my life in the big city. I kinda like being in the country." Of course, it's easy to counter all that profundity with some of the school's more popular sayings, such as this gem: "We don't need girls. We're doing just fine with yours."

If You Apply To ➤ | **Hampden-Sydney:** Early decision: Nov. 15. Early action: Jan. 15. Regular admissions and housing: Mar. 1. Financial aid: May 1. Does not guarantee to meet demonstrated need. Campus interviews: recommended, informational. No alumni interviews. SATs or ACTs: required. SAT IIs: recommended. Accepts the Common Application and electronic applications. Essay question: A prominent person you would interview; significant experience or achievement; why you have saved a personal object or item; experience with those of different race, background, or culture.

Hampshire College

P.O. Box 5001, Amherst, MA 01002-5001

Part of a posse of nonconformist colleges that includes Bard, Bennington, New School University, and Sarah Lawrence. Instead of conventional majors, students complete self-designed interdisciplinary concentrations and independent projects. Gains breadth and resources from the Five College Consortium.

Passion reigns at Hampshire College. It's found in just about everything students do—from devising their own courses to starting new clubs to debating the most current social issues. There's no one way to do things at Hampshire, and the students revel in the freedom they have to direct the path of their educations. "I am forced to choose between my interests but encouraged to combine them," says one student who, not surprisingly, is triple-majoring in theatre, social action, and women's studies. Without the yoke of traditional majors and the nail-biting stress of regular grades, Hampshire offers a virtually boundary-free exercise in intellectual nirvana.

Located in the Pioneer Valley of western Massachusetts, Hampshire's eight-hundred-acre campus sits amid former orchards, farmland, and forest. Buildings are eclectic and contemporary, and the school is most proud of its bio-shelter, arts village, and multisports and multimedia centers.

Instead of grades, Hampshire professors hand out "narrative evaluations," which consist of written evaluations and critiques. Degrees are obtained by passing a series of examinations—not tests, but portfolios of academic work, evaluations, and students' self-reflections on their academic development. The first hurdle, known as Division I, begins with project-based courses in each of five multidisciplinary schools: natural science; social science; cognitive science; interdisciplinary studies; and humanities, arts, and cultural studies. A typical test in Division I is a

Website: www.hampshire.edu
Location: City outskirts
Total Enrollment: 1,267
Undergraduates: 1,267
Male/Female: 42/58
SAT Ranges: V 600–700
   M 560–660
ACT Range: N/A
Financial Aid: 57%
Expense: Pr $ $ $ $
Phi Beta Kappa: No
Applicants: 2,483
Accepted: 54%
Enrolled: 34%
Grad in 6 Years: 58%
Returning Freshmen: 83%
Academics: ✐ ✐ ✐ ✐
Social: ☎ ☎ ☎

(Continued)

Q of L: ★ ★ ★
Admissions: (413) 559-5471
Email Address:
   admissions@hampshire.edu

Strongest Programs:
Film and Television
Photography
Environmental Studies
Communication
Cognitive Science
Creative Writing

Hampshire just changed its curriculum—independent first-year projects are now done as part of structured classes. There are no grades here, though. Instead, profs hand out "narrative evaluations," which consist of written evaluations and critiques.

single project or paper, two courses, or an experiment presented to one or two professors. Hampshire also recently changed its curriculum. There is a new first-year program that takes the required independent projects and moves them inside courses, where they are better supported by faculty.

The second hurdle, Division II, is each student's "concentration"—the rough equivalent of a major elsewhere. The concentration consists of individually designed courses, independent work, and often fieldwork or internships. Division III, or "advanced study," begins in the fourth year. Students are asked to complete a sizable independent study project centered on a specific topic,

"Challenging, empowering, liberating, in the sense that it allows students to study what they love."

question, or idea, much like a master's thesis. Because of the division system, there are as many curriculums at Hampshire as there are students; each individual must devise a viable, coherent program specific to himself or herself. Not surprisingly, competition is virtually nonexistent, and the academic climate is "challenging, empowering, liberating, in the sense that it allows students to study what they love," says a philosophy major. The common denominator is a heavy workload, an emphasis on self-initiated study, close contact with faculty advisors, and the assumption that students will eventually function as do graduate students at other institutions. "We Hampshire students will be the ones at a party talking about our exciting work," says a sophomore. (One popular campus T-shirt says Hampshire is "The Undergraduate Graduate School.")

Given the emphasis on close-working relationships with faculty and those "narrative evaluations," the importance of qualified, attentive faculty is not to be underestimated. Students at Hampshire heap praise on their professors. "The mentoring relationships I have formed with my professors will last well after I graduate," raves a literature major. The Hampshire academic year has fall and spring semesters, each four months long; an optional January term; and internships and other real-world experience are encouraged during all three. Despite Hampshire's entrepreneurial nature, a large percentage of grads do go on to graduate school, and many Hampshire students begin their own businesses in fields such as computer programming, construction, or film production.

Hampshire's flexibility is ideal for artists, and the departments of film and photography are dazzling, which is also the reason they are overcrowded. Communications, creative writing, and environmental studies are also good bets, and Hampshire was the first college in the nation to offer an undergraduate program in cognitive science. A popular program called Invention, Innovation, and Creativity exposes students to the independent reasoning and thinking essential to the process of inventing.

For courses in modern and classical languages, students must travel to another school in the Five College Consortium,* as Hampshire doesn't offer a full foreign language instruction. The school does, however, offer Yiddish. Although the school's library is a quiet and pleasant place to study, it has only 114,000 volumes.

"The mentoring relationships I have formed with my professors will last well after I graduate."

Still, if you count the library resources at all five institutions, students have ready access to more than eight million volumes. There is no extra cost to use the other schools' facilities or the buses that link them. And use them they do—Hampshire students take twelve hundred classes per year at the other schools.

Hampshire draws students from across the country who tend to be "free-loving, innovative-thinking scholars who challenge institutions and bureaucracy," says an English major. Another student reports that Hampshire students are "progressive, passionate, critical people who like barefoot picnics at sunset." For a school that's so focused on social issues, the minority community is relatively small—3 percent of students are African-American, 5 percent Hispanic, and 4 percent Asian-American—and most students would like to see these numbers rise. "Hampshire is very progressive, with many self-declared anarchists, Marxists, Greens and (a few) Libertarians," says an education major. The school is "100 percent politicized in every way," says a philosophy major. "'Political correctness' doesn't even begin to describe it."

First-year students live in co-ed dorms, about 20 percent in double rooms. Many single rooms are available for older students, who may move to one of more than one hundred "mods"—apartments in which groups of four to ten students share the responsibility for cleaning, cooking, and maintaining their space. "The dorms and apartments were quickly and cheaply built, and have problems," warns a senior. Special quarters are available for nonsmokers, vegetarians, and others with special preferences; it's not easy to move off campus.

On weekends, some students head for Boston, New York, Hartford, or, in season, the ski trails of Vermont and New Hampshire. But there are plenty of cultural resources within the Five College area, and the free buses to Amherst (the ultimate college town), Northampton, and South Hadley (all about twenty minutes away) are always crowded. From edgy record stores to ethnic restaurants and boutiques, the area abounds with diversions. The annual Spring Jam brings live bands to campus, and throughout the year there's almost always a party going on, including the drag ball and the much-anticipated Halloween bash—an intense, all-campus blowout complete with fireworks. A tradition called "Div

"Hampshire is very progressive, with many self-declared anarchists, Marxists, Greens and (a few) Libertarians."

Free Bell" celebrates the completion of Division III requirements—and graduation—with soon-to-be alumni ringing a bell outside the library, surrounded by friends.

Hampshire is no place for competitive jocks, since many sports are co-ed and primarily for entertainment (there never was a football team here). The school offers paid instructors in a handful of sports, but most students organize their own clubs (men's and women's soccer and basketball are the biggies, and there's also the competitive Red Scare Ultimate Frisbee Team) and intramural teams. The outdoors program offers mountain-biking, cross-country skiing, and kayaking; equipment may be borrowed for free. The school also has its own climbing wall and cave, a gym with solar-heated pool, and a co-ed sauna.

"Hampshire is where all the wacky and wonderful people reside," says a sophomore. There's a niche for every type of student, and even those pigeon holes are blown apart quite regularly. When you can make up your own education, and do it with great faculty and the option of studying at several other top-notch schools, there's little Hampshire students can't accomplish. "You set limits with yourself, and then push those limits and strive even higher," says one student, who adds: "This is the only place where I could see myself being happy."

Overlaps
Bard, Sarah Lawrence, NYU, Oberlin, Skidmore

If You Apply To ➤ **Hampshire:** Early decision: Nov. 15. Early action: Dec. 15. Regular admissions and financial aid: Feb. 1. Housing: May 1. Guarantees to meet demonstrated need. Campus and alumni interviews: recommended, informational. SATs or ACTs: optional. SAT IIs: optional. Accepts the Common Application and electronic applications. Essay questions: personal statement, and sample of academic work or persuasive critical essay on a complex issue.

Hartwick College

Oneonta, NY 13820

Hartwick is known for its cozy atmosphere and ability to take good care of students. Combines arts and sciences with a nursing program. The campus is beautiful but small-town upstate New York has proven to be a hard sell in recent years.

Website: www.hartwick.edu
Location: Small city
Total Enrollment: 1,400
Undergraduates: 1,400
Male/Female: 43/57
SAT Ranges: V 520–610
    M 510–620
Financial Aid: 78%
Expense: Pr $ $ $ $
Phi Beta Kappa: No
Applicants: 1,853
Accepted: 89%
Enrolled: 23%
Grad in 6 Years: 57%
Returning Freshmen: 77%
Academics: ✎ ✎ ✎
Social: ☎ ☎ ☎ ☎
Q of L: ★ ★ ★
Admissions: 607-HARTWICK
Email Address:
    admissions@hartwick.edu

Strongest Programs:
Anthropology
Biology
Geological and Environmental
    Sciences
English
Management
Sociology
Chemistry

Hartwick College has strived in recent years to transform itself. The school has chosen to become smaller in order to better focus on its ever-improving liberal arts profile. Hartwick emphasizes study abroad—especially for freshmen—crystallizing the school's philosophy that learning isn't about rote memorization, it's about creating knowledge and developing skills. The students here take full advantage of what's offered, and feel at home on this close-knit campus. "There is a real openness to build one-on-one relationships," says a senior.

Hartwick's campus has a New England feel with its ivy-covered, redbrick buildings and white cupolas, gables, and trim. The campus setting on the Oyaron Hill, overlooking the city and the Susquehanna Valley beyond, provides a breathtaking view, though the steepness of the campus may have some wishing for the legs of a mountain goat. More recent additions include a $12 million science center that offers lab space for biotechnology, ecology, environmental sciences and policy, and science communications. Other perks: a tissue culture lab, electron microscopes, a greenhouse, an herbarium, a cold room, a biotechnology "clean lab," and a graphics imaging lab.

Hartwick's liberal arts and sciences framework ensures that its students are exposed to what one administrator terms "a broad swath of human knowledge." The most popular major is management, followed by psychology and biology. Students are enthusiastic about political science and English, as well as life sciences, which one student accurately terms an "up-and-coming" program. Art and music also are praised, while modern and classical language and philosophy are works in progress. Student–faculty collaborations are the norm, as is the emphasis on learning through real-world experiences, from working in a Jamaican hospital to interning with the New York Mets.

Hartwick's general education program is divided into five areas: continuity (Western tradition), interdependence, science and technology, critical thinking and effective communication, and choices. Among the voluminous requirements are two Great Books courses, a course in Western and non-Western culture, foreign language, two decision-making seminars, a course in the creative or performing arts, and a senior research thesis. Another example of Hartwick's academic enrichment is the honors program that provides students with the opportunity to design and carry out a coherent program of study characterized by challenges exceeding those offered in typical course work required for graduation. The course offerings are necessarily limited by Hartwick's small size, but the Individual Student Program (ISP) enables students to create their own major dealing with a particular interest. Students may take courses at the nearby State University College at Oneonta (SUCO).

"The college is competitive and rewarding at the same time for students who work hard," says one student. Hartwick offers other unconventional learning options, many of them in off-campus locations. Students have traveled to all parts of the world while pursuing their Hartwick education—first-year students are especially encouraged to leave the "Bubble on the Hill," as some call Hartwick. The Awakening Challenge, completed by freshmen as part of orientation, is also an option for management majors who want to test their leadership skills. The four-week January term is also a favorite time to explore the world beyond Oneonta.

The faculty wins universal praise from the students. "The professors demand a lot of their students, but they also show appreciation for hard work," says a psychology major. Private tutoring and help sessions are offered, along with an innovative freshman early warning program that identifies struggling students early and offers counseling. "Our professors expect only the best from us," says a sociology major. Academic advising wins rave reviews from most students. "It is awesome," says one student. "Even the department chairman is really caring. He is willing to help students on several fronts."

Hartwick has traditionally attracted a somewhat less academically oriented student body than most of the colleges with which it competes, but it has improved its academic position in recent years, thanks to a focused recruitment program. Twenty-two percent of students come from the top tenth of their class. Sixty-four percent are from New York State, especially upstate, and most of the rest come from New England or the mid-Atlantic states. Hartwick has worked hard to improve the diversity of its student body. Now, 70 percent of the students are white; 5 percent are African-American, 3 percent Hispanic, and 1 percent Asian-American. Students at the Wick are generally from "fairly well-to-do" families and tend to be socially active and politically sedate, though one student says most are fairly liberal. Hartwick college awards merit scholarships that range from $4,000 to $20,000, and there are thirty athletic scholarships for Division I men's soccer and women's water polo.

In general, the dorms receive mixed reviews, but the administration is hoping for more positive reactions because all residence halls have been renovated and improved recently. Upperclassmen covet a place in one of the four townhouses described by one as "the yuppie version of on-campus living." Freshmen, sophomores, and juniors are required to live on campus, though the latter may move into one of the fraternity or special-interest houses. Each dorm has designated quiet hours, though they may not always be observed. Hartwick's 920-acre environmental campus, Pine Lake, has cabins that are heated by pellet stoves and a lodge where environmentally inclined students can live in rustic style. One student says that it is "very selective, but well worth the application process." On-campus students eat at a single dining commons, where the food has been dubbed "not so bad." Some wish that campus security would make its presence known a bit more than they do.

From campus it's only a short walk, bike ride, or bus ride downhill into the small city of Oneonta, with its tantalizing profusion of bars. But the underage Hartwick students usually don't get past the front doors of these taverns, and the administration is tough about enforcement on campus. No alcohol is allowed in dorm rooms. Tamer entertainment includes Sunday night movies as well as occasional lecturers and comedians, and just hanging out at the student union. The Greek system attracts 15 percent of the men and 17 percent of the women. Popular campus-wide bashes include a Last Day of Classes party, the Holiday Ball, and Winter and Spring Weekends, the latter of which features the notorious "Wick Wars," a school-wide sports competition. There's also the Breakfast of Champions before final exams when professors and administrators serve students breakfast between 11 p.m. and 2 a.m. Walking to class each day provides great hill workouts for your ski legs, and skiing is popular throughout the region. Another nice diversion is Pine Lake, which offers cross-country trails, swimming, boating, and fishing. Nearby Cooperstown offers entertainment for baseball and history buffs.

Oneonta is big on soccer, and Hartwick fits that bill. The Mayor's Cup Soccer Tournament weekend is a big event. Hartwick is nationally ranked at the Division I level in soccer; the remainder of the teams compete in Division III. The women's water polo team has been a real success story by recently winning the Eastern

Hartwick's environmental campus, Pine Lake, has cabins that are heated by pellet stoves and a lodge where environmentally inclined students can live in rustic style.

The Awakening Challenge, completed by freshmen as part of orientation, is also an option for management majors who want to test their leadership skills.

Collegiate Conference Tournament championship. The women's field hockey team reached the NCAA semifinals, and conference championships have been won by men's basketball, swimming, and baseball, and by the women's basketball, soccer, and lacrosse teams. Intramurals are popular as well.

Change is good, the sages say, and the folks at Hartwick would definitely agree. By refocusing its efforts on recruiting higher-caliber students and emphasizing top-notch experiential learning, Hartwick is shedding its image as a party school. Even some of the T-shirts sold on campus broadcast the students' attitudes about their education: one simply says "Smartwick."

If You Apply To ➤

Hartwick: Early decision: Jan. 15. Early action: Jan. 1. Regular admissions: Feb. 15. Financial aid: Feb. 1. Campus interviews: recommended, informational. Alumni interviews: optional, informational. SATs or ACTs: SATs preferred. SAT IIs: optional. Accepts the Common Application and electronic applications. Essay question: significant experience; issue of concern; influential person; character in fiction or history; topic of your choice.

Harvard University

Byerly Hall, 8 Garden Street, Cambridge, MA 02138

An acceptance here is the gold standard of American education. Gets periodic slings and arrows for not paying enough attention to undergraduates, some of which is carping from people who didn't get in. It takes moxie to keep your self-image in the midst of all those geniuses, but most Harvard admits can handle it.

Website: www.fas.harvard.edu
Location: City outskirts
Total Enrollment: 18,036
Undergraduates: 6,684
Male/Female: 54/46
SAT Ranges: V 700–800
   M 700–790
ACT Range: 30–34
Financial Aid: 70%
Expense: Pr $ $ $ $
Phi Beta Kappa: Yes
Applicants: 18,161
Accepted: 11%
Enrolled: 79%
Grad in 6 Years: 97%
Returning Freshmen: 96%
Academics: ✏ ✏ ✏ ✏ ✏
Social: ☎ ☎ ☎
Q of L: ★ ★ ★ ★
Admissions: (617) 495-1551
Email Address:
   college@fas.harvard.edu

Over the past 350-plus years, the name Harvard has become synonymous with excellence, prestige, and achievement. At this point, Harvard University is the benchmark against which all other colleges are compared. It attracts the best students, the most academically accomplished faculty, and the most lavish donors of any institution of higher education nationwide. Sure, some academic departments at Hah-vahd are smaller than others, but all have faculty members who have made a name for themselves, many of whom have written the standard texts in their fields. Olympic athletes, concert pianists, and Rhodes Scholars blend in nicely here, ready to embrace the challenges and rewards only Harvard's quintessential Ivy League milieu can offer.

Spiritually as well as geographically, the campus centers on the famed Harvard Yard, a classic quadrangle of Georgian brick buildings whose walls seem to echo with the voices of William James, Henry Adams, and other intellectual greats who trod its shaded paths in centuries past. Beyond the yard's wrought-iron gates, the campus is an architectural mix, ranging from the modern ziggurat of the science center to the white towers of college-owned houses along the Charles River. Loker Commons, a student center beneath the new Annenberg freshman dining hall, provides a place for students to meet and philosophize over gourmet coffee or burritos of epic proportions. The Barker Center for humanities has emerged from the shell of the Union, the old freshman dining hall, and the Maxwell Dworkin building, which houses the computer science and engineering departments, has also been completed.

Harvard's state-of-the-art physical facilities are surpassed only by the unparalleled brilliance of its faculty. Under its "star" system, Harvard grants tenure only to scholars who have already made it—usually someplace else—and then gives them free rein for research. It seems like every time you turn around, a Harvard professor is winning a Nobel Prize or being interviewed on CNN; every four years, half the government and econ departments move to Washington to hash out national policy. But one of Harvard's finest qualities is also one of its biggest problems. "You can have unlimited contact with professors, but it must be on your initiative," notes a biology major. "But, this is not a small liberal arts college where people will reach out to you." That's not to say profs are completely uncaring. Most teach at least one undergraduate course per semester, and even the luminaries occasionally conduct small undergraduate seminars (including those reserved for freshmen, which can be taken pass/fail). Harvard also sponsors a faculty dining program, encouraging professors to eat at the various residential houses and chew over ideas as well as lamb chops.

Harvard's best-known departments tend to be its largest; economics, government, biology, English, and biochemistry account for a large chunk of majors. But many smaller departments are gems as well: East Asian studies is easily tops in the nation. And under the leadership of Henry Louis Gates, the African-American studies department has assembled the most high-powered group of black intellectuals in American higher education. Smaller, interdisciplinary honors majors, to which students apply for admission, boast solid instruction and happy undergraduates, too. These programs—social studies, history and science, history and literature, and folklore and mythology—are the only majors that require a senior thesis, although many students elect to do one in other departments.

Harvard's visual and environmental studies major serves filmmakers, studio artists, and urban planners, and concentrations in women's studies and environmental sciences have been well received. Students can also petition for individualized majors, typically during the sophomore year. All students must choose some sort of major at the end of their freshman year, a year earlier than most schools. The field of concentration can be changed later, but Harvard expects its students to hit the ground running. Regardless of the department, students uniformly complain about the overuse of teaching fellows (graduate students) for introductory courses in mathematics and the languages. TFs aren't all bad, though, says a junior: "They can give good advice, having just been in our position." Besides, it's easier to ask "dumb questions" of mere mortals than of the demigod-like professors.

"You can have unlimited contact with professors, but it must be on your initiative."

Back in the mid-1970s, Harvard helped launch the current curriculum reform movement. The core curriculum that emerged ranks as perhaps the most exciting collection of academic offerings in all of American higher education. The best and brightest freshmen can apply for advanced standing if they have enough Advanced Placement credits. And should you not find a class you are looking for, admittedly highly unlikely, Harvard offers cross-registration with several of its graduate schools and the Massachusetts Institute of Technology.

In formal terms, the core requires students to select eight courses, or a quarter of their program, from a list of offerings in six different "modes of inquiry": foreign cultures, historical studies, literature and arts, moral reasoning, sciences, and social analysis. For the three or four most popular courses, enrollment is limited by the number of seats in the various large auditoriums on campus; sometimes places in these lectures are determined by lottery. Freshmen also face quantitative reasoning and foreign language requirements, as well as a semester of Expository Writing (Expos), taught mainly by preceptors.

For many students, the most rewarding form of instruction is the sophomore and junior tutorial, a small-group directed study in a student's field of concentration that is required in most departments within the humanities and social sciences. Teaching of the tutorials is split between professors and graduate students, and the

(Continued)
Strongest Programs:
Economics
Biology
Social Studies
Government
English
African-American Studies
East Asian Studies
Anthropology
Music
History of Science

Students can also petition for individualized majors, typically during the sophomore year.

It seems like every time you turn around, a Harvard professor is winning a Nobel Prize or being interviewed on CNN; every four years, half the government and econ departments move to Washington to hash out national policy.

weight of each party's responsibility varies with the subject and the professor. Juniors and seniors seek out professors with whom they want to work.

The oft-made claim that "the hardest thing about Harvard is getting in" is right on target. Failing out takes real effort. Once on campus, the possibilities are endless for those who are motivated. Then again, Harvard can feel uncaring and antisocial. While it offers unparalleled resources—including fellow students—brilliant over-achievers who desire the occasional ego-stroke might be better off at a small liberal arts college. Although most students feel little competition, the academic climate is still intense. "The courses at Harvard are very demanding," says a social studies major. "If you choose to be competitive, you'll find the competition can be cut-throat." Sooner or later, all roads lead to Widener Library, where incredible facilities lie in wait (and where snow-covered steps make prime sledding runs in the winter).

Harvard does have one thing its $19 billion endowment can't buy: a diverse, high-powered, ambitious, and exciting student body. You will meet smooth-talking government majors who appear to have begun their senatorial campaigns in kindergarten. You will meet flamboyant fine arts majors who have cultivated an affected accent all their own. You will sample the intensity of Harvard's extracurricular scene, where more than 6,600 of the world's sharpest undergrads compete for leadership positions in a luminous galaxy of extracurricular opportunities. "Most of the social life takes place on campus, and there are a million things

"Yes, despite what you may think, Harvard people have parties and Harvard people date!"

to do," says a history/government double major. "Yes, despite what you may think, Harvard people have parties and Harvard people date!" Stressed-out students can count on help from a variety of quarters, including the various deans' offices, the Bureau of Study Counsel, the Office of Career Services ("dedicated to working with Harvard students and alums for the rest of their lives," claims a senior), and counselors associated with each residential house. All students participate in week-long orientation, and the First-Year Urban and Outdoor Programs help students acquaint themselves with one another and the Boston area.

No one can tell you exactly what it takes to gain admission to Harvard (and if anyone tries, apply a large grain of salt), but here's a hint: 90 percent of the current student body ranked in the top tenth of their high-school class and two-thirds went to public high school. Though there are a few old-money types who probably spit up their baby food on a Harvard sweatshirt, their numbers are smaller than one might imagine on this liberal campus. (Many enter as sophomores when no one is looking.) Undergrads come from all fifty states and scores of foreign countries, although the student body is weighted toward the Northeast. Minority groups account for nearly a third of the enrollment. There are no merit or athletic scholarships to ease the pain of Harvard's hefty tuition, but a generous financial aid policy recently added $2,000 annually to every student aid package. Under a new financial aid policy, students whose families earn less than $40,000 a year will receive full scholarships.

In the past, female students benefited from "dual citizenship" in both Harvard and Radcliffe colleges, receiving degrees ratified by the presidents of both colleges. However, Radcliffe has been phased out as a separate institution; everyone is now considered a Harvard student, though students can still take advantage of Radcliffe's network of professional women, researchers, and alumnae.

Every first-year class lives and eats as a single unit in Harvard Yard, a privilege made more enticing by recent renovation of all the freshman dorms. Freshmen now eat in Annenberg Hall, the new name for beautifully renovated Memorial Hall. For their last three years, students live in one of twelve residential houses, built around their own courtyards with their own dining halls and libraries. All the houses are co-ed, and each holds between three hundred and five hundred students. Designed as learning communities, the upperclass houses come equipped with a complement of resident tutors, affiliated faculty members, and special facilities from art studios to squash courts. Each house has a student council, which plans programs and parties and arranges the fielding of intramural teams. Students are now randomly assigned (with up to fifteen friends) to one of the houses, but some houses still retain a personality from the days of old when each stood for a particular ideology, interest, or economic class. "Harvard housing is beautiful," says a history of science major. "Freshmen have amazing rooms and upperclass houses are great."

The nine houses along the Charles River feature suites of rooms, while the three houses at the Radcliffe Quad, a half-mile away, offer a mixture of suites and single rooms. Some students value the greater privacy of the Quad houses' singles; others consider it equivalent to a Siberian exile, especially during harsh Cambridge winters. The older dorms provide spacious wood-paneled rooms, working fireplaces, and the gentle reminders of Harvard's rich traditions. Most rooms are also wired for direct Internet access. With all these features and amenities, it's no wonder few students move off campus.

What socializing there is at Harvard tends to occur on campus and in small groups. "It's certainly normal to spend Friday and Saturday nights studying," says a philosophy major. With the exception of the annual all-school Freshman Mixer and the annual theme festivals each house throws, parties tend to be private affairs in individual dorm rooms. Though Harvard does enforce the drinking age at university events, in individual houses, it's up to the resident tutors. For some, the key to happiness in Harvard's high-powered environment is finding a niche, a comfortable academic or extracurricular circle around which to build your life. Outside activities include about eighty plays performed annually, two newspapers and several journals, and plenty of community service projects.

The possibilities of Harvard's social life are increased tenfold by Cambridge and Boston, where there are many places to have fun. Harvard Square itself is a legendary gathering place for tourists, shoppers, bearded intellectuals, and coffeehouse denizens. The American Repertory Theater by Robert Brustein, transplanted from Yale in the mid-1980s, offers a season of professional productions and nearly as professional student shows. Cambridge also enjoys an exceptional selection of new and used bookstores, including the Starr Bookshop (behind the *Lampoon* building), McIntyre & Moore, Grolier Books, and, of course, the Harvard Bookstore and the mammoth Harvard Co-op,

"It's certainly normal to spend Friday and Saturday nights studying."

known universally as "the Coop." Boston itself features Faneuil Hall, the Red Sox, the Celtics, and fifty-two other colleges. "Cambridge/Boston is the ultimate college town," says an English major. "Everything is geared toward the students."

Harvard's athletic facilities are across the river from the campus, and their incredible offerings often go unnoticed by students buried in the books. Both the men's and women's squash and crew teams are perennial national powers, and the men's ice hockey team draws a crowd of a few dedicated fans. The women's lacrosse team is strong, as are tennis, swimming, and sailing. As for football, the team has been doing better in recent years, but the season always boils down to the Yale game, memorable as much for the antics of the spectators and marching band as for the fumbles of the players. Intramural sports teams are divided up by house, and each fall, league champs play teams from Yale the weekend of the game. Another fall highlight is the annual Head of the Charles crew race, the largest event of its kind in the world, where as many as two hundred thousand people gather to watch the racing shells glide by.

Nowhere but Harvard does the identity of a school—its history, its presence, its pretense—intrude so much into the details of undergraduate life. Admission here opens the door to a world of intellectual wonder, academic challenges, and faculty minds unmatched in the United States—but then drops students on the threshold. "I have quickly gained exposure to major theories in literature, psychology, anthropology, social sciences, and evolutionary biology," says a junior. "I gauge myself by how many allusions in *The New Yorker* I understand." That's the way Harvard is; what other kind of place could produce statesmen John Quincy Adams and John F. Kennedy, pioneers W. E. B. DuBois and Helen Keller, and artists T. S. Eliot and Leonard Bernstein? But beware: it is only the most motivated and dedicated student who can take full advantage of the Harvard experience. Others who attempt to drink from the school's perennially overflowing cup of knowledge may find themselves drowning in its depths.

Overlaps

Princeton, Yale, Stanford, MIT, Brown

If You Apply To ➤

Harvard: Early action: Nov. 1. Regular admissions: Jan. 1. Financial aid: Feb. 1. Housing: May 1. Guarantees to meet demonstrated need. Campus interviews: optional, informational. Alumni interviews: optional, evaluative. SATs or ACTs: required. SAT IIs: required (any three). Accepts the Common Application. Essay question: uses Common Application questions.

Harvey Mudd College: See page 136.

Haverford College

Haverford, PA 19041-1392

Quietly prestigious college of Quaker heritage. With an enrollment of about eleven hundred, Haverford is half the size of some competitors but benefits from its relationship with nearby Bryn Mawr. Close cousin to nearby Swarthmore but not quite as far left politically. Exceptionally strong sense of community.

Website: www.haverford.edu
Location: Suburban
Total Enrollment: 1,105
Undergraduates: 1,105
Male/Female: 47/53
SAT Ranges: V 640–740
  M 640–720
Financial Aid: 41%
Expense: Pr $ $ $ $
Phi Beta Kappa: Yes
Applicants: 2,598
Accepted: 32%
Enrolled: 37%
Grad in 6 Years: 92%
Returning Freshmen: 96%

An overarching honor code covering everything from the classroom to the dorm room defines student life at Haverford College. Students schedule their own final exams, take unproctored tests, and police underage drinking on their own. "The honor code is Haverford's best feature and students take it very seriously," says a junior history major. Haverford may be smaller and less well known than some of its peers, but it holds its own against the finest liberal arts colleges in the country, especially for students who want to work hard and play hard (65 percent of Fordians were varsity athletes in high school, and they take many Haverford teams to championships). In response to the oft-heard dig "I've never heard of Haverford," one student says he and his friends have adopted a slogan from humor columnist (and Haverford alum) Dave Barry: "We haven't heard of you either!"

Founded under Quaker auspices in 1833, Haverford functions much like a family. The campus consists of 204 acres just off Philadelphia's Main Line railroad, and resembles a peaceful, well-ordered summer camp. The densely wooded campus has an arboretum, duck pond, nature trails, and more than four hundred species of shrubs and trees. Architectural styles range from nineteenth- and early-twentieth-century stone buildings to a sprinkling of modern structures here and there. The combination enhances the sense of a balanced community, bringing together two traditional Quaker philosophies: development of the intellect and appreciation of nature. The 140,000-square-foot, $50 million Koshland Center for Integrated Natural Sciences (for the departments of astronomy, biology, chemistry, physics, math, and more) was recently added near the heart of campus, providing a place for interdisciplinary teaching, learning, and research.

Haverford's curriculum reflects commitment to the liberal arts. Biology, English, history, philosophy, and political science are the most popular majors. There are ten areas of concentration—which are different from minors—that are attached to certain majors, including peace and conflict studies and mathematical economics. Unusual offerings include a philosophy seminar called "From Zen Buddhism to Contemporary Public Black Intellectuals" and a course called "Happiness, Virtue, and the Good Life." Comparative literature and East Asian studies are new, growing majors. Haverford's general education requirements call for three courses in each of three divisions: social sciences, natural sciences, and humanities. One of these nine courses must fulfill a quantitative reasoning requirement, and students also must study a foreign language for a year and complete a semester each of coursework in freshman writing and social justice.

The bicollege system that includes Bryn Mawr College, a nearby woman's school, allows Haverford students to major in subjects such as art history, engineering, growth and structure of cities, and environmental studies. Also, by combining resources with Bryn Mawr and nearby Swarthmore, Haverford offers students an extensive language program. The unique relationship between Bryn Mawr and Haverford dates to the days when Haverford was all-male, over two decades ago. However, students at each institution can still take courses, use the facilities, eat, and even live in the dormitories of the other. Haverford and Bryn Mawr students cooperate on a weekly newspaper, radio station, orchestra, and other clubs and sports, and a free shuttle bus connects the campuses. Cross-registration is also available at Swarthmore and the University of Pennsylvania. Study abroad programs in one of thirty-three countries attracts 35 to 40 percent of juniors.

Since there are no graduate students at Haverford, undergraduates often help professors with research, and several publish papers each year. In fact, Haverford's biggest strength may be its faculty members, 64 percent of whom live on campus and are said to be very accessible. A junior political science student notes that one professor personalized a ninety-student class by dividing it up into groups of ten and having

"The honor code is Haverford's best feature and students take it very seriously."

each group over for a pre-exam dessert. "The teaching here is the absolute best!" raves a junior history major. "Most classes are taught in a conversation style. The profs are simply amazing." Perhaps because of the intense classroom interaction, the workload is sizable, although students say they don't worry about each others' grades and try to squeeze in nonscholarly pursuits, too. "Everyone always has work to do but we're willing to drop it and throw a Frisbee," a political science student says. Advising is ever-present: freshmen are matched with professors who work with them from their arrival until they declare majors two years later, while upperclass "Customspeople" are resources and mentors for living groups of nine to sixteen first-year students.

One of Haverford's most distinctive features is the honor code that governs all aspects of campus life. "I can take my final exam at 3 a.m. on Founder's Green" says a junior who says the honor code "means we look out for ourselves." The code, administered by students and debated and re-ratified each year at a meeting called Plenary, helps instill the values of "integrity, honesty, and concern for others." While

(Continued)
Academics: ✎ ✎ ✎ ✎ ✎
Social: ☎ ☎ ☎
Q of L: ★ ★ ★ ★ ★
Admissions: (610) 896-1350
Email Address:
   admitme@haverford.edu

Strongest Programs:
Biological and Physical
   Sciences
English
History
Political Science
Economics

Students root for the Black Squirrels, and cheer with this gem: "Fight, fight, inner light—kill, Quakers, kill!'

the social honor code encourages students to "voice virtually any opinion so long as it is expressed rationally," that can mean self-censorship, says a philosophy major. "Sometimes you feel like you are walking on eggshells to avoid offending anyone," the student says. In good Quaker tradition, the faculty makes decisions by consensus rather than formal voting, and students also play a large role in college policy.

Only 14 percent of the Haverford's students hail from Pennsylvania, but a large percentage are East Coasters nonetheless. Approximately 15 percent of students are Asian-American, 6 percent are Hispanic, and 5 percent are African-American. Though the college is nonsectarian, the Quaker influence lives on in the form of an optional meeting each week. And politics lean toward the liberal: "People say that is it easier to come out as a gay male on campus than a Republican male," quips a junior.

Haverford's residence halls are spacious and well maintained, and 64 percent of available rooms are singles—even for freshmen—so it's not surprising that 98 percent of all students live on campus. All dorms are co-ed, but students may request single-sex floors. Freshmen are guaranteed housing, and even sophomores, who draw last in the lottery, can usually get decent rooms. The extremely popular, school-owned Haverford College Apartments sit on the edge of campus. These include one- and two-bedroom units, each with a living room, kitchen, and bathroom. Upperclassmen in the apartments may cook for themselves, but all others living on campus (and all freshmen regardless of where they live) must buy the meal plan, which includes weekend board. "Some of the dorms are incredible. The apartments are the best freshman housing anywhere," says an economics student. Crime is virtually nonexistent, owing to the school's location in the ritzy Philadelphia suburbs, "surrounded by luxury-car dealerships and expensive stores." Muses a philosophy major: "I've even seen people leave their laptops in the library and go to dinner."

> "Everyone always has work to do but we're willing to drop it and throw a Frisbee."

The Haverford College Apartments, owned by the college, are said to be some of the best dorms around, especially for freshman living. They feature one- and two-bedroom units, each with a living room, kitchen, and bathroom.

While the community spirit at Haverford works well for academics and personal development, it doesn't always carry over to the social scene. Without fraternities and sororities, Haverford and Bryn Mawr hold joint campus parties. These alcohol-soaked affairs can get tiresome after freshman and sophomore years, which is why students tend to spend at least part of their junior years abroad. The alcohol policy respects the law of the commonwealth of Pennsylvania—no drinking if you're under twenty-one—and is connected, as well, to the honor code. "Students drink underage on every college campus, and our policy creates a realistic and safe space that keeps students from getting hurt and entrusts them with their own responsibility," explains a political science major. For nondrinkers, there are frequently free movies, concerts, and other activities on campus. Other traditional events include the weekend-long pre-exams Haverfest—Haverford's approximation of Woodstock—as well as the winter Snowball dance and Taste the Rainbow drag ball. Life in the close-knit, introspective environment that is Haverford can get stifling, but there are easy escapes: downtown Philadelphia is twenty minutes away by train. New York City, Washington, the New Jersey beaches, Pocono ski areas, and Atlantic City are only a couple hours away by car. Many students participate in the Eighth Dimension, which coordinates volunteer opportunities. "Students try to get out there as much as possible," says a history student.

> "People say that is it easier to come out as a gay male on campus than a Republican male."

The football team at the Ford has been undefeated since 1972, when the administration eliminated it, so soccer, a sport in which Haverford played in the first intercollegiate game more than eighty years ago, has become most popular for both men and women. Track and cross-country are also strong, with the men's and women's teams winning regional championships in the last few years, along with the volleyball team. Every year, Haverford and archrival Swarthmore vie for the Hood Trophy, awarded to the school that wins the most varsity contests between the two. "The Swarthmore vs. Haverford basketball game is an annual excuse to yell and scream," says one student. Haverford also boasts the number-one varsity college cricket team in the country because, well, it's the only school with one! Intramural sports are popular, especially because participation counts toward the six quarters of athletic credit Haverford requires during the freshman and sophomore years. In spite of all the rivalries, these Quakers have struggled to justify their peace-loving heritage with the desire to bash opponents' brains out on the court or the field. For now, students root for the Black Squirrels, and cheer with this gem: "Fight, fight, inner light—kill, Quakers, kill!"

Haverford's small size is both the reason many students choose this oft-overlooked school—and the source of their frustration after a couple of terms here. With just over eleven hundred students, "other people will tell you who you hooked up with while drunk at a party before you can remember it," sighs a junior. "You can never be anonymous."

Overlaps

Swarthmore, Brown, Wesleyan, Williams, Amherst

If You Apply To ➤ **Haverford:** Early decision: Nov. 15. Regular admissions: Jan. 15. Financial aid: Jan. 31. Guarantees to meet demonstrated need. Campus interviews: recommended (required for those living more than 150 miles from from campus), informational. Alumni interviews: recommended, informational. SATs or ACTs: required. SAT IIs: required (writing and two others). Accepts the Common Application and electronic applications. Essay question: personal statement that reveals something other application materials have not covered and how the honor code would change you or help you grow.

University of Hawaii at Manoa

2530 Dole Street, Room C200, Honolulu, HI 96822

Who wouldn't want to go to Hawaii for college? To make it work, aim for one of UH's specialties, such as Asian studies, marine science, and travel industry management. Bear in mind the measly 55 percent graduation rate. Too many luaus and not enough studying can be a bad combination.

One of the goals of the University of Hawaii at Manoa is to "serve as a bridge between East and West." This multiculturalism is evident in everything from course offerings to the student body. And while you may be thinking about surfing as much as studying, don't be fooled: it will take more than a great tan to earn your degree here.

The UH campus occupies three hundred acres in the Manoa Valley, a residential Honolulu neighborhood. The architecture is regionally eclectic, mirroring historical and modern Asian Pacific motifs, and is enhanced by extensive subtropical landscaping. "There are many plants and trees that make our campus more environmentally friendly," says a sophomore. UH offers bachelor's degrees in eighty-eight fields. Among the best are astronomy, Asian and Pacific area studies, languages and the arts, ethnomusicology, and tropical agriculture. It should come as no surprise that marine and ocean-related programs are also first-rate. The university also takes pride in its programs in engineering, geology and geophysics, international business, political science, and travel industry management. Both medical and law schools are gaining reputations for excellence. UH also offers a B.A. degree in information and computer science. Beyond these few specialties, programs are adequate but hardly worth four years of trans-Pacific flights for students

Website: www.hawaii.edu
Location: Center city
Total Enrollment: 17,004
Undergraduates: 11,785
Male/Female: 46/54
SAT Ranges: V 480–580
    M 510–630
ACT Range: 20–24
Financial Aid: 30%
Expense: Pub $
Phi Beta Kappa: Yes
Applicants: 8,714
Accepted: 76%
Enrolled: 44%
Grad in 6 Years: 55%
Returning Freshmen: 82%

from the mainland. The math department is cited by several students as the school's weakest department.

Students describe the academic climate as "fairly competitive" and somewhat laid-back. Despite the relaxed atmosphere, core requirements are extensive. All students must take a semester in expository writing and math, two courses in world civilization, two years of a foreign language or Hawaiian, and three courses each in the humanities, social sciences, and natural sciences. Freshman seminar classes offer small-group learning in a variety of subjects. Desirable classes and times are said to be difficult to get into for freshmen and sophomores. You may need to talk to profs, one student advises. Another problem seems to be that certain classes are only offered one semester a year. The academic advising is described as "good" but requires that students take the initiative to seek guidance.

> "Hawaii is a unique place where diversity is recognized and accepted. There are many mixed-race students and many interracial couples."

Hawaii stands out among major American universities in that 78 percent of the students are of Asian descent. Caucasians account for 20 percent, and African-Americans and Hispanics, 1 percent each. The different groups seem to get along well, according to students. Mainland Americans account for about 7 percent of the students, and another 3 percent are foreign. "Hawaii is a unique place where diversity is recognized and accepted. There are many mixed-race students and many interracial couples," a senior says. Hot campus issues include gay rights, campus parking, and Hawaiian sovereignty. Especially promising students can compete for more than 108 merit scholarships, and a total of 310 athletes get grants-in-aid.

Only 21 percent of the student body live in campus housing, which is parceled out by a priority system that gives preference to those who are from across the sea. Students recommend the four towers, Ilima, Lehua, Lokelani, and Mokihana; the rooms are small, and the hallways are happening. "Students never know what to expect," one student explains. If you're thinking about off-campus housing, take note: the administration warns that housing in Honolulu is scarce and expensive. Once you are accepted into housing, continuous residency is not that difficult to obtain. Cafeterias are located throughout the campus and serve "edible" fare.

Because of all the commuters, UH is pretty sedate after dark. "On the whole, UH seems to be an academically focused campus, meaning that school is for on campus

> "On the whole, UH seems to be an academically focused campus, meaning that school is for on campus and socializing is for off campus."

and socializing is for off campus," a psychology major says. Many students hit nearby dance clubs or movies, or else head for home. Four percent of the men and two percent of the women join the tiny Greek system. Drinking is not allowed in the dorms. A couple of local hangouts provide an escape, and the campus pub, Manoa Garden, is also an option. Lest anyone forget, some of the world's most beautiful resorts—Diamond Head and all the rest—are less than a twenty-minute drive away. Waikiki Beach? Within two miles' reach. And round-trip airfare to the neighboring islands—including Maui, Kauai, and the Big Island—is not unreasonable.

About the only thing that generates excitement on campus are the athletic teams, the Rainbow Warriors, with football, volleyball, basketball, baseball, and swimming among the top draws. The Rainbow women's teams are also well supported, especially the championship volleyball team. The Homecoming Dance is one of the most popular events of the year. But what students really look forward to is Kanikapila, a festival of Hawaiian music, dance, and culture. Don Ho, eat your heart out.

(Continued)
Academics: ✍ ✍
Social: ☎ ☎
Q of L: ★ ★ ★
Admissions: (808) 956-8975
Email Address: ar-info@hawaii.edu

Strongest Programs:
Astronomy
Asian and Pacific Area Studies
Languages
Travel Industry Management
English as a Second Language
Ethnomusicology
Tropical Agriculture
Geosciences

Hawaii stands out among major American universities in that 78 percent of the students are of Asian descent.

Because of all the commuters, UH is pretty sedate after dark.

Overlaps
Hawaii Pacific, UH–Hilo, University of Washington, UCLA, University of Southern California

Students seeking warm weather and great surfing won't be disappointed at UH, but mainlanders should think twice about it unless they are set on one of the university's specialized programs. It's up to you, one student says, to get the best out of UH. "Many do not recognize the high quality of education possible through choosing challenging courses and instructors who urge achievement and high-quality work." And if you can catch a few waves in the process, so much the better.

<table>
<tr><td>

If You

Apply

To >

</td><td>

UH: Rolling admissions: May 1. Financial aid: Mar. 1. Housing: May 1. Guarantees to meet demonstrated need. Campus interviews: optional, informational. No alumni interviews. SATs or ACTs: required. Achievement tests: optional. No essay question.

</td></tr>
</table>

Hendrix College

1600 Washington Avenue, Conway, AR 72032

Along with Millsaps and Rhodes, Hendrix is in the class of mid-South liberal arts colleges. Hendrix is the smallest and most progressive of the three and has a strong emphasis on international awareness. Small-town Arkansas is a tough sell, and the college accepts the vast majority of students who apply.

For a school in the heart of the Bible Belt, Hendrix College is surprisingly liberal. Academics are demanding but students are laid back—even radical—in their political and social views. Ironically, healthy dialogue about tough issues such as gay rights, the environment, and capital punishment draws students together. "Students at Hendrix tend to be quite open-minded and experimental in all aspects of life. This leads to a diverse, if odd, student body," says a senior philosophy major.

Hendrix's compact and comfortable campus stretches for 160 acres between the Ouachita and the Ozark mountains. College land boasts more than eighty varieties of trees and shrubs, and more than ten thousand budding flowers each spring. The main campus—with its own lily pool, fountain, and gazebo—occupies about one-fourth of the total acreage. The redbrick buildings are a mix of old and new, and a pedestrian overpass connects the main campus to the college's athletic facilities and a wooded fitness trail.

> **"Students at Hendrix tend to be quite open-minded and experimental in all aspects of life. This leads to a diverse, if odd, student body."**

The campus is undergoing a building boom. An art facility is being built south of campus with $3 million from an anonymous donor, and a new home for the Hendrix-Murphy Foundation Programs in Language and Literature recently opened. A new student center and a new athletic and wellness center are on tap next.

Hendrix is strong in many areas, but natural and social sciences are definitely the school's forte—35 percent of students major in biology or psychology, the school's two most popular majors. Students also give high marks to English, history, religion, philosophy, and politics. "The humanities and social sciences are also strong, with a very low faculty/student ratio, which allows for a lot of one-on-one attention," says a senior. Less inspiring are the college's education and physical education programs, and, students say, the sociology department. Doing well at Hendrix means keeping up with the workload. "The courses are very difficult and challenge students to think about what they are studying," says a sophomore history major. This means plenty

Website: www.hendrix.edu

Location: Small town

Total Enrollment: 1,093

Undergraduates: 1,082

Male/Female: 45/55

SAT Ranges: V 570–690
   M 550–670

ACT Range: 25–31

Financial Aid: 51%

Expense: Pr $

Phi Beta Kappa: Yes

Applicants: 1,071

Accepted: 83%

Enrolled: 35%

Grad in 6 Years: 68%

Returning Freshmen: 86%

Academics: ✍ ✍ ✍

Social: ☎ ☎ ☎ ☎

Q of L: ★ ★ ★ ★

Admissions: (501) 450-1362

Email Address:
   adm@hendrix.edu

Strongest Programs:
Chemistry
Mathematics
History

of time in the $10 million library, but students say the intensity fosters collaboration rather than competition. "Expectations are high, but competition between students is seen as in poor taste and frowned upon by students themselves," a philosophy student says.

At Hendrix, undergraduate research takes priority, especially within the sciences, and students get the chance to present original papers at regional and national symposia. Hendrix offers exchange programs in Austria and England, sends aspiring ecologists to Costa Rica for two weeks and budding archaeologists to Israel, and allows other students to get course credit for internships at U.S. embassies and organizations such as the National Institutes of Health and Agency for International Development. Hendrix-in-London sends fourteen students and a professor to abroad for a semester. About 40 percent of Hendrix students participate in study abroad. The school is also a member of the Associated Colleges of the South* consortium, and offers five-year programs with Columbia, Vanderbilt, and Washington University in St. Louis for aspiring engineers.

Hendrix freshmen participate in a five-day orientation program, which includes a two-day, off-campus trip emphasizing outdoor experiences, urban exposure, or volunteer service. The school implemented a new curriculum recently, including a common Foundations of World Cultures course for freshmen. Professors from many departments teach the course, which considers the lasting importance and global influence of Western and non-Western traditions. Students are also required to complete one course from a category called Challenges of the Contemporary World, and to complete courses in seven learning domains—scientific inquiry, historical perspectives, social and behavioral analysis, literary studies, expressive arts and values, beliefs, and ethics. Additionally, the school changed from a three-term system to a semester calendar. More recently, a major and minor in environmental studies and a minor in Africana studies were added.

Recently, a major and minor in environmental studies and a minor in Africana studies were added.

Two thirds of Hendrix students are from Arkansas, and 73 percent are white, but students say diversity isn't a big issue on campus. Instead, students celebrate diversity unrelated to skin color, with events such as the Miss Hendrix drag show and pageant, where proceeds are given to charity. "Hendrix students are highly concerned with the environ-

"Expectations are high, but competition between students is seen as in poor taste and frowned upon by students themselves."

ment, globalization, and corporation reforms," says a junior. "A liberal/progressive stance is the norm on campus." Adds one sophomore: "Hendrix students are very unique and very open-minded to new ideas, opinions and actions." The college offers a variety of merit scholarships to academically qualified students, but there are no athletic scholarships.

All but one of Hendrix's dorms are single-sex, and freshmen are required to live on campus, which students say adds to the sense of community. "They are a community and really become home," says a sophomore. Eighty percent of students live on campus, but some seniors get permission to move into nearby college-owned apartments. "The hardest thing at Hendrix is getting off-campus permission, not getting an on-campus room," says a junior.

At Hendrix, undergraduate research takes priority, especially within the sciences, and students get the chance to present original papers at regional and national symposia.

The two Fs that dominate social life at most Southern schools—football and fraternities—are conspicuously absent at Hendrix. Students are proud of their independence; the annual Hendrix Olympics allows them to celebrate the absence of Alphas, Betas, and Gammas from campus. Other major affairs include the Toga Party, Oktoberfest, and Beach Bash, as well as the annual Toad Suck Daze, a rollicking carnival that features bluegrass music. Last but not least is the Shirttail Serenade, in which first-year men from each dorm croon out a song-and-dance routine in their shirts, ties, shoes, socks—and underwear—for freshman women. The latter rate each performance on the basis of singing, creativity, legs, and so on, and respond two days later with their own Long Shirts/Short Skirts Serenade.

Conway offers shops and restaurants, but it is not seen as a college town and gets mixed reviews from students, who consider it more conservative. Most social life takes place on campus, or on the campuses of two other nearby colleges. "We are working to improve relationships between Conway and Hendrix. One way happens to be through volunteering," says a sophomore. Faulkner County, where the school is located, is officially "dry," so students must travel thirty miles to Little Rock for booze—or find older peers to help out. "Underage students find little difficulty in getting alcohol if they choose to," says a sophomore. Other popular road trips are Memphis (two hours by car) and Dallas and Oklahoma City (each a five-hour drive), for concerts and the like. For those who stay in town, the Volunteer Activities Center coordinates participation in projects on Service Saturdays.

> **"A liberal/progressive stance is the norm on campus."**

In the absence of a football team to cheer for, basketball, soccer, baseball, and softball are hot sports on campus. Rhodes College is the chief rival. For outdoor buffs, the college sponsors trips around Arkansas for canoeing, biking, rock climbing, and spelunking.

Musician Jimi Hendrix—whose mug inevitably adorns a new campus T-shirt each year—once asked listeners "Are you experienced?" After four years at Hendrix College, with small classes, an emphasis on research, and a laid-back atmosphere in which to test their beliefs and boundaries, students here can likely answer "Yes!"

Overlaps

University of Arkansas, University of Central Arkansas, Rhodes, Tulane, Washington University (MO)

If You Apply To >

Hendrix: Rolling admissions. Financial aid: Feb. 15. Housing: May 1. Does not guarantee to meet demonstrated need. Campus interviews: recommended, evaluative. Alumni interviews: optional, evaluative. SATs or ACTs: required. SAT IIs: optional. Accepts the Common Application and electronic applications. Essay question.

Hiram College

P.O. Box 96, Hiram, OH 44234

At only 1,190 students, Hiram is the smallest of the prominent Ohio liberal-arts colleges. Less nationally known than Wooster or Denison, Hiram attracts the vast majority of its students from in-state. Many classes are taught in seminar format, and an extensive core curriculum ensures a broad education.

Hiram College's secluded campus breeds a strong sense of community among its students. "Hiram has a unique character," extols one junior. "Because of its small size...students get noticed, not lost in the shuffle." But for all their emphasis on closeness, Hiram students are hardly homebodies—more than 50 percent study abroad in locales ranging from Europe to Australia to Costa Rica. The school's flexible schedule makes it even easier to split campus for a while. Clearly, these Hiram Dawgs are loyal to their school but always willing to learn new tricks.

Set on a charming hilltop campus that occupies the second-highest spot in Ohio, Hiram is blessed with an abundance of flowers and trees as well as a nice view of the valley below. The prevailing architectural motif is New England brick, and many Hiram buildings are restored nineteenth-century homes. The college

Website: www.hiram.edu
Location: Rural
Enrollment: 1,190
Undergraduates: 1,190
Male/Female: 43/57
SAT Ranges: V 520–640
　M 500-620
ACT Range: 20–27
Financial Aid: 86%
Expense: Pr $ $

renovated Bowler Hall, the oldest standing structure on campus, investing $1.5 million to transform it into a modern, air-conditioned dorm while retaining its eleven-foot ceilings and Victorian charm. A $6.2 million science facility provides ample space for students studying biology, one of the most popular majors, along with education, premed, psychology, and management.

Future tycoons don't get the same fieldwork opportunities as budding doctors and researchers, though. Hiram's bio majors work at a 260-acre, college-owned ecology field study station a mile away, with a specialized lab, a seventy-acre beech and maple forest, artificial river, and numerous plant and animal species. Other sciences, especially chemistry, are also strong at Hiram. Weaker areas are music, physics, and French. Recent additions to the curriculum include a major in biochemistry, biomedical humanities, and a minor in international studies.

Hiram offers several unusual summer opportunities, most notably the Northwoods Station up in the wilds of northern Michigan, where students choose courses ranging from photography to botany and geology to writing. And Hiram is the only affiliate college of the Shoals Marine Lab, run by Cornell University and the University of New Hampshire, which offers summer study in marine science, ecology, coastal and oceanic law, and underwater archaeology.

Hiram's core curriculum is extensive. All students must complete two courses from each of the college's four divisions (fine arts, humanities, natural sciences, and social sciences), plus the Freshman Colloquium, a writing and speaking skills seminar, and an upper-division interdisciplinary requirement. First-year students are also enrolled in a seminar with a focus on Western intellectual traditions and an emphasis on writing.

The Hiram Plan allows students to cover a breadth of material in three courses during each semester's longer twelve-week session, and to focus on a seminar-style class during the additional three-week term. Even nonseminars are small, though; 75 percent of Hiram's courses have twenty-five or fewer students, allowing for an impressive degree of faculty

"Because of its small size...students get noticed, not lost in the shuffle."

accessibility. "At Hiram, students have every professor's home phone number, and they encourage us to call their office or home whenever we have any questions," says a junior.

Hiram goes to great lengths to offer outstanding travel abroad programs. Professor-led trips make it to all corners of the globe and all participating students get academic credit. Students can also study at Hiram's Rome affiliate, John Cabot International University, and transfer their credits. Hiram's unique academic calendar allows ample opportunity for off-campus endeavors of all types, including the Washington Semester* at American University, which Hiram helped found.

Eighty percent of Hiram students are in-staters, and many of the rest hail from New York and Pennsylvania, though the administration is working to broaden the college's geographic base. Minority students are present, too, with African-Americans constituting 8 percent and Asian-Americans and Hispanics together comprising another 2 percent. International students, minorities, and gays are said to feel welcome, as "We are known for our diversity," says a history major. Hiram heads off race-related conflict with a dorm program called Dialogue in Black and White that encourages open discussion on multicultural issues. There's also a one-credit course that has as its final project the creation of a plan of action on campus race relations. In addition to need-based financial aid, Hiram awards merit scholarships ranging from $3,000 to $15,000. Hiram lures good students with irresistible financial aid. "My financial aid package at Hiram is unbelievable," says a junior. "After applying to larger, cheaper public universities, I came to realize it would actually cost me less to attend Hiram."

Phi Beta Kappa: Yes
Applicants: 1,022
Accepted: 79%
Enrolled: 32%
Grad in 6 Years: 66%
Returning Freshmen: 77%
Academics: ✑✑✑
Social: ☎ ☎ ☎
Q of L: ★ ★ ★
Admissions: (800) 362-5280
Email Address:
admission@hiram.edu

Strongest Programs:
Biology
Chemistry
English
History
Psychobiology
Environmental studies
Communications
English/Creative Writing

Hiram is a bit isolated, and there are few distractions in town, so students must make their own fun.

Almost all Hiram students—93 percent—live on campus, and everyone who wants a room gets one. "Ours are much better than some I have seen at other schools," says a junior. Community lounges in each hall boast big-screen TVs and computer labs. Most halls are co-ed, and students choose between twenty-four-hour quiet, twenty-four-hour noise, or a happy medium. Upperclassmen who like their location can stay in the same room year after year. Most students live in two-person suites; the popular (and larger) triples and quads are scarcer and thus harder to get. Dorm dwellers are required to buy the meal plan, which does not always receive five-star reviews, but two gourmet dinners each term liven up the menu.

"At Hiram, students have every professor's home phone number, and they encourage us to call their office or home whenever we have any questions."

Hiram goes to great lengths to offer outstanding travel abroad programs. Professor-led trips make it to all corners of the globe, and all participating students get academic credit.

When the weekend rolls around, don't expect to find all Hiram students gathered around a keg. There are dorms designated as totally dry, and the college has cracked down on underage drinking. Still, students admit that it's easy for underage students to get alcohol if they really want to drink.

Hiram is a bit isolated, and there are few distractions in town, so students must make their own fun. Typically, that means hanging out in each other's rooms, or if they're twenty-one, at CJ's Down Under, an on-campus pub that serves pizza (and features karaoke on Tuesdays). The Student Programming Board plans concerts, comedians, speakers, movies, and both formal and informal dances. "We always have tons of things happening on campus," says one student, noting the college also sponsors trips to events. Cleveland's Jacobs Field is a short road trip away. Cleveland's Rock and Roll Hall of Fame can get students rockin' all year round, and Cedar Point amusement parks get them rollin' in good weather, along with Geauga Lake and Sea World. Sometimes the college offers free tickets to concerts, plays, and ballets in town. Every semester also brings a surprise Campus Day,

"My financial aid package at Hiram is unbelievable."

when classes are cancelled and a slew of activities are planned. Other diversions include an excellent golf course three miles away, a college-owned cross-country ski trail, and good downhill slopes about an hour distant.

Hiram is hardly a mecca for budding athletic superstars, but it does have a decent Division III sports program. Football, baseball, and soccer are among the most popular men's teams, while soccer, volleyball, and softball attract women. A fitness center is open to all.

Without being extreme, Hiram has a distinct personality. Those looking for a school where anonymity will be ensured need not apply. People here are so close that they share an equivalent of the secret handshake. "Everyone smiles at you as you pass—faculty, staff, a senior football player, a freshman chemistry major, the lady that vacuums in the morning, the gardener," says a junior. Indeed, those seeking a friendly, all-American institution with a touch of internationalism might want to give Hiram a serious look.

Overlaps

Wooster, John Carroll, Mount Union, Miami University (OH), Wittenberg

If You Apply To ➤

Hiram: Rolling admissions. Early decision: Dec. 1. Regular admissions: Feb. 1. Financial aid: Mar. 1. Does not guarantee to meet demonstrated need. Campus interviews: recommended (required for scholarship consideration), evaluative. Alumni interviews: optional, informational. SATs or ACTs: required. SAT IIs: optional. Accepts the Common Application and electronic applications. Essay question: last book you read; government spending; space exploration a good thing or not; most significant invention ever; your choice.

Hobart and William Smith Colleges

Geneva, NY 14456

Coordinate single-sex colleges overlooking one of New York's Finger Lakes. Because of the two-college system, relations between the sexes are more traditional than at most schools. Greek life and the men's lacrosse team set the pace of the social scene. Geneva is an old industrial town.

Website: www.hws.edu
Location: Small city
Total Enrollment: 1,893
Undergraduates: 1,893
Male/Female: 46/54
SAT Ranges: V 540–620
  M 540–630
Financial Aid: 66%
Expense: Pr $ $ $ $
Phi Beta Kappa: Yes
Applicants: 3,108
Accepted: 65%
Enrolled: 26%
Grad in 6 Years: 78%
Returning Freshmen: 85%
Academics: ✍ ✍ ✍
Social: ☎ ☎ ☎
Q of L: ★ ★ ★
Admissions: (315) 781-3472
Email Address:
  admissions@hws.edu

Strongest Programs:
Creative Writing
Environmental Studies
Architectural Studies
Biology
Political Science
History
Economics
Psychology

The new Stern Hall, set to open in fall 2004, will house economics, political science, anthropology, sociology, and Asian languages and cultures.

Students at Hobart College for men and William Smith College for women have the best of both worlds—each school has its own dean, admissions office, and student government, but their "coordinate system" means students eat together, study together, and even live together in co-ed residence halls. "It's like being at an all-girls' school with men around all the time!" says a senior. There's an easy-going sense of community here on the shores of upstate New York's Seneca Lake. "The campus is a beautiful and exciting place to be a part of," a sophomore says.

The H-WS campus stretches for two hundred tree-lined acres, with a "beautiful forest and farmlands and a wildlife preserve," says a studio art major. Architectural styles range from Colonial to postmodern, with stately Greek Revival mansions and ivy-clad brick residences and classrooms. The new Stern Hall, set to open in fall 2004, will house economics, political science, anthropology, sociology, and Asian languages and cultures. Many dorms were recently upgraded and two new residence halls are in the works. Development along Seneca Lake will include a new boathouse for the nationally ranked sailing team.

The colleges' innovative curriculum begins with an interdisciplinary first-year seminar capped at sixteen students, which emphasizes writing and critical thinking. Instead of traditional distribution requirements, students complete a major and minor or a double major, one from a traditional department and one from an interdisciplinary program. Some of the newest majors include international relations, European studies, and media and society. The list of new minors includes Holocaust studies and men's studies. "Curriculum is writing intensive and professors hold their students to high academic students," says a senior who created an individual major in movement science. Perhaps that's because small classes are the norm; nearly two-thirds have twenty-five or fewer students.

"It's like being at an all-girls' school with men around all the time!"

The colleges take pride in their creative writing, environmental studies, and architectural studies programs, the latter especially unusual for a small school. Administrators hope a planned "Finger Lakes Institute" at the college will become a center for the study and preservation of the lakes and the study of the region's future economic development. Hobart and William Smith also encourage students to take a term away from campus, with programs in twenty-eight cities ranging from Copenhagen, Rome, and Edinburgh to Sao Paolo, Taipei, and even New York and Los Angeles. Qualified students may also participate in the honors program— done by about thirty seniors—the Venture Program,* and independent research.

New Yorkers make up half of H-WS's student body; more than a third are graduates of private schools. Though hardly diverse—African-Americans constitute 5 percent, Hispanics 4 percent, and Asian-Americans 3 percent—the campus abounds in good intentions. Departments of women's, African-American, and third world cultural studies are small but flourishing, less surprising when you know that H-WS President Mark Gearan directed the Peace Corps before arriving on campus. Major issues on the left-leaning campus include gender equity ("all freshmen are first-years"), students say. Students also get riled up about the lack of a student union building and the administration's ban on fraternity parties. H-WSers are "very independent, very reactionary," explains a senior. "They take matters into their own hands."

Ninety percent of H-WS students live on campus, in "comfortable"and "roomy" dorms, where first-years may opt for single-sex or co-ed dorms, and usually get their first choice. Favorites include Geneva (Hobart) and Hirshon (William Smith), while Durfee, Bartlett, and Hale halls, known as "Miniquad" and formerly the most avoided living spaces on campus, are again popu-lar among Hobart men. Sophomores, who may find themselves on the short end of the stick in the housing draw, typ-ically live in a large co-ed complex known as J-P-R (for Jackson, Potter, and Rees halls). Juniors and seniors may choose from suites, twenty-one on-campus houses, or the "Village at Odell's Pond," where townhouses have four to five bedrooms and two bathrooms each. Housing is guaranteed for four years, so only sixty-five or seventy-five seniors typically live off campus, says an arts and education major.

> **"Curriculum is writing intensive and professors hold their students to high academic students."**

Six Hobart fraternities claim 15 percent of the college's men, who aren't permit-ted to pledge until sophomore year, and there are no sororities at William Smith (so much for the Socratic mean), so Greek life is an option, not an imperative. For men who'd rather not join in, Bampton House (the men's honors house) and McDaniel's House are good bets. Women may choose smaller residence halls, like Blackwell and Miller houses, which contribute to a feeling of community without rigid structure. William Smith has also retained a number of traditions typical of women's colleges, most notably Moving Up Day, in which seniors symbolically hand over their leader-ship role to juniors. (Hobart, not to be left out, has a similar event called Charter Day.)

Geneva is the embodiment of "small-town America," a junior says. Forget bright lights; the best you'll do here are a few coffee shops, a pool hall, a video-rental store, and an upscale grocery within walking distance of campus—and even those don't stay open late. But students say they feel welcomed by the town, and they show their thanks by volunteering. The annual Celebrate Service, Celebrate Geneva Day brings more than five hundred students and faculty members together for community service projects, ranging from tutoring to working in soup kitchens to home building with Habitat for Humanity. Students also look forward to the two-day Folk Fest, a music-, food-, and craft-filled party now held in the fall. There's a "zero tolerance" policy for underage drinking, and those who aren't twenty-one will find it tough to buy alcohol on cam-pus, but "it's relatively easy" for anyone to get a beer at off-campus pubs, says a senior. On weekends, "the outdoor recreation pro-gram hosts a variety of activities in the Adirondacks and surrounding areas," says a biology and environmental science major. "Rochester, Ithaca, and Syracuse are all about forty-five minutes away, providing easy weekend travel." Some intrepid souls really looking to escape trek as far as New York City, Washington, D.C., and Toronto, Canada.

> **"It has become more academic and less party-oriented in the four years I've been here."**

Sports are the most popular diversion from studying here. Each spring, the campus comes alive with mania for men's lacrosse, which has a long-standing rivalry with Syracuse. The team won 16 straight NCAA Division III championships before joining Division I in 1995, and made it to the NCAA playoffs in 1998, 2000, and 2002. The William Smith field hockey team won national titles in 1997 and 2000, and the lacrosse and soccer teams reach their Final Fours nearly every year. Sailing is strong and *US SAILING* recently named Hobart and William Smith Col-leges Sailing Head Coach Scott Iklé National Coach of the Year. Football, soccer, ice hockey, and basketball are becoming increasingly popular.

> *Administrators hope a planned "Finger Lakes Institute" at the college will become a center for the study and preservation of the lakes and the study of the region's future economic development.*

> ### Overlaps
> **Union, Skidmore, Hamilton, St. Lawrence, University of Vermont**

Hobart and William Smith Colleges may not be as well known as some other northeastern schools—a popular campus T-shirt explains, "Not Williams...Not Smith...William Smith!"—but that may be changing, students say. "It has become more academic and less party-oriented in the four years I've been here," says a senior. "The administration is seeking to make this a top-tier institution."

Hollins University

(formerly Hollins College)
P.O. Box 9707, Roanoke, VA 24020

Hollins is among a trio of western Virginia women's colleges—along with Sweet Briar and Randolph-Macon. Hollins is in the biggest city of the three, Roanoke, and has long been noted for its program in creative writing. Social life often depends on road trips to Washington and Lee and Virginia Tech.

Website: www.hollins.edu
Location: City outskirts
Total Enrollment: 1,153
Undergraduates: 847
Male/Female: 0/100
SAT Ranges: V 530–660
 M 490–610
ACT Range: 21–28
Financial Aid: 59%
Expense: Pr $ $ $
Phi Beta Kappa: Yes
Applicants: 686
Accepted: 80%
Enrolled: 37%
Grad in 6 Years: 68%
Returning Freshmen: 79%
Academics: ✑ ✑ ✑
Social: 🐿 🐿 🐿
Q of L: ★ ★ ★ ★
Admissions: (540) 362-6401
Email Address:
 huadm@hollins.edu

Strongest Programs:
English/Creative Writing
Psychology
Visual Arts/Film

Don't tell the students at this small liberal arts university that the time for single-sex education has passed, or you may find yourself being shown the door. When president Jane Rasmussen forecast financial disaster and suggested that the university consider going co-ed, she was unanimously ousted by the school's trustees. Make no mistake, the students here are fiercely loyal to the original mission of this small university and will fight to keep it intact.

Described by the *New York Times* as "achingly picturesque," the neoclassical redbrick buildings at Hollins date back to the mid-nineteenth century. Modernization is occurring, though, when the Wyndham Robertson Library—Virginia's first national literary landmark—recently joined the campus. The cafeteria was also renovated and the old library will be turned into a center for art history, studio art, film, and photography. A visual arts center is nearing completion as well.

Whether it's the award-winning writing program, the highly prized honor system, or the student-administered Independent Exam System, which allows students to take exams when they choose (within limits) and without faculty supervision, Hollins has much to offer. The academic program is rigorous but not brutally so. "Classes are difficult and workloads are fairly heavy, however the professor availability makes everything manageable," a senior history student says. The history, political science, English—particularly creative writing—and psychology departments are the strongest on campus, students say. Art is also a popular choice; a link to Christie's in London offers a yearlong opportunity to learn about galleries and auction houses, with strong emphasis on writing and research. Math and science programs tend to suffer because the emphasis here is on liberal arts, according to students.

Hollins changed its general education requirements in the fall of 2001 to emphasize the integration of areas of knowledge and the acquisition of specific skills. Students must now take at least eight credits in humanities, social sciences, fine arts, and natural and mathematical sciences and must demonstrate competence in written and oral communications, quantitative reasoning, and information technology. Two terms of physical education are also mandatory. Self-motivated students are encouraged to design individualized majors. Hollins does offer a combined-degree program in engineering and architecture, and, as a member of the Seven-College Exchange* consortium, allows students to cross-register at other participating institutions.

(Continued)
Dance
Biology
Communications Studies

Those with wanderlust may spend semesters at Hollins's extended campuses in England, France, Mexico, Spain, or Japan; 50 percent of all students spend some time abroad. They may also study in Ireland, Austria, Greece, or Italy; a service-learning program takes altruistic (or sun-seeking) students to Jamaica every year. The January term offers a break for on-campus projects, travel, or internships; alumnae help arrange housing in Washington and other cities. Classes here are small—more than three-quarters have twenty-five or fewer students, and none have more than fifty.

"Hollins is filled with hippies, geeks, Christians, ghetto girls, antisocials, 'pearl-girls,' and so many more. Hollins students, I believe, are far more diverse than at rival institutions," says a sophomore.

Back when Hollins was seen as a finishing school, its women were once disparaged as "Hollie Collies." Now they are seen as a mix of types, though not so much of ethnicities. The student body is 80 percent Caucasian, 6 percent African-American, 2 percent Hispanic, and 1 percent Asian-American. "Hollins is filled with hippies, geeks, Christians, ghetto girls, antisocials, 'pearl-girls,' and so many more. Hollins students, I believe, are far more diverse than at rival institutions," says a sophomore. Half of the students are Virginians, and 30 percent graduated in the top tenth of their high-school class.

"We have the most outspoken, nonconformist students here who are always looking for improvements in the administration and school as to make it better for the next class."

"We have the most outspoken, nonconformist students here who are always looking for improvements in the administration and school as to make it better for the next class," says a sophomore. Students vie for four hundred merit scholarships worth up to $18,200, though student athletes must find other means for footing the bill.

Dorms at Hollins range from the modern Tinker and Randolph to century-old houses on the Front Quad called East, West, and Main. The latter have wide front porches and halls, high ceilings, and hardwood floors in some of the "large, spacious, airy" rooms, says an economics major. Some rooms also include brass doorknobs, walk-in closets, and even fireplaces. The administration encourages students to live on campus and 90 percent do. Security is described as "on the ball," and students feel more than safe at their campus in the mountains.

A link to Christie's in London offers a yearlong opportunity to learn about galleries and auction houses, with strong emphasis on writing and research.

The city of Roanoke has a small museum, ethnic restaurants, a farmers' market, and artsy stores, says a junior. Students give back through a group called SHARE, which organizes volunteer work through the Society for the Prevention of Cruelty to Animals, Habitat for Humanity, and organizations serving local children and the elderly. "There are no clubs for us to dance at, and the bar scene is disappointing," says a student, although the college does offer discounted cab vouchers so that students who imbibe don't drink and drive.

Hollins shuns sororities, but sporadic student efforts to bring them to campus draws lively debate. The school organizes schoolwide mixers and maintains several traditions—one student says there are too many to name—such as the annual Tinker Day sometime after the first frost. Classes are canceled, everyone eats Krispy Kreme Donuts in PJs, and the whole school dresses up in "wacky costumes" and hikes to the top of Tinker Mountain for songs, performances, and a lunch of fried chicken and cake.

"Better dead than co-ed!"

On Ring Night, juniors receive their class rings from seniors, and on Hundredth Night seniors put on skits to celebrate the hundredth night before graduation. Drinks are available in the on-campus snack bar, but it's almost impossible for underage students to be served at college events because everyone knows everyone, and two forms of ID are required anyway. Road-tripping remains the preferred social option, and favored destinations are Hampden-Sydney College, Virginia Tech, the University of Virginia, and Washington and Lee.

The Hollins Outdoor Program offers hiking or spelunking in the beautiful Shenandoah Valley and Blue Ridge Mountains. The on-campus stable complements the school's equestrian program, which brought home a 2002 Intercollegiate Horse Show Association championship. Women's tennis won the Old Dominion Athletic Conference in 2002, and the swim team has won national Division III championships. In addition to the lacrosse, field hockey, golf, soccer, basketball, and tennis teams, Hollins offers fencing.

Loyal students continue to cry "Better dead than co-ed!" Hollins University has known all along what many private and public school educators and parents are rediscovering—that single-sex education is terrific for the right kind of student. Hollins has made a specialty of educating women for a long time and not only turns out independent women with a grounding in the liberal arts but provides a cozy, enjoyable atmosphere in which to learn. "We have a great sense of community and bonding between faculty, staff, and students. It makes us united in everything," a satisfied senior says.

Overlaps

Randolph-Macon, Mary Baldwin, Sweet Briar, Mary Washington, Virginia Tech

If You Apply To ➤

Hollins: Rolling admissions: Feb. 15 for priority. Early decision: Dec. 1. Financial aid: Feb. 1. Does not guarantee to meet demonstrated need. Campus interviews: recommended, informational. Alumni interviews: optional, informational. SAT or ACT: required. SAT IIs: recommended. Accepts the Common Application and electronic applications. Essay question: choose one: significant experience and its effect on you; volunteer service you have performed; how you express your creativity or have used it to solve problems; a woman you admire outside your family.

College of the Holy Cross

Worcester, MA 01610

A tight-knit Roman Catholic community steeped in church and tradition. Many students are the second or third generation to attend. Set high on a hill above gritty Worcester, an hour from Boston. Sports teams compete with (and occasionally beat) schools ten times HC's size.

Website: www.holycross.edu
Location: City outskirts
Total Enrollment: 2,773
Undergraduates: 2,773
Male/Female: 46/54
SAT Ranges: V 580–680
   M 630–670
Financial Aid: 58%
Expense: Pr $ $ $ $
Phi Beta Kappa: Yes
Applicants: 5,035
Accepted: 42%

Students at Holy Cross, a Roman Catholic college in the heart of New England, are devoted to the Jesuit tradition of becoming "men and women for others." They're a "happy, driven" bunch, says a senior. Peers and professors alike offer support and spiritual guidance, and bonds forged in the lab or on the field are strengthened through activities like SPUD (Student Programs for Urban Development), which provides community service opportunities. The classroom focus is critical thinking and writing, but the school's proximity to nine other colleges in the Boston area means Crusaders focus on their social lives, too. "One might think that HC, being a conservative school, would be cliqueish," says a junior. "However, that is not the case—everyone is friendly."

Located on one of the seven hills overlooking the industrial city of Worcester, the 174-acre Holy Cross campus is a registered arboretum. The school's landscaping has won a half-dozen national awards, including two first-place prizes, as the best-designed and planted campus in the nation. Architectural styles range from classical to modern, including Smith Hall, a 56,000-square-foot building for the departments of philosophy and religious studies that was just completed. The facility also houses centers for interdisciplinary and special studies—such as deaf studies and gerontology—and for religion, ethics, and culture. The biology department's O'Neill Hall has been renovated and expanded.

Other Holy Cross award winners are its small classes—69 percent of those taken by freshmen have twenty-five or fewer students, the rest have fifty or less—which help faculty members keep in touch with undergraduates. "We don't have any TAs or grad students teaching," says a sophomore. "Students are expected to put in two to three hours of studying for every hour spent in class," adds a senior. Crusaders come from a variety of backgrounds and hometowns, though most are Irish Catholics from the northeast who want "to learn and excel," says a political science major. "Cooperation is encouraged to improve the learning experience."

Students give high marks to HC's premed, English, history, and economics and accounting programs. As might be expected, philosophy and religious studies are strong, and concentrations in Latin American studies and peace and conflict studies are popular, as these are the disciplines central to Jesuit missionary work. Holy Cross recently added community-based learning courses, which include two to two-and-a-half hours of weekly service with local volunteer, education, or health organizations, in addition to time in the classroom. Students say they tend to avoid the extremely difficult chemistry and physics departments and note that music, theater, and fine arts suffer because of their small size. However, as the student/faculty ratio in these departments is about 2–1 and tutorials are encouraged, carefully chosen seminars can be excellent.

For a decade, nearly a quarter of Holy Cross's first-year students have enrolled in the First Year Program, which attempts to answer a question adapted from Tolstoy, "How then shall we live?" The FYP includes seminars, each limited to fifteen students; shared readings; cocurricular events; and a common dorm. Aside from

> "Students are expected to put in two to three hours of studying for every hour spent in class."

the FYP, Holy Cross's general education requirements comprise twelve courses in seven areas: arts and literature, religious and philosophical studies, natural and mathematical sciences, social sciences, language studies, historical studies, and cross-cultural studies. Ideas and thinking are the focus rather than preparation for a specific vocation.

Holy Cross is part of the Worcester Consortium,* which offers registration privileges at the region's most prestigious colleges and universities. Aspiring teachers will find education courses and student-teaching opportunities at local primary and secondary schools and a teacher certification program accredited by the Massachusetts Department of Education. Would-be engineers can choose Holy Cross's 3–2 dual-degree programs with Columbia or Dartmouth; a partnership with nearby Clark offers a B.A. and M.B.A., or a B.A. and master's in finance, in five years. Off-campus opportunities include academic internships in the community and the Washington Semester.* HC's honors program enables a small number of juniors and seniors to enroll in exclusive courses and thesis-writing seminars, while the Fenwick Scholars program helps students design and carry out independent projects. Through the Venture Program* and partnerships with

> "The college is concerned with increasing diversity, and has developed a task force for that purpose."

foreign universities, students may spend their junior year in one of eighteen programs in twelve European, Asian, and African nations. About one-fifth do so.

The religious influence at Holy Cross is somewhat greater than at other Jesuit schools—most students are Roman Catholic, one-third are in-staters, and less than half attended public high school—but daily Mass is not required. The chaplain's

(Continued)

Enrolled: 33%
Grad in 6 Years: 89%
Returning Freshmen: 98%
Academics: ✑ ✑ ✑ ✑
Social: ☎ ☎ ☎ ☎
Q of L: ★ ★ ★ ★
Admissions: (508) 793-2443
Email Address:
  admissions@holycross.edu

Strongest Programs:
Biology/Premed
History
Economics
English
Psychology
Political Science
Philosophy/Religious Studies

Holy Cross recently added community-based learning courses, which include two to two-and-a-half hours of weekly service with local volunteer, education, or health organizations, in addition to time in the classroom.

office does offer an optional five-day silent retreat four times a year, in which student volunteers follow the spiritual exercises of Jesuit founder St. Ignatius Loyola. African-Americans make up 3 percent of the student body, Asian-Americans comprise 4 percent, and Hispanics account for 5 percent. "The college is concerned with increasing diversity, and has developed a task force for that purpose," says a biology major. "The college is also working on controlling underage drinking." There are no sororities or fraternities.

Eighty-seven percent of Holy Cross students live in the residence halls, where freshmen and sophomores have double rooms, and juniors and seniors may opt for two- and three-bedroom suites—with living rooms and bathrooms, but no kitchens. Floors are single-sex; buildings are co-ed. Most first-years live on "Easy Street," the row of five dorms (Healy, Leahy, Hanselman, Clark, and Mulledy) on the college's central hill next to the Hogan Campus Center. Wheeler, Loyola, Alumni and Carlin house mostly upperclassmen. Each dorm has its own T-shirt, and they compete against each other for prizes in athletic and other contests, says a philosophy major. Doors have combination locks, which means no worries about forgetting your keys when you walk to the shower. Students say they feel safe on campus. "Public safety officers make rounds often," says a junior. "Holy Cross is pretty well enclosed into itself" despite its location in Worcester, a gritty industrial center and New England's second-largest city.

While Worcester isn't Boston, the town doesn't deserve its lousy reputation, students say. An hour from Beantown, Cape Cod's beaches, and the ski slopes of the White Mountains, Worcester "has everything you need—movies, clubs, restaurants, groceries, bars," says a junior. A school shuttle service takes students to the orchestra, the Worcester Centrum for athletic events and rock concerts, and the town's museum. Nightlife is good, especially with so many other schools nearby. HC abides by Massachusetts liquor law: Students under twenty-one can't drink at the campus pub. If they're caught with alcohol, they're put on probation and parents are notified. Still, as with most schools, students who seek to imbibe can find booze, regardless of their age. Since students are discouraged from having cars, most take advantage of concerts, hypnotists, comedians, and other events organized by the Campus Activities Board. The college also organizes trips to New York City and Providence, Rhode Island.

> **"Holy Cross is pretty well enclosed into itself."**

Tradition is big at Holy Cross, from Alumni Weekend to HC by the Sea, a week in Cape Cod at the end of the year. Midnight breakfasts provide sustenance as students cram for finals, while the 100 Days weekend begins the senior class countdown to graduation. Spring Weekend has brought headliners like Run DMC and the Pat McGee Band to campus. Would-be matchmakers can set up their roommates on dates at the "Opportunity Knocks" dance. And of course, given the high percentage of Irish Catholic students, St. Patrick's Day is an occasion for celebration. Students cheer with religious zeal when the Crusaders battle Boston College at HC's football stadium, which holds 23,500 screaming fans. Men's basketball and women's field hockey, soccer, and basketball teams have recently won Patriot League Championships.

Holy Cross is keeping the faith—its emphasis on Catholicism and the Jesuit tradition, that is—even as administrators place a renewed emphasis on academics. Four new tenure-track faculty, designated Edward Bennett Williams Fellows, are charged with teaching and pursuing research in English, religious studies, sociology, and philosophy that bears directly on the college's mission as a Jesuit institution focused on the liberal arts. Still, students here haven't forgotten how to have fun, as a campus T-shirt proclaims: "Purple Reign all the way!"

Holy Cross: Early decision: Dec. 15. Regular admissions: Jan. 15. Guarantees to meet demonstrated need. Campus and alumni interviews: recommended, evaluative. SATs or ACTs: required. SAT IIs: required (writing and two others). Accepts the Common Application and electronic applications. Essay question: a familial custom, practice, or tradition that's influenced you; would you travel forward or backward in time, what period you would visit, and why; how a Jesuit education will benefit you; or what makes your hometown unique.

Hood College

401 Rosemont Avenue, Frederick, MD 21701

The newly co-ed Hood faces a challenging task in building a co-ed environment. A major asset: Hood's strategic location, one hour from Baltimore and D.C. Hood's distinctive core curriculum stresses thematic study, and a Freshman Colloquium program ensures that all students have a common touchstone.

Newly co-ed Hood College has given new meaning to the term "legacy" in college admissions. This small liberal arts college lets the children and grandchildren of alumni pay the same tuition for their freshmen year as their elders. If Granny was Hood Class of '50, that means the tab is only $500! The new tuition policy is only one of the creative steps that Hood has been taking to reinvent itself in the wake of declining enrollment and serious financial problems in the late 1990s. The big change came in 2003 when Hood began admitting men as regular residential students (males had been commuting students since 1971). Now members of both sexes have the opportunity to partake of Hood's traditional mix of professional and liberal arts offerings on a campus strategically located in an historic Civil War setting.

Hood was founded as a women's college in 1893. Its strikingly beautiful fifty-acre campus, which features redbrick buildings and lush, tree-shaded lawns, sits in the Civil War town of Frederick. Hood is within an hour and a half of nearly thirty colleges, within minutes of a major National Cancer Institute research complex, high-tech firms, small and large businesses, and both Washington, D.C., and Baltimore. On campus, technology programs, which are already important, will get a further boost with the new Hodson Science and Technology Center.

> "There are so many cultures and ethnicities and traditions to be shared."

Students see their school's biggest strength as its people: students, staff, and faculty. "There are so many cultures and ethnicities and traditions to be shared," says one junior. "I love living here. I'm having the time of my life." All incoming students participate in the Freshman Colloquium, a series of intellectual, social, and cultural events that focus on a different topic each year. Sophomore Experience helps students pick a major and plan a career. The honor system also is an important part of a Hood education. The academic honor code permits unproctored exams and self-scheduled finals; the social code allows for self-governed residence halls where students call the shots in place of resident assistants.

Hood's required core curriculum is divided into three parts. Foundation courses include English, foreign language, computation, physical education, and fitness. Methods of Inquiry offers courses that acquaint students with scientific thought, historical and social/behavioral analysis, and philosophy. The Civilization section requires coursework in modern technology and Western and non-Western civilization at the junior-senior level. Even with these comprehensive requirements, there is still a great deal of flexibility; creative interdepartmental majors are often approved.

Website: www.hood.edu
Location: Small city
Total Enrollment: 1,693
Undergraduates: 820
Male/Female: 12/88
SAT Ranges: V 493–620
  M 473–590
ACT Range: 18–24
Financial Aid: 90%
Expense: Pr $ $
Phi Beta Kappa: No
Applicants: 530
Accepted: 78%
Enrolled: 43%
Grad in 6 Years: 62%
Returning Freshmen: 80%
Academics: ✑ ✑ ✑
Social: ☎ ☎ ☎
Q of L: ★ ★ ★
Admissions: (301) 922-1599
Email Address:
  admissions@hood.edu

Strongest Programs:
Biology
Management
Psychology
Education
Communication Arts
Social Work/Sociology

Hood's major strength lies in the sciences, especially the biology department, with its special emphases on molecular biology, marine biology, and environmental science and policy. A new semester-long coastal studies program takes students along the East Coast on a biological educational mission. Education, especially early childhood, is a program of note, as are psychology, communications, English, and management. The graduate school of mostly commuting students is as large as the undergraduate program. The Summer Research Institute allows twenty or so students to work with faculty members on research projects, and provides the students with a stipend.

"I love living here. I'm having the time of my life."

Hood has a unique financial aid program for legacy students—their first-year tuition will be the same as that paid by their parent or grandparent who attended the college.

Students say the learning environment is more rigorous than competitive. "The professors here are amazing," raves one mathematics and computer science major. In general, Hood students are "interested in their education and are serious and hardworking," says a sophomore. Hood students praise the competence and accessibility of the faculty. "The teachers want their students to succeed and are very accessible when students need help," says a math major. Only labs are taught by graduate assistants, and 93 percent of freshmen classes have twenty-five or fewer students. A computer network links every dorm room and academic building to the campuswide information system, and students have twenty-four-hour Internet access.

If you really want to stimulate the brain cells, the four-year honors program features team-taught courses and a sophomore-year seminar on the ethics of social and individual responsibility with student involvement in a community-service project. One-tenth of students complete internships that include overseas jobs for language and business majors and legislative and cultural positions in Washington, D.C. With the outstanding resources of the Catherine Filene Shouse Career Center (including a national electronic listing for resumes), students have a leg up on their next step in life—69 percent of graduates go straight into jobs after graduation; 16 percent enroll in graduate or professional schools. A unique French-German major is available to Hood students at the college's center at the University of Strasbourg in France. Other study abroad destinations are Korea, Japan, South America, and South Africa.

"The teachers want their students to succeed and are very accessible when students need help."

The Hood student body is 64 percent Caucasian, and one student says that characterizing her classmates is difficult because "we all come from such different financial, cultural, ethnic, and personal backgrounds. The only thing I can say for sure is that we come here to learn." Twelve percent of the student body are African-American, while Hispanics and Asian-Americans each make up 2 percent. Nineteen percent are from foreign countries. Twenty percent of Hood students are from out of state, with a large contingent from the Northeast. Students say major issues on campus include diversity, sexuality, and alcohol. Hood provides numerous merit scholarships, which can range from $500 to full tuition. And then, of course, there's that unbeatable deal for legacies.

The academic honor code permits unproctored exams and self-scheduled finals; the social code allows for self-governed residence halls where students call the shots in place of resident assistants.

Hood's residence halls are well liked, with good-sized rooms that are air-conditioned. One of the dorms, Shriner Hall, has been renovated. The lottery system is based on seniority, and 56 percent of students live on campus. Freshmen can expect to be assigned to doubles (seniors and juniors can compete for singles), and languages majors may choose to live in French-, Spanish-, or German-language houses.

Social life among the students is centered around the dorms, as each has its own personality as well as its own house council, rules, and social activities. Students report that there are parties every weekend, along with movies, dances, or other forms of entertainment. The Whitaker Campus Center, with its pool tables, snack bar, bookstore, and meeting rooms, offers a great gathering place for residents and commuters twenty-four hours a day. "If you don't like to stay on campus, there are restaurants, bars, clubs, malls, and coffeehouses within ten minutes of the college (by car)," explains an English major. About an hour in the car brings students to the multiple diversions in Baltimore and Washington, D.C. Campus alcohol policies follow state law and the honor code, but in general drinking is not a big deal at Hood. "At parties and events, you have to show ID to get alcohol," one senior says. "However, in the dorms at other times, it is possible for underage students to get alcohol from those 'of age.'" Students also frequent scenic Frederick, which is described as small, safe, and beautiful but without too much in the way of entertainment.

With a one-hundred-year history, Hood is rife with traditions. Some of the most important ones include Class Ring dinner and formal, a performance of Handel's *Messiah*, and Spring Parties, a weekend of carnival activities and dances. In sports, tennis, swimming, and basketball are tops. Students also brag that Hood has never lost a football game since 1893 (or, they might add, played one).

While Hood has undergone the major change from a women's college to a coeducational institution, its mission remains the same: to prepare students to face the challenges of a fast-changing society and professional environment. Century-old traditions are sure to remain, while new ones are sure to be made.

If You Apply To ➢ **Hood:** Early action: Dec. 1. Regular admissions: Feb. 1. Guarantees to meet demonstrated need of 38%. Campus interviews: recommended, evaluative. No alumni interviews. SATs or ACTs: required. SAT IIs: recommended. Accepts the Common Application and electronic applications. Essay question: leadership; issue or topic of concern.

Hope College

P.O. Box 9000, Holland, MI 49422

Hope has an in-between size—bigger than most small colleges but smaller than most universities. Evangelical in orientation, but less than a fourth of the students are members of the Reformed Church in America. In addition to the liberal arts, Hope offers education, engineering, and nursing, and more research opportunities than schools of its kind.

Each fall since 1897, Hope College freshmen have spent three grueling hours engaged in "the Pull," an epic tug-of-war against the sophomores, who stand assembled on the opposite end of a 650-pound rope across the 15-foot-wide Black River. This well-known annual tradition evokes the daily struggle Hope students face: maintaining their faith in a world eager to challenge it at every turn. The heritage of Hope's Dutch founders remains strong and visible on campus, but you don't have to be a member of the Reformed Church in America to appreciate the charms of this conservative Christian college.

The college, founded in 1866, is situated on six blocks near downtown Holland, the tulip capital of the nation (population 60,000) and a short bike ride from the shores of Lake Michigan. There's a lush pine grove in the center of campus, which features an eclectic array of buildings in architectural styles ranging from nineteenth-century Flemish to modern. A new $36 million Science Center opened in fall 2003 and construction of an athletic field house and a global communications center is on tap.

(Continued)

Grad in 6 Years: 74%

Returning Freshmen: 88%

Academics: ✍ ✍ ✍

Social: ☎ ☎ ☎

Q of L: ★ ★ ★

Admissions: (616) 395-7850

Email Address:

admissions@hope.edu

Strongest Programs:

Biology

Chemistry

Dance

Education

English

Music

Political Science

Psychology

Religion

A new $36 million Science Center was scheduled to open in fall 2003. Construction of an athletic field house and a global communications center is on tap.

Among Hope's academic offerings, the sciences (especially biology, physics, and chemistry) stand out, with excellent laboratory facilities and faculty who are eager to involve students in their funded research. During the school year, undergraduates often conduct advanced experiments and even publish papers; come summer, more than seventy-five biology, chemistry, mathematics, computer science, and physics and engineering majors participate in research full-time. Not surprisingly, many science majors go on to medical and engineering schools and Ph.D. programs. For those otherwise

"The professors are what make Hope the outstanding institution it is."

inclined, Hope's offerings in political science, psychology, music, dance, and education are solid, too. Hope's Department of Communication is one of the Speech Communication Association's two nationwide Programs of Excellence. And Hope is one of only fourteen colleges and universities in the nation with accredited programs in art, dance, music, and theater. The First-Year seminar and GEMS (General Education in Math and Science) courses are two new fully implemented courses. Offerings in anthropology and journalism continue to be limited, administrators say. The bachelor's-level nursing program, offered with Calvin College since 1982, became an independent Hope-only degree in 2003.

Most Hope students select a major from one of the college's thirty-nine fields, although the truly adventurous may design their own composite major. Hope's general education program, designed around the themes "knowing how" and "knowing about," includes a first-year seminar, which provides "an intellectual transition into Hope." Courses in expository writing, health dynamics, math and natural science, foreign language, religious studies, social sciences, the arts, and cultural heritage are also required; some must have a focus on cultural diversity. Students also complete a senior seminar, and a two-credit freshman seminar linked with academic advising. "Hope is a very strong school academically. However, the climate of classes is comfortable," a sophomore religion major says. Professors get high marks, too. "The teaching is absolutely exceptional," the same student says. "The professors are what make Hope the outstanding institution it is."

Hope offers off-campus programs through the Great Lakes Colleges Association,* including semesters at other U.S. colleges and options combining classes and internships. Students may also study abroad in Austria, England, Greece, Japan, or Israel. The modern and classical language departments offer students proficient in a second language the chance to use their skills in volunteer work and research with faculty members, while the Visiting Writers Series gives students an opportunity to interact with noteworthy authors.

Less than a fourth of Hope's students belong to the Reformed Church in America, but the student body is overwhelmingly Christian, white, conservative—and female. Thrice-weekly chapel is voluntary, but administrators say it's typically filled to capacity. "It definitely is a Christian campus. People have very high morals and want to find ways to have genuine fun," says a senior. Seventy-four percent of students hail from Michigan; African-Americans, Hispanics, and Asian-Americans make up just 5 percent of the student body. "The biggest social issue is that we aren't very diverse," says an accounting major, while another student feels "the biggest debate at Hope is over the Christian nature of the college." Homosexuality is another sensitive issue on campus. "Homosexual students often struggle to find a place in a student body that does not readily accept them," says one junior. Despite all of these issues students still feel that "one word that describes the campus community is friendly."

Hope's housing options include on-campus apartments, small houses called cottages, and traditional dorms, arranged in freshman clusters or co-ed by suite. First-year students are assigned dorms and roommates; upperclassmen get first pick in the annual lottery. Only seniors and married students may live off-campus, one reason why dorms are "very crowded," says a senior. "Housing is great except you are supposed to have seventy-five credits before you can live off campus," says a senior. "I believe after your sophomore year you should be able to be off campus." On-campus students eat in one of two large dining halls, where the fare—especially homemade bread and desserts—is tasty. "The food is very diverse!" says a junior.

Most of Hope's social life takes place on campus. The Social Activities Committee brings in comedians, bands, and hypnotists, shows movies in campus auditoriums, and plans the Spring Festival carnival, Winter Fantasia dance, and May Day celebration. Seven fraternities and six sororities, all local organizations, claim 26 percent of the men and 28 percent of the women, but Hope's campus is officially dry. While there are no echoes of *Animal House* on campus, "it's easy to find alcohol at off-campus parties, especially fraternity parties," admits one student. Students caught drinking must perform community service, although plenty of students do that anyway, through activities like charity walks in Holland, a "very touristy town" with "great downtown shopping" and a "simple, slow-paced lifestyle." Holland is also the site of spring's Tulip Time, one of the largest U.S. flower festivals.

Perhaps not surprisingly, social preferences here lean more toward sports, games, and coffeehouses than to keg parties. But when Hope's cozy campus and the quaint town of Holland get too close for comfort, students find relief at the beaches of Lake Michigan or drive 30 minutes to Grand Rapids, which offers some large-city amenities and good weekend rental deals at the ski slopes. Chicago and Detroit are other typical destinations for those trying to hit the road.

On the field and on the court, Hope's Flying Dutchmen are fearless and talented Division III competitors. The men's football team has won several conference championships in recent years, while the men's swim team recently finished fourth nationwide. Last year, Hope athletes and teams qualified for

"It definitely is a Christian campus. People have very high morals and want to find ways to have genuine fun."

eleven NCAA championship tournaments. The college also won the Commissioner's Cup of the Michigan Intercollegiate Athletic Association for the sixth time in the past eight years; the trophy recognizes the school with the conference's best cumulative sports program for men and women. Especially important are any competition against Calvin (a century-old rivalry) and football versus Albion and Kalamazoo.

Without losing sight of its Christian roots, the campus is expanding, political issues are becoming more openly discussed, and students are getting involved in the community. "From the president of the college to the maintenance staff, Hope is a community," says one happy student. "People intentionally seek out students to support, encourage, and challenge in and out of the classroom."

Hope's Department of Communication is one of the Speech Communication Association's two nationwide Programs of Excellence.

Overlaps

Michigan State, Western Michigan, University of Michigan, Grand Valley State, Calvin

If You Apply To ➤

Hope: Rolling admissions. Meets demonstrated need of 85%. Campus interviews: optional, informational. No alumni interviews. SATs or ACTs: required. SAT IIs: optional. Accepts the Common Application. Essay question: something important to you; a memorable experience that has influenced your life.

Houghton College

Houghton, NY 14744

The mid-Atlantic's premier evangelical Christian college. Women outnumber men nearly two to one and enjoy perks such as a 386-acre horseback-riding facility. All students are required to take a Biblical literature class, and most go to chapel three times a week.

Website: www.houghton.edu
Location: Rural
Total Enrollment: 1,325
Undergraduates: 1,325
Male/Female: 36/64
SAT Ranges: V 530–640
  M 520–630
ACT Range: 22–28
Financial Aid: 70%
Expense: Pr $
Phi Beta Kappa: No
Applicants: 956
Accepted: 93%
Enrolled: 32%
Grad in 6 Years: 72%
Returning Freshmen: 86%
Academics: ✍ ✍ ✍
Social: ☎ ☎ ☎
Q of L: ★ ★ ★ ★
Admissions: (800) 777-2556
Email Address:
  admission@houghton.edu

Strongest Programs:
Music
Biology
Bible
English
Education
Psychology

The school recently received state approval to start new graduate music programs in performance, composition, and conducting.

Houghton College, located in the bucolic New York town that shares its name, offers a solid, growing academic program and strong athletic teams, but remains committed to its core mission as a Christian liberal arts school. Run by the Wesleyan Church of America, Houghton celebrates its Christian heritage and tries to ensure that students do the same. Applicants must explain in their essays why they want to go to a Christian college, and thrice-weekly chapel attendance is a must. These strict mandates help create true community on campus. "I feel stretched, loved, supported, and honestly blessed to be at such a special place with such a warm, loving community of friends and mentors," says a sophomore.

Houghton's scenic hilltop campus covers thirteen hundred acres of rural beauty, surrounded by vast expanses of western New York countryside. The academic buildings are a mix of area fieldstone and brick with ivy-covered walls. Students can go online with the laptops they get at matriculation; through Houghton's Educational Technology Initiative, the computer's price is included in the tuition bill. The thirty-six-unit Houghton Apartment complex for upperclassmen and the Perkins Townhouses were recently added to the campus.

Students say Houghton's academic climate is rigorous, but not overwhelmingly so. "The level of competition is really up to the individual student, and courses are difficult, without being impossible," says a political science major. The school's most popular programs are education and biology, but business, music, and math also draw crowds. The accounting and computer science departments are less inspir-

> **"I feel stretched, loved, supported, and honestly blessed to be at such a special place with such a warm, loving community of friends and mentors."**

ing. Unusual minors such as equestrian studies—which takes advantage of Houghton's 386-acre riding facility—and linguistics have been joined by newer programs such as intercultural studies. The school recently received state approval to start new graduate music programs in performance, composition, conducting, and performance. Across departments, faculty get high marks for teaching and accessibility. "Freshmen through seniors have the opportunity to work with brilliant and interested teachers, most of whom live nearby and who take an active role in their students' lives," says a junior English major.

Houghton students must complete general education requirements known as Integrative Studies, designed to provide a context and framework for the entire educational program. Freshmen must take Biblical Literature, Principles of Writing, and a course titled FYI (First-Year Introduction), aimed at easing the transition to college. The First-Year Honors Program allows about twenty-five students to spend the spring semester of their freshman year in London studying under two Houghton professors.

In recent years, Houghton has begun to emphasize off-campus study, with programs in Paris, Tanzania, Honduras, Australia, and many locales in between. Students who want to get away within the U.S. can spend a semester at any Christian College Consortium* member school or participate in the American Studies program in Washington, D.C., sponsored by the Council for Christian Colleges and Universities.* The Oregon Extension program lets thirty Houghton students spend the fall studying in the Cascade Mountains while Houghton's extension campus in Buffalo offers internships and provides living quarters for students completing student teaching assignments. A 3–2 engineering program with Clarkson University (NY) is available, too.

Fifty-five percent of those who enroll at Houghton are from New York. The minority community is tiny, accounting for only 4 percent of the student body. Hot-button issues include the morality of war, international sensitivity, and gender-inclusive language. Closer to home, "the other big issue is the use of Styrofoam in the cafeteria...bad for the environment," says a junior English major. The increasing use of technology sparked a campus debate when the school's board blocked access to some Internet sites with sexually explicit materials or references. "There were students on both sides of the censorship issue, and eventually some of the restrictions were loosened," says a junior.

> **"The level of competition is really up to the individual student, and courses are difficult, without being impossible."**

Houghton's single-sex dorms, sixteen townhouses and thirty-six apartments are "well cleaned and carefully maintained." Students are required to live in the residence halls as freshmen and sophomores. There, in-room visitation is only allowed at weekly "open houses," but dorm lounges are open daily to members of the opposite sex. After their first two years, some students move off campus—77 percent of the total were dorm-dwellers at last count—but many opt for college-approved townhouses where regulations are self-imposed. This isn't exactly surprising, considering the other rules students voluntarily obey here, including abstention from tobacco, alcohol, drugs, and swearing, and optional Sunday church and Tuesday prayer meetings.

Houghton's boondocks village is truly small, lacking even a traffic light, says a junior. "It's us, a gas station, a coffeeshop, and a pizza place," the student says. "Students are very involved in service projects," such as Big Brothers Big Sisters and nursing home visitation, because the area surrounding the college is one of the poorest in New York State. Social life consists of on-campus movies, coffeehouses, concerts, and picnics. Because the student body is two-thirds female, dating can be a challenge. "You make your own fun at Houghton, or you go off-campus—usually Buffalo, Rochester, Olean, or Latchworth State Park," says a political science major. The college even has its own ski trails. The town of Houghton is "dry," and because college policy forbids alcohol,

> **"You make your own fun at Houghton, or you go off-campus."**

consumption is virtually nonexistent, says a freshman. "The student body does not put an emphasis on or find enjoyment in drinking," she notes. Students eagerly anticipate annual celebrations for Homecoming, Christian Life Emphasis Week, and the Christmastime Madrigal Banquets.

Soccer is the spectator sport of choice at Houghton, especially since there is no football team. The women's squad won the Region IX Championship in 2001 to advance to the NAIA National Tournament for the third time in four years. The women's basketball and volleyball teams also advanced to their respective national tournaments recently. The school's sports facilities have undergone extensive renovation and now include new tennis courts, an all-weather track, and lighted soccer and field hockey fields.

Students don't come to Houghton for the surrounding town, which is thirty minutes by car from the nearest mall, or for the weather, which can be brutal once winter sets in. But they do come, and for good reason, says a sophomore: there's little to distract them from their studies, their campus's natural beauty, and their

The thirty-six-unit Houghton Apartment complex for upperclassmen and the Perkins Townhouses were recently added to the campus.

Overlaps

Messiah, Roberts Wesleyan, Gordon, Grove City, Cedarville

connection to God. "I feel valued here," says a junior. "I love the community surrounding Houghton, and the people I have met—students, faculty, and staff—have made me feel welcomed and loved."

<table>
<tr><td>

If You

Apply

To >

</td><td>

Houghton: Rolling admissions. Financial aid: Mar. 1, Nov. 15. Housing: May 1. Does not guarantee to meet demonstrated need. Campus interviews: recommended, evaluative. No alumni interviews. SATs or ACTs: required. SAT IIs: optional. Music majors apply directly to music program. Accepts electronic applications. Essay question: when and how Christ became personal; how you are cultivating spiritual growth; why Houghton; opinion of the college's policies on drugs, alcohol, and tobacco; how a liberal arts college will contribute to your goals.

</td></tr>
</table>

Howard University

2400 Sixth Street NW, Washington, DC 20059

The flagship university of black America and the first to integrate the black experience into all areas of study. Strategically located in D.C., Howard depends on Congress for most of its funding. Preprofessional programs such as nursing, business, and architecture are among the most popular.

Website: www.howard.edu
Location: City center
Total Enrollment: 10,522
Undergraduates: 6,982
Male/Female: 36/64
SAT Ranges: V 440–680
    M 430–680
ACT Range: 20–29
Financial Aid: 43%
Expense: Pr $
Phi Beta Kappa: Yes
Applicants: 7,488
Accepted: 56%
Enrolled: 33%
Grad in 6 Years: 57%
Returning Freshmen: 85%
Academics: ✍ ✍
Social: ☎ ☎ ☎
Q of L: ★ ★ ★
Admissions: (202) 806-2763
Email Address:
    admission@howard.edu

Strongest Programs:
Biology
Psychology
Business
History
Communications

Perhaps it's no surprise that Howard University is located in the nation's capital, near the monuments and memorials erected to honor this country's history and heritage. This historically black school strives to educate its students about great achievements of African-Americans and honor the African-American perspective in the context of a traditional curriculum. Buoyed by the arrival of president (and alumnus) H. Patrick Swygert, Howard has strengthened its financial position and has begun implementation of a second strategic plan structured around "Leadership for America and the Global Community." The four-part plan focuses on strengthening academic programs and services, promoting excellence in teaching and research, increasing private support, and enhancing national and community service.

Founded in 1866 by General Oliver Howard primarily to educate freed slaves, the university now operates five campuses and serves nearly eleven thousand students. The eighty-nine-acre main campus houses most classrooms, dorms, and administrative offices, as well as the university center, the Founders, undergraduate and Medical and Dental libraries. The Howard Law Center, with a new library,

"Come to Howard ready to study."

is on the west campus near Rock Creek Park; the Divinity School is on a twenty-two-acre site in northeast Washington; and there's also a 108-acre campus in suburban Beltsville, Maryland, and a campus in Silver Spring. Architecturally, the main campus is a blend of old and new, with numerous sculptures and murals created by Jacob Lawrence, Richard Hunt, Elizabeth Catlett, and the late Romare Bearden. The campus is an easy bus ride from the attractions of the nation's capital, all the more visible now thanks to a campuswide window-replacement initiative. Auditoriums, office spaces, classrooms, galleries, and computer labs across campus have undergone large-scale renovation in recent years; the physics, chemistry, and fine arts facilities have also been completely redone.

Contrary to the advice of early black leaders such as Booker T. Washington, who argued in favor of technical training, Howard has promoted the liberal arts since its inception. This focus has served the school well; Howard's law school counts former Supreme Court Justice Thurgood Marshall among its alumni, and

Nobel Prize–winning author Toni Morrison went here, too. The school has excellent programs in business, computer sciences, and psychology. Other intriguing academic options are accelerated programs for a B.S. on the way to a medical or dental degree, coursework in the institute of jazz studies, programs in zoology and engineering (especially electrical engineering), and programs in communication science and disorders. The most popular major is biology, followed by political science, psychology, information sciences, and radio and television. New programs in ancient Mediterranean and international studies have become robust. Weaker departments include physical education, interior design, and recreation.

(Continued)
Fine Arts
Political Science

All students must complete general education requirements, which vary by school or college but uniformly encompass eighteen credits in science, social sciences, humanities, computer literacy, math, languages, and one Afro-American studies course. Freshman seminars and various other special programs for first-year students are available in the undergraduate schools such as communication, engineering, and arts and sciences. Seniors in arts and sciences must weather a comprehensive exam to graduate.

Founded in 1866 by General Oliver Howard primarily to educate freed slaves, the university now operates five campuses and serves nearly eleven thousand students.

In general, students say that the workload at Howard is demanding. "Some courses are more rigorous than others. But overall this school is tough," says a junior. Another student adds, "Come to Howard ready to study." Most students agree that professors are ready and willing to help when asked, though academic advising is not Howard's strength. "Sometimes you may get professors who do not know how to break down anything," explains a psychology major. "Then it is your job to talk up and ask questions. You must ask questions because a closed mouth does not get fed!" Students who need a break **"It's a very competitive school, from grades to fashion."** from the academic scene seek out internships in town or across the country. Many also study abroad at one of the more than two hundred institutions in thirty-six countries where Howard grants credit.

Eighty-seven percent of Howard students are African-American, and 11 percent hail from foreign countries. Most come from decidedly middle-class backgrounds. Although Howard seems to be a very cohesive community, career-minded and highly motivated men and women fit in best, students say, and most are politically liberal. "It's a very competitive school, from grades to fashion," says a junior. Hot issues include women's empowerment, student government, and fraternities and sororities. Fraternities and sororities do not have their own housing or dining facilities, and only 2 percent of men and 3 percent of women go Greek. Howard awards more than one hundred athletic scholarships in a variety of sports, and more than fifteen hundred merit scholarships. A deferred-payment plan also allows families to pay each semester's tuition in three installments. But even with financial aid, costs are steep; President Swygert hopes that will change as he encourages more alumni to give back to their alma mater.

Eighty-seven percent of Howard students are African-American, and 11 percent hail from foreign countries.

Interestingly, Howard is one of a handful of universities in the nation supported partly by federal subsidies; these days, the school gets about 55 percent of its budget from Congress. Bethune Hall, a $14 million housing complex, has helped ease the space crunch, but less than half of Howard's students are accommodated on campus. "It is quite difficult to get a room at times," says a sophomore economics major. "Housing at Howard is average in regards to availability, maintenance, and **"Housing at Howard is average in regards to availability, maintenance, and comfort."** comfort," says one student. Freshmen get room assignments, while upperclassmen take their chances in a lottery. The halls are co-ed, and the eleven residential computer labs have more than two hundred state-of-the-art machines for student use. Many students live off campus purely to avoid the mandatory meal plan. Still, the administration is doing its best to bring students back, and Drew, Meridian Hill, Baldwin, Carver, Truth, and Crandall halls have recently gotten facelifts.

Weekends bring an assortment of social happenings to campus, many of which take place in the student center. On-campus parties and sports events are always big draws, but the bars of Georgetown and Adams Morgan, the restaurants and clubs in the "New U" Street corridor, and the MCI Center arena (home to the NBA's Wizards and NHL's Capitals)—most accessible by public transit—also beckon. Though small in numbers, the Greeks are "an integral part of the university." Athletics are also an important presence on campus, particularly varsity basketball, soccer, football, and volleyball, and the highlight of the season is always the grudge match with Hampton University to decide which school is the "true HU." The women's cross-country team captured the MEAC championship recently. Students list Howard's Homecoming as one of the best annual events, along with various Greekfests, concerts, and talent shows that alumni, current students, and members of the community enjoy together.

Among America's historically black colleges and universities, Howard stands out as the standard-bearer, a longtime center of excellence and leadership. Its scholarship and collections of artworks, rare books, manuscripts, and photographs are a repository of the African-American experience and offer students unique educational opportunities.

Overlaps

Hampton, Clark Atlanta, Spelman, Morgan State, Florida A&M

If You Apply To ➤

Howard: Early action: Nov. 1. Regular admissions: Feb. 15. Financial aid: Feb. 18. Meets demonstrated need of 54%. Campus and alumni interviews: not available. SATs or ACTs: required. SAT IIs: required (writing only). Audition tape or portfolio required for fine arts applicants. No essay question unless applying for scholarship consideration by Early Action deadline.

University of Illinois at Urbana-Champaign

901 West Illinois, Urbana, IL 61801

Half a step behind Michigan and neck-and-neck with Wisconsin among top Midwestern public universities. U of I's strengths include business, communications, engineering, architecture, and the natural sciences. More than 90 percent of the student body hails from in-state.

Website: www.uiuc.edu
Location: Small city
Total Enrollment: 39,999
Undergraduates: 28,947
Male/Female: 53/47
SAT Ranges: V 550–670
 M 600–720
ACT Range: 26–30
Financial Aid: 40%
Expense: Pub $ $
Phi Beta Kappa: Yes
Applicants: 21,484
Accepted: 60%
Enrolled: 49%

Homecoming weekend was invented at the University of Illinois, and whether cheering for the Illini, pledging one of seventy-five Greek houses, or celebrating Moms', Dads', or Siblings' Weekends, students here stir up a vibrant mix of school spirit and good times. This may look and feel like a laid-back Midwestern campus, but students work hard for the degrees they receive, especially in prestigious departments such as engineering and business administration.

Befitting the oldest land-grant institution, the Illinois campus was built in farm country between the twin cities of Champaign and Urbana. The park-like campus was designed along a mile-long axis where trees and walkways separate stately white-columned Georgian structures made of brick. Physically challenged students tend to appreciate the campus because it is flat and well-equipped with ramps and widened doorways. A new 250,000 square-foot computer science center has recently opened, and so has an incubator facility, "The Enterprise Works @ Illinois," which provides

> "Students at the University of Illinois are the underdogs who are willing to fight."

faculty and students the opportunity to benefit from the commercialization of their research. Also new is the Spurlock Museum, with artifacts from diverse cultures and varied historical time periods.

Illinois has eight undergraduate colleges and more than one hundred fifty undergraduate programs; if nothing strikes your fancy, you may design your own. Requirements include six to nine hours of composition, three hours of quantitative reasoning, proficiency in a foreign language, and six hours each of cultural studies, natural sciences and technology, humanities and arts, and social and behavioral sciences. Engineering, architecture, business, education, and the sciences—especially agriculture and veterinary medicine—get high marks from students and lots of resources from administrators. The academic climate "varies by college," says a senior. "Engineering and Business tend to be highly competitive, while Liberal Arts and Sciences and Applied Life Studies are more relaxed." Whatever their academic pursuits, the students are fiercely loyal. "Students at the University of Illinois are the underdogs

"People used to say that Champaign was a drinking town with a football problem."

who are willing to fight," says a senior. "We're so tired of being out in the cornfields and looked over (compared to Berkeley and Michigan) that we work extremely hard to get where we want."

Partially because of its size, Illinois can afford to support excellent programs across the university, including the expansion of undergraduate minors campuswide. For a huge university, registration can be relatively painless, thanks to an online system allowing course selection from one's own computer. Nevertheless, freshmen and sophomores, who register last, may have trouble getting into certain general education classes, like foreign languages. Professors and academic advisors can usually help if classes you need are full, but "if you don't get into the College of Education by your sophomore year, you won't graduate in four years," says a sociology major. "Accounting is a five-year major, and engineering is hard to do in four."

The impressive Illinois library system, the largest public university facility of its kind worldwide, makes it easier to keep up with class work. Aside from engineering and business, other notable programs at Illinois include the Beckman Institute for Advanced Science and Technology, an interdisciplinary center designed to bring biological and physical sciences together to pursue new insights in human and artificial intelligence. The National Center for Supercomputing Applications at Illinois developed Mosaic, the predecessor to Netscape's Navigator World Wide Web browser. The undergraduate honors program includes faculty mentoring, intensive seminars, advanced sections of regular courses, and access to special resources. More than fourteen hundred undergraduates travel and study abroad each year, roaming one hundred countries around the globe, while the Ronald E. McNair Scholars Program helps fund independent, original research by minority, low-income, and first-generation college students who are completing bachelor's degrees.

Illinois has its share of stellar faculty, including eleven National Medal of Science winners and twenty-six members of the National Academy of Sciences. "I have experienced professors with a passion in their areas as well as a sincere concern for the well-being of their students," says a sophomore. Even freshmen stuck in large lectures (750 seats) will find some personal attention in the associated discussion sections, led by graduate teaching assistants. Freshmen Discovery Courses, seminars limited to twenty students, enable first-year students to interact closely with full professors. First semester freshmen can ease into the rigors of college level work in one of the Learning Communities.

Eighty-nine percent of Illinois undergrads are homegrown. But since Illinois stretches from the wealthy north suburbs of sophisticated Chicago to the unspoiled rural hills bordering Kentucky and encompasses classic farm towns as well as factory

(Continued)
Grad in 6 Years: 80%
Returning Freshmen: 92%
Academics: ✍ ✍ ✍ ✍ ✍
Social: ☎ ☎ ☎
Q of L: ★ ★ ★
Admissions: (217) 333-0302
Email Address:
undergraduate@admissions
.uiuc.edu

Strongest Programs:
Accounting
Advertising
Agricultural Economics
Architecture
Engineering
Business
 Administration/Business
 Management
Insurance/Risk Management
Psychology

First semester freshmen can ease into the rigors of college level work in one of the Learning Communities.

towns, students do come from multiple backgrounds and fit less into the stereotypical "Midwest" mold than one might think. African-Americans and Hispanics combine for 13 percent of the student body, and there's an equal number of Asian-Americans, due in large part to the administration's effort to attract high-achieving students through the President's Award of financial support for state residents. But even this moderate amount of diversity in the student body hasn't dampened the controversy over the mascot, Chief Illiniwek, which is seen by many as an insensitive symbol. There are those on the other side who see it as honoring Native Americans. However, one junior says, "Most people prefer to stay out of political issues" at Illinois.

Thirty-eight percent of students live in the U of I's twenty-two co-ed and single-sex residence halls, which range in size from 51 to 660 beds and are arranged in quadrangle-like groups. Beware that some dorms are quite a hike from classrooms, veterans warn. Daniels Residence has been renovated. All bedrooms have fast Internet connections, and many residence halls house living/learning programs, such as WIMSE (Women in Math, Science, and Engineering) and Unit One (academic support and educationally focused programming). Each residence hall is a mini-neighborhood, with dining halls, darkrooms, libraries, music practice rooms, computers, and lounges creating a sense of community. "For some halls, the rooms are a little small," says a sophomore. "After your freshman year, there really is no trouble getting a room." The dorms have unique personalities: "Champaign dorms are loud, party places, while Urbana is more focused on school. ISR has engineers, Allen is alternative, LAR is quiet, PAR is relaxed and fun, and FAR has air-conditioning in the rooms," reports one student. The food is good when the chefs keep things interesting. "Each night, the dining services offer a 'specialty restaurant' option serving pasta, meats, etc. These are usually the best foods offered," says a senior. Many sophomores live in fraternity or sorority houses; Illinois claims to have the largest Greek system anywhere, with more than seventy-five chapters drawing 23 percent of men and 25 percent of women as pledges. Many juniors and seniors move to off-campus apartments.

Illinois attracts many socially oriented students who love parties and intramural sports, which may be why the Greek influence is particularly strong. Independents don't have to suffer boredom, though, as there are also more than 850 registered student clubs and organizations ranging from the rugby team to ethnic advocacy groups. On most weekends, the Illini Union showcases bands, comedians, and hypnotists in its central

"Urbana-Champaign is very alive and there are many student organizations that go out and have contact with the community."

cafe. The impressive Krannert Center for the Performing Arts, with four theaters and more than 350 annual performances, serves as the area's cultural center, while Assembly Hall hosts national touring acts, including popular rock bands such as Pearl Jam, James Styx, and Kenny Chesney, and folk singers like James Taylor. Students get a discount at both facilities. Chicago and the shores of Lake Michigan beckon when the weather warms up, and Mardi Gras makes for a good road trip in the dead of winter. Though drinking is prohibited in the dorms, nineteen-year-olds can get into bars—and can also get alcohol fairly easily. "People used to say that Champaign was a drinking town with a football problem," reports a student. For those who itch for the stimulation of a big city, the campus is just about equidistant from Chicago, Indianapolis, and St. Louis.

The Illini basketball team won Big Ten championships from 2001 to 2004, and the football team made it to the Sugar Bowl in 2002. The intramural program is extensive mainly because of the university's excellent sports facilities: sixteen full-length basketball courts, five pools, nineteen handball/racquetball courts, a skating rink, a baseball stadium, and the $5.1 million Atkins Tennis Center, with six indoor and eight outdoor courts. The men's tennis team swept the Big Ten men's championships in 2002 and 2003. Illinois has a strong athletic program for disabled students, including wheelchair basketball, which Illinois invented.

Don't be scared off by the enormity of the University of Illinois. Its size is probably its greatest asset, offering a multitude of opportunities to those who seek them out. "Urbana-Champaign is very alive and there are many student organizations that go out and have contact with the community," says one student. Though state budget cuts have pushed tuition up and made freshman classes larger, students still leave with a great education and memories of good times outside the classroom.

If You Apply To >

Illinois: Regular admissions: Jan. 1. Financial aid: Mar. 15. Does not guarantee to meet demonstrated need. Campus interviews: optional, informational. No alumni interviews. SATs or ACTs: required. Apply to particular schools or programs; music, dance, and theater applicants must audition. Accepts electronic applications. Essay question: personal statement.

Illinois Institute of Technology

10 West 33rd Street, Chicago, IL 60616

Forget about cheerleaders, homecoming games, and the other trappings of college life. IIT is about learning technology, getting a degree, and landing a job. IIT is all engineering with a little bit of architecture thrown in for good measure. If your goal is a technical job in the Chicago area, this is your place.

Engineers unite at the Illinois Institute of Technology, where classwork and real-world experience promise to propel students to the top of their fields. After all, when you're taught by Nobel laureates, engaged in comprehensive undergraduate research, and able to take advantage of state-of-the-art labs, the check's in the mail. With all this midnight oil burning, students at IIT can escape to downtown Chicago for some much-deserved fun and culture.

IIT's home is an urban, 120-acre campus designed by Ludwig Mies van der Rohe, the influential twentieth-century architect who directed the architecture school for twenty years. Founded in 1890, the school is just three miles south of Chicago's Loop, one mile west of Lake Michigan. Miesian-style buildings are adorned by trees and grassy open parks. Comiskey Park, home of the White Sox, is located directly across from the campus. The S.R. Crown Hall, home of IIT's College of Architecture, is considered a landmark. In fact, a major campus renewal is currently in progress, with the McCormick Campus Center and State Street Village Residential Complex as the newest additions. A new biomedical research center is planned for the main campus.

Engineering sets the tone at IIT. All engineering departments are outstanding. Computer engineering is the most popular major, followed by computer science, architecture, electrical engineering, and mechanical engineering. The sciences, physics in particular, are first-rate; high-energy physicist and Nobel laureate Leon Lederman teaches freshman—yes, freshman—physics. Computer literacy is demanded of all students. In addition, all freshmen take an introduction to the professions seminar, which includes discussion of innovation, ethics, teamwork,

"The courses usually require three hours of time outside class for every lecture hour."

Website: www.iit.edu
Location: Urban
Total Enrollment: 6,199
Undergraduates: 1,905
Male/Female: 81/19
SAT Ranges: V 550–650
    M 630–730
ACT Range: 25–31
Financial Aid: 33%
Expense: Pr $ $
Phi Beta Kappa: No
Applicants: 2,309
Accepted: 67%
Enrolled: 16%
Grad in 6 Years: 62%
Returning Freshmen: 85%
Academics: ✍ ✍ ✍ ½
Social: ☎ ☎
Q of L: ★ ★
Admissions: (312) 567-3025
Email Address:
    admission@iit.edu

communication, and leadership. Multidisciplinary, group-based learning is big at IIT. Every student must complete two semester-long inter-profession projects that sharpen real-world skills. New academic options include majors in biomedical engineering and information technology and management. An environmental engineering degree was recently discontinued. Weaker offerings include the social sciences and, not surprisingly, the humanities.

The architecture curriculum emphasizes a team approach that mixes third-through fifth-year students under the supervision of a master professor. Guided by an academic reorganization, the physical sciences have been bolstered, grouped together with career-oriented fields such as psychology, political science, and computer information systems.

New academic options include majors in biomedical engineering and information technology and management.

Along with humanities and social science courses, students must fulfill general education requirements that include mathematics, computer science, natural science, and engineering; writing is emphasized across the curriculum. IIT's academic climate is pretty unforgiving, students say. Both the workload and the competition are fierce. "You always have a lot of work to do, especially with homework and labs," says an electrical engineering major. Adds another student: "The courses usually require three hours of time outside class for every lecture hour." Professors always teach their own classes at IIT, while TAs are available for labs and extra help. Most students praise the faculty for their knowledge and tendency to offer as much help as is needed. More than half of the classes have 25 or fewer students, and 94 percent have 50 or fewer.

In addition to meeting outside of class to go over problem sets or for career direction, IIT students and professors often work side-by-side on research projects. Engineering students have the use of sophisticated labs, and independent research labs in Chicago are also available. The five-year co-op program, another possibility for hands-on experience, helps lead IIT grads into high-paying jobs after graduation. There are study abroad programs that include France, Spain, Scotland, and Germany.

"Students at IIT study a lot," reports a psychology major. A majority of IIT students graduated from public high school in the top quarter of their class. Out-of-state students account for 46 percent of the undergraduate population, and a sizable 17 percent are from foreign countries. African-Americans and Hispanics together constitute 13 percent of the student body, and Asian-American students constitute another 16 percent. Students say International Fest is one of the year's most popular events, and IIT offers a multitude of cultural awareness workshops and sponsors "awareness" weeks and months on different topics to help avert potential problems. A three-day workshop on topics including race relations, international diversity, homophobia, and sexism is required of all new students. A director of women's services and diversity education helps address needs of minority groups on campus, including women, who constitute a mere 19 percent of the student body. Politics and political correctness don't really stir up campus because "we are so conservative and diverse," says an aerospace engineering major. IIT offers an unlimited number of merit scholarships, ranging from $3,000 to more than $23,000, and athletic scholarships in a number of sports. IIT's ROTC program has grown and matured into one of the finest in the nation and even hosts a popular annual formal ball.

"We are so conservative and diverse."

As befits the school's urban location, a chunk of students commute. The 63 percent of students who live in residence halls report that rooms are "kind of small" but comfortable. Six of the seven dorms are co-ed, with one hall for women only. The McCormick Student Village is popular, and South and North are said to be the nicest dorms. Fowler has the biggest rooms, but no air-conditioning; the rest of the dorms have A/C. Some students live in apartments in the area or on Chicago's North Side; others inhabit one of the eight fraternities, which claim 19 percent of the men. Sororities nab 10 percent of the women, and many students say the social aspect of Greek life is a welcome addition to campus. The dining hall has several meal plans and a special vegetarian menu. Breakfast and lunch can also be eaten in the cafeteria at the student union, while the

"Chicago is awesome—there is always something to do."

campus pub serves lunch and dinner. Engineers and architects—notorious late-night studiers—have to hit the library early, since it closes at 10 p.m. Though students tend to feel safe on campus, the surrounding area is a different story. "It is difficult to get to a doctor, pharmacy, or grocery store and feel safe unless you have a car," says a student.

IIT's six-block campus is contiguous to Chicago's "Gap" community, where historic but rundown homes are being rehabilitated to form one of the city's hottest new urban residential areas. Most students love exploring Chicago; the city skyline is beautiful and a veritable museum, with buildings designed by the likes of Frank Lloyd Wright, Louis Sullivan, and, of course, van der Rohe. "Chicago is awesome—there is always something to do," a sophomore says, but adds that it can be a bit pricey. Thus, the university provides free shuttle bus service to downtown on weekends. Lake Michigan is within jogging distance, and Chinatown is a walk away for lunch or dinner.

For students who stick around on weekends, "you have to create your own social life," a sophomore says. The Union Board offers movies, concerts, and comedians, and the Bog brings in bands on Thursdays and Saturdays. Students can also plan events like a formal on the Odyssey, a sightseeing boat, or an outing to the Chicago Symphony. The eight-day Winter Festival and the Spring Formal are other popular annual events. Returning sophomores are invited to a weekend retreat in Lake Geneva, Wisconsin, for some bonding time and to celebrate making it through their first year. As for alcohol, the school follows the twenty-one-year-old law and students say it generally works. In sports-crazy Chicago, IIT athletic teams are not much of a draw. Students praise the men's baseball and swimming teams along with women's volleyball, which compete in the NAIA Division I. Men's and women's soccer teams were recently started. The intramural program is strong, but students hate the fact that the facilities close at 5 p.m. on weekends. The Olympics occur every year at IIT when Greek Week and Sports Fest kick off, featuring Olympic-type competition for all students.

Shipping off to Chi-town to take on the mammoth workload at IIT means hitting the books for hours upon hours and a fair share of all-nighters. But the payoff is undeniable. Students who take advantage of this small school's ever-improving engineering departments are sure to have their pick of careers after graduation. And with the innumerable diversions offered in the Windy City, students at IIT revel in the best of two worlds: a challenging academic climate and a great city to let off all that steam.

Overlaps

University of Illinois–Chicago, University of Illinois–Urbana-Champaign, Purdue, Northwestern, MIT

If You Apply To ➤

IIT: Rolling admissions. Financial aid: Mar. 15. Housing: Jul. 1. Does not guarantee to meet demonstrated need. Campus interviews: recommended. Alumni interviews: optional. SATs or ACTs: required. SAT IIs: optional. Accepts the Common Application and electronic applications. Essay question: Influential person; significant personal experience; prominent figure you would interview; what you would tell the world in five minutes; most important modern invention.

Illinois Wesleyan University

210 East University, Bloomington, IL 61702-2900

IWU is an up-and-coming small college with a low-key Methodist affiliation. The curriculum is basic liberal arts with additional divisions devoted to fine arts and nursing. Offers an optional three-week term in May that allows students to travel or explore an interest.

Website: www.iwu.edu
Location: Small town
Total Enrollment: 2,107
Undergraduates: 2,107
Male/Female: 43/57
SAT Ranges: V 580–670
  M 590-690
ACT Range: N/A
Financial Aid: 56%
Expense: Pr $ $ $
Phi Beta Kappa: Yes
Applicants: 3,248
Accepted: 46%
Enrolled: 39%
Grad in 6 Years: 82%
Returning Freshmen: 92%
Academics: ✍ ✍ ✍ ½
Social: ☎ ☎ ☎
Q of L: ★ ★ ★ ★
Admissions: (309) 556-3031
Email Address:
  iwuadmit@iwu.edu

Strongest Programs:
Biology/Premed
History/Prelaw
English
Psychology
Mathematics
Music

Illinois Wesleyan University has its sights set on a special breed of student—the kind that isn't afraid to be many things at once. Students here are very much encouraged to pursue multiple interests. In fact, 14 percent of the student body has two or more majors while also finding time for sports, music lessons, and other activities. IWU is a mecca for students who have preprofessional interests, especially those with unusual interest pairings like management and music.

Founded in 1850, IWU occupies a seventy-two-acre campus site in a north side residential district of Bloomington. The heart of the campus is the central quadrangle, and tree-lined walkways connect buildings that range in style from gray stone Gothic to ultramodern steel and glass. A $23 million library recently opened along with a renovated student center.

The College of Fine Arts houses the three separate schools of music, art, and drama; music is the standout, having turned out such talents as opera star Dawn Upshaw. Among the top-notch programs in the College of Liberal Arts are biology, English, chemistry, and math. Students say the foreign language departments need improvement.

In addition to the usual fall and spring semesters, IWU has an optional three-week May term. The courses during this term must have one of five features—curricular experimentation, nontraditional approaches to traditional subject matter, student-faculty collaboration, crossing of disciplinary boundaries, or experimental learning through travel, service, or internships. About half the students take a May term class, and about one-fourth take off-campus travel courses. The university's study abroad program offers students the opportunity to travel to countries such as England, Denmark, and Japan. The business administration department offers a Portfolio Management course, in which students buy and sell orders overseen by a Client Board composed of University Trustees. IWU hosts an annual student research conference that attracts people from all disciplines.

> **"Academic advisors will give you as much or as little help as you want."**

The school's general education requirements emphasize critical thinking, imagination, intellectual independence, social awareness, and sensitivity to others. All first-year students must take a Gateway Colloquium, a topic-based, seminar-style class of fifteen that stresses critical reading, writing, discussion, and analytical skills and introduces students to the intellectual life of the university. Methodist founder John Wesley would no doubt be surprised to hear some of the topics, which range from Jesus at the Movies to Jewish Humor. For those not up to a whole term of popcorn or jokes, there is Oh la la! The French Mystique in American Pop Culture, Elegant Weirdness, and What is Poetry For? Students do jockey for high grades, especially since the institution of a plus/minus grading system. Career counseling is excellent, says a student, adding that in planning your college career, "Academic advisors will give you as much or as little help as you want."

Students at IWU are mostly the homegrown variety, with 87 percent hailing from Illinois. Although IWU began admitting African-American students in 1867, the campus is still predominantly Caucasian. African-Americans account for only 3 percent of the student body, Hispanics 2 percent, and Asian-Americans 3 percent. A multicultural task force has been formed to address the issue of diversity. "Most of the 'hot button' issues have a voice on campus (gays and lesbians, abortion, Christian groups, etc.), but I would not say we are a Madison or Berkeley of the 1960s here. The community around the college is conservative, but the administration is very PC," says

> **"The community around the college is conservative, but the administration is very PC."**

an observant student. The university has placed great emphasis on educating students about sexual harassment. Part of freshman orientation is spent role-playing harassment situations. Active participation in groups like Circle K, the Alpha Phi Omega service fraternity, and Habitat for Humanity provides evidence for the social consciousness of the IWU campus.

Housing is guaranteed for four years, and 85 percent of the students live in the dorms, which receive stellar marks from residents. "The dorms are very comfortable and nice as dorms go. All have been recently renovated and their locations are almost all convenient—no class more than a five-minute walk," says a student. "Better living conditions than I'll have after graduation," quips an English lit major. Students must be twenty-one to live off campus. Most students say campus security is good, though common sense is a must.

Thirty-one percent of the men and women go Greek because fraternities and sororities are the focus of IWU's social life. Non-Greeks also use the system for social life, which translates into "lots of parties," according to one senior. A new alcohol policy allows only of-age students to have beer and wine in their dorms. Each fall during Homecoming, the fraternities and residence halls compete in the Titan Games to get appropriately psyched. Other annual festivities include the Far Left Carnival, the Gospel Festival, and Earthapalooza (on Earth Day). The Student Senate also sponsors guest speakers; Spike Lee, Bonnie Blair, and Maya Angelou have addressed audiences in recent years.

Thanks to the proximity of Illinois State University in nearby Normal, IWU offers more than the typical small college-town atmosphere. The total area school population of about twenty-five thousand helps to offer students at tiny IWU "the best of both worlds," says a senior. A sophomore says, "There are more restaurants per capita than anywhere else in the country." The best road trips are to Peoria or Urbana-Champaign (home of the University of Illinois), or to Chicago or St. Louis, each two-and-a-half hours away.

In the IWU arena, baseball and football are well and good, but basketball really gets students going; the men's team placed third in Division III in 2001. Although you wouldn't think of IWU as a jock factory, it was the launching pad for many a professional athlete, including longtime basketball star Jack Sikma and Doug Rader, former manager of the California Angels. In 2002, the football team shared the CCIW championship

> **"There are more restaurants per capita than anywhere else in the country."**

for the second straight year. The Titan softball team won the conference championship in 2003. The men's golf team captured league titles in 2002 and 2003. Women's golf won the Conference Championship in 2002. Women's volleyball and softball also rouse the fans, as does women's basketball. The Fort Natatorium houses a whopping fourteen-lane swimming pool, and the swim team had its share of stars along with the track team. Intramural sports include volleyball, badminton, and co-ed inner-tube water polo.

One of the Midwest's better-kept secrets, Wesleyan is at once cozy and diverse, loaded with opportunities for ambitious students and for those with traditional as well as offbeat interests. This is a place that, according to one double major,

Students here are very much encouraged to pursue multiple interests. In fact, 14 percent of the student body has two or more majors while also finding time for sports, music lessons, and other activities.

The business administration department offers a Portfolio Management course, in which students buy and sell orders overseen by a Client Board composed of University Trustees.

Overlaps

University of Illinois, Northwestern, Washington University (MO), University of Chicago, Notre Dame

"continues to emphasize the pursuing of a variety of passions and talents to their fullest within an intellectually and socially nourishing environment."

If You Apply To ➤ | **Illinois Wesleyan:** Regular admissions: Feb. 15. Financial aid: Mar. 1. Does not guarantee to meet demonstrated need. Campus interviews: recommended, evaluative. No alumni interviews. SATs or ACTs: required. SAT IIs: optional. Accepts the Common Application and electronic applications. Essay question: significant event; talents and abilities; or topic of your choice.

Indiana University

300 North Jordan Avenue, Bloomington, IN 47405

Though men's basketball is IU's most famous program, it may not be its best. That distinction could easily go to the world-renowned music school or to the distinguished foreign language program. IU enrolls three times as many out-of-staters as University of Illinois.

Website: www.indiana.edu
Location: Small city
Total Enrollment: 38,903
Undergraduates: 30,752
Male/Female: 47/53
SAT Ranges: V 490–600
  M 500–610
ACT Range: 22–27
Financial Aid: 62%
Expense: Pub $ $ $
Phi Beta Kappa: Yes
Applicants: 21,264
Accepted: 81%
Enrolled: 33%
Grad in 6 Years: 69%
Returning Freshmen: 88%
Academics: ✍ ✍ ✍ ✍
Social: 🐦 🐦 🐦 🐦
Q of L: ★ ★ ★ ★
Admissions: (812) 855-0661
Email Address:
  iuadmit@indiana.edu

Strongest Programs:
Accounting
Business
Chemistry
Journalism/Communications
Languages
Music
Optometry

With more than thirty-five thousand students on its enormous campus, Indiana University is the prototype of the large Midwestern school. Indeed, the school has billed itself "America's New Public University." With strong academics, a thriving social scene, and some of the best sports teams around, this top-notch public institution is a testament to Hoosier determination.

Located in southern Indiana's gently rolling hills, the eighteen-hundred-acre campus boasts architecture from Italianate brick to collegiate Gothic limestone to the distinctive style of world-famous architect I.M. Pei. Other unique campus features include fountains, gargoyles, an arboretum of more than 450 trees and shrubs surrounding two reflecting pools, a limestone gazebo, and the Jordan River, a pretty creek that runs alongside a shaded path. The most recent campus addition is the 117,000-square-foot Theatre/Neal-Marshall Education Center. The new facility will house the African-American Cultural Center as well as new research studios, classrooms, and offices.

IU's ten schools offer many majors and minors, cross-disciplinary study, an individually designed curriculum, intense honors and research programs, and year-long study in twenty-seven countries (and sixteen languages). The highly touted business school, with its respected international studies component, is second only to arts and sciences in popularity. The internationally known

> **"There is a balance with room for both competitive overachievers and laid-back, carefree individuals."**

Kinsey Institute for the Study of Human Sexual Behavior is housed on IU's campus, and the music school is tops in its field, setting the, ahem, tone for much of the campus. Many of the communications programs have been merged into the communications and culture department, and the university has added a major in informatics. IU has also introduced a new two-year online M.B.A. program known as "Kelley Direct." Students don't complain about many departmental weaknesses but note that large introductory lectures, especially in the sciences, are a hazard of IU's size. The GradPact program guarantees that Indiana will pay all fees if a qualifying student has to stay on campus for more than four years. "IU is a four-year institution," says one economics major. "If a student takes longer than that, they probably have three majors, changed their majors, or are bad planners." Despite its size, Indiana prides itself on its liberal arts education—freshmen are admitted not to preprofessional schools but to the "university division." Majors are declared after one or two years, and the university discourages premature specialization. IU's communications and culture department advances the study of communication as a cultural practice, while the Environmental Science Joint Program is an undergraduate degree program that specifically considers the environment as a scientific entity.

(Continued)
Fine Arts

General education requirements vary from school to school but usually include math, science, arts and humanities, social and behavioral sciences, English and writing, culture, and a foreign language. Students describe the academic climate as rigorous but not cut-throat. "With four thousand different courses per semester, a variety of intensity levels exist," says a marketing major. "There is a balance with room for both competitive overachievers and laid-back, carefree individuals." Students say they regularly share ideas with each other, and group projects are commonplace. Faculty members bring their research results directly to students, and some profs bring undergrads into their labs to assist with ongoing projects. Students say the quality

"There is a large separation between the Greek community and the rest of the social body."

of teaching is excellent. "The professors here are remarkable," says an art history/telecommunications major. As for advising, many students seem surprised by the personal attention they receive at such a large university, and they soon learn that many available resources are helpful to those students who seek them out. Some students, though, complain of confusing bureaucracies and problems parking. The new Fee Lane Parking Structure should help.

Sixty-nine percent of IU students are from in-state, while the remainder hail from every state and more than one hundred foreign countries. Out-of-staters face much more rigorous minimum admissions standards, including rank in the top quarter of their high-school class and SAT scores in the 1050 to 1100 range. African-Americans comprise 4 percent of the student body, Hispanics 2 percent, and Asian-Americans 3 percent. By and large, students do not seem to dwell on political or social issues.

The highly touted business school, with its respected international studies component, is second only to arts and sciences in popularity.

The school's rolling admissions system enables students to know their fate only a month after their application is filed. And while IU does not guarantee to meet the full demonstrated need of every student, it admits on a need-blind basis and offers the Early Approximate Student Eligibility (EASE) program to help prospective freshmen gauge how much financial aid they will get. Merit scholarships are awarded to qualified students; applicants must be in the top 10 percent of their graduating class and have a minimum combined SAT score of 1200. There is also an "NCAA maximum" program of roughly 236 full athletic scholarships encompassing ten men's sports and nine women's.

Housing ranges from Gothic quads (co-ed by building) to thirteen-floor highrises (co-ed by floor or unit, except for one all-women dorm), and halls are considered "clean and comfortable." One student explains the housing situation this way: "All dorms have laundry facilities, cafeterias, computer clusters, and undergraduate advisors, and some even have special amenities like language-speaking floors." A junior adds, "There is no trouble getting a room, but preference of dorm may be harder." Academic floors (requiring a GPA of 3.1 or better) are popular with more serious students who are not interested in intense nightlife. Housing is guaranteed to all incoming freshmen, and those who stay in the university housing system won't ever face rent increases. Based on results from a student survey, some dining halls have been modernized to resemble mall food courts with outlets offering international and healthful menus sprinkled among the fast-food options. Alcohol is prohibited in the dorms, which may explain why 57 percent of the student body lives off campus. Most off-campus residents choose apartments or small wooden houses with big front porches within walking distance of the campus or of the IU bus system.

As for advising, many students seem surprised by the personal attention they receive at such a large university, and they soon learn that many available resources are helpful to those students who seek them out.

Although campus organizations host numerous events, the most active on-campus groups, in terms of social life, seem to be the Greeks. About 16 percent of IU men and 18 percent of IU women are in the Greek system, and membership is a status symbol. Some complain of a polarized atmosphere. "There is a large separation between the Greek community and the rest of the social body," says a senior. Every fall there is a thirty-six-hour Dance Marathon to raise money for Riley's Children's Hospital in Indianapolis. The Little 500 bike race, which was modeled after the Indianapolis 500, is one of the most highly attended events of the year at Indiana. With concerts, ballets, recitals, and festivals right on campus, students are not lacking for things to keep them busy. The IU student union is the largest in the nation, and the range of extracurricular organizations is also impressive. The Office of Diversity Programs, Committee on Multicultural Understanding, and Students Organized Against Racism are a few more ways students can make a difference on campus. "Bloomington is a great small college town," says one senior. There are many excellent bars, shops, and restaurants, including one of the few Tibetan restaurants in the country. Locally, the area offers some impressive rock quarries (often used as illegal but refreshing swimming pools), miles of public forests, and three nearby lakes. Spelunkers will find heaven down below in the many nearby caves. Chicago, Cincinnati, Indianapolis, St. Louis, and even New Orleans are popular road trips.

Intramurals pale in comparison with varsity athletics here; basketball is an established religion in the state of Indiana. The Hoosiers basketball program is entering a new era now that the combative and controversial coach Bobby Knight is long gone. Although students and faculty are all eligible for tickets, they've got to get requests in early—and even those lucky enough to get tickets don't count on going to more than a quarter of home games. In 1998 and 1999, Indiana Hoosiers soccer team won back-to-back NCAA championships. In recent years, women's golf and women's tennis have both claimed at least a share of the Big Ten championship, and even the football team is beginning to draw red and white crowds. Recently, women's water polo has attained varsity status. Purdue is IU's traditional athletic rival, and teams play for the Old Oaken Bucket, found on a farm in southern Indiana in 1925 and alleged to have been used during the Civil War.

IU is a huge university, but it seems as if IU has it all. Students graduate proud of their school, with a degree that is highly-respected in Indiana and outside the state.

Overlaps

Purdue, Ball State, University of Illinois, University of Iowa, Miami University (OH)

If You Apply To ➤ **Indiana:** Rolling admissions. Campus interviews: recommended, informational. No alumni interviews. SATs or ACTs: required. SAT IIs: optional. Accepts the Common Application and electronic applications. No essay question.

International Colleges and Universities

Do you thrive on new experiences? Like to meet new people? Want to learn about different cultures? You can do all that at a college or university in the United States, but if you really want to jump in with both feet, think about attending a school in a foreign country. This section highlights the opportunities available in Canada and Great Britain, by far the most common destinations outside North America for degree-seeking undergraduates.

The absence of a language barrier is the most obvious reason why Canada and Britain are the preferred destinations for overseas degree study. Plenty of students do a junior-year-abroad where the language is Spanish or

Swahili, but only a handful can realistically expect to earn an entire degree in a foreign tongue. A smattering of American universities do exist in places ranging from Paris to Cairo, but most are small and the majority of their enrollment is students from other countries seeking an American-style education. If you're willing to venture halfway around the world, Australia is an English-speaking destination that might be worth a look for its combination of beautiful scenery and bargain-basement tuition.

Look for coverage of Australian institutions in a future edition of the *Fiske Guide*. The following sections examine Canada and Britain in more detail, followed by full-length articles on selected institutions.

Canadian Colleges and Universities

Horace Greeley told ambitious young men of his generation to "go West." Today his admonition to young men and women seeking a quality college education at a fraction of the usual cost would probably be to "go North"— to Canada. A growing number of American students are discovering the educational riches that lie just above their northern border in this huge land of thirty million people that is known for its rugged mountains, bicultural politics, spirited ice hockey, and cold ale. What's drawing them is easy to discern.

The top Canadian universities are the academic equals of most flagship public universities and many leading privates in the United States, but the expense of a bachelor's degree is far lower, even taking travel into account. Canadian campuses and the cities in which they are located are safe places, and, unless one opts for a French course of study, there are no language and few cultural barriers. Canadian schools are strong on international exchange programs, and their degrees carry weight with U.S. graduate schools.

Canada has ninety institutions of higher learning, ranging from internationally recognized research universities to the small undergraduate teaching institutions in the country's more rural areas; the country ranks second after the U.S. in the percentage of citizens attending university. Most of the larger universities are located in highly urban centers, but some are situated in smaller towns where they dominate the life of the community. Most are almost literally next door to the United States, within one hundred miles of the Canada–U.S. border. In this guide, we feature four of Canada's strongest universities: the University of British Columbia, McGill University, Queen's University, and the University of Toronto.

Institutions of higher learning in Canada were established from the earliest days of French settlement in the mid-seventeenth century, making them some of the oldest in North America. The precursors to the public universities in Canada were the small, elite, denominational colleges that sprang up in Quebec, in the Maritimes, and later in Ontario. A few private denominational colleges and universities still exist in Canada, but most have been subsumed into affiliations or associations with the larger universities. Education in Canada, including university education, became the exclusive jurisdiction of provincial governments. As the Canadian West was developed, the large Western provinces of British Columbia, Alberta, Manitoba, and Saskatchewan set up provincially chartered universities similar to land-grant colleges in the U.S.

One of the key differences between Canadian and U.S. universities is that Canadian universities (and this is what they are, not "colleges") are primarily funded from public monies. Despite steady tuition increases in the past five years, the average Canadian student still only pays on average about $2,500 in Canadian dollars, or U.S. $1,700. Although non-Canadians may be charged up to six times the domestic rate, most costs are still lower than out-of-state tuition in the U.S. Tuition at the four universities described below ranges from U.S. $5,500 to $9,200.

Canadians have come to expect easy and affordable access to a uniformly high quality of education whether they live in Halifax or Vancouver. After diminishing government funding in the past several years, a now booming economy, a large government surplus, new federal initiatives grants for innovations and scholarships, and the universities' own aggressive fund-raising campaigns bode well for the continued growth and quality of Canadian higher education in the immediate future.

Federal and provincial loans and grants that are readily available to Canadian students are generally not available to students from the U.S. and other countries. However, the majority of universities with competitive admissions, particularly those featured in the *Fiske Guide*, offer merit-based awards and scholarships to students of all nationalities. American students who attend leading Canadian schools can apply their U.S. student assistance funds, including Stafford Loans and Pell Grants as well as the recently implemented HOPE Scholarship and Lifetime Learning tax credits.

The requirements for obtaining a degree are set by each institution, as are the admission requirements and prerequisites. Unlike the U.S., Canada does not offer nor require its own students to take a Canadian college entrance test. Some Canadian universities admitting students from the United States will require SAT or ACT scores along with high-school marks from academic subjects in the last two or three years of high school. In general, top universities are about as selective as their American counterparts.

Application fees vary by institution, as do deadlines. Canadian universities are aware of the May 1 deadline operative in the U.S., and they try to accommodate. Applications to the University of Toronto and Queen's University in Ontario are handled centrally through the Ontario Universities' Application Service. McGill handles applications directly and accepts both Web-based and paper applications. British Columbia has its own application; it can be mailed, but encourages students to apply online. Canadian universities differ widely in the amount of credit and/or advanced standing they offer for Advanced Placement Examinations or International Baccalaureate Higher Level Examinations.

The following admission requirements apply to applicants from an American school system. The University of British Columbia bases admission decisions on the average on eight full-year academic courses over the last two years of high school, and there are also specific program requirements for students entering the science-based faculties. SAT test results are not required, but if students submit them, the results can be helpful in the evaluation process. McGill bases its assessment of American high school graduates on the overall record of marks in academic subjects during the final three years of high school, class standing, and results obtained in SAT I and SAT II and/or ACT tests. Queen's wants applicants with a minimum score of 1200 on SAT I (with at least 580 in the verbal section and 520 in the mathematical one) and looks at class rank. There are also program-specific requirements for programs where mathematics and/or biology, chemistry, and physics are a requirement. Toronto's Arts and Science faculties want a high grade-point average and good scores on the SAT I and on three SAT II subject tests. ACT and CEEB Advanced Placement Examination scores are also considered.

It is hard to beat Canadian universities for the quality of student life. Although many students commute, most of the universities in Canada offer on-campus housing; some even guarantee campus housing for first-year students. Universities offer active intramural and intercollegiate sports programs for both men and women, and the usual student clubs, newspapers, and radio stations provide students with opportunities to get involved and to develop friendships. As in the United States, student-run organizations are active participants in university life, with leaders serving on university committees and lobbying on issues ranging from creating more bicycle paths to keeping tuition low. Few Canadian campuses are troubled by issues of student safety or rowdiness. In the larger urban centers, Canadian campuses reflect the rich cultural diversity of Canada's cultural mosaic, and most encourage their students to gain international experience by spending a term or a full year abroad.

Americans wondering about the currency of a Canadian degree in the U.S. should be reassured that top American and multinational countries—the likes of Archer Daniels Midland, Chase Manhattan, IBM, Microsoft, Nortel Networks, and Solomon Smith Barney—actively recruit on Canadian campuses, as do American graduate schools. According to the Institute of International Education in New York, more than seven thousand Canadians are currently enrolled in graduate schools in the United States.

The one thing that is different for U.S. and other international students intending to study in Canada is that they will have to obtain a Student Authorization, equivalent to a visa, from Canadian immigration authorities. Getting a Student Authorization is fairly straightforward for American citizens, but this slight bureaucratic hurdle is a reminder that Canada, for all of its similarities in language and culture with the United States, is still another country. For many American students who have chosen to study in Canada, this is part of the draw—they get to enjoy all the excitement of studying abroad in a foreign country with few of the cultural and none of the linguistic barriers to overcome. One of the most pleasant differences American students soon discover is how far their American dollar goes in Canada with the favorable exchange rate.

The Association of Universities and Colleges of Canada has a website at www.aucc.ca. Another good source of scholastic information is the website of the Canadian Embassy in Washington D.C. at www.canadianembassy.org/studyincanada.

Canadian universities are currently playing host to about three thousand American students on their campuses, and as a result of funding cutbacks and internationalization policies in the early 1990s, they have become increasingly active in recruiting students from south of the border. This is but one more reason why it makes sense for more young Americans to check out the "Canadian option." Canada, eh?

Vancouver, British Columbia, Canada V6T 1Z1

Natural beauty is the first thing that draws Americans to Vancouver—and Canada's premier western university. A similar scale to places like University of Washington but with two major differences—no big-time sports to unite the campus and limited dorm life.

What do two prime ministers of Canada, three provincial premiers, an astronaut, a world-renowned opera singer, and a Nobel Prize winner have in common? Give up? They are all graduates of the University of British Columbia. Founded in 1908, UBC offers students solid programs in business and science, ready access to beaches and mountains, and a diploma with instant name recognition. Though the massive campus can sometimes feel isolating, students are nevertheless happy to be here. After all, not everyone can lay claim to such illustrious company.

Located just twenty-five minutes from downtown Vancouver, UBC's striking Point Grey campus covers a peninsula that borders the Pacific Ocean and is bounded by an old-growth forest. Mountains—perfect for skiing—loom in the distance. Architectural styles are a mix of Gothic and modern, and students can enjoy a leisurely stroll through the university's botanical gardens. Recent campus additions include the two new intercultural student residences, the Chapman Learning Commons, and a campus-wide wireless network. A new life sciences center opens this year.

According to the UBC administration, the university's mission is to "offer students an intellectually challenging education...that prepares them to become citizens of...the twenty-first century through programs that are international in scope, interactive in process, and interdisciplinary in content and approach." Strong programs include microbiology, international relations, economics, and business administration. Asian studies is highly regarded, and theatre majors benefit from the Chan Centre for the Performing Arts. Other popular majors include psychology and computer science. The administration admits that some home economics and agricultural science courses could be strengthened, and one student grumbles about his 8 a.m. philosophy lecture: "Who can focus on the big questions at that time of the morning?"

> **"It requires a lot of hard work to achieve an A at UBC."**

Freshmen benefit from a wide array of first-year programs, including Imagine UBC, a first-day orientation. Arts Foundation is a series of three courses that offers an enriched, integrated approach to broad interdisciplinary themes in arts and humanities. Qualified students can take advantage of Science One, featuring team-taught courses in biology, chemistry, math, and physics. Student exchange programs are available through 145 partner universities around the globe, and co-op programs in engineering, science, arts, commerce, and forestry give students an opportunity to earn while they learn. In addition, honors and double-honors programs are available to super-brains and budding geniuses.

The academic climate is exactly what you would expect from a university of UBC's stature. "It requires a lot of hard work to achieve an A at UBC," says a senior. Most classes have less than fifty students, though mammoth lectures are not uncommon for freshmen. Faculty receive mixed reviews, depending largely on the department. "Most profs are focused on their students and will help whenever possible," says a senior. A junior, however, grumbles that many professors "are either too old and need to be retired...or too young and without experience." Academic

---

Website:
  www.welcome.ubc.ca
Location: Suburban
Total Enrollment: 38,634
Undergraduates: 28,030
Male/Female: 44/56
SAT Ranges: N/A
ACT Range: N/A
Financial Aid: N/A
Expense: Pub $
Phi Beta Kappa: No
Applicants: 18,646
Accepted: 49%
Enrolled: 53%
Grad in 6 Years: 90%
Returning Freshmen: 92%
Academics: ✍ ✍ ✍ ✍ ½
Social: ☎ ☎
Q of L: ★ ★ ★
Admissions: (604) 822-8999
Email Address: international
  .reception@ubc.ca

Strongest Programs:
Economics
Microbiology
Business Administration
Computer Science
Computer Engineering
Asian Studies
International Relations

Qualified students can take advantage of Science One, featuring team-taught courses in biology, chemistry, math, and physics.

advising is a mixed bag, with some students complaining that finding a knowledgeable advisor can be time-consuming.

With nearly forty thousand students attending, it's no surprise that UBC's student population is a melting pot. "Everyone can fit in because the student body is so diverse and large," says a senior. The typical UBC student is bright, hardworking, and gregarious. Though government subsidies make UBC a relatively affordable institution, at least one student says "those with tons of money" will fit in best. A history major divides his

"Everyone can fit in because the student body is so diverse and large."

classmates into two categories: commuters "who come in their fancy new cars with cell phones" and "those who live on campus and enjoy the community spirit." Minorities are well represented on campus (Asians make up the largest contingency), and the university encourages diversity through a series of special programs. Hot political issues include homosexual rights, abortion, and sexual harassment. UBC offers seventy-five merit scholarships to qualified students and athletic scholarships in seventeen varsity sports.

Only 15 percent of the students—mostly freshmen and sophomores—live in college housing, which is described as "quite nice and well maintained." The rest must fend for themselves against Vancouver's pricey rental market or commute from home. On-campus options include co-ed complexes (primarily for freshmen), university apartments, and family units for upperclassmen. Theme houses are another alternative, and offer like-minded students the opportunity to mingle. Dorm food encourages dieting, although "there are a couple of low-cost/good-food places that are always busy," reports a senior. Security is adequate, and features a walking escort service and nightly shuttle, though "most people just walk to where they want to go."

On such a large campus, isolation is a real threat. "You need to get in touch with other students quickly when you get here or you could feel lost on such a big campus," says a freshman. A senior adds, "To get the full value of UBC, you must willingly seek out clubs to join. Otherwise, you can feel lost and alone." Social life

"You need to get in touch with other students quickly when you get here or you could feel lost on such a big campus."

largely "depends on the crowd you hang with," according to one student. For partying types, there are the requisite beer bashes and toga parties, courtesy of UBC's small but active Greek scene—one of the few places where underage drinkers can sneak a sip of booze. Alcohol-free alternatives include university-sponsored events, such as movies and guest speakers. Popular campus events include Storm the Wall, long-boat racing, and the Arts County Fair.

Vancouver offers students countless opportunities for fun and contribution. "We can do anything we want in Vancouver," says a senior. "Most people go downtown for social events, bars, and shopping." Beautiful weather draws students outdoors and to nearby beaches and mountains for in-line skating, snowboarding, and swimming. Varsity and intramural competition are favorite pastimes; popular sports include soccer, basketball, hockey, volleyball, and skiing. The swimming teams are perennial championship winners (six consecutive years), and other recent championship teams include women's golf, men's basketball, and women's soccer.

"If you're not confident and outgoing...you might be lost or lonely [at UBC]," admits a junior. Indeed, spending four years at this mammoth university can be isolating for the shy student. But for those willing to take control of their social lives, UBC offers an impressive academic milieu.

Overlaps

Simon Fraser, McGill University, University of Toronto, University of Washington, UC–Berkeley

British Columbia: Early admission: Feb. 28 (domestic). Housing: May 1 (for non-Canadians). Does not guarantee to meet demonstrated need. No campus or alumni interviews. SATs: recommended. SAT IIs: optional. No essay question.

McGill University

Montreal, Quebec, Canada H3Z 2E2

The Canadian university best-known south of the border. Though instruction is in English, McGill is located in French-speaking Montreal. Americans will not find the degree of extracurricular life available in the U.S. Only the self-motivated need apply.

Strong preprofessional programs and a diverse student body are just two of the drawing cards of McGill University. But beware: this is not a place for those in need of attention. "McGill is a very independent school," says a senior. "It is not a place for the student who needs lots of personal contact." With such notable alumni as singer Leonard Cohen, musician Burt Bacharach, astronaut Julie Payette, and actor William Shatner (Star Trek's Captain Kirk), it's easy to see why enterprising men and women from around the world flock to McGill University.

Montreal's climate alternates between hot summers and freezing winters. A junior describes McGill's eighty-eight-acre campus as "an oasis in the heart of the city." Located in downtown Montreal amidst the hustle and bustle, the campus provides students with ample greenspace and a welcome respite from the decidedly urban atmosphere of the

> "It is not a place for the student who needs lots of personal contact."

city. Campus buildings range from "Gothic-like" structures with vines growing up the sides to more modern (read: ugly) constructions ("You can ignore them if you try hard," says a senior). Trees and greenery dot the campus landscape, and the sprawling recreation trails of Mount Royal rise to its immediate north. The new Montreal Genomics and Proteomics Centre building and new Trottier Information Technology Building have recently been completed.

Though the most popular majors are psychology and political science, there is no denying that the university's strengths lie in preprofessional programs such as medicine, law, and engineering. The management program is renowned, and students cite political science, religious studies, and philosophy as sure bets. The sciences receive uniform praise, and the school has recently opened its School of Environment, where environment-related courses are offered. For those who want to escape Montreal's brutal winter, there are internships, field studies in Barbados and Africa, exchange programs with more than five hundred partner universities around the world, and study abroad options via the Canadian University Study Abroad Program (CUSAP).

To fulfill the university's general education requirements, students must first choose which discipline (or faculty) to enter; popular choices include psychology, English, political science, mechanical engineering, and economics. A senior says, "It is important to consider the university on the basis of which faculty you would be interested in, because they vary greatly and operate almost as independent units." On average, students must earn 120 credits to graduate with a four-year degree. Freshmen must accumulate six to twelve credits in three of four disciplines,

Website: www.mcgill.ca
Location: City center
Total Enrollment: 29,810
Undergraduates: 22,915
Male/Female: 42/58
SAT Ranges: N/A
ACT Range: N/A
Financial Aid: 35%
Expense: Pub $ $
Phi Beta Kappa: No
Applicants: 16,952
Accepted: 55%
Enrolled: 47%
Grad in 6 Years: N/A
Returning Freshmen: N/A
Academics: ✍ ✍ ✍ ✍ ½
Social: ☎ ☎ ☎ ☎
Q of L: ★ ★ ★ ★
Admissions: (514) 398-3910
Email Address:
admissions@mcgill.ca

Strongest Programs:
Medicine
Law
Engineering
Management
Environmental Studies
Music

including languages, math and science, social sciences, and humanities, and declare a major before their sophomore year. Upon entering their major, students have a menu of course options that includes honors programs and double majors.

Regardless of the major, students can expect classes to be demanding. "Academics are taken very seriously here," asserts a junior. "People here want to go on to top grad schools and push themselves to get the marks they need to do so." Classes tend to be large—especially for freshmen—and students must be willing to seek out professors and advisors. "Students looking for small classes and personalized education...would not fit in at McGill," warns a political science major. Professors receive high marks for their knowledge and accessibility outside of class. "Except for a few bad experiences, the quality of instruction I've seen here has been very high," says a senior. "Professors here are well-informed and passionate." Academic advising is a bureaucratic tangle, but career counseling receives high marks. "Career and placement service runs lots of programs, so all you have to do is sign up," says one student. McGill's 6.1 million library holdings are reportedly adequate, though "not outstanding."

> **"People here want to go on to top grad schools and push themselves to get the marks they need to do so."**

Though the most popular majors are psychology and English, there is no denying that the university's strengths lie in preprofessional programs such as medicine, law, and engineering.

McGill students are a diverse lot—more than 150 countries are represented here—and the only common thread among students seems to be their fierce independence. They tend to be "mature, outgoing, independent, politically savvy, and socially conscious," according to a senior. "People are very liberal, open-minded, and accepting." Qualified students are eligible for 1,807 scholarships of $3,000 to $10,000. There is also a work-study program for those in need of financial assistance. There are no athletic scholarships. "Once you have started at McGill, they will do everything they can to help you graduate," says a grad student.

The university's six traditional and fourteen alternative residence halls house 8 percent of the student population, primarily freshmen from out of town. Dorms run the gamut from "cement box room" to "gorgeous studio flat." Party animals will feel free to crank up the stereo in Molson or McConnell, while bookworms might be better suited for Gardener. Douglas denizens enjoy their hall's quaint charm, and women who want to skip the co-ed scene can find a room in Royal Victoria College, an all-female dorm. "Almost every building has its own cafeteria and the food is generally good," says a senior. Off-campus apartments are a popular alternative for upperclassmen, who take advantage of Montreal's clean, affordable housing. Despite its urban location, the McGill campus is safe and security is considered more than adequate. "There are student organizations like 'Walksafe' and 'Drivesafe' that will walk or drive students to their residences at night regardless of where they are or where they are going," reports one student.

"McGill students are serious about academics but they love to party!" says one student. Though there are "considerable on-campus social activities, with many clubs and associations," many students venture off campus and into the bars and clubs of Montreal for fun and adventure. "Montreal's rich musical, artistic, and young culture is intoxicating," says a sophomore. A junior adds, "Montreal is a major cosmopolitan city. It is a blast to live in." Drinking is a popular pastime, but underage drinkers are few and far between since the legal age in Quebec is eighteen. "Alcohol is served on campus, but students are asked to show their IDs to prove their age," reports a modern languages major. Well-attended campus events include Homecoming, Winter Carnival, and Frosh Week activities. Popular roadtrips include New York City, Ottawa, and Toronto. Ski slopes are less than an hour away.

> **"Montreal's rich musical, artistic, and young culture is intoxicating."**

Drinking is a popular pastime, but underage drinkers are few and far between since the legal age in Quebec is eighteen.

Football, basketball, and ice hockey are the most popular varsity sports. According to one student, hated opponents include "our crosstown rivals at Concordia" and "our archenemies at Queen's University, in Kingston, Ontario. Both schools are very old and this is a long-standing traditional rivalry." Intramurals offer would-be jocks an opportunity to blow off steam after classes and on weekends. "As you walk through campus, you are sure to pass by a soccer, flag football, or rugby game on one of the numerous fields," says a student. New athletic facilities are a welcome addition for varsity athletes and "those of us who just like to work out," says a senior.

Overachievers and independent types do best here. "Slackers would be happier elsewhere," quips a senior. Large classes, brutal winters, and mountains of red tape are part of the McGill experience. Nevertheless, most seem happy to be here. "No one is here to hold your hand and make decisions for you," says a student. "But not to worry. You will have a great time—guaranteed!"

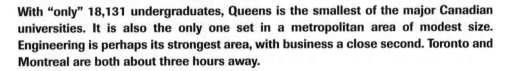

Overlaps

Concordia, University of Toronto, Queen's University, University of British Columbia, University of Montreal

If You Apply To ➢

McGill: Regular admissions: Jan. 15. Housing: Apr. 18 (American students). Does not guarantee to meet demonstrated need. No campus or alumni interviews. SATs or ACTs: required. SAT IIs: required (three, depending on program). Web applications preferred. No essay.

Queen's University

Kingston, Ontario, Canada K7L 3N6

With "only" 18,131 undergraduates, Queens is the smallest of the major Canadian universities. It is also the only one set in a metropolitan area of modest size. Engineering is perhaps its strongest area, with business a close second. Toronto and Montreal are both about three hours away.

Students at Queen's University approach work and play with equal zeal and enjoy a potent mix of school spirit and intellectual drive. Success requires energy and a willingness to get into the thick of things. "People who aren't interested in being a part of the school community are better off at a school that isn't such a big family," warns a sophomore. Solid academics, a pervasive school spirit, and longstanding traditions make life at this storied university unique—and demanding. "Getting into Queen's is just the first challenge," says a senior. "Succeeding at Queen's is another battle."

The 161-acre Queen's campus is located on the north shore of Lake Ontario, just minutes from the heart of Kingston, Ontario ("the limestone city") and directly between Montreal and Toronto. "Almost all buildings are constructed using limestone," explains a senior. Historically significant buildings have been maintained and "there are some modern buildings with a lot of glass to provide a bright and welcoming atmosphere." Ample greenery and open spaces provide students a place to stretch out under the sky and hit the books. A new $57 million chemistry building features a 250-seat multimedia lecture theater and environmentally friendly labs that consume less electricity and produce less waste.

Established in 1841 by Royal Charter of Queen Victoria, Queen's offers undergraduate degrees in a variety of faculties, including arts, science, engineering, commerce, education, music, nursing science, and fine art. Academics are unilaterally solid, but the most demanding are engineering and commerce. The bachelor of commerce program was the first of its kind in Canada and provides students with an internationally focused liberal business education, enhanced by new leadership modules and the integration of technology. The newly restructured School of

Website: www.queensu.ca
Location: City center
Total Enrollment: 18,649
Undergraduates: 15,483
Male/Female: 44/56
SAT Ranges: N/A
ACT Range: N/A
Financial Aid: N/A
Expense: Pub $ $
Phi Beta Kappa: No
Applicants: 39,135
Accepted: 34%
Enrolled: 24%
Grad in 6 Years: 95%
Returning Freshmen: 96%
Academics: ✐ ✐ ✐ ✐ ½
Social: ☎ ☎ ☎ ☎
Q of L: ★ ★ ★ ★
Admissions: (613) 533-2218
Email Address:
   admissn@post.queensu.ca

(Continued)
Strongest Programs:
Engineering
Commerce
Music

Computing offers Bachelor of Computer degrees in biomedical computing, cognitive science, and software design, as well as B.A. and B.S. degrees.

General education requirements vary by program, but all students can expect to complete a rigorous series of core and elective courses. Students participating in the Queen's International Study Centre are whisked away to the university's England campus, where they enjoy small classes and integrated field studies while residing in a fifteenth-century castle. In addition, there are exchange programs with universities around the world.

The academic climate is challenging and competitive, which comes as no surprise to students. "Queen's is fairly competitive," says a junior, "but not bloodthirsty." The general consensus among struggling students is that As are hard to come by. "After working your butt off and reading stacks of textbooks, your grades pale in comparison to the marks of students at other universities," gripes a biology major. Classes tend to be large for freshmen and sophomores, but

"People who aren't interested in being a part of the school community are better off at a school that isn't such a big family."

Twenty-five percent of the student body live in one of eleven residence halls, and all freshmen are guaranteed a place to hang their hat.

dwindle in size as one approaches graduation. The majority of classes are taught by full professors who receive praise for their accessibility and intelligence. "The teachers I have had have been thorough, challenging, and concerned about my success," says a junior. Office hours and special "wine and cheese" functions give students ample opportunity to mingle with faculty. Students report that there is little trouble getting into desired classes, and "there is lots of counseling available for students who need it."

Queen's students are an industrious, intelligent group, and most are used to academic success. "The Queen's student seems to take on the leader role and is more likely to succeed," asserts one student. School spirit runs high and campus issues include rising tuition fees—and just who is responsible for the cost. Students come from every Canadian province and eighty countries, and a sociology major says that "Queen's is very PC and inclusive, regardless of gender, race, religion, or sexual orientation." A large percentage of the student body is active in extracurriculars, and school spirit is a must. Though there are no athletic scholarships, more than eight hundred merit awards of $1,000 to $12,000 are handed out annually. "I have had great help through scholarships and financial aid," relates a senior. "There is quite a lot of money for you...you just have to go after it."

Twenty-five percent of the student body live in one of eleven residence halls, and all freshmen are guaranteed a place to hang their hat. "The residences are very comfortable and the custodial staff is in every day, becoming your parents away from home," says a junior. Co-ed and single-sex dorms are available. A mandatory meal plan gives freshmen a wide variety of foods to choose from, including

"After working your butt off and reading stacks of textbooks, your grades pale in comparison to the marks of students at other universities."

The newly restructured School of Computing offers Bachelor of Computer degrees in biomedical computing, cognitive science, and software design, as well as B.A. and B.S. degrees.

pasta, salad, pizza, and a soup-and-salad bar. The surrounding city also offers a plethora of dining options. "Kingston is known in our house as the 'city of restaurants,'" says a student. "They are everywhere." After freshman year, most students pack their bags and head off campus to the "student village," where comfortable apartments are available. In fact, 80 percent of Queen's students live within a fifteen-minute walk of campus. Though always a concern, safety is practically a non-issue on campus. Students report that they feel quite safe and that security is more than adequate.

Make no mistake about it, Queen's students know how to have a good time. "Social life is huge at Queen's," says a student. Adds another, "Campus pubs and city pubs have both found their niche." On Thursday nights, students flock to campus bars such as Afie's for a drink or two (or three), while Saturday nights are reserved for city bars and nightclubs. The legal drinking age is nineteen, and kiddies will have a tough time skirting the law. "The bouncers in Kingston actually have a couple of brain cells and can spot a fake ID from ninety kilometers away," says a senior. Nonalcoholic alternatives include school-sponsored movies and extracurricular clubs (there are more than 220!). "Extracurricular activities are a must, not an option!" says one student. Frosh Week is a favorite event with "cheers

"Queen's is very PC and inclusive, regardless of gender, race, religion, or sexual orientation."

that even the most blasé of students will be shouting out with pride by the end of the week." The school is steeped in Scottish tradition, and it's normal to see kilt-wearing bandsmen at important campus events.

Once the capital of Canada, Kingston is described as the "very much a university town." There are several universities in the area (including the Royal Military College), and downtown provides students with places to shop. "Kingston itself has several clubs, three malls, a number of museums, numerous gyms, and three or four movie theaters," says a student. The city's relative isolation makes it the favored stomping ground for students without wheels. Town-gown relations are good, and students are very active in the community. Toronto and Montreal (less than three hours away) are popular roadtrips.

With forty-one varsity teams, Queen's athletic program is not only the largest in Canada, but also ties with Harvard University for the largest program in North America. Popular sports include men's and women's rugby, women's squash, rowing, golf, and women's lacrosse. The annual "kill McGill" football game against rival McGill University draws pigskin-crazed students from every corner of campus; homecoming is reputed to be a raucous affair featuring "alumni from the 1920s parading around the football field during halftime." Intramural competition is fierce, too, and nearly every student is involved on some level. A student says, "There is so much school spirit, sometimes it makes you sick."

Life at Queen's University is one of extremes. "Students who are able to balance work and pleasure fit in best here," says a junior. The pressure to succeed can be tough and expectations are high. But for those who pull it off, the rewards are well worth the effort. "Queen's has its own culture," says a student. "Don't be afraid to engage it."

Overlaps

University of Toronto, University of Western Ontario, McGill University, University of Waterloo, University of Ottawa

If You Apply To ➢

Queens: Regular admissions: Feb. 28. Financial aid: Mar. 15. Does not guarantee to meet demonstrated need. Campus interviews: optional, informational. No alumni interviews. SATs: required. SAT IIs: required (for engineering candidates only). No essay question.

University of Toronto

Toronto, Ontario, Canada M5S 1A3

U of T is the largest institution in the *Fiske Guide* and one of the biggest in the world. It is also, for most readers, in a foreign country. If ever there were a place where go-getterism is a necessity, this is it. In the absence of American-style school spirit, U of T students cut loose to find their fun in the city of Toronto.

Website: www.utoronto.ca

Location: City center

Total Enrollment: 63,109

Undergraduates: 40,341

Male/Female: 44/56

SAT Ranges: N/A

ACT Range: N/A

Financial Aid: 50%

Expense: Pub $ $

Phi Beta Kappa: Yes

Applicants: 75,382

Accepted: 59%

Enrolled: 28%

Grad in 6 Years: 77%

Returning Freshmen: 95%

Academics: ✍ ✍ ✍ ✍ ½

Social: ☎ ☎ ☎

Q of L: ★ ★ ★

Admissions: (416) 978-2190

Email Address:

ask@adm.utoronto.ca

Strongest Programs:

Arts

Science

Engineering

Medicine

Education

"Even though fifty thousand people attend U of T, all undergraduate Arts and Sciences students choose a college to belong to," explains a junior. "This college has nothing to do with their academic studies, but allows them to meet people from various programs and take part in social events.

Students at the University of Toronto avoid getting lost in the shuffle by taking part in a unique residential college system that allows them to model their educational experience after their own personalities. Each college has a distinct character and appeal, yet blends seamlessly into the university's overall academic milieu. "Someone who wants to be involved in university life will have great opportunities here," says a student.

The University of Toronto is so large that it spans three campuses. The St. George campus is situated in downtown Toronto and features Gothic architecture and historic buildings, though one students describes the setting as "very much similar to a nuclear power plant." Two suburban campuses—one in Mississauga and one in Scarborough—feature more modern structures. Newer facilities include the Joseph L. Rotman School of Management building and a new residence hall for graduate students.

Students apply directly to one of nine colleges, seven of which are on the St. George campus. Each college has its own set of admissions requirements, but international applicants can expect to submit SAT I and three SAT II scores. Advanced Placement testing is also considered. Strong programs include engineering, medicine, and education. First-Year Seminars are taught by the faculty's leading scholars and provide freshmen with cross-disciplinary discussions in intimate class settings. In addition, there are study abroad programs around the world, internships, co-op programs, and specialized cross-disciplinary courses. Sophomores can choose from nearly one hundred research opportunities outside the classroom, where they work side by side with the university's most renowned professors. Newer programs include an architectural studies major and programs in forest conservation and health and disease.

"There is definitely no such thing as an easy A," asserts a senior. Indeed, the academic climate is challenging. Still, students tend to work together to achieve their goals. A sophomore says, "Students are generally willing to help each other out with assignments." Students report that class size can be a problem and it's not uncommon to have more than one hundred classmates, even in upper-level courses. Still, most large classes break into smaller tutorials, and even freshmen are taught by full professors. "The quality of teaching is excellent," says one student. "Most professors really do care and take time to help out students and get to know them better." With so many students vying for classes, it can be difficult to get desired courses. "In special cases, instructors are usually willing to admit extra students who really need to get into the class," says a

"There is definitely no such thing as an easy A."

senior. Academic advising is described as "comprehensive" and "readily accessible to students." U of T's extensive library system holds 12.8 million volumes and "most are open seven days a week," according to one happy bibliophile.

"U of T is a very urban, active school and the students tend to be focused, chic, determined, and goal-oriented," says a junior. Though Toronto is becoming increasingly popular with outsiders, students from Ontario still make up 89 percent of the student body. International students comprise 5 percent, and students say that the university is "a very inclusive and accepting environment." Political correctness is "a given at this university, not an issue," says a freshman. Top students (and there are many!) vie for twenty-four hundred admission scholarships and two thousand in-course awards. There are no athletic scholarships.

Eleven percent of the student body are residential students, and all are affiliated with one of the nine undergraduate colleges, which act as "local neighborhoods." "Even though fifty thousand people attend U of T, all undergraduate Arts and Sciences students choose a college to belong to," explains a junior. "This college has nothing to do with their academic studies, but allows them to meet people from various programs and take part in social events. It breaks the students into smaller communities." Each college has its own residences, which reflect the unique character of its students. St. Michael's College maintains a rich Roman Catholic tradition, while University College has a largely Jewish student body. Students of New College enjoy air-conditioned dorm rooms, and Victoria College houses

"The quality of teaching is excellent."

more than 750 students. The dorms are "clean, comfortable, and have a great social atmosphere," says a student. There are various dining options (mostly residence-specific), and all are well regarded. Campus security is adequate, according to most, and students say that they feel safe on campus.

Social life is quite active and takes place both in the city, where nightclubs beckon, and on campus. "There are pub nights and other social events held on campus," says a junior. "Hart House (which is the social and recreational center) has pool tables, an athletic wing, restaurants, and common rooms." The legal drinking age is nineteen, and students report that "alcohol abuse is not tolerated on campus." For those wishing to party without the aid of chemicals, there are university-sponsored events, including movies, guest speakers, and countless extracurricular clubs. Frosh Week gives students an excuse to get rowdy and enjoy themselves.

Students find plenty of reasons to love Toronto, their home away from home. "We are near museums, the art gallery, the bar and club district, and Lake Ontario," says one satisfied senior. "There are quite a few shops in the area and the Eaton Centre is just a subway ride away." Shopping is a favorite pastime, as are movies and excursions to the shores of Lake Ontario. Students also support a wide array of volunteer programs. "There is a lot to do here in terms of social activity," says one senior.

Toronto fields numerous varsity sports teams; popular sports include hockey, basketball, and soccer. Still, "school spirit is a little low," says a junior. "I believe that this is because so many people commute and only come to school for classes." Rivals include Queen's University and Western Ontario. Intramural competition is popular, and many students can be found cheering the Toronto Raptors, the city's professional basketball team.

A junior acknowledges that those coming to U of T "must be prepared for a large campus with thousands of students," but goes on to say that "most people are friendly and so relationships are easy to form." Though the mammoth campus can seem daunting at first, those who are willing to take their aca-

"There is a lot to do here in terms of social activity."

demic lives by the reins will be rewarded with an exceptional educational experience and a wealth of friends. "People who enjoy academic activities should come here," asserts a sophomore. "We have everything!"

"U of T is a very urban, active school and the students tend to be focused, chic, determined, and goal-oriented," says a junior.

Overlaps

York University, Queen's University, McGill University, University of Western Ontario

If You Apply To ➤ | **University of Toronto:** Early decision: Feb. 1. Regular admissions: Mar. 1. Guarantees to meet demonstrated need (for Canadian residents). No campus or alumni interviews. SATs or ACTs: required. SAT IIs: required. Accepts the Common Application. No essay question.

British Colleges and Universities

If going to college in Canada takes nerve, you'll need even more moxie to venture overseas. Give it some thought. At the most popular overseas destination, Great Britain, about two thousand five hundred Americans are currently enrolled in undergraduate degree programs, and another thirty thousand per year are doing semester- or year-long study abroad. Studying in Britain is not as cheap as in Canada—count on a total bill of $20,000 each year or more, not including travel—but Britain offers a richer international experience and a sense of history that cannot be had on this side of the Atlantic.

Britain makes the most sense for students interested in subjects such as English, history, foreign language, and anything related to international studies. If medieval history is your passion, why not go to school where the remains of that long-ago world still dot the landscape? If you're looking for a career in international business, consider a country where the global village has been a way of life. Though Britain is an English-speaking country, it offers far better instruction in European languages than you can get in the U.S. No matter what your academic interests, your classes will include a cross-section of nationalities that would be the envy of any North American institution. Most importantly, study in Britain has the potential to be a life-changing experience that will broaden your horizons and deepen your understanding of the world.

If you do consider Britain, there is one important wrinkle that may come as a surprise. You may picture yourself in England, the most populous region of Great Britain that includes London as well as fabled universities such as Oxford and Cambridge. But here's the rub: the English have a different system of higher education than that of the U.S. that makes degree study impractical in many cases. In England, undergraduate degrees are completed in three years, not four, and students are generally assumed to have completed thirteen years of schooling rather than twelve. As a result, the most selective English universities are reluctant to admit American high school graduates—some refuse to admit any—and the students who do get in will find themselves thrust into a world more appropriate for juniors and seniors in college.

The answer? Look to Scotland, England's less populous neighbor, where universities offer four-year degrees that are much better suited to the needs of American high school graduates. For those who are hazy on their geography, Scotland lies north of England. Together with Wales, they make up the island of Great Britain. Throw in Northern Ireland and the moniker changes to the United Kingdom. Scotland, which was an independent nation until 1706, has an illustrious intellectual history and has produced the likes of David Hume, Adam Smith, Rudyard Kipling, Robert Lewis Stevenson, J. K. Rowling, and the world's most famous ogre, Shrek.

Most people assume that the American version of higher education was imported from England. Not so. The American-style liberal arts institution came directly from Scotland in the person of John Witherspoon, a graduate of the University of Edinburgh who was lured to the U.S. in 1768 to head Princeton University. With the model of his alma mater in mind, Witherspoon transformed Princeton from a small-time school for ministers into a broad-based institution that taught philosophy, history, geography, science, mathematics, and theology. In the process, he became the most influential educator of his time and charted the path upon which the American university system has continued, more or less, to this day.

Though the American and Scottish systems share the same heritage, they are not identical. Any American who is considering Britain—whether in England or Scotland—should be aware of the differences that lie "across the pond." The most important: while American universities generally encourage students to sample a variety of fields before choosing a major, British institutions expect students to know their major before they set foot on campus, in part because British students take their general education courses in high school. As a result, college course work focuses almost exclusively on the student's major field, and American-style distribution requirements are all but unheard of. For students who want to get out of those nasty math or foreign language requirements, a British institution will probably fill the bill. But anybody who wants to change majors after a year or two may encounter difficulty.

Students in Britain take only two or three courses at a time, all of which are generally related to their major. This may sound like easy street to harried American students who are expected to take four or five courses per semester. But because British students tend to take courses only in subjects that seriously interest them, all classes are taught at a high level, even introductory ones. Though students in Britain get fewer hours in class, they are expected to put in more hours of study per course outside of class.

Education aside, American students will need to adjust to a different tenor of life in Britain. To put it bluntly, don't expect the comforts of home. There are no posh food courts or fitness facilities that look like a ritzy health club. The student body will not come out on a Saturday afternoon for the big game—there are no big games. Dorms are generally the domain of first-year students; expect to find a "flat" (apartment) for your upper-class years. Generally speaking, there will be no campus "bubble" to cloister you away from the real world—a good thing if you want an authentic sample of life in your new home.

Before we go further, here's a word to moms and dads. We know that you get queasy at the thought of sending your little cherub across a three-thousand-mile ocean. Take a chill pill. Safety fears are based on illusions, not facts. Even in the age of terrorism, a flight to Britain is quicker and safer than driving ten hours to get to First

Choice U. Once you're in Britain, the cities are at least as safe as those in the U.S., and the small towns have a crime rate roughly equivalent to that of the town of Mayberry on *The Andy Griffith Show*. The best part for parents: you'll need to visit at least once (and preferably several times).

As noted earlier, the price tag for all this cross-cultural enrichment is about one-third less than that of a selective private institution in the U.S., not including travel. The dark lining to the silver cloud is that academic scholarships are scarce and institutional financial aid is all-but nonexistent. Federal aid such as Stafford loans and Pell Grants can be transported in some cases, but most families will find themselves paying the full freight. And because exchange rates fluctuate, the bill can vary significantly depending on whether the dollar is weak or strong. For a searchable database of the few scholarships available for study in Great Britain, visit the British Council at www.britishcouncil-usa.org/learning.

We said earlier that English universities are probably not the best choice. The University of Cambridge (www.cam.ac.uk) is particularly blunt about "the possible mismatch between the broad liberal arts curriculum of the North American high school and the specialist emphasis of British degree courses." In a recent year, Cambridge accepted only three students from U.S. high schools. The University of Oxford (www.ox.ac.uk) does offer a glimmer of hope for a select few superachievers; Oxford considers American students who graduate in the top two percent of their class, and in a recent year it enrolled about thirty. Even so, the odds of admission to Oxford are lower than at any college in the U.S., including Harvard. The vast majority of American undergraduates at both Oxford and Cambridge are there for a second bachelor's degree after earning one from an American institution. Students with their hearts set on the Oxbridge institutions should consider them for graduate school, where both do admit Americans in significant numbers.

Students will get a similar story at the third-most recognized name in English higher education, the London School of Economics (www.lse.ac.uk), which enrolls about thirty-six hundred undergraduates. The LSE says it will not normally consider U.S. students until they have a year of higher education under their belts. Less selective English institutions are more receptive to Americans but no better equipped to meet their needs.

Students would be better served to look at Scotland's University of St. Andrews, which has a decades-long history of catering to American undergraduates. About a sixth of the U.S. students who earn a bachelor's degree in Great Britain do so at St. Andrews (www.st-and.ac.uk), a highly selective institution that considers applicants with a GPA of approximately 3.3 or higher, a combined SAT score of at least 1300, or an ACT of 29 or better. Also notable is the University of Aberdeen, a Scottish university that has stepped up its American recruitment by hiring a former dean of admissions at Hamilton College and Ohio Wesleyan University. St. Andrews and Aberdeen are profiled with full-length articles below.

Other notable Scottish institutions include the University of Edinburgh (www.edinburgh.ac.uk), which is set in one of Europe's most vibrant and interesting cities. With an undergraduate population of about sixteen thousand, Edinburgh has roughly one hundred degree students from the United States. Adam Smith's old haunt, the University of Glasgow (www.glasgow.ac.uk), is an option of similar size. Glasgow is less international than Edinburgh or St. Andrews but is believed by some to provide a more authentic Scottish experience. For more Scottish or English institutions, head to www.britishcouncil-usa.org/learning.

British universities evaluate applicants largely on the basis of academic credentials, with less weight on extracurricular activities and personal qualities than in the U.S. British universities tend to prefer SAT over ACT though they generally will accept either. For the application essay, the British usually ask about commitment to your intended major and why you want to study it. They often view American-style personal essays as fluff.

Students applying to more than one U.K. institution should use the Universities and Colleges Admissions Service (UCAS, www.ucas.ac.uk), which functions like the Common Application group in the U.S. (Students applying to only one British institution should generally use its own form.) The UCAS form asks you to list all your courses, and the grades you received in them, as well as your SAT and/or ACT scores. It also includes an essay and a letter of recommendation. Most institutions will accept applications through the spring, though we recommend that you apply by the deadline for British students, January 15. The deadline for applying to Oxford and Cambridge, or to apply to any program in medicine, is October 15 for entrance the following fall. Many institutions have rolling admissions, another reason to apply early. One note on terminology: In Britain, a program of study is called a course. The British word for what we call courses is "module."

College in Britain is not for the faint of heart, but those with the initiative to go will be richly rewarded. After college in Britain, students will have the skills and savvy to succeed almost anywhere in the world.

Aberdeen, Scotland AB24 3FX

Aberdeen is a leading Scottish institution that has stepped up its efforts to recruit Americans. Major attractions include engineering, life sciences, and anything related to Europe. Located on Scotland's picturesque east coast, the city of Aberdeen combines charm with the bustle of a small city.

Website: www.abdn.ac.uk
Location: Urban
Total Enrollment: 13,234
Undergraduates: 10,260
Male/Female: 45/55
SAT Ranges: N/A
ACT Range: N/A
Financial Aid: N/A
Expense: Pub $
Phi Beta Kappa: No
Applicants: N/A
Accepted: N/A
Enrolled: N/A
Grad in 6 Years: N/A
Returning Freshmen: N/A
Academics: ✍ ✍ ✍ ½
Social: ☎ ☎ ☎
Q of L: ★ ★ ★ ★
Admissions: (+44)1224
   272090
Email Address:
   sras@abdn.ac.uk

Strongest Programs:
Engineering
English
French
Geography
History
Medicine
Politics and International
   Relations

The University of Aberdeen was founded in 1495—three years after a certain well-known explorer sailed from Spain to the New World. Students seeking the flavor of old Europe will not be disappointed; with plenty of cobblestone streets and buildings made of ancient stone, the university has a distinctly medieval aura. But Aberdeen is more than just a history theme park. With a full-time U.S. recruiter and exchange programs with twenty-four American universities, Aberdeen is one of the few British universities with a critical mass of Americans. And why not? It offers top-notch academics, a curriculum that is unusually flexible by U.K. standards, and a slice of life far richer than any U.S. institution can muster. "I love the diversity at the University of Aberdeen," says a history major, "It is great to be surrounded by people from other countries and to hear their points of view."

Aberdeen is perched at a latitude roughly the same as Juneau, Alaska, but because of the Gulf Stream, winter temperatures are generally milder than those on the east coast of the United States. December days are short in winter, but sky-gazers are often treated to glimpses of the fabled Northern Lights. Most university buildings are concentrated in a quiet enclave known as "Old Aberdeen." The campus is crowned—literally—by a sixteenth-century tower in the shape of an imperial crown. Lightly traveled streets pass through the campus, and the multitude of green lawns and picturesque courtyards are ideal for lounging on sunny days.

Aberdeen is divided into five divisions: arts and divinity; education, medicine and medical sciences; science and engineering; and social sciences and law. Popular majors include English, French, geography, history, and a joint politics and international relations major. A new interdisciplinary program in physical sciences mixes scientific study with writing, commu-

"One of the finest points about Aberdeen is that you are always lectured to by full professors starting in the first year."

nication, and computer and Internet-related skills. Engineering is also strong, especially programs related to the oil industry. (The City of Aberdeen is headquarters for the thriving oil extraction business in the North Sea.) The life sciences are a major draw—with zoology being the most popular of them—and the university offers unique programs in marine resource management and tropical environmental science. Aberdeen's medical program, like most of those outside the U.S., is an all-in-one program that allows students to work on their undergraduate and medical degrees simultaneously—usually over five years. Be aware that the competition registers somewhere between intense and manic, and be sure to apply by October 15 of your senior year.

Aberdeen is a medium-sized university by U.S. standards, and courses in the first two years generally consist of lectures supplemented by smaller weekly discussion sections. "One of the finest points about Aberdeen is that you are always lectured to by full professors starting in the first year," declares an English major. "I have found my professors very approachable, friendly, and helpful," chirps a history major. Unlike in the U.S., professors typically team-teach introductory "modules," with each covering the topics that are his or her specialty. Perhaps the biggest academic difference from state-side institutions is that students generally take only three subjects at a time in the first two years, though extensive reading and research outside of class is generally taken for granted. "Often we are expected to come to class prepared to discuss certain topics, but given no minimum reading assignment—the professor gives out a list of selected readings from which we can choose," says a history major. As at most U.K. institutions, grades are typically determined by end-of-the-term evaluations with few intermediate assignments. At the end of their second year students must typically pass exams in order to advance to "honors level," the equivalent of the junior and senior years of college in the States. These advanced students typically take two year-long classes that may meet as many as four times per week with both lectures and interactive instruction. Upper-level scientists typically spend long hours in the lab. One nice feature: there is generally no limit to the number of students who can sign up for a particular course, thereby giving students the freedom to sign up for anything that strikes their fancy.

"Wandering around campus, you are bound to hear at least three different languages being spoken in a day."

There is generally no limit to the number of students who can sign up for a particular course, thereby giving students the freedom to sign up for anything that strikes their fancy.

Americans find the academic climate to be relatively relaxed. "On the whole, I would say that students here are less serious about academic work than they were at my home institution, though in any course there is the usual mix those few who really care, the middle majority, and the few who couldn't care less," says an exchange student. Several upperclassmen report a significant increase in the rigor of class work in the final two years.

Aberdeen has about 225 degree students from the States. Overall, 87 percent of the students hail from the U.K. while the remaining 13 percent arrive from overseas. "Wandering around campus, you are bound to hear at least three different languages being spoken in a day," reports a first-year student, adding that "the people here are extremely friendly and outgoing." The political climate on campus is relatively subdued—several students describe the tenor as "conservative"—though there were protests during the recent conflict in Iraq and its aftermath. Upon their arrival at the university, students partake of Freshers Week. No classes are held, and various student organizations sponsor informational meetings. Aberdeen is a selective institution for U.S. students, though less so than University of St. Andrews. The bill for an Aberdeen education depends on your course of study. Students in the humanities and social sciences can expect to fork over in the neighborhood of $20,000 for all expenses except travel, depending on the exchange rate, while scientists will pay closer to $25,000. No scholarships are available for U.S. students, but those eligible for federal student loans can use them for study at Aberdeen.

The drinking age in Britain is eighteen, so social life at Aberdeen revolves around legal consumption rather than drinking on the sly.

Housing at Aberdeen is less than ideal. A majority of the international students (along with first-years from the U.K.) live in Hillhead Halls of Residence, an aging complex of houses and flats that is about a fifteen-minute walk from the campus. "Rumor has it that Hillhead was designed after a Swedish women's prison," claims fourth-year history major. That may or may not be true, but it is undeniable that the accommodations are Spartan at best. (Renovations are due in the coming years, which should improve the situation.) Students may elect catered rooms (two meals per day) or self-catering, wherein they cook their own food with kitchen facilities generally located down the hall from the rooms. Many students choose to move off-campus

"Rumor has it that Hillhead was designed after a Swedish women's prison."

after their first year, and a variety of housing options are available within walking distance of the campus. Only a few students own cars, and parking can be dicey.

One staple of American college life will not be necessary at Aberdeen: a fake ID. The drinking age in Britain is eighteen, so social life at Aberdeen revolves around legal consumption rather than drinking on the sly. "Most people go out on most nights if only for a pint at the pub," reports an exchange student, "More often than not, one pint turns into a whole night out, but that's tricks." Nights out often start at the student union, which was recently named best in the U.K., though it is located a fifteen-minute walk or short bus ride away in the downtown area. After the union, you may find yourself doing what Britons call "the pub crawl," which means sampling the refreshment of several pubs before heading home in the wee hours. For those who find themselves inebriated in a distant part of the city, the university has a standing deal with a local cab company to take home any student who needs a ride with the tab put on the student's university bill.

Campus social events consist mainly of periodic formal balls, to which the men wear kilts and the women wear evening gowns. Perhaps the biggest campus event of the year is the Torcher's Parade, which is held every spring and features floats made by various student organizations. Sports are mainly for playing rather than watching at Aberdeen. Individual sports rather than team intramurals are the staple of weekend warriors, and students can purchase passes for various athletic facilities depending on their interests. Among the most successful of Aberdeen's intercollegiate teams are field hockey, "football" (soccer), crew, golf, and table tennis.

Aberdeen is a city of about two hundred thousand. "A fantastic college town!" raves a biology major, who notes that student discounts are available at a wide variety of establishments. The city has plenty of old-world charm, and outdoorsy types will love the dramatic scenery that is everywhere in northeast Scotland. Picturesque cliffs overlooking the North Sea are within an easy bus or train ride. Fifteen miles south of Aberdeen is breathtaking Dunnattar Castle, a fourteenth-century ruin set high on a rocky outcrop that was the set for Mel Gibson's film rendition of *Hamlet*. Within a half-an-hour ride inland is the edge of the legendary Scottish Highlands.

"It is such a carefree atmosphere with that special touch of Scottish tradition."

Famous castles are in all directions, including the royal family's summer hideaway, Balmoral. For the Scottish version of the big city, Glasgow and Edinburgh are several hours by train or bus. Two hours on a plane will get you to most places in western Europe.

Though Aberdeen may lack some of the conveniences of home, most Americans are happy they came. "Between classes on a sunny day, students will buy something from the bakery and sit on the grass in the midst of five hundred year-old buildings and cobblestone streets. It is such a carefree atmosphere with that special touch of Scottish tradition," says a satisfied history major. If you're the kind of person who likes to meet new people and learn about different cultures, take a chance. You, too, may thrive on the Aberdeen air.

If You Apply To ➤ | **Aberdeen:** Rolling: Jun. 30 (Medicine: Oct. 15). Campus Interviews: informational. SATs or ACTs required. UCAS essay only. Overlaps: Dundee, Edinburgh, Glasgow, St. Andrews, Stirling.

University of St. Andrews

St. Andrews, Scotland KY16 9AJ

St. Andrews is the most popular destination for Americans who want to study in Britain. Often compared to Princeton, St. Andrews is small by British standards and middle-sized by American ones. Major drawing cards include English, international relations, medieval history, and modern languages.

Harvard likes to brag about the fact that it was founded back in 1636. Think that's old? Try 1413—the date Pope Benedict XIII issued a Papal Bull recognizing the University of St. Andrews. Set in an ancient seaside town on the eastern shore of Scotland, St. Andrews is an ideal spot for adventuresome Americans who want a world-class education and an introduction to life outside North America. With 550 U.S. students in degree programs and another 250 in residence each year for study abroad, St. Andrews has the highest proportion of Americans of any major university outside North America. Yet success here requires a go-getter mentality. Support services are available, but students on this side of the Atlantic are accustomed to being treated like adults. "They don't hold your hand—you're going to be dropped in and it's sink or swim," says one U.S. student.

St. Andrews is the only institution in the the *Fiske Guide* that saw a heretic burned at the stake beneath its most prominent landmark. In 1528, a Protestant reformer named Patrick Hamilton was the victim of a botched burning imposed by the local archbishop that dragged on through six hours and several relightings. Hamilton's initials are carved in the cobblestones where he died, and legend has it that any student who steps on them will fail exams. The spot is at

> **"This is not a university for an undecided major."**

the base of St. Salvator's Tower, which dates from 1450. An adjoining quadrangle is the hub of the university, but most academic buildings are interspersed through the town's narrow medieval streets. Town and university alike are made of ancient stone, and the ruins of a fourteenth-century castle and cathedral are adjacent. Narrow alleys, called "wynds" by the Scots, lead to secluded gardens and courtyards that add to the old world aura.

Though more flexible than most British universities, St. Andrews offers less latitude to explore a variety of subjects than would be found in a U.S. institution. "Most U.K. students have a very good idea of what they want to study. This is not a university for an undecided major," says a senior who is studying international relations and French. Students typically take three year-long classes in each of their first two years—the equivalent of introductory survey courses in the States. These "modules" generally consist of three lectures per week with one hundred or more students and a tutorial with ten to twenty. With satisfactory progress, students move on to honors level courses for the final two years, which are generally taught in seminar format. Fewer courses means less time in class and more emphasis on outside reading— "much more than in the States" says a UCLA study abroad student. Instead of a textbook or two, most modules have sizable reading lists that students must navigate largely on their own. Modules typically end with papers or exams that account for most of the grade, and there is a full week without classes prior to exams. More so than in the U.S., the onus is on the students to keep current with their work and seek help when necessary. Nevertheless, the faculty gets high marks and students like the fact that professors are often internationally known in their fields. "The faculty is very accessible and friendly," says a fourth-year student. "The academic counseling has been far superior to my counseling back home," notes a junior-year-abroad student.

Website: www.st-and.ac.uk
Location: Small town
Total Enrollment: 6,512
Undergraduates: 5,508
Male/Female: 48/52
SAT Ranges: N/A
ACT Range: N/A
Financial Aid: N/A
Expense: Pub $
Phi Beta Kappa: No
Applicants: N/A
Accepted: N/A
Enrolled: N/A
Grad in 6 Years: N/A
Returning Freshmen: N/A
Academics: 🖉 🖉 🖉 🖉 ½
Social: 🍷 🍷 🍷
Q of L: ★ ★ ★
Admissions: (+44)1334 463326
Email Address: intoff@ st-and.ac.uk

Strongest Programs:
Art history
Medieval history
English
International relations
Modern languages
Physics
Psychology

St. Andrews is the smallest of the leading British universities and among the few to be located in a small town. It is a liberal arts university with additional programs in divinity, medicine, and business. Signature offerings include art history, medieval history, English, international relations (IR), modern languages, physics, and psychology. IR is the biggest draw for Americans, and St. Andrews is a world leader in the study of international terrorism. "I thought doing international relations in the U.S. would be a bit silly," says one American. Standards in foreign language are higher than in the U.S.— an opportunity but also a challenge. "I got close to 700 on my SAT IIs in French and I was completely lost," says a second-year student. As at many U.S. universities, natural science students tend to work the hardest. Premed is a killer, and most scientists will have spent hour upon hour in the lab by the time they get to honors level. While there are few weak majors, several students report that access to information technology has been less than they expected. Computer labs can be booked solid near the end of the term, and students are better off bringing their own machine.

> "My four best friends are Russian, Scandinavian, English, and Irish/Slovakian."

St. Andrews is one of the world's most international universities—25 percent of the students come from outside the U.K. It is an oft-noted fact that more English students than Scottish are enrolled, and sizable contingents also come from Scandinavia, eastern Europe, Asia, and the Middle East. "My four best friends are Russian, Scandinavian, English, and Irish/Slovakian," says one American who attended English boarding school. The whole seems to mesh reasonably well, though one student notes that class differences are sometimes apparent. The English tend to be from upper-middle-class backgrounds and help give the campus a more conservative tenor than some Americans might expect.

In the U.K., St. Andrews is viewed as a Scottish alternative to Oxford and Cambridge, inviting enough to attract the likes of Prince William, the heart-throb son of Prince Charles and Princess Diana. Admission for U.S. students is highly competitive—on par with places like Cornell, Tufts, or Emory. A high proportion of the U.S. students at St. Andrews attended private schools. The Americans who thrive at St. Andrews tend to have international experience, though not all do. Many students are "diplobrats" whose parents have worked in international organizations such as the World Bank or the State Department. The Scots generally give Americans a warm welcome, despite a few reservations about U.S. foreign policy. Tuition varies depending on the course, but the total bill for a year at St. Andrews is likely to be about $25,000, depending on the exchange rate.

Housing is guaranteed for first-year students, and students can request a single or shared room. They also have the option of the university meal plan or "self-catering," in which they use kitchens in the dorms to prepare their food. Reviews of the food are mixed at best. "British cuisine is not world renowned. There is good reason for this," says one student. Nor should students expect the glitzy food courts or all-you-can-eat service typical in the States. Meals are served at specified times with limited portions. On the plus side, dorm life includes once-a-week maid service. After their first year, students generally move to one of the many apartments ("flats") near the university. "There is a bit of a scramble for flats in February, but most students are able to find good accommodations," reports an international relations and French major. Because there is no boundary between town and university, students are less sheltered from the real world than they might be on a typical U.S. campus. "This is a grown-up place," declares one student, "We don't live on a campus—we live in a town. It is more like real life."

A peek inside the student union reveals something never seen on a U.S. campus—a fully equipped bar with everything from vodka to vermouth (not to mention scotch). The drinking age is eighteen in Britain, and though there may not be

Fewer courses means less time in class and more emphasis on outside reading—"much more than in the States" says a UCLA study abroad student.

St. Andrews is one of the world's most international universities—25 percent of the students come from outside the U.K.

more alcohol than at an American institution, it is certainly more out in the open. There are twenty-eight pubs in St. Andrews, a town of about eighteen thousand, and imbibing in them is the main form of social life. Black-tie balls are also a staple, as are ceilidhs (pronounced "kaylees"), which feature traditional Scottish dancing that resembles a square dance. Soccer ("football") is the national sport, and students congregate to watch pro teams in the pubs or on the big-screen TV at the union. University sports are not nearly as big in the U.K. as in the U.S. and draw few spectators. "Interhall" competitions in soccer or rugby are the equivalent of intramurals. There is a pay-per-use sports center with facilities ranging from basketball to squash. Golf enthusiasts know that the game was invented in St. Andrews in the 1500s, and the fabled Old Course is a short walk from campus. (Students can get a year-long pass to play at the courses in town for about $150, though Old Course players must have a specified handicap rating.)

The nearest road-trip destination is the medium-sized city of Dundee, about thirty minutes away, which offers a mall, movie theaters, and a McDonald's. (Subway is the only American fast-food joint to crack the St. Andrews market—so far.) Scotland's two largest cities, Edinburgh and Glasgow, are about an hour away, and for outdoorsy types, the legendary Scottish Highlands are within easy reach.

As befitting a six-hundred-year-old institution, St. Andrews is rife with tradition. At dawn on May 1, hundreds of sleep-deprived and/or drunk students take an icy dip in the North Sea as part of May Morning, a tradition with roots in pagan times. The all-male Kate Kennedy Club also goes back centuries and was created in tongue-and-cheek honor of the daughter of the university's founder, a lass who was supposedly liberal in her sexual favors for St. Andrews students. The KK Club sponsors numerous social events throughout the year, most notably Raisin Weekend, which culminates in a massive shaving-cream fight in St. Salvator's Quad.

St. Andrews is not the U.S., and those who come here must be ready to adjust to different way of life (not to mention constant rain and winter nights that begin with sunset at 3:30 p.m.). But these are a small price to pay for Scotland in all its ancient glory. Mothers may tremble at the thought of their off-spring going overseas for college, but the U.K. is not that much further from the East Coast than Berkeley or Pomona.

The education from merely living in St. Andrews will far exceed anything learned in the classroom. U.S. institutions may trumpet their diversity, but nothing state-side compares to the richness of living abroad among the best and brightest from all corners of the globe. St. Andrews delivers it all against a hauntingly beautiful back-drop that will remain forever etched in the minds of all who come here.

Mothers may tremble at the thought of their off-spring going overseas for college, but the U.K. is not that much further from the East Coast than Berkeley or Pomona.

If You Apply To ➤	**St. Andrews:** Rolling: May 31. Interviews: not available. SATs or ACTs recommended. Essay: reasons for wishing to study at St. Andrews. Overlaps: N/A

University of Iowa

107 Calvin Hall, Iowa City, IA 52242-1396

A bargain compared to other Big Ten schools such as Michigan, Wisconsin, and Illinois. Iowa is world-famous for its creative writing program and Writers' Workshop.

Other areas of strength include health sciences, social and behavioral sciences, and space physics. Future scientists should check out the Research Scholars Program.

Website: www.uiowa.edu
Location: Small city
Total Enrollment: 29,897
Undergraduates: 20,487
Male/Female: 45/55
SAT Ranges: V 520–650
　M 540–660
ACT Range: 22–27
Financial Aid: 35%
Expense: Pub $ $ $
Phi Beta Kappa: Yes
Applicants: 13,079
Accepted: 84%
Enrolled: 38%
Grad in 6 Years: 64%
Returning Freshmen: 83%
Academics: ✍ ✍ ✍ ✍
Social: ☎ ☎ ☎
Q of L: ★ ★ ★
Admissions: (319) 335-3847
Email Address:
　admissions@uiowa.edu

Strongest Programs:
Creative Writing
Theater Arts
Dance
Music
Health Sciences and Health
　Care
Business
Physics
Psychology

The campus is changing face with many new buildings recently opened, and several more on the way. The biggest are a $47 million medical education and biomedical research facility, a $37 million athletic complex, and an art and art history building with a 20-million-dollar price tag.

At first glance, one might dismiss Iowa as a standard-issue Midwestern school. But beneath the bland exterior of fields and corn lies one of the most dynamic schools in the country—and one of the best buys to boot. Iowa has long been a major player in the creative worlds, particularly writing, and its small-town atmosphere is just one of many reasons students nationwide flock to this "budget Ivy League."

The 1,880-acre campus, located in the rolling hills of the Iowa River valley, is bisected by the Iowa River and merges with downtown Iowa City. Among the ninety primary buildings is Old Capitol, the first capitol of Iowa, a national historic landmark, and the symbol of the university. The primary architectural style of the campus buildings is Greek Revival and modern. The campus is changing face with many new buildings recently opened and several more on the way. The biggest are a $47 million medical education and biomedical research facility, a $37 million athletic complex, and an art and art history building with a 20-million-dollar price tag.

Iowa has a long tradition in creative arts. It was one of the first universities to award graduate degrees for creative work and is also the home of the first Writers' Workshop. The school also prides itself on its International Writing Program, which brings a wide array of prominent authors to the campus. "The English department is stellar," raves one English major. "It's possibly the best in the country—at least for

"Social life at the University of Iowa is a very big part of the draw for many students."

creative writing." Iowa's on-campus hospital is one of the largest teaching hospitals in the United States. The Health Sciences Center, affiliated with the hospital, encompasses five colleges: the College of Medicine, Dentistry, Pharmacy, Nursing, and Public Health. Undergraduates benefit from the strong health center course offerings in related health professions, such as physician's assistant or medical technician. Combined degree programs, which permit students to earn degrees across colleges, exist between liberal arts and a choice of the following: the College of Business Administration, Engineering, Nursing, and Medicine. New undergraduate programs include: a bachelor's degree in international studies, which includes a scholarship for study abroad for every student; a bachelor's degree in performing arts entrepreneurship; a certificate in American Sign Language and deaf studies; and a certificate in museum studies. The University Honors Program provides special academic, cultural, and social opportunities to outstanding students in the Colleges of Business Administration, Education, Engineering, Liberal Arts and Sciences, Nursing, and Pharmacy. Iowa's study abroad program gives students a chance to travel to more than forty different countries. Agriculture, veterinary medicine, forestry, architecture, and animal science are not offered at Iowa but are taught at its sister institution, Iowa State.

Each of the undergraduate colleges has its own general education requirements. Liberal arts students must take courses in rhetoric, natural science, social sciences, foreign language, interpretation of literature, historical perspectives, humanities, and quantitative or formal reasoning. Distributed general education, including courses in cultural diversity, foreign civilization and culture, and physical education, are also required. Iowa's academic climate is described by the students as moderately competitive and differing by major. Most classes have less than fifty students, although some introductory courses have more. The University of Iowa's Four-Year Graduation Plan guarantees that students who fulfill certain requirements will not have their graduation delayed by unavailability of a needed course. Students give most professors high marks. "The profs are very well informed and always willing to help," says a junior nursing student. There are often smaller sessions led by graduate students as a way to make the classroom experience more accessible. Academic and career counseling programs also get good reviews.

Sixty-seven percent of the undergraduates hail from Iowa with most of the rest coming from contiguous states, especially Illinois. African-Americans, Hispanics, and Asian-Americans account for about 8 percent of the student body; but, as the administration points out, the state of Iowa has only a 4 percent minority population. Yet students say the campus is extremely tolerant and that almost anyone can find their niche at Iowa. "There is definitely a great amount of diversity at the University of Iowa. Students here are all very nice and come from different backgrounds," says a freshman. Besides the 432 athletic scholarships available in ten men's sports and twelve women's sports, there are more than three hundred academic scholarships, ranging from $500 to $7,000. The Roy J. Carver Scholarships are awarded to eighty-two students who have overcome social or psychological barriers; it is one of the first awards that was bestowed on a former homeless man.

"Campus housing is great, and very popular."

Students say that campus residence halls are clean but very sociable and therefore not very quiet. All are co-ed by floor or wing. Some students say that "campus housing is great, and very popular," while others think the dorms are "as satisfactory as dorms can be." Students can choose to live in one of eight "learning communities," such as women in science and engineering or performing arts. A few students get sloughed off to temporary housing, so it is important to apply early. There are many praises for the custodial staff that keeps the buildings clean. Only 28 percent of the students live in university housing, and more than half live in apartments or houses adjacent to the campus. Students usually move off campus after sophomore year. "Off-campus housing is popular but the high rents are often an issue," says one student. The dining halls and "diverse" food selections meet with students' satisfaction. The student union, improved by a $10 million renovation, includes a pastry and coffee shop, two cafeterias, and the State Room Restaurant.

Ten percent of the men and 13 percent of women belong to fraternities and sororities, and these groups tend to play less of a role in the social life than they do elsewhere. "Social life at the University of Iowa is a very big part of the draw for many students," says one theatre arts major. "Downtown Iowa City, which is practically in the center of campus, is bursting with nightlife even during the week." There are two university theaters right on campus and many affordable cultural events take place at Hancher Auditorium. "The social life revolves around bars and movie theaters in town," says a sophomore. The Union Bar and Grill, Mickey's, Sports Column, and George's are all popular hangouts with students. The school officially follows the state policy regarding alcohol; the legal drinking age is twenty-one, but one freshman says too much underage drinking is a main complaint of students. The college admits binge drinking among students is a problem, but has received a six-year, $830,000 foundation grant to solve it. For those who tire of the local scene, Chicago, Kansas City, or St. Louis are all within six hours by car, a short road trip by Midwestern standards. Skiing is another hour away in Minnesota. Riverfest, held at the Iowa Memorial Union and on the banks of the Iowa River, is a weeklong, all-campus event celebrating the long-awaited spring. Another annual event the students look forward to is the Iowa City Jazz Festival.

"The English department is stellar."

As for sports, there's that big football stadium, which now has the team it deserves. Iowa has become a national power and regularly appears in New Year's Day bowl games. Hawkeye fans are serious about their team. But if you want a real powerhouse, look no further than the Hawkeye wrestling team, a perennial national champion. Both basketball teams and the softball teams have also claimed recent titles.

New undergraduate programs include a bachelor's degree in international studies, which includes a scholarship for study abroad for every student; a bachelor's degree in performing arts entrepreneurship; a certificate in American Sign Language and deaf studies; and a certificate in museum studies.

Overlaps

Iowa State, Northern Iowa, University of Illinois, Indiana University, University of Wisconsin

The University of Iowa not only boasts a beautiful campus with many improvements on the way, it offers students a seemingly endless range of academic programs, an abundance of social activities, and a friendly, welcoming climate. With its combination of quality academics, mammoth resources, renowned specialty programs, and extensive research opportunities, this Midwest school is anything but faceless. "Iowa has everything I want, including the program I want in nursing, a diverse campus, many extracurriculars and other opportunities," says a junior.

Iowa State University

100 Alumni Hall, Ames, IA 50011

Visit ISU and you'll see why they call it Silo Tech. Agriculture and engineering are the twin pillars of the curriculum, and the university is a magnet for prevets. Ames is a small city and ISU must still endure barbs from certain snobby people in Iowa City.

Website: www.iastate.edu
Location: Small city
Total Enrollment: 27,898
Undergraduates: 22,999
Male/Female: 56/44
SAT Ranges: V 510–650
    M 550–570
ACT Range: 22–27
Financial Aid: 49%
Expense: Pub $ $ $
Phi Beta Kappa: Yes
Applicants: 10,370
Accepted: 89%
Enrolled: 46%
Grad in 6 Years: 62%
Returning Freshmen: 83%
Academics: 🖉 🖉 🖉
Social: 🕿 🕿 🕿
Q of L: ★ ★ ★
Admissions: (515) 294-5838
Email Address:
    admissions@iastate.edu

Strongest Programs:
Engineering
Agriculture
Design

Love for Iowa State University runs as deep as its Midwestern roots. Strong programs in engineering, business, and agriculture attract students from around the globe. The close-knit, small-town atmosphere fostered at this school of nearly twenty-eight thousand keeps them here.

The university has lavished attention on its park-like campus, located on a 1,984-acre tract in the middle of Ames, population fifty thousand. The campus, which boasts a combination of dignified old buildings and award-winning new ones, is a landmark of landscape design with numerous shady quadrangles with floral plantings and artwork that create a garden-like quality. History and tradition prevail, from the campanile, which serenades the campus with its carillon bells, to the huge public art collection including sculptures by Danish artist Christian Petersen. The new Howe Hall, the home to aerospace engineering, boasts a virtual reality application center and a six-sided virtual reality cave. Along with Hoover Hall, the complex provides the teaching and researching home for the College of Engineering. Other new additions to campus include the Gerdin Building for the College of Business and the 4-H extension building for the College of Agriculture. Much of the campus is closed to cars, largely for the benefit of walking, bicycling, and in-line skating students, as well as the swans (named Sir Lancelot and Lady Elaine) and the ducks who reside on Lake LaVerne.

"We have some world class profs here who are doing important research."

When Iowa State opened in 1869 as a land grant university, agriculture and engineering ruled the academic roost. These days, though, the liberal arts are at least as popular, and the College of Liberal Arts and Sciences is the largest of ISU's nine colleges. Among the university's one hundred plus majors, the College of Agriculture still fields outstanding programs in animal science, agriculture technology, agribusiness, and agronomy. Other colleges include business, design, education, veterinary medicine, family and consumer sciences (formerly home economics), and the graduate college. New undergrad programs include a technical communications major and minors in food safety and emerging global diseases. Students find the academic climate competitive, but that can vary by program.

All undergraduates must take two semesters of English composition their freshman year and demonstrate proficiency in English prior to graduation. Other general education requirements, which vary by college, focus on gaining breadth in the natural and social sciences, but everyone takes a half-credit course on the use of the library and a one-credit course on skills such as time management and test-taking. A modem network allows students to link their personal computers with the university system, and hundreds of Iowa State pages now inhabit the World Wide Web.

Students can also use the AccessPlus system of electronic kiosks sprinkled around campus to check the status of their university bill or financial aid package, print an unofficial transcript, or get their current schedule. An honors program enrolls nearly three hundred outstanding freshmen each year, many of whom live in honors housing. A summer language program in France, Germany, and Spain is one of fifty programs that students can choose from work or study in thirty-five countries worldwide. Iowa State ranks in the top twenty for sending students overseas.

"We have a lot of farmers and small-town Iowans."

Despite the university's size, professors teach most classes with the exception of some freshman English options. Students learn from faculty stars like Pulitzer Prize–winning author Jane Smiley. "We have some world class profs here who are doing important research," one senior says. A Spanish student adds the teaching is "undoubtedly excellent." Academic and career counseling draw praise, too, and advisors are "always readily available" to help students.

Seventy-seven percent of ISU's students are Iowans, though all fifty states and 118 countries are represented in the student body. Foreign students comprise another 5 percent of the student body. Iowa State was the first co-ed land grant institution, but attracting minorities has proven more difficult: minority students account for just 8 percent of the student body. "We have a lot of farmers and small-town Iowans," says a senior. "This is a pretty white campus." To help remedy this situation, ISU launched a $25 million campaign aimed at increasing the number of scholarships available for minority students, student athletes, and student leaders. Freshman orientation has come to include the topics of race relations and cultural diversity, and entering frosh participate in learning teams through which groups of students with similar interests and career goals take courses together and live in the same dorms. In addition to need-based financial aid and a variety of athletic scholarships, many merit awards are available, ranging from $500 to $10,000.

Thirty-five percent of undergrads live in on-campus residence halls and apartments. The new Etan Residence Hall offers suite-style rooms. Single-sex and co-ed dorms are available, and rooms are said to be comfortable and well maintained. One student indicates that the janitors throw a picnic every spring. "There is a great community. Each hall is divided into houses and they do activities and stuff together," says one senior. Special floors are available for international students, teetotalers, and particularly studious undergraduates; separate housing is available for married students. But "if students apply late and turn in their housing info late, they may have to live in the den of a dorm floor for a few days until housing is found for them." Each year, the food service sponsors a Favorites from Home contest, in which recipes entered by students are selected and adapted to feed thousands. The college boasts new and improved dining at the Union Drive Student Services Building. Many upperclassmen live off campus; Greek life claims 13 percent of men and 12 percent of women.

"Ames is a perfect college town."

(Continued)
Veterinary Medicine

The university boasts college wrestling's only four-time undefeated champion.

Among the university's one hundred plus majors, the College of Agriculture still fields outstanding programs in animal science, agriculture technology, agribusiness, and agronomy.

Each year, the food service sponsors a Favorites from Home contest, in which recipes entered by students are selected and adapted to feed thousands.

Iowa State is not simply located in Ames—in many respects it is Ames. "Ames is a perfect college town," one senior says. Des Moines, the state capital, is about thirty minutes away, and Iowa City, Minneapolis, and Chicago are other easy and enjoyable road trips. Socializing tends to stay on campus, with big-name bands playing at Hilton Coliseum and parties always rocking. The campus is officially dry, but according to one sophomore most older students will buy alcohol for minors. The big event every spring is a two-day campus festival called VEISHEA (an acronym for ISU's original five colleges), which features parades, exhibitions, food, and a fun-run. Another tradition is campaniling, where students must kiss under the campanile at the stroke of midnight to be considered "true" co-eds. And students have learned not to walk over the Zodiac sign in the Memorial Union—it brings bad luck.

In sports, basketball is king; the men's and women's teams are usual invitees to the NCAA tournament. The university boasts college wrestling's only four-time undefeated champion. An astounding 80 percent of the students participate in one of the largest intramural sports programs in the nation. The Hawkeye rivalry is one of the strongest in the nation.

Iowa State's goal is to become the best land-grant university in the nation. To that end, students can choose from programs and services that help them meet their potential and are constantly challenged to do their best. While academically competitive, the campus is also known for its Midwest friendliness. "Students at ISU believe in a sense of community," one senior says. "Everybody is polite, friendly and has a sense of pride in regards to the university."

Overlaps

University of Iowa, University of Northern Iowa, University of Illinois, University of Nebraska, University of Minnesota

If You Apply To ➤

Iowa State: Rolling admissions. Admissions: Aug. 1. Financial aid: Mar. 1. Guarantees to meet demonstrated need. SATs or ACTs: required. No SAT IIs. Accepts electronic application. No essay question.

Ithaca College

953 Danby Road, Ithaca, NY 14850-7020

Students looking at Ithaca also apply to BU, Syracuse, and NYU. The common thread? Outstanding programs in the arts and media. Students also clamor to get into physical therapy. (Watch the November 1 deadline.) Cross-town neighbor Cornell adds curricular and social opportunities.

Website: www.ithaca.edu
Location: Small town
Total Enrollment: 6,431
Undergraduates: 6,190
Male/Female: 43/57
SAT Ranges: V 540–630
   M 550–640
Financial Aid: 68%
Expense: Pr $ $ $
Phi Beta Kappa: No
Applicants: 11,309

Just over the hill, in upstate New York, sits Ithaca: a small college with much to boast about. Known for its strong programs in the arts—including drama, television and film, and music—Ithaca emphasizes quality over quantity. It has committed itself to undergraduate education and strives to prepare its students for life outside its institutional walls. Its offerings mirror that of a large university, but the school maintains small classes and "hands-on" learning more commonly found at small colleges.

Ithaca College is located in the center of the Finger Lakes region, on a 757-acre plot with spectacular views overlooking the city of Ithaca. None of the streamlined, modern campus buildings are more than a few decades old, since the college moved to its present location in the 1960s. Many believe the campus is one of the country's most beautiful, including author Tom Wolfe, who dubbed the school "the emerald eminence at the fingertip of Lake Cayuga."

Through its five schools—music, communications, business, health sciences and human performance, and humanities and sciences—Ithaca offers more than one hundred majors and more than fifty minors. The newest include integrated marketing and art education; a major in culture and communication is being created in the Division of Interdisciplinary Studies. Students in the School of Business can study to receive a certificate in international business. With its prominent faculty and many opportunities for student performance, the college's reputation for music education and performance are almost unparalleled. The Park School of Communications has its own elaborate $12 million facility. The school has grown up alongside the broadcast industry and is known for programs in radio and TV production (the most popular major) and cinema and photography. The business school has grown rapidly over the past decade; all students now matriculate into the business administration major and declare one of six concentrations after the first or second year.

In the School of Health Sciences and Human Performance, the physical therapy program is a national drawing card and boasts nearly a 100 percent placement rate; five-year B.S./M.S. programs in physical and occupational therapy are available in conjunction with the University of Rochester. Ithaca also offers a dual teacher certification program in health and physical education and majors in therapeutic recreation and environmental studies. In addition, Ithaca boasts one of the nation's most complete sports studies programs, with majors including exercise science, clinical exercise science, athletic training, sports management, and sports communication.

Though not the most well known, humanities and sciences, with more than 2,400 students, is the largest school on Ithaca's campus. The school has refocused its general education program around human communities, and students now explore how communities form, function, and express meaning. The program emphasizes global and historical perspectives through courses in self and society; science, mathematics, and formal reasoning; and human expression. Among the strongest of nineteen humanities and sciences departments are the natural sciences, which offer research

"Professors always teach their own classes and are there for students if we need help."

and even publishing opportunities for undergraduates. The $23 million Center for Natural Sciences boasts state-of-the-art teaching and research facilities for biology, chemistry, and physics. To enhance student–faculty interaction, Ithaca redesigned Williams Hall, adding new computers and lab facilities for the departments of mathematics, computer science, and psychology. Theater arts offers solid acting and technical production programs, but the English and foreign language programs need work, students say. Health services administration, religious studies, audiology, and speech communications programs are no longer accepting new students.

Humanities and Sciences offers an optional freshman seminar combining rigorous study of a selected subject with transition-to-college topics such as personal, social, and academic responsibility. Topics include Mathematical Art with Computers and Who Are We? What Do We Think? Applied psychology and applied economics are popular majors that cross disciplinary lines. Ithaca students can go to Cornell or Wells College to take courses not offered on their campus, and vice versa. Other off-campus opportunities include internships and foreign-study programs in more than fifty countries in all corners of the world, including the Ithaca College London Center and semesters in Washington, D.C., and Los Angeles. Those wanting to "walkabout down under" can take advantage of a semester-long trip to Australia. Students spend one month each at Griffith, La Trobe and Murdoch universities and the University of Tasmania.

The majority of Ithaca's classes are small—more than three-quarters have twenty-five or fewer students—and praise for professors abounds. Students appear

(Continued)
Accepted: 56%
Enrolled: 24%
Grad in 6 Years: 73%
Returning Freshmen: 87%
Academics: ✍ ✍ ✍
Social: ☎ ☎ ☎ ☎ ☎
Q of L: ★ ★ ★
Admissions: (607) 274-3124
Email Address:
  admission@ithaca.edu

Strongest Programs:
Music
Physical Therapy
Theater
Communications
Natural Sciences
Psychology

While there may be a figurative place for everyone at Ithaca, only 65 percent find a place to hang their hat on campus.

especially impressed by the fact that all classes (even labs) are taught by full professors, not TAs. "Professors always teach their own classes and are there for students if we need help," says a sophomore.

A senior describes the student body as "laid back and friendly." Students generally hail from the Northeast with nearly half from New York and most from middle- to upper-middle-class backgrounds. The school has a large, well-organized Jewish community, but the African-American, Hispanic, and Asian-American populations are small, combining for less than 10 percent of the student body. Students say the campus is becoming more diverse, and the administration's focus of late has been unity, with Unity Relays and Unity Day bringing together students and faculty from all walks of campus life. The Center for the Study of Culture, Race, and Ethnicity offers academic courses and extracurricular activities that encourage students to learn from their own identities and those of the people around them. And the self-motivated thrive here. Nearly eighteen hundred merit scholarships are awarded each year, ranging from $3,000 to a full ride. There are currently no athletic scholarships offered.

> "With Cornell on the other hill, it allows the students a ton of access to social life, educational experiences, and cultural development."

The school has refocused its general education program around human communities.

While there may be a figurative place for everyone at Ithaca, only 65 percent find a place to hang their hat on campus. Students cite the housing situation as a major campus issue. Though they are guaranteed space in the residence halls, arriving freshmen can find themselves squeezed into triples that used to be doubles or packed into a common-room lounge. But don't despair: many lounges have TVs, fireplaces, and terraces, and overcrowding is usually remedied by Thanksgiving, students report. Dorm rooms are comfortable and well maintained. The new College Circle Apartments has added more than six hundred units to on-campus housing. By junior year, many students move off campus.

Since "Ithaca is gorges," there are plenty of opportunities to get out of those dorm rooms for hiking, biking, sledding, and skiing. Officially, Ithaca is a dry campus. On weekends, Ithaca students take advantage of an array of college-oriented activities on campus, in the town of Ithaca, and at next-door neighbor Cornell. "With Cornell on the other hill, it allows the students a ton of access to social life, educational experiences, and cultural development," a senior says. Students frequent restaurants, movies, clubs, and festivals downtown, or may road-trip to Cortland, Syracuse, and Binghamton, New York (each an hour away, with plenty of malls), or Philadelphia, Washington, D.C., New York City, or Canada, less than six hours' drive. Ithaca's Greek scene is low key, with three professional music frats and one social service sorority; only about 2 percent of men and women each join the organizations. Homecoming is an occasion for revelry as is the not-too-esoteric tradition of Terrace mudslides. All Ithacans also look forward to the annual Rocktober-fest, which features games, dunking booths, and revelry.

On the sports scene, the men's wrestling team is competitive nationally and football and baseball are competitive. Students really get into Ithaca's football rivalry against Cortland State, known as the "Cortaca Jug" match (or the Division III Super Bowl). Women's softball won the 2002 National Division III Championship. Sailing is a favorite warm-weather activity, and horseback riding is also available.

Students at Ithaca College thrive on its beautiful campus. With more than one hundred majors and fifty minors to choose from, students find themselves in a competitive and challenging academic atmosphere. While it may share a city with Cornell University, Ithaca has made its own name as a powerful educational institution.

Overlaps

Syracuse, NYU, Boston University, Penn State, University of Massachusetts

If You Apply To ➤

Ithaca: Rolling admissions. Early decision: Nov. 1. Regular admissions: Mar. 1 (Nov. 1 for physical therapy). Financial aid: Feb. 1. Meets demonstrated need of 42%. Campus interviews: recommended, informational. Alumni interviews: optional, informational. SATs or ACTs: required. SAT IIs: optional. Apply to particular school or program. Accepts the Common Application and electronic applications. Essay question: important personal, local, national, or international issue.

James Madison University

Harrisonburg, VA 22807

JMU has carved a comfortable niche among Virginia's superb public universities. With more undergraduates than UVA and more than double the number at William and Mary, Madison is strong in preprofessional fields such as business, health professions, and education.

James Madison University means business. Business programs continue to garner national attention and attract top-notch students from coast to coast. The university is growing at a phenomenal rate, causing some to feel growing pains, but students have much to cheer about, including an emphasis on undergraduate teaching and close student-faculty interaction. Indeed, at JMU it's not simply "business as usual."

JMU is in the heart of the Shenandoah Valley, two hours from Washington, D.C., and Richmond, Virginia. Three types of architecture make up the campus. The buildings on Front campus have red-tile roofs and are constructed of a distinctive limestone block known as bluestone. Back campus has more modern, redbrick structures. The recently constructed College of Integrated Science and Technology campus features modern beige buildings. The university straddles Interstate 81, an outlet to several major East Coast cities. Recent construction includes a health and human services building, and numerous facilities are getting upgrades. A $100 million bond issued from the state will bring a new physics and chemistry building, library, and arts center to campus, along with renovations to historical buildings.

James Madison University is recognized nationally for programs within the business major, while social sciences and education are also strong. The most popular majors at JMU are marketing, psychology, and integrated science and technology. The sciences are also strong bets at JMU, and undergraduates in the biology department have even employed recombinant DNA technology to help develop organisms that produce biodegradable plastics. Also worth noting is the geology and geography departments' summer geology field camp for undergraduates. Although the math department is cited as weak, its development of a mathematical modeling laboratory is used by select undergrads to solve real-world applied math problems. The academic atmosphere, according to one senior, is "balanced to promote individual competition, pushing students towards their goals, yet allowing for free expression and cooperation. The academics are made to be enjoyable." Programs in the health professions, business, information technology, integrated science and technology, and science have all been expanded, and the school has placed a new focus on teacher education, especially science teacher education.

> **"The academics are made to be enjoyable."**

The General Education Program requires each student to take courses in several clusters, including Skills for the 21st Century, Arts and Humanities, the Natural World, Social and Cultural Processes, and Individuals in the Human Community.

Website: www.jmu.edu
Location: Small town
Total Enrollment: 15,965
Undergraduates: 14,828
Male/Female: 41/59
SAT Ranges: V 540–620
 M 540–630
Financial Aid: 28%
Expense: Pub $ $ $
Phi Beta Kappa: No
Applicants: 15,639
Accepted: 58%
Enrolled: 42%
Grad in 6 Years: 78%
Returning Freshmen: 92%
Academics: ✐ ✐ ✐
Social: ☎ ☎ ☎ ☎
Q of L: ★ ★ ★ ★
Admissions: (540) 568-6147
Email Address:
 gotojmu@jmu.edu

Strongest Programs:
Psychology
Communication Sciences and
 Disorders
Integrated Science and
 Technology
Health Professions
Education
Business

Don't look for a lot of diversity among fellow students at JMU. Ninety-five percent attended public high school, and 71 percent are from Virginia.

Freshmen Adventures, held before and after the beginning of the freshman year, gives students an opportunity to meet while hiking, navigating, and looking forward to the coming term.

The idea is to offer students a basis for life-long learning by challenging them to become active in their own education and to explore the foundations of knowledge. Freshmen are offered a variety of programs to help smooth their transition into the university. Freshmen Adventures, held before and after the beginning of the freshman year, gives students an opportunity to meet while hiking, navigating, and looking forward to the coming term.

Now that Madison's enrollment has exceeded fifteen thousand, parking—or rather the lack of space for parking—is a constant complaint, although a new five hundred-vehicle parking deck has eased the situation. With undergraduates far outnumbering grad students, JMU's main mission is undergraduate teaching. "Teachers here are excellent," says a psychology major. Students say that faculty advising can be hit or miss. But if you are

"Whereas UVA is preppy and Virginia Tech is really casual, JMU is right in between—very accepting and not so exclusive."

willing to find the time, some students say that even weekly meetings with these gurus are possible. Career counseling has a website for students to check job positions with employers visiting campus. Those looking for a more intense intellectual experience can check out the honors program, which offers small classes and opportunities for independent study. Many upper-level programs encourage undergraduate participation with faculty research, another plus of this school. If JMU gets a little confining, students may opt for a semester in London, Paris, Florence, Salamanca, and Martinique.

Don't look for a lot of diversity among fellow students at JMU. Ninety-five percent attended public high school, and 70 percent are from Virginia. In fact, there's a general effort to keep out-of-state enrollment under thirty percent at JMU. African-Americans account for just 4 percent of the student body, and Hispanics and Asian-Americans combine for another 7 percent. Students are friendly and comfortable with each other. "Whereas UVA is preppy and Virginia Tech is really casual, JMU is right in between—very accepting and not so exclusive," says a senior majoring in psychology. As for political involvement, a finance major says, "You will have your occasional small group demonstrate about something." JMU offers 260 merit scholarships ranging from $500 to $2,000 and 342 athletic scholarships for men and women in a variety of sports.

Forty-two percent of the students live in the dorms, which run the gamut from the old high-ceiling variety to newer, air-conditioned models that come complete with carpet and a fitness center in the building. "I loved living on campus my first two years, and I miss it now," says a junior. While most upperclassmen opt to move off campus to nearby apartments or houses, they still feel like part of the campus community. And "anyone with twelve or more credit hours is guaranteed housing," one student notes. Students rave about the meal plan, which has a growing number of options to choose from, including a salad bar and low-calorie meals.

All work and no play makes for a dull James Madison. Fortunately, that is hardly the case. "Social life is big," says a senior majoring in finance. A classmate agrees: "Many Greeks hold parties on JMU's Greek row, but you do not have to be Greek to have fun!" Much of the social life is off campus, including in nearby apartment complexes. Although the school does not allow underage drinking on campus, "minors can find ways to drink" and have no problem getting served off campus. The Greek system attracts 11 percent of the men and 13 percent of the

"I loved living on campus my first two years, and I miss it now."

women, though most agree that going Greek is by no means mandatory. Greeks and independents alike participate in JMU's many annual rites, including Homecoming and Christmas on the Quad. As for road trips, the favorite destination seems to be the University of Virginia, almost an hour's drive to the south. Equally enticing, however, are the many natural delights of the Shenandoah Valley, including hiking, camping, and even skiing, all nearby. Most students find local Harrisonburg a friendly Southern town, though it doesn't necessarily embrace the college.

The fans here are known as the Electric Zoo and are enthusiastic about their sports teams, which are all Division I. In 2002, the baseball team grabbed the CAA regular-season championship. Archer Caleb Heller won the national collegiate title in the compound bow two years in a row. In the 2002–2003 school year, JMU won CAA championships in women's cross country, women's soccer, women's golf, and women's lacrosse.

Though JMU still has a ways to go before establishing itself as a front-rank national university, it is making considerable progress. The school is growing, but not outgrowing its Southern charm. "Everyone is so nice and polite! The people are wonderful and the area in general—the Shenandoah Valley—is a beautiful location to live in," says one happy junior.

If You Apply To ➤

JMU: Early action: Nov. 1. Regular admissions: Jan. 1. Financial aid: Mar. 1. Housing: May 1. No campus or alumni interviews. SATs or ACTs: required. SAT IIs: English required for course placement. Accepts electronic applications. Essay question: one-page personal statement.

Johns Hopkins University

3400 North Charles Street, Baltimore, MD 21218

The Hop's reputation as a premed factory can be misleading. It's apt, but Hopkins also has fine programs in international relations (with D.C. close at hand) and a variety of liberal arts fields. The national powerhouse lacrosse team is a major rallying point.

The pursuit of academic excellence and a need to achieve fuel the typical Johns Hopkins University student. This midsize Baltimore school has garnered widespread acclaim for its top-notch professors, incredible resources, and unparalleled research opportunities. Though the university has built a reputation on its top-notch premed program, the administration has been working for a number of years to make it clear that Johns Hopkins has plenty to offer those whose interests are decidedly non-medical. Students who attend this elite university know they are at the top of the game, and they burn the midnight oil to stay there. "When you put this many great minds together, people are going to push each other to do well," says one public health major. "But after Hopkins, you are prepared for anything the real world throws at you."

The arts and sciences and engineering schools are located on the picturesque 140-acre Homewood campus, located just three miles north of Baltimore's revitalized Inner Harbor. Tree-lined quadrangles, open lawns, and playing fields make for an idyllic setting on the edge of a major urban center. The architecture on this woody urban campus is mainly Georgian redbrick, with several recently built, more modern structures scattered throughout. The new Hodson Hall is home to high-tech classrooms, and a

"After Hopkins, you are prepared for anything the real world throws at you."

Website: www.jhu.edu
Location: Urban
Total Enrollment: 5,551
Undergraduates: 4,112
Male/Female: 59/41
SAT Ranges: V 630–720
    M 660–750
ACT Range: 29–31
Financial Aid: 55%
Expense: Pr $ $ $ $
Phi Beta Kappa: Yes
Applicants: 10,124
Accepted: 30%
Enrolled: 35%
Grad in 6 Years: 88%
Returning Freshmen: 94%
Academics: ✐ ✐ ✐ ✐ ½
Social: ☎ ☎ ☎

(Continued)

Q of L: ★ ★ ★
Admissions: (410) 516-8171
Email Address:
   gotojhu@jhu.edu

Strongest Programs:
English/Writing
History
Biomedical Engineering
Biology
Philosophy

new chemistry building will house several research programs. A recently opened recreation center offers indoor tennis, racquetball, and other fitness activities, and plans for a computer science building are underway.

As much as some try to deny it, premeds dominate the campus. Biomedical engineering tops the list of most popular majors (followed by international relations, biology, computer science and public health.) The university's hospital provides excellent research opportunities. "Many (students) are involved in some form of research," says a junior biomedical engineering student. "That's a big part of Hopkins." Medicine at JHU plays such a major role in campus life that students sometimes fear it "overshadows the vibrant undergrad life that exists at Homewood." But administrators say the school is paying more and more attention to the undergraduate programs. Biomedical engineers also enjoy a strong department, to which options such as biomechanics and biomaterials engineering has recently been added. Many say it's the hardest department at the school thanks to its intense workload. But that doesn't deter a Hopkins student. The math department receives criticism, but the school says improvements are in the works. The school has initiated a new major in environmental engineering, making it one of the forty institutions in the country to offer a bachelor's of science in the field. Also new is a major in Africana studies.

Whether it's science or the humanities, undergraduates praise the talents and accessibility of their professors. "Most professors here are leading experts and scholars in their respective fields," raves a junior neuroscience student. "Being taught subjects that were discovered or created by the professor teaching gives the student a whole new respect for the subject."

Although Johns Hopkins is a firm supporter of traditional scholarship, there are no university-wide requirements other than a four-course writing component. Each major has its own distribution requirements, and there are several creative seminar offerings for freshmen. Students can receive a B.A. in creative writing through the Writing Seminars program, where they study with authors and playwrights such as John Barth.

> **"Being taught subjects that were discovered or created by the professor teaching gives the student a whole new respect for the subject."**

The Humanities Center espouses a casual, interdisciplinary approach, and with maximum curriculum flexibility allowed them, undergraduates are free to range as broadly or focus as specifically as they want. Students can get a dual degree in music performance with the Peabody Conservatory. There also are broad "area majors," such as social sciences and behavioral sciences, humanistic studies, or natural sciences, and students can choose from a cluster of related disciplines to design their own program. Even the strictly structured engineering course plan stresses the importance of interdisciplinary and interdepartmental exposure.

Students also benefit from the well-developed graduate side of Johns Hopkins. The International Studies Program, for example, is enriched by its offerings at the university's Bologna Center in Italy, Nanjing Center in China, and at its Nitze School of Advanced International Studies in nearby Washington, D.C. Undergraduate research is also a hallmark of a Hopkins experience, with 70 percent of students having at least one research experience. The provost awards sixty grants of up to $2,500 each for undergraduates to do summer research.

Overall, students find the academic climate competitive and challenging. "The academic climate is competitive and very rigorous," warns a senior international studies major. "Don't come to Hopkins if you want to have a laid-back academic college experience." Hopkins is one of the toughest schools in the country, and the workload reflects that. "There are very few slackers here," one student says. Another complains that grade inflation is nonexistent. There is a premajor faculty advisor for freshmen, and arts and sciences students are encouraged to wait until at least their sophomore year to declare a major. A pilot program has nine groups of eight freshmen take a trio of classes together, providing a ready-made study and support group. Johns Hopkins also generously allows freshmen to take an entire semester on a pass/fail basis to ease them into the academic rigor of the place. After this "hon-eymoon" period, students buckle down to a Herculean workload. Some relief is offered, however—the optional January intersession—during which students can take courses or pursue independent study for one or two credits.

"Don't come to Hopkins if you want to have a laid-back academic college experience."

Hopkins students are remarkably talented and proactive, with 77 percent from the top tenth of their high-school class. The image Johns Hopkins students once had as antisocial bookworms might be changing. "There's a growing number of students who are as outgoing, fun, beautiful and social as they are brilliant," a junior says. "It makes for a wonderfully diverse crowd, socially and ethnically." Issues on campus have included the war on Iraq. Sixty-five percent of the school is Caucasian, 19 percent Asian-American, 5 percent African-American, and 4 percent Hispanic. "We're hip on diversity," says one junior. "Southern Society lives peace-fully with the Black Student Union, the Jewish Students Association and the Mus-lim Students Association cosponsor events, frat guys tolerate the Gay, Bisexual, Lesbian, and Transgender Alliance and vice versa." Geographically, most students come from the mid-Atlantic states and New England—only 13 percent come from Maryland.

The school has initiated a new major in environmental engineering, making it one of the forty institutions in the country to offer a bachelor's of science in the field. Also new is a major in Africana studies.

Hopkins's endowment is among the top twenty in the country at nearly $1.8 billion, and it strives to meet the full demonstrated financial need of nearly every admit. Hopkins generously rewards the extraordinarily talented with eighteen hefty Hodson Trust scholarships worth $20,000 annually, regardless of need, and renew-able annually for those who keep a 3.0 GPA. The Hodson Success Scholarship, based on need, replaces the loans in the aid packages of selected

"Baltimore is not wild and crazy, but it grows on you."

students from underrepresented minority groups. Twenty-four athletic scholarships are also awarded in women's and men's lacrosse, where Hopkins is a perennial national powerhouse. Word is that non-premeds are looked on with particular favor by the financial-aid office.

Freshmen and sophomores are required to live on campus in either single-sex or co-ed-by-floor dormitories. Twenty-five percent of the upperclassmen, once left to fend for themselves, are now guaranteed housing in one of six residence halls or university-owned "luxury" apartments. Juniors and seniors, however, often choose to scope out the row houses and apartment buildings that surround JHU. "All underclassmen get excellent dorms, with Ethernet and 24/7 maintenance, although rooms are on the small side," a junior says. All in all, half of Hopkins undergrads live in university housing.

A pilot program has nine groups of eight freshmen take a trio of classes together, providing a ready-made study and support group. Johns Hopkins also generously allows freshmen to take an entire semester on a pass/fail basis to ease them into the academic rigor of the place.

Students say Hopkins's social scene is off-campus but solid. With one-third of the students dispersed among the city's apartment buildings, rowdy dorm parties and all-campus events are few and far between. But fraternity parties can be found on the weekends, though only 17 percent of the men and 19 percent of the women belong. The twenty-one-year-old drinking limit is officially enforced, with violators facing disciplinary action. "Students can get alcohol at frat parties, but sometimes it's more difficult at local bars," one senior says.

But the biggest and most popular undergraduate social event of the year is the annual student-organized Spring Fair, which draws crowds from the surrounding communities as well. Downtown Baltimore and the famed Inner Harbor are not too distant, and some of the city's best attractions, such as the art museum, aquarium, and Wyman Park, are right near campus. Trendy Baltimore hotspots—like Canton, Fells Point, and Little Italy—draw big crowds. Students also head to downtown for plays, the symphony, films, clubs, restaurants, the zoo and major league sports; Camden Yards, home of baseball's Orioles, is the most commodious park in the country. "Baltimore is not wild and crazy, but it grows on you," says a junior. Of course, that urban reality means parking can be hard on campus, some students say. When things become tiresome, Annapolis and Washington, D.C., are less than an hour by car, and Philadelphia and New York are just a train ride away. In the warmer months, a trek out to the Delaware and Maryland beaches takes the mind off studying and for those who want to try their luck, Atlantic City is a two hour drive away.

When the stellar lacrosse team takes the road against opponents, students often take advantage of the opportunity to road trip with them. Undergrads come together—even leaving the library at times—to cheer on their nationally acclaimed Blue Jays and release some study tension. Football, men's and women's soccer, women's basketball and baseball were all Centennial Conference Champions in 2002–2003.

With one of the world's premier medical and scientific programs as well as first-rate programs in areas as diverse as writing, international studies, and philosophy and an increasing emphasis on the undergraduate experience, Johns Hopkins University is clearly among the best schools in the country. "Hopkins attracts incredible interesting people from all over and offers fantastic career-building experiences to undergrads," says a junior. For those seeking top-notch professors, incredible resources, and unparalleled research opportunities, Johns Hopkins is hard to beat. Students truly take pride in the fact that they belong to the cream of the academic crop—premed or not.

Overlaps
MIT, Penn, Duke, Cornell, Harvard

If You Apply To ➤

Johns Hopkins: Early decision: Nov. 1. Regular admissions: Jan. 1. Financial aid: Feb. 1. Housing: May 1. Does not guarantee to meet demonstrated need. Campus interviews: recommended, informational. Alumni interviews: Optional, informational. SATs or ACTs: required. SAT IIs: required (writing). Biomedical engineering students must apply to that program. Accepts the Common Application and electronic applications. Essay question: how you would have a day's adventure with $10. For engineering applicants: projects you enjoy, problems you enjoy solving, areas of engineering that interest you.

Kalamazoo College

1200 Academy Street, Kalamazoo, MI 49006-3295

The "K" Plan should appeal to both the nontraditional student and the practical-minded. Those with wanderlust get to travel the world while enjoying hands-on learning experiences. Those looking for a leg up on the job market get it through K-zoo's extensive internship program.

Website: www.kzoo.edu
Location: City outskirts
Total Enrollment: 1,322
Undergraduates: 1,322
Male/Female: 43/57
SAT Ranges: V 590–700
   M 600–690

Kalamazoo College is a small school in a small city in America's heartland. But college subsidies enable 85 percent of students to study abroad during their years here, making the school a launching pad to the world. In addition to international education, the school's "K" Plan emphasizes teaching, internships (80 percent of students have at least one), and independent research (as seniors, all students complete a year-long project, with one-on-one faculty supervision). Despite snowy winters, the environment is warm and supportive, thanks to the school's "beautiful campus, friendly people, and open minds," says a theatre major.

Life on Kalamazoo's wooded, sixty-acre campus centers on the Quad, a green lawn where students ponder their destinies and play Ultimate Frisbee with equal ease. With its rolling hills, Georgian architecture, and cobblestone streets, the campus has the quaint look more typical of historic New England than of nearby Kalamazoo, which, with surrounding communities, has 225,000 residents. Recent campus construction includes a renovated fine arts building opened in the fall of 2001.

Kalamazoo operates on the quarter system, and students must spend their entire first year on campus. Still, many freshmen begin the year with a "land-sea adventure," three weeks of rappelling and backpacking in the mountains of Canada, followed by sailing a brigantine ship down Lake Huron to Windsor, Ontario. By the end, they're convinced they can survive anything, including the rigors of a Kalamazoo education (and the long Michigan winters). Once safely ashore on campus, they begin to fulfill distribution requirements,

> **"All students have a faculty advisor whom they choose, so they can pick the type of person they want guidance from."**

including three courses each in language, cultures, social sciences, and literature and fine arts, and two courses each in philosophy or religion and in math, natural sciences, or computer science. Also required are a first-year writing seminar and a quantitative reasoning course, as well as a senior individualized project—an internship, artistic work, directed research, student teaching, or a traditional thesis, basically anything that caps off each student's education in some meaningful way.

After their freshman year, most of K-zoo's undergrads meet life's challenges with suitcase in hand, studying wherever their heart takes them, for the regular tuition price. A variety of off-campus programs are available, including those offered by the Great Lakes College Association.* Kalamazoo's new Center for Experiential Education is another resource for information on careers, internships, and study abroad. "All students have a faculty advisor whom they choose, so they can pick the type of person they want guidance from," says a junior. "Professors serve as advisors, and since they know the faculty and classes available better than anyone, they do a great job!" adds a senior.

Kalamazoo aims to prepare students for real life by helping them synthesize the liberal arts education they receive on campus with their experiences abroad. This has filled the school with overachievers, says a religion major. "The academic climate is rigorous, but the students are supportive of each other," adds a classical studies major. "The only competition is for yourself, to do better each time." Still, students do seek balance, says a theatre major: "There is a great sense of trying to complete work as well as have fun." The natural sciences are exceptionally good and students heap praise on the psychology and languages departments, although economics draws the most majors. Asian studies, music, and education are candidly cited as weaker by administrators. Professors give students lots of individual attention and are rewarded with some of Michigan's highest faculty salaries. "Our professors really care," says a junior. "They are passionate, and for the most part, classes are superb."

Founded in 1833 and formerly associated with the American Baptist Churches, Kalamazoo is the oldest college in Michigan. Twenty-four percent of students come from out of state, and minorities comprise 10 percent of the student body—3 percent African-Americans, 2 percent Hispanic, and 5 percent Asian-American. Many K-zoo students crave more diversity on campus. "It's been diversified somewhat, but not enough," says a religion major. "That's the ongoing goal." Other hot

> **"This makes it hard for relationships and sometimes you don't see your friends for six to nine months."**

topics are women's rights and homosexuality, students say, although debate is far from rancorous. "We have many groups whose ideas are opposing, yet are very respectful of each other's beliefs and activities," a junior explains.

(Continued)
ACT Range: 26–30
Financial Aid: 43%
Expense: Pr $ $
Phi Beta Kappa: Yes
Applicants: 1,422
Accepted: 70%
Enrolled: 32%
Grad in 6 Years: 69%
Returning Freshmen: 91%
Academics: ✍ ✍ ✍
Social: ☎ ☎ ☎
Q of L: ★ ★ ★ ★
Admissions: (616) 337-7166
Email Address:
  admission@kzoo.edu

Strongest Programs:
Biology/Health Science
Psychology
English
Economics

Many freshmen begin the year with a "land-sea adventure," three weeks of rappelling and backpacking in the mountains of Canada.

Seventy-five percent of students live on campus, but with two to three hundred students away each quarter because of the K Plan, a certain instability pervades all activities, from athletics to student government to living groups in the co-ed residence halls, where suites hold one to six students. "Students are always coming and going," one laments. "This makes it hard for relationships and sometimes you don't see your friends for six to nine months." Dorms aren't divided by class standing, but Trowbridge is a good choice for freshmen. Those who return from abroad with bags of dirty laundry will be glad to know that dorm washers and dryers are free. While there are no Greek organizations at K-zoo, theme houses offer a more community-oriented atmosphere, including family-style dinners. The central dining hall's food is no match for its decor: six "motif" rooms each reflect a single nationality, such as the English pub, with wood panels and stained-glass windows. Although dorms require key cards for entry, "security is a big joke," says a senior. "Granted, we live in a safe area, but if something ever did happen, security is pretty useless."

The city of Kalamazoo "thrives on college life," says one student. The city, the college, and Western Michigan University, across the street, "are intertwined, and students love to work outside through organizations like Habitat for Humanity," as well as in local churches and schools. On campus, students look forward to a casino night called Monte Carlo, Home-

> "Frisbee golf is the thing to play, and K's golf course is used by Kalamazoo students, some faculty, and some townies."

coming, Spring Fling, and the Day of Gracious Living, a spring day where, without prior warning, classes are canceled and students relax by taking day trips or helping beautify the campus. (One popular T-shirt: "The end of learning is gracious living.") Off campus, Kalamazoo offers the typical collection of restaurants, theaters, and bars; K-zoo students also benefit from the physical proximity of colleges such as Western Michigan, where they may use the library or attend cultural events, as the college lacks a central place for students to hang out. Students also appreciate the city's proximity to Lake Michigan's beaches and Chicago's urban playground.

For those who equate college with big-time athletics, Kalamazoo has something to offer—even if it's not nationally televised games or tens of thousands of screaming fans. The Kalamazoo Hornets have a long-standing rivalry with Hope College, culminating in the football teams' annual competition for the "infamous wooden shoes," where the Hornets are cheered on by fans known as "the stingers." Kalamazoo also has an outstanding men's tennis team, which has won conference titles for the past sixty-three consecutive years. However, an economics and business major reports that "Frisbee golf is the thing to play, and K's golf course is used by Kalamazoo students, some faculty, and some townies."

"Study hard, party hard" is not the official motto of Kalamazoo College, but it might as well be. At this increasingly selective school, graduates leave with solid liberal arts preparation, made more thoughtful by required senior-year individualized projects and by near-ubiquitous study abroad. Well-traveled, well-grounded, and well-prepared for real life, students here can proudly say "whoop-dee-doo for Kalamazoo."

Memo to out-of-staters: Lawrence is not flat as a pancake and does not resemble Dorothy's home in "The Wizard of Oz." University of Kansas has a gorgeous campus and is one of the premier college bargains in the United States. Strong programs in a full slate of professional schools.

With solid academics, outstanding extracurricular programs, winning athletics and a stellar social life, the University of Kansas is one of higher education's best buys—about 13 percent less than the national public university average. It might be in the center of the conservative Midwest, but KU itself is an oasis of tolerance and open-mindedness. Recently, KU has taken steps to become more selective and the results are evident: the academic achievements of each incoming class continue to rise. And those students who are extremely dedicated can plunge into a great honors program the school provides to court them in its efforts to raise its academic profile.

The one thousand-acre campus is set atop Mount Oread ridge—once a lookout point for pioneer wagon trains—and spread out on rolling green hills overlooking valleys. Let's face it—Kansas isn't the first place that comes to many people's minds when asked to think of the most beautiful scenery anywhere. Never mind the wooded and hilly Lawrence campus is one of the most gorgeous in the United States. Many of the buildings are made of indigenous Kansas limestone. But the real beauty of the campus lies in its landscape, particularly the breathtaking foliage that appears each autumn. There are nearly as many trees on campus—nineteen thousand at last count—as there are undergrads. Recent construction includes the Dole Institute of Politics—home to the world's largest Congressional archives and a World Trade Center memorial—and a $15 million engineering building named for KU graduate and former DaimlerChrysler chairman Robert Eaton. The Kansas Memorial Student Union just underwent a pricey renovation, and couch potatoes also have less reason to stay inside, with a new, 98,000-square-foot Student Recreation Fitness Center and the $8 million Anderson Family Strength and Conditioning Center for student athletes.

KU applicants apply to the individual school of their choice. Those not admitted to one of the professional schools will automatically be considered for admission to the College of Liberal Arts and Sciences, where 70 percent of the undergraduate population is enrolled. Students in most of the professional schools, with the exception of engineering, architecture, physical education, urban design and fine arts, spend their first two years completing the liberal arts requirements. The general education curriculum is intended to expose students to the foundations of the humanities, sciences, and social sciences. It also includes math, English, and oral communication, and requires courses in both Western and non-Western civilization. Foreign language and laboratory science courses are required as well for all B.A. candidates.

Of the fourteen graduate and professional schools, those most noted for undergraduate programs are architecture and urban design, allied health, fine arts, social welfare, pharmacy, nursing, education, business, and engineering. The journalism, architecture, and business programs receive rave reviews from students. The lower-rated programs include **"Students are very involved in almost every social and political issue."** math, Western civilization, and the oft-maligned physical education. Those in the top 20 percent of their high school class and with high SAT (combined score of

Website: www.ku.edu
Location: Small city
Total Enrollment: 28,849
Undergraduates: 20,610
Male/Female: 47/53
ACT Range: 21–27
Financial Aid: 34%
Expense: Pub $ $
Phi Beta Kappa: Yes
Applicants: 9,573
Accepted: 67%
Enrolled: 63%
Grad in 6 Years: 57%
Returning Freshmen: 81%
Academics: 🖊 🖊 🖊 🖊
Social: ☎ ☎ ☎ ☎
Q of L: ★ ★ ★ ★
Admissions: (785) 864-3911
Email Address: adm@ku.edu

Strongest Programs:
Architecture
Biological Sciences
Business and Economics
Engineering
Environmental Studies
Journalism
Nursing and Pharmacy
Social Welfare
Premed Studies
Spanish and Portuguese

To demonstrate their loyalty to the Jayhawks, thousands of students show up for the first basketball practice of the season at 12:01 A.M. on October 15. This nocturnal tradition is lovingly labeled "Midnight Madness."

more than 1,240) or equivalent ACT scores should definitely look into the Mount Oread Scholars program, which offers a dorm, networking, and small classes with top professors. The Indigenous Nations Studies Program—a graduate program that focuses on indigenous people's issues—offers an undergraduate class to introduce students to this new area of study. The biological sciences have been reorganized from six units to one, and the international studies program now offers students an opportunity to receive a comajor. The curriculum at the William Allen White School of Journalism has been streamlined into two tracks: strategic communications and news and information. On the Edwards' campus in Overland Park, students now can major in literature, language and writing or molecular biosciences.

Students describe the academic atmosphere as fairly competitive. Professors earn high marks for their teaching ability and dedication, while some students complain about the number of graduate students teaching courses. The most popular courses include biological sciences, engineering, psychology and journalism. Aside from the usual coursework, options include independent study or the more than seventy-five study-abroad programs in fifty-two countries, including Brazil, France, Germany and Ghana. Kansas provides several area study programs supported by language instruction in more than twenty languages. The top-ranked Latin American, Spanish and Portuguese studies programs, which benefit from an exchange with the University of Costa Rica, are three good examples. Undergraduates at KU may receive research awards to work with faculty members in publishing papers and poetry. And students are pleased with their library system, which includes a 3.5-million-volume main library, a research library, and science and engineering libraries. Select freshmen can apply for the University Honors Program, which provides academically motivated students with honors courses, special advising and opportunities for scholarships and research grants.

"The dorms offer a variety of living arrangements."

Sixty-eight percent of the students are from Kansas, and most of the rest are fellow Midwesterners (with lots from Chicago). The most vocal groups on campus are African-Americans, gays, and lesbians. Vocal yes, highly represented, no: African-Americans, Hispanics, and Asian-Americans combined account for only 10 percent of the students. Students often are involved in political issues; the hot topic right now is diversity. "Students are very involved in almost every social and political issue," a senior says. KU, with its famous steep hill and more affluent profile, is called "Snob Hill" by students at other Kansas schools who come from humbler origins. However, students think they're a pretty friendly lot. "Students at KU for the most part are active members of the KU and Lawrence community," a senior says. "They care about the institution and what is going on." Out-of-staters must have a 2.5 high school GPA or a 24 on the ACT to get in. KU gives out about five thousand academic merit awards ranging from $500 to a full ride. Freshman orientation begins with a series of one- or two-day summer sessions. And the seven days before classes are officially called Hawk Week, but are more commonly known as Country Club Week because of all the partying that goes on—though it's been less in recent years due to tougher liquor laws.

Only 18 percent of the students live in university housing, and both co-ed and single-sex dorms are available. Overall, students are pretty happy with the housing, much of which is being spruced up. "The dorms offer a variety of living arrangements," one student says. "Most are within a ten-minute walk to campus or on the bus route. They are cleaned every weekday." Students with 2.5 GPAs can live in one of the ten scholarship halls where fifty men or women live in a cooperative-type arrangement. Groups of twenty students can live in thematic learning communities on their residence hall floors—past themes include aerospace engineering and the

Recent construction includes the Dole Institute of Politics—home to the world's largest Congressional archives and a World Trade Center memorial—and a $15 million engineering building named for KU graduate and former DaimlerChrysler chairman Robert Eaton.

meaning of film. A vast majority of KU students live off campus in Lawrence apartments, which are considered expensive only by Kansas standards. A dining complex called Mrs. E's provides extended-hour access to food court-style meals for 2,500 residence-hall occupants.

The university's bus system is run entirely by students and is much appreciated by tenderfeet, especially because that great big hill seems to double in size during the cold, windy winters. Lawrence, with its myriad boutiques, restaurants, and bars, receives rave reviews from students. "Lawrence is a great town for college students," a junior says. "There is a great variety of restaurants, coffeeshops, bars and shopping. There are many ways to get involved with the community." City slickers can trek off to Topeka, the state capital, or to Kansas City, each less than an hour's drive. The KC airport makes for easy long-distance transportation, and the area is also served by Amtrak.

The Greek system, which attracts 15 percent of the men and 18 percent of the women, tends to be a major force in the on-campus social life, though tension does exist between Greeks and independents. Sorority rush is completely dry, but rumor has it that the frats are a little more lenient when it comes to alcohol. Overall, the social scene is very much alive and well. More than four hun-

> "Lawrence is a great town for college students."

dred organized groups keep things lively; other extracurricular activities include movies, poetry readings, and concerts. Scholarship halls, dorms, and other student groups sponsor large campus parties and events, but most of the social life takes place off campus.

KU varsity teams—the only ones in the nation that carry the name Jayhawks—compete in the tough Big 12 Conference. The basketball team is legendary, and James Naismith, who invented basketball, was KU's first coach—and the only one with a losing record. Beloved coach Roy Williams has departed but KU landed Bill Self, one of the top young coaches in America, and boasts that a new era for the team is underway. More than four hundred athletic scholarships are available to students.

The school year kicks off with Hawk Week, the official welcome for new students. The traditional "Rock Chalk Jayhawk" KU cheer is enough to bring a pang of nostalgia to the heart of even the most grizzled Kansas alum. To demonstrate their loyalty to the Jayhawks, thousands of students show up for the first basketball practice of the season at 12:01 a.m. on October 15. This nocturnal tradition is lovingly labeled "Midnight Madness." KU's most-hated rival is Missouri, and the winner of the annual football game takes possession of an "alumni spirit drum." Favorite road trips are determined by where the basketball team is playing. The women's basketball team is also worth watching, as are the men's and women's tennis teams and the women's swimming and diving team.

With KU's huge number of high-ranking academic programs, its national reputation (the nonbasketball one) has certainly improved. "KU is special to me because of all the individual attention that I get from my professors," a visual communications major says. The university continues to push up in the rankings, making Kansas one heck of a deal.

Overlaps

Kansas State, University of Missouri, Washington University (MO), University of Nebraska, University of Illinois

---

If You Apply To ➤

Kansas: Rolling admissions. Financial aid: Mar. 1. Housing: Feb. 15. No campus or alumni interviews. SATs or ACTs: required. SAT IIs: optional. Apply to particular school or program. Accepts electronic applications. Essay question: personal statement (only for scholarship consideration).

100 Funkhouser Building, Lexington, KY 40506-0032

The state of Kentucky is better known for horses and hoops than higher education, but University of Kentucky is working to change that. The basketball team is still a championship contender, but so too are programs in business, engineering, and health fields.

Website: www.uky.edu
Location: City center
Total Enrollment: 23,060
Undergraduates: 16,841
Male/Female: 48/52
ACT Range: 22–27
Financial Aid: N/A
Expense: Pub $
Phi Beta Kappa: Yes
Applicants: 8,320
Accepted: 73%
Enrolled: 32%
Grad in 6 Years: 53%
Returning Freshmen: 79%
Academics: ✑ ✑ ✑
Social: 🐎 🐎 🐎 🐎
Q of L: ★ ★ ★
Admissions: (859) 257-2000
Email Address:
    admissio@pop.uky.edu

Strongest Programs:
Business
Premed
Predentistry
Nursing
Engineering
Chemistry

You probably know that the University of Kentucky Wildcats are perennial attendees at the NCAA postseason basketball tournament. What you may not know is that the University of Kentucky's excellence stretches beyond its winning athletic teams—into outstanding medical and premedical programs, scientific research involving both professors and students, and a social calendar packed so full of Southern tradition that it would make even the most composed debutante's head spin.

The University of Kentucky campus, home to a major public research university as well as a community college, contains a mixture of old and new, modern and traditional buildings that date back to the late 1890s. The campus buildings indicate a transition beginning with the original redbrick structures to designs using contemporary glass and concrete as one moves south following the path of development. Most visitors would agree that the grounds are well-maintained, organized around the comfortable park-like spaces influenced by Frederick Law Olmsted's design. The campus contains a vast amount of mature trees and lawns set in a natural arrangement of open spaces, typical of the great land-grant universities. Of course, UK's location in the heart of one of the finest horse-breeding areas in the world makes it a natural place for the Gluck Equine Research Center, a headquarters for research into horse diseases. The new William T. Young Library is ranked thirtieth among public research libraries by the Association of Research Libraries.

> "My professors have always shown a genuine concern for my grades."

Students sing the praises of many departments at UK, but several unique programs stand out. The Lexington campus is home to the Gaines Center of the Humanities, which is unusual in its study of public higher education. Lexington also hosts the Patterson School of International Diplomacy, one of the smallest yet most respected schools of its type in the country. The chemistry department turned out three National Science Foundation fellowship winners in 1998–1999, a feat matched only by Harvard, Cornell, Rice, Princeton, and the Massachusetts Institute of Technology. Weaker areas include lower-level "monster" science classes, which one student describes as "extremely large and not at all personalized." Undergrads complain about trouble getting into courses they need, especially entry-level offerings. According to a marketing major, students "have difficulty if they are freshmen, because most of them have to take the same classes, and sometimes they don't get the right times—or the classes at all." It's hard to complete the engineering, health, business, and architecture programs in four years, students say. Term-time internships, known as co-ops, also complicate, but enliven, the picture.

Students praise UK's professors. "My professors have always shown a genuine concern for my grades," says a sophomore. TAs and full professors teach about the same number of freshman classes. The Central Advising Service, or CAS, is helping to improve the quality of academic guidance, though one student notes, "I do wish I had more assistance from my advisors on which classes to take."

To graduate, all students must take mathematics and a foreign language, as well as written and oral communication classes and a statistics, calculus, or logic course.

The core program, called University Studies, also requires exposure to natural and social sciences, humanities, an introduction to cross-disciplinary education, and experience with non-Western ways of thinking. Additionally, all freshmen are encouraged to take an academic orientation class called UK101, designed to help them adjust to college life. The academic climate is laid-back, but students shouldn't expect easy As. "When it comes to study time and classwork, the students are always competing with themselves to earn the best grades they can," explains a junior.

"UK students are typically self-assured, slightly competitive, and outgoing."

For upperclassmen, UK offers a number of joint programs with other colleges and universities, including Transylvania, Centre, and Georgetown (in Kentucky). There's also a cooperative program with the Army and Air Force ROTC. Students studying prevet at UK will find coveted slots reserved for them at Auburn and Tuskegee in the advanced veterinary medicine program, at in-state tuition rates. UK is a member of the Academic Common Market, which provides students in fifteen states the opportunity to pay in-state tuition at any of these states' schools if they want to enroll in a program not offered in their home state.

"UK students are typically self-assured, slightly competitive, and outgoing," says a psychology major (perhaps practicing analysis for her future career). The UK student body hails from all fifty counties in Kentucky, with 13 percent from out of state and 4 percent from foreign countries. The student body is predominantly white; African-Americans account for 6 percent of students, and Hispanics and Asian-Americans combine for a little more than 3 percent. Despite these small numbers, students say diversity is valued. "Respectfulness is an issue," says one student. "But Southern hospitality abounds." The university aims to be an "inclusive learning community," achieving academic excellence by working toward "social responsibility and community building, with particular focus on equity, fairness, and safety for each person," among other initiatives. Merit scholarships, ranging from $500 to a full ride, are offered to qualified students.

UK is a member of the Academic Common Market, which provides students in fifteen states the opportunity to pay in-state tuition at any of these states' schools if they want to enroll in a program not offered in their home state.

Kentucky's dorms are clean and convenient, as well as a great way to meet people, students say, though there's quite a range of what amenities you may get. Dorms are located on three parts of the campus—north, central, and south. North campus housing is old, but the halls are small, so they afford a chance to form close relationships. They're also within a short walking distance of classrooms, the student center, and the bookstore. South campus offers newer dorms with small rooms and air-conditioning, while Central campus offers the biggest rooms. Recommended for freshmen: Kirwan-Blanding Complex, since "everything seems to happen there." Getting a room is not a problem as long as you apply by the deadline. Also, since students are not required to live on campus, only 25 percent do.

"In Kentucky, basketball is like a second religion."

Students say that while Lexington is a great place to go to school, it's not a typical college town. "Lexington is almost 250,000 people strong," an upperclassman explains. "It's small enough to drive across town easily, but large enough not to see everyone you know when you go to Wal-Mart." Despite the lack of diversity on campus, Lexington abounds with a multitude of ethnic eateries, as well as theaters, shopping malls, and nightspots. On campus, students enjoy movies, presentations, seminars, and athletic events, the most popular being basketball games at the legendary Rupp Arena. Other campus activities include the Little Kentucky Derby, a week-long student-run festival that features a balloon race and concerts. Among the highlights of any student's career at UK are two one-month periods—one in the fall, one in the spring—when students spend afternoons at Keeneland Race Track enjoying the tradition of Kentucky horse racing.

All but 10 percent of classes at UK have fifty or fewer students, unusual for a state university.

About 15 percent of the men and 17 percent of the women go Greek, but fraternities and sororities offer the great majority of on-campus activities, as well as opportunities for volunteer work in the community. The university has a strict no-alcohol-on-campus policy that is enforced, but it doesn't tend to affect students with fake IDs. When it's time for a road trip, UK students head to Cincinnati and Louisville (one hour away), or to Atlanta and Chicago (six hours)—that is, if they're not taking leisurely Sunday drives through nearby Blue Grass country. And the best road-trip destinations are anywhere there's a steamy, noisy gym and a basketball team ready to play UK's always-strong Wildcats. Home games at Lexington's Rupp Arena—what one student calls "a magical experience"—are consistently packed.

"In Kentucky, basketball is like a second religion," agrees another true-blue Wildcat fan. Although screaming yourself hoarse for five guys hitting the hardwood may not be as genteel as cheering while sipping a mint julep at the track, for many students, the mix of collegiate craziness and old-world Southern hospitality found in Lexington is just what they want.

Overlaps

University of Louisville, Miami University (OH), Indiana, Ohio State, University of Tennessee

If You Apply To ➤

Kentucky: Rolling admissions: February 15. Financial aid: Feb. 15. Does not guarantee to meet demonstrated need. Campus and alumni interviews: optional, informational. SATs or ACTs: required. SAT IIs: optional. No essay question.

Kenyon College

Ransom Hall, Gambier, OH 43022-9623

Kenyon is a pure liberal arts college plunked down in the middle of the Ohio countryside. More mainstream than Oberlin, more serious than Denison, and more selective than Wooster, Kenyon is best-known for English and a small but distinguished drama program.

Website: www.kenyon.edu
Location: Rural
Total Enrollment: 1,551
Undergraduates: 1,551
Male/Female: 46/54
SAT Ranges: V 620–720
  M 610–690
ACT Range: 27–32
Financial Aid: 38%
Expense: Pr $ $ $
Phi Beta Kappa: Yes
Applicants: 2,954
Accepted: 51%
Enrolled: 31%
Grad in 6 Years: 82%
Returning Freshmen: 89%
Academics: 🖉 🖉 🖉 🖉
Social: ☎ ☎ ☎

Kenyon College maintains a pure liberal arts and sciences emphasis that's less and less common in the world of higher education. Students here are proud of what sets Kenyon apart from other liberal arts colleges. "The small student body and the friendliness of the students makes for a genuine community feeling," explains one student. "At Kenyon, you really feel like you are sharing a great college experience with great people."

The oldest private college in Ohio, Kenyon's eight-hundred-acre campus sits on a hillside overlooking a scenic view of river, woods, and fields in a secluded villa of roughly six hundred residents. The college's oldest building, Old Kenyon, dates from 1826, and is said to be the first collegiate Gothic building in America and the campus is on the National Register of Historic Places. The Brown Family Environmental Center includes a butterfly garden and extensive perennial gardens planted with community donations. There are plans for a new fitness, athletic, and recreation complex slated to be completed in the fall of 2005. The 265,000 square-foot center will include a swimming pool, indoor tennis courts, racquetball and squash courts, training and fitness rooms, a movie theater, and office space.

Kenyon's focus on the liberal arts makes for a challenging, but largely noncompetitive, learning environment. "The courses are rigorous, but not unreasonable," says a student. "The professors are always willing to help with problems." In fact, at

Kenyon, it's hard to find a weak department. "Smaller departments such as Classics and Math draw fewer students, but still offer great courses," says one student.

English, a nationally renowned subject at Kenyon since the 1930s, is the most popular major, and it, along with the drama department (which turned out Paul Newman), sets the tone of campus life. This is, after all, home to *The Kenyon Review*, a prestigious literary quarterly, and a school about which

(Continued)
Q of L: ★★★
Admissions: (800) 848-2468
Email Address:
   admissions@kenyon.edu

Strongest Programs:
English
Art
Biology
Dance
Drama
History
Economics
International Studies
Political Science

> Professors "are so enthusiastic about their subjects and they want to share that passion with the students."

alum E. L. Doctorow has said, "Poetry is what we did at Kenyon, the way at Ohio State they played football." Political science is said to be solid, drawing undecided majors with its introductory class, "Quest for Justice," because it "introduces the material in such a way that you're left hungry for a greater understanding of it!" says one devotee. The Integrated Program in Humane Studies, which incorporates English, history, political science, and art history, is also popular.

The hallmark of Kenyon's academic philosophy is an almost fanatical devotion to the liberal arts and sciences. "Academic life at Kenyon is rooted in three strong tenets," an administrator explains. "That students thrive when they can work closely with their professors; that they can best explore their own potential when they have enough flexibility to experiment; and that they learn most productively in an atmosphere of cooperation." Preprofessional opportunities include 3–2 engineering programs with several universities, and with high acceptance rates to graduate programs in law, business, and medicine, Kenyon's emphasis on arts and sciences is clearly yielding positive results. In fact, three out of four recent Kenyon grads took jobs when they finished, rather than continuing on to graduate or professional schools. The Career Development Center helps sort out grad schools and employment opportunities, both summer and post-graduation. Kenyon awards approximately sixty merit scholarships a year ranging from $13,500 to $27,000.

While there is no core curriculum at Kenyon, all students must complete at least one unit of credit in the college's four divisions: humanities, fine arts, social sciences, and natural sciences. Students must also complete requirements in quantitative reasoning and foreign language study. Change is constant at Kenyon, including changes in curriculum. American studies, which used to be a concentration, has now been designated as a major. A bevy of academic counselors, including upperclassmen and professors, help ensure that freshmen stay on the right track. About 20 percent of juniors are invited by their departments to read for honors, and about 15 percent graduate with departmental honors. The culmination of each student's coursework at Kenyon is the senior exercise, which may take the form of a comprehensive examination, an integrative paper, a research project, or some combination of these.

Classes are small at Kenyon—the majority have twenty-five or fewer students—and even the larger introductory courses use a two-part format in which students meet for lectures one week and split up for discussion sections with the professor the next. "The professors have all been very accessible and are quite capable teachers," asserts a student. "They are so enthusiastic about their subjects and they want to share that passion with the students," adds a sophomore.

English, a nationally renowned subject at Kenyon since the 1930s, is the most popular major, and it, along with the drama department, sets the tone of campus life.

Kenyon students "pride themselves on being well-rounded and continue to be well-informed," says a neuroscience major. Twenty-three percent of Kenyon students are Ohioans, and together, African-Americans, Hispanics, and Asian-Americans make up just 9 percent of the student body. "Although ethnic diversity is something Kenyon needs to work on at the moment, there really isn't a 'model' Kenyon student," says a junior. The anti-sweatshop and Free Tibet movements that

> "There really isn't a 'model' Kenyon student."

have been sweeping the nation's campuses have found their homes at Kenyon as well; on-campus political issues include the formulation of a new sexual harassment policy and underage drinking. "Large-scale movements such as those against sweatshops or in favor of eliminating the death penalty find support in groups like Amnesty International and Activists United, and environmentally conscious students have recently formed a group called REEL (Resource and Energy Efficient Living) that is making big changes on campus," says a student.

Ninety-eight percent of Kenyon students live on campus, with housing guaranteed for four years. Freshmen start in five dorms at the north end of campus, and most move south to recently remodeled housing the next year. Although renovations and expansions are always in the works, they are currently having some trouble keeping up with demand. Rooms are selected via a harrowing housing lottery, and typically upperclassmen "opt for one of the historic dorms—Old Kenyon, Hannah or Leonard, or one of the campus-owned apartments—the Aclands, Bexleys, or New Apartments." Most dorms are co-ed. Rather than their own houses, fraternities occupy sections of the south-campus dorms, making that area the center of the party scene. "In general, the school could improve its housing options, but it is nice that by the time you are a junior, you are basically guaranteed an apartment," says one student. Everyone, including those in the apartments with kitchens, must eat college chow; dining halls operate on each end of the campus, though only one is open on weekends.

The school's Greek system draws 34 percent of the men but only 10 percent of the women, and the frats throw lively parties that are open to all. Like most campuses, Kenyon is slowly moving away from the *Animal House* paradigm of social life. "Kenyon is a great place to have fun," says one freshman. "There is always something going on from the opportunity to participate in game shows to try and win a trip to the Bahamas, listening to student bands or bands that come from nearby schools, karaoke contests, or watching the movie that the Kenyon Film Society show," adds a peer. Gambier is a small town, with a couple of bars and no movie theaters, but there are a few

"It is nice that by the time you are a junior, you are basically guaranteed an apartment."

more options fifteen minutes away in Mount Vernon, to which the college runs a daytime shuttle bus. On-campus events and college-sponsored activities are growing more popular to help keep boredom at bay. With its deli, market, inn, restaurant, bank, and post office, Gambier is at least quaint. Students enjoy buying real maple syrup, fresh bread, and cheese from Amish farmers with stands on its main street on Saturdays.

Kenyon remains defined by its traditions, the most hallowed of which is renewed each year as incoming freshmen sing college songs to the rest of the community from the steps of Rosse Hall. Departing seniors sing the same songs at graduation. On Matriculation Day each October, after a formal ceremony, freshmen sign a book that contains the signatures of virtually every Kenyon student since the early 1800s. Other major events include Homecoming and the Summer Send-Off. To break February's icy cold, the school holds a formal ball called Philander's Phling, remembering founder Philander Chase; an alum donates money for the dance. There are two small ski areas near campus, but for those seeking adventure further from home, Columbus and Ohio State University are a forty-five-minute drive south. The adventurous sometimes road-trip to Cleveland (home of the Rock and Roll Hall of Fame), Cincinnati, Chicago, or even Canada.

In addition to its emphasis on academics, Kenyon was instrumental in establishing the North Coast Athletic Conference, which includes a number of academically strong Midwestern schools, including longtime rival Denison. A junior cites the annual hockey game versus Denison, when "both teams have to drive to Newark and a surprising number of fans from both colleges attend." The women's tennis and basketball teams are reigning champs, but the flagship sport is definitely swimming. Kenyon's swimming and diving teams dominate Division III competition, with the men's team having won a record twenty-four times in a row. The school leads the nation with forty-four NCAA Division III postgraduate scholarships. Soccer games against Ohio Wesleyan draw large crowds. Clubs sponsor everything from Frisbee to water polo.

Kenyon introduces the upper crust of the Eastern seaboard to rural Ohio, and often makes it hard for them to tear themselves away. For the many young artists, writers, and budding intellectuals here, it's hard to face the end of their four years. "The community atmosphere of Kenyon makes it a special place," says a senior. "At Kenyon, you are around a group of people who love being where they are."

If You Apply To ➢

Kenyon: Early decision: Dec. 1, Jan. 15. Regular admissions, financial aid, housing: Jan. 15. Meets demonstrated need of 44%. Campus interviews: recommended, evaluative. Alumni interviews: optional, evaluative. SATs or ACTs: required. SAT IIs: optional. Accepts the Common Application and electronic applications. Essay question: special interests, experience, or achievement.

Knox College

2 East South Street, Galesburg, IL 61401

This friendly and progressive Illinois college was among the first in the nation to admit African-Americans and women. Offers close interaction with faculty and pure liberal arts. More mainstream than Beloit and Grinnell and just more than half as big as Illinois Wesleyan.

Knox College, with the unconventional Prairie Fire as its mascot, has long made a name for itself by breaking away from the conventions of the day. Founded in 1837 as the Knox Manual Labor College in Galesburg, Illinois, this liberal arts college was the first in the state to graduate an African-American student and among the first in the nation to admit women. And through a warm and supportive academic community, the college continues to foster a strong sense of individualism.

Located in the heart of the Midwest—almost midway between Chicago and St. Louis—the eighty-two-acre campus has spacious, tree-lined lawns and a dynamic mixture of architecture that reflects the 145-year span of construction dates of existing buildings. Old Main, constructed in 1857, is a National Historic Landmark and the only building remaining from the 1858 Lincoln-Douglas debates. The campus will become completely wireless this year and a supercomputing lab has been added for math and computer science majors.

Students say the academic relationships at Knox are infused with a spirit of cooperation and equality. Beyond the classroom, students, faculty, and administrators make decisions on boards together, each with identical voting power. First-year students confront the core issues of liberal education in Preceptorial, a one-term seminar examining questions of ethics and truth through multidisciplinary reading and critical writing. But while many schools have small, intense classes for first-year students, Knox takes things a bit farther by mandating an advanced preceptorial for seniors. This class connects their expertise in their major to a broad topic.

The general education curriculum has undergone changes and students are now required to take one course in the arts, the natural and social sciences, and the humanities, as well as courses in writing, speaking, mathematics, information technology, foreign language, and human diversity. Knox also boasts the Ford Foundation Research Fellowship Program, which was created in the mid-1980s to encourage

Website: www.knox.edu
Location: Small city
Total Enrollment: 1,127
Undergraduates: 1,127
Male/Female: 47/53
SAT Ranges: V 550–690
  M 540–660
ACT Range: 24–30
Financial Aid: 73%
Expense: Pr $ $ $
Phi Beta Kappa: Yes
Applicants: 1,652
Accepted: 73%
Enrolled: 27%
Grad in 6 Years: 78%
Returning Freshmen: 87%
Academics: ✑ ✑ ✑
Social: ☎ ☎ ☎
Q of L: ★ ★ ★
Admissions: (309) 678-KNOX
Email Address:
  admission@knox.edu

Strongest Programs:
Biology

students to consider careers in college teaching and research. Ford Fellows work with selected faculty mentors to design and carry out a research project in an area of interest. Through this permanently endowed foundation, Knox is able to offer stipends for summer research to a full one-fifth of the junior class. Moves like these have helped Knox earn a national reputation for its independent undergraduate research. More than 85 percent of students do some type of independent study.

Strong departments include creative writing, math, psychology, political science, and the natural sciences, with biology attracting lots of research grant money. The school's literary journal, Catch, has won national awards. Students can take part in the Chicago Semester in the Arts, and dramatists also benefit from several theaters, including one with a revolving stage. Students cite the modern languages and philosophy as weak. Study abroad options include programs in more than twenty countries, and the college is a member of the Associated Colleges of the Midwest consortium.*

Knox operates on an honor system that allows students to take tests in any public area unproctored, but few students would even think of cheating. "The classes at Knox are intense yet very rewarding," says a junior. A creative writing major adds,

> **"On one of your first days on campus as a first year, your Faculty Advisor takes his or her advisees out to dinner."**

"Academics are the most important part of Knox life." Where faculty is concerned, students offer uniformly glowing reviews for their performance in the classroom and availability outside of it. "The professors at Knox are superb in every way," raves a music major. "Classroom teaching is outstanding and the outside contact with students is something I have only seen here. It's one of Knox's greatest elements." Nearly all classes have fewer than twenty-five students. Knox's trimester system packs a great deal of studying into a short period, but students are only required to take three courses per term.

Knox's student advising system is praised by students. "On one of your first days on campus as a first year, your Faculty Advisor takes his or her advisees out to dinner," says one sophomore. "Academic advising has been excellent for me, and advisors are always available to discuss anything ranging from future plans to personal problems," adds a junior. An early identification of premed freshmen guarantees six students admission to Rush Medical College in Chicago if they maintain a four-year B average. Knox also offers 3–2 or 3–4 programs in engineering, nursing, medical technology, law, and architecture.

One of the most popular forms of activism is "chalking," where students write messages in chalk on campus walkways.

The bulk of students (51 percent) are from Illinois, and 9 percent of students come from foreign countries. Students of color make up 14 percent of the student body (4 percent African-American, 5 percent Asian-American, and 4 percent Hispanic), and maintain an active profile on campus. "There is no typical student at Knox. Students come here with vastly different backgrounds, political leanings, interests, and goals," says a junior. A biochemistry major describes his peers as "individuals who have a drive for success." While Knox does not seem to be a terribly politically active school, there appears to be a commitment to diversity across campus. One of the most popular forms of activism is "chalking," where students write messages in chalk on campus walkways. "Political correctness is huge. We're

> **"Political correctness is huge."**

pretty conscious of the words we choose," says a sophomore. A senior points out freshmen are always called "first-years." Most students went to public high school, and 67 percent graduated in the top quarter of their class. Merit scholarships, from $5,000 to $15,000, are available, but athletic scholarships are not.

Housing is not a problem on the Knox campus; renovations have improved housing for most students, though some students complain that most rooms are not air-conditioned. One student describes the dorms as "spacious and organized into suites with large common areas." Co-ed living arrangements are available, although most freshmen live in single-sex suites with one or two upperclassmen as residential advisors. Students suggest freshman women would be happiest in Post Hall, while men should try to live anywhere in Old Quad. Older students may band together with friends or form a special-interest or theme suite. The five fraternities are residential; the two sororities are not. It takes a minor miracle for students to obtain permission to move off campus, which has become a common complaint among juniors and seniors. Food service, as at many colleges, gets a thumbs-down, with some students lamenting that it is difficult to get off the board plan. Security is "very visible on campus, driving around in their 'chariots of justice,' or golf carts," says a student.

Knox operates on an honor system that allows students to take tests in any public area unproctored, but few students would even think of cheating.

Galesburg is a small Midwestern railroad town, and some students say they had trouble adjusting to the sounds of locomotives. At one time this city of about thirty-five thousand was a center of abolitionism, and the honorary degree that the college bestowed on then presidential candidate Abraham Lincoln was his first formal title. Relations between the town and school haven't been the greatest, but students say that is changing. Nearby Lake Storey offers boating, water slides, and nature trails, and students looking for more excitement can travel to Peoria, about forty miles away. Slightly farther away, Chicago is about

"Personal responsibility is valued above all."

140 miles to the northeast. Weekends are filled with dances, campus activities, and fraternity parties. Thirty-seven percent of the men and 15 percent of women go Greek, but you don't have to join to find fun. The alcohol policy is liberal, and as one sophomore notes, "Personal responsibility is valued above all." One of the best all-time traditions is Flunk Day. At five-thirty on a spring morning, Old Main's bell rings and classes are canceled to make way for dunk tanks and Jell-O pits. One sophomore proudly notes "the newest tradition on campus is to steal a cafeteria tray during the first snow of the year and go sledding down the Knox Bowl."

Athletics generate a reasonable degree of enthusiasm. Both the men's and women's golf teams are strong—the men have won nineteen of the last twenty-three conference championships, most recently in 2002. Every fall, the football team endures lots of hard Knox against archrival Monmouth to bring home the highly prized Bronze Turkey Award, a throwback to the time when the game was played on Thanksgiving Day.

Knox may not be a well-known school, but students here have little else to complain about. Academics are the priority and students are encouraged to be individuals, but the close-knit atmosphere helps them form strong connections with different types of students and down-to-earth professors.

Overlaps
Beloit, Grinnell, Illinois Wesleyan, University of Illinois, Earlham

If You Apply To ➢   **Knox:** Early action: Dec. 1. Regular admissions: Feb. 1. Financial aid: Mar. 1. Meets demonstrated need of 95%. Campus interview: recommended, evaluative. No alumni interviews. SATs or ACTs: required. SAT IIs: optional. Accepts the Common Application. Essay question: Common Application.

Lafayette College

118 Markle Hall, Easton, PA 18042

Geographically close to Lehigh, but closer kin to Colgate and Hamilton. Does offer engineering, as do Swarthmore, Trinity (CT), and Union. Attracts relatively conservative, athletic students who work hard and play hard. A recent spate of building shows Lafayette's financial health.

Website: www.lafayette.edu
Location: City outskirts
Total Enrollment: 2,300
Undergraduates: 2,300
Male/Female: 50/50
SAT Ranges: V 560–650
    M 610–700
ACT Range: 25–29
Financial Aid: 96%
Expense: Pr $ $ $ $
Phi Beta Kappa: Yes
Applicants: 5,504
Accepted: 36%
Enrolled: 30%
Grad in 6 Years: 86%
Returning Freshmen: 96%
Academics: ✐ ✐ ✐ ✐
Social: ☎ ☎ ☎ ☎ ☎
Q of L: ★ ★ ★
Admissions: (610) 330-5100
Email Address:
    admissions@lafayette.edu

Strongest Programs:
Engineering
Economics/Business
Chemistry
Art
Biology
Psychology/Neuroscience
English
Government/Law
Geology

Lafayette College has done its homework and is earning higher and higher points among top students, as seen in the growing applicant pile. Gleaming new buildings and crackdowns on excessive student partying are just two of the visible reminders that the college is serious about continuing to rise higher and higher among the small elite liberal arts colleges. One of the few liberal arts schools of its size to offer engineering, Lafayette has also won respect for its technical and scientific programs.

Lafayette is situated on a stately hill in Easton, Pennsylvania, just one and one-half hours west of New York City and even closer to Philadelphia. The campus has an eclectic blend of architectural styles, and more than 125 species of trees. The main library holds 490,000 volumes, with a twenty-four-hour study area and online access to the card catalog from the comfort of dorm rooms. A

"The best thing about Lafayette is the professors."

$20 million expansion of the library will add thirty thousand square feet of open learning space—a common theme in many Lafayette buildings. The new $10 million Oeschsle Center for Psychology and Neuroscience features three remote observation labs that allow students to watch their subjects—be they fish or human—without the subjects knowing it. The ninety thousand-square-foot Acopian Engineering Center stays open all night and weekends, and features lots of open work spaces and glass walls to build a sense of shared purpose—and allow for extra mingling.

Lafayette's engineering, economics, and government and law programs are among the most popular majors, followed by English and psychology. Physics and chemistry are the toughest courses of study, and some students shun them as a result. A senior notes that the campus's music facilities aren't great "for someone really serious about music." The standard course load is four classes a semester, and all first-year students take an interdisciplinary seminar designed to engage them as thinkers, speakers, and writers. In the second semester of sophomore year, students take a second seminar, to promote scientific and technological literacy. All students must take an intensive writing course, as well as four units in both math and natural sciences and humanities and social sciences. Students working for a B.A. must meet a foreign culture requirement through foreign language classwork or study abroad, or complete a group of courses providing intensive exposure to a specific foreign culture. Lafayette was recently noted by the Institute of International Education as having the highest study-abroad participation among liberal arts colleges. The EXCEL program pays students who take research positions with faculty.

Engineering students, too, may explore a foreign culture through an unusual arrangement with the Free University of Brussels, which allows them to study abroad while maintaining normal progress toward their degrees. There is also cross-registration available with other schools in the Lehigh Valley Association of Independent Colleges.* Most students are happy back on their own campus, though. "The best thing about Lafayette is the professors," says student, adding that they "are genuinely interested in teaching students and making sure they succeed."

Students are described as "intelligent and hard working," and 69 percent of Lafayette students are from out of state. While 63 percent attended public high school, it sometimes doesn't seem that way. "Students come largely from professional homes where a college education was assumed to be the next step after high school," comments an English major. Affluent and conservative students seem to set the tone, and student activism is hardly the kind that makes the evening news. "Once I saw a group of students protesting the quality of the food," recalls a math major, "but within an hour or two, they were hungry enough to stop for lunch." African-Americans account for 7 percent of the student body; Hispanics and Asian-Americans combine for another 4 percent. Four hundred merit scholarships worth $7,500 to $12,500 each are available to qualified students, though there are no athletic scholarships.

The ninety thousand-square-foot Acopian Engineering Center stays open all night and weekends, and features airy open work spaces and glass walls to build a sense of shared purpose—and allow for extra mingling.

Ninety-seven percent of students live on campus, and housing is guaranteed for all four years. Possibilities include Greek houses as well as independent dormitories and college-owned apartments with a variety of living and eating arrangements. The school is busily renovating and modernizing some of the older dorms, but still, one student says the range of housing can run the gamut from from dingy to "Taj Mahal." Keefe Hall, a new dorm, is "more like a hotel," says a senior, while South College Hall, recently renovated, has more washers and dryers and "nicer and newer facilities," says a classmate. A sixty-person residence hall has special-interest floors organized around themes such as science and technology. There's a lottery system that determines which dorm a student will live in, but most get into the dorm of their choice. Ruef and South College are more social, while Watson Hall and Kirby House are quieter, students say. Most upperclassmen, including women and non-Greek males, join meal plans at fraternities or the social dorms. And this is hardly a "suitcase school": everyone stays around for the weekends, a senior says. Students feel safe on campus. In fact, some complain that campus security is "overzealous," playing grinch too often by breaking up parties and handing out parking tickets.

Overzealous or just plain conscientious, these efforts have resulted in whisking much of the social life off campus. Greek life attracts 24 percent of the men and 43 percent of the women. For students with cars, or those willing to hop a bus or train, the bright lights of Philadelphia, New York, and Atlantic City beckon on weekends; for a change of pace, there is also

"Once I saw a group of students protesting the quality of the food."

hiking the Appalachian Trail. Another big "draw" is touring the nearby Binney & Smith factory where Crayola crayons are made. The Lafayette Activities Forum plans plays, movies, concerts, and coffeehouses for those who wish to stay on campus. Parties are BYOB, and all sororities and some fraternities are dry. The arts program brings a range of performers to campus. Blue-collar Easton has become more "college-friendly," and is now gentrified with more stores and restaurants that cater to the college crowd. From College Hill and Downtown to the South Side, the city offers plenty of opportunities for volunteer work in schools, prisons, rehabilitation centers, hospitals and environmental sites, under the auspices of Lafayette's Community Outreach Center.

Affluent and conservative students seem to set the tone, and student activism is hardly the kind that makes the evening news.

Sports add much flavor to the Lafayette experience. The Lafayette Leopards women's lacrosse teams brought home Patriot League championships in 2000 and 2001, and the women's field hockey team won the championship in 2002. The annual football game against nearby Lehigh is intense—students claim it's the oldest rivalry in the U.S., and when the two teams play, extra bleachers must be installed to accommodate the crowd. Women's basketball and indoor track and field are also strong, as are football, men's track, and soccer. All Leopard varsity teams compete in Division I except for football, which is I-AA. For those not up to varsity level, there is an extensive intramural program, buoyed by the state-of-the-art, $35 million Kirby Sports Center. The most important nonathletic campus event of the year is All-College Day, a spring festival with beach balls, bathing suits, bands, and the like.

Overlaps

Bucknell, Lehigh, Colgate, Villanova, University of Pennsylvania

Students looking for tradition and close contact with professors—and who aren't afraid of some serious study—should take a look at Lafayette. They should expect some competition for a spot in the freshman class, though, as applications are going up every year.

<table>
<tr><td>If You Apply To ➢</td><td>Lafayette: Early decision and regular admissions: Jan. 1. Financial aid: Feb. 1. Housing: Jun. 1. Does not guarantee to meet demonstrated need. Campus interviews: recommended, evaluative. Alumni interviews: optional, informational. SATs or ACTs: required. Accepts the Common Application and electronic applications. Essay question: Common Application.</td></tr>
</table>

Lake Forest College

555 Sheridan Road, Lake Forest, IL 60045

The only small, selective private college in the Chicago area. The college generally attracts middle-of-the-road and conservative students. In the exclusive town of Lake Forest, students can baby-sit for corporate CEOs at night and get internships at their corporations during the day.

Website: www.lakeforest.edu
Location: Suburban
Total Enrollment: 1,341
Undergraduates: 1,319
Male/Female: 41/59
SAT Ranges: V 520–620
M 510–620
ACT Range: 23–28
Financial Aid: 70%
Expense: Pr $ $ $
Phi Beta Kappa: Yes
Applicants: 1,666
Accepted: 66%
Enrolled: 32%
Grad in 6 Years: 70%
Returning Freshmen: 79%
Academics: ✍ ✍ ✍
Social: 🐧 🐧 🐧 🐧
Q of L: ★ ★ ★
Admissions: (847) 735-5000
Email Address:
admissions@lakeforest.edu

Strongest Programs:
Business
Economics
Psychology
Politics
Biology

Lake Forest, lovingly referred to as the "Enchanted Forest" by many of its students, is a small liberal arts college that offers a laid-back learning atmosphere in a picturesque setting. The school's true bounty is most apparent in its improving academics, fueled by small classes and dedicated professors, and a familiar, close-knit atmosphere among the student body. "Classes are challenging and competitive, but the small class size allows students to form close bonds with professors, which makes for a more open atmosphere," a junior English and psychology major says.

With its mixture of century-old Gothic and modern glass structures, Lake Forest's 107-acre campus is storybook beautiful. Located on Chicago's North Shore, about thirty miles north of The Windy City, the campus has three parts: North, Middle, and South. Each has a mix of residence halls and academic facilities. The college is spending $18 million on a new library and information resources center. It recently renovated the Cleveland Young International Center, a special interest house for international students, international studies majors and students interested in studying abroad. Other newly renovated facilities include Nollen Hall and Deerpath Hall with such noteworthy enhancements as central air-conditioning and a fitness center. The wealth and seclusion of the city Lake Forest make the college a real dreamland—but also feed the insularity many students come with or begin to feel once on campus. Nature lovers can explore the wooded ravines on the many undeveloped acres leading to Lake Michigan.

> "My advisor goes out of his way to make sure I am taking the right courses and aids in finding me jobs for the summer. It is highly useful."

Students are expected to fulfill a variety of course requirements. A general education curriculum requires two credits of natural and mathematical sciences, two credits of humanities, two credits of social sciences, and two classes in cultural diversity. In addition, freshmen must take a seminar-style First-Year Studies course and seniors must complete a senior seminar or senior thesis. Students say academics are intense as they want them to be. "Unfortunately, it's hit or miss with competition," says a junior communications major. "While the courses here have the potential to be very rigorous, many of them aren't because the students seem, in general, to dictate the workload and difficulty of courses, which kind of re-creates a high school environment." Students who seek more academic autonomy value the Independent Scholar program, which allows undergrads to create their own majors across traditional disciplines. There's also the Richter Apprentice Scholars program, which encourages freshmen to join faculty members in conducting scholarly research—and then to consider careers in research and teaching. The First-Year Studies program is being improved to capitalize on the opportunities in Chicago.

Students say LFC's best departments are business, economics, English, and the sciences. The Student/Faculty Science Research Center provides plenty of lab and office space for students and faculty alike. The theater and music departments are said to be weaker, owing to limited faculty and facilities. The "Information Revolution" has inspired LFC to create a new program in communications, and students can benefit from the new Latin American studies major and classical studies minor as well.

"Lake Forest is a very upscale town with many beautiful big homes and buildings."

Comparative literature has been dropped. Students who don't like what's offered at Lake Forest can create their own classes, provided they find professors to teach them.

Lake Forest believes deeply in the value of study abroad, and many students participate in programs such as the Greece and Turkey Program, where archeological sites and museums provide cultural classrooms, or the marine biology program, which includes work at a tropical field station. A new study abroad program in East Asian Studies is part of the college's new Asia Center. The International Internship program has placed students in organizations including the Paris Cultural Affairs Department, UNESCO, UNICEF, and Eurospace. Lake Forest students also can be found in secondary schools and multinational corporations in both Paris and Santiago, Chile. The school is a member of the Associated Colleges of the Midwest* too, which offers programs in Russia, Zimbabwe, Japan, India, and central Europe, among other locales. Unlike part-time internships at other schools, Lake Forest interns work full-time in business, education, social and political activities, and at nonprofit agencies.

While Foresters like the small class sizes, flexible academic guidelines, and large doses of individual attention, nothing seems to compare to the quality of the faculty. "Classes are small and professors know you by name, call you at home and sit among students in the cafe. All the professors love what they do and care about the students," says a junior. "They want to be here, teaching at a small liberal arts school, and it shows," adds a freshman communications student. Students praise the Career Advancement Center for its symposia, workshops, and resume clinics. "My advisor goes out of his way to make sure I am taking the right courses and aids in finding me jobs for the summer. It is highly useful," says a junior biology major. When it comes to recruiting, Lake Forest prides itself on its interstate appeal. Fifty-eight percent of students come from outside the Land of Lincoln, with many from either New England or the mid-Atlantic states. International students account for 13 percent. African-Americans comprise 6 percent of the student body, Hispanics 3 percent, and Asian-Americans 5 percent. But students say there is diversity of all types on campus. "Our students are incredibly diverse for such a small campus," says a freshman communications student who adds that partially due to "the incredible financial aid, every walk of life is represented." One thousand merit scholarships—worth up to full tuition—are available to qualified students.

Few students have the megabucks to live off campus in affluent Lake Forest, so 81 percent live in the dorms, where housing is co-ed by floor or quad unit except for one single-sex dorm. "North campus is nice, but no parties," says an in-the-know senior. Middle campus dorms are seen as more "academic" while the South

Lake Forest recently renovated the Cleveland Young International Center, a special interest house for international students, international studies majors and students interested in studying abroad.

The First-Year Studies program is being improved to capitalize on the opportunities in Chicago.

campus is the older, wilder area. "Half of the students live on South campus, which is the party place," claims one student. Nollen, McClure and Cleveland-Young are completely substance-free. Every room has an Ethernet connection and each hall has a computer lab. Freshmen are assigned rooms by the Dean of Students, while upperclassmen fend for themselves through a lottery based on seniority. Deerpath is by all accounts the top spot, and a recently completed $7 million renovation added air-conditioning, an aerobics and fitness center, and a state-of-the-art computer network. An honors dorm is home to the brainy crowd. Students have complained about not having cable TV, and that is now available campus-wide. Everybody eats in a recently renovated central dining hall, the social beehive of the campus, where unlimited helpings are served. Through "Real Food on Campus" meals are prepared in front of students with fresh ingredients.

The party scene on LFC's campus has picked up with the arrival of fraternities and sororities, which attract 19 percent of men and 27 percent of women, though parties are open to all. Students report they can drink behind closed doors, and it's a breeze for underage students to get alcohol. Says a junior, "Many students are 'written up' for open alcohol, however, seldom are seriously punished for drinking underage." For students not interested in the frat scene, LFC offers movies, speakers, and coffeehouses with musical and comedy acts. Major events on the campus social calendar include the semi-formal Winter Ball and Spring Concert. Other festivities celebrate ethnic and cultural diversity, such as Semana Latina (Hispanic culture) and CelebrAsian. The Big Chill in February is something akin to a winter carnival, and for diehard traditionalists, there's always Homecoming weekend in the fall.

Though Chicago is only an hour away by train, it helps to have a car for maximum freedom to get downtown and to other suburbs. Students complain businesses in Lake Forest close early and residents are less than welcoming. "Lake Forest is a very upscale town with many beautiful big homes and buildings," says a junior. "There are mostly expensive stores and restaurants in town and the people of Lake Forest aren't very involved with the college." Neighboring communities such as Highwood have bars—most notably Rainbows and the Wooden Nickel—frequented by students. The recent construction of a coffeehouse now provides Foresters with a setting for informal, nonalcoholic mixing. Aside from pure socializing, seven student organizations are devoted to community organizations. One program sends students to the Appalachian Mountains in Virginia and Tennessee every spring break to help local townspeople repair substandard housing.

Lake Forest isn't exactly what you'd call a football factory, but the team was the Midwest Conference Champion in 2002 and advanced to the NCAA Tournament. The softball and men's and women's handball teams also fared well that year. More than 65 percent of LFC students participate in athletics at some level, from club to varsity sports.

While Lake Forest still has a substantial contingent of spoiled rich kids who are there just to drink their college years away, the college is also working hard to attract sharp minds who are searching for a safe, cloistered environment and professors who know all of their students by name. "It seems to be becoming a more recognizable, more respected institution," a junior says of Lake Forest. "This college is definitely going places!"

Overlaps

Boston University, Northwestern, American University, Hobart and William Smith, Denison

If You Apply To ➢

Lake Forest: Early decision: Jan. 1. Early action: Dec. 1. Regular admissions and Financial Aid: Mar. 1. Campus interviews: recommended, evaluative. No alumni interviews. SATs or ACTs: required. SAT IIs: optional. Accepts the Common Application and electronic applications. No essay question, but a graded paper must be submitted.

One of two small colleges in the nation that combines the liberal arts with a first-rate music conservatory. (Oberlin is the other.) Occupying a spot in northeastern Wisconsin, Lawrence is comparable to Beloit in size but not quite as nonconformist.

Lawrence University is an unpretentious school that can appeal to both the left and right side of students' brains. For those with an analytical bent, there is Lawrence's uncommon laser physics program. More creative types can take advantage of the school's renowned Conservatory of Music, one of only two at a small liberal arts college (the other is at Oberlin).

Lawrence's campus is on a wooded bluff above the Fox River, perfect for long walks, jogging, or simply meditating underneath the trees. It was chosen in 1847 by one of Appleton, Wisconsin's earliest settlers. The pristine eighty-four-acre campus reflects several architectural styles of the past 150 years, including classical revival, 1920s Georgian-inspired, and 1950s and 1960s institutional, unified by their limestone color. The award-winning Wriston Art Center and the Conservatory's Ruth Harwood Shattuck Hall of Music (both designed by Lawrence graduates) bring contemporary architectural touches to the campus. Youngchild Hall, which also houses science programs, recently received $11 million in upgrades, and a new $15.3 million dorm is being built.

The second coeducational college established in the nation, Lawrence was founded to educate German immigrants and Native Americans. While co-education was shocking, innovators at Lawrence didn't stop there. More than fifty years ago, administrators introduced the Freshman Studies program, a required two-term course focusing primarily on the great works of art, music, and literature of primarily the Western tradition. These days, general education requirements at Lawrence include freshman studies, distribution requirements and diversity, foreign language, and writing-intensive courses. Most departments now offer minors, and newly added programs include Japanese and an ethnic studies minor.

> "It's not unusual to find a classical violinist who majors in physics or a chemistry major who also minors in studio art."

At the school's Conservatory of Music, first-year music students are offered courses including theory and analysis, keyboard skills, sight-reading, ear training, and applied study in music. The Conservatory's instrument collection includes an 1815 Broadwood piano identical to Beethoven's Broadwood, and a Guarneri violin. There is also a first-rate jazz group along with classical and world music programs; it offers a bachelor's degree in music within its liberal arts environment, plus a unique five-year bachelor's and master's program that receives regular national acclaim. "Music is the unifying theme at Lawrence," says one student. "Almost everybody plays it or studies it or likes to listen to it and talk about it." A five-year program allows students to earn two degrees—one in music and one in another subject.

Overall, however, the most popular major is biology, followed by music performance and history. Students are encouraged to spend at least one of the year's three terms off campus. Lawrence is known for its London Study Center, which allows students to take classes "across the pond" while taking advantage of the city's many cultural activities. Other off-campus programs involve the Kurgan Technical Pedagogical Institute in Russia, Waseda University in Japan, and the Ecoles des Beaux

Website: www.lawrence.edu
Location: Center city
Total Enrollment: 1,323
Undergraduates: 1,323
Male/Female: 46/54
SAT Ranges: V 560–700
  M 580–700
ACT Range: 25–30
Financial Aid: 71%
Expense: Pr $ $ $
Phi Beta Kappa: Yes
Applicants: 1,629
Accepted: 68%
Enrolled: 20%
Grad in 6 Years: 67%
Returning Freshmen: 87%
Academics: ✍ ✍ ✍ ✍
Social: ☎ ☎ ☎
Q of L: ★ ★ ★
Admissions: (800) 227-0982
Email Address:
  excel@lawrence.edu

Strongest Programs:
Music
Drama
Biology
Physics
Psychology
English

Arts in France. Programs in marine biology research are held in the Cayman Islands. In all, forty off-campus programs are available.

Back on campus, Lawrence students appreciate their professors' expertise and experience. They say faculty members are accessible and highly encouraging of intellectual curiosity while still showing compassion for all of students' needs. "Their dedication to students is unsurpassed, and it is rare when students do not meet with their professors outside of class," a senior physics major says. Because of the three-term calendar, the academic climate is intimate and intense. "We are constantly conscious of our academic performance and take our classes very seriously," confides a sophomore. Students choose their own faculty advisors and meet with them at least once a term. The system gets top-notch reviews from students.

Most of Lawrence's students hail from Wisconsin or the Midwest. The majority attended public high school, and 76 percent graduated in the top quarter of their class. The student body is described as a diverse group of individuals. "It's not unusual to find a classical violinist who majors in physics or a chemistry major who also minors in studio art," notes one junior. Minority enrollment is only about 10 percent, with Asian-Americans the largest group at less than 3 percent. International students account for 9 percent of the student body, representing more than forty countries. The political climate on campus is somewhat liberal—there's a leftist newspaper—but "sometimes outside politics can have a hard time penetrating the campus," a sophomore says.

The dorms at Lawrence are well populated; all but 3 percent of students live on campus. That's because you have to get permission to move off, which is no easy feat. A full 30 percent of men and 22 percent of women go Greek at Lawrence, and that gives the men the opportunity to live in their houses. Sororities can claim a house through a new group-housing program. Two

"Dining is a mixed bag."

dorms are reserved for upperclassmen, and six small university-owned houses handle overflow. All halls are co-ed, by room or by floor, and all have laundry facilities, kitchens, televisions, Internet links, and lounges. Students praise the variety of housing choices. They report the older halls are more elegant, but the newer ones are more practical, with extra storage space and other amenities. "The dorms all have their own special reputations, but they are all clean, comfortable, well maintained, and close to everything," raves one sophomore. On-campus students have a choice of meal plans and eat in one of the two dining halls. "Dining is a mixed bag," says a student.

Social life at Lawrence stays almost entirely on campus. "There isn't much to do off campus, so having a car isn't entirely necessary for life at Lawrence," a sophomore says. Alcohol policies aren't enforced, according to many students. Although it's almost impossible for underage students to be served at the on-campus bar, the story is different at private parties and dorm rooms. A sophomore notes that "the university does not support or enable underage drinking, of course, but no one is here to baby-sit you either." Fraternity parties, room parties, conservatory concerts, film series, coffeehouses, and art openings keep students busy. "There is usually enough going on on campus to keep everyone busy enough," says a junior. Those over twenty-one frequent Pat's Tap and the Wooden Nickel in town. The school radio station also broadcasts a fifty-hour trivia contest in January, in which each hall has its own team, and students stay up for the entire weekend answering offbeat questions. Once spring finally arrives, students look forward to a popular arts festival aptly called Celebrate! Octoberfest is also a big event, held in conjunction with the city of Appleton.

And what would a Midwest fall Saturday be without football? The Lawrence team draws good crowds almost every weekend. Women's cross-country and soccer have brought home recent Midwest Conference championships. Men's basketball is notable, too. The sparkling recreation center helps students fend off midwinter blues, sometimes in very strange ways: five years ago, 187 "Larries" set a Guinness World Record by traveling 220 feet on a 120-foot toboggan in Appleton's Memorial Park. Participating in a rousing game of intramural broomball, which is ice hockey played on shoes with brooms as sticks and kickballs as pucks, is a must for students, even if all you do is watch.

Students rarely venture into Appleton for fun; although the campus can seem suffocatingly small, there's not much to do in the town. "Students do almost nothing in town," complains a senior who notes there are not enough cultural opportunities. The nearest grocery store is a five-minute drive away, as is the nearest theater, and many students see a car as a necessity. A music student says that most students don't go off campus often to do things, though administrators insist that townspeople frequently visit for theater, concerts, art exhibits, and lectures. Volunteerism is popular, however, and students regularly take part in activities such as tutoring at local schools. The best road trips are Milwaukee (two hours), Green Bay (half an hour), and Chicago (four hours). There are also weekend seminars at Bjorklunden, the college's 425-acre estate on the shores of Lake Michigan.

With its outstanding liberal arts curriculum, knowledgeable and caring faculty, an administration that treats students like adults, and a charming country setting, Lawrence University is easily one of the best little-known schools in the country. And for students with a musical ear, Lawrence's symphony of offerings sounds especially pleasant.

Overlaps

University of Wisconsin–Madison, Macalester, Oberlin, Northwestern, Grinnell

If You Apply To ➤

Lawrence: Early decision: Nov. 15. Early action: Dec. 1. Regular admissions: Jan. 15. Financial aid: Mar. 1. Guarantees to meet demonstrated need. Campus interviews: recommended, informational. Alumni interviews: optional, informational. SATs or ACTs: required. SAT IIs: Optional. Music applicants must audition. Accepts the Common Application and electronic applications. Essay question: movie, play, book or piece of music that has challenged your thinking; significant experience, achievement, or risk; or what you would do with a year of funding.

Lehigh University

27 Memorial Drive West, Bethlehem, PA 18015

Built on the powerful combination of business and engineering, Lehigh occupies a middle ground between the techie havens, such as Rennselaer and Drexel, and the liberal arts/engineering institutions such as Bucknell and Union. By graduation, students are primed for the job market.

Lehigh University's reputation as a factory producing skilled engineers has traveled far and wide. But the P.C. Rossin College of Engineering and Applied Science is only one of three undergraduate divisions at this multifaceted school. From the College of Arts and Sciences (the school with the highest enrollment and the most selective) to the College of Business and Economics, Lehigh combines the academic resources of a large research university with the collegial atmosphere of a much smaller institution. Students choose from a vast selection of courses; classroom work is challenging, but not overwhelming. "Lehigh perfectly combines competitive academics with a great social life," says a junior.

Grand old oaks shade the buildings on Lehigh's sixteen-hundred-acre campus, which is tucked into the side of an eastern Pennsylvania mountain. Architectural

Website: www.lehigh.edu
Location: City
Total Enrollment: 6,665
Undergraduates: 4,685
Male/Female: 60/40
SAT Ranges: V 593–660
  M 620–710
Financial Aid: 52%
Expense: Pr $ $ $
Phi Beta Kappa: Yes

(Continued)

Applicants: 9,087
Accepted: 40%
Enrolled: 31%
Grad in 6 Years: 84%
Returning Freshmen: 92.4%
Academics: ✍ ✍ ✍ ✍
Social: 🐨 🐨 🐨 🐨
Q of L: ★ ★
Admissions: (610) 758-3100
Email Address:
   admissions@lehigh.edu

Strongest Programs:
Engineering
Accounting
Finance
Sciences
Architecture

The Goodman Athletic Campus provides first-class practice and playing facilities for Lehigh's sports teams, including a 16,000-seat stadium, 5,600-seat basketball arena and fields and facilities for many of the school's twenty-four Division I varsity sports teams.

styles range from ivy-covered collegiate Gothic to modern glass and steel. The Goodman Athletic Campus provides first-class practice and playing facilities for Lehigh's sports teams, including a 16,000-seat stadium, 5,600-seat basketball arena and fields and facilities for many of the school's twenty-four Division I varsity sports teams.

Because so much of Lehigh's reputation rests on its consistently strong engineering program, the school is investing $75 million over the next few years to enhance critical academic programs such as optical technologies, nanotechnology, bioscience and biotechnology, optoelectronics, bioscience, and biotechnology. But it is also paying more attention to the arts and humanities. New majors, including business economics and supply-chain management, augment already-notable programs in the College of Business and Economics, such as accounting, finance, management, and marketing. The College of Arts and Sciences boasts strong psychology, political science, architecture, biology and English departments. Despite its emphasis on science and engineering, Lehigh also has active theater and music programs; nonmajors may join student ensembles, which have toured Europe, Asia, and the U.S.

Requirements vary by college, and engineers face the most. Regardless of major, all freshmen must take two semesters of English (the second is said to be better than the first). Special degree options include seven-year programs, offered with two Pennsylvania medical schools, that lead to bachelor's and medical or dental degrees, and a five-year arts and engineering program, leading to B.A. and B.S. degrees. Co-ops allow certain engineering students to spend eight months working for a major-related company—and getting paid to do so—while still graduating in four years. Lehigh is big on connecting disparate disciplines, with a four-year integrated business

"Lehigh perfectly combines competitive academics with a great social life."

and engineering curriculum, five-year programs leading to a B.A. or B.S. and a master's in education, plus teacher certification, and the combined education-M.B.A. program, geared to future school administrators. IPD—the acronym stands for Integrated Product Development—brings engineering, business, and arts students together to design and make products for sponsoring companies.

Lehigh also offers more than fifty study-abroad options in thirty-eight countries, some through the Lehigh Valley Association of Independent Colleges.* And every summer, the Martindale Scholars Program sends a dozen select juniors to another country, where they interview business and political leaders and write reports on the country's economy for a journal.

The workload at Lehigh is heavy, especially in engineering and business; students are ambitious, and many pursue double majors. "The courses are rigorous and challenge you both academically and personally," says a senior majoring in religion studies and earth and environmental studies. "People work hard and there are several stressful points in each semester when the library is packed," adds a senior civil engineering major. Except for first-year English classes, professors teach all courses, with teaching assistants handling weekly recitation sections. Fifty-two percent of courses have fewer than twenty students, and "Lehigh is very good at making it so that you can take all the courses you need, and most of those you want, in four years," says one student. (Those who can't, or don't want to, but manage to maintain a 3.75 GPA are eligible for a fifth year of study tuition-free.) For academic or career planning, professors "are more than delighted to help, but you need to approach them," a senior says.

Lehigh's two main libraries include a card catalog accessible from most computers on campus, including those in students' rooms; all rooms in campus buildings, including dorms, have high-speed Internet access. Also noteworthy is the International Multimedia Resource Center, which gets news broadcasts from more than twenty-five countries via satellite. Through the Lehigh Clipper Project, students accepted for early admission may take Web-based freshman courses without charge, getting a jump on graduation requirements.

Only 30 percent of Lehigh's students come from Pennsylvania, and many others hail from other Northeastern states; three-quarters are white, and the majority graduated from public high schools. "Right now I can look at most students and categorize them as upper middle class, white and bright."

> "Right now I can look at most students and categorize them as upper middle class, white and bright."

Racial and ethnic diversity is improving—African-Americans and Hispanics now constitute 6 percent of the student body, and Asian-Americans add 6 percent. And students say there are still different types of students on campus. "There are all kinds of students at Lehigh," a senior says. "It's a healthy environment." The campus, students say, is slightly conservative, but there have recently been some anti-war demonstrations, suggesting that may be changing.

Two-thirds of Lehigh students live on campus; freshmen and sophomores are guaranteed housing. "There are two types of freshman dorms: Lower Cents, small halls that are more close-knit at the end of a year, and the Freshman Quad buildings, which are large and introduce a lot of people in one year," one student says. "Most of the rooms are spacious, with a lot of storage," adds another. Sophomores and juniors generally live in Greek houses—38 percent of men join fraternities and 43 percent of women pledge sororities—or in apartment-style dorms, while seniors move off campus, where some apartments are closer to their classes than their old dorm rooms. Other options include the new Campus Square, a residential and commercial complex that houses 250 upperclass students, and special-interest housing. Lehigh's dining service has been honored with the Ivy Award, given by the restaurant industry to first-class restaurants as well as to educational institutions including.

Social life at Lehigh revolves around "the Hill," where most fraternities and a new sorority are located. Students look forward to the craziness of Greek Week carnivals each semester, with toga races, pie-eating contests, and reasonably continuous partying, ending in a huge, free picnic and live concert. Like many universities, Lehigh is struggling with an entrenched drinking culture; it's one of ten schools nationwide to get a grant from the Robert Wood Johnson Foundation to help curb alcohol abuse. New policies aim to make the campus a "healthier, safer living and learning environment" by changing Lehigh's culture—placing stricter rules on parties and tailgating, and expanding alcohol-free programming. "In the past four years the alcohol policy has become stricter, however, it is still pretty easy to be served underage," says a senior.

The bustling campus stands in contrast to the worn condition of Bethlehem, a once-great steel town. However, the town has drawn a number of emerging information-technology companies, many with ties to Lehigh professors and the university's mountaintop research park. Lehigh has also joined a $400 million redevelopment effort that will include a Smithsonian Institute Museum of Industry, a multiplex theater, and a large new

> "In the past four years the alcohol policy has become stricter, however, it is still pretty easy to be served underage."

hotel and conference center. While the university's immediate neighborhood, South Bethlehem, "has a pretty bad reputation," says a senior, "I love it, and feel very safe." By contrast, the student says, "North Bethlehem is beautiful and historic," with an active downtown and cultural district a short walk away. "There are many ethnic restaurants within walking distance," says a senior, adding "Lehigh's newest residence hall is built right on the edge of campus to help integrate the city and university."

Lehigh is big on connecting disparate disciplines, with a four-year integrated business and engineering curriculum, five-year programs leading to a B.A. or B.S. and a master's in education, plus teacher certification, and the combined education-M.B.A. program, geared to future school administrators.

For non-Greeks, or those who don't want to end the evening soaked in beer, there are 130 clubs and organizations on campus, and they sponsor concerts, comedians, performances, and other diversions, often at the striking Zoellner Arts Center, which hosts more than seventy-five performances per year, or the 5,600-seat Stabler Arena. Center-city Bethlehem is five minutes from campus, and one in four students volunteers in the community, often at the Boys and Girls Club or through America Reads. In late August, just before classes begin, the town hosts Musikfest. Shortly thereafter, Celtic Classic is underway. For those with wheels, Philadelphia is an hour's drive, and New York City is barely two. Skiers will appreciate the close proximity of the Poconos in the winter, while sun worshippers can enjoy the nearby Jersey shore in the early fall and late spring.

While Lehigh's varsity wrestling team has been strong for years, the biggest deal is still the annual sell-out football game against Lafayette. Lehigh is a Division I-AA powerhouse, winning titles in 2000 and 2001, and its rivalry with Lafayette is college football's most-played rivalry. "I hate football," says one Mountain Hawk (the Lehigh mascot), "but I go to this game." Women's swimming is also strong, bringing home two championships recently. Even weekend warriors will find something to cheer about in the Welch Fitness Center's weight room in Taylor Gym, two pools, a climbing wall and racquetball and squash courts.

Lehigh students proudly juggle rigorous classes and a packed extracurricular calendar. They give college life more than the old college try—and expect to succeed. "Students at Lehigh University set the perfect example of combining academic vigor and social interaction," a journalism major says. "The average Lehigh student not only has intelligence, but can communicate it as well."

Overlaps

Bucknell, Boston College, Penn State, Cornell, University of Pennsylvania

If You Apply To ➢

Lehigh: Early decision I: Nov. 15. Early decision II: Jan. 1. Regular admissions: Jan. 1. Financial aid: Feb. 15. Meets demonstrated need of 52%. Campus interviews: recommended, informational. No alumni interviews. ACTs or SATs: required. SAT IIs: recommended. Apply to particular colleges. Accepts the Common Application and electronic applications. Essay question: why Lehigh is a good match for you; respond to one of six topics.

Lewis & Clark College

0615 Southwest Palatine Hill Road, Portland, OR 97219-7899

The West Coast's leader in international and study abroad programs. Politically liberal, but not so far out as cross-town neighbor Reed. Portfolio Path to admission allows students to finesse standardized tests. With Mount Hood visible in the distance, there is a wealth of outdoor possibilities.

Website: www.lclark.edu
Location: Urban
Total Enrollment: 3,051
Undergraduates: 1,763
Male/Female: 40/60
SAT Ranges: V 600–690
  M 580–670
ACT Range: 25–29
Financial Aid: 55%

The nineteenth-century explorers Lewis and Clark struck out from middle America to find where the trail ended, and their travels took them to Portland, a lush, green paradise by the Willamette River. The college that bears the explorers' names gained notoriety for graduating a former White House intern named Monica Lewinsky. But it's the school's international focus—more than 7,500 Lewis & Clark students have explored the world since 1962—and its setting in a quiet, residential neighborhood not far from Portland's brewpubs, coffeehouses, and hiking trails, that continue to draw high achievers.

Lest students become too enchanted overseas, Lewis & Clark lures them back with a gorgeous campus perched atop fir-covered bluffs overlooking the river. The campus is an old estate, complete with elaborate gardens, fountains, and pools, where cement is almost nonexistent and the roads are instead paved with cobblestones. Newer structures, added among the traditional Tudor buildings, reflect the heritage of Native American tribes of the Northwest. Three new apartment-style residence halls were recently completed. The historic Albany Quadrangle was remodeled and expanded to include classrooms, meeting rooms and a temporary home for the Lewis and Clark Expedition Bicentennial activities. And Howard Hall, a new social sciences building, is being constructed.

"Our students tend to be liberal."

Lewis & Clark requires that all students achieve competency in a foreign language and international study; more than half of the students fulfill these requirements by studying overseas for a semester or more. Students may travel to countries including Australia, China, Colombia, Ecuador, Japan, Kenya, Germany, France, and Scotland, and may also study in a number of American cities—some study in two or three countries. Freshmen also take a class called Inventing America, where they analyze the formation of the United States. In addition to the international requirement, students must complete courses in scientific and quantitative reasoning, creative arts, foreign languages, and physical education.

Not surprisingly, among the most popular majors at Lewis & Clark is international affairs, along with psychology and English. A new major in computer science is being offered. Music and art are well regarded, but students report difficulty getting into certain courses—even for majors—because these departments are small. Honors programs are available in all majors, and 3–2 programs in engineering are also offered. The John S. Rogers Science Research Program teams students and faculty on research projects ranging from the adhesive power of geckos to molecular science.

Lewis & Clark offers a Portfolio Path to admission, where students present a package representing their talents and interests and don't have to submit SAT or ACT scores as a reward. In addition to essays and other items required of students who send in test scores, PP students supply three teacher recommendations and graded samples of high-school work, such as essays, lab reports, or samples of art or music. Some students who use this approach feel standardized tests don't do them justice, while others have "incredible test scores." The key to a good portfolio is a "well-rounded approach," administrators say. "The more creative, the better, but be sure it's not solely artwork or writing samples."

Given this open attitude, it's not surprising that L&C students are not cutthroat. The atmosphere is "challenging and motivational, but not oppressive," explains a student majoring in psychology and sociology/anthropology. "Courses are thorough, but not excessive." Freshmen and graduating seniors get priority in the registration process, helping ensure graduation in four years for those who declare majors early and plan a way to fit in all of the requirements. Grad students don't teach classes, and professors get high marks. "They are experienced, approachable, personal, insightful, helpful, and enthusiastic," says a sophomore. "The professors are my favorite thing about this school," adds a junior. Every year, students and faculty members organize three major symposia—one on international affairs, one on environmental affairs, and the other on gender studies.

Lewis & Clark tends to attract West Coasters seeking an emphasis on the liberal arts; it's also a haven for Easterners who see L&C's open and outdoorsy feel as the antithesis of the typical prep school or fancy suburban high-school scene. "Our students tend to be liberal," says a history major. "Hippy is a term that is often applied." Those who succeed are very independent, adds a junior: "So many students study abroad that often it is hard to make strong connections and keep them. People have to be flexible. Students are friendly, but do not tend to be highly sociable." The campus is 63 percent white; minorities account for 10 percent of the student body.

(Continued)
Expense: Pr $ $ $
Phi Beta Kappa: Yes
Applicants: 3,223
Accepted: 68%
Enrolled: 23%
Grad in 6 Years: 63%
Returning Freshmen: 83%
Academics: ✐ ✐ ✐
Social: ☎ ☎ ☎
Q of L: ★ ★ ★
Admissions: (503) 768-7040
Email Address:
admissions@lclark.edu

Strongest Programs:
International Affairs
Psychology
English
Biology

Lewis & Clark offers a Portfolio Path to admission, where students present a package representing their talents and interests and don't have to submit SAT or ACT scores as a reward.

Students pour their energies into social causes and community service. Antiwar protests were frequent on campus. "Everyone here is celebrated for what they bring," a senior says. "Very, very few people are not involved." The Center for Service and Work draws students to volunteer projects that aim to combat AIDS and homelessness, among other causes.

A residency requirement keeps students on campus their first two year; more than 60 percent live on campus, with the help of three new residence halls. Owing

"If a student wants to get a six pack, it just takes a little planning."

to the college's hilltop location, lucky dorm residents have views of Mount St. Helens, Mount Hood, or the Portland skyline—at least when it's not raining. Students involved in performing arts, foreign languages, outdoor pursuits, and other programs can live in theme wings. Dorms are comfortable and spacious: "Not five-star, but livable," says a sophomore. Despite L&C's location in a residential section of Portland, safety is a priority—residence halls have card-swipe entry systems and door alarms, and campus security has officers on duty twenty-four hours. Aside from the Fields Dining Room (a.k.a. the Airplane Hangar because of its high ceilings and width), students may eat at a student-run restaurant that also hosts study breaks, movie nights, and musical performances. "The food is edible and reasonably diverse," a senior says.

Fun-seekers at Lewis & Clark rely primarily on SOFA (Students Organized for Activities) for on-campus movies, contests, dances, and talent show. Yearly events include Casino Night in February, the Sunburn concert in the spring and the Homecoming dance in the fall. On the weekends, College Outdoors sponsors trips to Mount Hood (great skiing, about an hour distant) or the coastal beaches (an hour and a half). Seattle and Vancouver, B.C., three- and six-hours' drive, are favorite road trips, as are San Francisco and Las Vegas when there's more time. Despite the famous rains of the Pacific Northwest, the campus is officially dry; per Oregon law, no one under twenty-one may drink, except perhaps in a room with a closed door and a few friends. "If a student wants to get a six pack, it just takes a little planning," says one senior. The neighborhood immediately surrounding the college is pleasant, affluent suburbia, which means few stores, restaurants, or bars. The activity of downtown Portland—mostly on Hawthorne Boulevard in the southeast section, and in the Pearl District or on 23rd Street in the northwest quadrant—is fifteen minutes away on the city's public transit system or the campus shuttle service, the Pioneer Express.

As might be expected at a school in the outdoorsy Northwest, Lewis & Clark has excellent athletic facilities and a well-organized intramural program. The men's basketball team won the Northwest Conference in 2002 and the women's tennis team can brag about the individual conference champion in 2003. Men's football, men's and women's crew and women's track & field are also popular. Women can also now participate in varsity soccer.

Students at Lewis & Clark College enjoy a rather laid-back atmosphere. Many are outdoor enthusiasts who enjoy sports and are unafraid to champion social causes.

Like the school's namesakes, students are knowledge-seeking pioneers—ones who would have made Lewis and Clark, the explorers, proud.

A residency requirement keeps students on campus their first two year; more than 60 percent live on campus, with the help of three new residence halls.

Overlaps

University of Puget Sound, Willamette, Whitman, UC–Santa Cruz, University of Oregon

If You Apply To ➤ **Lewis & Clark:** Early action: Dec. 1. Regular admissions: Feb. 1. Financial aid: Mar. 1. Does not guarantee to meet demonstrated need. Campus interviews: recommended, evaluative. Alumni interviews: optional, informational. SATs or ACTs: required (except Portfolio Path). SAT IIs: optional. Accepts the Common Application and electronic applications. Essay question: significant person or experience; issue of local, national, or international concern; situation or experience that changed your values or opinion; character in a book to whom you can best relate.

Louisiana State University

110 Thomas Boyd Hall, Baton Rouge, LA 70803

In the state that invented Mardi Gras, students come to LSU for a great time and a good education. The latter can be had in business, engineering, and life science fields. Administrators are trying to make LSU a more serious place with higher admission standards and less underage drinking.

Whether it's the abundance of azaleas and Japanese magnolias, the smell of Cajun cuisine, the sororities' antebellum mansions, or the diehard football rivalry with Ole Miss, few schools evoke the spirit of the South like Louisiana State University. Students here enjoy tailgate parties, road trips to New Orleans, and festivals such as Groovin' on the Grounds—and somehow squeeze in classes, too.

LSU's campus includes more than 250 principal buildings on the main 650-acre plateau—most in the Italian Renaissance style, with tan stucco walls and red-tile roofs. They sit along the banks of the Mississippi River on the grounds of a former plantation. Lakes and huge oak trees diffuse the strong sun and help temper Louisiana's legendary humidity. "LSU is a special place because of its beauty and tradition. The large oaks and arches make this campus so unique," says a sophomore. Ever progressing, the life science building and Nicholson Hall, the physics building, were recently expanded.

The historic acceptance at LSU of New Orleans' theme "Laissez les bons temps roulez!" (Let the good times roll!) is shifting as administrators work overtime to make the school competitive. Formerly an open-admissions university for state residents, LSU has been tightening its standards, requiring all freshmen to have successfully completed 17.5 high school units in designated academic areas, including computer studies and a foreign language. For out-of-state applicants, grades and test scores are weighed equally. Students encounter a rigorous core curriculum, including 39 semester hours in six areas: English composition, analytical reasoning, arts, humanities, and the natural and social sciences.

> **"LSU is a special place because of its beauty and tradition."**

Students give high marks to LSU's music, honors, agriculture, French, design, theater, history, and geology departments, and note that while the sciences are solid, they're tough. Engineering and accounting are also highly regarded. And, as one of the nation's twenty-five sea-grant colleges (as well as a land-grant college), LSU's offerings in coastal studies and coastal ecology are notable as well. Students report varying levels of satisfaction with their profs. "I have received good instruction from professors in the Honors College, but have also had a few professors who have a difficult time relating the material to the students," says a freshman elementary education major. "I've had really great professors and some who seemed uninterested in the class," adds a junior finance student. Although some faculty members' preoccupation with research can be annoying, most are accessible to undergraduates. Indeed, contact with professors here is said to be better than average, and freshmen are often taught by full professors. The academic and career counseling programs generally get good reviews.

Nearly nine out of ten LSU Tigers are Louisiana residents, but don't try to paint them with the stereotypical Southern conservative brush. "The students here are very diverse. Everyone can find a group they can fit in with," says a dietetics major. Whites comprise 80 percent of the student body, African-Americans 10 percent, Asian-Americans 3 percent, and Hispanics 2 percent. Nearly twenty-five hundred

Website: www.lsu.edu
Location: Urban
Total Enrollment: 32,228
Undergraduates: 26,660
Male/Female: 47/53
ACT Range: 22–26
Financial Aid: 27%
Expense: Pub $ $
Phi Beta Kappa: Yes
Applicants: 10,376
Accepted: 77%
Enrolled: 66%
Grad in 6 Years: 58%
Returning Freshmen: 84.2%
Academics: ✍ ✍
Social: 🐿 🐿 🐿 🐿
Q of L: ★ ★ ★
Admissions: (225) 578-1175
Email Address:
  admissions@lsu.edu

Strongest Programs:
Chemical Engineering
Physics
Astronomy
English
Animal Science
Plant Biology
French Studies

merit scholarships are available to qualified students and standout athletes can vie for 460 athletic awards in 18 sports.

Housing is available to all students who apply, but just 22 percent of students live in campus residences. Upperclassmen tend to prefer off-campus housing. The dorms get mixed reviews, and students say the process of getting a room can be frustrating. All dorms are single-sex with visiting hours, and students report that rooms fill up quickly, so it's important to apply early. Students praise the diversity of the cafeteria food, but say some of it is overpriced. Campus security, with seventy full-time officers, is visible and improving, students say. Lighting has become an issue, but it is being addressed. "I feel very safe. There are emergency boxes every-where," a student says. The school has a nighttime transit system so students don't have to walk alone.

Though the administration is working hard to improve academic standards, make no mistake about it: LSU offers one of the wildest party atmospheres around. "Social life is a big part of LSU," a freshman says. One way to ensure a nonstop campus social life is to join one of the Greek organizations that draw 10 percent of the men and 16 percent of the women. The campus is officially dry, but students say the school can only do so much to stop underage drinking. "During football games, alcohol is very

"There are also rodeos, live bands, and other activities that make LSU unique."

prevalent on the campus and it's easy for underage people to drink since it's every-where," says a freshman. "I also often see empty alcohol containers on the ground, so there is alcohol on campus." Students report drinking off campus is also easy. The high number of student groups helps students find their niche in the large university. The student union offers a wide variety of events, including movies, plays, concerts, fashion shows, lectures, and banquets. "There are also rodeos, live bands, and other activities that make LSU unique," a sophomore says. Homecoming is one of the year's biggest events, and Mardi Gras is always a popular draw.

While Tiger football is king in Baton Rouge, LSU athletes have also earned their laurels in men's indoor and outdoor track, women's indoor track and women's soft-ball in recent years. When the Tigers are on the road, the campus tends to empty out as students follow the team or find their fun elsewhere, often to Oxford, Missis-sippi (home of Ole Miss), or South Bend, Indiana (Notre Dame). Students are pleased with life in Baton Rouge, and one junior says, "I love it so much, I plan to stay here after graduation!" As the state capital, the city offers numerous chances to get involved in politics or volunteer programs.

LSU offers a range of academic opportunities along with a traditional Southern feel. "And the school spirit is awesome!" says a freshman Tiger. No one is forced to spend their years at LSU shuttling between keg parties and the stadium, but it can be hard to resist the temptations of the Big Easy. The trees and traditions date back more than a hundred years, but the school is looking ahead—raising admissions standards and striving for smaller classes and more funding.

Overlaps

University of South-western Louisiana, Tulane, Loyola (LA), Southeastern Louisiana, Louisiana Tech

If You Apply To ➢

LSU: Rolling admissions. Financial aid: Nov. 15. Does not guarantee to meet demonstrated need. Campus interviews: optional, informational. No alumni interviews. SATs or ACTs: required. No SAT IIs. Accepts elec-tronic applications. No essay question.

Loyola University New Orleans

6363 St. Charles Ave., Box 89, New Orleans, LA 70118

There are at least four Loyolas in the nation, but only one where you can go to Mardi Gras and still get up in time for class. New Orleans is an ideal setting for this Roman Catholic university with strengths in business and the arts. More progressive than any other Deep South location.

Loyola University students lay claim to the best that New Orleans has to offer while basking in the attention of this community-focused liberal arts school. Its "peaceful, beautiful campus" provides a respite from the wild side of the Big Easy—while keeping the clubs and bars of the French Quarter just a historic streetcar ride away. Loyola's strong programs draw a wide range of students. "We take what is presented to us in the academic setting very seriously, but we know when to let go and have a good time as well," says one senior.

The school's attractive and well-kept twenty-acre main campus, in the University section of Uptown New Orleans, mixes Tudor, Gothic, and modern structures. It overlooks acres of Audubon Park and, beyond, the mighty Mississippi River. Two blocks up St. Charles Avenue, Loyola's Broadway campus has an additional four acres, home to the Loyola School of Law, the Twomey Center for Peace through Justice, the visual arts department, and a residence hall. The J. Edgar and Louise S. Monroe Library houses 500,000 volumes, a center for community literacy, an art gallery, two multimedia classrooms, and Internet connections for laptops every 7.5 feet.

> "We are sitting in the birthplace of jazz, and it shows."

Loyola offers comprehensive undergraduate degree programs in the College of Arts and Sciences. The communications major wins points with students; Loyola once owned the only TV and radio stations in New Orleans. "Every year, the communications department has winning advertising and public relations teams, and the newspaper constantly wins awards," according to one student. Also in demand is the international business program in the College of Business Administration and virtually any major in the College of Music. "We are sitting in the birthplace of jazz, and it shows," says a junior. A minor in entrepreneurship has been added in the business administration college, and a major and minor in forensic science are now part of the chemistry department.

There are no teaching assistants, and students love that most of their professors have doctorates. "Teachers are well prepared for class and always bring new and helpful ideas into the classroom," says one senior. Students take twenty-four credits of introductory courses and twenty-four more of advanced courses in English, history, math, philosophy, religious studies, social sciences, natural science, and humanities/arts. The library has won national acclaim, but Loyola students are still not addicted to it. "People are serious about their academics but it's obvious that here in New Orleans, life doesn't just revolve around class," says a communications student. First-year students participate in a three-day orientation and can take advantage of more than twenty-two learning communities designed around various majors. A new Executive Mentoring program lets freshman business students meet regularly with local business leaders to discuss their career and personal development. Loyolans also benefit from the New Orleans Consortium, with cross-registration and library access at other schools in the area. Study abroad programs take students to Belgium, Ireland, Mexico, France, Spain, London, Berlin, and China, and a new Office of International Programs supports students with wanderlust.

Website: www.loyno.edu
Location: Urban
Total Enrollment: 5,562
Undergraduates: 3,772
Male/Female: 36/64
SAT Ranges: V 540–650
 M 520–620
ACT Range: 23–28
Financial Aid: 54%
Expense: Pr $ $ $
Phi Beta Kappa: No
Applicants: 3,603
Accepted: 68%
Enrolled: 36%
Grad in 6 Years: 60%
Returning Freshmen: 82%
Academics: ✑ ✑ ✑
Social: ☎ ☎ ☎
Q of L: ★ ★ ★
Admissions: (800) 4-LOYOLA
Email Address:
 admit@loyno.edu

Strongest Programs:
Music Therapy
Music Business
Finance
International Business
Communications
English/Creative Writing
Psychology
Environmental Studies

Forty-six percent of Loyola students are Louisiana natives—historically, they have made up two-thirds of the school—and many of the remaining students are from the Southeast. Religion—specifically Roman Catholicism—has a significant influence on campus. Daily mass is voluntary, but many students attend. Hispanics constitute 10 percent of the student body, African-Americans 11 percent, and Asian-Americans 4 percent. Recent hot-button issues at Loyola have included the death penalty, gay rights, and that perennial student gripe, campus parking. Loyola awards nearly twenty-five hundred merit scholarships each year, ranging from $2,000 to full tuition, but there are no athletic scholarships.

Most Loyola students commute from home or off-campus apartments; 78 percent of first-years and 38 percent of the total undergrad population live on campus.

"We live in New Orleans. They can't be too strict."

The school has renovated two residence halls and recently opened its first substance-free hall. The rooms are "comfy," but it can be hard for sophomores to find space on campus, some students say. As for safety, always an issue in a big city, one public relations major says, "campus is one of the safest spots in New Orleans." Campus security officers patrol on foot, by bike, and in golf carts, SUVs, and mini-vans.

Loyola fields baseball and basketball teams in the Gulf Coast Athletic Conference, NAIA Division II. Basketball, men's flag football (no real pigskins at Loyola), and women's volleyball are popular pastimes. The women's volleyball has competed in the NAIA nationals the past two years, and men's cross country won the conference title in the same years.

Aside from sweating on the field, students volunteer their sweat equity with the Loyola University Community Action Program, a coalition of eleven organizations that provides community service opportunities. With the help of a new service learning office, about five hundred students make service learning part of their studies. Fraternities and sororities are rarities at Jesuit schools, but are popular at Loyola, with 24 percent of the men and 19 percent of women choosing to belong. Major campus-wide social events include the annual Riverboat Dance, Swamp Stomp, Loyolapalooza, and Loup Garou, a concert featuring big-name bands. February brings Mardi Gras, of course—the school shuts down that week. As for underage drinking, Louisiana law requires that you be at least 21 to buy alcohol, but only 18 to consume it in a private residence. While Loyola maintains that dorms are private residences, the school has also established a Coalition to Reduce Underage Drinking. But as one student says: "We live in New Orleans. They can't be too strict."

Students at Loyola know how to *"Laissez les bons temps roulez,"* French for "Let the good times roll." Whether they're working closely with caring professors or relaxing with friends amid Bourbon Street's boundless energy, students are satisfied with their choice. "Loyola's tight-knit atmosphere is very conducive to learning and growing," says a junior. "Its size, tradition, and ideals set a balance that I don't think I could find elsewhere."

Overlaps

Tulane, University of Texas–Austin, Boston University, Fordham, NYU

If You Apply To ➤

Loyola: Rolling admissions. Financial aid: Mar. 1. Housing: May 1. Does not guarantee to meet demonstrated need. Campus interviews: recommended, informational. Alumni interviews: optional, informational. Audition required for admission to the College of Music and the Department of Drama and Speech. Portfolio required for admission to the Visual Arts Program. SATs or ACTs: required. SAT IIs: optional (writing is for placement only). Accepts the Common Application and electronic applications. Essay question: discuss an "assumed truth" that you now question; what obstacles face your generation; topic of your choice.

Macalester College

UN Secretary General Kofi Annan, '61, typifies one of Mac's hallmarks: an internationalist view of the world. Carleton has a slightly bigger national reputation, but Mac has St. Paul, a progressive capital city. Mac is the only leading Midwestern liberal arts college in an urban setting.

Macalester College might have been plucked from San Francisco's Haight-Ashbury district and set down in the Great Plains. The school's "activist culture" seems more appropriate to the wild west of the 1960s than the Midwest in the twenty-first century, but as the saying goes, if it ain't broke, don't fix it. Students here get riled up over all sorts of issues with local, national, or international import—from sweatshops and fair trade to bombing Iraq and gay rights. But they reserve their loudest shouts of protest for Mac's top brass, who refuse to include them in decisions affecting campus life, such as which faculty get tenure. With its Scottish roots and international focus, Mac is worth a look—if you can brave the bitter winters.

Macalester is located in a friendly, family-oriented neighborhood in St. Paul, Minnesota, one mile from the Mississippi River, which divides St. Paul from Minneapolis. The campus is a block from Summit Avenue, a tree-lined street with the longest, best-preserved stretch of Victorian homes in the nation. The self-contained, 53-acre campus is arranged around 115-year-old Old Main, a splendid Victorian structure listed on the National Register of Historic Places. The unifying theme is redbrick, the better to set off the octagonal Weyerhauser Chapel, constructed of black glass. In the past decade, Mac has spent more than $98 million to improve campus facilities, including $18.5 million on the Campus Center, which opened in 2001. The center has 70,000 square feet of space for students to meet, work, and socialize, plus dining facilities with cuisine from around the world. The 41,500-square-foot Kagin Commons, built at a cost of $7.7 million, opened in 2002.

> "We are always pushed to the maximum of our abilities, yet the environment is laid back and encouraging."

Mac's general requirements include two courses in social sciences and two in natural sciences and math, plus one to two courses in fine arts and in humanities, and foreign-language proficiency. Two courses must address cultural diversity, in the U.S. and internationally. Every student also completes a capstone experience, such as an independent research project, performance, artistic work, or senior thesis. Mac's academic strengths include economics, religious studies, chemistry, and biology; the school's impressive science facilities include an observatory, an animal operant chamber, and labs for electronic instrumentation and laser spectroscopy. Administrators say weaker programs include Russian, linguistics, sociology, and urban studies.

Mac emphasizes collaboration and working together to handle the challenging workload, and students say most pressure to do well comes from within. "We are always pushed to the maximum of our abilities, yet the environment is laid back and encouraging," says a Japan studies major. "It is impossible to go here and not be intellectually fulfilled," agrees a

> "Mac students are all left-leaning—even the Republicans."

political science major. "The courses are always turning out to be tougher than I think they are going to be." Teaching is paramount, with professors often having students over for dinner or taking their students for drinks at a local watering hole.

Website: www.macalester.edu
Location: City outskirts
Total Enrollment: 1,840
Undergraduates: 1,840
Male/Female: 42/58
SAT Ranges: V 630–730
 M 620–710
ACT Range: 27–31
Financial Aid: 67%
Expense: Pr $ $ $
Phi Beta Kappa: Yes
Applicants: 3,713
Accepted: 44%
Enrolled: 27%
Grad in 6 Years: 82%
Returning Freshmen: 93%
Academics: ✍ ✍ ✍ ✍ ½
Social: ☎ ☎ ☎
Q of L: ★ ★ ★ ★
Admissions: (651) 696-6357
Email Address:
 admissions@macalester.edu

Strongest Programs:
Economics
Religious Studies
Chemistry
Biology

In the past decade, Mac has spent more than $98 million to improve campus facilities, including $18.5 million on the Campus Center, which opened in 2001. The center has 70,000 square feet of space for students to meet, work, and socialize, plus dining facilities with cuisine from around the world.

Macalester is the alma mater of UN Secretary General Kofi Annan, Class of 1961.

The Twin Cities provide ample internship opportunities, with more than 60 percent of students working part-time for pay or academic credit at a local business, law firm, hospital, financial institution, governmental unit or non profit agency.

"Few students regularly skip class," one student says. "You virtually never have to take a class with an adjunct professor, though I've found them to be especially sprightly." More than one hundred students do stipend-supported research with Mac professors each summer, and since a number of faculty members play intramurals, students may find professors dishing off passes on the basketball court. Fifty-three percent of students participate in study abroad, through approved independent programs or the Associated Colleges of the Midwest.* Mac students may also cross-register at five other Twin Cities colleges, or select cooperative-degree programs in engineering, nursing, and architecture with larger Midwestern schools.

Nineteen percent of Macalester students hail from Minnesota, and the rest come from every state, the District of Columbia, and seventy-eight other countries—eighty-eight if dual citizens and permanent residents are double-counted.

"Off-campus living is one of the best reasons to come here."

Despite Mac's small size, the student body is 3 percent African-American, 3 percent Hispanic, and 5 percent Asian-American—and a whopping 17 percent of the student body is international. Political debate is lively, and "race, gender, and Earth consciousness are always hot-button issues," says a political science major. "Mac students are all left-leaning—even the Republicans." Merit scholarships worth up to $10,000 each are available to brainy types; there are no athletic scholarships.

While Mac students may harbor radical political and social viewpoints, they live in traditional residences, with double rooms for the first two years, when they're required to live on campus, and suites for upperclassmen. Single-sex floors are guaranteed to those who want them; many students have single rooms, and some live in language houses. Residents of the kosher house prepare their own meals, while the opening of the new Campus Center has vastly improved chow elsewhere on campus. Sixty-six percent of students remain in college-owned digs, and more say they'd stay, if only they could get rooms. Still, "off-campus living is one of the best reasons to come here," says a senior. Nearby neighborhoods are welcoming to students, with low-cost houses and apartments, and families eager to have them move in.

Without Greek organizations and given the proximity of a major metropolitan area ("only a dollar bus ride away"), Mac's on-campus social life "is wanting," one student says. "Many students cling to their first-year friends until they graduate."

"Students at Mac are brightly skeptical about everything in the world—this is their distinguishing trait."

Thank goodness, then, for the close proximity of Minneapolis and St. Paul, with their bookstores, coffee shops, restaurants, bars, and movie theaters, plus dance and jazz clubs and professional sports teams. The Twin Cities also provide ample internship opportunities, with more than 60 percent of students working part-time for pay or academic credit at a local business, law firm, hospital, financial institution, governmental unit or nonprofit agency. The Mall of America is also nearby, though Mac students tend to tire of it quickly, and at least one warns that "it is impossible to get anywhere without a car—the public transportation in the Twin Cities is deficient." For those with wheels, the best road trips include Chicago; Madison, Wisconsin; and Duluth and Bemidji, Minnesota, "to see Babe the Blue Ox," reports a senior.

Popular events include Spring Fest and the annual Brain Bowl football game against in-state rival Carleton, "the only school we can't chant 'We are smarter than you!' to," says a communications major. Although men's and women's soccer recently brought home conference championships, joining the debate team in the winner's circle, the math and computer programming teams are the ones typically competing internationally. "Mac athletics are all about lazy fun in the sun," quips one student, noting that popular club sports include ice hockey, fencing, water polo, crew, and ultimate Frisbee.

Macalester students are an open-minded, friendly bunch, more politically and socially progressive than their peers at similar institutions. The school provides an atmosphere of high-powered scholarship and success, pairing academic rigor with global perspective. As the school's story travels, the skill and diversity of the student body is rising. Still, one student says, one thing hasn't changed: "Students at Mac are brightly skeptical about everything in the world—this is their distinguishing trait."

> **Overlaps**
>
> **Carleton, Grinnell, University of Chicago, Oberlin, Brown**

If You Apply To ➤ **Macalester:** Early decision: Nov. 15, Jan. 15. Regular admissions: Jan. 15. Financial aid: Feb. 8. Guarantees to meet demonstrated need. Campus interviews: recommended, evaluative. Alumni interviews: optional, evaluative. SATs or ACTs: required. SAT IIs: optional. Accepts the Common Application and electronic applications. Essay question: why Macalester—what you can add to the community; and an original piece of written work, on an experience, philosophy or significant event, or a topic of your choice.

University of Maine–Orono

Orono, ME 04469

A sleeper choice for out-of-staters amid better-known public universities such as UMass, UNH, and UVM. Not coincidentally, Maine is the least expensive of the four. A popular marine sciences program flourishes here, as do forestry and a range of preprofessional programs.

Maine is known for its hardy residents, whose insistence on braving harsh winters and the state's rugged wilderness has helped create community in hamlets like Freeport and Bar Harbor. Students find much of the same close-knit feeling at UMaine–Orono, where nearly nine thousand undergraduates help themselves to a range of strong academic programs at a reasonable cost. UMaine is not only the state's only land-grant university, it's also the only sea-grant as well, and attracts top students to its marine sciences program. UMaine has become more academically competitive over the past several years. "The emphasis has been on and will continue to be on development of the whole person," says a psychology major.

Situated on an island between the Stillwater and Penobscot rivers, UMaine's 660-acre campus centers on a large, tree-shaded grass mall. Architectural themes at this flagship of the state university system range from English academic to contemporary. Edith Patch Residence Hall is brand new, as well as Colvin Honors Center. The science building, Auburn Hall, has been renovated.

UMaine's five undergraduate colleges include education and human development; business, public policy, and health; engineering; liberal arts and sciences; and natural sciences, forestry, and agriculture. The newly formed Honors College, which has arisen out of one of the oldest honors programs in the nation, admits about two hundred students with SAT scores of 1200 or higher. Specific requirements vary from college to college, though all students must demonstrate writing proficiency and take two physical or biological science courses, eighteen credits in human value and social context, six credits in math (including statistics and computer science), and at least one ethics course. A capstone experience in the major is also mandatory.

The engineering programs are widely viewed as the most demanding on campus. Other best bets include forestry and agriculture, Canadian studies and marine

Website: www.umaine.edu
Location: Rural
Total Enrollment: 11,135
Undergraduates: 8,817
Male/Female: 45/55
SAT Ranges: V 480–590
  M 490–610
ACT Range: 20–26
Financial Aid: 60%
Expense: Pub $ $ $
Phi Beta Kappa: Yes
Applicants: 5,249
Accepted: 79%
Enrolled: 43%
Grad in 6 Years: 54%
Returning Freshmen: 79%
Academics: ✍ ✍
Social: ☎ ☎ ☎ ☎
Q of L: ★ ★ ★
Admissions: (207) 581-1561
Email Address:
  um-admit@umaine.edu

science. Majors in information systems engineering and surveying engineering technology have been added to the curriculum. The interdisciplinary Institute for Quaternary Studies collaborates with other research centers around the world in focusing on the Quaternary period, a time of glacial and interglacial cycles leading up to the present.

The university library, one of the state's finest, is the regional depository for American and Canadian government documents, and houses some of alumnus Stephen King's papers. Former U.S. Senator William S. Cohen, a UMaine faculty member before he became defense secretary in the Clinton administration, donated his personal papers to the university as well. The papers, which chronicle Cohen's twenty-four-year congressional career, will be used to develop a nonpartisan center on international policy and commerce focused on teaching, research, and public service, and named in Cohen's honor. They are also available to scholars interested in Cohen's career.

"The emphasis has been on and will continue to be on development of the whole person."

Students don't expect long lines at registration, which can be done over the phone, online, or with their departments, and report that graduating in four years is virtually certain, unless you pursue a double major or choose the engineering or music programs. "Engineering requires 130 credits to graduate, which is sixteen or seventeen a semester (average load is fifteen per semester), but it can be done in four years," a student says. "People who change majors late often need to stay an extra semester or year." The Academic and Career Exploration program lets students work with professionals in different areas before declaring their degree choices. "The school is becoming more competitive," a freshman says. "The classes are rigorous and require the student to work hard." Students report that the quality of teaching is high.

Outside the classroom, internships and co-ops are available in most fields, and there's a Semester-by-the-Sea and a Lobster Institute for nautical types. Juniors who want a reprieve from Maine's often brutal winters can head for Brazil, while the heartier types choose Canada, Scandinavia, and Ireland. Most students, however, are immune to the weather, since 84 percent are from Maine and many of the rest hail from other parts of New England. The campus is 93 percent white but viewpoints are diverse, students say. "It's a fairly liberal campus," a senior says. "People are respectful of differing opinions." Merit scholarships offer $500 to $13,410 a year for qualified students, and there are 193 athletic awards.

Big winter events are the "bed sled" race, in which students race beds down a campus hill, and the annual carnival, featuring a school-wide snow-sculpting competition.

Forty-three percent of UMaine students live off campus in Orono, nearby Bangor, or the sparsely populated area in between. Dorms are co-ed; some have gyms, computer labs, or apartment-style suites. "Dorms are a great way to meet new people," a business major says. "They are comfortable and, for the most part, well maintained." Some housing or wings are set aside for specific majors. Dining hall food is pretty good, although one student says it's "always the same week after week. It needs to be more mixed up." Greeks can eat in their chapter houses.

"The school is becoming more competitive."

Despite UMaine's relatively isolated location, the campus pulses with social life; nearly 250 student organizations plan plays, carnival nights, concerts, and comedy hours. Partiers find their niche off campus, at bars, clubs, and house parties. Big winter events are the "bed sled" race, in which students race beds down a campus hill, and the annual carnival, featuring a school-wide snow-sculpting competition. Come spring, students go all out for April's Bumstock Weekend, a three-day event featuring bands playing outdoors from dawn till dusk.

The newly formed Honors College, which has arisen out of one of the oldest honors programs in the nation, admits about two hundred students with SAT scores of 1200 or higher.

The mid-sized town of Orono—described by one senior as a "quiet little college town"—offers a few bars, a theater, and some other hangouts. Buses to Bangor, a fair-sized city ten minutes away, run every fifteen to twenty minutes. A car is helpful, although there are gripes about parking. UMaine students tend to be outdoor enthusiasts, and popular road trips include Acadia National Park, skiing at Sugarloaf USA, L.L. Bean's twenty-four-hour store in Freeport, and the real-life Mt. Katahdin, which appears on Bean's logo. More urban types enjoy Bar Harbor, Boston, or Montreal, just four hours away (and with a lower drinking age and cheaper drinks).

Hockey reigns here, especially when played against New Hampshire, Boston University, or Boston College, and the Black Bears are perennial champions. The football brought home the Atlantic 10 championship two years in a row, and baseball claims the America East championship. Intramurals cover a range of sports from swimming and wrestling to hoopball (golf with a basketball) and broomball (ice hockey with a dodgeball and a broom, played with shoes instead of skates).

UMaine is a big school with a small-school atmosphere. Combine the state's natural beauty with an increased emphasis on top-quality facilities and increased student-faculty interaction, and it's no surprise that this campus draws more diehard "Maine-iaks" each year.

If You Apply To ➤	**Maine:** Rolling admissions. Financial aid: Mar. 1. Meets demonstrated need of 32%. Campus interviews: optional, informational. No alumni interviews. SATs or ACTs: required. Accepts Common Application and electronic applications. Essay question: personal statement on academic goals and objectives or essay of student's choice.

Manhattanville College

2900 Purchase Street, Purchase, NY 10577

Though co-ed for more than thirty years, Manhattanville is still almost 70 percent female. Strong programs include art, education, and psychology. Among the few small colleges in the NYC area, Manhattanville is a quick train ride from the city. Portfolio system emphasizes competency rather than rote learning.

Manhattanville sees its mission as "educating students to become ethically and socially responsible leaders for the global community." The Portfolio System, Manhattanville's distinct approach to undergraduate education, requires students to create a body of work reflecting their entire college career. Students must craft a freshman assessment essay, a study plan and program evaluation, specific examples of work in writing and research, and a resume. The Portfolio System, however, is only one way Manhattanville encourages individuality and personal growth. Personal attention is another. "You can go in and have a Diet Pepsi with the president," says one senior. "You're not just a number."

Manhattanville College, which began as a Roman Catholic academy for girls on Houston Street in New York City, pulled up stakes in the 1950s for a 125-acre estate in Purchase, New York. Today, the campus is located in wealthy Westchester County, near the town of White Plains—home to several major corporations but just twenty-eight miles from the excitement of the Big Apple. The focal point of the campus, which was designed by Central Park architect Frederick Law Olmsted, is Reid Hall, a nineteenth-century replica of a Norman castle.

"Everyone knows your name."

Manhattanville's distribution requirements include courses in five areas: humanities, social sciences, fine arts, mathematics and sciences, and languages. Students

Website: www.mville.edu
Location: Suburban
Total Enrollment: 2,443
Undergraduates: 1,400
Male/Female: 31/69
SAT Ranges: V 530–780
   M 530–720
ACT Range: 20–24
Financial Aid: 70%
Expense: Pr $ $ $
Phi Beta Kappa: No
Applicants: 2,105
Accepted: 61%
Enrolled: 32%
Grad in 6 Years: 53%
Returning Freshmen: 78%
Academics: ✎ ✎ ✎
Social: ☎ ☎ ☎

(Continued)

Q of L: ★★★
Admissions: (800) 328-4553
Email Address:
admissions@mville.edu

Strongest Programs:
Management
Art
Psychology
Education

must demonstrate English writing competency as well. Freshmen complete the Preceptorial, a two-semester introduction to college-level work, as well as a library and information studies course. Manhattanville's strongest offerings include art and design (enhanced by the proximity of New York City's many museums and galleries), music, and education, while economics and psychology are also popular. M-ville's School of Education, which offers two five-year masters programs, boasts a near-perfect passage rate for the New York State Teaching Exam. The languages—French, Spanish, Asian studies, and classics—attract the fewest majors. Students, who used to avoid math and science because of the difficulty of the classes and the age of some labs, can now enjoy facilities that are independently ranked among the top one hundred wired colleges in the country. Students may also opt to design their own major. Career Services, which offers internship opportunities at over 350 locations in the New York metro area and beyond, is "phenomenal," securing placements at places such as MTV, Metropolitan Museum of Art, Fox News, U.S. Senate offices, MasterCard, Dedicated Records, PepsiCo, and the Westchester County Board of Legislators. The school has recently reestablished the physics program and established new minors in communication and social justice.

The academic climate at Manhattanville is fairly laid back, "yet not to the point where no one is really serious about classes," says a sophomore. The low student/faculty ratio and the quality of teaching get high marks. More than 90 percent of freshmen classes have twenty-five or fewer students. Perhaps that's why "everyone knows your name," according to an English/history major. The Board of Trustee's scholarships offer qualified students an

"Purchase is not a college town at all, but we are close to NYC."

Honors Preceptorial. An Honors Seminar and honors programs within majors are also available. The college also offers dual degree programs with New York Medical College (M.S. in physical therapy or M.S. in speech language pathology) and Polytechnic University (M.S. in computer science or M.S. in information technology). The college has exchange programs with Mills College and with American University's World Capitals Program, plus study abroad options in England, France, Germany, Ireland, Italy, Japan, Mexico, and Spain.

Forty-seven countries and thirty-two states are represented by Manhattanville's student body. Females outnumber males by a ratio of two to one. Twenty-nine percent of undergraduates come from outside of New York, while 13 percent come from overseas. Hispanics comprise the largest minority group at 15 percent, followed by African-Americans at 6 percent and Asian-Americans at 3 percent. The college does not guarantee to meet the need of every admit, but there are nearly one thousand merit scholarships available, ranging from $2,000 to $10,000.

Sixty-eight percent of Manhattanville's students live on campus in one of four dorms, which have lounges, communal kitchens, laundry rooms, cable TV, and Internet access. Freshmen are assigned rooms that are "quite comfortable" according to a first-year art major, while upperclassmen enter a lottery—and complain they never get what they want. Campus dwellers can choose fifteen- or nineteen-meal-a-week plans, and can also use their meal cards at Cafe de Ville (a deli-type eatery), the convenience store, and vending machines. Students can also order "room service" three times a semester. The dining hall has been renovated and offers fresh-baked goods and a well-stocked salad bar.

Manhattanville's hometown, Purchase, "is not a college town at all, but we are close to NYC," says a senior. With increasing numbers of male students enrolling, things seem to be picking up, and with no fraternities or sororities, off-campus parties are usually open to all. The student programming board is working to improve the social life, with weekend events such as dinners, formals in the castle, parties, comedy and talent shows, plays, and concerts. The student center has a movie theater.

"You can go in and have a Diet Pepsi with the president," says one senior. "You're not just a number."

Thirty student-run organizations help to fulfill the cultural, intellectual, and social interests of the student body, but off-campus bars still draw many students—whether of age or not. "It's really boring because so many kids leave on weekends," one student says. "There's hardly any parties, so if you want to study, go here." On-campus alcohol policies are said to be strict. "We don't really serve alcohol often on campus," says a political science major. "But of course, kids still drink." Road trips include Rye Beach in the warmer months and upstate New York or Vermont for skiing in the winter. The college offers a free van service that runs into NYC, and a new bus service takes students to nearby outlets

"There's hardly any parties, so if you want to study, go here."

with movies, theaters, videos, bowling, billiards, restaurants, clubs, and shopping. Every spring, students look forward to Quad Jam, "an all-day, all-night concert and carnival and party." There's a Fall Jam and midnight brunches during finals served by faculty and staff.

Manhattanville's president has invested heavily in athletics—especially men's and women's hockey and men's basketball—as a way of making the school better known and attracting more males. It now offers eighteen NCAA Division III sports. In just their second year, the women's ice hockey team was ranked fifth in the nation. Women's tennis, volleyball, and softball are solid, and men's soccer, ice hockey, lacrosse, golf, and baseball are also successful. In 2000, the men's tennis team won the Skyline Conference championship. Intramurals sometimes draw flak because of organizational problems, but overall, students enjoy them. Weekend warriors and letter-winners alike applaud the college's gym, fitness center, swimming pool, tennis courts, and athletic fields.

Manhattanville's size can be both an asset and an annoyance, say students. The familial atmosphere can get claustrophobic at times, but for those wishing to be part of a close but growing community, Manhattanville may be worth a look.

Overlaps

Fordham, NYU, Manhattan, Iona, Hofstra

If You Apply To ➤

Manhattanville: Early decision: Dec. 1. Rolling admissions, financial aid: Mar. 1. Housing: July 1. Meets demonstrated need of 39%. Campus interviews: recommended, informational. Alumni interviews: optional, informational. SATs or ACTs: required. SAT IIs: optional. Accepts the Common Application and electronic application. No essay question.

Marlboro College

Marlboro, VT 05344

Marlboro is a hilltop home to several hundred nonconformist souls. Each develops a plan of concentration that culminates in a senior project. One of the few colleges in the country that is governed in town-meeting style where student votes carry equal weight with those of the faculty.

Marlboro College is only a half-century old, but already the college is known far and wide as an innovator in liberal arts education. It was founded on the principles of independent and in-depth study just after World War II, when returning GIs renovated an old barn as the college's first building while living in Quonset huts. And today's Marlboro students are just as trail-blazing; they prepare for the next century by digging into self-developed Plans of Concentration, including one-on-one tutorials and a thesis or project judged by visiting outside examiners from "the best

Website: www.marlboro.edu
Location: Rural
Total Enrollment: 380
Undergraduates: 290
Male/Female: 41/59

(Continued)

SAT Ranges: V 580–680

  M 500–620

Financial Aid: 95%

Expense: Pr $ $

Phi Beta Kappa: No

Applicants: 308

Accepted: 80%

Enrolled: 40%

Grad in 6 Years: 40%

Returning Freshmen: 78%

Academics: ✐ ✐ ✐

Social: ☎ ☎ ☎

Q of L: ★ ★ ★ ★

Admissions: (800) 343-0049

Email Address:

  admissions@marlboro.edu

Strongest Programs:

World Studies

Writing and Literature

Environmental Studies/Biology

Sociology

History

Marlboro is its own little world, where students enter as novices and leave as pros.

Eastern colleges and universities." With three hundred students and thirty-eight faculty members, Marlboro is its own little world, where students enter as novices and leave as pros.

Positioned atop a small mountain, surrounded by maples and pines, and with a gorgeous view of southern Vermont, Marlboro's physical beauty is striking. Buildings are adapted from barns, sheds, and houses that stood on three old farms that today make up the 350-acre campus. Among the renovated structures, many with

"Everything at Marlboro screams 'interactive learning.'"

passive solar heating, are nine dormitories, a library, a science building, art studios and music practice rooms, a 350-seat theater, and a campus center. Above the athletic field is the college's astronomical observatory. The school recently completed a new art gallery and studio, photography lab, and sculpture studio, and it is working with a professor of architecture from Yale to develop a campus planning model.

While some schools see growth as a sign of their success, Marlboro intends to remain one of the nation's smallest liberal arts institutions. Administrators believe that the size stimulates dynamic relationships between students and faculty, making learning happen both inside and outside the classroom. This isn't a place where students can fade into the background: the institution relies on everyone to share their talents and skills. The same philosophy will apply to the college's Graduate Center; its first programs—a master of arts in teaching with Internet technologies and a master of science in Internet strategy management—are as innovative as the college's heritage.

The cornerstone of an undergraduate Marlboro education is the Plan of Concentration, which each student develops independently. Juniors and seniors "on plan" take most coursework in one-on-one tutorials with the faculty sponsors. Seniors present their thesis or project to their sponsors, who are backed up by outside examiners, experts in the student's field unaffiliated with the college. The administration boasts that by bringing in these outsiders for two- to three-hour oral examinations of its seniors, Marlboro has created its own accountability system, ensuring that neither students nor faculty at this isolated institution are cut off from the most current academic thinking. Faculty members often find the exams as stressful as the students, as it means their teaching is being judged by outsiders. The only other requirement is the Clear Writing course, usually completed freshman year. Marlboro's flexibility should not be confused with academic flabbiness, though. Grades are an integral part of the evaluation process, professors are stingy with As, and most students work hard.

Marlboro offers solid instruction in literature, writing, environmental science, sociology, psychology, and theater. Administrators and students alike praise the World Studies program, which provides an eight-month professional internship and/or study experience abroad. Music and math are said to be weaker, and since one professor can constitute an entire discipline at Marlboro because of the college's small size, a personality conflict may mean problems with a whole department. Even that can be remedied, though; in most years, students can choose among 250 courses and more than six hundred tutorials. Only six had more than twenty students. Students give most profs high marks and appreciate the low student/teacher ratio: "Everything at Marlboro screams 'interactive learning,'" says one student.

In the old independent Yankee spirit, Marlboro's library operates on the honor system, where students sign out their own books twenty-four hours a day. It is the same for the computer center, science, and humanities buildings. The school has only one security guard. "I feel really safe here," says one freshman. "Everyone is out at night and nobody's worried about assault—except maybe by bears." Indeed, the college operates on a New England town-meeting style of government involving students, faculty, staff, and their spouses in every aspect of policymaking. Students can veto the faculty members on hiring and retention decisions, and it takes a two-thirds vote of the faculty to override them.

Clearly, 1960s-era liberalism is still the dominant political tone on this campus. A big issue these days is parking: "Should students be able to park on campus, or are cars too hideously ugly to be seen at Marlboro?" asks a psychology major. Minority enrollment continues to be low (4 percent), in spite of the administration's program to recruit and support poor rural Vermonters. The college offers fifty merit scholarships of up to $5,000 every year, but no athletic scholarships for the single reason that there are no varsity sports.

The dorms are mostly co-ed, and students say they have a "rustic" appeal. "The rooms are huge, something I took for granted until I visited friends at other schools," says one dorm-dweller. Housing is based on credits, so freshmen have triples, sophomores have doubles, and upperclassmen have singles. Twenty-two percent of students live off campus in Brattleboro, twenty minutes away, and shuttle to and from campus in a school van.

Students agree that the town of Marlboro, highlighted by a post office and general store, isn't much to write home about. Most head to Brattleboro for its restaurants, bookstores, and coffeeshops. As might be expected, Marlboro has no Greek organizations; a new staff member was recently hired to coordinate the planning of student activities like poetry readings, trips to Boston and New York City, vans to local movie theaters, and pumpkin-carving contests. Snowball fights by the

> **"Everyone is out at night and nobody's worried about assault— except maybe by bears."**

library are a big draw in winter. On Community Work Day, students and faculty skip class and work together to improve the campus through various manual labor projects. The annual Cabaret and Halloween parties are unofficial costume contests showcasing student creativity.

The school mascot, the Fighting Dead Trees, is emblazoned on the shirts of the ever popular co-ed soccer team, and broomball, a variation of ice hockey played using shoes and brooms instead of ice skates and sticks and a kickball instead of a puck, is also always popular for athletes and spectators. The "incredibly dynamic" outing club ensures plenty of opportunities to enjoy the local wilderness, including hiking and cross-country skiing on runs that radiate from the center of campus. Excellent downhill skiing is only a few minutes' drive away.

This iconoclastic school continues to push the academic envelope and remains proud of doing and being the unexpected. And that suits students here just fine. Says a student, "Basically, we're a bunch of crazy, dedicated, love-struck, joyful, cynical, conscious freaks who go blasting around campus in a frenzy of creative and destructive energy."

While some schools see growth as a sign of their success, Marlboro intends to remain one of the nation's smallest liberal arts institutions.

Overlaps

Hampshire, Bennington, Bard, Earlham, Evergreen State

If You Apply To ➤

Marlboro: Early decision: Nov. 1. Early action: Jan. 15. Regular admissions: Mar. 1. Financial aid: Mar. 1. Housing: May 1. Guarantees to meet demonstrated need. Campus interviews: required, evaluative. Alumni interviews: optional, evaluative. SATs or ACTs: required. SAT IIs: recommended. Accepts the Common Application and electronic applications. Essay question: academic paper of student's choice (research paper, book report, expository essay) and autobiographical statement. Encourages "nontraditional" students.

Marquette is an old-line Roman Catholic university along the lines of St. Louis University and Loyola of Chicago. Milwaukee is not a selling point, and the university's clientele is mainly from the southern Wisconsin/northern Illinois corridor. About 80 percent of the students are Catholic.

Website: www.marquette.edu
Location: Urban
Total Enrollment: 11,042
Undergraduates: 7,644
Male/Female: 44/56
SAT Ranges: V 520–640
   M 530–650
ACT Range: 23–28
Financial Aid: 60%
Expense: Pr $ $ $
Phi Beta Kappa: Yes
Applicants: 7,593
Accepted: 82%
Enrolled: 30%
Grad in 6 Years: 76%
Returning Freshmen: 87%
Academics: ✍ ✍ ✍
Social: ☎ ☎ ☎
Q of L: ★ ★ ★
Admissions: (414) 288-7302
   or (800) 222-6544
Email Address:
   admissions@marquette.edu

Strongest Programs:
Dentistry
Physical Therapy
Law
Biomedical Engineering
Nursing
Journalism
Education

Marquette boasts a friendly collection of middle-class students, most of whom did well enough to graduate in the top half of their high school class.

At Marquette University, students practice what they preach. Rooted in traditional Jesuit doctrines, this university has not left its Roman Catholic origins behind. The college experience here includes an emphasis on civic responsibility, community service, and personal growth. "Marquette students really are a community. Everyone supports everyone else," says a senior. Innovative programs combine classroom theory with volunteer opportunities in Milwaukee and beyond.

Eighty acres of "concrete with interludes of grass and trees," Marquette University is located just a few blocks away from the heart of downtown Milwaukee. While offering the advantages of an urban setting, its campus does have plenty of open spaces suitable for everything from throwing a Frisbee to throwing a barbecue. Although most of the buildings are relatively modern, the campus is the site of the oldest building in the Western Hemisphere, the St. Joan of Arc Chapel, which was built in France in 1400 and later transported to Wisconsin. The new $30 million dental school building is completed, along with the $31 million Al McGuire Center athletic facility. Current construction includes the John P. Raynor, S. J. Library, more housing for upperclassmen and a thousand-car parking garage.

Marquette has added several new majors, including biological sciences, physics, statistics, physician's assistant studies, physiological sciences, management information systems, and social welfare and justice and military history. Students are no longer being admitted into the social work and dental hygiene majors, and some students complain that the university is notorious for dropping majors without warning. Through an affiliation with the Milwaukee Institute of Art and Design, two art minors, studio art and art history, are available. Marquette has its own art museum and an active theater program.

"Almost everyone has great pride and wants to be here!"

Recently, a new general education core curriculum was put into effect. The program is comprised of nine subject areas: diverse cultures, human nature and ethics, histories of cultures and societies, individual and social behavior, theology, literature/performing arts, mathematical reasoning, rhetoric, and science and nature. In addition to myriad study abroad programs in several countries, the university is the proud owner of the Les Aspin Center for Government located in Washington, D.C., which allows students to take courses in philosophy, political science, and theology, while simultaneously participating in an internship with a federal government agency.

Two-thirds of the classes have fewer than twenty-five students, but students usually manage to get into the ones they want. The administration encourages students to "put our beliefs into practice" through volunteer activity, which serves the elderly, the sick, and the poor in the Milwaukee area and elsewhere. "We do a lot of community service and work a lot with the city of Milwaukee," one student says. Administrators claim students contribute more than 100,000 hours of community service each year. Student religious organizations are active, and weekly Masses are held in the dorms by the resident priest. Roman Catholics understandably predominate in the student body, but religious practice is left to the individual. The academic climate is described as challenging and competitive. "When talking to peers, it is very looked down upon if one is getting less than a 'B' average overall," says a junior. Students are looking forward to improvements to the advisement systems. An honors program with small classes is available for about seventy highly motivated students in each year, while the Freshman Frontier program offers admission and intensive assistance to students "who did not reach full academic potential in high school."

Although the university actively recruits in thirty-five or so states and several U.S. territories, most of the student body is from the Midwest, 46 percent from Wisconsin itself. In general, Marquette boasts a friendly collection of middle-class students, most of whom did well enough to graduate in the top half of their high school class. African-Americans and Hispanics combine to make up 9 percent of the student body, while Asian-Americans make up another 4 percent. "Lack of diversity is a huge issue," a junior says. Marquette offers a very successful Educational Opportunity Program, which enables low-income, disadvantaged students, most of whom are minorities, to have the advantage of a college education. There are about 1,500 merit scholarships, ranging from $2,000 to nearly $20,000. "Don't let the money factor keep you from coming to MU. They will help you make a package feasible for you to get here," a senior chemistry major says.

More than half of Marquette students make their home on campus; all but two residence halls are co-ed, and there are several apartment options. Residency is required for freshmen and sophomores, but by junior year an overwhelming majority of students choose to move off campus, though housing is guaranteed for all undergraduate students through a lottery. The university works hard to keep the campus safe. "Although Marquette is located in an urban environment, public safety does an absolutely outstanding job ensuring that students are safe and know how to remain safe in the area," a senior says. In addition to residence hall guards, the school has blue-light emergency phones throughout the campus and operates a safety patrol escort program (to provide safe travel between the campus and surrounding residential areas) and an intracampus shuttle service complete with vans known as "limos."

"You never feel like a number."

Students don't characterize Milwaukee as a college town, but still say there are many good things about being there. For one, students say they have plenty of opportunities for community service. "Marquette has a great service-learning program that allows the students to take part," says one student. An old advertising slogan once claimed that "Milwaukee Means Beer," and few Marquette students would disagree. Marquette is stricter than most universities in enforcing the drinking age, but getting served off campus is not as difficult, and most students happily declare alcohol is there for the getting. Another well-loved tradition is the Miracle on Central Mall, the annual lighting of the campus Christmas tree and accompanying Mass. There are fraternities and sororities, but they attract less than 8 percent of the men and women.

Sports fans will be impressed with Milwaukee's Bradley Center, close to campus and home to Marquette basketball and the NBA's Milwaukee Bucks. Nature lovers can head to Lake Michigan, a forty-minute walk from campus, or to Kettle Moraine, a glaciated region ideal for hiking and cross-country skiing. Chicago is only ninety-five miles away. As the school grows, varsity sports are gaining a higher profile. In 2002–2003, the men's basketball and soccer teams and women's cross country seized championships. Track and field and soccer are the most popular sports on campus.

Still, no matter how dynamic the basketball team or how impressive the facilities, it's the family atmosphere that makes Marquette what it is. "It is very homey," says a satisfied senior. "Almost everyone has great pride and wants to be here!" Adds a classmate, "You never feel like a number."

Overlaps

University of Wisconsin, Notre Dame, University of Illinois, Northwestern, Purdue

University of Maryland–College Park

College Park, MD 20742

The name says Maryland, but the location says Washington, D.C. Students in College Park can jump on the Metro just the same as they do at Georgetown or American. Maryland is nothing if not big, and savvy students will look to programs such as the College Park Scholars for some personal attention.

Website: www.umd.edu
Location: Suburban
Total Enrollment: 34,740
Undergraduates: 25,179
Male/Female: 51/49
SAT Ranges: V 570–670
   M 600–700
Financial Aid: 26%
Expense: Pub $ $ $
Phi Beta Kappa: Yes
Applicants: 23,117
Accepted: 43%
Enrolled: 39%
Grad in 6 Years: 69%
Returning Freshmen: 92%
Academics: ✑ ✑ ✑
Social: ☎ ☎ ☎
Q of L: ★ ★ ★
Admissions: (301) 314-8385
Email Address: um-admit@
   uga.umd.edu

Strongest Programs:
Business
Criminology and Criminal
   Justice
Engineering
Communication
Computer Science
Government and Politics
Psychology

For good luck on exams, University of Maryland students rub the nose of Testudo, the school's terrapin mascot. But even without touching the revered statue, most students here feel lucky to be at a school with so many courses, such a diverse student body, and state-of-the-art research programs and institutes. "The student body is diverse and active in many extracurriculars. Students do not just attend classes but become part of the school," says one happy camper.

Maryland's Georgian brick buildings are arranged in graceful quadrangles around the grassy twelve-hundred-acre campus. With help from the state of Maryland and a large grant from the cable giant Comcast, a new athletic arena—the Comcast Center—has been constructed. A partnership with Target will build a new interview room at the Career Center. Students select a major from one of the twelve schools and colleges; Maryland has earned a strong reputation for its engineering, physics, and computer science departments, as well as the Robert H. Smith School of Business and Philip Merrill College of Journalism.

As might be expected at such a large school, bureaucracy is ever-present, starting with the general education requirements that comprise a third of every undergrad's total course load. These include classes in writing, math and the sciences, humanities and the arts, social sciences and history, as well as two upper-level classes outside the major, and one course focusing on cultural diversity. For students at the extremes of the academic spectrum, there's a "very impressive" honors program and an intensive educational development and tutoring program. Students participating in individual studies combine established majors and create their own programs; other options for those feeling fenced-in on campus include internships in nearby Washington, D.C., and Baltimore, and study abroad in locations such as Costa Rica, Israel, and Sweden. Maryland isn't so big that it can't get bigger. Several new offerings include graduate certificates in large-scale assessment and critical theory, degree programs in bioengineering and information management, concentrations in biology and chemistry, and a certificate program in lesbian, gay, bisexual, transgender studies. A joint M.B.A. program is being offered between the Smith School of Business and the Naval Postgraduate School, and an articulation agreement has been signed with the Laban-Bartenieff Institute of Movement Studies.

Maryland's curriculum "is rigorous, but not overwhelming," says a cell biology major. Lower-level courses tend to be large and impersonal ("easy to hide in, even easier to skip"), but the corresponding weekly discussion sections led by teaching assistants offer personal attention. The situation improves by junior year, when classes of twenty to forty students become the norm. "The teachers expect a lot of students, but they also give a lot back," says an elementary education major. "Courses do require a lot of reading." Faculty members are "knowledgeable and enthusiastic," but as might be expected given Maryland's size, students must seek them out for extra help, feedback, or assistance. The career center is "very helpful," according to a computer science major. He adds, "Academic counseling is always available. I had no problem planning my own program and getting it approved."

"The people are generally nicer and more open than at other schools."

Less than 25 percent of Maryland's freshmen may come from out of state; overall, 73 percent of students are Bay State natives, and New York and New Jersey are also well represented. Middle-class backgrounds predominate, and "the people are generally nicer and more open than at other schools," says a senior. Diversity is more than just a buzzword: 12 percent of students are African-American, 5 percent are Hispanic, and another 14 percent are Asian-American. Important campus issues include the equitable distribution of student activity fees between various clubs and organizations, local and national politics (given College Park's proximity to the capital), and the environment, students say. Students from families earning less than $21,000 a year receive all of their financial aid in the form of grants, with no loans required.

Thirty-nine percent of Maryland students—and more than 90 percent of freshmen—live on campus in single-sex or co-ed dorms; freshmen are guaranteed housing, and while many juniors and seniors seek off-campus accommodations, those who stay on campus all four years will find their digs improve as they gain seniority. (Upperclassmen also have the option of on-campus apartments and suites.) "There is a huge demand for campus housing," says a senior, adding, however, "there are lots of housing options around the university." Decisions on financial aid and housing are affected by acceptance date, so the earlier you apply, the better off you'll be. Freshmen generally live in high-rises or low-rises; South Campus features air-conditioning, carpeting, and new furniture. Safety features include triple locks on dorm-room doors, blue-light emergency phones, and walking and riding escort services to transport students after dark. "Security is good. We have a very defined campus, and we keep unauthorized visitors to a minimum," says a student.

An individual studies program allows students to combine established majors and create their own programs; other options for those feeling fenced-in on campus include internships in nearby Washington, D.C., and Baltimore, and study abroad in locations such as Costa Rica, Israel, and Sweden.

"Security is good. We have a very defined campus, and we keep unauthorized visitors to a minimum."

Social life at Maryland revolves around nonalcoholic events such as concerts, movies, and speakers, as well as around the traditional fraternity parties and football and basketball games. The university's reputation as a haven for those who prefer partying to studying is changing as students with better credentials apply, but it's still true that in the dorms, at local pubs, and in nearby Baltimore and Washington, D.C., there's always something happening. On campus, only students over twenty-one may drink, in accordance with state law; the policy works "50 percent of the time," says one student. "RAs monitor dorms," warns one student. Nine percent of the men and 10 percent of women go Greek, but they don't dominate the tone of campus life. At a school this big, extracurricular activities and participants come in every shape and size.

Despite College Park's highly social atmosphere, Maryland's suburban campus can feel too small. A few bucks and a few minutes on the Metro (Washington's subway system) brings Terps into downtown D.C. at a hare's pace. Back on campus, favorite annual events include Art Attack, in which local artists share their crafts and national touring artists perform an evening concert, and Homecoming.

Terrapin basketball fans are unsinkable and not always civilized, turning out en masse to cheer against Duke. The football program continued its impressive run last season by racking up ten regular season wins and a post-season bowl game victory. The men's lacrosse and baseball teams also draw crowds, as do women's lacrosse (which has won championships from 1995 through 2001) and field hockey.

The University of Maryland's overwhelming size is both a blessing and a curse for the increasingly capable undergraduates here. On one hand, they may choose from an ever-growing variety of courses, and they live and study among a diverse group of peers. On the other, largeness can translate into crowded dorms, long lines at registration, big classes, parking problems, and hassles everywhere. Still, a junior insists, getting lost in the shuffle "is totally avoidable. Talk to professors, join clubs, attend campus meetings, and people will know you."

Overlaps

Penn State, University of Maryland at Baltimore County, Towson State, Virginia Tech, University of Delaware

If You Apply To ➤

Maryland: Early action: Dec. 1. Regular admissions: Jan. 20. Financial aid: Feb. 15. Housing: May 1. No campus or alumni interviews. SATs: required. SAT IIs: optional. Accepts electronic applications. Essay question: how you've changed since high school, what does integrity mean to you, write about a question of your own. Students who do not meet academic standards may submit additional information for consideration.

Mary Washington College

1301 College Avenue, Fredericksburg, VA 22401

Mary Washington could easily be mistaken for one of Virginia's elite private colleges. MWC offers just as much history and tradition—for a much lower price. Once a women's college, it is still over two-thirds female. On the selectivity chart, MWC ranks behind only UVA and William and Mary among Virginia public universities.

Website: www.mwc.edu
Location: Small city
Total Enrollment: 4,835
Undergraduates: 4,275
Male/Female: 30/70
SAT Ranges: V 570–660
   M 560–640
ACT Ranges: 24–29
Financial Aid: 65%
Expense: Pub $
Phi Beta Kappa: Yes
Applicants: 4,303
Accepted: 59%
Enrolled: 35%
Grad in 6 Years: 70%
Returning Freshmen: 89%
Academics: ✍ ✍ ✍ ½
Social: ☎ ☎ ☎
Q of L: ★ ★ ★ ★
Admissions: (540) 654-2000

Strolling among Mary Washington College's elegant buildings of redbrick and white columns has led more than one pleased parent to declare, "Now this is what a college should look like." Indeed, for an aura of history and tradition, few schools stack up to this small college in Fredericksburg, a site of Civil War action and the boyhood town of George Washington. If the campus architecture puts some people in mind of the University of Virginia, it's no accident: MWC was the all-female branch of that august institution before going co-ed and cutting its ties in 1970. Of course, Mary Washington is not just beautiful, but smart, too. Easily mistaken for one of Virginia's elite private colleges, Mary Washington has gained a reputation as one of the premium public liberal arts colleges in the country and continues to attract bright students from around the globe.

Located in historic Fredericksburg, the campus features classical Jeffersonian buildings, sweeping lawns, brick walkways, and breathtaking foliage. Of course, beauty these days requires that you also be in shape, so a brand new 20,000-square-foot fitness and recreation center and upperclassman apartment complex are in the works.

Mary Washington's core curriculum emphasizes its strong liberal bent. Students select courses to meet specific goals in the arts, literature, natural and social sciences, and mathematics. English composition, five writing-intensive courses, and foreign language competency are also required. Students also must complete across-the-curriculum general education requirements in five areas: written communication, oral communication, race and gender, global awareness, and the environment. As for majors, business administration and psychology are the most popular. Also very strong is a unique program in historic preservation. Among the sciences, biology is the clear favorite. The administration concedes that the dance and Russian departments are weaker because declining enrollments forced cutbacks. But the theater department has seen resurgence of late, something both current and prospective students have noticed, administrators say.

"The quality of teaching I have received has been phenomenal."

Students are encouraged to take on research projects of their own design, with the college spending $60,000 a year to support student research. Several departments offer grants for work abroad or in the U.S, and many students study abroad during their junior year. The college's location, roughly an hour from both Washington, D.C., and the state capital, Richmond, is a handy asset for approximately 350 budding politicos who seek internships every year. Because of the rise in Mary Washington's popularity, some students are concerned about potential overcrowding. "Registration is always a hassle, as classes fill up early on," says a senior political science major. "However, many professors will allow you to force-add a class if you ask." But the force-add system doesn't always work, especially in the psychology department, which is notoriously strict. A senior says, "It is hard to finish the teaching program in four years. But on the whole, graduating on time is definitely possible."

The close ties between students and faculty are a great source of pride at Mary Washington, where classes usually have fewer than twenty-five students and rarely more than fifty. "The quality of teaching I have received has been phenomenal," says one historic preservation major.

In general, Mary Washington students are "enthusiastic and supportive of one another," a junior says. "They respect each other based on the MWC Honor Code. Students are hard working and ambitious in their pursuit of academic excellence and job opportunities," says another junior. They tend to be conservative and not socially active, although the male/female ratio has become an issue and talk of changing the school's name has students complaining. Mary Washington may act and look like a private school, but her state school status is showing just a bit. "As a public institution, the college has been affected by Virginia politics and many student organizations suffer from budget cuts" a student says. African-Americans make up 4 percent of the student population, Hispanics 3 percent, and Asian-Americans 4 percent. Sixty-five percent of the student body is from Virginia,

"Many complain there is nothing to do, but opportunities are not going to come knocking on your door."

and a large majority continues on to jobs after graduation, rather than graduate school. The college offers five hundred merit scholarships ranging from $250 to $10,000, but no athletic scholarships.

Students have great affection for MWC housing, as 70 percent reside on campus. "All dorms are similar and provide a great atmosphere for learning and socializing," says a senior. The seventeen residence halls offer many different living arrangements, including foreign language floors, service-learning options, and special theme units. Students hope a new apartment complex will make it easier to get a good room. "The housing selection day is horrible, as many students dread it because it seems impossible to get what you want," says a senior. But those who do find a room that suits them can "homestead," or retain that room for their remaining years.

Small and friendly, nearby Fredericksburg is a "quaint, historic town." While it lacks some of the nightlife of a larger community, it has plenty of museums offering Civil War exhibits and shops and restaurants offer discounts to students. For dance clubs and bars, it's not far to Richmond or D.C. Likewise, women frustrated

(Continued)
Email Address:
admit@mwc.edu

Strongest Programs:
Historic Preservation
Psychology
English
Biology
International Affairs
History
Political Science

Students are encouraged to take on research projects of their own design, with the college spending $60,000 a year to support student research.

Since the inception of the Capital Athletic Conference, MWC has won more conference championships than all other conference members combined. In 2002–2003, it claimed eleven of eighteen conference championships.

by the disadvantageous gender ratio can reach UVA in an hour and a half, and Georgetown in even less. Both the scenery of the Chesapeake Bay and hiking in the Blue Ridge Mountains are roughly an hour away, due east and west, respectively. On campus, plenty of events are held by various student organizations. Although there are parties both on and off campus on any given weekend, alcohol does not dominate the social scene, and there are no fraternities or sororities. A band plays the campus snack bar most Thursday nights, and the student council often sponsors dances. "Many complain there is nothing to do, but opportunities are not going to come knocking on your door," says a senior.

"I couldn't imagine a more positive, supportive, fun atmosphere."

Even though Mary Washington doesn't have a football team, other sports are alive and well. Since the inception of the Capital Athletic Conference, MWC has won more conference championships than all other conference members combined. In 2002–2003, it claimed eleven of eighteen conference championships. Nonvarsity types also use the seventy-six-acre sports and field complex, complete with an Olympic-size pool, for a variety of intramural and club sports, including men's and women's rugby and crew.

Mary Washington students take an uncommon interest in college traditions. Several annual outdoor parties, including Grill on the Hill and Weststock, never fail to attract a large crowd. All third-year students brace themselves for Junior Ring Week, during which they are the victims of practical jokes prior to receiving their rings from the school's president. Another tradition is Devil-Goat Day, an all-day competition pitting odd- and even-yeared classes against each other in events such as sumo wrestling, jousting, and the Velcro wall. Homecoming is observed with the usual round of sporting events (particularly soccer), dances, and dinners. The Multicultural Festival is also popular.

With a first-rate liberal arts education in an intimate environment and at a public school price, Mary Washington College is a smart choice for anyone seeking the most bang for their buck. It offers a pleasing blend of beautiful architecture, first rate faculty, and serious, down-to-earth students who appreciate it all. "I couldn't imagine a more positive, supportive, fun atmosphere," a junior says.

Overlaps

University of Virginia, William and Mary, James Madison, University of Richmond, Virginia Tech

If You Apply To ➢ **Mary Washington:** Early action: Jan. 15. Regular admissions: Feb. 1. Financial aid: Mar. 1. Meets demonstrated need of 10%. No campus or alumni interviews. SATs or ACTs: required. SAT IIs: recommended. Accepts the Common Application and electronic applications. Essay question: personal statement; your sense of honor or how you would benefit under the college's honor system.

University of Massachusetts–Amherst

Amherst, MA 01003

A liberal mecca in cosmopolitan and scenic western Massachusetts. UMass boasts strong study abroad programs and an international flavor. Science and engineering are also strong. Ready access to privates Amherst, Hampshire, Mount Holyoke, and Smith via the Five College Consortium.

Website: www.umass.edu

The University of Massachusetts at Amherst, a leading land grant university with more than a century of tradition, offers students a dizzying array of majors and extracurricular options and the chance to take courses at nearby private colleges that are among the best anywhere. Students can live in one of the nation's top college towns, take advantage of an extensive research program and strong honors program, and enjoy an endless supply of social opportunities—without emptying their wallets.

UMass's sprawling 1,463-acre campus is centered on a pond full of ducks and swans, while architectural styles range from Colonial to modern. The school is located on the outskirts of Amherst, a city that combines the energy of a bustling cosmopolitan center with the quaintness of an old New England town. Students agree that Amherst caters to college life. New additions on campus include the Animal Care Facility; the Engineering and Computer Science Complex; and an addition to the School of Management building.

Of UMass's nine undergraduate colleges and schools, offerings in management and engineering are top-ranked. Polymer science is notable, as is the English department, which features such names as Pulitzer Prize–winning poet James Tate and John Edgar Wideman, a two-time PEN/Faulkner Award winner and MacArthur "Genius Grant" Award recipient. Political science, creative writing, and international studies also draw praise. Biology, math, computer science, and the natural sciences are regarded as especially tough. Students report little difficulty getting into courses they want or are required to take. Engineering students may face a bit of a challenge in finishing in four years; they are required to take 130 credit hours while most programs require 120 credit hours.

All undergraduates must complete two courses in writing; six Social World courses, including literature, arts/liberal arts, historical studies, social and behavioral sciences, and an interdisciplinary elective; three courses in biological and physical science; one basic math skills course; and a course in analytic reasoning. Freshmen must also complete

"We have five different living areas to suit every taste and personality."

the College Writing Program, taught in sections of twenty-four or fewer. The school's honors program, Commonwealth College, offers qualified students special courses and sponsors interdisciplinary seminars, student gatherings, service projects, a newsletter, and a housing option. Students seeking to stand out from the "Masses" might consider the interdisciplinary major in social thought and political economy or the bachelor's degree in the Individual Concentration program, a design-it-yourself major. The study abroad program offers options in thirty different countries, including Japan, the Netherlands, and Australia; about 15 percent of a typical class takes advantage of the program. The Center for Student Business offers one of the most unique programs at UMass, allowing students to staff and manage nine campus businesses, and learn how to work with others and resolve conflicts professionally.

UMass's intellectual and political climate is extraordinarily fertile for a state university, perhaps in part because of its membership in the Five College Consortium.* This special alliance allows students to attend UMass and take courses at the other four consortium schools: Amherst College, Smith, Hampshire, and Mount Holyoke. Students say that generally, the quality of teaching at UMass is excellent. "The classes are competitive and well set up for learning," a computer science major says. Full professors teach most courses, and some of the larger ones are broken down into smaller sections with graduate-level teaching assistants. Academic and career counseling receive mixed reviews, and it is usually up to students to pursue career help.

The majority of UMass students are white public school graduates from Massachusetts, especially because out-of-state enrollment is capped at 25 percent of students. Most make a beeline for the job market after graduation. Four percent of undergraduates are African-Americans, while 7 percent are Asian-American and

(Continued)

Location: Small town
Total Enrollment: 24,062
Undergraduates: 18,606
Male/Female: 49/51
SAT Ranges: V 500–620
   M 510–630
Financial Aid: 46%
Expense: Pub $ $
Phi Beta Kappa: Yes
Applicants: 20,499
Accepted: 57%
Enrolled: 28%
Grad in 6 Years: 61%
Returning Freshmen: 83%
Academics: ✍ ✍ ✍ ½
Social: ☎ ☎ ☎ ☎
Q of L: ★ ★ ★
Admissions: (413) 545-0222
Email Address:
   mail@admissions.umass
   .edu

Strongest Programs:
Linguistics
Polymer Science and
   Engineering
Psychology
Computer Science
Chemical Engineering
Electrical and Computer
   Engineering

"We have 24,000 students here," a senior reports, "so we have 'em all—the jocks, the artsy-fartsies, the hippies/earthy crunchies, the nerds. Most of them, however, being from Massachusetts, tend to use the word 'wicked.'"

another 3 percent are Hispanic. The university has established cultural centers on campus providing activities and support for students from different backgrounds, but affirmative action is still an issue, students report. "There are always rallies about better programs and aid for minorities," says a senior. Students from other New England states are treated as Massachusetts residents for admission purposes if

"I've never had trouble getting a room."

their own state schools don't offer the programs they want. Students have also cried out against state budget cuts, which have cost the school programs. "We have 24,000 students here," a senior reports, "so we have 'em all—the jocks, the artsy-fartsies, the hippies/earthy crunchies, the nerds. Most of them, however, being from Massachusetts, tend to use the word 'wicked.'"

UMass has the sixth-largest residence-hall system in the country. Forty-two dorms, organized in five residential areas, house 60 percent of students. Freshmen can choose single-sex or co-ed living and also submit a list of their preferred living areas, but they're required to live on campus through sophomore year. About half of the freshmen end up in the Southwest Area, a "huge, citylike complex" with five high-rise towers and eleven low-rise residence halls. The university is expanding its Residential Academic Programs, which allow first-year students with similar interests to live and study together in specialized interdisciplinary courses to ease their transition into campus life. Approximately 35 percent of freshmen participate. Upperclassmen tend to move off-campus. "We have five different living areas to suit every taste and personality," says one satisfied senior. "I've never had trouble getting a room."

UMass offers an abundant social life, marked by noisy dorms, overflowing frat houses, and frequent off-campus parties. "Social life is hot!" a senior raves. Both on campus and off, alcohol policies are strict and well enforced; underage drinking is many times confined to students' rooms, if they can get away with it. First-time underage offenders are sent to alcohol-education programs. The school is losing its reputation as "ZooMass." Nearly two dozen fraternities and sororities occupy 3 percent of the men and 7 percent of the women, but they are somewhat out of the

"Social life is hot!"

mainstream. A free public transportation system allows maximum mobility not only among the Five Colleges but also to nearby towns, which are graced with a number of exceptional bookshops. The annual Spring Concert around the pond is a daylong event where musicians such as U2, Bob Dylan, and the Beastie Boys have performed.

Settled in the Pioneer Valley and surrounded by the Berkshire foothills, Amherst is close to good skiing, hiking, and canoeing areas. It's also ninety miles west of Boston, a hundred and fifty miles north of New York City, and twenty-five miles south of Vermont and New Hampshire, making a car very useful (and very expensive if you get too many tickets from overzealous campus cops, students say). Varsity sports are popular, and UMass has been a model for achieving gender equity in athletics. "Midnight Madness," the first men's basketball practice of the season, held annually at midnight with everyone invited, is a hot campus ticket. The football team has won conference championships, as have men's baseball and swimming and women's basketball, crew, cross-country, field hockey, softball, soccer, tennis, lacrosse, and track. Two on-campus gyms offer facilities for the recreational athlete, and two Olympic-size skating rinks mark the recent reintroduction of intercollegiate hockey to the university.

UMass is big enough to offer a vast number of academic and extracurricular opportunities, but at times can feel impersonal and overwhelming. But with special residential programs that group students with similar languages, cultures, and lifestyles, students can easily find a home in Amherst.

The study abroad program offers options in thirty different countries, including Japan, the Netherlands, and Australia; about 15 percent of a typical class takes advantage of the program.

Overlaps

Boston University, Northeastern, University of Connecticut, Boston College, University of New Hampshire

Massachusetts Institute of Technology

Room 3-108, 77 Massachusetts Avenue, Cambridge, MA 02139

If you're a science genius, come to MIT to find out how little you really know. No other school makes such a massive assault on the ego (with little in the way of support to help you pick up the pieces). Technology is a given, but MIT also prides itself on leading programs in economics, political science, and management.

MIT is, in a word, excellence. With a student body that averaged near-perfect scores on the math portion of their SATs, and verbal scores not far behind, this is a place that restores faith in the American educational system. Engineering, science, and math are MIT's specialties, but students come here to learn about everything—and learn they certainly do.

MIT is located on 154 acres that extend more than a mile along the Cambridge side of the Charles River basin facing historic Beacon Hill and the central sections of Boston. The main campus of neoclassical architecture carved from limestone was designed by Welles Bosworth and constructed between 1913 and 1920. Since then, more modern designs in brick and glass have been added. The buildings give off a utilitarian aura; most are even known by number instead of by name. Athletic playing fields, recreational buildings, dorms, and dining halls are closely arranged on the campus and provide a sense of unity. Sculptures and murals, including the works of Alexander Calder, Henry Moore, and Louise Nevelson, are found throughout the campus. New undergraduate and graduate residence halls opened recently, as did the Zesiger Sports and Fitness Center.

Originally called Boston Tech and now frequently referred to as "the Tute," MIT stresses science and engineering studies with a "concern for human values and social goals." Every science and engineering department is superb. The biology department is a leader in medical technology and the search for designer genes. Nevertheless, pure sciences tend to play second fiddle to the engineering fields that, along with computer science, draw the bulk of the majors. Electrical engineering and computer science are almost universally credited as tops in the nation. Students in these two areas may now pursue a five-year-degree option, where they can obtain a professional master's degree upon completion of their studies. Biomedical, chemical, and mechanical engineering; physics; and the tiny aeronautics department are also highly praised programs. The most popular majors include biology, mechanical engineering, chemical engineering, and management. The humanities are strong here as well, though not on par with more technical programs.

MIT has always attracted top nontechnical professors, including such luminaries as linguist Noam Chomsky. Economics, political science, management, urban studies, linguistics, graphics for modern art, and holography—plus anything that can be linked to a computer—are strong, and the tiny minority who major in these subjects receive enough personal attention to make any college student envious. "Some professors really know how to engage the interest of the student," says a senior.

Website: http://web.mit.edu
Location: Urban
Total Enrollment: 10,340
Undergraduates: 4,112
Male/Female: 58/42
SAT Ranges: V 680–760
  M 730–800
ACT Range: 30–34
Financial Aid: 71%
Expense: Pr $ $ $ $
Phi Beta Kappa: Yes
Applicants: 10,549
Accepted: 16%
Enrolled: 59%
Grad in 6 Years: 92%
Returning Freshmen: 98%
Academics: ✑ ✑ ✑ ✑ ✑
Social: ☎ ☎ ☎
Q of L: ★ ★ ★
Admissions: (617) 253-4971
Email Address:
  admissions@mit.edu

Strongest Programs:
Engineering
Science
Architecture
Economics
Management

MIT is tops in technology, but also strong in the social sciences. The administration worries that engineers of the future will need to possess not only first-rate technical skills but also a better understanding of the social system in which they will be operating. As one dean put it, "Too many MIT graduates end up working for too many Princeton and Harvard graduates." The general education program does require undergraduates to take at least eight courses that stress such fundamental academic themes as literary traditions and the origins of political institutions. Perhaps to ensure that they will be able to make their future discoveries known, students must also complete a two-phase writing requirement. Technical types are also able to choose a minor in a non technical field in subjects ranging from philosophy to women in society. There's also a four-class physical education requirement as well as a mandatory swimming test to be passed by the end of freshman year.

> "It will take you right up to what you think your limits are, and then MIT will shatter them and make you realize how great your potential is."

One of MIT's most successful innovations is the Undergraduate Research Opportunities Program (UROP), a year-round program that facilitates student-faculty research projects. Considered one of the best programs of its kind in the nation, it allows students to earn course credit or stipends for doing research. The Experimental Study Group allows freshmen and sophomores to set a self-paced course of study as they learn through tutorials instead of in the traditional lecture format. Many students even have access to the world-renowned professors and the Nobel Prize winners, who carry lighter teaching loads to allow them time for students and research. Faculty advising is "pretty good for freshmen," one student says, but after that, "it's as good as you make it." The library system, which includes a recently expanded architecture facility, is vast and contains more than two million volumes, including some one-of-a-kind manuscripts on the history of science and technology. One library is even open twenty-four hours a day, and "some students spend the majority of their time (awake or asleep) there," one student reports.

A mandatory pass/fail grading system helps freshmen adjust to "MIT brain-stretching": freshmen receive grades of P, D, or F in all subjects they take. P means C-or-better performance; Ds or Fs do not receive credit or appear on the permanent record. Grades or not, most MIT students set themselves a breathtaking pace. "MIT is intense and will take you for quite a ride," a biology/premed student says. "The courses demand your full attention and a lot of extra work," another says. Some relief from "tooling" (that is, studying) is found through the optional January period of independent activities offering noncredit seminars, workshops, and activities in fields outside the regular curriculum as well as for-credit subjects. Participation in the engineering co-op program, junior year abroad, or cross-registration at all-female Wellesley College are other helpful ways to get young noses away from the grindstone. Academic and psychological counseling are well thought of by students. A student-run hotline provides all-night peer counseling. Many upperclassmen return to school at least two weeks before classes start "to help integrate the freshmen."

While MIT somewhat justly earned an image as a "conservative, rich white boys' school" in the past, there is certainly enough racial if not gender variety to beat the rap today. African-Americans account for 7 percent of the student body, Hispanics 13 percent, and Asian-Americans a hefty 30 percent. If anything, women may feel "a different tone, as the campus is three-fifths male." Ninety-seven percent of students come from the top tenth of their high school class, and average SAT and ACT scores are simply mind-boggling. "The average MIT student can be characterized as having a passion and singular drive for what they really want in life," offers a chemical engineering major. MIT helps financially needy students pay the superhefty tuition bill,

Technical types are also able to choose a minor in a non technical field in subjects ranging from philosophy to women in society. There's also a four-class physical education requirement as well as a mandatory swimming test to be passed by the end of freshman year.

and it also guarantees to meet demonstrated need. It does not give purely merit or athletic scholarships, but it has its own parent-loan fund with favorable interest rates to augment the federal-loan programs.

All freshmen are now required to live in dorms, eliminating the harried housing gauntlet. Cat lovers will be glad to learn that the MIT administration, which once cracked down on surreptitiously harbored kitties in dorm rooms, has backed off its no-pets-except-fish policy and permitted students to bring their beloved cats with them. Cats, however, face one admissions requirement not yet extended to undergraduates: they must be spayed or neutered. Guaranteed housing is either single-sex or co-ed; the dorms are in the middle of campus, and most of the fraternities and living groups are a mile or less away across the Charles. Ninety-three percent of the undergraduates live on campus, and mandatory meal plans exist, depending on the living group. Some dorms have kitchens, and the meal plan is optional. Dorms without kitchens have a required meal plan. Frat-types feast on spreads prepared by their full-time cooks, and the Kosher Kitchen, provides some refuge for others.

MIT's social scene is varied. There's Greek life, to which 26 percent of the men and 8 percent of the women belong. Then there are campus movies and lectures. There's the ubiquitous workload, worming its way into the uneasy consciousness of a techie's every waking hour. And there's the great city of Boston, with its many restaurants, clubs, parks, shopping opportunities, and more than fifty other colleges. On-campus dances, parties, and dorm activities keep other students busy. Most on-campus drinking for over-twenty-one students is relaxed and accepted, "as long as the alcohol does not result in unlawful behavior or cause any problems," a student explains. For those with the urge to roam, the multifaceted greater Boston metropolis lies only a few subway stops away.

"MIT is intense and will take you for quite a ride."

When the MIT megabrains take a break, practical jokes, or "hacks" (described by one student as "practical jokes with technical merit"), are sure to follow. In past years, popular hacks have included disguising the dome of the main academic building as a giant breast, unscrewing and reversing all the chairs in a five hundred-seat lecture hall, and, of course, welding shut Harvard's gates. Hacking can also involve late-night explorations by students in the tunnels and shafts that run through restricted parts of the campus, a practice that's definitely frowned upon by the school.

When not studying or hacking, these engineering jocks often turn into real jocks: MIT fields the second-highest number of intercollegiate varsity sports in the country with thirty-nine (Harvard has forty-two). Athletic accomplishments in the past three years include Constitution Athletic Conference championships in men's cross-country; the New England Women's 8 title in crew; and national championships for the air pistol and women's sports pistol teams. Hockey is popular, and even more popular is the extensive, well-organized intramural program, with sports ranging from Ping-Pong, billiards, and bowling to the more traditional basketball and volleyball. Everyone has access to MIT's extensive athletic facilities. Supposedly, there are more clubs and organizations at MIT than at any other school in the country, and a sampling of the offerings explains why. The Rocket Society, the Guild of Bell Ringers, a singing group called the Corollaries, and the Exotic Fish Society are only a few of the diverse interests on this campus.

Though students often wonder what life at a so-called typical college would have been like, chances of survival and even satisfaction at MIT are excellent. Students are able to comprehend the incredible experience of attending one of the nation's leading academic powerhouses. A biology major puts it bluntly: "It will take you right up to what you think your limits are, and then MIT will shatter them and make you realize how great your potential is."

One of MIT's most successful innovations is the Undergraduate Research Opportunities Program (UROP), a year-round program that facilitates student–faculty research projects. Considered one of the best programs of its kind in the nation, It allows students to earn course credit or stipends for doing research.

Overlaps
Harvard, Stanford, Princeton, Yale, Cornell

If You Apply To ➤

MIT: Early action: Nov. 1. Regular admissions: Jan. 1. Financial aid: Feb. 1. Guarantees to meet demonstrated need. No campus interviews. Alumni interviews: recommended, evaluative. SATs or ACTs: required. SAT IIs: required (writing, history, or science and math). Accepts electronic applications. Essay question: reaction to difficult experience; how has your world shaped your dreams. Looks for aptitude in math and science.

McGill University: See page 333.

McGill University: See page 333.

University of Miami

P.O. Box 248025, Coral Gables, FL 33124-4616

Football is the main reason UM is on the map, but it isn't the only reason. Renowned programs in marine science and music are big draws; business is also strong. Housing takes the form of a distinctive residential college system that offers living/learning opportunities.

Website: www.miami.edu
Location: Suburban
Total Enrollment: 13,963
Undergraduates: 8,955
Male/Female: 45/55
SAT Ranges: V 530–630
   M 540–650
ACT Range: 22–28
Financial Aid: 54%
Expense: Pr $ $ $ $
Phi Beta Kappa: Yes
Applicants: 13,088
Accepted: 53%
Enrolled: 15%
Grad in 6 Years: 62%
Returning Freshmen: 82%
Academics: ✍ ✍ ✍
Social: ☎ ☎ ☎ ☎
Q of L: ★ ★ ★
Admissions: (305) 284-4323
Email Address:
   admission@miami.edu

Strongest Programs:
Marine Science
Music
Business
Political Science
Biology/Premed

Year-round sunshine and the colorful Miami culture could make even the most dedicated students forget why they are at college. But at the University of Miami, students can have their fun and get a solid education at the same time. Trash-talking has been replaced by a renewed focus on academics, though the 'Canes have lost none of their south Florida swagger.

Twenty minutes from Key Biscayne and Miami's beaches, and ten minutes from downtown Miami, the university's 260-acre campus is located in tranquil suburbia. With its own lake in the middle of the campus (and on the cover of most brochures), the campus is architecturally varied, from postwar, international-style structures to modern buildings, most with open-air breezeways to let in the warm, salty winds. The state-of-the-art Francis L. Wolfson School of Communications building recently opened.

Miami has one of the nation's top programs in marine biology, and was the first university to offer a degree in music engineering. Miami's main strengths are in the preprofessional and professional areas. The school also boasts an unusual program in jazz, and students recommend any of the strong premed offerings. Chemistry majors have access to a nuclear magnetic resonance spectrometer, an essential tool for modern chemistry. The school's six-year medical program for outstanding students, and dual degree (grad/undergrad) programs in law, marine science, business, physical therapy, biomedical engineering, and medicine receive high marks. Women's studies and philosophy are said to be weaker. Business management is the most popular major, followed by visual and performing arts, biology, health professions, and engineering.

"The coursework is challenging," says a student, "especially if you have a scientific or engineering type major." Students give professors high marks for knowledge and accessibility. Full professors teach most courses. "The quality of teaching I have received is second to none," a sophomore says. "I have received that personal attention I wanted from my classes and professors." Though many have a preprofessional bent, students at Miami receive a broad liberal arts education. Distribution requirements vary from school to school, but general education requirements include proficiency in English composition, mathematics, and writing across the curriculum (courses that involve a substantial amount of writing). In addition, a certain number of credits must be earned in each of three areas of knowledge: natural sciences, social sciences, and arts and humanities. Students looking for a change of pace can take advantage of Miami's summer semester program in the Caribbean. In addition, the study abroad program offers more than forty study abroad options in countries such as Australia, Israel, France, Japan, the Netherlands, and Argentina.

Highly motivated students in any field can apply to the school's comprehensive honors program, which enrolls students who were in the top tenth of their high school class and have a combined SAT score of at least 1360. About 15 percent of each freshmen class enrolls. UM still attracts its share—though it's declining—of beach bums who drop by for a couple of classes in the morning, spend the rest of the day at the shore, and almost never see the inside of the library. That's a shame, though; the facility is one of the best in the region, with more than two million bound volumes and another three-million-plus on microform.

Thirty-eight percent of UM's students come from out of state, mostly from the Northeast, Ohio, and the Chicago area. UM is unique among universities of its caliber in the incredible diversity of its student body; Hispanics account for a substantial 31 percent of the total, African-Americans 11 percent, and Asian-Americans 6 percent. Nine percent are foreign-born. Students say that diversity is one of UM's best assets. "We have students from all fifty states and more than 110 foreign countries," says an English/political science major. "When I lived on campus at U of M, I think the most wonderful experience was hearing three different languages spoken by groups of students on my way from the dorm to the classroom." The school's large

> **"The coursework is challenging, especially if you have a scientific or engineering type major."**

number of Hispanics is traceable to the influx of Cuban and other Caribbean refugees into southern Florida, and at times it seems that Spanish is the mother tongue on campus. The Latin influence mixes colorfully with that of the wealthier New Yorkers, many of whom view their time at "Sunshine U" as an extended vacation. The one characteristic everyone seems to share is the hope of getting high-paying jobs after graduation. Nearly two thousand merit scholarships and athletic awards in several sports ease the school's hefty price tag for qualified students.

Miami offers a distinctive system of five co-ed residential colleges, modeled after those at Yale University. Each college is directed by a master—a senior faculty member who organizes seminars, concerts, lectures, social events, and the monthly community dinner. Faculty members often host study breaks in their homes and provide guest speakers from all walks of life to discuss current issues. Generally, students give the dorms average marks; less than 40 percent of students live on campus, and others bunk in off-campus apartments or Greek houses. Still, all dorm housing at Miami is co-ed, and students can choose apartment-style housing when they tire of the residential colleges' closeness. Scrounging up grub on campus is easy; the residential colleges have their own cafeterias with a variety of plans, from five to twenty meals, and there is a kosher alternative.

On the weekends, Miami students frequent nearby bars or the Campus Rat, home also to the popular Fifth Quarter post-football-game parties. On-campus alcohol policies are relatively strict for underage students, sometimes including parental notification for offenses. Fraternities still manage to thrive, accounting for 12 percent of the men and providing a space for most of the underage drinking at UM (although not during rush, which is dry). The sororities, with no housing of their own, attract 13 percent of the women. Many of the fraternities and sororities are small (averaging about thirty members), but they often join forces in throwing parties.

Students who tire of Miami's relentless sunshine can get a change of pace through more than forty education and exchange programs around the world. They include studying marine science in Australia and Middle East studies in Israel.

About 15 percent of freshmen are admitted into the college's honor program, which offers small seminars and research-oriented classes with top professors.

If keg parties aren't your scene, though, UM offers a plethora of other social opportunities. Those who shun sand between their toes bike down to the boutiques in Coconut Grove, Bayside, or South Beach, or attend on-campus events, such as International Week, Sportsfest, and the Cardboard Boat Races. "The majority of students at Miami fit into the trendy, clubbing profile," explains a psychology major.

> **"The majority of students at Miami fit into the trendy, clubbing profile."**

"They like trendy up-to-date clothes, and going to clubs in order to see and be seen." Public transportation runs in front of the residential colleges, but most students recommend a car in order to get "the full Florida effect." Parking can be a problem, though, says a senior: "If you want a parking space, you need to get to school by 8:00 a.m., and parking decals are way too expensive." The best road trips are Key West, Key Largo, and, of course, UM football games, especially those against Florida State.

Though hurricane season hits most of the Southeast coast in late summer, in Miami, 'Cane season lasts straight through New Year's. Under the tutelage of head coach Larry Coker, the 'Canes are a contender for the national championship nearly every season. Although football is undisputed king of the hill on campus, men's baseball, basketball, and tennis and women's track and field have also captured recent championships. A $14 million rec center, with juice bar and spa, and the annual intramural Sportsfest, also draw crowds.

It's hard to imagine a school in the Sunshine State without a generous allotment of fun, and UM is no exception. Life really is a beach for students at the University of Miami, although its days as a beach-bum hideout are long over. These days, UM students are just as likely to search long and hard for the perfect instrumental phrase or mathematical proof as they are to scope out the perfect wave. "It is the whole college experience at U of M," says one sophomore. "It is so fulfilling and rewarding."

Overlaps

University of Florida, NYU, Boston University, UCLA, Florida State

Miami University (OH)

301 S. Campus Avenue, Oxford, OH 45056

Rather than disappear into the black hole of Ohio State, top students in the Buckeye state come here to feel as if they are going to an elite private university. MU has a niche like William and Mary's in Virginia—though MU is twice as big. Miami's top draw is business, and its tenor is conservative.

Website: www.muohio.edu
Location: Rural
Total Enrollment: 16,730
Undergraduates: 15,384
Male/Female: 46/54
SAT Ranges: V 550–640
 M 580–660

This Miami is about one thousand miles from South Beach, but that doesn't mean it's without sizzle. The academic kind, of course. Miami University is actually tucked into a corner of Ohio and is gaining national recognition as an excellent state university that has the true look and feel of a private, with a picture-perfect campus and high-caliber student body.

The university is staked out on two thousand wooded acres in the center of an urban triangle of approximately three million people, encompassing Cincinnati and Dayton, Ohio, and Richmond, Indiana. The campus is dressed in the modified

Georgian style of the Colonial American period and it remains as impeccably groomed as its nattily attired students. New additions to campus include an academic center, a training facility for athletes, a child-care facility for faculty and students, an addition to the Student Health Services Center for the Counseling Services, a bell and clock tower at one of the entrances to campus, and a baseball field. The chemistry and administration buildings have received major overhauls.

Miami University was founded in 1809 to provide a classical liberal education, and has never strayed from its central commitment to liberal arts. All undergraduates must complete the Miami Plan for Liberal Education, which **"Teaching is Miami's biggest strength."** provides them with a background in fine arts, humanities, social sciences, natural sciences, and formal reasoning. Popular majors include marketing, elementary education, accounting, finance, and psychology. For those with an inclination toward forestry or the paper industry, the university's unique pulp and paper science technology degree is in a league of its own—literally. It's only one of eight in the nation for undergraduates.

University requirements, or foundation courses, provide for a broad education, and all undergraduates must complete foundation courses in English composition, fine arts, humanities, social sciences and world cultures, biological and physical sciences, and mathematics, formal reasoning, or technology. Additional requirements include twelve credits of an advanced liberal education focus consisting of nine credits of thematic and sequential study outside of the student's major, and three credits of the Senior Capstone Experience, which ties in liberal education with the specialized knowledge of their major. In addition, the university's provost has launched the First-Year Initiative, a review of the lives of first-year students.

The academic atmosphere at Miami is competitive but not cut-throat. "The classes are challenging, and a great majority of students put academic performance first, making peer interaction a big plus," says one English major. Most students are conscientious about their grades, says a senior who has "never taken a class here lightly." The professors at Miami are described as "exceptional." "Teaching is Miami's biggest strength," raves one senior. Fifty percent of classes have less than twenty-five students, and most are taught by full professors, though graduate students do pop up. Many students complain that it's very hard to get required classes, especially foundation courses. "I've had to force-add classes or wait to take them in the summer," gripes a speech communications major.

About 40 percent of the student body are studying abroad at any given time. The Dolibois European Center in Luxembourg offers a semester or year-long program in the liberal arts and an opportunity to live with a foreign family. Other exchange opportunities include universities in Denmark, Japan, Mexico, Austria, and England as well as summer programs in France, Italy, Germany, Russia, Mexico, Luxembourg, the Caribbean, and Asia. There are new majors in mechanical and electrical engineering. Undergraduate research gets a lot of attention at Miami—the competitive Undergraduate Research Scholars program gives one hundred students a stipend, free tuition, and an expense account to complete a ten-week academic project. More than one thousand undergrads participate in research activities each year, and there also are several leadership programs.

"Miami is made up of a lot of preps who are well-dressed and have money to spend," says one student. Another adds that "a lot come from upper-middle-class families where Mom and Dad pay for everything." Eighty-eight percent of the student body is white, 4 percent African-American, and 2 percent each Hispanic and Asian-American. Seventy-two percent of students are from Ohio, and the campus has a reputation for conservatism. In recent years, Miami has begun an effort to attract more students of color with programs such as the Minority Professional

(Continued)
ACT Range: 24–29
Financial Aid: 32%
Expense: Pub $ $ $
Phi Beta Kappa: Yes
Applicants: 12,204
Accepted: 77%
Enrolled: 38%
Grad in 6 Years: 80%
Returning Freshmen: 90%
Academics: ✑ ✑ ✑ ✑ ½
Social: 🍷 🍷 🍷
Q of L: ★ ★ ★
Admissions: (513) 529-2531
Email Address:
   admission@muohio.edu

Strongest Programs:
Economics
Accountancy
Music
Chemistry
Botany
Microbiology
International Studies
Architecture

More than nine hundred undergrads study abroad each year—giving Miami University the distinction of being No. I in the nation for the number of students taking advantage of opportunities in other countries.

Leadership Program. In another effort to foster better race relations, the university holds a series of forums designed to identify and solve issues within the African-American community.

Forty-five percent of the student body call the campus home. A few of the dorms remain single-sex and are accompanied by visitation rules. Most upperclassmen find good, cheap off-campus housing by their senior year, but remain very involved on campus. Campus security is said to be good, and students report that they feel safe.

Miami has a lively on- and off-campus social life, although students complain that social restrictions on campus are on the rise. "Many get busted for underage drinking. If you get caught, you have to take a substance-abuse class and do one hundred hours of community service," explains one student, but it's still "relatively easy" to get served. A lot of socializing takes place in the restaurants, bars, and clubs of Oxford. Twenty-four percent of the men and 27 percent of the women involved in fraternities or sororities. In fact, Miami is known as the "mother of fraternities" because several began here.

The town of Oxford "is as good as it gets." One students explains: "The students comprise two-thirds of its population, and most of its shops cater to the students. [Oxford] is a wonderful and distinct college town." Cincinnati is about thirty-five miles away. The well-organized intramural program provides teams for just about every sport (including the ever-popular korfball and broomball), and the Student Recreational Sports Facility is well used. Other annual events include Make a Difference Day in cooperation with Oxford, homecoming, and continued rivalries with Ohio University.

The Redhawks field a number of competitive athletic teams. Swimming, tennis, and volleyball are among Miami's best varsity sports, but football and men's basketball reign as the most popular spectator sports. For women, soccer and swimming teams do well. Ice hockey, which is one of the top ten programs in the country, is also extremely popular, and the women's precision ice skating team is the only one

"[Oxford] is a wonderful and distinct college town."

at collegiate level in the nation. For cycling enthusiasts, the annual 20/20 Bike Race is one of the largest collegiate events of its kind in the country. Miami has been dubbed the "Cradle of Coaches"—at last count, more than one hundred Miami grads were actively coaching or engaged in administrative work at the collegiate level.

Miami University of Ohio, with its strong emphasis on liberal arts and its opportunities for research, travel abroad and leadership, is looked upon as one of the rising stars among state universities. It recently broke with tradition and pegs its tuition at the out-of-state level—with automatic discounts for Ohio residents. The school effectively combines a wide range of academic programs with the personal attention ordinarily found only at much smaller institutions.

Overlaps

Ohio University, Ohio State, Indiana University, University of Dayton, Notre Dame

If You Apply To ➤

Miami: Early decision: Nov. 1. Regular admissions: Jan. 31. Financial aid: Feb. 15. Housing: May 1. Does not guarantee to meet demonstrated need. Campus interviews: optional, informational. No alumni interviews. SATs or ACTs: required. SAT IIs: optional. Accepts the Common Application and electronic applications. Essay question: a fictional or historical figure or work that has influenced you; a teacher who has influenced you; a national or international concern that is important to you; a significant academic achievement, a risk or an ethical dilemma you have faced.

1220 Student Activities Building, Ann Arbor, MI 48109-1316

The most interesting mass of humanity east of UC–Berkeley. UM is among the nation's best in most subjects, but undergraduates must elbow their way to the front to get the full benefit. Superb honors and living/learning programs are the best bet for highly motivated students.

One of the nation's elite public universities, Michigan offers an excellent faculty, dynamite athletics, an endless number of special programs, and the most interesting collection of students east of Berkeley. "Michigan is a special place because it has a deep history and reputation," says a senior. "It is an excellent school and no matter what degree you have, it is respected."

Situated on 3,129 acres, Michigan's campus is so extensive that newcomers may want to come equipped with maps and a compass to find their way to class. The university is divided into two main campuses. Central Campus, the heart of the university, houses most of Michigan's nineteen schools and colleges. North Campus, which is two miles northeast of Central, is home to the College of Engineering, School of Music, School of Art and Design, College of Architecture and Urban Planning, and the new Media Union. Other campus areas include the Medical Center complex containing seven hospitals and fifteen outpatient facilities, and South Campus, featuring state-of-the art athletic facilities. Architecturally, the main drag of campus features a wide range of styles, from the classical Angell Hall to the Gothic Law Quad.

Academically, students describe the courses as challenging and rigorous but not cut-throat competitive. "Although some students are overly ambitious, most are willing to share their notes and study together," says a senior. The university ranks among the best in the nation in many fields of study, mainly because it attracts some of the biggest names in academia to teach and research in Ann Arbor. The College of Literature, Science, and the Arts is the largest school at Michigan. The College of Engineering and School of Business are well-respected, and the university's programs in health-related fields are also top-notch. Students report that professors are "knowledgeable." One student says, "The professors here are intelligent and seem to enjoy teaching." Students claim excellent academic and career advising is available, but only

> **"Michigan is a special place because it has a deep history and reputation."**

for those who seek it. The administration, however, notes the advising office, which registers nearly twelve thousand clients each year, offers individually tailored services and workshops. The Career Planning and Placement Office processes about 120,000 transactions each year, provides individual and group career counseling/planning and individual job placement, and works with 950 companies annually in recruiting UM graduating students.

One of Michigan's most distinct characteristics is its special academic programs, which seek to offer the best of both worlds—personalized attention and a large university setting. Approximately 627 active degree programs, including about 226 undergraduate majors as well as individualized concentrations, are offered, mainly through the College of Literature, Science, and the Arts. Some of these special programs include double majors, accelerated programs, independent study, field study, and internships. In addition, students can choose from several small interdisciplinary programs. The instructors live and teach in the residential hall in the Residential College and the Lloyd Hall Scholars Program. The Comprehensive Studies

Website: www.umich.edu
Location: Suburban
Total Enrollment: 38,103
Undergraduates: 24,412
Male/Female: 50/50
SAT Ranges: V 570–670
  M 610–710
ACT Range: 26–30
Financial Aid: 54%
Expense: Pub $ $ $
Phi Beta Kappa: Yes
Applicants: 24,109
Accepted: 52%
Enrolled: 43%
Grad in 6 Years: 83%
Returning Freshmen: 95%
Academics: ✍ ✍ ✍ ✍ ✍
Social: ☎ ☎ ☎
Q of L: ★ ★ ★
Admissions: (734) 764-7433
Email Address:
  ugadmiss@umich.edu

Strongest Programs:
Premed
Engineering
Art and Design
Architecture
Music
Film and Television
Journalism/Communications
Business

Program allows students to become part of a community of scholars who work in programs designed to best realize an individual student's potential.

The University of Michigan's honors program, considered to be one of the best in the nation, offers qualified students special honors courses, opportunities to participate in individual research or collaborative research, seminars, and special academic advisors. A preferred admissions program guarantees 150 top high school students admission to Michigan's professional programs in dentistry, biomedical engineering, social work, architecture, or pharmacy, provided they make satisfactory progress during their first years. The Undergraduate Research Opportunities Program enables students to work outside the classroom with a small group of students and a faculty member of their choice. The most popular majors at University of Michigan are business administration, mechanical engineering, psychology, English, and political science, but students say the statistics department needs improvement. Michigan also offers a number of foreign language majors not found many other places, including Arabic, Armenian, Persian, Turkish, and Islamic studies. The newest addition to the undergraduate program is the organizational studies major.

"The dorms are a tad small but livable with a little bit of work."

The University of Michigan's honors program, considered to be one of the best in the nation, offers qualified students special honors courses, opportunities to participate in individual or collaborative research, seminars, and special academic advisors.

No courses are required of all freshmen at Michigan, but all students are required to complete some coursework in English (including composition), foreign languages, natural sciences, social sciences, and humanities. Students in the College of Literature, Science, and the Arts must also take courses in quantitative reasoning and race or ethnicity. In addition, the university offers a series of seminars designed specifically for freshmen and sophomores, which are taught by tenured and tenure-track faculty.

Off-campus opportunities abound at the UM. Students have the chance to visit and study abroad in more than thirty different countries, including Australia, China, Costa Rica, Finland, France, Greece, India, Ireland, Japan, Russia, Sweden, and Turkey. Some specific programs include a year abroad in a French or German university, a business program in Paris, summer internships in selected majors, and special trips organized by individual departments.

The University of Michigan's admissions office sifts through some of the best students in the country, with 69 percent of the students in the top tenth of their high school class. Two-thirds of the undergraduates are from Michigan. The student body is remarkably diverse for a state university. In fact, Michigan's Program on Intergroup Relations, Conflict, and Community was recognized by former President Clinton's Initiative on Race as one of fourteen "promising practices" that successfully bridge racial divides in communities across America. Minorities now comprise one-fourth of UM's total enrollment, an all-time high. African-Americans and Hispanics combined make up 13 percent of the student body, and Asian-Americans make up another 12 percent. There is a large and well-organized Jewish community at Michigan, and gays and lesbians are also organized and prominent. While the student body is more conservative today than it was a decade ago, it is still "most noticeably liberal," says a history major, and political issues flare up from time to time on campus.

"There are coffeehouses, bars, sporting events, movie theaters, and a lot more."

Michigan really socks it to out-of-staters with a $13,000-plus surcharge. However, the university guarantees to meet the demonstrated financial need of all admitted Michigan residents.

Michigan really socks it to out-of-staters with a $13,000-plus surcharge. However, the university guarantees to meet the demonstrated financial need of all admitted Michigan residents. Students can also vie for merit scholarships of up to $25,000 as well as 408 athletic scholarships for men and women. Dormitories at the University of Michigan traditionally have well-defined personalities. Sixties-inspired types and "eccentrics" find the East Quad the "most open-minded dorms" (the Residential College is here). The Hill dorms are "more sedate." For those seeking alternative housing arrangements, a plethora of special-interest housing is available, including substance-free residence halls. On-campus housing is comfortable and well-maintained. "The dorms are a tad small but livable with a little bit of work," says a history major. Overcrowding is a thing of the past thanks to a major renewal and improvement project; residence halls were actually under capacity last fall. Housing is guaranteed for all incoming freshmen, leaving many upperclassmen to play the lottery. For the student who wants to live off campus, the UM housing office provides information, listings, and advice for finding suitable accommodations. Other alternatives include fraternity and sorority houses, and a large number of college- and privately owned co-ops.

Detroit is a little less than an hour away, but most students become quite fond of the picturesque town of Ann Arbor. "It's a great city with something for everyone," says a political science major. "There are coffeehouses, bars, sporting events, movie theaters, and a lot more." A surprising variety of visual and performing arts are offered in town and on campus. Underage drinking is not allowed, and a senior has a stern warning for any potential schemers: "Your fake ID will be taken. Plan on it. Do not be surprised, no matter how good it is." An annual art fair held in Ann Arbor draws craftspeople from throughout the nation and Canada. Many lakes and swimming holes lie only a short drive away and seem to keep the large summer-term population happy. As one junior says, "We are ranked high enough to be known for our academic success, but we still have a reputation for having a good time." Michigan

"It is an excellent school and no matter what degree you have, it is respected."

winters, though, are known for being cold and brutal. Seventeen percent of the undergraduates go Greek, though these groups are the bane of campus liberals. Many students also volunteer in the community. One senior explains, "Most students get involved, especially if it has something to do with helping kids."

Football overshadows nearly everything each fall as students gather to cheer "Go Blue." In 1999, the Wolverine football team won the Big Ten Conference championship, as did the baseball, men's cross-country, men's and women's gymnastics, women's indoor track, and softball teams. Attending football games is an integral part of the UM experience, students say, and "you shouldn't be allowed to graduate if you haven't gone to a hockey game," quips a sophomore. Intramurals, which were invented at the University of Michigan, provide students with a more casual form of athletics.

The University of Michigan strives to offer its students a delicate balance between academics, athletics, and social activities. On one hand, this is American college as it's characterized in movies like *Animal House*—football and fraternities. But it's also a college with a fine faculty and top-rated programs, intent upon making America competitive in the twenty-first century. For assertive students who crave spirit and action as well as outstanding academics, Michigan is an excellent choice.

Overlaps

Michigan State, Northwestern, Cornell University, Duke, Penn

If You Apply To > **Michigan:** Rolling admissions. Regular admissions: Feb. 1. Financial aid: Mar. 15. Guarantees to meet demonstrated need of in-state students. Campus and alumni interviews: optional, informational. SATs or ACTs: required. SAT IIs: optional. Essay question: personal statement. Apply to particular school or program. Policies and deadlines vary by school.

250 Administration Building, East Lansing, MI 48824

Most people don't realize that Michigan State is significantly bigger than University of Michigan. (Classes via videotape don't help the situation.) Students can find a niche in strong preprofessional programs such as hotel and restaurant management, prevet, business, and engineering.

Website: www.msu.edu
Location: City outskirts
Total Enrollment: 44,937
Undergraduates: 34,559
Male/Female: 47/53
SAT Ranges: V 520–640
  M 540–660
ACT Range: 23–28
Financial Aid: N/A
Expense: Pub $ $
Phi Beta Kappa: Yes
Applicants: 25,210
Accepted: 67%
Enrolled: 41%
Grad in 6 Years: 69%
Returning Freshmen: 89%
Academics: ✍ ✍ ✍
Social: ☎ ☎ ☎ ☎
Q of L: ★ ★ ★
Admissions: (517) 355-8332
Email Address:
  admis@mus.edu

Strongest Programs:
Music Performance
Engineering
Packaging
Chemistry
Education
Hospitality Business
Accounting and Finance
Criminal Justice

Michigan State began as an agricultural school, and like most seeds planted in well-tended fields, the school's "cash crop"—a solid education in a friendly and fun-loving atmosphere—grows stronger each year. The school's focus has broadened to include would-be engineers, entrepreneurs, hoteliers, and doctors of the veterinary, traditional, and osteopathic persuasions, in addition to future farmers. The more than forty thousand students who now populate East Lansing may come from the gritty Motor City or from pretty Traverse City in the Lower Peninsula, or from farms or mining towns in the Upper Peninsula. But they have one thing in common: "Everyone has a smile for you here," says a communications major. "I noticed it from the first day."

The older heart of the MSU campus, north of the Red Cedar River, boasts ivy-covered brick buildings, some built before the Civil War and listed on the National Register of Historic Places. This area houses five colleges and includes the MSU Union and ten residence halls. Across the Red Cedar is the medical complex, the modern residence hall complexes, and not one but two eighteen-hole golf courses. On the southernmost part of campus are University Farms, where researchers keep up MSU's reputation as a premier land grant university through work in agricultural and animal production. New additions and renovations on campus include a six-story biomedical and physical science building and the National Superconducting Cyclotron Laboratory. The seemingly endless verdant acres of MSU's campus offer all the positive aspects of a large city and the safety of a town, along with lots of peaceful little spots to get away from the pressure of classes and hubbub of the crowd.

"Everyone has a smile for you here. I noticed it from the first day."

As a land grant university, MSU traditionally has been strong in agriculture and preveterinary science. However, psychology, accounting, finance, engineering, education, and criminal justice are also among the school's top drawing cards. Math is cited as weaker than most. Several new programs have been introduced, including majors in professional writing, technology systems management, plant pathology, and jazz studies. MSU boasts the nation's first School of Packaging, and student trainees from the Hotel, Restaurant, and Institutional Management program staff the university hotel. General education requirements include math, tier I and II writing courses, a 2000 and 3000 level social sciences course, two courses in arts/humanities, and one physical and biological science course with a lab. There is a strong international component, too. With eighty study abroad programs located in over forty countries around the world, it's not surprising that MSU sent more than thirteen hundred students to terms away last year, more than any other U.S. university.

The academic climate at MSU can be as daunting as its size. "The students here generally are very motivated in their academic endeavors," says an education major. The computerized enrollment system has done away with long registration lines, and advisors can help with overrides for classes that are technically full. Most lectures are given by professors. "Teaching is very high quality," an international relations major reports. Labs and smaller recitation sections are led by TAs, students say. Also controversial among students is the technique of teaching some classes via cassettes or videotapes, followed by twenty-minute discussion sessions with graduate assistants and one writing session per week. Academic advising gets high marks: "The advisors are very helpful, you just have to take the initiative to seek out their help," says a sophomore.

A sophomore describes MSU students as "friendly, outgoing, highly intelligent" people. Relationships across ethnic and racial lines are calm, students say. The campus may not get as heated as U of Michigan "down south" in Ann Arbor when it comes to political issues, but such issues as abortion and affirmative action can rouse activists here as well. MSU shows that diversity on campus can work. Indeed, African-Americans and Hispanics account for 12 percent of students, and Asian-Americans make up 5 percent. Each year hundreds of students receive scholarships for outstanding academic performance that range from $200 to $22,580. Athletic scholarships lure devotees of many different sports.

"The university and the city work hard on relations and many students are active in the community."

With a capacity of nearly eighteen thousand, MSU's residence system is the largest of any university in the nation. Almost half of all undergrads live on campus. MSU has divided its massive college into two smaller residential colleges, James Madison (organized around the social sciences) and Lyman Briggs (emphasizing the natural sciences and math). Each houses fewer than one thousand students and aims to create the feeling of a small undergraduate institution. Three much bigger living-learning complexes, each with about four residence halls, are also available, giving residents access to libraries, faculty offices, classrooms, counseling, cafeterias, and recreation areas. "The dorms are very nice, but very different depending on the side of campus you live on," says one student. An honors college brings the brightest freshmen together, houses them separately if they wish, and assigns them a special advisor. Other living/learning programs, known by their catchy acronyms, include RISE (focus on the environment), ROIAL (arts and letters), ROSES (science and engineering), and STAR (Support-Teamwork-Achievement-Resources).

Freshmen and sophomores usually live in "clean and well-maintained" residence halls with populations from 250 to more than twelve hundred. The halls offer various living options, including single-sex or co-ed, high-rise or low-rise, smoking or nonsmoking, and extra quiet or alcohol free. "I had a positive experience living in the dorm," says a junior, who adds, "The rules tended to be strict." Room and board includes various meal plans at any of the cafeterias sprinkled throughout the residence halls, all of which receive good reviews. For juniors and seniors, apartment living often becomes the thing in college-owned facilities or in East Lansing. But parking places are in chronically short supply. Fraternity and sorority members mostly live in their own off-campus houses. And despite its bucolic surroundings, campus safety is as much of an issue here as anywhere: Michigan State has its own police force, green light emergency phone system, and riding and walking escort services for those who need to travel at night.

With so many people concentrated in one spot, it's no wonder the residence halls and active Greek system (9 percent of men and women) sponsor popular MSU social events. As at most schools, the rule on alcohol is no one under twenty-one is served but a zero-tolerance policy, meaning that police can Breathalyze any student suspected of being under the influence, gives the rule teeth here. Popular leisure-time activities include picnics, pizza-eating contests, hall Olympics, hayrides, and ice-skating outings. The annual Michigan Festival brings big-name performers such as R.E.M., Elton John, and the Red Hot Chili Peppers to campus. The town of East Lansing, where the Land Shark and Rick's are popular hangouts, is a short walk from campus and many students do volunteer work in the community. "The uni-

MSU boasts the nation's first School of Packaging, and student trainees from the Hotel, Restaurant, and Institutional Management program staff the university hotel.

The halls offer various living options, including single-sex or co-ed, high-rise or low-rise, smoking or nonsmoking, and extra quiet or alcohol free.

The older heart of the MSU campus, north of the Red Cedar River, boasts ivy-covered brick buildings, some built before the Civil War and listed on the National Register of Historic Places.

versity and the city work hard on relations and many students are active in the community," says a junior.

Weekends are dominated by Big Ten athletic competitions, with the Michigan–MSU rivalry especially fierce. A sophomore proudly describes the pregame ritual: "During the week before the U of M–MSU football game, students guard our mascot Sparty, the largest free-standing ceramic statue in the world, and protect him from sneaky Wolverines." More than a few times, the Spartans have upset their archrivals in football and basketball; they even won the 2000 NCAA championship. The marching band is also a national award winner.

Nintety-one percent of the student population is from the state of Michigan. But that doesn't mean everyone is alike. MSU's position in the "middle of the mitten" brings students from the UP or the LP, from the suburbs of Motown and the tiniest small towns, lending the bonus of cultural diversity to complement the academic diversity of this big, beautiful campus.

Overlaps

University of Michigan, Western Michigan, Central Michigan, Grand Valley State, Eastern Michigan

If You Apply To ➤ **MSU:** Rolling admissions. Financial aid: May 1. Guarantees to meet demonstrated need. Campus and alumni interviews: optional, informational. SATs or ACTs: required. SAT IIs: not accepted. Accepts the Common Application and electronic applications. No essay question.

Middlebury College

Middlebury, VT 05753

One of the few small liberal arts colleges where applications have surged significantly in the past ten years. Students are drawn to the beauty of Midd's Green Mountain location and strong programs in hot areas such as international studies and environmental science. Known worldwide for its summer foreign language programs.

Website: www.middlebury.edu
Location: Small town
Total Enrollment: 2,297
Undergraduates: 2,297
Male/Female: 49/51
SAT Ranges: V 680–750
 M 670–740
ACT Range: 29–32
Financial Aid: 36%
Expense: Pr $ $ $ $
Phi Beta Kappa: Yes
Applicants: 5,299
Accepted: 27%
Enrolled: 41%
Grad in 6 Years: 88%
Returning Freshmen: 96%
Academics: 🎓🎓🎓🎓½
Social: 🎭🎭🎭
Q of L: ★★★

The nickname of Middlebury College—"Club Midd"—may bring to mind a tropical resort, but this school's rigorous workload is far from a four-year vacation. The campus, with its picturesque sunsets, excellent skiing, and rural Vermont charm, is a paradise for those interested in environmental studies, second and third languages, and a tight-knit community where highly motivated and intelligent students and faculty truly care about each other. "To be able to get a top-notch education in such an inspiring place is an opportunity that I consider myself incredibly lucky to have," says a sophomore English major. "Every day that I walk by the admissions building, I say a silent 'thank-you' for giving me this."

The college's 350-acre main campus overlooks the village of Middlebury, Vermont, which a senior calls a "typical quaint Vermont town." The eighteen-hundred-acre mountain campus, site of the Bread Loaf School of English, the Bread Loaf Writers' Conference, and the college's Snow Bowl, is nearby. Old Stone Row cuts across the campus, where buildings with simple lines and rectangular shapes evoke the mills of early New England. (Middlebury was founded in 1800.) Academic halls and dormitories of marble and limestone sit in quadrangles with views of the Adirondacks and Green Mountains. New additions include: Ross Commons, a residential and dining facility; an improved field house, with expanded seating and a new floor; the Duke Nelson Intramural Sports Facility; and the Peter Kohn Field, with an all-weather artificial turf. Next up are a new library, dining hall, and two residence halls.

Even with the recent building boom, Middlebury's priorities remain inside the classroom. Between June and August, Middlebury banishes English from its campus and hundreds of students live, learn, and, hopefully, think only in their chosen language, some wearing T-shirts that proclaim "No English spoken here." The language departments continue their excellent instruction during the school year; especially notable are German, Chinese, and Japanese. Although there is no foreign language requirement, just about everyone studies another language, if only to take advantage of Middlebury's campuses in France, Germany, Italy, Spain, and Russia. The school is also a member of the Maritime Studies Program.* There are ninety college-approved programs in total, and about 60 percent of juniors take advantage of them. Other highly touted Middlebury departments include English (the second-most popular major, bolstered by its connections to the famed Bread Loaf writer's conference), economics, and psychology. "Middlebury's academics are very rigorous and students are kept quite busy. But the fact is that you enjoy what you're learning so much that it usually doesn't feel overwhelming," says a sophomore English major. Teamwork also helps; "everyone here is totally willing and eager to help out a classmate at any time," says a senior political science student. Students cite math and film departments as limited. New programs include a neuroscience major and a course in Portuguese that will eventually be developed into a major.

> **"To be able to get a top-notch education in such an inspiring place is an opportunity that I consider myself incredibly lucky to have."**

Midd kids must take a discussion-based, writing-intensive First-Year Seminar with only fifteen people; the instructor serves as advisor to those enrolled until they declare a major. By the end of sophomore year, students must complete a second writing-intensive course. In addition to a ten- to sixteen-credit major, students must also satisfy distribution requirements in seven of eight academic areas: literature, the arts, philosophical and religious studies, history, physical and life sciences, deductive reasoning and analytical processes, social analysis, and foreign language. Students also take four cultures and civilizations classes, and two noncredit courses in physical education. With all of these requirements, it's no wonder students and faculty become close. "The quality of teaching is terrific!" says a sophomore philosophy and religion joint major. "Even if I have not been completely interested in the subject matter, my professors are so enthusiastic that it motivates me at least to take the course seriously."

> **"Everyone here is totally willing and eager to help out a classmate at any time."**

Seventy-four percent of Middlebury's students graduated in the top tenth of their high school class, and students of color constitute 14 percent of the student body. The school's partnership with New York City's Posse Foundation brings ten inner-city students to the school each year. Lack of parking is a familiar complaint, and students are concerned about the environment and the war in Iraq. A substance-free social house now offers living space. Middlebury's small, close-knit community can also make the place claustrophobic. Says a literary studies major, "Sometimes you just want to be anonymous, and it's absolutely impossible."

Few Middlebury students live off campus (5 percent), since tuition includes guaranteed housing for four years. A variety of "palatial" co-ed dorms offer suites, augmented by college-owned group houses, the Environmental House (where residents cook all of their own food), academic interest houses, and more "standard" situations. Rooms for upperclassmen are distributed by lottery, based on seniority, a system which a sophomore calls "somewhat of a chaotic nightmare." It's easy to get a single room, even as a sophomore, students report. The meal plan is served at five dining halls, which set high marks for both their decor and their victuals.

(Continued)

Admissions: (802) 443-3000
Email Address: admissions@ middlebury.edu

Strongest Programs:
Political Science
Language Study
Environmental Studies
Biology
Economics
English/Literary Studies
International Studies
Dance and Theater

New programs include a neuroscience major and a course in Portuguese that will eventually be developed into a major.

Students at Middlebury play as hard on the weekends as they work during the week. Most stay on campus for school-sponsored movies, discussions, or parties at the Greek-like co-ed social houses. Kegs are outlawed in the dorms but permitted at parties, which must be registered and also offer non-alcoholic drinks and snacks. Security keeps watch on these parties, but underage students still find ways to imbibe, students say. The college's Grille provides an alternative, with performers throughout the week and weekend.

"Sometimes you just want to be anonymous, and it's absolutely impossible."

Off campus, Middlebury is "the quintessential New England town, straight out of Normal Rockwell" that is "oriented almost exclusively to the college." It has necessities such as fast food, a grocery store, drug store, hardware store, and clothing shops, but the administration regularly airlifts or buses in culture and entertainment. February can be grim because the snow here comes early and stays late, so road trips are popular. The progressive city of Burlington is 45 minutes away, while Montreal is a three hours' drive, Boston four, and New York City five. Middlebury's own Snow Bowl ($100 for the season) and proximity to most Vermont ski slopes make this a paradise for ski fanatics, a breed Middlebury attracts in predictably large numbers.

Middlebury athletics draw rabid fans, especially when on cheering the powerful ice hockey teams—men's and women's—that compete in Division III against archrival Williams. Men's swimming and men's and women's lacrosse are also strong, having brought home conference championships recently. The administration shows its support, too, by favoring student athletes in admissions. Perhaps the biggest outdoor activity of all is the three-day Winter Carnival, an annual extravaganza including parties, cultural events, an all-school formal, sporting competitions, snow sculpture, and ice-skating at an outdoor rink. Townspeople support the school's hockey games, and students give back through volunteer work with children, women, the elderly, and local schools. "Community service is a big part of who we are here at Midd," says a sophomore.

"Community service is a big part of who we are here at Midd."

Students have noticed physical changes at Middlebury over the past few years, with more in the works, including a library due to open soon. But some things have remained the same—namely, the combination of "excellent academics with endless extracurricular opportunities," says a sophomore. "Academics are very important to us, but we realize that there's a lot to learn in life that can't be found in textbooks," a sophomore says.

The school's partnership with New York City's Posse Foundation brings ten inner-city students to the school each year.

Overlaps

Dartmouth, Williams, Yale, Amherst, Brown

If You Apply To ➤ **Middlebury:** Early decision I: Nov. 15. Early decision II: Dec. 15, Part I; Jan. 1, Common Application and essays. Regular admissions: Dec. 15, Part I; Jan. 1, Common Application and essays. Guarantees to meet demonstrated need. Campus and alumni interviews: optional, evaluative. The ACT or any three SAT IIs, AP exams or IB exams as long as those submitted include a writing test, a quantitative test, and one of the student's choice. Accepts the Common Application and electronic applications. Essay question: one Common Application essay; and describe an experience in which your values were tested.

Millsaps College

1701 North State Street, Jackson, MS 39210

Millsaps is the best liberal arts college in the deep, deep South. Its largely preprofessional student body typically has sights set on business, law or medicine.

Typically compared to Hendrix, Rhodes, and Sewanee, though less selective than the last two.

Millsaps College, long recognized as a finishing school for well-bred Southern belles and gentlemen, is also the best liberal arts institutions in the deep South. Its Heritage Program, an interdisciplinary approach to Western culture, is nationally recognized. "We're half spoiled little rich kids who sleep through classes and half academically minded students who are here on scholarships," explains a sophomore. "Since the school is so small, a great sense of community is established—and that includes all faculty, up to the president!"

Millsaps is situated in the center of Jackson, but owing to the city's small size, it offers the serenity of a less urban environment. The Bowl—according to legend, the crater of an extinct volcano—marks the center of campus, surrounded by an eight-foot wrought iron fence. Dotting the rest of campus is a mix of modern and traditional buildings, dominated by the 122-foot, copper-sheathed Millsaps Tower at the east entrance. The Campus Life Complex opened in January 2000, with offices for student organizations, a coffee house and cafeteria, fitness facilities, and a stage for outdoor events.

Millsaps requires students to complete 128 semester hours to earn a degree, all but eight of which must be taken for a letter grade. All students must also complete ten multidisciplinary courses designed to develop their skills in reasoning, communications, quantitative thinking, valuing, and decision-making—including four in the humanities and four in the sciences and math. Students begin the humanities sequence with either Heritage or Topics of the Ancient World. "The Heritage program, an option for incoming freshmen, is incredible," says one freshman. All freshmen also take a one-hour Perspectives class, led by an academic advisor, to aid in adjusting to college life, and all new students take the Introduction to Liberal Studies seminar, which emphasizes critical thinking and writing. Mandatory freshman and senior seminars provide perspective on the work in between.

> "We're half spoiled little rich kids who sleep through classes and half academically minded students who are here on scholarships."

Among the best programs at Millsaps are English—"We have the leading Eudora Welty scholar," says a freshman—and education, where students get involved with the Jackson Public Schools from introductory-level classes. The Else School of Management, Millsaps' business school, offers strong programs in accounting, business administration (the most popular major), and economics. Premed courses, including those in biology and chemistry, are also well-regarded. New courses include Superscience!, Living History: A Journey through the Civil Rights Movement, and Geographic Information Systems and Mediterranean Archaeology. Physics and political science suffer somewhat because each has only two faculty members, administrators say.

No course at Millsaps has more than fifty students, and three-quarters have twenty-five or less. "The quality of teaching is superb," raves a junior. "Freshmen are always taught by full professors." Off campus, students may do research for credit at Tennessee's Oak Ridge National Laboratory or at the Gulf Coast Research Laboratory, or they may intern for credit with local businesses or in government offices. Each year, about twelve upperclassmen are accepted into the Ford Teaching Fellows Program, letting them work closely with a faculty member to learn about teaching—and paying them for their time in the classroom. Students eager to see how government works may participate in the Washington Semester,* while those seeking passport stamps may spend summers in London, Paris, Munich, Florence, Nice, the Yucatan, or Costa Rica. Cooperative programs are also available through

Website: www.millsaps.edu
Location: City center
Total Enrollment: 1,251
Undergraduates: 1,158
Male/Female: 45/55
SAT Ranges: V 550–640
  M 530–650
ACT Range: 23–29
Financial Aid: 55%
Expense: Pr $ $
Phi Beta Kappa: Yes
Applicants: 913
Accepted: 87%
Enrolled: 32%
Grad in 6 Years: 68%
Returning Freshmen: 81%
Academics: ✍ ✍ ✍
Social: ☎ ☎ ☎
Q of L: ★ ★ ★
Admissions: (601) 352-1050
Email Address:
  admissions@millsaps.edu

Strongest Programs:
Accounting
Business Administration
Economics
Biology/Premed
Classics
Education
English
History

Students may do research for credit at Tennessee's Oak Ridge National Laboratory, the Gulf Coast Research Laboratory, or intern for credit with local businesses or in government offices.

the Associated Colleges of the South* consortium, of which Millsaps is a founding member. For students seeking careers in the medical field, Julian and Kathryn Wiener Premedical Summer Research Fellowships are also available.

Millsaps has broadened its recruiting efforts, and 44 percent of students now come from out of state. They're also getting smarter: 39 percent of a recent freshman class graduated in the top tenth of their high school class. While Millsaps was the first college in Mississippi to voluntarily adopt open admission for minority students, it's still far from diverse. African-Americans now account for 11 percent of the student body, Asian-Americans 3 percent, and Hispanics 1 percent. "Since this is a small, private, Methodist-based school, our rivals in the area tend to be much more conservative than we are," says a political science major. "As far as other liberal arts schools in the south, the actual students here seem to be much more grounded." Merit scholarships are available, but student-athletes must look elsewhere for funding as there are no athletic scholarships.

"The dorms are all quite different and have various levels of quality."

Most Mississippians view Millsaps as a hotbed of liberalism—noting that the school's co-ed dorms confirm their worst fears. Freshmen, however, are still required to live in single-sex halls. Seventy-eight percent of students stay in campus housing—mostly, grouses a sophomore, because they lose a third of their scholarship money if they leave. "The dorms are all quite different and have various levels of quality," the student reports. "Housing selection is a lottery done by classes." Junior and senior men may live in one of four fraternity houses; there is no sorority housing, even though the Greek system claims 50 percent of men and 50 percent of women. The food on campus gets good reviews. "The cafe always takes suggestions and even holds recipe competitions for new dishes," explains a junior.

The social scene at Millsaps revolves around the fraternity houses, which are usually open and rocking from Wednesday through Saturday nights. Greek rush is now held after fall midterms instead of during the first hectic week of school, but that hasn't dampened the party spirit. "The school tries to offer lots of on-campus events, and the frats seem to spike up the social atmosphere," says one student. The school's alcohol policy says only students of age may drink, and then only in their rooms—but students say the rule is only loosely enforced. "It's very easy for underage students to get alcohol, especially at the frat houses," says a freshman. Easy road trips include New Orleans and Memphis; closer to campus, ten miles to the north, is a huge reservoir, popular for weekend water sports. Major Madness is a favorite annual event, offering a week of open mic nights, hypnotists, and comedians, and culminating in a weekend-long festival in the Bowl, with food, games, and live music.

Millsaps competes in NCAA Division III, as a member of the Southern Collegiate Athletic Conference (SCAC), so it isn't nearly as sports-crazy as most Southern campuses. For the men, football, basketball, baseball, and soccer draw the largest crowds; basketball, soccer, softball, and volleyball are the most popular among women's teams. "We have a rivalry with Mississippi College that lots of Millsaps folks are hard-core about, and lots of MC folks couldn't care less about," quips a sophomore. "Or, as a friend of mine says, 'A one-sided rivalry—isn't that called hatred?'"

In a state renowned for its legendary blues and warm deltas, Millsaps College remains a well-kept secret. Small classes ensure plenty of time to get to know fellow students and faculty members. Emphasizing "scholarly inquiry and intellectual growth," in the words of the Honor Code, Millsaps is built around "a spirit of personal honesty and mutual trust." And that's one tradition that never gets old.

Most Mississippians view Millsaps as a hotbed of liberalism—noting that the school's co-ed dorms confirm their worst fears. Freshmen, however, are still required to live in single-sex halls.

Overlaps

University of Mississippi, Mississippi State, Rhodes, Mississippi College, University of the South

If You
Apply
To ≫

Millsaps: Early action: Dec. 1. Rolling admissions: Jun. 1. Financial aid: Mar. 1. Housing: May 1. Guarantees to meet demonstrated need. Campus interviews: recommended, informational. No alumni interviews. SATs or ACTs: required. SAT IIs: optional. Accepts the Common Application and electronic applications. Essay question: community, state, national, or world issue in which you've gotten involved; what fictional character would you be and why; the most memorable or significant experience of your life.

Mills College

5000 MacArthur Boulevard, Oakland, CA 94613

One of two major women's colleges on the West Coast. Mills has the Oakland area to fall back on, including UC–Berkeley, where students can take classes. Mills is strongest in the arts and math, though it does offer small programs in preprofessional areas such as communications and business economics.

At Mills College, women receive more than just a liberal arts education. Students are expected to graduate with a deeper understanding of social issues and a broad knowledge base that ensures they will be technologically savvy and artistically aware of the world around them. As one junior says, "The students here want more out of their education than being a number and having TA's instead of professors. Students are here because they want to learn, not because they think they need to go to college."

The school's fascinating history started in 1852, when it began as a young ladies' seminary serving the children of California gold rush adventurers who were determined to see their daughters raised in an atmosphere of gentility. Now, the combination of student diversity and educational opportunity guarantees that no one can graduate without having her horizons well expanded. It is a place where issues are debated and analyzed, and many students are politically active in such groups as NOW, Young Women's Political Caucus, and League of Women Voters. To foster its relationship with the surrounding community, the James Irvine Foundation has awarded the college a three-year grant to support the "Multicultural Engagement: Mills and Oakland" initiative.

The park-like 135-acre campus boasts both historic and modern architecture set among rolling meadows, woods, and a meandering creek. Residence halls and classrooms are located within easy walking distance of one another.

The college has completely revamped its general education curriculum. The program is designed to graduate students who are able to write clearly, think across disciplines, work productively with others, analyze, and reason clearly; who are technology savvy, artistically sensitive, adept in scientific and historical thinking; and aware of multiculturalism, the influence of social institutions, and the

> **"Students are here because they want to learn, not because they think they need to go to college."**

issues facing women in society. To that end, the college takes a broad view of a student's major, choosing instead to ensure she has a wide base of knowledge in her first year.

The general education requirements fall into three categories: skills, perspectives, and disciplines. Students are expected to master writing, reasoning, and computer skills. Women will gain an interdisciplinary perspective, as well as a deeper understanding of gender issues and multiculturalism. The disciplinary experiences range from the arts to natural sciences. Instead of having specific courses that fulfill

Website: www.mills.edu
Location: City outskirts
Total Enrollment: 1,206
Undergraduates: 763
Male/Female: 0/100
SAT Ranges: V 500–640
  M 480–620
ACT Range: N/A
Financial Aid: 100%
Expense: Pr $ $ $
Phi Beta Kappa: Yes
Applicants: 484
Accepted: 85%
Enrolled: 33%
Grad in 6 Years: 60%
Returning Freshmen: 81%
Academics: ✐ ✐ ✐
Social: ☎ ☎ ☎
Q of L: ★ ★ ★
Admissions: (800) 87-MILLS
Email Address:
  admission@mills.edu

Strongest Programs:
English
Computer Science
Dance
Psychology
Music
Studio Art
Political, Legal, and
  Economic Analysis

each requirement, students are able to choose from a variety of classes or draw from college-level courses they took in high school.

The first-year English course has been developed to introduce students to college-level writing. A unique seminar program allows students to work closely with one or two professors in an intensive collaborative classroom. The college also has designed an Electronic Collaborative Learning Center, which gives faculty and students the opportunity to use technology and computer literacy in teaching. Classes range from small to smaller; 95 percent of the classes taken by freshmen have twenty-five students or less. One junior boasts that freshmen often are taught by full professors, but at the least classes are led by assistant professors—not by teaching assistants or adjuncts. The professors are highly regarded, friendly, and accessible. With a remarkable 61 percent of them women, there's no shortage of excellent female role models. "The courses are as rigorous as students choose to make them," a women's studies major says.

English, history, psychology, art, and dance are all praised by Mills students, but most agree the natural sciences are the most improved; premed students enjoy a 75 percent acceptance rate at med schools. Popular among prelaw students is the interdisciplinary program in administration and legal studies. The fine arts department is Mills' traditional stronghold, and electronic and computer music specializations within the music program are worthy of note, as is the fact that Mills was the first women's college to offer a major in computer science. Students and the administration consider that pioneering move to have been a

"It's not as nurturing as you might think."

good investment in what is now among the best mathematics and computer science programs around. Newer majors include public policy, environmental science, and a joint bachelor's/master's program in economics. Foreign languages are somewhat limited, although students can make up for it through cross-registration at Berkeley. What administrators cited as the two weakest programs, German and dramatic arts, have been dropped from the curriculum.

Mills students are encouraged to explore beyond the Oakland campus, and many take advantage of the excellent programs abroad and exchanges with other American schools. A year at a women's or co-ed college in the East is especially popular. Mills has concurrent cross-registration agreements with UC–Berkeley and most Bay Area universities, with five-year engineering programs with several of the same schools. Opportunities for internships abound. Students take advantage of the fully automated 6-million-dollar F.W. Olin Library, with access to the huge facilities at Berkeley.

Two-thirds of Mills women are from California, and most attended public school. Asian-Americans and Hispanics make up 18 percent of the student body, and African-Americans make up 10 percent. Sixty-three percent of students ranked in the top quarter of their graduating class. An influential subgroup of the student body is "resumers," women returning to college after a break of several years. Merit scholarships ranging from $2,000 to $23,000 are available to qualified students, but there are no athletic scholarships.

Four Mediterranean-style old dorms and three California-modern hill dorms offer a plethora of spacious single rooms. "Most halls are very charming and have their own unique style," a junior says. Only 57 percent of the students live on campus, so there's not much of a housing crunch. Students can freely take advantage of cooperative housing, college-owned apartments, and French- and Spanish-language wings. Older dorms are more homey, with high ceilings and long windows. Each of the older dorms has its own dining room, in which traditions are very important.

Each Wednesday night a sit-down candlelight dinner is served, and each year students feast on a Christmas dinner of Cornish game hens and flaming plum pudding. Another old-dorm dining tradition is the candle passing ceremony: a candle is passed around the table until the honored woman blows it out. Students living in the three newer dorms eat together at the commons. And there isn't a place on campus where the food is not excellent.

Fears about a stunted social life on this tiny campus quietly linger throughout. "It's not as nurturing as you might think," a senior says. Building an active social life requires an "open and adventurous spirit." And what the campus may lack in social options can be found in Berkeley and San Francisco, only a short distance away. One junior says it's easy to get involved in volunteer work in the middle-class neighborhood that surrounds the college.

With a bus stop on campus, it is easy to get around Oakland and into San Francisco to take advantage of the dining, dancing, and cultural resources of both cities. Farther away, there's skiing in the Sierra Nevadas and the temptations of scenic Reno. Road trips to Tahoe are popular. Sports include the successful crew, cross-country, and soccer teams. Participation in student government and other campus organizations is strong. Other activities include Amnesty International and environmental activism. "Students are very proactive and socially aware," a junior confirms.

With the bustling Bay Area as their backyard, students at Mills College have the opportunity for work and for play. And with an educational program that emphasizes skills critical for understanding today's society and succeeding in the real world, the college's women are sure to graduate as independent thinkers capable of making it on their own.

If You Apply To ➢ **Mills:** Regular admissions: Feb. 1. Early action: Nov. 15. Financial aid: Feb. 1. Meets demonstrated need of 48%. Campus interviews: recommended, informational. Alumnae interviews: optional, informational. SATs or ACTs: required. SAT IIs: recommended. Accepts the Common Application. Essay question: submit sample of graded analytical paper or essay from the past year.

University of Minnesota–Morris

600 East 4th Street, Morris, MN 56267-2199

The plains of western Minnesota is an unlikely place to find a liberal arts college— and a public one at that. Morris is cut from the same cloth as UNC–Asheville, St. Mary's of Maryland, and Mary Washington. The draw: private-college education at a public-university price.

The University of Minnesota–Morris is far more comprehensive than its small size might indicate. Founded by a Roman Catholic nun as a school for Native Americans, Morris has since grown into a full-fledged university with solid academics, a dedicated faculty, opportunities for collaborative research, and options for study abroad. One of the four University of Minnesota campuses, Morris has become a quality public liberal arts college where personal attention is commonplace.

The school lies on one hundred thirty acres in west-central Minnesota, which for some students means "mootown." The campus is composed of twenty-six traditional brick-and-mortar buildings loosely arranged around a central mall. A recent $28 million addition to the science building doubled the size of the science and math facility.

In the classroom, Morris students must complete at least ninety credits of general education coursework outside their major in subjects ranging from writing, foreign

Website: www.mrs.umn.edu
Location: Small town
Total Enrollment: 1,910
Undergraduates: 1,910
Male/Female: 40/60
SAT Ranges: V 540–640
  M 520–640
ACT Range: 22–27
Financial Aid: 66%
Expense: Pub $ $
Phi Beta Kappa: No
Applicants: 1,299

(Continued)

Accepted: 82%

Enrolled: 45%

Grad in 6 Years: 56%

Returning Freshmen: 79%

Academics: ✐ ✐ ✐ ½

Social: ☎ ☎

Q of L: ★ ★ ★

Admissions: (800) 992-8863

Email Address:
admissions@mrs.umn.edu

Strongest Programs:
Biology
Elementary and Secondary
    Education
Psychology
Music
Computer Science

One of the college's
innovations is Morris
Academic Partners, in
which select students
receive a stipend to
conduct their own research
with a faculty member.

Once a year, Morris
coordinates a three-day
Multicultural Student
Leadership retreat to
foster civility and respect
on campus.

language, mathematical and symbolic reasoning, and artistic performance to historical perspectives, human behavior, communication, fine arts, physical and biological sciences, and the global village. Freshmen are also required to take a diversity seminar. Among major fields, the sciences and math are highly regarded, as is Morris's psychology department, which is known for breakthrough studies of daydreams. Pre-professional programs for wannabe doctors, lawyers, veterinarians, pharmacists, and physical therapists are recognized, too.

One of the college's innovations is Morris Academic Partners, in which select students receive a stipend to conduct their own research with a faculty member. The merit-based Undergraduate Research Opportunities Program offers financial rewards to students for research, scholarly, or creative projects undertaken in collaboration with a faculty member. Because of that program, students at Morris produce a greater percentage

"I can always get the help I need from academic or career counseling."

of undergraduate research than other campuses in the University of Minnesota system. Students in the English Language Teaching Assistant Program travel to schools in foreign countries to assist English teachers. The study abroad program at Morris allows students to live and learn in Africa, the Middle East, Asia, the South Pacific, and Europe. Majors in statistics and anthropology have been added, along with a minor in African-American studies.

Class size at Morris is generally small by public university standards: 90 percent have fifty or fewer students. The quality of teaching is "outstanding," says a management major. "Professors are always more than willing to sit down with you and discuss things," adds a freshman. Faculty also receive high marks from students for their individualized approach and willingness to get to know students as people, not just numbers on a class list. Every freshman is assigned an academic advisor who must approve his or her schedule. "I can always get the help I need from academic or career counseling," says a sophomore.

Morris draws 84 percent of its students from Minnesota, and 66 percent of incoming freshmen graduated in the top quarter of their high school class. They are an active bunch, and proud of their academic standing, as illustrated by a popular jeer at archrival Duluth: "It's better to fail at Morris than graduate from Duluth!" Minorities and international students comprise 19 percent of the student population at UMM, including a large contingency of Native Americans. The school is partnered with the Anti-Defamation League's World of Difference Institute, dedicated to decreasing prejudice and increasing intergroup understanding and communi-

"It's better to fail at Morris than graduate from Duluth!"

cation. The campus also hosts an annual three-day leadership retreat in which students join together and delve into issues of human diversity. UMM offers a wide variety of merit and athletic scholarships. And in keeping with its heritage, Morris automatically grants free tuition to Native Americans.

Forty-seven percent of Morris freshmen live on campus in one of five residence halls. Upperclassmen either move off campus or enter a lottery for space in a campus apartment complex. The dorms feature a twenty-four-hour visitation policy with kitchenettes on every floor and a TV lounge on the ground level. "I found living in the freshman dorms to be a pleasurable experience," says student. "It was a quick and easy way to meet people." Students find campus safe, and say even the dining halls aren't a danger zone: "There are salad bars for lunch and dinner, and food service is more than willing to fix a special lunch," says a math major.

The phrase "make your own fun" might well have been invented here, since students are left to their own devices when it's time to relax. "There are always activities taking place on campus," says one student. "Activities occurring off campus usually involve close friends getting together." That's because the drinking age is strictly enforced on campus and in local bars. Some students use weekends to participate in community service. Others head for home with laundry bags in tow.

For those who stick around campus, more than ninety clubs and student organizations are available, focusing on everything from juggling to geology. Morris sponsors several outstanding music groups, including a jazz ensemble that was selected to play at the 1994 Jazz Festival in Amsterdam. Intramural sports are also a big hit, especially basketball, volleyball, wrestling, and football. Morris competes in Division III, and crowds gather to cheer on the basketball, football, baseball, and women's soccer teams, among others.

"There are always activities taking place on campus."

UMM may seem isolated to some students, but those who want to challenge their minds for four years will find plenty to occupy their time. Students itching to escape can take advantage of the successful study abroad programs, while those wanting to stay can immerse themselves in the numerous research opportunities available at Morris.

If You Apply To ➤

Morris: Early action: Nov. 15. Regular admissions: Mar. 15. Guarantees to meet demonstrated need. Campus interviews: recommended, informational. No alumni interviews. SATs or ACTs: required. SAT IIs: optional. Accepts the Common Application and electronic applications. Essay questions: how will you make your presence known on campus in your first year; your academic interests and research goals; something more about yourself that isn't in the application.

University of Minnesota–Twin Cities

240 Williamson, 231 Pillsbury Drive SE, Minneapolis, MN 55455

Not quite as highly rated as U. of Wisconsin or U. of Michigan, but not quite as expensive, either. In a university the size of U. of Minnesota, the best bet is to find a niche, such as the honors program in the liberal arts college. Strong programs include engineering, management, and health fields.

The University of Minnesota, like the nearby Mall of America, can be overwhelming, with its seemingly limitless variety of offerings and gargantuan size. With more than one hundred fifty majors, UM offers an abundance of academic choices. Be advised, however, that "Snow *Week*" is not a joke, a euphemism, an oxymoron, or anything of the sort, nor is it intended to be misleading. It's a weeklong festival that takes advantage of what the winter sky does best most of the winter in Minnesota—sprinkle down the white stuff for everyone's enjoyment.

The vast Twin Cities campus actually consists of two campuses with three main sections, and within each the architecture is highly diverse. The St. Paul campus encompasses the colleges of agriculture, food, and environmental sciences, natural resources, human ecology, veterinary medicine, and biological sciences. The Minneapolis campus is divided by the Mississippi River into an East Bank and a West Bank that are home to the other colleges and most of the dormitories, as well as most of the fraternities and sororities. Both campuses offer a blend of traditional and modern architecture, with columned buildings seated next to sleek geometric structures. The two campuses are five miles apart and linked by a free bus service. Academic facilities are excellent, beginning with the five-million-volume library system, which is the fourteenth largest in North America. Every one of the colleges has its own library, many of which are good places to study. A 695-acre arboretum

Website: http://admissions .tc.umn.edu
Location: Urban
Total Enrollment: 46,677
Undergraduates: 28,103
Male/Female: 48/52
SAT Ranges: V 540–660
  M 550–670
ACT Range: 22–28
Financial Aid: 45%
Expense: Pub $ $ $
Phi Beta Kappa: Yes
Applicants: 14,746
Accepted: 74%
Enrolled: 47%
Grad in 6 Years: 54%
Returning Freshmen: 84%
Academics: ✍ ✍ ✍ ✍

(Continued)

Social: ☎ ☎ ☎

Q of L: ★ ★ ★

Admissions: (612) 752-1000

Email Address:
  admissions@tc.umn.edu

Strongest Programs:
Engineering
Psychology
Journalism
Biology
Theater/Dance
Business

is used for research and teaching. New additions include an architecture building, dance center, microbial and plan genomics building, and remodeled student union.

Minnesota offers more than one hundred fifty undergraduate majors in twenty-eight separate schools. The Institute of Technology is notable for the options it offers for tutorials and internships; its electrical and mechanical engineering programs are particularly strong and well subscribed. Engineering is the most popular major on campus and has a good reputation, as do political science, management, psychology, law, and journalism. Undergraduates also have access to more esoteric fields, from aging studies and biometry to therapeutic recreation and mortuary science. Anthropology, foreign languages, and math could be better, students say.

While efforts to limit class size have been stepped up and the university is focusing more on undergraduates, classes still top out at three hundred plus, with introductory classes typically the largest. "You have to work hard and be willing to compete if you want to make yourself known at such a large school," says one junior. Helpful teaching assistants are abundant, and the excellent honors program in the liberal arts college allows close contact with faculty members as well as leeway to enroll in certain graduate courses and seminars. Students say the academic climate varies by school. "If you prepare for classes and keep up, you'll usually do fine," says a student.

While undergraduates have had a difficult time enrolling in courses, the use of computer registration has made life a lot easier. One junior reveals, "If a class is closed and somebody really needs it, they can usually get a magic number from the department to be able to register for it." The administration attributes the school's

> **"You have to work hard and be willing to compete if you want to make yourself known at such a large school."**

low six-year graduation rate to the fact that students are likely to center their lives in spheres outside the university—in work and off-campus homes. However, the four-year plan guarantees graduation in four years provided students follow program requirements, including frequent academic counseling and specific coursework. "Career counseling is the best," says a senior.

Professors receive high marks from most students as being approachable and knowledgeable. "Since this is one of the best research institutions, our professors are the best in their fields," one student boasts. Students find plenty of internship opportunities at the many corporations and government agencies in the Twin Cities area. The university is on a semester system, and almost all classes have a pass/fail option (limited to no more than a quarter of a student's courses).

Sixty-five percent of students at the university come from the top quarter of their high school class, and 72 percent are from Minnesota. Minorities constitute 20 percent of the students, with 4 percent African-American, 2 percent Hispanic, and 8 percent Asian-American. Tuition hikes are a main gripe of students but there is need-based financial aid, seven hundred merit scholarships worth up to $48,000 each year, and athletic awards in all major sports.

Dorm life at Minnesota follows the big school, wait-in-line theme. Twenty-four percent of all undergraduates and three-quarters of freshmen live in residence halls, as there are now eight traditional halls and one new apartment-style facility, with at least one more on the way. Dorm rooms are hard to obtain, and parking spaces for all those commuters are almost as scarce. Students who have rooms get the chance to keep them for the next year. The administration ensures that new freshmen who apply for housing by May 1 have a room. "Residence halls are great places for freshmen and sophomores. These living areas are designed with programs to fit lower-division students," a sophomore says. Once you're there, you're required to join a meal plan. Opinions vary on the quality and variety of food. But "fresh fruit and veggies are always available," notes a junior. Lest anyone fear the dietitians are

Academic facilities are excellent, beginning with the five-million-volume library system, which is the fourteenth largest in North America.

excessively health-obsessed, she adds, "They have the *best* chocolate chip cookies." Campus security is adequate. "I think students feel very safe," says a junior, who praises the campus escort system, under which a student can request a security guard to accompany him or her for up to a mile on forays off campus.

Many students live in apartments and have a thriving social life away from campus. Underage drinking is banned, and students say the policy usually works. The downtown areas of the Twin Cities are easy to get to by bus, and there are scores of good bars, restaurants, nightspots, and movie theaters. This is an athletically inclined bunch of students, as both intramural and varsity sports are popular. Wrestling, baseball, and golf have brought home championship trophies recently, and the hockey team was top in the nation. Students always

Dorm rooms are hard to obtain, and parking spaces for all those commuters are almost as scarce.

"The campus is very social. It's easy to make friends."

hope the current season will be one in which the gridiron Gophers take home the roses in a bowl victory, but short of that, a win over Michigan for custody of the Little Brown Jug is cause for celebration. Minnesota's rivalry with the University of Wisconsin is considerable, especially since U. of M. has a large Wisconsin population. Intramural competition can go on well past midnight.

Here, being "under the weather" can be a good thing, as campus designers found a way to get around, or make that under, wet or wintry conditions—by linking many of the campus buildings with tunnels. For those who love it, there is the aforementioned Snow Week, and happy skiers and skaters are colorful spots all over the state's white backdrop. In the spring and summer, Minnesota's famed ten thousand lakes offer swimming, boating, and fishing. "The campus is very social," says a nursing student. "It's easy to make friends." She cites the union's bowling alley, pool tables, movie theater, and live music dance club as good places to meet people, adding, "There are about five hundred student groups on campus, and it's really easy to get involved. I have no idea what anyone gets out of road trips." The Carnival Weekend put on by the Greeks each April to raise funds for charity is a huge event. Spring Jam is described by one student as "Homecoming in spring—but better," and Campus Kick-off Days in the beginning of the fall quarter is much anticipated.

Anonymity is almost a given at a university of this size, but then size does have its virtues in the countless array of campus resources. UM is ideal for those who appreciate an urban setting and a good, old-fashioned, button-up-your-overcoat winter. "Students here are very confident and open-minded because we are in a large metropolitan area," says a junior. And as for the name "Snow Week" being perhaps a bit of an understatement, remember that Minnesotans are experts at dealing with winter, and students go full throttle academically and socially all year round.

Overlaps

University of Wisconsin–Madison, University of Minnesota–Duluth, University of Wisconsin–Eau Claire, University of St. Thomas, Marquette

If You Apply To ➤

Twin Cities: Rolling admissions: Dec. 15 (priority). Housing: May 1. Campus and alumni interviews: optional, informational. SATs or ACTs: required. Accepts electronic applications. No essay question.

University of Missouri at Columbia

130 Jesse Hall, Columbia, MO 65211

Mizzou is renowned for one of the top journalism schools in the nation, but engineering, business, and education are also standouts. Enrolls only about half the

Website: www.missouri.edu
Location: Small city
Total Enrollment: 26,124
Undergraduates: 19,698
Male/Female: 48/52
ACT Range: 24–29
Financial Aid: 87%
Expense: Pub $ $
Phi Beta Kappa: Yes
Applicants: 10,215
Accepted: 88%
Enrolled: 50%
Grad in 6 Years: 65%
Returning Freshmen: 84%
Academics: ✍ ✍ ✍
Social: ☎ ☎ ☎ ☎
Q of L: ★ ★ ★
Admissions: (573) 882-7786
Email Address:
   MU4U@missouri.edu

Strongest Programs:
Journalism
Biology
Psychology
Education
History
Physical Therapy
Food Science and Nutrition
Geology

number of out-of-state students as archrival University of Kansas. Columbia is a quintessential college town.

In 1839 the residents of Boone County, Missouri, raised enough money to create the state university in Columbia. Today, as Missouri's flagship university evolves into a top research institution, it continues to uphold the belief of its founders in the great value of higher education that is accessible to all. The school continuously wins awards for its innovative programming. Students at Mizzou enjoy research opportunities and hands-on experience, and are hosts of companies attracted during recruitment fairs. Students say Mizzou covers all the bases.

The oldest public university west of the Mississippi, Mizzou's spacious, tree-filled campus is flanked by mansion-like fraternity and sorority houses. The Francis Quadrangle Historical District, with nineteen National Historic Landmark buildings, is the core of the Red Campus (so named for the predominant color of brick). Central to this area are the sixty-foot granite columns of the original Academic Hall—the building was destroyed by fire in 1892. To the east of the columns is the original tombstone of Thomas Jefferson. The White Campus consists of vine-covered limestone buildings, symbolized by the Memorial Union Tower. The newest landmark is Tiger Plaza, a concrete and brick plaza that includes a bronze tiger sculpture mounted above a cascading waterfall and pool. Mizzou is in the midst of a plan to upgrade or replace all nineteen residence halls; the first phase was the construction of the Virginia Avenue Housing and Dining Facility. Other projects include a new basketball arena, an expansion to the Brewer Fieldhouse, and a new Life Sciences Center.

With more than two hundred fifty degree programs and twenty schools and colleges, Mizzou offers a comprehensive set of choices for basic and advanced study. Aspiring journalists can get hands-on experience working on the *Columbia Missourian*, the six-thousand-circulation local daily paper edited by J-school faculty members and students, or at KOMU-TV, the nation's only university-owned commercial television station. KBIA, MU's National Public Radio station, is popular among students and listeners alike. Agriculture is also nationally ranked, especially in the areas of agricultural economics and applied research for farm communities. The College of Engineering maintains several notable undergraduate segments, including biological and civil engineering. The College of Business is highly competitive and features a five-year bachelor's/master's accounting program. A bachelor of health science in diagnostic medical ultrasound has been added to the curriculum, as have minors in leadership and public service and a certificate program in geographic information science. Students can now pursue joint degrees in animal science and veterinary medicine. So sought after are Mizzou students that nearly three thousand companies and organizations—including two hundred Fortune 500 corporations—are regular recruiters.

Committed preprofessionals will be glad to know that MU offers highly able and directed freshmen guaranteed admission to its graduate-level programs in medicine, law, veterinary medicine, nursing, and health-related professions. Mizzou is also one of the leading public research institutions in the country for the number and range of lab and scholarly opportunities it offers undergraduates. Undergraduate research projects range from breast cancer research to plant genomics. The school has received millions of dollars over recent years from the National Science Foundation and others to continue expanding research opportunities. MU sends more students abroad each year—more than five hundred—than any other higher education institution in the state.

MU undergraduates must fulfill a strong "distribution of knowledge" requirement in order to graduate. General education courses include English, mathematics, and American history or political science. Students also must complete twenty-seven hours in three content areas: social and behavioral sciences, physical and biological sciences and mathematics, and humanistic studies and fine arts. All students must take a course in computer literacy, although the content of those courses varies by degree program. Two writing intensive courses and a senior capstone experience also are required. Full professors teach the lecture courses at Mizzou, supplemented by a weekly discussion session led by a teaching assistant to go over material presented in class. "Most faculty are really concerned with students being successful and actually learning—especially once you are in your major," a sophomore reports.

Students say the courses at Mizzou are challenging but not impossible if you are willing to work hard. "Mizzou is academically strong without being overly competitive," a business journalism major says. "It is possible to balance your classes and the rest of your collegiate life." Owing to MU's size, classes can fill up quickly, but professors do give overrides for students who must take certain credits at specific times. Missouri guarantees the availability of

"Mizzou is academically strong without being overly competitive."

coursework to complete a degree in four years. The study-conscious will find plenty of room and resources in the MU library system, which holds more than three million books, almost seven million microfilms, and more than sixteen thousand periodicals.

The Mizzou campus is home mostly to Missourians (86 percent), though every state in the union and more than one hundred foreign countries are represented. African-Americans account for 6 percent of the student body, while Asian-Americans and Hispanics combine for 5 percent. To boost its minority population, MU has established several scholarship programs designed especially for them. It's also opened a Black Culture Center and an Asian Affairs Center. The new Diversity Week program features workshops, speakers, and other events.

Fifty-three percent of MU students live on campus, and freshman under age twenty are required to do so. Residence halls have double rooms and are often crowded and noisy—and thus are fun places to be, though single-sex halls, a few single rooms, and round-the-clock quiet floors are also available. The university has embarked on a Residential Life Master Plan to upgrade or replace all nineteen residence halls. The project will be broken into four phases, each taking three to four years to complete. Dorm choice is first come, first serve and half of the halls offer co-ed living by floor or wing. Students can also choose to live in one of twenty-five Living-Learning Communities, where residents share a common interest, such as engineering, arts, or nursing. About 75 percent of students choose a Freshman Interest Group—there are eighty-five to choose from—where fifteen to twenty students with shared academic interests live in the same residence hall and enroll in three classes together. Dorm dwellers are required to purchase meal plans, but credits can be used at all-you-can-eat dining halls, coffee bars, and take-out stands, among many options. The fraternity and sorority houses are livable (the frat houses less so), although not all members can fit; 20 percent of Mizzou men and 25 percent of women go Greek.

Students at Mizzou, a champion of tough alcohol policies, have adopted the school's stance and agreed to ban alcohol from all fraternities and sororities, making it one of the largest Greek systems in the nation to go dry. The rule will be lifted when alumni come home to visit. Students say MU's social life is packed with options, including movies, shopping, eating out, the usual Greek parties, and great parks and hiking areas on the outskirts of town. Columbia is "the quintessential college town," says one sophomore. It offers the benefits of a large city—a versatile bar scene, lots of pizza joints, coffee shops, and expensive boutiques—and the friendly atmosphere of a small town. Students support the town by engaging in community service and the community caters to them in return; their concern even goes beyond the borders of campus to the plight of the wild tiger and the

Mizzou is in the midst of a plan to upgrade or replace all nineteen residence halls; the first phase was the construction of the Virginia Avenue Housing and Dining Facility.

Aspiring journalists can get hands-on experience working on the Columbia Missourian, the six-thousand-circulation local daily paper edited by J-school faculty members and students, or at KOMU-TV, the nation's only university-owned commercial television station.

preservation of its habitat. At Mizzou, service goes hand-in-hand with learning; about 10 percent of undergrads are enrolled in eighty-five courses through the Office of Service Learning, logging in more than a hundred thousand volunteer hours in a recent year. Road trips to St. Louis, Kansas City, and Lake of the Ozarks offer a change of scenery.

Mizzou's Tigers compete in the Big 12, and basketball and football games draw big crowds. In fact, the entire town turns out in black and gold for any football game. Kansas is their biggest rival. An indoor practice facility for football, baseball, softball, and soccer and a track/soccer complex offer seating for two thousand fans. MU's popular intramural program has nearly two dozen sports and two skill divisions, so bloodthirsty competitors and weekend warriors alike can get what they want.

The University of Missouri continues to grow academically while sticking with its longtime traditions like homecoming—a party Mizzou students know how to throw best. Students are challenged at every turn by quality teaching and ample research opportunities. For those seeking opportunity for growth in a dynamic college town, Mizzou is a great choice.

If You Apply To ➤

Mizzou: Rolling admissions. Financial aid: Mar. 1. Campus and alumni interviews: not available. SATs or ACTs required; ACTs preferred. No SAT IIs. Accepts electronic applications. No essay question.

Montana Tech of the University of Montana

1300 West Park Street, Butte, MT 59701-8997

If you go to Montana for college, you're probably interested in either rocks or trees. Montana Tech covers the former, with strong programs related to mining and petroleum engineering. Montana Tech is a third bigger than New Mexico Tech and about the same size as Colorado School of Mines.

Students at Montana Tech like to dig into their work and aren't afraid to get their hands dirty. Plunked down in the midst of Western mining country, Montana Tech, as you might expect, shines in land-related engineering fields like petroleum, mining, and geophysics. Students get a hands-on education geared toward "things metallic" (as the school's motto loosely translates). In fact, the school's mascot is Charlie Oredigger, and students are affectionately dubbed "diggers."

Situated on a shoulder of "the richest hill on earth" (some of the greatest copper, molybdenum, zinc, and manganese deposits in the world), Montana Tech's fifty-acre campus is composed of sixteen buildings of classic college brick architecture. This is exemplified by Main Hall, constructed in 1900, and the Engineering, Laboratory, and Classroom building (the ELC), built in 1987 and modernized to the tune of $850,000. Other unique features on campus include the Museum Building, which houses one of the country's largest mineral collections; an Earthquake Studies Office, which records tremors throughout southwestern Montana; and the Montana Bureau of Mines and Geology, a research arm of the college that produces geological and mineralogical maps and publications. Recent campus additions include a residence hall and renovations to the student union and a chemistry/biology building with all new labs.

Tech's degree programs emphasize the study of minerals, energy, and the environment, but students graduate with a well-rounded education. Strong degree programs include environmental engineering, business information and technology, and general engineering (formerly engineering science). Efforts have been made in recent years to strengthen the basic sciences underlying the engineering programs, and faculty is constantly upgrading classes technologically to prepare better job and graduate school candidates. The school also works to place upperclassmen in summer jobs in their fields. Everyone faces general education requirements including communications, humanities, social sciences, mathematical sciences, and life sciences, although students say the nonscience offerings are weak. For those who want more than just a straight science experience, Tech has a major in science and technology that attempts to relate liberal arts to today's increasingly technological society. Newer additions to the curriculum include a B.S. in general science and general engineering. Montana Tech also continues to add degree programs in software engineering, nursing, and biological sciences.

"With the small student-teacher ratio, free tutoring, and numerous computers on campus, help is always available."

Academic work at Tech is rigorous, with gym the only subject that can be taken pass/fail. "The academic climate is competitive and we do have rigorous courses," says a sophomore. "But with the small student/teacher ratio, free tutoring, and numerous computers on campus, help is always available." Faculty members have a genuine interest in teaching and work hard to accommodate students. In addition, the typical professor holds a terminal degree. "It is very rare for anybody but professors with Ph.D.s to teach," says a child psychology major. Freshmen are taught mostly by full professors and never by graduate students. Students must sit down with their academic advisors each term to discuss their schedules. "Tech prides itself on helping their students and they do a good job," says one senior.

Eighty-five percent of Tech's students are from Montana, and the majority were the "brains or the nerds from high school," according to a sophomore. Residents and nonresidents alike must be in the top half of their high school class or graduate with a 2.5 GPA and score at least 22 on ACT composite or 1030 on the combined SAT to gain admission. Student diversity stems from the 3 percent foreign enrollment. Minorities account for a mere 2 percent of the student population. The student body is conservative and "nerdy," a junior business major says. Students vie for merit scholarships, ranging from $250 to $20,000. There are forty-eight athletic scholarships distributed among football, basketball, volleyball, and golf. Registration and incidental fees are waived for some Montana state residents, including war orphans and those of at least one-fourth Native American blood.

Twelve percent of the students live in Prospector Hall, which is "comfortable and spacious," but those who can't fit are often forced to live in married student housing. Prospector includes modern baths, carpeting, exercise rooms, and kitchens, and it is "in the middle of everything." Each room is wired with a microcomputer connected to the campus mainframe. The school likes freshmen to live on campus, but the vast majority of upperclassmen live either in the many nearby apartments or in houses with reasonable rents. The campus is said to be safe, without much crime. "I've never heard of any problems," says a senior. "We live in Montana, remember." For students without cars, there's a bus service that runs into town.

Butte (population 40,000) gets a fair enough rating as a college town, although it is suffering from a collapse of the mining industry. One native, a mechanical engineering major, says the community takes a lot of pride in the school. Social activities—many of which are sponsored by clubs—take place both on and off campus. Underage drinkers have a difficult time getting served in town, but, like any school, can find alcohol if they want it, students say. The ratio of men to women is evening

(Continued)
Social: ☎ ☎
Q of L: ★ ★ ★
Admissions: (406) 496-4178
Email Address:
   admissions@mtech.edu

Strongest Programs:
Engineering
Information Technology

Tech's degree programs emphasize the study of minerals, energy, and the environment, but students graduate with a well-rounded education.

Butte (population 40,000) gets a fair enough rating as a college town, although it is suffering from a collapse of the mining industry.

out: 55 percent male to 45 percent female. On weekends, students who don't go home attend music or comedy shows on campus, see movies, go to a game, or frequent the bars in town. Butte's setting—nestled in the slopes of the Continental Divide—is magnificent for skiing, fishing, hiking, and camping. Yellowstone Park is a favored road trip.

The student union features a dining area, game room, bookstore, student-owned FM radio station, and a television where students are known to tune in to cartoons in the afternoon. St. Patrick's Day is widely celebrated on and off campus, and on M-Day, part of a three-day festival before spring finals, students whitewash the large stone "M" on a hill above campus and host the largest bonfire in the state.

Athletics at Tech, which competes in the NAIA, are up-and-coming, and jocks are generally considered "cool." The most popular varsity sports are football and women's basketball; one T-shirt reads, "Tech Football: A Miner Miracle." But other

"Athletics is big here." varsity teams, including men's and women's cross-country teams and women's volleyball, are also strong. Tech students take advantage of the excellent intramural program and the facilities of the modern physical education complex. Tech's biggest rival is Western Montana College, and freshman football players from WMC face off with those from Tech in an annual boxing match known as the "Smoker." "Athletics is big here," says a liberal studies major. "Everyone really supports the teams, especially if they are playing a rival of ours."

Montana Tech's students know why they've chosen their school: they want a solid grounding in earth-related engineering disciplines at a reasonable cost. Though state budget cuts have reduced the number of credits required to graduate, the school still boasts an impressive 95 percent job placement rate for graduates. Tech doesn't offer your typical college experience, but for would-be miners and geophysicists, its programs offer mountains of opportunity.

Overlaps

Montana State, University of Montana, Carroll College, Colorado School of Mines, Gonzaga

If You Apply To ➤

Montana Tech: Rolling admissions. Campus and Alumni interviews: optional, informational. SATs or ACTs: required; ACTs preferred. Accepts common and electronic applications. No essay question.

Morehouse College: See page 34.

Morehouse College: See page 34.

Mount Holyoke College

50 College Street, South Hadley, MA 01075-1488

One of two women's colleges, with Smith, that are members of the Five College Consortium in western Massachusetts. Less nonconformist than Smith and Bryn Mawr. MHC is strongest in the natural and social sciences, and one among the few colleges to have a program devoted to leadership.

Website: www.mtholyoke.edu

The women of Mount Holyoke will be the first to tell you that the nation's first all-female college is not a girls' school without men, but a women's college without boys. The women who choose MHC value tradition, leadership, and achievement, and eagerly support one another as each strives to meet her goals. Students rave about the quality of teaching and the small classes, and while they complain about the heavy workload, most bring that challenge upon themselves as they seek intellectual fulfillment. "I'm encouraged to explore and be adventurous, to learn about myself and the world," says a junior. "Also, no one fits into one specific category. Athletes are also involved in student government and other organizations—it's a total mix."

Mount Holyoke is located in the heart of New England, on eight hundred acres of rolling hills dotted with lakes and waterfalls. Modern glass-and-stone buildings stand alongside more traditional ivy-covered sandstone structures. Highlights include the Japanese Meditation Garden and Teahouse, an art building with studios and a bronze-casting foundry, an eighteen-hole championship golf course, and an equestrian center. A renovation and expansion of the music hall includes a new two-story addition

> **"I'm encouraged to explore and be adventurous, to learn about myself and the world."**

that has a forty-seat classroom, three studio offices, and a student lounge. Also updated were the art building and the Blanchard Campus Center, which now holds a cyber cafe, coffee bar, art gallery, and game room. The new Unified Science Complex continues to advance the college's reputation as a leader in scientific education.

Despite improvements to the campus, curriculum at this 163-year-old institution remains decidedly traditional. Students are required to complete 128 total credits to graduate, thirty-two in their major and sixteen in their minor. Required courses include three humanities courses, two courses from science and mathematics disciplines (with at least one lab), two social science courses, and one course in multicultural perspectives. A small number of exceptional students are invited into the First-Year Honors Tutorial Program, where two or three students are paired with a professor to delve deeply into a given topic. The college also offers more than twenty-five first-year seminars each fall, and more than a dozen in the spring, covering topics and disciplines from biology to women's studies. These courses' focus are aimed at developing skills in analysis and critical inquiry through speech and writing. Some also include field trips to museums or events in Boston and New York.

Mount Holyoke produces more female Ph.D.s in chemistry and biology than any other liberal arts college. The top-of-the-line chemistry labs, along with a solar greenhouse, a scanning electron microscope, several nuclear magnetic resonance spectrometers, and a linear accelerator, provide the students with state of the art equipment necessary to be the best. Five-year dual-degree programs enable students to combine degrees from MHC with B.S. degrees in engineering from the University of Massachusetts, Dartmouth, or Caltech, or with master's degrees in public health from UMass. A sociology major comments, "All departments are strong. Even smaller departments are bolstered by the five-college offerings."

Although some of Mount Holyoke's intro courses have fifty or more students, most have twenty-five or fewer. Since the required curriculum is so diverse, there is little trouble getting into the smaller classes and finishing in four years. A junior confirms this general opinion: "While professors often put caps on classes to keep them small, the course offerings are diverse enough for a student to be able to find a class she wants." No matter the size of the class, the students rave about the teaching, which is considered above and beyond expectations. One biology student says, "I have never been taught by anything but a full professor and their enthusiasm for teaching can't help but rub off on the students." The school's honor code makes possible self-scheduled, self-proctored final exams. After those tests is the optional January winter term, where many students opt for a two-credit, nontraditional course, or an off-campus internship in New York or Washington, D.C. About 30 per-

(Continued)

Location: Small town
Total Enrollment: 2,194
Undergraduates: 2,191
Male/Female: 0/100
SAT Ranges: V 600–700
   M 580–670
ACT Range: 26–30
Financial Aid: 68%
Expense: Pr $ $ $ $
Phi Beta Kappa: Yes
Applicants: 2,936
Accepted: 52%
Enrolled: 38%
Graduate in 6 Years: 81%
Returning Freshmen: 93%
Academics: ✍ ✍ ✍ ✍
Social: ☎ ☎ ☎
Q of L: ★ ★ ★ ★
Admissions: (413) 538-2023
Email Address:
   admission@mtholyoke.edu

Strongest Programs:
English
Biology
Psychology
Economics
International Relations

Mount Holyoke produces more female Ph.D.s in chemistry and biology than any other liberal arts college.

cent of MHC students seeking a complete change of scenery spend all or part of junior year in another country. The Twelve-College Exchange Program* offers opportunities in more than twenty-five locales, while Mount Holyoke also has its own study abroad programs. Those interested in the sea may be interested in the Maritime Studies Program.*

Mount Holyoke attracts students from all over the nation and the world; however, 21 percent are Massachusetts natives. African-Americans make up nearly 5 percent of the student body, Asian-Americans 10 percent, and Hispanics 4 percent. "People are fairly politically-minded and it is very important to be politically correct," says one student. The Student Coalition for Action is a very large and popular campus group dedicated to social change. Merit scholarships are available, ranging from $5,000 to $15,000.

Ninety-three percent of Mount Holyoke's students live in the nineteen residence halls, each of which has its own dining facility. According to a student, "Dorms are nice, comfortable, and well-maintained." Most dorms are also very homey, with living rooms, TV lounges, and baby grand pianos; all serve milk and cookies (as well as healthier fare, like hummus and vegetables) every night at 9:30 p.m. Students from all four classes live together and housing is guaranteed for all four years. Some residence halls also offer apartment-style living.

"All departments are strong. Even smaller departments are bolstered by the five-college offerings."

Students find the Five College Consortium* one of Mount Holyoke's greatest assets. A free bus service runs every 20 minutes between MHC and UMass, Amherst, Smith, and Hampshire, multiplying a Holyoke woman's access to academic, social, and cultural opportunities. "There are five colleges in the area, so there is always something to do," says one sophomore. The majority of social opportunities are on campus, such as parties, plays, concerts, speakers and cultural events. If on campus activities aren't appealing, road trips to Boston, Vermont, and New York City are also popular. Closer to campus, the South Hadley Center has eateries, a pub, shops, and apartments, though students say that Amherst and Northampton provide more shopping options. If you are 21, you are allowed to buy and have alcohol on campus; however, if you are underage and caught drinking "a warning or a counseling session may be required," says a sophomore.

Perhaps more than their counterparts at Smith and Wellesley, Mount Holyoke women have made a virtue out of the school's most visible "vice": the lack of men. Women fill all leadership positions, thanks to a strong and supportive community spirit, and boys are just down the road at Amherst or UMass. Like most happy families, Mount Holyoke students take pride in tradition. Upon arrival, each first-year student is assigned a secret elf (a sophomore), a big sister (a junior), and a disorientation leader (a senior). Each class also has a color and a mascot, and class spirit is huge, especially for the annual Junior Show. Every fall on Mountain Day, students wake up to ringing bells, classes are canceled (even the library is closed), and everyone treks up Mount Holyoke to picnic and see the foliage.

For those breaks in studying, the athletics at Mount Holyoke, such as crew, riding, field hockey and lacrosse are popular. The successful equestrian team has brought home championships recently. The college encourages athletic participation at all levels with a demanding eighteen-hole golf course, jogging trails, and two lakes. The twenty-acre equestrian center includes a fifty-seven-stall barn, two riding areas, a training and show area, and seating for three hundred. Crew regattas and rugby take the place of football games, and students come out in force when the opponent is another of the Seven Sisters.

The traditions of academic excellence, modern upgrades, and easy access to New York and Boston provide a small college atmosphere with nearby cultural education.

MHC may be described as a sorority without the associated "snobbery" and "exclusivity." The challenging, supportive environment "allows women to be in all different positions of leadership with no barriers," according to a student.

<table>
<tr><td>

If You

Apply

To ➣

</td><td>

Mount Holyoke: Early decision: Nov. 15. Regular admissions and financial aid: Jan. 15. Guarantees to meet demonstrated need. Campus and alumnae interviews: recommended, evaluative. ACTs or SATs: optional. SAT IIs: optional. Accepts the Common Application and electronic applications. Essay question: why Mount Holyoke is a good match for you; and a personal essay. Also requires a two- to five-page paper written in the 11th or 12th grade, with a teacher's comments.

</td></tr>
</table>

Muhlenberg College

2400 Chew Street, Allentown, PA 18104-5586

There is a definite Muhlenberg type: serious, ambitious, and buttoned-down. Muhlenberg is the only eastern Pennsylvania/New Jersey liberal arts college with a serious religious affiliation—Lutheran. Strong in premed, prelaw, preanything.

When a popular school pseudonym is "The Caring College" rather than some line referring to booze or babes, you know you're in for a different experience. That's the case with Muhlenberg College, a small liberal arts school that nurtures its students. Muhlenberg holds its students to rigorous academic standards, and they know it. From its solid Lutheran roots to its current standing as a top premed school, Muhlenberg shows students it really does care. "Academic excellence is, by far, the top priority," says a junior, "but the people are warm, friendly, compassionate, and truly care about making Muhlenberg the best possible place for everyone."

Set on eighty park-like acres, the Berg campus is a combination of older Gothic stone structures and newer buildings in a variety of architectural styles. Prominent facilities include a lovely chapel, the high-tech Trexler Library, a forty-acre biological field station and wildlife sanctuary, and a forty-eight-acre arboretum with more than three hundred species of wildflowers, broadleaf evergreens, and conifer trees. The campus also boasts a football stadium and all-weather track, and the fity-thousand-square-foot Trexler Pavilion for the Performing Arts that has a dramatic forty-five-foot glass outer shell and houses a variety of performing spaces. Two new dorms, Robertston and South, recently opened overlooking Lake Muhlenberg, and the communications building recently reopened with new radio and television studios.

Muhlenberg's regional reputation rests on its premedical program, which continues to attract large numbers of students. An agreement with Philadelphia's Drexel University College of Medicine guarantees seats for up to six Muhlenberg students each year. The college's theater arts program is also a national draw, and a few alumni have even gone on to star on Broadway. Science lab equipment at Muhlenberg is cutting-edge, and a comprehensive natural science major allows for a sampling of it all. The Living Writers course is offered every other year and has brought a number of noted authors to campus, including Robert Pinsky,

"Academic excellence is, by far, the top priority."

Jay Wright, and Alice Fulton. Muhlenberg sends study groups to Washington, D.C., and students may spend semesters abroad in countries from England, France, Spain, and Germany to Argentina, the Czech Republic, Japan, Australia, and Scotland. Programs sponsored by the International Student Exchange are also available, and Muhlenberg is member of the Lehigh Valley Association of Independent Colleges.*

Website:
 www.muhlenberg.edu
Location: City outskirts
Total Enrollment: 2,450
Undergraduates: 2,450
Male/Female: 44/56
SAT Ranges: V 545–645
 M 556-656
Financial Aid: 65%
Expense: Pr $ $ $
Phi Beta Kappa: Yes
Applicants: 3,822
Accepted: 35%
Enrolled: 41%
Grad in 6 Years: 81%
Returning Freshmen: 93%
Academics: ✐ ✐ ✐
Social: ☎ ☎ ☎
Q of L: ★ ★ ★ ★
Admissions: (484) 664-3200
Email Address: admissions@
 muhlenberg.edu

Strongest Programs:
Premed/Biology
Prelaw
English/Writing
Theatre Arts and Dance
Business
Psychology

The college offers three honors programs, the Muhlenberg Scholars Program, the Dana Associates Program, and the new R.J. Fellows Program, which focuses on the ramifications of change. Each is limited to fifteen students per entering class. They carry an annual $3,000 stipend and culminate in an in-depth mentored senior research project. Psychology is Muhlenberg's most popular major, followed by business, biology, theatre arts, and communications. Sociology is making a comeback with energetic new faculty, while the Russian studies and preseminary programs are not as strong. "Also, the theatre department has begun to grow in recent years

> **"We have a diverse pool of interests, which creates a lively campus in terms of politics and social awareness."**

because of an increase in interest," one student says. General education requirements are organized into two major groups: Skills (writing, oral expression, reasoning, and foreign language) and Perspectives (literature and the arts, meaning and values, human behavior and social institutions, historical studies, physical and life sciences, and other cultures.) Each freshman is assigned a First-Year Advising Team, usually consisting of four students (a student mentor, a student advisor, and two academic advisors) and a faculty member. One Spanish/premed double major says her science advisor helped pick classes to prepare her for medical school, while her Spanish advisor explained how language skills would serve her well as a doctor.

The fun-filled, three-day freshman orientation program carries one requirement: learning the alma mater and then hightailing it to the president's house to serenade him. All freshmen also take a writing-intensive, discussion-intensive First-Year Seminar, with enrollment capped at fifteen. About two-thirds of freshman courses have fewer than twenty-five students, and since there are no graduate students, there are no teaching assistants. "They are truly concerned with the students' well-being." says a natural science major. "Several different professors, upon hearing that I was not leaving campus during Easter break, invited me to Easter dinner with their families."

Greek life does not dominate the social scene—and it's becoming less important now that rush doesn't occur until sophomore year.

There is a definite Muhlenberg type: serious, ambitious, and buttoned-down. Muhlenberg draws 30 percent of its students from Pennsylvania, and many from adjacent New Jersey. The campus is 92 percent white, but "we have a diverse pool of interests, which creates a lively campus in terms of politics and social awareness," says a biology major. Cultural appreciation is emphasized as Muhlenberg strives for a more ethnically and religiously varied campus. Students stay involved in the community by volunteering as tutors and with groups such as Habitat for Humanity and Planned Parenthood. A political science professor has started a student-run polling institute, which is raising campus awareness and activism.

Muhlenberg encourages on-campus living and guarantees housing to all undergraduates except transfers, so 88 percent of students live in campus residences. All dorms have computer labs, study lounges, and vending machines. Prosser's co-ed

> **"It is easy to get together a group of friends, go somewhere, or make your own fun,"**

wing makes it a good choice for freshmen, while upperclassmen praise the Muhlenberg Independent Living Experience, or MILE, townhouses. Two new dorms, Robertson and South, house 140 students in single, air-conditioned rooms overlooking Lake Muhlenberg. Other popular choices include Taylor and Benfer, where students live in eight-person suites that have their own bathrooms. "The dorms are kept clean and are comfortable," recalls one senior. Freshmen choose from a seven- or five-day meal plan, where options include a salad bar, pasta station, soup-and-bread line, brown-bag lunches, "wellness" entrees, and the ever-popular ice cream machine. For some a measure of having "arrived," Starbucks has a coffee bar in the student union.

Most social life at Muhlenberg takes place on campus. The Muhlenberg Activities Council (MAC) provides comedians every Thursday evening—recent visitors have included Jimmy Fallon and Dave Chappell—current movies in the Red Door Cafe, live band concerts (Counting Crows headlined a recent show), and new movies on the lawn. "For those who enjoy different entertainment it is easy to get together a group of friends, go somewhere, or make your own fun," says one student. City buses stop five minutes from campus for trips to Allentown proper and area malls. There also are daily bus runs to New York City (for clubbing and theater), Philadelphia (for nightlife and cheese steaks), and Baltimore and Washington, D.C. Outdoorsy students can pick up the Appalachian Trail for a little hiking.

Twenty-six percent of men and women each pledge their undergraduate years to fraternities and sororities, but Greek life does not dominate the social scene—and it's becoming less important now that rush doesn't occur until sophomore year. Alcohol is forbidden if you're underage, per Pennsylvania law and the school's "no tolerance" policy, but "for those who know how to ask, it isn't difficult to obtain alcohol," a sophomore says. Big social events include East Fest, homecoming, Deck Party, the Scotty Wood basketball tournament, the Mr. Muhlenberg awards—which parody the Miss America pageant—and the Henry Awards, the college's version of the Oscars. There's also a candlelight ceremony where freshmen write down their college goals, reexamining them the day before graduation.

For the athletically inclined, intramural sports arouse a great deal of passion. Football, men's and women's golf, women's softball, and women's soccer are strong, winning Centennial Conference championships and NCAA tournament bids. Muhlenberg's Life Sports Center offers a pool, basketball court and other all-purpose courts, and a jogging track. Also popular is Frisbee golf; there's an eighteen-hole course on campus, where play goes on during all seasons and all hours of the day and night. Any contest against Johns Hopkins draws crowds, students say.

Muhlenberg has produced Fulbright Fellows and Udall Scholars, but it also ensures that every student excels at his or her own pace. "The students and staff at Muhlenberg are what continues to make me reluctant to leave and excited to return," a student says. "The warm and friendly feeling on campus makes me feel at home." Guess that slogan does fit after all.

The college offers three honors programs, the Muhlenberg Scholars Program, the Dana Associates Program, and the new R.J. Fellows Program, which focuses on the ramifications of change.

Overlaps

Lafayette, Skidmore, Dickinson, Gettysburg, Franklin and Marshall

If You Apply To ➤ **Muhlenberg:** Early decision: Jan. 15. Regular admissions and financial aid: Feb. 15. Housing: May 1. Meets demonstrated need of 90%. Campus interviews: recommended, evaluative (required, along with a graded paper, if students choose not to submit SAT scores). Alumni interviews: optional, informational. SATs or ACTs: optional. SAT IIs: optional. Accepts the Common Application and electronic applications. Essay question: significant experience or achievement; issue of personal, local, national, or international concern; influential person; influential fictional character, historical figure, or creative work; topic of your choice.

University of Nebraska at Lincoln

12 Administration Building, Lincoln, NE 68588-0415

Everybody knows Nebraska football, but in other areas UNL has a lower profile. Fewer out-of-staters attend Nebraska than, say, University of Kansas or Iowa. Agriculture is still the biggest drawing card, and the music program is also strong. Because of the state's demographic makeup, diversity is limited.

Website: www.unl.edu

Location: Center city

Total Enrollment: 22,988

Undergraduates: 18,118

Male/Female: 52/48

SAT Ranges: V 500–640
   M 520–660

ACT Range: 21–27

Financial Aid: 38%

Expense: Pub $ $

Phi Beta Kappa: Yes

Applicants: 7,631

Accepted: 78%

Enrolled: 61%

Grad in 6 Years: 54%

Returning Freshmen: 82%

Academics: ✍ ✍ ✍

Social: 🍷 🍷 🍷 🍷

Q of L: ★ ★ ★

Admissions: (800) 742-8800

Email Address:
   nuhusker@unl.edu

Strongest Programs:

Agribusiness and Agronomy

Animal Science

Architecture

Audiology and Speech
   Pathology

Music

Textiles, Clothing, and Design

Food Sciences

Journalism

Says one junior, "Nebraska is a very conservative state. Thus, on campus, there is a constant struggle between conservative Christian groups and the free-thought activist culture that colleges are known for."

Right downtown in the capital of the Cornhusker State is the University of Nebraska at Lincoln, a school that is making twenty-first century additions to its campus and its curriculum. Nearly 23,000 students call UNL home, and their school pride is contagious. On crisp fall weekends, when spirits are high and the Big Red football arcs through the air, Huskers cheer and paint the town of Lincoln red and white in a show of appreciation for their alma mater. In fact, on home-game Saturdays, the stadium is the third largest "city" in the state, holding 5 percent of the population. Away from the stadium, in the classrooms, UNL has even more reason to cheer with top programs ranging from music to agriculture to journalism. "The entire state revolves around the university, especially the football program and much of the research," a junior says.

UNL spreads across two campuses. The East Campus is home to the colleges of agricultural sciences and natural resources, human resources and family sciences, law, and dentistry. Most entering students end up on the larger City Campus, where the architectural style ranges from the modern Sheldon Art Gallery designed by Philip Johnson to the architecture building, which is on the National Register of Historic Places. There are also several malls, an arboretum, and a sculpture garden. This is the home of six of the eight undergraduate colleges: architecture, arts and sciences, journalism and mass communications, business administration, fine and performing arts, engineering and technology, and the teachers college. As part of a major construction effort on campus, several new facilities have been added, including the Haymarket Park Baseball Complex, Othmer Hall Chemical Engineering Building, the Van Brunt Visitor Center, and the Ross Media Arts Center. Schmid Law Library has been renovated, and the Barkley Speech building has been expanded.

> "The entire state revolves around the university, especially the football program and much of the research."

Nebraska's College of Agricultural Sciences and Natural Resources, known for its outstanding programs in food science and technology, agribusiness, and animal science, is housed in a 19-million-dollar complex. The school of music's opera program has received national attention, and the performing arts programs benefit from the 18-million-dollar Lied Center for the Performing Arts, which seats 2,300. Education, business administration, and engineering and technology are some of the most popular majors. New programs include a bachelor's degree program in professional golf management and master's programs in agriculture, telecommunications engineering, and architectural engineering. Doctoral

> "Classes are challenging, but not overly stressful."

programs are now available in survey research and methodology and integrative biomedical sciences. Students can no longer receive a master's in vocational and adult education at UNL. UNL can be academically challenging, if students want it to be. "Classes are challenging, but not overly stressful," says one English major. "There's a common feeling that learning is important, in and out of the classroom."

Nebraska's Comprehensive Education Program provides students with a common set of educational experiences across the majors and colleges. It has four components: Information Discovery and Retrieval (one course), Essential Studies (nine courses), Integrative Studies (ten courses), and Co-Curricular Experience. To help freshmen get oriented, a one-semester University Foundations class covers the inner and outer workings of the campus, organized around academic subjects. Big Red Welcome combines entertainment and food in a carnival setting to welcome new students, and the SIPS program (Summer Institute for Promising Scholars) is a six-week preorientation session for incoming minority students. The J.D. Edwards Honors Program gives computer science and management students internships to complement their coursework. The Undergraduate Creative Activity and Research

Experience Program provides a stipend for students after freshman year who want to participate in research with a professor.

Getting into courses in the most popular areas, especially education, business, and engineering, can be a problem, students say; preregistration is a must. Graduate students teach a quarter of the courses, but top professors can be found inside the classroom. "I can't rave enough about the professors I've had," a broadcasting major says. "The faculty is very knowledgeable and professors go out of their way to help students." Students also can study abroad in places such as Costa Rica, Germany, Mexico, and Japan.

The UNL student body is mostly conservative and from the Cornhusker State. Asian-Americans make up 5 percent of the student body, with African-Americans and Hispanics 4 percent combined. Says one junior, "Nebraska is a very conservative state. Thus, on campus, there is a constant struggle between conservative Christian groups and the free-thought activist culture that colleges are known for."

Twenty-five percent of students live in the university's single-sex or co-ed dorms, and there's usually no trouble getting a room. Dorm lotteries favor those wanting to stay in the same room or on the same floor. Students say the dorms are clean and well-maintained, though the freshman dwellings can be a bit cramped. Each room also is wired for the Internet. Freshmen, who must live on campus, are welcomed to the residence halls through the FINK program, which is friendlier than it sounds (the acronym stands for Freshman Indoctrination of New Kids). "I love the dorms," a sophomore says. "They certainly aren't the Ritz, but they're very suitable for college students."

UNL is big and there's a group or activity for everyone; fraternity and house parties, roller skating, the movies, eating out, visiting coffee shops and bars (for those of age), and road trips to Omaha or Kansas City are just some of the activities that keep students busy. For many, the fall semester revolves around football weekends and postseason bowl games. "The entire state shuts down on football Saturdays," one junior says. Fraternities draw 15 percent of UNL men and sororities attract 17 percent of the women. They offer both social events and a chance to get involved in the Lincoln community. Homecoming, Greek Week, and Ivy Day are among the most-anticipated campus events, as is The End, new alcohol-free programming at the end of each semester during "dead week" and finals week. For those who want to indulge, plenty of bars are within walking distance of UNL, providing relief to students dissatisfied with the dry campus. So committed is the administration to keeping a distance between students and alcohol that it has obtained a grant to combat high-risk drinking among students. "UNL is a dry camps—and it sucks!" one student complains. "The university has been cracking down on frat house and dorm drinking."

"The city of Lincoln is also pushing an anti-fake-ID campaign. Any and all underage drinking is done away from campus." Some say Lincoln itself is a great college town, with shopping, theaters, restaurants, and movies. "Lincoln is nice because it is a combination of a larger city and a smaller town," a junior says. "Although it is a 'college town,' it is not as desolate as many 'college towns' and could survive without UNL students economically." That said, Omaha is only forty-five minutes away. Pachyderm enthusiasts will be delighted by the Nebraska Museum of Natural History's outstanding collection of prehistoric elephant skeletons. Beyond the sidewalks are miles of flat road and plains ideal for biking, cross-country skiing, and snowmobiling.

Besides football, some of UNL is gaining a reputation as a powerhouse in other sports. Men's track and baseball and women's volleyball, gymnastics, track, and softball have all brought home Division I titles. The football team played for the 2001–2002 national championship (and lost to an undefeated Miami Hurricanes

For many, the fall semester revolves around football weekends and postseason bowl games.

"I can't rave enough about the professors I've had."

On home-game Saturdays, the stadium is the third largest "city" in the state, holding 5 percent of the population.

squad). The biggest football rivalries are with Colorado and Oklahoma. Husker fans proclaim that if forced to choose between going to Oklahoma and going to hell after death—well, it would be a tough choice.

At Nebraska, future agriculture experts mingle with techno-whizzes, while teachers-in-training brush elbows with architecture mavens. "The students at UNL are a diverse group of people," says a junior. "Everyone can find a niche which they fit into perfectly, whether it be Greek life, a campus ministry, their residence hall floor, intramural sports, or any one of the 350 campus organizations." Whether studying overseas, immersing themselves in an internship, or going wild on Saturday afternoon, students here know how to make the most of their time as Cornhuskers.

If You Apply To ➢

Nebraska: Rolling admissions: June 30. Campus interviews: recommended, informational. Alumni interviews: optional, informational. SATs or ACTs: required, ACTs preferred. SAT IIs: optional. Accepts electronic applications. No essay question.

New College of Florida

(Formerly New College of the University of South Florida)
5700 North Tamiami Trail, Sarasota, FL 34243-2197

New College is the South's most liberal institution of higher learning—apologies to Guilford. With an enrollment of 634, New College is about one-third the size of a typical liberal arts college. The kicker: New College is a public institution and one of the nation's best buys.

Website: www.ncf.edu
Location: Suburban
Total Enrollment: 650
Undergraduates: 650
Male/Female: 36/64
SAT Ranges: V 640–730
  M 590–680
ACT Range: 26–30
Financial Aid: 73%
Expense: Pub $ $
Phi Beta Kappa: No
Applicants: 494
Accepted: 65%
Enrolled: 50%
Grad in 6 Years: 72%
Returning Freshmen: 77%
Academics: ✐ ✐ ✐ ✐
Social: ☎ ☎ ☎
Q of L: ★ ★ ★
Admissions: (941) 359-4269
Email Address:
  admissions@ncf.edu

The New College of Florida blossoms with a madhatter's world of unique students, edge-of-the-envelope traditions, and the ability to create an academic future entirely of your design. This thirty-five-year-old school has done away with grades and GPAs, so students compete with themselves, not with their classmates. Students are encouraged to "know that they are part of something completely different, out of the norm, definitely unique, irreproducible, and in many ways amazing," extols one sophomore. The mere existence of the place is proof that it's possible to find success through individualism.

New College began in 1960 as a private college for academically talented students, but when inflation threatened its existence in the mid-1970s, it offered its campus to the University of South Florida. Today, NCF serves as Florida's independent honors college, but is an academically independent entity. New College's campus is adjacent to Sarasota Bay and consists of historic mansions from the former estate of circus magnate Charles Ringling, abutting modern dorms designed by I.M. Pei. The central quad is filled with palm trees, and sunsets over the bay are spectacular. New College shares its campus with the Sarasota branch of USF, which offers upper-level courses in business, education, and engineering. Newer facilities include two seventy-bed apartment-style residence halls, a building with a library, office, and classroom space for the natural sciences, and a marine biology research center.

The administration once had absolutely no required core curriculum, but now has added a liberal arts and math and computer literacy requirement to provide "each student with the depth and breadth of knowledge characteristic of a good liberal arts education." Under the new rules all undergraduates must complete the liberal arts curriculum and the mathematics and computer literacy requirements. The liberal arts curriculum offers 111 courses, of which students must complete eight by graduation, including at least one in each division. The school calendar, however, is still unique: the two fourteen-week semesters are separated by a month-long January Interterm, during which students devise and carry out their own research or conduct group projects. Students work out a "contract" with their advisor each semester and receive written evaluations instead of grades. The seven semester-long contracts and three independent study projects lead to an area of concentration, capped by a senior thesis and an oral baccalaureate examination.

Students "know that they are part of something completely different, out of the norm, definitely unique, irreproducible, and in many ways amazing."

Due to the highly individualized nature of the curriculum, getting into some classes can be a challenge, especially for science majors looking to fulfill requirements for grad school admission, says one student. The workload can be intense, and the shape of any student's program depends heavily on the outlook of his or her faculty sponsor, and students say advising—both academic and career-oriented—is readily available.

New College doesn't offer the specialized courses of a large university, but there's still plenty to choose from, especially for students interested in the social sciences, the humanities, and the physical sciences, where an eleven-hundred-gallon sea water system is available for lab experiments in animal behavior and physiology. Anthropology wins raves, and many students gravitate toward biology, psychology, political science, and sociology. The computer science concentration was dropped, and a partial concentration in theatre was added. Visual arts is said to be weak, and it remains to be seen whether the interdisciplinary international studies program will really pull professors together from various departments, administrators say. Regardless of discipline, the Jane Bancroft Cook Library makes up for its small size— less than three hundred thousand volumes—with a language lab, videotape viewing area, an interlibrary loan program with the entire state university system of Florida, and a classroom equipped for teleconferences.

Students praise the personalized attention they receive from New College professors; graduate students and teaching assistants don't lead classes here. During a typical semester, about half of the students are engaged in one-on-one tutorials, and most other classes are seminars. All disciplines provide the opportunity for original research and students also may conduct field research around the globe, including the study of coral reefs in Honduras, Buddhism in India, and history in Europe. "The quality of teaching is one of the best aspects of New College," says a junior. The academic climate at New College is rigorous, though without grades, "encourages the student to compete with him/herself."

"The quality of teaching is one of the best aspects of New College."

In keeping with the revolution theme, students on this relatively cosmopolitan campus tend to be creative liberal types with '60s nuances. Seventy-five percent of students hail from Florida, perhaps because New College has yet to make a national name for itself. Minorities account for 15 percent of the student body. Social and political issues run the gamut from animal rights and Tibetan independence to vegan issues and helping Mexican migrant workers. "Political inactivity is more a statement than the reverse," says one sophomore. "Political correctness is not much of an issue, as everyone is PC." A new Diversity and Gender Center explores race and gender relations and reconciliation through lectures, movies, and weekly discussions. Merit scholarships ranging from $800 to $10,000 are available to 170 qualified students.

All disciplines provide the opportunity for original research and students also may conduct field research around the globe, including the study of coral reefs in Central America, Buddhism in India, and history in Europe.

Seventy-one percent of students live in campus housing. Rooms in the Pei dorms "are huge and each has a private bathroom and many have balconies," says a biology major. "He built them so that they could be used as hotel rooms if the school failed." The Dart dorms, two apartment-style halls, accommodate 140 students in two-bedroom, two-bath suites with a kitchen, living area, and—of course—air-conditioning (as essential as food and water in the Sunshine State). Rooms are chosen by lottery; though in the past older students were encouraged to move off campus to make room for new students, the new dorms are drawing them back, students report. As for security, the campus is considered safe. "Sarasota consists of retirees and New College, so safety is not a great concern," says a sophomore.

On campus, social life is T-shirts-and-shorts relaxed. "Walls," free-form parties every Friday and Saturday night, can last until 4 or 5 a.m. the following morning. Loudspeakers line Palm Court and students sign up to reserve a night and play whatever music they want. The PCPs (Palm Court Parties) are "blown-out-of-proportion Walls" that occur during Halloween, Valentine's Day, and graduation. It's not hard for underage students to drink. While some students call Sarasota "old-timers ville," it does offer plenty of cultural enrichment (and beautiful beaches). The Ringling Museum of Art and the Asolo State Theater adjoin the campus, and many New College instrumentalists perform with the Florida West Coast Symphony, Sarasota's professionally led symphony orchestra. In the past, students have raised their own fees to fund plays, films, and programs like AIDS awareness. The open road to Tampa, Gainesville, Key West, New Orleans, Atlanta, and even Washington, D.C., ("to protest stuff"), beckons when Sarasota becomes too quiet.

"Political inactivity is more a statement than the reverse."

New College is definitely not a haven for jocks; it fields no varsity teams, somewhat of an oddity in football-crazy Florida. The yearly faculty–student softball game is popular, and anyone can play. Students also look forward to the Crucial Barbecue in January with music and mud wrestling, the Male Chauvinist Pig Roast, the Semi-Normal, a semiformal event on the bay, and the Bowling Ball, a formal-dress occasion at a bowling alley. While the school has a twenty-five-meter swimming pool, students complain than it closes at 10 p.m. The nearby ocean (which does not close) is a bigger draw. "Sarasota is beautiful, warm, and has great beaches," says one student.

The classes at NCF are seminar-like, the atmosphere is hippie beach, and the students are one-of-a-kind. The school's reputation for eccentricity doesn't impede students' academic motivation or their love for learning—whether they're learning belly dancing, biology, origami, or psychology. A sophomore sums up the New College experience this way: "One sunny afternoon at the New College, complete with fierce hugs, shared snacks, passionate debate, and unconditional kindness…restores your faith in humanity."

Overlaps

University of Florida, Grinnell, Hampshire, University of South Florida, Eckerd

If You Apply To ➤

New College: Rolling admissions: May 1. Financial Aid: Mar. 1. Housing: May 1. No campus or alumni interviews. SATs or ACTs: required. SAT IIs: optional. Accepts the Common Application and electronic applications. Essay question: why New College; views on an important issue.

University of New Hampshire

Grant House, 4 Garrison Avenue, Durham, NH 03824-3510

UNH is a public university that looks and feels like a private college, and its tuition hits the pocketbook with similar force. Expensive though it may be, UNH draws more than half of its students from out of state. Strong in the life sciences, especially marine biology, and in business and engineering.

Students at the University of New Hampshire know how to get their hands dirty, and this solid public institution provides them with countless opportunities to do so. Whether studying marine life in the nearby Atlantic waters or human life on another continent, UNH students enjoy the myriad of research options available to them.

The university's wide-open grassy campus hosts a blend of modern facilities and ivy-covered brick buildings. The sprawling lawns are surrounded by three thousand acres of farms, fields, and woods. During the past few years, UNH has invested in large-scale construction and renovation projects, including a new suite-style residence hall, which opened in November 2002. Holloway Commons, completed in fall 2003, is a new dining and conference facility. Murkland Hall, housing the College of Liberal Arts, and Congreve Hall, a student resident hall, both recently reopened after extensive renovations.

Interdisciplinary programs enhance UNH's emphasis on traditional academic programs and the many research opportunities offered by its seven undergraduate schools. Business and engineering are the most respected programs, and the English department has a fine creative writing program.

> **"You can make your courses as competitive as you can handle."**

The Whittemore School of Business and Economics now includes options in entrepreneurial venture creations, information systems, international business, and economics, management, marketing, and accounting; students can also design their own track. Marine biology is also considered stellar, due to UNH's proximity to the water. Environmental studies, chemistry, kinesiology, and nursing all are strong as well. The university now offers a major in computer engineering, and economics now has a B.S. major as well as a B.A. Two new minors, one in aerospace studies and one in animal behavior, were also recently approved. Qualifying students can begin an honors program featuring small classes in freshman year. The lack of professional schools such as law, medicine, or pharmacy has been noted as a weakness.

The university's general education requirements apply across the board and mandate completion of ten courses from eight categories: writing skills; quantitative reasoning; biological, physical, and technological sciences; historical perspectives; foreign cultures; fine arts; social science; and works of philosophy, literature, and ideas. Freshman composition is mandatory as part of a four-course writing intensive requirement. Classes are relatively small, almost always fifty students or fewer, and TAs only facilitate discussion sections or labs. "UNH has

> **"The professors are all knowledgeable people who are here to help you become the best you can be."**

an excellent academic climate," says a senior. "You can make your courses as competitive as you can handle." "The professors are all knowledgeable people who are here to help you become the best you can be," according to a statistics major.

UNH prides itself on producing undergraduates with research experience. The Undergraduate Research Opportunities Program provides about one hundred research awards each year for undergraduates to work closely with faculty on original

Website: www.unh.edu
Location: Small town
Total Enrollment: 14,248
Undergraduates: 11,496
Male/Female: 43/57
SAT Ranges: V 500–590
  M 510–610
Financial Aid: 52%
Expense: Pub $ $ $
Phi Beta Kappa: Yes
Applicants: 10,376
Accepted: 77%
Enrolled: 34%
Grad in 6 Years: 72%
Returning Freshmen: 85%
Academics: 🏛 🏛 🏛
Social: ☎ ☎ ☎ ☎ ☎
Q of L: ★ ★ ★ ★
Admissions: (603) 862-1360
Email Address:
  admissions@unh.edu

Strongest Programs:
History
Psychology
Sociology
Biological Sciences
Marine and Agricultural
  Sciences
Engineering

The school's nickname is the University of No Holidays, since an exceptionally generous winter break limits the number of days off during other seasons. Skiing, camping, fishing, and hiking in nearby forests are favorite seasonal pastimes, and the Outing Club is among the most popular student activities.

projects. A recent undergraduate research conference drew two hundred participants. Budding scientists and sociologists have opportunities to work at research centers for space science and family violence; other students can take advantage of the Institute for Policy and Social Science Research, the Center for Humanities, the Institute for the Study of Earth, Oceans, and Space and the Center to Advance Molecular Interaction Sciences. The Interoperability Lab enables students to work with professors and businesses on cutting-edge problems of computing equipment compatibility. The Isle of Shoals Marine Laboratory, which operates several research projects with Cornell University,

"Housing is excellent. They are beautiful, comfortable, and a great environment."

is just seven miles off the coast. And then there's UNH's Technology, Society, and Values Program, designed to address the ethical implications of the computer age. UNH's study abroad program offers exchange programs with more than 170 U.S. colleges via the Center for International Education. Students can even earn a dual major by combining foreign study and classes in international affairs with those of any other program.

While UNH is New Hampshire's major public institution, it has long been popular with out-of-staters, who make up 42 percent of its students. The school is working on becoming more diverse; only 4 percent of the student body are minorities, which students cite as an area of concern. A special task force at the university is working on keeping the minority students in school until graduation and in helping them network. Social issues at UNH include alcohol awareness and—as might be expected in a place with such lush natural beauty—the environment. The school offers more than 3,700 merit scholarships ranging from $500 to $7,500; awards are also available for athletic prowess.

Fifty-one percent of UNHers live in the school's thirty-one single-sex and co-ed dorms. "Housing is excellent," says a sophomore, "they are beautiful, comfortable, and a great environment." The dorms offer special-interest groupings, lounges, fireplaces, TV lounges, study rooms, and kitchenettes. A 360-student suite-style dorm and new dining hall are have been built, and Murkland Hall, which dates back to 1926, is recently renovated. Freshmen and sophomores are guaranteed dorm rooms; most upperclassmen live off campus or in Gables and Woodside, on-campus apartment complexes, though one senior recommends staying on campus as long as possible to avoid "missing too much fun." Students also gripe that parking is difficult on campus. "Campus security is very good," says one student. "If assistance is needed, there are call boxes at each path, and well-lit walkways."

Less than a five-minute walk from campus is the beautiful little town of Durham, which caters to the student clientele. Along Main Street, Durham has many restaurants, coffeehouses, a grocery store, an ice cream parlor, and a few bars, which have been divided into separate sections (for legal consumers of alcohol and everyone else). "What we can't find here, we can hop onto the bus and go fifteen minutes to Portsmouth," says one student. Greek groups claim 5 percent of UNH men and women. The Greeks also throw parties, which are subject to the university's no-tolerance alcohol policy that evicts from on-campus housing underage students caught with alcohol more than once. For nondrinkers, the university offers weekend social events including concerts, dances, movies, and coffeehouses. Popular road trips include Boston and the White Mountains, or apple picking at a nearby farm. Late nights at L.L. Bean have also become commonplace, and Homecoming, Greek Week, Winter Carnival, Casino Night, and Spring Fling draw crowds every year. And every four years, New Hampshire takes the spotlight when the state holds the nation's earliest presidential primaries.

UNH teams that regularly enjoy national rankings and generate strong spectator interest include men's and women's ice hockey, which recently won the NCAA

UNH prides itself on producing undergraduates with research experience.

Championship, and students celebrate the first UNH goal of each game by inexplicably throwing a large fish onto the ice. Women's gymnastics, men's and women's basketball, and football are also impressive. The university has a strong intramural sports program involving thousands of students.

When there's no game to watch or postgame revelry to indulge in, nature provides UNH students with more than enough to do—if they can find time off. (The school's nickname is the University of No Holidays, since an exceptionally generous winter break limits the number of days off during other seasons.) Skiing, camping, fishing, and hiking in nearby forests are favorite seasonal pastimes, and the Outing Club is among the most popular student activities. "I feel at home at UNH," a senior says.

New Hampshire's only major public university offers a huge variety of programs. That's one reason it attracts so many students from out of state. The laid-back atmosphere and multitude of both academic and social opportunities makes the UNH experience worth every dime.

If You Apply To ➤ | **New Hampshire:** Early action: Dec. 1. Regular admissions: Feb. 1. Financial aid: Mar. 1. Housing: Feb 1. Campus interviews: optional, informational. No alumni interviews. SATs or ACTs: required. SAT IIs: optional. Does not guarantee to meet demonstrated need. Accepts the Common Application and electronic applications. Apply to particular school or program. Essay question: risk you have taken, meaningful photograph, or topic of your choice; recent activities if previous applicant or have been away from school.

The College of New Jersey

(formerly Trenton State College)
P.O. Box 7718, Ewing, NJ 08628-0718

TCNJ is a public liberal arts institution in the mold of William and Mary or UNC–Asheville. Also offers business and education. More than nine-tenths of the students are homegrown Garden Staters. A smaller, more personal alternative to Rutgers.

The College of New Jersey is an up-and-coming public institution with special focus on undergraduates, an emphasis more commonly found at a private school. TCNJ offers professors focused on teaching and a campus physically similar to one found down the road at Princeton University—without the Ivy League price tag. Formerly a teachers' college, TCNJ strives to provide students opportunities in a host of other fields. The small size makes for closeness among students and faculty.

TCNJ is set on 289 wooded and landscaped acres in suburban Ewing Township, six miles from Trenton. The picturesque Georgian Colonial architecture centers on Quimby's Prairie, surrounded by the original academic buildings of the 1930s. A flock of Canada geese makes its home in one of the two campus lakes.

To graduate, students must earn 120 credits for all B.S. programs in the School of Business, B.A. programs except for teacher preparation, and the Bachelor of Science in Nursing. In addition, the list of majors and study abroad opportunities continues to grow. The First Year Experience program is a required two-semester sequence consisting of two courses—From Athens to New York, and Society, Ethics, and Technology. It is designed to ease students into the demanding reality of college life with an approach that integrates academics, individual development, and social understanding. Ten hours of community service is part of the requirement. Says an alum who's returned to work in admissions: "Every student is expected to

Website: www.tcnj.edu
Location: Suburban
Total Enrollment: 6,848
Undergraduates: 5,973
Male/Female: 41/59
SAT Ranges: V 560–650
  M 580–680
Financial Aid: 33%
Expense: Pub $ $ $
Phi Beta Kappa: No
Applicants: 5,988
Accepted: 51%
Enrolled: 41%
Grad in 6 Years: 80%
Returning Freshmen: 96%
Academics: ✍ ✍ ✍ ✍
Social: ☎ ☎ ☎
Q of L: ★ ★ ★

get involved and leave the college a better place for having been here." Also required of incoming freshmen: Expectations, a one-day program to help students and parents understand what they can expect from the college and what the college expects of them; the ten-week College Seminar, to smooth the transition to college; Welcome Week, which gives freshmen a chance to meet their classmates and become acquainted with the campus; and Summer Readings, which exposes students to the kind of scholarship and dialogue they can expect at The College of New Jersey. Recent choices include *Race Matters* by Cornel West and Ralph Ellison's *Invisible Man*. Other requirements include two semesters each of rhetoric and mathematics, twenty-six credits of Perspectives on the World, and three semesters of foreign language (arts and sciences students only).

Consistent with the school's origins as a teachers' college, elementary education is popular, and the business school is strong, as are the natural sciences. Sociology, health, and physical education are considered weak. Academically, TCNJ is competitive and getting more so. Not everyone sees the school's rising star as a benefit. "Becoming an Ivy League–type school," one student complains, means that they are "getting rid of the fun on campus." The college offers a combined, four-and-one-half-year B.S./M.A. in law and justice, taught jointly by TCNJ and Rutgers; a seven-year B.S./M.D. degree program with the University of Medicine and Dentistry of New Jersey; and a seven-year B.S./O.D. degree with SUNY College of Optometry. TCNJ also offers foreign study in eleven countries and is a member of the International Student Exchange Program, giving students access to 131 colleges and universities across the U.S., including Alaska, the Virgin Islands, Puerto Rico, and Guam. The college has no teaching assistants, and faculty members get high marks. Getting into their courses, though, can be frustrating, and students can find their hopes of graduating in five years disappearing as fast as spots in classes during registration.

> **"Every student is expected to get involved and leave the college a better place for having been here."**

The school has no cap on out-of-state admissions, but only 5 percent of TCNJ's students are non-Jerseyans; 63 percent of the freshmen graduated in the top tenth of their high school class, and 65 percent attended public high school. The college has aggressively pursued minority students, and today, African-American, Hispanic, and Asian-American students account for 17 percent of the student body. "If you don't leave this school very well educated in political correctness, then you were obviously unconscious," says a marketing major who praises the school for its diversity. The school has begun ongoing symposia on the Middle East and Afghanistan in the wake of September 11. Merit scholarships range from $500 to $12,000. "TCNJ brings in many of the best New Jersey students who are accepted to Ivy League schools but cannot afford them," says a senior.

Dorm housing, which is described as "very good" and "well-maintained," is only guaranteed for freshmen and sophomores, though 60 percent of all students (and 95 percent of first-years) live on campus. Freshmen hang their hats in either Travers-Wolfe, a two-building, ten-story hall, or Lakeside, a four-building complex. After that, students can enter the lottery for about 2,100 upperclass spaces in the apartment-style townhouses, Community Commons, the recently built residence hall, or try one of several local apartment complexes. Although suburban Ewing doesn't really cater to students, funky New Hope, PA, and preppy Princeton, NJ, are just up the road; restaurants, bars, movie theaters—and this being New Jersey, many malls—are within a short drive. State alcohol policies are strictly enforced, and the underage shouldn't hope to imbibe at the campus bar, the Rathskeller. Six percent of men and 8 percent of women belong to fraternities and sororities, which provide many of the off-campus parties. Campus programming includes dances, concerts

---

(Continued)

Admissions: (609) 771-2131

Email Address:
admiss@vm.tcnj.edu

Strongest Programs:
Biology
Chemistry
History
Elementary Education
Music
Psychology
Business
Computer science

The picturesque Georgian Colonial architecture centers on Quimby's Prairie, surrounded by the original academic buildings of the 1930s.

The college has aggressively pursued minority students, and today, African-American, Hispanic, and Asian-American students account for 17 percent of the student body.

(Billy Joel, Fiona Apple), and movies. Road trips to Philadelphia and New York, each about an hour away and accessible by train, are also highly recommended.

The College of New Jersey's twenty-one varsity teams are big fish in the small pond of NCAA Division III; since 1979, they've won dozens of Division III crowns and runner-up titles. In the 2001–2002 school year, thirty-four athletes won fifty-three All-American awards. Students rally around the football and basketball squads, especially when archrival Rowan comes to town, and the women's field hockey, lacrosse, and soccer teams have a faithful following. TCNJers also look forward to several annual events, including homecoming, a Family Fest Day, and—the springtime favorite—Senior Week.

The College of New Jersey is one of the nation's "budget Ivies," with reasonable tuition and a location that offers media types, artists, and budding scientists a relaxed suburban haven within shouting distance of the editors, producers, directors, curators, and pharmaceutical companies of New Jersey, Pennsylvania, and New York.

> ### Overlaps
> **Rutgers, Villanova, University of Delaware**

> ### If You Apply To ➤
> **TCNJ:** Early decision: Nov. 1. Rolling admissions: Feb. 15. Does not guarantee to meet demonstrated need. Campus interviews: recommended, informational. No alumni interviews. SATs or ACTs: required, SATs preferred. SAT IIs: required (writing). Accepts electronic applications. Essay question: what your reflections on college will be on the day before graduation; how a societal event from the past four years has affected your life; a challenge you overcame; your career goal and how a biology degree from TCNJ will help in achieving it (biology majors only; in addition to one of the other three topics).

New Jersey Institute of Technology

University Heights, Newark, NJ 07102

NJIT is one of the few public technical institutes in the Northeast. It occupies a middle ground between the behemoth Rutgers and smallish Stevens Institute. Offers engineering, architecture, and management. At nearly four to one, NJIT's gender ratio is particularly skewed.

The New Jersey Institute of Technology provides a no-frills technological education that prepares students for a future in an ever-changing global workplace. NJIT's challenging programs emphasize education, research, service, and—not surprisingly—economic development. It's an enticing combination for students seeking a high-tech, low-cost education.

NJIT's urban forty-five-acre campus is dotted with twenty-four buildings of diverse architectural styles, ranging from Elizabethan Gothic to contemporary design. Some of New Jersey's greatest cultural institutions are just blocks away, including the Newark Museum, Symphony Hall, and the New Jersey Center for the Performing Arts. Construction is nearly constant on campus, the latest encompassing a student services mall, renovation of labs, a dorm, and a new Building Sciences Complex.

NJIT is composed of the Newark College of Engineering, the School of Architecture (the only state-supported one in New Jersey), the School of Management, the College of Science and Liberal Arts, and the Albert Dorman Honors College. More than one hundred entering freshmen made up the Dorman class in 1998, and enrollment in the college is almost five hundred students. Top applicants are offered a spot in Dorman as NJIT freshmen, and they can stay as long as they keep

Website: www.njit.edu
Location: Urban
Total Enrollment: 8,828
Undergraduates: 5,730
Male/Female: 79/21
SAT Ranges: V 490–590
   M 550–650
Financial Aid: 70%
Expense: Pub $ $ $ $
Phi Beta Kappa: No
Applicants: 2,591
Accepted: 58%
Enrolled: 40%
Grad in 6 Years: 45%
Returning Freshmen: 80%
Academics: ✍ ✍ ✍
Social: ☎

(Continued)

Q of L: ★★
Admissions: (973) 596-3300
Email Address:
admissions@njit.edu

Strongest Programs:
Architecture
Computer Science
Engineering
Environmental Science

NJIT is still primarily a commuter school, with students living at home to cut costs, so getting a room is no problem.

Top applicants are offered a spot in Dorman as NJIT freshmen, and they can stay as long as they keep their grades up. Perks of Dorman membership include guaranteed dorm rooms, research opportunities, and acceptance into the B.S./M.S. program after completion of five courses for the undergraduate major.

their grades up. Perks of Dorman membership include guaranteed dorm rooms, research opportunities, and acceptance into the B.S./M.S. program after completion of five courses for the undergraduate major. Engineering, architecture, and computer science garner the most student praise, while mechanical and electrical engineering are especially challenging. The administration acknowledges that social sciences and humanities offerings could be better. Every incoming student gets a personal computer, which can be purchased after graduation at a reduced rate. To graduate, students must fulfill general education requirements in areas ranging from English to management. All freshmen take calculus I and II, English composition, computer science, physical education, and Freshman Seminar, a course that introduces students to university life. NJIT has worked with Rutgers to create a number of joint-degree programs from biology to history.

"The academic climate is extremely competitive."

Most NJIT courses have fifty students or fewer. While some say the atmosphere can be low-pressure in certain fields, an electrical engineering student relates his experience this way: "The academic climate is extremely competitive. It requires hours of study just to keep up." The administration assists students if they are having a difficult time, arranging for leaves of absence or extra semesters with a lighter courseload. "Graduating in four years would be miraculous at NJIT," especially for some engineering students, says one. Some have problems getting into classes, with enrollment caps, that are offered only once a year. But one student confides that if a freshman has all of the prerequisite courses, he or she has a good chance of graduating on time.

Students give teaching quality average to high marks. Since most profs have worked in industry, they can offer job information along with academic assistance. Academic advising isn't as helpful as it could be, say some students. "My advisors just look at the courses I choose and make sure that I am supposed to be taking them. I wish they knew more," says one junior. Career counseling, though, is helpful in preparing students for the job hunt. NJIT's most-favored academic option is the co-op program, which enables juniors to get paid for two six-month periods of work at technical companies.

"I love housing. We get free cable, fast Internet connections. We have very big rooms."

As New Jersey's comprehensive technological university, NJIT attracts a wide range of students with different interests. But, one sophomore laments, "We need women." African-Americans comprise 11 percent of the student body, while Hispanics represent 12 percent. Asian-Americans account for 22 percent, and 10 percent hail from out of state or from foreign lands. World Week—with cultural performances and ethnic foods—is a popular spring event. Tolerance is not a problem here as it is on some other campuses. One student praises the Educational Opportunity Program, saying, "If it weren't for them, I would not be here. They make it easy to be a minority." But students say it's a shame that ethnic groups tend to stick together and not mingle; as one puts it, "There's not a feeling of oneness." Political issues do come up, such as peaceful political protests against the war in Iraq. NJIT has a chapter of Tau Beta Pi, the national engineering honor society. The university does not guarantee to meet the financial aid of all admits, but offers merit scholarships to qualified students. The college works with local businesses to recruit qualified minority scholars, offering them scholarships and summer jobs.

NJIT is still primarily a commuter school, with students living at home to cut costs, so getting a room is no problem. NJIT's four residence halls can accommodate one-third of the students. Twenty-three percent of students live on campus. "I love housing," says a junior. "We get free cable, fast Internet connections. We have very big rooms." He does advise, however, that you should get your application in on time in order to get one of those roomy rooms. Freshmen and students living furthest away get first crack at the rooms, and those who get in are guaranteed space the next year. Consensus has it that the best freshman dorms are Redwood Hall and Cypress. Upperclassmen move into fraternity houses or nearby off-campus apartments. The dorms and frats both have kitchen facilities, which many students welcome because the food service fare at times draws a few grumbles from students left with grumbling stomachs after dinner. "Because of its urban location, safety is always a consideration at NJIT. However, students praise the security efforts the school has undertaken. "Public safety officers are always around," says an electrical engineering major.

The large number of commuters and the four-to-one male/female student ratio definitely put a crimp in the social life. There are some outlets, though. About 7 percent of the men and 5 percent of the women join the Greek system. One of the best annual campus events is Spring Week, which includes bands, **"Public safety officers are always around."** novelties, and a semiformal. Diwali, the Indian festival of lights, and Chinese New Year also give undergrads pause to party. "We have a lot of barbecues that bring people together," says an architecture major. Another option is the beach, an hour away, with windsurfing and sailing equipment courtesy of NJIT. Most students agree that the administration's strict alcohol policies work.

NJIT students take pride in their athletic prowess. The varsity teams are Division II, except for soccer, which just moved up to Division I. Men's soccer and baseball and women's swimming are the most popular sports on campus, followed by basketball, swimming, and tennis. The outstanding athletic facilities are open to all, and include an indoor running track, fitness center, racquetball and squash courts, a six-lane pool, and areas for weight training, archery, or aerobics. Outdoor facilities include lighted tennis courts, a sand volleyball court, and a multiuse soccer stadium seating one thousand. A proud (and sweaty) tradition is the Hi-Tech Soccer Classic, which pits NJIT athletes against rivals from MIT, RPI, and Stevens Institute of Technology.

"Students here are hard-working, smart, and aggressive," says an engineering management student. NJIT people have chosen their school because they want a top-notch technical education without the topflight price tag. Academics are the priority here, and if the social life is less than electrifying, students deal with it. After all, they know highly skilled jobs will beckon after graduation. Getting through is a challenge, but there's ample compensation available for NJIT alums in the technologically dependent workplaces of today—and tomorrow.

Overlaps
Rutgers, Rensselaer, Drexel, Stevens Institute of Technology, Rowan

If You Apply To ➤

NJIT: Rolling admissions. Does not guarantee to meet full demonstrated need. Campus interviews: optional, informational. No alumni interviews. SATs: required. SAT IIs: optional. Architecture applicants must submit portfolio of work.

University of New Mexico

P.O. Box 4895, Albuquerque, NM 87196-4895

UNM is shaped by the encounter between Hispanic, Native American, and white culture. Studies related to Hispanic and Native cultures are strong, and in a land of

picture-perfect sunsets, photography is a major deal. Technical programs are fueled by government labs in Albuquerque and Los Alamos.

Website: www.unm.edu
Location: Urban
Total Enrollment: 24,705
Undergraduates: 16,806
Male/Female: 43/57
SAT Ranges: V 510–630
    M 480–600
ACT Range: 19–24
Financial Aid: 74%
Expense: Pub $ $
Phi Beta Kappa: Yes
Applicants: 6,232
Accepted: 77%
Enrolled: 59%
Grad in 6 Years: 45%
Returning Freshmen: 76%
Academics: ✍ ✍ ✍
Social: ☎ ☎ ☎
Q of L: ★ ★ ★
Admissions: (505) 277-2446
Email Address:
    apply@unm.edu

Strongest Programs:
Southwest Hispanic Studies
Photography
Lithography
Geology
Environmental Studies
Laser Optics
Latin American Affairs

UNM's heritage goes back to 1889 when New Mexico wasn't even a state, and the university's strengths are still rooted in the rich history of the American Southwest. New Mexico excels in areas such as Latin American affairs and Southwest Hispanic studies. Lest you think it is a typical state school, consider that many students are commuters or of nontraditional age. UNM also boasts New Mexico's only law, medical, and architecture and urban planning schools, as well as its only doctor of pharmacy program.

Seated at the foot of the gorgeous Sandia Mountains, in the lap of Albuquerque, the beautifully landscaped campus sports both Spanish and Pueblo Indian architectural influences, with lots of patios and balconies. The duck pond is a favorite spot for sunbathing, and the mountains, which rise majestically to the east, are visible from virtually any point on campus. The student union building has been remodeled and the Frank Hibben Center has been completed—while students appreciate the new space, they complain about the construction it takes to create it.

"New Mexico is very open and accepting, so is the university."

UNM offers more than four thousand courses in eleven colleges and two independent divisions, running the gamut from arts and sciences, education, and engineering to management, fine arts, and the allied health fields. Academic and general education requirements vary, but the core curriculum mandates three English courses focused on writing and speaking, two courses in each of the humanities, social and behavioral sciences, and physical and natural sciences, and one course in each of the fine arts, a second language, and math. Those reluctant to specialize can spend a few semesters in the broad University College, which also offers the most popular degree, a bachelor of university studies. Freshmen are encouraged to participate in the Freshman Forum and Core Legacy Courses. Engineering and fine arts freshmen can join interest groups who share suites in a new dorm. The Tamarind Institute, a nationally recognized center housed at UNM's School of Fine Arts, offers training, study, and research in fine-art lithography. Anthropologists may root around one of New Mexico's many archeological sites, and engineers may join in major solar-energy projects. Other popular majors include biology, education, psychology, and nursing and business management. Environmental science has been added as a major, while the bachelor's in fine arts in theatre and dance has been dropped. The bachelor's of science degree in occupational and physical therapy has been changed to a master's degree program. Despite the school's large size, a computerized registration system keeps track of course requests, notifying students who register early when additional sections of courses they need are created.

The newly remodeled student union building includes chain restaurants and a restaurant that serves food from different cultures every week.

By virtue of its location, UNM enjoys a diverse mix of cultures, even though more than 87 percent of students are state residents. A large minority student enrollment—33 percent Hispanic, 3 percent African-American, and 3 percent Asian-American—reflects this cultural diversity. A cultural awareness task force and student diversity council work to keep race relations from becoming rancorous, while the new student orientation program includes a cultural awareness component, and a full-time human awareness coordinator develops diversity-related programs for the residence halls. UNM also hosts the Arts of the Americas, a broad cross-cultural program that involves U.S. and Latin American artists in festivals, classes, and exhibits. "New Mexico is very open and accepting, so is the university," says one junior. Many classes, and several complete degree programs, are offered in late afternoon and evening sessions, and about half of the student body takes advantage of these after-hours options.

Many UNM students commute, and students say finding parking spots continues to be difficult as a result. Only 10 percent of students live on campus. "This is a commuter campus," one senior says. "The dorms are nice but not too many students live there," preferring instead to look for apartments. An escort service, emergency phones, good lighting, and police who patrol around the clock help students feel safe. Students are happy with the variety of food available to them, and note that the newly remodeled student union building includes chain restaurants and a restaurant that serves food from different cultures every week.

Albuquerque—sometimes referred simply as ABQ—is New Mexico's largest city, and it offers a variety of cultural attractions, including the nation's largest hot-air balloon fiesta, a growing artists' colony, and concert tours to charm the ears. Santa Fe is an hour away. Those with cars or pickup trucks take advantage of the state's natural attractions: superb skiing in Taos, the Carlsbad Caverns, the Sandias, as well as excellent hiking and camping opportunities. For the historically inclined, numerous Spanish and Indian ruins are within an easy drive. And for those who yearn for more exotic locales, study abroad programs beckon from Mexico, Brazil, Venezuela, Costa Rica, and Scotland.

> "The dorms are nice but not too many students live there."

Alcohol, though banned on campus, is readily available, according to most students, especially at Greek parties. Other students find their fun off campus in Albuquerque's clubs and restaurants. "Social life takes place both on and off campus," a junior says. For the more socially conscious, the college sponsors Spring Storm, an outing of roughly a thousand students who volunteer around the city on a Saturday. Annual social events include Welcome Back Days in the fall and Nizhoni Days, a celebration of Native American culture. Each spring the whole campus turns out for a four-day fiesta with food and live music.

The men's basketball and football squads and the women's softball, soccer, and volleyball teams usually draw crowds. Scholarships are available for male and female athletes in sports ranging from skiing and wrestling to swimming, golf, and track and field.

UNM's campus and educational emphases keep in mind the Indian pueblos that surround the school. For those not concerned about having a "complete" college experience, and for students balancing college with a part-time job, UNM offers a sun-drenched location that satisfies—precisely because its academic climate is as relaxed as the rolling desert dunes. As one senior says, "It just feels right. It's home now."

The duck pond is a favorite spot for sunbathing, and the mountains, which rise majestically to the east, are visible from virtually any point on campus.

Overlaps

New Mexico State, Eastern New Mexico, Highlands, Arizona State

If You Apply To ➢ **UNM:** Regular admissions: Jun. 15. Financial aid: Apr. 1, Mar. 1 (priority). Does not guarantee to meet demonstrated need. No campus or alumni interviews. ACTs or SATs: required, ACTs preferred. SAT IIs: optional, required for home-schooled students or those at nonaccredited high schools. Accepts electronic applications. Essay question: your educational and career goals and any other information the admissions committee should know.

New Mexico Institute of Mining and Technology

Campus Station, Socorro, NM 87801

New Mexico Institute of Mining and Technology has evolved so much since its founding that it has outgrown its name. Founded as the New Mexico School of Mines, the college now emphasizes computer science, chemical and electrical engineering, and

information technology. New Mexico Tech continues to expand and change with the times, as evidenced by its growing reputation in antiterrorism training and research.

Website: www.nmt.edu
Location: Rural
Total Enrollment: 1,588
Undergraduates: 1,256
Male/Female: 62/38
ACT Range: 23–29
Financial Aid: 55%
Expense: Pub $
Phi Beta Kappa: No
Applicants: 343
Accepted: 84%
Enrolled: 75%
Grad in 6 Years: 38%
Returning Freshmen: 74%
Academics: ✐ ✐ ✐
Social: ☎ ☎
Q of L: ★ ★
Admissions: (505) 835-5424
Email Address:
    admission@admin.nmt.edu

Strongest Programs:
Earth Science
Electrical Engineering
Physics

Tech's tree-lined campus, seventy-six miles south of Albuquerque, is dotted with picturesque, white adobe, red-tiled buildings, and plenty of grassy open spaces that "capture the spirit of the Southwest." The Jones Hall Annex houses classrooms, labs, and offices. NMT owns twenty thousand acres adjacent to the town of Socorro (population 9,000), including Socorro Peak, which provides a mother lode of research and testing facilities. A thunderstorm lab sits on another mountaintop twenty miles away. Not surprisingly, mountain bikers, runners, astronomers, hikers, campers, rock climbers, geologists, rock hounds, and scenery enthusiasts feel right at home here.

NMT offers a number of excellent programs in three main areas: science, engineering, and natural resources. The departments of earth and environmental science, petroleum, and environmental engineering are among Tech's best, as is the program in hydrology, but administrators admit that the mineral engineering department could be bolstered. Freshmen can participate in the First Year Experience Program, in which they are grouped by major under a peer facilitator. New programs have been added in information technology and engineering mechanics. The arts are not what NMT is about, so don't look for an excess of stellar offerings. The closest thing to a well-regarded program in the soft sciences is technical communication.

The student body is said to contain its share of nerds—75 percent, calculates one senior. "However, they tend to be extremely smart," he adds. As might be expected, then, students are drawn to Tech's spacious library, which holds 255,000 books. Computer facilities are, naturally, quite good. And teaching gets high marks, though because of Tech's relatively small size, most courses in the technical fields are offered sequentially, and students who don't take a cluster all the way through may wait several semesters before the necessary course is offered again. To graduate, students must take courses in calculus, physics, chemistry, English, technical writing, humanities, social sciences, and foreign language. Students say it's tough to finish all requirements in four years. A chemical engineering major says students get frustrated because "they never have enough time to finish projects and homework."

Tech's student/faculty ratio is quite low for a technical school, and though professors are research-oriented, they do take teaching seriously. Class sizes vary, though 93 percent have fifty or fewer students. Jobs with mineral industries, research laboratories, and government agencies are available through the five-year cooperative work–study program. Undergraduates can also work part-time at research divisions on campus, including the New Mexico Bureau of Mines and Mineral Resources, the Petroleum Research and Recovery Center, the Energetic Materials Research and Testing Center, and the National Radio Astronomy Observatory's VLA and VLBA facilities. The terrorism training and research comes through

A bit of legwork can turn up decent and "incredibly cheap" housing off-campus.

"This is a small Western town with a deep Hispanic and Indian culture—it's very relaxed."

NM Tech's association with the Energetic Materials Research and Testing Center. As 99 percent of the faculty does research and most hire undergraduates, opportunities for scientific investigation and independent study are plentiful. Quality advising, on the other hand, is not: "Some advisors really care about their students and try to help, while others sign your forms and can't wait to get back to their research," gripes a biology major.

Only 17 percent of Tech's undergraduates are from out of state, and 2 percent are foreign nationals. Hispanics account for 20 percent of the student body, African-Americans 1 percent, and Asian-Americans 3 percent. Thirty-eight percent of students are female—a high number for a technical school. "The issues mostly are about how someone got a better grade than so and so," says a chemical engineering student. Tech's housing facilities have improved and expanded since the days when women resided in the school's trailer park. Students can now live in suites with private bedrooms, a kitchen, and a living room. Forty percent of students live on campus, which one resident describes as "comfortable but a little crowded." A bit of legwork can turn up decent and "incredibly cheap" housing off-campus. Plus, dorm-dwellers are required to buy the meal plan, and the food is said to be less than appealing. Luckily, and not surprisingly, the Mexican food available makes the town taco heaven.

Otherwise, the town, Socorro, is far from being a student paradise. A mining-turned-farming area in one of the most sparsely populated areas in the Southwest, it can only be described as tiny. Boredom may be a problem here, especially if you are under twenty-one, says a senior, though he admits that in its own way, Socorro "grows on a person." The good news is the spectacular weather, where something called rain is in danger of becoming a distant memory, and the nearby desert and spectacular mountains provide a wealth of outdoor opportunities. According to one Techie, "This is a small Western town with a deep Hispanic and Indian culture—it's very relaxed." Still, even those who enjoy the scenery and their classmates' company see a direct correlation between sanity and access to a car, which can take them to Albuquerque and El Paso, or the Taos ski slopes.

With no Greek system and little excitement in Socorro, it's no wonder students at Tech have always had to work to make their own fun. The alcohol policy—"in your room only, over twenty-one only"—works in residence halls with active resident advisors. But a senior says, "It is very easy for minors to find alcohol." There are no varsity sports at Tech, but the men's and women's rugby and soccer teams do travel to challenge other schools. Many students also enjoy an extensive intramural program and the school's eighteen-hole golf course. And in the absence of teams to cheer for, Tech's most popular annual events are 49ers Weekend, a homecoming tribute to the miners of yore with gunfighters and a bordello/casino, and Spring Fling, a mini-homecoming. Fall Fest, a new event, welcomes new and old students back to campus.

With just over twelve hundred undergraduates, New Mexico Tech boasts one of the most intimate and up-to-date technical educations—and certainly some of the best weather—in the nation. NMT is an island of intensity in the otherwise calm New Mexico desert, but those who make it through four years leave with a top-notch technical education at a rock-bottom price.

Not surprisingly, mountain bikers, runners, astronomers, hikers, bikers, campers, rock climbers, geologists and rock hounds, and scenery enthusiasts will be at home here.

Overlaps

New Mexico State, University of New Mexico, Colorado School of Mines

If You Apply To ➤

New Mexico Tech: Rolling admissions: Aug. 1. Financial aid: Mar. 1. Meets demonstrated need of 90%. Campus interviews: recommended, informational. No alumni interviews. SATs or ACTs: required. SAT IIs: optional. Accepts electronic applications. No essay question.

(formerly New School for Social Research)
65 West 11th Street, New York, NY 10011

Eugene Lang College is home to about four hundred street-savvy, free-thinking students. New York City is the campus, and Lang offers little sense of community. In keeping with the New School's traditional ties to Europe, an internationalist perspective predominates. Strong in the arts and humanities.

Website: www.newschool.edu
Location: Urban
Total Enrollment: 408
Undergraduates: 408
Male/Female: 32/68
SAT Ranges: V 570–673 M
470–633
Financial Aid: N/A
Expense: Pr $ $ $ $
Phi Beta Kappa: No
Applicants: 403
Accepted: 80%
Enrolled: 32%
Grad in 6 Years: 85%
Returning Freshmen: 85%
Academics: ✍ ✍ ✍
Social: ☎
Q of L: ★ ★ ★
Admissions: (212) 229-5665
Email Address:
lang@newschool.edu

Strongest Programs:
Writing
Fine Arts
Education Studies
Cultural Studies

Students seeking a typical college experience—large classes, rowdy football games, and rigid academic requirements—need not apply to Eugene Lang College. That's because Lang College has no majors, no departments, and not a single varsity sport. Instead, this small, urban liberal arts college offers individualized academic programs, small classes, and a campus that reflects the quirky and kinetic atmosphere of Greenwich Village. Students control their destiny at this school. Says a student, "Our unique tradition of innovative intellectualism is what makes the New School so special to students and valuable to the public as an institution."

Lang fits right in amid the brownstones and trendy boutiques of one of New York's most vibrant neighborhoods. The majority of Lang's classrooms and facilities are located in a single five-story building between Fifth and Sixth Avenues on West 11th Street, although New School University occupies fifteen buildings in the Village. NYU and the excitement of Greenwich Village and Washington Square Park are just a few blocks away.

The New School was founded in 1919 by a band of progressive scholars that included John Dewey, Charles Beard, and Thorstein Veblen. A decade and a half later, it became a haven for European intellectuals fleeing Nazi persecution, and over the years it has been the teaching home of many notable thinkers, including Buckminster Fuller and Hannah Arendt. Created in 1978, the undergraduate college was renamed in the late '80s for Eugene Lang, a philanthropist who (surprise, surprise!) made a significant donation to the school.

The two most distinctive features of Lang College are the small classes—fewer than sixteen students—and the practice of having undergraduates design their own program of study with no required majors or distribution of courses. As freshmen, students choose from a broad-based menu of seminars, and as sophomores they

"Our unique tradition of innovative intellectualism is what makes the New School so special to students and valuable to the public as an institution."

select from five overarching areas of concentration: writing, literature, and the arts; social and historical inquiry; mind, nature, and values; cultural studies; and urban studies. In their final year at Lang, students take on advanced "senior work" through a seminar or independent project in order to return to a broad plane of thought for a new perspective on the more specialized work of their middle years. The standard courseload is at least four seminars a semester, with topics such as From Standup to Shakespeare and the History of Jazz. All first-year students must take one year of writing and a series of workshops focusing on nonacademic concerns and library research skills. Because each student pursues an individualized educational program, cooperation, not competition, is the norm. "Teachers and students have a lot of freedom to shape the nature, pace, and expectations of courses," says a student. "The general atmosphere is more communal than competitive."

Lang's top offerings include political and social theory, anthropology, history, literature, and literary theory. Its city location lends strength to the urban studies and education programs. Writing is highly praised, especially poetry, and theater is strong. The natural sciences and math are weak areas, though courses are offered through an arrangement with nearby Cooper Union. While introductory language courses are plentiful, upper-level language offerings are limited. And the college has beefed up its offerings on the history and literature of Third World and minority peoples, which were already better than those at most colleges. The professors at Lang are well versed and engaging, according to many students. "We get an exceptional degree of personal attention from highly trained and involved professors who are prominent and respected in their fields."

The main academic complaint is that the range of seminars is somewhat limited by the small size of the school, but outside programs offer more variety. After their first year, students may enroll in courses outside Lang from a limited number of approved classes in other divisions of New School University. A joint B.A./B.F.A. with Parsons School of Design has proven very popular. There's also a B.A./B.F.A. program in jazz and a B.A./M.A. in media studies with the New School's communications department. A newer addition is the exchange program with Sarah Lawrence College, established to provide motivated students with additional academic opportunities. Advanced students also have the option of taking courses in the Milano Graduate School of Management and Urban Professions and the graduate faculty offerings in the social sciences. The New School's library is small, but students have access to the massive Bobst Library at nearby New York University.

> "Teachers and students have a lot of freedom to shape the nature, pace, and expectations of courses. The general atmosphere is more communal than competitive."

Lang College attracts a disparate group of undergraduates, but most of them can be described as idealistic and independent. "The students at Eugene Lang are mostly neo-hippies or activists," says one student. Some are slightly older than conventional college age (some have transferred from other schools) and are used to looking after themselves. Twenty-one percent of the students are African-American or Hispanic, another 3 percent are Asian-American, and 4 percent are foreign. A junior says that most of his classmates "want the freedom of an interdisciplinary education at a small school in a big city." Forty-two percent of Lang's students are from New York City and many cite the school's location as one of its best features. "Whatever is desired can be found somewhere in New York City," says a junior. "It's a nice place to be if you want to party or be a stone-cold intellectual." Lang College admits students regardless of their finances and strives to meet the demonstrated need of those enrolled. However, the school does not guarantee to meet the demonstrated financial need of all admits. A deferred-payment plan allows students to pay tuition in ten installments, and there are various loan programs available. There are no academic-merit or athletic scholarships.

Dorm life at Lang engages only about half of the student body, though the rooms are in good shape. One student offers this assessment: "Union Square is comfortable and fun to live in. Loeb Hall is the newest and is mostly for freshman. Marlton Hall is in sort of a drab location...and is just old and generally uncomfortable." Off-campus dwellers live in apartments in the Village, if they can afford it, or in Brooklyn or elsewhere in the New York City area. Eighty percent of freshmen live on campus. A meal plan is available, but most students opt for the hundreds of delis, coffee shops, and restaurants that line Sixth Avenue.

The social network at Lang is quite small, and like many things, is left up to the student. "Since we generally live off campus, our lives are off campus as well," says one student. The social activities found on campus generally involve intellectual pursuits such as poetry readings and open-mic nights, as well as typical college activities like the student newspaper and the literary magazine. A popular annual festival

The New School was founded in 1919 by a band of progressive scholars that included John Dewey, Charles Beard, and Thorstein Veblen. A decade and a half later, it became a haven for European intellectuals fleeing Nazi persecution.

Because each student pursues an individualized educational program, cooperation, not competition, is the norm.

A popular annual festival allows students to write, cast, design, direct, rehearse, and perform in plays—all in one twenty-four-hour period.

allows students to write, cast, design, direct, rehearse, and perform in plays—all in one twenty-four-hour period. Occasionally, students organize dances and parties, like the Spring Prom, a catered affair with live music that is "a satirical offshoot of the high school tradition." Students generally avoid drinking on campus, and when they do imbibe, alcohol is "far from the central focus of activity," asserts a junior.

Students relish the freedom they are given at Eugene Lang College. For a student who yearns for four years of "traditional" college experiences, Lang would be a disappointment. But for those desiring an intimate, seminar-style education in America's cultural center, with an emphasis on reading, analytical writing, and critical discussion, Lang offers all of the stimulation of the city it calls home.

Overlaps
Sarah Lawrence, NYU, Bard, Hampshire, Fordham

If You Apply To ➢

Eugene Lang: Early decision: Nov. 15. Regular admissions: Feb.1. Meets demonstrated need of 80%. Campus interviews (or by telephone): required, evaluative. No alumni interviews. SATs or ACTs: required. SAT IIs: optional. Essay question: explain how your community has affected your thinking; discuss a social, economic, or political issue of personal importance; and personal statement. Seeks "independent" students.

New York University

22 Washington Square, New York, NY 10011

Don't count on getting into NYU just because Big Sis did. From backup school to the hottest place in higher education, NYU's rise has been breathtaking. The siren song of Greenwich Village has lured applicants by the thousands. Major draws include the arts, media, and business.

Website: www.nyu.edu
Location: Urban
Total Enrollment: 38,096
Undergraduates: 19,490
Male/Female: 40/60
SAT Ranges: V 600–700
  M 610–710
ACT Range: 27-32
Financial Aid: 51%
Expense: Pr $ $ $ $
Phi Beta Kappa: Yes
Applicants: 30,101
Accepted: 33%
Enrolled: 42%
Grad in 6 Years: 78%
Returning Freshmen: 91%
Academics: 🖉 🖉 🖉 🖉 ½
Social: ☎ ☎ ☎
Q of L: ★ ★ ★
Admissions: (212) 998-4500
Email Address:
  www.nyu.edu/ugadmissions

With the world at its doorstep, New York University says to its outsized student body: Jump right in! Firmly planted in the heart of Greenwich Village, arguably one of the most eclectic and energizing neighborhoods in New York City, NYU is blossoming. Its growing student body, fantastic new facilities, and multiple opportunities for high-level internships and research projects have made it a top option for a rising number of high-caliber students. "This school is becoming more academically elite and attracting so many great professors," reports a junior. "And there's a great energy here that is not wrapped up in dull academics, but has an eye toward the real world."

It doesn't get more real world than New York City. NYU has campuses and centers throughout New York, but is centered at Washington Square. Trendy shops, galleries, clubs, bars, and eateries crowd neighboring blocks; SoHo, Little Italy, and Chinatown are just blocks away. Modern and historic NYU academic buildings mix with nineteenth-century brick townhouses surrounding Washington Square Park (the closest thing NYU has to a quad), where parades of rappers, punks, Deadheads, and trendoids surround a replica of the Arc d'Triomphe in Paris. The new Kimmel Center for University Life houses meeting space for NYU's more than three hundred student clubs, plus areas for the frequent recruitment fairs and lectures featuring national and international leaders. A student center with a one-thousand-seat theater is under construction.

> "This school is becoming more academically elite and attracting so many great professors."

The city scene is a defining part of the NYU experience. So, too, is the wide range of academic programs. The Tisch School of the Arts trained such famed directors as

Martin Scorcese, Spike Lee, and Oliver Stone, and current undergrads continue to win many national student filmmaker awards. Tisch also boasts excellent drama, dance, photography, and television departments, and it's not uncommon to see students who haven't yet finished B.F.A. degrees performing in Broadway shows.

Future bulls and bears of Wall Street find a home at the Stern School of Business, where they benefit from a center for Japanese and American business and economic studies. Another favorite department among students (and New York corporations who recruit them after graduation) is accounting, known for its high job-placement rate. The arts and sciences are strong, with English, journalism, history, political science, and applied math winning highest marks. There's an increased emphasis on foreign exchange and study abroad, with campuses in London and Buenos Aires; programs in Paris, Madrid, Florence, and Prague; and exchanges with universities in Chile, Mexico, Sweden, Denmark, and Germany. The Gallatin Division provides flexible schedules and freedom from requirements for those wishing to engage in independent study or develop their own programs. There are new concentrations in digital communications and media, recorded music, leadership and management studies, and international relations. The Speaking Freely program encourages undergraduates to learn languages in their residence halls.

Finding a cheap New York apartment may be easier than sailing through NYU's academics. "Students can expect a fairly heavy load," says an economics major. A senior observes that "NYU sometimes absorbs the high-stress environment of the city." Everyone is very focused on career preparation—it's never enough to just concentrate on your classes. Premed, prelaw, and prebusiness students may encounter packed schedules and competitive classes, while Gallatin and Tisch students may have lots of spare time, students say. "It's hard to avoid the pressure," says a student majoring in drama and political science, with nine hours of acting class a day, and writing-intensive academic courses, too. At least the NYU library is accommodating—it's one of the largest open-stack facilities in the country, with more than three million volumes.

"NYU sometimes absorbs the high-stress environment of the city."

Under the Morse Academic Plan, freshmen and sophomores take courses including foreign language, expository writing, foundations of contemporary culture, and foundations of scientific inquiry. The language offerings, though, go beyond the typical Spanish-French-German—among the choices are Cantonese, Hindi/Urdu, Modern Irish, Swahili, and Tagalog. Like other large universities, NYU inflicts "gargantuan" introductory courses on freshmen, and graduate students lead foreign language sections, writing workshops, and the recitations that accompany lectures. Still, students say teaching is top-notch. Professors "are all accomplished writers and lecturers and are well-known, kind, personable, and hard workers," a junior says. Those qualifying for freshmen honors seminars study in small classes under top faculty and eminent visiting professors.

The variety of degree options here may tempt students to hang around the Village for more than four years. There's a five-year program offering a B.A. and a master's in science, and a seven-year dental program. NYU also has a five-year joint engineering program with New Jersey's Stevens Institute of Technology, and a B.A./M.D. program in which a student is admitted to NYU Medical School at the time of college acceptance. Freshmen selected as University Scholars travel abroad each year. Point to a spot on a world map and you'll likely hit on a country hosting NYU students. Local internships range from jobs on Wall Street to assignments with film industry giants. The career center is "amazingly personal and well-run," says an econ major, and has thousands of listings for on-campus jobs, full-time jobs, and internships. "Career counseling is fabulous," says a junior.

"Career counseling is fabulous."

(Continued)
Strongest Programs:
Drama / Theater Arts
Dance
Business
Art and Design
Film and Television
Music

So you've gotta take a foreign language. But at NYU, the offerings go beyond the typical Spanish-French-German— among the choices are Cantonese, Hindi/Urdu, Modern Irish, Swahili, and Tagalog.

Lesson one: Leave your car at home. You won't need it. New York's extensive subway and bus system (once you learn it!) will tote you from Greenwich Village to the Upper West Side to Brooklyn without the hassle of competing with hair-raising cab drivers.

Thanks in part to the university's investment of new dorms, a majority of students (53 percent) now come from outside New York State and NYU enrolls the highest number of foreign students of any U.S. university. Thirty-nine percent of NYU students are from New York State, primarily the city and nearby suburbs. African-Americans make up 6 percent of the student body, Asian-Americans 14 percent, and Hispanics 7 percent. On this generally liberal campus, gender issues, social justice, the Israeli–Palestinian conflict, and rights of all kinds—gay, lesbian, transgender, animal, human, and workers'—are important now, students say.

An unusual psychological counseling program run by students, Peers Ears, tries to ensure that amid all the hubbub and the pressure of city living, students don't go off the deep end. New students are urged to attend an all-campus freshman orientation program, a program specifically designed for their school, or both. Students also meet with academic advisors—usually professors in their major department—at least once a semester. Advisors review course selections and give students permission to register, while also helping them stay on track toward graduation.

For concerned parents and students, the Office of Student Life, Protection, and Residence Halls hosts a series of workshops on keeping safe at NYU, and programs like the NYU Trolley and Escort Van Service provide door-to-door service for students until 3:00 a.m. "Security on campus is taken very seriously," says a student. "Overall, students feel safe." The police are such a strong presence that one freshman already knows that the campus is located in New York City's Sixth Police Precinct. All residence halls have two people on duty at their entrances twenty-four hours a day, and visitors, including parents, must sign in and leave proper identification.

While NYU students once had to fend for themselves in New York's outrageous housing market, the university now guarantees four years of housing to all freshmen (and most transfers) who seek it. About a dozen dorms, ranging from old hotels to a converted monastery, provide a wide range of accommodations. Most rooms have private baths and are larger, cleaner, newer, and better equipped than many city apartments, enticing 56 percent of students to stay on campus.

"I'm a senior and I still have a meal plan."

There are no freshman halls, and rooms are assigned by lottery each spring. Amenities include central air-conditioning, computer centers, musical practice rooms, kitchens, and even, in some buildings, small theaters. The university provides free shuttle buses to dorms that are further uptown than the Union Square area. The cafeterias offer extensive choices—from wraps to sushi to Burger King. "I'm a senior and I still have a meal plan," says one student. Of course, downtown's array of ethnic restaurants also offer amazing food at cheap prices. One student says the school was named the most vegan-friendly in the nation by People for the Ethical Treatment of Animals.

Students can't say enough good things about NYU's social life. "It's New York, come on," says a student majoring in playwriting. Another adds: "The social scene *is* the city." On campus, there are concerts, movies, fraternity and sorority events (just 4 percent of the men and 2 percent of the women go Greek), and more than three hundred clubs. The springtime Strawberry Festival includes free berries, cotton candy, outdoor concerts, and carnival amusements like a jumping bubble. Many students march in the city's Halloween Parade, which literally takes over Greenwich Village, while most spring and fall weekends find a city-sponsored street fair somewhere nearby. The Violet Ball, a dinner/dance held each fall in the atrium of Bobst Library, is an excuse to get dressed up. As for alcohol, underage students caught with it in public areas of dorms may lose their housing. The rest take their chances with the notoriously strict bouncers at bars and clubs around Manhattan. "They card like crazy," says one junior.

While sports have not exactly been NYU's strength, the women's basketball, men's and women's fencing, and women's soccer teams all brought home the 2003

University Athletic Association Championships. Other Division III powers include men's volleyball, soccer, and golf, as well as women's tennis, volleyball and swimming. More than seven thousand students participate in intramural sports, including arm wrestling. The newer Palladium Athletic Facility boasts a big swimming pool and a thirty-foot indoor climbing wall. Road trips to Philadelphia, Boston, or Washington are few and far between. "Why road trip when you are in NYC?" asks an educational theater major.

"I don't think I can separate NYU from the city," says a senior. Though it might seem hard to concentrate on school work as the heartbeat of New York City thumps day and night, NYU students seem to thrive on all that energy.

If You Apply To >

NYU: Early decision: Nov. 15. Regular admissions: Jan. 15. Financial aid: Feb. 15. Does not guarantee to meet demonstrated need. Campus interviews: optional, informational. No alumni interviews. SATs or ACTs: required. SAT IIs: recommended (writing and two others); required for applicants to the B.A./M.D. program. Accepts the Common Application (with NYU supplement) and electronic applications. Apply to particular schools or programs. Essay question: important person, place, or event in your life; describe the future; a value or ideal that is important to you; influential creative work.

University of North Carolina at Asheville

1 University Heights, Asheville, NC 28804-8503

The "other" UNC happens to be one of the best educational bargains in the country. At just over three thousand students, UNCA is about half the size of fellow public liberal arts college William and Mary and one thousand students smaller than Mary Washington. Picturesque mountain location in a resort city.

Whether it's the lush environment or the money you're saving, the University of North Carolina at Asheville will have you seeing green. This public liberal arts university offers all of the perks that are generally associated with pricier private institutions: rigorous academics, small classes, and a beautiful setting. And it does it for a fraction of the cost. The university continues to integrate experiential learning into its traditional curriculum, emphasizing internships and service-learning experiences. Any way you look at it, UNCA is a bargain that may have your friends turning green with envy.

Located in the heart of North Carolina's gorgeous Blue Ridge Mountains, the 265-acre campus lies in the middle of one million acres of federal and state forest near the tallest mountain in the East and the most heavily visited national park in the country. The campus was built in the 1960s, and much of the brick architecture reflects the style of that decade, although half of the buildings were added within the past few years. The Botanical Gardens at Asheville, adjacent to the main campus, features thousands of labeled plants and trees, and serves as a wildlife refuge and study center for botany students. The new Governors Hall houses 184 students and features Internet connections for each resident, local telephone and cable TV service, and contemporary furniture and amenities based on student input.

> **"With the small class sizes and amount of personal attention you receive, you are well prepared to succeed."**

The university is dedicated to providing a liberal arts education that "teaches students to become their own best and lifelong teachers." The newly implemented

Website: www.unca.edu
Location: Small city
Total Enrollment: 3,391
Undergraduates: 3,351
Male/Female: 42/58
SAT Ranges: V 530–640
  M 520–630
ACT Range: 21–27
Financial Aid: 40%
Expense: Pub $ $
Phi Beta Kappa: No
Applicants: 1,937
Accepted: 67%
Enrolled: 33%
Grad in 6 Years: 51%
Returning Freshmen: 78%
Academics: ✍ ✍ ✍ ✍
Social: ☎ ☎ ☎
Q of L: ★ ★ ★ ★
Admissions: (828) 251-6481
Email Address:
  admissions@unca.edu

general education curriculum is known as Integrative Liberal Studies. The program is characterized by first-year and senior capstone liberal arts colloquia; a humanities core that addresses development and beliefs of Western and non-Western cultures; topical cluster courses in natural and social sciences; and courses in written communication, critical thinking, diversity, and information literacy. There are also requirements for foreign language study as well as health promotion and wellness.

The academic climate is demanding and students admit that it can be competitive at times. "Classes are rigorous," says a senior, "but with the small class sizes and amount of personal attention you receive, you are well prepared to succeed." Political science, humanities, and literature receive near-unanimous praise, and one student says the once-struggling math department "is undoubtedly the strongest on campus." The most popular majors are psychology, management, environmental studies, sociology, and literature. Students cite chemistry and physics as being weaker than other offerings.

"I don't think I can voice how awesome the teaching has been during my four years here."

Asheville also offers 2–2 programs with NC State in engineering, forestry, and textile chemistry; study abroad is an option in Europe, Asia, Africa, and South America. The UNCA honors program offers special courses—as well as cultural and social opportunities—to motivated students who can make the grade. There are also ample opportunities for undergraduate research; in fact, nearly half of all students will have had an undergraduate research experience by graduation. A new interdisciplinary studies major allows students to develop an individual degree program that transcends the scope of a single academic major. Professors are given high marks and noted for their passion and experience. "I don't think I can voice how awesome the teaching has been during my four years here," says a senior. "They make class interesting and are always helping students outside of class."

The head count at Asheville has risen dramatically over the past decade, but only 10 percent of the student body come from out of state. (The school limits its out-of-state admits to 18 percent.) A student says, "The school is located in the Bible Belt, but all political attitudes thrive here." Environmental causes, gay and lesbian issues, campus issues such as parking, and multiculturalism are a few of the buzzwords on campus. "The big subject right now is diversity in the student population," says a student. Currently, the college is 2 percent African-American, 1 percent Hispanic, and 2 percent Asian-American, but Asheville is making special efforts to bring more students who are "underrepresented" to the campus. Asheville offers 153 athletic scholarships in a variety of sports, as well as 375 merit scholarships ranging from $100 to $12,500.

Asheville also offers 2–2 programs with NC State in engineering, forestry, and textile chemistry; study abroad is an option in Europe, Asia, Africa, and South America.

The majority of the students commute from nearby communities, while 35 percent reside on campus. Students can choose from air-conditioned suites in Mills Hall, double occupancy in the Founders Residence Hall, or singles in the wooded Governors Village complex. There is no lottery, and freshmen are mixed in with upperclassmen. "There is plenty of room to live and relax in all dorms," notes a senior. "The newer dorms go first in reservations." For meals, students may eat dining-hall fare or grab a bite at Cafe Ramsey. Vegetarian entrees are available at most meals, in addition to a salad and sandwich bar. Crime is nearly nonexistent on campus, thanks to the school's rural location. Still, emergency phones are available throughout the campus for an added measure of safety.

After class, there's lots to do, especially for the many Asheville students with a hankering for the great outdoors. The college is surrounded by the Blue Ridge Mountains and the Smokies, where students can hike and rock climb; water buffs can go rafting on the nearby French Broad River. For students with cars, the Blue Ridge Parkway is a short drive away, while Spartanburg and Charlotte are one and two hours away, respectively. Real big-city action takes extra effort, though, since Atlanta is a four-hour trek. Asheville offers a tame but inviting nightlife, with popular hangouts like Boston Pizza and MacGuffy's. Most parties take place off campus, especially since RAs stalk underage drinkers in the dorms. "There is no tolerance for unsafe, underage, or unwise drinking," says a student. Five percent of the men and 4 percent of the women belong to fraternities and sororities, but their presence is not influential. There are more than seventy campus organizations, including a student newspaper, *The Blue Banner*.

Involvement is no problem for the athletic teams. The Bulldogs boast Big South conference championship teams in volleyball and men's basketball. Women's tennis has captured the league crown three times, and the soccer team has imported recruits from Germany and England. Most recently, women's cross-country has brought home conference trophies. Intramurals are at least as popular as the varsity sports. The Justice Center Sports Complex houses a pool, weight room, racquetball courts, and dance studio.

Apart from athletics, several campus-wide events bring the school together each year, including Founders Day in October, Homecoming, a spring fling, and a mock casino night with an auction. Greenfest, a semester-based environment and beautification project, is also very popular. "There are lots of annual events, but the one I feel makes

> "The school is located in the Bible Belt, but all political attitudes thrive here."

our campus unique is the annual Greenfest," says a student. "All groups on campus—faculty, staff, and students—come together for two or three days to help make a designated section of campus more beautiful."

All the ingredients for a superior college experience lie in wait at Asheville: strong academics, dedicated professors, and an administration that continues to push for excellence. "The people make Asheville special," notes a senior. "From the chancellor to the custodians, Asheville's people are committed every day to making this college a warm and inviting place." It's a place to get the kind of liberal arts education usually associated with private colleges—but for a lot fewer greenbacks!

The university is dedicated to providing a liberal arts education that "teaches students to become their own best and lifelong teachers." The newly implemented general education curriculum is known as Integrative Liberal Studies.

Overlaps
Appalachian State, UNC–Chapel Hill, North Carolina State, UNC–Wilmington, UNC–Greensboro

If You Apply To ➤

UNC–Asheville: Early action: Oct. 15. Regular admissions: Mar. 15. Financial aid: Mar. 1. Does not guarantee to meet demonstrated need. Campus interviews: optional, evaluative. No alumni interviews. SATs or ACTs: required. SAT IIs: optional. Accepts electronic applications. No essay question.

University of North Carolina at Chapel Hill   BEST BUY

CB 2200, Jackson Hall, Chapel Hill, NC 27599-2200

Close on the heels of UVA as the South's most prestigious public university. With more than 80 percent of the spots in each class reserved for in-staters, admission is next to impossible for out-of-staters who aren't 6'9" with a forty-three-inch vertical jump. Chapel Hill is the quintessential college town.

Welcome to "the Southern part of heaven," a place where the sky is Carolina Blue and the academics are red-hot. As the flagship campus of the state university system and the oldest public university in the United States, UNC–Chapel Hill has earned its place among the South's most prestigious universities. The atmosphere here is uniquely Southern, a rowdy mixture of hard work, sports fanaticism, and tradition that seems to attract bright, fun-loving students from everywhere.

Website: www.unc.edu
Location: Suburban
Total Enrollment: 26,028
Undergraduates: 15,961
Male/Female: 40/60

(Continued)

SAT Ranges: V 580–680
  M 600–690
ACT Range: 24–30
Financial Aid: 29%
Expense: Pub $ $
Phi Beta Kappa: Yes
Applicants: 17,141
Accepted: 35%
Enrolled: 57%
Grad in 6 Years: 80%
Returning Freshmen: 95%
Academics: ✍ ✍ ✍ ✍ ✍
Social: ☎ ☎ ☎ ☎
Q of L: ★ ★ ★ ★
Admissions: (919) 966-3621
Email Address:
  uadm@email.unc.edu

Strongest Programs:
Journalism
Information and Library
  Science
Philosophy
Business
Sociology
Political Science
Classics
Drama

UNC's honors program is nationally recognized as being one of the best in the country.

UNC's campus occupies 730 acres lush with trees and lawns laced by thirty miles of brick-paved walkways. The architecture ranges from Palladian, Federal, and Georgian to postmodern, and redbrick is the prevailing motif. The original administration building is a replica of the central section of Princeton's gorgeous Nassau Hall, then sleek efficiency defines the latest architectural additions to campus, which include buildings for medical biomolecular research and for bioinformatics.

Chapel Hill offers sixty-nine undergraduate degree programs. Some of the strongest are sociology, philosophy, chemistry, business, political science, journalism and mass communications, classics, and biology. One of the most popular on-campus offerings is the small honors seminars open to all undergraduates. UNC's honors program is nationally recognized as among the best in the country. The Carolina Leadership Development Office deserves recognition, in the estimation of one sophomore, who says, "It administers programs, including the North Carolina Fellows Program (a highly selective four-year leadership development program), the Emerging Leaders Program, and the Womentoring Program, which matches female students with female faculty members who serve as mentors." The dramatic art department runs a repertory company with professional actors, as well as sponsoring ten or more student productions a season.

"I've always felt challenged and enriched by classes."

General education requirements, which must be completed in the first two years, include multiple semesters of English composition, foreign languages, physical education, natural and social sciences, aesthetics, and history as well as single courses in mathematical science, philosophy, and cultural diversity. The low-pressure, low-tension academic atmosphere, unusual at a school of UNC's caliber, lets students set their own scholarly pace. "I've always felt challenged and enriched by classes," says one student. Academic and social life are governed by a student-run honor system.

Registration is by Web or telephone, and seniority determines first access. If you get closed out of a class, "Be persistent," advises a freshman. "E-mail the professor. You can get in!" For those tired of the classroom rush, Research Triangle Park, a nearby research and corporate community and home of the National Humanities Center, employs many students as research assistants. UNC offers more than 230 study abroad programs in sixty-four countries. The Carolina faculty is, for the most part, top-notch. Professors keep regular office hours and welcome those students who seek them out. Academic counseling, once less than stellar, has been revamped.

Under state guidelines, 82 percent of UNC's freshman class must be state residents, and the admissions office has no problem filling this quota with the cream of the North Carolinian crop. Thus, unless you're an athlete, out-of-state admission is extremely tough. Some Carolinians spend their childhoods talking about "when I get to Chapel Hill." A good number of them can't afford or don't want to pay for an Ivy League or private-school education. Big social and political issues on campus include multiculturalism, gender roles, local and national elections, and religious issues. A "diversity assessment process" was recently launched to focus on such issues as race and cultural differences. African-Americans account for 11 percent of the student body, Asian-Americans 6 percent, and Hispanics 2 percent. This sports-minded school awards athletic scholarships in all of the major sports. Students also can vie for 250 merit scholarships, ranging from $1,000 to $15,000. The university also offers a need-based loan program with low interest and repayment periods running as long as ten years after a student leaves school—quite a deal when you consider that UNC's tuition is already a bargain. The student government runs a part-time employment service that provides about five hundred student jobs.

"The pickiest of the picky could be happy with Carolina dining services."

Forty-three percent of undergraduates live in university housing, and, "Our housing system is pretty darn good!" avows a senior. Freshmen and returning students are guaranteed university housing, and returning students may reserve their rooms for the upcoming academic year. Housing on the north side of campus offers old but comfortable dorms; the south side offers high-rise cell blocks of cramped four-room suites, which are a good hike from classroom buildings (not to worry—there's a free campus shuttle). Students may opt to be part of a living/learning community; house themes include foreign languages, substance-free, wellness, and women's issues. In fall, 2002, four state-of-the-art dorms—complete with classrooms—were opened. "The pickiest of the picky could be happy with Carolina dining services," says a freshman. "If you don't see it, you can request it. Great vegetarian options. Lots of variety." Campus security is praised. "It is all around, without making students feel uncomfortable," writes an education major. "The university takes precautionary measures instead of reacting measures." These include free bus and shuttle rides, emergency call boxes, and a fully accredited campus police department.

"'College town' in the dictionary should show a picture of Chapel Hill," boasts one senior. Franklin Street, the main drag in town that runs across the northern boundary of campus, offers Mexican and Chinese restaurants, ice cream parlors, coffee houses, vegetarian eateries, bakeries, a disco, and a generous supply of bars. Fraternities and sororities may account for only 12 percent each of the student population, but they exert an influence far beyond their numbers. They don't, however, have a monopoly on fun, or on drinking. "Students over 21 can have alcohol in the dorms. If underage students are caught, they can be fined or punished. Some people get caught, lots don't. It's a game of chance. Getting served at the bars when underage is not nearly as easy," reports a journalism major. "Fallfest" kicks off the school year with an emphasis on the idea that you don't have to drink to have fun. Students look forward to several annual festivals: Apple Chill, Festifall, the Carolina Jazz Festival, and the North Carolina Literary Festival, which recently featured author Calvin Trillin. Students are involved in the community, many through a unique service-learning program for which they receive academic credit.

The varsity sports teams are extremely popular, especially football. The word "popular" doesn't do justice to the basketball games. A contest between the top NCAA rated Tar Heel Basketball Team with NC State makes any Carolina fan's heart beat faster, but Duke takes the prize as the most hated rival of all. The slam-dunking Tar Heels play in the 21,750-seat Smith Center, named for retired coach Dean Smith, who just happens to be the winningest college basketball coach of all time. The school has taken almost two hundred ACC championships since the league was founded in 1953. Men's

"'College town' in the dictionary should show a picture of Chapel Hill."

and women's basketball, lacrosse, field hockey and men's soccer have won national championships, but the team with one of the best records in college sports history is women's soccer, which has won seventeen national championships since 1981. Women also brought home national championships in field hockey and basketball, and conference championships in volleyball and track. A strong intramural program draws heavy participation. Those not quite so competition-minded can enjoy the $4.9 million student recreation center, which includes a weight-training facility, an area for aerobic dance, and the student wellness center. Those who crave fresh air can take advantage of the Outdoor Education Center, which offers mountain bike trails, an eighteen-hole Frisbee golf course, rope courses, and the longest zipline in the U.S.

Often touted as one of the best college buys in the country, the University of North Carolina at Chapel Hill gives students everything they want, both academically and socially. The two-hundred-year history of this school creates an atmosphere of extreme pride, a love of tradition, and monumental school spirit. As one freshman who is full

Under state guidelines, 82 percent of UNC's freshman class must be state residents, and the admissions office has no problem filling this quota with the cream of the North Carolinian crop.

The student government runs a part-time employment service that provides about five hundred student jobs.

Overlaps

North Carolina State, East Carolina, UNC–Wilmington, Appalachian State, UNC–Greensboro

of that school spirit after a terrific first year says, "Southern hospitality blended with a high level of thinking, an overwhelming dose of friendliness and pep, and a spectacularly gorgeous campus make Chapel Hill my favorite place in the world."

University of North Carolina at Greensboro

1000 Spring Garden Street, Greensboro, NC 27412

UNCG is a medium-sized alternative in the UNC system—half the size of Chapel Hill and three times bigger than Asheville. UNCG began its life as a women's college and remains about two-thirds female. Residential College program offers a first-rate living/learning option.

Website: www.uncg.edu
Location: Center city
Total Enrollment: 13,918
Undergraduates: 10,751
Male/Female: 33/67
SAT Ranges: V 460–570
 M 470–570
Financial Aid: 35%
Expense: Pub $
Phi Beta Kappa: Yes
Applicants: 7,065
Accepted: 76%
Enrolled: 39%
Grad in 6 Years: 48%
Returning Freshmen: 74%
Academics: ✍️ ✍️
Social: ☎ ☎
Q of L: ★ ★ ★
Admissions: (336) 334-5243
Email Address: undergrad_admissions@uncg.edu

Strongest Programs:
Music
Dance
Creative Writing
Theater
Education
Nutrition
Psychology

At the University of North Carolina at Greensboro, an aggressive campaign is underway to make the school more "student centered." Living Learning Communities have been developed to help meet the needs of freshmen and make the matriculation experience less daunting. The administration is also taking steps to make all students feel at home. "Being a student at UNCG is so much more than going to class, studying, and getting a degree," says a senior. "There's so much opportunity to get involved here and many ways to make your total college experience valuable and lots of fun."

Set on two hundred acres sprinkled with magnolia and dogwood trees, Greensboro's well-landscaped campus features a mix of Colonial, Georgian, brick, and modern architecture. Still standing is the original university building, the Victorian-style Julius Foust Building; built in 1892 and now on the National Register of Historic Places, it is located on a knoll in the center of the campus's original ten acres. The Elliot University Student Center has been expanded and renovated, and a $39 million science building has opened its doors.

> **"Being a student at UNCG is so much more than going to class, studying, and getting a degree."**

Within the College of Arts and Sciences, psychology, fine arts, and literature are strong. The university's program in human environmental sciences is also highly regarded, and business and nursing are the most popular majors. The School of Music has three ensembles, a symphony orchestra, three choral groups, and has won the National Opera Association's production competition three of the past five years. There are some unusual interdisciplinary programs, such as therapy training, which combines classes from the dance, education, fine arts, and theater departments. Greensboro's program in human environmental sciences is North Carolina's largest. New majors include special education and African-American studies, an interdisciplinary program. The general education requirements allow students to complete core requirements in as few as thirty-six semester hours, provided they have met requirements in global perspectives, writing across the curriculum, and speaking across the curriculum.

The academic climate is rigorous and "very competitive," says a sophomore. Students take their education seriously, and so do the professors. "The teachers push you as well as support you," says a junior. Enrollments in introductory courses sometimes swell to more than one hundred, but preregistration is done through an online computer system. Those who make it into the residential college program enjoy the atmosphere of an intimate "academic community" with class sizes usually ranging from fifteen to twenty students. The school's residential college is among the nation's oldest living/learning programs. The honors program allows talented students the opportunity to tackle a broad interdisciplinary program through small seminars, while undergraduate research assistantships allow sixty-five students to work with faculty in all fields. To emphasize the importance of writing both as an essential skill and as a tool for learning, all students must take writing-intensive courses.

A summer orientation program allows freshmen to get their feet wet before classes begin. Each academic year starts off with the Fall Kickoff, when campus organizations line College Avenue with the trappings of their activities, creating a festival atmosphere. UNCG has more than 170 student organizations, including club sports, religious groups, service organizations, media groups, national societies, and professional organizations.

Eight percent of undergrads come from outside North Carolina, mostly from the South. African-Americans account for 20 percent of the student body, and the Neo-Black Society is very active on campus. Hispanics and Asian-Americans combine to make up 5 percent of the student body. According to a junior, "The students

"The students at UNCG are an eclectic group. Here a student is independent, political, friendly."

at UNCG are an eclectic group. Here a student is independent, political, friendly. There are so many different types, unlike private or well-known universities." Outstanding students can vie for hundreds of scholarships, which range from $1,000 to $12,000; 180 athletic scholarships are also offered.

Thirty-six percent of the undergraduates live in Greensboro's twenty-three residence halls, but students note that getting a room can be a challenge. "The past few years have been cramped and we have been experiencing a housing shortage," says a student. "But the rooms are OK." The Tower Village Apartments provide suite-style living on campus for three hundred lucky students who get private bedrooms. Rooms in the older buildings are spacious, those in the quad are more attractive, and the most modern, high-rise dorms offer cramped—but air-conditioned—quarters. Four of the twenty-three dorms are single-sex, and at the beginning of the year, each residence hall votes on guidelines establishing the visitation policy for members of the opposite sex. For those who still want to avoid institutionalized living, off-campus housing is plentiful and cheap. Students who live on campus choose from a variety of meal-plan options in the university dining hall or in specialty shops. Administrators boast that the newly renovated student center is one of the nicest centers in the state.

Eight fraternities and ten sororities attract 5 percent of the men and 5 percent of the women. For others, dances, coffee houses, concerts, movies, and other social activities pick up some of the social slack. "Greensboro is a wonderful, old Southern town," reports one student. Bars, restaurants, and stores are within walking distance, and the twenty-three-thousand-seat Greensboro Coli-

"Greensboro is a wonderful, old Southern town."

Overlaps

UNC–Chapel Hill, East Carolina, UNC–Charlotte, North Carolina State, Appalachian State

seum, a scant two miles away, regularly plays host to rock bands and athletic events. Weekend trips are to the beach (three hours) or the mountains (two hours). "UNCG is a good college for fun. It is not a party school but there is always something going on," a communication studies major says.

UNCG teams compete in Division I, and the university offers a comprehensive athletic program as part of the Southern Conference. Men's basketball and tennis and women's soccer have all brought home conference championships and continue to field solid squads. Intramurals are also popular.

Some students say that Greensboro is becoming somewhat of a commuter school, though it may be too early to tell. Others say the only problem is that the school, living in the shadow of its big sister at Chapel Hill, lacks the reputation it deserves for providing a first-rate education in such diverse fields as liberal arts, nursing, and education.

<table>
<tr><td>If You
Apply
To ➢</td><td>UNC–Greensboro: Regular admissions: Mar. 1. Financial aid: Mar. 1. Housing: May 1. Does not guarantee to meet demonstrated need. Campus interviews: optional, informational. No alumni interviews. SATs or ACTs: required. SAT IIs: optional. Electronic application accepted. No essay question.</td></tr>
</table>

North Carolina State University

Box 7103, Raleigh, NC 27695-7103

It is hard for NC State not to have an inferiority complex next to high falutin' neighbors like Duke and UNC. But having them in the neighborhood is also a blessing—just ask the thousands of graduates who have gotten jobs in the Research Triangle. Engineering and business are the most popular programs.

Website: www.ncsu.edu
Location: City suburbs
Total Enrollment: 29,854
Undergraduates: 22,971
Male/Female: 44/56
SAT Ranges: V 530–630
  M 560–670
ACT Range: 23–28
Financial Aid: 36%
Expense: Pub $
Phi Beta Kappa: Yes
Applicants: 11,835
Accepted: 66%
Enrolled: 49%
Grad in 6 Years: 64%
Returning Freshmen: 90%
Academics: ✏ ✏ ✏
Social: ☎ ☎ ☎
Q of L: ★ ★ ★
Admissions: (919) 515-2434
Email Address: undergrad
  _admissions@ncsu.edu

Strongest Programs:
Design
Statistics

Whether you're looking for a stellar education in engineering and textiles or a top-rated basketball program, North Carolina State is one of the bright leaves of the Tobacco Belt. NCSU offers students the benefits of a large school—reputable professors, a diverse student body, and plenty to do on weekends—while making sure that no one feels left out. Says one junior, "No matter how weird or crazy you are, there is someone just like you on campus."

The 107-year-old, nineteen-hundred-acre campus consists of redbrick buildings, brick-lined walks, and cozy courtyards dotted with pine trees. There is no dominant style, but more of an architectural stream-of-consciousness that reveals a campus that grew and changed with time. Newer facilities include a dining hall and toxicology building.

NCSU excels in the professional areas of engineering, pulp and paper science, statistics, design, agriculture, and forestry, which are the largest and the most demanding divisions. Not surprisingly, given its location in the heart of textile country, the

"No matter how weird or crazy you are, there is someone just like you on campus."

school also boasts a first-rate textile school, the largest and one of the best such programs in the country. Business tops the list of most popular majors, followed by engineering and accounting. Even the most technical of majors requires students to take a broad range of liberal arts courses, although the humanities are far from the biggest game on campus. English and sociology get poor marks from students. University-wide general education requirements include two semesters each of English composition, math, and science, as well as foreign language proficiency and electives in the humanities and social sciences. Freshmen are required to take English and math, and there are numerous seminars and orientation courses in each area of academic interest.

An important feature of NC State's approach to education is the cooperative education program, through which students in all schools can alternate semesters of on-site work with traditional classroom time. There are also domestic and international exchanges with more than ninety-seven countries and a Residential Scholars program in which academic standouts live together and participate in weekly activities such as guest lectures. A First Year College program provides guidance and counseling for incoming students to introduce them to all possible majors. Many classes at NC State are large, but the faculty gets high grades for being accessible, interested in teaching, and friendly. Says a junior, "On a scale of one to ten, I would rate the quality of teaching here as an eight. I was taught by full professors as a freshman." Aside from the regular hassles that come with attending a large school, the academic atmosphere is relatively relaxed. Free tutoring in most subjects is made possible by grants from state industries. The library contains six million volumes and is considered a good place to do research, but it's also a hot social spot.

(Continued)
Engineering
Pulp and Paper Science
Agriculture
Forestry
Textiles

The university benefits greatly from its relationships with Duke, the University of North Carolina at Chapel Hill, and private industry through the state's high-tech Research Triangle Park. The students at NC State are largely hardworking, bright North Carolinians. Some 87 percent are in-state students. "Students at NC State are very friendly, open, and down-to-earth," says a student. Nearly two-thirds graduated in the top quarter of their high school class, and 89 percent attended public high school. Ten percent of the student body is African-American, while Hispanics and Asian-Americans make up another 7 percent. Amid the public school diversity, conservatism abounds, and the largest political organization is the College Republicans. Jocks and sports fans are visible, and the university offers more than four hundred scholarships for men and women in twenty-two sports. Those with outstanding academic qualifications can compete for one of 108

An important feature of NC State's approach to education is the cooperative education program, through which students in all schools can alternate semesters of on-site work with traditional classroom time.

"I was taught by full professors as a freshman."

merit scholarships that range from $1,000 to $23,000 per year. To be considered for merit awards, students must file a separate application in the early fall of their senior year in high school.

As for housing, 33 percent choose to stay on campus in one of twenty dorms. All students are guaranteed rooms for all four years. Sullivan and Lee are recommended for freshmen because they provide a mixture of academic and social activities. Most of the older dorms lack air-conditioning, and are described as "well maintained" though students admit that some of the dorms are ancient and need major reconstruction. Rooms range in size from spacious to cramped. Students report that dorm dwelling is actually more expensive than several off-campus units. Two big issues, students report, are parking and financial aid. One students says, "The financial-aid packets have caused me nothing but stress." If you don't mind such minor annoyances, off-campus housing and social activities are plentiful. A small percentage of students are housed in fraternities and sororities, and the international house is also an option.

"Students at NC State are very friendly, open, and down-to-earth."

The dining hall feeds all freshmen and anyone else who cares to join the meal plan. It's an all-you-can-eat deal, and students can use their meal cards at numerous campus snack bars and sandwich shops.

As with many other schools, alcohol policies are not strictly enforced. The twenty-one fraternities and five sororities attract about 7 percent of the men and 9 percent of the women. The Greek scene provides much of the entertainment, but dorm and suite parties are also popular. Public transportation affords easy access to downtown, with its shops, restaurants, theaters, and nightspots. The university is well integrated into Raleigh, and its proximity to three all-women's colleges helps alleviate the imbalance of the three-to-two male/female ratio. Annual events include Wolfstock (a band party) and an All-Nighter in the student center. Many

The library contains six million volumes and is considered a good place to do research, but it's also a noisy social center.

students also like to head to the beach, which is less than two hours away, or to the ski mountains, which are about a three-and-a-half-hour trip.

With home close by for so many students, the campus does tend to thin out on weekends. Those who stay can cheer on the home teams, which do well in men's tennis, swimming, soccer, football, and men's and women's cross-country and track and field. But needless to say, basketball reigns supreme. The Wolfpack plays in the high-powered Atlantic Coast Conference. "We have an ongoing rivalry with the University of North Carolina," says a junior. Some crazy NC State fans have stormed nearby Hillsborough Street following game-day victories. The annual State versus Carolina football game usually packs the stadium, and the never-ending fight to "Beat Carolina!" permeates the campus year round. Intramurals also thrive, and a particularly popular event is Big Four Day, when NC State's intramural teams compete against their neighbors at Duke, Wake Forest, and UNC–Chapel Hill.

North Carolina State seems to have overcome many of the obstacles associated with large land-grant universities. It has attracted a dedicated and friendly student body independent enough to deal with the inevitable anonymity of a state school, but spirited enough to cheer the Wolfpack to victory. NC State works well for both those who can shoot hoops and those who can calculate the trajectory of the same three-point shot.

If You Apply To ➤ **NC State:** Rolling admissions: Feb. 1. Early action: Nov. 15. Financial aid: Mar. 1. Does not guarantee to meet full demonstrated need. No campus or alumni interviews. SATs or ACTs: required. SAT IIs: recommended (math) for placement only. Accepts electronic applications. Essay question: optional, benefits of a college education and how NC State fits into your plans.

Northeastern University

360 Huntington Avenue, 150 Richards Hall, Boston, MA 02115

Northeastern is synonymous with preprofessional education and hands-on experience. By interspersing a co-op job with academic study, students can rake in thousands while getting a leg up on the job market. With Boston beckoning, campus life is minimal.

In a rocky economy, there's nothing like solid, hands-on work experience to send a resume to the top of the pile. And that's what Northeastern is all about. With a strong emphasis on combining liberal arts requirements with up to eighteen months of challenging work placements, students come out of this school not only well rounded, but ready to take on real-world responsibilities. Of course, being in the middle of Boston also means that NU students get plenty of experience having a great time in one of the country's top college towns.

Northeastern's sixty-seven-acre campus is an urban oasis located in the heart of Boston, just minutes away from Fenway Park, shopping centers, nightclubs, cafes, Symphony Hall, and the Museum of Fine Arts. The campus's green spaces are interspersed with brick walkways, outdoor art, and a sculpture garden. Older buildings sport utilitarian gray-brick architecture while newer structures are of modern glass and brick design. During inclement weather, students can be found traversing the underground tunnel system that connects many campus buildings. A $37 million health sciences building and two apartment-style residence halls are the latest campus additions.

In order to enhance students' academic and co-op experiences, Northeastern University has switched from its academic quarter system to a semester calendar. The calendar consists of fifteen-week semesters in the fall and spring and two shorter sessions in the summer. Full-time undergraduates will typically take classes for eight semesters and complete a total of three six-month co-ops during their five years at Northeastern. For students in the College of Arts and Sciences, there are many alternatives to the co-op, such as internships, study abroad, and undergraduate research opportunities. Each of the six colleges presents its own core curriculum, but all freshmen must complete English and diversity requirements. Freshmen are also required to attend the summer orientation program. Newer programs include an M.S. in physician assistant studies and B.S. degrees in architecture, information sciences, and computer engineering. An honors program is open to top students in all departments. One freshman who just completed the first year of the honors program reports that "the academic climate has been competitive."

> **"The academic climate has been competitive."**

For six months worth of work, students average nearly $12,000, which is sometimes used to defray college-related costs. Most of the jobs are in the Boston area—though there are sixteen hundred employers participating worldwide—and related to the student's major. More than half of Northeastern's grads, especially those in the more high-tech and business-related fields, receive job offers from their co-op employers. Students warn, however, against becoming overly reliant on co-op advisors for good jobs or good advice. Plus, some students say that when the economy is on a downswing, co-op jobs are tougher to come by. Besides the money they can earn in co-op programs, outstanding students can compete for 2,575 merit scholarships that range from $400 to $32,000, and there are 326 athletic scholarships for eight women's sports and seven men's sports.

Undergrads say that most of their teachers are concerned with their needs, and most of Northeastern's classes have thirty-five or fewer students. A senior says, "Most professors avoid straight lecturing and use more interactive teaching methods." Scheduling can be difficult, as students sometimes find that courses they want are offered only when they're scheduled to be away on a job.

Northeastern, which was founded as a YMCA educational program, has traditionally served local students from diverse socioeconomic backgrounds. But that has changed—now, only 37 percent of the students are from Massachusetts. African-Americans comprise 6 percent of the population, while Hispanics make up 5 percent of the student body, Asian-Americans 8 percent, and foreign students 7 percent. NU students find there is more than lip-service to diversity. Students are "pretty liberal thinkers," says a finance and political science student. But because so many participate in the co-op program, many "don't have a good connection to the university," says one student. Northeastern has partnered with SquashBusters, a program in which urban middle and high school students receive tutoring and mentoring. They erected a new building, the SquashBusters Clubhouse, which is open to NU students for their own games.

> **"Most professors avoid straight lecturing and use more interactive teaching methods."**

Although 91 percent of freshmen live on campus, upperclassmen have a much harder time finding a place to sleep on campus. Some of the dorms have been showing their age, but NU recently completed several new residence halls, including the West Village complex, a thirteen-story apartment megaplex that houses up to six hundred students. "They're building dorms like crazy!" says one student. Off-campus options include privately owned apartments or suites located adjacent to the residence halls. Students speak highly of NU Public Safety.

(Continued)
Grad in 6 Years: 50%
Returning Freshmen: 84%
Academics: ✍ ✍
Social: ☎ ☎
Q of L: ★ ★
Admissions: (617) 373-2200
Email Address:
    admissions@neu.edu

Strongest Programs:
Business
Health Professions
Engineering
Business Administration
Art
Architecture
Psychology
Computer Science
Criminology

The biggest sports series of the year is the Beanpot Hockey Tournament, which pits Northeastern against rival teams from Harvard, Boston College, and Boston University.

Created in 1908, Northeastern's co-op program was one of the nation's first, and has since become one of the best in the country.

The co-op program puts a strain on campus social life. There are many clubs and activities, but the continuous flow of students on and off the campus tends to be disruptive. "I may see a friend one quarter in class and then not again for six months. It's hard to stay connected," a student explains. Fraternities and sororities attract 4 percent of NU men and women. Those who are not in the Greek system find Boston with all its attractions to be a fully acceptable substitute.

In the winter, students head to the ski slopes of Vermont, and in balmier weather they're off to the beaches of Cape Cod and the North Shore. Not surprisingly, in the city the Celtics made famous, the basketball team attracts adoring fans,

"They're building dorms like crazy!" especially after having produced the late Celtic star Reggie Lewis. But the biggest sports series of the year is the Beanpot Hockey Tournament, which pits Northeastern against rival teams from Harvard, Boston College, and Boston University. Northeastern's female pucksters have frequently prevailed as champs. And the fleet-footed men's and women's track and cross-country teams, who work out in the newly renovated Bernard Solomon Indoor Track Facility, regularly leave their opponents blinking in the dust. The competitive nature of the sports teams, especially toward those also in the Boston area, is epitomized by one T-shirt that reads, "No—we don't want to B.U."

Perhaps now, more than ever, a school that truly prepares students to enter the working world is needed. The point for students, says one international affairs major, is to "gain professional experience in their fields and get a better idea of their future goals." By the time Northeastern students graduate, they have built up a broad reservoir of experiences that they know will serve them well once they start scouring those job listings.

Overlaps

Boston University, Boston College, Syracuse, University of Massachusetts at Amherst, University of Connecticut

If You Apply To ➤ **Northeastern:** Rolling admissions and financial aid: Feb. 15. Housing: May 1. Does not guarantee to meet demonstrated need. Campus interviews: optional, informational. No alumni interviews. SATs or ACTs: required. SAT IIs: optional. Accepts the Common Application. Essay question: issue of concern and its impact on you; fictional or nonfictional character with admirable values; experience, achievement, or event that has affected your life.

Northwestern University

1801 Hinman Avenue, P.O. Box 3060, Evanston, IL 60204-3060

The most selective university in the Midwest. The Big Ten is not the Ivy League, and NU has more school spirit than its Eastern counterparts. Much more preprofessional than its nearby rival University of Chicago and than any of the Ivies except Penn. World renowned in journalism.

Website:
www.northwestern.edu
Location: Suburban
Total Enrollment: 16,032
Undergraduates: 7,946
Male/Female: 47/53
SAT Ranges: V 640–730
  M 660–750

On Sunday nights before finals begin at Northwestern University, students are encouraged to let off steam with a campus-wide "primal scream." The ear-shattering event illustrates two big themes at NU: students work really hard, but they know how to have some fun, too. Regarded as the most elite school in the Midwest, this top-tier university boasts some of the most well-respected preprofessional programs in the country. Plus, Northwestern is ideally located just outside of Chicago. "I love being at a place where I can learn and have a great social life," says one student.

Northwestern is situated on 231 acres about a dozen miles north of the Chicago Loop. Evanston is "gorgeous," students say, its leafy shores looking out on the sailboat-filled Lake Michigan in warm weather, and "lake effect" snow combining with the real thing to make it a Currier & Ives painting in winter. The newer buildings are located adjacent to a fourteen-acre lagoon, part of an eighty-five-acre lakefill addition built in the '60s. This area provides students with a prime location for picnicking, fishing, running, cycling, rollerblading, or just daydreaming. Among the new additions to the campus are the McCormick Tribune Center, a state-of-the-art broadcast and multimedia center; the 84,000-square-foot Center for Nanofabrication and Molecular Self-Assembly; and the Ford Motor Company Engineering Design Center, slated for completion this year.

"I love being at a place where I can learn and have a great social life."

As for the academic climate, Northwestern offers a choice of some widely known programs; among the six undergraduate schools, the School of Communications, the Medill School of Journalism, the School of Music, and the McCormick School of Engineering and Applied Science have national reputations. The School of Communications has excellent departments across the board, from theater and radio/TV/film to communicative disorders. The School of Journalism offers invaluable experience and the opportunity to make important job contacts through ten-week internships at 52 newspapers, 41 magazines, and 19 television stations across the nation. There's also a four-year accelerated B.S.J./M.S.J. program. A dazzling electronic studio centralizes Medill's state-of-the-art broadcast newsroom and the communication school's radio/TV/film department. The McCormick School of Engineering and Applied Science is particularly strong in all aspects of engineering, and five-year co-op options are available. The physical and social sciences are the strongest of the liberal arts. There is now a bachelor of music offered, and a five-year journalism/art degree.

Fine arts programs in the music school, particularly in the brass and wind departments, enhance the university's offerings. A newer major in dance has already drawn attention from students. Northwestern also emphasizes interdisciplinary education, and there are many accelerated and combined-degree programs. Special academics programs like the Center for the Writing Arts, which sponsors one or more professional writers of national prominence to teach undergraduate courses, conduct seminars, and present readings and discussions of their own work, are highly praised. Interdisciplinary programs, ranging from American culture, integrated arts, mathematical methods in the social sciences, and integrated sciences, are offered in eighteen fields. The

"The quarter system makes the academic climate at NU intense."

Weinberg College of Arts and Sciences has a Junior Tutorial Program, in which small groups of undergrads in a variety of fields work with senior faculty members on advanced topics.

Each of the undergraduate schools determines its own general education requirements, but the distribution requirements are similar. Each school requires a graduate to have coursework in "the major domains of knowledge"—science, mathematics and technology, individual and social behavior, historical studies, values, the humanities, and the fine arts.

Unlike most schools on a ten-week quarter system, Northwesterners take four (not three) courses each quarter, except in engineering, where five are permitted. A student says, "The quarter system makes the academic climate at NU intense. It feels like people are constantly studying for midterms or finals." Students can also take a break from the campus through any of twenty field-study programs and programs abroad in twenty-eight countries. Perhaps one reason students study so hard is the motivation provided by their professors. "The quality of teaching is out of this world," says one student. Another gushes, "One of my professors had the last class at her home!" Virtually all undergraduate courses, including required freshman

(Continued)
ACT Range: 28–33
Financial Aid: 60%
Expense: Pr $ $ $ $
Phi Beta Kappa: Yes
Applicants: 14,283
Accepted: 33%
Enrolled: 43%
Grad in 5 Years: 93%
Returning Freshmen: 96%
Academics: ✑ ✑ ✑ ✑ ✑
Social: ☎ ☎ ☎
Q of L: ★ ★ ★
Admissions: (847) 491-7271
Email Address:
  ug-admission@
  northwestern.edu

Strongest Programs:
Engineering
Economics
Journalism
Communications Studies
Psychology
Theater
Music Performance

seminars (of ten to fifteen students) in arts and sciences, are taught by regular faculty members. Introductory courses are larger than most, but the average 100-level class size is about thirty students. Overall, the student/faculty ratio is 7 to 1. In response to student complaints, the university has expanded the advisory system, assigning students a counselor for all four years. Medill has its own career services office, and one of the staff members there "can magically turn crappy resumes into gold with a few simple suggestions," quips a journalism major.

All buildings are connected to the campus's fiber optic system, so students can access the library and Internet from their rooms. They are supported by student consultants who live in each residence hall and are on call 24/7 to provide computer support. The library contains 4.15 million volumes. Its resources online include the catalog, more than seven hundred journals, and more than two hundred databases and indexes.

Seventy-four percent of the student body come from outside Illinois borders, and 82 percent graduated in the top tenth of their high school class. Minorities represent 37 percent of the student body, with Asian-Americans accounting for 13 percent, African-Americans 6 percent, and Hispanics 5 percent. Some call the political atmosphere on campus "apathetic," but others say groups are becoming much more active. "Political correctness

"The quality of teaching is out of this world."

isn't an issue because if a person isn't PC, many student groups will jump all over them," says an economics major. The abundance of preprofessionals has added to Northwestern's image as "young corporate America," and the acceptance rate for medical school applicants is 63 percent while that of graduates at schools of business and law hovers around 90 percent. There are no academic merit scholarships, but NU does guarantee to meet the full demonstrated need of every admit, and it provides 345 scholarships for its athletes. Loans for middle-income families are available through the university.

With the addition of two residence halls in the past few years, there is now ample on-campus housing. "Rooms are spacious compared to other schools," says a senior. "My friends are always in awe of how big they are." However, housing is guaranteed only to freshmen and those with demonstrated need. Dorms range from small single-sex houses to large co-ed buildings, the most popular of which are organized in suites of eight students around a common living room. Students may join thematic or nonthematic residential colleges, which bring students and faculty members together during faculty "firesides" or simply over meals. The newer Slivka Hall houses the engineering residential colleges; there also are special dorms for students in communications, international studies, humanities, commerce and industry, performing arts, and public affairs. Fraternities and sororities also have their own houses. Students can choose to eat at the coffeehouse or at any one of the many dining halls on campus. A variety of meal plans are available, including one that provides Sunday brunch and one offering Kosher food. Evanston offers some comfortable apartments to the 35 percent who live off campus, but rents are high and zoning laws prohibit occupancy of a house or apartment by more than three unrelated people. As for security, one student says, "Even though the campus is located so close to Chicago, I feel extremely safe."

Students agree that Evanston is not a great college town, and in fact there has traditionally been hostility between townspeople and students. "Our administration and the city government are always fighting," says one student. Another student feels the tension is lessening, and says, "One mayoral candidate ran on an 'anti-NU' platform and was soundly defeated." The town has built a new complex with a cineplex, hotel, and shopping mall.

For a night out, of course, there is that "toddlin' town," Chicago, right across the border. For those who don't think Chicago is their kind of town, Evanston will do nicely with its many excellent restaurants and trendy bars. Much of the social life on campus is centered around the Greek system, and 30 percent of the men and 40 percent of the women go Greek. For non-Greeks, on-campus entertainment opportunities are numerous, including theater productions, concerts, and movies. The school's alcohol policy is tough, but not always effective. "They don't really want us to have it, but students get it anyway," says one student. The student government and Activities and Organizations Board sponsors an array of campus-wide events, such as the very popular thirty-hour Dance Marathon and Dillo (Armadillo) Day, an end-of-the-year party with numerous bands

"Rooms are spacious compared to other schools."

and other activities. "It's just hippie fun," raves a student. Another tradition is upheld when representatives of student organizations slip out in the dead of night to paint their colors and slogans on a centrally located rock. As a bonus to the social atmosphere as well as to educational hands-on experience, the campus has its own radio station, television studio, and award-winning newspaper, and, says one administrator, "Certainly any student who wishes to act, produce, direct, conduct, build scenery, or play in a musical ensemble has ample opportunity to do so."

Football and tailgate parties are a traditional way of bringing alumni back and rousing the students to support the only non-state school in the Big Ten. The men's golf team brought home consecutive Big Ten championships in 1999, 2000, and 2001. The women's tennis team did that, too, and won again in 2002 and 2003. Other competitive women's teams include volleyball, softball, field hockey, swimming, and NU's newest varsity sport: women's lacrosse. As far as facilities, NU is on par with many schools its size and larger, with the beautiful Norris Aquatics Center/Henry Crown Sports Pavilion and the Nicolet Football and Conference Center, used for conditioning of varsity athletes. The student-sponsored intramural program provides vigorous competition among teams from dorms and rival fraternities.

With a strong work ethic, and an equally strong desire for play, Northwestern students bask in their school's balance of challenging academics, preprofessional bent, and myriad opportunities to get off campus to learn and let loose. "I'm able to have fun in a learning environment," says a biomedical engineering major. "The friends I've made here also make this a place that will be hard to leave."

Every so often, a traveling chef will stop by NU and whip up dishes. Past chefs have specialized in Chinese, Kosher, or Indian foods.

Overlaps

Stanford, Duke, Cornell, University of Pennsylvania, University of Michigan

If You Apply To ➢

Northwestern: Early decision: Nov. 1. Regular admissions: Jan. 1. Financial aid: Feb. 1. Housing: May 27. Guarantees to meet demonstrated need. Campus and alumni interviews: optional, informational. SATs or ACTs: required. SAT IIs: recommended. Accepts electronic applications. Essay question: varies every year, pick one of four.

University of Notre Dame

220 Main Bldg., Notre Dame, IN 46556

The Holy Grail of higher education for many Roman Catholics. ND's heartland location and 85 percent Catholic enrollment make it a bastion of traditional values. Offers business and engineering in addition to the liberal arts. ND's personality is much closer to Boston College than Georgetown.

Founded 159 years ago by the French priest Edward Sorin, the University of Notre Dame has come a long way from its fledgling days in a rustic log cabin. While it is

Website: www.nd.edu

(Continued)

Location: City outskirts
Total Enrollment: 11,311
Undergraduates: 8,261
Male/Female: 53/47
SAT Ranges: V 620–720
  M 650–730
ACT Range: 30–33
Financial Aid: 70%
Expense: Pr $ $ $ $
Phi Beta Kappa: Yes
Applicants: 9,744
Accepted: 34%
Enrolled: 20%
Grad in 6 Years: 95%
Returning Freshmen: 98%
Academics: ✍ ✍ ✍ ✍
Social: ☎ ☎ ☎
Q of L: ★ ★ ★
Admissions: (574) 631-7505
Email Address:
  admissio.1@nd.edu

Strongest Programs:
Theology
English
Philosophy
Chemical Engineering
Program of Liberal Studies
Business
Chemistry
Accounting

Nearly 85 percent of the students are Catholic, leaving some skepticism about the comfort level of those who are not.

described as "a Catholic academic community of higher learning," students need not be affiliated with the Roman Catholic Church. According to the administration, "What the university asks of all its scholars is not a particular creedal affiliation, but a respect for the objectives of Notre Dame and a willingness to enter into the conversation that gives it life and character." A soft spot for football doesn't hurt, either.

With 1,250 acres of rolling hills, twin lakes, and woods, the university offers a peaceful setting for studying. The lofty Golden Dome that rises above the ivy-covered Gothic and modern buildings and the old brick stadium, where in the 1920s Knute Rockne made the Fighting Irish almost synonymous with college football, are national symbols. Newer parts of campus are housing for visiting faculty and a new theology/philosophy building named Edward A. Malloy Hall in honor of Notre Dame's president, who also is a full professor of theology.

Liberal education is more than just a catchphrase at Notre Dame. No matter what their major, students must take the First Year of Studies, one of the most extensive academic and counseling programs of any university in the nation. The core of the program is a one-semester university seminar that is limited to twenty students per section and is writing intensive. The remainder of each freshman's schedule is reserved for the first of a comprehensive list of general education requirements: one semester each in writing and mathematics and two semesters in natural science, as well as one semester chosen from theology, philosophy, history, social science, and fine arts. The First Year of Studies program also includes a strong counseling component in which peer advisors are assigned to each student, as are academic advisors and tutors if necessary. Administrators are quick to point out that, due in part to the success of the first-year support program, a whopping 98 percent of the freshmen make it through and return for sophomore year—the highest retention rate in the nation.

> "The workload is very demanding. It requires the student to have very good time-management skills."

In the College of Arts and Letters, highly regarded departments include English, theology, and philosophy, while physics and chemistry are tops in the College of Science. Within the engineering school, chemical engineering rules. The College of Business Administration's accountancy program is ranked among the nation's best, and the chemistry labs in the Nieuwland Science Hall have first-rate equipment. While weak departments are hard to come by at Notre Dame, some students complain about the creative arts programs. The academic climate at Notre Dame is said to be fairly rigorous. "The workload is very demanding," says a senior. "It requires the student to have very good time-management skills." And while the atmosphere is competitive, students agree that it is not cut-throat by any measure. Faculty members are praised for being dynamic, personable, knowledgeable, and accessible. "The professors here care a great deal about their students and it shows," says a biology major. Students report it can be hard to get all the classes they want during a particular semester, but say it's not difficult to graduate in four years.

Notre Dame offers a variety of special academic programs and options. One of the most popular is the Program of Liberal Studies (PLS), in which students study art, philosophy, literature, and the history of Western thought within their Great

> "The professors here care a great deal about their students and it shows."

Books seminars. The Kaneb Center for Teaching and Learning, the university's most recent commitment to teaching, is based in DeBartolo Hall, an eighty-four-classroom complex with state-of-the-art computer and audiovisual equipment. The Arts and Letters Program for Administrators combines a second business major with liberal learning, and the College of Science also allows students the option of pursuing majors in two departments. In addition, Notre Dame offers programs in military and naval science, aerospace studies, and an international study program that allows students to travel to numerous countries.

With a predominantly lay board of trustees and faculty, Notre Dame remains committed to "the preservation of a distinctly Catholic community." The president and several other top administrators are priests of the Congregation of the Holy Cross, and each dorm has its own chapel with daily Masses. Nearly 85 percent of the students are Catholic, leaving some skepticism about the comfort level of those who are not. Students feel Notre Dame nurtures their faith as well as their minds. The main social issues discussed on campus include abortion, gender and racial issues, homosexuality, and faith. Diversity is also a concern, and some students feel it is a big problem. Minority enrollment is growing. African-Americans and Hispanics make up 11 percent of the student body and Asian-Americans another 4 percent. Despite its relative cultural homogeneity, Notre Dame recruits from all over the country; 88 percent of the students are from outside Indiana. The university offers competitive academic scholarships to students with outstanding high school records and financial need, and 404 athletic scholarships are available.

Dorm life at Notre Dame appeals to three-quarters of the students. "Notre Dame dorm life is extraordinary," says a junior. "The dorm rooms are all very well-kept and very comfortable." Students are assigned to a dorm for their freshman year, and are encouraged to stay in the same one until graduation. Fraternities are banned, and freshmen are spread out among all campus dorms. The single-sex dorms really become surrogate fraternities and sororities that breed a similar spirit of community and family. Parietal rules (midnight on weekdays, 2 a.m. on weekends) are strictly enforced. Boarders eat in either the North Quad or South Quad cafeterias, and must buy a nineteen-meal plan. For those who tire of institutional cuisine, the Huddle offers plenty of fast-food options as well as a pay-as-you-go snack bar. Students can also reserve the kitchen to cook their own meals.

Notre Dame has been open to female applicants since 1972, and with a nearly perfect gender split in the undergraduate student body, the ratio is now comparable to many other formerly all-male schools. ND's social life isn't as rambunctious as it once was, thanks to the policy that forbids alcohol at campus

"Notre Dame dorm life is extraordinary."

social events. The rules relating to alcohol in the dorms are a bit more relaxed. For those who choose not to indulge, there are several groups dedicated to good times without alcohol. Most activities take place on campus and include parties, concerts, and movies. Each dorm holds theme dances about twice a month, and there's always the annual Screw Your Roommate weekend, where students are paired with the blind dates selected by their roomies. Another popular event is the An Tostal Festival, which comes the week before spring finals and guarantees to temporarily relieve academic anxiety with its "childish" games such as pie-eating contests and Jell-O wrestling. The annual Sophomore Literary Festival is entirely student-run and draws prominent writers and poets from across the country. Students are involved in the community through volunteer work. The best outlet for culture is nearby Chicago, about ninety minutes away.

With its proud gridiron heritage, there's nothing like the Fighting Irish spirit. From Knute Rockne and the Gipper right on down to modern-day greats such as Joe Montana, the spirit of Notre Dame football reigns supreme. Though the team has struggled as of late, most on campus believe its only a matter of time before the team regains its former glory. It wasn't intentional—at least that's what they say—but the giant mosaic of Jesus Christ on the library lifts his hands toward the heavens as if to signal yet another Irish touchdown. Tailgate parties are also celebrated events, occurring before and after the game. Aside from football, Division I Notre Dame offers one of the strongest all-around athletic programs in the country with

Newer parts of campus are housing for visiting faculty and a new theology/ philosophy building named Edward A. Malloy Hall in honor of Notre Dame's president, who also is a full professor of theology.

No matter what their major, students must take the First Year of Studies, one of the most extensive academic and counseling programs of any university in the nation.

nationally ranked teams in women's soccer, volleyball, basketball, tennis, softball, and fencing, and men's tennis, lacrosse, fencing, baseball, and cross-country. Diehard jocks who can't make the varsity teams will find plenty of company in ND's very competitive intramural leagues. The Bookstore Basketball Tournament, which is the largest five-on-five, single-elimination hoops tournament in the world with more than seven hundred teams competing, lasts for a month.

Everyone at the university, from administrators to students, is considered part of the "Notre Dame family." Traditions are held in high esteem. For those looking for high-quality academics, a friendly, caring environment with a Catholic bent, and an excellent athletic scene, ND could be the answer to their prayers.

Overlaps

Boston College, Duke, Northwestern, Georgetown, Harvard

If You Apply To ➤

ND: Early action: Nov. 1. Regular admissions: Jan. 9. Financial aid: Feb. 15. Housing: May 1. Guarantees to meet demonstrated need. No campus or alumni interviews. SATs or ACTs: required. SAT IIs: optional. Accepts electronic applications. Essay question: personal example of courage; personal example of ideas motivating actions or actions changing ideas; personal statement.

Oberlin College

101 North Professor Street, Carnegie Building, Oberlin, OH 44074-1075

The college that invented nonconformity. From the Underground Railroad to the modern peace movement, Obies have been front and center. As at Reed and Grinnell, Oberlin's curriculum is less radical than its students. Oberlin is especially strong in the sciences, and its music conservatory is among the nation's best.

Website: www.oberlin.edu
Location: Small town
Total Enrollment: 2,861
Undergraduates: 2,848
Male/Female: 45/55
SAT Ranges: V 630–740
  M 610–710
ACT Range: 26–31
Financial Aid: 54%
Expense: Pr $ $ $
Phi Beta Kappa: Yes
Applicants: 5,934
Accepted: 33%
Enrolled: 37%
Grad in 6 Years: 76%
Returning Freshmen: 88%
Academics: ✍ ✍ ✍ ✍ ½
Social: ☎ ☎ ☎ ☎
Q of L: ★ ★ ★ ★
Admissions: (440) 775-8411
Email Address:
  college.admissions@oberlin.edu

New and contrasting ideas are a way of life at Oberlin College: a liberal arts school that invented nonconformity. Tucked away in a small Ohio town, Oberlin was the first American college to accept women and minorities, and it was a stop on the Underground Railroad. That pioneering spirit has not faded. With diverse academic challenges ranging from cinema studies to neuroscience, Obies thrive on higher thinking and exploring their myriad talents.

Oberlin's attractive campus features a mix of Italian Renaissance buildings (four designed by Cass Gilbert), late-nineteenth- and early-twentieth-century organic stone structures, and some less interesting 1950s barracks-type dorms. The buildings rise over flatlands typical of the Midwest, which do little to stop brutal winter winds. The Allen Art Museum, sometimes mentioned in the same breath as Harvard's and Yale's, is one of the loveliest buildings on campus, with a brick-paved, flower-laden courtyard and a fountain. A new science center was dedicated in October 2002.

Oberlin is especially strong in the sciences, and its music conservatory is among the nation's best. Oberlin has been a leader among liberal arts colleges seeking to promote their science offerings; biology and chemistry are two of the college's strongest departments, and undergraduates may major in interdisciplinary programs like neuroscience and biopsychology. Students rave about the religion

"Students here want to make a difference."

department, where profs are "at the top of their game." Oberlin's conservatory of music holds a well-deserved spot among the nation's most prominent performance schools; the voice, violin, and TIMARA (Technology in Music and Related Arts) programs are especially praised. English is also lauded, and—not surprisingly at such a liberal school—interdisciplinary and self-created majors, such as black, Latin American, Russian, Third World, and women's studies, are popular. East Asian studies have long been outstanding at Oberlin as well; a study-abroad program at China's Yunnan University is available, and the two-year Shansi fellowship in an Asian country is a popular and sought-after post graduate goal. The college has added a cinema/film studies major and dropped a 3–2 engineering with the University of Pennsylvania.

Oberlin's students are as serious about their schoolwork as they are about politics, justice, and other social causes. Courses are rigorous; heavy workloads and the occasional Saturday morning class are the norm. Still, this is no "smackdown" school. One student describes the environment as "pretty laid back, not competitive. Oberlin kids ask a lot of questions, which is how their professors like it." "Students here want to make a difference," one student says. "I don't see the student apathy here that exists at other colleges." The pressure is somewhat minimized by the credit/no-entry policy, which allows students to take an unlimited number of grade-free courses (if they can get in). Plus, anything below a C is scratched from a student's transcript. Generally, however, students at Oberlin are gifted and want to challenge themselves. Recognizing that, most departments offer group and individual independent study opportunities and invite selected students to pursue demanding honors programs, especially during their senior year. Professors are "very engaging and make us have some extensive conversations/discussions, not just lecture at us," says a history and classics major.

There are no requirements for freshmen at Oberlin, but general education requirements include proficiency in writing and math and nine credit hours in each of the three divisions—arts and humanities, math/natural sciences, and social sciences—plus another nine credit hours in cultural diversity courses, which include a foreign language. Students are also required to take one-quarter of the semester hours needed to graduate outside their major's division, and to participate in three January terms, during which they pursue month-long projects, traditional or unique, on or off campus. About twenty-five

"EXCO classes range from beer-making to sexual information to martial arts to the Beatles discography."

different freshman/sophomore colloquia are available, with enrollment limited to fifteen students each, and though the majority of other classes are limited to twenty-five students, the computerized registration system makes it easy to get in.

One of Oberlin's more unusual offerings is EXCO, an experimental college that offers students and interested townsfolk the chance to teach one another. "EXCO classes range from beer-making to sexual information to martial arts to the Beatles discography," notes one student. Many learning opportunities are available beyond the town of Oberlin as well, with about 40 percent of students taking advantage of semesters at the Oberlin Center of European Studies in Strasbourg, France, or programs in China, London, France, Germany, and Dublin through the Great Lakes Colleges Association.* Sea lovers can travel to Mystic Seaport.* Back on campus, the Mudd Library has more than 1.5 million volumes and is a superb facility for research and studying or socializing; the famous A-level is the place to be on weeknights. Even more special is the music conservatory, with its 153 practice rooms, substantial music library, and more Steinway pianos under one roof (175 grands, twenty-one uprights) than anywhere else in the world. Qualified students can earn both a B.M. and a B.A. in a five-year dual degree program.

Obies are "eclectic and individualistic," says one student. "Students speak their minds and are very involved." Two-thirds come from public school and 76 percent are white. Still, 83 percent of students are from out of state, hailing primarily from the mid-Atlantic states. African-Americans account for 7 percent of the student body, Asian-Americans 6 percent, and Hispanics 4 percent. Initiatives to increase

(Continued)
Strongest Programs:
Neuroscience
Environmental Studies
Creative Writing
East Asian Studies
Music Performance
Biology
Chemistry

Tucked away in a small Ohio town, Oberlin was the first American college to accept women and minorities.

East Asian studies have long been outstanding at Oberlin as well; a study-abroad program at China's Yunnan University is available, and the two-year Shansi fellowship in an Asian country is a popular and sought-after post-graduate goal.

diversity at Oberlin include advisors from various ethnic and racial backgrounds and a multicultural resource center with a full-time director. The campus is politically active, with issues of sexuality, race, and gender coming to the fore. One senior says, "Students are serious about any number of issues, but most are more far-reaching than just on campus." A popular annual event is the Drag Ball, sponsored by the Lesbian Gay Bisexual Union, in which half the student body shows up in full drag. The event includes a runway competition and a disco string orchestra, and it brought MTV's cameras to campus a few years ago. The annual Folk Fest attracts artists like Dar Williams. Students can drive to the majestic Severance Hall in Cleveland for some more serious tunes.

Seventy-two percent of Oberlin's students live on campus. They choose from among twenty-five dorms, several of which focus on foreign languages. "Some dorms are better maintained than others," notes one student. "Avoid the co-ops, they can be quite messy." Students are guaranteed housing, but your choices get better as you gain upper-class standing. Only one dorm is single-sex; all dorms are four-class except Barrows, which is reserved for freshmen. The best dorms are said to be the program houses, including French House, African Heritage House, Russian House, and Third World House. Seniors and lucky juniors can land the preferred singles (thanks to their standing or good lottery numbers), but many move into cheaper off-campus apartments, although only a fraction are allowed off the college's meal plan. Oberlin's dining hall system includes six dining rooms in four buildings, chosen through another lottery. An appetizing alternative to institutional fare can be found at one of the six co-ops that comprise the Oberlin Student Cooperative Association (OSCA), a $1-million-a-year corporation run entirely by students. Co-opers plan and prepare their own meals, and though only 12 percent of the student body actually live in these houses, almost 25 percent take their meals there, enjoying everything from homemade bread to whatever's left in the pantry before the next food shipment arrives.

> **"Students are serious about any number of issues, but most are more far-reaching than just on campus."**

Six dining co-ops comprise the Oberlin Student Cooperative Association (OSCA), a $1-million-a-year corporation run entirely by students.

Social life, like so much of the Oberlin experience, is what you make of it, students report. One student proclaims, "I'm never bored." Another student admits, "Usually there's more to do than I have time for." House parties, plays, movies, and conservatory performances are planned every other night. And since there's no Greek system, nothing is exclusive. As for drinking, underage students can finagle booze, and of-age students are allowed to imbibe in their rooms.

The "tiny but complete" town of Oberlin offers the essentials, students say, including "a small-town movie theater, two bookstores, pizza places, banks, grocery stores, and a bakery with great doughnuts." Town–gown relations are symbiotic; "There's a lot of give and take on many levels," a philosophy major opines. Hospitals and a mentoring program for college-bound kids attract many Obies. "The Center for Service and Learning takes care of volunteerism and I'd guess the majority of students engage in community service at some point," says a senior. If all else fails, Cleveland—including the Rock and Roll Hall of Fame and major league baseball— is thirty miles away. Other good road trips are Chicago (six hours) and Washington, D.C. (six-and-a-half hours).

Oberlin's new athletic director has taken charge of what many consider to be a lukewarm athletics program, with an eye on reversing the school's losing ways and building a loyal fan base. Women's lacrosse and tennis have both captured the NCAC championship in recent years; other decent teams include men's swimming, men's and women's soccer and track and field, and women's basketball. Participation in club sports, particularly rugby and Ultimate Frisbee, is on the rise, and there is now a golf team.

Overlaps

Wesleyan, Brown, Vassar, Grinnell, Swarthmore

Oberlin might be small in size, but its emphasis on global learning, undergraduate research, and a vibrant liberal arts education helps it bust those statistical seams. Students are more likely to discuss local poverty than the quality of cereal choices in the dining halls, and can be found playing a Steinway or plugging away at astronomy. No matter what you find Obies doing, they'll be doing it their way. Like a popular Oberlin T-shirt says: "Think one person can change the world? We do."

If You Apply To ➢

Oberlin: Early decision: Nov. 15, Jan. 2. Regular admissions: Jan. 15. Financial aid: Feb. 15. Housing: Jun. 1. Guarantees to meet demonstrated need. Campus and alumni interviews: recommended, evaluative. SATs or ACTs: required. SAT IIs: recommended. Accepts the Common Application and electronic applications. Essay question: Why Oberlin?

Occidental College

1600 Campus Road, Los Angeles, CA 90041

Oxy is a diverse, urban, streetwise cousin to the more upscale and suburban Claremont Colleges. Plentiful internships and study abroad give Oxy students real-world perspectives. Oxy's innovative diplomacy and world affairs program features internships in Washington and at the UN.

Occidental College is one of a handful of small colleges located in a big city, in this case LalaLand. Don't confuse small with backwater, though. After all, Oxy is within spitting distance from the glitz of Beverly Hills. Most students seem to appreciate the close-knit atmosphere and the decidedly cosmopolitan vibe. "It's so friendly," says one student. "It truly feels like a family."

Set against the backdrop of the San Gabriel Mountains, Occidental's self-contained Mediterranean-style campus is a secluded enclave of flowers and trees between Pasadena and Glendale, minutes from downtown Los Angeles. Inside this urban oasis resides a thriving community of high achievers who don't for a moment believe that the liberal arts are dead, or even wounded. Required first-year cultural studies seminars include topics in human history and culture, emphasizing learning skills, critical thought, and a wide range of human activities, including art, philosophy, politics, and literature. Students must also complete one year each of English writing, foreign language, and science (with lab), one semester each of fine arts, math, and preindustrial-era coursework, and three semesters of world cultures courses. Most students consider the core program, with its small classes and intimate labs, worthwhile. Upper-level classes often enroll fewer than a dozen students, and if students can't graduate

"One thing that makes Oxy stand out is its outstanding, dedicated faculty."

in four years because classes were closed or were not offered, Oxy will pay for any necessary extra semesters. All this makes for lots of hard work. A senior says, "We're passionate, motivated, and inspired members of a diverse and global community, who enjoy learning in and out of the classroom and never stop having fun."

As rigorous as its requirements are, Occidental encourages diverse learning experiences through internships, independent study, and study abroad. Oxy's innovative diplomacy and world affairs program features internships in Washington and at the UN. Students also can propose an Independent Pattern of Study to avoid a fixed distribution of courses. Independent study on special projects is possible

Website: www.oxy.edu
Location: Urban
Total Enrollment: 1,832
Undergraduates: 1,808
Male/Female: 41/59
SAT Ranges: V 580–670
   M 580–680
Financial Aid: 77%
Expense: Pr $ $ $
Phi Beta Kappa: Yes
Applicants: 4,172
Accepted: 43%
Enrolled: 26%
Grad in 6 Years: 79%
Returning Freshmen: 91%
Academics: ✍ ✍ ✍ ✍
Social: ☎ ☎ ☎
Q of L: ★ ★ ★ ★
Admissions: (323) 259-2700
Email Address:
   admission@oxy.edu

Strongest Programs:
Economics
English
Music
Chemistry

under an honors program for outstanding students, and all departments offer honors courses. For aspiring techies, there is a computer science "emphasis," but no major. There is, however, a cognitive science major that combines math, philosophy, computers, and psychology. As for quality, many of Occidental's academic departments are excellent, with English, music, chemistry, and an innovative diplomacy and world affairs program among the strongest, and economics the most popular. Perhaps because of Oxy's small size, the American studies, classics, and women's studies departments have less prowess, and there are no communications or foreign language majors. However, owing to Oxy's location, the television and film program is said to be strong.

Faculty members are readily available in and out of the classroom, and teaching is one of Occidental's strong points. "I have been inspired, motivated, challenged, and sometimes even scared by my professors," says one student. "One thing that makes Oxy stand out is its outstanding, dedicated faculty." Emphasis is on ideas and their application, not memorization of meaningless facts. The great majority of classes have twenty-five or fewer students, and the university will not cancel classes because of small enrollment. As academic advisors are responsible for about four students per class (sixteen total), personal relationships develop quickly. "Professors take a personal interest in their students, which profoundly affects the students' learning," says a history major. For those going stir-crazy on campus, Oxy has study abroad programs in Western Europe, Japan, China, Mexico, Nepal, Zimbabwe, Hungary, Costa Rica, and Russia. For politicos, there's Oxy-in-Washington and Oxy-at-the-UN. There are also 3–2 engineering programs with Caltech and Columbia University, exchange programs with Spelman and Morehouse colleges in Atlanta,

"It's so friendly. It truly feels like family." and cross-registration privileges with Caltech and Pasadena's Art Center College of Design. Students may also take advantage of a 4–2 biotechnology program with Keck Graduate Institute (of the Claremont Colleges).

Occidental students represent forty-four states and twenty-six foreign countries. Whites comprise only slightly more than half of the student population; African-Americans make up 7 percent, Hispanics 14 percent, and Asian-Americans 15 percent. Perhaps not surprisingly, students tend to be liberal. Says one freshman, "There are always people protesting about something." Since 1989, students here have won three Rhodes scholarships, three Marshall scholarships, five Truman scholarships, three Fullbright fellowships, and a handful of other significant awards. Administrators say "excellence and equity in education" is Oxy's top priority, though admission is not need-blind. Still, the college does offer a varying number of merit scholarships each year, ranging from $5,000 to $27,000. There are no athletic scholarships.

Students rave about Oxy's friendly and supportive environment but also complain that the school's smallness can lead to gossip and cliques. Upperclassmen on the "O-team" plan freshman orientation the week before school starts. Housing is guaranteed; freshmen are required to live on campus and eat in the dining hall, though there are plenty of hole-in-the-wall eateries nearby, including Burger Continental (BC's), Auntie Em's, and the Big O. The eleven residence halls are small—fewer than one hundred and fifty students each—and co-ed by floor or room. One student raves, "Some of the dorms are a little old but the wonderful community makes up for it!" Seventy percent of students live on campus in dorms ranging from "'five-star hotel' to 'this isn't too bad.'" What you get depends on your luck in the housing lottery, but everything is at least clean and well maintained. In fact, university housekeeping will clean your room for you three times a week. Students from all four classes live together, many in special-interest houses like the Multicultural Hall, the Environmental Quad, the Women's Center, or the Substance-Free

Oxy's innovative diplomacy and world affairs program features internships in Washington and at the UN.

Quad. A few students live off campus, although students characterize the surrounding neighborhood of Eagle Rock as "definitely not a college town." Student escorts, shuttles, and a twenty-four-hour campus security system contribute to the feeling of safety.

While the bright lights of L.A. often beckon on weekends, on-campus social life can still be satisfying, students say, with Greek and other parties always an option and free tickets to the theater usually available. "The parties put on by student government departments are always well attended and usually have a theme," says a junior. Fraternities and sororities, though declining on the Oxy social ladder, attract 7 percent of men and 5 percent of the women, but they are neither selective nor exclusive; students choose which to join, rather than being chosen, and the frats must invite everyone to their functions. Alcohol policies are in effect, however; as one student puts it, "There is drinking on campus, of-age and underage, as is the case at all colleges, regardless of what anyone says." The Senior Smack offers graduates-to-be the chance to smooch whomever they've wanted to during the past four years. Other big events include parties such as Sex on the Beach and Da Getaway—a Roaring Twenties bash where students gamble with fake money and Charleston 'til they drop. Here's a tip: Keep your birthday a secret, or on that unhappy day a roaring pack of your more sadistic classmates will carry you out to the middle of campus and mercilessly toss you in the Gilman Fountain. It's a tradition, after all.

When students become weary of the incestuous social life in the "Oxy fishbowl," they head for the bars, restaurants, museums, and theaters of downtown Los Angeles, where, one student notes, "you can find almost anything except snow." What! No snow? Never fear, the ski slopes of the San Gabriel Mountains are not far away. Neither is Hollywood nor the beautiful beaches of Southern California. When they tire

"Some of the dorms are a little old but the wonderful community makes up for it!"

of California, students try their luck in Las Vegas—or trek south of the border, into Tijuana. A car—your own or someone else's—is practically a necessity, though the college runs a weekend shuttle service to Old Town Pasadena. The weather is warm and sunny, but the air (cough! cough!) is often thick with that infamous L.A. smog.

Oxy's sports teams compete in Division III and draw a modest following. Football is the most popular, followed by men's basketball and soccer. Men's track and field is strong, and any match against rivals Pomona, Pitzer, Claremont McKenna, Scripps, and Harvey Mudd draws a crowd. The most popular intercollegiate sport of all, according to one student, is studying, but beach volleyball has fans, too. And don't forget that L.A. is home to the NBA's Lakers, the NHL's Kings, and baseball's Dodgers.

Occidental's creative, motivated, and diverse students are not here for the bright lights and beautiful people of Los Angeles; those are just fringe benefits. Instead, students are drawn to this intimate oasis of learning by professors who hate to see anyone waste one whit of intellectual potential. And students here are only too happy to live up to these lofty expectations.

Here's a tip: keep your birthday a secret, or on that unhappy day a roaring pack of your more sadistic classmates will carry you out to the middle of campus and mercilessly toss you in the Gilman Fountain. It's a tradition, after all.

Overlaps
Stanford, Pomona, Yale, Berkeley, UCLA

If You Apply To ➤ **Oxy:** Early decision: Nov. 15. Regular admissions: Jan. 15. Financial aid: Feb. 1. Guarantees to meet demonstrated need. Campus interviews: recommended, evaluative. Alumni interviews: optional, evaluative. SATs or ACTs: required. SAT IIs: recommended. Accepts the Common Application and electronic applications. Essay question: significance of a personal picture or photo or a teacher who had most influence, or situation where you worked with someone different from yourself.

Oglethorpe University

4484 Peachtree Road NE, Atlanta, GA 30319

Small wonder that brochures for Oglethorpe trumpet Atlanta as the college's biggest asset. In a region where most liberal arts colleges are in sleepy towns, Oglethorpe has the South's most exciting city at its fingertips. With only 1,112 undergraduates, Oglethorpe puts heavy emphasis on community.

Website: www.oglethorpe.edu

Location: City outskirts

Total Enrollment: 1,115

Undergraduates: 1,037

Male/Female: 35/65

SAT Ranges: V 560–680
   M 540–650

ACT Range: 23–29

Financial Aid: 33%

Expense: Pr $

Phi Beta Kappa: No

Applicants: 602

Accepted: 90%

Enrolled: 35%

Grad in 6 Years: 61%

Returning Freshmen: 81%

Academics: ✍ ✍ ✍

Social: ☎ ☎ ☎

Q of L: ★ ★ ★ ★

Admissions: (404) 364-8307
   or (800) 428-4484

Email Address:
   admission@oglethorpe.edu

Strongest Programs:
Biology
Accounting
Business Administration
English
Psychology

Each Christmas, students at Oglethorpe University take part in a unique tradition. The Boar's Head Ceremony celebrates a student who, years ago, halted a stampeding wild boar by ramming his copy of Aristotle down the animal's throat. Though some may find it boorish, students at this small Southern school claim that it fosters a sense of family.

Founded in 1835, the school is named for the idealistic founder of the state of Georgia, James Edward Oglethorpe. In a region where most liberal arts colleges are in sleepy towns, Oglethorpe has the South's most exciting city at its fingertips. Its 118-acre campus is located near suburban Buckhead, a ritzy area about ten miles north of downtown Atlanta. The heavily wooded, slightly rolling terrain is perfect territory for walks or long runs, and the beautiful campus has served as the backdrop for several movies and TV shows. Oglethorpe's academic buildings and some residence halls are in the English Gothic style; every year the campus plays host to the Georgia Shakespeare Festival.

Oglethorpe's strengths are business administration, English, biology, accounting, and psychology. Weaker bets are the fine arts and foreign language departments, though the latter does offer courses in Japanese, German, French, and Spanish. And whatever isn't offered at Oglethorpe can usually be taken through cross-registration at other schools in the Atlanta area.

Aspiring engineers may take advantage of 3–2 dual-degree programs with Georgia Tech, the University of Southern California, Auburn, and the University of Florida. The school also offers courses and additional resources as a member of the Atlanta Regional Consortium for Higher Education.* Oglethorpe also offers a wide variety of study abroad programs, including a semester at Seigakuin University in Japan and sister-school exchanges in Argentina, the Netherlands, Germany, France, Russia, and Monaco. According to administrators, Oglethorpe "emphasizes the preparation of the humane generalist" and "rejects rigid specialization." That doesn't mean the curriculum's a cakewalk, though. "The classes are very challenging, especially the core curriculum, but some students do very well," says a marketing major. "It depends on the student as to whether or not they will strive for the best or settle for mediocre."

The university's guiding principle is the Oglethorpe Idea, which says students should develop academically and as citizens. This philosophy is based on the conviction that education should help students make both a life and a living. All students take the sequenced, interdisciplinary Core Curriculum program at the same point in their college careers, providing them with a model for integrating information and gaining knowledge. In addition to the ability to reason, read, and speak

"All classes are taught by full professors and the teaching quality is excellent, there is a lot of one-on-one attention."

effectively, the core asks students to reflect upon and discuss matters fundamental to understanding who they are and what they ought to be. The core requires Narratives of the Self (freshmen), Human Nature and the Social Order (sophomores), Historical Perspectives on the Social Order (juniors), and Science and Human Nature (seniors), plus a fine arts core course in music and culture or art and culture, and coursework in modern mathematics or advanced foreign language.

Oglethorpe's faculty may be demanding, but they're also friendly and helpful. "All classes are taught by full professors and the teaching quality is excellent, there is a lot of one-on-one attention," a freshman says. Another student adds, "It's a small school so the professors know you by face and name and always encourage a visit to their office." Classes are generally small, and most students notice few problems at registration. Advising services are said to be helpful. The library's holdings are minuscule, though—just over 131,000 volumes.

What's an Oglethorpian like? The vast majority are smart, semiconservative offspring of middle- and upper-middle-class Southern families. Three-quarters ranked in the top quarter of their high school class; most come from public schools and more than half are native Georgians. "We have students from all over so there is a lot of diversity as far as backgrounds go; however, Oglethorpe is not diverse in race," says a senior. Oglethorpe prides itself on being one of the first Georgia colleges to admit African-American students, and today 26 percent of the students are members of minority groups: roughly 17 percent are African-American, 3 percent are Asian-American, 3 percent are Hispanic, and 3 percent hail from abroad. There's a level of comfort with racial differences, students report. Some students complain that their peers can be rather cliquish, but say that all in all, everyone gets along well.

Sixty-six percent of Oglethorpe's students choose to live on campus—and love it. "The dorms are big and have nice furniture," says an accounting major. Most rooms are suites with private bathrooms, and some singles are available. Some students commute to campus; a quarter live in Atlanta—not a college town, but where the wild life is. "There are lots of events on campus and there are lots of events off campus in the city of Atlanta," one student explains. Fraternities and sororities, which claim 33 percent of the men and 22 percent of the women, throw parties that draw big numbers. Officially, the campus is dry, but underage students can find alcohol if they try, students agree. It's rumored that Oglethorpe barflies do more hopping than Georgia bullfrogs, and bars, clubs, and cafes abound within ten minutes of campus.

> "It's a small school so the professors know you by face and name and always encourage a visit to their office."

Those who tire of the Oglethorpe scene can find excitement on the campuses of the dozen or so other colleges in the area ("Georgia Tech boys can be spotted from a mile away with their skinny, pale legs and baseball caps," says a student) or in downtown Atlanta, which at least one student considers "a great place to come to college." Atlanta proper offers everything you can imagine—arts, professional sports (including basketball's Hawks, football's Falcons, and baseball's Braves), and entertainment (ride the Great American Scream Machine at Six Flags). Facilities built for the 1996 Olympics also provide a diversion. Oglethorpe always has a big contingent going to Savannah for St. Patrick's Day and to New Orleans for Mardi Gras. The campus celebrates its origins once a year during Oglethorpe Day. Students looking for warmer weather, though, head down to sunny Florida.

Intramurals are important at Oglethorpe, sometimes more so than varsity sports. Perhaps Atlanta's diversions or the relatively small number of students on campus cause varsity sports to be a weak draw. Still, the Stormy Petrels men's golf team has brought home a Southern Collegiate Athletic Conference title, and basketball games against cross-city rival Emory are popular. The Georgia landscape makes possible a plethora of outdoor activities, including hiking at nearby Stone Mountain and boating or swimming in Lake Lanier (named for Georgia poet Sidney Lanier—Oglethorpe class of 1860).

Oglethorpe prides itself on being one of the first Georgia colleges to admit African-American students, and today 26 percent of the students are members of minority groups.

Aspiring engineers may take advantage of 3–2 dual-degree programs with Georgia Tech, the University of Southern California, Auburn, and the University of Florida.

Overlaps
University of Georgia, Emory, Georgia State, Georgia Tech, Mercer

Though Oglethorpe may lack widespread name recognition, its students get all the attention they need from a caring faculty on a close-knit campus. And being in a large city like Atlanta provides anything else that might be lacking, ranging from great nightlife to internships and postgraduate employment with big-name corporations. In a sea of large Southern state schools, Oglethorpe stands out as a place where students come first.

<table>
<tr><td>

If You

Apply

To ≫
</td><td>

Oglethorpe: Rolling admissions. Early action: Dec. 15. Financial aid: Mar. 1. Does not guarantee to meet demonstrated need. Campus interviews: recommended, evaluative. Alumni interviews: optional, informational. SATs or ACTs: required. SAT IIs: optional. Accepts the Common Application. Essay question: more about you.
</td></tr>
</table>

Ohio State University

3rd floor, Lincoln Tower, 1800 Cannon Drive, Columbus, OH 43210

Ohio State may be the biggest university in the Big Ten, but it is far from the best. OSU has never achieved the reputation of a Michigan or a Wisconsin—partly because it has three major in-state rivals (Miami, Cincinnati, and Ohio U) that siphon off many top students.

Website: www.osu.edu
Location: City center
Total Enrollment: 50,731
Undergraduates: 37,605
Male/Female: 55/45
SAT Ranges: V 520–630
   M 590–660
ACT Range: 23–28
Financial Aid: 40%
Expense: Pub $ $ $
Phi Beta Kappa: Yes
Applicants: 20,122
Accepted: 72%
Enrolled: 44%
Grad in 6 Years: 62%
Returning Freshmen: 86%
Academics: ✍ ✍ ✍
Social: ☎ ☎ ☎ ☎
Q of L: ★ ★ ★
Admissions: (614) 292-OHIO
Email Address:
   askabuckeye@osu.edu

Strongest Programs:
Business
Premed
Engineering

Think big. Think very big. Think very, very big. Envision a school with almost fifty thousand students and too many opportunities to count. What might come to mind is Ohio State University, located in the heart of the state's capital, offering nineteen colleges and more than 10,444 courses in 175 undergraduate majors. If those numbers aren't staggering enough, consider the fact that OSU has thirty-four varsity teams, forty-four intramural sports, and fifty-one sports clubs. While students cite the school's size as both a blessing and a curse, all seem to agree that at OSU, the sky is the limit for those with a desire to sample its academic and other resources.

This megauniversity stands on 3,200 wooded acres rubbing the edge of downtown Columbus on one side. On the other side, across the Olentangy River, is farmland associated with the College of Agriculture. OSU's architectural style is anything but consistent, yet it's all tied together in one huge redbrick package. "One part of the campus maintains a nostalgic air while another is relatively modern," observes a student. The grounds are nicely landscaped, and a centrally located lake provides a peaceful setting for contemplation.

Business, education, geography, industrial design, and engineering are among the school's most celebrated departments. OSU bills itself as the place to go for computer graphics and has a supercomputer center to back up its claim. It also boasts the

"One part of the campus maintains a nostalgic air while another is relatively modern."

largest and most comprehensive African-American studies program anywhere and turns out more African-American Ph.D.s than any other university in the nation. Furthermore, the university has the nation's only programs in welding engineering and geodetic science, and the state's only program in medical communications. Although immensely popular, students report that the English program needs improvement.

The university's fundamental commitment to liberal arts learning means all undergrads must satisfy rigorous general education requirements that include at least one course in math, two each in writing and a foreign language, three in social science, four in natural science, and five in arts and humanities. To top it all off, students must complete a capstone requirement that includes a course on Issues of the Contemporary World. A quarterly selective admissions program has replaced OSU's old open-door policy, but a conditional-unconditional admissions policy allows some poorly prepared students to play catch-up in designated areas. Some 10,500 students receive merit-based scholarships while 560 athletes receive scholarships in seventeen sports.

(Continued)
Education
Geography
Industrial Design
Linguistics
Psychology

Freshmen, who are grouped together in the University College before entering one of the degree-granting programs, find most introductory lectures huge. Teaching assistants, not professors, hold smaller recitation sections and deal on a personal level with students. "Ohio State is becoming more and more competitive," says an early child development major, "but it is far from overwhelming if you attend class and keep up with the coursework." Students find that class sizes are whittled down as they continue in their fields of study. OSU's honors program allows twenty-five hundred students to take classes that are taught by top professors and limited to twenty-five students each. Internships are required in some programs and optional in others, and possibilities for study abroad include Japan and the People's Republic of China. A personalized study program enables students to create their own majors.

Inside OSU's ivy-covered halls and modern additions are some of the best up-to-date equipment and facilities, including a "phenomenal" library system with two dozen branches and nearly four million volumes—all coordinated by computer. Professors "are well-informed about their subjects," according to students. "Teachers are passionate about working with students," says a senior. Complaints about long registration lines have been answered by BRUTUS, Ohio State's Touch-Tone telephone registration system, which saves on time but does little to ease class overcrowding.

OSU has the nation's only programs in welding engineering and geodetic science, and the state's only program in medical communications.

Eighty-five percent of Ohio State's students come from Ohio, and the balance come largely from adjacent states. Every type of background is represented, most in huge numbers. Paradoxically, this school with its nationally recognized African-American studies program has a student body that is 8 percent African-American; Hispanics and Asian-Americans make up another 7 percent. Several programs are aimed specifically at "enhancing" efforts to attract and retain minority students, including a statewide Young Scholars Program that yearly guarantees admission and financial aid to seventh graders once they complete high school.

The residence halls that house 24 percent of the Ohio State masses are located in three areas: North, South, and Olentangy (that is, those closest to the Olentangy River). Freshmen—required to live either at home or in the dorms—are scattered among each of OSU's twenty-seven residence halls. "The dorms are very comfortable," says a student. "Plus, you get a lot of living options."

"Ohio State is becoming more and more competitive."

Upperclassmen, when they don't head for off-campus life in Columbus, find the South campus section among the most desirable (it's more sociable, louder, and full of single rooms). The Towers in the Olentangy section have gained more popularity since their conversion to eight-person suites. All in all, students have a choice of single-sex, co-ed (by floor or by room), or married-couples apartments if they want to live in campus housing. Computer labs are located in each residence area. A system of variable room rates based on frills (air conditioning, private bath, number of roommates), as well as a choice of four meal-plan options, give students flexibility in determining their housing costs. Dormitory students have a choice of five dining halls, but others cook for themselves or eat in fraternity houses.

A system of variable room rates based on frills (i.e., air conditioning, private bath, number of roommates, etc.), as well as a choice of four meal-plan options, give students flexibility in determining their housing costs.

Such a large student market has, of course, produced a strip of bars, fast-food joints, convenience stores, bookstores, vegetarian restaurants, and you-name-it along the edge of the campus on High Street, and downtown Columbus is just a few minutes away. The fine public transportation system carries students not only throughout this capital city but also around the sprawling campus. In addition to the usual shopping centers, restaurants, golf courses, and movie theaters, Columbus boasts a symphony orchestra and ballet, and its central location in the state makes it easily accessible to Cleveland and Cincinnati. Outdoor enthusiasts can ski in nearby Mansfield, canoe and sail on the Olentangy and Scioto rivers, hike around adjacent quarries, or camp in the nearby woods.

Ohio State is a bustling place on weekends. "Student involvement is overwhelming," says one student. Various social events are planned by on-campus housing groups—floors, dorms, or sections of the campus. The Michigan–Ohio State football game inspires the best partying of the year, and other annual events include a Renaissance Festival and River Rat Day. Two student unions run eateries as well as movies on Friday and Saturday nights, and High Street's zillion bars, saloons, restaurants, and discos come to life. Campus policies prohibit underage drinking in dorms, but one partier discloses, "I can get served in almost any bar on campus." Just 5 percent of men and 6 percent of women on this vast campus belong to one of the 61 fraternities and sororities. By one account, these students make the Greek system "a way of life and isolate themselves from the rest of the student population."

Ohio State operates the largest and most expensive college sports program in the country—a $79-million-a-year operation led by the only athletic director in the country with his own Bobblehead doll for sale. The Buckeyes field teams in thirty-seven sports, from women's rifle to men's football. Nonrecruited students should not expect to make any varsity team as walk-ons. But despair not, your chances of eventually graduating with a degree are much better than the varsity athletes (for male basketball players the odds are one in four), and you can take advantage of an ambitious intramural program that boasts a dozen basketball courts and twenty-six courts for handball, squash, and racquetball. "It rained one day and two hundred softball games were rained out," one student reports. For diehard basketball fans, the first official day of practice, Midnight Basketball, is a favored ritual.

OSU's sheer size is sometimes overwhelming to be sure, but students say they "thrive on the challenge and excitement of a big university." They enjoy "the freedom to pick and choose courses, programs, activities, and friends to fit their needs." For those who really want to be a Buckeye, jump in with both feet and heed the old campus saying: "Welcome to the Nut House."

Overlaps

University of Cincinnati, Kent State, Ohio University, Bowling Green State, Case Western Reserve

If You Apply To ➤

OSU: Rolling admissions. Meets demonstrated need of 12 percent. Campus interviews: recommended, informational. No alumni interviews. SATs or ACTs: required. SAT IIs: optional. Accepts the Common Application and electronic applications. Essay question.

Ohio University

Chubb Hall 120, Athens, OH 45701-2979

OU is half the size of Ohio State and plays up its homey feel compared to the cast of thousands in Columbus. The Honors Tutorial College is a sure bet for top students

who want close contact with faculty. Communications and journalism top the list of prominent programs.

Once known as the prototypical party school, Ohio University is shedding the image for that of a competitive public institution with a classical touch befitting the name of the town it calls home. Students and faculty members are still forced to chide well-meaning outsiders who confuse the school with its neighbor to the north, Ohio State. Students here will be quick to tell you that the schools have very different personalities, OU being much smaller and more liberal.

Established in 1804 as the first institution of higher learning in the old Northwest Territory, Ohio University is located in Athens, about seventy-five miles from Columbus, the state capital. Encircled by winding hills, the campus features neo-Georgian architecture, tree-lined redbrick walkways, and white-columned buildings all clustered on "greens," which are like small neighborhoods. Long walks are especially nice during the fall foliage season. Current campus beautification projects include a $25 million renovation of Grover Center, an athletic mall, and a life sciences facility. In 2002, the university restored an art deco movie theater, The Athena. In addition, a $20 million renovation and expansion was completed of Bentley Hall.

One of the focal points of an Ohio University education and something that sets the school apart from run-of-the-mill state institutions is the Honors Tutorial College. This unique program is modeled on the tutorial method used in British universities, notably Oxford and Cambridge. It is ranked as one of the best programs on campus. Students in the honors program take an individualized curriculum in a major field, including weekly tutorials with profs on a one-on-one basis. Most participants finish their degrees in three years and then go on to attend leading graduate programs with close to a 100 percent acceptance rate. Students are eligible for such special privileges as paid research apprenticeships, priority class registration, special library policies, and exemption from most university general education requirements. Other top areas are the College of Communication and its three offspring: the schools of telecommunications, visual communication, and journalism, which feature the latest graphics and computer equipment. The Global Learning Community Certificate is an innovative program that prepares students for leadership opportunities in a rapidly changing world. There is a new online journalism program available as well as a variety of certificate programs.

General education requirements involve a minimum of one course in math or quantitative skills, two courses in English composition, one senior-level interdisciplinary course, plus thirty quarter hours in applied sciences and technology, social sciences, natural sciences, humanities, and cross-cultural perspectives. To lighten the load, you can take electives such as The Language of Rock Music (so you can communicate better with Mom and Dad?). Study abroad offers worldwide destinations for anywhere from two weeks to one year, though only 2 percent of students study abroad. Co-op programs are available for engineering students, and nearly anyone can earn credit for an internship.

Regarding their profs, students are generally pleased with what they've found. "Professors can always be reached and are easy to talk to," says a sophomore. Freshmen usually are taught by full professors with TAs handling study sessions. Classes of one-hundred-plus students do exist, but the average class size for freshmen is about twenty-five. Getting into classes is diffi-

> **"Professors can always be reached and are easy to talk to."**

cult. "It has been difficult for seniors to get into tier three classes that they must take to graduate, although the system is being overhauled and will soon be more accessible," comments one student. Faculty advising is generally hit or miss. The academic climate at OU is debatable, depending on the classes and major you choose.

Website: www.ohiou.edu
Location: Rural
Total Enrollment: 20,528
Undergraduates: 17,343
Male/Female: 45/55
SAT Ranges: V 500–600
  M 500–610
ACT Range: 21–26
Financial Aid: 42%
Expense: Pub $ $ $
Phi Beta Kappa: Yes
Applicants: 13,195
Accepted: 75%
Enrolled: 37%
Grad in 6 Years: 70%
Returning Freshmen: 84%
Academics: ✏️ ✏️ ✏️
Social: 🍺 🍺 🍺 🍺
Q of L: ★ ★ ★
Admissions: (740) 593-4100
Email Address: admissions
  .freshmen@ohiou.edu

Strongest Programs:
Engineering
Journalism
Business
Communications
Film

You'll find many classmates from the Buckeye State; 85 percent are Ohioans. "The students here are average, Midwestern people," writes a senior. "They are fun-loving but also value a good academic performance." Almost everyone attended public high school and 18 percent graduated in the top tenth of their class. The student body is overwhelmingly Caucasian. Three percent are African-American; Hispanics and Asian-Americans combine for 3 percent. The university has established an Office of Multicultural Programs. However, a senior writes, "Campus is fairly liberal, although there is a strong conservative minority." Ohio offers numerous merit scholarships and 379 athletic scholarships.

Campus housing is plentiful (forty dorms) and well liked. Almost everyone lives on campus for two years then moves into neighboring dwellings. Freshmen and sophomores live in one of three residential neighborhoods, or greens. Campus housing comes with a variety of options: co-ed, single-sex, quiet study, academic interest, and even an international dorm. At the "mods," six men and six women occupy separate wings but share a living room and study room. Upperclassmen usually move to fraternity or sorority houses, nearby apartments, or rental houses. Four different meal plans are available at four cafeterias and include fast-food counters next to regular dorm-food fare. "Dorms are great communities for students," says a sophomore.

The social life is adequate. "I would say most people stay in Athens during the weekends, our social life is incredibly vibrant," says a history and economics major. Uptown features bars and clubs, campus and community activities such as plays, and guest speakers and performers. Some students also choose to participate in Greek life. Twelve percent of men and 14 percent of women join their ranks. The administration and some students have tried to downplay OU's party-school image

"Campus is fairly liberal, although there is a strong conservative minority."

by strictly enforcing the alcohol policy. But despite their efforts, students say that drinking is a problem and that binge drinking is not uncommon. Athens's fabled Halloween celebration, "a huge block party" with people from all over the Midwest, wouldn't be missed by many students. The International Street Fair features food and music from the different cultures on campus. "Athens is the ideal college town," says one student. "I always see someone I know when I am out and I always meet someone new." Volunteer opportunities, such as Habitat for Humanity and a local homeless shelter, are available through the Center for Community Service. Students also love to hike and camp at the nearby state parks or trek to Columbus.

Sports are a big draw at Ohio. Any competition pitting the Bobcats against hated Miami of Ohio draws a rowdy crowd. In 2001, the women's field hockey, swimming and diving, and soccer teams won NCAA Division I championships, as did the men's wrestling team. The Athens Criterium bicycle race draws competitors from throughout the nation.

There is something for nearly everyone at OU, from those interested in the classics to those with a practical bent. "I love OU," says one student. "It offers all the opportunities of a large university—activities, classes, organizations—with the feel of a small community."

Overlaps

Ohio State, Miami University (OH), Bowling Green, Kent State, University of Cincinnati

If You Apply To ➤

OU: Regular admissions: Feb. 1. Housing: May 1. Does not guarantee to meet demonstrated need. Campus and alumni interviews: optional, informational. SATs or ACTs: required. SAT IIs: optional. Essay question: optional personal essay.

Ohio Wesleyan University

South Sandusky Street, Delaware, OH 43015

OWU serves up the liberal arts with a popular side helping of business-related programs. In a region of beautiful campuses, Ohio Wesleyan's is nondescript. Like Denison, OWU is working hard to make its fraternities behave. Attracts middle-of-the-road to conservative students with preprofessional aspirations.

Ohio Wesleyan University is a small school with a big commitment to providing its students with a well-rounded education. Hallmarks at OWU are strong preparation for graduate and professional school, a solid grounding in the liberal arts, and an emphasis on having fun outside the classroom. Once known for its raucous students, this small university has overcome its hard-partying past and now offers its students a rewarding college experience.

Situated smack in the center of the state, OWU's spacious two-hundred-acre campus is peaceful and quaint, with eleven buildings on the National Register of Historic Places. The architecture ranges from Greek Revival to Colonial to modern, with ivy-covered brick academic buildings on one side of a busy thoroughfare and dormitories and fraternities on the other side of the highway. Stately Stuyvesant Hall, with its majestic bell tower, is the main campus landmark. The R.W. Corns Center, which houses the economics department, information systems, and the writing center, has recently been renovated, and the science center is undergoing additional construction and improvements.

Preprofessional education has always been OWU's forte, and in 1998, the school placed all of its prehealth graduates in medical, dental, or veterinary schools. New additions to the curriculum include majors in neuroscience and East Asian studies, and the highly popular zoology and microbiology departments are interesting alternatives to the traditional premed route. The Woltemade Center for Economics, Business, and Entrepreneurship caters to budding entrepreneurs, and the music and fine arts programs offer both professional and liberal arts degrees. Students say the French department lacks "pizzazz."

A member of the Great Lakes College Association* consortium, Ohio Wesleyan offers numerous innovative curricular programs. The most prominent is the National Colloquium, a year-long series of lectures on a timely issue. Recent speakers have included David Wetherell, president and CEO of CMGI, and novelist Gloria Naylor. The honors program offers qualified students one-on-one tutorials and a chance to conduct research with faculty members in areas

> **"All students are taught by full professors, regardless of year."**

of mutual interest. The Special Languages program offers the opportunity for self-directed study and tutoring by native speakers in languages such as Arabic, Chinese, Japanese, and modern Greek. Students can travel to Mexico for a community-service experience during spring break, while fine arts, theater, and music majors can spend a semester in New York City to study with professionals there.

"Courses are very challenging, but not impossible," says a senior. To graduate, OWU students must take a year of foreign language; three courses in each of the social sciences, natural sciences, and humanities; one course in the arts; and one course in cultural diversity. Students must also pass three mandatory writing classes to sharpen their written communication skills, but these aren't burdensome. Students universally laud OWU's faculty for ability and accessibility. "Professors are amazing," says a student. "[They are] dedicated and really work with the students." The school highly values opportunities for students to interact closely with its

Website: www.owu.edu
Location: Small town
Total Enrollment: 1,886
Undergraduates: 1,886
Male/Female: 48/52
SAT Ranges: V 550–660
　M 550–660
ACT Range: 23-29
Financial Aid: 58%
Expense: Pr $ $ $
Phi Beta Kappa: Yes
Applicants: 2,257
Accepted: 78%
Enrolled: 33%
Grad in 6 Years: 58%
Returning Freshmen: 79%
Academics: ✍ ✍ ✍ ½
Social: 🐨 🐨 🐨 🐨 🐨
Q of L: ★ ★ ★
Admissions: (740) 368-3020
Email Address:
　owuadmit@cc.owu.edu

Strongest Programs:
Psychology
Zoology
Economics and Management
Sociology/Anthropology
English
History
Politics and Government
Biology

thoughtful and dedicated faculty. "All students are taught by full professors," a senior says, "regardless of year."

Forty-seven percent of students come from Ohio; another big contingent consists of students from mid-Atlantic and New England states, while recruits from Chicago and California are increasing. Students agree that diversity is valued on campus, but African-Americans make up only 5 percent of the student body, Hispanics 2 percent, and Asian-Americans 2 percent. "There is a large international student population," says a senior. "OWU has students from all different backgrounds." Fifty-eight percent of students receive some type of financial aid, and merit scholarships recognizing academic or artistic ability ranging from $5,000 to $24,000 plus room and board are available.

All but one of the dorms are co-ed, and rooms are mostly apartment-style, four-person suites or doubles. Fraternities, unlike sororities, offer a residential option. Special-interest houses, such as Creative Arts House, House of Black Culture, House of Spirituality, and Women's House, are available, as is Welch Hall, which is for students with GPAs over 3.2. "I think that the housing is good but overbooking new students creates problems with the returnees getting the rooms they want," says a sophomore. Seniors are now permitted to live off campus, a policy change that has received praise. Each meal eaten on the college plan subtracts a certain number of points (far too many in the opinion of most students) from students' accounts, but there are numerous culinary choices, from all-you-can-eat in the three dining halls to pizza and snacks from the college grocery store.

> **"Ohio Wesleyan is a place where the education goes well beyond the classroom."**

Does the buttoned-down seriousness of recent years mean that OWU has forsaken its heritage of raucous partying? Administrators certainly hope so. Trying to stamp out drunken binges, OWU slaps fines of up to $150 on all underage students caught drinking and puts them on probation after the fourth offense. Nevertheless, one student says, "Most of the time when students drink and get loud, they get caught. That might not be the case if you drink quietly in your room." Part of OWU's commitment to mend its partying ways includes dry rush for all fraternities and an armband policy at parties. Greek membership, however, still attracts 44 percent of men and 34 percent of women. Among OWU's best-loved traditions are Fallfest and Monnett Weekend in the spring—campus-wide bashes for students, parents, and alumni that include bonfires, a Fun Run, and open houses for the Greeks. Romantics will enjoy the President's Ball the weekend before finals in the winter, and the famous Little Brown Jug harness race provides offbeat fun.

> **"The family atmosphere and the opportunities that the college provides you in a diverse environment enrich the entire college experience."**

Delaware, a town of twenty-five thousand, is "very peaceful and friendly," reports one junior. Another student notes, "There is some involvement of the students in the community." Approximately 85 percent of the students volunteer in the community for Habitat for Humanity and other charitable organizations. Ohio's capital and largest city, Columbus, is only thirty minutes away by car and offers many job and internship opportunities. Lakes, farms, and even ski slopes are within a few hours' drive.

OWU sports rank in the top ten in the nation, according to the Sears Director's Cup Standings, which rates top all-around programs. The women's Battling Bishops basketball team has proven successful, and men's indoor and outdoor track have won NCAC championships. Sports fever carries over into single-sex and co-ed intramurals, and a massive annual game of Capture the Flag begins at eleven one night and lasts until the wee hours.

Overlaps

College of Wooster, Denison, Wittenberg, Miami University (OH), Ohio State

It's clear that Ohio Wesleyan University has much to offer its students, including close student–faculty interaction, quality academics, and a social atmosphere that fosters a sense of community. "Ohio Wesleyan is a place where the education goes well beyond the classroom," explains one student. "The family atmosphere and the opportunities that the college provides you in a diverse environment enrich the entire college experience."

University of Oklahoma

1000 Asp Avenue, Room 127, Norman, OK 73019

Football aside, OU has historically been outclassed by neighbors like the University of Texas at Austin and the University of Kansas. But the signs of the improvement are there. Check out the Honors College, which boasts a living/learning option. OU is strong in engineering and geology-related fields.

Ranking first among the Big 12, the University of Oklahoma has more to brag about than football. Thanks to an aggressive self-improvement kick and one of the largest honors programs among public universities, OU is dedicated to providing students with the opportunity to develop their intellectual potential to the fullest. "Our college is a new place in the last five years," says a senior English education major. "The administration's goal is for OU to be just as prestigious and stimulating as any Ivy League or private institution." A bit presumptuous, perhaps, but not bad for a school of whom a former president once said, "We want a university the football team can be proud of."

Located about eighteen miles south of Oklahoma City, OU's two-thousand-acre Norman campus features tree-lined streets and predominantly redbrick buildings. Many are historic buildings in the Cherokee or Prairie Gothic style. The campus houses twelve colleges; six medical and health-related colleges are located on the OU Health Sciences Center campuses in Oklahoma City and Tulsa. Newer facilities on the Norman campus include the $17 million addition to the College of Law Center, dedicated

> "Any incoming freshman wondering how to survive the first year should seriously consider taking Gateway as a ticket to ensured success."

in spring 2002; a $17 million renovation of the Norman Campus Student Union, a beautification campaign including tiered gardens, and an $18 million expansion of the Lloyd Noble Center. Last year, the sixth faculty-in-residence apartment facility was also completed. The Sam Noble Museum of Natural History, which opened in mid 2000, is the largest university-based museum of natural history in the nation, with more than five million artifacts.

All Oklahoma freshmen start out in the university college before choosing among several degree-granting institutions, including the colleges of architecture, arts and sciences, education, business administration, and fine arts. The engineering

Website: www.ou.edu
Location: Suburban
Total Enrollment: 26,792
Undergraduates: 20,193
Male/Female: 50/50
ACT Range: 23–28
Financial Aid: 58%
Expense: Pub $ $
Phi Beta Kappa: Yes
Applicants: 7,248
Accepted: 89%
Enrolled: 60%
Grad in 6 Years: 54%
Returning Freshmen: 84%
Academics: ✑ ✑ ✑ ✑
Social: ☎ ☎ ☎
Q of L: ★ ★ ★
Admissions: (405) 325-2252
Email Address:
  admrec@ou.edu

Strongest Programs:
Meteorology
Finance and Accounting
History of Science
Chemistry and Biochemistry

school offers specializations in geological, aerospace, petroleum, and environmental engineering. The petroleum program ranks among the best in the nation and is home to numerous recent national Black Engineers of the Year. OU has the state's only comprehensive fine arts college, with one of the nation's oldest collegiate ballet programs. In the College of Arts and Sciences, the natural sciences, notably chemistry, are strong. The state-of-the-art $50 million Energy Center houses some of the brightest energy-related programs under the sun. The College of Geosciences brings together Oklahoma's strong programs in meteorology, geology and geophysics, and geography.

OU offers majors in a wide variety of fields such as Native American studies, African-American studies, energy management, Chinese, and public administration. Interestingly, the OU Native American studies program teaches more American Indian languages than any other institution in the United States. Future forecasters can stay on to get their master's degrees in professional meteorology, while the College of Education's rigorous, nationally accredited five-year teacher-certification program, Teacher Education Plus (TE-PLUS), incorporates field experience, mentoring, and instruction from thirty full-time professors. New programs offered include a master's and Ph.D. in bioengineering, a master's and Ph.D. in environmental engineering, and master's in knowledge management and professional engineering. Bachelor's degrees in mathematics and real estate are no longer offered.

A university-wide education curriculum, comprised of five core areas, has been approved by the Oklahoma State Regents for Higher Education. The general education requirements consist of three to five courses in symbolic and oral communication, including English composition, two courses in natural science, two courses in social science, four humanities courses, an upper-division general education course outside the major, and a one-course Senior Capstone Experience. OU also offers optional Gateway to Learning classes for freshmen, which provide a survey of the university's academic opportunities, services, and resources. One participant comments, "Any incoming freshman wondering how to survive the first year should seriously consider taking Gateway as a ticket to ensured success at the University of Oklahoma." Another rich opportunity is the Presidential Travel and Study Abroad Scholarships, which provide $75,000 for students and faculty to study and conduct research around the globe.

OU offers optional Gateway to Learning classes for freshmen, which provide a survey of the university's academic opportunities, services, and resources.

For the academically ambitious, the Honors College offers small classes with outstanding faculty members, independent reading and research for credit, and interdisciplinary studies. It also has its own dorm, which houses two hundred of the program's twelve hundred students. Along with the Honors College, top students can apply for admission to the Scholarship-Leadership Enrichment Program,

"Our college is a new place in the last five years."

through which well-known lecturers from outside the university give seminars for academic credit. With all of these opportunities for the bright and highly motivated, plus its reasonable price tag, it's no wonder OU attracts one of the highest concentrations of National Merit Scholars of any school in the nation.

Though OU is one of the smaller Big 12 schools, it can still overwhelm. A freshman orientation program, involving both students and faculty, tries to ease the transition to college, and when it's time to hit the books, students can check out wireless laptops from the library if they don't yet have their own. Class size is not generally a problem; advisors and professors can usually get students into most courses, even if they're officially closed, and with a little upfront planning and dedication to the coursework required for your major, students report little trouble graduating in four years. Students also give the faculty high marks and note that even freshmen are taught by full profs, though 20 percent of undergraduate courses

OU's student body is primarily homegrown, with only 21 percent from outside the Sooner state.

are led by graduate students. An English education major notes that students should utilize both faculty and departmental advisors; the former can offer perspective on their academic field, while the latter know OU's bureaucracy and logistics. Each college also offers advisors and support organizations, such as Project Threshold and the Minority Engineering Program.

OU's student body is primarily homegrown, with only 21 percent from outside the Sooner state. Minorities account for 26 percent of the student body; African-Americans and Native Americans make up 6 percent each, Asian-Americans 5 percent, and Hispanics 4 percent. Foreign students comprise 4 percent. The Center for Student Life has hosted programs such as A Day of Dialogue on Race, but political correctness, acceptance of alternative lifestyles, and the power of the Greek system appear to be more pressing issues these days. OU awards 12,484 merit scholarships, ranging from $100 to $7,838, and 364 athletic scholarships in eight sports.

The university's residence halls provide a happy home to only 21 percent of the undergraduate students. Says one sophomore, "The dorms are pretty good in size and close to campus but they are getting old." Most halls have been renovated; some feature air-conditioned buildings with color-TV lounges and recreation rooms. (Of course, there are also basic box accommodations with no frills attached.) Most halls are co-ed by floor, and many of the lounge areas on the halls have been refurbished. Off-campus housing is affordable (most students choose this option); though fraternities draw 17 percent of the men and sororities 25 percent of the women, only 10 percent of students live in Greek housing.

Students love the town of Norman, Oklahoma's third-largest city, which provides restaurants and shops plus numerous volunteer opportunities. "It is a great college town," notes one student. "The town caters to college kids with coupons and specials." Fraternity parties are the highlight of weekends at OU, as are annual events such as the road trip to Dallas for the OU–Texas game, the first-of-the-football-season Big Red Rally, the Medieval Festival, and the University Sing, a talent show.

OU sports big-time athletics. The football team went undefeated in 2000–2001 and brought home a national championship under second-year coach Bob Stoops. In 2003–2004, they played for another national championship. Other strong teams include men's gymnastics, men's basketball, men's wrestling, and women's softball and basketball.

There's a dedication and spirit of family evident in Norman, Oklahoma, these days, and not just among fans of Sooner football, says a senior. "A remarkable faculty, staff, and president are working to make OU a top-notch university, and help students do the same," she explains. OU students have a favorite saying: "Sooner born and Sooner bred, when I die, I'll be Sooner dead!"

The petroleum program ranks among the best in the nation and is home to numerous recent national Black Engineers of the Year.

Overlaps

Oklahoma State, University of Texas, Texas A&M, Texas Tech, Baylor

If You Apply To ➤

OU: Early action: rolling. Early decision: rolling. Regular admissions: Jun. 1, Nov. 1. Financial aid: Jun. 1, Nov. 1. Housing: rolling. Does not guarantee to meet demonstrated need. Campus interviews: optional, informational. No alumni interviews. SATs or ACTs: required. No SAT IIs. No essay question.

Box 1226, Eugene, OR 97403-1226

UO may be the best deal in public higher education on the West Coast. Less expensive than the UC system and less selective than the University of Washington, UO is a university of manageable size in a great location. The liberal arts are more than just a slogan, and programs in business and communication are strong.

Website: www.uoregon.edu
Location: Small city
Total Enrollment: 20,044
Undergraduates: 16,047
Male/Female: 46/54
SAT Ranges: V 492–610
    M 494–608
Financial Aid: 45%
Expense: Pub $ $
Phi Beta Kappa: Yes
Applicants: 12,431
Accepted: 84%
Enrolled: 44%
Grad in 6 Years: 60%
Returning Freshmen: 84%
Academics: ✍ ✍ ✍ ½
Social: ☎ ☎ ☎
Q of L: ★ ★ ★ ★
Admissions: (541) 346-3201
    or (800) BE A DUCK
Email Address: uoadmit@
    oregon.uoregon.edu

Strongest Programs:
Architecture
Music
Creative Writing
Business
Chemistry
Journalism and
    Communication
Psychology
Education

Students at the University of Oregon say their school boasts "the world's coolest website." But they're not referring to the university's virtual presence on the Internet: they mean Autzen Stadium, home of their football team, the (mighty) Ducks. Sure, the joke's a little hokey, but its offbeat humor is typical of the laid-back, slightly eccentric attitude that prevails here in Eugene, where bicycles are the main form of transportation, recycling is a requirement, and littering is déclassé.

UO's buildings date from as early as 1876 to as late as 1999 and are surrounded by the university's lush 295-acre arboretum-like campus, which boasts two thousand varieties of dew-kissed trees. Most academic buildings were built before World War II and represent a blend of classical styles, including Georgian, Second Empire, Jacobin, and Lombardic. Residential facilities range from nineteenth-century Colonials to modern high-rises. Renovations of the Autzen football stadium have increased its seating capacity to fifty-four thousand. Other recent renovations include the Museum of Art and the Lundquist College of Business.

While a liberal arts emphasis underlies Oregon's entire curriculum, general education requirements are not highly structured. The calendar is composed of quarters,

> Students "are open minded and liberal politically. Every big political issue is an issue on our campus."

and students must take two terms of English composition, two years of foreign language (for a B.A.), one year of math (for a B.S.), and one term of a race- or gender-sensitive course, plus six courses in each of three areas: arts and letters, social sciences, and natural sciences. Freshman seminars introduce students to top professors in small-group settings, and profs have to apply to teach them, a process students applaud. Freshman Interest Groups help new students acclimate to campus life through informal meetings and activities with upperclassmen.

Oregon's professional schools—journalism, architecture and allied arts, education, law, business, and music—are highly regarded, with journalism, education, and architecture drawing the most student praise. The school of Architecture and Allied Arts is the home of Oregon's only accredited degrees in architecture, landscape, and interior architecture. Of the more than thirty-five departments in the College of Arts and Sciences, students give high marks (and high enrollments) to psychology and biology, and the science departments within this particular college offer many opportunities for research. Newer majors include family and human services and marriage and family therapy.

Highly motivated undergraduates may join the Honors College, a small liberal arts college with its own courses, and outstanding liberal arts majors may spend five years on campus to earn their master's degree in the Graduate School of Management. The student-run ESCAPE (Every Student Caring about Personalized Education) program provides credit for community volunteer work, while on-campus internships allow students to earn credit for work with university organizations and academic departments. The Green Chemistry Laboratory and Instrumentation Center, the first in the nation to use nontoxic materials in experiments, opened in 2002. Pine Mountain Observatory, a field-study resource for astronomy and physics students located high in the Cascade Mountains, and the Oregon Institute of Marine Biology give students a chance for intimate studies in their major.

A telephone and Web registration program has improved the registration process. "The online registration system called Duckweb allows for an immediate update of openings in a class, so you can constantly check back," one student notes. A senior recalls, however, that "getting into classes as a freshman is very difficult because you register last and classes fill up quickly." As you move up, though, so does your registration priority, and signing up gets easier. "The counseling here is the students' responsibility but it's extremely helpful," says a senior.

Blend two vegetarians, one track star, a frat brother, two tree huggers, three hikers, and one conservative. What have you got? Ten UO students. Some students say UO is one of the last collegiate strongholds for people who "are open minded and liberal politically." "Every big political issue is an issue on our campus," says one student. "We have a lot of protestors." In general, every part of the white Anglo-Saxon spectrum is well represented, with an especially heavy dose of the athletically inclined. There is a noticeable contingent of international students, who account for 6 percent of the student body. Asian-Americans account for another 6 percent, African-Americans 2 percent, and Hispanics 3 percent. The 19 percent of students who come from out of state are mostly from California. Numerous merit scholarships of up to $5,000 and 215 athletic scholarships are awarded to qualified students.

Since there are no residence requirements and few dorms, only 21 percent of all undergrads live on campus. There are a number of thematic living arrangements— a cross-cultural dorm, an academic-pursuit residence hall, and a music dorm. Students recommend Walton, Carson, and University Inn. Rooms in the residence halls tend to be small but clean and comfortable, and they have Internet connections. "The good news is the dorms are in excellent condition," states a video production major. "The bad news is they weren't that great to start with." Any student can sign up for the meal plan in the two main dining halls; restaurants in the student union and off-campus fast food round out the menu. "Lots of people complain about the food, but I liked it because there was so much to choose from," one junior recalls.

Eugene, the second-largest city in Oregon, is "a college town—the locals all love the Ducks and come to campus activities like plays and cultural nights," a student says. Popular hangouts include Old Taylor's and Rennies, and community- and public-service projects also draw crowds. The one drawback to all this fun is Oregon's weather: it rains and rains. "Eugene gets some sunny days in early fall, late spring, and summer," reports a veteran. Still, the moist climate rarely dampens enthusiasm for the many expeditions available through the university's well-coordinated outdoor program, from rock climbing to skiing. An hour to the west, the rain turns to mist on the Pacific Coast; an hour to the east it turns to snow in the Cascade Mountains. Students can also escape the weather year-round in the new recreation center, complete with rock climbing wall and juice bar.

Ten percent of UO men and women join Greek organizations, which provide living space and interesting social diversions. Oregon's twenty-one-year-old drinking age means that alcohol is banned from college-owned dorms, but students claim this rule can be broken. "It is not easy for underage students to be served—we live in a college town and bars are expecting the little people," says a journalism major. Major events include the Eugene Celebration, the Oregon Country Fair, the Martin Luther King, Jr. Festival, and weekly street fairs attended by local vendors. University Day, which happens twice a year, offers students an opportunity to clean up their campus. The Willamette Valley Wine Festival is a fun road trip.

Second only to parties, athletic activities head the list of favorite free-time activities. The Ducks' biggest athletic rival is the Oregon State Beavers, and each

Blend two vegetarians, one track star, a frat brother, two tree huggers, three hikers, and one conservative. What have you got? Ten UO students.

When students aren't on the tracks and fields themselves, they're trooping down to the stadium to join the Quacker Backers in cheering on the successful basketball and football teams.

year the Civil War game in football is huge. When students aren't on the tracks and fields themselves, they're trooping down to the stadium to join the Quacker Backers in cheering on the successful basketball and football teams. Track is also prominent; Nike is headquartered in nearby Beaverton.

A recent University of Oregon Orientation Week T-shirt sported a picture of a duck and the simple exhortation "Let your future take flight." UO offers ample opportunities for those with lofty ambitions to succeed. Indeed, UO's caring faculty, excellent academics, and abundance of social activities reveal that UO is all it's quacked up to be.

If You Apply To ➤ **UO:** Rolling admissions. Financial aid and housing: Mar 1 (priority). Meets demonstrated need of those who meet eligibility and priority deadline of Mar. 1. No campus or alumni interviews. SATs or ACTs: required. SAT IIs: required if home schooled or graduate of nonstandard high school (English, math, one of choice). Accepts the Common Application and electronic applications. Essay question (required for students with GPA below 3.25): Why do you want to attend college?

Oregon State University

Corvallis, OR 97331-2106

The biggest dilemma facing the typical eighteen-year-old Oregonian is whether to be a Beaver or a Duck. Choose Beavers and get small-town life with professional programs in business, engineering, and life sciences. Choose Duck and hang with the ex-hippies in cosmopolitan Eugene.

Website: www.osu.orst.edu
Location: Small city
Total Enrollment: 18,034
Undergraduates: 14,877
Male/Female: 52/48
SAT Ranges: V 470–590
    M 480–610
ACT Range: 20–26
Financial Aid: N/A
Expense: Pub $
Phi Beta Kappa: No
Applicants: 9,588
Accepted: 88%
Enrolled: 36%
Grad in 6 Years: 58%
Returning Freshmen: 80%
Academics: ✍ ✍
Social: ☎ ☎ ☎
Q of L: ★ ★ ★
Admissions: (541) 737-4411
Email Address:
    osuadmit@orst.edu

With a wide range of academic programs, Oregon State University could very well be the setting of its own movie, titled *Planes, Trains, and Submarines*. You see, Oregon State is one of just a handful of universities in the country with land, sea, and space grant designations. Though the school might be happy to forget its many years of being called Moo U, that doesn't mean its agriculture department should go unnoticed. In fact, many of the contributions made by Oregon State researchers center on the field of agriculture. Still, there's more to OSU than fruits and vegetables. The school is strong in many departments, including biotechnology, forestry, and engineering.

Located in the pristine but rainy Willamette Valley, OSU's campus is a mix of older, ivy-covered buildings and more modern structures. In addition to the five-hundred-acre main campus, OSU owns thirteen thousand acres of forestland near campus and numerous agricultural tracts throughout Oregon. Thousands of azalea and rhododendron bushes welcome springtime on campus with their colorful blooms, and summers are unfailingly sunny. (All that rain during the rest of the year has to be good for something, right?) Recent additions to the campus map include a forest resource lab, a residence hall, and a baseball field.

OSU's College of Liberal Arts ranks with Business and Engineering as the largest on campus, but there are many more preprofessionals than poets. With the exception of history and English, the liberal arts—including such standard fare as sociology, psychology, economics, and philosophy—play second fiddle to more practical, technical fields. The departments of engineering (with their up-to-date electrical and computer engineering building) and forestry are major drawing cards, and even though agriculture doesn't lure as many students as it used to, those who do come find excellent programs. Business administration is the most popular major, followed by exercise and sport science, liberal studies, general science, and psychology. The business school offers some of the finest business-related programs in the state, while the health and human performance program—a euphemism for home economics—recently has expanded its offerings. Newer degree programs include ethnic studies and environmental engineering.

OSU's extensive Baccalaureate Core requires courses in a variety of areas, including skills; perspectives; and difference, power, and discrimination. One writing-intensive course is required, as well. Perhaps the core's most innovative facet is its "synthesis" requirement, in which upperclassmen take two interdisciplinary courses on global issues in the modern world. The campus's global awareness is also evident in the new international degree, which can be coupled with any other course of study. Thus, students can earn a B.S. in forestry and a B.A. in international studies in forestry simultaneously. The level of academic pressure varies by major, but even those in the various honors programs say they don't feel overworked. "The academic climate here fosters learning," says a business major. "The courses are challenging but manageable." Another adds, "The students here seem to be team-oriented." Students have good access to professors, but classes tend to be crowded. "We have great professors and instructors," says a senior.

Of particular note is OSU's Experimental College, where undergraduates spice up their semesters with noncredit courses in a range of imaginative subjects—everything from wine tasting to the art of bashing, a medieval war technique. Those who can afford a semester abroad may study at universities in England, France, Australia, Mexico, New Zealand, China, and Japan—or participate in individual exchange programs in still more countries. (Oregon State returns the favor, playing host to about fifteen hundred foreign students from more than ninety nations each year.) The university's small town location (population 45,000) makes it difficult to find much career-oriented, part-time employment, and term-time internships are hard to come by. (OSU operates on a quarter system.) Students in almost all majors, however, can participate in the cooperative education program, which allows them to alternate terms of study with several months of work in a relevant job.

Statistically, Oregon State certainly doesn't offer the most diverse student body. Nineteen percent graduated in the top 10 percent of their high school class. Seventy-nine percent of the students are from Oregon, and the 12 percent minority population is mostly Asian-American. Foreign students account for another 3 percent of the total. Communication between different racial and ethnic groups is poor, students report, despite a new ethnic studies program. Other big issues are underage drinking and tuition increases. Most Oregon Staters are conservative and "very all-American—not cowboys and not city slickers, but very middle-of-the-road in all respects," a business major observes. Says an engineering major, "The college has its intelligentsia, its social butterflies, its determined athletes, and any combination of those."

Freshmen are expected to live in college housing, though fraternity pledges have the option of living in their houses. Co-ed and single-sex options are available in the comfortable and well-maintained dorms, which house about a third of the students. "The residence halls are comfortable and well maintained, for the most part," says a forestry major. "They also offer many opportunities to get involved and meet new people." In addition to standard rooming situations, a new "wellness" hall offers an exercise room and low-calorie meals. Students can also choose life in one of eight cooperatives or the plentiful off-campus apartments. Foraging for food on your own generally beats so-so dorm grub; the better chow at frat and sorority houses is one motivation for students to go Greek, which about 15 percent of the men and 11 percent of the women do. Alcohol still flows freely at Greek affairs, but recent crackdowns by the administration and local police have begun to curb the most wanton debauchery.

(Continued)
Strongest Programs:
Agriculture
Biotechnology
Forestry
Engineering
Business

Freshmen are expected to live in college housing, though fraternity pledges have the option of living in their houses.

Of particular note is OSU's Experimental College, where undergraduates spice up their semesters with noncredit courses in a range of imaginative subjects—everything from wine tasting to the art of bashing, a medieval war technique.

Says an engineering major,
"The college has its
intelligentsia, its social
butterflies, its determined
athletes, and any
combination of those."

Cheering for the Beavers' nationally ranked wrestling team, which has had four top ten national finishes in the last five years, demands a lot of students' time and energy here, as does participation in the well-rounded intramural program. Benny Beaver, the school's former (and somewhat benign) mascot has been replaced by a more aggressive beaver that students have dubbed the "angry beaver." Other talented varsity squads include women's gymnastics, basketball, and volleyball, and men's football and baseball; the basketball team has the eighth-winningest program of all time among NCAA Division I schools. As for rivalries, one student says, "Civil War games between OSU and U of Oregon are a big part of every season."

Another popular student activity is complaining about the Willamette Valley weather: "People in the valley don't tan, they rust," warns one native. One reward for this sogginess, however, is the abundance of flowers that bloom in every color and shape each May. Many students consider Corvallis a good-size town; a number of bars and cheap theaters cater to their entertainment needs. Beautifully rugged beaches are less than an hour away, and some of the best skiing in the country can be found in the Cascade Mountains, two hours east. Hiking and rafting are nearby, too, and trips to powwows in the area and camping on the coast provide other good times. Popular campus traditions include the Greeklife Sing (featuring musical numbers staged by fraternity and sorority members) and the annual Fall Festival.

Oregon State University continues to build on its solid reputation as an agricultural institution, marching into the millennium as an old and faithful part of the state's university system. OSU doesn't scream for attention. Instead, it's content to be a "nice" college, in "a safe and pleasant little town," where professors are "helpful" and, even if everyone doesn't know your name, they'll lend you an umbrella whenever the skies open up.

Overlaps

**University of Oregon,
Portland State,
Western Oregon,
University of
Washington,
Washington State**

If You Apply To ➤ **Oregon State:** Early action: Nov. 1. Regular admissions: Mar. 1. Financial aid: Feb. 1. Does not guarantee to meet demonstrated need. Campus interviews: optional, informational. No alumni interviews. SATs or ACTs: optional. No SAT IIs. Accepts the Common Application and electronic applications. No essay question.

University of the Pacific

3601 Pacific Avenue, Stockton, CA 95211

The pretentious name dates from a time when there were no other universities near the Pacific. UOP is the only small, independent university in California north of L.A. UOP offers an eye-popping array of programs for an institution its size, including business, engineering, pharmacy, and education.

University of the Pacific looks like several hundred acres of New England plunked down in California wine country. With its stately combination of redbrick and ivy, it could be mistaken for an East Coast liberal arts college. But instead of a blanket of snow, UOP is surrounded by the lush greenery of the San Joaquin Valley. On campus, this increasingly competitive bastion of learning offers its more than thirty-two hundred undergrads a solid and diverse academic program and scores of things to do when not hitting the books.

With majestic evergreens and flowering trees, UOP is home to six undergraduate schools and the College of the Pacific, the university's liberal arts and sciences

Website: www.uop.edu
Location: Suburban
Total Enrollment: 5,886
Undergraduates: 3,233
Male/Female: 42/58
SAT Ranges: V 510–610
  M 540–650
ACT Range: 22–26

division. There is also a school of law in Sacramento and a superlative school of dentistry in San Francisco. A new program in dental hygiene is one of several accelerated programs in which students may earn a joint degree between liberal studies and a professional program over five or six years. Strong departments abound in the schools of engineering, pharmacy, and business (with special programs in the arts/entertainment management and entrepreneurship) as well as the sciences, English, and international studies. Prepharmacy is the most popular major, followed by biology, psychology, business, and engineering. The university-wide general education program is divided into two main components: the liberal learning program (interdisciplinary courses spread across three categories of learning) and the Mentor Seminars. All freshmen are required to take Mentor Seminars I (Timeless Issues, including: What is appearance/What is reality? What do we come to think, to know? and Why be good?) and II (Today's Decisions, focusing on public-policy decisions students could face in their lifetime). A senior political science major calls the Mentor Seminars "very worthwhile and useful." Another seminar (Ethical Application of Knowledge) is required during the junior or senior year. A number of internship and co-op programs are available, and students are guaranteed to have some type of experiential learning. Students may also design their own majors with faculty approval. An extensive study abroad program offers two hundred choices in dozens of countries, and international studies majors are required to complete one. An art history program was recently dropped.

> "Teachers are caring, insightful, and help their students to think critically."

The academic climate varies by department, with students citing the science fields as the most rigorous. An English major says the climate is "extremely laid-back" while a medicine/chemistry major disagrees, saying the climate is "fairly competitive." Studying accounts for anywhere from ten to forty hours a week. The university guarantees graduation in four years (assuming the student follows all university guidelines), or it will pay for the extra schooling. Professors at UOP get raves for accessibility and personal attention. "Teachers are caring, insightful, and help their students to think critically," says one senior. Classes average twenty-two students, and the TAs teach only the labs.

Eighty-six percent of UOP students are Californians. Hawaii and Colorado are also strongly represented, while foreign students make up 3 percent of the student body. As for ethnic diversity, Asian-Americans account for 26 percent, while African-Americans and Hispanics together make up 6 percent. Students come from a mix of economic backgrounds; 69 percent receive financial aid. The school is middle-of-the-road to conservative, though politics in general play a small role on campus. One senior notes, "Our school is very conservative and rarely faces current issues unless forced to." But the school recently received a three-year diversity grant and has a new Pride Center for gay and lesbian students.

Though not unusually expensive by national standards, the university price tag can seem steep when compared to the University of California system. So UOP has stepped up efforts to compete using merit scholarships, which range from $6,500 to $15,000, as well as 210 scholarships to athletes in a long list of sports. The financial aid packages generally get good reviews.

The campus has many new additions, including a student fitness center, science lab building and health sciences building. Freshmen and sophomores are required to live on campus, and the few complaints mostly center on aging facilities, some of which are undergoing much-needed renovations. Grace Covell Hall, with 350 people, is the largest residence, and two new residence halls recently opened. Sixty-two percent of undergrads make their home on campus. In terms of quality of life, however, residential life is praised for plentiful social programming.

(Continued)

Financial Aid: 69%
Expenses: Pr $ $ $
Phi Beta Kappa: No
Applicants: 3,736
Accepted: 71%
Enrolled: 26%
Grad in 6 Years: 69%
Returning Freshmen: 87%
Academics: ✍ ✍ ✍
Social: ☎ ☎ ☎
Q of L: ★ ★ ★ ★
Admissions: (209) 940-2211
Email Address:
   admissions@uop.edu

Strongest Programs:
Biology
Communications
Music
Predental
Prepharmacy
Business
International Studies
Engineering

A new program in dental hygiene is one of several accelerated programs in which students may earn a joint degree between liberal studies and a professional program over five or six years.

The school occasionally hosts big-name concerts and other campus-wide events. Students complain, however, that much social life centers on the Greek scene; 20 percent of men and 21 percent of women go Greek. With three meal plans, two dining halls, and one fast-food-type facility, residents are well fed.

For weekend excitement, UOP students love to hit the road: within about two hours, they can be skiing, shopping in San Francisco, or surfing in Monterey. Stockton itself (population 250,000) offers shopping and plenty of fast-food joints, as well as numerous volunteer opportunities. But students say it is too large to be a college town, and parts of it are not safe for students.

Social opportunities on campus are offered by ASUOP (Associated Students of UOP), the Residence Hall Association, intramural and club sports, conservatory and drama/dance programs, Division I athletics, campus movies, sororities and fraternities, and more than one hundred student clubs. The school is now enforcing state law, prohibiting all students under twenty-one from drinking. Students caught violating that policy must take an online course in alcohol education. The majority of Greek houses are designated substance-free, following a national trend enforced by their national organizations. But a senior says the policies are pointless: "They have little effect except making people sneak their alcohol around." Annual campus festivities include Diversity Week, International Spring Festival, and the popular Fall Festival and Greek Week. In sports, the men's and women's swimming, men's golf, women's softball, and women's volleyball squads were all Big West champions in 2001–2002.

Pitted against the state's immense public university system, UOP stands out for offering major university opportunities in a small-college setting. And the administration is striving to place more focus on its student body, which is becoming more top-notch and diverse. "The small atmosphere, small classes, and great faculty support" make the school a special place, says one happy senior.

<table>
<tr><td>

Overlaps

UC–Davis,
UC–Berkeley,
California Polytechnic,
Santa Clara, University
of San Francisco

</td></tr>
</table>

If You Apply To > **UOP:** Early action: Dec. 1. Regular admission: Jan. 15. Financial aid: Feb. 15. Housing: Jun. 1. Does not guarantee to meet demonstrated need. Campus interviews: optional, informational. No alumni interviews. SATs or ACTs: required. SAT IIs: optional. Accepts the Common Application and electronic applications. Essay question: significant experience; what will make your college experience a success; special personal or academic situation.

University of Pennsylvania

1 College Hall, Philadelphia, PA 19104-6376

Though an Ivy League institution in name, Penn has more in common with places like Georgetown and Northwestern—places where the liberal arts share center stage with preprofessional programs. At Penn, that means business, engineering, and nursing. Penn has something else other Ivies don't: school spirit.

Website: www.upenn.edu
Location: Urban
Total Enrollment: 21,729
Undergraduates: 9,133
Male/Female: 51/49
SAT Ranges: V 640–730
 M 660–750

Though best known for dangerous experiments with kites and keys, Founding Father Benjamin Franklin pulled off a number of other remarkable stunts in the mid-eighteenth century, not the least of which was founding the University of Pennsylvania. Frustrated with the philosophizing and intellectual dithering of the earliest New England colleges, Franklin wanted Penn to provide a practical education for citizens and merchants, and over the next 250-odd years the school did just that. Penn established the nation's first medical school, the first business school, the first journalism curriculum, and the first psychology clinic. In her inaugural address, a former president paid tribute to Franklin as "the ultimate visionary and pragmatist." "Franklin thought education should be for the body as well as for the soul—that it should enable a graduate to be a breadwinner as well as a thinker, that it should produce socially conscious citizens as well as conscientious bankers and traders," she said.

Uncle Ben would be proud of the way his university has surged in recent years. Once relegated to the bottom of the Ivy League (and confused with Penn State), Penn is now the first choice for top students who see no conflict between high-level academics and having a life. The undergraduate School of Arts and Sciences—once on the university's back burner—is now central not only to its undergraduates but also to the remaining three undergraduate schools that tap into its programs and course offerings.

Penn is situated in a tree-shaded, totally self-contained 260-acre nest called University City, which is adjacent to downtown Philadelphia. Its 116 buildings range from Victorian Gothic to postmodern. There are very old structures, such as College Hall, with red and green foliage creeping up its facade, and newer ones, such as Wharton's Steinberg-Dietrich Hall, which stretches out just west of the Schuylkill River. While many students thrive on Philadelphia's cultural abundance, the school is located in the west part of town, considered to be the most dangerous. The area is slowly gentrifying, but it's still an area of major concern for many. "Penn's biggest problem is probably its close surroundings of West Philadelphia and the security issues this poses," said a sophomore.

Penn's reputation is primarily wrapped up with its twelve graduate schools, especially the prestigious Wharton School for business administration, the Annenberg School of Communication, and the well-known law, medical, and veterinary schools. Three of four undergraduate schools—engineering, nursing, and the undergraduate division of Wharton—are also professionally oriented and offer an education that's hard to beat anywhere. The undergraduate College of Arts and Sciences (a.k.a. "The College") has come into its own in the past decade or so, and provides students with high-quality instruction as well as the chance to run into a Nobel laureate here and there.

Finance is the most popular undergrad major, followed by history and communications. Economics is also a strong department, and even the natural sciences draw praise from students. Penn's anthropology department ranks with Chicago's as perhaps the best in the country, while programs in management and technology are also outstanding. Penn has earned applause in the field of cognitive and computer sciences because of its special program linking psychology, linguistics, and computers with philosophy. Another popular crème de la crème interdisciplinary major, Biological Basis of Behavior, combines psychology, economics, and anthropology. Undergrads also single out folklore and the legal studies concentration as good arts and science bets. Students are allowed to design their own individualized majors, and they can hop from school to school—undergraduate or graduate—in doing so. In addition to the self-designed majors, Penn has constructed its own innovative and marketable joint majors. Design and structural technology or management and technology, for example, lead to dual arts and engineering or business and engineering degrees in four years.

At the Wharton School, officials have introduced the Joseph Wharton Scholars program, which emphasizes breadth in the arts and sciences and includes a language requirement. In fact, all undergraduates must attain proficiency in one of the forty-five foreign languages taught at Penn. Another added plus that comes with a Penn undergraduate education is the opportunity for early entry (submatriculation)

> "Penn students seem to find a way to balance out the competitive atmosphere."

Penn's anthropology department ranks with Chicago's as perhaps the best in the country, while programs in management and technology are also outstanding.

(Continued)
ACT Range: N/A
Financial Aid: 48%
Expense: Pr $ $ $ $
Phi Beta Kappa: Yes
Applicants: 16,658
Accepted: 29%
Enrolled: 49%
Grad in 6 Years: 90%
Returning Freshmen: 96%
Academics: ✐ ✐ ✐ ✐ ✐
Social: ☎ ☎ ☎
Q of L: ★ ★ ★
Admissions: (215) 898-7507
Email Address: info@
   admissions.ugad.upenn.edu

Strongest Programs:
Business
History
English
Economics
Anthropology
American Studies
Cognitive and Computer
   Science
Nursing
Art and Design

Thousands of faculty and students give expression to Benjamin Franklin's adage that service to humanity is "the great aim and end of all learning." They work with local public school students as part of academic coursework in disciplines as diverse as history, anthropology, and mathematics.

into the university's graduate programs. Juniors may apply to any master's program (continuing into the Wharton M.B.A. program is especially popular) and begin completing graduate requirements during their senior year. Penn offers no co-op programs and discourages full-time internships for credit, remaining true to the Ivy League belief that learning is best done in the classroom. Those who want to explore more exotic classrooms may study abroad at Penn's programs in Italy, Scotland, Japan, France, England, China, Nigeria, Spain, Germany, and Russia, among others. Freshmen are encouraged (but not required) to participate in a seminar program that explores various areas of academic interest, and also in the Penn Reading Project, which involves student and faculty discussion of a common text.

Professors at Penn take their research responsibilities seriously, leaving graduate teaching assistants to manage all but the lectures and office hours for some lower-level classes. Freshman seminars and general honors courses (usually more demanding versions of introductory courses) provide exceptions to the rule. "The quality of teaching has been really good, and as a freshman, I had several full professors," says a sophomore. "I have found the teachers to be very accessible and willing to help." The academic program at Penn is well supplemented by its huge and busy library, which houses more than three million volumes.

Despite all the preprofessional programs, Penn never lets its undergraduates stray too far from the liberal arts. All Penn students fulfill distribution requirements, which vary by school. All Wharton undergraduate students take a core curriculum that consists of courses in social structures, language, arts and culture, and science and analysis. Engineering requires students to take seven humanities courses, and the College of Arts and Sciences requires ten courses from seven sectors. There also is a writing requirement, and all freshmen are encouraged to take at least one course in the Freshman Seminar Program, designed to give students an opportunity to work closely with a faculty member. Strict academic policies and demanding professors exacerbate the academic pressure, but while students find the school competitive, not all are complaining. "Personally, I have found it to be a good competition," says one sophomore. "It keeps me on my toes." Unlike some other schools, Penn strikes a good balance between academics and social life. A senior adds, "Penn students seem to find a way to balance out the competitive atmosphere. We definitely strive to do well, and this involves a serious commitment to coursework. But we don't let this inhibit our Penn experience by keeping us in the library nonstop." Each year students evaluate every class themselves and publish their findings in a guide. Thousands of faculty and students give expression to Benjamin Franklin's adage that service to humanity is "the great aim and end of all learning." They work with local public school students as part of academic coursework in disciplines as diverse as history, anthropology, and

"Off-campus living is just an extension of student neighborhoods, as we tend to stay in large groups."

mathematics. There are tons of opportunities to volunteer—from tutoring to Big Brother/Big Sister to the Ronald McDonald House. Back in the classroom, one classics professor uses modern Philadelphia and fifth-century Athens to explore the interrelationships among community, neighborhood, and family.

Undergraduates may work hard during the week, but in contrast to most Ivy League achievers, they leave it behind them on weekends.

Penn is a diverse campus; 20 percent of the population is Asian-American, and African-Americans and Hispanics combine for 10 percent. But students are not diverse in their brainpower—they're all smart. Ninety percent of the students rank in the top tenth of their high school class. Nearly 60 percent come from public high school. Penn's Diversity Awareness Program for freshmen helps students from various backgrounds blend more harmoniously. Freshman orientation includes skits that depict students in various situations of possible conflict and include discussions about each situation.

Penn admits students regardless of need but does not offer any merit, athletic, or academic scholarships. Through its innovative Penn Plan, the university strives to ensure that virtually every family with a college-bound son or daughter, no matter what its income, can benefit from financial assistance. For some this means subsidized loans and other traditional forms of aid. Other possibilities under the Penn Plan, however, include prepayment and borrowing options designed with the rate of inflation in mind and aimed at families in the higher-income brackets. In all, Penn students have six payment-plan options.

Nearly all freshmen and 55 percent of all undergraduates live on campus and enjoy a wide range of living options. Dorms are co-ed. The Quad seems to be the hot spot, described as "beautiful, self-enclosed, and social" and "the greatest place in the world for freshmen." Upperclassmen reluctantly move to the high-rises across campus that look like "prefabricated twenty-four-story monsters" but do offer more space, as well as kitchens. Students may also apply for a number of small College Houses, which provide a greater community experience. There are living-learning programs for those who are interested in the arts, Asian studies, etc., and want to be surrounded by others with the same interests. Rather than compete in the lottery for rooms, many juniors and seniors simply head off campus—"for the freedom, plus it's a lot cheaper," a junior says. Some end up in nearby renovated

"Penn has a vibrant social scene."

three-story houses in the neighborhood. "Off-campus living is just an extension of student neighborhoods, as we tend to stay in large groups," explains a senior. Like housing, the meal plans are optional (though strongly recommended in the freshman year as an important source of social life), and the food isn't all that bad for institutional fare, though there is no food served on weekends.

Undergraduates may work hard during the week, but in contrast to most Ivy League achievers, they leave it behind them on weekends. "Penn has a vibrant social scene," a junior says. "A lot of the social life takes place on campus because of the Greek system and the many student-run clubs, such as a capella singing groups and comedy and theater groups," says a sophomore. After an underage student suffered from alcohol poisoning, the university stiffened its alcohol policy, but with only limited effectiveness, say students. More than two dozen fraternities attract 30 percent of the men and provide "your basic meat-market scene." Similarly, sororities claim 30 percent of the women. The frats' exclusive claim to the houses along Locust Walk, the main artery on campus, has been undone: after some controversy, it was determined that non-Greeks, too, must be able to live at the social nexus of the campus.

Two big annual events at Penn are Spring Fling, a three-day weekend "nothing short of absolutely incredible fun," and Hey Day, when juniors, donning Styrofoam hats and bearing the president of the university on their shoulders, march down Locust Walk to officially become seniors, taking chomps out of each other's hats as they go. A less formal tradition is the Quad Streak, when uninhibited undergraduates run through the crowd naked. Road trips include New York City, Washington, D.C., Atlantic City, and even Maine and Florida. Downtown Philadelphia, only a few minutes away by foot, cab, or public transportation, offers enough social and cultural activities to make up for the less-attractive aspects of city living. "Students constantly take advantage of all the social and academic opportunities the city has to offer," a senior says. "I don't know if I would call it a college town, because there is so much else going on here, but there is plenty for students to do!" Students frequent sporting events, malls, South Street ("a miniature Greenwich Village"), and, of course, myriad bars and dancing joints.

Penn is more sports-minded than most Ivy schools, and football is the biggie. The team has grown accustomed to sitting on the top of the Ivy League and has

Penn is more sports-minded than most Ivy schools, and football is the biggie. The team has grown accustomed to sitting on the top of the Ivy League and has sparked a widespread revival of school spirit.

Despite all the preprofessional programs, Penn never lets its undergraduates stray too far from the liberal arts.

sparked a widespread revival of school spirit. Tickets are free for those with a student ID. The Penn-Princeton rivalry is always a crowd pleaser. At the end of the third quarter of each home game, everyone in the stands begins belting out the lyrics of the Penn fight song, and when they get to "Here's a toast to dear old Penn," the students shower the field with burnt toast, "a moment that makes all Penn students proud," gushes a senior. Aside from football, recent Ivy championship teams include men's basketball and wrestling, and women's field hockey, basketball, and fencing. Nearly two dozen intramural sports bring thousands of less-seasoned athletes out to play each year, and all types of athletes benefit from the swanky track and weight-lifting facilities. Each spring, Penn hosts the prestigious Penn Relays, a track-and-field extravaganza that attracts the nation's best track athletes.

While its students work hard, Penn lacks the intellectual intensity of some of the top Ivies, and you can even detect some undercurrents of anti-intellectualism. But most accept it for what it is: a first-rate university where you can live a relatively normal life. Penn is one Ivy League university where no one apologizes for having fun!

Overlaps

Harvard, Princeton, Yale, Cornell, Brown

If You Apply To ➢   **Penn:** Early decision: Nov. 1. Regular admissions: Jan. 1. Financial aid: Feb. 15. Guarantees to meet full demonstrated need. No campus interviews. Alumni interviews: optional, informational. SATs or ACTs: required. SAT IIs: required (writing and two others). Essay question: how you and Penn are a good match and how you envision your freshman year; an influential person, a page of your autobiography, or influential quotation.

Pennsylvania State University

201 Old Main, University Park, PA 16802

Aside from UVA and UNC, there are precious few public universities more selective than Penn State. With a student body the size of a small city, the university is strong in everything from meteorology to film and television. The University Scholars Program is one of the nation's elite honors programs.

Website: www.psu.edu
Location: Small city
Total Enrollment: 41,445
Undergraduates: 34,829
Male/Female: 53/47
SAT Ranges: V 530–630
  M 560–670
Financial Aid: 72%
Expense: Pub $ $ $ $
Phi Beta Kappa: Yes
Applicants: 27,604
Accepted: 57%
Enrolled: 38%
Grad in 6 Years: 80%
Returning Freshmen: 91%
Academics: 🔔 🔔 🔔 🔔 ½
Social: 🐺 🐺 🐺 🐺 🐺
Q of L: ★ ★ ★

Living it up with more than thirty-four thousand classmates in Happy Valley is the perfect college experience for some, though it might not fit everyone's idea of a good time. Those who can muster the energy to take advantage of Pennsylvania State University's fabled school spirit and immense academic offerings may find a home here. "It is an amazing university founded on excellence" says one senior. "You feel the strongest internal pride and love for Penn State. A very personal bond is forged forever."

Sporting an eclectic architectural mix, including white-columned brick, stone, and some modern apartments, this land-grant university continues to experience growth as major renovation and expansion projects continue. Newer facilities at the University include the Pasquerilla Spiritual Center and a career services building. One junior says, "The university is technologically updated and savvy in its ability to accommodate more student interests."

Penn State maintains strong programs in the scientific and technical fields such as earth sciences, engineering, agricultural sciences, and life sciences, as well as nutrition and family studies. The meteorology program boasts alumni worldwide, including the founder of AccuWeather, an internationally renowned private forecasting firm that is headquartered here. The newer School of Information Sciences and Technology is designed to prepare students for the digital age in the business world. On the other end of the spectrum, the Agriculture College has extensive facilities that include huge livestock barns. Dairy products from the school's cows are sold at an on-campus store, and courses are offered in the production of its famous ice cream. Students can choose from 225 baccalaureate programs, 155 graduate fields, and the Dickinson School of Law, located near the state capital. At a school of Penn State's size, there are bound to be some weaknesses, but the curriculum is in a seemingly constant state of change; recently 23 majors were added, 128 changed, and 4 dropped.

"It is an amazing university founded on excellence."

(Continued)
Admissions: (814) 865-7641
Email Address:
   admissions@psu.edu

Strongest Programs:
Business/Marketing
Engineering/Engineering
   Technologies
Education
Communications
Social Sciences

General education requirements consist of forty-five credits that include several communications and quantification courses as well as humanities, arts, natural sciences, social and behavioral sciences, and health and physical education courses. The incorporation of critical thinking skills has been a priority in redesigning the general curriculum. About eighteen hundred of the university's best and brightest are invited to participate in the Schreyer Honors College, which offers opportunities for independent study and graduate work as well as honors options in regular courses. According to one upperclassman, "The courses are rigorous and challenging but allow you to be competitive with yourself and get the pick of classes." Students who are part of the honors college take both honors classes and regular university classes.

In addition, undergrads must enroll in "diversity-focused" courses that encourage awareness of minority concerns. One helpful program offered to freshmen is L.E.A.P. (Learning Edge Academic Program), which gives new students the benefit of a big university while making it seem small. Students in L.E.A.P. take a team approach by taking classes together and living together. But all this education can be put too good use with the "beyond superior" career counselors, one senior says. Another student says, "My advisor has been great. She helped me get my last job."

Some of Penn State's intro-level lecture courses draw up to four hundred students, yet most of the students seem to agree classes are excellent and require your full attention. A junior says, "The professors are knowledgeable and highly intellectual in their fields. If I have any complaint, it has been that the professors know their material too well, and the students have to work extra hard to

"You feel the strongest internal pride and love for Penn State. A very personal bond is forged forever."

keep up." For cramming outside of class, the Penn State library contains approximately 4.6 million volumes, and a branch library is open twenty-four hours every day for the after-hours crowd. A large number of students study abroad, and combined undergraduate/graduate degree options are available, as are co-op programs in engineering, distance learning, and student-designed majors.

Most undergraduates are residents of Pennsylvania, with 22 percent hailing from out of state and 2 percent hailing from outside the nation. Seventy-eight percent ranked in the top quarter of their high school class. Many students note that race and diversity issues are becoming more pronounced on a campus that is still pretty homogenous: Asian-Americans make up 5 percent of the undergrad population, and African-Americans and Hispanics combine for another 8 percent. A whopping 516 athletic scholarships are available, covering all NCAA-approved sports, as are a number of merit awards.

Freshmen must live in the dorms, which students say are affordable and extremely comfortable. More than 60 percent of students live off campus, often in downtown apartments. The meal plan operates on a point system where you pay for what you eat. More than half of Penn State's undergraduates spend their first two years at one of the university's eighteen campuses across the state, or at Penn State's Behrend College in Erie, which also offers four-year programs.

The meteorology program boasts alumni worldwide, including the founder of AccuWeather, an internationally renowned private forecasting firm that is headquartered here.

Penn State's students take advantage of the picturesque and peaceful locale by engaging in outdoorsy activities, including skiing at a nearby slope, and sailing, canoeing, hiking, and renting cabins in Stone Valley. State College offers some cultural events, such as symphonies, theatrical shows, and ballets, while the Bryce Jordan Convocation Center hosts top-notch performers, including Linkin Park, Dave Matthews Band, Nelly, Ricky Martin, and Faith Hill. The town may be small, but according to a biochem major, "a majority of the students get involved in community service to maintain and constantly improve town relations."

Partying at Penn State is almost as legendary as the football team, which registered two national championships in the '80s. Students mostly go to bars and parties off campus in State College, where "it's very difficult for underage students to be served at the bars," according to a student. "Students with fake IDs have almost a zero percent chance of gaining admittance." While the administration strives to keep booze out of underage hands on campus, "there are places students can get alcohol, mostly at other people's apartments," says a junior. The HUB, the campus union building, is open twenty-four hours, so students seeking nonalcoholic entertainment are encouraged to attend. The Greeks—which include 13 percent of Penn State men and 11 percent of women—have BYOB parties.

When thousands of alumni converge to cheer on their Nittany Lions in blue and white, the festivities include tailgate parties replete with marshmallow throwing, pregame parties, and postgame revelry. As a member of the Big Ten, Penn State's foes include Michigan and Ohio State, both of which make great road trips in addition to Philadelphia, Pittsburgh, and New York.

> **"A majority of the students get involved in community service to maintain and constantly improve town relations."**

Other popular events include the mid-July art festival, the Dance Marathon (which in 2002 raised $3.6 million for children with cancer), and, of course, Homecoming.

While the football team has struggled as of late, it's just one of twenty-nine varsity teams in town. In fact, Penn State teams have won nearly sixty national titles in a wide variety of sports, including men's and women's volleyball, women's soccer, field hockey, and fencing. There are three large gyms, a competitive-size pool, an indoor ice rink, and an extensive intramural program for the recreational athlete.

Penn State's nationally recognized academics, sense of pride, community spirit, and sports are a tough combination to beat. "Imagine a family of forty thousand— the excitement, pride, compassion, and sense of belonging which is unparalleled at any institution," says one proud Nittany Lion.

If You Apply To ➢ **PSU:** Rolling admissions. Financial aid: Apr. 15. Housing: Jan. 21. Meets demonstrated need of 6%. No campus or alumni interviews. SATs or ACTs: required. SAT IIs: optional. Accepts electronic applications. Essay question optional. Apply to particular school or program.

Pepperdine University

24255 Pacific Coast Highway, Malibu, CA 90263-4392

With apologies to Wellesley and Furman, Pepperdine has the most beautiful campus in America. Small wonder that its acceptance rate hovers at about one in three.

Students must come to Pepperdine ready to embrace an evangelical Christian emphasis much stronger than, say, the Roman Catholicism of U of San Francisco.

With picturesque surroundings, it's easy to confuse Pepperdine University with its nicknames—Pepperdine Resort and Club Med. Surrounded by the beautiful Southern California seashore, Pepperdine University might seem paradise found for students seeking sunshine rather than studies at this conservative, Christian-affiliated university, though students take their work and their worship seriously. "The philosophy of the school is that God and the academic experience must be married," says a senior telecommunications major. "This creates an intimate learning environment that prides itself on moral integrity and a high academic standard." Business and communications are the blessed programs, though other departments deserve recognition, too. Undergrads praise their educational opportunities, the strength of their school's spiritual community, and (God's good grace in creating cute little bikinis) for the vast sandy beaches beckoning below their hilltop campus.

There's no denying that Pepperdine's location—high in the Santa Monica Mountains, about twenty-five miles northwest of Los Angeles—is a strong selling point. The 830-acre Malibu campus, to which the school moved in 1972, overlooks the Pacific Ocean and features fountains, hillside gardens, mountain trails, and a twenty-minute walk to the beach. Cream-colored, Mediterranean-style buildings topped with red terra-cotta roofs dot the landscape. A 125-foot-tall white stucco cross stands near the center of campus, reminding students and faculty of the school's affiliation with the Churches of Christ.

Pepperdine was founded in 1937 by George Pepperdine, a devout Christian who had amassed a fortune through his mail-order auto parts supply company. The church's continued influence on the school pervades many aspects of campus life, from the prohibition of overnight dorm-room visits by members of the opposite sex to the requirement that students attend convocation—similar to chapel—fourteen times each semester. Students at Seaver College, Pepp's undergraduate school, must also take three religion courses. While drinking is officially prohibited on campus, the administration has lifted the ban on dancing, and now allows students to choose their own seats at convocation. Though restrictions like this would drive the average kid up a wall, most at Pepperdine like the "highly moral" atmosphere. Says one student: "In comparison to other schools, Pepperdine students generally have a more religious foundation and thus have high standards of moral integrity."

Seaver's academic programs aim to provide students "with a liberal arts education in a Christian environment and relate it to the dynamic qualities of life in the twentieth century." Individual classes are demanding, as is the required General Studies program, which includes a freshman seminar, a physical education course, three courses in Western heritage, two courses each in American heritage and English composi-

"The philosophy of the school is that God and the academic experience must be married."

tion, and one class each in a foreign language and non-Western culture. However, faculty members are said to be accessible and responsive—not surprising when the average class has seventeen students. "The quality of teaching is very personal and exceptional," says an art major. Another student adds: "Because it is a small school, professors don't accept excuses or laziness. They demand a lot from their students and expect a high standard and quality of work."

The Business Administration department is unequivocally the strongest and most popular department at Pepperdine, and it tends to set the tone on campus. The Communications department, with majors including advertising, public relations, and journalism, is also highly touted, especially now that it boasts radio and television broadcasting studios. Biology and computer science are said to be strong,

Website:
  www.pepperdine.edu
Location: Suburban
Total Enrollment: 7,476
Undergraduates: 3,068
Male/Female: 42/58
SAT Ranges: V 570–670
  M 580–680
ACT Range: 25–29
Financial Aid: 54%
Expense: Pr $ $ $ $
Phi Beta Kappa: No
Applicants: 5,393
Accepted: 36%
Enrolled: 35%
Grad in 6 Years: 68%
Returning Freshmen: 89%
Academics: ✏️ ✏️ ✏️
Social: ☎ ☎
Q of L: ★ ★ ★ ★
Admissions: (310) 506-4392
Email Address:
  admission-seaver@
  pepperdine.edu

Strongest Programs:
Business
Accounting
Communications
Natural Science

Pepperdine's location— high in the Santa Monica Mountains, about twenty-five miles northwest of Los Angeles—is a strong selling point.

and sports medicine, rare at the undergraduate level, is both popular and well respected. Although music studios and a $10 million humanities and visual arts center have been built to enhance the Fine Arts Division, students still say art and

"Because it is a small school, professors don't accept excuses or laziness."

music are relatively weak. Recent additions to the academic menu include minors in African-American studies, women's studies, and multimedia design. Juniors interested in European culture may spend a year at Pepperdine's own facilities near Heidelberg Castle, or in London or Florence. Other study abroad programs are available in Japan and Australia; locations for summer study include France, Spain, Israel, Asia, and Russia.

Back on campus, students trying to complete term papers can use one of the 292 public computer terminals and the collections of Pepp's eight-facility library system, which boast more than 515,000 volumes and 375,000 titles on microfilm. The well-organized campus Career Center allows students sign up for job fairs, interviews, and individual and group career-counseling sessions.

One might expect students at this religiously oriented school to be conservative, and politically, they most definitely are. Many come from well-to-do Republican, California families; there is also a relatively high percentage of wealthy international students. Students joke that there's never a shortage of Porsches and BMWs on campus, but there is a shortage of places to park them. Hispanics account for 10 percent of the students, Asian-Americans 7 percent, and African-Americans 7 percent. The Republican influence is felt far and wide. Pepperdine has received millions of dollars from conservative Pittsburgh financier Richard Mellon Scaife. One student sums up the political climate gently: "Pepperdine tends to shy away from political activism."

Some say flashy student vehicles fit into the small, very wealthy community of Malibu better than the students themselves; the city sees the university as a catalyst for development, and that hurts town-gown relations. Because the social scene in Malibu is pretty slack, with a 10 p.m. noise curfew and high price tags for everything, students typically head to L.A., Hollywood, Westwood, and Santa Monica for fun. "For a large proportion of students, academics and their social lives take priority over religious matters," says a public relations major. "Parties on weekends are

"Parties on weekends are well attended, and probably draw a larger portion of students than church on Sunday."

well attended, and probably draw a larger portion of students than church on Sunday." Twenty-four percent of men and 29 percent of

women join one of six national fraternities or eight national sororities, which are playing a larger role in social life. Along with student government, they sponsor dances, movies, and other typical college activities, including the occasional illicit drink. "Pepperdine enforces a 'dry' campus, but 'damp' would be a better way of describing the residential community," says one student. "I think most of us would like to see Pepperdine get out of the dark ages in these matters."

Except for commuters, students are required to live on campus if they are single and under twenty-one. That's a good thing, says one senior, who declares that Pepperdine's dorms are "comfortable, convenient, and really quite nice." The single-sex

dorms and apartments are connected to the campus computer network. Rooms are assigned on a first-come, first-served basis, and the housing stock consists of 22 dorms with 26 rooms each, a 135-room tower, and a 75-unit apartment complex for juniors and seniors. Freshmen are typically assigned to suites with bathrooms, living rooms, and four double bedrooms. Some consider these arrangements crowded, but a junior says they "connect freshmen instantly to seven suitemates and friends." Despite the above-average cost of living in the Malibu area, many upperclassmen choose to live off campus. The relatively new student union serves as the main campus social center, and annual events including Songfest, Family Weekend, and Midnight Madness draw crowds.

Sports receive a lot of attention at Pepperdine, with athletic scholarships offered in multiple sports, and a tennis pavilion and recreation center drawing varsity jocks and weekend warriors alike. The men's golf team and men's water polo team have recently won NCAA championships. Men's volleyball is always a contender for the national championship, and a Pepperdine men's tennis singles player has won the national title. Eleven club and intramural sports, including lacrosse, rugby, cycling, surfing, and soccer, keep students busy, as does the physical education department, with classes in everything from surfing to horseback riding.

Students here love to tease their well-manicured university with T-shirts proclaiming, "Pepperdine. 8 month party. 20K cover charge." But most seem to think the solid, values-oriented education they receive is worth the stiff price tag. Pepperdine faces a unique challenge in trying to marry the Christian focus of a Bible college with the academic rigor of a secular university—all in a location not known for the strength of its moral fiber.

If You Apply To ➤ **Pepperdine:** Early action: Nov. 15. Regular admissions: Jan. 15. Financial aid: Feb. 15. Housing: May 1. Does not guarantee to meet demonstrated need. Campus interviews: recommended, evaluative. No alumni interviews. SATs or ACTs: required. SAT IIs: optional. Accepts the Common Application and electronic applications. Essay question: current topics; ethical dilemma; or most embarrassing moment.

University of Pittsburgh

Bruce Hall, Second floor, Pittsburgh, PA 15260

With the city of Pittsburgh's rise in stature, Pitt has become a hot commodity. A state university in the mold of University of Cincinnati—not the state flagship, but strong in a host of mainly preprofessional programs. Unexpectedly, Pitt is among the nation's best in philosophy.

Pittsburgh has shaken off its idled steel-factory stigma and joined the ranks of the most livable cities in the U.S. The University of Pittsburgh has matured, too, becoming a formidable public research institution. The school offers numerous opportunities for students pursuing technical, medical, and engineering careers, but leaves a great deal of room for exploration in the liberal arts. Students are encouraged to be individuals and carve out their own academic niche, either with multiple majors or certificate programs. Combine this with a satisfying social life, and Pitt has discovered one formula for a rewarding college experience.

Pitt began as a tiny private educational academy in the Allegheny Mountains in 1787. Oh, how times have changed. The university, which became state-related in 1966, is now part of the landscape of shops, parks, museums, galleries, and apartment complexes that make up Oakland, the heart of Pittsburgh's cultural center. Spacious, light-filled, contemporary buildings and generic modern office buildings make up the Pitt campus, but the architectural delight is a forty-two-story, neo-Gothic academic building, appropriately called the Cathedral of Learning, a national historic landmark. The stately and towering cathedral, with its unique Nationality Rooms, attracts one hundred thousand visitors annually. And contrary to images you may hold of inner-city Pittsburgh, the campus borders a 456-acre

Website: www.pitt.edu
Location: City
Total Enrollment: 26,329
Undergraduates: 17,424
Male/Female: 47/53
SAT Ranges: V 530–630
  M 530–640
ACT Range: 22–29
Financial Aid: 70%
Expense: Pub $ $ $
Phi Beta Kappa: Yes
Applicants: 13,565
Accepted: 62%
Enrolled: 35%
Grad in 6 Years: 60%
Returning Freshmen: 85%
Academics: ✍ ✍ ✍

(Continued)

Social: ☎ ☎
Q of L: ★ ★
Admissions: (412) 624-PITT
Email Address: oafa@pitt.edu

Strongest Programs:
Nursing
Business
Engineering
Philosophy
International Studies
History and Philosophy of
    Science
Information Science
History of Art and Architecture

city park. The state has granted Pitt nearly $140 million for renovations and new construction.

With ten undergraduate schools and more than 280 degree programs, Pitt rightfully claims to accommodate students with diverse needs. The academically motivated can take advantage of the excellent University Honors College, which one sophomore gushes is "the best thing at Pitt. It can do so much for any students taking a serious interest in their education." It offers "small, intensive classes so students can work with professors and do independent research." Honors students publish the *Pittsburgh Undergraduate Review*, which receives submissions from students nationwide. Pitt's extensive research programs are its finest asset. The University of Pittsburgh is one of the top twenty institutions in the nation in terms of the federal research dollars that it attracts, and for good reason. Pitt astronomers discovered what appear to be two new planets orbiting a nearby star, and its physicians were the first to utilize gene therapy on a person with rheumatoid arthritis. The schools of engineering and nursing are excellent and attract high-caliber students. Premed students can even watch transplants at the famed University of Pittsburgh Medical Center, which is one of the world's leading organ-transplant centers. On the arts side, faculty and students in the music department consistently rake in more awards and fellowships than their counterparts at other U.S. universities.

Pitt now offers guaranteed admission into graduate programs in communication science, public and international affairs, dental medicine, law, medical school, and physical therapy for outstanding freshman applicants. In two national studies, Pitt had four programs—philosophy, information science, history and philosophy of science, and nursing—ranked in the top six of their fields, and several others rated very high on the list. The College of Arts and Sciences (CAS) has academic requirements that include skill requirements in writing, quantitative and formal reasoning, foreign languages, and distribution requirements in the humanities, social and natural sciences, and foreign cultures. Psychology ranks among the most popular majors, and a heavily subscribed option permits students to combine a business major with a CAS degree. The university has a new Center for International Studies and has added a B.S. in scientific computing. Qualified freshmen may enter the School of Engineering, the College of Business Administration, or the School of Nursing, as well as the College of Arts and Sciences.

> "I have never met a professor who is not willing to help a student outside of the classroom."

For undergraduates who want to travel, the university cosponsors the Semester at Sea Program,* where students visit ports around the world and take classes at the same time. Closer to home, Pitt is a partner in the Pittsburgh Supercomputer Center, one of five such centers nationwide established by the National Science Foundation. The center houses the fastest computer in the world, performing one trillion calculations per second. There is also the Engineering Co-op, a program in which students alternate terms of study with work experience. Students in the co-op may take more than four years to graduate.

Pitt students take advantage of the school's flexible scheduling, which includes a strong evening program and summer sessions, and take on double and even triple majors, ensuring themselves of plenty of education and a degree that's well worth the money.

First-year students undergo an extensive orientation that includes three days in the summer focused on academics, another three days before the term starts, and a one-credit orientation seminar. Class sizes are not out of control. Out of 1,917 courses, 61 percent have fewer than twenty-nine students enrolled, and only 6 percent have one hundred or more. Most students agree that professors are very

The University Honors College offers "small, intensive classes so students can work with professors and do independent research."

approachable. "I have never met a professor who is not willing to help a student outside of the classroom," says a biology major.

Eighty-six percent of all undergraduates are from Pennsylvania, including a substantial number from the Pittsburgh area. African-American students account for 9 percent of the student body, Asian-Americans 4 percent, and Hispanics 1 percent. Incoming freshmen discuss diversity during orientation, and a cultural diversity fair is held at the beginning of the school year. To top that off, every student must take a pledge to promote civility on campus. The university admits students without reference to financial need, and 70 percent of undergraduates receive need-based financial aid. Pitt also offers six hundred merit awards of $1,000 to a full scholarship to qualified students. Athletic scholarships are also offered in nineteen varsity sports.

Incoming freshmen discuss diversity during orientation, and a cultural diversity fair is held at the beginning of the school year.

While student housing may have been scarce in the past, Pitt is working to increase the amount of on-campus living space. Thirty-five percent of full-time undergraduates live in on-campus university housing, which features eleven co-ed and single-sex dorms with liberal visitation hours and all kinds of rooming situations, from singles to seven-person suites. The new Bouquet Gardens apartments have been expanded, and more student housing will open as part of the new north campus. Sutherland Hall boasts a view of Oakland and the rest of the city and offers its own computing lab. Suites in McCormick and Brackenridge halls have two-story windows in the living rooms. Lothrop Hall tends to attract the quieter students and features attractive singles. Many students opt to live off campus "because it can be less expensive and students can have more freedom," says a biology major.

Pitt's urban location provides a wide variety of social activities. Within minutes of campus are shops, parks, museums, and sporting events. "I would say Pittsburgh is a great college town in which students can always find something to do," a sophomore says. Though only 10 percent of the men and 6 percent of the women belong to the Greek system, the fraternities and sororities play a vital role on campus. Many students say alcohol policies on campus are pretty tough for underage students. "Students somehow find a way to bring alcohol to campus," one student confides. "However, the penalties are severe when students get caught." A senior notes that under-twenty-one students caught drinking are referred to the Pittsburgh police department. Students feel safe on campus, considering the extensive network of campus lighting, emergency phones, the shuttle bus route, and an on-demand van system. In addition, Pitt students can ride the city PAT bus system for free to nearby neighborhoods to shop and go to coffeehouses, bookstores, or movie theaters. Adjacent Schenley Park offers ice skating, golfing, a pool, jogging trails, and tennis courts. Ski slopes and mountain trails are not far away, and road trips

> **"I would say Pittsburgh is a great college town in which students can always find something to do."**

to Penn State and Philadelphia, Boston, and New York City are popular. Although the Pitt Panther football team has endured some unhappy (read: losing) seasons of late, the university is striving to change that by bringing in new coaches. Men's basketball is also popular, and competition is heated in Big East hoops.

Pitt boasts innumerable resources and opportunities for its students in the sciences and the arts, and is improving not only in its academics, but in the caliber of its student body. Pitt is raising its sights and, in many cases, breaking records. The university is molding its offerings to fit in with the new fields, such as bioengineering, that are dominating headlines.

Overlaps

Penn State, Duquesne, University of Maryland, Carnegie Mellon, University of Delaware

If You Apply To ➤

Pitt: Rolling admissions. Financial aid: Mar. 1. Housing: May. 1. Does not guarantee to meet demonstrated need. Campus interviews: recommended, informational. Alumni interviews: optional, informational. SATs or ACTs: required. SAT IIs: optional. Accepts the Common Application and electronic applications. Essay question: optional.

Pitzer College: See page 139.

Pomona College: See page 140.

Presbyterian College

503 Broad Street, Clinton, SC 29325

A South Carolina liberal arts college that competes head to head with Wofford for students who want their education served up with plenty of personal attention. Programs in business and engineering complement those in the liberal arts. Lacks the urban allure of Oglethorpe or Furman.

Website: www.presby.edu
Location: Small town
Total Enrollment: 1,217
Undergraduates: 1,217
Male/Female: 46/54
SAT Ranges: V 500–600
  M 510–610
ACT Range: 21–26
Financial Aid: 59%
Expense: Pr $ $ $
Phi Beta Kappa: No
Applicants: 1,034
Accepted: 79%
Enrolled: 39%
Grad in 6 Years: 72%
Returning Freshmen: 83%
Academics: ✑ ✑ ✑
Social: ☎ ☎ ☎
Q of L: ★★★★
Admissions: (864) 833-8230
Email Address:
  admissions@presby.edu

Presbyterian College has come a long way since its 1880 founding, when William Plumer Jacobs created the school to provide "education at a higher level" for the children of a local orphanage. Today, PC students can choose from among thirty-one major fields, though they continue to pursue personal, spiritual, and academic growth guided by the school's creed: "While we live, we serve." This small liberal arts institution remains focused on its mission of helping the less fortunate. "I am surrounded by the type of people I would one day like to become," says a sophomore. "PC definitely has a higher purpose, and I'm glad to be a part of it."

The PC campus sits on 234 acres in the South Carolina piedmont. The redbrick buildings are largely Georgian in style, with tall white columns and lots of shade trees; many structures are listed on the National Register of Historic Places. The campus resembles Thomas Jefferson's University of Virginia, with buildings grouped around three plazas that offer great space for reading, studying, or throwing a football. Recent

"I am surrounded by the type of people I would one day like to become."

additions include a dorm for seniors and the Bailey Football Stadium for PC's Division II team. Each year, the team faces off against rival Newberry College for the Bronze Derby.

All PC students complete a core curriculum that includes courses in English, natural and social sciences, math, foreign languages, religion, history, fine arts, and physical education. In addition, students must attend ten Cultural Enrichment Programs a year, ranging from drama, film, and musical performances to lectures and panel discussions. Academically, PC is rigorous, and one student advises newcomers to expect two hours of homework for each hour spent in class. "I have never learned so much while trying to study so hard," says an overwhelmed freshman.

"The courses are challenging and force students to think." Presbyterian doesn't use teaching assistants, and students say faculty members are among the school's strongest asset. "All of our professors teach introductory level classes, up through the more specialized upper-level courses," says a history major. "At PC, students aren't just a number. Professors here make a point to get to know their students," having them over for dinner and attending college events with them. The most popular majors are business administration, political science, and biology; administrators say fine arts and modern foreign language are comparatively weak, because they have the most adjunct professors.

Students who feel PC's close-knit campus is a little too small have numerous options for off-campus study. During the May "fleximester," the biology department offers research and study trips to the Galapagos or Hawaiian Islands. The Oxford Program, which began in 1992, takes students to Oxford's Corpus Christi College in England. PC has also arranged study abroad programs in France, Austria, Spain, Mexico, China, Japan, Australia, and New Zealand. The Hansard Society for Parliamentary Government in London offers scholarships to students wishing to study and intern in the U.K., while the Russell Program allows students who remain on campus to focus on the media and society, with guest lecturers such as journalist Bill Moyers and former White House Press Secretary Dee Dee Myers. The honors program is open to sophomores, juniors, and seniors with GPAs of 3.2 or above. It incorporates meetings with deans and dignitaries; a series of seminar classes in great issues, thinkers, and literary works; and independent research opportunities.

"PC definitely has a higher purpose, and I'm glad to be a part of it."

Fifty-five percent of the PC student body hails from South Carolina, and minorities are a small but increasing presence on campus: African-Americans make up 4 percent of the students, and Hispanics and Asian-Americans add 1 percent each. You don't have to be Presbyterian to attend PC, but it helps, since roughly one third of the students are. "Students tend to be more religiously active than at other institutions," says a history and English major. Most are "white, upper-middle class, and generally from the southeastern United States." To address the lack of cultural diversity on campus, administrators have created the Southeastern Intercultural Studies Center, to promote diversity and global citizenship. "Many students are trying to open fellow students' minds to such issues as race, homosexuality and mental illness," says a business major. But a sophomore says that's an uphill battle: "South Carolina is the land of debutantes and Southern gentlemen, so an emphasis is placed on politeness. Social justice groups concerning race, gender and sexuality are becoming more visible, though."

Ninety percent of PC students live on campus, where all dorms are air-conditioned, and students say most are quite nice. "You can choose from a hall bath, suite-style, apartment-style, and town homes," says a freshman. "Only seniors can live off campus, and many do not even participate in this. If you would like a room, you have one." There's one dining hall and a small cafe on campus, and the chow "has come a long way" since the school outsourced food service to Sodexho, says an elementary education major. "Although students still complain, the food is good and diverse and edible," the student says. "Vegetarians are well taken care of."

The Greeks have a strong presence in social activities at PC—44 percent of the men and 43 percent of the women join up. Still, the school has taken a firm stand against underage drinking, and three violations of that policy results in a two-semester suspension. Since the town of Clinton (population 10,000) is relatively small, a freshman says road trips frequently take students "to Greenville to go out to eat, or dance at the Blind Horse," to Columbia (home of the University of South Carolina), or to Charleston. PC is equidistant from South Carolina's mountains and beaches,

Recent additions include the Bailey Football Stadium for PC's Division II team. Each year, the team faces off against rival Newberry College for the Bronze Derby.

The Hansard Society for Parliamentary Government in London offers scholarships to students wishing to study and intern in the U.K.

providing many opportunities to enjoy the outdoors. In addition, many students join campus clubs, which typically have at least one off-campus retreat each semester. Community service is also popular; Student Volunteer Services is the largest organization on campus, and half of PC's community takes part in some type of service activity. "Students play with kids, spend time with the elderly, or mentor a child," says a business major. Some also lead youth groups at local churches. Students also look forward to the annual Spring Fling and Homecoming celebrations, the candlelight Christmas service, and the outdoor graduation ceremony under the oaks, with bagpipes and trumpets heralding students and faculty in full academic regalia.

> "Students tend to be more religiously active than at other institutions."

PC's ten varsity sports teams call themselves the Blue Hose, a reference to the stockings of their Scottish ancestors. While some students wear kilts during athletic events, most are more conservative, says a sophomore: "Football games are social events, and everyone dresses up in their Sunday best to attend." Recent conference champions include the men's golf, tennis, and baseball teams and the women's soccer, tennis, and volleyball teams. The thirty-one-acre recreational facility offers lighted softball, football, and soccer fields, volleyball and horseshoe pits, a driving range, a basketball court, a track, and an amphitheater.

PC students are proud of their school's history and tradition, which includes its very own tartan. They feel lucky to be part of an up-and-coming college that places equal emphasis on academic excellence and spiritual growth. "When walking down the sidewalk, you are guaranteed to receive a smile and a 'Hello' from everyone you pass," says a junior. "The PC community is a lot like a family. People around here care about what is going on in your life."

Overlaps

Clemson, University of South Carolina, College of Charleston, Wofford, Furman

If You Apply To ➤

Presbyterian: Early action: Dec. 5. Rolling admissions. Meets demonstrated need of 88%. Campus interviews: recommended, informational. No alumni interviews. SAT or ACT: required. Accepts the Common Application and electronic applications. Essay question: what Presbyterian College's motto means to you; a risk you've taken, and its result and impact; issue of personal, local, national, or international concern; influential person.

Prescott College

220 Grove Avenue, Prescott, AZ 86301

Not a place where students fresh out of high school typically go. Those who succeed here love the outdoors and are looking for an alternative college experience. College of the Atlantic is the only other college in the *Fiske Guide* remotely comparable. If you loved Outward Bound, consider Prescott.

Future *Survivor* contestants take note: This tiny outpost in the wilderness of central Arizona is a perfect spot for the nature lover who seeks adventure, wants to learn survival skills, and likes studying outdoors. Where else but Prescott College could you major in adventure education or take courses like mountain search and rescue, ecopsychology, and wilderness rites of passage? Before any Prescott student sets foot in a classroom, the college sends him or her to the outback for three weeks of hiking and camping. Wilderness Orientation is an introduction to everything Prescott stands for: hands-on experience, personal responsibility, cooperative living, and stewardship of the environment.

Website: www.prescott.edu
Location: Small city center
Total Enrollment: 1,031
Undergraduates: 834
Male/Female: 42/58
SAT Ranges: M 450–610
V 500–660
ACT Range: N/A

Founded in 1966, Prescott retains the air of a 1960s commune. A senior says, "The student body of Prescott College tends to be fairly liberal 'hippy' whereas those of rival institutions are more conservative 'normal.'" Surrounded by national forest, the college's "campus" consists of a two-block-long handful of buildings in the small town of Prescott. The largest of the college's buildings was once a convent; its chapel is now used for meetings, art shows, and performances. Behind the chapel, a student center houses the Organic Alley and community garden, which was once a volleyball court. The architectural style of the campus ranges from the historic to the modern. A recent library expansion doubled the space available for book storage and study. Other new additions include labs for students in the biology, geology, agroecology, and geographical information science programs.

Prescott bills itself as a college "for the liberal arts and the environment," and most students envision themselves becoming teachers, researchers, park rangers, or wilderness guides. Adventure education, a major including everything from alpine mountaineering to sea kayaking, is a specialty.

"The quality of teaching at Prescott College is first class."

Also popular is environmental studies, which provides offerings of impressive breadth and depth for such a small school. The major in social and human development, a hodgepodge of sociology, psychology, and New Age mysticism includes such unorthodox courses as Dreamwork Intensive. Integrative studies has been separated into Cultural and Regional Studies and Human Development, and is "home" for core humanities and liberal arts areas such as religion, philosophy, and social sciences, as well as an "incubator" for new programs such as peace studies. Among the college's few concessions to practicality is the Teacher Education Program, which offers students teaching credentials in elementary, secondary, special, and bilingual education, and English as a second language. Prescott does not offer a comprehensive program in advanced math, chemistry, physics, or foreign languages other than Spanish. The school also lacks a developed sociology curriculum, which, given the state of sociology on most campuses, is not a major problem.

Prescott's requirements for graduation are characteristically unorthodox. Instead of grades, faculty members give narrative evaluations. And rather than accruing credits, students design individualized "degree plans" that outline the competence (major) and breadth (minor) areas they will pursue, and the Senior Project (thesis) they will complete to demonstrate competence (graduate). Students must also obtain two levels of writing certification (college level and thesis level), and math certification, showing knowledge of college-level algebra.

Prescott's calendar is divided into three periods, each with one ten-week quarter and one four-week block. During the quarters, students follow a traditional schedule, studying liberal arts and spending time doing fieldwork and student teaching. During the blocks, students pursue intense immersion in one course, most likely in the field, perhaps the backcountry of Baja, California, the alpine meadows of Wyoming, or even a local service clinic. Students can even take a one-month rafting trip down the Colorado River for credit! Summers may be spent studying field methods in agroecology at Prescott's thirty-acre Wolfberry Farm. Though Prescott does not offer a traditional study abroad program, it encourages students to take courses at the Kino Bay Center for Cultural and Ecological Studies in Mexico.

While Prescott carefully studies the global problems of the environment, it does so in an intimate localized setting. Each class is limited to twelve to fourteen students and the classes are always taught by professors. There's no tenure track at Prescott, so publishing and research take a backseat to teaching. According to a student, "The quality of teaching at Prescott College is first class." The one complaint is that the excellent but small classes mean that it is difficult to graduate in four years.

(Continued)
Financial Aid: 66%
Expense: Pr $
Phi Beta Kappa: No
Applicants: 129
Accepted: 89%
Enrolled: 69%
Grad in 6 Years: 41%
Returning Freshmen: 69%
Academics: ✎ ✎ ✎
Social: ☎ ☎
Q of L: ★ ★ ★ ★
Admissions: (800) 628-6364
Email Address:
  admissions@prescott.edu

Strongest Programs:
Education
Environmental Studies
Psychology
Visual/Performance Arts
Interdisciplinary Studies

Prescott students get a taste of a unique college experience before they ever attend a class when they are sent on a three-week backpacking trip. This Wilderness Orientation is an introduction to everything Prescott stands for: hands-on experience, personal responsibility, cooperative living, and stewardship of the environment.

Prescott bills itself as a college "for the liberal arts and the environment," and most students envision themselves becoming teachers, researchers, park rangers, or wilderness guides.

Liberal politics predominate and one student declares, "There are always political issues on campus, primarily anti war rallies and environmental awareness." Prescott's unconventional approach entices many well beyond Arizona. Indeed, 35 percent of students come from the Northeast; only 6 percent are in-staters. The minority population is small, with African-Americans, Hispanics, and Asian-Americans making up only 5 percent of the total. Part of the problem is the college's meager supply of financial aid. Since the school's endowment is just one million dollars, needy students rely on government loans and grants.

Because the college has no housing, students fend for themselves in the town of Prescott, a rapidly growing community of approximately thirty-five thousand where almost everything is accessible by bicycle. The college assists with the apart-

"There are always political issues on campus, primarily anti war rallies and environmental awareness."

ment hunt by providing lists of available properties and by cosigning leases when necessary. As for the townsfolk, students describe them as retirees who are extremely conservative. Prescott recently set up a meal plan, though many students still eat at home or in town. However, the student-run cafe is rumored to be "very good, catering to special tastes such as vegetarian, vegan, and organic."

Prescott social life is informal and spontaneous. Aside from environmental activities, Prescott offers a nationally recognized literary magazine, *Alligator Juniper*, and a chapter of Amnesty International. Those looking for nightlife can hit Whiskey Row, the town bar scene, or drive to Flagstaff (ninety minutes) or Phoenix (two hours). Though the college offers no athletics, students often participate in city sports leagues. Prescott's personal touch extends to graduation, a unique experience where a faculty member speaks about each student personally and then the student speaks on his or her own behalf.

Prescott may not have a huge campus or financial resources that are typically associated with larger schools; however, the small classes and interesting programs appeal to a student that would not be interested in your "typical" college. An environmental studies senior says, "If you are liberal and like the outdoors, then this college is perfect for you."

Overlaps

Evergreen State, Hampshire, Marlboro, Warren Wilson, Antioch

If You Apply To >

Prescott: Regular admissions: Feb. 1, Sep. 1. Does not guarantee to meet demonstrated need. Campus interviews: recommended, informational. No alumni interviews. SATs or ACTs: optional. SAT IIs: optional. Apply to particular school or program. Essay question: autobiography, past academic experiences, and reasons for attending Prescott.

Princeton University

110 West College, Princeton, NJ 08540

More conservative than Yale and a third the size of Harvard, Princeton is the smallest of the Ivy League's Big Three. That means more attention from faculty and plenty of opportunity for rigorous independent work. Offers engineering but no business. The affluent suburban location contrasts with New Haven and Cambridge.

Website: www.princeton.edu

At Princeton, exclusivity is endemic. Admissions officers brush off countless valedictorians, athletes, and legacies with the contents of one thin envelope—sans mercy. The number of applicants accepted keeps inching downward; if the percentage gets much lower, it will be a single digit. Those who get in find other entrances barred. Only graduating seniors may pass through a northern campus gate, such a sacred tradition that no uniformed sentries are needed to enforce it—no upstart undergraduates would dare step through it. But the wait to squeeze in through that narrow gate is well worth it. Undergraduates at Princeton are surrounded by intellect and intensity and 250 years of finely honed educational tradition, delivered today by some of the nation's most brilliant, scholarly stars. And since Princeton has begun replacing all loans in its financial aid packages with grants, more bright scholars are able to afford the place.

Cloistered in the secluded but upscale New Jersey town, Princeton's architectural trademark is Gothic, from the cavernous and ornate university chapel to the four-pronged Cleveland Tower rising majestically above the treetops. Interspersed among the Gothic are examples of Colonial architecture, most notably historic Nassau Hall, which served as the temporary home of the Continental Congress in 1783 and has defined elegance in academic architecture ever since. A host of modern structures, some by leading American architects Robert Venturi and IM Pei, add variety and distinction to the campus, but the ambiance is still quintessential Ivy League at its best. Among the newest additions are a new genomics institute and a new humanities center.

Princeton is distinctive in its scale (among the Ivies, only Dartmouth has a lower total enrollment) and its emphasis on undergraduates. For a major research institution, the university offers its students unparalleled faculty contact. "Top-notch teachers are here to help you develop every step of the way," says an economics major. With fewer graduate students to siphon off resources or consume faculty time than at large research universities, undergraduates get the lion's share of both; at last count, 70 percent of Princeton's department heads taught introductory undergraduate courses. Freshmen explore various texts and ideas that have shaped Western culture in interdisciplinary seminars taught by senior faculty members. Lovers of literature can study with Joyce Carol Oates, Paul Muldoon, or Toni Morrison, and nearly every other department has a few stars of its own. At least one or two of the small discussion groups that accompany each lecture course are led by senior professors, and the seminar program for freshmen based in the residential colleges further enhances student–faculty interaction. Every liberal arts student must fulfill distribution requirements in epistemology and cognition, ethical thought and moral values, historical analysis, literature and the arts, quantitative reasoning, social analysis, and science and technology. Students must also take writing courses. During their junior year, liberal arts students work closely with a faculty

> "There are no factories, toxic-waste dumps, or smokestacks, contrary to popular belief."

member of his or her choice in completing two junior papers—about thirty pages of independent work each semester in addition to the normal courseload. Princeton is also one of the few colleges in the country to require every graduate to complete a senior thesis—an enterprise that serves as a culmination of their work in their field of concentration. As a result, "Seniors develop close personal relationships with their thesis advisor," says one student.

As one might expect, Princeton's small size means the number of courses offered is smaller than at other Ivies, but lack of quantity does not beget lack of quality. Princeton's math and philosophy departments are among the best in the nation, and English, physics, economics, molecular biology, public policy, and romance languages are right on their heels. Princeton is one of the few top liberal arts universities with equally strong engineering programs, most notably chemical, mechanical, electrical, and aerospace engineering, and computer sciences (which has its own facilities). In fact, the department of civil engineering and operations research has

(Continued)

Location: Small town
Total Enrollment: 6,537
Undergraduates: 4,613
Male/Female: 52/48
SAT Ranges: V 680–770
    M 700–793
Financial Aid: 50%
Expense: Pr $ $ $ $
Phi Beta Kappa: Yes
Applicants: 14,521
Accepted: 11%
Enrolled: 74%
Grad in 6 Years: 96%
Returning Freshmen: 99%
Academics: ✍ ✍ ✍ ✍ ✍
Social: ☎ ☎ ☎
Q of L: ★ ★ ★
Admissions: (609) 258-3060
Email Address: N/A

Strongest Programs:
Physics
Molecular Biology
Public Policy
Economics
Philosophy
Romance Languages
Computer Science
Math
English

Princeton's math and philosophy departments are among the best in the nation, and English, physics, economics, molecular biology, public policy, and romance languages are right on their heels.

split into two departments: civil and environmental engineering and operations research and financial engineering. One of Princeton's best-known programs is the prestigious Woodrow Wilson School of Public and International Affairs ("Woody Woo" to the students), which admits undergraduates on a selective basis. The university has undertaken a major effort to become a national center in the field of molecular biology, with a laboratory for teaching and research staffed by twenty-eight faculty members, including one who shared the Nobel Prize in medicine in 1995.

Princeton's semester system gives students a two-week reading period before exams in which to catch up, with first-term exams postponed until after New Year's, much to the dismay of many ski buffs and tropical sun worshipers. The university honor code, unique among the Ivies, allows for unproctored exams. The outstanding library facilities embrace five million volumes and provide five hundred private study carrels for seniors working on their theses; there are another seven hundred enclosed carrels in other parts of the campus.

About 10 percent of the student body take advantage of the opportunity to study abroad. Except for students with sufficient advanced standing to complete their degree requirements in three and a half years, leaves of absence must be taken by the year, not the semester, an impediment to "stopping out." The university does offer an intriguing five-year program that includes intense language in an Asian country. There is also a five-year program that leads to a B.S.E. and M.E. in mechanical and aerospace engineering. A limited number of courses can be taken on the pass/fail option and the University Scholars program provides especially qualified students with what the administration calls "maximum freedom in planning programs of study to fulfill individual needs and interests." Although the faculty gets high ratings for its academic advising, students are rather cool on the university's nonacademic counseling programs.

"Top-notch teachers are here to help you develop every step of the way."

The majority of Princeton undergraduates are "highly organized, highly competitive, goal-oriented" students, both in terms of academics—high school valedictorians make up 45 percent of each class—and extracurricular activities. African-American and Hispanic enrollment combined now stands at 14 percent, with Asian-American at 14 percent. While diversity is present, mixing is often not. "As an African-American, I can say that even the African-Americans are subdivided based on economics, place of origin, and whether you went to public or private school," explains one senior. And the campus remains socially conservative, with tweed and penny loafers adorning many students. Artists aren't a dominant social force on campus, but the administration hopes that renovations of the arts facilities, coupled with a $5.9 million expansion of the art gallery, will make the university more appealing to future Picassos and Baryshnikovs. Princeton undergraduates are admitted to the university without regard to their financial need, and those who qualify for aid get an appropriate package of benefits. There are no merit or athletic scholarships, but Princeton's financial aid package is generous to middle-class families. Each student's Princeton experience begins with a week of orientation; five hundred each year participate in Outdoor Action, a few days of wilderness activities immediately preceding orientation.

In an attempt to improve the quality of life for freshmen and sophomores, Princeton has grouped many of its dorms into residential colleges, each with its own dining hall, faculty residents, and an active social calendar. Under this system, nearly all the freshmen and sophomores live and dine with their residential college unit, alleviating the formerly fragmented social situation. However, by providing a separate social sphere for these students, the system "creates a gulf between underclassmen and upperclassmen." And all too often the upper-level eating clubs steal the thunder from the college's social events. As a result, "the underclassmen spend too much time pining for the day when they, too, can join the closest thing Princeton has to cliques," says one student.

The university's turn-of-the-century Gothic dorms may look like crosses between cathedrals and castles, but conditions on the inside are often less glamorous. Some halls have amenities, including living rooms and bay windows. Several new dorms have helped ease the space crunch somewhat, and a new residential college that will house both under- and upperclassmen is on the drawing board. Less than 3 percent of the students live off campus. The modern and roomy Spelman dorms, which come complete with kitchens, are the best on campus and fill up quickly every year with seniors who do not belong to eating clubs.

Ah, yes, the eating clubs. Princeton's most firmly entrenched bastions of tradition. Run by students and unaffiliated with the school, they line Prospect Avenue, and have, for more than a century, assumed the dual role of weekend fraternity and weekday dining hall. Of the eleven, six admit members through an open lottery, but the other five still use a controversial selective admissions process called bicker (because of the wrangling over whom to admit), to the embarrassment of the administration and most of the students. While many of the clubs opened their doors to women back when Princeton went co-ed, two of the oldest and most exclusive—the Ivy Club and the Tiger Inn—remained all-male until 1991, when a court decision compelled them to admit women. Now, all the clubs are co-ed.

Catering exclusively to upperclassmen, the clubs provide a secure sense of community for their members. More than half of all sophomores join one of the clubs at the end of the year, becoming full-fledged members by the fall of their junior year. Annual dues vary; the most expensive is the Ivy Club, which charges its members almost five thousand dollars a year. Unfortunately, the social options for those who choose not to join are limited. Some opt for life in independent dormitories or join the handful of Greek fraternities and sororities (not sanctioned by the administration) that have sprung up on campus over the past few years.

Princeton's campus is self-contained, but those who venture outside its walls will find the surroundings quite pleasing. "There are no factories, toxic-waste dumps, or smokestacks, contrary to popular belief," states one student. One side of the campus abuts quaint Nassau Street, which is dominated by chic (and pricey) boutiques and restaurants, most out of the range of student budgets, although coffee shops and affordable restaurants are becoming more prevalent. The other side of campus ends with a huge man-made lake that was financed by Andrew Carnegie so that Princetonians would not have to forgo crew. Students rarely venture much farther than New York or Philadelphia, each one hour away (in opposite directions) on the train. Few students complain about boredom, and many praise the affluent town of Princeton for the parks, woods, bike trails, and, most important, the quiet and safety it offers students. McCarter

"Seniors develop close personal relationships with their thesis advisor."

Theatre, adjacent to campus, is the nation's seventh-busiest performing arts center and houses Princeton's Triangle Club, which counted Jimmy Stewart and Brooke Shields as members. The roundup of annual campus events includes Communiversity Day, an international festival, and the P Party in the spring, which features a big-name band. Each year about two thousand students engage in volunteer activities such as tutoring, working in soup kitchens, or helping the elderly.

Princeton has the oldest licensed college radio station in the nation, plenty of journalistic opportunities, a prestigious debating and politics society (Whig-Clio) whose ranks included James Madison and Aaron Burr, and a plethora of arts offerings. The sports program includes several national championship teams, including men's lacrosse, men's heavyweight crew, men's lightweight crew, and women's softball. The women's rugby club is also outstanding, having won its second straight

A host of modern structures, some by leading architects Robert Venturi and IM Pei, add variety and distinction to the campus, but the ambiance is still quintessential Ivy League at its best.

national title as part of a fifty-nine-match winning streak. The men's basketball team is a phenomenal success, and has represented the Ivy League in numerous NCAA championship tournaments. Well-attended events are found on the intramural fields, where teams from the eating clubs and residential colleges compete. Every fall, the freshman and sophomore classes square off in Cane Spree, an intramural Olympics that has been a tradition since 1869.

It's easy to be humbled at Princeton. Even the most jaded students must be awed and inspired when they think of those who've traversed the campus paths before them: former U.S. presidents James Madison and Woodrow Wilson attended the university, as did writer F. Scott Fitzgerald, to name just a few luminaries. While some may find the ambiance too insular, not many turn down membership in this very exclusive—and rewarding—club.

<table>
<tr><td>

Overlaps

Harvard, Yale, Stanford, MIT

</td></tr>
</table>

<table>
<tr><td>

If You Apply To ➢

</td><td>

Princeton: Early decision: Nov. 1. Regular admissions: Jan. 2. Financial aid: Feb. 1. Guarantees to meet demonstrated need. Campus interviews: optional, informational. Alumni interviews: recommended, informational. SATs: recommended. SAT IIs: recommended (engineering applicants required to take either physics or chemistry and math I or II). Accepts the Common Application. Essay question: changes every year.

</td></tr>
</table>

Principia College

Elsah, IL 62028

Prin is a tiny college in a tiny town about an hour from St. Louis. All students have ties to Christian Science. Prin is mainly liberal arts, though it offers popular programs in mass communications and history. More than two-thirds of the students travel abroad.

<table>
<tr><td>

Website: www.prin.edu
Location: Rural
Total Enrollment: 550
Undergraduates: 550
Male/Female: 47/53
SAT Ranges: V 530–660
  M 520–660
ACT Range: 22–29
Financial Aid: 80%
Expense: Pr $ $
Phi Beta Kappa: No
Applicants: 230
Accepted: 83%
Enrolled: 60%
Grad in 6 Years: 77%
Returning Freshmen: 93%
Academics: ✍ ✍ ✍
Social: ☎ ☎ ☎
Q of L: ★ ★ ★ ★
Admissions: (618) 374-5181
  or (800) 277-4648 x2802

</td><td>

Principia College students shun smoking, drinking, and drugs for the high that comes from their common faith, Christian Science. Located an hour from St. Louis, this small liberal arts school is a haven for students who want to do everything and be everywhere, combining activities and interests that might be impossible at larger schools. "People aren't narrowly categorized," explains a sophomore business major. "I am able to train and play varsity football, get straight A's and be on the honor roll, work a student job, be involved in my house's activities, work on my spiritual side, and still have a life." Clearly, sleep is a secondary priority!

Principia's 2,600-acre campus, located on limestone bluffs above the mighty Mississippi River, was designated a National Historic Landmark in 1993. The dominant architectural influences are colonial American, Tudor, and medieval, and many

"The majority of students are true thinkers, seeks of truth, believers in issues, and overwhelmingly lively and creative."

buildings—including most dormitories—were designed by California architect Bernard Maybeck. A contemporary of Frank Lloyd Wright, Maybeck urged Principia trustees to bring the college to its current spot when they relocated from St. Louis in 1935. The College Chapel, whose bells ring out hymns every evening, is the symbolic center of campus.

Students say Principia's strongest programs include religion, business, biology, sociology, and studio art. Mass communication majors can hone their craft at the school's working television studio and FM radio station. The science center provides an aviary, greenhouse, thirteen lab rooms, and a computer weather center.

</td></tr>
</table>

Nonmajors tend to avoid the natural sciences because of their difficulty, and math, because it "has the most requirements," says a sophomore. In addition to ten to twelve courses in the major, students must complete one course each in foreign language and the arts, and two courses each in literature, history, religion and philosophy, social science, lab science, and math, computer science or natural science. Students must take four physical education courses and pass a swim test. The First-Year Experience includes a two-week writing seminar, held before fall courses begin, as well as a freshman housing program.

Principia operates on the quarter system, meaning that students get only ten weeks to master the material in each of their courses. Academics and grades are a focus, but "competition among students is rare," says a senior. "The courses and professors focus on individual growth." Prin's faculty members generally receive high marks. "Since this is such a small school, even the lower-level courses are taught by experts," says a physics and math major. All courses taken by freshmen have twenty-five or fewer students, providing intimate discussion forums and plenty of individualized attention.

Over a given four years, about 68 percent of Principia students participate in the five or six study abroad programs the school organizes each year. Each program enrolls eighteen to twenty-two students, either during a quarter or the six-week inter-term, from mid-November to January. Sites are determined by academic subject and focus, and have included countries from France, Germany, and Austria to Nepal, Indonesia, and Mongolia. Faculty

"We always joke that if Prin was in L.A., it would be perfect."

members and resident counselors have also taken Prin groups to U.S. locations such as Hawaii and Puerto Rico, and to San Francisco for business internships. A geology field-study course enables students to help excavate the remains of a woolly mammoth found on campus. And in 2001, the Prin Solar Car Team finished seventh in the Chicago-to-Los Angeles American Solar Challenge, beating schools such as MIT and Stanford.

Only 10 percent of Prin students hail from within Illinois, and although African-Americans, Asian-Americans and Hispanics each comprise less than 1 percent of the student body, an impressive 15 percent of Prin students arrive from abroad. About 15 percent of each year's new students are transfers from other colleges, and there is a small but growing contingent of nontraditional students, those over 23, who are returning to school or beginning college. "The majority of students are true thinkers, seeks of truth, believers in issues, and overwhelmingly lively and creative," says a philosophy major.

Virtually all students (99 percent) live in Prin's dorms, except for the few who are married or live locally with their parents. A sophomore says rooms are "very comfortable and spacious, larger than my room at home." The freshman dorms are "gorgeous," a senior agrees, noting that upper-class residences "have a family-like atmosphere." After the first year, most students become "house" members and stay in the same building—similar to a sorority or a fraternity—for the rest of their time at Prin. Still, a business major says, "it's fairly easy to switch dorms for a change." Students can submit recipes to the dining service, and in addition to the grill station and a sit-down pub and restaurant, "there is always a salad and fruit bar, plenty of cereals, desserts, and drinks to choose from."

Settled in the 1800s, Elsah, Illinois, is "far from being a college town," one student says. "We always joke that if Prin was in L.A., it would be perfect. In reality, our college is right next to a big river and some cornfields." The town of Edwardsville, about 30 minutes away, offers stores and restaurants, and the zoo and museums of St. Louis are about an hour distant, so those with cars make friends fast. As Christian Scientists, students eschew alcohol, tobacco and drugs, and Prin also asks them

(Continued)
Email Address:
collegeadmissions@prin
.edu

Strongest Programs:
Education
Studio Art
History
Biology/Natural Resources
Business Administration

A geology field-study course enables students to help excavate the remains of a woolly mammoth found on campus.

The Public Affairs Conference is the oldest student-run event of its type, bringing in big-name speakers such as Colin Powell and Jimmy Carter.

to sign a pledge of abstention from premarital and extramarital sexual relationships. So instead of partying, students keep busy at school-sponsored concerts, movies, dances, or intramural sporting events. Annual dorm celebrations, such as the Howard Luau and the Lowery Rumpus, draw crowds, as does the Whole World Festival, where international students show off their cultures' unique cuisine and clothing. The Public Affairs Conference is the oldest student-run event of its type, bringing in big-name speakers such as Colin Powell and Jimmy Carter.

Principia's Panthers compete in Division III, and rivals include Blackburn College and Washington University (MO), especially in baseball, soccer, football, and basketball. In recent years, Prin has produced All Americans in women's cross-country and indoor and outdoor track and field. Campus athletic facilities include a four-court indoor tennis center, a field house with gym and pool, and outdoor courts and running trails.

Prin's students take pride in their adherence to and love for Christian Science. While this makes for a conservative—even restrictive—campus climate, they don't seem to mind. The "school is far from home, and the small, tight-knit community gives me and others a comforting sense of family," says a senior. "Students here tend to be really open, friendly, and warm."

Overlaps

Indiana, UC–Santa Barbara, UCLA, Ball State, UC–Santa Cruz

If You Apply To ➤

Principia: Rolling admissions: Jan. 15 (scholarship candidates), March 1. Financial aid: March 1. Meets demonstrated need of 90%. Campus interviews: recommended, informational. No alumni interviews. SATs: required. SAT IIs: optional. Accepts electronic applications. Essay question: book, movie, painting poem or other creative endeavor that's affected you, and why; what makes you tick; your passion in life, and how college will help you attain or express it; or what integrity means to you, and how you apply it in your daily life. Only college in the world that admits only Christian Scientists.

University of Puget Sound

1500 North Warner, Tacoma, WA 98416

Ask anyone in Tacoma about UPS—the university, not the parcel service—and they'll tell you that Puget Sound delivers solid liberal arts programs with a touch of business. With easy reach of the Sound, the university specializes in all things Asia. Compare to Willamette and Whitman.

An ambitious building program and revised core curriculum are helping raise the profile of the University of Puget Sound, transforming it from a regional liberal arts college in sleepy Tacoma into an undergraduate institution with the potential for national recognition. As part of the new core, students will be required to demonstrate foreign language proficiency and pass two freshman seminars and a capstone seminar. What won't change are the school's emphasis on Asia (every three years, a nine-month Pacific Rim–Asian studies education tour takes thirty-five lucky students to eight Far Eastern nations) and its close-knit community.

Founded in 1888, UPS is cradled by the Cascade Range and the rugged Olympics, with easy access to the urban energy of Seattle and the natural beauty of Mount Rainier. The ninety-seven-acre campus boasts carefully maintained lawns, native fir trees, and plenty of other greenery, thanks to the omnipresent rain. Most buildings, with distinctive arches and porticos, were built in the 1950s and 1960s, and the administration building, Jones Hall, was completely renovated in 2001. The fifty-seven-thousand-square-foot Trimble Hall dorm was finished in 2002, with

Website: www.ups.edu
Location: Suburban
Total Enrollment: 2,846
Undergraduates: 2,592
Male/Female: 40/60
SAT Ranges: V 580–685
M 580–670
ACT Range: 25–29
Financial Aid: 57%
Expense: Pr $ $ $ $
Phi Beta Kappa: Yes
Applicants: 4,154
Accepted: 72%
Enrolled: 22%

suite-style apartments for two to six students each. In 2002–2003, an all-weather track was added to Payton Field and field dimensions were updated to accommodate soccer and lacrosse. In September 2003, UPS opened a new 3,850-square-foot Sculpture House, with facilities for welding, woodwork, and painting.

UPS students must complete an eight-course core curriculum, which includes a freshman seminar in writing and rhetoric, and another in scholarly and creative inquiry. In the first three years at Puget Sound, students also study five "Areas of Knowing"—fine arts, humanities, math, natural sciences, and social sciences. An upper-level integrative course, Connections, challenges traditional disciplinary boundaries and examines the benefits and limits of an interdisciplinary approach to learning. There's also a senior capstone course. Additionally, first-years may participate in writing seminars, a highly selective classics-based honors program, and the Business Leadership Program.

After navigating Puget Sound's requirements, students may pursue a bachelor of arts, bachelor of science, or bachelor of music degree. The most popular majors are business, psychology, and biology, followed by English and politics and government. The university has also developed a reputation as a jumping-off point to Asia—both literally and figuratively. Its curriculum stresses two of the fastest-growing fields in the region: Asian studies and Pacific Rim economics. Nearly one-third of Puget Sounders take at least one Asian studies course, and once every three years, there's that nine-month school-sponsored trip through Japan, Thailand, Korea, India, and Nepal, where participants study native art, architecture, politics, population, and philosophy. UPS has added a major and minor in science, technology and society, and minors in environmental studies and African American studies. The minor in psychology has been dropped, and the physical therapy program is now for graduate students only.

Regardless of the department or program, students say the academic climate here is competitive, though most competition is internal. "Students strive to do their best, and the course load is usually heavy," says an economics major. "The classes are small, and teachers go by their first names," adds a religion and theater major. Three-quarters of the classes taken by freshmen

"Freshman advising sessions will often be over pizza and soda, with the help of both a professor and an upperclassman."

have twenty-five students or fewer, and all but 1 percent of the rest have fifty students or less. "Freshman advising sessions will often be over pizza and soda, with the help of both a professor and an upperclassman," a junior says. "The Academic and Career Advising center helped me blend my interests in technology and business to develop a four-year plan double majoring in business and computer science."

While UPS may not be as well-known outside the Pacific Northwest, only 30 percent of its students hail from Washington. African-Americans and Hispanics make up 5 percent of the student body. Asian-Americans constitute 10 percent, and an active Hawaiian student organization sponsors a number of events, including a massive annual luau. "The campus falls left of center politically, but just barely," says a religion major. "The school and students enjoy open communication about controversial topics," a religion and theater major agrees. Puget Sound offers 872 merit scholarships, ranging from $1,000 to $9,000, for achievement and promise in general academics and specific areas such as music, art, and debate. There are no athletic scholarships.

Sixty-four percent of Puget Sound students live on campus, and housing is guaranteed for freshmen, who are sprinkled among the ten dorms. Students say Phibbs and Todd are the best choices for first-years; all rooms have high-speed Internet access and voicemail. "Rooms are big and have nice wooden furniture," says a senior. After the first year, students may go Greek and live in chapter housing,

(Continued)

Grad in 6 Years: 74%
Returning Freshmen: 88%
Academics: ✑ ✑ ✑ ½
Social: 🕿 🕿 🕿
Q of L: ★ ★ ★ ★
Admissions: (253) 879-3211
Email Address:
   admission@ups.edu

Strongest Programs:
Asian Studies
Business Administration
Biology
Psychology
English
Politics and Government
International Political Economy

The university has also developed a reputation as a jumping-off point to Asia—both literally and figuratively. Its curriculum stresses two of the fastest-growing fields in the region: Asian studies, and Pacific Rim economics.

pursue a single room in the dorms, or apply for one of sixty university-owned theme houses, which focus on substance-free lifestyles, social justice, or outdoor adventures. Other options include four foreign language houses. Aside from the main campus dining area—which is open around the clock and offers Mexican, Chinese, and Italian stations plus salad and deli bars—students, faculty, and staff can chow down at the Pizza Cellar, "which has great ice cream and milk shakes," and at the student-run Diversions Cafe.

Twenty percent of men and 29 percent of women at UPS go Greek, though fraternities and sororities don't dominate the social scene. "Most off-campus events are house parties and quiet get-togethers," a senior says. "Weekends reflect participation in sports, theater and musical performances, and downtime from a busy week." Popular school-sponsored activities include the Log Jam BBQ, which kicks off the school year, and Foolish Pleasures, a festival of short student-produced films. UPS follows

> **"The school and students enjoy open communication about controversial topics."**

state and federal laws when it comes to alcohol, meaning those under twenty-one can't drink, but determined students can usually find booze anyway. Tacoma's "art scene is terrific, and the numerous restaurants are a definite perk," says an economics major, but "it is a city I would love to live in and raise a family," not a college town. Still, there's no concern about boredom. With the mountains and beaches so close—Seattle is thirty minutes away by car, Portland is two hours south, and Vancouver, British Columbia, is three hours north—road trips are de rigueur. That's especially true during ski season, and UPS rents out all the necessary equipment.

Students are fond of saying that Puget Sound's Division III varsity teams, the Loggers, "Kick Axe." Among the teams that have brought home conference championships in recent years are women's volleyball, men's golf and cross-country, and men's and women's soccer and swimming. The school's archrival is Pacific Lutheran University, and students turn out to cheer during the annual UPS–PLU gridiron match-up.

Students at the University of Puget Sound may look like they just stepped out of an American Eagle Outfitters catalog, but don't let the slacker-chic casual clothes fool you. UPS means business and serious study for students seeking immersion in the liberal arts and the natural beauty of the outdoors. "The location, student autonomy, quality of education and size of the student body make this college a wonderful place," says a senior. "The people here have become my friends, and have taught me how to be a student and a good person at the same time."

Overlaps

University of Washington, Lewis and Clark, Whitman, Willamette, Colorado College

If You Apply To ➤

Puget Sound: Early decision: Nov. 15, Dec. 15. Regular admissions and financial aid: Feb. 1. Housing: May 1. Meets demonstrated need of 43%. Campus interviews: recommended, evaluative. Alumni interviews: optional, informational. SATs or ACTs: required. SAT IIs: optional. Accepts the Common Application and electronic applications. Essay question: topic of your choice or one of the following: original work's effect on your thinking; what you wish you'd known before entering high school, experiences with diversity; your ideal admission committee; how your hometown has shaped your outlook on life; goal you hope to accomplish in your lifetime; qualities of your ideal roommate and what about you will be most difficult for your roommate to handle.

1080 Schleman Hall, West Lafayette, IN 47907-1080

Purdue is Indiana's state university for science and technology—with side helpings of business, health professions, and liberal arts. Compare to Kansas State and Big Ten rival Michigan State.

Successful Indiana colleges have three things in common: a strong agricultural program, a powerhouse basketball team, and a conservative student body. Purdue University has all of these—plus one of the nation's strongest engineering programs, and the distinction of having awarded more bachelor's degrees in the field than any other institution. Purdue is also home to the nation's first computer science department, and its programs in pharmacy, nursing, and management are likewise strong. Budding classicists, dramatists, and vocalists probably should look elsewhere, as liberal arts are not Purdue's forte. But those seeking small-school friendliness with big-school spirit may be very happy here. "It's a big campus with a plethora of activities, majors, schools, and people," says a sophomore. "It just feels like home, even though I'm not originally from here," a junior agrees.

Purdue is the main attraction in the small industrial town of West Lafayette, where the population triples when students return each fall. The campus features redbrick and limestone buildings arranged around lush shaded courtyards. New buildings include the School of Management's Rawls Hall, a visual and performing arts, and the Earhart Dining Hall, named for famed aviator Amelia Earhart, who was once a career counselor here. The Ross-Ade Stadium, home to Boilermaker football, has been renovated as well.

Students apply to and enroll in one of Purdue's ten schools, and academic requirements vary with the school and the major. Typically, they include English, math, a lab science, and perhaps speech or foreign language proficiency. Management is the most popular program, followed by electrical and computer engineering, communications, elementary education, and computer science. Students flock to the five-year engineering co-op program, one of the most competitive on campus, because it marries classroom study with real-world work. Purdue also offers a strong undergraduate program in flight technology, which includes hands-on training at the university's own airport. Purdue has graduated twenty-one astronauts, including Neil Armstrong and Gus Grissom. Also strong are programs in veterinary medicine and hospitality and tourism. The physical education major has been dropped.

Purdue students are focused on life after graduation; a junior says they tend to avoid the organizational leadership and supervision program "because there aren't a lot of jobs that you can get with it." And despite the university's size, about half of freshman classes are seminar-style, taught by graduate students and academic advisors who help answer students' questions and provide career advice. "Every year, I have had a good blend of large lectures (taught by professors), small classes (taught by TAs or professors), and labs," says an animal sciences major.

Purdue's student body is fairly homogeneous, with about two-thirds from Indiana and only 9 percent minority: 3 percent African-American, 4 percent Asian-American, and 2 percent Hispanic. Students are a "hard-working, mature, and skillful" bunch, says a speech pathology major, who are "willing to study a lot, open to all types of people, and into having fun and being polite." Although some complain that the campus looks like the world's biggest Abercrombie & Fitch catalog,

> **"It's a big campus with a plethora of activities, majors, schools, and people."**

Website: www.purdue.edu
Location: Small city
Total Enrollment: 38,564
Undergraduates: 30,908
Male/Female: 58/42
SAT Ranges: V 500–610
   M 530–660
ACT Range: 23–28
Financial Aid: 71%
Expense: Pub $ $ $
Phi Beta Kappa: Yes
Applicants: 22,872
Accepted: 76%
Enrolled: 37%
Grad in 6 Years: 64%
Returning Freshmen: 88%
Academics: ✍ ✍ ✍ ½
Social: ☎ ☎ ☎
Q of L: ★ ★ ★
Admissions: (765) 494-1776
Email Address:
   admissions@purdue.edu

Strongest Programs:
Engineering
Technology
Science
Agriculture

New buildings include the School of Management's Rawls Hall, a visual and performing arts center for the School of Liberal Arts, and the Earhart Dining Hall, named for famed aviator Amelia Earhart, who was once a career counselor here.

Boilermaker pride does stretch across boundaries of race, gender, and socioeconomic background. Numerous scholarships are available to academic and athletic standouts.

Thirty-six percent of students live in Purdue's dorms; the numbers may be so low because of rules governing male and female visitation hours. (The notion of a "co-ed dorm" here means that both sexes share a dining hall and a lobby.) Almost all freshmen live on campus, though they aren't required to, and Harrison Hall is said to be a good pick for newbies. "The rooms are clean and comfortable," says a sophomore. "The roommate-matching service worked really well my freshman year, too." Students say, however, that it's become harder to get a room as the student body has grown. Most upperclassmen find inexpensive housing just off campus, where walking and riding escorts, blue-light phones, and more than forty campus police officers help them feel safe.

Officially, Purdue is as dry as Death Valley, and "people have been kicked out of the residence halls for being caught with alcohol," says a sophomore. Still, underage students get served at the frats, or—as at most schools—when friends over twenty-one are buying. Those of age may also frequent Harry's Chocolate Shop—a longtime bar, not a candy store. Overall, Greek life draws 17 percent of men and 14 percent of women and offers many social opportunities. But there are other options, too, says an animal science major, including football, basketball, soccer, and baseball games. "There are movies for $2.50 on the weekends," the student adds. "There's also a bowling alley, arcade, and billiards room on campus." Purdue's more than 621 campus organizations range from the BBQ society to professional development clubs.

As far as college towns go, West Lafayette "may not be exciting, but it's still pretty fun," one student says. "There are lots of ways for students to get involved with the community: Food drives, mentoring children, Habitat for Humanity, volunteering in homeless and crisis centers, and working with religious groups." Chicago and Indianapolis are favored weekend destinations for students with cars, and each spring, a week of fun and parties leads up to the Grand Prix go-cart races.

"The rooms are clean and comfortable." Students also look forward to the Slayter Slammer, a free Labor Day weekend concert on the school's main hill, and the Bug Bowl, an annual celebration sponsored by Purdue's entomology department, including cricket-spitting and cockroach races.

Purdue's all-purpose athletic facility offers opportunities for weekend warriors and varsity athletes alike. Boilermaker pride manifests itself at Division I games of all types, especially when the opposing team is Indiana University, known derisively as "that school down south," in the annual struggle for the Old Oaken Bucket. Every year, the winner adds a link to a chain on the bucket, in the shape of either an "I" or "P." Women's volleyball and softball and men's and women's basketball are among the most popular sports on campus. Also notable is Purdue's rivalry with Notre Dame.

A strategic plan developed two years ago has Purdue focused on reaching "the next level of preeminence," through discovery, learning, and engagement—adding more professors and scholarship funding and decreasing the number of teaching assistants. What the happy students here have already discovered is that learning is fun when academics are mixed with a healthy dose of school spirit and general carousing. "I've made so many great friends here," sighs a sophomore. "It's so great to be at a large university and still run into people I know all over campus."

Purdue: Rolling admissions, financial aid and housing: Mar. 1 (priority consideration). Does not guarantee to meet demonstrated need. Campus and alumni interviews: optional, informational. Apply to particular schools or programs. SATs or ACTs: required. SAT IIs: optional (English composition, math, and lab science for home-schooled students). Accepts electronic applications. No essay question.

Queen's University: See page 335.

Randolph-Macon Woman's College

2500 Rivermont Avenue, Lynchburg, VA 24503

In its glory days, Randolph-Macon was one of the premier women's colleges in the nation. The coming of coeducation to places like Washington and Lee has cut into R-MWC's market, but it still manages to field fine programs in the liberal and fine arts. Unlike pastoral Sweet Briar, R-MWC has a suburban location.

Randolph-Macon Woman's College may not have men on campus, but devoted students say that's about all that it lacks. With rich traditions, homey dorms, and challenging, seminar-based classes, the school has preserved the best elements of its past, while evolving into an institution that remains relevant today. Students incorporate independent study, research, internships, and extracurricular activities into their individualized education plans, graduating not only with knowledge and strong friendships, but also with confidence, grace, and poise. "I immediately found a small, close-knit group of quirky intellectuals to be a part of, and now I think we are all attached at the hips—I hope for life!" says a sophomore. "That's a priceless thing."

R-MWC's one-hundred-acre campus sits in a lovely residential area of Lynchburg (population 80,000), on the banks of the James River. The old and majestic buildings, arranged in a semicircle, are covered with purple wisteria and surrounded by grand trees that burst into riotous bloom each spring. Glass corridors called trolleys link nearly all campus buildings. Main Hall, dating from 1893, offers student housing, classrooms, and faculty and administrative offices. The Maier Museum of Art houses works by Andrew Wyeth, Mary Cassatt, Georgia O'Keefe, and James McNeil Whistler, fertile ground for museum studies majors. A new playing field complex and bookstore opened in spring 2002, and architectural renderings have been completed for the physical education building and library renovations. The school's one-hundred-acre equestrian center is in the nearby Blue Ridge foothills.

All Randolph-Macon students complete general education requirements reflected in a matrix of study areas, with artistic expression, cultural inquiry, global issues, gender issues and quantitative literacy and analysis on one axis, and arts and literature, humanities, natural sciences and math, wellness, and interdisciplinary courses on the other. Freshmen take the one-semester First-Year Seminar, which explores the value of a single-sex liberal arts education, and examines ways to maximize academic success. R-MWC has established new interdisciplinary programs in American studies and environmental studies; students in the 3–2 Engineering Program can take advantage of the new engineering physics major, and aspiring nurses

Website: www.rmc.edu
Location: Residential
Total Enrollment: 764
Undergraduates: 764
Male/Female: 0/100
SAT Ranges: V 540–640
   M 510–620
ACT Range: 23–28
Financial Aid: 61%
Expense: Pr $ $
Phi Beta Kappa: Yes
Applicants: 723
Accepted: 85%
Enrolled: 33%
Grad in 6 Years: 63%
Returning Freshmen: 77%
Academics: 🖊 🖊 🖊
Social: ☎ ☎
Q of L: ★ ★ ★ ★
Admissions: (800) 745-7692
Email Address:
   admissions@rmc.edu

Strongest Programs:
Psychology
Biology
English
International Studies
Fine Arts

may select a partnership program with Johns Hopkins. "Most of the students are independent women with an active interest in their education and future," says an English literature and dance major. "No students attend this school just to have a good time."

The sciences get high marks at Randolph-Macon, with biology and psychology the most popular majors. English ranks third, helped by "visiting authors and poets reading on campus weekly," says a sophomore. Political science and international studies round out the top five choices. No matter which classes students choose, they will find devoted and skilled professors. "I think if I stand close to some professors long enough, I will absorb knowledge just from the smart-vibes they give off," quips a creative writing and history major. Students interested in research may compete to assist professors with ongoing projects. "Students take full advantage of office houses to speak with their professors," a junior says. "Students also expect a lot of feedback and advice—there is very much a 'mentor' aspect to professor–student relationships." Courses are rigorous—"If you get an A, you know that you have worked hard and earned it," says a sociology major—but there's little grade-grubbing.

> **"I immediately found a small, close-knit group of quirky intellectuals to be a part of."**

Though the R-MWC community is small, students need not worry about claustrophobia; worldliness is a part of life here. The Global Studies Initiative sponsors immersion programs in South Africa and Zimbabwe, peace studies in Nagasaki and Hiroshima, and a theater seminar in London and Stratford. Randolph-Macon also participates in the Seven-College Exchange,* giving students the chance to spend a year or semester at the University of Reading in England, the Universidad de las Americas in Mexico, or the University of Economics in Prague. And the college participates in American University's Washington Semester program and the Tri-College Exchange. Two-thirds of R-MWC students take off-campus internships, with organizations and businesses from the Chicago Lyric Opera to Washington's Kennedy Center for the Performing Arts and the Centre for European Policy Studies in Brussels.

Forty percent of Randolph-Macon women hail from Virginia. Minorities are a sizable presence, with Hispanics and Asian-Americans adding 3 percent each, and African-Americans making up 8 percent. The African-American Woman's Alliance encourages awareness of and respect for differences, and Randolph-Macon is also a member of the International 50, a group of colleges committed to multiculturalism.

> **"R-MWC attracts an abnormally intelligent crowd."**

"Opinions, convictions, political persuasions are not held against anyone, nor does anyone feel that have to walk on eggshells," says an English literature and education major. "Lesbianism on campus seems to be an issue with some people, but they're in the minority," agrees a sophomore. "Basically, everyone here has her own beliefs, and others tend to respect her for it. If you're closed-minded, though, don't come here—you will probably be ostracized." There are no athletic scholarships, and merit scholarships range from $4,000 to full tuition.

Eighty-seven percent of Randolph-Macon students live in the dorms, which are "wonderful," says a senior. "Rooms are fairly large, and we get a lot of storage space. The carpets and furniture are well-maintained, as are the hall bathrooms." Main Hall, once nicknamed "the Hilton," is the largest dorm, and its central location makes it the most convenient. All rooms are linked to the campus computer network and are wired for cable TV. Campus chow is so good, one student says, that "the community comes to our dining hall for lunch sometimes." Security officers patrol continuously between 4 p.m. and 8 a.m. and take pride in knowing students by name. Men may not walk around campus unaccompanied.

Weekends find as many as half of R-MWC's students heading off campus for parties at nearby schools with men such as Hampden-Sydney, the Virginia Military

(Continued)
Classics

The Maier Museum of Art houses works by Andrew Wyeth, Mary Cassatt, Georgia O'Keefe, and James McNeil Whistler, fertile ground for museum studies majors.

Security officers patrol continuously between 4 p.m. and 8 a.m. and take pride in knowing students by name. Men may not walk around campus unaccompanied.

Institute, and Washington and Lee. On campus, "we have dances, mixers, and other social events, if you are into that sort of thing," says a sophomore. "And then, if you're into going to IHOP in medieval garb at 3 a.m., you can do that, too. The best road trip is definitely to Charlottesville, where you can see Monticello and eat at Michie Tavern." Charlottesville, an hour away, is also home to the University of Virginia, another popular destination for those seeking frat parties and football. Students also make the three-hour trek to Washington, D.C., by car, bus, or train. Underage drinking is prohibited at R-MWC, in accordance with state and federal law. It still happens, though RAs patrol the dorms to catch violators, so students suggest imbibing behind closed doors.

The town of Lynchburg, which hosts two other colleges, is "very safe and very beautiful, but the fun is to be found elsewhere," says a junior. "If you like industrial towns with little to do, or you don't care about an active night life, then Lynchburg is the town for you," a sophomore grumbles. Most clubs in the area are twenty-one and over, and the few restaurants, stores and movie theaters close by 10 p.m. The college's upscale bookstore stays open late to satisfy students' caffeine cravings—and that's no inconsequential task. "R-MWC attracts an abnormally intelligent crowd, because you have lots of folks like me and my friends, who would rather drink milk from champagne glasses as we psychoanalyze Brutus and Cassius and translate *The Lives of Twelve Caesars* from Latin on Saturday nights," says an English and history major.

Randolph-Macon's Wildcats compete in Division III, and the school's top rival is nearby Sweet Briar. The equestrienne team brought home a conference championship in 2002–2003. But more than athletic contests, students look forward to college traditions, such as the Odd-Even rivalry (referring to the year in which students will graduate), Ring Week (in which a freshman anonymously decorates the door of a junior and leaves her small gifts all week, culminating with a scavenger hunt for her class ring), and the Pumpkin Parade (during which sophomores and seniors, not to be left out, scour campus in search of carved pumpkins). The Never-Ending Weekend each fall includes both a formal and the annual Tacky Party, for which tasteless attire is required.

The women of R-MWC aren't shy about their academic goals, career drive, or sense of campus unity and sisterhood. "I love participating in silly traditions with my friends, and crying when the school song is sung by our a cappella group," agrees an English literature and dance major. "I know I am making memories here that I will cherish always."

Randolph-Macon's athletic teams compete in Division III, and the school's top rival is nearby Sweet Briar. The equestrienne team brought home a conference championship in 2002–2003.

Overlaps

Sweet Briar, College of William and Mary, University of Virginia, Virginia Tech, Mary Washington

If You Apply To ➤

R-MWC: Early decision: Nov. 15. Rolling admissions and financial aid: Mar. 1. Does not guarantee to meet demonstrated need. Campus interviews: recommended, informational. Alumni interviews: optional, informational. SATs or ACTs: required. SAT IIs: optional. Accepts the Common Application and electronic applications. Essay question: inspirational fictional character, historical figure, or work of art, dance, music, theater, or literature; an experience where you "did the right thing" in spite of your feelings; or a topic of your choice.

University of Redlands

1200 East Colton, P.O. Box 3080, Redlands, CA 92373-0999

BEST BUY

If you like the thought of palm trees against a backdrop of snow-covered peaks, Redlands may be your place. Though a "university," Redlands is about the same size

as Occidental and a hair bigger than Whittier. The alternative Johnston Center makes an odd contrast with the buttoned-down conservatism of the rest of Redlands.

Website: www.redlands.edu
Location: City outskirts
Total Enrollment: 1,800
Undergraduates: 1,600
Male/Female: 47/53
SAT Ranges: V 490–610
   M 500–610
ACT Range: 21–27
Financial Aid: N/A
Expense: Pr $ $ $
Phi Beta Kappa: Yes
Applicants: 1,848
Accepted: 83%
Enrolled: 24%
Grad in 6 Years: 63%
Returning Freshmen: 78%
Academics: ✍ ✍ ✍
Social: ☎ ☎ ☎
Q of L: ★ ★ ★
Admissions: (800) 455-5064
Email Address:
   admissions@uor.edu

Strongest Programs:
Government
English
Creative Writing
Biology
Chemistry

About 10 percent of the students here opt for an experimental living/learning college where students create their own course of study and are judged by self- and professor evaluations rather than grades.

Amid the dozens of gigantic and well-known universities in the state of California stands the University of Redlands. With its innovative living/learning college and strong preprofessional emphasis, this versatile school is one of higher education's better-kept secrets, and a place where students receive all the personal attention they could want. One student describes it as a "small liberal arts college in sunny Southern California with great financial aid packages."

The University of Redlands' 140-acre campus, covered in majestic oak trees, is designed around "The Quad," a group of dorms that face one another. The two main landmarks are the Memorial Chapel and the administrative building. Redlands' facilities are a mixture of older, more historical columned buildings and more modern, renovated ones. The view from the college can only be described as breathtaking. Mountain ranges form the backdrop, and neighboring Big Bear Lake and Arrowhead ski resorts give endless getaway opportunities. Also nearby are the San Gorgonio Wilderness and Joshua Tree National Park. For those looking for big city adventures, Los Angeles is only an hour away.

One of Redlands' most distinctive attributes is its experimental living/learning college where students create their own course of study and are judged by self- and professor evaluations, rather than grades. The Johnston Center for Integrative Studies was established in 1969 to function as an "alternative" college within a traditional setting; about 10 percent of the students here take advantage of this opportunity. The program offers unusual academic freedom; there are no departments, majors, or distribution requirements. Instead, students "contract" with professors for their entire plan of study. At the beginning of each course, students make up the syllabus by consensus and then set their own research and writing goals. Each student develops four-year goals—which are reviewed by a student–faculty board for direction and breadth—within one or more broad areas: the social sciences, behavioral sciences, humanities, and fine and performing arts.

Compared with other Redlands students, Johnston undergrads are better qualified academically, with average SATs that are 50 to 75 points above the Redlands median. One student explains, "Johnston center students tend to be independent thinkers, self-motivated, and [don't] take classes just because they have to." Johnston's enrollment declined in the late '70s and '80s as students became very career-oriented and found that alternative education no longer fit their needs. Fortunately, student interests and needs have once again changed, and Johnston is seeing its highest enrollment in nearly two decades.

Aside from Johnston, Redlands is unusual among liberal arts institutions mainly in that it also offers professional programs. The schools of education and music provide strong career training, as does the excellent program in communicative disorders. Business is the most popular major, followed by integrative studies, psychology, government and political science, and English. The environmental studies program consists of courses in natural science, humanities, and social science focusing on values-based environmental problem solving. Students can receive degrees in environmental studies, environmental science, and environmental management. Redlands has also emerged as a national leader in science curriculum reform. An example is the introduction of Calculus in Context, which focuses on discovery-based learning principles. It has been so successful that in a recent year the percentage of students taking second-semester calculus nearly doubled from 45 to 85 percent.

The liberal arts foundation gives students the fundamental skills essential to effective learning and scholarship by challenging them to examine their own values and the values of society. With its 4–1–4 calendar, Redlands has students take one intensive course each January. Students may also choose among sixty study abroad options in Europe, Asia, Africa, and Latin America. The highly acclaimed freshman seminar program places small groups of first-year students with some of the school's best professors, while the selective honors program enables outstanding students to work individually with professors, who are very accessible outside of class and occasionally even come by the dorms for "fireside chats." "Freshmen are always taught by full professors," says one sophomore, and a writing major declares that at Redlands, "the professors are the school's biggest asset." Most students agree that Redlands' laid-back academic atmosphere is much appreciated.

Fifty-seven percent of the student body comes from within the state, creating a mellow, Southern California atmosphere on campus. The climate is a definite plus, with temperatures rarely below fifty degrees. The typical Redlands student tends to be fairly conservative, although one student reports that the minority of liberals are quite vocal. The racial makeup of the school is fairly

"Freshmen are always taught by full professors."

diverse, with Hispanics representing a solid 8 percent, Asian-Americans 7 percent, and African-Americans 4 percent. About half of the graduating class each year moves on to graduate schools, while the other half heads into the workforce. Redlands annually awards a variety of merit scholarships, ranging from $1,500 to full tuition. There are talent awards in art, writing, music, and debate, but there are no athletic scholarships.

Students have nothing but rave reviews for the dormitories in which 89 percent of the students live all four years. "Each dorm has a personality of its own," exclaims one student. "The dorms are comfortable and complete with Ping-Pong and pool tables," raves a sophomore. Most of the dorms are co-ed, though there is an all-woman dorm. Students agree that freshmen should check out Merriam Hall first. Other housing options include on-campus apartments and student-run co-ops. Students enjoy their food in the new dining hall, part of the $9 million Hunsaker University Center. Students can mingle in the "town square" atmosphere of the center's bookstore, cafe, and student-life offices.

The Southern California heat and smog can become unpleasant, and students with wheels often flee Redlands on weekends for healthier pleasure spots along the California coast or in the mountains. But overall, social life is centered around campus activities. Local fraternities and sororities claim 26 percent of men and 21 percent of women as members, and their parties are open to all, but

"Each dorm has a personality of its own."

even these parties are rarely raucous. Road trips to Hollywood, Palm Springs, San Francisco, the beach, and even Mexico are common. Despite the school's enforcement efforts, alcohol is fairly accessible. "It is very easy. Students operate bars out of their rooms," reports one student.

The sports program injects a measure of excitement into the social scene, and about seven out of every ten students join at least one intramural team. The swimming and water polo teams are enjoying a brand-new facility, and Redlands has won two recent national championships in women's water polo. But the team that has long been a national power in Division III is men's tennis. Football has made a resurgence, with the team winning the conference three times and advancing to the NCAA championships twice in the last seven years. Also competitive are men's basketball and Frisbee, and women's basketball, softball, and volleyball. But the team to watch is, to no one's surprise, the debate team—a perennial powerhouse.

The University of Redlands is a lot of different things to a lot of different people. With hardly more than one hundred faculty members, it manages to be a preprofessional institute, a liberal arts college, and an alternative school all in one.

Redlands is unusual among liberal arts institutions mainly in that it also offers professional programs.

The Southern California heat and smog can become unpleasant, and students with wheels often flee Redlands on weekends for healthier pleasure spots along the California coast or in the mountains.

Overlaps

UC–San Diego, University of San Diego, Occidental, UC–Riverside, Pitzer

The Johnston Center is clearly a path to travel for the innovative individualist, but even those who don't join Johnston will likely find what they want and need at Redlands.

<table>
<tr><td>If You

Apply

To ≫</td><td>Redlands: Regular admissions: rolling. Scholarship deadline: Dec. 15. Financial aid: Feb. 15 (for merit scholarship), Mar. 2 (need-based aid). Does not guarantee to meet demonstrated need. Campus interviews: recommended, evaluative. Alumni interviews: optional, informational. SATs or ACTs: required. SAT IIs: optional. Essay question: personal statement.</td></tr>
</table>

Reed College

3203 S.E. Woodstock Boulevard, Portland, OR 97202

Reed is like a West Coast version of Oberlin or Grinnell, mixing nonconformist students with a traditional (and rigorous) curriculum. Only two-thirds of first-year students graduate in six years, a function of Reed's demands and the fact that its students often live close to the edge.

Website: www.reed.edu
Location: City outskirts
Total Enrollment: 1,389
Undergraduates: 1,363
Male/Female: 46/54
SAT Ranges: V 660–760
 M 620–710
ACT Range: 29–32
Financial Aid: 57%
Expense: Pr $ $ $ $
Phi Beta Kappa: Yes
Applicants: 1,847
Accepted: 55%
Enrolled: 30%
Grad in 6 Years: 70%
Returning Freshmen: 85%
Academics: ✑ ✑ ✑ ✑ ½
Social: ☎ ☎ ☎
Q of L: ★ ★ ★ ★
Admissions: (503) 777-7511
Email Address:
 admission@reed.edu

Strongest Programs:
Biology
Chemistry
Psychology
English
Philosophy
History

Reed College is one of the most intellectual colleges in the country. In fact, this hotbed of liberalism has produced thirty-one Rhodes scholars, forty-eight Fulbright scholars, and two winners each of the Pulitzer Prize and the MacArthur "genius grant." Reed is a place where students complain that the libraries, which close their doors at midnight on Fridays and Saturdays, shut down too early. "I have finally found a place where other people are as intellectual as I am," gloats a senior math major. "Reedies discuss classes even when class is over, and read interesting books just for fun." They also don't get grades, instead receiving lengthy and detailed comments from professors that foster continued dialogue about their work.

Located just five miles from downtown Portland, Reed's one-hundred-acre campus boasts rolling lawns, winding lanes, canyon creek, and protected wetlands. Fish ladders have been installed to help salmon reach their spawning grounds, and non-native plants are being removed from the area to protect the natural habitat. In addition to the canyon, the campus hosts 125 different species of trees. Two thousand majestic arbors shade a mix of original campus buildings, constructed of brick, slate, and limestone in the Tudor Gothic style, as well as lodges in the homey Northwest Timber style, and some more modern facilities. The 23,000-square-foot Educational Technology Center and a $5.5 million library expansion were completed in August 2002.

Although Reed emphasizes personal freedom and responsibility, especially through its Honor Principle, the curriculum and requirements are traditional. All freshmen must complete Humanities 110, a year-long interdisciplinary course focused on society and culture in archaic and classical Greece and imperial Rome. The course, which has been taught for more than a half-century, draws on the expertise of twenty-five professors, including some of Reed's most senior and distinguished faculty. Students must also take courses in four "breadth" areas: literature, philosophy, and the arts; history, social science, and psychology; natural science; and mathematics, logic, linguistics, or foreign languages. Juniors must pass a qualifying examination in their major departments and all seniors must submit a thesis to graduate. On the due date, just after spring classes have ended, seniors march from the library steps to the registrar's office in the Thesis Parade, inscribe their names on a giant thermometer known as the Thesis Meter, and then throw the Renn Fayre, a weekend-long party that involves "a bug-eating contest, Glow Opera, and the ball drop," says a history major.

(Continued)
Physics

Despite Reed's small size—84 percent of the courses taken by freshman have twenty-five students or fewer, and it just gets better from there—the school offers unsurpassed intellectual opportunities in the liberal arts and sciences. The Gray Fund helps make

"I have finally found a place where other people are as intellectual as I am."

this possible by funding field trips and other cultural and social programs. Budding physicists and environmental scientists can work with college staff at the 250 kilowatt Triga nuclear reactor, after passing an eight-hour Atomic Energy Commission examination. Study abroad programs attract about 30 percent of each graduating class, taking students to a dozen countries, from Israel and Italy to Germany and China. Reed also offers domestic exchange programs with Howard, Sarah Lawrence, and the Woods Hole Oceanographic Institute. Dual-degree (3–2) programs include engineering, computer science, forestry, and environmental science.

All of these academic options tend to keep Reed students tied to their computers and study carrels. "Most Reedies are confirmed bookworms," says a senior. "Reedies can easily go from relativity to Aristotle to *The Simpsons* in a single sentence." A classmate agrees, characterizing students here as "driven, intelligent, passionate, idealistic, and committed to academic pursuit. Students here do not try to just 'get by,' and are not simply here for a degree." You'll never find a TA at the lectern here, or leading a group discussion, so students rarely attend class unprepared for the lively intellectual banter that typically ensues between inquiring and active minds. Over the years, a quarter of Reed's grads have gone on for Ph.D.s, the highest percentage of any liberal arts college in the country.

While Reed is located in Oregon, its quirky brand of intellectualism means only 18 percent of the students are in-staters. Six percent hail from abroad, and nine percent are minorities—4 percent each Asian-American and Hispanic, and 1 percent African-American. "Most of the students fit the sort of dorky, tragically hip social milieu," says a history major. "Of course, you have the more sporty, straight-and-narrow types, too. The thing to remember is that a Reedie comes in almost any shape or size, though not necessarily any political leaning." (An English major says social and

"Reedies can easily go from relativity to Aristotle to *The Simpsons* in a single sentence."

political debates here "are primarily between moderate liberals and far-leftists.") Reed's orientation program, called "Freshpeople," includes a three-day backpacking trip, organized forays into Portland, and community service projects. Hot-button issues on campus include racism, free speech, affirmative action, and the war in Iraq, says a sociology major. "Students tend not to be as politically active as they like to think they are, but most are very socially and politically aware," says a math major.

Sixty-five percent of Reed students live on campus in the co-ed or single-sex dorms, which usually house fewer than thirty people each. Some rooms feature such homey touches as fireplaces or balconies. Freshmen are guaranteed housing, and usually get divided doubles; upperclassmen get singles, though "recent resurgence in the desire to live on campus makes rooms hard to come by," says a history major. Old Dorm Block and Anna Mann are said to be most popular choices for first-years, and all rooms are connected to the campus computer network. For those who lose out in the housing lottery, or upperclassmen seeking a taste of postcollege independence, off-campus share houses are cheap and plentiful. On-campus students must buy the meal plan, and students say outside caterer Bon Appetit does a good job, with salad and sandwich bars and grill and entree stations available each day at lunch and dinner. Vegetarian and vegan choices are offered, too.

Over the years, a quarter of Reed's grads have gone on for Ph.D.s, the highest percentage of any liberal arts college in the country.

Students say Portland is a great college town—"big enough to accommodate just about any niche, but small enough where you feel part of a whole," says a senior. The vibe is similar to Seattle, with plenty of technology, coffee—and rain. "It's friendly (especially to pedestrians and bicyclists), and actually rather charming," says an English major. "The music and arts scene is lively, and the quality of the restaurant scene is seriously top-notch, but in a way that college students can be interested in (affordable!)." Aside from low-key parties and gatherings with friends on and near campus, Reed students love to road trip—whether to the mammoth Powell's bookstore downtown (about a fifteen-minute drive) or to Oregon's coastal beaches, mountains, or high desert, all about two hours away. The school also owns a ski cabin on Mt. Hood that sleeps thirty.

Where there are college students, there is also alcohol, though drinking is not a high priority here. Reed follows federal and state laws, meaning that those under twenty-one may not imbibe. However, use of alcohol or drugs is governed primarily by the Honor Principle, which "makes for an atmosphere in which those who use substances are safely in view," one student says. "The ideal environment is one in which you can trust students to make their own decisions, intelligently and maturely." While Reed doesn't have competitive athletics (except for women's rugby, which competes with other clubs in the area), students look forward to Paideia, a week-long program of wacky alternative classes before spring semester begins. Named for the ancient Greek festival of learning, Paideia's non-credit workshops from range from Skittle appreciation to a *South Park* marathon, and from how to get into law school to how to make Shrinky Dinks. The Halloween social is noted for its "utter zaniness" and "uninhibited bodily movements." The closest thing Reed has to an official school mascot is the Doyle Owl, a three-hundred-pound concrete sculpture that dorms regularly plot to steal from one another. But because residents of the Pacific Northwest place such a premium on outdoor activities and general fitness, students do appreciate the newly renovated sports center, with squash and paddleball courts, a swimming pool, weight room, and other facilities.

One thing is for sure—Reed is not the right choice for everyone. But if you're a firmly committed intellectual who leans left politically and prefers to spend Saturday nights with your nose in a book, this nontraditional Portland school is worth a look. The emblematic school T-shirt sold in the bookstore bears the slogan "Atheism, Communism, Free Love." A senior says that dates back to the 1970s, "when it was a literal statement of truth. These days, it's true in spirit, and more than a little self-parodying."

Overlaps

Oberlin, UC–Berkley, Brown, Stanford, NYU

If You Apply To ➤

Reed: Early decision: Nov. 15, Jan. 2. Regular admissions and financial aid: Jan. 15. Housing: June 15. Does not guarantee to meet demonstrated need. Campus and alumni interviews: recommended, evaluative. SATs or ACTs: required. SAT IIs: recommended. Accepts the Common Application and electronic applications. Essay question: personal statement of student's choice or from the Common Application; why Reed; and a graded writing sample.

Rensselaer Polytechnic Institute

110 Eighth St., Troy, NY 12180-3590

If you can spell Rensselaer, you've already got a leg up on many applicants. RPI is one of the nation's great technical universities, along with Caltech, MIT, Worcester

Polytech, and Harvey Mudd. The beauty of RPI is the chance for hands-on learning and synergy between technology and management.

Students at Rensselaer learn by doing. The research university gives them hands-on control of the learning process in everything from the renowned engineering programs to the new electronic arts major. While they may have been known as geeks in high school, the students come to Rensselaer to find a home among their own. "The students here are used to being the 'elite' in their respective high schools," one management freshman says. "Because everyone's pretty smart, you have to get used to being average again." Students at RPI use technology and their own imagination to make their mark on the world.

Set high on a bluff overlooking Troy, New York, Rensselaer's 260-acre campus mixes modern research facilities and classical, ivy-covered brick buildings dating to the turn of the century. Recently, the school completed a $9.3 million renovation of the student union, conceal- ing in its atrium a state-of-the- art wireless computing network that serves two hundred students on the building's two upper floors. Construction on two new major facilities—one for research in biotechnology and interdiscipli- nary studies, the other a center for electronic media and performing arts—has begun. A $7 million computer center contains one of the largest computer graphics laboratories in the nation; RPI is a national leader in the study and application of electronic media, and recently introduced a B.S. program in electronic arts.

> **"Because everyone's pretty smart, you have to get used to being average again."**

It would be an exaggeration to say that technology is "God" at RPI, though the school's conversion of a Gothic chapel into a computer lab does hint in that direc- tion. Even if it's not deified, technology remains omnipresent at this school, which pioneered the teaching of calculus via computer in the early '90s, and has been named one of Yahoo!'s most-wired campuses. Not surprisingly, all students are required to have their own laptop computer. Studio courses foster small-group interaction between students and professors, after which students return to their workstations for collaborative problem solving. RPI, which made its reputation as one of the nation's premier engineering schools, continues to excel in traditional favorites such as chemical and electrical engineering, as well as newer specialties like environmental and computer systems engineering. Computer science is the most popular major, followed by mechanical and electrical engineering, manage- ment, and the notoriously difficult, five-year architecture program. The nuclear engineering department has its own linear accelerator, while graduate and under- graduate students participate in research at the Center for Industrial Innovation.

RPI's Lally School of Management and Technology combines elements of a business school with the latest technical applications. Entrepreneurship is one of its specialties; budding entrepreneurs may participate in the Lally "Business Incu- bator," a support system for start-up companies run by Rensselaer students and alumni. RPI students are required to take courses in entrepreneurship or have an "entrepreneurial experience" before graduation. The B.S. program in information technology continues to attract top students, who often combine it with course- work in e-commerce or the arts. Majors in the humanities and social sciences are limited, and their quality is directly related to their applicability to technical fields. Some students dismiss those programs as "too easy." Still, all students must complete at least twenty-four credits in these areas, as well as at least twenty-four credits in physical, life, and engineering sciences, a minimum of thirty credits in their majors, and a writing or writing-intensive course. "Some- times sleep is not an option—the coursework is that rigorous," a senior majoring in bioinformatics says.

Website: www.rpi.edu
Location: City outskirts
Total Enrollment: 9,145
Undergraduates: 5,139
Male/Female: 74/26
SAT Ranges: V 580–680
 M 640–720
ACT Range: 24–28
Financial Aid: 77%
Expense: Pr $ $ $ $
Phi Beta Kappa: No
Applicants: 5,580
Accepted: 70%
Enrolled: 27%
Grad in 6 Years: 78%
Returning Freshmen: 91%
Academics: ✐ ✐ ✐ ✐
Social: ☎ ☎ ☎
Q of L: ★ ★ ★
Admissions: (518) 276-6216
Email Address:
 admissions@rpi.edu

Strongest Programs:
Architecture
Engineering
Humanities and Social
 Sciences
Information Technology
Management and Technology
Science

About two-thirds of Rensselaer students are undergraduates, a high percentage for a top engineering school; because of this, RPI has worked hard to ensure that classes are smaller and more attention is paid to individual needs. Professors are extremely knowledgeable, and the quality of teaching is excellent. "I've thoroughly enjoyed and obtained a great knowledge from my professors," a management major says. "There are none like them." Juniors and seniors enjoy self-paced courses and occasionally paid positions helping with faculty research. Career counseling is helpful, and academic advisors get mixed reviews. All of the effort pays off: 69 percent of a recent RPI senior class went on to jobs after graduation, and 27 percent entered graduate or professional school.

For students who can't wait to start working, popular co-op programs in more than a dozen fields help them earn both money and credit. Those who already know what field they'll pursue may enter a seven-year dual degree program in medicine, a six-year program in law, and four- and five-year master's programs in biology, geology, and mathematical science. Although most engineering schools discourage studying abroad, Rensselaer offers exchange programs in several European countries, most notably at Switzerland's renowned Federal Institute of Technology.

About half of RPI students are New Yorkers, and 91 percent ranked in the top quarter of their high school class. RPI is fairly diverse, with Asian-Americans comprising 12 percent of the student body, African-Americans 4 percent, and Hispanics 5 percent. A slogan warns male students to import their girlfriends, since males outnumber females three to one. Students tend to be bright, studious, and technically savvy. "Students here are the type that likes to take apart things and see how they work," one computer systems major says. "They differ from other students at rival schools because they look at reality more than theory." RPI is far from a center of political activism; students say they're just too busy. "Students are so apathetic that it's pathetic," one senior says. "They only care about their computers." The biggest campus issue may be choosing the Grand Marshal, who oversees a boisterous week-long carnival celebrating campus elections, during which professors are forbidden from giving tests.

"Sometimes sleep is not an option— the coursework is that rigorous."

Fifty-five percent of students live in university residence halls; freshmen are required to live on campus and, for the fall term, must buy the meal plan. The residence halls are well maintained and clean. "I have found the rooms to be comfortable," a freshman says. All bedrooms have fast Internet connections for every resident. In recently constructed Barton Hall, even the laundry room is wired for fast access to the Internet and RPI's campus network. Upperclassmen may keep their current room, enter the lottery to get something better, or live in college-owned apartments off campus, widely considered the nicest option. About half of RPI upperclassmen live in fraternity and sorority houses, where meals are served family-style; 35 percent of men and 20 percent of women go Greek.

Social life "is very good for the people who want it," one student says, but the male/female ratio is a major hassle, forcing lovelorn men to haunt Russell Sage (next door) or Skidmore (forty minutes away) in hopes of finding a mate. While the proactive can find something to do, a junior says, "many students like to play computer games and complain about not having a girlfriend." Other than Greek parties, weekend options at RPI include sporting events, live entertainment, concerts, movies, and a half-dozen local pubs—some of which students find easily accept fake IDs. Those under twenty-one can't have alcohol in the dorms, and fraternities aren't allowed to have "containers of mass distribution" (i.e., kegs) at parties; students are split as to whether those not of age are easily served. Extracurricular clubs, organized around such interests as chess, dance, judo, and skiing, are chartered and funded by a student-managed body that doles out more than $8 million annually.

Free shuttle buses run regularly from campus to downtown Troy, a former industrial revolution town, but there aren't many good reasons to make the trip. "Troy has been called 'a city of urban renewal without the renewal,'" one student says. "It is very much not a college town." Students and Greek groups do get involved with community service projects, though, and the town offers opportunities for internships. A six-screen movie theater is within easy reach, and for a taste of bigger-city nightlife, Albany is a half-hour drive. For scenic excursions, the Berkshires, Catskills, Adirondacks, Lake George, Lake Placid, the Saranac Lakes, Montreal, and Boston are popular destinations.

The athletic scene at Rensselaer revolves around hockey, hockey, hockey, the school's only team playing in Division I. One of the biggest weekends of the year is Big Red Freakout, when all festivities center around cheering on the beloved Big Red. "Hockey at RPI equals insanity," one student says. "If you go to one hockey game all season, go to the men's hockey season opener. The place is packed with rowdy RPI students who scream and chant in unison." "Hockey has huge events and draws a big crowd all the time," adds another. RPI offers eighteen full scholarships to hockey players each year. Other varsity teams play in Division III, and the football, baseball, men's and women's basketball, and women's ice hockey and field hockey teams are most popular. Each year, Rensselaer's football players vie with rival Union College for the coveted Dutchman's Shoes, while a fitness center helps even nonvarsity players sculpt six-pack abs.

Students at RPI learn cutting-edge technology in an atmosphere based on teamwork and collaboration. They thrive on figuring out how things work. They work hard—sometimes to the detriment of a social life. "Students at RPI are all a little bit nerdy, and proud of it," a computer engineering major says. "The types of things that might be looked at strangely at other colleges are accepted here."

Overlaps

Cornell, MIT, Carnegie Mellon, Rochester Institute of Technology, Worcester Polytechnic Institute

If You Apply To ➢ **Rensselaer:** Early decision: Nov. 15. Regular admissions: Jan. 1. Financial aid: Feb. 15. Meets demonstrated need of 68%. Campus and alumni interviews: optional, informational. SATs or ACTs: required. SAT IIs: optional (required for all accelerated program applicants). Accepts the Common Application and electronic applications. Apply to particular programs. Essay question: significant experience or achievement; influential person; or how your work will impact the twenty-first century; others depend on program.

University of Rhode Island

Kingston, RI 02881

URI is a smallish alternative to UMass and UConn. With Boston, Providence, and vacation hot-spot Newport within easy reach, there is plenty to do. Strong programs include engineering, marine science, and pharmacy. More than half of URI's students are out-of-staters.

Once known as a great party school, the University of Rhode Island is building a new reputation for challenging academics and friendly associations. In the years since President Robert Carothers cracked down on the wild drinking scene, the school has become more focused on Monday morning and less on Saturday night. "Over the years, URI has become more academically competitive," says one senior. "Many students are concerned about their academic performance."

URI's twelve-hundred-acre campus is located in the small town of Kingston. Surrounded by farmland and only six miles from the coast, it is also within driving

Website: www.uri.edu
Location: Small town
Total Enrollment: 14,180
Undergraduates: 10,784
Male/Female: 43/57
SAT Ranges: V 490–590
   M 500–610

(Continued)

ACT Range: NA

Financial Aid: 62%

Expense: Pub $ $

Phi Beta Kappa: Yes

Applicants: 11,072

Accepted: 69%

Enrolled: 31%

Grad in 6 Years: 58%

Returning Freshmen: 80%

Academics: ✍ ✍

Social: ☎ ☎ ☎ ☎

Q of L: ★ ★ ★

Admissions: (401) 874-7000

Email Address:
uriadmit@etal.uri.edu

Strongest Programs:

Pharmacy

Engineering

Marine and Environmental
  Sciences

Communicative Disorders

All new students take URI 101, a one-credit course intended to acquaint students with support services, co-curricular activities, and academic majors and career options.

distance of cities such as Providence, Boston, and New York. The main academic buildings, a mixture of modern and "old New England granite," surround a central quad on Kingston Hill. At the foot of Kingston Hill lies the athletic buildings and agricultural fields. Work on a new $54 million eight-thousand-seat convocation center—the largest building project ever at the University of Rhode Island—is now complete. The men's and women's hockey teams now enjoy a new $54 million sports complex featuring luxury boxes and a skating rink.

> **"It's a very competitive process to live on campus after freshman year."**

New students here are first enrolled in the University College, which offers courses in communication skills, fine arts and literature, natural and social sciences, letters, mathematics, foreign language, and culture requirements, while providing academic and career guidance. All new students take URI 101, a one-credit course intended to acquaint students with support services, cocurricular activities, and academic majors and career options. After a year or two in University College, students choose more specialized colleges, such as the well-regarded College of Pharmacy. The university also offers a marine and environment program, landscape architecture, and African and African-American studies. Some majors require students to stay for five or six years, but most students graduate in four years. New programs include majors in computer science, coastal and marine policy studies, and wildlife and conservation biology.

Freshmen often have full professors; more than 75 percent of professors have their doctorate. "I like knowing I have earned a grade as opposed to having it handed to me," says communications major. The university offers exchange programs with universities in Austria, England, France, Germany, Japan, Korea, Mexico, Spain, Venezuela, Quebec, and Nova Scotia. Students can also participate in the international engineering program, spend a year of the five-year program abroad, and major in both engineering and Spanish, German, or French. The Writing Center provides free tutorial assistance to anyone who wants feedback on any kind of college or extracurricular writing.

"There is a huge population of New Jersey and New York students here," says a junior. "Also there is a large population of fraternity/sorority members. I feel like going to class is like a fashion show." Indeed, students mostly hail from the Northeast, and URI gives preference to in-state students who meet requirements. About 52 percent of entering freshmen are from outside Rhode Island. Although students say the campus is becoming more diverse, at least 75 percent of undergraduates are white. Ninety percent of freshmen come from public schools. Students bemoan the lack of school spirit and general political apathy on campus.

Though most freshmen live on campus, 62 percent of all undergraduates do not. Because of ongoing renovations, on-campus housing is tight. "Half of the dorms look brand new and the other half are in extremely poor condition," says a computer science major. "It's a very competitive process to live on campus after freshman year," says a senior. The good news is that students live in a sizable off-campus community near the beach. Students complain about a chronic shortage of parking but say that even freshmen are allowed to have cars. There is ample public transit. The university now has a strict alcohol policy, and students note that underage drinkers have a hard time finding an adult beverage on campus. "The policies are strict. They do work," says a communications major. "Alcohol is only permitted if you are twenty-one. You may have one six-pack in your room." URI has ten meal plans available to commuters and dorm residents.

> **"There are many opportunities to get involved. Some attend the town council meetings while others organize beach cleanups."**

While the hearty New England winters are invigorating for some, many students wind up catching colds, earning URI the unflattering nickname Upper Respiratory Infection. Kingston is a sleepy New England college town. "The only thing of interest to students in Kingston is campus," says a senior. "There are many opportunities to get involved. Some attend the town council meetings while others organize beach cleanups," says a psychology major. URI is also within striking distance of both Rhode Island's famous beaches and the major New England ski slopes. Newport, with its heady social scene, is just twenty minutes away, and those feeling lucky can get to the Foxwoods Resort and Casino in forty-five minutes. Other fun road trips include Providence (thirty minutes), Boston (ninety minutes), and New York City (four hours). Travel is facilitated by the fact that there is an Amtrak stop on campus. Many natives find going home on weekends a pleasant diversion, but on campus there are always movies and guest speakers, plus the usual Greek parties. The campus coffeehouse hosts open mic nights, and movie theaters, clubs, and malls beckon just off campus. The student newspaper that covers it all has one of the most original names anywhere: *The Good 5¢ Cigar* (as in, "what this country needs"). Ten percent of men and 12 percent of women join the active Greek community.

Sports are big at Rhode Island, and basketball games are especially exciting. Midnight Madness (the team's first sanctioned practice of the year) is always well attended, and URI fans love it when the team defeats archrival Providence College. Another student favorite is Oozeball, an April volleyball tournament played in about two feet of mud. As befits the school's locale, sailing draws much interest, and the team regularly produces All Americans. Students can find unique opportunities running businesses like a flower shop, a sound and lighting group, and a coffeehouse in the Memorial Union under full-time supervision but with a lot of independence.

Centrally located in dense New England, URI students are close to the beaches and ski slopes, and within easy reach of some major cities. The administration works hard and the students feel at home. "It is so big and has so much to offer that most people will find what they are looking for," says a senior.

A Writing Center provides free tutorial assistance to anyone who wants feedback on any kind of college or extracurricular writing.

Overlaps

University of Massachusetts, University of Connecticut, Northeastern, Boston University, University of Delaware

If You Apply To ➢

URI: Early action: Dec. 14. Does not guarantee to meet demonstrated need. Campus interviews: recommended, evaluative. Alumni interviews: optional, evaluative. SATs or ACTs: required. Essay question: personal statement (optional).

Rhode Island School of Design

2 College Street, Providence, RI 02903

The nation's best-known arts specialty school, RISD sits on a hillside adjacent to Brown. The campus offers easy access to downtown Providence, but it can't match the location of rival Parsons in New York's Greenwich Village. Offers an artsy architecture major in addition to programs in the visual arts.

Founded in the late nineteenth century to address the country's need for more artisans and craftsmen, the Rhode Island School of Design has grown into a premier arts incubator. It's a place where today's artists and designers gather to share ideas and create tomorrow's masterpieces and architectural icons. RISD grants degrees in virtually every design-related topic, and like the varied curriculum, the students and

Website: www.risd.edu
Location: City center
Total Enrollment: 2,204
Undergraduates: 1,882

(Continued)

Male/Female: 36/64

SAT Ranges: V 540–650

 M 550–650

Financial Aid: 49%

Expense: Pr $ $ $ $

Phi Beta Kappa: No

Applicants: 2,524

Accepted: 32%

Enrolled: 50%

Grad in 6 Years: 90%

Returning Freshmen: 95%

Academics: ✐ ✐ ✐ ✐

Social: ☎ ☎

Q of L: ★ ★ ★ ★

Admissions: (401) 454-6300

Email Address:

 admissions@risd.edu

Strongest Programs:

Architecture

Illustration

Graphic Design

Industrial Design

their creations are as diverse as the colors on an artist's palette. "It is competitive but not mean-spirited," says a senior architecture major. "The environment really fosters production, creativity, and a high level of learning," says another student.

Though you might expect an art school like RISD to occupy funky, futuristic buildings, the predominant look here is Colonial New England. Set on the upgrade of College Hill, RISD sits at the edge of Providence's beautifully preserved historic district across the street from Brown University. Many campus buildings date from the 1700s and early 1800s; the mostly redbrick-and-white-trim group includes converted homes, a bank, and even an old church with the campus pub in what used to be its attic. The six-story Industrial Design building, designed by faculty member Jim Barnes, occupies the old Roitman furniture company warehouse. Its fifty thousand square feet are designed for wood- and metal-working and prototype making. Recently, the school purchased buildings to house graduate student studio spaces and plans are currently underway for a new RISD center complex.

While RISD looks traditionally New England on the outside, behind its historic walls lies something else entirely. Students give the architecture, graphic design, and industrial design programs top marks, while liberal arts are considered more of a "joke." One apparel major remarks, "I think most people try to avoid the art history programs." That said, bachelor's and master's liberal arts concentrations in art history, English and literature, history, philosophy, and social sciences are available, complementing offerings in furniture design and architecture and interior architecture (for grad students). Landscape architecture is no longer available to undergraduates. RISD also offers cross-registration at adjacent Brown University for students

> "The department faculty is made up of practicing artists in the field which really makes a difference."

seeking more diverse courses. The institute's highly specialized library contains 662,000 nonbook items (prints, etc.) and 106,000 volumes, and students are likely to be found at their personally assigned studio carrels. Perhaps RISD's most prized facility is its art museum that boasts more than 85,000 pieces, a superlative collection that includes everything from Roman and Egyptian art to works by Monet, Matisse, and Picasso.

To graduate, students must be in residence for at least two years, and must complete a final-year project. They must also finish 126 credit hours—54 in their major, 18 in the Foundation Studies program (an integrated year of "functional and conceptual experiences" that leads to "an understanding of visual language"), 42 in the liberal arts (art and architectural history, English, history/philosophy/social sciences, some electives), and 12 in nonmajor electives. Hands-on studio courses abound, and most classes have fewer than twenty students. Still, a sophomore says, "Sometimes classes fill very quickly because they are really interesting but there are always ample alternatives to choose from." During RISD's winter session, six weeks between the first and second semesters, students are encouraged to take courses outside their major. And each year about thirty juniors and seniors venture to Rome for the European Honors Program, which offers independent study, projects with critics, and immersion in Italian culture. There is also an International Exchange program where students study abroad at approved art institutions.

While students at RISD don't "hit the books" in the traditional sense, the in-studio workload is tremendous.

While students at RISD don't "hit the books" in the traditional sense, the in-studio workload is tremendous. "Our Freshman Foundation program is nicknamed the RISD boot camp," says a senior industrial design student. Students praise faculty members' knowledge and accessibility. "The quality of teaching is good," a junior says. "The department faculty is made up of practicing artists in the field which really makes a difference." Career and academic counseling both get high marks.

RISD students (referred to as "RISDoids" or "Rizdees") come to Providence to form a largely urban mix of styles and personalities. In a word, the school is diverse, and that can create tension. "We're artists," a sophomore says. "We don't believe in being politically correct...we're a bunch of weirdos!" Indeed, only 8 percent of students are native Rhode Islanders, not surprising given the state's small size. Many of the rest are from the vicinity of other East Coast cities, notably New York and Boston. Though highly selective—58 percent of freshmen were in the top quarter of their high school class—RISD will often take a chance on students who did not perform well in high school by

"Everyone here is really dedicated to what they are doing, lending a kind of general excitement that I have not seen anywhere else."

the usual academic criteria, but make up for that with special artistic talent. The racial makeup of the campus is fairly mixed, with Asian-Americans making up 12 percent of the student body, African-Americans 3 percent, and Hispanics 5 percent. Issues of ethnicity and sexuality top the campus agenda, though a sophomore says, "I see Brown as more political but RISD gets involved as well." Tuition and fees here are steep; though RISD offers some merit scholarships, athletic scholarships are nonexistent, and the school does not guarantee to meet financial need.

All noncommuting freshmen are required to live in co-ed dorms that one student says "are fine; there was no trouble to get a room." The dorms are comfortable and feature common studio areas and connections to the campus computer network, but a graphic design major says "apartments are easy to find and rival the cost of living in the dorms." The vast majority of upperclassmen move off campus to nearby apartments, many of which occupy floors of restored homes; RISD also owns an apartment building and some renovated Colonial and Victorian houses. All boarders buy the meal plan, which students say has improved as of late. "The food is actually pretty good," admits a senior.

Despite a student body that looks like it could have been plucked from the streets of New York's Greenwich Village, RISD is not the place to come for wild and funky nightlife.

Despite a student body that looks like it could have been plucked from the streets of New York's Greenwich Village, RISD is not the place to come for wild and funky nightlife. "The social life is mostly centered around friends you work in studio with," explains one sophomore. With three eight-hour studios each week, plus two other classes (and that's just freshman year), "typical social activity is running out for a cup of coffee. If you're desperate, there's always Brown University." Providence also provides some social outlets. The Taproom, shown on the campus' map, went dry years ago, and each year, those twenty-one and over vote on whether to allow drinking in their residences. But underage students can swill. "It is generally easy for underage students to be served," an architecture major says. Though RISD isn't much for traditions, one big annual event is the Artist's Ball, a November formal where dress is "formal or festive, which has been interpreted as everything from chain mail to buck naked," says a senior. When claustrophobia sets in, students can flee to the RISD farm, a thirty-three-acre recreation area on the shores of nearby Narragansett Bay. Boston and New York are one and four hours away by train, respectively.

Perhaps RISD's most prized facility is its art museum that boasts a hundred thousand pieces, a superlative collection that includes everything from Roman and Egyptian art to works by Monet, Matisse, and Picasso.

Though jocks are an endangered species at RISD, recreation opportunities abound. There is no intercollegiate sports program in the ordinary sense, though there is a hockey team, called the Nads (which, of course, leads to RISDoids hollering "Go Nads!"). Students do get involved in intramural sports, ranging from football and baseball to sailing and cycling. There's also a weight room for those who thrive on pumping iron.

Students come to RISD committed to their crafts, and most march to the beat of their own drummer as they rush from studio courses to gallery openings to exhibitions. But this professional preoccupation is not a problem. Students are confident the endless studio hours are starting them on the path to success. Says a student, "Everyone here is really dedicated to what they are doing, lending a kind of general excitement that I have not seen anywhere else."

Overlaps

Pratt Institute, Parsons School of Design, Maryland Institute College of Art, School of Visual Arts, Cooper Union

Rhodes College

2000 North Parkway, Memphis, TN 38112-1690

Goes head to head with Sewanee for the top spot in the pecking order of mid-South liberal arts colleges. While Sewanee has a gorgeous rural campus, Rhodes has Memphis. Economics and international studies head the list of strong programs.

Website: www.rhodes.edu
Location: City residential
Total Enrollment: 1,553
Undergraduates: 1,541
Male/Female: 44/56
SAT Ranges: V 590–700
  M 600–690
ACT Range: 26–30
Financial Aid: 37%
Expense: Pr $ $
Phi Beta Kappa: Yes
Applicants: 2,345
Accepted: 70%
Enrolled: 27%
Grad in 6 Years: N/A
Returning Freshmen: N/A
Academics: ✍ ✍ ✍ ½
Social: ☎ ☎ ☎
Q of L: ★ ★ ★ ★
Admissions: (901) 843-3700
  or (800) 844-5969
Email Address:
  adminfo@rhodes.edu
Strongest Programs:
Biology
Chemistry
Physics
International Studies
English
Economics
Political Science
Business Administration

Rhodes College sits happily in the city that gave us Elvis, Beale Street, barbecue and the blues, and since 1848, it's been instilling in Southern sons and daughters the timeless values of truth and trust. The school's honor code means exams are not proctored and backpacks are left unattended in the cafeteria. Its small size gives everyone an opportunity to take on leadership roles in campus clubs and organizations. "Every person on the campus, from the students to the faculty, visitors and staff, becomes a part of this family and community," says an international business major. "There cannot be many other schools where every professor, cafeteria worker, and dorm cleaning lady—and the deans—knows your name."

Rhodes was founded as a Presbyterian school in Clarksville, Tennessee. It moved to a one-hundred-acre campus in Memphis in 1925. Located in the residential midtown section, Rhodes is across from a 175-acre park housing the city's largest art museum, a golf course, and the Memphis Zoo, which now has two giant pandas. Whether new or old, most campus buildings are Gothic in style, of brownish orange stone with leaded-glass windows and slate roofs; thirteen of the school's original buildings are on the National Register of Historic Places. A $15 million apartment-style dorm opened in 2001 and a 40-million-dollar library will open in 2005.

To receive a Rhodes degree, students must compete 112 credit hours, at least half on campus. In the first year, students must take an English course that emphasizes critical reading, thinking, and writing. Also required is third-semester proficiency in a foreign language, three half-semester physical education classes (with pass/fail grading), three courses each in the humanities, social science, and natural science, and two courses in fine arts. Students must also choose one of two four-course sequences—Search for Values in the Light of Western History and Religion, or Life: Then and Now. The Search course takes students through the history and culture of Western civilization, with special emphasis on the Bible.

Academically, Rhodes is especially strong in the natural and social sciences, thanks to labs equipped with state-of-the-art equipment. A partnership with St. Jude Children's Research Hospital lets students conduct summer research there and continue their projects the following school year. Biology is the most popular major, followed by English, business administration, political science, and international studies. The political science department has won the National Intercollegiate Mock Trial Tournament four times. "A friend of mine recently visited a well-known grad school to check out a religious studies program," an English major says. "When she mentioned to professors there that she

"The challenge is choosing what to do from many great options."

went to Rhodes, they started listing off religious studies professors and pulling their books off the shelf—all were very well-known and respected."

Aside from traditional lecture-style classes, Rhodes offers seminars, honors programs, one-on-one Directed Inquiry tutorials, and interdisciplinary majors. Students who can't find what they want on campus may take advantage of the Greek and Roman studies program, which offers sizable scholarships for a twenty-four-day travel–study excursion to Greece. There's also study abroad at Oxford or through exchange programs in countries including France, Germany, Spain, Scotland, and Belgium. The Buckman International Fellows program offers summer internships abroad in Madrid, Hong Kong, and Johannesburg. Rhodes is a also member of the Associated Colleges of the South consortium* and a participant in dual-degree program for engineers with Washington University (MO).

Rhodes students want to get good grades, but the academic climate is laid-back. "Students and faculty challenge each other, both in and out of the classroom," says a junior. "Heated discussions often continue in the hallways, cafeteria and dorms." Eighty-one percent of all classes have fewer than twenty-five students, which means professors are more than talking heads. "I had a former dean and department chair in a 101 Econ class—he loves to teach it!" says a junior. "I've only had one professor who I felt was not very good, and departments take into account student opinions and evaluations when rehiring and hiring professors," a classmate agrees. Rhodes' computerized registration system helps students get the courses they need, though that can be a problem for those enrolled in the most popular majors.

"Like other small, Southern, liberal arts schools, the majority of students here are white and upper middle class," says a junior. "The stereotypical Rhodes student is very Southern, wealthy, and well-rounded," a classmate adds. "Students are well-traveled and well-spoken, and are extremely amiable and respectful." Twenty-seven percent of Rhodes students hail from Tennessee; African-Americans comprise 4 percent of the student body, Hispanics add 1 percent and Asian-Americans make up 3 percent. The Black Student Association has been proactive in bringing concerns to administrators. "We received national media attention last year for the demonstration and creation of a diversity statement and increased awareness of the situation," says an English major.

Three-quarters of Rhodes students live on campus where all dorms are air-conditioned and clean; most are single-sex. Freshmen have their own halls—Glassell for men, Williford for women—and upperclassmen vie for rooms in the yearly lottery. Housing at Rhodes "is like living in a castle," says a philosophy major. "Even though there is beautiful Gothic architecture outside, the interiors are modern and well-maintained," kept that way with a Web-based system that allows students to report clogged drains, dim lights, and other problems. Rhodes has a gated campus and security officers know students by name. A new director of food services has really improved campus chow, says one student: "We now have made-to-order pasta and stir-fry, panini sandwich makers, a pizza station, multiple and diverse salad bars, and yogurt and ice cream stations." Sandwiches and fast food are available at the grill.

"Every person on the campus, from the students to the faculty, visitors and staff, becomes a part of this family and community."

Lively and energetic Memphis "offers everything and anything that a college student could want—clubs and bars, the arts, volunteer opportunities, internships, you name it," says a junior. Live music and professional sports are also easy to find. Fraternities draw 51 percent of the men and sororities sign up 58 percent of the women. Chartered buses are provided to off-campus parties, many of which are sponsored by the Greeks, though independents are welcome to attend. More than half of Rhodes students, known as Rhodents, help elderly, homeless, and hungry

A $15 million apartment-style dorm opened in 2001 and a 40-million-dollar library will open in 2005.

Tennesseans. While it's illegal for underage students to drink, students say those who are determined can usually find booze. Everyone looks forward to the three-day Rites of Spring concert each April and to the Rites of Play carnival that precedes it, which brings underprivileged kids to campus for a day of food, fun, and games. At Rhodes, "a student typically doesn't have a problem finding something to do," a senior says. "The challenge is choosing what to do from many great options."

Rhodes fields eleven women's and ten men's varsity teams, all in Division III, and "the school is really investigating ways to enhance the athletic programs, both current and prospective," says an international business major. "It is a top priority." Women's cross-country brought home a conference championships in 2001 and women's golf did the same in 2001 and 2002. The $22.5 million Bryan Campus Life Center provides squash and racquetball courts, a suspended indoor track, and a sports arena, all the better for the 25 percent of students who participate in intramural athletics.

Rhodes College students are fond of saying "our ivy is in a league of its own," and they adore the school's solid academics and rich Southern tradition. "A successful student at Rhodes would be best characterized as a self-governing, self-motivated, and service-oriented individual," says a philosophy major. If y'all are looking for a cozy community where everyone will know your name, Rhodes may be the perfect place to spend four years.

If You Apply To ➤   **Rhodes:** Early decision: Nov. 1. Regular admissions and financial aid: Feb. 1 (Jan. 15 for competitive scholarships). Does not guarantee to meet demonstrated need. Campus interviews: recommended, evaluative. No alumni interviews. SATs or ACTs: required. SAT IIs: optional, required for home-schooled students. Accepts the Common Application. Essay question: significant person or experience and the effect on your life; circumstances and results of a risk you've taken; how you've dealt with an ethical dilemma; or how a quote from a favorite movie is personally meaningful.

Rice University

6100 Main Street MS-17, Houston, TX 77005-1892

One of the few elite private colleges that makes the list of best buys. Rice is outstanding in engineering, architecture, and music. With less than three thousand undergraduates, Rice is smaller than many applicants realize. In lieu of frats, Rice has a residential college system like Yale and the University of Miami.

Website: www.rice.edu
Location: Urban
Total Enrollment: 4,785
Undergraduates: 2,787
Male/Female: 53/47
SAT Ranges: V 650–750
  M 670–770
ACT Ranges: 28–33
Financial Aid: 30%
Expense: Pr $ $
Phi Beta Kappa: Yes
Applicants: 7,079

With top-notch programs in the liberal arts and sciences, a huge endowment, and a below-average tuition, Rice University is one of the best buys around. It is the dominant university in the Southwest and second only to Duke in the entire South. Add to that a strong football team, a spirited student body, and an impressive success rate for graduates, and you've got yourself an incredible deal.

Created under the will of legendary Texas cotton mogul William Marsh Rice nearly a hundred years ago, the school was modeled after such disparate institutions as progressive, tuition-free Cooper Union and the more traditional Princeton University. Despite its resemblance to other institutions, Rice maintains distinctive characteristics of its own. The predominant architectural theme of the campus, situated three miles from downtown Houston, is Spanish Mediterranean, and it's surrounded by a row of hedges—the singular buffer between the quiet campus and the sounds of the city. Recent campus additions include a new building for the Jones

Graduate School of Business, a new humanities building, and two new residential halls. Renovations to several other facilities have also been completed.

The students tend to put a lot of pressure on themselves. "The academic climate is very intense," reports a philosophy student. "Students tend to work together a lot, and each individual pushes him or herself to succeed." And no matter how much coursework is assigned, "you can always be assured that someone else will have more." Science and engineering are the strongest programs: Competition in the engineering and premed programs is especially intense, and each year a good number of students who start in these fields retreat to the humanities, which in general are less demanding. In fact, Rice has a long tradition of encouraging double, and even triple, majors in such seemingly opposite fields as electrical engineering and art history. Economics is the most popular major, followed by biological sciences, electrical and computer engineering, English, and psychology.

The university has traditionally excelled in the sciences and engineering, and SEs (as these students are called) still dominate the student body. Architecture is one of the finest undergraduate programs in the nation, and the space physics program works closely with NASA. Under the Mellon Fellow program, selected humanities and social sciences majors may work with a faculty mentor on an academic project that offers a summer research stipend. Some students give less than favorable reviews to economics and math courses, although it appears this is strictly driven by a lack of interest in these fields.

Under the area-major program, students can draw up proposals for independent interdisciplinary majors. An additional option is the "coherent minor" program, which can replace distribution requirements. Distribution requirements mean that science and engineering majors must take courses in

"The academic climate is very intense."

humanities; social science and humanities majors must take them in science; and music and architecture students must take them all. Class size rarely presents a problem. "Rice has an extremely liberal registration process and it is rare that a student get turned away from classes they want," claims one sophomore. Faculty members for the most part are friendly and accessible, sometimes providing upperclassmen with research opportunities. "The quality of teaching I have received is extremely high," one student reports. Students seem somewhat dissatisfied with the advising and counseling system. One student claims, "Most students wish they got more attention from faculty advisors in planning academic programs." Everyone operates under the honor system and most exams go unsupervised.

Those who want to take their education on the road can visit Swarthmore, and there are internships for engineering and architecture students. The library is stocked with most needed materials and, thanks to a renovation, has become more inviting. The career counseling program is a disappointment to many. But the administration reorganized the Career Services Center and now notes "limited data" as the only drawback.

Rice was founded to serve "residents of Houston and the state of Texas," but Texans no longer dominate the student body. Today, 46 percent of Rice students come from out of state, with high percentages transplanted from California, Florida, the Northeast, and other Southern states. Fourteen percent of the student body is Asian-American, 11 percent is Hispanic, and 7 percent is African-American. "The campus is fairly apolitical," according to a junior, "although the recent war led to numerous antiwar rallies and teach-ins, which were well attended." Because much of the university's $3.2 billion endowment is dedicated to keeping tuition low, Rice costs thousands of dollars less than most other selective, private universities. Rice guarantees to meet the full demonstrated need of every admit and there are a variety of merit scholarships available every year, ranging from $1,500 to full

(Continued)
Accepted: 24%
Enrolled: 42%
Grad in 6 Years: 92%
Returning Freshmen: 95%
Academics: ✑ ✑ ✑ ✑ ✑
Social: ☎ ☎ ☎
Q of L: ★ ★ ★ ★
Admissions: (713) 348-7423
Email Address:
  admi@rice.edu

Strongest Programs:
Architecture
Biosciences
Engineering
English
History
Music
Nanotechnology
Sociology

Rice is the dominant university in the Southwest and second only to Duke in the entire South.

tuition. There are also a number of athletic scholarships awarded to both men and women. Still, for all its riches, Rice is fairly provincial Texas.

Fraternities and sororities are forbidden on campus—Rice's founder did not approve of elitist organizations—but their functions are largely assumed by the eight residential colleges, Rice's version of dorms. Each college houses about 225 students who remain affiliated with it for all four years and develop a strong sense of community, even for those who later move off campus. Freshmen are randomly assigned to one of the eight co-ed dorms. Many freshmen enjoy rooms as spacious as their older colleagues and a dormer contends that "the housing has improved greatly in recent years." Air-conditioning is a standard weapon against Houston's muggy climate. Everyone is guaranteed a room for at least three of the four years, though students sit through a lottery system. About 27 percent of the students go packing, many seeking quieter surroundings and cheaper rents. Students can eat at any of the college dining halls, and cafeteria-hopping can be a "great way to meet people." Though the food receives average marks for college cafeteria food, students report that it's getting better with each year. Apparently the salad bar and frozen yogurt machines have won converts.

Houston has plenty of nightlife, but to enjoy it bring a car; mass transit is virtually nonexistent. Luckily, parking on campus is easy. Galveston's beaches on the Gulf of Mexico are only forty-five minutes away, and heading for New Orleans, especially in February, can make a great weekend trip.

Students don't have time to plan anything more formal on weekends than the traditional TGIF lawn parties on Friday afternoons, but campus-wide parties sponsored by one of the residential colleges spring up from time to time. Night of Decadence is Rice's Halloween party, where it is reported that the students appear in "lingerie or less." Drinking age or no, students are expected to unwind on the weekends. "For a bunch of nerds, we really know how to have fun...and drink," a political science major explains. If nothing else, there's always the campus movie.

"Rice has an extremely liberal registration process and it is rare that a student get turned away from classes they want."

Ardent football fans abound at Rice; tearing down the goalposts after home victories remains a happy tradition. A familiar chant echoes, "Two, four, six, eight, our players graduate." Other strong programs include baseball, women's cross-country, men's indoor track, and both men's and women's tennis. Rice students go really wild for intramurals—the most popular pits the colleges against each other in a Beer–Bike Race in which co-ed teams of twenty chug cans of beer and speed around a bicycle track, which gives them a chance to let off academic steam.

A majority of Rice students head straight to jobs after graduation, wasting no time in climbing those corporate ladders or hitching themselves to a dot-com. They've had a terrific academic experience and a decent social life for four years, and their wallets are still thick thanks to a pint-sized tuition. It is obvious that with top-notch programs in the liberal arts and sciences, a huge endowment, and a below-average tuition, Rice University is one of the best buys around

Overlaps

Stanford, Harvard, MIT, Duke, University of Texas

If You Apply To >

Rice: Early decision: Nov. 1. Early action: Dec. 1. Regular admissions: Jan. 1. Housing: May 1. Guarantees to meet demonstrated need. Campus or alumni interviews: recommended, evaluative. SATs or ACTs required. SAT IIs: required (varies by program). Essay question: important experience, achievement, or interest; issue of concern; or influential person or event.

28 Westhampton Way, Richmond, VA 23173

The former capital of the Confederacy is now crawling with Yankees—at least at the University of Richmond. Students come from points north to partake of warmer weather and Richmond's business-oriented curriculum. One of the few institutions with an entire school devoted to leadership.

The University of Richmond may be located below the Mason–Dixon line, but you can forget about finding the South's laid-back feel here. Students are busy conquering tough classes, serving the community, and completing research and internships—all while trying to maintain an active social life. Small classes and terrific faculty interaction are just a few of the perks of being a Richmond Spider—and they even make up for having an arachnid for a school mascot. "The academic climate is very rigorous. Most students are very serious about academics—although they still allow time for fun, too," one sophomore says.

If the enthusiasm about the teaching staff wasn't enough of a draw, the campus might be. The school's 350-acre campus is situated amid rolling hills, stately pines, and a ten-acre lake. Located about fifteen minutes from the center of Richmond, the university's academic buildings, residence halls, and athletic and student-life facilities are designed in traditional collegiate Gothic architecture. Currently, the Gottwald Science Center is being expanded to include another 28,000 square feet (including a new atrium), while the current 162,000 square feet will be updated to include the latest technology and scientific equipment. In the summer, Weinstein Hall, a 35,000-square-foot social science center, will be complete. Renovations were recently finished on the Robins Sports Center, the Boatwright Library, and, to accommodate a recent change in housing, several residence halls.

Richmond offers students a unique gender-based coordinate college system, which until recently included housing men and women on opposite sides of the lake. Now, both genders are being housed on each side of the lake, providing students with more social opportunities while still benefiting from the coordinate college system—Richmond College for men, and Westhampton College for women. The division allows more students to have an opportunity at leadership because each college has its own student government, traditions, and special programs.

Business is the most popular major, followed by biology, social sciences, international studies, and English, all of which are considered strong programs. The business school enrolls students who have completed two years in the School of Arts and Sciences, and it's exceptionally popular among eager, financially ambitious students. Richmond has an excellent feel for international studies and nearly 43 percent of the students study abroad. The Jepson School of Leadership Studies is, according to the administration, the nation's first school of its type and is dedicated to leadership in service to society.

Besides the excellent classes, students also rave about the faculty. Most classes are taught by full professors who are "dedicated to teaching" and are caring and accessible. A junior agrees, saying "The teachers provide a lot of individual attention." One-third of students study abroad and three-quarters of the students have at least one internship. Also, undergraduates are encouraged to do research—they can even get university funding for it.

The core curriculum at Richmond includes courses in expository writing, foreign language, and oral communications. They also have to complete several courses in "fields of study," which include courses in areas such as social analysis, historical and

Website: www.richmond.edu
Location: Suburban
Total Enrollment: 3,774
Undergraduates: 2,998
Male/Female: 49/51
SAT Ranges: V 600–690
   M 620–700
ACT Range: 27–30
Financial Aid: 30%
Expense: Pr $ $
Phi Beta Kappa: Yes
Applicants: 5,895
Accepted: 41%
Enrolled: 33%
Grad in 6 Years: 84%
Returning Freshmen: 93%
Academics: ✐ ✐ ✐
Social: ☎ ☎ ☎
Q of L: ★ ★ ★
Admissions: (800) 700-1662
Email Address:
   admissions@richmond.edu

Strongest Programs:
Business
Biology
Social Sciences/History
International Studies
English
Leadership Studies

While the classes are not easy, students seem to feel that the environment is supportive rather than competitive.

Currently, the Gottwald Science Center is being expanded to include another 28,000 square feet (including a new atrium), while the current 162,000 square feet will be updated to include the latest technology and scientific equipment.

Richmond offers students a unique gender-based coordinate college system, which until recently included housing men and women on opposite sides of the lake. Now, both genders are being housed on each side of the lake, providing students with more social opportunities while still benefiting from the coordinate college system—Richmond College for men and Westhampton College for women.

Overlaps

University of Virginia, William and Mary, Wake Forest, Boston College, Georgetown, Vanderbilt

literary studies, natural science, symbolic reasoning, and visual and performing arts. First-year students must also complete a core course that has focused intensive discussions, and is linked to campus activities such as musical performances.

While the classes are not easy, students seem to feel that the environment is supportive rather than competitive. A political science major says, "Students are competitive with themselves and hold themselves to a high standard but do not compete with each other. Usually you will see students in groups helping each other study." In the new Richmond Quest, the campus spends a year discussing a question posed by a student in class and through activities.

Most students attending Richmond are from out of state—only 16 percent are from Virginia. Although increasing diversity is a main mission of the school, the campus remains overwhelmingly white. Eighty-seven percent of students are white, 5 percent are African-American, 3 percent are Asian-American, and 2 percent are Hispanic. Race relations are addressed through diversity workshops for all new

"The people make UR such a special place. Everyone is so friendly and welcoming."

students, and the administration reports active student unions for multiculturalism, international students, and students of color. Richmond offers 55 merit scholarships ranging from half to full tuition, including benefits, and 168 athletic scholarships for eleven sports.

Ninety-two percent of the students live on-campus for all four years. Most residence halls and student apartments are newly built or recently remodeled and blend in tastefully with the older, more typically collegiate Gothic buildings. The students say the dorms are well-maintained and "homey." One sophomore states, "Some dorms even have fire places and bathtubs." Upperclassman have additional housing options, including townhouses and apartments. Students report feeling safe on campus, thanks to a campus police force, shuttle bus, and emergency phones.

In an effort to educate students on gender, programs such as WILL (Women Involved in Living and Learning) and Spinning Your Web, an orientation program for first-year men, have been created. All freshman women participate in Proclamation Night, where they write letters to themselves about their goals for college during a candlelight service, which they will read when they are seniors. Investiture Night is when the male freshmen are inducted into the university and sign the honor code. Junior year there is the During the Ring Dance, where junior women don white gowns and are presented with their class rings.

When the students are not participating in a Richmond tradition, the Greek life is very popular—32 percent of men and 49 percent women are involved with fraternities or sororities. For the students who are looking for alternative activities, there are comedians, movies, and bands on campus, and students can visit Tyler's Grill, a

"The academic climate is very rigorous. Most students are very serious about academics."

coffeehouse alternative established in the wake of an outcry over sexism in fraternity rush, or the Cellar, a student restaurant and bar. Another popular tradition happens at the end of year—the campus-wide pig roast. Many students spend time volunteering in on-campus activities or with local community groups. Restaurants, bars, and clubs in downtown Richmond are popular spots. While most Richmond students prefer to stick around on weekends, those with wanderlust can head to Virginia Beach, Washington, D.C., and the Blue Ridge Mountains.

Sports are just one more way to become involved at Richmond. The school has recently won several Atlantic 10 championships for women's swimming and track and field and men's baseball. The men's 2003 basketball team even advanced to the NIT tournament and won the Commissar's Cup. Games against rivals like William and Mary draw big crowds, and tailgating is regarded as a key social event. Intramural sports are popular, and the recently renovated Spider Sports Center includes Nautilus machines, cardiovascular free weights, and a wellness area.

The beautiful Virginia landscape is a definite drawing card, bolstered by the school's excellent reputation in academics—especially for business, international, and leadership studies—as well as its traditions, small class sizes, and knowledge-able professors. Says a senior, "The people make UR such a special place. Everyone is so friendly and welcoming. You feel at home when you are on campus."

<table>
<tr><td>If You Apply To ➤</td><td>Richmond: Early decision: Nov. 15, Jan. 15. Regular admissions: Jan. 15. Financial aid: Feb. 25. Does not guarantee to meet demonstrated need. No campus or alumni interviews. ACTs or SATs: required. SAT IIs: required (Writing and Math Ic or IIc). Accepts the Common Application and electronic applications. Essay question: how a nonrequired book or experience has affected intellectual development; how an intellectual activity proves intellectual curiosity.</td></tr>
</table>

Ripon College

300 Seward Street, P.O. Box 248, Ripon, WI 54971

Everything about Ripon is small—the town, the college, and just about all the classes. Ripon is more conservative than Beloit and Lawrence and is more similar in atmosphere to places like DePauw and Knox. With fewer than one thousand students, Ripon is the smallest of the five.

Ripon College is affectionately nicknamed the The Cookie College because it sits near a cookie factory. That sweetness pours over into the campus of the small col-lege. "Ripon College is a special place because of the close relationships and friend-liness of the students, staff, and faculty," says one delighted Red Hawk. It's a good thing Ripon students like each other so much, because the school enrolls just over nine hundred of them. And when it gets cold, students depend on each other and residents of their small town for just about everything.

Set on a hill in a tiny east-central Wisconsin town, just a block from Main Street, Ripon's 250-acre campus features tree-lined walks, wetlands, prairie, and woods, and a mixture of nineteenth- and twentieth-century architecture that gives the campus a "majestic" atmosphere. Recent upgrades to the campus include some residence hall renovations that were, according to some students, much needed.

Founded as a co-ed school in 1851, Ripon is a place where the curriculum is rooted in tradition, and there is little room for dabbling in trendy educational fash-ions. Academic work does take a high priority among Ripon students, and while the quiet, rural setting has both cultural and down-home Midwestern activities for those who seek them out, there isn't much danger of twinkling neon lights distract-ing anyone from his or her studies. The courses are rigorous but not unusually so, and just as anywhere else, there are competitive people. "Most professors advocate a diversity of ideas, and this diversity of ideas seeks to limit the extent to which stu-dents are academically plotted against each other," says a senior.

The chemistry and biology (especially premed) programs at Ripon are particu-larly strong and well known, and their students enjoy the benefits of the science center. Other departments that get high marks include English, history, politics and government, and psychology. The most popular majors are social sciences, history, business, biology, and psychology. The foreign languages could use some improve-ment, students say. Recently, majors were added in early childhood education and

<aside>
Website: www.ripon.edu
Location: Small town
Total Enrollment: 987
Undergraduates: 987
Male/Female: 50/50
SAT Ranges: V 570–640
 M 540–670
ACT Range: 22–26
Financial Aid: 75%
Expense: Pr $
Phi Beta Kappa: Yes
Applicants: 934
Accepted: 84%
Enrolled: 32%
Grad in 6 Years: 59%
(Continued)
Returning Freshmen: 88%
Academics: ✍ ✍ ✍
Social: ☎ ☎ ☎
Q of L: ★ ★ ★
Admissions: (920) 748-8337
Email Address:
 adminfo@ripon.edu

Strongest Programs:
Biology
</aside>

physical sciences. An accelerated degree program is available to students eager to finish college in three years. Some students seek out Ripon for its Division I forensics team, which consistently ranks in the nation's top twenty.

Distribution requirements cover natural sciences and mathematics, foreign language, writing skills, behavioral and social sciences, fine arts, humanities, global studies, and physical education. In addition, freshmen are required to take First-Year Studies. Ripon students delight in their small classes; two-thirds of classes have twenty-five or fewer students. If the student/faculty ratio wasn't the reason they applied here, it's one reason they stay. "Faculty dedication was most evident when, even in the face of significant pay cuts last year, the college witnessed a high morale among faculty," says a senior. Students and professors are regularly on a first-name basis, and critiques of the academic advising range from superb to just plain excellent. Students report no problems getting the classes they need. For temporary changes of scenery, study abroad is available through the college's own programs in Chicago and overseas (German majors may study in Bonn), in addition to programs sponsored by the Associated Colleges of the Midwest.* The Fisk Exchange program with Fisk University has improved diversity and race relations by fostering a relationship between Ripon and the predominately African-American Southern university.

> "Ripon College is a special place because of the close relationships and friendliness of the students, staff, and faculty."

Sixty-nine percent of the Ripon student body hails from Wisconsin, and others come from several states and foreign counties. The vast majority are white, upper-middle-class conservatives, with Asian-Americans, African-Americans, and Hispanics accounting for just 6 percent of the population. Twenty-one percent come from the top tenth of their high school graduating class. With enrollment down, officials are hoping to get the school recognized and grow the student body to one thousand students. The college offers numerous renewable merit awards ranging from $1,000 to full tuition. No athletic scholarships are available.

Freshmen are housed together and are given a choice between co-ed and single-sex halls, as are the upperclassmen. Ninety percent of the students live on campus. For most dorms, those students who want singles will have to pay a premium each term. "We are a residential college with dorms that are well maintained, except for the quads, which are under renovation," a senior says. All students eat in one large dining hall, and food is described as good and plentiful. "Their one downfall is covering everything in cheese, but it is Wisconsin," jokes a senior. Campus security measures include regular foot patrols and key cards for access to residence halls.

> "Social life is surprisingly strong."

The small Midwestern town of Ripon (population 7,500) is well known to history buffs as the birthplace of the Republican Party—which was founded at a meeting on the college campus on February 28, 1854, to be exact. One student says the town is "small but very involved." Where else do you find a community that holds a welcome back picnic for students at the beginning of the year? Students return the favor in the form of volunteer work. For students who want to get away on weekends, Chicago is a three-hour drive; Milwaukee is just eighty miles away.

For those staying in town, local bars offer a break from boredom for those twenty-one and older. The school's new BYOB policy allows of-age students to imbibe on campus, while those under twenty-one must skirt school rules to drink. Other social activities include an array of concerts, plays, and cultural activities, including free movies on Wednesday nights. A weekend of dancing and music in the spring attracts alumni back to the campus enclave. "Social life is surprisingly strong. Many high school students believe that the social life in the Midwest is sparse, but this is not the case in Ripon," notes one satisfied English major. Forty-nine percent

Some students seek out Ripon for its Division I forensics team, which consistently ranks in the nation's top twenty.

Frozen lakes and a blanket of snow are a natural part of the winter landscape, and students can cross-country and downhill ski, toboggan, skate, and attend dogsled and iceboat races.

of the men join fraternities and 27 percent of the women join sororities, and with all Greeks living in dorms and eating in the dining hall, there is little tension between them and nonmembers. Fraternity parties are the main form of campus social life, and Ripon is so darned friendly that independents are included in just about all Greek events.

Ripon is located in the wonderful North Woods territory, a spot in the state where the scattered trees begin to grow thicker and then give way to rugged pine forests. Frozen lakes and a blanket of snow are a natural part of the winter landscape, and students can cross-country and downhill ski, toboggan, skate, and attend dogsled and iceboat races. Nearby Green Lake boasts facilities for skiing and, when it's not winter ("for one month during the year," warns one student), facilities for water sports. Athletic matches against the rival team from Lawrence University usually draw excited crowds. Men's teams have been successful in recent years, snatching up conference championships in baseball (four times), football, soccer (twice), and tennis (twice). Men's basketball is also popular, along with women's basketball, volleyball, and softball.

The homey atmosphere is just one benefit of this small liberal arts college. Students appreciate the intimacy of their classes and the attention they get from their professors, and don't seem to mind that they can't just blend into the scenery or get lost in the back of the class.

Where else do you find a community that holds a welcome back picnic for students at the beginning of the year?

Overlaps

St. Norbert, University of Wisconsin, Carroll, University of Whitewater

If You Apply To ➤

Ripon: Rolling admissions. Regular admissions: Mar. 15. Financial aid: Apr. 15 Guarantees to meet demonstrated need. Campus interviews: recommended, evaluative. No alumni interviews. SATs or ACTs: required. SAT IIs: optional. Accepts the Common Application and electronic applications. Essay question (strongly recommended): discuss reasons for pursuing an education at Ripon.

University of Rochester

Rochester, NY 14627

The name may conjure up a nondescript public university, but Rochester is a top-notch private university in the orbit of Carnegie Mellon, Case Western Reserve, Johns Hopkins, and Washington U (MO). The university has a scientific bent and is known as a haven for premeds.

The University of Rochester is not afraid of change. In 1996, this distinguished private university implemented its unique Rochester Renaissance Plan, and it has never looked back. The five-year plan, which includes a 20 percent reduction in the size of the freshman class, more merit scholarships, a refocusing of the curriculum, and new investments in library and computer/networking resources and campus facilities, has been the major catalyst in a new, improved, user-friendly University of Rochester.

Cold weather and snow are a given at the University of Rochester, but anyone who visits will find a flourishing community thriving on a clandestinely snug little ninety-acre campus, which nestles up to a bend in the Genesee River. One student acknowledges that the university has "perpetually gray [read: winter] skies," but finds comfort that "it's great for winter sports or studying or even sleeping late on a snowy Saturday." Another student adds, "The nippy winter days are perfect for sitting inside and hitting the books." Although a few buildings are modern—the Wilson Commons

Website: www.rochester.edu
Location: Small city
Total Enrollment: 7,681
Undergraduates: 4,452
Male/Female: 51/49
SAT Ranges: V 590–690
  M 620–710
ACT Range: 26–30
Financial Aid: 70%
Expense: Pr $ $ $ $
Phi Beta Kappa: Yes
Applicants: 8,880
Accepted: 62%

(Continued)

Enrolled: 17%

Grad in 6 Years: 77%

Returning Freshmen: 95%

Academics: ✍ ✍ ✍ ✍

Social: ☎ ☎ ☎

Q of L: ★ ★ ★

Admissions: (716) 275-3221

Email Address: admit@
admissions.rochester.edu

Strongest Programs:
Premedicine
Engineering
Music
Optics
Biology
Psychology
Economics
Political Science

An unofficial Rochester tradition calls for each student to eat a "garbage plate" at the infamous dive called Nick's before graduating.

student center designed by I. M. Pei, for example—most of the older structures come in Greek Revival and Georgian Colonial styles. There is an aesthetically pleasing contrast between old and new, and the Eastman Quadrangle, with the library and original academic buildings, adds to Rochester's stately look. Recent construction projects include a 240,000-square-foot building to house the Institute of Biomedical Sciences.

Degree requirements vary slightly from college to college, but all are designed to ensure that students are exposed to the full range of liberal arts. The curriculum—appropriately but unimaginatively known as the Rochester Curriculum—focuses on three classic divisions of learning: humanities and arts; social science; and natural science, mathematics, and engineering. Students choose a major from one of these areas and also complete a cluster of three courses in each of the remaining two divisions. These clusters give students the opportunity for integrated study in diverse fields and the chance to participate in three very different types of learning. Freshmen have the option of taking seminar-style Quest courses, which teach them how to learn and how to make learning a lifetime habit. Quest courses can involve extensive work with original materials, existing and experimental data, and primary texts. Orientation Rochester-style includes a week-long fall festival called Yellow Jacket Days designed to help new students "become fully integrated in the university community."

The university's 175 degree programs span the standard fields of study, but Rochester takes special pride in its famed Eastman School of Music. It also excels in the engineering and scientific fields—competition is keen to "beat the mean" among science majors. A cognitive science program—a cooperative venture among faculty in computer science, psychology, and philosophy—is innovative and popular. The Institute of Optics, the nation's first center devoted exclusively to optics, is a leader in basic optical research and theory. The most popular majors include psychology, political science, economics, and biology. Students cite math and anthropology as being weak.

The academic climate at Rochester is challenging, owing much of that to its energetic professors, who are described as "extremely knowledgeable" and "enthusiastic about teaching undergraduates." No matter what their field of interest, students who are sufficiently advanced may combine undergraduate with graduate study. The Rochester Early Medical Scholars program offers highly qualified first-year students guaranteed admission to the medical school after four years. In addition, Rochester offers a tuition-free fifth year that allows students to explore interests outside their major. The Center for Work and Career Development receives

"Dorms are comfortable, modern, high-tech, very generously sized, and well maintained."

praise for its vigorous preparation of seniors for the job market. Students may also study abroad, and the university sponsors programs in a variety of places ranging from Russia to Singapore, not to mention what one student calls a "chance of a lifetime" British Parliament internship program. A work–study program called Reach for Rochester provides students with on- or off-campus jobs, summer employment options, and individually tailored "experienceships."

Fifty-one percent of the students hail from New York State. Many also come from New England, and there's been a large jump in the numbers from Florida, the Midwest, California, and overseas. Asian-Americans make up 11 percent of the student body, while African-Americans account for 6 percent, and Hispanics another 5 percent. "I can say that Rochester students are a hard-working, fun-loving, positive group that puts a high value on academics," says a student. Campus issues include political correctness and antisweatshop campaigns, though one student notes political involvement is "lower than might be expected" due to a "lack of free time." In an effort to attract scholars, the university offers in-state applicants and children of alumni a $5,000 annual grant. Its strongest applicants are awarded a Rush Rhees Scholarship, which ranges from $5,000 to $10,000 per year.

As far as housing is concerned, there's virtually nothing but praise from the 78 percent of students who live on campus. "Dorms are comfortable, modern, high-tech, very generously sized, and well maintained," a senior says. Some of the housing units offer such benefits as computer terminals, telephones with voicemail features, oak floors, and marble trim. All housing offers Internet access. New students are assigned to rooms—usually doubles—and upperclass students can usually get singles or suites through the lottery. Susan B. Anthony comes highly recommended. Dormitories are available single-sex, co-ed by floor, and co-ed by room. Though few students choose to live off campus, a new shuttle bus runs to and from the major off-campus living areas. Dormitory students may eat meals in the cafeteria, where a credit system ensures they pay per meal instead of in one lump sum. The fare served in the dining halls receives high ratings from students, especially the a la carte options such as tacos and burritos and the deli bar. Other meal options available include a kosher deli, the Common Ground Coffeehouse, and a submarine sandwich shop.

Twenty percent of the men and 14 percent of the women go Greek. "The Greek scene plays a large factor in social life here, but it is by no means the only social outlet," says one student. Yet, fraternities still contribute heavily to the social life of Greeks and independents alike by sponsoring parties and concerts. UR does have its own set of movie theaters that charge $3 or less per ticket, and campus concerts always draw a crowd. Despite the university's

> "I can say that Rochester students are a hard-working, fun-loving, positive group that puts a high value on academics."

best efforts to enforce a stricter alcohol policy, underage drinking still occurs. "This school's policy in no way curtails underage drinking unless students take it upon themselves to obey," one student says. Many students take the free campus shuttle into "Rochchacha," where they may entertain themselves on the beaches of Lake Ontario, in the International Photography Museum at the George Eastman House, or at the Rochester Philharmonic Orchestra. Favored out-of-town ventures are Niagara Falls, about seventy miles westward, and, for the more venturesome, Toronto, 125 miles farther westward.

Other popular activities include cappuccino at the student union, frequent ski trips, Yellow Jacket Days, and a spring fling known as Dandelion Day. The Viennese Ball and the Boar's Head Dinner are also popular events, as is the unforgettable Screw Your Roommate Dance. An unofficial Rochester tradition calls for each student to eat a "garbage plate" at the infamous dive called Nick's before graduating. Students are involved in the community through projects on and off campus, and Rochester was recently recognized nationally for its high percentage of student volunteers.

The varsity sports teams are coming of age at Rochester, which competes in the University Athletic Association. For those who want something to cheer about, the golf team, the basketball teams, men's and women's soccer, tennis, and cross-country are all quite successful. Intramurals are a popular outlet for "ex-jocks from high school who miss their glory days gone by." Even if intramurals aren't your bag, Rochester has an $8 million sports complex, complete with basketball, tennis, squash, and volleyball courts; lighted rooftop tennis courts; a Nautilus fitness center; the Speegle-Wilbraham Aquatic Center with an eight-lane pool; and an indoor track.

In the past, students bemoaned the fact that the school didn't have a wider academic reputation, but that's changing due, in part, to the Rochester Renaissance Plan. Improvements have been made in the curriculum, the facilities, and just about anywhere you look on campus. "Prospective students who are unsure where their academic careers will take them will have no problem finding what excites

The Institute of Optics, the nation's first center devoted exclusively to optics, is a leader in basic optical research and theory.

Overlaps
Cornell University, Brown, SUNY–Binghamton, Northwestern, Washington University

them intellectually," says a junior. "But more importantly, they will build relationships with others that will last their entire lives." Rochester seems to be winning its battle for a spot among the nation's leading private universities. Now if they could only do something about all that snow.

Rochester Institute of Technology

60 Lomb Memorial Drive, Rochester, NY 14623-5604

RIT is the largest of New York's three major technical universities—about double the size of Rensselaer. The school is strong in anything related to computers, business, and engineering, and in the city built by Eastman Kodak, photography is among the tops in the nation.

Website: www.rit.edu
Location: Suburban
Total Enrollment: 14,600
Undergraduates: 12,300
Male/Female: 68/32
SAT Ranges: N/A
ACT Range: 25–28
Financial Aid: 75%
Expense: Pr $ $
Phi Beta Kappa: No
Applicants: 8,500
Accepted: 69%
Enrolled: 38%
Grad in 6 Years: 61%
Returning Freshmen: 87%
Academics: ✍ ✍ ✍
Social: ☎ ☎ ☎
Q of L: ★ ★ ★
Admissions: (585) 475-6631
Email Address:
  admissions@rit.edu

Strongest Programs:
Photography
Computer Science
Engineering
Biotechnology and
  Bioinformatics
Crafts

Unlike many liberal arts colleges that prefer that students test the academic waters before deciding on a major or future job plans, RIT focuses on career-oriented and technology-based academics. And unlike many big universities where the academic luminaries shine from research-oriented graduate schools, RIT's spotlight is very definitely on undergraduates. Students seeking up-to-date technological training will be at home at RIT. Those who are geared up and ready to "go professional" will be happy to know that the school places 2,700 juniors and seniors in full-time paid positions through its co-op program.

While the town of Rochester may sometimes seem like a reluctant host to weekend fun-seekers, it can hardly deny that it is in fact a college town; RIT shares the city with six nearby colleges. RIT's main campus, located on thirteen hundred suburban acres six miles from downtown Rochester, has its own distinctive style—redbrick buildings with sharp, contemporary lines. The new 125,000-square-foot Computing and Information Sciences Building opened in 2003. The modern aesthetic is embodied in a seven-story high sculpture—one of the largest pieces of metal artwork in the world—just unveiled.

RIT specializes in carving out niches for itself with unusual programs, and majors are offered in more than two hundred fields, from basic electrical and mechanical engineering to packaging science and bioinformatics. Fortunately, applicants narrow the range of choices to a manageable size by applying to one of eight undergraduate colleges: applied science and technology, business, computing and information sciences, engineering, imaging arts and sciences, liberal arts, science, and the National Technical Institute for the Deaf (NTID). NTID students and faculty use a combination of communication methods including sign language, finger spelling, and visual aids, and the college boasts a placement rate of 95 percent. The nation's

"Students are dedicated and career-oriented, and many go for high degrees."

first undergraduate program in new media was recently instituted at RIT. It combines graphic design, printing, publishing, and information technology courses to prepare students for jobs in digital-based media such as the World Wide Web. The latest in the school's seemingly infinite offerings is a new biomedical engineering program, developed by the electrical engineering department.

Predictably, engineering is the most popular major, but one might be surprised to know that the third-most popular major is art and design. Information technology, business, and photography (Rochester, New York, is home to Eastman Kodak) also head the list. Academic programs include aerospace engineering, environmental management, hotel and tourism management, engineering technology, and a physician assistant program. The RIT School for American Crafts offers excellent programs in ceramics, woodworking, glass, metalcraft, and jewelry making, and students have the run of Bevier Gallery, where visiting artists provide firsthand instruction. The small College of Liberal Arts is cited as weaker than the other colleges. However, it has been updated with a new public policy program focused on science or environmental policy development in government and industry.

All students have a liberal arts requirement from the humanities, social science, and English departments. They must also take three physical education courses, but the emphasis is more on health and wellness than competitive sports. Unlike many universities, RIT allows freshmen to schedule significant coursework in their major early on, and spreads out liberal arts requirements over a more extended period. RIT's academic pressure is there, but not "out there," to where no one is getting any sleep. Still, RIT's quarter system makes the academic semester "short and fast," says a senior. "Students should have good time-management skills, as academics move quickly and classes can be intense." He describes the student body as "committed and a bit driven, but friendly as a whole." Teaching is excellent, and one student assures, "Freshmen have immediate and direct contact with full professors." Undergraduates being the school's top priority, the faculty develops new academic programs to fit career needs. Applied research initiatives with extensive ties to industrial partners are a new thrust of the administration. Academic counseling is very good, as is the co-op's office support for career counseling, says a senior.

Just over half the students are from New York State, the remainder coming largely from New Jersey, Pennsylvania, and Connecticut. Five percent of the student body is African-American, 3 percent Hispanic, and 7 percent Asian-American. Preprofessionalism is a common bond, but beyond that interests vary. The unique mix of art, engineering, business, and science students, along with the large number of deaf students, creates a diverse atmosphere on campus. If the men here could change anything, it would likely be the male/female ratio of more than 3 to 1. That accomplished, they might wish to raise the night life wattage in Rochester, along with the temperature in winter. RIT admits without regard to student financial need, and it meets the demonstrated need of 90 percent of the students for as long as the funds allow. RIT offers more than eighteen hundred renewable merit scholarships to each freshman class, ranging from $500 to $21,000, made without reference to need. Political debate on campus has sometimes centered on CIA-funded campus projects and issues surrounding the U.S.-led war on terrorism.

Sixty-five percent of RIT students live in college dorms and apartments, and students report that getting a room is not that difficult. Freshmen are required to live in the dorms, while upperclassmen can vie for campus apartments through a lottery. But that shouldn't be too tough because, according to the administration, RIT has the largest number of on-campus apartments in the country. Dorms are well maintained and offer a variety of living styles: single-sex, co-ed by room, or co-ed by floor. Special-interest floors range from nonsmoking to "mainstream" (with hearing-impaired students). Vegetarians, vegans, and carnivores will find choices on campus meal options to be reasonably diverse. Those who choose to live off

RIT specializes in carving out niches for itself with unusual programs, and majors are offered in more than two hundred fields, from basic electrical and mechanical engineering to packaging science and bioinformatics.

"Freshmen have immediate and direct contact with full professors."

RIT allows freshmen to schedule significant coursework in their major early on and spreads out liberal arts requirements over a more extended period.

campus take advantage of areas serviced by the school shuttle bus. Seven percent of men and 5 percent of women choose to go Greek and live and eat in RIT's seventeen fraternity and seven sorority houses. Campus security is "courteous and responsive," reports one student.

The dorms and academic buildings are supposed to be dry, but alcohol in rooms is not unheard of. The only facilities within walking distance of this sedate suburban campus are a variety of shopping plazas, including one of the largest between New York and Cleveland. Students take road trips to Buffalo, Syracuse, Rochester, and Canada. For those without transportation, there's always something to do on campus. Drama and other creative arts are less common than parties and movies, but a fine jazz ensemble and a chorus perform regularly. RIT has just added the first ESPN Entertainment Zone area on a U.S. campus as part of student union renovations. Brick City Bash, a favorite way to celebrate the end of a long winter, is held each spring. Men's hockey is the overwhelming sports favorite, a real crowd pleaser that draws even the campus commuters and local residents to the rink. Men's soccer and roller hockey have been recent conference champions. Other sports such as men's basketball and lacrosse and women's volleyball, hockey, and basketball are popular.

Organized and focused, RIT students have their eye on the future. "Students are dedicated and career-oriented, and many go for high degrees," says an imaging science major. And best of all, with all the co-op education opportunities, "They graduate with lots of lab/field/hands-on experience."

Overlaps

Rensselaer Polytechnic, University at Buffalo, Clarkson, Syracuse, Cornell University

If You Apply To ➤

RIT: Early decision: Dec. 15. Regular admissions: Feb. 1. Financial aid: Mar. 1. Meets demonstrated need of 90%. Campus interviews: recommended, informational. No alumni interviews. SATs or ACTs: required. SAT IIs: optional. Accepts the Common Application and electronic applications. Essay question: how does your desired academic program relate to your future career plans?

Rollins College

1000 Holt Avenue, Box 2720, Winter Park, FL 32789-4499

Rollins is the marriage of a liberal arts college and a business school. A haven for Easterners who want to their ticket punched to Florida, Rollins attracts conservative and affluent students and world-class water-skiers. Rivals include Eckerd in St. Petersburg and the University of Miami.

Website: www.rollins.edu
Location: Suburban
Total Enrollment: 2,505
Undergraduates: 1,723
Male/Female: 40/60
SAT Ranges: V 530–620
M 530–630
ACT Range: 22–26
Financial Aid: 42%
Expense: Pr $ $ $ $
Phi Beta Kappa: No
Applicants: 2,307

Central Florida is home to many of the world's greatest attractions. There's Walt Disney World, Sea World, and Universal Studios, to name a few. And for those seeking a quality education, the area offers an attraction of another sort: Rollins College. Here you can dig your toes in the sand while studying theater or biology, and enjoy making waves as well as making grades.

Although founded in 1885, Rollins' commitment to Spanish Mediterranean–style architecture was established in the 1930s. Capitalizing on its location on beautiful Lake Virginia, campus planners have succeeded in combining the natural beauty of the lakeside with consistent architecture. Recent additions include the Harold and Ted Alfond Sports Center, Rinker Building, McKean Gateway, and the Cahall–Sandspur Field.

Receiving a bachelor's degree at Rollins leads all students through three areas of general education requirements: skills (writing, foreign language, public speaking, mathematical methods, decision-making); cognitive (Western and non-Western culture, natural world); and affective (expressive arts and literature). For freshmen acclimating to college, the fall-semester Rollins Conference Course eases the transition by placing them into groups of sixteen to discuss themes such as imaginary voyages, contemporary ethical issues, and the environment. Each group has a professor-advisor and two upper-class peer mentors. Students also have the opportunity to pursue independent research, travel abroad, and take service-learning classes where they earn credit by volunteering in the community.

Students give the psychology department their highest marks, and also praise history, English, theater, biology, and international studies. The chemistry department turned out the winner of the 1987 Nobel Prize. Some students say they avoid the sciences, but only because instructors are so tough and science majors are so competitive. "There has to be a strong desire to be a science major and a determined career path for the future," says an English major. The Annie Russell Theatre hosts productions staged by the active theater department, which takes pride in having set the stage for such stellar actors as alumni Buddy Ebsen and Tony Perkins. An Accelerated Management Program allows qualified freshmen to gain guaranteed admission to the Roy E. Crummer Graduate School of Business when they enter Rollins, leading to B.A. and M.B.A. degrees in five rather than six years.

While the workload at Rollins varies by major, academics are important. "The professors are very demanding and the students take their academics very seriously," says a junior. Despite the challenging classes, the students seem to agree that the other students "are always there to help them out." The teaching staff also receives high praise. "All teachers have an open door policy," states a junior. A senior agrees, "Teachers are flexible, available, and encouraging." That's made easier by the fact that there aren't any TAs here; teaching is the responsibility of professors. Many students take advantage of Rollins' study abroad program, which offers programs in Sydney, Australia, Munster, Germany, and Asturias, Spain, for regular tuition costs, as well as internships in London.

"All teachers have an open door policy."

Rollins draws 48 percent of its students from outside Florida. The student body is more than three-quarters Caucasian, 4 percent African-American, 8 percent Hispanic, and 3 percent Asian-American. While many of the students come from well-to-do families, adequate financial aid is available for the BMW-deprived, with merit scholarships for qualified students and athletic scholarships given to male and female standouts in eight sports.

Sixty-three percent of the college's students live on campus in comfortable co-ed dorms. "The dorms are very spacious," says a senior. For those students who miss Mom picking up after them, a junior notes that "all dorms are maintained five days a week by a professional cleaning service." Students agree that bookworms should choose Ward, while McKean is the social center. Some students live in special-interest houses or move off campus. Dining facilities are located in the campus center and food is charged on a credit card system, so students eat when they want and pay only when they eat. All the students seem to agree the food is good. One sophomore says, "Well, it's not my mom's cooking, but it comes close."

"All dorms are maintained five days a week by a professional cleaning service."

The high-powered Greek scene claims 40 percent of the women and 38 percent of the men at Rollins, so there's always a party somewhere. And with Cocoa Beach, Orlando, Miami, and the Florida Keys nearby, "there are always activities off-campus as well." says a senior. The administration has clamped down on the social scene, with party monitors checking IDs and a student activity director attending each on-campus party. No open containers of alcohol may be carried on the campus

(Continued)

Accepted: 63%
Enrolled: 32%
Grad in 6 Years: 60%
Returning Freshmen: 86%
Academics: ✍ ✍ ✍
Social: ☎ ☎ ☎ ☎
Q of L: ★ ★ ★
Admissions: (407) 646-2161
Email Address:
  admission@rollins.edu

Strongest Programs:
International Business
Psychology
English
Economics
Education

Fox Day is "a sacred tradition"—the president cancels classes for the day by placing a fox statue on the front lawn.

The Annie Russell Theatre hosts productions staged by the active theater department, which takes pride in having set the stage for such stellar actors as alumni Buddy Ebsen and Tony Perkins.

grounds, and if you're caught with one, "you will be written up by an RA or campus security," according to a biology major.

Fox Day is "a sacred tradition"—the president cancels classes for the day by placing a fox statue on the front lawn. Students look forward to the tradition every spring and, though they never know exactly which day the president will choose, almost everyone heads for the beach once the day arrives. Many students volunteer with programs such as Habitat for Humanity and tutoring at local schools. Orlando's offerings include entertainment complexes like Downtown Disney and Universal Citywalk, and amusement parks such as Walt Disney World, Epcot Center, Universal Studios.

Sports are an integral part of the Rollins scene; tennis, golf, and water-skiing are favorites. The women's tennis team recently placed fourth in the NCAA national championships and the women's golf team captured second place in their sport.

Students at Rollins may not realize how lucky they are. They have gorgeous new facilities to complement the natural beauty of Florida's sun and surf, plus a lake in their own backyard. Their biggest gripes are a lack of on-campus parking and a campus safety force too eager to hand out citations for expired meters or underage drinking. It's true that high tuition costs and a lack of diversity have some students concerned. But for those who want to put off entry into the "real world" just a bit longer, Rollins could be an ideal oasis in which to spend the next four years.

If You Apply To ➤

Rollins: Early decision: Feb. 1. Regular admissions: Feb. 15. Does not guarantee to meet demonstrated need. Campus interviews: recommended, informational. No alumni interviews. SATs or ACTs: required. SAT IIs: recommended. Accepts the Common Application and electronic applications. Essay question: significant experience or achievement; issue of personal, local, or national concern and its importance; significant person.

Rose-Hulman Institute of Technology

5500 Wabash Avenue, Terre Haute, IN 47803

Co-ed since 1995, Rose-Hulman offers the rare combination of technical education and personal attention. Only Caltech, Clarkson, and Harvey Mudd offer comparable intimacy in a technical environment. Nearby Indiana State and St. Mary's of the Woods help mitigate the skewed gender ratio.

Website: www.rose-hulman.edu
Location: City outskirts
Total Enrollment: 1,800
Undergraduates: 1,700
Male/Female: 82/18
SAT Ranges: V 570-670
  M 640-720
ACT Range: 27-31
Financial Aid: 92%
Expense: Pr $ $ $ $
Phi Beta Kappa: No
Applicants: 3,207
Accepted: 60%

Understand one thing: The Rose-Hulman Institute of Technology is a haven for young engineers, but the school is hardly a refuge for the pasty nation. Though some Hulman students gleefully describe themselves as "big dorks," this small tech school fosters a sense of unity and takes pride in giving back to its community. "The students at Rose are the best of the best," says one mechanical engineering major. "They have a strong work ethic, desire to learn, and want for hands-on experience. There are few slackers here." With fewer than sixteen hundred undergraduates and only eleven majors, the Rose-Hulman Institute of Technology doesn't have much room for weakness.

Established in 1874, Rose-Hulman is the oldest private engineering school west of the Allegheny Mountains. It gets its name from Chauncey Rose, an entrepreneur who brought the railroad to Indiana, and the Hulman family, owners of the Indianapolis Speedway, who gave their fortune to the institution in 1970. Its two-hundred-acre campus boasts an idyllic setting of trees and two small lakes. The campus recently completed a new building, the Hatfield Hall Performing Arts Building.

Coursework is "rigorous and tough but the atmosphere isn't really competitive," according to a senior. Hard classes forge tight bonds among Rose students and "students often work to help each other succeed," explains an engineering major. The work requires much effort out of class in both groups and independent studies, but the teaching staff of full professors helps ensure success. Not only is every "professor a Ph.D., but they honestly care about the students, not just the class," enthuses a senior. Majors such as optical engineering (the only undergraduate program of its kind in the country), bioengineering, engineering physics, double majors, and even a humanities minor help round out the curriculum. Programs such as Fast Track Calculus enable students to accelerate in areas where they demonstrate special aptitude. Students in every program except math must work in a team and complete a project for an outside company, and all are required to take College and Life Skills, which covers study skills, time management, and resume writing. Rose-Hulman Ventures gives students the chance to form companies after graduation.

Most of Rose-Hulman's degree programs are in engineering, but there is also chemistry, computer science, biology, math, and physics. It was the first private college to offer a bachelor's degree in chemical engineering, and this department remains among its strongest. Electrical and mechanical engineering are also popular with students, but for every student, a fifth of their academic program will consist of classes in the humanities and social sciences. Bioengineering, software engineering, and engineering physics are also majors. Rose-Hulman's library system is excellent in technical fields, but for anything else, students must trek to nearby Indiana State University, where they have free access. Even though the classes are tough, the technology classes are popular

"Students often work to help each other succeed."

Ninety-two percent of the students are white, 3 percent African-American, 2 percent Hispanic, and 2 percent Asian-American—and all are used to academic success, as 90 percent were in the top tenth of their high school class. Most students say that diversity is not an issue overall though the student body does not consider itself politically active. The increase in the female population is now enough to warrant the existence of sororities and several women's sports teams. Rose-Hulman also offers nearly one thousand merit scholarships each year, worth $2,000 to $18,000. The scholarships don't cover tuition but "support remains constant as long as your GPA does," according to a senior.

Sixty percent of the student body choose to live on campus and freshman are required to do so. Sleeping, studying, and relaxing occur in the dorms, which are described as "well-maintained with an amazing staff." Greek life is big at Rose—45 percent of the men are in fraternities and 60 percent of the women are in sororities. Even though it's a dry campus you can get alcohol if you try hard enough; however, "if an RA sees it, they dump it," says engineering major.

Terre Haute is not the most endearing college town. It is an old industrial town that, according to the students, smells bad due to a paper mill. Since there are three colleges nearby, including St. Mary's of the Woods and Indiana State, there are plenty of malls and eateries in the area to serve local students. Volunteer activities include the Lighthouse Mission and Bikes for Tykes. The most popular road trips are to Indianapolis, Chicago, St. Louis, and even Florida if you're really feeling adventurous. On campus, there are mixers, Greek parties, and traditions like the homecoming bonfire and spring carnival.

Lest anyone envision Rose-Hulman students as pale lab dwellers, be aware that athletics are very popular. More than 90 percent of the students are involved in intramurals, and even faculty members get into the act. Varsity teams play in Division III of the NCAA with football, soccer, and baseball among the most popular sports for men. The women enjoy playing soccer, basketball, and volleyball. The

(Continued)

Enrolled: 23%

Grad in 6 Years: 82%

Returning Freshmen: 93%

Academics: ✍ ✍ ✍

Social: ☎

Q of L: ★ ★

Admissions: (812) 877-8213

Email Address: admis.ofc@ rose-hulman.edu

Strongest Programs:
Civil Engineering
Chemical Engineering
Mechanical Engineering
Electrical Engineering
Computer Engineering

It was the first private college to offer a bachelor's degree in chemical engineering, and this department remains among its strongest.

Students in every program except math must work in a team and complete a project for an outside company, and all are required to take College and Life Skills, which covers study skills, time management, and resume writing.

men's basketball team and women's softball teams took home the 2002 SCAC championships. The Indianapolis Colts even use the facilities for their month-long summer camps.

Academics remain the focus at this Midwestern technical school. While students may find the classes tough, they thrive in this environment and strive to take advantage of the small classes and faculty interaction. Ultimately, says one student, it's this "personalized attention and sense of being at home" that makes Rose-Hulman special.

Rutgers–The State University of New Jersey

65 Davidson Road, Piscataway, NJ 08854-8097

Rutgers is a huge institution spread over three regional campuses and twenty-nine colleges or schools. Rutgers College on the New Brunswick campus is the most prominent. Literally everything is available: engineering, business, pharmacy, the arts, and the nation's largest women's college (Douglass College in New Brunswick).

Website: www.rutgers.edu
Location: Small city
Total Enrollment: 51,480
Undergraduates: 38,576
Male/Female: 45/55
SAT Ranges: V 520–630
  M 550–670
Financial Aid: 57%
Expense: Pub $ $ $
Phi Beta Kappa: Yes
Applicants: 42,276
Accepted: 54%
Enrolled: 28%
Grad in 6 Years: 69%
Returning Freshmen: 88%
Academics: ✑ ✑ ✑ ✑
Social: ☎ ☎ ☎
Q of L: ★ ★ ★
Admissions: (732) 932-INFO
  (New Brunswick); (856)
  225-6104 (Camden); (973)
  353-5205 (Newark)

Strongest Programs:
Accounting

Life at Rutgers University is all about choice. Choices between the more than one hundred undergraduate majors and four thousand courses offered among its campuses in New Brunswick, Newark, and Camden. Choices about which of the more than four hundred student organizations to join. Even choices about which library to visit, as there are eighteen branches with holdings of more than three million volumes university-wide. "Rutgers's best quality is its wide variety of majors, classes, and social activities," says one junior.

Rutgers University has three regional campuses in Camden, Newark, and New Brunswick. Rutgers–New Brunswick, which has the largest concentration of students, is composed of five smaller campuses located along the Raritan River. The campuses are connected by a free university bus system and students travel among campuses to take classes. Rutgers–Newark is in a downtown section of Newark, giving the campus neighborhood a collegiate feel. The smallest campus in the Rutgers system is in Camden, located one stop away from the shopping and cultural offerings of downtown Philadelphia. The RUNet 2000 project, a $100 million infrastructure initiative in progress, promises to transform student–faculty interaction through access to voice, video, and data from just about any location on campus.

Among the nearly one hundred majors, the three most popular are psychology, biological sciences, and accounting. Especially strong academic programs include accounting, history, political science, and chemistry. The workload is steady for most students; science majors and pharmacy students can expect the heaviest load. "The courses here require a great deal of thought and outside preparation if you want to be successful," says a political science major. Recently added majors include cell biology and neuroscience; genetics and microbiology; biomedical engineering; evolutionary

> **"Rutgers's best quality is its wide variety of majors, classes, and social activities."**

anthropology; and allied health technology. As at any big state university, registration can sometimes be a headache. But Rutgers now has telephone registration at its New Brunswick campus, and students say the situation has improved.

In an effort to reverse the traditional exodus of New Jersey high school superstars from the state, Rutgers offers a variety of honors programs, including special seminars, internships, independent projects, and research opportunities with the faculty. Rutgers also provides its undergraduates with a chance to study abroad in Britain, Costa Rica, France, Germany, India, Ireland, Israel, Italy, Mexico, Switzerland, and Spain. Biology students have the run of the 370-acre Rutgers Ecological Preserve and Natural Teaching Area. In addition, Rutgers is also home to more than one hundred specialized research centers and institutes dedicated to the study of topics ranging from ancient Roman art to mountain gorillas. Professors generally get high marks. "I completely revere most of my professors," says a junior. "They are intelligent, well respected in their fields, and present dynamic lectures."

Although the administration has been trying to increase the number of out-of-staters, about 90 percent of Rutgers students hail from New Jersey. Nevertheless, the student population is as diverse as that of the state, with a good proportion of students from cities, suburbs, farms, and seaside communities. Minorities account for nearly half the students: 11 percent are African-American, 9 percent are Hispanic, and 19 percent are Asian-American. "I feel I've grown so much here and learned so much about being a member of a rich and diverse community," explains one senior. The school's administration takes pride in their Committee to Advance Our Common Purpose, for students who want to reduce prejudice and promote diversity on campus. In the past, the committee developed a World Wide Web page for multicultural resources and submitted a proposal for the creation of an Intercultural Relations Study Group.

"I completely revere most of my professors."

For those seeking a broad-based education, the university has eight liberal arts schools spread out among its campuses. Seven colleges cater to the needs of students wanting a preprofessional school (business, nursing, life and environmental studies, fine and performing arts, engineering, and pharmacy). The school does not guarantee to meet the full demonstrated need of every admit. About four hundred students receive athletic scholarships in a wide range of sports, and more than 6,500 receive merit awards. Students say they have noticed budget cuts in terms of tuition increases, fewer course offerings, shorter hours at buildings around campus, and fewer administrators.

On-campus housing in New Brunswick accommodates 47 percent of full-time students. "There has been a big push recently to renovate the dorms, so most of them are really nice," says a history major. Another student says, "With the exception of a few mediocre dorms for freshmen, most are extremely large and have air-conditioning; some have free cable TV; and a good number are directly hard-wired with fiber-optic cables into the Internet." Current on-campus housing options include conventional dorms, special-interest areas, and apartment complexes with kitchens and living rooms. The university also offers a special dormitory for students who are trying to overcome addictions to drugs and alcohol.

"The courses here require a great deal of thought and outside preparation if you want to be successful."

The city of New Brunswick is an attractive place to go for a drink or dinner on the town. Just don't stray too far from the campus. True, Rutgers has its own police department that possesses the same training and powers as the New Jersey state police. "I personally don't feel safe in New Brunswick, so I restrict my outings to on-campus locations," one student admits. For those who want to hit the road for fun, New York City and Philadelphia are each only about an hour drive, and students flood the

The city of New Brunswick is an attractive place to go for a drink or dinner on the town. Just don't stray too far from the campus.

Jersey shore in springtime. The Rutgers College Program Council offers trips ranging from white-water rafting to mountain climbing to skiing. "The variety of activities at Rutgers provides you with the opportunity to have fun any way you desire," says one student. "There are lots of on-campus social activities," a senior explains. "Movies, coffeehouses, local and bigger bands, lectures, parties. Off-campus activity includes frat parties and bars." In the past five years, students enrolled in the Citizenship and Service Education Program at Rutgers contributed more than ninety thousand hours of service to communities across New Jersey. "Students definitely get involved in the surrounding community and do a lot of volunteer work," says a senior.

The Greek system, which attracts only a small percentage of men and women, is entirely off campus. While the school neither owns nor administers any of the Greek organizations, it does have a university office for Greek affairs, which oversees the welfare of those belonging to fraternities and sororities. Students say a lot of the nightlife for the New Brunswick campuses takes place at the Greek houses. Reportedly, it is "difficult to drink in dorms," but underage students drink if they really want to. Each college has its own student center with pinball machines, pool tables, bowling alleys, and a snack bar. Major social events include Reggae Day at Livingston, Agricultural Field Day at Cook, and Oktoberfest for the campus as a whole. Pioneer Pride Night is Camden's big party. During homecoming, tailgate parties are held in the stadium parking lot, featuring tons of food (including roast pigs and whole sides of beef), continuous music, and thousands of revelers.

"I feel I've grown so much here and learned so much about being a member of a rich and diverse community."

Varsity, intramural, and club sports fill whatever gap is left by the social scene. In fact, the university fields the highest number of athletes—more than one thousand— of any university in the nation. The Rutgers baseball team is competitive, as are many other sports, including football, basketball, tennis, lacrosse, soccer, cross-country, and track. Women's basketball, fencing, soccer, softball, field hockey, tennis, and track teams are also strong. A member of the Big East in football, Rutgers faces a tough schedule that includes Boston College, Miami, Syracuse, and West Virginia. Big East Conference competition makes up for not getting to play Princeton, which in 1980 bowed out of what was then the oldest football rivalry in the nation.

Rutgers has a plethora of people and programs characteristic of large state universities. It also has a lot more, including loyal support from the state's legislature and private sector, and tuition at an affordable price. Says one satisfied student: "From the diversity of its majors and courses to the hundreds of student organizations on campus, Rutgers gives me a chance to explore a world of options."

If You Apply To ➢

Rutgers: Rolling admissions: Dec. 15. Financial aid: Mar. 15. Housing: June 15. Does not guarantee to meet demonstrated need. No campus or alumni interviews. SATs or ACTs: required. No SAT IIs. No essay. Apply to particular school.

University of St. Andrews: See page 345.

St. John's College

Annapolis campus: P.O. Box 2800, Annapolis, MD 21404-2800
Santa Fe campus: 1160 Camino Cruz Blanca, Santa Fe, NM 87505-4599

Books, books, and more books is what you'll get at St. John's—from Thucydides to Tolstoy, Euclid to Einstein. St. John's attracts smart, intellectual, and nonconformist students who like to talk (and argue) about books. Easy to get in, not so easy to graduate.

The two campuses of St. John's College may be a thousand miles apart, but they share an all-consuming quest for knowledge in the classical tradition. St. John's has no lectures and no traditional professors. Instead, classes are led by tutors, who guide students as they seek knowledge from one another and from great philosophers and thinkers, from Thucydides and Tolstoy to Euclid and Einstein. St. John's may be the most intellectual college in the country, making even erudite Chicago look like a party school. "I am here to get an education, and become a responsible human being, and not just earning a degree so that I can go off and make money," says a sophomore.

Physically, the two St. John's campuses are more than just three time zones from one another. The Colonial brick structures of the small urban campus in Annapolis, where the central classroom building dates from 1742, are squeezed into the city's historic district. With the Maryland state capitol and the U.S. Naval Academy in the neighborhood, this campus exudes an old-world ambiance. The other campus occupies 250 acres on the outskirts of sun-drenched Santa Fe. The adobe-style buildings standing silhouetted against the Sangre de Cristo Mountains offer beautiful views of the city below. Though it's far from public transportation, students at St. John's in Santa Fe can get back to nature in a nearby national forest. Students may attend both campuses during their academic careers, and about a quarter do so.

St. John's has no professors in the usual sense because the Great Books—about a hundred and fifty of the most influential works of Western civilization—are the teachers. Both campuses follow a curriculum that would have delighted poet and educator Matthew Arnold, who argued that the goal of education is "to know the best which has been thought and said in the world." The St. John's curriculum, known as "the program," has every student read the Great Books in roughly chronological order. All students major in liberal arts, discussing the books in seminars, writing papers about them, and debating the riddles of human existence they raise.

At St. John's there are no registration or scheduling hassles; the daily course of study for all four years is mapped out before a student sets foot on campus. It includes four years of mathematics, two years of ancient Greek and French, three years of laboratory science, a year of music, and, of course, four years of Great Books seminars. Freshmen study the Greeks and Romans, sophomores advance to the Renaissance, juniors cover the seventeenth and eighteenth centuries, and seniors do the nineteenth and twentieth centuries. Readings are from primary sources only: Math from Euclid and Ptolemy, physics from Einstein, psychology from Freud, and so on. For about seven weeks in the junior and senior years, seminars are suspended and students study a book or topic one-on-one with a tutor. The assumption is that the Great Books can stand on their own, representing the highest achievements of human intellect. Students are proud that the educational program has changed little in forty, sixty, or eighty years (but it depends on

> **"It's all rigorous. Some of it—studying calculus in the raw by reading Newton and Leibniz—is downright Olympic."**

Annapolis Website:
  www.sjca.edu
Location: City center
Total Enrollment: 549
Undergraduates: 465
Male/Female: 55/45
SAT Ranges: V 660–750
  M 550–685
Financial Aid: 62%
Expense: Pr $ $
Phi Beta Kappa: No
Applicants: 450
Accepted: 71%
Enrolled: 39%
Grad in 6 Years: 70%
Returning Freshmen: 79%
Academics: ✍ ✍ ✍ ✍ ½
Social: 🍺 🍺 🍺
Q of L: ★ ★ ★ ★
Admissions: (410) 626-2522
Email Address:
  admissions@sjca.edu

Santa Fe Website:
  www.sjcsf.edu
Location: City outskirts
Total Enrollment: 531
Undergraduates: 444
Male/Female: 55/45
SAT Ranges: V 630–720
  M 560–650
ACT Range: 26–30
Financial Aid: 67%
Expense: Pr $ $
Phi Beta Kappa: No
Applicants: 358
Accepted: 80%
Enrolled: 55%
Grad in 6 Years: 58%
Returning Freshmen: N/A
Academics: ✍ ✍ ✍ ✍ ½

(Continued)

Social: ☎ ☎ ☎
Q of L: ★ ★ ★ ★
Admissions: (505) 984-6060
Email Address:
admissions@sjcsf.edu

Strongest Program:
The Great Books Program

who you ask), and hopefully, says a freshman in Sante Fe, the school "will always change with reluctance."

Overall, students say the junior year, with its advanced curriculum in math and the natural sciences, is the most challenging, though competition is minimal. "About the only thing I've noticed is that almost everyone here is very smart, and very dedicated," says a freshman. "We talk about class outside class," says a junior. There are no multiple-choice tests and no formal exams, but small classes make it impossible to slide by. "It's all rigorous," a junior says. "Some of it—studying calculus in the raw by reading Newton and Leibniz—is downright Olympic. Academically, we each do what we can and roll with the punches. Having no written tests removes a lot of the anxiety, but none of the difficulty." Math, languages, and lab sciences are very strong, "but the music class sophomore year could use a bit more structure," says another student.

Though the curriculum is far more structured and classical than any other college, the method of presentation is as radical as that of any alternative school. Tutors would be professors at any other institution; at St. John's, they are considered only the most advanced students in class. Like true Renaissance men, tutors must be able to teach any subject in the curriculum, and in a few years' time, they do. Many never publish at all; they put teaching above all else. "Tutors are there to help us discover things on our own," says a freshman from Annapolis. Instruction is entirely by small discussion groups, and student–faculty relations are excellent. "Students get disappointed when classes are cancelled, and complain that tutors do not assign enough papers," one student says.

Students are proud that the educational program has changed little in forty, sixty, or eighty years (but it depends on who you ask).

Many St. John's students find they need a year off between sophomore and junior years; some switch from Annapolis to Santa Fe or vice versa, not only for a change of scenery, but also for a change of climate. The Santa Fe campus, founded in 1964 to increase the school's size without sacrificing the virtues of a small campus, is more relaxed than the comparatively uptight Annapolis campus. As dutiful as the cadets at the Naval Academy across the street, Annapolis Johnnies come as close as students can to learning every waking hour of the day. "Students here are very thoughtful, informed, and always ready to discuss whatever they're currently studying, both in and out of the classroom," says a sophomore.

Though the reasons students choose St. John's are never simple, the common thread is a fierce love of learning. "Students are looking for something more than anything they can find at another college, or any textbook," says an Annapolis freshman. "We're after the 'why' of knowledge, not just the 'what.'" Most students are bright, opinionated, and have no use for the status quo. "The one thing we all have in common is a passion for what we study," says a sophomore on the same campus. "All St. John's students feel strongly about the importance of the books we read." There's not much of a political scene, a Santa Fe freshman says, calling those issues trite: "I'd rather discuss eternal ideas than passing events." Admission of qualified students is first-come, first-served. After all spaces fill up (the school has a strict cap on enrollment), admissions begin for the following semester. A fifth of the students are transfers from more conventional colleges—a true act of devotion, since St. John's requires all students to begin as freshmen. Minorities represent 8 percent of the student body in Sante Fe and 7 percent in Annapolis; there's little racial tension, though the same can't be said for intellectual snobbery.

There are no fraternities or sororities here, though a favorite T-shirt has the St. John's name and motto printed in Greek.

Sixty-five percent of students in Annapolis and 75 percent in Santa Fe, including most freshmen, live on campus. Annapolis dorms are co-ed, and some buildings date to the mid-nineteenth century; a sophomore calls them "somewhat cramped, but well-maintained." Because of high demand for campus housing, plans are underway to build another residence. The age of existing buildings shows in the showers, where "the water often changes temperature," says one student. Upperclassmen typically live off campus in apartments and group houses; those who stay in the dorms usually get single rooms. The Santa Fe campus has a collection of small two-story dorms, housing twenty students each, located seven-thousand-feet above sea level. Views from the rooms rival those of some luxury hotels, as the nearby mountains turn blood red at sunset. In Santa Fe, most students get singles or divided double rooms, though demand for housing there also outstrips supply.

Santa Fe undergraduates plunge into the outdoorsy activities made possible by their mountaintop location, while Annapolis students limit their adventures to intramural teams with names like the Druids and the Furies. The annual croquet tournament against the U.S. Naval Academy attracts five thousand spectators in spring finery, who consume mass quantities of wine and cheese. "Most of the time, we win," says one Johnnie. Road trips to Washington, D.C., Baltimore, New York, and Assateague State Park are options for students with cars; the annual spring break trip to the Santa Fe campus is known as Wagons West. In Santa Fe, some students venture south of the border on weekends

> While intramurals are popular, fencing is the only intercollegiate sport at Santa Fe, and there are none at Annapolis.

> "Students get disappointed when classes are cancelled, and complain that tutors do not assign enough papers."

to Juarez, Mexico, and others head to the hot springs of White Sands, New Mexico. Nearby blues and jazz clubs are also popular, though one student cautions that town shuts down around 9 p.m. "Santa Fe is small, artsy, and expensive," sighs a sophomore. "It's good for lectures, restaurants, and concerts, but the rest of the activities are beyond my budget."

Drinking is a favored release for Johnnies, who have of course read Plato's *Symposium* and are familiar with the likes of Rabelais. Although no one under twenty-one may be served at college-sponsored events, which are patrolled to prevent underage drinking, youngsters tip their share of brew at smaller gatherings and in their rooms. Only students who are extremely rowdy or disruptive are reported to the dean's office to face penalties. "People are too busy working to have much of a social life," says a freshman in Santa Fe. "Parties are common, but laid-back," a classmate agrees. "You're just as likely to find someone at a party with Aristotle in their hand as a beer." Did we mention that there are no fraternities or sororities here, though a favorite T-shirt has the St. John's name and motto printed in Greek?

Popular annual events on both campuses include Lola's, a casino night sponsored by the junior class to raise money for Reality, a three-day festival of food, games, and general debauchery thrown for the seniors the weekend before commencement. "A big part of Reality is the Spartan Mad-Ball game, which pits the freshmen and seniors against the sophomores and juniors in a free-for-all," says a junior. "The only rule is no one can use motorized devices or excessively sharp objects." There's also Fasching, a 1930s-style formal dance; the Ark party, held to celebrate the sophomores' completion of the Old Testament; and Oktoberfest, which takes students to the ski basin for "good beer and German trappings," says a sophomore. Senior Prank is a day-long surprise party for the whole college community. While intramurals are popular, fencing is the only intercollegiate sport at Santa Fe, and there are none at Annapolis.

A Santa Fe freshman says he chose St. John's because it's "a quiet place to study among similarly minded peers," lamenting "the idiocy of less-dedicated students who ruin the community." And indeed, the motley crew of environmentalists, Goths, and ultraconservatives that had happily coexisted here has been replaced in some measure with "good-grade rich kids" who complain about the amount of work, says a sophomore. "I don't agree," one student says. "If you want to cruise, go somewhere else." As many colleges and universities try desperately to grow and change, St. John's cherishes its tradition—including the mandate that seniors wear formal academic dress to their oral examinations, which are open to the public. As they march by, midshipmen often chant, "I don't want a real degree, that's why I

Overlaps

Annapolis: Chicago, Vassar, Bryn Mawr, Oberlin, Smith

Santa Fe: Chicago, Reed, Oberlin, Sarah Lawrence, Carleton go to SJC." Johnnies take it all in stride. "We think it's pretty funny," says one. "At least we can dress ourselves."

If You Apply To ➤

St. John's: Rolling admissions: Mar. 1 (priority consideration). Financial aid: Feb. 15 (priority, Annapolis); Mar. 1 (priority, Santa Fe). Campus interviews: recommended, evaluative. Alumni interviews: recommended, informational. SATs and ACTs: optional. SAT IIs: optional. Accepts the Common Application (with supplemental essays) and electronic applications. Essay questions: evaluate strengths and weaknesses of your formal education, and explain why you wish to attend St. John's; describe reading habits and experience with books, and discuss one aspect of a book that's shaped your thoughts; and describe the value of an experience from which you've derived exceptional benefit. Optional essay discussing additional relevant information, such as health or family situation, special talents or hobbies, religion, accomplishments or postcollege plans. Gives special attention to essays.

St. John's University and College of St. Benedict

St. John's campus: P.O. Box 7155, Collegeville, MN 56321-7155
St. Benedict campus: 37 South College Avenue, St. Joseph, MN 56374-2099

St. John's is a throwback to the way college was fifty years ago: men and women on separate campuses and copious amounts of school spirit. Roman Catholics comprise about 80 percent of the students and monastery brothers make up 20 percent of the faculty.

Website: www.csbsju.edu
Total Enrollment: 4,118
Undergraduates: 3,969
Male/Female: 48/52
SAT Ranges: V 530–650
  M 560–660
ACT Range: 22–28
Financial Aid: 60%
Expense: Pr $ $
Phi Beta Kappa: No
Applicants: 2,375
Accepted: 86%
Enrolled: 48%
Grad in 6 Years: 77%
Returning Freshmen: 90%
Academics: 🖉 🖉 🖉
Social: ☎ ☎ ☎
Q of L: ★ ★ ★
Admissions: (800) 245-6467 (St. John's) or (800) 544-1489 (St. Benedict)
Email Address: admissions@csbsju.edu

Strongest Programs:
Biology

Remember when women's colleges had nearby brother schools, when dorms were single-sex, and when visitors of the opposite gender were only welcome at certain times? Those days are alive and well at St. John's University and the College of St. Benedict, though students don't seem to mind. These two single-sex campuses are three miles apart, but they share a common heritage and mission: that students and faculty work together to better understand and use the liberal arts, guided by principles of the Catholic faith. The schools' small size and strong sense of tradition give rise to tight-knit community. "Everyone smiles or says hello to one another and opens doors for each other, even if they don't know them," says a junior economics major. "There is a great sense of community, and everyone is so warm and welcoming."

Owned and operated by the largest Benedictine monastery in the world, St. John's occupies 2,400 pristine acres in rural Minnesota, an area filled with forests, lakes, and the wide-open spaces perfect for outdoorsy types. Alongside an ancient quadrangle erected by monks is a strikingly modern church designed by Marcel Breuer, with a towering bell banner and three-story stained-glass window. In recent years, St. John's has invested nearly $20 million in its facilities, overhauling the football stadium, renovating Warner Palaestra, and building a 48,000-square-foot science center. Down the road in St. Joseph sits St. Benedict, which offers an impressive combination of contemporary and carefully restored turn-of-the-century buildings. New residences have been built on both campuses, and students can travel between them on a free shuttle bus.

"The professors are always willing to help, and you can often find them at school on the weekend."

St. John's and St. Benedict have a joint academic program through which students take classes together on both campuses. The core curriculum reflects the Benedictine focus on the humanities, sciences, and fine arts, and requires two cross-disciplinary courses: a first-year symposium and a senior seminar. Students must also demonstrate proficiency in math and a foreign language, take courses emphasizing global and gender perspectives, writing, discussion, and quantitative reasoning, and fulfill disciplinary requirements in the fine arts, humanities, natural and social sciences, and the Judeo–Christian heritage.

An honors program serves exceptional freshmen, and skilled sophomores may also apply. The most popular major is management, which benefits from a computer-simulation program that places students in charge of corporations and lets them try their hand at free-market enterprise. Also popular are communication, biology, psychology, and nursing. Students give high marks to science programs such as chemistry and the new environmental studies major, as well as to nutrition and music. The medieval studies program benefits from the Hill Monastic Manuscript Library, one of the foremost microfilm collections of centuries-old handwritten manuscripts. Much to students' dismay, the schools have eliminated their optional January term, which had provided time for short trips abroad, or for internships, research projects, and part-time work.

No class here has more than fifty students, and some fill up fast. Students say it can be tough for nursing, education, and music majors to graduate in four years, especially if they come to those fields late. Generally, though, students who need to take a course can petition for a seat if it's closed—and if there's enough demand, the schools may even offer another section. The small classes also encourage strong student–faculty ties. "The professors are always willing to help, and you can often find them at school on the weekend," says a senior. "I have really been submerged in a broad variety of knowledge," agrees a sophomore. Monastery brothers make up 20 percent of the St. John's faculty, and sisters make up a contingent of the St. Benedict professors. For those who tire of the Minnesota winters, which can start in September and run until April, international study programs are offered in twelve countries, from Austria and Australia to South Africa and Spain. Each program is limited to about thirty students, and about half of CSB and SJU students take part. The university sends more students to study abroad each year than any other small liberal arts college.

Though 70 percent of students at St. John's and St. Benedict are Roman Catholic, few resemble priests in training. In fact, the vast majority goes to work after graduation, and 15 percent go on to graduate or professional school. Eighty-three percent are from Minnesota, and most are white, public school alumni from middle-class backgrounds. African-Americans and Hispanics each constitute 1 percent of the student body, and Asian-Americans add 2 percent, though the administration is trying to increase minority enrollment. Politically, "abortion and war are two big issues," says a management major. Also up for debate, says a psychology and communication major, are "the sexual abuse scandal within the Catholic church, and various issues that surround the church and what it stands for." Generally, though, the tone of discourse remains respectful. Merit scholarships ranging from $2,000 to $12,000 are available to qualified students.

Eighty-two percent of students live on campus; freshman and sophomores are required to stay in the dorms, which are staffed partly by the monks at St. John's and sisters at St. Benedict. But lest you think a nun is watching your every move, "students have enough freedom in dorm rooms to make them comfortable," says a philosophy major. "The dorms are spacious, clean, and well-kept," says a sophomore. Each room has a sink, plus an Internet connection for each student. Other options include small off-campus houses for half a dozen students each, an experimental Christian community of five units for 110 students, and college-owned apartments, including an earth-sheltered complex on the shore of a lake. Campus dwellers can choose from among four dining halls, and the on-campus bakery "makes good breads, cookies, and other treats," says an economics major. Upperclassmen typically live off campus in a nearby town and commute by car or college bus.

(Continued)
Chemistry
Computer Science
Economics
English
Mathematics
Music
Political Science

St. John's has invested nearly $20 million in its facilities, overhauling the football stadium, renovating Warner Palaestra, and building a 48,000-square-foot science center.

Each year, students look forward to the Festival of Nations, the mother–daughter brunch and father–daughter dance, the Senior Farewell, and spring break trips involving community service or missionary work. Also popular is the annual Pinestock Folk Festival, which welcomes the new season with a day of concerts.

Since there are no fraternities or sororities here, students have learned to make their own fun. SJU's Stephen B. Humphrey Fine Arts Theater and CSB's Benedicta Arts Center host a wide variety of cultural events. For those seeking typical college fun, "the Joint Events Council plans dances, game shows, concerts and a number of other activities," says a sophomore. "Off-campus, there are many things to do in St. Cloud and also in St. Joseph, such as parties, coffee shops, restaurants, shopping, and movies." St. Cloud (population 50,000) is fifteen minutes away by car, and the Twin Cities are about an hour away; both are among students' favorite road trips. Each year, students look forward to the Festival of Nations, the mother–daughter brunch and father–daughter dance, the Senior Farewell, and spring break trips involving community service or missionary work. Also popular is the annual Pinestock Folk Festival, which welcomes the new season with a day of concerts featuring national acts, such as Ben Harper and Better than Ezra.

> "There is a great sense of community, and everyone is so warm and welcoming."

Religion may be the most dominant program on campus, but football is a close second. The team is a perennial Division III powerhouse, and its rivalry with St. Thomas is as strong as ever. Curiously enough, a team of guys, known as The Rat Pack gets students psyched up for games. St. Benedict basketball and soccer teams and the football, ice hockey, Nordic skiing, and golf teams at St. John's recently have brought home conference championships. Nonvarsity students can participate in the intramural program.

Students at these two Catholic schools are "are here for a good education," says a sophomore. "They work hard and they want to be here." A classmate describes them as "very friendly, warm, and open," comparing the campus community to "a big happy family." Those who attend St. John's and St. Benedict revel in the schools' small-town setting, their traditions, and the grounding that comes from their shared Catholic values. With small classes, ample opportunity for independent research and study abroad, and a strong sense of community, these students are a contented lot.

Overlaps

University of St. Thomas, University of Minnesota–Twin Cities, Gustavus Adolphus, St. Cloud State, St. Olaf

If You Apply To ➤

St. John's and St. Benedict: Early action: Dec. 1. Rolling admissions: Feb. 1 (priority consideration). Financial aid: Mar. 15. Housing: May 15. Meets demonstrated need of 85%. Campus interviews: recommended, informational. No alumni interviews. SATs or ACTs: required. Accepts the Common Application and electronic applications. Essay question: issue of personal, local, national, or international concern; another person you would be for one day and why; how your culture and ethnic identity has fostered your appreciation of difference; a significant experience, achievement, risk, or ethical dilemma; or a topic of interest to you.

St. Lawrence University

Canton, NY 13617

St. Lawrence is perched far back in the north country, closer to Ottawa and Montreal than to Syracuse. Isolation breeds camaraderie, and SLU students have a special bond similar to that at places like Dartmouth and Whitman. Environmental studies is the crown jewel.

Website: www.stlawu.edu
Location: Village

St. Lawrence University beckons those seeking an education that exercises both body and mind. Located deep in upstate New York, this school's excellent liberal arts curriculum is complemented by a close-knit community—and one of the best environmental studies programs in the nation. Students take full advantage of their pristine and rugged surroundings, and many prefer to find their thrills on the ski slopes and hiking trails rather than the dance floor or concert hall.

The St. Lawrence campus—which has undergone $80 million in construction and renovation over the past few years—is just ninety minutes from Ottawa, the Canadian capital. Hiking trails, a river, and a golf course surround thirty buildings, which sit centered on a thousand acres. Many buildings date from the late nineteenth century, and though their exteriors have been preserved, their interiors are fully modernized. Winter temperatures average between twenty and thirty degrees, but the good news is it's only a ten-minute walk between the two most distant buildings. A whole new world of athletic facilities has sprung up: a fitness center, field house with a track, tennis courts, and climbing wall, soccer and baseball fields, and a new boathouse for the crew team. After all that exercise, students can go chow down in their new dining hall. The building boom doesn't stop there—a 120-unit senior townhouse-style residence and a new student center have opened.

St. Lawrence offers a classical liberal arts education, emphasizing quality over quantity. Enrollment has been reduced to improve the student/faculty ratio, keep classes small, and allow for more team teaching. The sciences will undergo a $60 million construction and renovation project to help them meet the needs of an innovative curriculum. St. Lawrence is well known for its environmental studies. Among the unique offerings are outdoor education courses in music and writing, and a student-run, self-sustainable residence. General education requirements can be satisfied through one of two tracks. The "standard track" requires one course in the natural sciences, one in social sciences, one in humanities, and one in any non-Western topic, plus two courses in "classical liberal arts" (math or symbolic logic, arts, and language). The "alternative track" is based on St. Lawrence's Cultural Encounters program, which includes core courses, foreign language study, science and mathematics, one semester of study abroad, and a senior seminar.

The university's First-Year Program—small, interdisciplinary, two-semester courses taught by professors from all departments, who then become academic advisors—is "a good stepping stone to get you into the college environment," says a junior. Psychology is the most popular major, followed by English, economics, biology and government, but many students prefer less conventional programs, such as Renaissance music. Administrators say the music department is small but growing steadily with the recent addition of an instrumental music faculty position.

Striving "to make the world our classroom," St. Lawrence augments its on-campus offerings with numerous study abroad programs. More than half of the students head overseas to such places as Kenya, Japan, Costa Rica, China, Australia, Denmark, or India, or stay right nearby for the new "Adirondack semester" at Saranac Lake. Students may also take advantage of group-sponsored exchange programs in Canada or Washington, D.C. Frequent trips to Ottawa for cultural and political events are part of the academic and extracurricular agendas. There are also five-year programs with other universities in engineering, nursing, and management. Some lucky students will have the opportunity to participate in the St. Lawrence University Fellows Program, which supports faculty/student research done in the summer.

St. Lawrence students speak highly of their professors and say administrators have worked hard to increase the school's academic rigor over the past few years. That results in some disconnects: "The academic climate is mixed, split between those who are excited by their academics

"I have had the opportunity to study with exceptional instructors who motivate me, interest me, and care about my future."

and those who don't care," says a senior. "But the coursework is pretty demanding." Small classes make for a lot of attention and assistance from professors. "I have had

(Continued)
Total Enrollment: 2,293
Undergraduates: 2,150
Male/Female: 47/53
SAT Ranges: V 520–620
  M 520–620
ACT Range: 22–28
Financial Aid: 69%
Expense: Pr $ $ $ $
Phi Beta Kappa: Yes
Applicants: 2,867
Accepted: 65%
Enrolled: 33%
Grad in 6 Years: 72%
Returning Freshmen: 87%
Academics: ✍ ✍ ✍
Social: ☎ ☎ ☎
Q of L: ★ ★ ★
Admissions: (315) 229-5261
Email Address:
  admissions@stlawu.edu

Strongest Programs:
Psychology
Sociology
Environmental Studies
Math
Speech and Theater
English

The university's First-Year Program—small, interdisciplinary, two-semester courses taught by professors from all departments, who then become academic advisors—is "a good stepping stone to get you into the college environment," says a junior.

the opportunity to study with exceptional instructors who motivate me, interest me, and care about my future," an English and government major reports. Most "Larries" agree that there is no cut-throat competition here. The emphasis on shared learning is furthered by the school's residential college system, through which students living in the same dorm take a common interdisciplinary course team-taught by professors from multiple disciplines. To complement their year-long common course, first-year students live together in one of twelve residential "communities" with forty to fifty students each.

St. Lawrence students are a conventional bunch with a streak of outdoorsy non-conformity. The student body is predominantly white, with African-Americans, Hispanics, and Asian-American students constituting 5 percent of the student body. Qualified students vie for merit scholarships worth up to $15,000, and talented puck-pushers may take advantage of athletic scholarships in hockey.

Dorm life at St. Lawrence is your standard bed, dresser, chest of drawers, and desk-with-a-light. "There has been a steady improvement in the state of the dorms over the last four years," says a senior majoring in economics. Most rooms are well maintained, though students complain it sometimes takes a while for repair requests to be addressed. Most dorms also have co-ed wings, and students generally live in doubles. Freshmen are placed in their residential colleges. The new town-house complex made finding housing easier for the 95 percent that stay on. Seniors occasionally gain permission to live off campus. Campus living also has its rewards: the food served in the dining hall frequently features student recipes. Twenty-three percent of the women and 15 percent of the men live and eat in sorority and frater-nity houses. Other options for grub include the campus pub in the student center, a cafe in the physical education building, and a convenience store.

The social life at SLU centers on campus because—thanks to the school's small size—most students know each other. The university provides activities, such as a nonalcoholic campus nightclub, a new pool hall, four different current movies each week, and the campus coffeehouse—a great place to hear a band, acoustic guitarist, or comedian. Still, students say, "most of the social life revolves around Greek houses,"

"There has been a steady improvement in the state of the dorms over the last four years."

where independent students are welcome, too. No hard liquor or kegs are allowed on campus, and the school has clamped down on underage drinking. However, at St. Lawrence, to "make a run for the border" doesn't mean heading for Mexican fast food; the purchasing age for liquor in Ontario is a mere nineteen years old.

Canton is a charming town of restored Victorian buildings and storefronts offering everything from bagels to handmade jewelry to bars and restaurants. As a college town, however, it rates "nonexistent," says a sociology major. Potsdam, ten minutes away, has more to offer.

On campus, the university's Winterfest is an annual two-week celebration of the season. During Peak Weekend, the SLU Outing Club tries to "put St. Lawrence students on every peak in the Adirondacks." Most St. Lawrence students enjoy sports; the school's fine athletic facilities, including an indoor field house, nine squash courts, indoor tennis, a pool, a three-story climbing wall, and ropes course, cater to varsity athletes and weekend warriors alike.

St. Lawrence's on-campus golf course doubles as a running route and a cross-country skiing trail during the winter. Hiking and rock climbing are other outdoor exercise options, as is canoeing the St. Lawrence River. In varsity sports, men's hockey is the top draw, especially when played against archrival Clarkson. Champi-onship teams include women's soccer, basketball, and track; men's soccer, basket-ball, track, and lacrosse; and softball. Intramurals are the thing to do for almost everyone, with competition ranging from softball to hockey to volleyball.

With administrators raising the academic bar and a lengthy round of renovation and construction about to conclude, St. Lawrence is a school on the rise. It could be the ideal school for those seeking a small, caring environment—and wanting to get back to nature.

<table>
<tr><td>If You
Apply
To ➤</td><td>St. Lawrence: Early decision: Nov. 15, Jan. 15. Regular admissions and financial aid: Feb. 15. Guarantees to meet demonstrated need of 33%. Campus interviews: recommended, evaluative. Alumni interviews: optional, informational. SATs or ACTs: required. SAT IIs: optional. Accepts the Common Application and electronic applications. Essay question: significant experience, achievement or risk; issue of concern; influential person; influential fictional or historical figure.</td></tr>
</table>

St. Mary's College of Maryland

St. Mary's City, MD 20686

A public liberal arts institution of the same breed as Mary Washington, UNC–Asheville, and William and Mary. St. Mary's historic but sleepy environs are ninety minutes from D.C. and Baltimore. With the Chesapeake Bay close at hand, St. Mary's is a haven for sailors.

Despite its religious-sounding name, St. Mary's is a public institution that has been designated the state's "honors college." Fifteen years ago, St. Mary's was just another complacent public college with a dazzling waterfront. But now, with rising test scores, increased state support, and growing numbers of applications, suffice it to say that St. Mary's is out to make waves. It also has the advantage of being one of the East Coast's prettiest schools, with its own beautiful marina located right on the St. Mary's River and plenty of opportunities to stroll along the shore and watch gorgeous sunsets.

St. Mary's got its start in 1840 as a women's seminary intended as a monument to the colonial birthplace of the state. The campus, built on a peninsula in southern Maryland where the Potomac River meets the Chesapeake Bay, is a mix of Colonial and modern architecture clustered directly on the waterfront. The college has taken advantage of its setting by establishing an outstanding center for marine research along the river. It's also part of an eleven-hundred-acre national historic landmark commemorating Maryland's first Colonial settlement; archeological digs dot the campus and provide opportunities for research. Spiffy new residence halls have just opened, and the athletic facility is undergoing a transformation that includes the addition of an Olympic-size pool and fitness center.

Students may sail through the bay, but not the academics; the curriculum is continuously improved and the courseload is getting tougher. "The academic climate is fairly rigorous," reports one student, though "students can balance the more difficult courses with the easier ones so at no point is any one semester too difficult." Students have excellent departments to choose from, especially biology, which places many of its grads into top graduate schools and research positions. The strong music department includes prize-winning pianist Brian Ganz as head of the piano faculty. St. Mary's has also created an independent student-designed major for more free-thinking types. A state-of-the-art science center, with fifty-five thousand square feet of classrooms, labs, and research space, benefits the already strong science departments. Neuroscience and biochemistry were recently added to the list of majors.

Website: www.smcm.edu
Location: Rural
Total Enrollment: 1,823
Undergraduates: 1,823
Male/Female: 40/60
SAT Ranges: V 570–680
   M 560–660
Financial Aid: 63%
Expense: Pub $ $ $ $
Phi Beta Kappa: Yes
Applicants: 1,884
Accepted: 59%
Enrolled: 38%
Grad in 6 Years: 81%
Returning Freshmen: 91%
Academics: ✐ ✐ ✐ ✐
Social: ☎ ☎ ☎
Q of L: ★ ★ ★ ★
Admissions: (800) 492-7181
Email Address:
   admissions@smcm.edu

Strongest Programs:
Biology
English
Economics
Political Science
Psychology

Course requirements include: English composition; second semester–level proficiency in a foreign language; Legacy of the Modern World, a history survey course; literature; mathematics; physical science; biology; behavioral science; policy science; Values Inquiry, an upper level philosophy course; and a lab. Also required is a Senior Experience. The school offers study abroad programs, including Oxford's Center for Medieval and Renaissance Studies; exchange programs in Germany, China, and France; and participates in the National Student Exchange. Closer to home, biology students can cruise the bay on the college's research boat. The Nitze Scholars Program, both highly respected and very selective, has further boosted St. Mary's academic standards. The good news is that all classes are taught by faculty, the even better news is the student/faculty ratio is just 12 to 1. "My teachers have all been very knowledgeable of the subjects and were enthusiastic in attempting to spark my interests," a student reports.

St. Mary's students are "probably the most well-rounded and culturally aware population I have ever met," says a student. Eighty-five percent of the student body hails from Maryland, and 80 percent comes out of public schools. More minority students are also finding their way to the peninsula; 7 percent of the school are African-American, 3 percent Hispanic, and 4 percent Asian-American. The big social issue on campus, according to students, is the environment. The political atmosphere here is described as fairly liberal and laid back. St. Mary's offers 298 scholarships for academic merit that range from $1,000 to $7,000, but there are no athletic scholarships.

Seventy-nine percent of students live on campus. Options include five residence halls, three of which are co-ed, and a newly constructed complex of co-ed residential suites. Best of all are the eighty-one two-story townhouses that allow upperclassmen with sufficient credits to do their own cooking. "Everyone looks forward to having enough credits to get into a townhouse," remarks an anxious sophomore. Older students get preference if they decide to retain a room or want one nearby, and students select rooms based on the number of academic credits they have acquired. Those who do live off campus have enticing options, including old farmhouses and riverside cottages available for rent. Students who tire of cafeteria food can join the vegetarian co-op or just go catch their own fish and crabs.

St. Mary's secluded location—about an hour and a half from either Washington, D.C., or Baltimore—means there's little nightlife off campus. The seclusion gets mixed responses from students: "St. Mary's is a pretty close community. Weekend social life is usually centered around a few parties that everyone attends," one student comments. Campus organizations, including a film society, sponsor several events a week. The main

"It's virtually impossible to graduate without knowing how to sail."

source of fun, of course, is the surrounding water and its sporty offerings. "It's virtually impossible to graduate without knowing how to sail," says one student. The waterfront also becomes the focus of campus-wide activities, including World Carnival, an Earth Day celebration, and the cardboard boat race held each fall. More than 70 percent of students become involved in community service.

Although certainly not known for its athletics, Division III St. Mary's has recently taken off. The co-ed and women's sailing teams, coached by a former member of the U.S Sailing Team, have won several national titles, including the 2002 Intercollegiate Sailing Association Co-ed Dingy North American Championship. Women's sailing and men's lacrosse are also strong, the women having taken the 2002 Capital Athletic Conference Championship. The Ultimate Frisbee golf club team has a heated rivalry with Navy and even attracts considerable alumni interest.

St. Mary's is bent on establishing itself as one of the country's premier public liberal arts colleges. Though its small size and isolation can seem stifling at times, most students appreciate the close bonds that are created at this school. With its

Overlaps

University of Maryland–College Park, University of Maryland–Baltimore County, Washington College (MD), William and Mary, McDaniel College

unique blend of learning and life on the waterfront, says one student, "It's like your parents are paying for you to live at a vacation resort for eight months of the year."

| If You Apply To ➤ | **St. Mary's:** Early decision: Dec. 1. Regular admissions: Jan. 15. Financial aid: Mar. 1. Does not guarantee to meet demonstrated need. Campus interviews: recommended, informational. Alumni interviews: optional, informational. SATs or ACTs: required, SAT preferred. SAT IIs: optional. Accepts electronic applications. Essay question: title of autobiography; most significant invention; describe ideal college; your most significant learning experience. |

St. Olaf College

1520 St. Olaf Avenue, Northfield, MN 55057-1098

Lutheran to the core, the well-scrubbed undergraduates at St. Olaf are a stark contrast to the grunge of crosstown rival Carleton. The music program is world famous, and a whopping 60 percent of the students study abroad. Daily chapel is not mandatory, but many students go.

Northfield, Minnesota, which bills itself the city of "Cows, Colleges, and Contentment," is home to St. Olaf College—and the blondest student body this side of Oslo. This small Midwest school, founded by Norwegian Lutheran immigrants, was named for the country's patron saint and aims to be "an excellent liberal arts college of the church." One student describes her peers at St. Olaf as "Minnesota nice," adding, "You can't go anywhere without saying hi to people. Even if you don't know a person, there is still a feeling of belonging to the same community. We are friendly, outgoing, hardworking, and we love to have fun."

St. Olaf's meticulously landscaped 350-acre campus, featured in several architectural journals, is located on Manitou Heights, overlooking the Cannon River valley and the city of Northfield. More than ten thousand trees, native prairie, and a wetlands wildlife area surround the thirty-four native limestone buildings that form the campus. The student union, the Buntrock Commons, offers dining and food services, a bookstore, post office, conference and banquet facilities, movie theater, and game room.

All students at St. Olaf complete a general education requirement that covers three areas: foundation studies, core studies, and integrative study. A first-year seminar emphasizing writing, a foreign language, math, oral communication, and physical education fulfill the first area. Two courses in each of six disciplines— Western culture, multicultural studies, art, literary studies, biblical studies, and theological studies—with two courses in natural sciences and two in social sciences, complete the second requirement. A course in ethical issues and perspectives fulfills the third area. Typically, fourteen to sixteen courses satisfy the general education requirements; some courses may fulfill requirements in more than one area.

"I like the community feeling a lot. It's one of the best things at Olaf."

Students give the nod to biology and chemistry, and the college also boasts a solid premed program; economics, psychology, English, and math are also popular majors. The music department draws high praise; it offers many performance opportunities with five school choirs, a band, and an orchestra. The choirs are often featured at church services and other religious events, and can regularly be heard singing with the Minnesota Orchestra. Weaker academic departments include

Website: www.stolaf.edu
Location: Small town
Total Enrollment: 3,041
Undergraduates: 3,041
Male/Female: 41/59
SAT Ranges: V 590–690
M 580–690
ACT Range: 25–30
Financial Aid: 58%
Expense: Pr $ $ $
Phi Beta Kappa: Yes
Applicants: 2,624
Accepted: 73%
Enrolled: 41%
Grad in 6 Years: 80%
Returning Freshmen: 93%
Academics: ✍ ✍ ✍ ✍
Social: ☎ ☎ ☎
Q of L: ★ ★ ★ ★
Admissions: (507) 646-3025
Email Address:
admissions@stolaf.edu

Strongest Programs:
Biology
Psychology
Economics
English
Mathematics

family resources and sociology. In the last quarter-century, the college has cultivated an international agenda for its students and faculty, and has created the largest international studies program in the country among liberal arts colleges. Programs are available in forty-eight countries.

The Finstad Office for Entrepreneurial Studies conveys knowledge about the challenges, risks, rewards, opportunities, and responsibilities of being an entrepreneur. Research is available in the sciences and psychology, and the Center for Integrative Studies allows students to form their own majors. All students get faculty advisors, and the vast majority of students graduate in four years. Students who participate in the intensive, nontraditional program—the two-year Great Conversation course in classic works—live together in one dorm to facilitate late-night study sessions. Additionally, because the program in international studies is an important part of the school's curriculum, more than 60 percent of students take advantage of study abroad opportunities, including those offered through membership in the Associated Colleges of the Midwest* consortium.

Faculty members at St. Olaf are highly praised by students. "The professors at St. Olaf are phenomenal," a sophomore says. "They don't lecture. They teach." Instructors participate in and out of the classroom, reportedly having as many as ten hours of open office time a week. Still, just because professors want to see them succeed doesn't mean students can coast. "I find the coursework demanding and usually spend two to three hours on homework for every hour of class. Sometimes more," one student says. There's also an annual study break where professors serve their stressed-out pupils ice cream.

Diversity is by far the hottest topic at St. Olaf. The student body is extremely homogeneous: 85 percent are white—a situation the administration says it is working to change through workshops and other awareness programs. African-Americans and Hispanics make up 1 percent of the student body each, while Asian-Americans account for 4 percent. Most students are high achievers from Midwestern public schools, drawn in part by hundreds of merit scholarships ranging from $500 to $9,000 per year. Despite their similar backgrounds, students say they have their differences. "Unfortunately, there is a typical or stereotypical Ole. They are typically blond, well-off, and very attractive. At the same time, two people who may look like they are similar may have very different views," a sophomore says.

Ninety-six percent of students live in on-campus housing, with college-owned houses available off campus, and freshmen are assigned double rooms in twenty-student "corridors," each with two junior counselors. Dorms are co-ed by floor, and each has its own personality. Rooms are selected by lottery, which students consider very fair. "I like the community feeling a lot," says an English major. "It's one of the best things at Olaf." Students eat in a large modern cafeteria, where the food is considered above average for

college fare. Every December, the dining hall serves a special meal of traditional Norwegian cuisine, including lutefisk, which "tastes awful," according to one junior philosophy major.

Opinions diverge on St. Olaf's social life. Some students blame peer apathy for the lack of things to do, noting "it's what you make of it." Others grouse about the dry campus or students' efforts to circumvent it, yet "most students seem to make very satisfying friendships that extend beyond the drinking scene," according to one student. "If you're looking for adventure and excitement, this is not the place to be," advises a freshman. Most weekend activities are on campus, including a nightclub called Lion's Pause and a coffeehouse, the Alley. The fine arts department provides many music, theater, and dance performances. And because there are no fraternities or sororities at St. Olaf, any large-scale weekend partying usually occurs off campus at the few bars in town, or even better, at crosstown rival Carleton College. The Student Activities Committee sponsors frequent dances, speakers, and cultural events, covered by student fees and at-the-door ticket sales. Daily chapel services, though not mandatory, are heavily attended, and studying is always another weekend option.

In the city of Northfield, there is little of social interest for St. Olaf students aside from Carleton, Olaf's liberal neighbor and chief rival. The most talked-about annual event, running more than seventy-five years, is the four-day Christmas Festival during which choirs, orchestras, and bands combine in televised concerts celebrating the birth of Jesus. Many students volunteer in Northfield and report a friendly rapport with the community. "They work in town, volunteer at the food shelf and at the schools, and have other programs to help out with the town," reports a senior. Nonetheless, for those with wanderlust, buses leave regularly for the twin cities of Minneapolis and St. Paul, which are less than an hour drive, where one can experience a shopper's paradise at the huge Mall of America. Chicago is also a popular road trip.

St. Olaf has outstanding Division III athletic programs. Women's cross-country and men's baseball secured recent conference titles. The diving program is strong as well. There is also an extensive intramural program, and broomball—ice hockey played with brooms instead of sticks, and shoes rather than skates—is the sport of choice in the winter. The St. Olaf football team competes against Carleton for the honor of having the statue in the town's square face the winning campus. The chorus of the school's fight song is "Um Ya Ya," which has become a popular chant on campus.

"I really like Olaf," says a student. "I've met some incredible people, been challenged, engaged, and excited about my academic pursuits, and I can't talk up the community vibe enough." For those yearning for a school where spirituality and scholarship exist on the same exalted plane, St. Olaf is a good bet. It's a place where students work hard, are encouraged by good teachers, toughened by Minnesota winters, and nourished by strong moral values—in addition to hearty Scandinavian food.

Overlaps

Gustavus Adolphus, Carleton, Luther, University of Wisconsin–Madison, University of Minnesota

If You Apply To ➢ **St. Olaf:** Rolling admissions. Early decision: Nov. 15. Early action: Dec. 15. Financial aid: Feb. 15 (priority). Guarantees to meet full demonstrated need. Campus interviews: recommended, informational. No alumni interviews. SATs or ACTs: required. SAT IIs: optional. Accepts the Common Application and electronic applications. Essay question: define an ideal community; meaning of diversity; what you would like to research.

Saint Louis University

221 North Grand Boulevard, St. Louis, MO 63103-2097

This is not your father's SLU. The campus and surrounding neighborhood have been spiffed up in the past two decades, and SLU's campus is a pleasant oasis from the bustle of midtown St. Louis. In addition to strengths in premed and communication, SLU has an unusual specialty in aviation.

Within sight of Saint Louis's famed Gateway Arch, the historical gateway to the American West, sits Saint Louis University, the first university established west of the Mississippi River. SLU offers students a "slew" of programs, from aviation and engineering to public service, social work, and meteorology. The school's academic

Website:
www.imagine.slu.edu
Location: Urban

(Continued)

Total Enrollment: 11,272

Undergraduates: 7,178

Male/Female: 46/54

SAT Ranges: V 530–640

M 530–655

ACT Range: 23–28

Financial Aid: 71%

Expense: Pr $ $

Phi Beta Kappa: Yes

Applicants: 6,281

Accepted: 72%

Enrolled: 34%

Grad in 6 Years: 71%

Returning Freshmen: 87%

Academics: ✍ ✍ ✍

Social: ☎ ☎

Q of L: ★ ★ ★

Admissions: (314) 977-2500

Email Address:

admitme@slu.edu

Strongest Programs:

Biology

Psychology

Communications

Finance

Management Information
   Systems

Marketing

SLU attracts scholars from around the globe with one of the world's most complete microfilm collections of Vatican documents.

atmosphere is shaped by its Roman Catholic—specifically Jesuit—tradition; administrators ensure that each student receives personal care and attention and expect graduates to contribute to society and lead efforts for social change.

The SLU campus has undergone an $870 million renovation and features pedestrian walkways, lush greenery, fountains, and sculptures, as well as the signature Saint Louis University gates at all entrances. Cupples House, a beautiful old mansion in the middle of campus, houses nineteenth-century furniture and an art gallery—and is just steps from the futuristic glass structure of the law school. Numerous renovations and campus additions have been completed over the last two years, including the former Compton Heights Hospital reopened as Salus Center, which now includes the School of Public Health; the renovated Childgarden Building, which is now the Academic Resources Center; and the Saint Louis University Museum of Art. Renovation and expansion has also been done on the Busch Memorial Center and the SLU Cancer Center.

In keeping with its strong Jesuit commitment to education in the broader sense, all SLU undergrads must complete distribution requirements in international cultures, fine arts, English, literature, science, social/behavioral science, mathematics, and history. Additionally, students must take philosophy and theology courses, such as SLUVision, which integrates community service with the philosophy and theology component. The most popular majors are biology, psychology, communications, marketing, and finance while premed also gets high marks from students. As might be expected, philosophy and theology are outstanding. Weaker spots are hard to find, however, one sophomore insists that, "students tend to stay away from majors that are not going to bring in a lot of revenue in their future careers." SLU attracts scholars from around the globe with one of the world's most complete microfilm collections of Vatican documents. Parks College, America's first certified college of aviation, offers degree programs in aviation science where students can become professional pilots. The College of Arts and Science's meteorology program provides students with an opportunity to study with specialists in satellite, radar, and mesoscale meteorology. The College of Public Service offers majors in communication disorders, educational studies, and urban affairs, which encourage students to put research into action.

> "The courses are rigorous enough to be challenging, but not too much to be overwhelming."

Nearly two-thirds of SLU freshmen come from the top quarter of their high school class, and a criminal justice major reports that "the courses are rigorous enough to be challenging, but not too much to be overwhelming." "The teachers expect a lot out of their students, but the students get a lot in return," says a senior. Students report few problems getting into classes, despite the fact that most enroll less than fifty, and say that graduating in four years is the norm. Study abroad is an option, too; SLU has one of the most charming and largest European campuses of an American university in Madrid, Spain. More than 830 SLU students currently study outside of the United States.

Fifty-six percent of SLU students hail from the Show-Me State; the balance represents all fifty states and more than seventy-three foreign countries. African-Americans comprise 7 percent of the student body, Asian-Americans 4 percent, and Hispanics 2 percent. Race relations tend to be nonconfrontational, and political correctness does not seem to be an issue for most students. There are some, however, who feel, "SLU is very political." One student comments, "SLU is a Jesuit institution, so issues of human rights and right to life are very prominent." One junior feels, "This is an excellent opportunity to learn about the world. Conformity is not encouraged." The Residential

> "This is an excellent opportunity to learn about the world. Conformity is not encouraged."

Life department trains diversity advocates who serve as programmers and facilitators for the dorms; they get more in-depth training about diversity, racism, and oppression. Generally, students come from private, religiously affiliated high schools, and are a friendly bunch dedicated to community service. The school offers 110 athletic scholarships, along with merit scholarships worth up to $28,150.

Speaking of residential life, 51 percent of students choose from a variety of housing options, including recently renovated residence halls. However, housing is not guaranteed. Upperclass members can move into courtyard-style apartments, which are newly furnished because they opened last year, reports a junior. SLU has all the advantages and problems usually associated with being in the middle of a city. But most students feel safe on campus because the school has officers on twenty-four-hour patrol ("bicycles, cars, and walking," says a junior) and ID checks at dorm doors. "I have never felt unsafe when I am on campus, but I do feel a little uncomfortable on the outskirts," one student reports.

Social life at SLU includes campus events, such as movies in the Quad, dances, and Greek parties, and options in downtown St. Louis, such as comedy clubs and sporting events. Road trips to Kansas City, Chicago, and nearby schools like the University of Illinois and Indiana University are also popular. Greek life at SLU—highly unusual for a Jesuit institution—claims 16 percent of the men and 17 percent of the women. Alcohol doesn't play a big role; open containers aren't allowed on campus, and only students who are of age can drink in their own rooms without underage roommates present. "A lot of students use fake IDs and can get into bars pretty easily," claims one junior. Spring Fever and Fall Festival, both annual events, feature bands, club-sponsored booths, and vendors. True to tradition, Sunday evening mass is usually packed, and many students participate in community service and outreach projects.

SLU has no varsity football team, but other Billiken squads more than compensate for this deficit. What's a Billiken? A history major says, "It was a common good-luck charm in the early 1900s." A popular sportswriter of the time said the charm resembled the then football coach, and the name stuck. The SLU men's soccer team has won a record ten NCAA national championships, and the men's basketball team brought home the Conference USA championship in 2000 and regularly contends for an NCAA Tournament berth; games against Marquette or Cincinnati draw crowds. The women's soccer team recently won their first outright conference championship. For weekend warriors, the Simon Recreation Center boasts a forty-meter pool, six racquetball courts, and loads of equipment.

"The teachers expect a lot out of their students, but the students get a lot in return."

St. Louis University may not have the marquee name or reputation of some of its larger Jesuit peers, but its winning students' devotion and increasing its national visibility by combining a caring faculty with athletic excellence and friendly and diverse undergraduates. One sophomore describes SLU as "small enough that I don't feel lost. Big enough that it's not like high school again." No wonder students are proud to "Just SLU it!"

Parks College, America's first certified college of aviation, offers degree programs in aviation science where students can become professional pilots.

Overlaps

Washington University (MO), Marquette, University of Missouri, Truman State, Loyola

If You Apply To ➤ | **SLU:** Rolling admissions. Financial aid and housing: May 1. Meets demonstrated need of 75%. Campus interviews: recommended, informational. Alumni interviews: optional, informational. SATs or ACTs: required. SAT IIs: optional. Apply to particular programs. Accepts the Common Application and electronic applications. Essay question: letter for future college roommate; description of your autobiography; why Saint Louis University?

University of San Francisco

2130 Fulton Street, San Francisco, CA 94117-1080

Talk about prime real estate: USF is next door to the legendary Haight-Ashbury district, catty-corner to Golden Gate park, and within five miles of the Pacific Ocean. Though USF is a Jesuit institution, only about half of its students are Roman Catholic. Pacific Rim studies is a stand-out.

Website: www.usfca.edu
Location: Urban
Total Enrollment: 8,194
Undergraduates: 3,863
Male/Female: 35/65
SAT Ranges: V 510–610
    M 510–610
ACT Range: 21–26
Financial Aid: 51%
Expense: Pr $ $ $ $
Phi Beta Kappa: No
Applicants: 3,590
Accepted: 82%
Enrolled: 28%
Grad in 6 Years: 65%
Returning Freshmen: 81%
Academics: ✎ ✎ ✎
Social: ☎ ☎ ☎
Q of L: ★ ★ ★ ★
Admissions: (415) 422-6563
Email Address:
    admission@usfca.edu

Strongest Programs:
Business Administration
Hospitality Management
Psychology
Communication
Nursing
Biology
Pacific Rim Studies

In the heart of one of the nation's most liberal cities is a thriving Jesuit university that has become an integral part of its community. Instead of shunning the city's reputation, the University of San Francisco embraces it. With an incredibly diverse student body and an emphasis on preprofessional programs such as nursing and business, students encounter a broad set of cultures, academic challenges in a liberal arts setting, and the chance to put all that experience to good use. In keeping with its Jesuit Catholic tradition, the university's mission is to educate future leaders "who will fashion a more just and humane world."

USF's fifty-five well-kept acres, spotted with beautiful basilica-type buildings and modern facilities, are, as one student puts it, "wedged into the heart of San Francisco." The campus stands atop one of San Francisco's seven hills, adjacent to Golden Gate Park, overlooking San Francisco Bay and the city skyline. Students in the Adult Education Degree Program have a newly remodeled home; a new School of Business is under construction. The Loyola Village provides apartment- and townhouse-style rooms for an additional 350 students, alleviating a housing crunch that has plagued the university in recent years.

Liberal arts are the centerpiece of USF, both in terms of numbers of students and academic quality. There is also a strong emphasis on preprofessional programs, especially nursing, health studies, communications, and business. The Center for the Pacific Rim allows students to do interdisciplinary majors with an Asian focus, as does the Asian studies program. The forty-four-unit core curriculum requires students to take courses in six major categories: foundation of communication; math and sciences; humanities; philosophy, theology, and ethics; social sciences; and visual and performing arts. The St. Ignatius Institute program offers an integrated four-year curriculum based on the great books of Western civilization presented in an unusual seminar/lecture combination. The St. Ignatius program is not restricted to top students, and its participants are able to study in Oxford and Innsbruck.

Some of the preprofessional majors are demanding, and students say that competition is common but not cut-throat. "Certain students are competitive, but the majority are not," says a biology major.

"The students who go here are very open-minded about the world."

Extensive and mandatory academic advising ensures that students' courseloads are manageable. "Faculty really take their time in helping students pick and choose the classes they should be taking," says a sports science major. Teaching quality is high, and professors generally maintain high standards.

The university operates on the basis of fall and spring semesters, with five weeks off at Christmastime. Students interested in speeding up their education can enroll in optional three-week courses in January at extra cost. There's also a joint B.A./B.S.–J.D. program. The average class size is about twenty-five, so "the instructor isn't a faint vision at the bottom of the lecture hall," reports one student. A new visual arts program provides courses in art education, graphic and fine art, drawing, painting, art history, and museum studies. Five computer labs are available to students, and every residence hall is equipped with high-speed Internet connections.

"The students who go here are very open-minded about the world," a marketing major says. "They are also very aware of the world outside the campus. I wouldn't consider them radicals or very political, yet they are heavily involved in outside programs." Community-minded students can taken advantage of volunteer programs with Outreach Ministries. Social causes do rally some students, but political correctness is key. "Being in San Francisco, there are many social/political issues which students are actively aware of, such as the war," a sophomore says. "Other issues aren't really issues here because of the tolerance of others among students, such as race, sexual preference, religion." Sixty-nine percent of the students are from California and an astounding 65 percent of the student body is female. Diversity is far from lacking; Asian-Americans account for 26 percent of the population, African-Americans 5 percent, and Hispanics 12 percent. One of the university's missions is to "prepare men and women to shape a multicultural world with creativity, generosity, and compassion." A student remarks, "As a black student, I feel very comfortable at the University of San Francisco. Students from different backgrounds mix." Admissions are need blind, and the university makes an effort to provide financial aid to accepted students, although it's not guaranteed. There are 156 athletic scholarships available for men and women, as well as fifty-seven merit scholarships that cover about half the total cost.

San Francisco is notorious for its ridiculously tight housing market, but still, 40 percent of undergraduates take their chances. Upperclassmen who don't live at home often leave campus to brave the city's high rents and tight rental market. The perennial campus housing crunch has been somewhat eased with the opening of the 136-unit Loyola Village apartment complex, primarily to graduate, married, and upper-division students. Students who do want dorm rooms (some with views of San Francisco Bay) have several choices: an all-women dorm, a co-ed-by-floor dorm that "caters to a younger population," three co-ed halls that are said to foster "a more liberal lifestyle," and the quiet, renovated co-ed Lone Mountain Hall for upperclassmen. "Dorms are livable but I wouldn't consider them comfortable," notes a junior. On-campus students eat in a commons, where various meal plans are offered (though some grumble about the cost).

> "Faculty really take their time in helping students pick and choose the classes they should be taking."

USF's greatest asset is undoubtedly its location. San Francisco is a cosmopolitan city. "It is definitely a busy city with a great, diverse community," says a student. Students can take advantage of the city's reliable public transportation, including the famous cable cars, to get to a variety of cultural attractions, ranging from Chinatown to the symphony. Nightlife is great for those who want to dance at the clubs or meet in the bars. "Social life usually takes place off campus," a sophomore says. "After all, it is San Francisco." Campus activities include the Hawaiian Club's annual luau and the Barrio Festival held by the Filipino-American Club. The College Players is the oldest continuously performing college theater group in the West. Fraternities and sororities attract 1 percent of men and women, and though underage drinking is officially prohibited, the policy "doesn't really work," a senior says. The academic fraternities—the accounting frat, the honors frat, etc.—add social options to the mix. There are frequent forays to the California beaches, Los Angeles, and Lake Tahoe.

Varsity athletics provide a popular diversion, and USF touts a conference-winning national powerhouse in soccer. Basketball and baseball are among the most popular sports for male athletes, while the women have formed strong volleyball and basketball teams. Athletes are pleased with the health and recreation center, which touts an Olympic-size swimming pool, exercise rooms, and courts.

The core mission of USF is to use the Jesuit tradition, which views "faith and reason as complementary resources in the search for truth and authentic human development," as the backdrop for a solid liberal arts and preprofessional education.

Students can take advantage of San Fran's reliable public transportation, including the famous cable cars, to get to a variety of cultural attractions, ranging from Chinatown to the symphony. Nightlife is great for those who want to dance at the clubs or meet in the bars.

The Center for the Pacific Rim allows students to do interdisciplinary majors with an Asian focus, as does the Asian studies program.

The perennial campus housing crunch has been somewhat eased with the opening of the 136-unit Loyola Village apartment complex, primarily to graduate, married, and upper-division students.

Overlaps

UC–Berkeley, University of San Diego, University of Southern California, Santa Clara, Stanford

With a diverse student body that encourages social interaction and a home city that virtually demands it, students at USF make sure they have fun while they learn and grow.

If You Apply To ➤

USF: Rolling admissions. Early action: Nov. 15. Regular admissions: Feb. 1. Financial aid: Feb. 15. Does not guarantee to meet demonstrated need. Campus and alumni interviews: optional, informational. SATs or ACTs: required. SAT IIs: writing required for placement only. Accepts the Common Application and electronic applications. Essay question: personal statement that includes how students can contribute to the university mission.

Santa Clara University

500 El Camino Real, Santa Clara, CA 95053-1500

Popular because of its Bay Area location, Santa Clara is one of the few middle-sized universities in California that is not impossible to get into. A well-developed core curriculum keeps students focused on the basics, and Santa Clara offers engineering and business in addition to the liberal arts.

Website: www.scu.edu
Location: Suburban
Total Enrollment: 8,060
Undergraduates: 4,643
Male/Female: 45/55
SAT Ranges: V 550–650
  M 560–660
ACT Range: 23–28
Financial Aid: 32%
Expense: Pr $ $ $ $
Phi Beta Kappa: Yes
Applicants: 5,842
Accepted: 70%
Enrolled: 27%
Grad in 6 Years: 81%
Returning Freshmen: 92%
Academics: ✍ ✍ ✍
Social: ☎ ☎ ☎ ☎
Q of L: ★ ★ ★ ★
Admissions: (408) 554-4700
Email Address:
  ugadmissions@scu.edu

Strongest Programs:
Psychology
Marketing
Finance
Economics
Management
Philosophy

Steeped in history and tradition, Santa Clara University was founded with a Jesuit mission that emphasizes a commitment to academics and the community. Classes stay small and intimate, while the revised curriculum focuses on an expanding global society. The class schedule is based on quarters (ten weeks), so classes are challenging, but not too competitive. According to one senior, the environment and school "promotes group work and learning as a community."

SCU's Old World charm includes 104 acres complete with lush green lawns, palm trees, and luscious rose gardens, accented by authentic Spanish architecture. The Mission Gardens, with many olive trees, are a beautiful escape from the pressures of school. The famous classic mission church was rebuilt most recently in 1926 in the design of the six previous churches that were destroyed by disasters ranging from fires to floods. Recent changes to the campus include a new residence hall and pedestrian mall.

The core curriculum, whose theme is Community and Leadership for a Global Society, is meant to give the students broad knowledge in three main themes: community, global societies, and leadership. Courses include composition, Western culture, world culture, the United States, ethics, religious studies, mathematics and the natural sciences, technology, social sciences, and foreign language. There is also an emphasis on professional programs like engineering and business. Students can opt for the 3–2 engineering program, which allows them to get a bachelor's and master's degree in five years and the Leavey School of Business is renowned along the West Coast, with accounting, agribusiness, and retail management being particularly strong. In the College of Arts and Sciences, psychology remains popular, as do biology, communications, and English. The Combined Sciences program

"The quality of teaching is good and professors are really there to help the students rather than research."

allows students who desire a broad curriculum to include courses from both the natural and social sciences. New majors include environment sciences, environmental studies, and German.

For those students looking for more of a challenge, the honors program places forty-five to fifty selected freshmen in special classes, and an endowed scholarship sponsors one student's junior year at Mansfield College, Oxford University. Also, an extensive study abroad program, in which approximately one-third of the students participate, allows travel and study in Europe, Central and South America, the Caribbean, Canada, Africa, Asia, New Zealand, and Australia.

As at any small school, resources and facilities are limited. Students used to report that the library is not always adequate for research needs, forcing many to go to nearby Stanford to get the materials they need; however, a portion of a $350 million fund-raising campaign will be donated to a new library. Students complain that finding a seat in some of the classes is a challenge. "Communications is the biggest major and therefore the hardest classes to get into," says one student. But a senior explains that if your first choice isn't available "there is always a required course available to take instead." Bottom line: stay flexible and you'll likely graduate on time.

"[Professors] seem to enjoy teaching and go out of their way to be available to the students."

Small classes taught by full professors mean "the quality of teaching is good and professors are really there to help the students rather than research," says a senior. A classmate agrees, "They seem to enjoy teaching and go out of their way to be available to the students." The academic climate is described as challenging. "One course only lasts ten weeks. It is gone in a flash and if you miss something there isn't much time to catch up," says a student. "It keeps you on your toes!"

More than half the students are Roman Catholic, and religion, while not intrusive, is a factor in many aspects of campus life. Campus ministry provides counseling and opportunities for spiritual development, and many students are active in local volunteer organizations. "SCU students tend to be very out-going and involved. They are focused on academics yet they also do extracurricular activities," says a marketing major.

Sixty-one percent of the student body is comprised undergraduates from California and the rest are from the West Coast or at least the West—Oregon, Hawaii, Washington, and Arizona. Split fairly evenly between parochial and public schools, seventy-five percent of the students are from the top quarter of their graduating class. The diversity on campus is impressive; the minority students nearly equal the number of white students. Twenty percent of the students are Asian-American, 2 percent are African-American, and 13 percent are Hispanic. The Santa Clara Community Action Program, a student volunteer outreach program, provides community-service opportunities for the entire campus. "There are clubs on campus concerned with social justice, like SCAP and the GREEN club, which send volunteers to help out in the community," says one freshman. A variety of academic and athletic scholarships are available to those who qualify.

"SCU students tend to be very out-going and involved. They are focused on academics yet they also do extracurricular activities."

Since housing is guaranteed to nearly all who apply, "housing can be a pain when trying to find where you'll live next year," says a senior. Almost all freshmen and sophomores live on campus, but soon they are packing up and heading for apartments. Most residence halls are co-ed by floor. A communication major describes the dorms as "a good size with lots of amenities" and another student agrees. "The dorms are quite large and well equipped with internet, phone, and cable." The Freshman Residential Community program gives incoming students the opportunity to room with others pursuing the same course of study. Participating students are housed at the Graham residence complex, and not only study the core curriculum, but virtually eat, sleep, and breathe it. Casa Italiana provides about sixty students with the opportunity to develop an in-depth understanding of Italian language, culture, and cuisine. A substance-free living program houses seventy students at Campisi Hall.

In April 2001, the Greek organizations (rare at a Jesuit institution in the first place) began a three-year dissolution process after a decision by the administration

Only twenty miles away is Santa Cruz for those who want to bask in the sun. San Francisco is forty-five minutes away and other short road trips to popular hot spots include Napa Valley, Monterey, and Palo Alto.

For those students looking for even more of a challenge, the honors program places forty-five to fifty selected freshmen in special classes, and endowed scholarship sponsors one student's junior year at Mansfield College, Oxford University.

to phase them out. Don't let this fool you, social activity is alive and well. With such beautiful weather and great California locations and events nearby, how could anyone resist partying and road trips? Only twenty miles away is Santa Cruz for those who want to bask in the sun. San Francisco is forty-five minutes away and other short road trips to popular hot spots include Napa Valley, Monterey, and Palo Alto. Those who chose to party on or near campus can take advantage of the schools attempt at enforcing "no drinking and driving" by providing the students with transportation called the Bronco Bus. Alternate forms of leisure activity include a fitness center that is open for longer hours and The Bronco, a sports and recreation bar where over-twenty-one students can drink beer or wine.

Santa Clara sports compete in and with the Division I teams and players that are among the best in the nation. For two consecutive years, the women's basketball team won the West Coast Conference championship. The women's soccer team won the West Cost Conference in 2001 and 2002 and the NCAA Women's Soccer Championship in 2002. For those not up to intercollegiate sports, club sports and intramurals are quite popular. "Soccer is a big deal here, so the games are always a hit," according to a senior.

Santa Clara University is a warm place—in every sense of the word—a comfortable and beautiful setting where morality and ethics are infused into the curriculum of strong academics. It's this blend of traditional values and progressive academics that turns out people who want to make a difference in the world.

Overlaps

UC–Davis, UCLA, UC–San Diego, UC–Santa Barbara, UC–Berkeley

If You Apply To ➤

SCU: Early admissions: Nov. 15. Regular admissions: Jan. 15. Financial aid: Jan 1. Housing: Guaranteed for freshman. Does not guarantee to meet demonstrated need. Campus interviews: optional, evaluative. No alumni interviews. SATs or ACTs: required. Accepts the Common Application and electronic applications. Essay question: what inspires you or an experience you will never forget.

Sarah Lawrence College

1 Mead Way, Bronxville, NY 10708-5999

The free-spirited sister of East Coast alternative institutions. Though SLC is co-ed, women outnumber men nearly three to one. Strong in the humanities and fine arts with a specialty in creative writing. Full of quirky, head-strong intellectuals who hop the train to New York City every chance they get.

Website:
www.sarahlawrence.edu
Location: Suburban
Total Enrollment: 1,556
Undergraduates: 1,226
Male/Female: 25/75
SAT Ranges: V 610–710
M 530–650
ACT Range: 24–29
Financial Aid: 51%
Expense: Pr $ $ $ $
Phi Beta Kappa: No

It seems the only rule at Sarah Lawrence College is that rules are made to be broken. This elite liberal arts school prides itself on individualism and self-expression. "At SLC the climate is open to make it what you will," says one junior. Freedom and exploration are valued more highly than any tradition, and it's this commitment to the individual and the mind that makes Sarah Lawrence College a creative place to learn. "The students here are left-winged, right-brained people," says one student.

Founded in 1926, the college sits on a quaint, forty-acre campus. English Tudor buildings and mansions of converted estates intermingle with more modern structures. The landscape is hilly and green, with more than one hundred types of trees and abundant rock outcroppings. The school's founders believed that there should be as little physical separation as possible between life and work, so classrooms, dormitory suites, and faculty offices are all housed in the same ivy-covered buildings.

It's tough to find two Sarah Lawrence students studying the same thing, because every student has an individually designed program of study, and almost no subject is out of bounds. Instead, you'll find uniquely combined concentrations, such as American history and cultural anthropology or sculpture and literature. Grades are recorded for transcript purposes only; more emphasis is placed on written faculty evaluations. Some students become overwhelmed here, but those who stay find that the combination of close faculty supervision and an endless slate of choices provide an experience unavailable elsewhere. "There are no mandatory classes, so each class is chosen by the student," says a freshman studying international relations.

Students will become intimately acquainted with the written word at Sarah Lawrence—one of the few things that everyone does here. Writing begins in the first year and continues relentlessly "across the curriculum" for the next three years. All first-year students take a First-Year Studies Seminar in one of more than thirty subjects. Each student meets with a professor individually each week to discuss his or her independent projects, academic plans, and transition to college. Undergraduate students must complete 120 credit hours in at least three of four academic areas. Other than that, undergraduates write their own academic ticket, with the help of their "academic guru" (called a "don" from the Latin for "gift").

At Sarah Lawrence, students take three courses each semester. Courses can last a semester or the full year, depending on the nature of the course. Students also work on independent projects with faculty members in individual, one-on-one conferences every two weeks for each of these classes. Perhaps because of the close personal contact with professors, the registration process is rigorous: students interview their prospective teachers to determine whether the course fits their academic plan, and to make sure the instructor is someone they respect and want to study with. Students get very involved with the individual projects that result from the seminar/conference system, which is modeled after Oxford University's and said to be intense. Getting into popu-

"The students here are left-winged, right-brained people."

lar classes can be a problem, but the administration guarantees students at least two of their first three course choices each semester. A senior says that some students "avoid the maths and sciences, just because most have had bad experiences in the past or because they equate them with stressful quizzes and tests."

The Sarah Lawrence writing program is one of the strongest in the country. Other highly rated fields include literature, visual arts, and psychology. The psychology department offers fieldwork at the college's Early Childhood Center. The film department has been upgraded with expanded offerings in filmmaking and film history, and environmental studies and computer science have expanded offerings as well. The premed program, more structured than other offerings, places nearly all of its eligible graduates into medical schools while science students have the opportunity to use the state-of-the-art science center, with 22,500 square feet of classrooms, labs, and computer workspaces. However, students report that math and science are weak and that the Russian, Japanese, and German departments have only one professor in each discipline. New additions to the curriculum include African art, geography, Latin American history, African history, and Islamic studies.

Since individual attention is the cornerstone of the Sarah Lawrence educational philosophy, even grading is done personally. Teachers give students written evaluations twice a year, though conventional grades also go on record. The library, though small (224,000 volumes and more than one thousand periodicals), is a delight, with an area for eating and a pillow room for cozy studying and occasional dozing. For the travelers, there are academic years in Cuba, Oxford, Paris, Florence, and a London theater program for study at the British American Drama Academy.

(Continued)

Applicants: 2,667
Accepted: 40%
Enrolled: 31%
Grad in 6 Years: 72%
Returning Freshmen: 91%
Academics: ✍ ✍ ✍ ✍
Social: ☎ ☎
Q of L: ★ ★ ★
Admissions: (914) 395-2510
Email Address:
  slcadmit@slc.edu

Strongest Programs:
History
Literature
Psychology
Writing
Visual and Performing Arts

Grades are recorded for transcript purposes only; more emphasis is placed on written faculty evaluations.

One popular dorm contains four townhouses, each with seven single rooms. In fact, accommodations are so good that there's been a bit of a housing crunch lately.

Perhaps because of the close personal contact with professors, the registration process is rigorous: students interview their prospective teachers to determine whether the course fits their academic plan, and to make sure the instructor is someone they respect and want to study with.

Overlaps

NYU, Vassar, Barnard, Smith, Oberlin

Sarah Lawrence students are not your run-of-the-mill young American men and women. "People come from all walks of life, and thusly come in fighting for what they think is right," says a student who describes her major as "arts and the administration thereof." And what about campus issues? "Every issue is a big social and political issue," reports a senior. Eighteen percent of SLC's students come from New York State—the bulk from nearby New York City—and most of the rest are from somewhere along either the East or West Coast. African-Americans make up 5 percent of the student body, Asian-Americans 4 percent, Hispanics 4 percent, and foreign students 16 percent. The school is working to increase diversity among students as well as faculty. Following a growing trend in higher education, the college will no longer require students to submit SAT scores as part of the admissions process—effective with the graduating high school class of 2005.

Eighty-seven percent of Sarah Lawrence students live on campus, where freshmen usually get doubles in the newer dorms and upperclassmen are guaranteed singles in the prettier, older dorms or college-owned houses. One popular dorm contains four townhouses, each with seven single rooms. In fact, accommodations are so good that there's been a bit of a housing crunch lately. "We are so spoiled by housing here, it's ridiculous," says one sophomore. Off-campus students on a budget often commute from Westchester County's lower-rent districts or from their folk's homes in New York City. The cooks on campus know their audience; "There is always a vegetarian option and more times than not, there is a vegan option," reports a student. "Sometimes the carnivores have to go a little out of their way to fulfill their needs." In that case, the student center's greasy spoon fills in the gaps. Most dorms also have their own kitchens.

> "People come from all walks of life, and thusly come in fighting for what they think is right."

New York City, just a half-hour train ride away, is a drain on weekend social and cultural life. SLC's large theatrical contingent takes advantage of the art and culture of the Big Apple. For those who stick around over the weekend, there are free dances and movies, plays, poetry readings, guest lectures, and several tea and coffeehouses. When it comes to big dances, we're not exactly talking white gloves and carnations. "Dating is a joke on this campus," scoffs one cynic. "If you want to find true love—go somewhere else." For those who love to party Sarah Lawrence style, there is the end-of-the-year mega party, Bacchanalia, and the oldest college AIDS benefit in the country, the Deb Ball, along with the Sleaze Ball. Other traditions include Coming Out Week and May Fair, which brings community children to campus for games and food. Drinkers, largely ignored in the past, are now subject to tough rules regarding on-campus consumption. This may be a creative person's paradise, but the fact is, many Sarah Lawrence artists are not exactly the starving artist types, the price tag at Sarah Lawrence being definitely designer label. On the other hand, Bronxville is seen as populated by a lot of June Cleaver–types in Humvees, and as a rich suburb that has neglected to throw out the welcome mat to students.

> "We are so spoiled by housing here, it's ridiculous."

You hardly have to be a jock to fit in here, however athletes who are into crew and tennis will find some competition. There are some women who are sporty, and they are into volleyball and swimming mostly. And there are some who are horsey, as well, and into equestrian sports. The men who are into sports can often be found on the basketball courts.

The Sarah Lawrence community is an intimate one, and students say this is both a challenge and a blessing. "Sarah Lawrence is one of the few schools where students really have the chance to set their own pace," says one senior. "It's really hard to be competitive without grades shoved in your face. The courses themselves will always push a student that extra lap around the field, especially since the conference system insures that a student has individual time with professors."

If You Apply To ➤

Sarah Lawrence: Early decision: Nov. 15. Regular admissions: Jan. 15. Financial aid: Feb. 1. Meets full demonstrated need of all admitted students who file on time. Campus interviews: recommended, evaluative. Alumni interviews: optional, informational. SATs or ACTs: required. SAT IIs: optional. Accepts the Common Application and electronic applications. Essay question: a significant social, economic, or political issue; recent scientific advance; or a passage from art or literature and why it is important to you.

Scripps College: See page 143.

Skidmore College

815 North Broadway, Saratoga Springs, NY 12866

Like Vassar, Connecticut College, and Wheaton (MA), Skidmore is a successful convert to coeducation. Strong in the performing arts with an unexpected emphasis on business, Skidmore is top-notch when it comes to internships, study abroad, and student research. Instead of green lawns, Skidmore has the woods.

Founded in 1903 as the Young Women's Industrial Club of Saratoga, Skidmore College still excels in the fine and performing arts that were then deemed proper for ladies—but little else remains the same. In 1961, as enrollment surpassed 1,300 and many of the college's turn-of-the-century Victorian buildings grew obsolete, Skidmore traded its Victorian campus in the heart of Saratoga Springs for 650 acres on the northwest edge of town. Since then, the campus has grown to forty-nine buildings on 850 acres, and the student body has doubled in size (and welcomed men). What hasn't changed? "The people, the education, and the massive amount of beautiful girls!" says a male government major.

While contemporary in style, the buildings on Skidmore's Jonsson campus—named after the donor who made it possible—are human in scale. They reflect the Victorian heritage of Skidmore's original Scribner campus in their aesthetic details. The campus was carefully planned to preserve natural beauty, with a feeling of freedom and a wide horizon. From the covered walkways that unite residential, academic, and social centers on campus, the prevailing views are of the surrounding mountains, woods, and fields, and into the central campus "green." Teachers and students often meet informally, and academic resources are easily accessible. Recent improvements to the campus include the Frances Young Teaching Museum and Art Gallery, which opened in fall 2000 and the renovation of the Case College Center.

> "The feeling at Skidmore is, get out of college what you want."

Skidmore's mandatory core groups require courses under broad themes. Students start with Foundation classes in expository writing and quantitative reasoning, followed by Interdisciplinary courses titled Liberal Studies 1 and Liberal Studies 2. LS1, The Human Dilemma, is team-taught by professors from many departments, and combines lectures, performances, readings, and discussions to examine the issues and questions of human life. Students have many options for LS2, which

Website: www.skidmore.edu
Location: City outskirts
Total Enrollment: 2,557
Undergraduates: 2,506
Male/Female: 41/59
SAT Ranges: V 580–670
　M 580–660
ACT Range: 25–28
Financial Aid: 43%
Expense: Pr $ $ $ $
Phi Beta Kappa: Yes
Applicants: 5,606
Accepted: 46%
Enrolled: 25%
Grad in 6 Years: 75%
Returning Freshmen: 91%
Academics: ✏️ ✏️ ✏️ ✏️
Social: ☎ ☎ ☎
Q of L: ★ ★ ★
Admissions: (800) 867-6007
　or (518) 580-5570
Email Address:
　admissions@skidmore.edu

Strongest Programs:
Drama

must be completed by the end of sophomore year and connect back to LS1. Also required are four Breadth courses—one each in arts, humanities, natural sciences, and social sciences—and two Culture-Centered Inquiry courses. One must be a foreign language, and the other may focus on either non-Western culture or cultural diversity.

Skidmore's programs in business and art are among its best and most popular majors. English, psychology, and biology are also well enrolled, perhaps because of their applicability to graduate study in medicine. Biology majors also may conduct fieldwork in the marsh at the northern end of campus. Through the Hudson-Mohawk Association of Colleges and Universities, students may take courses at Rensselaer Polytechnic Institute, Union College, and SUNY–Albany. There's also a cooperative program in engineering with Dartmouth College, a Washington semester with American University, a semester at the Marine Biological Laboratory in Woods Hole, Massachusetts, a master of arts in teaching with Union, and M.B.A. programs with Clarkson University and Rensselaer.

Skidmore augments liberal arts and sciences offerings with preprofessional training. Studio art and art history majors frequently enroll in business classes, where they work in groups with business majors and make presentations for actual executives. Another much-praised option is junior year abroad, especially when spent in a Skidmore-run program in France, England, Spain, or India. A new program for Beijing, China, is in development for fall 2004. Students who just can't get enough time on campus may compete for summer grants to fund collaborative research with professors, or attend one of the school's incredible summer programs. In addition, the University Without Walls offers older students a flexible and inexpensive route to a bachelor's degree through remote coursework, tutorials, and internships.

Students start with Foundation classes in expository writing and quantitative reasoning, followed by Interdisciplinary courses entitled Liberal Studies 1 and Liberal Studies 2.

The academic climate at Skidmore is fairly laid back, though courses in all disciplines can be rigorous. "The courses are as rigorous as you want them to be," says a music major. "The feeling at Skidmore is, get out of college what you want." That said, it may be hard to get into the courses you want, says a government major. "As a freshman some courses are hard to get into." "You can, however, generally talk to a professor and get into the class eventually," assures another student.

Given Skidmore's hefty price tag—only a bit less than Harvard's—it's not surprising that the students are typically well-off and from the Eastern seaboard,

"The dorms are very nice—better than I've seen at other schools."

especially New York, New Jersey, and New England. "Everyone at Skidmore brings different characteristics to the college," says a business major. Hispanics constitute 5 percent of the student body, Asian-Americans another 5 percent, and African-Americans 2 percent. More than two decades of effort to recruit men has also paid off; two of every five students are male.

Students also look forward to the Diva Night party, hosted by a group devoted to sexuality awareness, "where everyone dresses to show off their sexuality and is always great fun," a government major says.

Seventy-seven percent of Skidmore students live in the dorms, where they are guaranteed rooms for four years, though it can be difficult to get the room of your choice according to some students. Most buildings have carpet, air-conditioning, and cozy window seats. "The dorms are very nice—better than I've seen at other schools," one student says. "Heating and air-conditioning are sometimes a problem," a sophomore says. Dorms are integrated by class and are co-ed by floor or suite, with kitchenettes and lounges on every floor. The double rooms in South Quad tend to be livelier than those in North Quad. Sophomores aren't permitted to live off campus, but they "always dread room selection" because space limitations force them away from the main part of campus. Juniors and seniors typically get single rooms in the centrally located dorms, or move to apartments—on campus in Scribner Village, or off campus in Saratoga.

With no fraternities or sororities, Skidmore students flock to dorm parties, especially if there's live music. They're also eager participants in road trips to Albany, New York City, Boston, and Montreal. A campus event card is distributed to students over twenty-one who plan to drink on school grounds, though a business major notes that there are more than thirty bars within two blocks of campus. "They are fairly lax. If you get caught too many times you will get in trouble," a sophomore says. Another student states, "Campus policies are strict and require students to adhere to the law." Skidmore's more traditional activities, which have lingered even after a quarter-century of coeducation, include Junior Ring Week, when juniors receive their class rings and a dance is held in honor of their initiation. Every year, there are also two or three formal dances at the Hall of Springs, which a senior calls "basically the fanciest reception hall ever." Students also look forward to the Diva Night party, hosted by a group devoted to sexuality awareness, "where everyone dresses to show off their sexuality and is always great fun," a government major says.

The nearby Adirondacks make Skidmore a haven for backpackers and skiers, while the old resort town of Saratoga, with its healing springs and antique shops, offers plenty of culture, including the Saratoga Performing Arts Center and the country's oldest thoroughbred racetrack. Saratoga is also the summer home of the New York City Ballet,

> "There are no athletic rivalries, because sports are not real big here."

the New York City Opera, and the Philadelphia Orchestra. Students reach out to the community through Benefaction, a volunteer group connected to several local agencies and schools. Still, a senior quips, "The people of Saratoga don't necessarily like the college kids, but there are tons of bars and great places to eat."

Skidmore's Thoroughbreds compete in Division III; men's and women's tennis and the equestrian team have claimed several conference championships in recent years. "There are no athletic rivalries, because sports are not real big here," says a government major. Students who do compete play mostly in the intramural sports program, which has more than twenty teams, a student commissioner, and 250 acres of playing fields. Varsity athletes and intramural jocks alike enjoy the four-hundred-meter, all-weather track and the athletic center, which includes a gym, fitness center, and locker rooms.

Skidmore continues to win the hearts of liberal, motivated students with its flexibility, openness, and receptivity to change and growth. Its small size means they have the opportunity to really get to know each other, says a business student. "The community and the comfort level here are so high," a women's studies major says, "sometimes, it's like being in a bubble."

Founded in 1903 as the Young Women's Industrial Club of Saratoga, Skidmore College still excels in the fine and performing arts that were then deemed proper for ladies—but little else remains the same. Like Vassar, Connecticut College, and Wheaton (MA).

Overlaps

Vassar, Connecticut College, Wesleyan, Tufts, Hamilton

If You Apply To ➤

Skidmore: Early decision: Dec. 1, Jan. 15. Regular admissions and financial aid: Jan. 15. Meets demonstrated need of 85%. Campus interviews: recommended, evaluative. Alumni interviews: optional, evaluative. SATs or ACTs: required. SAT IIs: recommended. Accepts the Common Application. Essay question: significant experience; important issue of personal, local, or national concern; important person; or significant fictional or historical character.

Smith College

College Lane, Northampton, MA 01063

The most left-wing of the nation's leading women's colleges. Liberal Northhampton provides big-city social life, and the Five College Consortium adds depth and breadth all around. With a total enrollment of more than three thousand, Smith is the biggest of the leading women's colleges, and the only one to offer engineering.

Website: www.smith.edu
Location: Small city
Total Enrollment: 3,121
Undergraduates: 2,601
Male/Female: 0/100
SAT Ranges: V 590–700
  M 580–670
ACT Range: 24–30
Financial Aid: 63%
Expense: Pr $ $ $ $
Phi Beta Kappa: Yes
Applicants: 3,047
Accepted: 53%
Enrolled: 42%
Grad in 6 Years: 80%
Returning Freshmen: 90%
Academics: ✑ ✑ ✑ ✑ ½
Social: ☎ ☎ ☎
Q of L: ★ ★ ★ ★
Admissions: (413) 585-2500
Email Address:
  admission@smith.edu

Strongest Programs:
Government
Art
Psychology
Biological Sciences
Economics

Heaven only knows what Sophia Smith would think of the women's college she founded in 1871 with the hope it would be "pervaded by the Spirit of Evangelical Christian Religion." There are still evangelicals at Smith, but today they join the rest of their schoolmates in crusading against societal injustices such as racism, classism, sexism, and heterosexism. Though the all-female school remains strongly committed to its liberal arts mission, it is also focused on placing women at the forefront of science and technology. Students here have an opportunity to become leaders in the male-dominated field of engineering, or pursue interdisciplinary fields such as landscape studies.

Smith is located in the small city of Northampton, an artsy oasis in the foothills of the Berkshire Mountains. The 125-acre campus resembles a medieval fortress from the front gate, but inside it sparkles with many gardens, Paradise Pond, and a plant house. Buildings cover a range of styles from late eighteenth-century to modern, and the college has successfully retained its historic atmosphere while keeping facilities up to date. The new $35 million Brown Fine Arts Center opened in the spring of 2003. In September 2003, the first campus center, a sixty-thousand-square-foot facility, and a new $4 million fitness center both opened their doors. The school also expects to break ground on a permanent engineering building sometime in 2005.

Be ready to hit the books with your newfound sisters at Smith. "Smith College is a strong academic institution because it is composed of strong, intelligent women," says one junior. Smith's student-run honor system, which covers everything from exams to library checkout, is widely praised and enforced. Students generally refrain from discussing grades, choosing instead to focus on helping one another.

Government is the favorite major on campus, followed by psychology, art, English, and economics. One in four Smith women majors in science and thereby enjoys numerous opportunities to assist professors with their research. The STRIDE program allows freshmen and sophomores to become paid research assistants to professors. Science students also benefit from a spacious, state-of-the-art science center. Two electron microscopes are available for student use, and, through the Five College Consortium,* students have access to one of the best radio astronomy facilities in the world. Smith's art history department is among the best in the nation and enjoys access to the college's superb museum. One of the more popular new fields is landscape studies. In keeping with its commitment to diversity, the school has added a major in East Asian studies and a minor in African studies.

> **"Advisors can be the key to encouraging students bent on studying a specific field to expand their horizon."**

With the exception of a mandatory writing course, Smith women have unusual freedom to plan a course of study. They must take half of their credits outside of their major. "Because Smith does not require its students to take classes in each of the main departments, advisors can be the key to encouraging students bent on studying a specific field to expand their horizon," explains one junior. Qualified students may enter the Smith Scholars program and embark on one or two years of independent or extra college research for full credit. About 250 older students are enrolled in the Ada Comstock Scholars program for women going back to college. The Picker Program in Engineering and Technology—which accepted its first class in 2001—is the first of its kind at a women's college. The program offers students the opportunity to pursue an ambitious engineering program that will focus on computer, electrical, and environmental engineering. Administrators hope the curriculum will lead to greater gender parity in engineering.

All courses are taught by full professors and students seem to be pleased with the quality of teaching. "Professors are very approachable and always ready to meet with you to go over drafts of papers or just to chat," one economics major says. Smith's four libraries have almost two million holdings among them, making it one of the largest collections of any liberal arts college in the country. Students can study for a semester or two at one of twelve well-known New England colleges through the Twelve-College Exchange Program,* or take advantage of the innovative Maritime Studies Program.* Students are also enthusiastic about

"Smith students are outspoken and opinionated. Many students are very politically and socially active."

the opportunity to take part in Smith's well-known study abroad program, which includes opportunities for study in a number of countries. The Praxis program lets each student participate in at least one summer internship funded by the college.

With an endowment of more than half a billion dollars, Smith has deeper pockets than many of its competitors. And though it's got a hefty price tag, the school manages to recruit a diverse group of women who aren't afraid to say what they think. "Smith students are outspoken and opinionated. Many students are very politically and socially active," a philosophy major says. Nobody disputes that Smith is a liberal place, with the social issues of the day dominating conversations, though some students are surprised to find themselves in such a freewheeling atmosphere—one where potentially divisive topics such as lesbianism are nonissues. On this politically correct campus, students debate the finer points of women's rights, racism, sexual freedom, politics, and police brutality. Ninety percent of the students ranked in the top quarter of their high school class. Seventy-eight percent of Smithies are from out of state or abroad. African-Americans account for 5 percent of the student body, Asian-Americans 10 percent, and Hispanics 6 percent.

Housing at Smith, which consists of houses, not dorms, is unabashedly adored. "Smith housing is one of the greatest assets of the college because it helps foster a sense of community," one junior says. Students note that they often eat breakfast in their pajamas and that the bathrooms are probably much cleaner than if there were men around. Each of the thirty-five houses, accommodating from thirteen to one hundred students, is a self-governing unit, responsible for everything from visiting hours to weekend parties and concerts. Accouterments in each house include a living room, a TV room, and a study room, many with a fireplace and a grand piano. The head resident, selected by the administration, is the leader of the house, but the elected house council runs day-to-day affairs.

The atmosphere is less that of a sorority than of an extended family. Except for one senior house, classes are mixed in each house, and first-year students easily mingle with seniors. Incoming students can indicate a preference for size and location of their first house, and changes are possible by entering a lottery. All undergraduates except for Ada Comstock Scholars must live on campus—a bone of contention among some juniors and seniors. Two alternatives offered are a vegetarian cooperative and an apartment complex. Meals are a variation on the same community theme, though budget cuts have forced consolidation of dining facilities, causing much grief on campus. The food is highly praised. Professors are often

The Picker Program in Engineering and Technology—which accepted its first class in 2001—is the first of its kind at a women's college. The program offers students the opportunity to pursue an ambitious engineering program that will focus on computer, electrical, and environmental engineering.

One in four Smith women majors in science and thereby enjoys numerous opportunities to assist professors with their research.

invited to Thursday dinners, which are served family-style, by candlelight, to add a touch of graciousness midweek.

You will not be greeted with a rocking social scene at Smith, but there are plenty of parties to be had and great places to visit. "Its usually not difficult to find a party on campus during the weekend," a junior says. Meeting men (or non-Smith women) is made easier by the five-college system. In addition, each house throws an average of two parties a semester. For special weekends, a whole fraternity may be invited from Dartmouth or another nearby college, an arrangement that is only slightly more civilized than the typical college bar scene. Students must be twenty-one to drink alcohol at campus parties; IDs are checked and hands are stamped. Students say the alcohol policies are getting stricter. There is a free bus service to the other four members of the consortium, which among them offer a broad range of social and cultural opportunities.

Northampton, known as NoHo after New York City's SoHo neighborhood, is a college town of about thirty thousand that is known for funky bohemianism. The town is home to multiple subcultures, and is generally tolerant of everyone. "Northampton is awesome," a senior exclaims. "Especially if you're into folk music and earth-friendly alternative living systems with a liberal outlook." Smith also offers time-honored traditions like Mountain Day, when the president cancels class for a day of hiking and female bonding, complete with brown-bag lunches. The New England countryside has numerous special charms, including ski slopes only ten minutes away. The best road trips are to Boston (two hours) or New York City (three hours).

Smith has a long tradition of success in athletics; the college was the first women's college to join the NCAA, and still places a premium on recruiting scholar-athletes. Top teams include cross-country, track and field, crew, softball, soccer, field hockey, and tennis. Smith's multimillion-dollar sports complex includes indoor tennis and track facilities, a six-lane swimming pool, and a riding ring. Interhouse competitions include everything from kickball to inner tube water polo. Service Organizations of Smith (SOS) arranges for students to volunteer in about six hundred placements in Northampton, the surrounding communities, and on campus.

The strict evangelism is gone, and today's Smith women are far from Sophia Smith wannabes. But her namesake and spirit lives on at this eclectic, open-minded institution where women don lab coats, power suits, combat boots, and even white dresses at graduation. "It is as if when I came here, I could start being the person I always was but never could be before," says one happy sophomore. This unique institution readies women to be and do just about anything. "Together, we are Smith," surmises a junior.

Overlaps

Mount Holyoke, Wellesley, Bryn Mawr, Brown, Harvard

If You Apply To ➤ **Smith:** Early decision: Nov. 15 and Jan. 2. Regular admissions, financial aid and housing: Jan. 15. Guarantees to meet demonstrated need. Campus interviews: recommended, evaluative. Alumnae interviews: optional, evaluative. SATs or ACTs: required. SAT IIs: recommended (writing and two others). Accepts the Common Application and electronic applications. Essay question: significant academic or intellectual experience; significant person; a situation in which your beliefs were challenged; place you would like to have a summer internship.

Sewanee is like a little bit of Britain's Oxford plunked down in the highlands of Tennessee. More conservative than Rhodes and Davidson, Sewanee is a guardian of the tried and true. Affiliated with the Episcopal Church, Sewanee still draws heavily from old-line Southern families.

Tradition is the word at University of the South, known simply as Sewanee after the university-owned village town in which it is located. Episcopal bishop Leonidas Polk founded the university in 1857 and envisioned it as a distinguished center of learning in the South. Through the years, a host of customs have emerged: honors students wear gowns to class, dress up for football games, and adhere to an honor code. With proceeds from Tennessee Williams's estate, the university holds a prestigious annual conference to promote the art of writing and seats a theater complex bearing his name.

Sewanee is located atop Tennessee's Cumberland Plateau between Chattanooga and Nashville. The university's stately English collegiate Gothic buildings of native-mountain, beige-and-pink sandstone are home to both a college of arts and sciences and a seminary. Be prepared to do a good amount of walking around the campus, whose buildings are often widely spaced on the ten thousand acres fondly known as "the Domain." Noteworthy structures include the St. Luke's and All Saints Chapel, and Convocation Hall, built in 1886. Owned by Southern Dioceses of the Episcopal Church, the university calls its semesters Advent and Easter and the student body is overwhelmingly Christian. A new residence hall is being completed that will include room for 119 students with single or double rooms and a few suites. Each room will be air-conditioned and have high-speed Internet access. Oddly enough, dogs and cats can be found all around the campus, and rumor has it that they are the reincarnated souls of deceased professors.

Sewanee's undergraduate core curriculum remains diverse—students must complete thirty-two full courses, including twenty-one courses outside their major field, with an overall grade point average of at least 2.0 for all academic work. Classes include English and one other course in literature or English and a writing-intensive course; foreign language at the third-year level; math; a lab science; history; religion or philosophy; fine arts; and physical education. A First Year program of small, interactive seminars, which cover topics from seventeen departments, was added to the curriculum. The professors of these courses become the student's advisors, which makes the transition to college life easier. In keeping with the European tradition, Sewanee seniors take comprehensive exams in their majors as part of their graduation requirements. While students take the test, their friends decorate their cars and prepare for celebrations.

Sewanee's English department is nationally recognized. In fact, the university publishes *Sewanee Review*, the nation's oldest continuously published literary quarterly, and sponsors the Sewanee Writers' Conference through the gift of (you guessed it) Tennessee Williams's estate. The students also express their approval of the history program, political science, and economics. There is also a natural resources department that focuses on geology and forestry. The preprofes- **"Every professor here holds a Ph.D."** sional programs are not only popular but widely regarded; 89 percent of premed, dentistry, and veterinary students go on to professional schools. Students report that the weaker departments include Italian and Japanese, primarily due to their

Website: www.sewanee.edu
Location: Village
Total Enrollment: 1,449
Undergraduates: 1,340
Male/Female: 48/52
SAT Ranges: V 560–660
  M 550–650
ACT Range: 24–28
Financial Aid: 38%
Expense: Pr $ $ $
Phi Beta Kappa: Yes
Applicants: 1,699
Accepted: 71%
Enrolled: 31%
Grad in 6 Years: 76%
Returning Freshmen: 82%
Academics: ✑ ✑ ✑ ✑
Social: ☎ ☎ ☎
Q of L: ★ ★ ★ ★
Admissions: (800) 522-2234
Email Address:
  admiss@sewanee.edu

Strongest Programs:
English
History
Psychology
Mathematics
Natural Resources

small size. A cooperative master's degree program in environmental science with Duke and Yale is also offered. Of the study abroad opportunities, the summer British studies program at Oxford is especially popular.

The environment at Sewanee reflects the old customs and standards that add uniqueness to campus life. The women have a voluntary dress code that includes wearing dresses or skirts and men wear jackets and ties to class. Professors as well as the numerous honors students (members of the Order of Gownsmen) wear black academic gowns to class. An honor code is strictly observed, and lying, cheating, or stealing usually results in expulsion.

According to the students, the small classes and wonderful professors are "the best part of Sewanee." One impressed junior says, "Every professor here holds a Ph.D." A freshman adds, "You can talk to professors in person and they are accessible." Most Sewanee students understand what is expected of them academically and say that classes are rigorous and competitive, though not cut-throat.

Eighty percent of the students are out-of-state, and many hail from Southern families. The student population is 92 percent white, with African-Americans the largest minority group at 5 percent. Students complain of the lack of diversity, but Sewanee is attempting to draw in more minorities through scholarships, including the Tutu Scholars program for students from South Africa. Sewanee awards 114 merit scholarships (ranging from $5,000 to $30,000), but there are no athletic scholarships. A financing plan enables families to pay tuition in ten monthly installments. Students who maintain a 3.0 cumulative GPA may have the loan portion of their award replaced by a grant.

The town of Sewanee is "a good location for a school," according to a junior, who adds, "You can be extremely active with the community through volunteer activities." A political science major says, "Sewanee is the town and the town is the university." Ninety-six percent of the students live on campus in single-sex dorms, although renovated halls are now co-ed, and there are three co-ed language houses. Dorms are readily available and the students rave about the recent upgrade to air-conditioning in the rooms. The few seniors who move off campus must live in university-approved housing. Many students complain about the quality of the food.

"You can talk to professors in person and they are accessible."

Social life is mostly on campus with occasionally jaunts to Chattanooga, Memphis, or Nashville. For the most part, Greeks provide an important social outlet with 45 percent of the men and 43 percent of the women participating. Drinking is a fact of life here. There are "parties every weekend at the frat houses," says a freshman. Annual Fall and Spring Party Weekends, homecoming weekend, the Shakespeare Festival, and a blues fest are popular campus happenings. For students who want to get out of town, the beautiful rural setting, complete with lakes, waterfalls, and even caves and caverns, make outdoor activities popular.

Sports are popular at Sewanee, where virtually no one gets cut from varsity sports squads. The most popular sport on campus is probably football—not so much because of the sport, but because games are social events where everyone shows up in coats and ties and dresses. Participating in the NCAA Division III, the equestrian team recently won their region and placed at the nationals. Men's soccer also won conference in 2001 and field hockey won their conference in 2002. Other popular sports for men include football, track, soccer, and baseball while women prefer field hockey, soccer, track, softball, and equestrian activities. The cheer here is: "Sewanee, Sewanee, leave 'em in a lurch. Down with the heathens and up with the Church. Yea, Sewanee's right."

While the location may seem a bit remote, the beautiful location seems to provide plenty of activities for the students. For the most part, though, students are

Overlaps

Vanderbilt, Rhodes, Davidson, Washington and Lee, Furman

here to learn, "Sewanee is a great place to become a leader and actually make a difference in the school," and are impressed with quality of teaching, saying, "a close faculty/student relationship goes beyond academic life into social aspects."

If You Apply To >

Sewanee: Early decision: Nov. 15. Regular admissions: Feb. 1. Financial aid: Mar. 1. Campus and alumni interviews: optional, informational. SATs or ACTs: required. SAT IIs: optional. Accepts the Common Application and electronic applications. Essay question: an issue of great concern and importance; or personal statement.

University of South Carolina

Columbia, SC 29208

In the state that started the Civil War, USC is still trying to fight off the image of being one step behind UNC–Chapel Hill. The university has paid big money to attract star professors and boasts one of the top international business programs in the nation. Criminal justice is also a specialty.

Whether it's football or international business, the students at the University of South Carolina are game—they're the Gamecocks and they've got plenty of fighting spirit. Sure, South Carolina's a somewhat crowded state university, but these Gamecocks rarely feel cooped up. The bevy of courses offered and plenty of interesting academic programs to explore make for a campus that seems to have a lot more space than it actually does. Which is not to say that South Carolina's an impersonal school—this is the South, after all. Gamecocks may lay claim to their school, but old-fashioned Southern charm still rules the roost.

Carolina's large modern campus is located right in the heart of Columbia, a city of more than 450,000 and the capital of the state. Government buildings and downtown businesses are all within walking distance of the campus and serve as fertile hunting grounds for internship opportunities. Mild winters are typical. Snow—even a few flurries—is a traffic-stopping event. The old section of the campus, which dates back to the school's founding in 1801, includes the glorious oak-lined Horseshoe, composed of numerous nineteenth-century buildings, ten of which are now listed in the National Register of Historic Places.

The University of South Carolina offers seventy-nine professional, liberal, and technical bachelor's degrees to its undergrads. Biology is the most popular major, but the school is also known for its psychology, nursing, English, and criminal justice programs.

Students in the huge marine science program enjoy a splendid seventeen-thousand-acre facility located about three hours from the main campus. The university is also the beneficiary of an excellent film library. Much of the economy of South Carolina is tied to foreign trade, and, fittingly, the university has developed a top-notch international business program. Art students have access to the latest cameras, editing stations, and computers, as well as kilns and other equipment necessary for their studies.

Among the liberal arts, English is one of the best departments in the region, and the natural sciences are strong. The four-level, one-thousand-square-foot music building features studios, classrooms, a music and performance library, chamber and music rooms, recording studios, and a 250-seat lecture hall. A unique minor

Website: www.sc.edu
Location: City center
Total Enrollment: 25,140
Undergraduates: 16,567
Male/Female: 46/54
SAT Ranges: V 500–610
   M 510–620
ACT Range: 21–26
Financial Aid: 38%
Expense: Pub $
Phi Beta Kappa: Yes
Applicants: 12,016
Accepted: 70%
Enrolled: 70%
Grad in 6 Years: 60%
Returning Freshmen: 82%
Academics: 🖉 🖉 🖉
Social: ☎ ☎ ☎
Q of L: ★ ★ ★
Admissions: (803) 777-7700
Email Address:
   admissions-ugrad@sc.edu

Strongest Programs:
Biology
English
International Business
Psychology
Criminal Justice
Nursing

called medical humanities is designed for future medical students; it provides an understanding of the ethical, sociocultural, legal, economic, and political factors that affect medical practice.

Many classes are predictably large, and freshmen should not be surprised to find themselves taught by graduate students in "microphone classes" where they are known only by their Social Security numbers. In the past, registration has been a hassle, but students now have the option of using the Internet to register, making the task less troublesome. Required courses vary by college, but degree-seeking students must take a comprehensive two-year core curriculum, which generally forces freshmen to take English, numerical and analytical reasoning (math or philosophy), humanities and social sciences (history and fine arts), natural sciences (lab science), and a foreign language. Also required for freshmen is University 101, a three-hour seminar designed to help freshmen adjust to the university. The university has a top-notch library, with numerous special collections, including the world's most comprehensive collection of F. Scott Fitzgerald research materials, and a recent acquisition of Ernest Hemingway materials. While responsibility for faculty contact rests squarely on the students, the student–teacher relationship seems good here. "I have had excellent advisors and they are very interested in my academic career," says a student.

> "I have had excellent advisors and they are very interested in my academic career."

Eighty-one percent of the student body is from South Carolina. Nearly a quarter are from the top tenth of their high school class. Seventeen percent are African-American, and Asian-Americans and Hispanics account for 4 percent combined. "Relations are good, but the integration could be better," reports a journalism major. Groups like SEED (Students Educating and Empowering for Diversity) tend to be popular. USC offers thousands of merit scholarships, ranging from $500 to nearly $17,000, and hundreds of athletic scholarships.

The advice to prospective students: apply immediately or at least before Christmas if you want a room on campus. Forty-seven percent of the students live on campus, and everything here works on a first-come, first-served basis—freshmen as well as upperclassmen must compete for space. The best rooms in the stately old Horseshoe section of campus cost considerably more than one-room, two-bed arrangements in dorms with bathrooms in the hall. Nearly every choice of living space is available, and the surest way to beat the housing system is to get into the Honors College, which entitles you to some of the best rooms. On-campus dining options are numerous, including a sub shop, baked potato bar, Mexican food bar, frozen yogurt, and a pizza delivery service. USC employs both all-you-can-eat meal plans and cash cards of various denominations.

Fall football weekends are always a big deal, and fans have reason to cheer as Coach Lou Holtz has brought new life (and post-season bowl bids) to the program. The USC–Clemson rivalry is one of the oldest and most colorful in college sports. The festivities begin weeks in advance and include a blood drive where the two schools compete to donate the most blood, the annual Tigerburn parade and bonfire, and lengthy all-night tailgating parties. Winter weekends bring basketball—now in the new Carolina Center—and when warm weather hits, Myrtle Beach is three hours away. For hiking, skiing, camping, or just getting away, the mountains are located just four hours to the north; but those interested in watching top-ranked swimming and tennis teams should stick around the campus. Club sports have been eclipsed by the varsity teams, but intramurals are still strong.

Athletic victories and losses are equally good excuses for setting up weekend-long parties on campus, but stricter campus policies regarding alcohol have cramped the traditional Carolina style. As one undergrad notes, "It's easy for underage students to get alcohol from older students, but real hard to get served in bars."

The USC–Clemson rivalry is one of the oldest and most colorful in college sports. The festivities begin weeks in advance and include a blood drive where the two schools compete for the most blood, the annual Tigerburn parade and bonfire, and lengthy all-night tailgating parties.

The advice to prospective students: apply immediately or at least before Christmas if you want a room on campus.

However, another student claims, "If you have any kind of ID, you can get served." In South Carolina, drunkenness can be punished by the city police and the university. About 17 percent of the men and 17 percent of the women join the fraternities and sororities, and these organizations orchestrate much of the nightlife. On campus, university-sponsored events include movies, dances, theater, orchestra, and comedy shows. And with more than two hundred political, religious, social, and service clubs on campus, everyone can find something to get involved in. For those inclined to stray off campus, Columbia offers theaters, a comedy club, a performing arts center, and Five Points, which includes a strip of six different bars. The new Strom Thurmond Fitness and Wellness Center is available for students wanting to take advantage of indoor-outdoor pools, an indoor track, volleyball and basketball courts, a climbing wall, and racquetball courts.

Of course, with such a large school, the potential of becoming a "little fish in a big pond" is great. Students who aren't ready to take initiative would be wise to look elsewhere. But students who enjoy a lively, sports-oriented collegiate life and are ready to take responsibility for their academic involvement may find that no place could be finer.

> **Overlaps**
>
> **Clemson, College of Charleston, Winthrop, UNC–Chapel Hill, University of Georgia**

If You Apply To > **South Carolina:** Regular admissions: Feb. 15. Financial aid: Apr. 1. Meets demonstrated need of 64%. Campus interviews: optional, informational. No alumni interviews. SATs or ACTs: required. No SAT IIs. Accepts electronic applications. No essay question.

University of Southern California

University Park, Los Angeles, CA 90089-0911

USC's old handle: "The University of Spoiled Children." USC's new handle: highly selective West Coast university with preeminent programs in arts and media. The difference: a deluge in applications of historic proportions as students flock to L.A. and the region's only major private university.

The University of Southern California has many fine programs, but if the entertainment or communications business is one's desired destination, USC's ticket is guaranteed to take a graduate there. Programs in journalism/communications, drama, and music are top-notch. And with a little help from its friends Steven Spielberg, George Lucas, and Johnny Carson, who made possible the addition of a high-tech, state-of-the-art cinema/TV complex, USC is able to boast a stellar cinema/television department. Let's not overlook how many employers might get the warm fuzzies at the mention of USC's superstar sports teams. Whatever one's major, a USC diploma is like money in the bank.

The USC campus occupies 150 park-like acres but is a mere ten-minute drive from the heart of Los Angeles. An immaculate mix of traditional ivy-covered and modern structures dotted with fountains and reflecting pools, the campus provides a richly foliated and well-shaded refuge from city asphalt and the Southern California sun. Despite its decidedly urban location, the campus itself is a veritable urban oasis, and security is tight compared to most other college campuses, as USC police patrol several blocks around the school in addition to USC-owned grounds. A new internationally themed residence hall opened recently, and students once again have access to Doheney Memorial Library following a major renovation.

Website: www.usc.edu
Location: City center
Total Enrollment: 30,682
Undergraduates: 16,145
Male/Female: 50/50
SAT Ranges: V 600–700
  M 640–720
ACT Range: 27–31
Financial Aid: 50%
Expense: Pr $ $ $ $
Phi Beta Kappa: Yes
Applicants: 28,362
Accepted: 30%
Enrolled: 32%
Grad in 6 Years: 76%
Returning Freshmen: 94%
Academics: ✍ ✍ ✍ ½

Social: ☎ ☎ ☎
Q of L: ★ ★ ★
Admissions: (213) 740-1111
Email Address:
   admitusc@usc.edu

Strongest Programs:
Business/Marketing
Visual and Performing Arts
Social Science and History
Communications
Engineering

The "once a Trojan, always a Trojan" mantra seems to hold water with many USC alums, and many students find that their continued school spirit has paid off in their job search after college.

USC is a California school through and through, as most of its alumni go on to lucrative jobs in L.A.'s private sector.

The campus isn't the only thing that's changing. Curriculum restructuring of the last three years has transformed USC into an interdisciplinary smorgasbord. The school is now home to several unique programs for freshmen, including Learning Communities, a seminar-sized group of students interested in the same broad topic who study and take classes together. The group meets up to six times throughout the semester and is guided by a faculty advisor responsible for advising and mentoring the students during their first year at the school. Recent Learning Communities were arranged around such topics as Image and Culture: From the Trojan Wars to Star Wars and Medicine and Technology. The Thematic Option, or "Traumatic Option" as it's commonly called by students, is USC's version of a freshman honors program. Admission is tough, requiring a near-perfect GPA and a 1360 SAT score. Participating students have smaller classes and are exposed to a more cohesive group of core courses than most freshmen.

For upperclassmen, simplification of the general education requirements during the last two years has allowed many to major and minor in a variety of disparate subjects, something that was previously impossible to do without sticking around for a fifth year. In fact, the administration touts the high numbers of students with interdisciplinary academic records, and it's not uncommon to meet an art history major with a biomedical sciences minor. The school recently created the Renaissance Scholars program, which recognizes students excelling in academic breadth. To be eligible for the prize, you must major or minor in two or more disparate fields of study and graduate with a 3.5 or higher GPA. Last year, the school awarded seventy-nine prizes.

USC is a California school through and through, as most of its alumni go on to lucrative jobs in L.A.'s private sector. If you want to make connections in the film and music industry, this is the place to do it. To say that USC loyalty among alumni is strong is an understatement. The "once a Trojan, always a Trojan" mantra seems to hold water with many USC alums, and many students find that their continued school spirit has paid off in their job search after college.

Despite being stereotyped as spoiled, upper-middle-class kids, USC's student body is pretty diverse: 51 percent are Caucasian, 21 percent Asian-American, 12 percent Hispanic, and 6 percent African-American. Sixty-four percent hail from California, though the university has more foreign students—nearly six thousand—than any other college in the country. Tuition isn't cheap, but the university offers a need-blind admissions policy and guarantees to meet demonstrated financial need for all students for all four years. The school also awards hundreds of academic scholarships, ranging from partial to full tuition.

Students complain little about university-sponsored housing, which is available both on and off campus. Students say that finding housing is a fairly painless process, and freshman housing is all but guaranteed. Dorms, both co-ed and single-sex, are large, comfortable, well maintained, even luxurious by most standards. Swimming pools, tennis courts, carpeting, air-conditioning, dishwashers; you name the convenience and you can find it in a USC dorm. But you pay for what you get, and housing—on or off campus—is expensive. About 37 percent of undergraduates live on campus. Dining halls serve croissants and gourmet coffee among other delicacies. Safety both on and off campus is a big concern, as the area around campus is questionable at best. Most students agree that campus security patrols are excellent, though long waits for campus cruiser escorts are common.

Though L.A. can hardly be described as a "college town" in the traditional sense, no one complains about a lack of social options. In addition to community service, downtown L.A. offers a vast array of internships and a hopping social scene for budding professionals. Although fewer than 20 percent of students go Greek, the scene tends to dominate the social landscape at USC. Jaded upperclassmen say that the frat parties are easily avoided by taking trips into Hollywood or Santa Monica.

Famous Venice Beach is just a few miles from campus, and in the winter months, students can reach the San Gabriel Mountains (and its ski resorts) in less than an hour (by car, not by skis).

On campus, sports are pretty much the biggest thing going. Football mania has reached a new level since the team brought home a share of the national title. Two of USC's biggest school-wide traditions revolve around the ol' pigskin. The first is Troy Week—the week leading up to the UCLA game—which culminates with a pep rally and concert in the middle of campus. Ask any USC student what the best road trip of the year is, and they'll tell you that the massive Trojan migration to San Francisco for the Stanford or Berkeley game is where it's at. Throngs of USC undergrads, alumni, and fans gather together in Union Square for a huge pep rally, featuring the band, cheerleaders, and university personalities. USC water sports teams are solid, with winning teams in men's and women's water polo and crew, and swimming.

USC is a place where everything seems large and prosperous, and is getting to be more so all the time. It's keeping academics on the upswing, and has an energetic student body that works hard, concentrating simultaneously on studies, careers, parties, and athletics in equally substantial portions. For those planning on remaining in L.A., the connections you'll forge could possibly be your ticket to success.

If You Apply To ➤

USC: Regular admissions: Jan. 10. Financial aid: Jan. 21. Guarantees to meet demonstrated need. Campus and alumni interviews: optional, informational. SATs or ACTs: required. SAT IIs: recommended. Accepts electronic applications. Essay question: story about yourself; important experience (or why USC, for transfer and foreign students).

Southern Methodist University

P.O. Box 750181, Dallas, TX 75275-0181

SMU is all but the official alma mater of the Dallas business and professional elite. The university is best known for business, performing arts, and upscale conservatism. Though tuition is moderate by national standards, SMU is pricey compared to rivals Texas Christian and Rice.

Southern Methodist University has that whole Southern hospitality thing down pat—even if you're not Methodist, and you don't come from around these parts. Once known a "Southern Millionaire's University," SMU is fast becoming a place for serious scholars, both in historically strong areas like business and the arts, and in more academic and technical disciplines, such as political science, history, and engineering. "The student population does give off a sense of uppity-ness and snobbery," says a political science and math major. "However, there are so many people from different backgrounds that you can always find the right group for you."

The campus is located in the affluent suburb of Highland Park, "five minutes from downtown Dallas and within thirty minutes of everything else," says a senior. Flower beds, fountains, and neatly trimmed lawns surround stately brick buildings, most in the collegiate Georgian style. Dallas Hall, with its four-story rotunda, is the centerpiece. New buildings for the library, life sciences, engineering and student services, as well as a new art museum and football stadium, are helping enhance student life. An expansion of the fitness and recreation center is underway, as is a new business education center.

Website: www.smu.edu
Location: Suburban
Total Enrollment: 10,955
Undergraduates: 6,210
Male/Female: 46/54
SAT Ranges: V 540–630
  M 550–650
ACT Range: 23–28
Financial Aid: 35%
Expense: Pr $ $ $
Phi Beta Kappa: Yes
Applicants: 6,152
Accepted: 66%
Enrolled: 22%
Grad in 6 Years: 70%

(Continued)
Returning Freshmen: 86%
Academics: ✍ ✍ ✍
Social: ☎ ☎ ☎ ☎
Q of L: ★ ★ ★ ★
Admissions: (214) 768-3417
Email Address:
  enroll_serv@mail.smu.edu

Strongest Programs:
Business
Drama
Dance
Political Science
History
Natural Sciences/Premed
Engineering

New buildings for the library, life sciences, engineering and student services, as well as a new art museum and football stadium, are helping enhance student life. An expansion of the fitness and recreation center is underway, as is a new business education center.

While SMU is a university, administrators believe that "the liberal arts are central to the goals of higher education." To that end, the general education curriculum includes courses in cultural formations (interdisciplinary humanities and social sciences options, emphasizing writing), perspectives (one course in each of arts, literature, religious and philosophical thought, history, politics and economics, and behavioral sciences), information technology (understanding technology and its social, legal, and ethical implications), human diversity, and foreign language. In all, the school offers nearly seventy undergraduate majors, and many students pursue more than one.

SMU is training ground for Dallas' business and professional elite. Its Cox School of Business offers the most popular majors, business and finance. Engineers have access to an extensive co-op program, thanks to the proximity to more than eight hundred high-tech companies, including Nokia and Nortel, which have facilities in the Dallas suburbs. The John Goodwin Tower Center for Political Studies, named for the former senator, focuses on international relations and comparative politics, while the on-campus Tate Forums provide informal question-and-answer sessions with national and international figures. The Meadows School of the Arts, also home to the Temerlin Advertising Institute, shines just as brightly. Its facilities include the Bob Hope and Greer Garson theaters, funded by their namesake performers. The fifty-thousand-square-foot Garson includes a thrust stage for the study and performance of classical plays.

SMU's humanities programs are notable, too; English, history, and political science stand out. The annual literary festival brings to campus poets and playwrights such as Adrienne Rich and Edward Albee for readings and seminars with aspiring authors. SMU also publishes Southwest Review, one of the four oldest continuously published literary quarterlies in the nation.

"SMU opened its arms to me, and made it feel like home."

Communications programs have been strengthened with new curricula, faculty, and state-of-the-art studio facilities; the top spokesman for the long-distance phone company MCI, Brad Burns, is an SMU grad. A junior says the program in corporate communications and public relations "does a good job providing students with ways to apply course material to the real world, through projects with clients and writing articles."

SMU prides itself on small classes; most course sections have fifty students or fewer. The Honors Program is even better, enabling about six hundred students to take seminars on topics not offered broadly, with enrollment in each course capped at twenty students. "The school offers many programs to both challenge and encourage students," says a marketing major. "Professors want to help you do well." Teaching assistants are available for extra help, students say, but they never teach classes. Twenty-two study abroad programs are available in places ranging from Austria to Australia; about four hundred students participate each year. SMU also operates a second campus near Taos, New Mexico, at historic Fort Burgwin, a mid-nineteenth-century army outpost.

Although it was founded by what is now the United Methodist Church, SMU is nondenominational and welcomes students of all faiths. In fact, while 28 percent of students are Methodist, 20 percent are Roman Catholic, and the remainder report affiliations with various Protestant denominations, as well as Judaism, Buddhism and Islam. Texans make up 62 percent of the SMU student body, and most students "are especially spirited and outgoing," says an accounting major. "Everyone wants to get involved." Politically, "the campus is largely Republican," says a marketing major. "While the average student at SMU is an upper-middle-class to upper-class white Christian, this is not a prerequisite. The minority population continues to rise, led by a large Hispanic surge." Indeed, Hispanics account for 8 percent of the student body, while African-Americans and Asian-Americans add 6 percent each. While campus diversity has increased, ethnic groups still tend to stick together, a division some attribute to the Greek system. Administrators are working to increase understanding among races, with activities such as Intercultural Student Orientation. Also helping boost diversity is SMU's

"I have found lifelong friends, supportive faculty and staff, and a place I'll want to return in years to come."

own student-loan program, for middle-income families who do not meet federal guidelines for need-based loans. More than 4,500 merit scholarships are awarded each year, ranging from $292 to $22,568, and 272 athletic scholarships are available, in seven men's and nine women's sports.

Forty-eight percent of SMU's students live on campus, and freshmen are required to do so. Most upperclassmen find off-campus apartments or dwell in Greek houses, as 38 percent of the women join sororities and 37 percent of the men pledge fraternities. All thirteen residence halls are co-ed by floor, and theme floors are also available, focused on honors, wellness, or the arts. "Housing on campus is top-of-the-line," says a senior. "There are singles and doubles, community and en suite baths, all with air-conditioning, recent renovations, two Internet jacks and a phone." The Inner City Experience house allows students to live and provide community service in East Dallas, a struggling section of the city. SMU has two buffet-style cafeterias, with salad and sandwich bars, make-your-own-pasta stations, two different hot entrees, and a variety of desserts. Meal plans also include dollars that can be spent at off-campus restaurants and coffee shops.

Fourteen student-athletes also took their talents to the 2000 Olympic Games, where SMU swimmers won gold and silver medals, and a high jumper won bronze.

When the weekend comes, almost two hundred student groups sponsor speakers and other diversions. "Although a lot of people go off-campus on the weekends, during the week you can find ten different clubs hosting some event or serving food or having a dance," says a political science major. "Nightlife takes place in nearby bars, clubs, and restaurants," since the campus is dry, says a marketing major. (Regardless of their age, students say it's easy to find beer at the fraternity houses. Those under twenty-one caught drinking are referred to the Judicial Council.) Highlights of the campus calendar include the Mane Event, honoring the Mustang mascot, and the Celebration of Lights, when students gather to admire Christmas lights at Dallas Hall. Formals and other Greek parties are by invitation only, and

"Housing on campus is top-of-the-line."

students are often bussed to them. SMU's neighborhood "has the feel of a small town, but the convenience of a big city," says one student, noting that museums, amusement parks, big-league sports, entertainment, and shopping are all within a quick drive. Cars can be a headache, as on-campus parking is limited, but they're necessary for road trips to New Orleans (for Mardi Gras), Shreveport (for gambling), and Austin (where the Sixth Street bars and music halls stay open until the wee hours).

Football games are a big deal here—after all, this is Texas—and SMU students get riled up for the annual battle against Texas Christian University. If their Mustangs are losing—which has happened often recently, spurring much frustration—students can be heard chanting "That's all right. That's okay. You're going to work for us some day." When the Mustangs play at home, there's Tailgating on the Boulevard, a festival with tents, family activities, music, and food on the main quad. SMU competes in the Division I-A Western Athletic Conference, and fourteen student-athletes also took their talents to the 2000 Olympic Games, where swimmers won gold and silver medals, and a high jumper won bronze.

Southern Methodist isn't for everyone. As one recent grad says, "Does SMU have its fair share of social-climbing luxury car drivers? Sure." But that's only part of the story. While it helps to be Greek and goal-oriented, this is no longer simply a finishing school for southern millionaires. "SMU has given me the chance to be a leader,

Overlaps

University of Texas–Austin, Vanderbilt, Tulane, Texas Christian

get involved, succeed in classes, enjoy social events on- and off-campus, and better prepare myself for the real world," says a wistful senior. "I have found lifelong friends, supportive faculty and staff, and a place I'll want to return in years to come."

<table>
<tr><td>**If You Apply To** ➤</td><td>**SMU:** Early action: Nov. 1. Regular admissions: Jan. 15 (priority). Financial aid: Feb. 1. Housing: May 1. Meets demonstrated need of 79%. Campus interviews: optional, informational. SATs or ACTs: required. SAT IIs: optional. Accepts the Common Application and electronic applications. Essay question: give the title of your autobiography, then choose one of the following: a page or two from that autobiography; the origin of your e-mail address and how it reflects your personality; and some of the things you are thinking, laughing or talking about these days.</td></tr>
</table>

Southwestern University

1001 E. University Avenue, Georgetown, TX 78626

Camouflaged beneath a nondescript name, Southwestern is a private-college alternative to Austin and Trinity (TX). Southwestern is about half the size of the latter and prides itself on individual attention and down-to-earth friendliness. Strong programs include communications and international studies.

Website:
 www.southwestern.edu
Location: Suburban
Total Enrollment: 1,266
Undergraduates: 1,266
Male/Female: 41/59
SAT Ranges: V 570–660
 M 570–670
ACT Range: 24–29
Financial Aid: 55%
Expense: Pr $ $
Phi Beta Kappa: Yes
Applicants: 1,572
Accepted: 61%
Enrolled: 36%
Grad in 6 Years: 70%
Returning Freshmen: 87%
Academics: ✍ ✍ ✍
Social: ☎ ☎ ☎
Q of L: ★ ★ ★
Admissions: (512) 863-1200
Email Address: admission@ southwestern.edu

Strongest Programs:
Biology/Premed
Psychology
Communication
Business

Smack in the heart of the Lone Star State, Southwestern University is a small liberal arts school in a state that is known for thinking big is better. The focus here is not only on classroom studies, but students' total development as contributors in the post-grad world, and despite an enrollment of less than thirteen hundred students, SU proves that big things come in small packages.

Southwestern is situated on seven hundred acres at the edge of the rolling Texas Hill Country. The oldest college in Texas, Southwestern maintains its affiliation with the United Methodist Church. The campus boasts turn-of-the-century Texas limestone buildings in a Romanesque architectural style. There are plenty of wide-open spaces, including a nine-hole golf course and outdoor tennis courts. Construction of new apartment-style residence halls was recently completed, as was a new greenhouse that serves as a research facility for students and faculty.

Rigorous classes mean hard work is the norm at Southwestern. But competition isn't the bottom line. "The courses are intense and there is definitely a strong pressure to succeed," says an economics major. Another biology major agrees that "the pressure to do well is more self-instigated rather than as a result of a competitive student body." Preprofessional degrees, biology, religion/philosophy, and business are considered the school's strongest programs and are quite popular with students. Non-Western language studies are getting a boost through the Language Learning Center. While engineering may not be Southwestern's strongest program, the 3–2 Engineering program allows students to do a dual degree program that includes three years at Southwestern and approximately two years at an engineering school—participating universities include Arizona State, Texas A&M, and Washington University.

Graduation requirements include eight hours of Foundation courses, thirty hours of Perspectives on Knowledge courses, and English Composition. There's also a stipulation that students take a foreign language through sophomore year and two hours of a fitness or recreational activity. The study abroad program is very strong, and about half the students here take advantage of opportunities in London, Jamaica, Mexico, Hungary, Honduras, and Germany. Several student exchange programs are offered as well. Internships are available, including those to study politics, foreign policy, journalism, and architecture in Washington, D.C. The New York Arts program offers students the chance to work with professional artists, designers, actors, and filmmakers in the Big Apple. Undergraduate research is encouraged in all majors. The biology department offers a summer research program to students interested in working with a faculty member, which also provides a $3,000 student stipend. In addition, Southwestern has been a member of the Associated Colleges of the South* consortium for more than a decade.

(Continued)
Political Science
International Studies

Classes are small, usually fewer than twenty-five students, so one-on-one attention and connections between professors and students is the norm. "Professors are really interested in a student's progress and activities both in and out of the classroom," says a

"The courses are intense and there is definitely a strong pressure to succeed."

student. Professors even occasionally invite students to their homes. "They know students by name and are eager to form strong relationships with them," says a junior. Perhaps because of their respect for their profs, Southwesterners take their academics seriously, and staying in to study is a legitimate excuse for not going out.

The student body is 78 percent Caucasian, 13 percent Hispanic, 3 percent Asian-American, and 3 percent African-American. Ninety percent of the students are Texans, with large numbers from the metropolitan areas of Houston, Dallas, and San Antonio. Most students are from middle-class families "so you don't get a good sense of diversity while you are walking around campus." one student reports; however, the campus "embraces diversity to the point that sometimes students who are in the majority are the ones who feel uncomfortable." SU's tuition is markedly less than at institutions of similar quality in other parts of the nation, and the university has several special tuition payment plans, including a new loan program for all families. The school also offers merit scholarships to each class, ranging from $1,000 to a full ride. There are no athletic scholarships.

Over the past few years, Southwestern has changed a number of programs to keep up with the times. It developed sexual harassment and alcohol policies involving students, faculty, and staff as advisors, and created a Gender Awareness Resource Center on campus to offer programs on gender communication and acquaintance

Professors "know students by name and are eager to form strong relationships with them."

rape. All new students go through an afternoon diversity workshop called Facing Differences, which focuses on relating in spite of racial, ethnic, cultural, and other differences. The Bridge Builders helps students to examine their own views on issues such as racism and sexism with their Tunnel of Oppression program.

Georgetown is a small town that does not fit into the "college town" category and does not provide a lot of housing for the student population. Therefore, 80 percent of the students live on campus—in fact, freshman are required to live at the college. Dorms are considered "comfortable" and "convenient" and tend to "knit the community together." Most rooms of the co-ed and single-sex European-style residence halls are suite-like, and on-campus apartments also are available. Housekeepers clean up several times per week. Different meal plans are available, and students can also eat in the student union snack bar.

The social life on campus tends to center around the Greek system, to which 36 percent of the men and 34 percent of the women belong. The frats host house parties on the weekends, but the fine arts department sponsors concerts and plays for students who would rather skip the Greek scene, and there are campus-wide picnics with carnival-style entertainment. During Homecoming, students look forward to Sing!, a variety show where students produce short musical skits and acts about Southwestern.

Preprofessional degrees, biology, religion/philosophy, and business are considered the school's strongest programs and are quite popular with students.

Classes are small, usually fewer than twenty-five students, so one-on-one attention and connections between professors and students is the norm.

The study abroad program is very strong, and about half the students here take advantage of opportunities in London, Jamaica, Mexico, Hungary, Honduras, and Germany. Several student exchange programs are offered as well. Internships are available, including those to study politics, foreign policy, journalism, and architecture in Washington, D.C.

For the real action, many students travel thirty minutes south to Austin's great restaurants, concerts, and live music shows on Sixth Street. Another popular campus activity is "rolling," where students pack as many people in a car as they can and drive very slowly on the back roads with blaring music. MallBalls begin and end the year with food, frivolity, music, and games on the Academic Mall. The official school policy prohibits underage drinking, but it's "fairly easy to obtain alcohol from frat parties or friends," a junior says.

Intramural sports are popular and Southwestern is a member of the Southern Collegiate Athletic Conference in the NCAA's Division III. Baseball, women's basketball, soccer, and golf have all won conference championships. Crowds gather anytime SU plays San Antonio's Trinity University because of a strong rivalry between the two schools.

In a state where everything tends to be considered huge and overwhelming—the individual attention, beautiful campus, and students who are "laid-back back and open with their beliefs" make this small college a big hit.

If You Apply To ➣

SU: Rolling admissions: Feb. 15. Early decision: Nov. 1 Financial aid: Mar. 1. Does not guarantee to meet demonstrated need. Campus interviews: recommended, evaluative. Alumni interviews: optional, evaluative. SATs or ACTs: required. SAT IIs: optional. Accepts the Common Application and electronic applications. Essay question: a personal experience or achievement that has changed you; most important challenge for your generation; biggest misconception people have of you.

Spelman College: See page 36.

Stanford University

Stanford, CA 94305-3005

If you're looking for an Eastern version of Stanford, try Duke (with a touch of MIT mixed in). Stanford's big-time athletics, preprofessional feel, and laid-back atmosphere differentiate it from Ivy League competitors. In contrast to the hurly-burly of Bay Area rival Berkeley, Stanford's aura is upscale suburban.

Think the only difference between Stanford and the Ivy League is a couple hundred extra sunny days each year? Think again. From the red-tiled roofs to the lush greenery and California vibe, Stanford is a world away from the Gothic intellectual culture of the Ivies. Virtually all the great Eastern universities began as places to ponder human existence and the meaning of life, using European institutions as their models. Stanford, by contrast, built its academic reputation around science and engineering, the fields characterized by American ingenuity, and only later cultivated excellence in the humanities and social sciences. Stanford is, without a doubt, the nation's first great "American" university.

The differences between Stanford and other institutions with which it competes for the country's top high school seniors are evident everywhere, from the architecture to the curriculum. The school's mission-style buildings look outward to the world at large, rather than inward to ivy-covered courtyards. And unlike Yale and Princeton, Stanford—founded in 1885 by Leland and Jane Stanford—has been co-ed from the beginning. During its centennial, the school became the first U.S. university to successfully launch a billion-dollar capital campaign; as of August, 2002, Stanford's endowment was $7.6 billion. Some architectural critics say the campus looks like the world's biggest Mexican restaurant, even though Frederick Law Olmsted, designer of New York City's Central Park, planned many buildings. The campus stretches from the foothills of the Santa Cruz Mountains to the edge of Palo Alto in the heart of Silicon Valley, smack in the middle of earthquake country. Recently, the university opened a new student health center and the Mechanical Engineering Research Laboratory, in addition to a bevy of campus-wide renovations and improvements.

Biology and human biology, the quintessential premed preparation, are the most popular programs on campus, followed by economics and computer science. Stanford has also developed a particularly interesting set of interdisciplinary majors, which let students fashion a course of study by culling classes across departments. The School of Humanities and Sciences has a major in archaeology. Other programs include overseas seminars, taking place the three weeks before the fall quarter, for those not otherwise able to study overseas. They are held in China, Belgium, Russia, and South Korea. For those students who are able to study abroad, programs are offered in Australia, Japan, Chile, England, Russia, Germany, Italy, and France. In fact, more than one-quarter of each graduating class takes advantage of these programs. Closer to home, the Stanford-in-Washington program allows sixty students to live, study, and intern in the nation's capital each quarter. The Haas Center for Public Service offers service-learning courses in a wide range of disciplines, while the communications department sponsors the Rebele internship, which offers paid positions with various California newspapers.

Stanford's general education requirements are extensive. All students take a three-quarter Introduction to the Humanities, designed to hone skills through close reading and critical investigation of a limited number of works, as well as three courses in the humanities and social sciences. Students must also fulfill **"Teaching at Stanford is first class."** requirements in natural sciences, applied science and technology, and mathematics, as well as take one course in at least two of three areas: world culture, American culture, and gender studies. The new Stanford Introductory Studies program includes Freshman Seminars, courses limited to sixteen students to enable close discourse with professors. Recent topics have included The Operas of Mozart, Understanding the '60s, and Jewish American Literature. Stanford manages the "sophomore slump" with programs like Sophomore College, a three-week program that brings 430 incoming sophomores together several weeks before fall quarter begins, to work with faculty on intensive group projects. Sophomore Dialogues are small seminar courses for second-year students only; 120 will be offered this year. There's also Summer Research College, designed to create community among undergraduates engaged in full-time summer research on campus.

Don't let Stanford's California location fool you into thinking that studying is optional—it's more like a full-time job. "Everyone works very hard but it is not competitive in the sense that students are competing with each other." One student compared his classmates to ducks—"They look peaceful on the surface, but they're paddling like mad underneath." Stanford's faculty ranks among the best in the nation, with most departments boasting a nationally known name or two. Professors are considered outstanding scholars with outstanding credentials and freshman are often taught by full professors as opposed to graduate students or adjunct professors. According to one student, "Teaching at Stanford is first class. Professors tend to be very passionate about their work and about working with those students willing to pursue interest in their fields." The only negative comments expressed by

(Continued)
Enrolled: 69%
Grad in 6 Years: 93%
Returning Freshmen: 98%
Academics: ✍ ✍ ✍ ✍ ✍
Social: ☎ ☎ ☎ ☎
Q of L: ★ ★ ★ ★ ★
Admissions: (650) 723-2091
Email Address:
  admission@stanford.edu

Strongest Programs:
Biology
Computer Science
International Relations
Engineering
Political Science
Economics

"The social life is very campus- and residence-based. There is a noticeable Greek life presence, but parties are almost always open to the entire student body."

students concern the level of support academic advisors provide to freshmen. While most students are more than satisfied with both faculty and peer academic advisement, the help within the department advising may be "hit or miss." If you can deal with the hustle and bustle a larger campus environment tends to foster, this should not pose much of a problem.

Despite its upscale image, Stanford tends to have the same demographic profile as its state-supported neighbor in Berkeley. Sixty-nine percent of a recent freshman class attended public high school; 88 percent graduated in the top 10 percent of their class. Forty-seven percent of students are from out of state, while foreigners account for 5 percent of the student population. Minority enrollment is above average, with Asian-Americans accounting for 24 percent of the student body, Hispanics 11 percent, and African-Americans 10 percent. One student describes classmates as, "fun, sporty, sometimes spoiled, and dedicated."

About 20 percent of Stanford's students take advantage of its liberal stop-out policy, which lets students take some time off along the way, rather than staying in school for four straight years. Admissions are need-blind, and the university guarantees to meet the full demonstrated financial need of every domestic admit, with the exception of international students. While there are no merit scholarships, 74 percent of students receive some sort of internal or external financial aid; the university also awards three hundred athletic scholarships annually in thirty sports, ranging from football and basketball to gymnastics and diving.

Freshmen must live on campus, and Stanford guarantees housing for four years; 94 percent of students stay on campus, with most of the others attending Stanford-in-Washington or other off-campus study programs. One percent of students commute from home, in part because of the lack of affordable off-campus options in extraordinarily expensive Silicon Valley. As students gain seniority, a lottery system decides where they'll live. "Dorms are nice and well taken care of, although room size and facilities vary a lot," according to one senior. The multimillion-dollar Governor's Corner complex, for example, includes all-oak fixtures, homey rooms with views into the foothills, microwave ovens in the kitchenettes, and Italian leather sofas in the lounges. Those living in residence halls must sign up for a meal plan. Students describe campus security as "good," and most feel very safe. When academic pressures become too great, students seek refuge in the outdoors. Nearby hills are perfect for jogging and biking, and a small lake is great for sailing and windsurfing (the most popular spring physical education class). Trips to the Sierra Nevada mountains (four hours away) or to the Pacific coast (forty-five minutes) are popular, as are jaunts to San Francisco, much more of a college town.

Like most things at Stanford, activities and social life vary a great deal, although most take place on campus, because that's where students live. As tradition goes, freshmen aren't "true Stanford students" until they've been kissed at midnight in the quad

"Dorms are nice and well taken care of, although room size and facilities vary a lot."

by a senior. Full Moon on the Quad occurs at the first full moon, and features a bevy of giggling first-year students eager to receive their initiation (courtesy of a well-timed entrance by upperclassmen/women). Greek organizations claim 17 percent of the men and 12 percent of the women, and provide their share of happy hours and weekend beer bashes, which are open to all. Another Stanford tradition is the Viennese Ball, a February event that may make you wish you'd taken ballroom dancing lessons. Halloween finds students partying at the Mausoleum, the Stanfords' final resting place. According to one student, "The social life is very campus- and residence-based. There is a noticeable Greek life presence, but parties are almost always open to the entire student body."

Stanford has a proud athletic tradition that includes 70 NCAA championships since 1990. Cardinal teams recently won their ninth consecutive Director's Cup as the best overall collegiate athletic program in the country. Stanford holds eighty-three national NCAA championships (fifty-seven since 1985, which ranks number one among NCAA Division I schools). The football team has pulled off its share of upsets, and the annual contest against Cal (Berkeley) is the "Big Game." In 2002, Stanford won NCAA championships in women's tennis, women's and men's water polo, and women's volleyball. For those not inclined to varsity play, Stanford offers a full slate of intramurals, and its vast sports complex includes twenty-six tennis courts, two gymnasiums, a stadium, an eighteen-hole golf course, and four swimming pools.

Stanford's sunny demeanor and infectious West Coast optimism offer an appealing alternative to the gloom and gray weather that seem to hang over some of its East Coast counterparts, with the same high-caliber academics and deep athletic traditions that have made them great. The "sense of mutual responsibility" and "lack of intense fraternity presence" make Stanford a special place, says a senior. Sentiments that no doubt would make Leland and Jane Stanford proud.

Overlaps
Harvard, MIT, Yale, Princeton, Duke

If You Apply To ➤ **Stanford:** Regular admissions: Dec. 15. Guarantees to meet demonstrated need. No campus or alumni interviews. SATs: required. SAT IIs: strongly recommended. Accepts electronic applications. Essay question: reflect on a risk you have taken; attach a photograph of importance and explain its significance.

State University of New York

As the largest university system in the world, the State University of New York provides more than four hundred thousand students with a vast landscape of educational opportunities—both figuratively and literally. Encompassing sixty-six campuses and twenty-one thousand acres of property, SUNY's staggering physical presence is exceeded only by the scope of its academic offerings.

The statistics of SUNY (pronounced "SOOney") are awesome. The university has an annual operating budget of billions, greater than the gross national product of many countries and larger than the budget of more than a dozen American states. It has more than four thousand academic programs and 24,500 faculty members and maintains more than 2,200 buildings. Every year it awards approximately sixty-five thousand degrees, from associate to Ph.D., in thousands of different academic fields. And—you're not going to believe this one—it has more than one million living graduates.

Such figures are all the more remarkable because until 1948 New York had no state university at all. That year, the legislature created the State University around a cluster of thirty-two existing public institutions, the best of which focused on the training of teachers, to handle the flow of returning World War II veterans. But a "gentleman's agreement" not to compete with the state's private colleges (which for generations had enjoyed a monopoly on higher education in New York) hindered SUNY's movement into the liberal arts. Not until Nelson A. Rockefeller became governor in 1960 and made the expansion of the university his major priority did SUNY begin its dramatic growth.

SUNY has now ripened into a network of four research-oriented "university centers," thirteen arts and sciences colleges, six agricultural and technical colleges, five "statutory" colleges, four specialized colleges, thirty locally sponsored community colleges, and four health science centers. The fruits of the labor, though practiced in as high-cost a state as there is, have become legitimately advertised as among the best bargains in the nation, particularly at the undergraduate level. Annual costs at institutions like SUNY–Albany are still barely more than half of what it costs to attend such hoary and prestigious publicly supported flagship campuses as California at Berkeley and the University of Michigan. Nevertheless, the SUNY system faces continuing budget cuts, and New York State's investment per capita in higher education as a whole is forty-seventh in the country.

Prospective students apply directly to the SUNY unit they seek to attend. Forty-six of the colleges, though, use a "common form" application that enables a prospective student to apply to as many as four SUNY campuses at the same time. The central administration runs a SUNY Admissions Assistance Service that helps rejected students find places at other campuses. Students who earn associate degrees at community or other two-year colleges are guaranteed the chance to continue their education at a four-year institution, though not necessarily at their first choice. The level of selectivity varies widely. Most community colleges guarantee admission to any local high school student, but the university centers, as well as some specialized colleges, are among the most competitive public institutions in the nation. As part of a recent "standards revolution," SUNY trustees voted to adopt a new budgeting model designed to financially reward campuses that increase enrollment. Undergraduates at all liberal arts colleges and university centers pay the same tuition, but the rates at community colleges vary (and are lower). Out-of-state students, who make up only 4 percent of SUNY students, pay about double the amount of in-state tuition.

Mainly for political reasons, the State University of New York chose not to follow the model of other states and build a single flagship campus the likes of an Ann Arbor, Madison, or Chapel Hill. Instead, it created the four university centers with undergraduate, graduate, and professional schools and research facilities in each corner of the state. When they were created in the 1960s, each one hoped to become fully comprehensive, but there has been a certain degree of specialization from the beginning. They also decided not to establish a Division I football program, something that has lowered their visibility to out-of-state students.

Albany is strongest in education and public policy, Binghamton is best known for undergraduate arts and sciences, and Stony Brook is noted for its hard sciences. Buffalo, formerly a private university, maintains a strong reputation in the life sciences and geography but comes the closest of any of the four to being a fully comprehensive university. Critics of the system say that the decision to forgo a flagship campus guarantees a lack of national prominence, and the lack of big-time football or other sports programs has affected SUNY's reputation as well. Still, many insist that somewhere in the labs and libraries of these four university centers are lurking the Nobel Prize winners of this century. To these supporters, it's only a matter of time before SUNY achieves excellence in depth as well as breadth.

The thirteen colleges of arts and sciences likewise vary widely in size and character. They range from the 26,000-student College at Buffalo, whose 125-acre campus reflects the urban flavor of the state's second-largest city, to the rural and highly selective College at Geneseo, where half as many students nearly outnumber the year-round residents of the small local village. Still others are suburban campuses, such as Purchase, which specializes in the performing arts, and Old Westbury, which was started as an experimental institution to serve minority students, older women, and others who have been "bypassed" by more traditional institutions.

With the exception of Purchase and Old Westbury, which were started from scratch, the four-year colleges are all former teachers' colleges that have, for the most part, successfully made the transition into liberal arts colleges on the small, private New England model. Now they face a new problem: the growing desire of students to study business, computer science, and other more technically oriented subjects. Some have adjusted to these demands well; others are trying to resist the trend.

SUNY's technical and specialized colleges, while not enjoying the prominence of the colleges of arts and sciences, serve the demand for vocational training in a variety of two- and four-year programs. Five of the six agricultural and technical colleges—Alfred, Canton, Cobleskill, Delhi, and Morrisville—are concerned primarily with agriculture, but also have programs in engineering, nursing, medical technology, data processing, and business administration. The sixth, Farmingdale, offers the widest range of programs, from ornamental horticulture to aerospace technology. A new upper-division technical campus at Utica-Rome now provides graduates of these two-year institutions with an opportunity to finish their education in SUNY instead of having to head for Penn State University, Ohio State, the University of Massachusetts, or destinations in other directions.

Four of the five statutory schools are at Cornell University—agriculture and life sciences, human ecology, industrial and labor relations, and veterinary medicine—while the internationally known College of Ceramics is housed at Alfred University, another private university. In addition to Utica-Rome, the specialized colleges consist of the College of Environmental Sciences and Forestry at Syracuse, the Maritime College at Fort Schuyler in the Bronx, the College of Optometry in New York City, and the Fashion Institute of Technology, whose graduates are gobbled up as fast as they emerge by employers in the Manhattan Garment District.

The twenty-nine community colleges have traditionally been the stepchildren of the system, but the combination of rampant vocationalism and the rising cost of education elsewhere is rapidly turning them into the most robust members of the family. Students once looked to the community colleges for terminal degrees that could be readily applied in the marketplace. Now, with the cost of college soaring, a growing number of students who otherwise would have been packed off to a four-year college are saving money by staying home for the first two years and then transferring to a four-year college—or even a university center—to get their bachelor's degree.

Following are full-length descriptions of SUNY–Purchase, which is the liberal arts institution best known beyond New York's borders, SUNY–Geneseo, and the four university centers.

SUNY–Albany

1400 Washington Avenue, Albany, NY 12222

SUNY–Albany won't win any awards for campus beauty, but it does have some attractive programs. Albany is strong in anything related to politics, public policy, and criminal justice. Study abroad programs in Europe and Asia are also a strength. Less than 5 percent of the students are out-of-staters.

Founded in 1844 to train teachers, SUNY–Albany offers outstanding education and public policy programs that attract undergrads from around the nation who are eager to take advantage of vast resources. Preprofessional programs are strong, and students here work hard to make the grade.

Designed by Edward Durrell Stone, who also designed the Kennedy Center and Lincoln Center, SUNY–Albany's campus is modern and suburban. Almost all the academic buildings are clustered in the center of the campus, while students are housed in five symmetrically situated quads so similar in appearance that it usually takes a semester to figure out which one is yours. (Hint: the quads are named for periods in New York history—Indian, Dutch, Colonial, State, and Freedom—and progress clockwise around the campus.) The new Empire Commons houses twelve hundred upperclassmen and the $78 million life sciences building is nearing completion.

Most of the preprofessional programs are among the best of any SUNY branch. Students in the public administration and social welfare programs may take advantage of their proximity to the state government to participate in internships. Biology, physics, sociology, and psychology are other notable majors, and undergrads are clamoring for admittance to the university's business administration program, which is especially strong in accounting. The New York State Writers' Institute is the newest and least traditional of Albany's offerings, and with William Kennedy as head of the institute, the university's dream of becoming distinguished for its creative writing has nearly come true. The School of Nanosciences and Materials is another recent campus addition and the first of its kind in the nation.

All undergraduates must fulfill Albany's thirty-credit general education program, which includes courses in disciplinary prospectives, national and international perspectives, mathematics and statistics, pluralism and diversity, communication and reasoning

> **"We are given a lot of work and there is a lot of pressure to get all the work done."**

competencies, and foreign language. If this liberal arts exposure whets your appetite for interdisciplinary study, try your hand at human biology, information science, or urban studies. The more career-minded can sign up for one of forty B.A./M.A. programs or opt for a law degree with the bachelor's in only six years. Many students take advantage of SUNY–Albany's superior offerings in foreign study. The university was one of the first in the nation to develop exchange programs with Russia (and China, for that matter).

Undergraduates may also study in several European countries as well as in Brazil, Costa Rica, Israel, Japan, and Singapore. Project Renaissance brings together groups of

Website: www.albany.edu
Location: Suburban
Total Enrollment: 16,988
Undergraduates: 11,796
Male/Female: 50/50
SAT Ranges: V 510–610
  M 520–620
Financial Aid: 56%
Expense: Pub $ $
Phi Beta Kappa: Yes
Applicants: 17,328
Accepted: 56%
Enrolled: 22%
Grad in 6 Years: 63%
Returning Freshmen: 84%
Academics: 🖎 🖎 🖎 🖎
Social: ☎ ☎ ☎
Q of L: ★ ★ ★
Admissions: (518) 442-5435
Email Address:
  ugadmissions@albany.edu

Strongest Programs:
Criminal Justice
Atmospheric Science
Physics
Accounting
Business
Political Science
Social Welfare
Computer Science

one hundred freshmen with a team of senior faculty, librarians, computer specialists, and assistants in a shared academic and living community. Participants engage in a year-long, unified course of study covering twelve hours of the university's general education requirements, and have access to special perks including housing and faculty mentors. The academic climate is challenging but not cut-throat. "We are given a lot of work and there is a lot of pressure to get all the work done," says a student.

One undergraduate describes his peers as "intelligent, assertive, hardworking, urban—generally pretty fast company." Albany students tend to spend a lot of time thinking about their future. But, lest you get the wrong impression, "They're also highly motivated to party at every available moment," another adds. The student body comprises "bits and pieces of every Long Island high school and a dash of upstate, topped off with a Big Apple or two." All but 7 percent of the students are native New Yorkers. African-American and Hispanic enrollment now stands at 15 percent combined, while Asian-Americans make up another 6 percent. Racial issues are hot, but a senior says, "No problems, just a lot of diversity." Fifty-five percent of the students are from the top quarter of their high school class. SUNY–Albany makes available 708 merit scholarships of $1,000 to $6,000 each.

> **Students are "intelligent, assertive, hardworking, urban—generally pretty fast company. They're also highly motivated to party at every available moment."**

Fifty-eight percent of students live in university housing, which is described as "average." Freshmen and sophomores are required to live in dorms. The co-ed quads are exceptionally friendly, surprisingly quiet, and comfortable. "They are compact and force unity and friendship," says one undergrad. Each floor of these dorms is divided into four- to six-person suites. But the word from most students is that the best dorms are in the Alumni Quad on the downtown campus. "Alumni has much more attractive rooms and ambiance overall," says a business major. Many students move off campus because "the transportation system to and from campus is convenient and the cost of apartments is as cheap (or cheaper) than living on campus," says a junior. Students on the main campus take their meals at any of the four dorms or at the campus center that includes a popular food court and bookstore, while downtowners haunt the cheap local eateries as well as their own cafeterias. "The dining facilities need work," says an economics major.

While most people are serious about their work, a SUNY–Albany weekend starts on Thursday night for many. Students go to parties or go bar-hopping about town. Students warn that alcohol policies forbidding underage drinking are strict and well enforced. "It is easy for underage residents to drink on campus, but if you're caught there are severe penalties," says a student. Fraternities and sororities attract 4 percent of the men and 5 percent of the women, and have become the main party-throwers on campus. Albany students tend to be traditional, but rites-of-spring festivals, mandatory after enduring the miserable upstate winters, have produced Guinness records for the largest games of Simon Says, Twister, and Musical Chairs. Fountain Day brings thousands of students together for the spring turn-on of the infamous podium fountain. Mayfest is a huge all-school concert party that brings in well-known as well as up-and-coming bands.

> **"The transportation system to and from campus is convenient and the cost of apartments is as cheap (or cheaper) than living on campus."**

The natural resources of the upstate region keep students busy skiing and hiking. Treks to Montreal and Saratoga are popular. Plus, the student association owns and operates Dippikill, a private camp in the Adirondacks. Men's basketball, tennis, wrestling, and football and women's softball, volleyball, and basketball are strong, and the school is a member of Division I. Meanwhile, intramurals engender a great deal of student enthusiasm, and participation numbers in the thousands. Athletic scholarships are offered in a dozen different sports such as soccer, tennis, and golf, to name a few.

SUNY–Albany is not the concrete, sterile diploma mill it may appear to be. It's a place of opportunity for those willing to put in the hours and hard work. As one veteran warns, "You can find an outlet here for even the most obscure interest, but this is not a school that will educate you when you're not looking."

<table>
<tr><td>If You Apply To ≫</td><td>SUNY–Albany: Early action: Dec. 1. Regular admissions: Mar. 1. Financial aid: Mar. 15. Does not guarantee to meet demonstrated need. Campus interviews: recommended, informational. No alumni interviews. SATs: required. No SAT IIs. Accepts the Common Application and electronic applications. Optional essay question: personal statement.</td></tr>
</table>

SUNY–Binghamton University

P.O. Box 6001, Binghamton, NY 13902-6000

If one hundred thousand screaming fans on a Saturday afternoon tickles your fancy, head two hundred miles southwest to Penn State. Binghamton has become the premier public university in the northeast because of its outstanding academic programs, such the Binghamton Scholars and Discovery Initiative, and its commitment to undergraduates.

Known among its students as the Ivy of the SUNY system, Binghamton offers a challenging academic pace without the cut-throat edge. "You feel challenged but not intimidated," a junior says. Its Watson School of Engineering and Decker School of Nursing are top-notch programs that are putting the university on the map. "The caliber of the students here is much greater than that of any other SUNY school and right on par with the best private institutions," says a computer engineering major.

Binghamton University is situated on more than eight hundred acres of open grassy areas that include a large nature preserve, trails, fountains, and a pond. The campus features modern, "functional" buildings (all structures have been built since 1958). Some students say that from an aerial view the circular campus bears a striking resemblance to the human brain—a total coincidence and not a secret plan of the architects, the administration asserts. Recent construction includes the renovation of University Union West, the construction of an Institute for Child Development and Physical Facilities North. The new Events Center includes a six-thousand-seat multipurpose arena with a two-hundred-meter running track. Two new residence halls, Hunter and Mary, are open, with others on the way.

The first thing that greets students who do gain admission is the general education program. This comprehensive curriculum requires new students to take courses in five areas: language and communication, creating a global vision, sciences and mathematics, aesthetics and humanities, and wellness. Engineering receives high marks from students, as do the Decker School of Nursing, which offers an accelerated bachelor's degree program for students with degrees in other fields, and the school of management, which offers a five-year B.S./M.B.A. program. In addition, qualified students enrolled in any undergraduate program may pursue the baccalaureate/M.B.A. in a five-year program. Biological science, chemistry, and English win rave reviews in Harpur College. Interdisciplinary fields of study include women's

Website:
  www.binghamton.edu
Location: Suburban
Total Enrollment: 13,099
Undergraduates: 10,328
Male/Female: 48/52
SAT Ranges: V 550–640
  M 590–690
ACT Range: 24–29
Financial Aid: 68%
Expense: Pub $ $
Phi Beta Kappa: Yes
Applicants: 18,315
Accepted: 42%
Enrolled: 27%
Grad in 6 Years: 80%
Returning Freshmen: 91%
Academics: 🖉 🖉 🖉 🖉 ½
Social: ☎ ☎ ☎
Q of L: ★ ★
Admissions: (607) 777-2171
Email Address:
  admit@binghamton.edu

studies, medieval studies, Asian and Asian-American studies, Middle East and North African studies, and Latin American and Caribbean area studies. If these don't satisfy a student's intellectual cravings, the Innovational Projects Board will oversee and help students design not only their own majors but courses as well.

Internship possibilities exist, as do numerous study abroad programs. Undergraduate students are also encouraged to participate in faculty research projects. The Binghamton Scholars Program offers students of exceptional merit a chance to participate in a special four-year program that includes experiential and capstone courses. The Discovery initiative, boasted as the only one of its kind in the country, offers students opportunities for self-assessment, skill-development, academic advising, tutorial assistance, career preparation, and collaborative learning. The Global Studies Integrated Curriculum (GSIC) offers students from any school or major a chance to explore global issues from a broad range of perspectives, to develop skills and knowledge relative to a particular world culture, and to pursue collaborative research related issues. A bioengineering program has been added to the curriculum in the hope of attracting more students—especially women—to the Watson School of Engineering and Applied Science.

> "The caliber of the students here is much greater than that of any other SUNY school and right on par with the best private institutions."

Professors receive high marks from students, who say they're readily accessible and helpful. Graduate teaching assistants (mainly those in the natural sciences) hold smaller group meetings to supplement large lecture courses that sometimes seat close to five hundred students. Binghamton's strong academic reputation has been enhanced by a tough grading policy in which students are given an F rather than no credit, and pluses and minuses as well as straight letter grades. The academics aren't for the faint of heart. "The courses are challenging and demand that students work hard and stay dedicated to their studies," a senior says. "Students are competitive but not to a point where they won't help someone with an assignment so they can stay ahead."

Recent construction includes the renovation of University Union West, the construction of an Institute for Child Development and Physical Facilities North. The new Events Center includes a six-thousand-seat multipurpose arena with a two-hundred-meter running track.

Although Binghamton is a top-notch public arts and sciences school, word of this is slow to cross state lines. The university attracts large numbers of New Yorkers (92 percent) who come seeking a lower-cost alternative to good private liberal arts colleges. The traditional upstate–downstate divisions of New York State politics are reflected in the student body, with upstaters complaining about provincial peers who think that "New York City is the only city in the world." African-Americans make up 7 percent of the student body, Hispanics 7 percent, and Asian-Americans 20 percent. "The students here are extremely diverse," one junior says. "They come from all walks of life, all parts of the world."

> "The students here are extremely diverse. They come from all walks of life, all parts of the world."

To help make the university seem a little smaller, residence halls are grouped into five residential areas. Dickinson is the oldest and most stately, but each area has its own personality and reputation. Fifty-six percent of the students live on campus. "The residence halls on campus cannot be beat," boasts a biology major. The majority of juniors and seniors move off campus, where housing is plentiful and "moderately priced." Those who stay on campus say that the residence halls are "good-sized and comfortable." Dining halls have plenty of options, including sushi. "My mother has degrees in cooking, and I still enjoy the dining hall food," a mechanical engineering major says.

A bioengineering program has been added to the curriculum in the hope of attracting more students—especially women—to the Watson School of Engineering and Applied Science.

Binghamton enforces the state's twenty-one-and-over drinking law. "Like any college town, underage students find alcohol, but it's very, very difficult on campus," one student says. This has not damaged the social life for nondrinkers, however, as there is plenty of fun to be had at neighborhood bars, movies, concerts, quiet dinners off campus, and occasional campus-wide parties in the residence areas. In an effort to decrease drinking, the school is participating in the "Just the Facts" program, which offers students alternatives to drinking that include free movies, games, a coffee bar, and musical groups. Late Nite Binghamton offers free activities on campus from 10 p.m. until 2 a.m. every Friday and Saturday. Annual events among the dorms include the Passing of the Vegetables to bring in the winter season, Stepping on the Coat to usher in spring, and dorm wars. Spring Fling brings in bands, and Picnic in the Park is the annual senior barbecue.

Binghamton the town gets mixed reviews from the students, but students agree that townies are friendly and there is a growing trend of community service and volunteer work. There is a fraternity and sorority presence on campus—a total of thirty-three—with about 10 percent of the men and 10 percent of the women as members. "There's something for everyone here," according to one sophomore. "We have frats and sororities, but it's not the entire campus. There's also a downtown with bars and clubs, if

"My mother has degrees in cooking, and I still enjoy the dining hall food."

that's your thing." Few students take major road trips on the weekends, but for those who need an escape, Syracuse, Ithaca, Cortland, and Oneonta are about an hour by car. The toughest part about road trips may be finding a parking space when you get back—permits currently outnumber spaces by about three to one.

Several Binghamton teams have brought home conference championships in recent years, and varsity sports have made the move to the NCAA Division I in 2001. Students say their football team is undefeated. Then again, Binghamton doesn't have a football team. What they do have is co-rec football, where teams of three men and three women (always a female quarterback) stir up intense rivalries, and "traying" (downhill snow sledding on trays).

Binghamton students find a spirit of cooperation amid a challenging academic environment. The school's reputation for value and excellence attracts an overwhelming number of highly qualified students to its classrooms. One student says, "It fits me perfectly—socially, academically, and politically."

Overlaps
NYU, SUNY–Albany, SUNY–Stony Brook, Cornell University, SUNY–Buffalo

If You Apply To ➤

Binghamton University: Early action: Nov. 15. Regular admissions: Feb. 15. Financial aid: Mar. 1. Guarantees to meet full demonstrated need. No campus or alumni interviews. SATs or ACTs: required. SAT IIs: optional. Accepts electronic applications. Essay question: thoughts about violence; or why pursue a degree.

SUNY–University at Buffalo

15 Capen Hall, Buffalo, NY 14260

Glamorous it is not, but the University at Buffalo offers solid programs in everything from business and engineering to geography and English. The majority of students come from western New York and a high percentage commute from home. The largest of the SUNY campuses.

While part of the mammoth State University of New York system, the University at Buffalo makes sure it doesn't get overlooked. Its resources are large enough to warrant two campus, North and South. Considered one of the nation's most wired

Website: www.buffalo.edu
Location: Suburban

(Continued)

Total Enrollment: 26,168
Undergraduates: 17,054
Male/Female: 55/45
SAT Ranges: V 500–600
    M 520–630
ACT Range: 21–27
Financial Aid: 69%
Expense: Pub $ $
Phi Beta Kappa: Yes
Applicants: 16,057
Accepted: 61%
Enrolled: 31%
Grad in 6 Years: 56%
Returning Freshmen: 86%
Academics: 🖉 🖉 🖉 🖉
Social: ☎ ☎
Q of L: ★ ★
Admissions: (716) 645-6900
Email Address:
    ub-admissions@buffalo.edu

Strongest Programs:
Business Administration
Psychology
Engineering
Biological Sciences
Social Sciences
Architecture
Communication
English

*UB's considerable efforts
in increasing awareness of
diversity include a
Committee on Campus
Tolerance, Office of
Student Multi-Cultural
Affairs, and Multi-Cultural
Leadership Council.*

campuses, UB makes sure its students are at the cutting edge of technology. Once a private university, UB maintains a strong reputation in the life sciences and geography and is the most comprehensive of the SUNY schools. "If you want to be the best in science, it's the place to be," according to one student.

The North campus of the University at Buffalo, less than twnety-five years old and home to most undergraduate programs, stretches across eleven hundred acres in the suburbs just outside the city line and boasts buildings designed by world-renowned architects such as I. M. Pei. Meanwhile, the South campus, along Main Street, favors collegiate ivy-covered buildings and the schools of architecture and health sciences, including the highly rated programs in medicine and dentistry. New apartment-style complexes provide housing for 2,170 students. In 2003, UB's campus was showcased on MTV's "Fraternity Life" and "Sorority Life." The Multi-disciplinary Center for Earthquake Engineering Research has a ten-thousand-square-foot addition, and construction is underway for the Center of Excellence in Bioinformatics and the Alfiero Center.

On the academic front, the engineering and business management schools are nationally prominent, and architecture is strong. Occupational and physical therapy programs are also quite good. The English department is very strong and notable for its emphasis on poetry. Well-known poets visit the campus frequently, and students not only compose and read poetry, but study the art of performing it as well. French, physiology, geography, and music are highly regarded, but other humanities vary in quality. UB offers the only accredited professional degree programs in architecture and pharmacy in the SUNY system. Complaints occasionally surface about the lack of major programs in journalism and broadcasting, although courses in both disciplines are offered.

UB has a multitude of special programs, joint degrees (such as a five-year B.S./M.B.A.), and interdisciplinary majors, as well as opportunities for self-designed majors and study abroad. Students accepted into the honors program enjoy smaller classes, priority in class registration, individual faculty mentors, and special scholarships regardless of need. Freshmen are encouraged to take University Experience 101, which orients students to UB's academic life, general social experience, and resources. General education requirements are standardized and include courses such as writing skills, math sciences, natural sciences, foreign language, world civilizations, and American pluralism. The university's newest programs include majors in biochemical pharmacology, architecture and planning, English as a second language, geography, educational technology, computer science, and exercise science. Also available are programs for geriatric and acute care nursing.

"If you want to be the best in science, it's the place to be."

"UB is a college for everyone," says a sophomore. "It is a wonderful college with more courses to take than one can fit into their years." Class size can be a problem, especially for freshmen. Scheduling conflicts are not unusual, and required courses are often the most difficult to get into. But registration now is available online or by phone. Students seem to accept that some degree of faculty unavailability is the necessary trade-off for having professors who are experts in their fields at a school where graduate education and research get lots of the attention. "Every teacher has their ability to change you," one communications/sociology major says. "UB professors seem to do it with ease and passion." The academically oriented student body spends plenty of time in UB's six main libraries, or one of the several branches, which are for the most part comfortable and well-stocked at three million volumes.

Once upon a time, a large majority of UB's student body went straight into the job market after graduation, but today a third go on to graduate school. With only 2 percent of the students from out of state, the biggest contingent of homegrown New York Staters, apart from the locals, is from New York City and Long Island.

"Political correctness is an issue only because we are so liberal and have such a diverse population," one senior says. African-Americans and Hispanics combined account for 12 percent of the student body, and Asian-Americans represent another 10 percent. UB's considerable efforts in increasing awareness of diversity include a Committee on Campus Tolerance, Office of Student Multi-Cultural Affairs, and Multi-Cultural Leadership Council.

Twenty-one percent of students live on campus; the rest commute from home or find apartments near the Main Street campus. Students warn that potential renters should shuffle off to Buffalo a couple of months early to secure a place. UB has added several new apartment-style complexes over the last few years for those who wish to live on campus. Those complexes feature cable, high-speed Internet connections, and central air-conditioning. "The housing is actually quite well-maintained and comfortable," a student says. Most of the on-campus dwellers are housed on the Amherst campus. The Main Street campus dorms are smaller, older, and of

"Every teacher has their ability to change you."

a more traditional collegiate design, which upperclassmen tend to prefer. Three all-freshmen dorms house extremely sociable freshmen. Security on campus is generally good, with a full-time police station comprised of trained officers, and emergency call lights all around. The cafeteria food gets good reviews, especially since the reopening of the newly renovated Ellicott Food Court on the North campus.

The large number of commuters and the split campus put a damper on social life, but students seem to manage. "Buffalo is definitely a college town," says one student. Road trips are often taken to Niagara Falls, Toronto, Rochester, and Cleveland. Friday-night happy hour centers on beer and the chicken wings that spread the fame of Buffalo cuisine. Also popular are the Albright-Knox Art Gallery, with its world-renowned collection of modern art, and the Triple-A baseball Bisons, who play downtown. The two major pro teams, the Buffalo Bills in football and the Sabres in hockey, are both top draws. Open drinking is banned in the dorms, but that doesn't stop students from staging "progressive parties" with a different drink in each room (and we don't mean Cherry Coke and Sprite). Off-campus bars are another favorite spot for underagers.

UB offers the only accredited professional degree programs in architecture and pharmacy in the SUNY system.

Having a car might be a great idea, though parking can be a problem on campus. Students without cars can get trapped when the intercampus bus stops running after 2:00 a.m. on weekends. The winters are cold in Buffalo but students can take refuge inside a series of tunnels that connect the buildings. But the flip side is that the outlying areas of the city offer great skiing, skating and snowmo-

"Political correctness is an issue only because we are so liberal and have such a diverse population."

biling—and the ski club even offers free rides to the slopes. UB supports more than five hundred other student organizations ranging from jugglers to math enthusiasts. Students can preview their honeymoons by darting over to Niagara Falls, just half an hour away, or flee the country altogether by driving to nearby Canada, where the drinking age is lower.

School spirit is sometimes generated at the Student Union and UB's impressive sports complex, which boasts the fourth-largest pool in the world, a ten-thousand-seat arena, squash and racquetball courts, and other amenities. The men's and women's cross-country teams are among Buffalo's championship-caliber squads, as are women's basketball and men's and women's swimming. Intramural sports are popular, and earthy types appreciate the annual Oozefest—a mud-bound sports competition that is part of SpringFest.

UB, the largest of the SUNY schools, depends upon its students to make the most out of the comprehensive education it offers. While some complain about the two campuses, others find that the education they've received more than compensates.

Overlaps
SUNY–Albany, SUNY–Binghamton, SUNY–Stony Brook, Cornell University, NYU

"The school is a great size, with great diversity," boasts one senior. "There is always something to do. It was the best four years of my life."

SUNY–College at Geneseo

1 College Circle, Geneseo, NY 14454

Geneseo is a preferred option for New Yorkers who want the feel of a private college at a public university price. Similar in scale to William and Mary and Mary Washington in Virginia, smaller than Miami of Ohio. Offers business and education in addition to the liberal arts.

Website: www.geneseo.edu
Location: Small town
Total Enrollment: 5,668
Undergraduates: 5,387
Male/Female: 35/65
SAT Ranges: V 580–650
  M 590–660
ACT Range: 25–28
Financial Aid: 85%
Expense: Pub $ $
Phi Beta Kappa: No
Applicants: 8,535
Accepted: 49%
Enrolled: 27%
Grad in 6 Years: 80%
Returning Freshmen: 91%
Academics: ✍ ✍ ✍ ½
Social: 🏛 🏛 🏛
Q of L: ★ ★ ★ ★
Admissions: (585) 245-5571
Email Address:
  admissions@geneseo.edu

Strongest Programs:
Business
Communicative Disorders and
  Sciences
Education
English
Natural Sciences
Music

For those seeking a public alternative to small private liberal arts colleges, SUNY–Geneseo offers a comprehensive educational experience that emphasizes strong professional programs and a traditional liberal arts core. "Geneseo has a great reputation as a competitive, successful institution at a fair price," says a junior. "It has managed to keep its small size and unique atmosphere throughout the years." Students are quick to point out that faculty and staff go out of their way to ensure that each student is treated as an individual.

The campus is located in the scenic Genesee Valley, with its spectacular sunsets, in western New York State. "The scenery is beautiful, and the sunsets are incredible here," one freshman says. The architectural style is a mix of Gothic and modern buildings, all nestled in a tree-lined, small community that has been designated a National Historic Landmark Community by the U.S. Department of the Interior. New student resident townhouses have been completed recently.

Geneseo operates on the semester system, and the college's offerings balance between several professional programs and the traditional liberal arts. Special education is the most popular major, followed by biology, management, psychology, and English. The John Wiley Jones School of Business boasts a strong program; 3–2 M.B.A. programs are available with Pace, SUNY–Buffalo, and Syracuse; and 3–3 programs are available with the Rochester Institute of Technology. History, English, and biology are also good, and, true to its roots as a teachers-training institution, Geneseo has an outstanding education program that offers a teaching certificate. There is

"Geneseo has a great reputation as a competitive, successful institution at a fair price."

also a 3–2 program in engineering. The flexible core curriculum requires two interdisciplinary humanities courses and two courses in each of four categories: natural sciences, social sciences, fine arts, and critical reasoning; as well as one course in non-Western traditions. The general education core requirements include Numeric and Symbolic Reasoning and Critical Writing and Reading as well as American History and foreign language requirements.

On the whole, students feel at home in Geneseo's competitive academic climate. "The courses are very rigorous but students strive to do well more for themselves than for competitive reasons," a junior says. Says another student, "Grades seem to be a priority here. I always seem to be doing more work than my friends at other schools." The quality of teaching draws raves. "Professors strive to provide students with as much knowledge as possible without exceeding their comprehension level," a student says. "Professors also make themselves readily available." Students do complain that courses, especially upper-level ones, are hard to get into. "Getting the courses you want is not always an easy process," an English major says. However, students find few problems graduating within four years. "If someone needs a class, the dean is very helpful in working with students who were closed out," another student says.

(Continued)
Psychology

Ninety-eight percent of the students are from New York State, and 93 percent of them attended public high school. Eighty-one percent graduated in the top quarter of their high school class. "The students here are very intelligent and competitive," a psychology major says. "They are also

"The scenery is beautiful, and the sunsets are incredible here."

very involved in campus life." Asian-Americans make up 5 percent of the campus, following by Hispanic students at 3 percent and African-Americans at 2 percent. The school offers nearly 350 merit scholarships, ranging from $500 to $5,000.

Fifty-eight percent of the students, including all freshmen, live in on-campus housing, which is guaranteed for all four years. Rooms are determined by lottery, and many students remain on campus until their junior or senior years because of the well-maintained living conditions. Campus security is described as "excellent" by many. Says a freshman: "Geneseo seems like the safest place. Most areas, especially heavy traffic areas, are always lit. And emergency phones are all over campus."

Fifty-eight percent of the students, including all freshmen, live in on-campus housing, which is guaranteed for all four years. Rooms are determined by lottery, and many students remain on campus until their junior or senior years because of the well-maintained living conditions.

Small and idyllic, the neighboring village is considered by many students a perfect setting. "Seventy percent of residents are affiliated with the college, making it a 'college town,'" a junior says. Hiking and skiing are both nearby, and beautiful Conesus Lake is only a ten-minute drive away. As for the social life, there's always plenty to do both on and off campus. For those aching to hit the road, Rochester lies thirty miles to the north, and Buffalo sixty miles west. Ten percent of the men and 12 percent of the women belong to fraternities and sororities, which keep life on campus from getting too humdrum. The administration has a strict alcohol policy that is definitely enforced, students say. "Students find ways to get alcohol from surrounding areas, but for many, that doesn't work either," a freshman says.

Sports are extremely popular, and Geneseo fields several excellent teams. Women's and men's basketball, women's soccer, and men's ice hockey are very strong. Intramurals are popular, and there are nearly two hundred other student-run organizations, including a newspaper and radio and television stations.

Students at Geneseo don't call it the "Harvard on the Hill" for nothing. Academics are challenging and for only the most serious students. Professors know how difficult it is to be accepted to the college and treat their students accordingly, by expecting a lot from them. Says one junior, "In the past five years,

"If someone needs a class, the dean is very helpful in working with students who were closed out."

the college has emphasized a well-rounded education and an increased drive to bring the best students to Geneseo." Indeed, only the most dedicated need apply.

Overlaps

SUNY–Binghamton, SUNY–Buffalo, SUNY–Fredonia, James Madison, University of Rochester

If You Apply To ➤

SUNY–Geneseo: Early decision: Nov. 15. Regular admissions: Mar. 15. Financial aid: Feb. 15. Housing: May 1. Does not guarantee to meet demonstrated need. Campus interviews: recommended, informational. No alumni interviews. SATs or ACTs: required. Essay question: how sports develop good character; the effects of heredity and the environment on a person; which of the five senses you wouldn't want to give up; unpublished sample of your writing.

SUNY–Purchase College

735 Anderson Hill Road, Purchase, NY 10577-1400

One of the few public institutions that is also an arts specialty school. The visual and performing arts are signature programs, though Purchase has developed some liberal arts specialties in areas like environmental.

Website: www.purchase.edu
Location: Suburban
Total Enrollment: 4,018
Undergraduates: 3,866
Male/Female: 43/57
SAT Ranges: V 500–610
    M 480–580
Financial Aid: 40%
Expense: Pub $ $
Phi Beta Kappa: No
Applicants: 6,427
Accepted: 33%
Enrolled: 32%
Grad in 6 Years: 35%
Returning Freshmen: 77%
Academics: ✍ ✍ ✍ ½
Social: ☎ ☎ ☎
Q of L: ★ ★ ★
Admissions: (914) 251-6300
Email Address:
    admissn@purchase.edu

Strongest Programs:
Acting
Art History
Dance
Environmental Science
Film
Liberal Studies
Music
Women's Studies

SUNY–Purchase College is a dream come true for aspiring artists of all kinds—an academic environment that provides a strong sense of community and support, yet celebrates individuals for their unique talents and contributions; it's OK to be an individual here. A senior says the best thing about Purchase is "the freedom to focus on whatever you want without feeling pressured to join anything to fit in."

Set on a five-hundred-acre wooded estate in an area of Westchester's most scenic suburbia, Purchase has a campus described by one student as "sleek, modern, ominous, and brick." The college has earned a national reputation for its instruction in music, dance, visual arts, theater, and film. Almost all the faculty members in the School of the Arts are professionals who perform or exhibit regularly in the New York metropolitan area, and the spacious, dazzling facilities rank among the best in the world. Purchase College boasts of the Neuberger Museum, the sixth-largest public college museum. The four-theater Performing Arts Center is huge, and dance students, whose building contains a dozen studios, whirlpool rooms, and a "body-correction" facility, may never again work in such splendid and well-equipped surroundings. Recent campus improvements include townhouse-style student apartments that allow more than four hundred additional students to hang their hats on campus.

Mingling with highly motivated and talented performers and artists can make some students in the liberal arts and sciences feel a little drab and out of place. "Dancers, actors, visual artists, and music students pull the most weight as far as campus life is concerned," says a student. Still, Purchase is a fine place to study humanities and the natural sciences, particularly literature, psychology, art history, environmental sciences, and biology. Most of the shaky liberal arts and sciences programs are confined to some majors in the social sciences and language and culture, where offerings are limited.

Students in the liberal arts and sciences spend one-third of their time at Purchase fulfilling the general education requirements, which include ten knowledge areas. Students now take mathematics, natural sciences, social science, American history, Western civilization, other world civilizations, the arts, humanities, foreign language, and basic communications. In addition to these core requirements, they also must take critical thinking and information management as skill areas, and everyone must complete a senior project. Students in the arts divisions usually have many more required courses, culminating in a senior recital or show. There are two

"Dancers, actors, visual artists, and music students pull the most weight as far as campus life is concerned."

separate sets of degree requirements, one for the liberal arts and sciences and one for the performing and visual arts. B.F.A. students in the performing and visual arts are required to sample the liberal arts; B.A. and B.S. students in the liberal arts and sciences are required to sample fine arts courses. The college also offers several certificate programs including computer science, arts management, and early child development. New majors include creative writing, journalism, dramatic writing, women's studies, and new media. A new B.F.A. program in dramatic writing was added most recently.

The atmosphere at Purchase varies between programs. "Our classes are rigorous and competitive but on a level that demands a lot from all students," reports a senior. Students tend to be very serious about their own personal achievements. Professors tend to be accessible and friendly. "My professors and advisor were more than helpful. They were amazing," claims a senior. Eighty-two percent of the students are from New York State, most from New York City and Westchester County. Others are from Long Island, New Jersey, and Connecticut, but all are different and very political (that means very liberal). Minorities make up 22 percent of the student body. "Our student body is full of scholars and artists, most of whom are heavily driven by our politically active campus," says a women's studies/sociology major. Indeed, the largest student organization on this politically active campus is the gay and lesbian union. "We are diverse but politically we are a very liberal college," says a senior. "We believe

"My professors and advisor were more than helpful. They were amazing."

strongly in animal rights, civil rights, women's rights, etc." In addition to need-based aid, merit scholarships are awarded each year on the basis of academic achievements, auditions, and portfolios.

The living facilities have undergone renovations, but continue to receive mixed reviews. A sophomore says, "There is a housing shortage, which results in three people living in two-person rooms." The two eating facilities offer decent fare, and for those who tire of institutional cuisine, there is a student-run co-op that specializes in health food. Forty-two percent of the student body commutes from nearby communities, though housing in the surrounding suburbs is expensive and hard to find.

The campus is a neighbor to the world headquarters of IBM, Texaco, AMF, General Foods, and Pepsico, but while sharing the "billion-dollar mile" with a few Fortune 500s might excite students at some other SUNY schools, "it doesn't do much for us except provide convenient antiapartheid demonstration locations," admits one Purchase activist. No college town exists per se at Purchase, so "we tend to think of our campus as our community," a senior psych major attests. "In my opinion, Purchase is not a 'college town,' however, students do participate in volunteering in the community," says another student. The Big Apple provides a regular weekend distraction that inhibits the formation of a tight campus community. Since the campus shuttle bus runs only once on the weekend, students started their own van service, which goes into Manhattan three times a day. Still, "a car is a definite must at Purchase," counsels one student. The Performing Arts Center is host to at least two stu-

"The closest we come to Greek are the two guys from Athens who go here."

dent or faculty performances every weekend, and there is a constant flow of New York artists and celebrities. Notes a literature major, "Most of the social life on campus takes the form of parties thrown by apartment residents," and the over-twenty-one crowd often frequents the Pub. Fraternities and sororities are definitely out. "The closest we come to Greek are the two guys from Athens who go here," quips a staunch independent. Besides, as one artist explains, "individuality is far more important to the artist than being part of a group." Despite the unconventional aura of the place, Purchase is not without its traditions. There's an annual autumn dance, a Spring Semiformal, and an April Showers campus festival, and on Halloween there are ghost stories told at a historic graveyard on campus.

Purchase is a member of the NCAA (Division III), and the few competitive teams include men's basketball and women's volleyball. Intramural programs and an excellent athletic facility exist, but informal Frisbee tossing remains more popular than organized sports. Says a student: "Our 'teams' are our dancers, our vocalists, our musicians, and our theater companies."

"We are diverse but politically we are a very liberal college," says a senior. "We believe strongly in animal rights, civil rights, women's rights, etc."

Overlaps

SUNY–New Paltz, NYU, SUNY–Oneonta, SUNY–Albany, SUNY–Stony Brook

Despite a conspicuous lack of a college-town atmosphere, Purchase is a perfect place to study the arts and still be able to indulge in academics of all kinds, or vice versa. Those willing to put up with what a senior calls "an isolated campus full of ugly architecture," may find that Purchase offers the opportunity for a personalized, diverse education unique within the SUNY system.

If You Apply To ➢

SUNY–Purchase College: Rolling admissions. Does not guarantee to meet demonstrated need. Campus and alumni interviews: optional, informational (required of theatre design/technology and film program applicants). SATs or ACTs: required. SAT I preferred. SAT IIs: optional. Accepts the Common Application and electronic applications. Essay question: personal or historical event of impact; personal influences; describe a time you took a leadership role. Apply to particular school or program. Auditions held for acting, dance, and music.

SUNY–Stony Brook

118 Administration Building, Stony Brook, NY 11794-1901

Strategically located ninety minutes from New York City, Stony Brook has risen a few notches in the SUNY pecking order. The natural sciences, engineering, and health fields are the major drawing cards. Situated in the lap of Long Island luxury, Stony Brook offers easy access to beachfront play lands.

Website: www.stonybrook.edu
Location: City outskirts
Total Enrollment: 21,989
Undergraduates: 14,224
Male/Female: 52/48
SAT Ranges: V 520–610
  M 560–660
Financial Aid: 64%
Expense: Pub $ $ $
Phi Beta Kappa: Yes
Applicants: 16,849
Accepted: 54%
Enrolled: 27%
Grad in 6 Years: 57%
Returning Freshmen: 85%
Academics: 🎓 🎓 🎓 🎓
Social: ☎ ☎ ☎
Q of L: ★ ★
Admissions: (631) 632-6868
Email Address:
  enroll@stonybrook.edu

Strongest Programs:
Anthropology
Biology
Computer Science
Engineering Science
English

SUNY–Stony Brook boasts the best of both worlds: a small-college community with the power of a leading research institution. The public university has made a name for itself with its top-notch programs in the hard sciences. It has also become known for its highly competitive learning environment and the high quality of its professors.

The school's location on Long Island's plush North Shore (Gatsby's stomping grounds) is a wonderful drawing point. Sitting on about one thousand wooded acres just outside of the small, picturesque village of Stony Brook, and only ninety minutes from New York City and half an hour from the beaches of the South Shore, the campus is a conglomeration of redbrick Federal-style buildings interspersed with several modern brick and concrete designs. Campus beautification is a priority, and much of the uninspiring campus concrete has been replaced by grass and trees. Current construction projects include a new undergraduate apartment complex, an eight-thousand-seat outdoor stadium and an Asian-American Center that promises to be the nation's largest. Also being built is a Student Activities Center.

Coming of age in the high-tech era, Stony Brook quickly became widely known and respected for its science departments. Facilities are extensive, and the science faculty includes a number of internationally known researchers. The comprehensive university hospital and research center make health sciences strong, especially physical therapy. The hospital, which has been ranked among the nation's best for teaching, attracts grants to the campus and offers a lot of opportunities for various research programs for undergrads as well as graduate students. Students report that engineering is also strong; new majors in that field include biomedical engineering and chemical and molecular engineering. There are complaints that the emphasis on science overshadows the school's best social science and humanities programs, but efforts have been made to boost the arts with a fine arts center, complete with studios and a reference library. The center complements Stony Brook's beautiful five-theater Staller Center for the Arts. The music department faculty boasts the American pianist Gilbert Kalish. Journalism and philosophy are cited as weak. "The academic climate is excellent and very competitive," one student says. Courses "are rigorous and require much time and commitment."

The College of Arts and Sciences, the College of Engineering and Applied Sciences, and the Health Science Center previously had their own general education requirements, but recently the school decided to streamline the general education program. All of the schools cover writing and quantitative reasoning skills, literary and philosophic analysis, exposure to the arts, disciplinary diversity, the interrelationship of science and society, and three culminating multicultural requirements, including one course each in the European tradition, non-Western cultures, and American pluralism. Everyone in the arts and sciences must also satisfy a language requirement. Freshmen also take a one-credit course; its purpose is to provide them with knowledge about the university and give them a forum for discussing a variety of issues. New majors include athletic training, and students can now minor in jazz music and adapted aquatics. Students wishing to receive a degree in physical therapy will find it's been retooled as a doctoral degree program.

(Continued)
Nursing
Geology
History

"The academic climate is excellent and very competitive."

Liberal arts students are less stressed academically than their peers in the sciences, but this may change somewhat with additions of major writing-intensive courses. As professors delve into their own research projects, undergraduates must struggle for the attention of their teachers. Students who do take the considerable initiative to contact professors report that they are often met with responsive attitudes. "The teachers are very good," one freshman says. "The majority of them are vital learning tools." Since freshmen are the last to register, they sometimes have to wait a semester or two to get into the most popular electives.

An Undergraduate Research and Creative Activities program (URECA) offers undergraduates the opportunity to work on research projects with faculty members from the time they are freshmen until they graduate. Women in Science and Engineering (WISE) is a multifaceted program for women who show promise in math, science, or engineering. There's also the Federated Learning Communities (FLC) program, in which students take a preplanned block of courses in one general area, such as The United States in Perspective, which then becomes their minor. A residential studies program links dormitories to fields of study, and interested students may live in one of the six living/learning Centers: science and engineering, health and wellness, international studies, service learning, environmental studies, and interdisciplinary arts. Some students take advantage of one of Stony Brook's wonderful travel programs (France, England, Italy, Japan, and Tanzania are some possibilities), while others choose established internships in the fields of policy analysis, political science, psychology, foreign language, and social welfare. Combined B.A./M.A. or B.S./M.S. programs are available in engineering, the teaching of math, and management and policy.

Current construction projects include a new undergraduate apartment complex, an eight-thousand-seat outdoor stadium and an Asian-American Center that promises to be the nation's largest.

Stony Brook students are 93 percent in-staters, and about half commute from Long Island homes. Sixty-three percent graduated in the top quarter of their high school class, and more than half of Stony Brook's graduates go on to graduate and professional schools. African-Americans and Hispanics comprise 18 percent of the student body and Stony Brook enrolls 23 percent Asian-Americans. The university has created a Campus Relations Team, composed of university police officers who educate the community on topics ranging from personal safety to rape prevention to drug and alcohol awareness. Students are also required to take classes focusing on different cultures. The university does not meet the demonstrated financial need of all accepted applicants. Approximately 64 percent of those who apply, however, do

"Dorms are comfortable and well-maintained, just like a four-star hotel."

receive financial aid. About four hundred merit scholarships ranging from $500 to full tuition are given out each year, in addition to a variety of athletic scholarships.

Stony Brook, which has one of the largest residential facilities in the SUNY system, has in the last several years completed a major rehabilitation, giving students access to state-of-the-art fitness centers, computing facilities, Internet access, and widescreen TVs. Nearly half the student body lives in university housing. "Dorms are comfortable and well-maintained, just like a four-star hotel," a senior says. Commuters are given a social facility of their own, "the commuter commons." While residential freshmen must take a meal plan, upperclassmen who live on campus either opt for a flexible food-service plan or pay a nominal fee to cook for themselves. The suites come equipped with dishwashers and ranges, and each hall has a lounge and kitchen area, all of which, students say, could be kept a lot cleaner. Kosher and vegetarian food co-ops keep interested students well supplied with cheap eats. Four additional residences have also been completed and come fully furnished with full kitchens, high-speed Internet access, and cable TV.

Most activities take place on campus, since there isn't too much to do in Stony Brook. "There are plenty of activities taking place on campus, but students often come up with their own fun things to do," a senior says. The university has fairly strict policies on alcohol consumption, although underage students report no problems getting served. Other students say that access to alcohol for underage students isn't quite so easy. The longtime ban on fraternities and sororities has been lifted, so a fledgling Greek system (with no houses) is another option. Current and classic movies are screened during the week, and other entertainment is available in the form of frequent concerts, plays, and other performances. Annual festivals in the fall and spring and the football game with Hofstra are among the biggest social events of the year. Because many students go home on the weekends, Thursday is the big party night.

The students who remain on the weekends often go beachcombing on the nearby North Shore or the Atlantic Ocean shore of Long Island, or head into New York City. Cars are desirable, but many students make do with trains, and a station is conveniently located at the edge of campus. The local community is a "beautiful, wealthy area of Long Island," says one student. "It's not much of a college town, because there are so many things to do on campus." Nearby Port Jefferson offers small shops and interesting restaurants. Sports facilities have been upgraded, and all twenty varsity teams compete in Division I. Intramurals provide one of the school's greatest rallying points, and competition in oozeball (a mud-caked variant of volleyball) is especially fierce.

Though Stony Brook is not old enough to have ivy-covered walls, it does offer some of the best academic opportunities in the SUNY system. Students have to maneuver around lots of rough spots, including increasing class sizes and decreasing course offerings. Yet despite these budget-crisis-induced problems, students share in the promise of Stony Brook's future. In the meantime, they boast of their school's diversity and creativity as well as the feeling of hospitality that pervades campus life.

Overlaps

NYU, SUNY–Binghamton, Cornell University, SUNY–Buffalo, Penn State

If You Apply To ➤

SUNY–Stony Brook: Rolling admissions. Early Action: Nov. 1. Housing: Jun. 30. Does not guarantee to meet demonstrated need. Campus interviews: recommended, informational. No alumni interviews. SATs or ACTs: required. SAT IIs: recommended. Accepts electronic applications. No essay question.

Stetson University

Campus Box 8378, DeLand, FL 32720

Stetson keeps company with the likes of Baylor and Furman among prominent Deep South institutions with historic ties to the Baptist Church. The common thread is conservatism, and business is easily the most popular program. Stetson is also strong in music and has a specialty in sport and integrative health sciences.

Stetson University has long been committed to the value of a liberal arts education, emphasizing majors with a cross-disciplinary influence. The school also nurtures community by keeping classes small and appealing to students with similar geographic and religious backgrounds—that is, Southern and Baptist. That said, Stetson is no longer affiliated with the church, so chapel worship services have been replaced by nondenominational presentations on ethics and social responsibility. And regardless of where they come from, Stetson urges students to take off their hats and stay awhile—so much the better if those hats are of the cowboy variety, since the school takes its name from the maker of the famed ten-gallon hat.

Located halfway between Walt Disney World and Daytona Beach, Stetson's 165-acre campus features mainly brick structures in styles from Gothic to Moorish to Southern Colonial. While there are eccentric wood buildings scattered about, the theme is decidedly old-fashioned, replete with royal palms and oak trees. In recent years, an addition to the duPont-Ball Library has provided distance-learning technology, plus space for more books.

While students apply to Stetson as a whole, they enroll in one of its three schools: music, business administration, or arts and sciences. General education requirements include two freshman English courses and one course each in religious heritage, oral communications, math, civilization, contemporary culture, and fine arts. Students must also take one to two courses in the natural sciences and one to two in the social sciences and demonstrate proficiency in computers and in a foreign language. All students in the college of arts and sciences must complete a research project before graduation; those who choose to do so in the summer may win a stipend from the Stetson Undergraduate Research Experience (SURE) program.

Recent additions in the college of arts and sciences include a creative writing program and majors in sport management and integrative health sciences, which have replaced the sport and exercise science major. Other highlights include concentrations in Russian studies, aquatic biology, and digital arts, which prepares students for careers in computer graphics and teaches them how to translate music and video into multimedia content on the Internet. In the business school, the major in computer information systems and minor in management information systems have morphed into a new program in electronic business technology. In fact, business is Stetson's most popular program, with finance and accounting particularly strong. Would-be money managers benefit from the Roland George Investments program, where they work with an actual cash portfolio worth $1.7 million. The Prince Entrepreneurial Program is a mentoring initiative that connects students with successful business owners. Stetson's music department is notable (no pun intended) for programs in brass instruments, organ, and voice. The school's education department has partnered with Walt Disney and the Osceola County School Board to develop a state-of-the-art school and teaching academy in the Disney-created city of Celebration, Florida.

Stetson's honors program allows eighty-five students to take interdisciplinary courses and create their own majors. Administrators say 63 percent of the classes

Website: www.stetson.edu
Location: Suburban
Total Enrollment: 2,508
Undergraduates: 2,142
Male/Female: 42/58
SAT Ranges: V 510–620
   M 500–610
ACT Range: 21–27
Financial Aid: 70%
Expense: Pr $ $ $
Phi Beta Kappa: Yes
Applicants: 2,000
Accepted: 74%
Enrolled: 39%
Grad in 6 Years: 60%
Returning Freshmen: 80%
Academics: ✍ ✍ ✍
Social: ☎ ☎ ☎
Q of L: ★ ★ ★
Admissions: (386) 822-7100
Email Address:
   admissions@stetson.edu

Strongest Programs:
Accounting and Finance
Music Education and
   Performance
Biology and Environmental
   Science
Psychology
Political Science
English and Communications
Health Science and
   Rehabilitative Studies

taken by freshmen have twenty-five students or fewer, and the rest have fifty or less, which, a junior says, improves the quality of instruction: "Freshmen almost always are taught by full professors. For a majority of my classes, I have received a high quality of teaching." Still, it can be hard for freshmen and sophomores to get the courses

"The dining is very edible and diverse." they want because Stetson is trying to keep class sizes down. Students with wanderlust may choose to study in England, Mexico, Russia, Germany, Spain, France, and Hong Kong, or spend a summer focused on language in Mexico or business in Austria. There are also internship opportunities in Germany, England, and Latin America, and each year, professors lead off-campus study trips during semester breaks, taking students to such places as Turkey, Greece, and the Czech Republic.

Stetson's Academic Quality Initiative is working to make the school more competitive by raising admission standards. For now, though, there are three main types of people on campus, says a history major: "Very smart and motivated; rich kids who aren't as smart; and average students (the majority). Rollins College most likely has the same climate due to its price tag, but I sometimes think I'm in high school again." A finance major disputes that, saying that "courses are fairly rigorous, especially as you get into the upper-division courses of your major." Three-quarters of Stetson's "Hatters" are native Floridians; they're generally conservative and tend to lean Republican, though students report little interest or involvement in student government—or any other causes or issues. African-Americans constitute nearly 4 percent of the student body, Hispanics make up 5 percent, and Asian-Americans add 2 percent.

Eighty percent of Stetson students live in the dorms, which are "very nice, especially compared to the state schools," says a finance major. Singles are reserved for juniors and seniors. All but two of the dorms are co-ed, and students say the nicest options are Emily Hall, Chaudoin, Stetson, and Conrad. Still, they say more people would move off campus if the school didn't assess a financial penalty for doing so. The cafeteria resembles a food court, and includes a make-your-own stir-fry station. "The dining is very edible and diverse," says a junior. Students may buy seven, fifteen, or twenty-one meals a week; credits are also good at the campus coffee shop, the Hat Rack.

Stetson's fraternities attract 36 percent of the men, and sororities draw 27 percent of the women. Greek groups tend to have a disproportionate influence on campus social life because alcohol is prohibited in the dorms, and the town of DeLand ("deadland") is almost as dry as the campus. DeLand, with only "a few small bars, and one club," is no Tallahassee or Gainesville, says one student. "It's a 'college town' because our school is about the only thing there," agrees another. The town does have many elderly residents, though, providing opportunities for students to participate in community service. For fun, students rely on Orlando (forty minutes away) and Daytona (twenty minutes), where they can hit the beach, stroll the Universal Studios CityWalk, or watch the Daytona 500. Other options include Disney World, Epcot Center, and Cape Canaveral.

Back on campus, the Council for Student Activities brings in big-name acts, such as *Saturday Night Live*'s Jimmy Fallon or the band Sister Hazel. Music majors also stage concerts, and students look forward to annual events such as Greenfeather, a week when student groups compete to raise money for charity. When your birthday rolls around, don't forget to wear your bathing suit—it's a tradition for fellow students to toss you into the mid-campus Holler Fountain. When it comes to sports, Stetson's varsity teams compete in Division I, and the men's soccer and women's softball teams brought home conference championships in 2001. The new Hollis Wellness Center includes a field house, outdoor pool, game room, dance studio, and exercise room.

All students in the college of arts and sciences must complete a research project before graduation; those who choose to do so in the summer may win a stipend from the Stetson Undergraduate Research Experience (SURE) program.

Stetson's fraternities attract 36 percent of the men, and sororities draw 27 percent of the women. Greek groups tend to have a disproportionate influence on campus social life because alcohol is prohibited in the dorms.

Overlaps

University of Florida, University of Central Florida, Florida State, Rollins, University of Miami (FL)

Stetson students bask in the one-on-one attention freely given at this small Sunshine State university. Whether they conquer Wall Street after graduation, travel the world to test their language skills, create new realities on the World Wide Web, or simply make a joyful noise, Hatters take along fond memories, close friendships, and a solid academic grounding.

If You Apply To ➤ **Stetson:** Early decision: Nov. 1. Rolling admissions: Mar. 15. Financial aid: Feb. 14. Meets demonstrated need of 60%. Campus interviews: recommended, evaluative. Alumni interviews: optional, informational. SATs or ACTs: required. SAT IIs: optional. Accepts the Common Application and electronic applications. Essay question: significant experience or achievement with special meaning; issue of personal, local, or national concern and its importance to you; influential person; or why a commitment to a spiritual life, environmental responsibility, diversity, community service, gender equity, or ethical decision making are important. Applicants wishing to be considered for a Sullivan Creative Writing Scholarship must answer the question: "Why write?"

Stevens Institute of Technology

Castle Point on the Hudson, Hoboken, NJ 07030

Stevens ranks with Clarkson and Worcester Polytech among East Coast technical institutes that offer intimacy and personalized education. Youth-oriented Hoboken is a major plus and a quicker commute to Manhattan than most places in Brooklyn.

Forget the stereotypical image of the sterile engineering school devoid of wackiness and a social life. It bears no resemblance to Stevens Institute of Technology. Just across the Hudson River from Manhattan, Stevens students pursue a valuable engineering degree in an atmosphere of fun and camaraderie. "We have our dork moments where computers are the most important thing, but we also like to have fun," admits a junior.

Stevens' fifty-five-acre park-like campus is punctuated by an eclectic mix of architecture. Many of the residence halls and administrative buildings are redbrick, while classrooms and labs range from historical ivy-covered brownstones to modern glass-and-steel structures. Campus construction includes the Lawrence T. Babbio, Jr., Center for Technology Management, scheduled to be completed in 2004, and the DeBaun Field, which has been recently resurfaced with NexTurf.

Stevens was the first college in the country to offer the degree of mechanical engineering, and it now offers majors in the fields of business, engineering, computer science, and even the humanities (degrees are offered in English and American lit, history, philosophy, and science and technology studies). But engineering, be it mechanical, biomedical, chemical, civil, electrical, environmental, or computer, is the indisputable king of the campus. New majors include computational science and science and technology. The school tries to ensure that all students are computer fluent, not just literate, by the time they leave. Hence, all freshmen receive a new personal notebook computer.

Stevens is organized into three schools: the Charles V. Schaefer, Jr., School of Engineering, the Wesley J. Howe School of Technology Management, and the Arthur E. Imperatore School of Sciences and Arts. This organization is intended to allow Stevens to better meet the changing technological needs of business and industry by fostering collaboration across academic departments. A guiding concept at the school is "technogenesis," which encourages students to put their research and innovation into practice. For the first two years in the engineering

Website: www.stevens.edu
Location: Urban
Total Enrollment: 4,599
Undergraduates: 1,757
Male/Female: 75/25
SAT Ranges: V 560–650
   M 640–710
Financial Aid: 85%
Expense: Pr $
Phi Beta Kappa: No
Applicants: 2,049
Accepted: 49%
Enrolled: 39%
Grad in 6 Years: 61%
Returning Freshmen: 90%
Academics: ✍ ✍ ✍
Social: ☎ ☎
Q of L: ★ ★ ★ ★
Admissions: (201) 216-5194
Email Address:
   admissions@stevens.edu

Strongest Programs:
Chemical Engineering
Computer Engineering
Mechanical Engineering
Electrical Engineering

school, students must follow a core curriculum stressing courses in the sciences and in broad areas of engineering, followed by technical electives that culminate in a senior design project. The business program and the applied sciences each have their own curriculum guidelines. In addition, students must complete four semesters of calculus, eight semesters of humanities, and six semesters of physical education. But never fear, there are ways to get around this predestined courseload. For example, students not quite up to the intensity of Stevens's academic prescription may arrange for a five-year decelerated program without extra tuition charges. Freshmen follow a core program in their chosen curriculum. Juniors can attend the school's program in Scotland or can study abroad in one of more than fifty countries through the International Student Exchange Program. Stevens has initiated a cooperative education program, which offers all students a chance to earn on-the-job training (and earn more than $53,000 in some cases) over a five-year period. Stevens also has an active recruiting program with major corporations, entrepreneurial firms, and the government.

> "We have our dork moments where computers are the most important thing, but we also like to have fun."

Students are more than pleased with their professors' teaching ability. "Freshmen are always taught by full professors," a junior says. All courses are usually taught in "recitations" of fewer than twenty-five students. Exams are taken under a successful student-run honor system. Given the subject matter, no one considers the workload unreasonable, and tutorial help is readily available. Students are competitive and focus heavily on their GPAs, but study groups abound. Stevens students have to remember to unwind after all that academic stress, or "they'll go crazy," says a computer science major.

A guiding concept at the school is Technogenesis, which encourages students to put their research and innovation into practice.

Stevens draws 60 percent of its students from the greater New York area. Seventy percent come from public high school, and 50 percent graduated in the top tenth of their class. Minorities are well represented on campus; 24 percent are Asian-Americans, 10 percent are Hispanic, and 5 percent are African-American. Female student enrollment is 25 percent, a high percentage for a technical school. Admissions staffers look more closely at high school grades, especially in math and science, than at test scores; interviews are recommended; and letters of recommendation from teachers and essays are also highly recommended. Students praise the school's financial aid policy, and with 85 percent of the student body receiving some sort of aid, most speak from experience. In addition to need-based funding, Stevens also awards academic merit scholarships, ranging from $1,000 to full tuition.

Students not quite up to the intensity of Stevens's academic prescription may arrange for a five-year decelerated program, without extra tuition charges.

Eighty-five percent of students live in the dorms, forgoing the almost impossible, very expensive housing hunt in the Hoboken area. Students say housing at Stevens is adequate and well maintained, and each room is hooked into the campus-wide wireless computer network. The seven undergraduate residence halls are conveniently located at the center of campus. As for looks, Tech Hall stands out among the crowd. It is an ultramodern dorm with carpets, telephones, and private bathrooms in each room. Rooms are assigned by lottery or by squatter's rights. After the first year, students can, and often do, move into fraternities, old brownstones off campus, or nearby university-owned apartments. "Some dorms are extremely nice while others are not maintained," explains one junior. As for dining services, students report that the cafeteria food isn't anything to write home about, although there is a variety to choose from. One student dryly remarks that "there is not much of a selection for vegetarians, but sandwiches and pasta are great."

Those who don't go home can take advantage of the extensive pleasures of Manhattan, just across the Hudson, or kill time until the evening fraternity parties, which are the most popular of the on-campus weekend activities. About one-third of the student body go Greek, but they don't define the campus social scene. Students also benefit from the revitalization of Hoboken. "It's a beautiful town and many people go out to eat on Washington Street," says a business major. The dorms are substance-free, but the frats are nearby to quench one's thirst. "Drinks are served to anyone in frats," quips a freshman.

Being at a small school with a lot of engineers also gives students a chance to be editor of the college newspaper or deejay on the campus radio station without being edged out by a journalism or communications major. Fifteen minutes and a cheap PATH train ticket will land you in the middle of Manhattan's Greenwich Village. Beaches and ski slopes are within a ninety-minute drive.

Sports are popular at Stevens, especially intramurals, for which "everyone gets together on ridiculously named teams and blows off steam," in games such as floor hockey and bombardment. But Stevens is working hard on the varsity field, too. Over the past two years, teams have brought home about a dozen pennants. The women's swim, soccer, and volleyball teams are playing stronger than ever while men's lacrosse, soccer, baseball, and fencing teams are also scoring high.

So the male/female ratio at Stevens is a problem and the workload is pretty intense. But the end result of a stint at this small school is usually a lucrative job or a spot at a top graduate school, a close band of friends, and a sharp awareness of cutting-edge technology. When you add in a killer view of Manhattan and the myriad experiences that wonderful city has to offer, it makes a top-notch engineering education seem like icing on the cake.

Overlaps
Rensselaer Polytechnic, Cornell University, Carnegie Mellon, MIT, Caltech

If You Apply To ➤ | **Stevens:** Early decision: Nov. 1. Regular admissions and financial aid: Feb. 15. Housing: Jun. 1. Does not guarantee to meet demonstrated need. Campus and alumni interviews: required, evaluative. SATs: required. SAT IIs: recommended. Accepts electronic applications. Essay question: personal statement.

Susquehanna University

Selinsgrove, PA 17870

Susquehanna offers welcome relief from the plodding, unimaginative education at many universities. The university's innovative core curriculum includes personal development and transition skills (e.g., computer proficiency) in addition to more conventional topics. Best known for its business program.

"Susquewho?" That's the question many students ask when they're first introduced to this undergraduate institution. While it may not be a household name, Susquehanna University is making a reputation for itself. Challenging courses, friendly faculty, and an increasing emphasis on global community make SU a good place to expand your mind and enjoy lush scenery. "SU is gorgeous year-round," says a junior. "It's a place that makes me feel at home and puts me at ease when I'm stressed."

Susquehanna's campus is beautiful, with more than two hundred lush acres located on the banks of the Susquehanna River. Most of the fifty buildings on campus are brick, with Georgian the predominant architectural style. Selinsgrove Hall, built in 1858, and Seibert Hall, built in 1901, are on the National Register of Historic Places. The campus is compact and serene. Recent additions to the campus include a sports complex featuring a field house, fitness center, football stadium, and playing fields.

"SU is gorgeous year-round."

Website: www.susqu.edu
Location: Small town
Total Enrollment: 1,933
Undergraduates: 1,829
Male/Female: 43/57
SAT Ranges: V 520–610
  M 520–620
Financial Aid: 70%
Expense: Pr $ $ $
Phi Beta Kappa: No
Applicants: 2,375
Accepted: 75%

(Continued)

Enrolled: 28%

Grad in 6 Years: 77%

Returning Freshmen: 88%

Academics: ✐ ✐ ✐

Social: ☎ ☎ ☎

Q of L: ★ ★ ★ ★

Admissions: (800) 326-9672
    or (570) 372-4260

Email Address:
    suadmiss@susqu.edu

Strongest Programs:
Biology/Biochemistry
Business
Music
Psychology
English
Communication
Environmental Science

Susquehanna's unusual core curriculum consists of three components: personal development (wellness/fitness and career development); transition skills (including computer proficiency, logical reasoning, and foreign languages); and world perspectives (social sciences, humanities, and sciences).

SU's best academic programs are in business and the sciences. The Sigmund Weis School of Business is not only one of the most striking buildings on campus, but also a prestigious accredited business program that attracts the most majors on campus. The Weis School also sponsors a semester in London exclusively for its junior business majors. The business school, along with the other majors, encourages SU students to take summer internships as a crucial part of their education and future job search. Susquehanna is becoming increasingly recognized for its science programs, especially biology, biochemistry, and environmental science. Weaker departments at SU include classical languages and art, which are hampered by their small size and lack of funds. A new graphic design major and a minor in anthropology have been added to the curriculum.

Susquehanna's unusual core curriculum consists of three components: personal development (wellness/fitness and career development); transition skills (including computer proficiency, logical reasoning, and foreign languages); and world perspectives (social sciences, humanities, and sciences). All freshmen must take a writing seminar (or its honors equivalent) that involves small-group readings and discussion of a particular author. Reading centers around a common contemporary work, with the author often visiting campus to partake in the seminar. A seven-week orientation experience is offered to first-year students; topics include study skills, stress management, and interpersonal communication. Freshmen also have access to the Susquehanna Education in Leadership program, which begins with an all-day retreat and is followed by four seminars throughout the fall semester that focus on leadership styles, listening skills, time management, dealing with conflict, and team building.

For about fifty students a year, the academic experience is defined by the Susquehanna Honors Program. Unlike other programs in schools of similar size, SU's program does not separate its students from the rest of the campus. Instead, it allows students to take most of their classes in other classes with the general student body, thus creating a balance between freedom of choice and a challenging education. Honors students or not, most agree that SU offers a rigorous academic climate. "Depending on the major you select, your courseload can be moderately easy to close to impossible," says a math major.

"It's a place that makes me feel at home and puts me at ease when I'm stressed."

Student–faculty interaction is one of Susquehanna's strong points, and students have high praise for their professors. "The faculty is committed to Susquehanna's concept of education: student-centered, undergraduate only. They are committed to their students," says a senior. SU students may also take classes at nearby Bucknell University and study abroad on almost every continent. The school also offers several study programs in Washington, D.C., as well as a 3–2 engineering program with the University of Pennsylvania and a cooperative dentistry program with Temple University. An assistantship program for outstanding first-year students combines a $10,500 scholarship with hands-on work with a professor or staff member (ten hours per week). Past positions have included academic research, university publications, the Writers' Institute, and marketing research.

SU students are down-to-earth, hardworking kids. Sixty-three percent are from Pennsylvania, and 85 percent attended public high school. At a school in which 92 percent of the students are white, and which is "dominated by middle- and upper-class conservative Republicans," most agree that ethnic diversity is lacking. A communications major offers, "Diversity and multiculturalism are big issues. The university wants the student body to be more diverse."

Residence halls are described as "comfortable." A senior says, "Dorm rooms are big with great closets. All housing is pretty equal." Students must get permission to live off campus, and the 20 percent of students who have that privilege are selected by lottery. Cafeteria food is considered average, although a senior claims the "quality has declined sharply over the past three semesters." Campus security receives mixed reviews. "I feel safe because I'm on a small campus," says a student, "not because of campus security."

Greeks dominate the nightlife of Susquehanna, where 26 percent of the men and 27 percent of the women belong to fraternities or sororities. Students twenty-one and over are allowed to drink on campus, but most acknowledge that underage drinking is "as easy as asking." Favorite campus traditions include a candlelight Christmas service, a pumpkin that mysteriously appears at Halloween, and a Thanksgiving dinner at which faculty members serve traditional fare to the students. Sports are popular among Susquehanna students, especially when the football team plays Lycoming College. Recent MAC championships were won by men's golf and baseball and women's indoor track.

Outside the university, Selinsgrove is "a small, rural, quaint town" with several restaurants and stores. A biochemistry major says, "We are not located in a 'college town.'" For those with cars, New York and Philadelphia are three hours away, and Penn State is an hour away. SU began by preparing students for the ministry and the university's commitment to the community has remained strong. Each year, two-thirds of the student population volunteer on major community service projects.

At Susquehanna, "the professors care about their students," a biochemistry major says. A classmate adds that the "personal atmosphere, great faculty–student relationships, and beautiful campus" make Susquehanna worthwhile—and make it a name worth remembering among strong regional colleges.

Sports are popular among Susquehanna students, especially when the football team plays Lycoming College.

Overlaps

Bucknell, Gettysburg, Dickinson, Muhlenberg, Penn State

If You Apply To >

Susquehanna: Rolling admissions: Mar. 1. Early decision: Dec. 15. Financial aid: Mar. 1 (preferred), May 1. Meets demonstrated need of 26%. Campus interviews: recommended, evaluative. Alumni interviews: optional, informational. SAT I or ACT: required; optional for students in top 20% of their class. Accepts the Common Application and electronic applications. Essay question: significant experience; issue of concern; accomplishments since high school (if applicable); or graded high school paper.

Swarthmore College

500 College Avenue, Swarthmore, PA 19081-1397

Don't mistake Swarthmore for a miniature version of an Ivy League school. Swat is more intellectual (and liberal) than its counterparts in New Haven and Cambridge. The college's honors program gives hardy souls a taste of graduate school, where most Swatties invariably end up.

Swarthmore College's leafy green campus may be just eleven miles from Philadelphia, but students don't always have either the time or the inclination to make the jaunt. That's because they have opted for one of the country's most self-consciously intellectual undergraduate environments. Swatties are bright, hard-working and eclectic in their interests, and campus life is fabled for its intensity. But it's not the intensity that comes from huge amounts of course work (a la Yale) so much as the self-imposed drive of talented students who want to do lots of things simultaneously—from academics to social protest to rugby—and to do so at a high level. "We don't have a lot of half-way people around here," said one denizen. "We are intense about everything we do. To us, work is part of the fun."

Website:
  www.swarthmore.edu
Location: Suburban
Total Enrollment: 1,479
Undergraduates: 1,479
Male/Female: 48/52
SAT Ranges: V 670–770
  M 680–760
Financial Aid: 49%

(Continued)

Expense: Pr $ $ $ $
Phi Beta Kappa: Yes
Applicants: 3,886
Accepted: 24%
Enrolled: 40%
Grad in 6 Years: 93%
Returning Freshmen: 96%
Academics: ✐ ✐ ✐ ✐ ✐
Social: ☎ ☎ ☎
Q of L: ★ ★ ★ ★
Admissions: (610) 328-8300
Email Address: admissions@
  swarthmore.edu

Strongest Programs:
Biology
Economics
English Literature
Sociology/Anthropology
History
Political Science
Physics

Swarthmore's student/faculty ratio is quite low, so there is a lot of personal attention given to students in addition to the standard student advisor/counseling programs offered.

Swarthmore's 357-acre campus is a nationally registered arboretum, distinguished by rolling wooded hills. Multistory buildings with natural stone exteriors from local quarries, shaped roofs, and cornices are the norm, fostering a quiet, collegiate atmosphere. A $77 million science center was recently completed, providing students and faculty with eighty thousand square feet of new lab space, state-of-the-art lecture halls, and flexible workstations that are more computer-friendly.

Swarthmore's student/faculty ratio is quite low, so personal attention is the norm. Students are required to take three courses in each of its three divisions—humanities, natural sciences and engineering, and social sciences—and at least two of the three must be in different departments. Students must also complete twenty courses outside their majors, demonstrate foreign language competency, and fulfill a physical education requirement, which includes a swimming test. Swarthmore has introduced freshman seminars that have low enrollment and emphasize close interaction with faculty members in a seminar format. The acclaimed Honors Program at Swarthmore features

"There is a unique willingness to learn to view the world from different perspectives."

small seminars or independent study, collegial relationships betweens student and professor, and written and oral examinations by external reviewers at the end of the senior year accompanied by festive banquets. About a third of Swat's juniors and seniors take the honors option, after demonstrating—through their academic records—that they can handle the work.

The college has boosted the number of departments in which students may pursue honors to include studio and performing arts, as well as study abroad. More than half of Swarthmore students study abroad in countries such as France, Japan, Poland, and Spain, and the Office of Foreign Study helps arrange programs in other countries. Cross-registration is also offered with nearby Haverford, Bryn Mawr, and Penn, and a semester exchange program includes Harvey Mudd, Middlebury, Mills, Pomona, Rice, and Tufts. Through the Venture Program,* students who tire of staring at the chalkboard may take time off for short-term jobs in areas of academic or professional interest.

While the academic climate at Swarthmore is intense, it is not competitive. There is no class rank or dean's list, and there is a big emphasis on group projects. "I have study groups in just about every course I take," said a senior. The administration has encouraged this spirit of collegiality by sprinkling small lounges and cappuccino bars around the dorms and academic spaces, and it even publishes the code needed to get access to the faculty lounge (1864). Aside from teaching, Swarthmore professors also serve as advisors, each helping a small group of students choose their classes each semester. Students are likewise assigned to Student Academic Mentors, who shepherd them through the transition to college and the first year on campus. A common slogan at Swarthmore, "Anywhere else it would have been an A," typifies the academic standard to which all students are held.

Consistent with their school's Quaker roots, the student body at Swarthmore pays huge attentioin to social and political issues, and the new Eugene Lang Center for Civic and Social Responsibility has made Swarthmore a national force in the area of service learning. The school encourages students to be as educated as possible on issues of cultural, racial and socioeconomic pluralism, and the entire community is brought into decisions on issues such as the socially responsible investments and pay scale of campus workers. When faced with complex and highly charged issues, one sophomore notes, all side are generally given a voice. Nevertheless, the vast majority of expressed opinion is "liberal," according to one conservative senior. Another freshman adds, "The environment is more toward the left, and so there are very few issues with political correctness."

Swarthmore is home to a diverse student body; only 11 percent are native Pennsylvanians. The student body is 54 percent Caucasian, 7 percent African-American, 16 percent Asian-American, and 9 percent Hispanic. A "Diversity Workshop" exists for all first-year students in the week after orientation. Swarthmore's Quaker roots come through in the concern and respect students have for others.

Most social life at Swarthmore takes place on campus, and it often begins late, since students hit the books until 10 or 11 p.m., and then head out for fun. Annual activities include Primal Scream, a tradition where everyone screams at midnight the night before exams; the Mile Run, where everyone decorates the McCabe Library with toilet paper around shelves (Scott Tissue is an alumnus and contributor); and last, but certainly not least, Screw Your Roommate, where roommates pair each other with other roommates and are forced to meet each other in "really crazy" manners. More regular activity options range from parties, dances, and movies to performances and concerts by student troupes. There's also a student-run cafe and Pub Night every Thursday.

"The environment is more toward the left, and so there are very few issues with political correctness."

When it comes to alcohol, Swarthmore follows Pennsylvania law, which states that you must be twenty-one to drink. The unofficial campus policy is "act like an adult, and we'll treat you like one," says a junior. Swarthmore's two fraternities attract 6 percent of the men; women are out of luck, since there are no sororities. The Greeks and other campus groups volunteer in both Philadelphia and the nearby smaller town of Chester.

"Swatties are an eclectic group of passionate learners from all walks of life," says a sophomore.

Students' biggest complaints include lack of sleep and too much work. With so much going on campus, according to another freshman, "It's often very difficult to just take a break from it all. You are on your toes, in all respects, all of the time." It's no wonder, considering all of the options available to them. The village of Swarthmore, known as the "'Ville," has some stores, a pizza shop, and the usual college town staples. The environment fosters a feeling of safety and security due to its suburban local, but while it's "really cute," says one student, "it isn't a place for off-campus social activity." For that, students hop the commuter rail into Philadelphia from the on-campus station, where many temptations await, including concerts, dance clubs, museums, and four different professional sports. The King of Prussia mall, with a megaplex movie theater and department stores including Nordstrom and Bloomingdale's, isn't far, either.

With Swarthmore's focus on academics, athletics aren't a high priority—the school competes in Division III. The school recently scrapped its football program because the need to recruit enough males to remain competitive in the "increasingly professional Division III environment" was undermining efforts to recruit students with other interests and talents. However, the University desires to improve the quality of athletics and the facilities devoted to athletics. Women's sports are the true powerhouses, with swimming, tennis, and basketball bringing home conference championships in 2001, and badminton and rugby are also strong. Any victory over archrival Haverford will have Swatties swelling with pride. Intramurals are also popular, with the rugby team's Dash for Cash fund-raiser a favored annual event. Players streak through the halls of the main administration building, where spectators—including faculty and administrators—hold out money for them to grab. In the Crum Regatta, student-made boats float in nearby Crum Creek—Swarthmore's answer to the America's Cup.

"It's often very difficult to just take a break from it all. This place is so intense."

Swarthmore imbues its "intense, quirky, passionate, and activist" students with the sense that they can accomplish anything to which they dedicate their hearts and minds. "It's such a great place to expand your horizons and discover what it is that you love to do." Adds a senior, "It's not a place to come if you do not want to push yourself."

For those interested in a college career where you can truly make a difference, Swarthmore may be the right choice. It's an institution where the administration supports the student body completely and students are given a voice in a variety of issues ranging from faculty hiring decisions to making campus-wide policies. It's this open-door communication policy that make Swarthmore the right fit for many in their academic careers.

If You Apply To ➤

Swarthmore: Early decision: Nov. 15, Jan. 1. Regular admissions: Jan. 1. Financial aid: Feb. 15. Guarantees to meet demonstrated need. Campus or alumni interviews: recommended, evaluative. SATs or ACTs: required. SAT IIs: required (writing and two others; math required for engineering students). Accepts the Common Application and electronic applications. Essay questions: why Swarthmore, activities or personal interests to which you feel particularly committed, and two-page personal statement.

Sweet Briar College

Box B, Sweet Briar, VA 24595

Sweet Briar offers the pure women's college experience—served up with plenty of tradition and gift-wrapped in one of the nation's most beautiful campuses. SBC is the country girl next to in-state rivals Randolph-Macon and Hollins. Academic standouts include English and the life sciences.

Website: www.sbc.edu
Location: Rural
Total Enrollment: 688
Undergraduates: 688
Male/Female: 0/100
SAT Ranges: V 530–660
M 490–610
ACT Range: 22–27
Financial Aid: 49%
Expense: Pr $ $
Phi Beta Kappa: Yes
Applicants: 420
Accepted: 86%
Enrolled: 42%
Grad in 6 Years: 73%
Returning Freshmen: 82%
Academics: ✍ ✍ ✍
Social: ☎ ☎
Q of L: ★ ★ ★ ★
Admissions: (434) 381-6142

Indiana Fletcher Williams, who founded Sweet Briar College in 1901, envisioned a school that would educate young women "to be useful members of society." These days, the college—in the heart of beautiful, rural Virginia—produces more career women than homemakers. A few men even make an appearance as nondegree or exchange students. But this remains a place where, in the words of a popular bumper sticker, "Women are leaders and men are guests." Says a government major: "Professors and students develop intense, wonderful, special relationships, built around a solid and challenging academic experience."

Set on thirty-three hundred acres of rolling green hills, dotted with small lakes and surrounded by the Blue Ridge Mountains, Sweet Briar's campus of early twentieth-century redbrick charmers is a picture of pastoral beauty. Sweet Briar House, now the president's residence, was once the eighteenth-century home of the college's founder, and is listed on the National Register of Historic Places. The Florence Elston Inn and Conference Center includes high-tech meeting rooms.

Sweet Briar's general education program has four components: an English course called Thought and Expression, Skills Requirements (oral and written communication, and quantitative reasoning), Experience Requirements (self-assessment, physical activity, and a major), and Knowledge Area Requirements (various courses, including Western and non-Western culture, foreign language, the arts, and economics, politics, and law). Seniors must pass a culminating exercise in their majors, which may include comprehensive exams. Students give high marks to Sweet Briar's programs in government, English (especially creative writing), history, and chemistry.

The sciences benefit from state-of-the-art equipment such as a digital scanning electron microscope, modular laser lab, and a gas chromatograph/mass spectrograph. English is the most popular major. The philosophy, religion, classical studies, German, and Italian departments have only one or two professors each, rendering them weaker, administrators say. Students may take classes in these disciplines at nearby Lynchburg College and Randolph-Macon Woman's College. Students may now major in business or communications.

"Professors and students develop intense, wonderful, special relationships, built around a solid and challenging academic experience."

Sweet Briar's academic climate is "collegial, challenging, and vibrant," says a senior. "Academics are treated as top priority, making SBC a place conducive to studying, learning, and excelling." Most professors have terminal degrees in their fields, and the quality of teaching is exceptional, students report. "The low student/ professor ratio allows teachers to know their students better, and gives students the opportunity to really enjoy the teaching," says a Spanish and business major. And with 40 percent of the faculty living on campus, "You get to know the faculty's spouses, kids, and dogs," says one woman. The Sweet Briar Honor Pledge, which states that "Sweet Briar women do not lie, cheat, steal, or violate the rights of others," makes possible self-scheduled exams and take-home tests. An honors program and self-designed majors allow some students to further challenge themselves.

Sweet Briar's Junior Year in France is the oldest and best known of its study abroad programs. And the younger Junior Year in Spain program is gaining in popularity, as are exchanges with Germany's Heidelberg University and Oxford University in the U.K. It's also common for faculty to offer short courses abroad during semester breaks, such as a theater course in London or an antiquities course in Italy. Students can also spend time on other campuses through the Seven-College Exchange, the Tri-College Exchange, or 3–2 liberal arts and engineering programs. Classes end in early May, providing ample opportunity for internships. Sweet Briar's unusually strong alumnae network is helpful in arranging positions and housing in cities across the country.

Thirty-nine percent of Sweet Briar's student body hail from Virginia, and the school is becoming more diverse, with 4 percent African-American, 2 percent Hispanic, and 2 percent Asian-American. An increasing number of older "turning point" students also contribute a valued perspective. "We're very concerned with gay and lesbian rights, as well as racial and gender equity," declares an international affairs major. "You can be 'politically different,' and you and your opinion will be respected," agrees a freshman. Various merit scholarships are available for up to $15,000 each.

Eighty-nine percent of Sweet Briar's students live in the college's vintage dorms, which are more like stately antebellum homes with sweeping wooden staircases, fireplaces, and furnished parlors. Thanks to lots of attention from the college, they have aged gracefully, with "hardwood floors and functioning ceiling fans," says a senior. With a few exceptions, students are required to live on campus all four years. Freshmen are advised to choose Reid, Grammer, or Randolph, though every hall has a fair share of students from all four classes. Student leaders are given the first shot at singles, and upperclassmen choose rooms in a lottery. Several dorms have twenty-four-hour male visitation, and administrators are considering the addition of newer, more independent housing for upperclassmen. All residents eat in the common dining hall.

"We're very concerned with gay and lesbian rights, as well as racial and gender equity."

When the weekend rolls around, the Sweet Briar Social Committee's annual fee is put to good use, covering mixers with other schools, theatrical performances, formal dances, and yearbooks. The committee's events attract men "like flies from all over,"

(Continued)
Email Address:
admissions@sbc.edu

Strongest Programs:
Psychology
Biology
Chemistry
Government
English/Creative Writing
History
Art History
Modern Languages and
    Literature

Ninety-two percent of Sweet Briar's students live in the college's vintage dorms, which are more like stately antebellum homes with sweeping wooden staircases, fireplaces, and furnished parlors. All now have air-conditioning.

The Sweet Briar Honor Pledge, which states that "Sweet Briar women do not lie, cheat, steal, or violate the rights of others," makes possible self-scheduled exams and take-home tests.

one student says—and if students don't like the ones who show up, frat parties beckon at Washington and Lee, Hampden-Sydney, and the University of Virginia (an hour away). Other popular road trips include Washington, D.C., and Virginia's beaches (three hours). Campus alcohol policies are "very strict," a sophomore says, and heavy drinking is rare—remember, these women are trying to preserve an image of gentility! SBC students volunteer at local schools and with Habitat for Humanity.

> **"You can be 'politically different,' and you and your opinion will be respected."**

And the Sweet Briar Outdoor Program (SWEBOP) has introduced hundreds to the joys of backpacking, canoeing, and white-water rafting with weekly expeditions. Students also lovingly nurture traditions such as Founder's Day, lantern bearing, step singing, and "tapping" for clubs. Students receive their class rings at the annual junior banquet; they are worn on the left pinkie.

SBC's Vixens compete in Division III, where the fencing team won a Virginia State Championship in 2001. Swimming, tennis, and field hockey are also popular, having brought home Women's College Conference championships recently. And backed by the largest private indoor ring in the country, the equestrienne squad has snagged eight national championships. That's led to another Sweet Briar slogan: "Where women are athletes, and men are spectators."

Sweet Briar has transcended its reputation as a finishing school for well-bred daughters of Virginia. Women now come here for a well-balanced mix of academics, friendliness, and career preparation. While some complain about the remoteness of the school's rural location, most say the beauty of the campus and the sense of family that prevails are more than satisfactory compensation.

Overlaps

Hollins, Randolph-Macon Woman's College, Mary Washington, Mount Holyoke, William and Mary

If You Apply To ➤ **Sweet Briar:** Early decision: Dec. 1. Regular admissions: Feb. 1. Financial aid: Mar. 1. Housing: May 1. Does not guarantee to meet demonstrated need. Campus interviews: recommended, evaluative. Alumni interviews: optional, evaluative. SATs or ACTs: required. SAT IIs: recommended (three required for home-schooled students). Accepts the Common Application and electronic applications. Essay question.

Syracuse University

201 Tolley Administration Bldg., Syracuse, NY 13244-1140

Syracuse has recast itself to make undergraduate education a top priority. Offerings such as the Gateway program provide small classes for first-year students. World-famous in communications, Syracuse is also strong in engineering and public affairs. Big East basketball provides solace during long winter nights.

Anyone who has watched college sports is familiar with the bright orange color associated with Syracuse University. They have seen the screaming fans and the stadiums overflowing with cheering hordes. Beyond all the athletic fanfare is fanfare of another sort: Syracuse is constantly striving to meet its goal of becoming a student-centered research university. By fostering close relationships between students and faculty, expanding course offerings, and pouring loads of money into facility upgrades, Syracuse's reputation as an academic assembly line with killer sports teams is rapidly changing.

The Syracuse campus is located on a hill overlooking the town of Syracuse in central New York State. The Carrier Dome sits on the hillside like an oversized alien

Website: www.syr.edu
Location: City center
Total Enrollment: 14,830
Undergraduates: 10,936
Male/Female: 44/56
SAT Ranges: V 560–640
  M 590–670
Financial Aid: 73%
Expense: Pr $ $ $ $

spacecraft. The character and mixture of architectural styles depict a continuously changing campus, which is grassy, full of trees, and bordered by residential neighborhoods. Fifteen of SU's 140 buildings are listed in the National Register of Historic Places. Many schools and colleges have restructured facilities to accommodate more faculty/student research, as well as social interaction between the two groups. All the dorms are wired with a high-speed communications network. The university is embarking on a multimillion-dollar campus-wide upgrade. Some of the improvements include a new School of Management building to be completed in 2005.

Offerings such as the Gateway program provide small classes for first-year students. World-famous in communications, Syracuse is also strong in engineering and public affairs. The academic programs are diverse. The Newhouse School of Public Communications, which has produced such media celebrities as NBC Sports announcer Bob Costas and Steve Kroft of *60 Minutes*, is undoubtedly Syracuse's flagship. It offers a new dual program where students can major in any one of the eight Newhouse majors and have a dual major in information management and technology. Also well-known is the Maxwell School of Citizenship and Public Affairs, whose faculty members teach sought-after undergraduate economics, history, geography, political science, and social sciences. Teaming with NASA, the school now has a $3 million virtual aerospace engineering facility—one of three in the nation—where students have helped design a new reusable space launch vehicle. SU students have also participated in NASA's reduced-gravity student flight programs. The College of Arts and Sciences is the largest college at Syracuse, and offers recognized programs in creative writing, philosophy, geography, and chemistry. Students and the administration cite mathematics and foreign languages as weaker SU programs. The most popular majors are psychology, political science, television/radio/film, management technology, and architecture.

General education requirements vary, but all students are expected to take writing courses. Several schools and colleges subscribe to the Arts and Sciences core requirements, which include coursework in the sciences, math, social sciences, humanities, and contemporary issues. Entering freshmen must complete a writing seminar, and each school and college offers a small-group experience course, known as the Freshman Forum, to share common first-year experiences and stimulate discussion of academic and personal issues. The Gateway program allows freshmen to take introductory classes with senior faculty members in a small classroom setting. For upperclassmen, Syracuse offers a strong honors program based on seminars and independent research. New additions include a degree in music industry, the first in the nation, a fifth-year master's in music education, a B.S. in acting with an emphasis on stage management, and a minor in Latino–Latin American studies.

Despite the school's large size, students say professors are friendly and accessible. "Not only do these professors have Ph.D.s to back up their knowledge in their teaching fields, they hold extensive office hours, give out home phone numbers, even arrive early to class to give students an opportunity to speak with

"Students do not have difficulty getting into the course they would like to, or are required to take."

them," a junior says. Career counseling is praised, but academic advising receives mixed reviews. Classes are usually small (fewer than twenty-five students) and registration can be easy. "Students do not have difficulty getting into the course they would like to, or are required to take," assures one junior.

Admissions standards differ among the various schools and are most rigorous in the professional schools, especially architecture, communications, and engineering. Forty-four percent of Syracuse's undergraduates come from the top 10 percent of their high school class, and 78 percent attended public high school. African-

(Continued)
Phi Beta Kappa: Yes
Applicants: 14,144
Accepted: 62%
Enrolled: 30%
Grad in 6 Years: 77%
Returning Freshmen: 91%
Academics: ✍ ✍ ✍
Social: ☎ ☎ ☎
Q of L: ★ ★ ★
Admissions: (315) 443-3611
Email Address:
  orange@syr.edu

Strongest Programs:
Aerospace Engineering
Architecture
Art
Communications
Computer Engineering
Chemistry
Drama
Geography
Information Management and
  Technology
Inclusive Education
Religion
Physics
Political Science
Policy Studies
Social Work

Americans and Hispanics account for 6 and 4 percent of the student body, respectively, and Asian-Americans make up another 5 percent. "We represent all fifty states and over one hundred countries," says a junior. "This is such a unique student population which makes SU's atmosphere great!" Big issues range from environmental issues to the war in Iraq. But, as one computer science major says, "Syracuse is not a hotbed of political interest." Forty-four percent of the students are from New York State, and most of those hail from New York City and Long Island. There are about three hundred athletic scholarships in sports ranging from football and basketball to crew and lacrosse. Merit scholarships are also available, ranging from $6,000 to $12,000.

Housing on campus is clean and comfortable, and is provided all four years in modern and well-maintained halls. Seventy-five percent of the undergraduates live in university housing. Syracuse is continually upgrading dorm facilities, and students appreciate the efforts. Freshmen and sophomores are required to live in the dorms, and should check out Brewster-Boland, Day, and Flint halls. The upperclass Skytop Apartments were recently refurbished from floor to ceiling. Living and dining in fraternity or sorority houses is another option because 12 percent of the men and 16 percent of the women go Greek. As for campus safety, SU has a series of emergency alarms throughout the campus, and a card-key access system in all dorms. Bus service is available for students studying late at the library or in labs.

Students generally enjoy the town of Syracuse, which offers a variety of off-campus retreats. Many students are involved in the community through internships in the corporations and SU education students give more than forty thousand hours in community service in Syracuse. Downtown is within easy reach on foot or by convenient public transportation. Once there, opportunities include an excellent art museum, a resident opera company, a symphony, and a string of movie theaters and restaurants. If you tire of the city life, several quaint country towns, complete with orchards, lakes, and waterfalls, are nearby, as are several ski resorts. The Turning Stone casino is a big draw. The six-story Carousel Mall, about ten minutes away, has an eighteen-theater cinema. Erie Boulevard is home to big chain stores, and the city's Armory Square is flanked with coffee shops, a great music store, clubs, and eateries.

The social life tends to stay on campus for freshmen and sophomores and move off campus for upperclassmen. There are always activities available such as movies, bowling, skating, and dancing. Students over twenty-one spend many an evening barhopping on Marshall Street, a lively strip near campus. For underage students, there is a campus club where student bands play and nonalcoholic drinks and snacks are free. Drama productions are frequent on the weekends, and popular road trips include Ithaca, Niagara Falls, Montreal, and Rochester.

The spacious Carrier Dome rocks every time the Orangemen take the field or the court. Football games against Miami and a basketball rivalry with Georgetown make for great fun and much enthusiasm during the year. In 2003, the men's basketball team rewarded its fans with the ultimate prize—a national Division I championship.

"We represent all fifty states and over one hundred countries. This is such a unique student population which makes SU's atmosphere great!"

The "painters" are famous at SU—they are the students who paint each letter of the school's name on their bare chests and run through rain, sleet, or snow to each home game in the Carrier Dome. Though the Dome seats thirty-three thousand for basketball—enough to shatter NCAA attendance records—tickets must still be parceled out by a lottery, to the disdain of some. Though receiving less attention, the men's lacrosse team has won a national championship, and the women's rowing team won a conference championship.

From special partnerships with NASA to opportunities to study abroad or help out right at home, students at Syracuse know they've got something unique. The place itself can be enough to inspire school spirit. "In the past year I have watched myself mature into the person I was destined to be and Syracuse University and all it has to offer generated this incredible process and experience," explains one marketing major.

<table>
<tr><td>If You Apply To ➣</td><td>Syracuse: Early decision: Nov. 15. Regular admissions: Jan. 1. Financial aid: Feb. 1 (regular admissions). Housing: May 1. Campus interviews: recommended, informational. Alumni interviews: optional, informational. Recommendations and essays: important. SATs or ACTs: required. SAT IIs: optional. Apply to particular program; can apply to single, dual, or combined programs. Accepts the Common Application. Essay question: career and academic aspirations; comment on the Syracuse Compact.</td></tr>
</table>

University of Tennessee at Knoxville

Knoxville, TN 37996-0230

UT is in the middle of the pack among its southeastern rivals—behind UNC, U of Georgia, and Florida; ahead of Arkansas, Alabama, and Ole' Miss. As the only major public university in Tennessee, UT comes close to being all things to all students. Strong in business, engineering, and communications.

University of Tennessee students put a premium on school spirit, athletics, and academics—usually in that order. In the fall, more than one hundred thousand boisterous fans pack into one of the nation's largest on-campus football stadiums to watch the Volunteers play against national powerhouses like Florida, Alabama, and Arkansas. Also competitive are the SEC-dominating women's basketball and soccer teams and men's baseball teams. Amid this excitement, it's easy to forget that UT prides itself on having a strong academic program.

Set in the foothills of the Great Smoky Mountains, UT is in the heart of east Tennessee's urban hub and only a few miles away from Oak Ridge, Tennessee, home to the prominent Oak Ridge National Laboratory. The 511-acre campus has an array of architectural styles ranging from Gothic to Georgian to modern. Particularly noteworthy is the John C. Hodges Library—the largest one in the state—built in the shape of a ziggurat. Newest construction on campus includes a geography building and an addition to the Claxton Education Building.

Many strong academic programs are in preprofessional fields, most notably business, architecture, accounting, and engineering. On the liberal arts side, psychology and communications are popular majors. Several majors in French, German, and Spanish incorporate a concentration in international business. A cooperative arrangement with nearby Oak Ridge National Laboratory—the federal government's largest nonweapons lab—bolsters science and technology offerings, and involves more than four hundred students and faculty in majors as diverse as English and physics. The honors program at UT is a campus-wide program that offers qualified students scholarships, honors courses, seminars, and a chance to complete an original research project in collaboration with a faculty member. Students who participate in the Whittle Scholars Program are encouraged to pursue their leadership skills through campus and community organizations, and are given the opportunity to travel to a variety of different countries including Argentina, Australia, France, Mexico, and the Netherlands. The humanities, foreign languages, and philosophy programs are reportedly weak.

Website: www.tennessee.edu
Location: City center
Total Enrollment: 25,890
Undergraduates: 20,009
Male/Female: 49/51
SAT Ranges: V 500–610
  M 500–620
ACT Range: 21–26
Financial Aid: 21%
Expense: Pub $
Phi Beta Kappa: Yes
Applicants: 10,171
Accepted: 62%
Enrolled: 61%
Grad in 6 Years: 56%
Returning Freshmen: 75%
Academics: ✐ ✐ ✐
Social: 🍷 🍷 🍷 🍷
Q of L: ★ ★ ★
Admissions: (865) 974-2184
Email Address:
  admissions@tennessee.edu

Strongest Programs:
Business
Engineering
Communications

Competition varies, depending on the class, as does course difficulty. "UT has both laid-back and rigorous courses with the difficulty increasing each year," says a junior. UT faculty gets a mixed rating. "Most of my freshman classes were taught by teaching assistants and graduate students," said a chemistry major. Students report occasional problems with registration because preference is given to seniors, but none that would extend a four-year stay. "During the past two years, courses were difficult to get into because there were too many students attending UT," says a senior. Advising also gets mixed reviews, depending on the field of study, and students are expected to meet with their advisors each semester before registering. UT's general education requirements are fairly extensive and include two courses each in English composition, math, humanities, history, social sciences, and natural sciences, plus intermediate proficiency in a foreign language or multicultural studies. Business majors are immersed in a broad liberal arts program, including a foreign language requirement, during their first two years of study.

> "During the past two years, courses were difficult to get into because there were too many students attending UT."

Several majors in French, German, and Spanish incorporate a concentration in international business.

Eighty-two percent of the student body is made up of homegrown Tennesseans, and 26 percent of the undergrads graduated in the top tenth of their high school class. Minority enrollment is low; African-Americans account for only 6 percent of the students, while Asian-Americans and Hispanics combine for 4 percent. Students also warn that the campus's size can lead to a phenomenon called the "Big Orange Screw," in which the impersonal bureaucratic system makes students' lives miserable. Financial aid opportunities are generous: more than three thousand merit scholarships are available, from $500 to full rides. An additional 360 athletic scholarships are awarded in sixteen sports.

Students warn that the campus's size can lead to the "Big Orange Screw," in which the impersonal bureaucratic system makes students' lives miserable.

Dorm rooms are average, and 67 percent of UT students live off campus. "They could be bigger, but couldn't they all?" says one psychology major. "They're better compared to most." The dorms are for the most part comfortable and well maintained, and about the only hitch is that some don't have air-conditioning (which can be brutal in August). Each of the dorms has a residence hall association, which for a token fee provides check-out of sports equipment, games, cooking utensils, and other useful items. The university goes out of its way to ensure the security of the campus and the students. To this end, UT has installed remote alarm units that allow students to report a crime from anywhere on campus. "There are cops everywhere," a junior says. "As long as you're not stupid, you're fine."

Students say that the social life is "very active" both on and off campus. The social calendar is dotted with numerous major events, including River Fest on the nearby Tennessee, Saturday Night on the Town, and the Dogwood Arts Festival. Greek life is growing more popular—14 percent of men and 18 percent of women go Greek. Alcohol flows freely, even for underage students. But nothing compares to the sea of orange that engulfs the campus on Saturday afternoons in the fall. More than one hundred thousand people jam the football stadium to see their Vols take on Southeast Conference rivals ("Alabama is a four-letter word" in these parts). Denizens liken football to religion in Knoxville. Coach Pat Summit's Lady Vols basketball team has won a record-breaking number of NCAA championships in recent years and enjoys tremendous crowds (drawing more fans than many NBA teams). Women's soccer enjoyed a successful 2001 season, ranking in the top twenty nationally for much of the fall.

The University of Tennessee is well known for its athletics, and administrators and students are hoping that it can develop the same reputation for academics. Though some may be turned off by the oft-sluggish bureaucracy, many will find the myriad of opportunities here at the "Big Orange" to be well worth the squeezing.

Overlaps

Middle Tennessee State, Tennessee Tech, Auburn, Georgia, University of Memphis

University of Texas at Austin

BEST BUY

John Hargis Hall, Austin, TX 78712-1157

UT is on anybody's list of the top ten public universities in the nation. The Plan II liberal arts honors program is one of the nation's most renowned. Though it is also the capital of Texas, Austin ranks among the nation's best college towns.

The University of Texas at Austin has come a long way from where it began as a small school with only one building, eight teachers, two departments, and 221 students. Today, the UT campus is Texas-sized—home to 52,000 students. From its extensive academic programs to its powerful athletic teams to its location in one of the nation's ultimate college towns, the University of Texas has it all.

A four-hundred-acre oasis near downtown Austin, replete with rolling hills, trees, creeks, and fountains, the campus features buildings ranging from "old, distinguished" limestone structures to "contemporary" Southwest architecture. Statues of famous Texans line the mall, and the fabled UT Tower is adorned with a large clock and chimes (a lifesaver for the disorganized). From the steps of the tower, one can see the verdant Austin hills and the state capitol. The outstanding library system at the University of Texas has more than seven million volumes located in nineteen different libraries across campus, and is the sixth-largest academic library system in the United States.

UT–Austin is the nation's largest single-campus university. Many classes are extremely large, and smaller sections fill up quickly. Says a fine arts major, "Sometimes there is difficulty getting into classes, but it usually has to do with not getting the desired summer school, which offers

"Austin is a very student-friendly town. Student discounts are abundant and everywhere feels like a college hangout."

slightly reduced class sizes, in order to graduate in four years. "A few majors actually require five years of school, but an extra year only strengthens your knowledge and educates you more completely," rationalizes an architecture major. UT is a research-oriented institution, so the professors are often busy in the laboratories or the library. They do, however, have office hours. "The UT professors are intelligent and communicate well with their students," says a senior. Academic counseling draws praise.

The list of academic strengths at University of Texas is impressive for such a large school. Undergraduate offerings in accounting, architecture, botany, biology, business, foreign languages, and history are first-rate. The engineering and computer science departments are excellent and continue to expand. The English department is huge (ninety-five tenure-track professors) and students give it high marks, but say the art/photography department needs improvement. A new molecular biology building and a new telescope have been completed for the prestigious Institute for Fusion Studies, which already boasts one of the world's largest telescopes.

The Plan II liberal arts honors program, a national model, is one of the oldest honors programs in the country, and one of the best academic deals anywhere. It

Website: utexas.edu
Location: Urban
Total Enrollment: 52,261
Undergraduates: 39,661
Male/Female: 51/49
SAT Ranges: V 540–650
  M 570–630
ACT Range: 22–28
Financial Aid: 52%
Expense: Pub $
Phi Beta Kappa: Yes
Applicants: 22,179
Accepted: 61%
Enrolled: 59%
Grad in 6 Years: 72%
Returning Freshmen: 91%
Academics: ✍ ✍ ✍ ✍ ½
Social: 🐘 🐘 🐘 🐘
Q of L: ★ ★ ★ ★
Admissions: (512) 475-7399
Email Address:
  admit@utxdp.dp.utexas.edu

Strongest Programs:
Liberal Arts
Computer Science
Business
Biological Sciences
Psychology
Electrical Engineering
Applied Learning and
  Development
Economics
Natural Sciences
English

offers qualified students a flexible curriculum, top-notch professors, small seminar courses, and individualized counseling and provides them with all of the advantages of a large university in a small-college atmosphere. Business and natural sciences honors programs are also available. Engineering majors can alternate work and study in the co-op program, while education and health majors hold term-time internships. Being in the capital city should have its advantages, and it does. Almost two hundred UT undergrads work for lawmakers in the Texas State House, only a twenty-minute walk from campus. A strong Reading and Study Skills Lab services students in need of remedial help. Students say the academic climate overall is competitive and rigorous. "You must keep up with your studies in order to be successful," a junior admonishes. Freshmen can take University 101, which covers everything from major requirements to healthy lifestyle choices and cultural diversity. In addition, the colleges within the university have established basic requirements for all majors: four English courses, with two writing-intensive; five courses in social sciences; five courses in natural sciences and math; and one course in the fine arts or humanities. Urban studies, biomedical engineering, and women's gender studies are new programs.

Four out of every five UT students are Texans. Students say there is no dominant political pattern on campus—despite the fact that historically UT has been integral in the careers of big-time (conservative) Texas politicians. The liberals are anything but hiding out on this huge campus. "Austin draws a unique crowd," says a senior.

"A few majors actually require five years of school, but an extra year only strengthens your knowledge and educates you more completely."

"There are a lot of vegetarians, and Austin gets a lot of hippies and musicians." Political issues can get students pretty riled up on one side or the other here, such as the war in Iraq and tuition deregulation. Hispanics account for 12 percent of students, Asian-Americans 14 percent, and African-Americans 3 percent. Race has been a controversial issue due to court decisions outlawing affirmative action. The university now offers special "welcome programs" for African-American and Hispanic students, with social and educational events and peer mentoring. The university also provides thousands of merit scholarships based on academic performance, ranging from $2,000 to $7,000, as well as athletic scholarships in a range of sports.

University housing can accommodate only 6,500 students. It can range from functional to plush, and dormies have a variety of living options based on common social and educational interests. "The community showers are always clean," a junior reports. As for food, bigness is an asset here as well; the word "variety" hardly does justice to the array. "There are so many options for food," says an advertising major. "Two all-you-can-eat cafeterias, a dining hall food court with different choices such as tacos, Chinese, chicken, make-your-own sandwich, stores with sushi, smoothie bars, bakeries, candy stores, pizza places, Greek food, and so much more. The student union has a food court with over nine places to eat. The meal plan extends all around campus and off (surrounding places and delivery)." Most students live off campus; apartments and condos close to campus are lovely—and very expensive. More reasonably priced digs can be found in other parts of town, a free shuttle ride away. But be forewarned: UT life requires lots of walking, especially for commuters, with 110 buildings and bus stops and parking lots scattered about. You might not even need to go to the gym!

As the state capital, Austin is not a typical college town, but it is one of the best ones. "Austin is a very student-friendly town. Student discounts are abundant and everywhere feels like a college hangout," says a senior. Nightlife centers on nearby Sixth Street, full of pubs and restaurants of all types, and a well-known music scene with everything from jazz to rock to blues to folk. Numerous microbreweries have opened their doors in the past few years. Halloween draws an estimated eighty

Although only 10 percent of the men and 14 percent of the women go Greek, members of fraternities and sororities are "probably highest on the social totem pole," says one student. The chapters tend to be choosy, have high visibility, and have increased in size dramatically over the past year.

thousand costumed revelers to Sixth Street (and sometimes up its lampposts). Annual festivals include 40 Acres, a sprawling carnival of all the campus organizations, and Eeyore's birthday party, where students pay homage to the A. A. Milne character with food and live music. Two pep rallies get students psyched before the Longhorns play Texas A&M or Oklahoma, their biggest rivals. And Texas Independence Day provides an occasion for celebration in March.

On campus, the Texas Union sponsors movies and social events and boasts the world's only collection of orange-top pool tables. For those more interested in octaves than eight-balls, the Performing Arts Center has two concert halls that attract nationally known performers. Students hang out at the union's coffee shop or cafe and the on-campus pub draws top local talent to the stage (but you must be twenty-one to drink). When the weather gets too muggy (quite often in spring and summer), students head for off-campus campgrounds, lakes, and parks. The most popular road trips are to San Antonio or Dallas. For Spring Break, the students travel to Padre Island, if not New Orleans. Although only 10 percent of the men and 14 percent of the women go Greek, members of fraternities and sororities are "probably highest on the social totem pole," says one student. The chapters tend to be choosy, have high visibility, and have increased in size dramatically over the past year.

Athletics is the lifeblood of most Texans. In fact, the UT Tower is lit in Longhorn orange whenever any school team wins. The students look forward to the annual Texas–Oklahoma football game played in the Cotton Bowl in Dallas, and the Texas A&M–UT game is an incredibly noisy experience you have to see to believe. "Football games pull the student body together and give us a chance to show our school spirit," says one student. Basketball is also popular, and the men's and women's teams regularly reach their respective NCAA tournaments. The baseball program has many alumni in the major leagues, and the annual spring game between UT's baseball alumni and the current college squad is quite a contest. The men's golf and outdoor track and field teams were conference champions in 2003, as were women's softball, basketball, and indoor and outdoor track and field teams. Other top programs nationally for men and women include swimming and diving and track and field. UT's intramural program is the largest in the nation and offers weekend athletes access to the same great facilities that the big-time jocks use.

The University of Texas may seem overwhelming because of its imposing size, but students say the school spirit and sense of community found here make it feel smaller. UT also prides itself in having one of the most reasonably priced tuitions in the country, and provides the one of best all-around educational experiences a student could ask for.

The outstanding library system at the University of Texas has more than seven million volumes located in nineteen different libraries across campus, and is the sixth-largest academic library system in the United States.

Overlaps

Texas A&M, Baylor, Texas Tech, Rice, Southwest Texas State

If You Apply To ➤ | **UT:** Rolling admissions: Feb. 1. Financial aid: Feb. 15. No campus or alumni interviews. Apply either to institution as a whole or particular program. SATs or ACTs: required. SAT IIs: recommended (for placement purposes). Essay question: an event that gives insight into your character; a fictional character who has affected you; an event that influenced your academic interest.

Texas A&M University

College Station, TX 77843-0100

Coming to A&M is like joining a fraternity with forty thousand members. In addition to fanatical school spirit, A&M offers leading programs in the national sciences,

business, and engineering. To succeed in this mass of humanity, students must find the right academic niche.

Website: www.tamu.edu
Location: Small city
Total Enrollment: 45,083
Undergraduates: 36,775
Male/Female: 51/49
SAT Ranges: V 520–630
　M 550–660
ACT Range: 22–27
Financial Aid: 30%
Expense: Pub $ $
Phi Beta Kappa: No
Applicants: 17,284
Accepted: 68%
Enrolled: 59%
Grad in 6 Years: 75%
Returning Freshmen: 90%
Academics: ✑ ✑ ✑ ✑
Social: ☎ ☎ ☎
Q of L: ★ ★ ★
Admissions: (979) 458-0427
Email Address: acmail@
　admin-rec.tamu.edu

Strongest Programs:
Engineering
Business
Veterinary medicine
Agriculture
Architecture

In a state that is known for big things, Texas A&M is one of its biggest. This school of forty-three thousand students is huge; it boasts a massive endowment and more traditions than Vatican City. Since its inception as a military academy, Texas A&M has become known for its top-notch engineering program and its unsurpassed school spirit. When they're not studying for rigorous technical courses, Aggies are likely to be found at "yell practice" before each home football game or cheering for their teams at other high-energy athletic events. For the sake of their lungs, it's a good thing that A&M students have much to cheer about.

Texas A&M is now the largest university campus in the country—something that is apparent to students every time they walk to class. The A&M campus combines historic brick buildings from the turn of the century with newer structures in more modern styles, and it is pulled together by its heavy cover of live oak trees. Newer buildings include the George Bush Presidential Library and Museum Complex, featuring open lawns and a pond with bridges for pedestrians and bikers, a chemical engineering building, and a football complex.

Texas A&M is best known for its agriculture and engineering colleges, and for veterinary medicine, although the university is cultivating a strong liberal arts program and an even stronger business school. Aggies also stand by science programs, especially chemistry and physics. Technical programs of virtually all kinds are heartily supported at A&M, especially nuclear, space, and biotechnical research. A&M has become a sea grant college due to its outstanding research in oceanography, and is also a space grant college. Add that to the college's land grant status, and the whole universe seems covered by A&M. Coursework sometimes takes students far from Aggieland. Participants in the Nautical Archaeology Program conduct research all over the world, delving into time periods from prehistory to the recent past. The Academy for Future International Leaders trains fifteen students per year in international business and cultural issues, followed by a summer international internship. The school is trying to build up its weaker programs in fine arts. New majors include music and telecommunication media studies, and new minors are Africana Studies, dance, outdoor education, and urban and regional planning.

Incoming Aggies can expect some heavy coursework in general education requirements, which consist of speech and writing, mathematics/logical reasoning, science, humanities, social science, physical education, and citizenship (political science and history). They are also expected to have at least two years of a foreign language, complete a cultural diversity requirement, and demonstrate computer literacy. Students generally agree that academics are taken seriously at A&M. "Some classes are hard, some are not, but it really all depends on how much time you put into them," says a senior marketing major. And the professors also receive rave reviews. "Every teacher I have encountered has gone above and beyond the call of duty that you would expect from a large university such as Texas A&M," a classmate reports. Because of the school's size, it's sometimes hard to enroll in a required class. "You just have to go to the professor and get forced in," one student advises.

Texas A&M is best known for its agriculture and engineering colleges, and for veterinary medicine, although the university is cultivating a strong liberal arts program and an even stronger business school.

"College Station is a model college town."

A large majority of students is from Texas, and 82 percent are white. The school's departments of Multicultural Services and Student Life offer numerous programs to enhance minority student recruitment and retention. Still, for many students, the one unifying characteristic of the A&M experience is the university spirit. "Aggies look out for other Aggies. Everyone is an Aggie," a senior history major says. To help trim the cost of earning a degree, an athlete can compete for one of hundreds of scholarships parceled out each year, while an academic scholar can vie for one of thousands of merit awards, ranging from $500 to $10,000.

Thirty-eight single-sex and co-ed dorms range from the cheap and not-so-comfortable to the expensive and cushy (with air-conditioning and private bathrooms). "All dorms are full. In fact they are generally too full," one senior observes. "Freshmen must request a dorm as soon as they are accepted in order to get a dorm of choice or any dorm for that matter." Because of the ever-growing student population, the school's dorms provide only enough space for a quarter of those enrolled. Most upperclassmen end up living in the numerous apartments and houses in College Station or its twin city, Bryan. These students needn't fear being cut off from campus life, though, as the entire town is filled with fervent Aggies. Several meal plans are offered in the dining halls, and there are snack shops all over campus.

Although College Station may appear uninspiring at first glance, most of the students fall in love with it. "College Station is a model college town," a senior explains. "Every restaurant has an 'Aggie special,' the radio stations play our 'war hymn' at times throughout the day." Students are actively involved in the community, including the largest single-day service project in the nation annually, the Big Event. Although the Texas Alcohol Board is stationed in town, "those who choose to drink have no problem getting alcohol." Those with more sophisticated tastes can drive an hour and a half to either Houston or Austin or three hours to Dallas. Greek participation involves 4 percent of the men and 6 percent of the women. More than seven hundred organizations are available to meet whatever interests you may have.

> "Every teacher I have encountered has gone above and beyond the call of duty that you would expect from a large university such as Texas A&M."

Athletics, whether on the varsity level or for recreation, are tops on anyone's list here. Football fans rock Kyle Field with cries of "Gig 'em, Aggies," or "Hump it, Ags." After touchdowns are scored, Aggie fans kiss their dates, and the annual game against the University of Texas stirs up the Aggies and their fans all season long. Men's baseball routinely fields outstanding teams, and the women's golf and soccer teams have brought home a few championships of their own. The well-organized and extensive intramural program includes hundreds of softball teams. Tennis has become a popular sport as well. Aggie jokes abound, much to the chagrin of A&M students, who don't take too kindly to being the object of ridicule. Example: "How do you get a one-armed Aggie out of a tree?" "Wave."

Favorite traditions include "Twelfth Man," in which all students stand for the entirety of every football game as a symbol of their loyalty and readiness to take part, and the Aggie Muster, a memorial service for A&M alumni around the world who died within the year. There's also the three-hundred-plus member Fightin' Texas Aggie Band and the senior "boot line" at the end of the halftime show. The treasured Corps of Cadets, one of the largest military training programs in the country, is structured like a military unit; students lead other cadets. While less than 10 percent of the school belong to the Corps, it remains the single most important conservator of the spirit and tradition in Aggieland. Although the administration has banned the traditional on-campus bonfire before the football game against the University of Texas because of a tragic incident a few years ago, students have organized their own bonfire—albeit smaller—and now continue the tradition off campus.

Texas A&M, while extremely large, is uniquely familial. Being a student here is being a part of something seemingly so much bigger, which is what the Aggie Spirit embodies. Students get the best of two intense worlds at A&M—a large school with tons of people surrounded by a small community. A&M's no longer just a military school, it's a potpourri of varied educational opportunities worth cheering. Boasts

Favorite traditions include "Twelfth Man," in which all students stand for the entirety of every football game as a symbol of their loyalty and readiness to take part, and the Aggie Muster, a memorial service for A&M alumni around the world who died within the year.

Overlaps

University of Texas, Texas Tech, Baylor, University of Houston, Rice

one senior, "We have the same traditions as were created years ago and, young or old, Aggies know them all."

Texas Christian University

TCU Box 297013, Fort Worth, TX 76129

The personalized alternative to the behemoth state universities of Texas. Tuition is about $5,000 less than that at archrival SMU. Though affiliated with the Disciples of Christ, the atmosphere at TCU goes lighter on religion than, say, Baylor. Strengths include the fine arts, business, and communications.

Website: www.tcu.edu
Location: Suburban
Total Enrollment: 8,074
Undergraduates: 6,851
Male/Female: 42/58
SAT Ranges: V 510–620
  M 520–630
ACT Range: 21–27
Financial Aid: 40%
Expense: Pr $
Phi Beta Kappa: Yes
Applicants: 6,137
Accepted: 71%
Enrolled: 33%
Grad in 6 Years: 64%
Returning Freshmen: 81%
Academics: ✍ ✍ ✍
Social: ☎ ☎ ☎
Q of L: ★ ★ ★
Admissions: (817) 257-7490
Email Address:
  frogmail@tcu.edu

Strongest Programs:
Business
Nursing
Communications
Fine Arts
Psychology
Premed

You know a school has spirit when its students paint themselves purple to cheer raucously for a horny frog. Texans know these folks are TCU fans cheering for the home team (known officially as the Texas Christian University Horned Frogs) at a Saturday afternoon football game. There's a true sense of solidarity and school spirit here. "Students at TCU really have a sense of community and of mutual support," says a sophomore.

The spacious 237-acre campus is kept in almost perfect condition and features a small lake, several fountains, and a jogging track. Nearby is a lovely residential neighborhood not too far from the shops and restaurants of downtown Fort Worth. The campus features an eclectic mix of architecture, ranging from neo-Georgian to contemporary. Newer facilities include the Taylor Recreational Track and the Walsh Center for Performing Arts, a 56,000-square-foot performance hall and theater complex.

Students can choose their majors from about eighty disciplines, with the core curriculum counting for forty-seven semester hours. The core emphasizes critical thinking and is divided into three areas: foundations (writing and math); explorations (natural and social sciences, cultural heritage, language, and literature); and physical education. There are freshman seminar courses, along with a new student orientation and Frog Camp (an optional summer camp that emphasizes team building and school spirit).

> **"Students at TCU really have a sense of community and of mutual support."**

TCU's stand-out programs are business, nursing, communications, psychology, and fine arts. Some business majors manage a $1.5 million investment portfolio that is one of the largest student-run investment funds in the nation. The university also offers an innovative dance program with a ballet major and a strong theater internship program. The most recent addition to the curriculum is a major in ranch management. The communications program offers hands-on experience at the two fully operational TV studios, a five-thousand-watt radio station, and a Center for Productive Communication. The campus also features a geological center for remote sensing, a nuclear magnetic resonance facility, an observatory, and an art gallery, along with a state-of-the-art electrical engineering lab.

The academic climate at TCU is challenging but not overwhelming. "TCU students are definitely concerned about academics and grades, but there is also a feeling of support and open cooperation between students," says an English major. Professors are well liked and respected. "In my freshman year, I had three different department chairs for three different freshman level classes," enthuses one student. Academic advising received high marks, too. "My advisor is so eager to help," says a student. "I think he really enjoys giving me advice."

TCU's student body is fairly homogeneous; 70 percent are from Texas, many from affluent, conservative families. TCU is affiliated with the Christian Church (Disciples of Christ), but the atmosphere is not overtly religious. This is hardly an activist campus, but it is definitely correct to be politically correct. In fact, "TCU should be called PCU," says a junior. The undergrad student body is 6 percent Hispanic, 5 percent African-American, and 2 percent Asian-American. TCU offers more than thirteen hundred academic merit scholarships and more than three hundred athletic scholarships for talented athletes.

Just under half the student body lives on campus, and dorm life is a good experience. Cable and free Internet access are available in all rooms. Students describe them as comfortable and clean. An escort service, Froggy 5-0, takes you wherever you want to go on campus. "There are also plenty of lights and emergency phones," one freshman says, "so students feel physically safe."

Many juniors and seniors move off campus, and fraternity and sorority members may live in their Greek houses after freshman year. Dorm residents must take the meal plan, which does not receive very high marks. The alcohol rules on campus are fairly strict for minors: resident advisors even perform occasional "fridge checks" looking for alcohol in students' rooms. "If you're caught you are ticketed and have to go to Alcohol Abuse meetings," one student says. "But we're all smart enough to find a way around it," another retorts.

Greek life is important at TCU; 34 percent of the men and 38 percent of the women join Greek organizations. They party in the esprit de corps tradition, but there's plenty of fun left in Fort Worth and on campus to keep the non-Greek frogs hopping. "Fort Worth is awesome," says a junior. "Downtown has tons of bars, clubs, theaters, comedy shows and is safe to walk around in. The

> **"In my freshman year, I had three different department chairs for three different freshman level classes."**

stockyards let you get in touch with the inner country in you, and no one should miss a visit to Billy Bob's, the world's largest honky tonk." Dallas is only forty-five minutes to the east. Parents' Weekend, Siblings' Weekend, Homecoming, and the traditional lighting of the Christmas tree are all special events. Road trips include Austin, San Antonio, the Gulf Coast, and Shreveport, Louisana.

As for athletics, the school recently joined the ranks of Conference USA. The football team's resurgence has given championship-hungry fans a reason to cheer, and big rivalries include SMU and Rice. Championship teams in the past few years include football, men's basketball, and men's and women's tennis. On-campus sports facilities feature two indoor pools, weight rooms, a track, and tennis, basketball, sand volleyball, and racquetball courts.

There's a quiet sense of accomplishment at TCU, and an appreciation for the personal attention that is given to the students. TCU provides multiple opportunities to prosper both academically and socially. "We all really love our school and what it stands for," says one student. Like the beloved Horned Frog, TCU graduates have taken a giant leap toward their futures.

TCU's stand-out programs are business, nursing, communications, psychology, and fine arts.

TCU's student body is fairly homogeneous; nearly three-quarters are from Texas, many from affluent, conservative families.

Overlaps

Southern Methodist, Texas A&M, University of Texas, Baylor, Texas Tech

Texas Tech University

Lubbock, TX 79409

A child of the remote west Texas plains, Texas Tech is finally emerging from the shadow of Texas A&M. Though engineering is its specialty, Tech is a full-service university. It takes big-time sports to be on the map in Texas, and the Red Raiders are making a splash in both football and basketball.

Website: www.ttu.edu
Location: Suburban
Total Enrollment: 27,569
Undergraduates: 22,768
Male/Female: 54/46
SAT Ranges: V 480–590
   M 500–610
ACT Range: 21–26
Financial Aid: 62%
Expense: Pub $ $ $
Phi Beta Kappa: Yes
Applicants: 13,101
Accepted: 69%
Enrolled: 35%
Grad in 6 Years: 52%
Returning Freshmen: 82%
Academics: ✍ ✍ ✍
Social: ☎ ☎ ☎
Q of L: ★ ★ ★
Admissions: (806) 742-1480
Email Address: nrs@ttu.edu

Strongest Programs:
Agriculture Education and
   Communications
Chemistry
Computer Science
Electrical Engineering
Family Financial Planning
Finance
Human Development and
   Family Studies
Technical Writing

Texas Tech University has advanced far beyond the mere branch of Texas A&M that it was supposed to be—a boon to students looking for a solid education with a laid-back vibe. A comprehensive capital campaign has helped ensure that research capabilities, faculty, and facilities keep pace with Tech's Texas-sized ambitions. Founded in 1923, it has managed to grow and compete with the older Texas schools. "It endures and excels," says a political science and psychology major. "We receive far less support from the state...but we have guts, endurance, and personality."

After two years of governmental infighting over its status as an A&M branch, Tech finally opened its doors as an independent institution in 1925. Fewer than one thousand students came to the West Texas city of Lubbock to study liberal arts, agriculture, engineering, and home economics. Today, Tech's 1,839-acre campus hosts more than twenty-five thousand students, undergraduate programs in hundreds of disciplines, and schools of medicine and law. Expansive lawns and impressive landscaping complement red-roofed Spanish Renaissance–style buildings. "Campus is very peaceful," says an agricultural economics major. "There is a soothing breeze." A $500 million fund-raising effort helped finance the construction of a new English, philosophy, and education building, as well as new science labs.

Even if new money is going toward building projects, the smorgasbord of academic options hasn't been given short shrift. Tech students may still choose from more than a hundred and fifty degree programs. Anything in the agriculture school is a good bet, says a senior. The accounting department and various engineering programs are also well regarded, though a senior cautions that in the popular business school, "everyone is just a number because the classes are so huge." Weak spots include art history, German, and Latin American and Iberian studies, administrators say.

> **"We receive far less support from the state...but we have guts, endurance, and personality."**

Tech's general education requirements include courses in written and oral communications, math, natural science, technology and applied science, humanities, visual and performing arts, social and behavioral sciences (including U.S. history, political science, and individual or group behavior), and multiculturalism. The Tech Transition program helps ease students into college by helping them understand the philosophy and scope of higher education. Most freshman classes average less than fifty students, and the academic climate varies by program, students say. "The academic climate is demanding," says a senior. "The professors are demanding and expect high standards from each student." Teaching is average to very good, and many feel that the quality of instruction improves "as you get deeper into a program," according to one student. Still, professors are "willing and excited to help," says a management major.

Outstanding students may enroll in Tech's Honors College, where they sit on committees, help with recruiting, make decisions about course content, and evaluate faculty. They also work on research projects, either independently (with a professor's guidance), or as part of a student–faculty team. Recent study topics have included pain management, wind engineering, and sick-building syndrome. Those yearning to leave behind the hardscrabble plains of Texas may study abroad.

The Tech student body is overwhelmingly white and homegrown; only 5 percent of students hail from outside the Lone Star State. Asian-Americans account for 2 percent of the total, African-Americans 3 percent, and Hispanics 11 percent. "Tech students care about and love this university, but are not obsessed and brain-washed about it like students at Texas A&M and the University of Texas," says a senior. A majority of students are "conservative and conformist, but there are, thankfully, several who are more open and free-thinkers," adds a classmate. Forget about political correctness—or even political consciousness, students say. "Most people here are only concerned with what Greek organization to join, and where the best drink specials are," one student sighs.

> **"The academic climate is demanding. The professors are demanding and expect high standards from each student."**

Twenty-six percent of students live in the residence halls, which are "well maintained, but not that comfortable," an agricultural communications major says. Freshmen are required to live on campus; upperclassmen generally flee the dorms for apartments in Lubbock (population 200,000), where the cost of living is low. Co-ed, single-sex, and quiet study dorms are available; one men's dorm lacks air-conditioning, which might be considered cruel and unusual punishment given the West Texas heat. Tech police officers—plus blue-light emergency telephones and late-night shuttle buses—help students feel safe. "You couldn't get a flea's whisker through the door most of the time," says a freshman.

Since three-quarters of Tech students live off campus, that's where the social life is, students say. Most bars and clubs admit anyone eighteen and over, but only those older than twenty-one may drink. Alcohol is banned on campus, though students say it's pretty easy for underage students to be served at off-campus parties. Forty-four fraternities and sororities attract 13 percent of the men and 18 percent of the women, but the Greek presence is complemented by "lots of other social, religious, and academic clubs," says a family studies major. Lubbock offers plenty of opportunities to get involved through community service organizations or Bible study at one of many local churches. "It's a great college town, without the big-city stress," explains a business major. Still, because Lubbock is the biggest city for miles, "any road trip is a good road trip," says a senior. The best destinations? Away games played by the school's Red Raiders; the bright lights of Dallas (320 miles); or the ski slopes and hiking trails of New Mexico, a three- to four-hour drive.

The Division I Red Raider teams compete in the Big 12 Conference. Tech has some intense rivalries, notably with Texas A&M and the University of Texas. Women's basketball is strong, and the Lady Raiders have won the conference championship a number of times in the past few years. The men's basketball program has gotten a lot of attention since Tech hired explosive former Indiana coach Bobby Knight who, as of press time, has (more or less) been behaving himself. The football team always draws hordes of rabid fans (remember, this is the South!) to tailgate parties and games. When players take the field, the Masked Rider, replete with red and black cape and cowboy hat, motivates the crowd by galloping up and down the sidelines. Other popular sports include men's and women's golf, tennis, and track and field.

Texas Tech has a little bit of everything—or maybe a big bit, given its size—so long as you don't mind hot, dry weather, ever-present construction barricades, and taking some initiative to make friends and a name for yourself. "We have a big university, but it doesn't feel huge," says a senior. "There's lots of fun traditions and a lot of school spirit, plus lots of good programs to choose from for a major." For those seeking a dynamic education in a Southern setting, Texas Tech may be worth a look.

If You Apply To ➤

Texas Tech: Rolling admissions. Financial aid and housing: May 1. Does not guarantee to meet demonstrated need. Campus and alumni interviews: optional, informational. SATs or ACTs: required. SAT IIs: optional. Accepts electronic applications and the State of Texas Common Application for Admission to Public University. No essay question.

Trinity College

300 Summit Street, Hartford, CT 06106

While most small colleges have been treading water, Trinity has had a notable increase in applications and selectivity in recent years. Trinity is taking advantage of its urban setting through a $175 million community revitalization initiative. Trinity joins Lafayette, Swarthmore, and Smith among small colleges with engineering.

Website: www.trincoll.edu
Location: Urban
Total Enrollment: 2,298
Undergraduates: 2,098
Male/Female: 49/51
SAT Ranges: V 590–690
 M 600–690
ACT Range: 24–29
Financial Aid: 40%
Expense: Pr $ $ $ $
Phi Beta Kappa: Yes
Applicants: 5,417
Accepted: 36%
Enrolled: 28%
Grad in 6 Years: 84%
Returning Freshmen: 93%
Academics: ✍ ✍ ✍ ✍
Social: ☎ ☎ ☎ ☎
Q of L: ★ ★ ★
Admissions: (860) 297-2180
Email Address: admissions
 .office@trincoll.edu

Strongest Programs:
Economics

Students at Trinity College know what life is like beyond the campus borders. The small liberal arts college in the large, gritty city of Hartford, Connecticut, at first doesn't seem like a match made in heaven. But instead of insulating itself from the problems around it, Trinity is taking advantage of those surroundings by using Hartford as its classroom. The centerpiece of the college's community revitalization effort is the Learning Corridor, an eclectic mix of sixteen schools in the neighborhood surrounding the campus. On campus, academic standards continue to rise, and students graduate with a strong liberal arts background.

Splendid Gothic-style stone buildings behind wrought-iron fences decorate Trinity's one-hundred-acre campus. The large, grassy quadrangle is home to pick-up games of hackeysack and lazy relaxation on warm spring and fall afternoons. Along with revitalizing the neighborhood that surrounds it, Trinity's campus is undergoing its own revitalization. The Admissions and Career Services Center opened in July 2001 to be the first and last stop for students. The relatively new Summit residential complex provides comfortable living quarters in a community setting. La Voz Latina, Asian-American Students Association, and the Jewish cultural organization at Zachs Hillel House have new cultural houses. The college is also completing a $35 million Library and Information Technology Center.

Trinity's general education requirements include one course each in humanities, natural sciences, numerical and symbolic reasoning, and social sciences. Students must also demonstrate proficiency in writing and mathematics. The First-Year Program includes a seminar emphasizing writing, speaking, and critical thinking; the seminar instructor serves as students' academic advisor. Freshmen may also choose one of three guided-studies programs in the humanities, natural sciences, or the history, culture, and future of cities, which one student calls "phenomenal— very challenging and rewarding."

New majors at Trinity include public policy and law; women, gender, and sexuality; and environmental science, which benefits from the 256-acre Field Station at Church Farm in Ashford, Connecticut. In 2001, Trinity appointed Dr. Laurel E. Baldwin-Ragaven, a family-medicine specialist and a human-rights activist, as its first Luce Professor of Health and Human Rights. In addition to teaching, she works on Trinity's Human Rights Program, community service projects, and biennial conferences. Students also give rave reviews to Trinity's English, economics, and history departments, and say that the school's small but accredited engineering program is likewise strong. That department sponsors the Fire-Fighting Home Robot Contest, the largest public robotics competition in the U.S., open to entrants of any age, ability, and experience. Through the BEACON program, biomedical engineering students can take courses at UConn, the UConn Health Center, and the University of Hartford while conducting research at three area health centers. Trinity's close ties to the community also are apparent in the curriculum; students can take courses on urban development and history of the city of Hartford. Thirty Community Learning courses are offered each year that provide an out-of-classroom learning experience.

Faculty/student collaboration is a tradition at Trinity. Nearly 30 percent of a recent graduating class worked with professors on research and scholarly papers, and many students join their mentors to present findings at symposia. In the classroom, a laid-back vibe prevails. "The curriculum is as challenging as you make it," a senior says. "I would not describe the atmosphere as being too competitive, but students do put a lot of effort into their grades." Professors get high marks, as they do the lion's share of teaching—graduate assistants only lead review sessions before exams. The quality of teaching "is great," an American studies major says. "Ninety-six percent have the highest degree in their field."

Nearly two-thirds of Trinity's students seek internships with businesses and government agencies in Hartford (the insurance capital of the world), and some also take terms at other schools through the Twelve-College Exchange.* The Global Sites program enables students to study with Trinity professors in seven exotic locations, from South Africa and Trinidad to Chile and Nepal; a program in China began in spring of 2003. Other enticing choices include the Mystic Seaport term* for marine biology enthusiasts, studying Italian language and art history at Trinity's campus in Rome, or learning Spanish at the University of Cordoba. Back on campus, the Department of Theater and Dance offers an unusual integrated major, and

> "Trinity is a beautiful campus in the middle of a city, with friendly people, great professors, and a student body that knows how to work hard and play hard."

sponsors a study-abroad program with LaMaMa in New York City and Europe. Administrators caution that the educational studies department offers students a richer understanding of the field, but that to get teacher certification, students must tap into the Hartford higher education consortium.

Twenty percent of Trinity students are Connecticut natives; many of the rest hail from Massachusetts and other nearby states. One student describes the student body as "majorly preppy and label whores. They go to college because they're expected to." African-Americans and Asian-Americans each constitute 6 percent of the student body, and Hispanics add 5 percent. "Trinity is trying to further diversify the student body, and they are becoming increasingly successful with each academic year," a senior says.

Ninety-five percent of Trinity's students live in the co-ed dorms. The best bets for freshmen are said to be Jones or Jarvis because of their central location on the quad. "The housing is nice," says one junior. "The rooms are well-kept." After freshman year, rooms are assigned by lottery; seniors pick first, then juniors and sophomores, though everyone is guaranteed a bed. Options include singles, doubles, quads, units

(Continued)
Political Science
History
Biology
Chemistry
Engineering
Modern Languages

The Office of Community Service and Civic Engagement offers opportunities for students to work and learn in the city. Students have created and run organizations that provide housing, tutoring, meals, and other services to youth, families, and senior citizens.

with kitchens, and theme houses for those interested in music, community service, wellness, art, and quiet. Freshmen must eat in Trinity's dining hall; the Bistro, an upscale but reasonable cafe, is another choice for students on the meal plan. Others hibernate in the Cave, which offers sandwiches and grilled fare.

When it comes to Trinity's social scene, opinions are divided. Some students praise the Trinity College Activities Council, which brings in comedians and musical performers, and organizes parties, study breaks, and community-service days. The Underground Coffeehouse and the Bistro's weekly comedy nights are also popular. A college-sponsored "culture van" takes students to downtown Hartford, to catch a show at the Busnell or visit the Wadsworth Atheneum, the nation's oldest public art museum. But the action on Thursday, Friday, and Saturday nights is mostly on campus, mostly at the co-ed Greek houses (27 percent of men and 22 percent of women join up), and mostly soaked in beer. "Most of the social life is on campus," one student says. "Many go to clubs in the area, and we are only two hours from Boston and New York."

Hartford may not be the typical college town, but Trinity students are working to change that. "We are in a small city that offers great opportunities," a student says. The $175 million community revitalization campaign includes a $5.1 million grant from the W.K. Kellogg Foundation and draws on existing community resources. The initiative will generate $130 million in new construction. The Office of Community Service and Civic Engagement offers opportunities for students to work and learn in the city. Students have created and run organizations that provide housing, tutoring, meals and other services to youth, families and senior citizens.

On campus, drinking is officially taboo for students under twenty-one, and at official college functions, including the frat parties, students must present two forms of ID to be served. "Very few students venture off campus to bars," one student says, "but there are room parties on campus." Spring Weekend brings bands to campus for a three-day party outdoors, while the annual Tropical party finds a fraternity filling its backyard with sand to create a beach. Popular road trips include Montreal, Boston, New York City, and the beaches and mountains of Maine.

Trinity's Bantams compete in Division III, and both men's and women's squash are powerhouses, particularly when the opponent is Princeton or Harvard. (The men's squad has won the national championship for five years running, and the women's team claimed the title two years in a row.) Homecoming typically brings Wesleyan or Amherst to campus for a football game that Trinity loses, but students get their revenge by burning the opposing school's letter on the quad before the game. "There is a huge competitive spirit at Trinity that cannot be matched by any school, especially when it comes to drinking games," according to one student.

Trinity students have taken their civic responsibility to heart. They also are ahead of the curve in liberal arts education. At the same time, students aren't afraid to party. Says one student, "Trinity is a beautiful campus in the middle of a city, with friendly people, great professors, and a student body that knows how to work hard and play hard."

Overlaps

Tufts, Boston College, Wesleyan, Colgate, Middlebury

If You Apply To ➤

Trinity College: Early decision: Nov. 15, Jan. 15. Regular admissions: Jan. 15. Financial aid: Mar. 1. Guarantees to meet demonstrated need. Campus interviews: recommended, evaluative. Alumni interviews: optional, evaluative. SATs or ACT: required. SAT IIs: required (writing). Accepts the Common Application and electronic applications. Essay question: topic of personal significance.

Trinity University

715 Stadium Drive, San Antonio, TX 78212-7200

The Southwest's leading liberal arts college is also one of the few in a major city. Trinity is twice as big as nearby rivals Austin and Southwestern, and offers a diverse curriculum that includes business, education, and engineering in addition to the liberal arts. Upscale and conservative.

Trinity University is a small school with big bucks. Thanks to the oil boom of the 1970s, Trinity has one of the nation's largest and fastest-growing educational endowments for a school its size. The wealth is used unashamedly to lure capable students with bargain tuition rates and to entice talented professors with Texas-sized salaries. The result? A student body comprised of smart, ambitious men and women, and a faculty that is knowledgeable and caring. Students here enjoy challenges, but still manage a laid-back Texas attitude. "It's not 'work hard, party hard,'" says a student. "It's more like 'have fun while working.'"

Trinity was founded during Civil War times and was located in a small central Texas town. In 1952, the school moved to its current location, a residential area about three miles from downtown San Antonio, one of the most beautiful cities in the Southwest. The 117-acre campus, filled with the Southern architecture of O'Neill Ford, is located on what was once a rock quarry. Everything fits the school's somewhat well-to-do image, from the uniform redbrick buildings to the cobblestones in pathways that wind along gorgeous green lawns and through immaculate gardens spotted with Henry Moore sculptures. Trinity's most dominant landmark is Murchison Tower, which rises in the center of campus and is visible from numerous vantage points throughout San Antonio. Recent construction was completed on the new Northrup Hall, which will house the Modern Languages and English department as well as various administrative offices.

> "Every dorm room/suite has its own balcony, bathroom, microwave oven, and is large in size."

The school makes a strong effort to maintain its strict admissions standards, keeping a small enrollment, tightening the grading system, and recruiting high achievers with greater energy than is possible from larger universities. The university has set its sights on becoming the premier small liberal arts school in the Southwest. In fact, 80 percent of the students were in the top quarter of their high school class. "Students at Trinity were overachievers in high school. They were people who liked to get involved and they carry this commitment to involvement with them to college," says an engineering science major. Students report that the academics are very rigorous. "Trinity prides itself on the rigorous nature of the classes," confides a student.

The professors at Trinity are described as "knowledgeable" and "accessible." "Trinity's winning characteristic is the faculty. From first year to last, you might be in a class listening to the expert in a field—you can't help but be impressed and inspired," raves a senior. Another student adds, "Professors teach all the classes and labs and are always available during office hours to answer questions." Trinity has a highly praised education department, with a five-year MAT program and a good premed program. Other strong departments include English, economics, business, and engineering. The communications department offers students hands-on training with television equipment or the chance to produce a newscast. Accounting majors are offered a chance to serve an internship with the Big Four accounting firms in San Antonio, Houston, Dallas, or Austin while earning a salary and receiving college credit.

Website: www.trinity.edu
Location: Urban
Total Enrollment: 2,621
Undergraduates: 2,406
Male/Female: 48/52
SAT Ranges: V 580–690
  M 610–690
ACT Range: 27–31
Financial Aid: 40%
Expense: Pr $ $
Phi Beta Kappa: Yes
Applicants: 3,108
Accepted: 69%
Enrolled: 31%
Grad in 6 Years: 75%
Returning Freshmen: 88%
Academics: ✍ ✍ ✍ ½
Social: ☎ ☎ ☎
Q of L: ★ ★ ★
Admissions: (210) 999-7207
Email Address:
  admissions@trinity.edu

Strongest Programs:
Business
Economics
Computer Science
Communication
Modern Languages
Engineering

Trinity's approach to general education requirements is the Common Curriculum, an extensive list of mandatory courses including a first-year seminar dealing with liberal arts and sciences, as well as the ability to express themselves through presentations and writing. Students must also take courses from five fundamental areas, called "Understandings," which include world cultures, the role of values, and human social context. The common curriculum is popular with students, especially because full-time faculty teaches the courses. As a member of the Associated Colleges of the South* programs, Trinity approves a number of study abroad programs and encourages premed and prelaw students, as well as history and English majors, to take advantage of them. Another feature of Trinity's curriculum is an opportunity for students to participate in research projects with faculty mentors. Some students even present their findings at professional conferences or have them published in professional journals.

The classes at Trinity are small, most have fifty or fewer students, and freshmen are assigned to mentor groups of ten to fifteen students for academic and guidance counseling, as well as peer tutoring from upperclassmen. "The advisors do a good job of helping students because each advisor does not have more than ten advisees most of the time," says a sociology major. However, students say that the career counseling area could use a little work.

Seventy percent of the students at Trinity are Texans. The school is fairly diverse, with approximately 20 percent of the student body comprised of minority groups; Hispanics alone account for 11 percent, Asian-Americans another 6 percent, and African-Americans 2 percent. "The students at Trinity tend to have a lot of initiative and this is encouraged by the amount of positive interaction between the administration, the faculty, and the students," says one student. As with most universities, there is some attention paid to social and political issues. In fact, the recent war has become a "cause for political rallies with both sides represented on campus," according to a senior. Merit scholarships are available to academically gifted students, but student athletes must fend for themselves.

Trinity requires students to live on campus until their junior year, which continues to provide a "home away from home" bond for the students. In fact, 75 percent of the students live in the residence halls, which are described as beautiful and spacious. "Every dorm room/suite has its own balcony, bathroom, microwave oven,

"Students at Trinity were overachievers in high school."

and is large in size," says one student. "When they vacuum and clean the room, they leave mints." Dorms are co-ed, with one single-sex residence hall that is off limits to freshmen; all dorms are now wired for cable and the Internet. Most seniors move off campus so that they can have single rooms.

There seems to be some difference in opinion about San Antonio. Is it a tourist or college town? However, students agree it's a great place to go to college. With a number of colleges nearby, young people abound and frequent the many outdoor shops and cafes at the Riverwalk, as well as touristy hangouts such as Sea World. There are also many cultural and musical attractions. Students get involved in city life through the Trinity University Volunteer Action Center.

Typical social life is off-campus bars or parties or on-campus meeting places/ events such as lectures, coffeehouses, or bands. Most of the parties are within walking distance of the school and primarily hosted by the fraternities and sororities— but open to all students. Twenty-five percent of the men and 30 percent of the women in the student body join the local fraternity and sorority organizations. Country line dancing is also a popular activity, and the university sponsors an excellent lecture series that brings notable politicians and public figures to campus. Alcohol may not be consumed on campus except by those of legal age in one of four "wet" dorms. "Trinity is creating more wet dorms to discourage drinking and driving," according to an English major. While there are rules against drinking underage (if caught the RA or Student Council decides on the punishment) but like any university, if you try hard enough you can get a drink.

The beautiful, warm weather of San Antonio provides plenty of activities for the students year around, but there are also plenty of fun road trips that the students enjoy. The funky state capital of Austin is seventy miles north, and students also can road trip internationally to nearby Mexico. An annual event most students look forward to is Fiesta, a weeklong celebration of San Antonio's mixed culture that features bands, dancing, food, and drink. They also anticipate the Tigerfest dance and parade on homecoming weekend and Chili Cook-Off that pits Greek and other clubs against one another. The school year kicks off with a party at the school's bell tower, which students can climb to get a knockout view of San Antonio.

Sports are another popular activity at Trinity, where they compete in the Division III and SCAC Championships. Over the past six years, the school has won forty-six conference titles and six consecutive SCAC Presidents' Trophies, which are awarded to the school with the best overall athletic program. In fact, one student brags that "there are no rivalries in sports since we win at everything." Popular sports include football, track, soccer, swimming, basketball, and tennis.

Big state, big money, and a small university—all of these facts lead to a school that provides all the advantages of a larger university. If you are looking for a small community feel with top-notch professors, lots of social activities and sports, as well as intelligent and enthusiastic students, look no further than Trinity.

> **Overlaps**
>
> **University of Texas, Texas A&M, Rice, Tulane, Vanderbilt**

> **If You Apply To ➤**
>
> **Trinity University:** Early decision: Nov. 1. Early action: Dec. 15. Regular admissions: Feb. 1. Financial aid: Apr. 1. Housing: May 1. Guarantees to meet first-year students' demonstrated need. Campus interviews: recommended, evaluative. Alumni interviews: optional, informational. SATs or ACT: required. SAT IIs: optional. Accepts the Common Application. Essay question: describe a person, place, or event that has had a significant impact on you.

Truman State University

(formerly Northeast Missouri State University)
McClain Hall, Room 205, Kirksville, MO 63501

Truman changed its name to emphasize that it has more in common with private institutions than nondescript regional publics. Truman is looking for a public ivy niche like Miami of Ohio and William and Mary. A new residential college program will increase cocurricular learning.

Students expect a lot from Truman State University, Missouri's only public liberal arts and sciences institution. Happily, it delivers. Since paring down the number of majors offered from more than 140 to 43 when it sloughed off its regional school status in 1996, Truman has focused on its strengths. The result is a thriving academic climate stuffed with high achievers who have eyes for learning, not slacking. "Although we are in the middle of small town U.S.A., we still try to do very big things here," says a journalism major.

Truman is located in northeast Missouri, approximately two hundred miles from both Kansas City and St. Louis. The campus, which is loaded with flowers, is spread over 140 acres and includes thirty-nine buildings that reflect aesthetic details of the Georgian style. The oldest portion of the campus, which dates back to

> **Website:** www.truman.edu
> **Location:** Small town
> **Total Enrollment:** 5,867
> **Undergraduates:** 5,636
> **Male/Female:** 41/59
> **SAT Ranges:** V 560–680
>   M 550–660
> **ACT Range:** 25–30
> **Financial Aid:** 27%
> **Expense:** Pub $ $

(Continued)

Phi Beta Kappa: Yes
Applicants: 5,132
Accepted: 79%
Enrolled: 36%
Grad in 6 Years: 66%
Returning Freshmen: 85%
Academics: ✍ ✍ ✍
Social: ☎ ☎ ☎
Q of L: ★ ★ ★
Admissions: (660) 785-4114
Email Address:
   admissions@truman.edu

Strongest Programs:
Business
Accounting
Physics
Chemistry
English
Psychology
Russian
Political Science

1873, is based on Thomas Jefferson's University of Virginia. Recent renovations include an addition to the existing Ophelia Fine Arts Center, which now has a performance hall, black-box theater, and several classrooms; a campus mall with improved handicapped accessibility; and the $22 million science hall expansion that will be finalized in 2005.

Although Truman is a preprofessional school, the students must complete sixty-three hours of a Liberal Studies Program. The core consists of courses in fine arts, mathematics and science, religion, humanities, foreign language, and social science. Freshman are also required to complete a week-long orientation program called Truman Week in which they take a one-credit-hour class familiarizing themselves with the faculty and students. In their junior year, students must complete an interdisciplinary writing seminar developed by faculty members. Students rave about the political science department, citing it as "by far the best program at Truman." Other strong programs include English, biology, and economics. More than six hundred undergrads participate in research with faculty members. For study abroad opportunities, nearly five hundred students attend programs in roughly fifty countries through the College Consortium for International Studies and the Council on International Educational Exchange.

> **"Although we are in the middle of small town U.S.A., we still try to do very big things here."**

Truman receives high marks because "it places the right emphasis on education and faculty–student interaction," according to a biology major. Truman students say the classes are tough and competitive but, according to a sophomore, the students bring the challenge on themselves. "You are constantly pushing yourself to be a better student." A classmate says, "These students were leaders in high school and expect success." Still, a political science major says that while competitive, the students help each other with "groups that collaborate for communal benefit."

The professors foster an environment of learning by providing a lot of personal attention, including "writing letters of recommendation and frequently stopping by and visiting outside of classes," according to one student. Teaching is considered "high quality" and full professors teach nearly all classes. Although some complain about academic and career advising, one senior says, "The program has improved by leaps and bounds since my arrival four years ago."

Seventy-two percent of the student body is from Missouri and the number of freshman from out-of-state is limited to 25 percent of the incoming class. The majority of the student body was in the top quarter of their graduating class and a whopping 78 percent attended public school. Minority students make up 8 percent of the student body. Diversity is a big issue on campus and according to a sophomore, "The student organization center was created to work with the integrated student office and multicultural affairs center to

> **"You are constantly pushing yourself to be a better student."**

plan and host a Diversity Week." Truman offers 3,443 merit scholarships ranging from $250 to $12,622 and athletic scholarships are available in numerous sports.

On-campus housing is considered comfortable and well maintained, which is fortunate because 48 percent of Truman students live in the dorms. A senior says, "The dorms are comfortable and receive maintenance every summer and occasionally throughout the school year." The Residential College program creates an integrated living and learning environment within the residence halls, led by a senior faculty member called a College Rector. All are co-ed except for one all-female dorm. Most upperclassmen live off campus.

Truman is located in the town of Kirksville (population 17,000), and students say it's hardly a college town. "If not for the college, there would be no town," says a senior. Still, most students seem to agree that there are tons of opportunities to get

For study abroad opportunities, nearly five hundred students attend programs in roughly fifty countries through the College Consortium for International Studies and the Council on International Educational Exchange.

involved with the community—many students volunteer at local nursing homes and schools as tutors or mentors.

Kirksville may be small but that doesn't limit social life for students. A majority of the activities revolve around Greek life because these organizations claim 30 percent of the men and 21 percent of the women. Those who are not a Greek are represented by the student activities board, which has a large budget to sponsor concerts, movies, dances, and excursions. Other big events are Greek Week, homecoming, Dog Days (a carnival), and Special Olympics. If the students want to get off campus and in tune with nature, there are trails at Thousand Hill State Park, five miles from campus. Those craving a change of pace can take road trips to Columbia, St. Louis, and Kansas City.

When not competing academically, the students are swimming, hitting, and wrestling their way into NCAA Division II wins. Sports are popular at Truman, and the Bulldog basketball team never fails to draw a large crowd. Football does, too, but bragging rights for best squads on campus go to women's volleyball, swimming, and softball. Women's swimming recently won its third consecutive national championship, while the volleyball team finished second in the nation in 2002–2003. Overall, the Truman athletic department finished fourth in the Sears Directors' Cup.

Students at Truman are deeply engaged in their studies, but still know how to appreciate the lighter side of life. "It is not uncommon to hear a student get ecstatic not over receiving high marks on a paper, but due to the latest sale at J.Crew," a political science major says. With a state university price tag, Truman is, as its namesake would say, a fair deal.

The Residential College program creates an integrated living and learning environment within the residence halls, led by a senior faculty member called a College Rector.

Overlaps

University of Missouri at Columbia, St. Louis University, Southwest Missouri State, Washington University (MO), University of Illinois

If You Apply To ➤ **Truman State University:** Early action: Nov. 15. Regular admissions: Mar. 1. Financial aid: Apr. 1. Housing: May 1. Does not guarantee to meet demonstrated need. Campus interviews: recommended, informational. No alumni interviews. SATs or ACTs: required. Accepts the Common Application and electronic applications. Limit of 25 percent freshmen from out of state. Essay question: writing sample on topic important to you.

Tufts University

Bendetson Hall, Medford, MA 02155

Tufts will always be a second banana to Harvard in the Boston area, but given the Hub's runaway popularity among college students, second is not so bad. Best known for international relations, Tufts is also strong in engineering and health-related fields. In the Experimental College, students can take off-the-wall courses for credit.

Some academic superstars used to consider Tufts University a safety school, a respectable place to go if you didn't get into Penn or Cornell. But Tufts isn't so safe anymore, at least not when it comes to admissions. Applications are up dramatically, propelling Tufts into the ranks of the most selective schools in the country. With its strong academics, high-achieving student body, and an attractive setting, some would say that not much more separates Tufts University from its illustrious neighbors, Harvard and MIT, than a few stops on the T.

Tufts's 150-acre, tree-lined hilltop campus overlooks the heart of nearby Boston, and is a striking scene. The main campus, with its brick and stone buildings, sits on the Medford/Somerville boundary. Medford, the fifth-oldest city in the country, was a powerful shipbuilding center during the nineteenth century. Somerville, the

Website: www.tufts.edu
Location: Suburban
Total Enrollment: 8,876
Undergraduates: 4,791
Male/Female: 48/52
SAT Ranges: V 610–700
   M 640–720
ACT Range: 27–31
Financial Aid: 39%
Expense: Pr $ $ $ $

(Continued)

Phi Beta Kappa: Yes

Applicants: 12,366

Accepted: 33%

Enrolled: 30%

Grad in 6 Years: 87%

Returning Freshmen: 95%

Academics: ✍ ✍ ✍ ✍ ½

Social: ☎ ☎ ☎

Q of L: ★ ★ ★ ★

Admissions: (617) 627-3170

Email Address: uadmiss-inquiry@infonet.tufts.edu

Strongest Programs:

Engineering Technology
   Center

Center for Environmental
   Management

Center for Materials and
   Interfaces

Electro-Optics Technology
   Center

Experimental College

International Relations

historic Revolutionary powder house, lies adjacent to the Tufts campus, and in 1776, the first American flag was raised on its Prospect Hill. Recent construction includes a five-story parking garage and $20 million field house.

For years, Tufts has devoted resources to traditional areas of graduate strength—medicine, dentistry, law, and diplomacy—as well as new ventures, such as a Nutrition Research Center. Such additions had only a peripheral impact on the liberal arts and engineering colleges, but Tufts has made a noticeable commitment to facilities that primarily benefit undergraduates. Recent additions include the high-tech project development laboratory for student design projects, a $21 million addition to the Tisch library, which doubled its size, and the renovation of the chemistry research building, which allowed more lab space for undergraduate research. On the nonacademic but all-important quality-of-life side, Tufts renovated the Dewick/Macphie Dining Hall, which added a food court with thirteen individual prep stations, such as a noodle bar, wok station, and vegetarian grill; built a new intramural gymnasium; and hardwired all dormitory rooms for Internet, email, and voicemail access. Tufts is conspicuously committed to self-improvement.

Despite the recent flurry of expansion, undergraduate teaching is what attracts students. They get highly personalized attention from faculty, and they enjoy wide freedom to design their own majors, pursue independent study, and do research and internships for credit. Strong departments include international relations, political science, biology, engineering, drama, and languages, and there is an excellent child-study program. The most popular major is international relations, followed by biology, economics, English, and psychology.

While upper-level courses are reasonably sized (with an average of about twenty-five students), intro lectures can be quite large. Tufts has two popular programs in which students who need a break from being students can develop and teach courses: the thirty-one-year-old Experimental College, which annually offers more than one hundred nontraditional, full-credit courses taught by students, faculty, and outside lecturers; and the Freshman Explorations seminars, each taught by two upperclassmen and a faculty member to between ten and fifteen students. With topics ranging from media and politics to juggling, Exploration courses are a way for freshmen to get to know each other and ease into the college experience, since the teachers double as advisors.

Tufts students also get a healthy diet of traditional academic fare. Distribution requirements include a new World Civilization course in addition to art, English and foreign languages, social sciences, humanities, natural sciences, and math. Engineers only have an English requirement in addition to the standard math, science, and technically oriented curriculum, but they must complete thirty-eight credits compared to the liberal arts students' thirty-four. According to the administration, preparing students "to make the Global Village safe" is a central goal, and annually 35 to 40 percent of the junior class studies abroad. Ambitious students may enroll in five-year joint-degree programs with the university's School of the Museum of Fine Arts, the New England Conservatory of Music, and the famed Fletcher School of Law and Diplomacy, or they may pack their suitcases for engineering and liberal arts programs in England, Germany, France, Spain, and Russia. Back home, Tufts offers the Washington Semester,* the Mystic Seaport program,* an exchange with Swarthmore, and cross-registration at a number of Boston schools.

"Many students compete with themselves but not with each other."

The biggest homeland of the student body is Massachusetts (21 percent). New Jersey, New York, and California are also well represented, but students hail from all fifty states and sixty-one countries. The university's reputation in international relations also attracts a substantial number of foreign students (8 percent) and

With topics ranging from media and politics to juggling, Exploration courses are a way for freshmen to get to know each other and ease into the college experience.

Americans living abroad. Asian-Americans make up 14 percent of the population, Hispanics 6 percent, and African-Americans 5 percent. Political liberals outnumber conservatives. In general, Tufts undergraduates tend to be a little less competitive and a bit more easygoing than their counterparts at the Ivies. They are expected to do more than absorb, memorize, and regurgitate. Professors are looking for thoughtfulness, and "many students compete with themselves but not with each other," says one student. No merit or athletic scholarships are available, but several prepayment and loan options are, and in the past the school has met the full demonstrated need of all admits.

Accommodations in the Uphill and Downhill (the two quads joined by a great expanse of grass and trees) campus dorms vary from long hallways of double rooms to apartment-like suites, old houses, and co-ops. A good-natured rivalry exists between the two areas; Uphill is closer to the humanities and social sciences class-rooms and supposedly a little more social, while Downhill is nearer the science facilities. Freshmen and sophomores must live on campus in the dorms, while upperclassmen compete in a lottery. Students and administration agree that the addition of South Hall makes housing available to just about anyone who wants a room. Apartments are plentiful and, according to at least one student, affordable. Still, 20 percent of the students live off campus. All but one of the dorms are co-ed by floor, suite, or alternating rooms. Food plans for five, ten, fourteen, or twenty meals a week are offered to everyone but freshmen, who must choose one of the last two options. Kosher and vegetarian meals are available, and occasional special meals (e.g., Italian night and Mexican night) spice up standard college cuisine.

While suburban Medford is not very exciting for those of the college class, the T metro system extends to the Tufts campus, so it's easy to make a quick jaunt to "student city" (a.k.a. Boston) for work or play. Harvard Square is even nearer and provides plenty of restaurants, nightlife, and music stores. For those with valid IDs, the campus pub has become an "in" place to hang out, especially Monday through Thursday nights. Tufts, incidentally, has earned a national reputation for its programs to promote the "responsible" use of alcohol.

A small band of thirteen fraternities and three sororities provides many of the on-campus weekend parties, though only 15 percent of the men and 3 percent of the women join the Greek system, and there is talk of getting rid of it altogether. University-sponsored activities include concerts, plays (there are fifteen to twenty productions each year at Aidekman Arts Center), and parties, and there are two-dollar movies on Wednesday and weekend nights. Major campus events in the fall include Homecoming and Halloween on the Hill, the latter of which is a carnival for children in the community. At the end of finals week in December, the "students turn out by the hundreds and watch and participate in the Naked Quad Run!" confesses one student. In the spring, there is Tuftsfest, a month-long affair with festivals, interdorm Olympics, a semiformal dance, and Spring Fling, an end-of-year hurrah. Of all student activities, the largest by far, with more than five hundred students, is the Leonard Carmichael Society, the umbrella group for all volunteer activities. The students are involved in programs of adult literacy, blood drives, elderly outreach, teaching English as a second language, hunger projects, tutoring, low-income housing construction, and active work with the homeless and battered women.

The Tufts sailing team has won the Fowle trophy for the best overall collegiate sailing team in North America numerous times, and the baseball team is strong, too. As a Division III school, Tufts is no sports powerhouse, but many of its thirty-three varsity teams are competitive on the regional level, and the school boasts an impressive number of All-American athletes. The intramural gym and athletic facility upgrades make sports more accessible to jocks of all stripes.

In general, Tufts undergraduates tend to be a little less competitive and a bit more easygoing than their counterparts at the Ivies.

Tufts is in the midst of a modern-day renaissance, or what many universities know as a capital campaign. Money raised already is allowing Tufts to improve campus facilities and financial aid for students. This, along with a swelling applicant pool, makes Tufts a much hotter school than it was just a few years ago. And its proximity to Boston, an intellectual and educational mecca, makes it even more attractive than if it were it in, say, Detroit. Tufts gives every indication that it's going to keep scaling the university ranks until it reaches the summit—and that's not too far from Prospect Hill.

If You Apply To >

Tufts: Early decision: Nov. 15, Jan. 1. Regular admissions: Jan. 1. Financial aid: Mar. 1. Housing: June 1. No campus interviews. Alumni interviews: recommended, informational. ACTs or SATs and 3 SAT IIs: required. Guarantees to meet demonstrated need. Accepts the Common Application and electronic applications. Essay question: two Common Application essays or choose from following: how you were shaped by your environment; why have you chosen to be a leader; how have you demonstrated citizenship. Apply directly to either the College of Liberal Arts or Engineering.

Tulane University

6823 St. Charles Avenue, New Orleans, LA 70118

The map may say that Tulane is in the South, but Tulane has the temperament of an East Coast institution. The university is trying to shoehorn its way into the front rank of Southeastern universities, though it still trails Emory and Vanderbilt. High achievers should shoot for the Tulane Scholars program.

Website: www.tulane.edu
Location: Urban
Total Enrollment: 12,443
Undergraduates: 7,862
Male/Female: 47/53
SAT Ranges: V 610–730
 M 630–690
ACT Range: 28-32
Financial Aid: 73%
Expense: Pr $ $ $ $
Phi Beta Kappa: Yes
Applicants: 13,931
Accepted: 61%
Enrolled: 22%
Grad in 6 Years: 77%
Returning Freshmen: 86%
Academics: ✎ ✎ ✎ ½
Social: ☎ ☎ ☎ ☎
Q of L: ★ ★ ★
Admissions: (504) 865-5731
Email Address: undergrad
 .admission@tulane.edu

New Orleans—a diverse metropolitan city with much excitement and a rich history, not to mention the exotic foods, soulful jazz, and lively people. And nowhere is the playful flavor of this city more evident than on the campus of Tulane University. "New Orleans is the dream college town," says an enthusiastic junior. "The students more or less own the city." Aside from its prime location, Tulane offers all the charm of the South, and all the charge of a good education.

The school's 110-acre campus is located in an attractive residential area of uptown New Orleans, about fifteen minutes from the French Quarter and the business district. Tulane's administration building, Gibson Hall, faces St. Charles Avenue, where one of the nation's last streetcar lines still clatters past mansions. Across the street is Audubon Park, a 385-acre spread where students jog, walk, study, or feed the ducks in the lagoon. The buildings of gray stone and pillared brick are modeled after the neocollegiate/Creole mixture indigenous to Louisiana institutional-type structures. One particular point of pride is the university's thirteen Tiffany windows, one of the largest collections in existence. New buildings add modern comfort to the beauty of the traditional ones, including engineering and science buildings.

Tulane's strength lies in the natural sciences, environmental sciences, and the humanities; international studies in general and Latin American studies in particular are especially strong. The Stone Center for Latin American studies includes the 200,000-volume Latin American Library and offers more than 150 courses taught by eighty faculty members. An interdisciplinary program in political economy (economics, political science, and philosophy) stands out among the social sciences and is very popular with prelaw students. Those undergraduates ready to focus on a career may apply to Tulane's respected schools of engineering (biomedical engineering is particularly good), architecture, and business, as well as the highly acclaimed medical and law schools. Environmental studies majors benefit from the Tulane/Xavier Center for Bioenvironmental Research, where faculty members and students work together on research projects that include hazardous-waste remediation and the ecological effects of environmental contaminants.

Tulane offers several study abroad options, including one-semester programs to locations such as Japan to study sociology and culture, Mexico City to delve into the language, and London to study liberal arts. In addition, the Tulane/Newcomb Junior Year Abroad program is one of the country's oldest and most prestigious programs, in which the student is fully immersed in the language and culture of the particular country. For students looking to go to medical or law school, approximately 66 percent of graduates are accepted. Helping freshman make the transition are several programs. One is TIDES, where students can join

"New Orleans is the dream college town."

groups on such topics as Understanding Your Classmates, World Religions, and Cultures. Another offering for freshmen is the First Year Experience, one-credit courses on such subjects as Metacognition (Thinking about Thinking), Campus Life, and Women and Leadership.

Sixty-one percent of the classes at Tulane have fewer than twenty-five students, while an additional one-fourth have fewer than fifty, making it difficult for students to get into the classes of their choice. About 60 percent of those classes are taught by full professors. Graduate instructors are most likely to teach the beginning-level classes in English, foreign languages, and math, and are rarely found in the schools of business, architecture, or engineering. Overall, students praise Tulane's faculty, and the academic atmosphere can be very intense, depending on the class.

All Tulane liberal arts majors must complete a rigorous set of general education requirements. Besides demonstrating competency in English, math, and a foreign language, these requirements mandate that students take distribution requirements in the humanities and fine arts, the social sciences, and mathematics and the sciences. In the process of satisfying the requirements, students must take at least one course in Western and non-Western civilization, as well as a writing-intensive class, although freshmen with high SATs can place out of some classes. Each year the university's highly acclaimed honors program invites about seven hundred outstanding students, known as Tulane Scholars, to partake in accelerated courses taught by top professors. These select scholars also have the opportunity to design their own major and spend their junior year abroad.

While Tulane has a somewhat Southern feel, it is a sophisticated and cosmopolitan institution. Says one student, "There is a large Northeastern constituency here who have brought their Type-A personalities and racial tolerance down to a Southern city. If you're a Northerner, it's impossible to escape the Southern influence of the city, and if you're a Southerner, it's impossible to escape the Northern influence that exists on campus." Eighteen percent of the students are minorities, about half of whom are African-American. Tulane awards merit scholarships, ranging from $9,000 up to full tuition, and hundreds of athletic scholarships for student athletes.

Residence halls were not always given rave reviews in the past, yet students say they are improving. A number of modern residence halls were added within the past few years, and the rooms are cheerful and efficient. "Three years ago freshman housing was the oldest on campus, now it is among the newest," says a student. Except for local students, freshmen must live on campus and leave their cars at home. After freshman year, housing is by lottery, and choices include Stadium Place, a student apartment complex. Many students opt to move off campus, claiming that it's much cheaper than university housing, but others are concerned about the safety factor of living in New Orleans. Some men live in their fraternity houses,

(Continued)
Strongest Programs:
Premed
Prelaw
Political Economy
Biomedical Engineering
Engineering
Business
Anthropology
Latin American Studies

Says one student, "There is a large Northeastern constituency here who have brought their Type-A personalities and racial tolerance down to a Southern city. If you're a Northerner, it's impossible to escape the Southern influence of the city, and if you're a Southerner, it's impossible to escape the Northern influence that exists on campus."

Tulane offers several study abroad options, including one-semester programs to locations such as Japan to study sociology and culture, Mexico City to delve into the language, and London to study liberal arts.

but sororities only have social halls due to an old New Orleans law that makes it illegal to have more than four unrelated women living in one house. Freshmen have to stomach the cost of Tulane's meal plan, but alternatives exist at the University Center food court.

While schoolwork is taken seriously at Tulane, so are sports. The campus-wide acclaim for men's basketball borders on hysteria. Because the basketball arena seats only 3,600, students camp out to buy tickets for big games. Tulane basketball benefits from a new arena adjacent to the Louisiana Superdome. The football team isn't

"Three years ago freshman housing was the oldest on campus, now it is among the newest."

as talented, but draws a loyal following nonetheless. Women's and men's tennis, women's volleyball, and men's baseball had winning teams in recent years. Club sports are big, and students can also opt for weight work, squash, or swimming among other options at the Reily Recreational Center.

Social life at Tulane goes almost without saying. "New Orleans itself never stops partying!" boasts a junior. Fraternities and sororities are a presence—33 percent of the men and 37 percent of the women join—but do not dominate the social life. Though you're supposed to be twenty-one to buy alcohol or enjoy the bar scene in the cafes and clubs that dot the French Quarter, a sophomore explains that "alcohol is accessible." Mardi Gras is such a celebration that classes are suspended for two days and students from all over the country pour in to celebrate. An annual Jazzfest in the spring also draws wide participation. Road-trip destinations include the Gulf Coast, Mississippi, Houston, Atlanta, and Memphis.

While Tulane is rich in Southern tradition, it is a forward-looking school where the possibilities seem endless. And like its hometown, it is a diverse, energetic melting pot of interests and activity. Those seeking a dynamic education in a vibrant city need look no further. C'est si bon!

Overlaps

Washington University (MO), Emory, Vanderbilt, Boston University, NYU

If You Apply To ➤

Tulane: Early action: Nov. 1. Regular admissions: Jan. 15. Does not guarantee to meet demonstrated need. No campus or alumni interviews. SATs or ACTs: required. SAT IIs: recommended (home-schooled applicants only). Accepts electronic applications. Essay question: personal statement.

University of Tulsa

600 South College Avenue, Tulsa, OK 74104

Tulsa is a notch smaller than Texas Christian and Washington U, but bigger than most liberal arts colleges. The university has a technical orientation rooted in Oklahoma oil, but Tulsa has a much more diverse curriculum than Colorado School of Mines. Tulsa has an innovative program allowing undergraduates to do research.

Website: www.utulsa.edu
Location: Urban
Total Enrollment: 4,049
Undergraduates: 2,691
Male/Female: 48/52

The University of Tulsa has been working through some identity issues. It's a small, private, liberal arts school, but it wants to provide its students with a strong foundation on which to build a solid career. With an emphasis on undergraduate research, hands-on work experience, and a diverse array of course offerings, TU has managed to find a balance that works.

TU's 210-acre campus is just three miles from downtown Tulsa, and there's a striking view of the city's skyline from the steps of the neo-Gothic McFarlin Library.

The university's more than fifty buildings run the architectural gamut from 1930s-vintage neo-Gothic to contemporary, all variations on a theme of yellow Tennessee limestone dubbed "TU stone." Recently completed facilities include the eight-thousand-seat Donald W. Reynolds Center, which includes a basketball arena; the TU Legal Information Center, a $10.5 million renovation and expansion of the law library; a design studio featuring computer-aided design and a virtual slide library; and high-tech computer and teaching labs in several buildings. A new state-of-the-art tennis complex, which features eighteen courts, will soon be joined by a new track and student fitness center.

In addition to its well-established and internationally recognized petroleum and geosciences engineering programs, TU offers solid majors in finance, accounting, and computer science. The rapidly growing English department has some impressive resources at its disposal in McFarlin Library's special collections. The collections boast original works by nineteenth- and twentieth-century American and British authors, including books, letters, manuscripts, and even a stained necktie that once belonged to James Joyce, and more than fifty thousand items representing Nobel Laureate V. S. Naipaul's life and work from the 1950s to the present. TU's Naipaul Archive is the only comprehensive collection of Naipaul manuscripts, correspondence, and family memorabilia in the world. The elementary education program has been enhanced; film studies and arts management interdisciplinary programs were recently added.

In accordance with the Tulsa Curriculum, the cornerstone of the school's emphasis on liberal arts, all undergraduates take three writing courses, at least one mathematics course, and one or two years of foreign language, depending on the degree. In addition, each student completes at least twenty-five credit hours of general curriculum classes in aesthetic inquiry and creative experience, historical and social interpretation, and scientific investigation. All freshmen take one semester of Argumentation and Exposition, followed by Writing for the Professions (for business students and future engineers) or First Seminar (for everyone else). American Sign Language may be used to fulfill the language requirement for the College of Arts and Sciences. Professors are highly praised and include famed Russian poet Yevgeny Yevtushenko.

Fourteen interdisciplinary programs allow the pursuit of cross-departmental interests. Honors students take exclusive seminars, complete a thesis or advanced project, and can live together in a computer-equipped house. The Tulsa Undergraduate Research Challenge offers outstanding opportunities for cutting-edge scientific research, and has produced twenty-six Goldwater Schol-

"Residence halls on campus are very nice."

arship winners, eleven National Science Foundation Graduate Fellowships, and four Fulbright Grants. About half of all engineering students and 35 percent of business undergrads do research with faculty. Another portion of students travel abroad for programs including language immersion in Spain, studio art in Italy, business integration in Germany, and environmental study in Costa Rica.

Sixty-five percent of Tulsa's students are from Oklahoma; most others are from the Midwest and Southwest, with many hailing from Dallas and St. Louis. Twelve percent of the students are foreign, coming from the Middle East, East Asia, and Scandinavia. The student body is mildly diverse, with 8 percent African-American, 2 percent Asian-American and 3 percent Hispanic. "We have a more diverse campus than any other here in Tulsa," says one junior. Political issues do not seem to be prevalent and political correctness is not often an issue on campus. Rising tuition, however, is a prominent issue on campus. "Financial aid at TU is very good because of our endowment and strong community and alumni support," boasts a senior. Most students feel the support they receive has been constant, which makes the tuition hikes more bearable. Athletes can compete for 345 scholarships in sixteen

(Continued)
SAT Ranges: V 540–700
M 540–700
ACT Range: 22–30
Financial Aid: 64%
Expense: Pr $
Phi Beta Kappa: Yes
Applicants: 2,077
Accepted: 73%
Enrolled: 36%
Grad in 6 Years: 63%
Returning Freshmen: 80%
Academics: ✍ ✍ ✍
Social: ☎ ☎ ☎
Q of L: ★ ★
Admissions: (918) 631-2307
Email Address:
admission@utulsa.edu

Strongest Programs:
Engineering
Computer Science
Communicative Disorders
Psychology
Anthropology
Biological Sciences
Chemistry
History
Art

TU's Naipaul Archive is the only comprehensive collection of Naipaul manuscripts, correspondence, and family memorabilia in the world.

sports, ranging from women's crew to men's golf. TU also offers 1,736 merit scholarships, ranging from $2,000 to $22,000.

At Tulsa, freshmen and sophomores are required to live on campus, but only about half of the student population use campus housing. Students have plenty of "extremely livable" options, including three mixed-sex dorms (two co-ed by wing and the other co-ed by suite), one women's dorm, one men's dorm, fraternity and sorority houses, and campus apartments. All of the dorms are equipped with free cable television and connections to the campus mainframe and the Internet are available for a nominal charge. The single-sex dorms are quieter and more attractive to upperclassmen. Dorms get average to good reviews.

> **"Financial aid at TU is very good because of our endowment and strong community and alumni support."**

"Residence halls on campus are very nice," a senior says. "They are updated every few years and almost all have movable furniture." The school recently started a faculty-in-residence program in the LaFortune House and University Apartments. Faculty and their families live in the facilities and interact regularly with the students.

The social life at TU is based on the individual's motivation to participate, a trait not all students possess. "Our student association and other organizations bring different events to campus such as bands and speakers," one student says. "For road trips, a lot of students will go places like Dallas, Arkansas, or even Colorado over break," offers a sophomore. The Greek organizations claim 21 percent of TU men and 23 percent of the women, and the frats host campus-wide house parties. Student-initiated policies govern drinking on campus. Administrators say this self-policing has led to responsible imbibing.

Campus traditions include the ringing of the college bell in the Alumni Center cupola by each senior after his or her last class and Springfest. Other big events include Reggaefest, Homecoming, and Greek events such as the Kappa Sigma Olympics, the Sigma Chi Derby Days, and the Delta Gamma Anchor Splash. Nearby parks, lakes, and a huge recreational water park please outdoor enthusiasts. Downtown Tulsa offers symphony, ballet, opera, and an annual Oktoberfest. Students are very active in community service. "Students can get involved in a variety of community organizations such as churches, Habitat for Humanity, Big Brothers and Sisters, and Tulsa's Day Center for the Homeless," comments one senior.

Here in the state of Oklahoma, sports are important. Tulsa's men's basketball team and women's golf team both recently won conference championships. The school places a heavy emphasis on games against football rivals Oklahoma and Oklahoma State, and basketball games against Arkansas and OSU get students riled up.

TU is trying to do some things differently: be a small liberal arts school in a part of the country most known for sprawling public universities, and incorporate professional preparation with an emphasis on broad intellectual challenges. It's a philosophy that serves the school well and polishes its reputation beyond the Midwestern plains.

Overlaps

Texas Christian, Southern Methodist, Washington University (MO), University of Oklahoma, Oklahoma State

If You Apply To ➤

Tulsa: Rolling admissions. Meets demonstrated need of 90%. Campus interviews: recommended, evaluative. Alumni interviews: not available. SATs or ACTs: required. SAT IIs: optional. Accepts the Common Application and electronic applications. Essay question: challenge you have faced; how you would change the world; significant life event.

807 Union Street, Schenectady, NY 12308

Union is split down the middle between liberal arts and engineering. That means its center of gravity is more toward the technical side than places like Trinity, Lafayette, and Tufts, but less so than Clarkson and Rensselaer. Schenectady is less than exciting, but there are outdoor getaways in all directions.

Union College draws a disparate group of students from around the country. Future engineers rub elbows with liberal arts students in a student population of less than three thousand. To further complement this intimate social milieu, Union College is deemphasizing the Greek system and implementing a House System in order to give every student access to a social group. The Union Scholars program gives entering freshmen with unusual capabilities and talents a more extensive Freshman Preceptorial program and the chance to get involved in independent, faculty-sponsored research in their sophomore year. Each spring, students present scholarly projects in an atmosphere of a professional conference. It's a heady blend of academic involvement that draws praise from students and faculty alike.

The one-hundred-acre Union campus sits on a hill overlooking Schenectady. Its unified campus plan, designed in 1813 by French architect and landscaper Joseph Jacques Ramée, includes eight acres of formal gardens and woodlands. Ramée's vision took shape in brownstone and redbrick, with plenty of white arches, pilasters, and lacy green trees. The sixteen-sided Nott Memorial, a National Historic Landmark, is a meeting, study, and exhibition center for students and alumni.

Union's general education requirements fall into four groups. The History, Literature, and Civilization cluster includes the Freshman Preceptorial called Diversity and Dialog, plus two courses in history (ancient, European, or American), and two associated follow-up courses (two in literature, or one in literature and one in civilization). The team-taught Preceptorial focuses on critical reading, analysis, and writing, and each section is capped at sixteen students. The Social and Behavioral Science cluster requires an introductory course in anthropology, economics, political science, psychology, or sociology. The Mathematics and Natural Science cluster requires one math course and two courses in basic or applied science, one of which must have labs. The Other Languages, Other Cultures, Other Disciplines cluster includes three courses in a modern language, one term abroad, or three related courses in Africana studies, East Asian studies, or Latin American studies. As part of their education, Union tries to develop students' social conscience. The college has invested $10 million to revitalize an adjacent neighborhood, and many students volunteer through Big Brothers/Big Sisters and We Care About U Schenectady, which builds houses for the homeless. Also, all freshmen work on a community clean-up project during orientation.

"Our professors are amazing—they are here because they want to teach, as well as do research."

Students praise Union's programs in English, biology, political science, and psychology—all, except biology, among the five most popular majors on campus. "The chemistry, mathematics, and geology departments are superior," adds a biochemistry major. "We have state-of-the-art instrumentation, great funding to attend national and regional conferences, undergraduate research, small laboratory sections, and awesome faculty." Each spring, Union cancels classes one afternoon for the Charles Steinmetz Symposium, where students present scholarly projects in an atmosphere of a professional conference. More than three hundred students participated last year.

Website: www.union.edu
Location: City outskirts
Total Enrollment: 2,147
Undergraduates: 2,102
Male/Female: 53/47
SAT Ranges: V 550–650
  M 590–680
Financial Aid: 50%
Expense: Pr $ $ $ $
Phi Beta Kappa: Yes
Applicants: 3,828
Accepted: 45%
Enrolled: 33%
Grad in 6 Years: 84%
Returning Freshmen: 93%
Academics: ✐ ✐ ✐ ✐
Social: ☎ ☎ ☎
Q of L: ★ ★ ★
Admissions: (518) 388-6112
Email Address:
  admissions@union.edu

Strongest Programs:
Mathematics
Chemistry
Psychology
Political Science
English
Classics
Mechanical Engineering

Union's programs in engineering and computer science are legendary, especially for a liberal arts school, though they are smaller now that civil engineering has been phased out. The history department is home to Union's most esteemed lecturer, Stephen Berk, whose course on the Holocaust and Twentieth-Century Europe is a hot ticket. The Educational Studies program allows aspiring teachers to complete courses and fieldwork required for secondary-school certification in fourteen subjects, while including a strong liberal arts grounding. Interdisciplinary majors include Russian and Eastern European studies, industrial economics, and law and public policy. Administrators say philosophy and performing arts are weaker because of lower enrollment and resources.

Union operates on a trimester system, which students call a mixed blessing. On the downside, the system means thrice-a-year exams and a late start to summer jobs because school doesn't finish until June. "The trimester calendar really prevents a laid-back atmosphere," says one student. On the upside, some students feel that concentrating on just three courses a term helps them learn more. More terms also mean more opportunities for independent study and internships, either in the state capital of Albany, twenty minutes away, or in Washington, D.C. About 65 percent of each class studies abroad. Some choose a summer program examining national health care systems in England, Holland, and Hungary, while others study marine life in Bermuda, Woods Hole, or Newfoundland. A set of mini-terms abroad, during the winter and summer breaks, join engineering and liberal arts students on team projects in Brazil and Australia.

Back on campus, students give the faculty high marks. "Our professors are amazing—they are here because they want to teach, as well as do research," says a junior. "They are very concerned with our academic careers, often coming in on nights and weekends to either teach, counsel, or simply get to know us better." Sophomore and junior honors students can take interdisciplinary seminars team-taught by faculty from multiple departments, and may attend private meetings with visiting speakers.

Forty-six percent of Union's students come from New York State. "Students at Union are, by and large, superficial and unconcerned with their education," says a junior. "Students tend to be a little snobby," agrees a psychology and biology major. "It was hard to find a niche at first." Three percent of the student body is African-American, another 4 percent is Hispanic, and 5 percent is Asian-American. The school's Multicultural Affairs Council and the President's Commission on Diversity are working to boost these numbers, and an affirmative action officer and community outreach director have been hired to help with race relations. Regardless of background, a general indifference about key issues on campus and in the larger world seems to prevail.

Union offers seventy merit scholarships of $12,000 each, as well as a complement of loans, but no athletic scholarships. The Chester Arthur Undergraduate

"The chemistry, mathematics, and geology departments are superior."

Support for Excellence (CAUSE) award, which takes its name from the former U.S. president and most distinguished graduate, offers loans to students interested in public service, forgiven at 20 percent per year if the student pursues a service-oriented career.

Eighty percent of Union students live in the dorms, which are "well maintained for the most part, but some are downright cramped," says a junior. "Campus apartments are gorgeous," and reserved for upperclassmen. Underclassmen may choose from single-sex, co-ed, and theme houses; the new House System will bar Greek groups from offering housing. Students recommend West, which is co-ed by room, and thus very social, as well as Fox and Davidson, where freshmen and sophomores live in suites: four people to two bedrooms and a "huge" common room. All dorm rooms are linked to the Union computer network, and everyone eats at one of two dining halls.

Social life at Union "is like a skipping record—the same thing over and over and over again," a junior laments. "The school spends a lot of money to keep us entertained," with movies, a coffeehouse, dances, and guest speakers, "but it's often unsuccessful." The lack of things to do leads 21 percent of men and 25 percent of women to go Greek—significant fractions, but lower than in past years. The Greeks have actually been helped by the new alcohol policy, which restricts parties to no more than two kegs and no more than one hundred guests, a biochemistry major reports. "The head-count limit makes it difficult for people to get in, increasing the elite status of the Greek system," the student says. The policy also hasn't stopped the underage from guzzling beer. However, students found abusing alcohol or drugs have to attend a six-hour substance abuse program at a local rehab center. Local bars such as Van Dyck, Pinhead Susan's, and Bar One are said to be fun, but dingy. Montreal is a popular road trip.

Schenectady is an old-line industrial city that's becoming more high-tech, but it "is not a college town in the least," says a junior. What Schenectady lacks can be found in Saratoga Springs, which is lively with restaurants, jazz clubs, and horse racing, and in the Adirondacks to the north and the Catskills to the south. Fall Fest and Spring Fest feature all-campus picnics and live music. Party in the Garden is also popular, and only hard-core geeks miss the Division I ice hockey games against Rensselaer, Polytechnic Institute, or Cornell. The men may find they have some competition for audiences these days, though, since women's ice hockey is now Division I, too. Union's twenty-five other intercollegiate teams compete in Division III. Painting the Idol, a really ugly campus statue, "is something everyone does, and a great bonding experience."

Union College is a small, friendly place full of eager intellectual exchange, where students wish that the social life were as vibrant as the discussions in their labs and classrooms. "The faculty, academics, and undergraduate research opportunities are by far exceptional—for any college or university," says a junior. "We are very fortunate to obtain the well-versed and well-rounded education that we do."

Union's programs in engineering and computer science are legendary, especially for a liberal arts school, though they are smaller now that civil engineering has been phased out.

Overlaps

Hamilton, Lehigh, Lafayette, Skidmore, Colgate

If You Apply To ➤ | **Union:** Early decision: Nov. 15, Jan. 15. Regular admissions and housing: Jan. 15. Financial aid: Feb. 1. Guarantees to meet demonstrated need. Campus interviews: strongly recommended, evaluative. Alumni interviews: recommended, informational. SAT I or three SAT IIs (writing and two others) or ACT: required. Accepts the Common Application and electronic applications. Essay question: significant experience, achievement, risk, or ethical dilemma; issue of personal, local, national, or international concern; influential person, fictional character, historical figure, or creative work; or a topic of your choice.

Ursinus College

Box 1000, Collegeville, PA 19426

Ursinus is the smallest of the cohort of eastern Pennsylvania liberal arts colleges that includes Franklin and Marshall, Muhlenberg, and Lafayette. The plus side is more attention from faculty and more emphasis on independent learning. Although Philly is within arm's reach, the setting is quiet.

Ursinus College was established as a school where, in the words of namesake Zacharias Ursinus, students would "examine all things and retain what is good." For many years, the college emphasized solid training in practical fields ranging from business administration to sports science, but it is now returning with a

Website: www.ursinus.edu
Location: Suburban
Total Enrollment: 1,370

The Common Intellectual

Experience for freshmen,

which is taught by faculty

members from all

disciplines, is designed to

give students a common

basis for academic

discussions that will spill

over into the cafeteria and

dorms.

vengeance to its liberal arts roots. All new students and faculty members must now take part in a course called the Common Intellectual Experience that explores topics ranging from Plato to Buddhist scripture, and there is a requirement that each student have an Independent Learning Experience. Though Ursinus (pronounced Ur-SIGN-nus) is small, students are happy at this college in the suburbs of Philadelphia, thanks largely to close contact with professors and a cozy atmosphere where everyone knows everyone else.

Ursinus is located in Collegeville, about forty minutes west of Philadelphia, and only ten miles from the green, rolling hills of Valley Forge National Park. The 167-acre campus is mostly Pennsylvania fieldstone with a variety of restored buildings. The campus walkway includes the F.W. Olin Hall and the Berman Museum of Art. Ursinus completed a $16 million renovation and expansion of Pfahler Science Hall, which houses chemistry, computer science, mathematics, and physics. A $1 million bookstore was added to the back of the student center and a new, 143-bed student residence opened last year. A state-of-the-art fitness center and field house, the Floy Lewis Bakes Center, is complete.

The school offers twenty-six majors and forty-seven minors, with the sciences garnering the most praise. Ursinus has cultivated a strong major in East Asian studies, and it has a viable classics program as well as solid strength in history, English, and politics. Biology is still one of the most popular majors, though faculty members have shifted the emphasis of instruction from premed to research. Ursinus was the first college in Pennsylvania approved by the state to certify secondary teachers of Japanese. Other language programs are popular, but the number of economics and business administration majors has declined since the economists began requiring calculus. A quarter of each senior class has paid summer academic fellowships where they work full-time with a faculty mentor. For the academically motivated who want a change from the Philadelphia 'burbs, Ursinus offers opportunities around the globe as part of the Bradley University Consortium. The college also offers programs with its own faculty in Japan, Mexico, Spain, Italy, England, Costa Rica, and Germany. Students can study at other U.S. universities, including Howard and American in Washington, D.C. Prospective engineers may choose 3–2 programs at Columbia University and elsewhere.

Every freshman is issued a laptop computer. A new graduation requirement, the Independent Learning Experience, requires every student to either complete an independent research project, become an intern, study abroad, or student teach. The newest academic offerings include majors in neuroscience and art.

General education requirements under the Ursinus Plan revolve around the Common Intellectual Experience, which include a Freshman Seminar, English composition, two foreign language courses, two math or science courses, two courses in different social sciences, and two humanities courses. The Common Intellectual Experience for freshmen, which is taught by faculty members from all disciplines, is designed to give students a common basis for academic discussions that will spill over into the cafeteria and dorms. Honors students complete an independent research project that is evaluated by outside examiners. The library has 375,000 volumes, but the

"The academic environment at Ursinus is strenuous. You're going to work here."

school is connected to OCLC, a consortium of more that eighteen thousand libraries, and most books are accessible within a few days. Ursinus students may also use the Penn libraries.

Ursinus students work hard for their grades. "The academic environment at Ursinus is strenuous," a senior history major says. "You're going to work here." In fact, more than 30 percent of students at the school come from the top tenth of their class. Classes at the college are small and professors are outstanding. "All students are taught by professors, never graduate students. Professors get to know students and are always available outside the classroom," says one junior communications major. Academic advising also receives high marks; freshmen meet their advisors once a week during the first half of their first semester. "Advisors are there whenever you need them," one student says. Other students say Ursinus makes it easy to succeed. "Just about everyone graduates in four years, unless you are a real slacker," says a sophomore.

The school offers twenty-six majors and forty-seven minors, with the sciences garnering the most praise.

Sixty-two percent of the students at Ursinus are from Pennsylvania, with others hail from New York or New Jersey. Eighty-three percent of students are white, with African-Americans making up 8 percent, Asian-Americans another 4 percent, and Hispanics 3 percent. Racial tension is minimal. The school's excellent student life staff includes several key members who are African-American. Race relations, sexual harassment, and physical safety are covered in "Ursinus in Community," which begins with freshman orientation. "Ursinus is not a politically active school at all," a sophomore says. "Too laid-back." Merit scholarships are available each year, ranging from $5,000 to $25,000.

Housing options at Ursinus run the gamut from typical to modern, and 93 percent of students live in the dorms, adding to the college's community feel. "Rooms are big, especially for freshmen," a student raves. Upperclassmen quickly grab the Main Street houses, a string of Victorian-era homes across the street from campus, while many first-year men take up residence in Old Men's (BWC, short for Brodbeck-Wilkinsin-Curtis), which has generously sized rooms. The college recently finished renovations on two of the thirty Victorian-era student residences that the college owns. The college provides three meal plans (nineteen, fourteen, or nine meals per week), and students may choose to eat in the main dining room or Zack's snack bar. The

"All students are taught by professors, never graduate students. Professors get to know students and are always available outside the classroom."

campus is very safe, one student says; the security guards are always available for anything. "If it's raining, they will bring you an umbrella. If you're locked out of your room, they will get you in."

Collegeville is a tiny town, only eight blocks long, and Ursinus takes up six of them. While the town has little that the students want, it does have some of what they need, including late-night pizza delivery. The name, one student says, is a misnomer: "Collegeville is a small town, but it doesn't exist just because the college does." As for social life, students stick close to home. "Most parties are on campus," a student says. "Parties get crazy. Not many road trips." Campus social activities include free movies every night, lectures, and dances. Greek life draws 26 percent of the men and 38 percent of the women. Central Philadelphia is less than an hour away, and because many students have cars, they retreat to the Jersey shore during the warmer months. Finally, there are two mega-malls within a twenty-minute drive of Ursinus, including the King of Prussia complex, the second-largest mall in the country. Alcohol isn't difficult to come by, even for those not twenty-one. "The town bars card with a passion, yet upperclassman 'aid' the young," one senior says. However, "if you're being irresponsible, 90 percent of the time you will get in trouble."

Ursinus is mentioned in Trivial Pursuit for having a tree in the endzone of the football field.

Students here love sports, and 60 percent of the student body play on an NCAA Division III varsity team. For women determined to pursue careers in athletics, Ursinus is a well-known stepping stone to collegiate coaching posts; more than fifty colleges have hired Ursinus alumni, including the University of Virginia and Old Dominion. The lacrosse team is recognized as a perennial contender for the national championship, and the women's field hockey team is strong. Sadly, the longest-running football rivalry in the Philadelphia area against rival Swarthmore is no more; Swarthmore has dropped its program. Among other contributions in the world of sports, Ursinus is mentioned in Trivial Pursuit for having a tree in the endzone of the football field.

Ursinus may not be in the center of a great metropolitan area, or be big enough to have a big town built around it, but to the students who attend, the college offers a solid education within a close-knit community. Students step up to the academic challenges and rave about the faculty, many of whom, a student says, live within fifteen minutes of the campus. According to one happy philosophy major, "They treat you like family."

If You Apply To ➤

Ursinus: Early decision: Jan. 15. Regular admissions, financial aid, and housing: Feb. 15. Does not guarantee to meet demonstrated need. Campus interviews: recommended, informational. No alumni interviews. SATs: optional (required for students not in the top 10% of high school graduating class). SAT IIs: recommended. Accepts the Common Application and electronic applications. Essay question: significant experience; personal issue; or significant person.

University of Utah

250 SSB, Salt Lake City, UT 84112

While the true-blue Mormons generally head for BYU, University of Utah attracts a diverse crowd that is drawn to the region's only major city. A majority of students hail from the Salt Lake City region, and many live at home. Professional programs such as business, engineering, and communications are the most popular.

Website: www.utah.edu
Location: City outskirts
Total Enrollment: 26,193
Undergraduates: 22,648
Male/Female: 56/44
SAT Ranges: V 460–620
M 470–630
ACT Range: 20–27
Financial Aid: 30%
Expense: Pub $
Phi Beta Kappa: Yes
Applicants: 5,802
Accepted: 90%
Enrolled: 47%
Grad in 6 Years: 53%
Returning Freshmen: 73%
Academics: ✍ ✍ ✍
Social: ☎ ☎ ☎
Q of L: ★ ★ ★
Admissions: (801) 581-7281
Email Address: N/A

Strongest Programs:
Business
Psychology

Utah may be home of the Mormons, but the University of Utah is decidedly secular. In addition to being the flagship institution of the public Utah System of Higher Education, the university is a major national scientific research center. Founded in 1850, the University of Utah is unusual in its ability to offer students the advantages of living in a city while at the same time maintaining a connection with nature.

Set in the foothills of the Rocky Mountains near the shores of the Great Salt Lake, the university enjoys a picturesque location a half-hour drive from "the greatest snow on earth." Occupying fifteen hundred well-landscaped acres with nearly as many different kinds of trees as undergraduates, the campus is the state's arboretum. The architectural style of the university's structures ranges from nineteenth-century, ivy-covered buildings to state-of-the-art athletic facilities. The location, snow, and beautiful mountain location is partially why this city was chosen to host the Olympics. The Olympic village is now used as

"The best thing about students at U is that they are friendly to all, supportive of each other, and you can do whatever you want."

student housing equipped with quality furnishings and the latest technology. The U also recently broke ground on a new 150,000 square foot Health Sciences Center designed to become the new center for health profession education.

While the professional degrees are quite popular, the U does not skimp on general education requirements. Students must fulfill classes such as writing, American institutions, intellectual explorations, and quantitative reasoning. Renowned for its research in biomedical engineering, Utah hosted the first mechanical heart transplant. Students are impressed with majors such as nursing, medical, and law departments but other tracks such as business and engineering also receive positive reviews. The class environment is considered to be "challenging, but worth it" according to a freshman student. Programs such as the service learning program or the Undergraduate Research program give students the chance to join faculty members in research projects and allows them to receive either academic credit or a stipend for their participation. The Honors program allows students to receive even more individual attention in small classes.

To make it easier to sign up for classes, the school now has Web-based registration, with freshmen getting first priority. Introductory courses often enroll hundreds of students, and classes can be overcrowded. Utah's professors generally receive high marks from the students. "I would rate the teaching as pretty good, and for the most part, freshman are taught by full professors" says a nursing student.

Utah's students are a middle-class, fairly homogeneous lot; out-of-staters make up 15 percent of the student body, while minority students are barely represented, with African-Americans, Hispanics, and Asian-Americans making up 6 percent. Utah offers more than sixteen hundred scholarships for academic achievement, some reserved for state residents, along with three hundred athletic scholarships distributed among twenty-one NCAA Division I teams.

Those students that live on campus say that "the housing is very nice and all dorm facilities are kept clean and tidy." Seventeen percent of students live on campus in newly built apartments and dorms. If you live on campus, don't be afraid of the food; most seem to agree that it's good and plentiful. According to a computer animation major, "They have everything from a sushi bar to Pizza Hut."

Social life is low-key due in large part to the high number of commuters. Still, one student says, "The social life is wonderful and there are many on- and off-campus activities." The Outdoor Recreation Program offers excursions into nature and also has a storehouse of more than fifteen hundred different recreational items to rent to students. While the university sponsors symposiums and lectures and students do support a variety of movie houses and clubs with live acts, most socializing at this "suitcase school" takes place off campus. Favorite road trips take the students to Las Vegas, Seattle, or any of the nearby ski resorts (the school provides slopeside bus service). Only 3 percent of the men and 2 percent of the women go Greek, and the city council recently clamped down on Greek growth in order to keep the system small.

> "There is a community service center located in the heart of campus and lots of students get involved."

Salt Lake City may not rate as the nation's best college town, but a senior states that "there is a community service center located in the heart of campus and lots of students get involved." Adjacent to campus, the Latter-day Saints Institute of Religion sponsors dances and other social activities, though the conservative social attitudes may dampen the spirits of the party animals. The flourishing cultural scene is regional in scope and includes the respected Utah Symphony, several dance companies, opera, the NBA's Utah Jazz, the minor-league Utah Stingers, and, of course, the Mormon Tabernacle Choir.

Football and basketball are the most popular sports on campus and both draw an enthusiastic following. The women's gymnastics team has won ten NCAA titles in the past sixteen years, and the men's basketball team is always strong. Available athletic amenities include indoor tennis, racquetball, squash courts, saunas, swimming pools, an indoor track, and weight machines. Intramurals in nearly one hundred sports, a quarter of which are co-ed, are an important student activity. Any match against rival BYU usually sells out. Students also rave about the three-day Mayfest celebrated every spring, which brings the campus together for dances, plays, movies, speakers, and edible delights.

If you are looking for a diverse campus and an escape from what is typically a Mormon area—look no further. "The best thing about students at U is that they are friendly to all, supportive of each other, and you can do whatever you want" said a

(Continued)
Communications
Ballet/Dance
Chemistry
Engineering
Computer Science

The U also recently broke ground on a new 150,000 square foot Health Sciences Center designed to become the new center for health profession education.

The flourishing cultural scene is regional in scope and includes the respected Utah Symphony, several dance companies, opera, the NBA's Utah Jazz, the minor-league Utah Stingers, and, of course, the Mormon Tabernacle Choir.

Overlaps

Brigham Young, Utah State, Stanford, University of Arizona

computer animation major. Also, nationally recognized professional programs and an Honors program that is the third oldest in the nation help round out the overall college experience. Ultimately, if you just want to study and ski, this is the place. After all, why else would this have been the hub for the Winter Olympics?

If You Apply To ➤

University of Utah: Regular admissions: May 1. Financial aid: Feb. 15. Does not guarantee to meet demonstrated need. No campus or alumni interviews. SATs or ACTs: required; ACT preferred. No essay question.

Vanderbilt University

2305 West End Avenue, Nashville, TN 37240

More "southern" than Emory or Duke, Vandy has traditionally been a preferred choice in the Deep South suburbs of Atlanta and Birmingham. Along with Tulane, it is the only leading Southern private institution with both business and engineering (and one of the South's leading music programs to boot).

Website: www.vanderbilt.edu
Location: City outskirts
Total Enrollment: 10,712
Undergraduates: 6,146
Male/Female: 48/52
SAT Ranges: V 610–700
  M 640–720
ACT Range: 27–31
Financial Aid: 32%
Expense: Pr $ $ $ $
Phi Beta Kappa: Yes
Applicants: 9,836
Accepted: 46%
Enrolled: 34%
Grad in 6 Years: 84%
Returning Freshmen: 94%
Academics: ✍ ✍ ✍ ✍
Social: ☎ ☎ ☎ ☎
Q of L: ★ ★ ★ ★
Admissions: (615) 322-2561
Email Address:
  admissions@vanderbilt.edu

Strongest Programs:
Musical Arts
Education
English
Philosophy
Engineering

Vanderbilt University used to be a quiet, conservative school in the heart of the South. But no longer. Vanderbilt is working to diversify its student body and is gaining an impressive national reputation. Sure, football games still require dressing up and finding a date, but the flip side of that formality is a Southern ease and friendliness that make rigorous academics easier to swallow. In contrast to Duke, Emory, and Tulane, which are merely located in the South, Vanderbilt remains a bastion of Southern culture.

The 330-acre Nashville campus was named a national arboretum in the late 1980s. Art and sculptures dot the campus, and architectural styles range from gothic to modern glass and brick. Vandy's campus also includes sixty-acre Peabody College, the central section of which is listed on the National Register of Historic Places. As it tries to preserve its roots, the campus is also growing at an incredibly fast pace. Recent construction has left little of the campus untouched and includes additions to academic buildings, plus new lots and garages to ease the campus's tight parking situation. The engineering school has been overhauled, and many changes have taken place at the Sarratt Student Center, such as a new Stonehenge Cafe.

Vanderbilt undergraduates choose from among four schools—arts and science, engineering, music, and education/human development—with all undergraduates taking their core liberal arts courses in the College of Arts and Science. Specific distribution requirements vary from school to school, but most students get a good dose of writing, math, foreign language, humanities, and natural science courses. "I've taken a wide variety of liberal arts courses and come away with the impression that all of Vanderbilt's academic offerings are well above average," a junior reports. Freshmen in the College of Arts and Science benefit from one of the best writing programs anywhere, and the university's freshman seminars offer small settings and discussion on topics ranging from Country Music in Social Context to Women and Work in the U.S.

Popular majors include social sciences, engineering, psychology, biology, and mathematics. The Peabody College of education and human development—which requires its teacher licensure candidates to double major, usually in a liberal arts field—offers strong programs in elementary and special education, including the opportunity to spend a summer at England's Cambridge University and teach at a British school. Though Vandy has no undergraduate major in business administration, many students make do as economics majors with a business minor. There is also a 3–2 program with the Owen Graduate School of Business. Newer programs include a major and an honors program in women's studies, a minor in Italian studies, a revised history major, and a concentration in collaborative arts for pianists.

Vanderbilt's popular study abroad program features instruction in England, France, Italy, Siena, Ireland, Scotland, Mallorca, Palma de Mallorca, Germany, Spain, Balboa, Florence, China, Japan, and Australia. The optional May session allows students to spend four weeks on one concentrated project—helping some graduate with two majors in four years. Drama classes have been known to tour London theaters during the May term, while some students work at regional archeological digs. Thanks to a multiyear dorm renovation project, students in dorms are networked to the campus library computers. The state-of-the-art library also has one of the country's best videotape collections of network evening news, a special help to students majoring in history and political science.

When it comes to academic etiquette, Vanderbilt students are governed by the school's honor system, which makes unproctored exams possible. First instituted in 1875, this system governs all aspects of a student's academic conduct. Students rave about the faculty. "First rate. My experiences with professors have been extremely positive," says a biomedical engineering major. "Professors love interacting with students," adds a classmate. "I recently passed a professor in the dining room on campus and he interrupted his morning newspaper to talk to me about his fascination with Mark Twain."

While a mixture of conservative Republicans and fraternity and sorority types has set the tone at Vanderbilt in the past, students say the college is slowly becoming more liberal. "Probably the most infamous students are the affluent, socially oriented, designer-clad types," says a student. "But another group—the probably-affluent-but-not-flaunting-it, socially conscious, intellectually minded—is probably a better representation of the student body." The changes may be due to the fact that more students are coming from outside the state of Tennessee and the suburban

> **"I recently passed a professor in the dining room on campus and he interrupted his morning newspaper to talk to me about his fascination with Mark Twain."**

Birmingham–Atlanta corridor and public school graduates now constitute about 55 percent of the student body. Still, Vandy has a much more Southern feel than Duke, the South's other leading private university. The number of minorities is increasing (Asian-Americans constitute 6 percent, African-Americans 6 percent, and Hispanics 4 percent) as is their acceptance by the student body. One student says, "Racial and gender issues are very pivotal on this campus. Political correctness is very important for many people." Vandy's need-based financial aid program is complemented by numerous merit scholarships and more than two hundred athletic scholarships.

Eighty-four percent of Vandy's undergraduates live in the dorms. According to the students, the dorms are "typical to college" and "well maintained." Freshmen occupy singles or doubles in their own special dorms; other accommodations include ten-person townhouses, six-room suites, theme dorms (wellness, environmental awareness, philosophy, foreign language), and apartments. Seniors can live off campus but report that housing is not easy to find, and that the on-campus lottery system—in which seniors get first priority—is a better bet. There are thirteen different dining facilities on campus. Freshmen are required to buy the Dinner Plan, but the quality of the food and service gets rave reviews. Upperclassmen can purchase the Dinner Plan or use other dining facilities. Fraternity houses have cooks, but sorority kitchens are used only once a week. Campus security is tight.

> *The Peabody College of education and human development—which requires its teacher licensure candidates to double major, usually in a liberal arts field—offers strong programs in elementary and special education, including the opportunity to spend a summer at England's Cambridge University and teach at a British school.*

Fifty percent of the women and 34 percent of the men join the Greek system, which is a very active force on the campus. Interaction between the Greeks and non-Greeks is encouraged, although not always successfully, by making many functions open to the whole campus. "Fraternities have parties almost every weekend," a senior says. The Vandy Late Night Program provides free entertainment opportunities off campus from ice-skating to trips to the Grand Ol' Opry. Dating is big at Vandy; the most coveted invitation is the Accolade formal that precedes Homecoming, tickets to which are both expensive and limited. (Funds from the Accolade benefit scholarships for minority students.) Another favorite Vandy tradition is the Rites of Spring festival, a carnival and music festival that takes place on the main lawn. Though Vandy students drink as much alcohol as those at any other school, they have to work to get their hands on it. Open containers are banned in public and kegs are taboo. "The policy is fairly effective, but underage students can find loopholes," a worldly senior says.

Vanderbilt's proximity to Music City USA provides "something for pretty much everyone"—a rich supply of bluegrass, country, and rock music and an abundance of good restaurants and theaters—all within walking distance. Walk in one direction

"Racial and gender issues are very pivotal on this campus. Political correctness is very important for many people."

and there are fajitas and buckets of beer at the San Antonio Taco Company; walk the other way and it's CDs galore at Tower Records. For country music fans, the wax museum in town is a must-see, and there is an ever-increasing amount of brew pubs in the city. Beyond Nashville's borders are the Smokies, state parks with picnic facilities, beautiful lakes, and skiing in the winter. The best road trips are to Memphis (home of Elvis!), New Orleans (for Mardi Gras), the Kentucky Derby, and Atlanta.

In a noteworthy effort to overcome the "disconnect" between athletics and the rest of the university, Chancellor Gordon Gee recently abolished the athletics department and put both intercollegiate and recreational athletics under control of the central administration. Vanderbilt is the smallest—and the only private—institution in the competitive and football-crazy Southeastern Conference (Division IA). Among the campus sports events, basketball is the hot ticket, and both the men's and women's teams draw raves from Vanderbilt fans. Women's soccer has also done quite well, winning the conference for two years straight. Rivals include Alabama, Georgia, and Tennessee, though Vanderbilt almost always comes up on the losing end against these schools in football.

Vanderbilt is quietly building a reputation for excellence that extends beyond its Southern heritage. Its talented students, who enjoy working hard and playing harder, thrive in its uniquely Southern atmosphere. It's not a cheap alternative, exemplified by one of its slogans: "Vanderbilt: It Even Sounds Expensive." But for many, it's money well spent. One student says after he had visited all the schools on his list, he felt "most at home" at Vanderbilt. It's this easygoing charm that makes the Vandy experience so appealing.

Overlaps

Duke, Washington University (MO), Emory, University of Virginia, Northwestern

If You Apply To ➤ **Vanderbilt:** Early decision: Nov. 1, Jan. 15. Regular admissions: Jan. 15. Financial aid: Nov. 1 and Jan. 1 (early decision), Feb. 1. Housing: May 1. No campus or alumni interviews. SATs or ACTs: required (SAT preferred). SAT IIs: optional. Apply to particular school or program. Accepts the common application and electronic applications. Essay question: applicant's choice of topic.

Vassar College

Poughkeepsie, NY 12604

It is hard to imagine that Vassar once considered picking up and moving to Yale in the 1960s rather than become a co-ed institution. Thirty-five years after admitting men, still on its ancient and picturesque campus, Vassar is a thriving, highly selective, avante-garde institution with an accent on the fine arts and humanities.

Once known as the most liberal of the Seven Sisters, and still a bastion of the left, Vassar stands out among its small-college peers because of its curricular flexibility, proximity to city life, tolerance, and diversity. A Vassar diploma, whether held by a man or a woman, is well respected in the job market, and a strong Vassar GPA is highly regarded at graduate schools. But even more important is the experience behind the sheepskin and transcript.

The college's one-thousand-acre campus, just outside the town of Poughkeepsie, New York, is beautifully landscaped. Daffodils circle the two lakes in springtime and foliage is inescapable in the fall. Encircled by a fieldstone wall, the campus includes an astronomical observatory with one of the largest telescopes in the Northeast, a state-of-the-art chemistry building, a farm with an ecological field station, and an art center boasting 13,500 works from Ancient Egypt to modern art. The architecture is varied, with neo-Gothic overtones, and includes buildings designed by such notables as Marcel Breuer, Eero Saarinen, and James Renwick. In the past three years, a $25 million technological upgrade of the main library and a $12 million expansion of the athletic facilities was completed. In 2003, a Center for Drama and Film opened and two new townhouse complexes were finished for student living.

> "Professors are there for you all the time, they come to the races, grab lunch with students and live in the dorm—all while helping you with research papers."

There is great curricular freedom at Vassar because there is no core curriculum, which allows students to construct their own multidisciplinary area of interest. However, all students must take a Freshman Course, which includes a writing- and presentation-oriented seminar. The students must also complete a course that emphasizes quantitative analysis as well as either test out of or prove proficiency in a foreign language. Vassar strikes a happy balance between being a competitive and laid-back environment by keeping students sincerely motivated. "Vassar students are smart, friendly, creative, well-rounded, and intellectually curious," says one senior. The professors are accomplished in their fields, having written acclaimed books and edited major works, but they still make time for students—inside the classroom and beyond. "Professors are there for you all the time, they come to the races, grab lunch with students and live in the dorm—all while helping you with research papers" enthuses a senior.

Seminars and tutorials are the rule here, even for introductory courses. Popular classes fill up quickly, but on the positive side, friendships with faculty members develop easily (80 percent of the professors live on campus). Exams run on an honor system. Most people study in the Gothic-style library, with its delightful decor and twenty-four-hour study room for those all-night crams.

The biology building houses two electron microscopes and music students are spoiled by a grand collection of Steinway pianos, sprinkled all over campus, and their own superb library of scores and books. Vassar runs the Powerhouse Summer Theater program in which apprentices are accepted from around the country to take classes, perform Shakespeare, and work in some capacities with a professional

Website: www.vassar.edu
Location: Small town
Total Enrollment: 2,350
Undergraduates: 2,350
Male/Female: 40/60
SAT Ranges: V 650–730
  M 630–700
ACT Range: 28–32
Financial Aid: 55%
Expense: Pr $ $ $ $
Phi Beta Kappa: Yes
Applicants: 5,733
Accepted: 31%
Enrolled: 36%
Grad in 6 Years: 89%
Returning Freshmen: 96%
Academics: ✍ ✍ ✍ ✍ ½
Social: ☎ ☎ ☎
Q of L: ★ ★ ★ ★
Admissions: (845) 437-7300
Email Address:
  admissions@vassar.edu

Strongest Programs:
English
History
Psychology
Biology
Drama
Political Science
Art History

company from New York City. Also highly regarded, the Undergraduate Research Summer Institute (URSI) pays students a stipend to work one-on-one with faculty members on scientific research projects, either at Vassar or at off-campus sites. The Ford Scholars program offers similar opportunities for student–faculty collaboration in the humanities and social sciences. Vassar is also one of the few remaining colleges that allow students to study abroad and use their financial aid to support them. Approximately 30 to 40 percent of the students participate in the Vassar-sponsored away programs that include studying in countries such as England, Germany, France, Spain, Morocco, Ireland, and Italy. For domestic study, Vassar has an agreement with the Bank Street College in NYC for students interested in urban education. There are programs with the other eleven members of the Twelve College Exchange* or at any of four historically black colleges, as well as opportunities to participate in a drama production at the Eugene O'Neil Theater and a maritime studies program at the Mystic Seaport,* both in Connecticut.

"The dorms are being renovated and updated to include state-of-the-art technology and they are also beautiful, comfortable, and convenient."

Sixty-five percent of Vassar's students come from the top tenth of their class; only 26 percent are New York natives. Minorities account for a substantial subset of the student population: Asian-Americans make up 10 percent, African-Americans 6 percent, and Hispanics 6 percent. Vassar has a commitment to its ALANA Center, which supports and recognizes students of color and other ethnic and cultural groups, and students delight in the diversity found on campus. "The campus tends to be very politically active," says a student, citing "gay rights, U.S. foreign policy, economic issues, and even the community issues of the city of Poughkeepsie" as important to Vassar students.

Housing is guaranteed for four years and 98 percent of the students live on campus. According to a senior, "The dorms are being renovated and updated to include state-of-the-art technology and they are also beautiful, comfortable, and convenient." All but one of the nine dorms is co-ed. The word is that Lathrop is the best dorm for freshmen, but no halls are reserved strictly for first-year students. Juniors and seniors favor the college-owned townhouses (five-person suites) or the four-person Terrace Apartments, both with kitchens and living rooms, while some prefer the communal living in Ferry House.

The town around Vassar is not a your typical college town. Poughkeepsie is an old industrial town that leaves, as far as many of Vassar's more cosmopolitan students are concerned, much to be desired. Still, the town is the seat of Duchess County government so internships with law firms and political offices are easy to come by, a student says. Most of Vassar students do some kind of community work—there are clubs like Vassar Volunteers and PEACE, which get involved in community issues. However, most social activities—films, drama, and musical entertainment—are found on campus. There is also an on-campus dance club called Matthew's Mug that is packed on weekends and a coffeehouse for those not yet of legal age. Vassar is not a big drinking school and if you are caught, you may be required to attend alcohol counseling and your "party privileges and admittance into the campus dance clubs may be revoked," says a student. Nonalcohol-centered activities include worthwhile jaunts to Roosevelt's Hyde Park and the Culinary Institute of America (for gourmet meals). Typically road trips include visits to New York City and Boston if the students want a change from the on-campus activities.

"The passion and excitement everyone has for Vassar makes it the best place on Earth."

The annual gala formals bring high society to Vassar twice a year. There are many other social traditions, including the Founders Day carnival in May, which includes a Ferris wheel, outdoor movie, bands, and fireworks by the lake. Another favorite ritual is called Primal Scream—where all the students go out to the quad and scream at midnight the night before finals. Afternoon teatime—yes, tea—in the Rose Parlor of historic Main Building remains a popular ritual for unwinding after a day of classes.

Varsity athletics are experiencing a renaissance; tennis and volleyball are among the strongest offerings. The men's volleyball teams have won conference championships over the past few years, while the women's tennis, rugby, and volleyball squads have excelled. Women's crew is also ranked sixteenth in the nation.

Vassar's academically challenging environment is the perfect place for the passionate, intellectually curious student who is trying to learn about themselves and the world around them. "All the students, faculty, administrators act as one large family. Between the small number of students and the beautifully manicured campus, Vassar has been an amazing nurturing home," says a student. "The passion and excitement everyone has for Vassar makes it the best place on Earth."

Overlaps

Brown, Wesleyan, Yale, NYU, Tufts

If You Apply To ➤ **Vassar:** Early decision: Nov. 15, Jan. 1. Regular admissions and financial aid: Jan. 1. Guarantees to meet demonstrated need. No campus interviews. Alumni interviews: optional, informational. SATs or ACTs: required. SAT IIs: required (any three). Accepts the Common Application and electronic applications. Essay question: significant experience, achievement, person, or matter; also requests a graded copy of an analytical essay written in eleventh or twelfth grade; "your space" (optional).

University of Vermont

194 South Prospect Street, Burlington, VT 05401

For an out-of-stater sizing up public universities, there could hardly be a more appealing place than UVM. The size is manageable, Burlington is a fabulous college town, and Lake Champlain and the Green Mountains are on your doorstep. UVM feels like a private university, but alas, it is also priced like one.

Nestled within New England's gorgeous scenery (its acronym doubles for Universitas Viridis Montis, Latin for "University of the Green Mountains"), the University of Vermont is a groovy place that inspires students to hit the books as well as the nearby ski slopes. Although a public university, the high-caliber academics and ample research opportunities are reminiscent of a private university setting—and so is the tuition. The school's price tag, high even for Vermont natives, is offset by generous financial aid and attractive growth plans proposed by the school's leader. Students agree that the picturesque setting, close relationships with faculty, and the school's emphasis on undergraduate excellence create a winning recipe.

Perched on the placid shores of Lake Champlain, the UVM campus, a pleasant mix of Colonial, high Victorian Gothic, and functional modern buildings, is located in Burlington (the state's largest city and cultural mecca, virtually on Canada's doorstep). In the heart of the campus, each building surrounding the manicured park is recognized in the National Registry of Historic Places. New additions include the Health Science Research Facility, which will add 110,000 square feet of research space, the Living/Learning Center, a cybercafe in the library, and the $4.5 million Rubenstein Ecosystem Science Laboratory at the nearby Lake Champlain Basin. A two-hundred-bed apartment-style housing complex for juniors, seniors, and graduate students is scheduled for completion in the fall of 2004. There are also plans for an 825-bed suite-style housing facility in the center of campus.

Website: www.uvm.edu
Location: Small city
Total Enrollment: 10,314
Undergraduates: 7,601
Male/Female: 44/56
SAT Ranges: V 520–620
  M 520–620
ACT Range: 22–27
Financial Aid: 50%
Expense: Pub $ $ $ $
Phi Beta Kappa: Yes
Applicants: 9,776
Accepted: 71%
Enrolled: 26%
Grad in 6 Years: 70%
Returning Freshmen: 84%
Academics: 🖋 🖋 🖋 ½
Social: 🐻 🐻 🐻 🐻 🐻
Q of L: ★ ★ ★ ★ ★

(Continued)
Admissions: (802) 656-3370
Email Address:
  admissions@uvm.edu

Strongest Programs:
Environmental Studies
Business Administration
English
Health
Natural and Life Sciences
Philosophy
Psychology
Political Science

The Living and Learning Center is an imaginative residential–academic program where like-minded students live together in suites and create their own programs with a faculty advisor's help.

The Gund Institute for Ecological Economics has relocated to UVM from the University of Maryland. The institute develops policy and management practices to protect vital ecosystems worldwide.

Like the architecture, UVM's academic atmosphere is varied. "The academic climate is not cut-throat competitive," says one student, "but academic pressure is self-inflicted." There are no university-wide general education requirements at the seven undergraduate colleges, though most students must enroll in at least thirty credits (ten courses) in the arts, humanities, social sciences, languages, literature, mathematics, and the sciences. A three-credit Race and Culture course is also required. Premeds and physical therapy students benefit from UVM's fine medical school, and learning-disabled students are supported in all majors. Some of the most popular majors include business administration, psychology, English, biology/biological sciences, and political science. Weaknesses appear in a few social science areas, such as anthropology and the fine arts. Changes in the curriculum include new majors in nuclear medicine technology, environmental engineering, agriculture and resource entrepreneurship, and Italian studies.

"Our students are dedicated to the environment."

At UVM, you can design your own major. You can also participate in the Living/Learning Center, an imaginative residential–academic program where like-minded students live together in suites and create their own programs with a faculty advisor's help. Freshmen in Arts and Sciences may participate in the Teacher–Advisor Program (TAP), a special seminar where the professor also serves as the enrolled students' advisor. The internship program is popular, and co-ops are available in engineering, business, recreation management, and agriculture. About four hundred students per year partake in UVM study abroad programs in South America, Western Europe, Asia, and the Pacific Rim.

"Sometimes it can be difficult registering for classes, especially as a first-year student when upperclassmen have priority registration," says one student. By junior year, most students are in classes with twenty-five or fewer students, which helps foster relationships with UVM's outstanding faculty. "The quality of teaching is very high," reports one English/psychology major. And the profs are more than accessible: "Many teachers hold review sessions outside of class time to ensure the students are understanding the material," says a sophomore. Advisors get high marks, too.

UVM students have much in common: 94 percent are white, and most are New Englanders. Many complain at the relative lack of diversity on campus: Hispanic and Asian-American students make up 2 percent each, while African-Americans represent 1 percent of the student body. The campus political climate is unabashedly liberal, and recycling and other environmental concerns are big issues, say students. "Our students are dedicated to the environment," claims one senior.

"The quality of teaching is very high. Many teachers hold review sessions outside of class time to ensure the students are understanding the material."

"Political correctness is important to people up here, especially where we are in Vermont, a state known for it's liberal views on many tough issues," notes a junior. Nearly 2,700 merit-based scholarships are available to students who also demonstrate financial need, and UVM also offers 158 athletic scholarships.

There are twenty-six residence halls on campus, each with its own flavor. That's a good thing because freshmen and sophomores are required to live on campus and they select rooms by lottery. Dorms are situated in three residential areas separated by ten-minute walks. Other on-campus options include the Living and Learning suites, co-ops, and apartments. Redstone Campus is described as the rowdiest area, while the best freshman dorms are said to be Chittenden or Buckham, which feature tiny rooms and a great atmosphere. Still, almost all juniors and seniors rent apartments in town.

A popular campus T-shirt warns: "If you want to party, come to UVM. If you want to stay, study!" While students here buckle down when they have to, they also know how to have fun when the week's studying is done. Skiing takes the prize as the most popular pastime. College-sponsored movies, dances, bars, and coffeehouses are all big draws. Only 3 percent of men and 2 percent of women join Greek organizations. One annual festival of sorts is the Primal Scream, a collective scream on campus every midnight during finals week. Underage drinking isn't tolerated, though students agree that it does happen. Students, though, are "much more aware and cautious" and less likely to throw wild parties.

As a venue, students say Burlington is "the greatest college town!" It's stylish, with symphonies, art galleries, chic shopping, and lively bars and restaurants, as well as ample community service opportunities. "There is so much to do and everything is within walking distance," says a junior. But as much as they love their little city, students look forward to getting out of town. The Outing Club is one of UVM's most popular student organizations, as the nearby Green Mountains, White Mountains, and Adirondacks offer prime hiking, skiing, and backpacking. The best road trips are Montreal (ninety minutes) and Boston (four hours).

The hockey team competes in the ECAC, has ranked as high as second nationally, and is the pride and joy of UVM sports. Catamount games are always sold out; students get access to tickets before the general public, and there is a lengthy waiting list for community members. Soccer draws crowds in the fall—there is no football team. Men's and women's basketball are solid programs, as are field hockey and men's and women's track, and the ski teams are NCAA powerhouses. Students love intramural sports, especially tennis and broomball (ice hockey played with brooms, on shoes instead of skates).

"Groovy UV" is a generally laid-back campus, but students are curious, intellectual, and willing to work hard. And as UVM continues blending the high points of a small liberal arts school, such as one-on-one attention, with the traits of a prime undergraduate research institution, including generous funding for student projects, the end result is sure to be sweet.

> *One annual festival of sorts is the Primal Scream, a collective scream on campus every midnight during finals week.*

Overlaps

University of New Hampshire, University of Massachusetts, University of Colorado, Boston University, Ithaca

If You Apply To ➤

UVM: Early decision: Nov. 1. Regular admissions: Jan. 15. Financial aid: Feb. 10. Does not guarantee to meet demonstrated need. Campus and alumni interviews: optional, informational. SATs or ACTs: required. SAT IIs: optional. Apply to individual schools or programs. Accepts the Common Application and electronic applications. Essay questions: significant experience, outside interests, topic of your choice.

Villanova University

800 Lancaster Avenue, Villanova, PA 19085-1672

Set in an upscale suburb, Villanova is Philadelphia's counterpart to Boston College. As at BC, about 80 percent of the students are Roman Catholic (compared to a figure of about half at Georgetown). The troika of business, engineering, and premed are popular at 'Nova, as is nursing.

Villanova University takes pride in its Augustinian roots, even basing its admissions essay on one of St. Augustine's teachings about "right reason." The school has all the trappings of a typical Roman Catholic university, from strong academics to deeply rooted traditions and rivalries and students firmly dedicated to their faith. The emphasis on community creates an "inviting and friendly atmosphere," says a sophomore. "All are welcomed," adds a senior. "All feel comfortable, and all are here to enjoy college."

Website: www.admission
.villanova.edu
Location: Suburban
Total Enrollment: 10,489
Undergraduates: 7,375
Male/Female: 49/51

(Continued)

SAT Ranges: V 570–660
   M 590–690

ACT Range: 27–30

Financial Aid: 76%

Expense: Pr $ $ $ $

Phi Beta Kappa: Yes

Applicants: 10,897

Accepted: 49%

Enrolled: 31%

Grad in 6 Years: 85%

Returning Freshmen: 93%

Academics: ✍ ✍ ✍

Social: ☎ ☎ ☎

Q of L: ★ ★ ★

Admissions: (610) 519-4000

Email Address:
   gotovu@villanova.edu

Strongest Programs:

Finance

Communication

Nursing

Accounting

Engineering

Villanova was recently included on the list of the top twenty-five most connected campuses.

Villanova's lush campus of more than 250 acres once served as the estate of a Revolutionary War officer and is situated near Philadelphia. The campus continues to keep some of its historical roots with ivy-covered buildings, well-kept lawns, and secluded, tree-lined walkways. As Villanova continues to grow, a new health center has opened, the business school has been revamped, and future renovations such as a new gym and a performing arts center are being considered.

The troika of business, engineering, and communication are popular at 'Nova, as is nursing. Aside from the College of Commerce and Finance, undergraduates may enroll in the College of Engineering, the College of Liberal Arts and Sciences, or the College of Nursing. The programs that tend to be the most popular include finance, nursing, and engineering. In fact, the engineering school enjoys strong regional recognition. General education requirements vary by school, but all students take the two-semester Core Humanities Seminar, team-taught by members of the English, history, philosophy, and religious studies departments. These courses stress discussion, intensive writing, readings from primary texts, and close student–faculty relationships. They also let students study a topic or theme from several perspectives, with an emphasis on Christian thought and values.

Coursework at Villanova is considered "rigorous but the atmosphere is not overly competitive or cut-throat," according to one student. The students enjoy classes that are always taught by "professors, never TAs, who make a great effort to know your name and keep their door open," according to a student. There are few problems graduating within four years, and Villanovans register for classes online. However, those who don't log in early enough may find it tough to get into popular electives, though professors are helpful when students really need to get into their classes. The one-million-volume library is adequate for most needs. An honors program is available to about two hundred students, by invitation only.

Many of Villanova's students are from the East Coast and upper middle class families, and 84 percent are white. Apparently the efforts by the Multicultural Affairs office are paying off, as African-Americans, Hispanics, and Asian-Americans each comprise nearly 5 percent of the student body. In fact, a philosophy major says, "One of the primary social concerns on campus revolves around diversity. Although the student body is not noticeably diverse, it is accepting of other faiths, races, and ethnicities." More than a thousand merit scholarships are available, as are a wide variety of athletic scholarships.

"One of the primary social concerns on campus revolves around diversity."

Two-thirds of the student body lives in Villanova's dorms, which are guaranteed for three years and considered "to be well-maintained and comfortable." Everyone seems to agree that the new on-campus junior apartments are "unbelievable." Freshmen live primarily on the South Campus Circle, while upperclassmen take their chances in the lottery system. A senior says most seniors move off campus, despite steep rents and neighbors hostile to college types; doing so lets them skip the meal plan. About 10 percent of Villanova students are from the Philadelphia area, and they avoid the hassle entirely by commuting from home.

Even with the presence of some commuters, Villanova isn't a suitcase school. Weekend social life centers around campus events and parties, some sponsored by Greek groups, which claim 8 percent of the men and 25 percent of the women. Officially, the campus is dry, and Pennsylvania state law says no one under twenty-one can drink. Students do manage to drink somehow if they are really motivated, but the juniors and seniors seem to agree that "bars are tough on fake IDs" and you will get "fined or suspended if caught." Alternatives to drinking include movies and dances, usually held in the school's multimillion-dollar Connelly Center. On Fridays and Saturdays there is something called "Late Night at Villanova" where comedians, bands, or dance parties provide an opportunity for students to get together with friends in a safe environment. Despite the tough courses, the students seem to take pride in finding the time to socialize, which seems to be comprised heavily of community involvement. A junior says, "The students tend to be active and enjoy being part of the community. Involvement in campus organizations is extremely competitive because the majority of students are interested in furthering their involvement."

"All feel comfortable, and all are here to enjoy college."

Community service opportunities are plentiful, and Villanova has the largest student-run Special Olympics, in addition to Habitat for Humanity and Big Brother/Big Sister programs.

Those who tire of Villanova's suburban setting can be in Philadelphia in twelve minutes, thanks to local commuter rail. Also, trips to New York only take an hour and a half and road trips to Boston and the south are popular. The city's cultural and social opportunities include museums and pro sports, as well as events at numerous other colleges and universities, from La Salle and Temple to St. Joseph's, Drexel, and Penn.

When they're not out socializing, Villanova students are cheering for their Wildcats. Students frequently "unleash the Wildcat within" against their rivals. The women's track and field squad brought home the Big East title in 2000. In fact, men's track is strong, too, and both teams sometimes see their members going for Olympic gold against the best runners in the world. The football team plays to sold-out crowds in Division IAA. The school's fitness complex has a swimming center and an indoor track.

Despite the changes in the world around them, Villanova continues to be a Catholic university devoted to its students, community, and strong traditions, both spiritual and academically. While the school takes pride in tradition, it recognizes the technology improvements, continuing upgrades to facilities, and changing and improving educational programs will help their students remain competitive in the workplace and the world beyond.

Overlaps

Boston College, University of Notre Dame, Lehigh, Loyola (MD), College of Holy Cross

If You Apply To ➤

Villanova: Early action: Nov. 1. Regular admissions: Jan. 7. Financial aid: Mar. 8. Does not guarantee to meet demonstrated need. No campus or alumni interviews. SATs or ACTs: required. SAT IIs: required in French and Spanish only for placement. Apply to a particular school or program. Accepts electronic applications. Essay question.

University of Virginia

P.O. Box 400160, Charlottesville, VA 22904

Is it Thomas Jefferson? The Romanesque architecture? The Charlottesville air? Whatever it is, students nationwide go ga-ga for UVA, where competition for out-of-state admission has hit the Ivy League level. UVA combines old-line conservatism with a touch of rowdy frat boy.

Easily one of the most prestigious public schools in the nation, the University of Virginia blends rich tradition with progressive attitudes. Perhaps that's a mark of its founder. UVA is known to all in Charlottesville as Mr. Jefferson's University. Not just any Mr. Jefferson, mind you, but *the* Mr. Jefferson, author of the Declaration of Independence. Though he passed away more than a hundred and fifty years ago, he is referred to here as if he ran down to the apothecary shop for a bit of snuff and will be back in a moment. Of all his accomplishments, Jefferson was arguably

Website: www.virginia.edu
Location: Small city
Total Enrollment: 23,144
Undergraduates: 13,805
Male/Female: 45/55

(Continued)

SAT Ranges: V 600–700
  M 620–720
ACT Range: 25–31
Financial Aid: 22%
Expense: Pub $ $ $
Phi Beta Kappa: Yes
Applicants: 14,320
Accepted: 39%
Enrolled: 54%
Grad in 6 Years: 92%
Returning Freshmen: 97%
Academics: 🖉 🖉 🖉 🖉 🖉
Social: ☎ ☎ ☎ ☎
Q of L: ★ ★ ★ ★ ★
Admissions: (434) 982-3200
Email Address:
  undergradadmission@
  virginia.edu

Strongest Programs:
English
Foreign Languages
Physiology
Government
Economics
History
Biochemistry
Religious Studies

Mr. Jefferson founded UVA as a place where students could come together to "drink the cup of knowledge," but today's undergraduates seem to favor a different sort of brew.

proudest of UVA—he even asked that his epitaph speak to his role in creating the university rather than his presidency of the United States.

Located just east of the Blue Ridge Mountains in central Virginia, UVA's campus was designed by Jefferson himself, and still uses many of its original buildings. At the core of the university is Jefferson's "academical village," with its majestic white pillars, serpentine walls, and extensive brickwork. The village is built around a rectangular terraced green—called the Lawn—that is flanked by two rows of identical one-story rooms that are reserved for undergraduate student leaders. Five pavilions, each in a different style, accent each side of the Lawn. Both the rooms and the pavilions enter into a colonnaded walkway that fronts the Lawn. Behind the rows of buildings are public gardens. The Rotunda, a half-scale model of the Roman Pantheon, overlooks the Lawn. Clark Hall for environmental sciences is a new addition, the Health Science building was expanded, and construction has begun on an addition to the architecture school, a special collections library, a basketball arena, and a twelve-hundred-space parking garage.

Elite among public institutions of higher education, UVA holds its own against the best of the private schools, too. Students are accepted into the four-year schools of engineering, nursing, and architecture, but the vast majority enter the liberal arts college. According to students, the best departments are history, English, religious studies, and the School of Commerce. A planning commission on the fine and performing arts is working on improving those departments, and a proposed arts precinct will include a new museum, library, and concert hall. The most popular majors are economics, commerce, psychology, English, and biology. UVA's school of education offers a five-year program that culminates in a B.A. from the College of Arts and Sciences and a Master of Teaching degree from the education school. The International Residential College fosters close contact with faculty and special short courses.

After their second year, about three hundred Arts and Sciences students transfer into the commerce school, but competition for these spots is tough. Virginia requires students in the College of Arts and Sciences and the commerce school to master a foreign language. Arts and Sciences students must also take courses in humanities and fine arts, social science, natural sciences and mathematics, non-Western studies, and composition. All freshmen in the college are required to take English composition. The emphasis is on top-level academic programs taught within nationally recognized departments. With more than four million volumes and one of the nation's largest collections of online materials in six digital centers, the library is more than adequate. The computer science department also has a state-of-the-art virtual reality lab. Life is notoriously competitive at UVA. "Every aspect of life has a competitive edge to it," one senior says. "The students are ambitious, always striving for the best."

> **"Every aspect of life has a competitive edge to it. The students are ambitious, always striving for the best."**

A number of special programs are offered in addition to the regular curriculum. The most prestigious of these is the Echols Scholars program, which exempts students from distribution and major-field requirements and lets them loose to explore the academic disciplines as they see fit. The school invites up to two hundred freshmen (plan on total SATs solidly above 1400) into the program and houses them together for their first year. The Rodman Scholars program in the engineering school selects students based on financial need, leadership qualities, and scholarship. The Distinguished Majors program enables qualified students to pursue an independent study during their third and fourth years. Three residential colleges house approximately eleven hundred students, mostly upperclassmen, with a hundred faculty members participating (a handful even living in the student housing).

One focuses on international themes, with nearly one-quarter of the students hailing from other countries. Professors are said to be highly accessible and friendly. A senior says professors "have engaged me in research, hour-long discussions, and other academic pursuits." The University Seminar program features prominent faculty teaching twenty first-year students in a seminar learning environment. The school has added a coffee bar in the library and a fund subsidizing faculty–student lunches, both aimed at fostering informal conversations.

Virginia is noted for its honor system, which was instituted by students in 1842 after no one owned up to shooting a professor on the Lawn. "Students really do govern themselves and we are given a large amount of responsibility and opportunity," a foreign affairs major says. Don't take it lightly—the penalty for infractions is a swift dismissal from campus. A number of controversial cases recently produced a measure of reform, and discussions continue about the appropriateness of the single-sanction system and even the continued existence of the student-run honor system. But rest assured, some form of the honor code will remain a way of life here, as many students say they feel comfortable leaving backpacks and calculators unattended without worry of thieves. "Students here are kicked out if they are caught lying, cheating, or stealing, which makes for a really unique community of trust," a junior says.

Admission for out-of-state students—29 percent of the undergraduate body—is more competitive than for in-staters, but nearly everyone who gets in is highly qualified. Many students hail from Washington, D.C., and suburbs of northern Virginia, while most out-of-staters come from New York,

"Students really do govern themselves and we are given a large amount of responsibility and opportunity."

New Jersey, Pennsylvania, and Maryland. The student body is somewhat diverse: 9 percent are African-American, 11 percent are Asian-American, and 3 percent are Hispanic. The consensus here is that while race relations are not overly hostile, there is a sense that African-American students "self-segregate," as one student says. Among the eighty-five merit scholarships offered at Virginia are twenty-five to thirty highly prized Jefferson Scholarships, which are awarded annually by the alumni association and are good for full tuition, as well as room and board. Up to seven out-of-state African-Americans get renewable stipends of $10,000 a year. About 450 athletes are awarded athletic scholarships in fifteen sports. UVA recently announced that low-income students will receive grants and no longer be required to take out loans.

A conspicuous exception to the historic character of most of the Virginia campus is the Hereford College, a residential and dining complex that features contemporary architecture described by the *New York Times* as "proudly, almost defiantly modern." All first-year students live "on grounds," as do some top fourth-year leaders and honors students who qualify for coveted singles in the academic village. Fifty-four percent trek off campus but still stay involved with the university. Commuters praise the university's bus system, which is important because campus parking is extremely limited. Meal plans are required for first-year students, while many upperclassmen either cook for themselves or take meals at their Greek houses. Thirty percent each of men and women make up the Greek system, which has a fairly prominent role in campus social life.

Mr. Jefferson founded UVA as a place where students could come together to "drink the cup of knowledge," but today's undergraduates seem to favor a different sort of brew. Studious Virginians by day can metamorphose into the Rowdy Wahoos (a nickname derived from one of the college cheers about the fish that can drink twice its weight, usually shortened to Hoos) by night. As with most college students, drinking is a favorite pastime, and underage students have little problem obtaining alcohol, though the administration has been more strictly enforcing drinking rules. UVA has a dry rush, and guest lists are now required for all fraternity parties. The fraternities assume an obligation to provide social activities not only for their own members but for the campus at large, and the "big weekends" are still big, though far less legendary than in the early eighties. The student-run University Union and more than three hundred student organizations offer movies, concerts, social hours, and other extracurricular activities. Students also tend to immerse themselves in community service activities. One traditional local event is Foxfield, in which students dress up and host catered parties prior to attending a steeple-chase horse race. Other famous traditions include streaking the Lawn, doing the "Corner Crawl" on your twenty-first birthday, dressing up for football games (a relic from the days when UVA was all male and the games were an opportunity to meet women), and an annual visit by a hypnotist that draws more than ten thousand people. The nationally recognized Madison House is the umbrella group for a host of student volunteer groups.

Charlottesville "is the perfect college town." From a ton of amazing restaurants—the town is becoming famous for its gorgeous vineyards and wineries—to bars, shops, theaters, and other cultural attractions, this town is a great complement to campus. But if the city limits get old, students can road trip two hours to Washington or Richmond. Outdoorsy folks can hike, bike, ski, and sightsee in the nearby Blue Ridge Mountains and daydream along its famous Skyline Drive.

Big-time Atlantic Coast Conference basketball has long been an integral part of UVA life and students get fired up anytime their team takes the court. Gridiron action is hit-or-miss, but support for the Cavs runs deep. Intramurals attract a healthy number of students who are eager to show their stuff.

Students who attend UVA are generally thrilled with their situation: top academics, a fabulous social life, a stunning campus, and opportunities to learn with some of the best educators in the country. From its uniquely American roots and beloved legacy from Thomas Jefferson, the school has maintained its special traditions that make for "the best memories I have," says a fourth-year. And though it's unclear whether the eloquent Mr. Jefferson would approve of the rather coarse tone of a popular rhetorical question on campus—"Hoo's Your Daddy?"—he wouldn't argue with the answer.

Overlaps

William and Mary, Duke, Virginia Tech, University of Pennsylvania, Cornell University

If You Apply To ➤

UVA: Early decision: Nov. 1. Regular admissions: Jan. 2. Financial aid: Mar. 1. Does not guarantee to meet demonstrated need. Campus interviews: optional, informational. No alumni interviews. SATs or ACTs: required. SAT IIs: required (writing, math, and science, foreign language, or history). Apply to particular schools or programs. Accepts electronic applications. Essay question: varies.

Virginia Polytechnic Institute and State University

Blacksburg, VA 24061

Hokie Nation is tickled pink about the rise of its football team, which has become a consistent national power. Engineering has always been Tech's calling card; business and architecture are also popular. Blacksburg is a nice college town, but is far from the population centers near the coast.

Website: www.vt.edu

Although its full name is the Virginia Polytechnic Institute and State University, those in the know just call it Virginia Tech. Long-known for its solid engineering and architecture programs, this Southern university has recently garnered more national attention for its football team than its academics. It's no wonder students want to spend four years at the "Hokie Pokie."

Set on a plateau in the scenic Blue Ridge mountains, Tech's campus occupies three thousand acres and comes complete with a duck pond, hiking trails, and a two-hundred-year-old plantation that is a local landmark. Students enjoy unlimited outdoor recreation thanks to the proximity of the Jefferson National Forest, the Appalachian Trail, the scenic Blue Ridge Parkway, and the majestic old New River. The campus buildings are an attractive mix of gray limestone structures, Colonial-style brick, and modern cement buildings. Newer facilities include the 150,000-square-foot Advanced Communications and Information Technology Center (ACITC).

Virginia Tech is best known for its first-rate technical and professional training. For undergrads with an appetite for engineering, Tech has programs for every taste, including aerospace, ocean, biological systems, civil, chemical, computer, electrical, industrial and systems, materials, mechanical (the most popular), and mining. The Pamplin College of Business is also prominent, and the five-year architecture program is considered one of the nation's best. Though no longer Tech's centerpiece, the College of Agriculture and Life Sciences remains strong, especially in animal science. Students in the College of Natural Resources can choose from such concentrations

> "On campus you can do anything from handing in homework to checking grades to checking out what movies are playing, all by computer."

as environmental conservation, fisheries science, forestry, and wildlife management. The College of Education merged with the College of Human Resources, where Hospitality and Tourism is the best-known program.

Students in the sciences reap the benefits of their high-tech environment; other disciplines do not fare so well. The humanities have been hard hit by budget cuts. In particular, "religious studies, foreign languages, and philosophy are dwindling away," says a senior. One bright spot is internationally known poet Nikki Giovanni, who teaches creative writing and advanced poetry. The university also has a tradition of excellence in the performing arts, and the school's theater group has received more awards from the American College Theater Arts Festival than any other college in the Southeast.

Introductory class size tends to be large—sometimes well into the hundreds—and the budget ax has only made matters worse. Most of the big lecture classes are taught by full-time faculty, though discussions and grading are generally handled by TAs. Nevertheless, a communications major says her professors "keep you on the edge of your seat." An accounting major adds, "Freshmen are taught by professors and grad students." All students are required to take courses in English, math, humanities, and social and natural science. There is also a foreign language requirement, though high school coursework may cover this. The fifteen hundred or so students who participate in the university honors program are guaranteed access to top faculty and research opportunities. Tech is among the nation's leaders in the integration of computers into all facets of life. All freshmen are required to own a computer. Says an engineering major, "On campus you can do anything from handing in homework to checking grades to checking out what movies are playing, all by computer."

Each year, more than one thousand students take advantage of Tech's co-op opportunities available in almost all majors. The nationally acclaimed Small Business Institute program enables faculty-led groups of business majors to work with local merchants, analyze their problems, and make suggestions on how to increase profits. The Corps of Cadets, a tradition once on the verge of extinction, has made a comeback. Cadets earn a minor in leadership and can choose from three tracks: military/ROTC, civic professions, or a combination of the two.

(Continued)
Location: Small town
Total Enrollment: 27,662
Undergraduates: 21,468
Male/Female: 59/41
SAT Ranges: V 540–630
    M 570–650
Financial Aid: 66%
Expense: Pub $
Phi Beta Kappa: Yes
Applicants: 18,028
Accepted: 69%
Enrolled: 39%
Grad in 6 Years: 00%
Returning Freshmen: 90%
Academics: ✍ ✍ ✍
Social: ☎ ☎ ☎
Q of L: ★ ★ ★ ★
Admissions: (540) 231-6267
Email Address:
    vtadmiss@vt.edu

Strongest Programs:
Engineering
Architecture and Urban Studies
Business
Sciences
Human Resources and
    Education
Mathematics
Forestry and Wildlife
    Resources

Not surprisingly, the admissions office is inundated with out-of-state applicants, which means stiff competition for the 25 percent of the slots available to non-Virginians.

Students looking at pricey Northeastern technical schools will find Tech a real bargain. Not surprisingly, the admissions office is inundated with out-of-state applicants, which means stiff competition for the 25 percent of the slots available to non-Virginians. Tech's relative isolation from major cities is a drag on minority recruitment: African-Americans and Hispanics account for only 8 percent of the student body. Asian-Americans account for another 7 percent. Eighty percent graduated in the top quarter of their high school class. Students with financial need who apply for aid before the deadline receive priority consideration; those who apply later are likely to be out of luck. Tech hands out a few hundred athletic scholarships, and there are merit scholarships available to qualified students.

Tech housing is nothing to write home about, but adequate to meet the needs of most students. "Rooms are on the small side, but they provide all you need to live," says a freshman. Some twenty-five undergraduate dorms serve 8,400 students; 32 percent of the student body live on campus, though only freshmen and the Corps of Cadets are required to. Most upperclassmen live off campus in nearby apartment complexes. Dietrick's Depot, the largest dining hall on campus, was recently renovated. Three specialty lines supplement the standard dining-hall fare to create an intimate, cafe-style atmosphere. Students who are committed to a healthy lifestyle can opt to reside in the W.E.L.L. (Wellness Environment for Living and Learning), which will provide them with a substance-free atmosphere, and includes special healthy-living courses and is overseen by a specially trained wellness staff.

Leisure-time favorites include school-sponsored plays, jazz concerts, arts and crafts fairs, and dances. The nearby Cascades National Park is an especially popular retreat for lovers and camping jocks alike, and tubing down the New River is a ritual for summer students. Thirteen percent of the men and 15 percent of the women join fraternities and sororities, which set the tone of the social life. If going Greek isn't for you, don't worry, as one student says,

> **"I think Tech is pretty personal considering the number of students it serves."**

"Most students go downtown to shoot pool, dance, or go to a bar." The most important annual event is the Ring Dance (when the juniors receive their school rings), the German Club's Midwinter's Dance, and the Corps of Cadets military ball. Blacksburg offers the usual city fare and one student says the town "revolves around Tech." For real big-city action, Washington, D.C., and Richmond are four and three hours away by car, respectively.

A longtime member of the Big East, Tech recently made the jump to the Atlantic Coast Conference. Tech's varsity athletics program struggled for years to make the big time—and never succeeded—but the football team's recent appearances in postseason bowl games have cheered alumni and hiked applications by several thousand. The annual "big game" pits the backwoodsy Hokies against the aristocratic (snobby?) Cavaliers of the University of Virginia. Tech has one of the nation's most extensive intramural programs, with everything from football to horseshoes and underwater hockey—a recent rage—and more than four hundred softball teams each spring, many of them co-ed. Weekend athletes benefit from the addition of a fitness center.

Anyone looking for a high-tech education garnished with Southern hospitality will find Virginia Tech just right. "I think Tech is pretty personal considering the number of students it serves," says a junior.

Overlaps

University of Virginia, University of Maryland, Penn State, James Madison, George Mason

If You Apply To ➤

Tech: Early decision: Nov. 1. Regular admissions: Jan. 15. Financial aid: Mar. 11. Does not guarantee to meet demonstrated need. No campus or alumni interviews. SATs: required. SAT IIs: required (writing and math I or II). Accepts electronic applications. Essay question. Level of difficulty of high school curriculum stressed.

Wabash College

301 West Wabash, Crawfordsville, IN 47933

Wabash and Hampden-Sydney in Virginia are the last of the all-male breed. With steady enrollment and plenty of money in the bank, Wabash shows no signs of changing. Intense bonding is an important part of the Wabash experience, and few co-ed schools can match the loyalty of Wabash alumni.

At all-male Wabash College, students follow the Gentleman's Rule: "Wabash men are expected to behave like gentlemen at all times. This rule encompasses alcohol, relations with women, academics, and all other areas of college life," says a history and speech major. Indeed, stepping onto the Wabash campus is much like stepping back in history to a time when men were men and the world was theirs. Wabash was founded in 1832 by transplanted Ivy Leaguers who most certainly held a positive view of a man's future.

The Wabash campus is characterized by redbrick, white-pillared Federal-style buildings (three are originals from the 1830s). Located in the heart of tiny Crawfordsville, a small town of about fifteen thousand, Wabash is surrounded by grass and tall trees that are part of the gorgeous Fuller Arboretum. Recent additions to the campus are the Allen Athletics and Recreation Center, the Malcolm X Institute, Trippet Hall, and a biology and chemistry building.

The Wabash educational program has certainly proved itself over the years. This small college has amassed quite an impressive list of alumni: executives of major corporations, doctors, lawyers, and a large number of Ph.D.s. Most Wabash alumni are faithful to their school in the form of generous donations. On a per capita basis, the school's $302 million endowment makes it one of the wealthiest in the nation. This financial security enables Wabash to refuse any federal aid, with the exception of Pell Grants, which go directly to students.

History and psychology draw the most majors at Wabash, and the highest accolades go to the biology (premed) and chemistry departments, which are among the most challenging and produce many successful grads. In keeping with its reputation in the sciences, Wabash has an electron microscope and a laser spectrometer, a 180-acre biological field station, and a cell culture lab. Political science and the religion/philosophy department are also popular, but students say the speech department could be improved. A 42,600-square-foot fine arts center provides more studio space and practice rooms and is a pleasant addition to the music and art departments. The newest additions to the curriculum include international studies, gender studies, and multicultural American studies. And while Wabash still emphasizes its mission as a liberal arts college, the traditional programs have been augmented with cross-cultural immersion learning courses, internships, and collaborative research with faculty.

The studying at Wabash is intense. "Professors and other students really push you to achieve your fullest potential," says a senior, who quickly adds, "It's friendly competition." General education requirements include courses from a wide variety of fields—natural and behavioral sciences, literature and fine arts, mathematics, language studies, and a course on cultures and traditions. In

"All students, regardless of race, are Wabash brothers."

addition, a freshman tutorial is designed to improve class participation and reading and writing skills. A special writing center is available for all Wabash students who demonstrate a weakness in written communication skills. The ability to write well is definitely an asset here, as many tests feature essay questions. Juniors are encouraged

Website: www.wabash.edu
Location: Small town
Total Enrollment: 912
Undergraduates: 912
Male/Female: 100/0
SAT Ranges: V 530–620
   M 560–655
ACT Comp: 23–28
Financial Aid: 68%
Expense: Pr $ $
Phi Beta Kappa: Yes
Applicants: 1,287
Accepted: 50%
Enrolled: 42%
Grad in 6 Years: 68%
Returning Freshmen: 86%
Academics: ✍ ✍ ✍ ½
Social: ☎ ☎
Q of L: ★ ★ ★
Admissions: (800) 345-5385
Email Address:
   admissions@wabash.edu

Strongest Programs:
Religion
Premed
Prelaw
Economics
Biology

to study on continents throughout the world or in various domestic programs through the Great Lakes College Association.* Those who can't satisfy their high-tech interests at Wabash can opt for a 3–2 program in engineering with Columbia University or Washington University in St. Louis. Wabash also offers a tuition-free semester after graduation to train students to become teachers. Students use the words "outstanding" and "fantastic" to describe their professors. Advising is also considered excellent, and students say they have no problems getting into required courses.

Most of Wabash's students come from public high schools in Indiana, and 68 percent were in the top quarter of their high school class. Many were active in athletics and student government and continue that tradition in college. The campus is mostly conservative, though both Republican and Democratic student organizations are strong. The administration is working with a grant to improve diversity on campus. It has expanded the freshman orientation program to include diversity and community issues, focusing on making choices and accepting the consequences. However, students agree there's still a ways to go. African-American, Hispanic, Asian-American, and foreign students combined account for 15 percent of the campus population. "There tend to be very few pressures on campus caused by diversity," one sophomore says. "All students, regardless of race, are Wabash brothers."

Residential life for the temporary denizens of small-town Crawfordsville revolves around the ten fraternities, each with its own house. Sixty-seven percent of the students join up, and many end up living with their brothers. As an alternative to Greek life, there are three modern dorms, two of which have all single rooms.

Dorm residents must eat in the dining hall. Those living in the dorms (and the 6 percent who live off campus) may feel excluded from what

> "Professors and other students really push you to achieve your fullest potential. It's friendly competition."

there is of campus social life because the fraternities "ship in" sorority members from Purdue, Indiana, DePauw, and Butler for parties. "Many people make the mistake of thinking that since Wabash has no women...we don't have good parties," says a senior history major. A wise freshman, however, points out that "the absence of women on weekdays helps some to concentrate on their studies." As for drinking on campus, students agree that policies are loose. A sophomore says, "Alcohol is fairly accessible. The big difference is that at Wabash, students behave responsibly. No one is stupid enough to drink and then decide to drive around."

Wallies are tough in athletics. The football, baseball, basketball, swimming, and the cross-country teams are very competitive. When they're not studying or partying, students are likely to be found working out in the gym or running. Most nonvarsity athletes participate in intramurals, which encompass twenty-two sports, including pool and horseshoes. School spirit is abundant, especially when the opponent is long-standing rival DePauw. The annual Monon Bell football game against the hated "Dannies" (DePauw Tigers) is "a great game, steeped in tradition." Another popular, though less sweaty, event is Chapel Sing, where all the freshmen sing the lengthy school song in unison. "Actually, we yell until we go hoarse," one participant says.

Traditions have not changed much since the school's founding in the 1830s, and still play an important part in the lives of the men at Wabash. Here, a guy can be unapologetic about being a guy—in fact, he can be proud of it. And Wabash men know that not a few women appreciate a true gentleman these days. And while Wabash students know they won't have much involvement with women while they're in class or hitting the books, there are always the weekends to look forward to. Students here accept the workload and the social sacrifices to be part of the Wabash tradition.

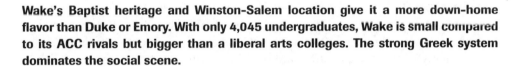

Wake Forest University

Winston-Salem, NC 27109

Wake's Baptist heritage and Winston-Salem location give it a more down-home flavor than Duke or Emory. With only 4,045 undergraduates, Wake is small compared to its ACC rivals but bigger than a liberal arts colleges. The strong Greek system dominates the social scene.

Already well-established as one of the top private schools in the Southeast, Wake Forest is working hard to transform that goodwill into a national reputation. The sciences are especially strong here, and students benefit from an intimate atmosphere that exudes an Old South charm.

Located in the Piedmont region of North Carolina, the school's 340-acre campus has an air of serenity, thanks to flower gardens, wooded trails, and stately magnolias. There are more than forty Georgian-style buildings constructed of old Virginia brick with granite trim. Each is connected to the campus computer network, and some also have multimedia classrooms. All of the new mortar and stone complements the school's lush surroundings, which includes the 148-acre Reynolda Gardens annex, with a formal garden, greenhouses, and a wooded area with trails. The garden features one of the first collections of Japanese cherry trees in the United States. New are the Kenneth D. Miller Center for athletics, a research facility for the Health and Exercise Sciences Department, and renovation of Calloway Hall, renamed The Calloway Center for Business, Math, and Computer Science.

To graduate from Wake Forest, students must complete a writing seminar, a first-year seminar, one semester of foreign language literature, and two half-semesters of health and exercise science. In addition, students take three courses in history, religion, and philosophy; two in literature; one in fine arts; three in social and behavioral sciences; and three in natural sciences, mathematics, and computer science. Students must also satisfy quantitative reasoning and cultural diversity requirements. There is some grumbling about grade deflation, and the nickname "Work Forest" is no joke. "The academic climate is very rigorous and competitive, but at the same time, it is bearable," reports a chemistry and Spanish major. "I have not taken any class where an 'A' has been handed out on a silver platter." For those who are up to it, there is a program leading to "Honors in Arts and Sciences" distinction. Students going for that take three or more honors seminars during freshman, sophomore, and junior years.

Communication is Wake Forest's most popular major, followed by business, psychology, political science, and biology. Graduate assistants teach labs, but full faculty members lead lectures and students give them high marks. "The quality of teaching is very good, and professors are accessible," says a sophomore. "Most are engaging, and very welcoming—I've yet to have a professor I really don't like." Two-thirds of the courses taken by freshmen have twenty-five or fewer students, and nearly all the rest have fifty or less. A junior economics major says the quality

Website: www.wfu.edu
Location: City outskirts
Total Enrollment: 6,410
Undergraduates: 4,045
Male/Female: 49/51
SAT Ranges: V 600–680
  M 620–710
Financial Aid: 34%
Expense: Pr $ $
Phi Beta Kappa: Yes
Applicants: 5,995
Accepted: 41%
Enrolled: 41%
Grad in 6 Years: 87%
Returning Freshmen: 94%
Academics: ✍ ✍ ✍ ✍
Social: ☎ ☎ ☎
Q of L: ★ ★ ★
Admissions: (336) 758-5201
Email Address:
  admissions@wfu.edu

Strongest Programs:
Health and Exercise Science
Chemistry
English
Psychology
Mathematics
Economics
Biology
Political science
Business
Romance Languages

of teaching at Wake Forest kept him from transferring to Harvard, Stanford, or Emory. The Richter Fellowships fund research collaboration between students and faculty members. And for those who feel claustrophobic in Winston-Salem, Wake

"The quality of teaching is very good, and professors are accessible."

Forest owns residential study centers on the Grand Canal in Venice and in London and Vienna, and more than half of the student body studies abroad. The school also offers study programs on virtually every continent aside from Antarctica.

Still, while Wake Forest students traipse around the world sampling foreign cultures, life on campus is fairly homogeneous. The student body is 87 percent white. "The Wake has been viewed by my peers as a university for white, upper class southern students," says a finance major. "Wake is maturing in terms of diversity, both ethnically and geographically." Only twenty-nine percent of Wake's students are native Tar Heels, though many of the rest hail from other Southern states. African-Americans represent 7 percent of the student body, while Hispanics, Asian-Americans, and other minorities together make up 5 percent. "Students, even though many of them are wealthy, are not necessarily snobby or arrogant," says a history major. "In fact, Wake students, beneath the veneer of preppy and pseudo-preppy clothing, are for the most part caring and conscientious people."

Three-quarters of Wake's students live on campus, where rooms are small. "The newer dorms are more spacious," reports a senior. Students are guaranteed housing for all four years, unless they move off campus and later decide to return. Campus safety isn't an issue, quips a junior: "We only fear midterms and finals." Dining options include a fairly typical cafeteria, a convenience store, the food court, and the Magnolia Room, which dishes out classier food, and thus costs more. Students use a school-issued debit card to pay for meals. Upperclassmen often choose to move off campus so that they can cook for themselves.

Fraternities and sororities dominate much of the social scene; 34 percent of the men and 52 percent of the women go Greek, but the "open party" system means independents are also welcome to join the festivities. Underage students say it's rela-

"Wake is maturing in terms of diversity, both ethnically and geographically."

tively easy to get alcohol at frat parties, though the school's Honor Code means that those who help facilitate illegal drinking, and those who imbibe when they shouldn't, face stiff sanctions if caught. Some of Wake's more wacky traditions include a midnight concert by the school orchestra every Halloween, with members in full costume, and the Lilting Banshees comedy troupe, which helps students laugh off their stressful workloads. "What made me love WFU so much when I came to visit was that everyone here was smart, but still normal," says a freshman. "They weren't so smart they were weird."

Winston-Salem is rich in culture, with a symphony, a Christmastime "Moravian love feast," and the well-known Carolina School of the Arts. In addition to the on-campus Museum of Anthropology, art museums—Reynolda House, Museum of American Art (an affiliate of the university), and Southeastern Center for Contemporary Art—are within a three-mile walk of campus. The town also has a strong music scene, with Ziggy's and The Garage the cornerstones of the local concert circuit. Students get involved in the community through volunteer activities, including Project Pumpkin, a trick-or-treat night on campus for underprivileged children. For those with cars, it's four hours to Carolina's beaches, and three hours to the Great Smoky Mountains National Park.

When it comes to sports, basketball is king. Wake's Demon Deacons compete in the incredibly tough Atlantic Coast Conference (where they captured the 2003 regular season title), cheered on by the Screaming Demons Fan Club. "We roll the quad in toilet paper after winning, turning it into a white fairyland." The football

Fraternities and sororities dominate much of the social scene; 34 percent of the men and 52 percent of the women go Greek, but the "open party" system means independents are also welcome to join the festivities.

Some of Wake's more wacky traditions include a midnight concert by the school orchestra every Halloween, with members in full costume, and the Lilting Banshees comedy troupe, which helps students laugh off their stressful workloads.

There is some grumbling about grade deflation, and the nickname "Work Forest" is no joke.

team draws big crowds, too, especially for games against Appalachian State. The Field Hockey Team won the NCAA championship in 2002. Of course, virtually any contest against in-state rival UNC–Chapel Hill is guaranteed to get students excited.

Wake Forest offers an enviable combination—the championship-caliber athletics and outstanding faculty and facilities of a state school, with the competitive academics and cozy feeling of an elite private college. Wake Forest's emphasis on information technology is indeed beginning to compute in the minds of college seekers who are willing to work hard for the rewards of a great college education.

If You Apply To ➤ **Wake Forest:** Early decision: Nov. 15. Regular admissions: Jan. 15. Financial aid: Mar. 1. Guarantees to meet demonstrated need. Campus interviews: recommended, evaluative. No alumni interviews. SATs: required. SAT IIs: optional. Accepts the Common Application and electronic applications. Essay questions: What is your academic passion, and discuss a work of art. Also answer briefly: best class you've taken; what would cause you to lead a march on Washington, D.C.; your best quality; why Wake Forest is the best college for you; favorite author.

Warren Wilson College

PO Box 9000, Asheville, NC 28815-9000

The best of schools where students combine academics, community service and on-campus work. Roots in the culture of Appalachia combine with a strong international orientation to give Warren Wilson its unique flavor. Setting in the mountains of Western North Carolina is tough to beat.

Warren Wilson has to be the only small, liberal arts college in the country where the president, an accomplished musician, pulls out his guitar and joins students for a weekly noontime Appalachian jam session in front of the student center. But that's only one of the engaging little quirks of this school, which promotes global perspectives, puts students to work on the campus farm, and makes service-learning a central part of the educational experience. Additionally, whitewater canoeing is the most important intercollegiate sport.

Founded by the Presbyterian Church in 1894 as the Asheville Farm School, Warren Wilson College initially provided formal schooling for "mountain boys." By 1966, it had evolved into a four-year, co-ed liberal arts college that, while still maintaining its Presbyterian ties, welcomes students of all backgrounds. WWC is located fifteen minutes from downtown Asheville in the lush Swannanoa Valley of the Blue Ridge Mountains. Its 1,132-acre campus features formal gardens, fruit and vegetable gardens, a three-hundred-acre farm, and a myriad of hiking trails. Consistent with campus culture, the wood and stone buildings are small in scale and done in an architectural style that emphasizes natural earth tones accented by extensive stonework by traditional Appalachian stone masons. The campus is also home to one of the most important Cherokee archeological sites in the Southern Appalachian Mountains, dating from as early as 5,000 B.C. Somewhat more recent campus additions include a six-thousand-square-foot art studio, four new dormitories, and a major science center. WWC is also home to North Carolina Outward Bound, an organization with which it has close ties, and the Mountain Area Child and Family Center, which serves as a laboratory school for students of education, psychology, and social work.

The heart of the WWC curriculum is its unique Triad Education Program, which combines liberal arts coursework, community service, and work. Students may

Website: www.warren-wilson.edu

Location: Small town

Total Enrollment: 844

Undergraduates: 778

Male/Female: 39/61

SAT Ranges: V 550–670
M 500–620

ACT Range: N/A

Financial Aid: 53%

Expense: Pr $

Phi Beta Kappa: No

Applicants: 753

Accepted: 79%

Enrolled: 30%

Grad in 6 Years: 46%

Returning Freshmen: 66%

Academics: ✍ ✍ ✍ ½

Social: ☎ ☎ ☎ ☎

Q of L: ★ ★ ★ ★ ★

Admissions: (800) 934-3536

Email Address: admit@warren-wilson.edu

choose from forty-three majors and concentrations. The most popular programs include environmental studies, global studies, psychology, outdoor leadership, and history. To graduate, students have to perform at least a hundred hours of service-learning through organizations such as Habitat for Humanity or environmental organizations. Warren Wilson is also one of only a half dozen four-year colleges in the nation that requires all residential students to work on campus. To fulfill their weekly fifteen-hour work requirement, students do electrical work, plumbing, and landscaping, tend the farm animals, and maintain the campus gardens.

> **"A large bit of the food comes from the school's own cattle and garden, so the food is more healthy than at most colleges."**

To meet general education requirements, WWC students take at least one class within each of the school's eight liberal arts areas: language and global issues, literature, history and political science, natural science, mathematics, social science, philosophy and religion, and artistic expression. They must also demonstrate competency in college composition. The First-Year Experience Program lays a foundation for academic success by introducing students to the study–serve–work trinity through small, interactive group activities. All first-year students enroll in the First-Year Seminar, which includes field experience and/or a service-learning component that takes students and faculty off campus for a day or a weekend.

All first-year students enroll in the First-Year Seminar, which includes field experience and/or a service-learning component that takes students and faculty off campus for a day or a weekend.

Almost every student spends some time getting the taste of a foreign culture. Juniors to take a semester-long course and then spend several weeks on an international "field experience"—with the cost built into their regular tuition—and qualified students may also study for a semester or two in countries such as Guatemala, Costa Rica, Italy, Scotland, Greece, and Vietnam. The college offers honors programs in biology, chemistry, English, environmental studies, math, and computer science. Internship opportunities are available in most undergraduate programs (fully 90 percent of students participate), and there are dual-degree programs in pre-environmental management, preforestry, engineering, and applied science. New programs include majors in Spanish, creative writing, and women's studies. The Appalachian Studies program serves as a catalyst for local cultural activities, including numerous musical groups. And where else does the music department offer you the choice of "finger-picking" or "flat-picking" guitar?

Students say that while the atmosphere is relaxed, hard work is the norm. "The courseload at WWC is challenging," says a psychology major, "but there isn't the need to compete against your peers." Outdoor Leadership and environmental studies receive high marks from students. "There are wonderful professors in each of these departments who are very concerned with the success of their students," says a junior. Business and economics aren't as well-received "because many students don't understand that it can be a strong program in a liberal arts context," according to one student. Physics could also use improvement. Although nearly all classes have twenty-five or fewer students, "it can be difficult to get into certain classes," says a junior. Without proper planning, "It can be difficult to graduate in four years."

> **"The courseload at WWC is challenging, but there isn't the need to compete against your peers."**

The typical WWC student is "committed to community service, extremely left-wing, fond of dropping everything to go to anarchist marches, and very outdoorsy," according to a creative writing major. Upon graduation, most go into service professions such as teaching or working for environmental or other non-governmental organizations. The first step for many is into the Peace Corps. Eighty percent of the student body hail from out of state and attended public school. Students of color account for only 5 percent of the student population, but a student asserts, "I see a sincere effort by the deans to give the international students and minority students more voice on campus." Hot campus issues include diversity, sexual assault, and global concerns such as the war in Iraq. A senior gripes, "These kids are sometimes so politically correct I want to vomit!" Sixty-nine merit scholarships ranging from $1,000 to $4,000 are available to qualified students. There are no athletic scholarships.

Eighty-seven percent of students live in campus housing, ranging from "superb" to "scary." "The freshman dorm is generally loud, ugly, and dirty," says one student. "Most other dorms are gorgeous houses that look like ski chalets or woodsy cabins." EcoDorm incorporates solar heating, natural ventilation, and is made of hardwoods milled on campus. Overall, housing is plentiful and well-maintained (thanks to the industrious student workforce). Dining is a treat, and there are plenty of edible options, including vegetarian and vegan meals. "A large bit of the food comes from the school's own cattle and garden, so the food is more healthy than at most colleges," says a history major.

"There is a strong sense of community here," says a student. "Just about all social life takes place on campus." Despite the absence of Greek organizations, students find plenty of ways to have fun and blow off steam, including open mic nights, concerts, and plays. The outing club is the largest on campus and sponsors weekly hiking, skiing, or other excursions. Students of legal drinking age are allowed to imbibe indoors, and students say it's very easy for underage students to obtain alcohol. Popular events include Mayhem, The Bubba (a huge party and bonfire), and homecoming, which features live bluegrass music, a barbeque, hay rides, and dancing,

"There are wonderful professors in each of these departments who are very concerned with the success of their students."

"Asheville rocks!" gushes a senior. "It isn't totally geared toward college students, so it actually has culture." Museums, cafes, theaters, music clubs, and the symphony are only fifteen minutes away. "The downtown scene is amazing for the relative small size of the town," says a student. Thanks to the college's service requirement, students take an active role in the community through volunteer work. WWC sponsors short-term service projects during vacation breaks, and students camp out overnight in order to qualify for the annual trip to Cumberland Island off the coast of Georgia. Popular roadtrips include Atlanta and the beaches of South Carolina, but the best excursions "are to protests and political events or camping and backpacking trips," according to a political science major.

In a state famed for its rabid sports fans, Warren Wilson students are decidedly laid back. "There are no big sports teams or other rivalries," says a freshman. "Students come here largely because they don't like those rivalries. There is a great sense of school spirit, nonetheless." The college is a member of the United States Collegiate Athletic Association and competes against small universities and colleges in the south. Popular sports include soccer, whitewater paddling (yes, it's a varsity sport here), mountain biking, and basketball. Students have access to a myriad of facilities, including soccer fields, basketball courts, an indoor pool, and a recently renovated fitness center.

Success at Warren Wilson is measured not only by grades but by community service and a sense of stewardship. "Students and professors really care about each other," says one student. Students who aren't afraid to get their hands dirty will see this small liberal arts college as a place that takes seriously the notion of thinking globally and acting locally. As the college motto puts it: "We're not for everyone...but then, maybe you're not everyone."

Not surprisingly, the typical WWC student is "committed to community service, extremely left-wing, fond of dropping everything to go to anarchist marches, and very outdoorsy," according to a creative writing major.

"Students here are very involved in all kinds of issues," says a freshman. A senior gripes, "These kids are sometimes so politically correct I want to vomit!"

Overlaps

Guilford, UNC–Asheville, Evergreen State, Earlham, Appalachian State

University of Washington

1410 N.E. Campus Parkway, Seattle, WA 98195

UDub wows visitors with its sprawling park-like campus in hugely popular Seattle. Washington is tougher than University of Oregon for out-of-state admission but not as hard as UC heavyweights Berkeley or UCLA. Location near the coast and mountains makes for strong marine and environmental studies programs.

Website:
  www.washington.edu
Location: Urban
Total Enrollment: 35,559
Undergraduates: 25,638
Male/Female: 59/41
SAT Ranges: V 510–630
  M 530–650
ACT Range: 22–27
Financial Aid: 30%
Expense: Pub $ $ $
Phi Beta Kappa: Yes
Applicants: 12,785
Accepted: 76%
Enrolled: 43%
Grad in 6 Years: 62%
Returning Freshmen: 91%
Academics: 🖊 🖊 🖊 🖊 ½
Social: ☎ ☎ ☎
Q of L: ★ ★ ★
Admissions: (206) 543-9686
Email Address: askuwadm@
  u.washington.edu

Strongest Programs:
Business
Art
English
Psychology
Drama
Engineering
Architecture
Environmental Studies

In recent years, the University of Washington has come on strong as a solid research institution, and with funds pouring in from Microsoft multimillionaires (including head honcho Bill Gates), this public university promises to become even stronger in the future. Students here understand that anonymity and size are the prices that must be paid for the wealth of opportunities that await them. Those looking for an extra, personal touch might want to investigate the school's two branch campuses in Tacoma and Bothell, where class sizes average twenty-five students. But if the Seattle campus is your focus, one senior hints, just "learn to work the system."

Washington's Seattle campus features a number of distinctive landmarks. Red Square sits atop the Central Plaza parking garage and features the Broken Obelisk, a twenty-six-foot-high steel sculpture gifted to the university by the Virginia Wright Fund.

Many of Washington's diverse undergraduate strengths correspond with its excellent graduate programs. The ultracompetitive business major, for example, benefits from the university's highly regarded business school and is the most popular undergraduate major, followed by biology, art, English, and accounting. Similarly, students majoring in public health, community medicine, pharmacy, and nursing profit from access to facilities and faculty at the medical school, an international leader in cancer and heart research, cell biology, and organ transplants. Also recommended for undergraduates are biological and life sciences (pumped up even more by a new physics/astronomy building), and most engineering programs, especially aero- and astronautical engineering, which are generously funded by Boeing and NASA. Reflecting the focus on natural resources in Washington's economy, the programs in fisheries and forestry are excellent, as are earth and atmospheric sciences, including oceanography. Washington has dropped its major in environmental studies and added a major in community and environmental planning.

"Political correctness is very big here and students find very creative ways to make their points."

Undergraduates in both professional and liberal arts programs must take five credits in English composition, seven credits in writing beyond composition, and one course in quantitative and symbolic reasoning. Students must also fulfill forty credits in general education requirements, including the arts, individuals and societies, and the natural world. Schools and colleges also have their own requirements that must be met. Many Washington professors are tops in their field, but students may have to be patient about seeing professors after class. As for academic advising, a student advises, "The key is to take the bull by the horns and find out which advisors are better than others." While students once complained that classes were difficult to get into, that problem seems to have been reduced, except for large 100- and 200-level courses. Ninety percent of the classes have fewer than fifty students. "It is very common to be taught by teaching assistants, but overall the quality is good in both senior-faculty and graduate-student teachers," a business major says.

For those interested in skirting the masses, UW sports an honors program that offers small classes on interesting subjects taught by fine professors. The academic environment at UW is "very much centered on learning. Part of that comes from the fact that this is a research institution." And if students get the itch to see some different scenery, there are sixty different study abroad programs

"There's simply no better way to learn than by combining challenging courses with real-world experience."

offered in twenty countries, including China, Denmark, and Russia. A program in experiential learning encourages students to find internships and participate in community service. This fits in with a variety of classes that give students the opportunity to volunteer as part of their coursework. A senior says, "There's simply no better way to learn than by combining challenging courses with real-world experience. When you're learning in the classroom, you can't always apply it. Experience adds to your learning, and it helps you remember it."

Part of the reason for UW's national anonymity is the fact that it turns away large numbers of out-of-state applicants, preferring to keep its focus on the home folks. Ninety percent of undergraduates are state residents, and an unusually large proportion are over the age of twenty-five. The student body is 59 percent white and 22 percent Asian-American, with Hispanics and African-Americans comprising 7 percent. Students say the school strives for diversity by offering Valuing Diversity workshops to foster increased awareness of and sensitivity to individual differences; one student calls it "the administration's way of giving lip service to issues they can't or won't deal with." The campus is very active politically, as one junior reports: "Political correctness is very big here and students find very creative ways to make their points."

Students say budget cuts have decreased the number of course offerings, and programs like Society and Justice. Merit scholarships are awarded to Washington residents with good high school records and test scores. Athletic scholarships are awarded to men and women in a wide variety of sports, including swimming, women's gymnastics, golf, tennis, and track and field. Freshmen are given special attention via the Freshman Interest Group (FIG) program, which offers freshmen a chance to meet, discuss, and study with other freshmen who have similar interests. Each FIG consists of twenty to twenty-four students who share a cluster of classes (which meet graduation requirements), and includes a weekly seminar led by a junior or senior peer advisor. Also of interest to freshmen are General Studies 101, an optional two-credit course designed to help students meet the demands and expectations of college life, and Freshman Seminars, one-credit courses with ten or twelve other freshmen.

Fifty-six percent of the students live in the school's seven co-ed dorms. Hagget provides a comfortable setting for freshmen, and McMahon is recommended for those inclined to party. Housing is also available for married students, and the fraternity and sorority organizations are home to another 11 percent of the men and 12 percent of the women. The rest live off campus in Seattle or other parts of King County. Each dorm has its own cafeteria and fast-food line based on a debit card system. The Husky Union Building also offers a dining hall, espresso bar, writing center, sun deck, and lounges. "Great" is how one student describes campus security, while others also report that they feel "100 percent safe" on campus.

While students once complained that classes were difficult to get into, that problem seems to have been reduced, except for large 100- and 200-level courses. Ninety percent of the classes have fewer than fifty students.

Given the large number of commuters, it's no surprise that most of Washington's social life takes place away from campus, except for the Greeks (members of a combined total of forty-eight fraternities and sororities). "The dorms and fraternities seem to contain the most social activity, and what they lack is made up for by the proximity to downtown Seattle," says one student. There are also free movies and drama productions for those who must find entertainment on campus. Both dormies and Greeks are not supposed to drink if they're under twenty-one. Sooner or later most students hit the "Ave," University Way, where shops and top restaurants await them.

And that's true of Seattle, too. A ten-minute bus ride connects students to a full array of urban offerings. The Seattle Center hosts outstanding operas, symphonies, and touring shows, while the Seahawks Stadium houses the NFL team. But who needs pro football with Washington's Huskies around? Husky Fever breaks out on every football weekend, and the stands are always packed for UW's top-rated team. Despite some off-the-field problems among football players, the Huskies are much loved on Saturday afternoons. The team won the Rose Bowl in 2001 and is consistently on the hunt for the PAC 10 athletic crown. While students get fired up for the trip to Pasadena, they're equally excited when Washington State comes to town to vie for the coveted Apple Cup. Other strong UW teams include women's basketball, crew, cross-country, and tennis, and men's crew, baseball, soccer, and tennis.

More than anything else, the great outdoors define the University of Washington. The campus offers breathtaking views of Lake Washington and the Olympic Mountains. Outdoor pastimes for students include boating, hiking, camping, and skiing, all found nearby, and Canada is close enough for road trips to Vancouver. The weather is consistently temperate, and natives insist that the city's reputation for rain is undeserved. Then again, the sports stadium has an overhang to protect spectators from showers.

While some students won't appreciate the no-nonsense and often impersonal academic programs and the lack of a centralized social life, many students can overlook these obstacles for the big picture of the up-and-coming University of Washington—one that takes in more than just the beautiful scenery.

Overlaps

Washington State, Western Washington, UC–Berkeley, University of Oregon, Puget Sound

If You Apply To ➤ **Washington:** Regular admissions: Jan. 15. Financial aid: Feb. 28. Housing: May 1. Does not guarantee to meet demonstrated financial need. Campus interviews: optional, informational. No alumni interviews. SATs or ACTs: required. SAT IIs: optional. Essay question: personal statement. Primarily committed to state residents.

Washington and Jefferson College

60 South Lincoln Street, Washington, PA 15301

Premed Central would be as good a name as any for W&J, where the proportion of students who go on to medical school is one of the nation's highest. Law school and business school are also popular destinations. The tenor of life is conservative and the Greek system dominates the social life.

Website: www.washjeff.edu
Location: Small town

With strong programs in business and English, and an emphasis on the sciences and technology—which includes a new technology building—students at Washington & Jefferson College are virtually guaranteed a top-notch liberal arts education.

Academics are competitive but students still know how to cut loose, making frequent trips to nearby Pittsburgh.

The campus, like the student body, is tight-knit: just over thirty buildings reside on fifty acres in a small town about thirty miles outside of Pittsburgh. W&J is the eleventh-oldest college in the country, and houses the eighth-oldest college building, which was built in 1793. Famous songwriter Stephen Foster was a student here until he got kicked out. The prevailing architectural style is traditional Colonial/Georgian, though modern structures have been added at a rapid pace during the past two decades. The new Howard J. Burnett Center houses the economics, business and accounting, modern languages, education and entrepreneurial studies departments, and the Office of Life-Long Learning. Cameron Stadium has been expanded and renovated. Also open for business is the Vilar Technology Center, and a new science center is in the planning stages.

W&J's formula for success starts with individual attention in small classes, three-quarters of which have twenty-five students or fewer. "These small group classes spark each student's intellectual curiosity," a junior says. Half of the students ranked in the top quarter of their high school class, and most agree the academic climate at W&J is tough, especially for those on the premed and prelaw tracks. "Students are expected to adhere to a high degree of academic quality, and, therefore, courses can be quite rigorous," an economics major says. "Students who have transferred to W&J from other colleges have commented that the courses require more time, effort, and attention than those at other institutions." Tenured professors, who are eager to help them understand the requirements and assist them if they fall behind in classwork, teach most classes. "The professors are not only extremely smart people, but they are also interesting to listen to," a sophomore says. "I honestly can say that I enjoy going to classes." There's no lack of good academic advisors, students say.

> "Students are expected to adhere to a high degree of academic quality, and, therefore, courses can be quite rigorous."

Graduation requirements call for students to complete thirty-four courses and demonstrate proficiency in writing, speaking, reading, quantitative reasoning, foreign language, and use of information technology. Students must take credits in culture and intellectual tradition, fine arts, language and literature, science and mathematics, and social sciences. Students must meet a reinstituted language requirement. A thematic major allows students to design their own course of study, while double majors produce such types as a biologist well versed in literature. Rare among liberal arts colleges are the 3–4 programs with the Pennsylvania Colleges of Optometry and Podiatry. More technically minded students can take advantage of the 3–2 engineering programs with Case Western Reserve and Washington University in St. Louis. Among the standard departments, premed or prelaw, chemistry, biology, political science, and history are popular. There are new majors in biochemistry, information technology leadership, environmental science, and a psychology program called Mind, Brain, and Behavior.

More than 90 percent of W&J graduates who apply to medical or health-related programs are accepted for admission, and the acceptance rate of W&J graduates to law schools is 90 percent. The new Information Technology Leadership program will prepare students to assume leadership roles in that field. Other new programs include environmental studies, Mind, Brain, and Behavior (mentioned above), and neuroscience.

During the January intersession, students find brief apprenticeships in prospective career areas, take a school tour abroad (marine biology trips to the Bahamas or Australia, English theater trips to London, history trips to Russia or China, and biology trips to Africa), or engage in nontraditional coursework. There is also a

(Continued)

Total Enrollment: 1,209
Undergraduates: 1,209
Male/Female: 52/48
SAT Ranges: V 500–600
  M 500–610
ACT Range: 21–26
Financial Aid: 69%
Expense: Pr $ $ $
Phi Beta Kappa: Yes
Applicants: 1,874
Accepted: 51%
Enrolled: 35%
Grad in 6 Years: 73%
Returning Freshmen: 82%
Academics: ✍ ✍ ✍
Social: ☎ ☎ ☎
Q of L: ★ ★
Admissions: (724) 223-6025
Email Address:
  admission@washjeff.edu

Strongest Programs:
Premed
Prelaw
Business Administration
Biology
English

Without a doubt, the social life at W&J centers around the Greeks, who attract 45 percent of the men and 48 percent of the women.

semester- or year-abroad option in Germany, England, Moscow, Russia, or Bogotá, Colombia. Other study abroad opportunities are also available in Australia, Europe, Asia, and Latin America.

Diversity is not a strong suit at W&J, but it is improving thanks to administrative diligence. Seventy-nine percent of the students hail from Pennsylvania and many are from neighboring states in the Northeast. Two percent of students are African-American, 1 percent Hispanic, and 2 percent Asian-American. No matter what their ethnicity, excellent students get a bargain at this somewhat pricey school if they win one of the several hundred academic scholarships that range from $5,000 to $23,860. There are no athletic scholarships, and the school doesn't guarantee to meet students' full demonstrated need, but the same package is promised for a student's four years at the college. One English and Russian major says, "The college makes every effort to financially help students get here and remain here for four years."

> "The professors are not only extremely smart people, but they are also interesting to listen to. I honestly can say that I enjoy going to classes."

Graduation requirements call for students to complete thirty-four courses and demonstrate proficiency in writing, speaking, reading, quantitative reasoning, foreign language, and use of information technology.

Students can live in either co-ed or single-sex dorms, and eight out of ten students prefer to live on campus. Students say the older dorms are fair. A ninety-six-bed suite-style residence hall has been completed, and more student housing is in the works. The choices get better with academic rank, and on-campus apartments are available based on GPA, activities, and need. The administration does have plans to build new townhouses and specialty housing. In order to live off campus, students need an excuse from a doctor. Students say campus security is increasing; police officers have been added to the security force.

Without a doubt, the social life at W&J centers around the Greeks, who attract 45 percent of the men and 48 percent of the women. A crackdown on alcohol and noise violations has somewhat quieted the school's tradition of enormous parties, but the Student Activity Board has begun filling the gap with more on-campus events, such as free movies, and a student-run coffeehouse provides another non-frat option. The school has ten national fraternities and four national sororities. A nonalcoholic pub called George & Tom's has become quite a popular diversion with comedy, musical, and novelty/variety acts. During the course of the year, the Spring Street Fair and Spring Concert are the most popular events.

Students head home on the weekends or explore dating opportunities at nearby colleges, most notably Penn State and the University of Pittsburgh. One of the most popular excursions is a thirty-minute commute to Pittsburgh. Still, not all students share the administration's appreciation for "the unique characteristics of the western Pennsylvania milieu." Many complain that there is nothing to do in this former steel/mining town, now hit by hard times. But new restaurants, such as Applebee's and TGI Friday's, are springing up. Townies tend to be a bit resentful of dressy W&J undergrads, but students try to assuage this attitude by actively volunteering in the community. "W&J and the city of Washington, Pennsylvania, have always had a close relationship," a sophomore says. "The two basically grew up together."

> "The college makes every effort to financially help students get here and remain here for four years."

Just about anyone has a shot at varsity sports. Men's and women's swimming, golf, volleyball, football, and hockey all boast their own successes. For the non-varsity type, there are numerous clubs to join, from the cycling association to the theater club.

The leadership at W&J is constantly revising what it will take to ensure graduating students have integrity, are competent, and are ready to meet the world's challenges. Students praise the education they receive and the professors who give it to them. "The student-centeredness of the school and the premium placed on

Overlaps

Allegheny, University of Pittsburgh, Penn State, Duquesne, College of Wooster establishing strong student/faculty relationships makes me certain that W&J is where I should be," a sophomore says. "Faculty and administrators do everything in their power to ensure that, in their four years at W&J, students have every opportunity to explore every opportunity."

<table>
<tr><td>

If You

Apply

To ➤

</td><td>

W&J: Early decision: Dec. 1. Early action: Jan. 15. Regular admissions: Mar. 1. Financial aid: Feb. 15. Guarantees to meet demonstrated need of 35%. Campus interviews: recommended, evaluative. Alumni interviews: optional, informational. SATs: required. SAT IIs: optional. Accepts the Common Application and electronic applications. Essay question: personal statement.

</td></tr>
</table>

Washington and Lee University

Lexington, VA 24450

Coeducation came to W&L and the pillars of the Colonnade did not come tumbling down. Nearly twenty years after the coming of women, W&L is the most selective small college in the South, rivaled only by Davidson. W&L supplements the liberal arts with strong programs in business, public policy, and journalism.

Washington and Lee University, which shares the town of Lexington, Virginia, with the Virginia Military Institute, is as genteel as a Southern school can be. The Fancy Dress Ball is a highlight of each year, and a "speaking tradition" results in at least casual communication between students and professors when they pass one another on the well-manicured grounds. And behind the frills and fun lies an honor system that students cite as one of their school's best features.

W&L's wooded campus sits atop a hill of lush green lawns, sweeping from one national landmark to another. Redbrick buildings feature white Doric columns and the prevailing architectural style is Greek Revival, although the physical face is changing. A parking garage, playing fields, and sorority houses were recently completed. The school boasts a new University Commons and art and music building, a new soccer stadium, and has finished renovations on Reid Hall, home of the journalism and mass communications department.

Though Washington and Lee is a school steeped in tradition, it is also working hard to find the future. Women's numbers are growing, as is their influence on the campus academic and social life. Although a standard liberal arts program remains the foundation of the school's curriculum, it offers excellent preprofessional programs, particularly business, economics, public policy, and accounting through the Williams School of Commerce, Economics, and Politics. Journalism and mass communications are popular, as are biology (for premeds) and English. W&L also has bachelor's degree programs in fields as diverse as Russian studies and marine science education, which allows students to work at the Duke University Marine Laboratory for a semester. The East Asian studies program has ties to universities in Taiwan and Japan. Students can take part in the Shepherd Program for the Interdisciplinary Study of Poverty, and a biochemistry major was recently added. A cooperative forestry major with Duke University has been dropped. More and more students are spending time abroad, and the new Global Stewardship Program is designed to increase international study opportunities.

General education requirements account for one-third of a student's courses. Distribution requirements at W&L include English composition; two literature

Website: www.wlu.edu
Location: Small town
Total Enrollment: 2,128
Undergraduates: 1,749
Male/Female: 53/47
SAT Ranges: V 640–720
  M 640–720
ACT Range: 28–30
Financial Aid: 28%
Expense: Pr $ $ $
Phi Beta Kappa: Yes
Applicants: 3,188
Accepted: 31%
Enrolled: 46%
Grad in 6 Years: 88%
Returning Freshmen: 95%
Academics: 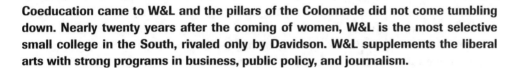 ✐ ✐ ✐ ✐ ½
Social: ☎ ☎ ☎
Q of L: ★ ★ ★ ★
Admissions: (540) 458-8710
Email Address:
  admissions@wlu.edu

Strongest Programs:
Business
History
Politics
English
Journalism

(Continued)
Economics

courses; three courses in fine arts, history, philosophy, and religion; three courses in science and math; three social science courses; five terms of physical education; proficiency in swimming; and two years of a foreign language. A class on the history of Washington and Lee University is immensely popular.

The academic climate ranges from intense to casual, depending on the student. "Competitive, but not aggressive," claims a history major. Classes tend to be small, and freshmen can count on getting full professors; there are no teaching assistants. "Professors truly want to see you succeed, and they will do everything to make sure you do," says a chemistry major. The famous honor system lends a relaxed feeling to the otherwise rigorous academic climate. Tests and final exams are taken without faculty supervision; doors remain unlocked, calculators stay on desks, and library stacks are open twenty-four hours a day. "I enjoy the small community and the freedom we enjoy due to the honor system," says a senior. Online registration helps quell any potential scheduling disasters. The modern library, like most W&L facilities, is superb and offers eight hundred individual study areas as well as private rooms for honors students. Well-qualified students can apply for the Robert E. Lee Undergraduate Research Program, which offers students paid fellowships for assisting professors in research or doing their own.

> "I enjoy the small community and the freedom we enjoy due to the honor system."

This is a friendly campus. "The speaking tradition is such that W&L students say 'hi' to people they pass on campus, which definitely contributes to the collegial atmosphere and sense of community here," says a premed student. Prospective students should be aware that there is little urgency on this campus to change the world. "The administration is getting a little more liberal," says one student. "But you would still be hard-pressed to find a more conservative school." Not that open-mindedness is absent. "Political correctness is definitely an issue, since women have just started to have a voice on campus, and the black and minority population is small," writes a French and Economics major. African-Americans account for a mere 3 percent of the student body, despite the school's argument that it is strongly committed to recruiting African-American students; Hispanics and Asian-Americans, meanwhile, combine for 4 percent. Fourteen percent of students are native Virginians, but the university's geographic diversity has not prompted much other differentiation. Co-education has been a godsend for the admissions office; applications are way up for the past several years, the median SAT scores of each freshman class are on the rise, and the acceptance rate is much lower than it was five or six years ago. The school offers 342 merit scholarships worth up to $30,700, but no athletic awards.

Students spend their first year at W&L in "quite comfortable and well-maintained" co-ed dorms, and some freshmen may reserve singles. Freshmen are required to buy the meal plan, and the food is said to be good. Upperclass dorms and apartments are available, and many students move into country houses when they are juniors or seniors. Sixty-four percent of students reside on-campus.

Eighty percent of the men join fraternities, which, along with newly created sororities that claim 72 percent of the women, dominate the social scene. Underage drinking is banned in the dorms and strictly avoided because it's against the honor code, but students insist "drinking is quite prevalent." W&L's social life focuses on Greek bashes, which often feature live bands, although the Fancy Dress Ball, or "$100,000 prom," also draws raves. A lot of creative energy goes into fraternity parties—one recently featured a real mechanical bull, another was decorated like the Playboy Mansion. "All the girls dressed up as Playboy bunnies, complete with tails," reports a senior. Another student sighs that fraternities pretty much have a monopoly on revelry here, but that some outgrow them. "They are cool at the beginning,

Tests and final exams are taken without faculty supervision; doors remain unlocked, calculators stay on desks, and library stacks are open twenty-four hours a day.

Students can take part in the Shepherd Program for the Interdisciplinary Study of Poverty, and interdisciplinary programs were recently added in women's studies and business journalism.

but they get repetitive." W&L's mock political convention for the party out of power, held every four years, has predicted past presidential nominees with uncanny accuracy. The Foxfield races near Charlottesville and the Kentucky Derby are popular road trip destinations.

With its scenic location in the midst of the Appalachian Mountains, the university provides an abundance of activities for nature lovers, including hunting, fishing, camping, skiing, and tubing on the rivers. Washington, D.C., Richmond, and Roanoke are easily reached by car for weekend trips, though, because there is seldom a dull moment, most students like to stay on campus during weekends. Lexington, a "quiet, friendly town that has much history to offer" also offers a few bars, two movie theaters, and several restaurants. Football sparks some interest in the fall, with its attendant tailgate parties, but W&L students live for the spring and the Lee Jackson Lacrosse Classic against VMI. W&L's teams won six conference championships in their most recent seasons. Popular participation sports include men's football, soccer, and lacrosse, and women's lacrosse, tennis, and field hockey.

Many graduates are proud to look back on their college careers and point to the progress their alma mater has made in the intervening years, but not those from Washington and Lee. The culture here doesn't embrace change, and students here grin and bear the teasing of those who say W&L really stands for "White and Loaded." But strong academics and respect for tradition have their appeal. After all, who wouldn't like a group of students who put sugar cubes or apples on the grave of Traveller, Robert E. Lee's horse, at exam time?

If You Apply To ➤

W&L: Early decision: Dec. 1. Regular admissions: Jan. 15. Does not guarantee to meet demonstrated need. Campus and alumni interviews: recommended, evaluative. ACTs or SATs: required. SAT IIs: required (writing and two nonrelated subjects). Accepts the Common Application and electronic applications. Essay question: significant experience or achievement with special meaning; best advice received; issue of personal, national, or local concern and its importance.

Washington University in St. Louis

Campus Box 1089, One Brookings Drive, St. Louis, MO 63130-4899

In the space of little more than a decade, Wash U has gone from Midwestern backup school to elite private university close on the heels of Northwestern. Wash U is strong in everything from art to engineering. The halo effect of the university's medical school attracts a slew of aspiring doctors.

One of higher education's rising stars, Washington University is arguably the best private school between Chicago and San Francisco. Though it's always been well-recognized regionally, Wash U has now firmly established itself as a truly national institution—with a relaxed Midwestern feel that differentiates it from the high-strung eastern Ivies. Applications have skyrocketed, and with a hefty endowment, strong preprofessional programs, and an emphasis on research, it's not hard to see why. "Students are Wash U are more laid back than those at comparable schools," says a senior majoring in art history and political science. "We enjoy being here, rarely feel overworked beyond that which is expected at a good school, and genuinely like each other."

The school's 169-acre campus adjoins Forest Park, one of the nation's three largest urban parks. Buildings are constructed in the Collegiate Gothic style, mostly

*Every spring, the whole
campus turns out for the
century-old Thurtene
Carnival, the oldest
student-run philanthropic
festival in the country.*

in red Missouri granite and white limestone, with plenty of climbing ivy, gargoyles, and arches. The campus is continually growing, with the recent opening of new residence halls for small groups who share common interests and goals. New buildings for lab sciences and biomedical engineering are complete and a new Earth and Planetary Sciences building is underway. Olin Library is being renovated and expanded by seventeen thousand square feet to make room for a cybercafe and twenty-four-hour study space. Architects are working on plans for a new University Center and new space for the visual arts.

Undergraduates enroll in one or more of Washington U's five schools—arts and sciences, architecture, art, business, or engineering. Double and interdisciplinary majors, such as environmental studies, are encouraged and easily arranged—so easily arranged, in fact, that about 60 percent of students earn either a major and minor, more than one major, and sometimes more than one degree. General education requirements vary by school and program. For liberal arts students, they include courses in quantitative reasoning, physical and life sciences, social or behavioral sciences, minority or gender studies, language or the arts, and English composition.

Washington U's offerings in the natural sciences, especially biology and chemistry, have long been notable, especially among premeds. The outstanding medical school runs a faculty exchange program with the undergraduate biology department, which affords bio majors significant opportunities to conduct advanced laboratory research. The University Scholars Program allows students to apply for undergraduate and graduate admission before entering college. If accepted, students can begin exploring their chosen career path earlier—though they aren't obligated to follow through if their interests change.

The freshman FOCUS program helps balance the preprofessional bent of some of Washington U's best programs with the school's desire to provide a broad and deep educational experience and a smaller class size. In FOCUS, students use a weekly seminar to explore topics of contemporary significance, such as law and society. The program lets first-year students work closely with professors—including at least one Nobel Prize winner—and sample offerings from various departments. Other notable options include the two-year Hewlet Program, which allows groups of students to focus on an interdisciplinary area, such as the connection between the mind and the brain.

As Washington U's applicant pool has gotten bigger, the admissions committee has become more selective—and classes have gotten tougher, students report.

**"Students are Wash U are more laid
back than those at comparable schools."**

"Courses are very demanding. A lot is expected on a daily and long-term basis," a junior says. "At the same time, the students themselves are laid back. There is a feeling of 'We're in this together' and cut-throat, get-ahead techniques are rare." Those who are struggling will find plenty of help, however, from teaching assistants who conduct help sessions to study groups of their peers. "I have truly been pleased by the commitment to and quality of undergraduate teaching and mentorship," a music/political science/educational studies major says. "Professors don't just want to lecture here, they want to fully engage undergrads in the material.

Diversity is an issue facing most schools, and Washington University is not immune. The school's population is relatively heterogeneous, with African-Americans comprising 8 percent, Hispanics 3 percent, and Asian-Americans 10 percent. There's also a large contingent from Eastern states like New York and New Jersey, many of whom are Jewish, leading to much debate about the Arab–Israeli conflict. Organizations such as STAR (Students Together Against Racism) and ADHOC (Against Discrimination and Hatred on Campus) also help enlighten students. "Intellectual debate is promoted on campus," a senior says. "WU encourages the free expression of ideas. Political correctness is not made out to be a huge issue."

Eighty percent of Wash U students live in the school's dormitories, known as residential colleges. Most are clustered in an area called South 40, a forty-acre plot next to campus. All dorms are co-ed and air-conditioned, and some have suites for six to eight students of the same gender. Freshmen are guaranteed rooms, and students who stay in the dorms after that are promised rooms for the following year, says a junior. It's becoming more popular to stay on campus for all four years, a psychology major reports, especially since upperclassmen may live in university-owned apartments. Some juniors and seniors do choose true off-campus digs in the nearby neighborhoods of University City and Clayton, where apartments are reasonably priced. Dorm-dwellers and others who buy the meal plan may use their credits in any of fourteen dining centers. "The food is better than home—don't tell my mother!" a senior raves. "There are tons of veggie and kosher options."

Washington U students pride themselves on being able to balance work and play, and on weekends, movies, fraternity parties, and concerts tear them away from their books. Every spring, the whole campus turns out for the century-old Thurtene Carnival, the oldest student-run philanthropic festival in the country. Student groups—especially fraternities and sororities, which attract 27 percent of the men and 21 percent of the women—build booths, sell food, and put on plays, and profits are donated to a children's charity. Another big event is Walk-In-Lay-Down (WILD) Theater, held the first and last Fridays of the academic year. Everyone brings a

> **"Courses are very demanding. A lot is expected on a daily and long-term basis."**

blanket to the main quad, assumes a horizontal position, and listens to live bands until the wee hours. Alcohol policies emphasize responsible drinking, though students under twenty-one aren't supposed to drink at all, per Missouri law. "Students can have alcohol, and as long as they aren't hurting themselves or others, people won't step in," says an English and finance major. "The university seems to realize college is a time for experimentation."

Aside from an active campus social life, Washington U offers incredible recreational options because of its location abutting Forest Park: a golf course, an ice-skating rink, a zoo, a lake with boat rentals, art and history museums, an outdoor theater, and a science center are all within a short walk. The St. Louis Rams, Blues, and Cardinals attract pro football, hockey, and baseball fans, and the city is also home to the addictive Ted Drewes frozen custard. The school runs a free shuttle service to parts of St. Louis not within walking distance, and community service programs such as "Each One Teach One," in partnership with the city's schools, attract a sizable number of students. "St. Louis is great," said an art history/political science major. "I expected a Midwestern cowtown surrounded by cornfields. Man, was I wrong!" The best road trips include Chicago; Nashville and Memphis, Tennessee; Lake of the Ozarks; and Columbia, Missouri—home of the University of Missouri.

Washington U competes in Division III, and its a women's basketball powerhouse, bringing home national titles from 1998 through 2001. The women's softball team won a University Athletic Association title in 2000, its first year as a varsity sport. Other strong programs include women's volleyball, with seven NCAA national champi-

> **"I expected a Midwestern cowtown surrounded by cornfields. Man, was I wrong!"**

onships and fourteen UAA championships in its history, and football, winner of the UAA title in two of the past three years. Intramural sports range from badminton, arm wrestling, and floor hockey to pocket billiards and Ultimate Frisbee.

With demanding courses and excellent programs in the sciences and art, Washington U is changing from being another sleepy little Midwest school to being a

Washington U students pride themselves on being able to balance work and play, and on weekends, movies, fraternity parties, and concerts tear them away from their books.

The outstanding medical school runs a faculty exchange program with the undergraduate biology department, which affords bio majors significant opportunities to conduct advanced laboratory research.

Overlaps
Duke, Harvard, Northwestern, University of Pennsylvania, Yale

competitive educational institution. The curriculum is becoming increasingly focused on global and international perspectives. But despite the rigor of academic life, students still find time to play. "Our students come from all over the world and have diverse interests," a senior says. "We want to share our ideas and experiences both inside and outside the classroom. We study hard and have fun too."

If You Apply To ➢

Washington U: Early decision I: Nov. 15. Early decision II: Jan. 1. Regular admissions: Jan. 15. Financial aid: Nov. 1 (early decision applicants), Feb. 15. Housing: May 1. Meets demonstrated need of 78%. Campus and alumni interviews: optional, evaluative. SATs or ACTs: required. SAT IIs: optional. Apply to one of five undergraduate schools. Accepts the Common Application and electronic applications. Essay question: personal statement.

Wellesley College

Wellesley, MA 02481

There is no better recipe for popularity than a postcard-perfect campus on the outskirts of Boston. That formula keeps Wellesley at the top of the women's college pecking order—along with superb programs in economics and the natural sciences. Nearly a quarter of the students are Asian-American, the highest proportion in the East.

Website: www.wellesley.edu
Location: Suburban
Total Enrollment: 2,287
Undergraduates: 2,287
Male/Female: 0/100
SAT Ranges: V 640–730
   M 630–710
ACT Range: 27–31
Financial Aid: 52%
Expense: Pr $ $ $ $
Phi Beta Kappa: Yes
Applicants: 3,047
Accepted: 43%
Enrolled: 44%
Grad in 6 Years: 90%
Returning Freshmen: 96%
Academics: ✍ ✍ ✍ ✍ ✍
Social: ☎ ☎ ☎
Q of L: ★ ★ ★ ★
Admissions: (781) 283-2270
Email Address:
   admission@wellesley.edu

Strongest Programs:
Economics
Political Science
Biological Sciences
Computer Sciences

Wellesley is not just the best women's college in the nation—it's one of the best colleges in the nation, period. With an alumnae roster that includes Senator Hillary Rodham Clinton, Madame Chiang Kai-shek, Madeleine Albright, and Diane Sawyer, Wellesley College should be at the top of the list for those who are seeking an all-women's education. Wellesley women excel in whatever field they choose, including traditional male bastions like economics and business. "It is a wonderful place to grow," says a senior.

Nestled in a corner of a wealthy Boston suburb, the Wellesley campus, one of the most beautiful anywhere, occupies five hundred rolling acres of cultivated and natural areas, including Lake Waban. Campus buildings range in architectural style from Gothic (with stone towers and brick quadrangles) to state-of-the-art science, arts, and sports facilities. A twenty-two-acre arboretum and botanical garden features a wide variety of trees and plants.

With its hefty endowment and lavish facilities, Wellesley offers a top-of-the-line educational experience. The most popular majors are English, psychology, economics, political science, and international relations, though economics is known as the biggest powerhouse. In fact, Wellesley has produced virtually all of the country's high-ranking female economists. Students in molecular biology work with faculty on DNA research, and a high-tech science center houses two electron microscopes, two NMR spectrometers, ultracentrifuges, two lasers, and other such equipment. A comprehensive renovation of the social science building added videoconferencing, computer labs, and a research facility.

In the past, theater studies was considered a weak department, but the school has gone to great lengths to remedy the situation by building a department students can brag about. The Ruth Nagel Jones Theater provides performance space for mainstage productions and experimental theater. The Davis Museum and Cultural Center houses eleven galleries, a cinema, and a cafe. The students at Wellesley will find an academic art museum to their benefit, along with more than a million volumes in the campus libraries. The five libraries sport a computerized catalog system that is accessible from on or off campus. Anything Wellesley women find lacking in their facilities or curriculum can probably be found at MIT, where they have full cross-registration privileges. Wellesley students can also take courses at Brandeis University and Babson College, or participate in exchange programs with Spelman College in Atlanta or Mills College in Oakland, California.

(Continued)
Chinese Language

Wellesley has distribution requirements that include three units drawn from language and literature and visual arts, music, theater, film, and video; one unit from social and behavioral analysis; a unit each from two of the following: epistemology and cognition, religion, ethics, and moral philosophy, and historical studies; and three units from natural and physical science and mathematical modeling and problem solving. In

"The classes can seem competitive, especially when the top women from high schools are placed together on the same campus."

addition, students must take a first-year writing class, a foreign language, and a course on multiculturalism. Academics are taken very seriously at Wellesley. "The classes can seem competitive," says a senior, "especially when the top women from high schools are placed together on the same campus." Professors are highly respected and make themselves available through email, voicemail, office hours, and by appointment. "The quality of teaching is excellent," says a senior. "All students are taught by professors and class sizes are small, so we get individual attention. Profs here are dedicated to teaching their students, and that makes a big difference."

A five-course technology studies concentration gives liberal arts students the skills necessary to understand and use technological innovations in their future studies as well as in the professional world. Grants from private foundations have allowed Wellesley to add other innovative programs, including independent research tutorials for advanced science students and fellowship funding for joint student–faculty projects. Students can participate in the Twelve-College Exchange, including the National Theater Institute, and the Maritime Studies Program, or they can travel and study abroad through one of Wellesley's recently expanded international programs, including the summer internship program in Washington, D.C.

Economics is known as the biggest powerhouse. In fact, Wellesley has produced virtually all of the country's high-ranking female economists.

Under the honor system, students may take their finals, unsupervised, at any time during exam week. Class sizes are almost always small (they average eighteen to twenty-three students per class). First-years (as they are exclusively called here) and upperclasswomen alike have faculty advisors. First-years also have a dean of first-year students to offer additional advice on courses and other academic matters. "There are good counseling resources available, but students must seek them out," explains a sophomore.

Once known as "a haven for rich white girls," Wellesley is now a picture of diversity. Forty-two percent of Wellesley's students are minorities. Although the Northeast is the best-represented geographical area (though only 18 percent are from Massachusetts), students also come from every state and more than seventy-five countries. Ninety-seven percent ranked in the top quarter of their

"We have such a diverse campus racially, culturally, geographically, and religiously that the major issues address creating a supportive environment for all."

high school class. Whatever their background, most have a fair amount of social aplomb. Issues on campus run the gamut from multiculturalism and racism to gender questions and national politics. "Political correctness is a huge issue," says a psychology and economics double major. "We have such a diverse campus racially, culturally, geographically, and religiously that the major issues address creating a supportive environment for all." There are no athletic or academic scholarships, but students don't seem to mind, rating the recently enhanced financial aid packages as "constant and fair."

Dorm life at Wellesley is a step ahead of most institutions, to say the least. Virtually every student lives on campus, in rooms that are described as "immaculate." Dorms feature high-ceilinged living rooms, hardwood floors, fireplaces, computers and laser printers, television annexes with VCRs, walk-in closets, kitchenettes with microwaves, and even grand pianos. The dorms are renovated every five years or so and all are well maintained, students say. "Nice dorms—most of them have early-twentieth-century architecture and beautiful windows to look out on a beautiful campus," says an anthropology senior. All residence halls are smoke-free.

There are no dorms specifically for first-years—all classes live on all floors. Peer tutors also live in each dorm. These students, called APT advisors, are trained to tutor in specific subjects and in study skills and time management. Juniors and seniors are granted single rooms. Two co-ops, one with a feminist bent, present an educational housing option. Meal cards are valid in every dorm, and at the campus snack bar, which is stocked with everything from milk and flour to Twinkies.

When it comes to weekend fun, Wellesley is in a prime location. Or more accurately, it's close to a prime location: Boston. Not even half an hour away, Boston is the place where Wellesley women can mingle with lots of other students—specifically male—from Harvard and MIT. Cambridge—with Harvard Square, MIT frat parties, and lots of jazz clubs—is accessible by an hourly school shuttle that runs on weekdays and weekends. There is also a trolley stop located a short walk from school. Cape Cod, Providence, and the Vermont and New Hampshire ski slopes are close by car.

The town of Wellesley is an upper-crust Boston suburb without many amenities for students. "The town is not a college town," gripes a junior, due to "unfriendly residents and expensive stores." For campus-bound students (like many first-years, who cannot have cars on campus), dorm parties and movies are the featured attractions. "Wellesley students decide their own social lives, and there is no one way or outlet," one student notes. Wellesley is a dry town, although the school is in the process of trying to get liquor licenses for the dorms. When alcohol is served, campus police check IDs. Students enjoy going to the student-run Cafe Hoop, the campus coffeehouse, to sip tea or share a fro-yo or a chocolate croissant. The closest thing Wellesley has to sororities are societies for arts and music, literature, Shakespeare, and general lectures. These societies also sometimes hold parties.

"It's a wonderful place to grow as individuals, as students, and as women."

Wellesley is chock-full of traditions, but the most endearing ones include Flower Sunday, step-singing (an all-campus sing-along on the chapel steps), the sophomore class planting a tree, a junior class variety show, Spring Weekend (with a big-name band and comedian), and a hoop-rolling contest by seniors in their graduation robes. The winner of this contest will supposedly be the first in her class to become a CEO, and she gets off to a flying start when her classmates toss her in the lake. Speaking of the lake, students mention their unofficial campus event, Lake Day, where students take breaks between (or from) classes to enjoy a festival held on the lawn near the lake.

Students balance their academic schedule with athletics to become "Healthy, Wellesley, and Wise." Lacrosse and tennis are among the top varsity sports and cross-country made the NEWMAC Conference championships for four consecutive years. Field hockey, soccer, and volleyball have also claimed championships. The sports "palace," recently renamed the Nannerl Keohane Sports Center in honor of Wellesley's eleventh president (who now runs Duke), offers an Olympic-size pool, squash, racquetball, and tennis courts, dance studios, a weight room, and an indoor track. Harvard's Head of the Charles crew race takes honors as the most popular spectator sport of the year. The big athletic rival is Smith College, another of the Seven Sisters group of great women's colleges.

When it comes to academics, Wellesley women are no joke. Their school is competitive with all but the top three Ivies. Many of them enjoy the quaint traditions of the school and appreciate the idyllic atmosphere for contemplation, but know they are poised to dominate whatever field they enter. The graduates of this incredible school are smart, self-confident, capable, and unstoppable in their drive to the top. As one contented senior says: "It's a wonderful place to grow as individuals, as students, and as women."

If You Apply To ➢

Wellesley: Early decision: Nov. 1. Regular admissions and financial aid: Jan. 15. Guarantees to meet demonstrated need. Campus and alumni interviews: recommended, evaluative. SATs and SAT IIs (writing and two others) or ACTs: required. Accepts the Common Application and electronic applications. Essay question: significant experience or achievement; issue of personal concern; influential person. Students participate on admissions board.

Wells College

Aurora, NY 13026

Wells is fighting to show that a women's college with under five hundred students can survive in rural upstate New York. A family atmosphere is the hallmark of Wells, right down to the dinner bell that calls everyone to the evening meal. Wells is big on interdisciplinary study and internships during its January term.

Traditions abound at Wells College, a small, all-women's school in upstate New York. Whether it's riding to graduation in an old Wells Fargo stagecoach or showing off in a hardcore basketball game between sophomores and seniors, the history of Wells is apparent at every turn. But Wells is no throwback. It aims to educate and empower women for leadership roles in the twenty-first century while instilling in its students an appreciation for the liberal arts and an awareness of global issues. Consider a popular slogan on campus: "You can do anything because you are a Wells woman."

A few dramatic additions on campus, such as the renovation and rededication of Weld House in the Greek revival style, have maintained the classic collegiate atmosphere created by the school's massive, old, ivy-covered buildings. The rolling 365-acre lakeside campus has been named to the National Register of Historic Places. With Cayuga Lake affording beautiful sunsets, boating, and fishing opportunities, students can juxtapose the rigor of their studies with relaxation in a gorgeous environment. Students will soon be able to enjoy a $17.5 million state-of-the-art science building as well.

The liberal arts provide the basic framework for a Wells education. In addition to standard distribution requirements, all students must complete two courses in a foreign language, one course in formal reasoning, three courses in the arts and humanities, three courses in natural or social sciences, and four courses in physical education. Students are also required to do three internships and a senior thesis. Wells 101, a core course required for all freshwomen, covers the basics of college writing, speech, and analytical thinking. The most popular majors (psychology, biology, English, sociology, and the performing arts) are generally the strongest academic departments, according to students. Those who major in biology are able to use the local environment—Cayuga Lake and surrounding lands—for ecology and botany fieldwork. A minor in Japanese has been added to the foreign language

Website: www.wells.edu
Location: Small town
Total Enrollment: 437
Undergraduates: 437
Male/Female: 0/100
SAT Ranges: V 530–650
  M 500–590
ACT Range: 22–26
Financial Aid: 79%
Expense: Pr $
Phi Beta Kappa: Yes
Applicants: 404
Accepted: 86%
Enrolled: 31%
Grad in 6 Years: 63%
Returning Freshmen: 75%
Academics: ✍ ✍ ✍
Social: ☎ ☎
Q of L: ★ ★ ★ ★
Admissions: (800) 952-9355
Email Address:
  admissions@wells.edu

Strongest Programs:
Biological and Chemical Sciences

offerings. Accredited elementary and secondary education programs are available, and interdisciplinary minors are offered in such fields as management studies, secondary education, communications, public policy, and international studies.

Wells also offers a variety of integrated majors, all of which require coursework across traditional disciplinary boundaries. Specialized areas include American studies; foreign languages, literature, and cultures; history; and sociology and anthropology. Qualified students may design their own majors. Wells also offers 3–2 dual degree programs in community health and business administration with the University of Rochester, 3–4 in veterinary medicine with Cornell, and in engineering with Case Western Reserve, Cornell, Columbia, and Clarkson. For a change of pace, students can take one nonmajor course per semester on a pass/fail basis and cross-register to take up to four courses at nearby Cornell University or Ithaca College.

"I meet with my thesis advisor at least two times a week, often to just talk about life."

The college operates on a semester calendar, with January used as a time for internships, study abroad, independent study projects, or Leadership Week. In addition, Wells College sponsors a popular corporate affiliate program aimed at preparing women for the business and financial professions through special courses and lectures, portfolio management experience, and corporate internships. Foreign study is available for either a semester or a year.

Because the average class size is only twelve, students often lead discussions while the professor focuses the direction of the conversation. An honor system is enforced by the student-run collegiate association, and take-home and self-scheduled tests are the rule rather than the exception. "Counselors and advisors are easy to find at Wells," says a senior. "I meet with my thesis advisor at least two times a week, often to just talk about life. Career Services is active and open for students to drop in for advice." But there is a downside: the small classes make it "more obvious if you have been falling behind," warns a sophomore. And another drawback of its teeny size is that it's sometimes harder to get into a class at registration time, says a history major.

The women pride themselves on their open-mindedness and variety of philosophies, and the school is slowly becoming more diverse. "Most of the students here are motivated, highly intelligent, liberal upstate New Yorkers," says a freshman majoring in history. "I think we differ from other schools because we have a strong sense of self." Seventy percent of the students are state residents. Asian-Americans make up 4 percent of the student body, African-Americans 5 percent, and Hispanics 4 percent. A wide range of courses with a minority focus, workshops on racial

"Career Services is active and open for students to drop in for advice."

issues, and a support network for new minority students is used to educate students about diversity. Homosexual rights are a big issue on campus, and students say the gay population has increased of late. The school does not guarantee to meet the full demonstrated financial need of every admit, but a majority of the students receive need-based aid and there are two merit scholarships of up to $20,000 awarded over four years.

The students pride themselves on their open-mindedness and variety of philosophies, and the school is slowly becoming more diverse.

All students are guaranteed housing on campus, and 82 percent take advantage of this option. "The dorms are some of the most beautiful I've ever seen," raves a freshman. "One dorm used to be a mansion, and they all have professionally decorated lounges." The dorms range from the founder's nineteenth-century mansion to a modern dorm setup with a suite system. Weld House, with two computer labs, is the newest. Upperclass women participate in a lottery for housing (most prefer singles), and freshwomen are usually assigned doubles. Each dorm has a lake view, and some boast bay windows and winding staircases. There is virtually no off-campus housing in Aurora, where the total population is equal to the tiny student body at Wells. Meals, which can vary in quality, are served in a magnificent Tudor-style dining hall complete with two working fireplaces. The school is so small that "security knows all of us and will always approach unescorted people and ask them where they belong," a senior says.

The college owns a great deal of waterfront property and maintains a dock and boathouse for its students, which translates into plenty of opportunities for camping and fun in the water. Meanwhile, the ski slopes of Greek Peak are less than an hour away, and the golf course and tennis and paddle courts are usually full of lively players. A field house provides indoor tennis courts, a pool, and other facilities. Aurora itself offers almost no entertainment. There is a market, bank, post office, flower shop, sandwich shop, and "not much else!" according to a psychology major. But Ithaca to the south and Syracuse to the east provide more diversions, and a Wells van runs between the school and Ithaca several times a day. When students exit on weekends, they usually travel to nearby Cornell University or Ithaca College, where fraternity parties and mixers are the main attractions. As far as drinking is concerned, no one under twenty-one is served on campus or at the local bars, but students say it's still possible for an underage student to get alcohol.

On the first and last day of classes, professors serve the seniors a champagne breakfast; sophomores give them roses on the last day of classes and dance around the sycamore tree.

"The dorms are some of the most beautiful I've ever seen."

The soccer and field hockey teams do well, and lacrosse, tennis, swimming, and newly added softball are popular. The college's penchant for tradition carries over into athletics in the Oddline/Evenline competition, which culminates in a basketball game between the freshwomen and the sophomores. Intramurals are available for those with the initiative, but they take a backseat to the more popular and numerous nonsports clubs.

The school is very high on traditions. Bells are rung every evening to announce dinner and when the first snow of the season falls, and alumnae may request that they be rung on the occasion of their marriage. On the first and last day of classes, professors serve the seniors a champagne breakfast; sophomores give them roses on the last day of classes and dance around the sycamore tree.

With its mix of tradition and modern thinking, the accepting yet challenging atmosphere at Wells shows that good things come in small packages. "A Wells woman is open-minded, creative, intelligent, and fun loving," says an American studies major. "She knows when to be serious and when to be totally silly. She cares more about being herself than worrying what others think. She is involved, she is curious, she wants to make a difference in the world." In a word, she's a reflection of the Wells College spirit.

Overlaps
Cornell, Mt. Holyoke, SUNY, Smith, Syracuse

 If You Apply To > **Wells:** Early action and early decision: Dec. 15. Regular admissions: Mar. 1. Financial aid: Feb. 15. Meets demonstrated need of 92%. Campus and alumni interviews: recommended, informational. SATs or ACTs: required. SAT IIs: optional. Accepts the Common Application and electronic applications. Essay question: write about a significant achievement or experience; a person who influenced you; an issue of personal, local, or national concern.

Wesleyan University

North College, Middletown, CT 06457

Usually compared to Amherst or Williams, Wesleyan is really more like Swarthmore. The key difference: Wesleyan is twice as big. Wes students are progressive, politically minded, and fiercely independent. Exotic specialties like ethnomusicology and East Asian studies add spice to the scene.

One of the top small liberal arts colleges in the country by any measure, Wesleyan boasts engaging faculty members who care deeply about student performance and students who are driven by an innate desire to learn for learning's sake. Whether they're engrossed in academics, debating and demonstrating over various issues, or engaged in community service, Wes students seem to do things with a passion and intensity that helps set this school apart from tamer institutions. "Wes students take an in-your-face approach to life," says a government major.

This New England college offers more academic and extracurricular options than almost any school its size, and the Wesleyan experience means liberal learning in a climate of individual freedom. "Students work very hard, but the academic climate is not competitive," an American studies major says. Another student agrees, saying "The courses are rigorous, but the climate is supportive and conducive to sharing ideas." The freedom at Wesleyan requires motivated students who stay on task despite the laid-back atmosphere. There are abundant opportunities open to students willing to take advantage of them, which is precisely what these doers do.

It begins with the Wesleyan campus architecture, which is as diverse as the student body. The nucleus of this stately university is a century-old row of lovely ivy-covered brownstones that look out over the football field. The rest of the buildings can be described as "eclectic" and range from mod-looking dorms of the '50s and '60s to the early-nineteenth-century architecture of many academic buildings to the beautiful and modern Center for the Arts. The Wesleyan-owned student residences look freshly plucked from Main Street, U.S.A. The most recent additions to campus include classroom renovations and the initiation of a ten-year program to renovate facilities and classrooms across the campus, including an addition to the athletic center and the new Center for Film Studies.

Wesleyan has used its considerable wealth to attract highly rated faculty members who are expected to be scholar-teachers: academic supermen who juggle groundbreaking research, enthusiastic lectures, and personal student attention at the same time—and they seem to pull it off. "The quality of teaching is extremely high," says a junior, "but more remarkable is the active interest the professors take in the students." Among Wesleyan's strongest departments are music, economics, biology, American studies, and English, which for years has been the most popular degree. But even the smaller departments attract attention. Ethnomusicology, including African drumming and dance, is a particular specialty; students can be found reclining on the wide, carpeted bleachers at the World Music Hall or watching a dozen musicians play the Indonesian gamelan. The film department is first-rate. The East Asian Studies Center has both a strong program and an authentic Japanese tea room. Even the math department, which has been a source of criticism for years, has made significant changes to emphasize problem solving in small groups rather than interminable lectures dedicated to theory.

Wesleyan's curriculum renewal program ensures the relevance of liberal arts education in the twenty-first century by adding more professors for first- and second-year students, clustering courses to help students reach their academic goals, and requiring an electronic portfolio from each student. Students are expected in their first two years to take a minimum of two courses in each of three areas—humanities and the arts, social and behavioral sciences, and natural sciences and mathematics. During their second two years, students must take one course in each of the three areas. At the end of their freshman year, Wesleyan students can apply to major in one of three competitive, interdisciplinary seminar colleges: the College of Letters (literature, politics, and history with a leftist bent), the College of Social Studies (politics, economics, history with a conservative bent), and the Science in Society program (concerned with the

"Wes students take an in-your-face approach to life."

humane use of scientific knowledge, a la Buckminster Fuller). New students can take First-Year Initiative courses designed just for them. The university also implements a Web-based course selection and registration system to ease the process, but a sophomore grumps, "Registration is more complicated and frustrating than it should be."

The key to Wesleyan's success seems to be the fostering of an intellectual milieu where independent thinking and an appreciation of differences are omnipresent.

Wesleyan students are marked by an unusual commitment to debate, from political to cultural to intellectual. Chalking on the sidewalks is a cherished tradition (the student assembly even supplies the chalk free of charge), though not long ago the president declared a moratorium on the practice because of some negative references to specific faculty members. "One thing about Wesleyan, people aren't afraid to speak their mind or challenge someone else's idea," a student reports. "This creates an environment that is constantly debating and discussing things." It is hands-down an activist campus. One sophomore lists rallies and protests alongside parties and concerts as part of the campus social life. "This is a politically aware and active campus," a history major says. "Anything and everything can be an issue." Another student adds, "You'll have a hard time finding a more politically correct and socially active campus than Wes." But students level their smarts against topics close to home, mostly the university administration. "There's an energy on this campus, for me it's a spirit of creativity and political energy," a sophomore explains. In recent years, a significant number of Wesleyan alumni have gone on to make their mark in the entertainment industry and the high-tech world on the West Coast.

Wesleyan strives to keep its classes small and only 6 percent of the courses have fifty or more students. Some students claim they sometimes have trouble getting into the "hot" courses. "With popular classes, you have to be persistent, but you can get in," a history major says. If beseeching is not your style, studying abroad may be a temporary tonic to registration headaches. Programs are available in Israel, Germany, Africa, Japan, Latin America, France, Spain, and China. Students can also participate in the Venture Program,* study at Mystic Seaport,* or take a semester at another Twelve-College Exchange* school. Internships are popular, and students can also take advantage of 3–2 engineering programs with Columbia and Caltech.

Wesleyan likes to describe itself as "a small college with university resources." The libraries have more than a million volumes, practically unheard of at a school this size. Students claim that whenever you happen to walk past the brightly lit, glass-walled study room of Sci-Li (the science library), you're apt to see numerous students huddled over their books. Wesleyan's excellent reputation and strong recruiting network attract students from all over, ensuring the clash of viewpoints that makes it such a vital place. Of the student body, enrollment figures indi-

"You'll have a hard time finding a more politically correct and socially active campus than Wes."

cate the makeup as 8 percent African-American, 6 percent Hispanic, and 8 percent Asian-American. Students report that diversity is cherished at Wes. "Wesleyan is extremely liberal," notes a junior. "Nevertheless, it has its share of conservatives, which adds to the diversity of the student body." Another student adds, "Wes students are tolerant because there's an open dialogue both in and outside of the classroom that creates a high level of awareness and acceptance." Seventy-three percent graduated in the top tenth of their high school class. No academic or athletic merit scholarships are offered, but Wesleyan does guarantee to meet the financial need of all admits. Freshman orientation, which gets rave reviews, consists of a week of standard preregistration fare, plus comedy nights, movies, and square dancing.

For housing, most freshmen are consigned to the newly renovated singles or doubles in the campus dorms. Popular opinion indicates that the Butterfield complex is the choice for quiet study, while Clark Hall is where the party people go. Ninety-four percent of undergraduates live in university housing, and housing is guaranteed for

A sophomore describes the typical Wesleyan student as "sarcastic, dramatic, poetic, athletic, creative, proactive, open-minded, caring, loud, and polite."

*New students can take
First-Year Initiative courses
designed just for them.*

four years. Juniors and seniors enjoy numerous housing options: townhouses for four or five students, fraternities, college-owned houses and apartments, or special-interest houses organized around concerns such as ecology, feminism, or minority student unity. Upperclass students who want to live off campus must apply for permission. Those who move off have the option of eating at home, in the school grill, or at the fraternity eating clubs. Everyone else takes meals in Mocon, the glass-walled main dining hall, or two smaller cafeterias, and complains about the mandatory meal plan.

Middletown is a small city within easy driving distance of Hartford and New Haven, but it is off the beaten track of steady public transportation. Often students contend that "it may have everything you need, but nothing you want." Still, Wes students contribute a great deal of time to community service, and help maintain a peaceful, beneficial relationship with the town. And Wesleyan's rural surroundings afford the much-appreciated opportunity to jog through the countryside, swim at nearby Wadsworth Falls, or pick apples in the local orchards. Good road trips include New York and Boston, each two hours away, and decent ski areas and beaches just under an hour away. Wesleyan sports tend to be for scholar-athletes rather than spectators. In any sport, annual encounters with "Little Three" rivals Williams and Amherst get even the most bookwormish student out of the library and into the heat of the action. The Ultimate Frisbee club (the

"Wes students are tolerant because there's an open dialogue both in and outside of the classroom that creates a high level of awareness and acceptance."

"Nietzsch Factor," named after a former star player's dog, not the philosopher) almost always whips challengers, and intramurals are extremely popular. Athletics are enhanced by a complex that comes complete with a two-hundred-meter indoor track, a fitness center, and a fifty-meter pool.

Although two former fraternities have turned into co-ed literary societies, Greek life at the remaining three is a jock preserve. Only 5 percent of the men and 1 percent of the women go Greek. Wesleyan's enforcement of the twenty-one-year-old drinking age is moderate compared with most schools. Consistent with the university's encouragement of independence, students bear a large part of the responsibility for policing themselves. "To the university's credit, they are really stressing alcohol awareness, so to speak," says a neuroscience and behavioral studies major. Students who throw a party for seventy-five or more people must attend a workshop that stresses safe drinking. Still, most students concur that it is quite easy for the under-aged to imbibe. "You can get alcohol if you want to," notes a sophomore. It seems, however, that drinking alcohol is a minor event when compared to the multitude of other things happening on campus. Activities abound from comedy performances to a cappella groups, films, plays, bands, lectures, parties, and events planned by the more than two hundred student groups. "There's tons going on right on campus," raves a sophomore, "so much that you feel like you're missing out if you leave." Major events on the social calendar include Spring Fling and Fall Ball—two outdoor festivals—and Uncle Duke Day and Zonker Harris Day, two similar events with a more psychedelic, 1960s flavor, in which students pay tribute to the infamous Doonesbury characters.

With so much to do and learn, students at Wesleyan take it all in stride. The key to Wesleyan's success seems to be the fostering of an intellectual milieu where independent thinking and an appreciation of differences are omnipresent. So different, in fact, that a sophomore describes the typical Wesleyan student as "sarcastic, dramatic, poetic, athletic, creative, proactive, open-minded, caring, loud, and polite." And if you're still not convinced, take it from a veteran: "We would make any liberal arts college proud, but you can only find us here."

Overlaps
Brown, Yale, Columbia, Amherst, Harvard

West Virginia University

P.O. Box 6009, Morgantown, WV 26506-6009

With the exception of a few Pennsylvanians who migrate south to Morgantown, out-of-staters find little reason to consider WVU. The honors program is a must for top students, and the university has good programs in professional fields ranging from journalism to engineering.

While West Virginia University continues to be the state's flagship land grant college, its academic mission has broadened. With a hundred and seventy degree programs, three hundred student organizations, and sixteen intercollegiate varsity athletic programs, it's no wonder students flock to this large university. And while the university recently received the dubious distinction of being among the nation's premier party schools, students say they work just as hard as they play. "Our students are very proud of WVU," a junior says. The party-school designation "is just because people see what a huge support the student body is to all our programs." With strong academic programs and student organizations, the school has become a solid choice for scholars, researchers, and athletes, too.

WVU is situated in the picturesque mountains of north central West Virginia, a few miles from the Pennsylvania border and overlooking the Monongahela River. A driverless rail system bridges the school's two campuses—the older Morgantown and the more modern Evansdale, which are a mile and a half apart. Ten of the ivy-covered Morgantown buildings, dating mainly from the nineteenth century, are listed on the National Register of Historic Places; many of their interiors have been restored or renovated. The newest facility is the eight-floor, 190,000-square-foot Life Sciences Building, which houses the psychology and biology departments. Other new additions include a brand new, high-tech library adjoined to the Wise Library and the Student Recreation Center, which has received national recognition for its design.

WVU's degree programs span thirteen schools, the best of which are engineering (particularly energy-related) and the allied health sciences (medical technology, physical therapy, nursing, and occupational therapy). The most popular majors are business and economics, engineering, psychology, journalism, and biology; unusual options include a six-year PharmD, and a B.S. in forensic identification, developed in conjunction with the FBI. Regardless of major, students must complete the liberal studies program, which helps them "acquire knowledge, make critical judgments in a logical and rational manner, and communicate their findings clearly." Graduates are expected to possess knowledge and experience in three broad clusters—arts and humanities, social and behavioral sciences, and mathematics

> "Morgantown is perfect. It creates opportunities for students with jobs, activities, and even political action."

and natural sciences—as well as broaden their understanding of people different from themselves. New programs include master's degrees in creative writing and integrated marketing communications, a fully online program. Physical therapy is

Website: www.wvu.edu
Location: Small city
Total Enrollment: 23,492
Undergraduates: 16,692
Male/Female: 54/46
SAT Ranges: V 460–560
  M 470–580
ACT Range: 20–25
Financial Aid: 57%
Expense: Pub $ $
Phi Beta Kappa: Yes
Applicants: 9,147
Accepted: 94%
Enrolled: 46%
Grad in 6 Years: 56%
Returning Freshmen: 77%
Academics: ✍ ✍
Social: ☎ ☎ ☎ ☎
Q of L: ★ ★ ★
Admissions: (304) 293-2121
Email Address:
  wvuadmissions@arc.wvu
  .edu

Strongest Programs:
Forensic and Investigative
  Science
Biometric Systems
Engineering
Political Science
Pharmacy
Psychology
Allied Health

While WVU is a big school, administrators say that about two-thirds of the classes taken by freshmen have thirty or fewer students.

Morgantown is a small city with a college-town feel and plenty of community-service opportunities, students say.

Sixty percent of students are in-staters, and a sizable contingent arrives from western Pennsylvania and southern New Jersey— so many that the university has been dubbed "New Jersey University: West Virginia campus."

Overlaps

Marshall, Fairmont State, Penn State, University of Pittsburgh, Virginia Tech

now a doctorate program, and there's now a doctorate program in nursing. A bachelor's degree in interdisciplinary studies is also available. Undergrads can now major in women's studies.

While WVU is a big school, administrators say that about two-thirds of the classes taken by freshmen have thirty or fewer students. Students say the quality of teaching is generally very good, but academic advising is lacking. "The first two years of school are very important and many times students are led astray by faulty advisors," one political science and economics major says. Classes are challenging, but the atmosphere is supportive. "Overall, the academic climate of WVU is relatively laid back," a junior says. "In many courses, I have found that what I get out of the course is contingent upon what I put into it." Operation Jump-Start helps students adjust to college with New Student Convocation, dorm-based Freshman Interest Groups, and Resident Faculty Leaders, who live next door to the dorms and serve as mentors and friends. A pass/fail course called Orientation to University Life also helps students understand the academic, social, and emotional expectations of the college experience, covering study skills, university and community support services, goal setting, and career planning. On the other end of the spectrum, an honors program offers small classes and early registration to students with a 3.5 high school GPA and 1360 on the SAT (or a 3.8 and a 1240).

Though West Virginia attracts students from most U.S. states and nearly one hundred foreign countries, it is primarily regional. Sixty percent of students are in-staters, and a sizable contingent arrives from western Pennsylvania and southern New Jersey—so many that the university has been dubbed "New Jersey University: West Virginia campus." African-Americans comprise 4 percent of

"Students love the school and the state."

the student body, and Hispanics and Asian-Americans are just over 1 percent each. But the biggest complaint among students is the lack of available parking. The university offers approximately 3,500 merit scholarships, ranging from $1,000 to $11,000, along with athletic scholarships in all sixteen intercollegiate sports.

Twenty-one percent of WVU's undergraduates live on campus, where dorms are fairly mediocre but filling up fast because of the increase in students flocking to the university. Most are co-ed; the older ones are known for their character; the newer residential complexes on the Evansdale campus have larger rooms and luxuries like air-conditioning. Many upperclassman opt for nearby apartments. Nine percent each of men and women who go Greek may live in their chapter house. Each dorm has its own cafeteria, and students may buy meal plans regardless of where they live. Fraternities and sororities have their own cooks.

Morgantown is a small city with a college-town feel and plenty of community service opportunities, students say. "Morgantown is perfect," a mechanical and aerospace engineering major says. "It creates opportunities for students with jobs, activities, and even political action. The possibilities are endless." The school has worked hard to curtail underage drinking, banning alcohol in the dorms and limiting each frat to three social events per semester with three hundred members and guests. Students report that it's now near impossible for those under twenty-one to be served on campus, and say off-campus bars have also cracked down. That said, social life is still centered on campus, often focused on the free food, movies, bands, and comedians offered Thursday through Saturday by the school-sponsored Up All Night program. Spring Fest and Fall Fest provide stress relief each semester, and Mountaineer Week showcases the customs of Appalachia. For those with cars, road trips to Columbus, Washington, D.C., or Pittsburgh are quick and easy. Football rivalries with Miami, Virginia Tech, Syracuse, Notre Dame, and Pitt (the "Backyard Brawl") take students farther afield.

Aside from Mountaineer football, which has again achieved national prominence, West Virginia fields a very competitive rifle team, and its wrestling team has been named Eastern Wrestling League Champions two years in a row. The gymnastics team has also brought home a league championship. Track and soccer is also strong among women.

WVU students take pride in their university. They study hard and play hard. After all, they go to a top-notch state university that offers strong programs in whatever their field. "Students love the school and the state," one student raves. "They truly 'bleed blue and gold.'"

| **If You Apply To** ➢ | **West Virginia:** Rolling admissions (priority date Mar. 1). Financial aid: Feb. 15 (for freshman scholarships), Mar. 1. Does not guarantee to meet demonstrated need. Campus and alumni interviews: optional, informational. SATs or ACTs: required. SAT IIs: optional. Accepts the Common Application and electronic applications. No essay question. |

Wheaton College

501 College Avenue, Wheaton, IL 60187

Wheaton is at the top of the heap in evangelical education, rivaled only by Pepperdine (with its Malibu digs) and traditional competitors such as Calvin and Hope. Students pledge to live a Christian life and renew the vow every semester. Wheaton's low tuition makes it a relative bargain.

There is no denying that Wheaton College is one dedicated place: dedicated to learning, spiritual growth, and a deep love for Jesus Christ. One of the finest evangelical schools in the country, Wheaton is also a liberal arts college that encourages its students to dip into a wide range of academic pursuits, travel the world, and help the less fortunate. "There is a genuine commitment among the students to Christ. They care about the world and their studies because they see how it is connected to their faith," explains an economics major.

Wheaton's eighty-acre campus is an oasis of sorts: Blanchard Hall, built in the last century, looks like a castle perched atop the front campus hill. Down the hill from the main campus is the $13.5 million Billy Graham Center, a museum and library that has become a cornerstone in research on American evangelicalism. The mall area provides room for strolls through the verdant campus, which sits right in the middle of one of Chicago's oldest and most established suburbs. The sports and recreation center recently benefited from new basketball courts, a climbing wall, and a weight-lifting facility.

Wheaton bills itself as a "Christian, liberal arts institution that is committed to the principle that truth is revealed by God through Christ, in whom is hidden all the treasures of wisdom and knowledge." The school's deep dedication to the Christian faith only strengthens its commitment to education. Christian perspective is integrated into disciplines across the curriculum, which is built around requirements that include studies in faith, reason, society, nature, literature, and the arts. Students are also expected to be competent in knowledge of the Bible, public speaking, English, foreign language, and mathematics. Twelve credit hours of Bible studies and theology are required of all students, and all freshmen must

> "There is a genuine commitment among the students to Christ. They care about the world and their studies because they see how it is connected to their faith."

Website: www.wheaton.edu
Location: Suburban
Total Enrollment: 2,872
Undergraduates: 2,395
Male/Female: 50/50
SAT Ranges: V 620–710
    M 610–700
ACT Range: 26–31
Financial Aid: 50%
Expense: Pr $
Phi Beta Kappa: No
Applicants: 1,968
Accepted: 55%
Enrolled: 56%
Grad in 6 Years: 85%
Returning Freshmen: 94%
Academics: ✍ ✍ ✍
Social: ☎ ☎ ☎
Q of L: ★ ★ ★ ★
Admissions: (630) 752-5005
    or (800) 222-2419
Email Address:
    admissions@wheaton.edu

Strongest Programs:
English

take the Freshman Experience Seminar. Students describe professors as exceptional. "The professors are amazing—experts in their fields and committed Christians. They care about their students and invest heavily in their lives," says a sophomore.

Any fears about the gap between Christianity and science have been overcome at Wheaton, where most of the natural sciences are strong—biology and chemistry in particular. English, business/economics, elementary education, communications, and music are the most popular majors. In addition to major programs in the liberal arts and sciences, students can opt for the 3–2 liberal arts/nursing program or liberal arts/engineering double degree. Wheaton recently added an international relations major. Studying abroad in East Asia, England, France, Germany, Spain, Russia, Latin America, or the Holy Lands is an option for Wheaton undergraduates, as is spending a semester at one of twelve other evangelical schools in the Council for Christian Colleges and Universities.* The Human Needs and Global Resources (HNGR) program coordinates studies in Third World development with six-month internships in a development project in a Third World country.

The High Road Wilderness Program provides an Outward Bound–type experience. There is also the Black Hills Science Station for summer study in botany and zoology and the Northwoods Honey Rock Campus for leadership training. More than a dozen other options are offered through the Council for Christian Colleges and Universities.* Students in science, math, and computer science have the opportunity to perform research at Argonne National Laboratory.

Christian perspective is integrated into disciplines across the curriculum, which is built around requirements that include studies in faith, reason, society, nature, literature, and the arts.

A majority of Wheaties share a fairly similar middle-class, public school background. Sixty-five percent graduated in the top quarter of their high school class, a fact that adds to both the intellectual energy and the academic pressures. Minorities make up 12 percent of the student body, and about one-fifth of the students are from Illinois. For the most part, people at Wheaton are educated about issues, and discussions of interest include abortion, euthanasia, and genetic cloning. "There is always a push for greater awareness of unity/diversity so that we might become more integrated," says an anthropology major. "Another issue unique to our campus is the religious political issue of the role of women in the church. This year there was the peace movement, but that is always a recurrent theme." Whatever the discussion or point of view, an international relations major says, "Wheaton does not put a lot of emphasis on being politically correct, but it does want people to be considerate of others while voicing their opinions." A large number of students spend time volunteering in inner-city Chicago, tutoring, visiting nursing homes, visiting AIDS patients, and running church youth groups.

Students are generally pleased with their dorm rooms, though they can range from beautiful to ready for a little renovation. Saint and Elliot are said to fit into the

"The professors are amazing—experts in their fields and committed Christians."

latter category. Many juniors and seniors live in college-owned apartments on campus, but only 12 percent of undergraduates live off campus or commute. The single-sex dorms are only open to students of the opposite gender on certain days of the week during set hours. Wheaton offers a beautiful dining hall with fireplaces and a variety of spaces in which to eat. Students praise the food, which ranges from the exotic to good old "comfort food" like biscuits and gravy.

"Wheaties," who are also known as "Breakfast of Champions," have lots of sports traditions, including when teams trade uniforms or otherwise invade each others' territories.

Two common elements of college that are noticeably absent from the Wheaton experience are Greek organizations and alcohol. Almost all students adhere to the community covenant of no drinking, anywhere, any time on campus. Wheaton's social scene is active, albeit mostly on campus. The College Union organizes activities like movies, late-night skating parties, and weekly coffeehouses. The school's administration has loosened its ban on social dancing, pleasing students. Also popular are treks to the movies, and a quick forty-five minute train ride transports

Wheaton undergrads to Chicago's Loop, which offers restaurants, blues clubs, museums, shopping, and professional sporting events. Major annual events include Fall and Spring fests, the talent show, the annual Air-Jam, and the class film festival. In a nod to changing times, Wheaton's Board of Trustees recently held a swing dance—the first of its kind at the college—that attracted one thousand rug-cutters, signaling an end to the prohibition of dancing.

The calm of Wheaton's mild-mannered Christian ambiance is periodically shattered by the interclass scramble for the Bench, a reinforced slab of concrete that is the subject of an ongoing and often rough-and-tumble game of keep-away. "Wheaties," who are also known as "Breakfast of Champions," have lots of other sports traditions, including when teams trade uniforms or otherwise invade each others' territories. "Swimmers, for example, dress up really crazily and run around at football games at half time," reports a sophomore. A gentler Wheaton tradition is that engaged couples climb to the top of Blanchard Hall and ring the bell. Wheaton athletic teams, known for seventy years as the Crusaders, are

"There is always a push for greater awareness of unity/diversity so that we might become more integrated."

now the Thunder. Critics claimed the old mascot glorified medieval Christians who killed thousands of people in the name of Jesus. The new mascot was chosen from thirteen hundred suggestions because it sounds strong and is one of the natural phenomena associated with God. Men's and women's soccer and football and women's basketball games are favorite events.

The school's motto, "For Christ and His Kingdom," demonstrates its deep commitment to the nurturing of one's mind and soul. The school is coming from a definite point of view, and yet, "No topic is off limits" at Wheaton, a sophomore says. "It is this openness of dialogue that keeps Wheaton such a dynamic place of growth." And with an alumni roster that reads like a "Who's Who" among American Evangelical Protestants, it's clear that Wheaton's impact remains with students for the rest of their lives.

Overlaps

Taylor, Calvin, Northwestern, Grove City

If You Apply To ➤

Wheaton: Early action: Nov. 1. Regular admissions: Jan. 15. Financial aid: Feb. 15. Campus interviews: optional, evaluative. No alumni interviews. SATs or ACTs: required. SAT IIs: informative. Essay question: personal statement and additional essay.

Wheaton College

Norton, MA 02766

Wheaton is the most recent convert to coeducation among prominent East Coast institutions, and women still outnumber men by nearly two to one. Though in Massachusetts, Wheaton is actually closer to Providence than Boston. One of the few moderately selective institutions in the area.

It's been well over a decade since Wheaton College first admitted men, but the traditions and academic excellence that helped the college make its name endure. The first night of freshman year, for example, is still marked by a candlelight ceremony in the chapel. Students keep their candles until Sentimental Night, when, as seniors, they float them on Peacock Pond. And a woman who walks with a date three times

Website:
    www.wheatoncollege.edu
Location: Suburban
Total Enrollment: 1,521

(Continued)

Undergraduates: 1,521
Male/Female: 37/63
SAT Ranges: V 590–670
  M 550–650
ACT Range: 26–29
Financial Aid: 58%
Expense: Pr $ $ $ $
Phi Beta Kappa: Yes
Applicants: 3,534
Accepted: 44%
Enrolled: 27%
Grad in 6 Years: 70%
Returning Freshmen: 88%
Academics: ✍ ✍ ✍
Social: ☎ ☎ ☎
Q of L: ★ ★ ★ ★
Admissions: (508) 286-8251
Email Address: admission@
  wheatoncollege.edu

Strongest Programs:
Social Sciences
Fine Arts
Humanities
Chemistry
Hispanic Studies (Spanish)
Italian
French
Mathematics
Computer Science

When they're not hitting the books, Wheaton students love to put on their dancing shoes— whether for the Boston Bash party on a boat in Boston Harbor, for the Valentine's Dance, or for any number of events at Rosecliff, a mansion in Newport, Rhode Island.

around the pond may still push the hapless fellow in if he doesn't deign to kiss her. Wheaton also continues to attract students with solid programs in the social sciences, fine arts, and humanities. "Wheaton students are leaders," one junior says. "We know how to take action and get things done. We enjoy energizing others and raising student awareness and activity."

Wheaton's rural location offers few distractions from intellectual pursuits. Its 385-acre campus blends Georgian brick buildings and modern structures set among beautiful lawns and shade trees. The two halves of the campus are separated by the aforementioned pond, which probably qualifies as the only heated duck pond on any American campus. In 2002, Wheaton completed a $20 million renovation and construction project, which included the creation of the Mars Arts and Humanities Building. Beard Hall, a new one-hundred-bed dormitory, is now open to students and boasts wireless Internet connections throughout. Parking has increased by two hundred spaces, and Wheaton plans on redoing the landscaping throughout campus.

Students say Wheaton's best programs include psychology, political science, psychology, and English. Programs in the arts are well recognized, impressive given the school's small size, and the chemistry department is also strong, producing both Wheaton's Rhodes Scholarship winners in 2000–2001 and two Fulbright scholars. The major in Hispanic studies benefits from its affiliation with a study-abroad program in Cordoba, and a Mellon Foundation grant supports native speakers in Spanish and other languages. Those interested in interdisciplinary or cross-disciplinary work may design an independent major, or add classes taken at other schools in the Twelve-College Exchange Program.* Students may also take classes not offered at Wheaton at nearby Brown University. For those tired of studying on land, Wheaton offers the Maritime Studies Program.* Dual-degree programs offer motivated students the chance to earn a bachelor's degree in engineering or graduate degrees in business, communication, religion, or optometry in conjunction with schools like Dartmouth, Emerson, and Clark.

Back on campus, Wheaton has implemented a new curriculum for the class of 2007, which will emphasize foundation courses and encourage students to explore the liberal arts through connections between and among classes. The curriculum will link experiential learning to each department and require a capstone senior project. Core classes include English, quantitative skills, foreign language, natural science, and non-Western history. Students also choose a first-year seminar from among twenty-four sections, each focused on "controversies" that have generated debate or heralded changes in how they experience or understand the world.

Wheaton's small classes encourage close ties between students and faculty. "All classes are taught by professors," an economics and Hispanic studies major says. "The quality of teaching is exceptional. Professors always challenge students and

"All classes are taught by professors. The quality of teaching is exceptional."

are always very enthusiastic about their subjects." Aside from a faculty advisor, students get a staff mentor and two peer advisors, known as preceptors. Classes are demanding, a mathematics majors says. "The academic climate at Wheaton is very competitive. Professors demand a lot from their students." The Filene Center for Work and Learning gets high marks from students seeking internships—and jobs after graduation.

About a third of Wheaton's students come from Massachusetts, and nearly two-thirds went to public high schools. The student body is largely Caucasian, with African-Americans accounting for 3 percent, Hispanics 4 percent, and Asian-Americans 3 percent. Political viewpoints are especially diverse, which lends to an open atmosphere, a junior says. "We are so diverse in our political stands that students are generally comfortable expressing views." Those efforts have been helped by Wheaton's decision to go co-ed, which sparked a dramatic increase in applications and enrollment. The administration has undertaken a massive capital campaign, using some of the proceeds to hire more minority scholars—and recruit more minority students.

As might be expected on this small, secluded campus, virtually everyone lives in one of Wheaton's dorms or houses (one all-women, twenty-six co-ed). Gebbie Hall, the all-female dorm, regularly hosts panels, presentations, and colloquia on gender issues. The fifty-one residents of this self-governing hall are selected on the basis of applications that ask about their commitment to gender equality. All students are guaranteed housing for four years; freshmen live in doubles, triples, or quads, and upperclassmen try their luck in the lottery system. "The dorms are comfortable," but overcrowded with the increase in freshmen, a junior English major says. The bright and spacious dining halls offer unlimited chow, and the biggest winners of all are the ducks, who thrive on the leftover bread students toss into Peacock Pond.

Social life at Wheaton includes dances, concerts, lectures, and parties on campus, or road trips to Boston (thirty-five miles away) and Providence (fifteen miles). The town of Norton, just outside campus, draws some students with a Big Brother/Big Sister program, hospital visits, and opportunities to tutor and mentor children, but otherwise has few redeeming qualities. "Norton is the farthest from a college town that you could be," a junior says. "It has a CVS, bank, and pizza parlors. It is a nice town, but Wheaton makes up for lack of Norton nightlife with campus programming." For that, students head to the college's student center, which offers a cafe, dance studio, and sun deck for afternoon study breaks. There are no sororities and fraternities here, which helps cut down on underage drinking, though students say that as on most campuses, those who want to find alcohol will do so. Nondrinkers won't feel ostracized, though. "Our long-standing honor code reminds students about respect and community living," a senior says.

When they're not immersed in classwork, Wheaton students love to put on their dancing shoes—whether for the Boston Bash party on a boat in Boston Harbor, for the Valentine's Dance, or for any number of events at Rosecliff, a mansion in Newport, Rhode Island. Spring Weekend has the Head of the Peacock boat race, where students build ships and race them across the pond, as well as live bands and outdoor barbecues. When it rains, students get dirty as they slide around the craters on Wheaton's lawns, an activity known as "dimple diving."

Wheaton competes in Division III of the NCAA, and its strongest teams include men's and women's soccer—both of which have won numerous championships—men's and women's indoor track, baseball, softball, and men's and women's lacrosse. The athletic facility boasts an eight-lane swimming pool, a field house, and an 850-seat arena for basketball or volleyball.

Students at Wheaton understand that there is an education that needs to be attained in college in addition to an academic one. That explains why so many students are involved in campus planning and college operations. Students here take pride in their achievements inside and outside the classroom, while striving to preserve the school's friendly, small-town feel.

Wheaton has implemented a new curriculum for the class of 2007, which will emphasize foundation courses and encourage students to explore the liberal arts through connections between and among classes.

Overlaps

Skidmore, Connecticut College, Clark, Boston University, Bates

If You Apply To ➤ **Wheaton:** Early decision: Nov. 15, Jan. 15. Regular admissions: Jan. 15. Financial aid: Jan. 15. Campus interviews: required, evaluative. Alumni interviews: recommended, informational. SATs or ACTs: optional. SAT IIs: optional. Accepts the Common Application and electronic applications. Essay question: significant experience or achievement; issue of personal, local, national, or international concern; influential person; influential fictional character, historical figure, or creative work; or a topic of your choice.

Whitman College

345 Boyer Avenue, Walla Walla, WA 99362-2083

Whitman has quietly established itself as one of the West's leading liberal arts colleges. Don't sweat the umbrella: Walla Walla is in arid eastern Washington. Whitman's isolation breeds community spirit and alumni loyalty. True to its liberal arts heritage, Whitman has no business program.

Website: www.whitman.edu
Location: Small city
Total Enrollment: 1,454
Undergraduates: 1,454
Male/Female: 42/58
SAT Ranges: V 610–710
    M 610–700
ACT Range: 26–31
Financial Aid: 94%
Expense: Pr $ $ $ $
Phi Beta Kappa: Yes
Applicants: 2,411
Accepted: 50%
Enrolled: 31%
Grad in 6 Years: 87%
Returning Freshmen: 93%
Academics: ✍ ✍ ✍ ✍
Social: ☎ ☎ ☎
Q of L: ★ ★ ★ ★
Admissions: (509) 527-5176
Email Address:
    admission@whitman.edu

Strongest Programs:
Politics
Biology
History
English
Psychology
Music
Environmental studies

Down-to-earth friends and easy-going outdoor fun are just a Frisbee-throw away at this environmentally-minded liberal arts school for the academically minded. Somehow, in these wheat fields and vineyards of southeastern Washington, a small school is outgrowing its confines to produce a crop of students who are engaged in the world and intently focused on the well-being of their peers. It must be something in that Blue Mountain air.

Whitman was founded in 1836 by Marcus and Narcissa Whitman, who first established a medical mission and school to serve the Cayuse Indians and immigrants on the Oregon Trail. Everything important is within walking distance of campus, including the main drag of Walla Walla ("Walla Squared"), which recently won a national Best Main Street award. If a picturesque setting is your thing, you'll feel right at home at Whitman, with its 117-acre campus blending Colonial buildings and modern facilities, all covered in New England ivy. The campus stands in contrast to the rolling expanse of Northwestern terrain nearby, inhabited primarily by farmers and ranchers. Beyond Walla Walla (which means "many waters" in the Cayuse Indian language), and as far as the eye can see, are scenic mountains, rivers, fields, and forests. Recent college construction includes completion of the new Reid campus center, a new science building, and an expansion of Penrose Library.

Professors at Whitman are "brilliant, well spoken, and caring," a politics major says. It's not unusual for students to pop into professors' offices, regardless of their posted help hours, and just sit down for a chat. Many students consider their teachers friends, not just people droning in front of a lectern. "The quality of teaching is one of the reasons I chose Whitman," says a senior. "I have developed close, long-term relationships with several of my professors." The school's small size translates into relatively limited course offerings, but students with far-flung interests can find a supportive faculty mentor and put together combined or individually planned majors. The school also funds several faculty–student research teams. Seniors get first dibs at registration, but most professors allow students to enroll in full classes if students approach them.

Many students agree that academics at Whitman are challenging, but underlying that rigor is a general sense of peer support. "We work our behinds off, but help each other out along the way," says a biology major. Impressive academic departments are politics, biology, psychology, English, and history, and Whitman has the most active small-college theater program in the country. Recent additions to the curriculum include majors in religion, rhetoric, and film studies. The program in biochemistry, biophysics, and molecular biology offers a major at the interface of the physical and biological sciences. There is also a new minor in Latin American Studies.

> **"I have developed close, long-term relationships with several of my professors."**

All Whitman students must complete the General Studies Program, which is designed to allow for flexibility based on a student's background, interest, and aptitude. The program is divided into the first year core and distribution requirements. The program helps first-year students learn to read analytically and write effectively.

Also, all students take at least six credits in social sciences, humanities, fine arts, and science; at least one class in quantitative analysis; and two courses that fulfill the requirement in alternative voices. Seniors must pass comprehensive written and oral exams in their major—the first college or university in the nation to require undergrads to do so.

Seniors must pass comprehensive written and oral exams in their major—the first college or university in the nation to require undergrads to do so.

Whitman boasts an extensive Asian art collection and expanded Asian studies and art history programs, which are supplemented by the College Summer Studies program in China. The library, with 355,000 volumes, is a great place to catch up on the latest campus news as well as to study. Whitman has 3–2 or 3–3 programs in engineering (with the University of Washington, Caltech, Columbia, Washington University, and Duke), international studies and international business (Monterey Institute of International Studies), computer science and oceanography (University of Washington), and law (Columbia). A student here could actually end up certified to teach in New York State through Whitman's teacher certification programs with the Bank Street College of

"We work our behinds off, but help each other out along the way."

Education (there's one with the University of Puget Sound School of Education, too). Off-campus semester programs include the Chicago Urban Studies Program, the Philadelphia Center, the Washington Semester Program, and Biosphere 2.

Whitties are "open and interesting," says a sophomore. Forty-four percent come from Washington, the rest are primarily from the suburbs of Western cities, notably San Francisco and Portland. Seven percent are Asian-American, while African-Americans and Hispanics combined make up only 5 percent of the students. The campus is pretty liberal in its political bent, and big issues range from abortion to vegetarianism, environmental issues, capital punishment, and Greek life. Liberal, but open-minded. "The students are willing to accept new people, things, and ideas," says one philosophy major. Whitman awards merit scholarships based on academic performance each year, ranging from $5,500 to $10,200, but there are no athletic scholarships. Ninety-one percent of students are offered aid equal to their demonstrated need.

Students rave about the campus housing, in which all freshmen and sophomores are required to live. "Residence life does a phenomenal job of making students feel welcome," writes a politics/Asian studies major. "Their excellent programming combined with immaculate dorms and multiple housing options makes many juniors and seniors want to live on campus." In fact, 74 percent of the entire student body does live on campus. Prentiss Hall and

"The students are willing to accept new people, things, and ideas."

Lyman House, both built in 1926, have received multimillion-dollar face-lifts. There's also theme housing for students interested in foreign languages, fine arts, writing, community service, Asian studies, environmental studies, or the outdoors, as well as a multiethnic house. Forty-five percent of the men belong to the four fraternities, which have their own houses. The four sororities, which claim 48 percent of the women, stake out sections in the all-female residence hall. In a break from tradition, the Bon Appetit company runs the food service, featuring cafe and bistro styles of food.

Outdoor attractions are important in this area of the country, where autumn is gorgeous, winter sporadically snowy, and spring delightfully warm. Walla Walla (population 30,000) is located in the center of agricultural southeastern Washington near the Blue Mountains. The town has several shops and restaurants, but that's not what this part of the country is about. Go outdoors! Hiking, biking, and backpacking are minutes away, and white-water rafting and rock climbing are popular on weekends. Two ski centers and other recreational areas are within an hour's drive of campus. Seattle (260 miles) and Portland (235 miles) are a welcome change of scenery.

Whitman scrapped varsity football in the late 1970s, but the "Missionaries" maintain an active interest in physical exertion. Highly popular intramural football

The school's small size translates into relatively limited course offerings, but students with far-flung interests can find a supportive faculty mentor and put together combined or individually planned majors.

(where both men and women participate) has filled the void nicely, and 75 percent of the student body competes in the vigorous intramural club program. Rock climbers can challenge themselves on two walls, one outdoor and one indoor. Men's snowboarding does very well, as does track and field, skiing, swimming, tennis, and lacrosse. The Alpine and cross-country ski teams won both men's and women's conference titles in recent years.

The campus is an oasis of activity. Students mention the very active drama department, which stages about twelve productions a year, as important to on-campus life. The lack of a football team doesn't stop Whitties from celebrating homecoming, as well as the Ultimate Frisbee Onionfest and the Beer Mile (chug a cold one at each lap.) In the spring, Whitman shows its intellectual side with Renaissance Faire. There are also free movies and a student coffeehouse featuring weekly live music from various local or out-of-town bands. The alcohol policy is very loose, students say; generally, if you've got it in your room, keep the door shut. Walla Walla supports a resident symphony, community theater, numerous art galleries, two rodeos, and a hot-air balloon festival in the spring.

> **"Residence life does a phenomenal job of making students feel welcome."**

You don't have to own a Frisbee to get into Whitman. But if you throw one, you will most likely find someone who'll toss it back to you. Says a student, "[Whitman] is everything I wanted in a school. There are no words or surveys that can show what Whitman is all about."

If You Apply To ➤

Whitman: Early decision: Nov. 15. Regular admissions: Jan. 15. Financial aid: Apr. 7 (Dec. 20, Feb. 1 for early decision). Meets demonstrated need of 94%. Campus interviews: recommended, evaluative. No alumni interviews. SATs or ACT's: required. SAT IIs: recommended (English composition with essay). Accepts the Common Application and electronic applications. Essay question: significant experience; important issue; influential person; fictional/historical figure; creative work; topic of choice.

Whittier College

13406 East Philadelphia, P.O. Box 634, Whittier, CA 90608-4413

Whittier's Quaker heritage brings a touch of the east to this suburban campus on the outskirts of L.A. Less selective than Occidental and the Claremont Colleges, Whittier lures top students with an arsenal of academic scholarships. Beware the sneaky October 15 deadline for the best of them.

Founded in 1887 by members of the Society of Friends, Whittier College is fast becoming a global training ground. Whittier students can be found all around the world, studying in thirty foreign countries and even designing their entire curriculum. And when they return to the Whittier campus, they have access to caring faculty and a close-knit environment.

Located just eighteen miles away from downtown Los Angeles, the college is perched on a hill overlooking the town of Whittier, California, with the San Gabriel Mountains rising up from the horizon. The seventy-three-acre campus is a pleasant mixture of modern buildings tucked between the red-roofed, white-walled Spanish traditionals. Its landmark building, Deihl Hall, has been updated to include a digital audio/video computer lab for languages. Renovation and expansion of the Bonnie Bell Wardman Library is complete. A four-foot high granite monument stands on the north campus lawn, honoring Whittier's most famous alum, former president Richard Nixon.

Whittier officially ended its affiliation with the Quakers in the 1940s, but the prevailing spirit of community hearkens back to their traditions. Faculty wins high marks for their concern and accessibility. One junior says, "The climate is competitive in most of the fields but it depends on your major. The courses (mostly) are excellent due to the proficient faculty." Freshman are taught by full professors, "which raises the standards and challenges your thinking," a business major says. "For the most part, the quality of the teaching has been very intense, but very rewarding." While classes are somewhat competitive, students still work together. "Whittier students tend to be open and friendly," says a student majoring in comparative cultures. "You aren't afraid to sit with someone you haven't met before."

Whittier offers its students two major programs: the liberal education program and the Whittier Scholars Program. About 80 percent of the students take the revised liberal education track, in which they fulfill distribution requirements in writing skills, mathematics, natural

> "The quality of the teaching has been very intense, but very rewarding."

sciences, global perspectives, comparative knowledge, and creative and kinesthetic performance. The emphasis of the liberal education program is on an interdisciplinary focus, globalism, and critical and quantitative thinking. These liberally educated Whittierans next choose a major from among twenty-six departments, the strongest and most popular of which include English, biology, psychology, political science, and business administration, and programs that focus on teaching certification.

Whittier's strongest reputation lies in the Whittier Scholars Program, a path taken by 20 percent of the undergraduates who choose to bypass the traditional liberal education program. They are relieved of most general requirements and start from square one with an "educational design" process. With the help of an academic advisor, the scholars carve their majors out of standard offerings by taking a bit of this and a bit of that. Majors have included such names as symbol systems, visual studies and business, and dynamics of politics and urban life. The program is highly regarded (even by those who don't elect to take it) because of the more active role it allows students to play and the freedom it affords them in pursuing their interests. All students, no matter which curriculum they choose, must fulfill a year-long freshman writing requirement. In an attempt to help freshmen develop both their critical thinking skills and their ability to communicate clearly in writing, Whittier lets students choose their preferences from a variety of seminars. They are also encouraged to take an additional writing course, mathematics, and lab science during their freshman year. First-years also must attend a series of speakers who discuss topics relevant to student coursework and must take part in the Exploring Los Angeles series, which includes trips to museums and cultural events.

Study abroad options include programs in Denmark, India, Mexico, and Asia, and undergraduates may also take foreign study tours during the January interim. Forty percent of the students come from California, and the rest are from all over the United States and the world. Diversity plays a major role on this campus. While African-Americans make up only 5 percent of the students, Hispanic enrollment is an impressive 26 percent, and other minorities constitute 16 percent. The Black Student Union and Hispanic Student Association are vocal on campus. An on-campus cultural center focuses on diversity programming and resources. "Tolerance is a big watchword on campus," a junior says. "You can get severely disciplined or expelled for being intolerant." In addition to need-based aid, the college grants some students merit scholarships, ranging from $3,000 to $20,000.

Thirty-eight percent of the students seek off-campus shelter, but the Turner Residence Hall entices many students to stay on campus and vie for a chance to get a

(Continued)
Applicants: 1,485
Accepted: 76%
Enrolled: 27%
Grad in 6 Years: 50%
Returning Freshmen: 74%
Academics: ✍ ✍ ✍
Social: ☎ ☎ ☎
Q of L: ★ ★ ★ ★
Admissions: (562) 907-4238
Email Address:
admission@whittier.edu

Strongest Programs:
Child Development
Education
Social Work
Psychology
Business
Biology
Political Science
English

room with a panoramic view of Los Angeles and access to the campus computer network in every room. Most freshmen are assigned rooms, though Whittier Scholars, athletes, and members of Whittier's social societies tend to cluster in selected dorms and houses. All dorms are equally suited for freshmen, says one student, because each is its own little community. All campus residents must take at least ten meals at the Campus Inn dining hall, where the food is said to be typical college fare. "The dining facilities are of average quality, but the menu is diverse," a junior says. The Spot (Whittier's popular campus coffeehouse) was recently expanded to include a state-of-the-art nightclub called—what else?—the Club.

Nine social societies (they're not called fraternities or sororities here) attract 12 percent of the men and 17 percent of the women but hardly dominate the social scene. However, their dances, which frequently feature live entertainment, are welcomed by all. For many, entertainment takes the form of road trips, everything from Disneyland to the California beaches. Other common destinations include Las Vegas, Mexico, Joshua Tree, Hollywood, San Diego, and northern California. Whittier itself is a spot for community-minded students to get involved. "Whittier is a friendly town," one junior says. "The college is involved a lot with the community."

Whittier has a fairly strict alcohol policy and underage drinking is not permitted. Students say it's difficult for underage drinkers to get served at campus events.

"Tolerance is a big watchword on campus. You can get severely disciplined or expelled for being intolerant."

"Underage students are not allowed to even be in the same proximity as alcohol," a senior says. Popular annual events include a Spring Sing talent show, the football game against archrival Occidental College—dubbed the Battle of the Shoes—and Sportsfest, which is a campus-wide competition in which dorms compete in a variety of athletic, intellectual, and wacky games and events. A favorite among students is Mona Kai, a Hawaiian party put on by the Lancer Society where tons of sand are shipped in for the event. Also favored is the Midnight Breakfast served by professors during second-semester finals. The most important campus landmark is the Rock, which sits near the front of campus and is given a fresh coat of paint by countless aspiring artists. The beach is a frequent destination, and for nightlife, Los Angeles looms large. The local community, known as Uptown Whittier, offers quaint shops, restaurants, and cobblestone sidewalks but little in the way of entertainment.

Men's lacrosse is the most successful sports team on campus; their only loss last season was while competing in the NCAA Division III championships. Men's football and soccer, women's soccer, softball, and track are the most popular. Facilities have gotten an upgrade, including a new football field and a fully equipped fitness center.

The students at Whittier have created a supportive, intimate environment where people work together and celebrate their diversity. "It's a small, friendly place where everybody knows everybody," a junior math major says. With the opportunity to design their own majors, students are active in their own education.

If You Apply To ➢ **Whittier:** Rolling admissions. Early action: Dec. 1. Regular admissions: Feb. 1. (priority). Financial aid: Feb. 15. Does not guarantee to meet demonstrated need. Campus interviews: recommended, evaluative. No alumni interviews. SATs or ACTs: required. SAT IIs: optional. Accepts the Common Application and electronic applications. Essay question: achievement in twenty-five years; agenda for conversation with president of United States; one thing to change about high school experience; issue of concern; person you emulate.

Willamette is strategically located next door to the Oregon state capitol and forty minutes from Portland. Bigger than Whitman, smaller than U of Puget Sound, and more conservative than Lewis and Clark, Willamette offers extensive study abroad enhanced by ties to Asia.

Willamette University, founded in 1842, was the first university in the Pacific Northwest. Students can take advantage of their proximity to the state's legislative offices and a nearby hospital for internships, jobs, or off-campus learning experiences. Students at WU find a more personal atmosphere than larger universities nearby. "Willamette is special because there is a true passion for this institution," a senior says. The campus has become increasingly diverse, to the point where it's one of the most diverse of college campuses—public or private—in the region.

The sixty-one-acre campus lies across the street from the Oregon state capitol building and the state Supreme Court, providing a perfect avenue for student internships and political involvement. Willamette is home to full trees (thanks to Oregon's omnipresent rain), small wildlife, and occasionally steelhead salmon, which splash around in the Mill Stream that runs between WU's redbrick academic buildings. New additions include the Mary Stuart Rogers Music Center and a $3.5 million expansion to the art building. The new Day and Jean Montag Student Center features a convenience store, TV room, a wide selection of board games, a laundry room, a place to rent movies, and space for conferences, studying, and meetings. The university has embarked on a multiyear plan to transform dorms into residential colleges. The goal is to make the campus more of a series of neighborhoods, to further build and nurture community.

Willamette (pronounced "Will-AM-it") offers bachelor of arts and bachelor of music degrees, and most popular majors are English, psychology, and politics—especially strong because of the school's location in Oregon's capital. Students say other good bets include biology and chemistry. All students complete the freshman World Views seminar, four writing-centered courses, two courses in quantitative and analytical reasoning, study in a language other than English, and course work in six modes of inquiry—the natural world; the arts; arguments, reasons, and values; thinking historically; interpreting texts; and understanding society. Students also take capstone senior seminars, often culminating in research or thesis projects. More than half of the student body participates in a robust study abroad program, and WU also benefits from its proximity to the U.S. campus of Tokyo International University.

Classes are small; 81 percent of those taken by freshmen have twenty-five or fewer on the roster. Students work hard but don't compete for grades. "The Willamette experience is designed for students who are dedicated and willing to work hard to achieve their goals," a student says. "While the courses may be difficult, we are not here to compete with others; rather, we are here to gain the best education possible to prepare us for the future." Outside the classroom, the computerized card catalog and spacious study lounges in the Mark O. Hatfield Library (named for the former U.S. senator) make it easier to shoulder the workload. If students aren't reading or writing papers, numerous undergraduate research opportunities beckon. Support has more than doubled with the creation of the Carson Undergraduate Research Awards, the Science Collaborate Research Program, and a humanities center.

"Willamette is special because there is a true passion for this institution."

Website: www.willamette.edu
Location: Center city
Total Enrollment: 2,420
Undergraduates: 1,750
Male/Female: 46/54
SAT Ranges: V 550–680
   M 560–660
ACT Range: 25–30
Financial Aid: 65%
Expense: Pr $ $ $
Phi Beta Kappa: Yes
Applicants: 1,640
Accepted: 83%
Enrolled: 26%
Grad in 6 Years: 80%
Returning Freshmen: 91%
Academics: ✐ ✐ ✐½
Social: ☎ ☎ ☎
Q of L: ★ ★ ★ ★
Admissions: (503) 370-6300
Email Address:
   libarts@willamette.edu

Strongest Programs:
Politics
Biology
Economics
English

Students give Willamette's professors high marks. "If I were to grade the quality of teaching at Willamette, I would have to give it an A+, because so many professors are dedicated to the students in all aspects of academic life," a film studies major says. "These professors not only teach in the classroom, but also dedicate their time to help students outside of the classroom." The student/faculty ratio is 10 to 1.

Thirty-nine percent of Willamette students are native Oregonians, and much of the remainder come from Western states, notably California and Washington. The school is 57 percent white, with African-Americans making up 2 percent of the student body, Hispanics 5 percent, and Asian-Americans 7 percent. Foreigners and other non-Caucasian students comprise 29 percent. Women's issues, race relations, and the war in Iraq spark discussion on campus. "Students are respectful of others and socially aware," a sophomore says. "We have thoughtful, provocative social and political dialogue." Willamette offers talent and academic merit scholarships each year, ranging from $2,500 to full tuition; there are no athletic awards.

Seventy-one percent of students live in campus housing, which is social and convenient to classes and parties; doing so is required for freshmen and sophomores. "Students cannot live off campus until junior year; most students seem to stay on campus anyway," a sophomore reports. "I think that is a great testament to the quality of on-campus housing." All housing is co-ed, and theme wings or floors

> **"If I were to grade the quality of teaching at Willamette, I would have to give it an A+."**

are available, focused on community service, the outdoors, wellness, or substance-free living. Thirty-two percent of men and women go Greek, and some live in fraternity and sorority houses. The student-owned and -operated Bistro offers a coffeehouse atmosphere and is a popular alternative to cafeteria fare. "The dining facilities? They are great. Otherwise, the president of the university, faculty, staff, or even the governor of the state wouldn't eat here," a senior says. "The food is good and is focused around what the students want." When it comes to security, students feel very safe and take advantage of the college's escort service when they need it.

Most of Willamette's social life takes place on campus, whether it's free movies and lectures, open-mic nights at the Bistro, dance parties (salsa or swing), or performances from the music and theater departments. The Ram Brewery draws big crowds on Thursdays. Annual social highlights include the spring Wulapalooza, celebrating art and music, and the Hawaiian Club Luau, where students chow down on spit-roasted pig. Each fall, students from Tokyo International organize the Harvest Festival. Other wacky traditions including being Mill-Streamed—dumped into the campus brook on your birthday. When it comes to drinking, Willamette abides by state law, which says no one under twenty-one can imbibe—but students say anyone who wants booze can find and consume it behind closed doors.

Downtown Salem is a short walk from campus, and while students say it isn't a college town, it does have movies, shopping, restaurants, and coffeehouses. Also nearby are the Cascade Mountains and rugged beaches of Lincoln City and Coos Bay (an hour's drive), skiing and snowboarding on Mount Hood or in the high desert town of Bend (three hours), and the cosmopolitan cities of Portland (forty minutes) and Seattle (about four hours

> **"We have thoughtful, provocative social and political dialogue."**

north). San Francisco is an eight- to nine-hour drive. Willamette students remain true to the school motto, "Not unto ourselves alone are we born," when they go "Into the Streets" for a day of service each fall.

Willamette competes in Division III, and football, women's rowing, and track—women's and men's—are strong. Women's and men's cross country and track and field and men's golf have claim to recent championships. The university made history in October 1997, when junior soccer star Liz Heaston kicked her way into the record books as the first woman to play intercollegiate football. The annual football game against Pacific Lutheran usually has conference championship implications, and games against Linfield are also well attended.

Willamette may be the best little school you've never heard of, especially if you're from outside the California–Oregon–Washington corridor. "There are few other schools where I would have the support, attention, and opportunities to enjoy my two majors, study abroad for a semester, intern for a legislator, work on campus, volunteer in the community, participate in the Greek system, and graduate in four years with three hundred equally involved and committed students," marvels a sophomore. The school's close-knit community is strengthened by its emphasis on service, and by warm, supportive faculty members, who push students to achieve.

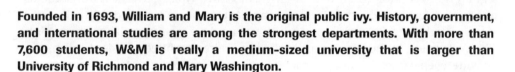

If You Apply To ➤ **Willamette:** Early action: Nov. 1, Dec. 1. Regular admissions and financial aid: Feb. 1. Does not guarantee to meet demonstrated need. Campus interviews: recommended, evaluative. Alumni interviews: optional, evaluative. SATs or ACTs: required. SAT IIs: optional. Accepts the Common Application and electronic applications. Essay question: how did you learn about Willamette; why Willamette is a good match for you; and choice of one: how you strive to serve others; source of racial tension; how does music reflect who you are; define success; responding to failure; personal experience.

College of William and Mary

P.O. Box 8795, Williamsburg, VA 23187

Founded in 1693, William and Mary is the original public ivy. History, government, and international studies are among the strongest departments. With more than 7,600 students, W&M is really a medium-sized university that is larger than University of Richmond and Mary Washington.

Though the physical campus might seem stuck in a time warp, students say everything about William and Mary—from the amazing faculty to the picturesque grounds—is up to date. Traditions abound, yet this historic public university—the second oldest in the nation—continues to evolve in its pursuit of academic excellence. The W&M formula of blending the old and the new has been working for more than three hundred years, and it's only getting better with age.

A profusion of azaleas and crape myrtle adds splashes of color to William and Mary's finely manicured campus, located about 150 miles southeast of Washington, D.C. The campus is divided into three sections and includes a lake and wooded wildlife preserve, which is filled with trails and widely used by the science departments. The Ancient Campus is a grouping of three Colonial structures, the oldest being Wren Hall, which has been in continuous use since 1695 and is one of the most visually pleasing buildings in American higher education. The Old Campus, where the buildings date from the '20s and '30s, is a little farther out, and next to it is New Campus, where ground was first broken in the '60s. The W&M campus boasts one of the most romantic spots of any in the nation: Crim Dell, a wooded area with a small pond spanned by an old-style wooden bridge. The 95,000-square-foot university center includes a bookstore, auditorium, game room, post office, conference rooms, and student lounge. Students say the center has enhanced campus social life by providing bands and comedians with a great performance space.

Website: www.wm.edu
Location: Small city
Total Enrollment: 7,645
Undergraduates: 5,694
Male/Female: 44/56
SAT Ranges: V 620–730
     M 630–710
ACT Range: 27–31
Financial Aid: 90%
Expense: Pub $ $
Phi Beta Kappa: Yes
Applicants: 8,917
Accepted: 35%
Enrolled: 35%
Grad in 6 Years: 91%
Returning Freshmen: 96%
Academics: ✍ ✍ ✍ ✍ ✍
Social: ☎ ☎ ☎
Q of L: ★ ★ ★
Admissions: (757) 221-4223

(Continued)

Email Address:
admiss@wm.edu

Strongest Programs:
Business Administration
Government
History
English
Biology

William and Mary created Phi Beta Kappa in December of 1776, and the honor code demands much from the college's students. There are no "easy A" classes at the college, and the academic climate is demanding and competitive. "Everyone here was a great student in high school," says a junior, "so there is this tacit level of competitiveness that drives people in the classroom." Still, most agree that it's a healthy rivalry.

Fittingly, the history department, a joint sponsor with Colonial Williamsburg of the Institute for Early American History and Culture, is among William and Mary's best departments. Business, psychology, government, biology, and English are the most popular majors. The accounting program ranks in the top twenty nationwide, causing one envious government major to grumble that "accounting majors don't seek employment, employers seek them." State-mandated restructuring eliminated "master's only" programs in English, government, mathematics, and sociology, but undergraduate programs haven't yet felt the pinch. There are summer and year-long study abroad programs around the globe, from Europe to China, the Philippines, Australia, and Mexico, and summer field schools in archeology, including one in St. Eustatius in the Caribbean. The College's International Relations center is internationally acclaimed. About 12 percent of freshmen are designated Monroe Scholars and receive a $2,000 summer research stipend, which is typically used after their sophomore or junior year. One student used his to distribute his band's CD; another traveled to Paris to sketch and study.

"Everyone here was a great student in high school."

Relations between students and professors are excellent. "Professors cultivate a genuine interest and students go home thinking and applying these things to our daily lives," says a student, who goes on to complain that the college "fired a few really good professors as a result of budget cuts," leading many to question the college's priorities. More than half of all classes have twenty-five or fewer students, although a few introductory lectures may have a couple hundred. Virtually every class is taught by a full professor, and TAs are used for grading or lab purposes only. The college established freshman seminars, limited to fifteen students each, that provide even closer faculty interaction. A computerized registration system has taken the headaches out of the once hellish scheduling process.

Graduation requirements are thorough and include proficiency in a foreign language, writing, computing (concentration-specific), and physical education. More specific distribution requirements include a course in mathematics and quantitative reasoning, two courses in the natural sciences, two in the social sciences, one each in literature and history of the arts and creative and performing arts, and one course in philosophical, religious, and social thought. The Center for Honors and Interdisciplinary Studies allows outstanding students four semesters of intensive liberal arts seminars, with lectures by top scholars from around the country, and also facilitates interdisciplinary majors like American studies, environmental science, and women's studies.

Because W&M is a state-supported university, 64 percent of its students are Virginians. Competition for the nonresident spots is stiff, with many out-of-staters from the mid-Atlantic and farther north. Ninety-nine percent of freshmen ranked in the top quarter of their high school class. The college has made a major effort to recruit and retain more minorities; Asian-Americans now account for 7 percent of the students, Hispanics make up 3 percent, and African-Americans contribute 5 percent. An ongoing series of programs in the residence halls addresses safety issues as well as diversity and gender communication. W&M has its share of eagerly recruited jocks; nearly three hundred athletic scholarships are offered each year in eighteen sports. Nearly two hundred academic merit scholarships are awarded annually for $200 to $6,500.

William and Mary created Phi Beta Kappa in December of 1776, and the honor code demands much from the college's students.

Seventy-five percent of the undergraduates live on campus in mostly co-ed dorms that range from stately old halls with high ceilings to modern buildings equipped with air-conditioning. All freshmen are guaranteed a room on campus (with both cable and Internet connections), but after that students try their luck with the infamous lottery ("stressful but efficient"). Some students, usually sophomore men, draw the Dillard Complex—two dorms located a couple miles off campus. "The residence halls are sufficient and comfortable...far from the prison-like places I've seen at some schools," says one student. Special-interest housing is available—there are seven language houses and an International Studies House—and life in a fraternity or sorority house is also an option. Students give the three campus cafeterias mixed reviews, but all freshmen must purchase a nineteen-meal plan. Others have a variety of options, including cooking in the dorms and dinner plans open to Greeks and non-Greeks alike in sorority and fraternity houses.

W&M isn't known as a social school, but "it never gets dull," says an international relations major. "Our students are so inventive that it's a guaranteed great time." Thirty-one percent of the men and 33 percent of the women join Greek organizations, which host most of the on-campus parties. The few local bars pick up the rest. Although the college has implemented measures to prevent binge drinking and promote safety, underage drinkers still obtain alcohol. "I would be lying if I said no 'underagers' consumed alcohol," says one student. "However, because most social events take place near campus, there's never driving to events." The Student Association sponsors mixers, band and tailgate parties, and a film series. Campus security is regarded as tight, although crime is not a big issue. "Everyone feels completely safe—even in the wee hours of the night," says a senior.

"Our students are so inventive that it's a guaranteed great time."

Anyone who gets restless can always step across the street to Colonial Williamsburg to picnic in the restored area, walk or jog down Duke of Gloucester Street (called "Dog Street"), or study in one of the beautiful gardens. Substantial job opportunities exist for students at Colonial Williamsburg, Busch Gardens, and other tourist-oriented attractions in the area. Although the "tourons" can be trying, says one student, "We can access most of the tourist stuff for free," says an upperclassman. Volunteer opportunities abound and many students participate. Richmond and Norfolk, each an hour's drive, are top road trips; the University of Virginia, although an archrival, is also popular; and Virginia Beach, a favorite springtime mecca, is a little farther away.

Traditions are the stuff of which William and Mary is made, and perhaps the most cherished is the annual Yule Log Ceremony in Wren Hall, where students sing carols and hear the president, dressed in a Santa Claus outfit, read the Dr. Seuss story *How the Grinch Stole Christmas*. Grand Illumination is a great Christmas fireworks display, and on Charter Day, bells chime and students celebrate the distinguished history of their three-hundred-year-old institution. On Sorority Acceptance Day, the pledges must all cross the sunken garden barricaded by fraternity men, and romantics will be happy to learn that any couple who kisses at the top of Crim Dell Bridge will be married by the end of the year. The 13 Club, a secret society of students dedicated to the college, provides students and professors with a helping hand (like missed class notes) or a pat on the back when they're feeling low—all delivered anonymously. One activity, though illegal, is always popular: jumping the wall at the Governor's Mansion at the end of Dog Street.

William and Mary isn't a football powerhouse like most Southern state schools, but the athletic program is strong nonetheless. The men's cross-country team won the league championships in 2001–2002 and 2002–2003. Women's soccer, volleyball, tennis, and track and field have also won championships. Men's gymnastics

About 12 percent of freshmen are designated Monroe Scholars and receive a $2,000 summer research stipend, which is typically used after their sophomore or junior year. One student used his to distribute his band's CD; another traveled to Paris to sketch and study.

Grand Illumination is a great Christmas fireworks display, and on Charter Day, bells chime and students celebrate the distinguished history of their three-hundred-year-old institution.

has dominated the state, winning twenty-seven consecutive championships. The football team plays in Division I-AA and always stirs enthusiasm, especially on homecoming weekend, while basketball and soccer are other popular men's sports. Intramurals, from skydiving to Ultimate Frisbee, attract two-thirds of the student body, and a $6 million recreational athletic complex provides excellent facilities. The old gym is now the home of the graduate school of business and undergraduate student services, including admissions and career planning.

William and Mary's traditions stretch back to the dawn of this nation, and its grand old campus and stirring history make it a distinguished and cherished part of many student's lives. And on the last day of classes, seniors return to the Wren. They climb the old stairs and reach for a cord to ring the building's bell high above to announce to the world, here we come!

If You Apply To ➤ **William and Mary:** Early decision: Nov. 1. Regular admissions: Jan. 6. Financial aid: Feb. 15. Housing: Feb. 14. Meets demonstrated need of 82%. Campus interviews: optional, informational. ACTs or SATs: required. SAT IIs: recommended (math, English and one other). Accepts the Common Application and electronic applications. Essay question: personal statement.

Williams College

Williamstown, MA 01267

Running neck-in-neck with Amherst on the selectivity chart, Williams occupies a campus of surpassing beauty in the foothills of the Berkshires. Williams has shaken the preppy image, but still attracts plenty of well-toned all-around jock-intellectuals. The splendid isolation of Williamstown is either a blessing or a curse.

Whether they're hiking mountains with the deans or engaging in deep debates with professors over coffee, students at Williams College adore the close ties they nurture at this premier liberal arts school. It's a place with an abundance of school spirit, and a stunning natural backdrop of gentle mountains and wooded countryside. Williams beckons students to take in the same picturesque setting that moved Henry David Thoreau during his travels through the Massachusetts wilderness. When they're not gazing at the purple mountains' majesty, students at Williams are digging into their studies to earn the diplomas that will open doors for them after they leave this idyllic institution.

Nestled in the small village of Williamstown, the college takes full advantage of the Berkshires' rich history and natural resources. The verdant surroundings beg for the skiing, cycling, and backpacking for which Williams students are famous. Williams buildings constitute a virtual museum of architectural styles, from the elegantly simple Federal design of the original West College to contemporary designs by Charles Moore and Carlos Jimenez. Many of the buildings of brick and gray stone are arranged around loosely organized quads that provide both a sense of enclosure and of openness to nature. Students can also take advantage of MASS MoCA, a center for visual, performing, and media arts.

Williams's greatest strengths are in art history, environmental science, history, political science, economics, English, chemistry, and biology, all of which contribute directly to an acceptance rate of about 90 percent at business, law, and medical schools. Says one senior, "With one of the finest college art museums in

America and one of the best impressionistic collections in the world, we have tremendous resources for an outstanding [art history] program." Students agree that the Romance languages are weak, but interdisciplinary programs in Afro-American studies, area studies, and women's studies are increasingly popular. The college recently strengthened the requirements for such majors, and is developing new team-taught courses such as Culture, Society, and Disease. Environmental studies, based in the two-thousand-acre, college-owned Hopkins Forest, makes full use of the campus's natural resources. For future engineers, 3–2 B.A./B.S. programs are offered in conjunction with Columbia and Washington universities.

The Williams curriculum places an emphasis on interdisciplinary studies and personalized teaching. Almost all classes have fewer than fifty students; two-thirds have less than twenty-five. The distribution requirements consist of three courses in each of three areas—arts and languages, social studies, and sciences and mathematics—two of which must be completed by the end of the sophomore year. Students must take at least one course on cultural pluralism, two writing-intensive classes, and one quantitative and formal reasoning course. Entering first-years have the option of taking the First-Year Residential Seminar, in which they live together in the same residential unit and take a team-taught or interdisciplinary course together.

Students must complete four winter study projects during the January intersession. There is also Free University, in which students teach one another anything from Chinese cooking to the jitterbug. In recent years, students have explored India, the Soviet Union, West Africa, and Western Europe with the college's unusual and relatively inexpensive faculty-guided tours. Opportunities for off-campus study are also available during the fall and spring. The many options include Williams at Mystic Seaport,* the Twelve-College Exchange,* and an innovative program in conjunction with Exeter College of Oxford University in England.

Williams's faculty is "far above the rest," says a freshman. "You are in contact with experts in their fields." But the profs are not just talking heads. Most professors live right in Williamstown, giving students the opportunity to see them not just in class, but at the bank, on Main Street, and even in their homes. Additionally, the college provides a stipend with which advisors sometimes take their advisees out to lunch or dinner.

Students "have an uncanny ability to be involved in multiple extracurricular activities while also maintaining their academic studies."

Academic and career counseling is comprehensive, students say. The alumni network is "amazing," a senior says, with grads offering loads of help to their undergrad kin. The computer center is impressively equipped, and Sawyer Library reportedly has ample accommodations to offer the wearied but inspired. The entire campus, including all residences, is networked, providing access from student rooms to the Internet.

The typical Williams student is a bright, enthusiastic, extremely energetic, well-rounded extrovert—and they're not pretentious, one student insists. "They have an uncanny ability to be involved in multiple extracurricular activities while also maintaining their academic studies," another adds. In-state residents only account for 15 percent of the student body, while foreign and minority students make up nearly one-third. Williams clearly looks for diversity in prospective students; students who are strong in more than one area tend to stand out. "People are very open here," says a psychology major. But a classmate warns, "Sometimes it seems hard to relate to people if you aren't an athlete or a social partier." Political correctness does crop up on campus, where issues including gender roles and sexual identity are discussed. Nearly a third of the students are bona fide preppies; the rest just look that way. The campus uniform seems to include relatively little makeup for women and Williams sweatshirts and jeans for all. The school's mascot is a purple

(Continued)

Email Address:
   admission@williams.edu

Strongest Programs:
Art
Environmental Science
History
Political Science
Economics
Art History
English
Natural Sciences

The typical Williams student is a bright, enthusiastic, extremely energetic, well-rounded extrovert—and they're not pretentious, one student insists.

One dormitory was once a fine old inn, with fireplaces and mahogany paneling; several others look as if they should have been.

Except for the much-feared tofu pie, the food is considered quite good for institutional fare, and nearly everyone buys the meal plan, which is usable in any of the five campus dining halls.

cow, so cows and purple naturally dominate clothes and signs. There are no athletic or merit scholarships at this expensive school, but Williams guarantees to design a financial aid package that meets the full demonstrated need of every admit.

"Phenomenal" and "definitely above the norm" is how students describe the housing at Williams. "The dorms here are pretty and students love it," says a history major. The rooms are spacious and well maintained, and housing is guaranteed for all four years. One dormitory was once a fine old inn, with fireplaces and mahogany paneling; several others look as if they should have been. "Every dorm has lots of common space with couches, TVs, VCRs, and fireplaces, and some even have ballrooms," says an English major. Living options range from two modern complexes to the lovely row houses that were fraternities before Greek organizations were abolished in 1962. New arrivals

"Every dorm has lots of common space with couches, TVs, VCRs, and fireplaces, and some even have ballrooms."

reside in first-year-only dorms known as "entries," where the highly praised junior advisor system works to provide advice and support. Says a history major, "The minute you get here you know about twenty other people with whom to hang out." Small co-op houses are available for students who want to cook and play house. Upperclassmen, virtually ensured a single, may enter the housing lottery individually or in groups. The college permits only a handful of students to move. The best first-year dorm is said to be the quad. Beware: thin walls are a complaint. Food is another area where Williams's resident overachievers are pampered. Except for the much-feared tofu pie, the food is considered quite good for institutional fare, and nearly everyone buys the meal plan, which is usable in any of the five campus dining halls.

Williams's Berkshires setting can seem isolated at times, yet civilization—Albany, New York—is only an hour away. Even the most focused of scholars would find the peaceful Williamstown backdrop a refreshing distraction. "Williamstown has a lot of character," a biology major says. The Clark Art Institute, within walking distance of campus, possesses one of the finest collections of Renoir and Degas in the nation, as well as a great library. The modern college music center attracts top classical musicians, and the college theater is home to a renowned summer festival that often features Broadway stars. Films, lectures, and concerts abound on most weekends, as do the usual number of parties. "One of the reasons I chose Williams was because the campus social life actually exists on campus," a senior says.

Fraternities and sororities have no place at Williams, but that hasn't created a dearth of drinking opportunities. The administration has taken a tougher stance on drinking. "Our policy has recently become a lot stricter, so now it's very hard for underage students to drink at a party, and the consequences are more severe," says one senior. Still, students say it's possible to get booze "if you know the right people." Aside from imbibing, students find plenty of other things to do. The college brings in lots of cultural groups, popular concerts, and speakers, and there are always student performances or organized activities. An organization called Connections strives to distract keg-seeking students and emphasize alcohol-free alternatives, of which there are many. All parties must serve food and nonalcoholic beverages whenever alcohol is present.

"The minute you get here you know about twenty other people with whom to hang out."

Sports are more like a religion than an extracurricular activity, and Williams has become a perennial winner of the Division III Sears Cup, awarded annually to the school with the strongest overall athletic program. Everyone seems to play on some team, and any contest with archrival Amherst ensures a big crowd. After all, Amherst was founded in 1821 by a defecting Williams president and part of the

Fiske Guide to Colleges 2005

student body. And the insults tend to go beyond the athletic field and consistent high scores. T-shirts can be seen around campus offering the following sentiment regarding its rivals in the Little Three: "The good: Williams. The bad: Wesleyan. The ugly: Amherst." The men's and women's swim teams are nationally ranked, and the men's tennis, basketball, and cross-country teams have been among the top in the nation. Women's tennis, field hockey, and lacrosse teams are also strong contenders. The men's indoor track and field team has won 122 straight Quad Cup competitions. The Taconic golf course, rated among the best collegiate facilities, has been host to several national college championships. The college helps maintain a cross-country ski trail located ten miles from town, and two alpine ski resorts within ten miles of campus are also popular. The one knock against the Williams sports program is the charge from some quarters that women's sports get less support than men's. Homecoming is always popular at Williams, as are Mountain Day, Winter Carnival, and Spring Fling. Every winter there is also a campus-wide snow sculpting contest.

When you're nestled by gorgeous purple mountains and have access to a wide range of academic options, as well as top-notch faculty, somehow the overall "smallness" of the Williams setting doesn't matter so much. These Ephs (that's pronounced Eefs, as in school founder Ephraim Williams) know they've got a good thing going. "Complaints are few and far between," reports a senior. "We love it!"

If You Apply To ➤ **Williams:** Early decision: Nov. 15. Regular admissions: Jan. 1. Financial aid: Feb. 1. Guarantees to meet demonstrated need. Campus and alumni interviews: optional, informational. SATs or ACTs: required. SAT IIs: required (any three). Accepts the Common Application and the electronic application. Essay question: experience that defined a value.

University of Wisconsin–Madison

140 Peterson Building, 750 University Avenue, Madison, WI 53706-1490

UW draws nearly 40 percent of its students from out of state, the highest proportion among leading Midwestern public universities. Why brave the cold? Reasons include top programs in an array of professional fields and several innovative living/learning programs.

At the University of Wisconsin at Madison, two things are a sure bet: very cold weather and red-hot academics. On a campus where the mercury often dips below zero, you're likely to be too busy studying to notice. With 27,000 undergraduates and enormous resources, Madison offers something for virtually everyone. All that's required is a desire to learn—and a very warm coat.

Described by one student as "architecturally olden with a modern touch," Madison's mainly brick campus is distinctive. It spreads out over 903 hilly, tree-covered acres and across an isthmus between two glacial lakes, Mendota and Monona, named by prehistoric Indians who once lived along their shores. From atop Bascom Hill, the center of campus, you look east past the statue of Lincoln and the liberal arts buildings, down to a library mall that was the scene of many a political demonstration during the '60s. Farther east you see rows of State Street pubs and restaurants and the bleached dome of the Wisconsin state capitol. On the other side of the hill, another campus, dedicated to the sciences, twists along Lake Mendota. But students from

Website: www.wisc.edu
Location: City center
Total Enrollment: 40,196
Undergraduates: 27,533
Male/Female: 48/52
SAT Ranges: V 520–650
    M 550–670
ACT Range: 25–29
Financial Aid: 55%
Expense: Pub $
Phi Beta Kappa: Yes
Applicants: 16,290
Accepted: 77%

both sides of the hill drink beer elbow to elbow in the old student union, the Rathskeller, where political arguments and backgammon games can rage all night. Outside on the union's veranda, students can look out at the sailboats in summer or iceboats in winter.

The icy wind that blows off the lakes in winter is vicious, and the academic climate is not exactly tropical either. Coursework is demanding, and in many ways akin to graduate school elsewhere. Predictably, grading is tough and inflexible and often figured on a strict curve. "There are a lot of smart people studying here," notes one student with a firm grasp of the obvious. A list of first-rate academic programs at Madison would constitute a college catalog elsewhere. There are seventy programs considered in the top ten nationally. Some highlights include education, agriculture, communications, biological sciences, and social studies. The most popular majors are history, engineering, political science, psychology, and business, in that order. The math department is cited as lacking faculty, and letters and science could use better advising, according to some. Due to overcrowding, some popular fields, such as engineering and business, have had to restrict entry to their majors by requiring high GPAs. But with a smaller freshman class, students are finding it a bit easier to get into the courses of their choice. Several improvements made over the last few years have helped to relieve the overload. First, an automated system makes the headaches of registration a bit less severe. Second, the Grainger Hall of Business Administration, a $35 million complex, quadrupled the space in the current school of business. The biotechnology building supports research and undergraduate teaching.

Distribution requirements vary among the different schools and academic departments, but they are uniformly rigorous, with science and math courses required for B.A. students, and a foreign language for virtually everyone. All students must fulfill a two-part graduation requirement in both quantitative reasoning and communication. For students who prefer the academic road less traveled, options include the Institute for Environmental Studies and the Integrated Liberal Studies (ILS), which consists of related courses introducing the achievements of Western culture. An elite Medical Scholars program allows fifty select high school seniors guaranteed admission to the Madison medical school after completing three years of undergraduate work. A variety of internships are available, as are study abroad programs all over the world, including Europe, Brazil, India, Israel, and Thailand.

Professors at Madison are certainly among the nation's best, with Nobel laureates, National Academy of Science members, and Guggenheim fellows scattered liberally among the departments. The English program boasts such young, vibrant faculty as highly acclaimed writers Lorrie Moore and Debra Spark. Along with downsizing, Madison has taken a number of steps to strengthen the freshman experience in particular. They have emphasized smaller classes of fifteen to twenty students to help entering freshmen adjust to college-level coursework; more comprehensive orientation and mentoring for freshmen; and more student–faculty contact. Advising has received a booster shot, too. For undergrads who find it difficult to choose one of the vast array of majors available, the university has developed a plan called Cross-College Advising System, which features a ten-member team of academic staff advisors. The idea is to help students refine their educational and career goals, so their interests, majors, and professional aspirations mesh into a complete package. Upon admission, every student is assigned an advisor to meet with at least three times in the first year.

If there is one common characteristic among the undergraduates, it is aggressiveness. "It's easy to get lost in the crowd here, so you have to be fairly strong and

"It's easy to get lost in the crowd here, so you have to be fairly strong and confident. No one holds your hand."

"Anyone can fit in, you just have to find your own niche."

"There are a lot of smart people studying here," notes one student with a firm grasp of the obvious.

confident," declares one student. "No one holds your hand." The flip side is that "anyone can fit in, you just have to find your own niche." Almost two-thirds of the students are from Wisconsin. The school is a heartland of progressive politics, and Madison's reputation as a haven for liberals remains intact. "Students here are called liberal because they are eager and willing to change and are continually looking for newer and better ideas," explains an activist. The university has implemented a racial-awareness program to make the campus more hospitable to minorities. African-Americans and Hispanics currently make up 4 percent of the student body, while Asian-Americans constitute another 4 percent. CIA recruiting, women's rights, and tuition increases have all been issues recently. Thousands of academic merit scholarships ranging from $500 to $7,000 are awarded each year, and most of the sports on campus offer full scholarships. Need-based financial aid packages meet 100 percent of need for all in-staters, but out of-state applicants get no guarantees. The two-day orientation program, known as SOAR, welcomes incoming freshmen in groups staggered throughout the summer.

Housing, once the bane of many a student's existence, is no longer a problem now that housing is guaranteed for all. For a school this size, that's quite an accomplishment. Dorms are either co-ed or single-sex and come equipped with laundry facilities, game rooms, and lounges. Most also have a cafeteria. The student union also offers two meal plans, and there are plenty of restaurants and fast-food places nearby. Campus safety is always an issue, but the school offers a variety of services for those on campus. There

> **"Students here are called liberal because they are eager and willing to change and are continually looking for newer and better ideas."**

are escort services for those walking and those needing a ride, and a free shuttle system that operates seven days a week. Madison (a.k.a. Madtown) has been the stomping ground for many fine rock 'n' roll or blues bands on the road to fame.

There are more film clubs than anyone can follow, and everyone has a favorite bar. "This is Wisconsin, don't forget, and everybody drinks a lot of beer. If you don't drink, then you'll have to be quite comfortable with that," says one teetotaler, "because peer pressure can be quite overwhelming." About 10 percent of the men and 18 percent of the women go Greek. "Frat parties are a very popular break from the bar scene," reports one expert on both options. One old standby that is still as popular as ever is the student union, which hosts bands, shows, and so forth and provides a great atmosphere in which to hang out. Nature enthusiasts can lose themselves in the university's twelve-thousand-acre nature preserve. Ski slopes are close at hand, but be prepared to confront thermometers that read twenty below zero.

The students at this Big Ten school show "tons of interest" in sports, especially hockey and football, and especially when the Badgers try to rout the University of Minnesota's Gophers. Bucky Badger apparel, emblazoned with slogans ranging from the urbane to the decidedly uncouth, is ubiquitous. However, the much-acclaimed marching band known as Fifth Quarter may outdo all the teams in popularity. The Badgers are recent Big Ten champions in a number of sports, notably women's cross-country and men's basketball and indoor and outdoor track. The men's soccer team won the NCAA Division I championship recently, a feat that will undoubtedly draw attention to the school's athletic program.

All in all, Madison is a school that students sum up as "diverse, intellectual, fashionable, and moderately hedonistic." And these are the qualities that attract bright and energetic students from everywhere. "You feel you're accepted for who you are no matter what," says one student. "It's so nice to just be yourself." Perhaps one of the best and most well-rounded state schools around, Madison is truly a best buy.

If there is one common characteristic among the undergraduates, it is aggressiveness.

Overlaps

University of Michigan, Northwestern, University of Illinois, Indiana, Boston University

If You Apply To ➤

Wisconsin: Rolling admissions: Feb. 1. Financial aid: Mar. 1. Guarantees to meet the demonstrated need of in-state admits. Campus interviews: recommended, informational. No alumni interviews. SATs or ACTs: required (ACTs required for Wisconsin residents). SAT IIs: optional. Essay question: personal statement. Special consideration given to students from disadvantaged backgrounds. Apply to particular school.

Wittenberg University

P.O. Box 720, Springfield, OH 45501

Wittenberg is an outpost of cozy Midwestern friendliness. Less national than Denison or Wooster, Witt has plenty of old-fashioned school spirit and powerhouse Division III athletic teams. Top students should aim for the honors and fellows programs, the latter providing a chance for undergraduate research.

Website: www.wittenberg.edu
Location: City outskirts
Total Enrollment: 2,240
Undergraduates: 2,055
Male/Female: 45/55
SAT Ranges: V 560–645
   M 558–642
ACT Range: 25–29
Financial Aid: 77%
Expense: Pr $ $ $
Phi Beta Kappa: Yes
Applicants: 3,175
Accepted: 73%
Enrolled: 28%
Grad in 6 Years: 72%
Returning Freshmen: 83%
Academics: 🐘 🐘 🐘
Social: ☎ ☎ ☎
Q of L: ★ ★ ★
Admissions: (800) 677-7558
Email Address:
   admission@wittenberg.edu

Strongest Programs:
Biology
Political Science
English
Psychology
Chemistry
Education
Fine Arts
Theater

Founded in 1845 by German Lutherans, Wittenberg University remains true to its faith by emphasizing strong student–faculty relationships—and making sure that students don't become too comfortable in the campus bubble. In fact, before granting their diplomas, Wittenberg requires students to complete thirty hours of community service in the surrounding town of Springfield (population 70,000). "There are great traditions and amazing ways to get involved here," says a junior, who adds that students' biggest complaint is that "it's over in four years!"

The Wittenberg campus is classic Midwestern collegiate, with a mixture of Gothic and 1960s-style buildings on one hundred rolling acres in southwestern Ohio. The redbrick Myers residence hall, with picturesque white pillars and an open-air dome dating from the nineteenth century, stands at the center. Matthies House provides a home for the Wittenberg Honors Program, while construction of Hollenbeck Hall, a state-of-the-art learning center, was recently finished. There's also a new $15 million humanities center, and a $24 million science center.

Wittenberg's general education requirements emphasize a solid liberal arts background. The school's Wittenberg Plan includes sixteen learning goals, ranging from experience with writing and research to exposure to the natural sciences and foreign languages. Students select courses from a variety of disciplines to meet the goals, and also must fulfill requirements in religion or philosophy, non-Western cultures, and physical education. All first-year students take the interdisciplinary Common Learning Course, focused on contemporary social issues and taught by faculty advisors. Wittenberg is also currently developing a new "First Year Experience." New additions to the curriculum include a communications major and a $2 million Freeman Grant, which will allow students pursuing East Asian studies to take a term abroad. The honors program is being upgraded; there is also a University Scholars Program for outstanding freshmen, while the Wittenberg Fellows Program provides opportunities to work on research with faculty members. The school is putting more emphasis on community service and leadership as part of campus life.

> **"There are great traditions and amazing ways to get involved here."**

Wittenberg students give high marks to the school's education department, which a freshman calls "one of the best in the country," as well as to programs in biology, English, and business—so perhaps it's not surprising that the most popular majors on campus are biology, education, and management, in that order. "Inside the classroom at Witt, instruction is engaging, and often a different spin on 'known truths' is presented that stimulates independent thinking and critical thinking skills," says a business management major. "Consequently, outside of the classroom group discussions and interaction between peers is utilized. Coursework is competitive and challenging, but not meant to seem—or be—impossible." Administrators say weak spots include philosophy, geography, and physics.

Despite Wittenberg's small size, students say they have no trouble registering for needed courses and graduating in four years—though a junior warns it's hard to complete requirements for an education degree if students don't choose that program freshman year, and a classmate says music majors often take longer. Still, if students declare their major on time and complete the proper coursework in the correct order, the college guarantees a degree in four years—and will pay for any additional necessary courses. Wittenberg also encourages students to take a semester or a year away from campus, either in the U.S. or abroad. Options include the International Student Exchange Program, field study in the Bahamas or Costa Rica, work with the National Institutes of Health in Washington, D.C., or a term at the United Nations in New York. Wittenberg also offers 3–2 engineering programs with Columbia, Case Western Reserve, and Washington University in St. Louis.

Sixty percent of Wittenberg students are native Ohioans, and many others are from nearby states like Pennsylvania, though 4 percent are from other countries. African-Americans comprise 7 percent of the student body, and Hispanics and Asian-Americans add 2 percent each. The school's multicultural affairs director is working to boost those numbers through changes in minority recruiting and advis-

"Instruction is engaging, and often a different spin on 'known truths' is presented that stimulates independent thinking and critical thinking skills."

ing. "Some of the issues on campus are gay rights, human rights, and alcohol usage," says an early childhood education major. "We are a very active campus politically. Both conservative and liberal students have a strong voice in the school paper and in debates," says a senior. Wittenberg offers an unlimited number of merit scholarships, ranging from $5,000 to full tuition, but no athletic scholarships.

Wittenberg students are required to live on campus their first two years. After that, most chose nearby houses and apartments owned by the school. Just opened are two brand new apartment complexes that can house one hundred students. "The dorms have all been updated with Internet access, some with air-conditioning and cable TV," says a sociology and women's studies major. "Rooms are a decent size, with lots of space for storage. Sophomore students have first pick on rooms, and then the freshmen are assigned to the remaining rooms," so almost everyone gets a double when he or she first comes to campus. Greek groups draw 15 percent of the men and 32 percent of the women; members may live in chapter houses. Marriott provides the chow in Witt's dining hall, which has been rated the company's best college food service. Choices range from burgers to made-to-order breakfasts to monthly theme dinners. Also, "There are many choices for people with special dietary needs," notes a senior.

When the weekend rolls around, social life centers around parties in houses, dorm rooms, and apartments on and near campus. Greek groups, the Union Board, and the Residence Hall Association also bring in guest speakers and movies, comedians, and concerts. The administration just recently clamped down and said no kegs on campus. Students are not universally saying "cheers" to that rule, which really is being enforced. Favorite annual events include Greek Week, homecoming ("the alumni involvement is incredible"), and Wittfest in May, "a music festival with games, food, prizes, and socializing before finals," says an early childhood education major. "It is like a big block party—everyone goes!" adds a junior. While Springfield has movie theaters, a mall, restaurants, and a $15 million performing arts center,

The honors program is being upgraded; there is also a University Scholars Program for outstanding freshmen, while the Wittenberg Fellows Program provides opportunities to work on research with faculty members.

Wittenberg students give high marks to the school's education department, which a freshman calls "one of the best in the country," as well as to programs in biology, English, and business—so perhaps it's not surprising that the most popular majors on campus are management, biology, and education, in that order.

students with cars do like to get out of town. Popular road trips include Dayton (thirty minutes), Columbus (sixty minutes), and Cincinnati (ninety minutes), and for those with more time, Washington, D.C., New York City, and Windsor, Canada (to gamble). Nearby state parks also offer swimming, camping, and picnics in the warmer months, and skiing in the winter.

While not as well known as many of its bigger Midwestern brethren, Wittenberg's athletic teams are competitive in Division III. Recent championship teams include men's football, basketball, and track, and women's field hockey, volleyball, softball, and basketball. Rivalries with the College of Wooster (football and basketball) and Allegheny College (football) really get students riled up. Even weekend warriors may take advantage of the Bill Edwards Athletic and Recreational Complex, which boasts a stadium and eight-lane track, football and soccer fields, twelve lighted tennis courts, and a weight room, plus a pool and racquetball courts.

> **"We are a very active campus politically. Both conservative and liberal students have a strong voice."**

Wittenberg stands out among small liberal arts colleges for several reasons, one of which is that Wittenberg students defy stereotyping. "Our students are pretty easygoing," says an English major. "You would have a hard time finding a 'typical' student. We have a little bit of everything, and there is a place for everyone." And that's pretty refreshing to college-seekers who aren't always impressed by designer labels—especially for people.

If You Apply To ➤

Wittenberg: Early decision: Nov. 15. Early action: Dec. 1. Rolling admissions and financial aid: March 15. Does not guarantee to meet demonstrated need. Campus interviews: recommended, informational. No alumni interviews. SATs or ACTs: required. SAT IIs: recommended. Accepts the Common Application. Essay question: significant experience or relationship; or issue of concern.

Wofford College

429 North Church Street, Spartanburg, SC 29303-3663

Wofford is about one-third as big as Furman and roughly the same size as Presbyterian. With more than a few gentleman jocks, Wofford is one of the smallest institutions to compete in NCAA Division I. Fraternities and sororities dominate the traditional social scene.

Wofford College is a study in contrasts. The school's average SAT score is greater than the size of its student body. It's spitting distance from both Georgia and North Carolina, but two-thirds of the students are South Carolina natives. And perhaps most unusually, Wofford offers the rigorous academics of a small liberal arts college with rough-and-tumble Division I athletics. Wofford students take pride in the Wofford Way, combining a well-rounded curriculum with career-related internships and study abroad. What makes this place special? "Students and faculty who are serious about studies, but never too busy to have a conversation over sweet tea," says a senior.

Wofford is near the heart of Spartanburg, a mid-size city in the northwest corner of South Carolina. Founded in 1854, it's one of fewer than two hundred existing American colleges that opened before the Civil War—and it still operates on its original 140-acre campus. Azaleas, magnolias, and dogwoods surround the distinctive, twin-towered Main Building and four original faculty homes. "In the spring, everyone sunbathes and plays Frisbee on the lawn and barbecues out," a senior says. "Southern hospitality means that everyone will say 'hey' whether you know them or not!" President Dunlap is working to create more indoor and outdoor gathering places for students and faculty; to that end, new plazas have been created in outdoor gathering places. The Roger Milliken Science Center is being renovated, blending a 1959 structure with 110,000 square feet of new space for the chemistry, biology, psychology, and physics departments. Ground has been broken for the Russell C. King Field and Switzer Stadium, a baseball facility. The historic Main Building—built in 1854—is being renovated in time for the college's sesquicentennial.

"In the spring, everyone sunbathes and plays Frisbee on the lawn and barbecues out."

Students rave about Wofford's programs in biology and economics. About two dozen of the school's 260 graduates go on to graduate medical or dental programs within two years of graduation. Dr. Warren Derrick, director of pediatrics at the University of South Carolina (and Wofford alum) guides premeds with case-based lectures every Friday. For aspiring entrepreneurs, Wofford's alumni network has clout: more than twelve hundred of its fifteen thousand living graduates serve as presidents or owners of corporations or organizations. Prospective engineers may apply for 3–2 programs with Clemson or New York's Columbia University. Religion, English, and foreign language, and study abroad programs, also get high marks, especially for the one lucky junior chosen as the Presidential International Scholar. This student is sent around the world, all expenses paid, to study an issue of global importance for a year.

In keeping with Wofford's reinvigorated spirit, the college now offers more than thirty new courses and interdisciplinary course sequences. Some are "learning communities," such as a Spanish language course taught in conjunction with a Latin American and Caribbean history course, and a sociology course focusing on the local Hispanic community. Wofford also boasts a unique program called the Novel Experience, part of the first-year orientation. The program consists of a common reading, which is then discussed during a meeting of twenty-two humanities classes at different restaurants throughout Spartanburg.

Professors have high standards, and students feel pressure to meet them because they have personal relationships with the faculty, says a finance major. Many invite students to their homes for dinner at least once a semester, a Spanish and French major says. "The quality of teaching at Wofford is top-notch. Our professors are highly qualified and because our student/teacher ratio is so low, we get to know our professors personally. Most of my professors are passionate about their subject and this is infectious for the students."

Most Wofford students (89 percent) are white, and more than three-quarters graduated from public high school—half in the top tenth of their class. They're generally polite, friendly, and politically conservative, and they seek balance between studying and socializing. "Wofford students are South Carolinian, for the most part, and it seems that college ties to the state will maintain this demographic," a senior says. "There is a desire for a more diverse population." African-Americans comprise

"Southern hospitality means that everyone will say 'hey' whether you know them or not!"

8 percent of Wofford's total, Asian-Americans 2 percent, and Hispanics 1 percent. The school has implemented a summer program, led by a female African-American faculty member, to attract more Spartanburg County minorities and women to the sciences. The biggest political issues on campus are not boosting diversity or gay rights, but controlling underage drinking and mitigating the Greek influence.

Eighty-eight percent of Wofford's students live in the dorms, where first-year women get doubles in Greene Hall, and their male counterparts have similar digs in

(Continued)
Accepted: 78%
Enrolled: 28%
Grad in 6 Years: 75%
Returning Freshmen: 87%
Academics: ✍ ✍ ✍
Social: ☎ ☎
Q of L: ★ ★ ★
Admissions: (864) 597-4130
Email Address:
    admissions@wofford.edu

Strongest Programs:
Life Sciences (Biology and
    Psychology)
Prelaw
Business
English
Computer Science

The historic Main Building —built in 1854—is being renovated in time for the college's sesquicentennial.

Marsh Hall. "Usually after freshman year, students get suites with cubes—little rooms just big enough for a desk and bed," says a junior. "However, there are some sophomores who have to live in the freshman dorms each year." Students aren't too keen on the college cafeteria—other than as a social outlet—but they praise the Canteen, a lunchtime option that serves Southern cooking. Campus safety is good—so good, in fact, that "students' dorm-room doors are always unlocked, and many feel safe walking across campus at night," says an English major.

The Greek system is a huge force in Wofford's social life, with fraternities attracting 54 percent of the men and 61 percent of the women. Each fraternity has a house, and most host parties on every Friday and Saturday—with some kicking off the weekend on Thursday. "The 'Row' is fun, but can get old," says an accounting major. "And if you are not in a fraternity, it gets old fast." The frats are a source of steady booze for most Wofford students, even those under twenty-one. "It is not hard to get alcohol underage," despite the fact that South Carolina law says you can't have it, explains a senior. "If you get caught, it is generally because you are blatantly drunk, or have alcohol on you."

Off campus, Spartanburg is home to Converse College and a few other schools, but students say it's not a great college town in terms of music or the arts. For that, students head to Greenville, Atlanta, and Charlotte, "all an easy drive," says a finance major. And almost every Wofford student participates in some type of volunteer work. Terrier Play Day brings kids from the community to campus for a

> "Most of my professors are passionate about their subject and this is infectious for the students."

fair with booths and games. Bid Day, when the fraternities tap their new members, is another annual tradition, involving "lots of mud, and then a bath in the college fountain." Every year before finals, student musicians and readers perform a Festival of Nine Lessons and Carols, perhaps praying as well for luck on their exams. The Greeks clean up their acts in time for Spring Weekend, a sort of campus Olympics.

Historically, Wofford competed in the NAIA, later moving to Division II of the NCAA. By 1995, the school found itself stuck between two worlds—academics more similar to schools in Division III, but a football tradition dating back to 1889, and rivalries with powerhouses like Furman and Davidson. So the school stepped up to Division I-AA, hoping the extra revenue and exposure from playing in big-time televised games would help it recruit better athletes. The strategy seems to have paid off. But some things haven't changed. Wofford's biggest football rival remains the Citadel, and "every other year, practically the whole school packs up and heads to Charleston for the game weekend," says a senior. The school's golf team is also stellar, and baseball is up-and-coming, with plans underway for a new field. Women's soccer and basketball are also strong, with soccer player Jenny Nett recently winning First Team Academic All-America honors.

Wofford's chaplain has a saying: "You don't come to Wofford, you join it." And students say that's true, citing the close-knit community and intimate student–faculty relationships fostered by the school's small size. "Everyone knows everyone else, and we all work together," says an accounting major. "I can't walk to class without seeing tons of people I know," agrees an English major. "Everyone speaks to everyone, and Wofford students genuinely care about each other—and the college."

Overlaps
Furman, Clemson, University of South Carolina Honors College, Wake Forest, Presbyterian

If You Apply To ➤

Wofford: Early action: Nov. 15. Regular admissions: Feb. 1. Financial aid: Mar. 15. Housing: May 1. Does not guarantee to meet demonstrated need. Campus interviews: recommended, informational. Alumni interviews: optional, informational. SATs or ACTs: required. SAT IIs: optional. Accepts the Common Application and electronic applications. Essay question: event, interest, experience, goal, or person who reveals something about you.

Wooster, OH 44691

Though not well-known to the general public, Wooster is renowned in academic circles and a number of foreign countries. Getting admitted is not difficult, but graduating takes work. All students complete an independent study project in their last two years. More intellectually serious than competitors such as Denison.

Instead of teaching students *what* to think, the College of Wooster focuses on teaching students *how* to think. From the first courses of the freshman year seminar to the final day when seniors hand in their hard-won theses, the college paves each student's path to independence. This all happens within a tight-knit community that many students compare to a family. The one-to-one attention from faculty who really "probe and stimulate the students' minds" makes Wooster an intellectual refuge in the rural countryside of Ohio.

Located in the city of Wooster, Ohio, C.O.W.'s hilltop campus is spread over 240 acres, many designed in the English-Collegiate Gothic style and constructed of cream-colored brick. More recent buildings are trimmed in Indiana limestone or Ohio sandstone. The central arch and two towers of Kauke Hall, the central building in Quinby Quadrangle (the square around which the college grew), make it stand out. The Gault Library for Independent Study offers a private carrel for each senior in the humanities and social sciences. The $2 million Longbrake Student Wellness Center opened in spring 2002 and includes a student lounge. The Burton D. Morgan Hall provides a new home for economics, education, psychology, and information technology departments. Other new additions include the Gault Center for Admissions and Bornhuetter Hall, a new dorm.

What goes on behind the facades of Wooster's attractive buildings is more impressive than the structures themselves. The required first-year seminar in critical inquiry, limited to fifteen students per section, invites students to engage in issues, questions, or ideas drawn from classical readings. The seminar is linked to the Wooster Forum, a series of first-semester lectures and events focused on a single, broad issue. "Everyone wants to succeed academically," a senior says. "They also help each other succeed. It's competitive, but against yourself—not against other students."

Wooster's curriculum is built around the required Independent Study, which lets students explore subjects they're passionate about with faculty guidance. Independent Study has become such a part of C.O.W. that each year seniors celebrate I.S. Monday—the day they turn in their projects—with a campus-wide parade. "We are led around campus by the bagpipers," says a senior. "The whole campus shows up." Completion of the I.S. earns you a Tootsie Roll, to eat or keep for posterity next to your diploma. "It's a day all Wooster graduates will always remember!" a senior says. The college even awards $60,000 each year for student research, travel, materials purchases, or conference registration fees.

In addition to the critical inquiry seminar, three semesters of Independent Study, and six cross-discipline courses, Wooster mandates courses in writing, global and cultural perspectives, religious perspectives, and quantitative reasoning; foreign-language proficiency; and seven to nine courses in the students' major. Students praise faculty members for their devotion to teaching and mentoring; only a few introductory courses have teaching assistants, who run review sessions and offer extra help. "Professors are excellent, are always available to students, and know each of their students personally," one student says. It's not uncommon for

Website: www.wooster.edu
Location: Small town
Total Enrollment: 1,856
Undergraduates: 1,856
Male/Female: 47/53
SAT Ranges: V 550–650
  M 550–650
ACT Range: 23–29
Financial Aid: 56%
Expense: Pr $ $ $
Phi Beta Kappa: Yes
Applicants: 2,392
Accepted: 72%
Enrolled: 30%
Grad in 6 Years: 65%
Returning Freshmen: 86%
Academics: ✍ ✍ ✍ ½
Social: ☎ ☎ ☎
Q of L: ★ ★ ★
Admissions: (330) 263-2322
E-mail Address:
  admissions@wooster.edu

Strongest Programs:
Economics/Business
  Economics
Biology
Art
History
English
Sociology/Anthropology
Communication
Mathematics/Computer
  Science
Political Science
International Relations

science majors to coauthor faculty papers, while students in the Jenny Investment Club manage a portion of the college's assets, with professors serving as advisors. Wooster's small size hasn't placed it at a technological disadvantage; WoosterNet links every academic and administrative building and residence hall, and labs and kiosks offer twenty-four-hour access to more than 150 microcomputers and terminals.

Wooster's most popular majors are history, English, sociology/anthropology, economics/business economics, communication, mathematics, computer science, political science, biology, art, and international affairs. The foreign language departments are small but provide "individual attention to each student," a senior says. A new interdepartmental program in biochemistry and molecular biology has been added, along with a formal writing program and an interdisciplinary program that provides for a half-dozen or so new courses team-taught by faculty from different disciplines. For those who tire of rural Ohio, a leadership and liberal learning program includes a seminar class and a week-long acquaintanceship, where participants shadow a prominent politician, executive, or other professional. Wooster also sponsors overseas programs on five continents, by itself and through the Great Lakes Colleges Association.*

Each year, Wooster's admissions office strives to assemble a diverse group of scholars, and as the college's reputation spreads, it's becoming more selective, with acceptance rates falling and freshman-retention rates improving. Still, diversity mainly extends to academic and extracurricular interest; 81 percent of the students are white. Half are from Ohio. African-Americans constitute 5 percent of the student body, and Asian-Americans and Hispanics are just 1 percent each. That said, C.O.W. students aren't politically apathetic. Gay rights, women's issues, the Middle East conflict, U.S.–Afghanistan relations, and even free-trade coffee pepper campus table talk. "There is a niche for everyone, even on such a small campus," one sophomore says. A theater major says the student body is "quite diverse in terms of background, attitudes, interests, academic involvement, and social style."

Ninety-seven percent of students live on campus in nine co-ed and two single-sex dorms, where rooms are small but maid service is regular. Housing varies; one political science major said the quality ranges from "really nice" to "crappy." Students stay connected with the community through the Wooster Volunteer Network. Students seriously committed to service may apply to live in one of the college's twenty-six residential program houses, each of which is

"Professors are excellent, are always available to students, and know each of their students personally."

affiliated with a community group. Food in the two campus dining halls is getting better, more parking has been added, and all dorms are now wired for cable television. Given Wooster's location "in the middle of corn fields," security isn't an issue, students say, although emergency phones are strategically located just in case.

Wooster social life is campus-based, thanks in large part to the school's remote location. Students do travel to nearby colleges such as Denison, Oberlin, Kenyon, and Ohio State to combat cabin fever. Other popular road trips are Cleveland's Flats or warehouse district, and just across the border to Windsor, Canada, where there's legal gambling and a lower drinking age. That's important to some because "it is getting harder and harder for underage students to be served" on campus, says a senior. C.O.W. has no national Greek organizations, but local "sections" draw 7 percent of men and "clubs" attract 8 percent of women. One major weekend hangout is the Underground, a bar and dance club that hosts well-known bands, as well as the campus's bowling alley, pool hall, and game room. Wooster and about a quarter of its students are affiliated with the Presbyterian Church. The school's Scottish heritage can be seen in its band, which performs in bagpipes and kilts, and in its Scottish dancers, who trot on stage during the fall's Scot Spirit Day. Other annual traditions include the outdoor Party on the Green, a fall concert, and the formal Winter Gala, where students, faculty, and staff dance the night away to the sounds of a swing band. When it snows—which it does quite often in Wooster—the student body descends upon the central arch and fills it with snow.

Wooster fields a number of competitive Division III teams. Men's basketball is a spectator favorite—it and the men's baseball team have both come home with the North Coast Athletic Conference Championship title. Any match versus rival Wittenberg usually brings out the fan in Wooster students (you have to get the free tickets well ahead of time), and men's and women's soccer, swimming, and women's lacrosse have been strong in recent years.

The College of Wooster is nationally recognized for its commitment to independent study. Students are open minded, eager to learn, and able to think on their own. They make do with the long, cold winters by immersing themselves in study and finding ways to have a good time.

> ## Overlaps
> **Denison, Kenyon, Ohio Wesleyan, Wittenberg, Miami University (OH)**

> **If You Apply To** ⮞
>
> **Wooster:** Early decision: Dec. 1. Regular admissions and financial aid: Feb. 15. Housing: May 1. Meets demonstrated need of 100%. Campus interviews: recommended, informational. Alumni interviews: optional, informational. SATs or ACTs: required. SAT IIs: optional. Accepts the Common Application and electronic applications. Essay question: personal statement.

Worcester Polytechnic Institute

100 Institute Road, Worcester, MA 01609-2280

Small, innovative, and undergraduate-oriented, WPI is anything but a stodgy technical institute. The WPI Plan is hands-on and project-based. Teamwork is emphasized instead of competition. WPI is half the size of Rensselaer and a third as big as MIT.

As a pioneer in engineering education, one might expect the Worcester Polytechnic Institute to have already claimed its highest honors. But with its ever-expanding academic curriculum, surprising devotion to music and theater, and dedication to hands-on undergraduate experiences, WPI is not content to rest on its laurels. Its students must complete several extensive projects, endure seven-week semesters, and engage in real-world job experiences. But at the end of their tenure here, the practicality of their education makes WPI students valuable commodities in the job market.

WPI is the third-oldest independent science and engineering school in the nation. Its compact eighty-acre campus is set atop one of Worcester's "seven hills" on the residential outskirts of town. Worcester is an industrial city (third largest in New England) and the home of fourteen colleges, most notably WPI, Clark University, and Holy Cross. These schools are brought together by the Colleges of Worcester Consortium, Inc.* This program is a one-stop academic and social gathering place on the World Wide Web where students can discover what is happening on each campus associated with the consortium.

The city is also a base for the rapidly growing Northeastern biotechnology and biomedicine industry. The area is one of the nation's most successful high-technology regions, which supports WPI's project and research programs. WPI's campus borders two parks and the historic Highland Street District, where local merchants and students come together to form the neighborhood community. Old

Website: www.wpi.edu
Location: City outskirts
Total Enrollment: 3,831
Undergraduates: 2,767
Male/Female: 77/23
SAT Ranges: V 560–660
  M 620–710
Financial Aid: 75%
Expense: Pr $ $ $ $
Phi Beta Kappa: No
Applicants: 3,191
Accepted: 76%
Enrolled: 29%
Grad in 6 Years: 76%
Returning Freshmen: 91%
Academics: ✍ ✍ ✍ ½
Social: ☎ ☎ ☎
Q of L: ★ ★ ★ ★
Admissions: (508) 831-5826

(Continued)
Email Address:
admissions@wpi.edu

Strongest Programs:
Computer Science
Mechanical, Electrical, and
Computer Engineering
Biology/Biotechnology
Biomedical Engineering

English stone buildings, complete with creeping ivy, dominate the architecture, but modern facilities have moved in to claim their own space on the immaculately kept grounds. Recent changes include a high-speed Internet network, a student center, and extensive refurbishments in all dorms.

There are four terms per academic year at WPI, each lasting seven weeks, which students say changes the climate. "I would say the best thing and the worst thing about our courses is that they are only seven [weeks] long," says one student. "It makes you really focus on three courses, yet if you fall behind there is little time to play catch-up." "We learn time management early," says a technical writing major. The Interactive Qualifying Project has students apply technical knowledge to one of society's problems and the Major Qualifying Project represents a student's first chance to work on a truly professional-level problem. Courses provide the information students need to complete their projects, reemphasizing WPI's curriculum as one driven by knowledge and not credit. When students are not completing projects, they take three courses per term. It's difficult to graduate in four years in some majors such as chemical engineering, some say.

> "I would say the best thing and the worst thing about our courses is that they are only seven [weeks] long."

The intent of WPI's unique grading system and educational philosophy is to polish social skills, build self-confidence, produce well-rounded students, and nurture young people interested in using their knowledge to improve the work. WPI focuses especially on developing teamwork abilities. Many students see that as a real strength. "The courses are very rigorous and the atmosphere could be very competitive," says a biomedical engineering major. "But it is significantly toned down by the nature of our curriculum, which has projects as an eminent feature. Most of these are unique and they require group and team effort." The curriculum remains remarkably flexible for a high-powered engineering school. Standard course distribution requirements vary by major but include courses in engineering, math, and science. Every WPI student must complete a humanities and arts sufficiency project. To promote cooperation and cohesiveness, the only recorded grades are A, B, C, or No Record. Failing grades do not appear on transcripts, and the school does not compute GPAs or class ranks.

The WPI Plan is hands-on and project-based. Teamwork is emphasized instead of competition.

Technical writing, which was once seen as a somewhat anemic program, is growing swiftly. The most popular departments are, not surprisingly, computer science, electrical/computer engineering, mechanical engineering, biology/biotechnology, and civil/environmental engineering. "All departments have excellent reputations, yet the older ones are a little better established and equipped," says a physics major. There are also a number of interdisciplinary programs such as prelaw and international studies. Many biomedical engineering majors do their projects at Umass Medical and Tufts Veterinary, as well as at local hospitals. And WPI has a joint Ph.D. Program with Umass medical school. WPI also offers a rare fire protection engineering program and a system dynamics

> "All departments have excellent reputations, yet the older ones are a little better established and equipped."

major and minor. An aerospace major has been added, and the electrical engineering department, the biology and biotechnology department, and the department of management have updated many of their programs. Now math and science types can pick up middle or high school teaching credentials on the way. The theater technology major requires projects in set, lighting, or audio design, which means school shows often highlight cutting-edge production techniques. Nearly four hundred students participate in one of seventeen musical ensembles, one of the largest music programs among technological universities.

In light of an increasingly interdependent global economy, WPI offers a unique Global Perspectives Program that spans five continents. Nearly 70 percent of WPI students visit locations including Germany, Ireland, Spain, Australia, Costa Rica, Hong Kong, and Switzerland. The school's residential project centers in New York, San Francisco, Washington, D.C., England, Denmark, Holland, Italy, Puerto Rico, or Thailand provide students with the opportunity to tackle current problems for a sponsor and spend their term working independently on a specific sociotechnical assignment under the direction of one or more faculty members. The co-op program offers upperclassmen two eight-month work experiences and adds an extra half or full year to the degree program.

Eighty-two percent of students ranked in the top quarter of their high school class. African-Americans and Hispanics together account for only 4 percent of the students, and Asian-Americans represent an additional 7 percent. The school offers more than six hundred merit scholarships, ranging from $8,000 to a full ride each year, but there are no athletic scholarships.

Only first-year students are guaranteed spots in the university residence halls; however, the room-assignment process usually allows upperclassmen their first, second, or third choice. There are six co-ed halls, including a spacious 230-bed residence hall that houses students in suites of four or six, on-campus apartments, and smaller houses for more homelike living. Half of students move, sometimes to nearby, "reasonably priced, close to school, off-campus" apartments that are within a mile of the college grounds. But still, 83 percent of the students live on campus, and they can choose from the multiple meal plans of the dining halls.

Thirty-five percent of the men join fraternities, and 25 percent of the women enter sororities. Of-age students may have alcohol, provided it is kept in their rooms, but underage students do find a way to imbibe. In addition to Greek parties, there are student-organized coffeehouses, concerts, poetry readings, movies, and pub shows. "There's always something to do on campus," says a biotechnology major. Nearby colleges such as Holy Cross, Assumption, and Clark University are linked to WPI through shuttle buses, which provide even more social and academic opportunities. Boston and Hartford are both an hour's drive, as are ski resorts and beaches.

One of WPI's more notable campus traditions is the Goat's Head Rivalry, a grudge match between the freshman and sophomore classes that includes the Pennant Rush, a rope pull across Institute Pond, and a WPI trivia competition. The prize? A one-hundred-year-old bronze goat's head trophy (the winning class's year is engraved on it). There is also an annual festival of international culture and QuadFest, complete with carnival rides. Students say the new student center encourages cohesiveness across the campus and offers a viable alternative to the Greek domination of the social scene. One major gripe about WPI is its lopsided gender ratio.

While not particularly scenic, Worcester does offer a large number of clubs and restaurants and an art museum, as well as an upscale outlet shopping mall. A large multipurpose arena, the Centrum, is host to frequent concerts (like Phish and P. Diddy) and occasional visits from Boston's Bruins and Celtics and a minor league hockey team. The men's crew team, soccer team, golf team, cross country, and track had great seasons. The women's tennis and men's wrestling are titleholders, and women's soccer was added to the list of nineteen varsity sports. Crew is also popular with both sexes.

One of WPI's chants is fittingly mathematic: "E to the x, dydx, e to the xdx, cosine secant tangent sine, 3.14159, e, i, radical Pi, fight 'em fight 'em WPI!" If you know what any of that stuff means, you'll fit right in at WPI.

WPI also offers a rare fire protection engineering program and a system dynamics major and minor.

Nearly four hundred students participate in one of seventeen musical ensembles, one of the largest music programs among technological universities.

Overlaps

Rensselaer Polytechnic Institute, Northeastern, University of Massachusetts at Amherst, MIT, Tufts

WPI: Early decision and early action: Nov. 15. Regular admissions: Feb. 1. Meets demonstrated need of 62%. Campus and alumni interviews: optional, informational. ACTs or SATs and three SAT IIs (writing, math, and science): required. Accepts the Common Application and electronic applications. Essay questions: personal choice.

Xavier University of Louisiana

7325 Palmetto Street, New Orleans, LA 70125

Xavier's strategic location in New Orleans is its biggest drawing card. XU is bigger than a small college but smaller than most universities. Just more than 60 percent of the students are Roman Catholic. Competes with other leading historically black institutions such as Spelman, Morehouse, and Howard.

Website: www.xula.edu
Location: City center
Total Enrollment: 3,913
Undergraduates: 3,145
Male/Female: 24/76
SAT Ranges: V 440–550
   M 430–550
ACT Range: 18–23
Financial Aid: 48%
Expense: Pr $
Phi Beta Kappa: No
Applicants: 4,172
Accepted: 84%
Enrolled: 26%
Grad in 6 Years: 50%
Returning Freshmen: 73%
Academics: 🖉 🖉 🖉
Social: ☎ ☎ ☎
Q of L: ★ ★ ★
Admissions: (504) 483-7388
Email Address:
   apply@xula.edu

Strongest Programs:
Biology
Chemistry
Psychology
Business Administration
Prepharmacy
Premed
English

Breaking out of the ordinary is par for the course at Xavier University of Louisiana, the nation's only historically African-American Roman Catholic college. The goal at XU is to prepare students for great careers while providing a strong foundation in the liberal arts. With its stellar reputation for graduating a wealth of scientists, the school's primary focus is much loftier: "The promotion of a more just and humane society." But it's not all math books and Mass at XU—the school's location in New Orleans promises students a variety of social and cultural options unique to the Big Easy.

Founded in 1915, Xavier is located near the heart of New Orleans in a quiet neighborhood that is dotted with bungalows. The focal point of the campus is the Library Resource, which, with its green roof and stately neo-Gothic architectural style, has become a landmark for those traveling by car from the New Orleans airport to the French Quarter. A closed campus green mutes the urban feel of the encroaching city, and yellow brick buildings have been erected among the older limestone structures. Xavier's U-shaped administration building marks the geographic center of the campus. Recently added recreation areas are popular, and a new Art Village is a welcome addition for humanities majors.

"The departments that are important in setting the tone of the campus are biology, chemistry, and pharmacy."

"The departments that are important in setting the tone of the campus are biology, chemistry, and pharmacy," explains a student, "because more than half of Xavier's students major in these areas." It's true—in fact, nearly two-thirds of the student body majors in a science-related field. For the last three years, Xavier has led the nation in the number of undergraduate physical science degrees awarded to African-Americans, as well as the number of African-Americans placed into medical school. Xavier is also credited with educating 25 percent of all African-American pharmacists nationally. Forty-two percent of its alums go on to professional or grad schools. The university has built a national reputation as one of the most effective teaching institutions anywhere, and has been designated as one of only a few Model Institutions for Excellence by the National Science Foundation. Political science is a small but good department, and the psychology and education departments have been traditional strengths. Computer engineering is the newest major, and the school is trying to strengthen its small history and philosophy departments. Economics is no longer offered as a major, and departments consistently revise their curriculums to accommodate the evolving demands of the students. In addition to the many internships available, Xavier offers cooperative education programs in all fields and study abroad programs throughout Europe, Africa, Japan, and North, Central, and South America. The Center for the Advancement of Teaching works to improve pedagogy across the curriculum and encourages African-American students to become teachers and researchers.

Xavier's undergraduate curriculum is centered on the liberal arts. All students are required to take a core of prescribed courses in theology and philosophy, the arts and humanities, communications, history and the social sciences, mathematics, and the natural sciences. Freshmen also take a mandatory seminar titled The Student and the University. The academic climate is competitive and challenging. "There are a lot of students here who came from private or Catholic schools, which contributes to their outstanding educational background," says a psychology major. Priests and nuns teach and help run the school, though the faculty and staff are composed mainly of multiracial laypeople. "Teachers here are top notch and they expect the best from students," says a freshman. Another says that the "majority of teachers here are very thorough in what they teach, and they tend to follow a regular syllabus." Academic and career advising are well received, and registration doesn't present any major concerns.

> **"Teachers here are top notch and they expect the best from students."**

For a historically African-American Catholic college, Xavier's student body is quite diverse. More than 60 percent of the students are non-Catholic and 17 percent are not African-American. Students come mostly from the Deep South; half are from parochial high schools, and a high percentage are second- or third-generation Xavierites. More than one-third graduated in the top quarter of their high school class. While school and career are priorities, social issues such as abortion, contraception, and the environment are not forgotten. "Political correctness is a big issue here because it is a Catholic institution with moral religious values," says a sophomore. Merit scholarships are available for those who qualify, but financial aid is rated as just "okay." "I think they are a little stingy with the financial aid," gripes a pharmacy major.

Three of the four contemporary-looking residence halls are single-sex, and "housing is very limited," says a psychology major. "Many students live off campus because dorm rooms are scarce and the rules are very strict." Though the housing situation is far from perfect, students admit that dorm rooms are comfortable and well kept. New Orleans has one of the highest crime rates in the nation, so campus security is always an issue. Not everyone feels safe. "Security is abundant, but not very good," a senior gripes. A classmate adds, "The officers might be too obsessed with parking policies when spaces are limited."

> **"Political correctness is a big issue here because it is a Catholic institution with moral religious values."**

When students tire of microscopes and Mass, they can trek into the Crescent City for a good time. "Students often go out for a night on the town where they can enjoy good music, fine dining, or great clubs," says a biology/premed major. New Orleans is home to Mardi Gras, the French Quarter, and a boundless buffet of smoky clubs and one-of-a-kind eateries. "It is a major college town," says a student. Back on campus, fraternities and sororities play a leading role in extracurricular and social life, though less than 10 percent of the student body goes Greek. Popular events include Culture Fest, Spring Fest, and Homecoming. "These events contain fashion shows, concerts, balls, dances, Greek shows, food, and rides," explains a sophomore. Xavier is "a nonalcohol, nondrug school," reports a psychology major. Underage drinkers return to the city where nearly anything goes. Basketball for men and women—the Gold Rush and Gold Nugget teams—is the only varsity sport, and the teams are enthusiastically supported, especially when the opponent is rival Dillard.

"The departments that are important in setting the tone of the campus are biology, chemistry, and pharmacy," explains a student, "because more than half of Xavier's students major in these areas."

Students come mostly from the Deep South; half are from parochial high schools, and a high percentage are second- or third-generation Xavierites.

Overlaps
Spelman, Morehouse, Dillard, Howard, Southern University at Baton Rouge

With its small size and high-caliber academics, students at Xavier "really feel like they are a part of their classes," a senior says. The school's emphasis on prepro-fessional training, its good reputation for turning out scientists, and its spiritual underpinnings gives this liberal arts college a unique place among its peers.

Yale University

38 Hillhouse Avenue, New Haven, CT 06520

Yale is the middle-sized member of the Ivy League's big three: bigger than Princeton, smaller than Harvard. Its widely imitated residential-college system helps Yale strike a balance between research university and undergraduate college. Gritty New Haven pales next to Cambridge or Morningside Heights.

Website: www.yale.edu
Location: Urban
Total Enrollment: 11,270
Undergraduates: 5,339
Male/Female: 50/50
SAT Ranges: V 680–780
   M 690–780
ACT Range: 28–33
Financial Aid: 40%
Expense: Pr $ $ $ $
Phi Beta Kappa: Yes
Applicants: 15,466
Accepted: 13%
Enrolled: 66%
Grad in 6 Years: 95%
Returning Freshmen: 98%
Academics: 🖉 🖉 🖉 🖉 🖉
Social: ☎ ☎ ☎
Q of L: ★ ★ ★
Admissions: (203) 432-9613
Email Address:
   undergraduate.admissions@
   yale.edu

Strongest Programs:
Art and Architecture
History
English
Biology

Tradition is more than just a buzzword at Yale University. Founded in 1701 by Con-necticut Congregationalists concerned about "backsliding" among their counter-parts at a certain school in Cambridge, Massachusetts, Yale has long been recognized as one of the nation's—and the world's—finest private universities, and one of the few Ivy League schools focused on undergraduates. In recent years, the school has undertaken the Herculean task of renovating its aging campus. The uni-versity has begun the largest construction and renovation project ever undertaken at an American university. What hasn't changed are the students. Says a sopho-more: "Every student at Yale is truly remarkable. My friends include Olympic ath-letes, published authors, United Nations task force members, world-class pianists. Instead of talking about how great they are, Yale students want to discover the excellence of those they see every day."

Yale's campus looks like the traditional archetype—magnificent courtyards, imposing quadrangles, Gothic buildings designed by James Gamble Rogers, and Harkness Tower, a 201-foot spire once washed with acid to create its aged, stately look. A massive, $2.6 billion construction and renovation project, to be completed in 2010, is slowly transforming the university's historic buildings into state-of-the-art facilities. Renovations are complete for Berkeley College, Branford College, Say-brook College, and Timothy Dwight College—four of the twelve undergraduate residential colleges—as part of a $300 million effort to renovate and modernize all of the colleges, some of which date to the 1930s. Yale also has committed $1 billion to promote its basic science, engineering, and biomedical research programs. The class of 1954 Environmental Science Center opened last fall, and a $176 million, state-of-the-art facility is being constructed on Congress Avenue, which will pro-vide six floors of laboratories devoted to disease-oriented research. A new Center for Geronomics and Proteomics is also under construction.

Inside Yale's wrought-iron gates, academic programs are superb across the board. Arts and humanities programs are especially outstanding—just ask Meryl Streep or Jodie Foster, both School of Drama alumnae. The prominence of the arts makes for an interesting juxtaposition: while tradition is ever-present on campus, today's Yale attracts one of the most liberal and forward-thinking student bodies in the Ivy League. Still, the ancient Puritan work ethic remains. Graduating from Yale requires thirty-six credits, or nine courses a year, rather than the thirty-two courses required at most other colleges. Students say there's virtually no competition between students; the competition that is there is all internal. "It's as competitive as you make it," says a sophomore majoring in Portuguese. "Academics, much like Yale, depend on who you are and what you want to do." Adds a history major, "The courses are rigorous but most are also very interesting." New majors include biomedical and environmental engineering and environmental studies.

Although Yale has twelve graduate schools, Yale College—the undergraduate arts and sciences division—remains the university's heart. Virtually all professors teach undergraduates, and the professional schools' resources—especially architecture, fine arts, drama, and music—are available to them as well. Yale's superb history department offers the most popular undergraduate major, followed by English, engineering, biology, political science, and economics. History also has one of the most demanding programs, including a mandatory thirty- to fifty-page senior essay. The English department is routinely at the vanguard of literary theory,

"Every student at Yale is truly remarkable."

while an outstanding interdisciplinary humanities major includes the study of the medieval, Renaissance, and modern periods. While some science majors grumble about the walk up Science Hill, where most labs and science classrooms are, they agree it's worth the trip. The biological science department is excellent, where student interests range from biomedical engineering research to preparation for medical school. The Environmental Science Center recently opened, providing a home to the Yale Institute of Biospheric Studies. Architecture and modern languages, especially French and Chinese, are top-notch, and the school's Center for the Study of Globalization is directed by Strobe Talbott (class of '68), a former *Time* magazine reporter who served in the State Department during the Clinton administration. Elite students with a particularly strong appetite for the humanities can enroll in Directed Studies, which examines the literature, philosophy, history, and politics of Western tradition. Prospective DSers should be prepared for some serious bonding with their books—they don't call it "Directed Suicide" for nothing.

Despite its reverence for tradition, Yale doesn't require any specific courses for graduation, and it doesn't have a core curriculum. Instead, students must take three classes in each of four broad areas: language and literature (English and foreign, ancient, or modern); humanities and arts (other than literature); social sciences, including economics; and natural sciences and math. Instead of preregistering, students spend two weeks "shopping" at the beginning of each term, sampling morsels of the various offerings before finalizing their schedules. Yale also mandates intermediate-level mastery of a foreign language. Yale encourages studying abroad; about a hundred juniors a year participate in the Junior Term/Year Abroad program, while others study abroad during the summer, on a leave of absence or after graduation. Yale also sponsors the Yale World Fellowships, in which burgeoning world leaders spend a semester in a new global leadership program.

Despite its reverence for tradition, Yale doesn't require any specific courses for graduation, and it doesn't have a core curriculum. Instead, students must take three classes in each of four broad areas.

Introductory-level classes at Yale are usually large lectures, accompanied by small recitation and discussion sections, typically led by graduate teaching assistants. Some of the most popular courses, such as John Gaddis' Cold War history class, seem more like performances, students say. Upper-level seminars are small and plentiful, and underclassman can usually get into the ones that interest them. Of the one thousand classes offered each semester, 75 percent have twenty or fewer students, and 29 percent of classes have ten students or less. "Every major is designed to be successfully completed in four years," a freshman says. Faculty members are accessible and open to questions and concerns. "The quality of teaching is excellent," a junior says. "Most classes are taught by full professors and they are very accessible outside the classroom." Adds a sophomore majoring in architecture, "All my professors have been truly remarkable and incredibly accessible."

Yale's libraries hold more than ten million volumes, second in size only to Harvard's. Extensive renovations are underway to repair deterioration caused by age, heavy use, and environmental conditions. The new, 26,000-square-foot Irving S. Gilmore Music Library holds the university's extensive music collection and features electronic access to music information, a historic sound recording room, and a place to listen to records. The flashcube-shaped Beinecke Rare Book Library houses many extraordinary manuscripts, including a Gutenberg Bible and some music manuscripts penned by Bach, while the most frequently used books are found underground in the Cross Campus Library. Also located in CCL are rows of study carrels, "tiny beige boxes that look like phone booths with desks in them." To Yalies, these are "weenie bins," where many a tired student has dozed on an open book.

Only 6 percent of Yale students are Connecticut natives, but nearly 40 percent of the student body hails from the Northeast. Yale is also consistently more popular with women than many of its rivals, most notably Princeton; the student body is evenly split along gender lines. Most traditions unique to Yale—all-male singing groups like the Whiffenpoofs, drinking at "the tables down at Mory's"—have female counterparts, like Whim 'n Rhythm, if they haven't gone co-ed. Yale strives to increase the diversity of its student body; African-Americans make up 9 percent of the students and Hispanics 8 percent, while Asian-American enrollment is fairly large at 17 percent. Yalies are more liberal than their counterparts at Harvard and Princeton, and they aren't shy about expressing their opinions. "Political life is very strong on the Yale campus, but everyone is careful to respect the thoughts of others," a sophomore says. "The diversity of the student opinion only enhances the Yale experience." Recent rallying causes include the war in Iraq and the antisweatshop movement. Says a senior: "Students at Yale are less nerdy than those at Harvard, more diverse than those at Princeton, and smarter than those at any other Ivy or Stanford."

The residential colleges that serve as dorms—and as the focal points for undergraduate social life—are "one of the greatest attractions in a Yale education," says an ethics, politics, and economics major. "The residential college system at Yale is so incredible that no one wants to move off campus—you would miss so much!" raves

"Every major is designed to be successfully completed in four years."

an architecture major. Endowed by Yale graduate Edward S. Harkness (who also began the house system at Harvard) and modeled on those at Oxford and Cambridge, Yale's colleges provide intimate living/learning communities, creating the atmosphere of a small liberal arts college within a large research university. Each college has a library, dining hall, and special facilities such as photography darkrooms or tree swings—one is even said to have an endowment used solely for whipped cream. All colleges also have their own dean and affiliated faculty members, a few of whom live in the college, who can help undergraduates struggling to adapt to the rigors of college life. Residential college masters organize social and cultural events, including master's teas, where prominent public figures meet with groups of students. College-sponsored seminars, along with plays, concerts, lectures, and other events, add to the cultural life of the university as a whole. The biggest complaint, says an ethics, politics and economics major, is that the four years "go by so quickly."

Much of each residential college's distinctive identity comes from its architecture. Some are fashioned in a craggy, fortress-like Gothic style, while others are done in the more open Colonial style, with redbrick and green shutters as the prevailing motif. All colleges have their own special nooks and crannies with cryptic inscriptions paying tribute to illustrious Yalies of generations past. Most freshmen live together in the Old Campus, the historic nineteenth-century quadrangle, before moving into their colleges as sophomores, who, along with juniors, generally live in suites of single and double rooms. Many seniors get singles. Some upperclassmen move into New Haven, although 87 percent choose to stay on campus all four years.

In addition to identifying with their colleges, many Yale students identify strongly with extracurricular groups, clubs, and organizations, spending most of their waking hours outside class at the newspaper, radio station, or computer center. Particularly clubby are the a cappella singing groups, whose members do everything from drinking together on certain weeknights to touring together during spring break. Many of Yale's mysterious secret societies, such as Skull and Bones (which counts President George W. Bush and presidential hopeful John Kerry as members), have their own mausoleum-like clubhouses and issue invitations to those with the right qualifications. There's also the Yale Anti-Gravity Society and improv comedy groups.

Though studying takes the lion's share of their time, students here also find ways to unwind. The university doesn't have a strict policy on alcohol, students say. "The university's policy of helping kids with alcohol and drugs rather than criminalizing them is effective," a freshman says. Still, the drinking age of twenty-one is enforced at larger, university-sponsored bashes, pushing most socializing to private parties in the colleges or off-campus apartments. A handful of Greek organizations have yet to make their mark. For the artistically

> "Faculty members are accessible and open to questions and concerns. The quality of teaching is excellent."

inclined, local film societies offer numerous weekend screenings and York Square Cinemas show indie films, foreign films, and the occasional blockbuster. The Palace Theater and the Shubert Performing Arts Center host touring Broadway musicals, dance companies, musicians, and popular singers. The Tony Award–winning Yale Repertory Theater is an excellent, innovative professional company that depends heavily on graduate school talent but always brings in a few top stage stars each season. Natural history and art museums on and near campus, especially the British Art Center, are excellent. For those who want more excitement, the typical Yalie refrain on New Haven—"It's halfway between New York and Boston"—tells it all. Metro North trains run almost hourly to New York, and visiting Boston is nearly as easy. Storrs, Connecticut, home of UConn, is also a popular road trip.

For those wanting to stay close to home, "New Haven is a good college town," one math and philosophy major says. "It gets a bad rep, but it's quite nice. It has a plethora of nice restaurants, and there are several cultural events per month." The university and the city work closely together to promote economic and human development. "New Haven and Yale are inextricably linked; one could not survive without the other," a sophomore says.

Yale's superb history department offers the most popular undergraduate major, followed by English, engineering, biology, political science, and economics.

A summer jazz festival brings thousands to the historic town green, and there are outdoor ethnic food fairs and theatrical performances. The city's long-standing theatrical tradition—it was once the place to try out plays headed for Broadway—has been revived with the reopening of two grand old theater and concert halls a block from campus. Locals will swear that Pepe's on Wooster Street was the first (and best!) pizza parlor in the country, while Louis's Lunch was the first true hamburger joint. Relations between students and locals are improving, and more than two-thirds of Yale undergrads do volunteer work in town through Dwight Hall, the largest college community-service organization in the country.

Yale fields a full complement of athletic teams. The basketball team won an Ivy League title in 2002. The football team last won an Ivy championship in 1999, the same year it won the Harvard–Yale–Princeton crown. In 2002, Yale won three Ivy League championships in women's lacrosse and in men's and women's golf. The men's lightweight crew team also won the 2002 IRA, an intramural competition among the residential colleges. Each year, thousands of students take part in intramural competition among the residential colleges. The Lanman Center's 57,000-square-foot gym and an elevated indoor track have been added to the Whitney Gym, as have eighteen squash courts. Also new are the 20,000-square-foot Israel Fitness Center and the 22,000-square-foot Gilder Boathouse. The annual Harvard–Yale football game is the hottest event on campus.

"All my professors have been truly remarkable and incredibly accessible."

Yale is one of America's oldest institutions of higher learning, and students and graduates here take seriously the intonation, "For God, for country, and for Yale." For proof, just remember that among its alumni, Yale counts the presidents or former presidents of about seventy other colleges and universities, as well as the last three presidents of the United States. As the university celebrates its three-hundredth anniversary, its past and former students continue to make their mark on the world.

Overlaps

Harvard, Stanford, Princeton, Brown, Penn

If You Apply To ➤

Yale: Early action: Nov. 1. Regular admissions: Dec. 31. Financial aid: Feb. 1. Guarantees to meet demonstrated need. Campus interviews: optional, evaluative. Alumni interviews: recommended, evaluative. SATs or ACTs: required. SAT IIs: required (any three). Accepts the Common Application. Essay question: personal essay; meaningful interest or activity.

Consortia

Students who feel that attending a small college might limit their college experiences should realize that many of these schools have banded together to offer unusual programs that they could not support on their own. Offerings range from exchange programs—trading places with a student on another campus—to a semester or two anywhere in the world on one of the seven continents or somewhere out at sea.

The following is a list of some of the largest and oldest of these programs, some sponsored by groups of colleges and others by independent agencies. An asterisk (*) after the name of a college indicates that the institution is the subject of a write-up in *The Fiske Guide*. An asterisk following the name of a program in the college write-ups means that it is described below.

The **Associated Colleges of the Midwest** (www.acm.edu) comprises fourteen institutions in five states: Beloit,* Lawrence,* and Ripon* in Wisconsin; Carleton,* Macalester,* and St. Olaf* in Minnesota; the University of Chicago,* Knox,* Lake Forest,* and Monmouth in Illinois; Coe, Cornell,* and Grinnell* in Iowa; and Colorado College.*

The consortium offers its students semester-long programs to study art in London and Florence; culture and society in Florence, the Czech Republic, and Zimbabwe; language and culture in Costa Rica and Russia; and tropical field research in Costa Rica. Year-long programs include Chinese studies in Hong Kong, India studies, and study in Japan. The Arts of London and the Florence program are the most popular with students. Language study is a component of all the ACM overseas programs. Prior language study is required for the programs in Costa Rica, Japan, and Russia. Domestic off-campus programs include Humanities at the Newberry Library (an in-depth research project) or a semester in Chicago in the arts, urban education, or urban studies. Scientists can study at the Oak Ridge National Laboratory in Tennessee, or there's a wilderness field station in northern Minnesota.

Living arrangements vary with the program and region. Students in programs in Chicago live in apartments and residential hotels; Minnesota's wilderness enthusiasts must rough it in cabins, and Oak Ridge scientists are on their own. There are no comprehensive costs for any of the ACM programs, domestic or foreign, and tuition is based on the home school's standard fees. The programs are open to sophomores, juniors, and seniors majoring in all fields. The only programs that tend to be especially strict with admissions are the Oak Ridge, Newberry, and Russian arrangements. For information, contact Associated Colleges of the Midwest, 18 South Michigan Ave., Chicago, IL 60603, (312) 263-5000.

The **Associated Colleges of the South** (www.colleges.org), incorporated in 1991, is composed of twelve southern schools (Birmingham-Southern,* Centenary, Centre,* Millsaps,* Rhodes,* University of the South,* Furman University, Hendrix College,* Morehouse College,* Southwestern University, Trinity University,* and the University of Richmond*). Established to strengthen liberal education in the South, the consortium focuses on academic program development (with attention to international programs), and faculty, staff, and student development. Overseas courses are offered year-round. Affiliated and ACS-managed programs are offered at Oxford, in Central Europe, and in Brazil. For information, contact the Associated Colleges of the South, 17 Executive Park Dr., Suite 420, Atlanta, GA 30329, (404) 636-9533.

The **Atlanta Regional Consortium for Higher Education** (www.atlantahighered.org) comprises twenty public and private colleges and universities in the Atlanta area, as well as several specialized institutions of higher education. Members are Agnes Scott College,* Atlanta College of Art, Clark Atlanta University,* Clayton College and State University, Columbia Theological Seminary, Emory University,* Georgia Institute of Technology,* Georgia State University, State University of West Georgia, Institute of Paper Science and Technology, Interdenominational Theological Center, Kennesaw State University, Mercer University, Morehouse College,* Morehouse School of Medicine, Morris Brown College,* Oglethorpe University,* Southern Polytechnic State University, Spelman College,* and the University of Georgia.*

Students from member colleges and universities may register for approved courses at any of the other institutions, including those with highly specialized courses. The consortium's interlibrary lending program uses a daily truck delivery service to put more than ten million books and other resources at students' disposal.

The **Christian College Consortium** (www.ccconsortium.org) comprises thirteen of the nation's top evangelical liberal arts schools: Asbury, Bethel (MN), George Fox, Gordon,* Greenville, Houghton,* Malone, Messiah, Seattle Pacific, Taylor, Trinity (IL), Westmont, and Wheaton (IL).*

The consortium offers a "student visitors program" whereby students can spend a semester—with little paper pushing—at any of the member schools. More than one hundred students (not including freshmen) participate each year, and the cost is strictly the home school's regular fees. Other than a reasonably good grade average, there are no special requirements. Consortium schools share a wide array of international programs on a space-available basis, and the consortium has cooperative arrangements with Daystar University College in Nairobi, Kenya, and Han Nam University in Taejon, Korea.

The **Five College Consortium** (www.fivecolleges.edu) is a nonprofit organization that comprises Amherst,* Hampshire,* Mount Holyoke,* Smith,* and the University of Massachusetts at Amherst,* and is designed to enhance the social and cultural life of the thirty thousand students attending these Connecticut Valley colleges. Legally known as Five Colleges Inc., this cooperative arrangement allows any undergraduate at the four private liberal arts colleges and UMass to take courses for credit and use the library facilities of any of the other four schools. A free bus service shuttles among the schools.

The consortium sponsors joint departments in dance and astronomy, as well as a number of interdisciplinary programs, including black studies, East Asian languages, coastal and marine sciences, Near Eastern studies, peace and world security studies, Canadian studies, and Irish studies. Certificate programs are available in African studies and Latin American studies. There are five college centers for East Asian studies, women's studies research, and foreign language resources. Students from the four smaller colleges benefit from the large number of course choices available at the university. The undergrads from UMass, in turn, take advantage of the small-college atmosphere as well as particularly strong departments such as art at Smith, sculpture at Mount Holyoke, and film and photography at Hampshire. There is also a Five College Orchestra and an open theater auditions policy that allows students to audition for parts in productions at any of the colleges. The social and cultural aspects of the Five College Consortium are more informal than the academic structure. The consortium puts out a calendar listing art shows, lectures, concerts, and films at the five schools, as well as the bus schedules. In addition, student-sponsored parties are advertised on all campuses, and there is a good deal of informal meeting of students from the various schools.

For those students taking courses on other campuses, one's home-school meal ticket is valid on any of the five member campuses for lunch. Dinners are available with special permission. Taking classes at other schools is encouraged, but not usually for first-semester freshmen. The consortium is a big drawing card for all schools involved.

The **Great Lakes Colleges Association** (www.glca.org) comprises twelve independent liberal arts institutions in three states: Antioch,* Denison,* Kenyon,* Oberlin,* Ohio Wesleyan,* and the College of Wooster* in Ohio; DePauw,* Earlham,* and Wabash* in Indiana; and Albion,* Hope,* and Kalamazoo* in Michigan. Like ACM, the Great Lakes group offers students off-campus opportunities both in the U.S. and overseas.

For adventures abroad, there are African studies programs in Sierra Leone, Senegal, and Kenya. Students can spend a year studying in Scotland or Japan, or a semester comparing socioeconomic changes in Poland, the United Kingdom, and Germany (European Academic Term). GLCA cosponsors five programs mentioned in the ACM write-up above, but these sometimes cost more: a fall or a year at a People's Republic of China university; study in Hong Kong, Russia, or the Czech Republic; and programs at the Newberry Library in Chicago and Oak Ridge National Laboratory in Tennessee. Other domestic programs include a one-semester arts internship in New York City and a liberal arts urban-study semester in Philadelphia.

Primarily juniors participate, but the programs are open to sophomores and seniors. New York and Philadelphia are the most popular domestic plans, and Scotland is the largest of those abroad. There are language requirements to meet in several of the programs, such as a year of Mandarin for China, a year of Japanese for Japan, and two years of Russian for Russia. Sometimes, however, an intensive summer language program can be substituted. Contact GLCA, 2929 Plymouth Rd., Suite 207, Ann Arbor, MI 48105-3206, (313) 761-4833.

The **Lehigh Valley Association of Independent Colleges** (www.lvaic.org) is a twenty-three-year-old cooperative effort among six colleges in the same area of Pennsylvania: Allentown College of St. Francis de Sales, Cedar Crest College, Lafayette College,* Lehigh University,* Moravian College, and Muhlenberg College.*

Approximately four hundred students each year cross-register at member campuses, although the bulk of the activity occurs between schools that are closest to each other. A Jewish studies program, headquartered at Lehigh, draws on the faculties of Lehigh, Lafayette, and Muhlenberg. Faculty members travel from college to college in order to offer students a variety of courses in this field. The association's Consortium Professors program puts faculty on two other member campuses each year to teach unusual or special-interest courses. Several members exchange courses by video conference. Special seminars are arranged at central locations for selected students, with transportation provided. The association offers a cooperative cultural program sponsoring nationally known visiting dance companies. Students at each college are eligible for reduced-rate tickets to plays and other events on campuses of association schools. But the most frequently used service of the association is its interlibrary loan program, which permits students at one institution to use the research facilities of the others. Summer study-abroad programs take students to Germany, Spain, Mexico, or Israel.

The **Maritime Studies Program** of Williams College and Mystic Seaport Museum is an interdisciplinary semester designed for twenty-two undergraduates (primarily juniors, but some second-semester sophomores and seniors) who are eager to augment liberal arts education with an in-depth study of the sea. Participants take four Williams College courses (maritime history, literature of the sea, marine policy, and oceanography or marine ecology). Classes are taught with an emphasis on independent research in the setting of the Mystic Seaport Museum. Classroom lectures are enhanced by hands-on experience in celestial navigation, boat building, sailing, blacksmithing, and other historic crafts. Students spend two weeks offshore in deep-sea oceanographic research aboard a traditionally rigged schooner highlighting the purpose of the program: to understand our relationship with the sea—past, present, and future.

Most students are drawn from twenty affiliate colleges: Amherst,* Bates,* Bowdoin,* Colby,* Colgate,* Connecticut,* Dartmouth,* Hamilton,* Middlebury,* Mount Holyoke,* Oberlin,* Smith,* Trinity,* Tufts,* Union,* Vassar,* Wellesley,* Wesleyan,* Wheaton (MA),* and Williams.* Credit is granted through Williams College, and financial aid is transferable. Students from all four-year liberal arts colleges are encouraged to apply. Write to the Maritime Studies Program, Box 6000 Mystic Seaport Museum, Mystic, CT 06355-0990, (302) 572-5359.

Sea Semester (www.sea.edu, not to be confused with Semester at Sea) is a similar venture for water lovers, but it is designed for students geared more toward the theoretical and practical applications of the subject. Five twelve-week sessions are offered each year, and there are forty-eight students in each session. One prerequisite for the program is a course in college-level lab science or the equivalent. All majors are considered as long as they're in good academic standing, submit transcripts and recommendations, and have an interview with an alumnus in their area.

Students spend the first half of the term living on Sea's campus in the Woods Hole area and immersing themselves in oceanography and maritime and nautical studies. Independent-study projects begun ashore are completed during the sea component aboard either a schooner or a brigantine, which cruises along the eastern seaboard and out into the Atlantic, North Atlantic, or Caribbean, depending on the season. Six weeks on the ocean is when theory becomes reality, and the usual mission consists of enough navigation, oceanographic data collection, and recordkeeping to keep even Columbus on the right course.

Students from affiliated colleges (Boston U,* College of Charleston,* Colgate,* Cornell,* Drexel,* Eckerd,* Franklin and Marshall,* the U. of Pennsylvania,* and Rice University*) receive a semester's worth of credit directly through their school. Students from other schools must receive credit through Boston U. Write to the Sea Education Association, P.O. Box 6, Woods Hole, MA 02543.

Semester at Sea (www.semesteratsea.com) takes qualified students from any college and whisks them around the globe on a study/cruise odyssey. Based at the University of Pittsburgh, this nonprofit group takes 450 students each term (from second-semester freshmen to grads) and puts them on a ship bound for almost everywhere. The vessel itself is a college campus in its own right. Sixty courses are taught by two dozen professors in subjects ranging from anthropology to marketing, and usually stressing the international scene as well as the sea itself. What's more, art, theater, music, and other extras can be found on board. When students aren't at sea, they're in port in any of twelve foreign countries throughout India, the Middle East, the Commonwealth of Independent States (Russia), the Far East, Africa, South America, and the Mediterranean, and it's not uncommon for leaders and diplomats to meet them along the way.

Students must be in good standing at their home colleges to be considered, which often means a GPA of 2.5 or better. Some financial aid is available in the form of the usual federal grants and loans, and thirty eligible students can use a work/study plan to pay for half the trip. Most colleges do recognize the Semester at Sea program and will provide participating students with a full term's worth of credits. Information may be obtained by writing to Semester at Sea, University of Pittsburgh, 811 William Pitt Union, Pittsburgh, PA 15260, (800) 854-0195 or (412) 648-7490.

The **Seven-College Exchange** consists of four women's colleges (Hollins,* Mary Baldwin, Randolph-Macon Woman's,* and Sweet Briar*), one men's school (Hampden-Sydney*), and two coed schools (Randolph-Macon College and Washington and Lee*). The exchange program was more popular when it began almost two decades ago and was utilized mainly for social reasons. Today the exchange program is used mainly for academic reasons and enables students to take advantage of courses offered on the other campuses. Eligibility for participation is determined by the home institution, and except for special fees, rates are those of the home institution. Designed primarily for juniors, the program also considers sophomores and seniors as applicants. Several participating members sponsor study-abroad programs.

The **Twelve-College Exchange Program** comprises a dozen selective schools in the Northeast: Amherst,* Bowdoin,* Connecticut College,* Dartmouth,* Mount Holyoke,* Smith,* Trinity (CT),* Vassar,* Wellesley,* Wesleyan,* Wheaton (MA),* and Williams.*

The federation means that students enrolled in any of these schools can visit for a semester or two (usually the latter) with a minimum of red tape. Approximately three hundred students utilize the opportunity each year; most of them are juniors. Placement is determined mainly by available space, but students need also display good academic standing. While the home college arranges the exchange, students must meet the fees and standards of the host school. Financial-aid holders can usually carry their packages with them. Also available through this exchange is participation in the Williams College–Mystic Seaport Program in American maritime studies or study at the Eugene O'Neill National Theater Institute.

The **Venture Program** is based at Brown University, but has at various times counted many of the most prestigious East Coast and Midwestern colleges and universities in its membership. The eight current member institutions include Bates,* Brown,* Connecticut College,* Hobart and William Smith,* College of the Holy Cross,* Swarthmore College,* Vassar,* and Wesleyan.*

Venture, established in 1973, places students who want to take time off from college in short-term, full-time jobs in many fields of interest and geographic locations. Venture provides students with an opportunity to test academic, career, and personal interests on the job. There is no cost to students or employers for participation. Venture is supported by member institutions. About two hundred students apply to the program, and about half of them are eventually placed in positions. All students attending a member college are eligible to participate. Venture also works with students who want to take time off between high school and college. In 1987, the consortium initiated the Venture II program, which encourages graduating seniors from member schools to explore work opportunities in the not-for-profit sector. The consortium also operates the Urban Education Semester in collaboration with the Bank Street College of Education and Community School District Number 4 in New York City, introducing liberal arts undergraduates to issues and practice in urban education. All of Venture's programs aim to foster social awareness and responsibility among students and build connections between higher education and the community.

The **Washington Semester of American University** takes about 750 students each year from hundreds of colleges across the country (who meet minimum academic qualifications of a 2.75 GPA) and gives them unbeatable academic and political opportunities in the nation's capital. The program is the oldest of its kind in Washington.

Students take part in a semester of seminars with policymakers and lobbyists, an internship, and a choice between an elective course at the university or a self-designed, in-depth research project. Students live in dorms on the campus, and are guided by a staff of twenty American University professors.

Ninety percent of the students are drawn from 192 affiliated schools. Although admissions competition depends on the home school and how many it chooses to nominate, the average GPA hovers around a 3.3. Most who participate are juniors, but second-semester sophomores and seniors get equal consideration. The cost is either American University's tuition, room, board, and fees or that of the home school. Just over a third of the affiliated colleges are profiled in *The Fiske Guide*.

The **Worcester Consortium** is made up of ten institutions nestled in and about Worcester, Massachusetts: Anna Maria, Assumption, Becker Junior, Clark University,* Holy Cross,* Quinsigamond Community, Tufts University of Veterinary Medicine, the University of Massachusetts Medical Center, Worcester Polytechnic Institute,* and Worcester State. Member schools coordinate activities ranging from purchasing light bulbs to sharing libraries, and a bus transports scholars to the various campuses as well as public libraries. Academic cross-registration is offered, as are two special programs: a health studies option and a certificate in gerontology. The consortium calendar lists upcoming events on each campus and encourages community service with a special emphasis on college/school collaboration. The consortium also provides free academic and financial-aid counseling to low-income, first-generation students thinking about college. Write the Educational Opportunity Center, 26 Franklin St., Worcester, MA 01608.

Index

Acknowledgments

The *Fiske Guide to Colleges* Staff

Editor: Edward B. Fiske
Managing Editor: Robert Logue
Contributing Editor: Bruce G. Hammond
Production Coordinator: Julia Fiske Hogan

Writers: Lisa Levenson, Samantha Levine, Terri Needham, Diane Oriel, Susan Saiter, Jennifer Scruggs, Chrissa Shoemaker

The *Fiske Guide to Colleges* reflects the talents, energy, and ideas of many people. Chief among them are Robert Logue, the managing editor, and Julia Fiske Hogan, the production coordinator. I am also grateful for the continuing valuable contributions of Bruce G. Hammond, my coauthor on the *Fiske Guide to Getting into the Right College* and other resources in the field of college admissions. We are all grateful for the dedicated work of our intrepid team of writers, as well as the formidable editorial assistance of Todd Stocke, Peter Lynch, Carrie Obry, Morgan Hrejsa, Jill Amack, Michelle Schoob, Kelly Barrales-Saylor, Samantha Raue, and their talented colleagues at Sourcebooks. Special thanks are in order to Taylor Poole for creative job he has done in translating our words into a thoughtful and effective design.

In the final analysis, the *Fiske Guide* is dependent on the contributions of the thousands of students and college administrators who took the time to answer detailed and demanding questionnaires. Their candor and cooperation are deeply appreciated; and while I, of course, accept full responsibility for the final product, the quality and usefulness of the book is a testimony to their thoughtful reflections on their colleges and universities.

Edward B. Fiske
Durham, NC
April 2004

Editorial Advisory Group

Nancy Beane, Atlanta, GA
Eileen Blattner, Shaker Heights, OH
Kevin Callaghan, Montreal, Quebec
Susan Case, Wellesley, MA
Angela Connor, Raleigh, NC
Anne Ferguson, Shaker Heights, OH
Carol Gill, Dobbs Ferry, NY
Marsha Irwin, San Francisco, CA
Margaret Johnson, San Antonio, TX
Gerimae Kleinman, Shaker Heights, OH

William Mason, Southborough, MC
Jane McClure, San Francisco, CA
Susan Moriarty Paton, New Haven, CT
Judy Muir, Houston, TX
Alice Purington, Andover, MA
Jan-Russell-Cebull, Danville, CA
Rod Skinner, Milton, MA
Phyllis Steinbrecher, Westport, CT
Chris Teare, St. Thomas, VI

College Counselors Advisory Group

Marilyn Albarelli, Moravian Academy (PA)

Scott Anderson, Mercersburg Academy (PA)

Caroline Van Antwerp, Colorado Springs School (CO)

Christine Asmussen, St. Andrew's-Sewanee School (TN)

Bruce Bailey, Lakeside School (WA)

Samuel Barnett, SchoolFutures (VA)

Amy E. Belstra, Cherry Creek H. S. (CO)

Greg Birk, Kinkaid School (TX)

Susan T. Bisson, Advocates for Human Potential (MA)

Robin Boren, Dakota Ridge H. S. (CO)

Clarice Boring, Cody H. S. (WY)

John B. Boshoven, Community High School & Jewish Academy of Metro Detroit (MI)

Mimi Bradley, St. Andrew's Episcopal School (MS)

Nancy Bryan, Pace Academy (GA)

Claire Cafaro, Ridgewood H.S. (NJ)

Nancy Caine, St. Augustine H. S. (CA)

Mary Calhoun, St. Cecilia Academy (TN)

Mary Chapman, St. Catherine's School (VA)

Nedra A. Clark, Montclair High School (NJ)

Anthony L. Clay, Carolina Friends School (NC)

Kathy Cleaver, Durham Academy (NC)

Alison Cotten, Cypress Falls H. S. (TX)

Alice Cotti, Polytechnic School (CA)

Rod Cox, St. Johns Country Day School (FL)

Carroll K. Davis, North Central H. S. (IN)

Renee C. Davis, Rocky River H. S. (OH)

Mary Jo Dawson, Academy of the Sacred Heart (MI)

Christy Dillon, Crystal Springs Uplands School (CA)

Walta Sue Dodd, Bryan H. S. (NE)

Tara A. Dowling, Saint Stephen's Episcopal School (FL)

Dan Feldhaus, Iolani School (HI)

Ralph S. Figueroa, Albuquerque Academy (NM)

Emily E. FitzHugh, The Gunnery (CT)

Larry Fletcher, Salesianum School (DE)

Nancy Fomby, Episcopal School of Dallas (TX)

Daniel Franklin, Eaglecrest High School (CO)

Laura Johnson Frey, Vermont Academy (VT)

Phyllis Gill, Providence Day School (NC)

H. Scotte Gordon, Moses Brown School (RI)

Freida Gottsegen, Pace Academy (GA)

Molly Gotwals, Suffield Academy (CT)

Kathleen Barnes Grant, The Catlin Gabel School (OR)

Madelyn Gray, John Burroughs School (MO)

Amy Grieger, Northfield Mount Hermon School (MA)

Elizabeth Hall, Education Consulting Services (TX)

Andrea L. Hays, Hathaway Brown School (OH)

Rob Herald, Cairo American College (Egypt)

Darnell Heywood, Columbus School for Girls (OH)

Bruce Hunter, Rowland Hall-St. Mark's School (UT)

Deanna L. Hunter, Shawnee Mission East H. S. (KS)

John Keyes, The Catlin Gabel School (OR)

Sharon Koenings, Brookfield Academy (WI)

Joan Jacobson, Shawnee Mission South H. S. (KS)

Gerimae Kleinman, Shaker Heights H. S. (OH)

Laurie Leftwich, Brother Martin High School (LA)

Mary Jane London, Los Angeles Center for Enriched Studies (CA)

Martha Lyman, Deerfield Academy (MA)

Brad MacGowan, Newton North H. S. (MA)

Robert S. MacLellan, Jr., The Pingry School (NJ)

Margaret M. Man, La Pietra-Hawaii School for Girls (HI)

Susan Marrs, The Seven Hills School (OH)

Karen A. Mason, Wyoming Seminary (PA)

Lisa Micele, University of Illinois Laboratory H. S. (IL)

Corky Miller-Strong, Alexander Dawson School (CO)

Janet Miranda, Trinity Christian Academy (TX)

Richard Morey, Dwight-Englewood School (NJ)

Joyce Vining Morgan, Putney School (VT)

Daniel Murphy, The Urban School of San Francisco (CA)

Judith Nash, Highland High School (ID)

Arlene L. Prince, University Preparatory Academy (WA)

Deborah Robinson, Mandarin H. S. (FL)

Julie Rollins, Episcopal H. S. (TX)

William C. Rowe, Thomas Jefferson School (MO)

Bruce Scher, Barrington H. S. (IL)

David Schindel, Vail Mountain School (CO)

Kathy Z. Schmidt, St. Mary's Hall (TX)

Joe Stehno, Bishop Brady H. S. (NH)

Bruce Stempien, Weston H. S. (CT)

Paul M. Stoneham, The Key School (MD)

Audrey Threlkeld, Forest Ridge School of the Sacred Heart (WA)

Vincent S. Travaglione, La Jolla Country Day School (CA)

Ted de Villafranca, Peddie School (NJ)

Scott White, Montclair H. S. (NJ)

Linda Zimring, Los Angeles Unified School District (CA)

About the Author

In 1980, when he was education editor of the *New York Times*, Edward B. Fiske sensed that college-bound students and their families needed better information on which to base their educational choices. Thus was born the *Fiske Guide to Colleges*. A graduate of Wesleyan University, Fiske did graduate work at Columbia University and assorted other bastions of higher learning. He left the *Times* in 1991 to pursue a variety of educational and journalistic interests, including a book on school reform, *Smart Schools, Smart Kids*. When not visiting colleges, he can be found playing tennis, sailing, or doing research on the educational problems of South Africa and other Third World countries for UNESCO and other international organizations. Fiske lives in Durham, North Carolina, near the campus of Duke University, where his wife, Helen Ladd, is a member of the faculty. They are coauthors of *When Schools Compete: A Cautionary Tale* and *Elusive Equity: Education Reform in Post-Apartheid South Africa*.